2007 | WORLD DEVELOPMENT INDICATORS

Manufactured in the United States of America
First printing April 2007

Photo credits: Front cover, clockwise from top left, World Bank photo library, Alfredo Caliz/Panos Pictures, World Bank photo library, and Digital Vision.

If you have questions or comments about this product, please contact:

Development Data Group
The World Bank
1818 H Street NW, Room MC2-812, Washington, D.C. 20433 USA
Hotline: 800 590 1906 or 202 473 7824; fax 202 522 1498
Email: data@worldbank.org
Web site: www.worldbank.org or www.worldbank.org/data

ISBN 0-8213-6959-8

ECO-AUDIT
Environmental Benefits Statement
The World Bank is committed to preserving endangered forests and natural resources. The Office of the Publisher has chosen to print *World Development Indicators 2007* on recycled paper with 30 percent post-consumer waste, in accordance with the recommended standards for paper usage set by the Green Press Initiative, a nonprofit program supporting publishers in using fiber that is not sourced from endangered forests. For more information, visit www.greenpressinitiative.org.

Saved:
93 trees
4,354 pounds of solid waste
33,908 gallons of waste water
8,169 pounds of net greenhouse gases
65 million BTUs of total energy

2007 | WORLD DEVELOPMENT INDICATORS

PREFACE

You can't monitor development progress without good data. The point may seem obvious, but it bears repeating. What we know about development—successes and failures—depends on the availability and quality of data. Data are the evidence for evidence-based decisionmaking. When we talk about managing for development results, we are talking about using data to plan, implement, guide, and evaluate development programs. We won't know when we have achieved the Millennium Development Goals unless we have the data to measure progress.

Strong statistical systems, based on institutional autonomy, professional integrity, and commitment to high standards, provide the basis for producing credible statistics for informed decisionmaking. That is why we are working with our partners to improve international databases, which provide the data for *World Development Indicators,* and to strengthen national statistical systems, the ultimate source of the data.

Three years ago in Marrakech, Morocco, the Second Roundtable on Managing for Development Results endorsed a new strategy for improving development statistics, the Marrakech Action Plan for Statistics (MAPS). Since then, countries and donor agencies have united behind those joint goals.

Much has been accomplished. With support from the Partnership for Statistics in Development in the 21st Century (PARIS21), regional bodies, international agencies, and bilateral donors, 88 countries have adopted National Statistical Development Strategies to guide the maturation of their statistical systems. Many are also subscribers to the General Data Dissemination System. Based on these plans, countries and donors have begun to increase their investments in statistics.

MAPS also called for actions to improve the quality and availability of data needed in the near term to measure progress on national development plans and the Millennium Development Goals. An Accelerated Data Program, piloted in six African countries, is demonstrating that even existing data sets can yield valuable information.

Work on the next round of population and housing censuses has begun. The United Nations Statistics Division has initiated an intergovernmental process to increase support for censuses in developing countries.

Along with censuses, surveys are a major source of development statistics. In 2005 the International Household Survey Network was formed to coordinate activities and provide tools for documenting and archiving surveys, thus ensuring that investments in surveys will continue to pay dividends into the future.

All of these are important steps in building national and international statistical systems that respond to the demand for evidence to guide development. But more remains to be done, and the need is urgent.

The challenges to us—national and international statisticians, donors, data users, and everyone concerned with measuring results—are threefold:

- How to accelerate investment in statistics.
- How to produce statistics that meet the needs of users.
- And how to harmonize donor efforts in support of developing countries as they build their statistical systems.

Building statistical systems is a long-term process. So is our commitment. As we plan for the future, we are learning from our experience and realizing the results of past investments.

PREFACE

This year the preliminary results of the International Comparison Program are being released, providing new comparisons of price levels for more than 140 countries. The program, the largest single data collection effort ever undertaken, is a salutary example of what can be accomplished through global partnership, technical innovation, and systematic attention to building local statistical capacity. When the final results become available in next year's *World Development Indicators,* we will know more about the size of the world's economy and the welfare of its people than ever before. And what we have learned by working together through the program will help us to manage new large-scale efforts to improve development statistics.

As always, we welcome your comments and suggestions for making *World Development Indicators,* its databases, and related publications more useful to you.

Shaida Badiee
Director
Development Data Group

ACKNOWLEDGMENTS

This book and its companion volumes, *The Little Data Book* and *The Little Green Data Book,* are prepared by a team led by Eric Swanson and comprising Awatif Abuzeid, Mehdi Akhlaghi, Azita Amjadi, Uranbileg Batjargal, David Cieslikowski, Sebastien Dessus, Richard Fix, Masako Hiraga, Kiyomi Horiuchi, Raymond Muhula, M.H. Saeed Ordoubadi, Brian Pascual, Sulekha Patel, Changqing Sun, and K.M. Vijayalakshmi, working closely with other teams in the Development Economics Vice Presidency's Development Data Group. The CD-ROM development team included Azita Amjadi, Ramgopal Erabelly, Saurabh Gupta, Reza Farivari, and William Prince. The work was carried out under the management of Shaida Badiee.

The choice of indicators and text content was shaped through close consultation with and substantial contributions from staff in the world Bank's four thematic networks—Sustainable Development, Human Development, Poverty Reduction and Economic Management, and Financial and Private Sector Development—and staff of the International Finance Corporation and the Multilateral Investment Guarantee Agency. Most important, the team received substantial help, guidance, and data from external partners. For individual acknowledgments of contributions to the book's content, please see *Credits.* For a listing of our key partners, see *Partners.*

Communications Development Incorporated provided overall design direction, editing, and layout, led by Meta de Coquereaumont, Bruce Ross-Larson, and Christopher Trott. Elaine Wilson created the graphics and typeset the book. Amy Ditzel, Laura Peterson Nussbaum, and Zachary Schauf provided copyediting, proofreading, and production assistance. Communications Development's London partner, Peter Grundy of Peter Grundy Art & Design, provided art direction and design. Staff from External Affairs oversaw printing and dissemination of the book.

TABLE OF CONTENTS

FRONT

1. WORLD VIEW

2. PEOPLE

3. ENVIRONMENT

TABLE OF CONTENTS

4. ECONOMY

5. STATES AND MARKETS

6. GLOBAL LINKS

BACK

PARTNERS

Defining, gathering, and disseminating international statistics is a collective effort of many people and organizations. The indicators presented in *World Development Indicators* are the fruit of decades of work at many levels, from the field workers who administer censuses and household surveys to the committees and working parties of the national and international statistical agencies that develop the nomenclature, classifications, and standards fundamental to an international statistical system. Nongovernmental organizations and the private sector have also made important contributions, both in gathering primary data and in organizing and publishing their results. And academic researchers have played a crucial role in developing statistical methods and carrying on a continuing dialogue about the quality and interpretation of statistical indicators. All these contributors have a strong belief that available, accurate data will improve the quality of public and private decisionmaking.

The organizations listed here have made *World Development Indicators* possible by sharing their data and their expertise with us. More important, their collaboration contributes to the World Bank's efforts, and to those of many others, to improve the quality of life of the world's people. We acknowledge our debt and gratitude to all who have helped to build a base of comprehensive, quantitative information about the world and its people.

For easy reference, Web addresses are included for each listed organization. The addresses shown were active on March 1, 2007. Information about the World Bank is also provided.

International and government agencies

Carbon Dioxide Information Analysis Center

The Carbon Dioxide Information Analysis Center (CDIAC) is the primary global climate change data and information analysis center of the U.S. Department of Energy. The CDIAC's scope includes anything that would potentially be of value to those concerned with the greenhouse effect and global climate change, including concentrations of carbon dioxide and other radiatively active gases in the atmosphere; the role of the terrestrial biosphere and the oceans in the biogeochemical cycles of greenhouse gases; emissions of carbon dioxide to the atmosphere; long-term climate trends; the effects of elevated carbon dioxide on vegetation; and the vulnerability of coastal areas to rising sea levels.

For more information, see http://cdiac.esd.ornl.gov/.

Deutsche Gesellschaft für Technische Zusammenarbeit

The Deutsche Gesellschaft für Technische Zusammenarbeit (GTZ) GmbH is a German government-owned corporation for international cooperation with worldwide operations. GTZ's aim is to positively shape political, economic, ecological, and social development in partner countries, thereby improving people's living conditions and prospects.

For more information, see www.gtz.de/.

Food and Agriculture Organization

The Food and Agriculture Organization, a specialized agency of the United Nations, was founded in October 1945 with a mandate to raise nutrition levels and living standards, to increase agricultural productivity, and to better the condition of rural populations. The organization provides direct development assistance; collects, analyzes, and disseminates information; offers policy and planning advice to governments; and serves as an international forum for debate on food and agricultural issues.

For more information, see www.fao.org/.

International Civil Aviation Organization

The International Civil Aviation Organization (ICAO), a specialized agency of the United Nations, is responsible for establishing international standards and recommended practices and procedures for the technical, economic, and legal aspects of international civil aviation operations. ICAO's strategic objectives include enhancing global aviation safety and security and the efficiency of aviation operations, minimizing the adverse effect of global civil aviation on the environment, maintaining the continuity of aviation operations, and strengthening laws governing international civil aviation.

For more information, see www.icao.int/.

International Labour Organization

The International Labour Organization (ILO), a specialized agency of the United Nations, seeks the promotion of social justice and internationally recognized human and labor rights. As part of its mandate, the ILO maintains an extensive statistical publication program.

For more information, see www.ilo.org/.

International Monetary Fund

The International Monetary Fund (IMF) was established to promote international monetary cooperation, facilitate the expansion and balanced growth of international trade, promote exchange rate stability, help establish a multilateral payments system, make the general resources of the IMF temporarily available to its members under adequate safeguards, and shorten the duration and lessen the degree of disequilibrium in the international balance of payments of members.

For more information, see www.imf.org/.

International Telecommunication Union

The International Telecommunication Union (ITU), a specialized agency of the United Nations, covers all aspects of telecommunication, from setting standards that facilitate seamless interworking of equipment and systems on a global basis to adopting operational procedures for the vast and growing array of wireless services and designing programs to improve telecommunication infrastructure in the developing world. The ITU is also a catalyst for forging development partnerships between government and private industry.

For more information, see www.itu.int/.

National Science Foundation

The National Science Foundation (NSF) is an independent U.S. government agency whose mission is to promote the progress of science; to advance the national health, prosperity, and welfare; and to secure the national defense. It is responsible for promoting science and engineering through almost 20,000 research and education projects. In addition, the NSF fosters the exchange of scientific information among scientists and engineers in the United States and other countries, supports programs to strengthen scientific and engineering research potential, and evaluates the impact of research on industrial development and general welfare.

For more information, see www.nsf.gov/.

PARTNERS

Organisation for Economic Co-operation and Development

The Organisation for Economic Co-operation and Development (OECD) includes 30 member countries sharing a commitment to democratic government and the market economy. With active relationships with some 70 other countries, nongovernmental organizations, and civil society, it has a global reach. It is best known for its publications and statistics, which cover economic and social issues from macroeconomics to trade, education, development, and science and innovation.

The Development Assistance Committee (DAC, www.oecd.org/dac/) is one of the principal bodies through which the OECD deals with issues related to cooperation with developing countries. The DAC is a key forum of major bilateral donors, who work together to increase the effectiveness of their common efforts to support sustainable development. The DAC concentrates on two key areas: the contribution of international development to the capacity of developing countries to participate in the global economy and the capacity of people to overcome poverty and participate fully in their societies.

For more information, see www.oecd.org/.

Stockholm International Peace Research Institute

sipri

The Stockholm International Peace Research Institute (SIPRI) conducts research on questions of conflict and cooperation of importance for international peace and security, with the aim of contributing to an understanding of the conditions for peaceful solutions to international conflicts and for a stable peace. SIPRI's main publication, *SIPRI Yearbook,* is an authoritive and independent source on armaments and arms control and other conflict and security issues.

For more information, see www.sipri.org/.

Understanding Children's Work

As part of broader efforts to develop effective and long-term solutions to child labor, the International Labor Organization, the United Nations Children's Fund (UNICEF), and the World Bank initiated the joint interagency research program "Understanding Children's Work and Its Impact" in December 2000. The Understanding Children's Work (UCW) project was located at UNICEF's Innocenti Research Centre in Florence, Italy, until June 2004, when it moved to the Centre for International Studies on Economic Growth in Rome.

The UCW project addresses the crucial need for more and better data on child labor. UCW's online database contains data by country on child labor and the status of children.

For more information, see www.ucw-project.org/.

United Nations

The United Nations currently has 192 member states. The purposes of the United Nations, as set forth in the Charter, are to maintain international peace and security; to develop friendly relations among nations; to cooperate in solving international economic, social, cultural, and humanitarian problems and in promoting respect for human rights and fundamental freedoms; and to be a center for harmonizing the actions of nations in attaining these ends.

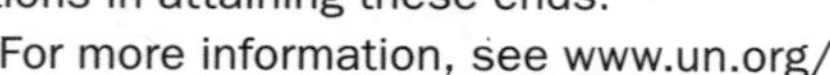

For more information, see www.un.org/.

United Nations Centre for Human Settlements, Global Urban Observatory

The Urban Indicators Programme of the United Nations Human Settlements Programme was established to address the urgent global need to improve the urban knowledge base by helping countries and cities design, collect, and apply policy-oriented indicators related to development at the city level.

With the Urban Indicators and Best Practices programs, the Global Urban Observatory is establishing a worldwide information, assessment, and capacity building network to help governments, local authorities, the private sector, and nongovernmental and other civil society organizations.

For more information, see www.unhabitat.org/.

United Nations Children's Fund

The United Nations Children's Fund works with other UN bodies and with governments and nongovernmental organizations to improve children's lives in more than 140 developing countries through community-based services in primary health care, basic education, and safe water and sanitation.

For more information, see www.unicef.org/.

United Nations Conference on Trade and Development

The United Nations Conference on Trade and Development (UNCTAD) is the principal organ of the United Nations General Assembly in the field of trade and development. Its mandate is to accelerate economic growth and development, particularly in developing countries. UNCTAD discharges its mandate through policy analysis; intergovernmental deliberations, consensus building, and negotiation; monitoring, implementation, and follow-up; and technical cooperation.

For more information, see www.unctad.org/.

United Nations Educational, Scientific, and Cultural Organization, Institute for Statistics

The United Nations Educational, Scientific, and Cultural Organization is a specialized agency of the United Nations that promotes "collaboration among nations through education, science, and culture in order to further universal respect for justice, for the rule of law, and for the human rights and fundamental freedoms . . . for the peoples of the world, without distinction of race, sex, language, or religion."

For more information, see www.uis.unesco.org/.

United Nations Environment Programme

The mandate of the United Nations Environment Programme is to provide leadership and encourage partnership in caring for the environment by inspiring, informing, and enabling nations and people to improve their quality of life without compromising that of future generations.

For more information, see www.unep.org/.

United Nations Industrial Development Organization

The United Nations Industrial Development Organization was established to act as the central coordinating body for industrial activities and to promote industrial development and cooperation at the global, regional, national, and sectoral levels. Its mandate is to help develop scientific and technological plans and programs for industrialization in the public, cooperative, and private sectors.

For more information, see www.unido.org/.

World Bank Group

The World Bank Group is the world's largest source of development assistance. Its mission is to fight poverty and improve the living standards of people in the developing world. It is a development bank, providing loans, policy advice, technical assistance, and knowledge sharing services to low- and middle-income countries to reduce poverty. The Bank promotes growth to create jobs and to empower poor people to take advantage of these opportunities. It uses its financial resources, trained staff, and extensive knowledge base to help each developing country onto a path of stable, sustainable, and equitable growth in the fight against poverty. The World Bank Group has 185 member countries.

For more information, see www.worldbank.org/data/.

World Health Organization

The objective of the World Health Organization (WHO), a specialized agency of the United Nations, is the attainment by all people of the highest possible level of health. The WHO carries out a wide range of functions, including coordinating international health work; helping governments strengthen health services; providing technical assistance and emergency aid; working for the prevention and control of disease; promoting improved nutrition, housing, sanitation, recreation, and economic and working conditions; promoting and coordinating biomedical and health services research; promoting improved standards of teaching and training in health and medical professions; establishing international standards for biological, pharmaceutical, and similar products; and standardizing diagnostic procedures.

For more information, see www.who.int/.

World Intellectual Property Organization

The World Intellectual Property Organization (WIPO) is an international organization dedicated to helping to ensure that the rights of creators and owners of intellectual property are protected worldwide and that inventors and authors are thus recognized and rewarded for their ingenuity. WIPO's main tasks include harmonizing national intellectual property legislation and procedures, providing services for international applications for industrial property rights, exchanging intellectual property information, providing legal and technical assistance to developing and other countries facilitating the resolution of private intellectual property disputes, and marshalling information technology as a tool for storing, accessing, and using valuable intellectual property information. A substantial part of its activities and resources is devoted to development cooperation with developing countries.

For more information, see www.wipo.int/.

World Tourism Organization

The World Tourism Organization is an intergovernmental body entrusted by the United Nations with promoting and developing tourism. It serves as a global forum for tourism policy issues and a source of tourism know-how.

For more information, see www.world-tourism.org/.

World Trade Organization

The World Trade Organization (WTO) is the only international organization dealing with the global rules of trade between nations. Its main function is to ensure that trade flows as smoothly, predictably, and freely as possible. It does this by administering trade agreements, acting as a forum for trade negotiations, settling trade disputes, reviewing national trade policies, assisting developing countries in trade policy issues—through technical assistance and training programs—and cooperating with other international organizations. At the heart of the system—known as the multilateral trading system—are the WTO's agreements, negotiated and signed by a large majority of the world's trading nations and ratified by their parliaments.

For more information, see www.wto.org/.

Private and nongovernmental organizations

Containerisation International

Containerisation International Yearbook is one of the most authoritative reference books on the container industry. The information can be accessed on the Containerisation International Web site, which also provides a comprehensive online daily business news and information service for the container industry.

For more information, see www.ci-online.co.uk/.

International Institute for Strategic Studies

The International Institute for Strategic Studies (IISS) provides information and analysis on strategic trends and facilitates contacts between government leaders, business people, and analysts that could lead to better public policy in international security and international relations. The IISS is a primary source of accurate, objective information on international strategic issues.

For more information, see www.iiss.org/.

International Road Federation

The International Road Federation (IRF) is a nongovernmental, not-for-profit organization with a mission to encourage and promote development and maintenance of better and safer roads and road networks. It helps put in place technological solutions and management practices that provide maximum economic and social returns from national road investments.

The IRF has a major role to play in all aspects of road policy and development worldwide. For governments and financial institutions, the IRF provides a wide base of expertise for planning road development strategy and policy. For its members, the IRF is a business network, a link to external institutions and agencies and a business card of introduction to government officials and decisionmakers. For the community of road professionals, the IRF is a source of support and information for national road associations, advocacy groups, companies, and institutions dedicated to the development of road infrastructure.

For more information, see www.irfnet.org/.

PARTNERS

Netcraft

Netcraft's work includes the provision of network security services and research data and analysis of the Internet. It is an authority on the market share of Web servers, operating systems, hosting providers, Internet service providers, encrypted transactions, electronic commerce, scripting languages, and content technologies on the Internet.

For more information, see www.netcraft.com/.

PricewaterhouseCoopers

PricewaterhouseCoopers provides industry-focused assurance, tax, and advisory services for public and private clients in corporate accountability, risk management, structuring and mergers and acquisitions, and performance and process improvement.

For more information, see www.pwcglobal.com/.

Standard & Poor's Emerging Markets Data Base

STANDARD
&POOR'S

Standard & Poor's Emerging Markets Data Base (EMDB) is the world's leading source for information and indices on stock markets in developing countries. It currently covers 53 markets and more than 2,600 stocks. Drawing a sample of stocks in each EMDB market, Standard & Poor's calculates indices to serve as benchmarks that are consistent across national boundaries. Standard & Poor's calculates one index, the S&P/IFCG (Global) index, that reflects the perspective of local investors and those interested in broad trends in emerging markets and another, the S&P/IFCI (Investable) index, that provides a broad, neutral, and historically consistent benchmark for the growing emerging market investment community.

For more information, see www.standardandpoors.com/.

World Conservation Monitoring Centre

WORLD CONSERVATION
MONITORING CENTRE

The World Conservation Monitoring Centre provides information on the conservation and sustainable use of the world's living resources and helps others to develop information systems of their own. It works in close collaboration with a wide range of people and organizations to increase access to the information needed for wise management of the world's living resources.

For more information, see www.unep-wcmc.org/.

World Information Technology and Services Alliance

The World Information Technology and Services Alliance (WITSA) is the global voice of the information technology industry. It is dedicated to advocating policies that advance the industry's growth and development; facilitating international trade and investment in information technology products and services; strengthening WITSA's national industry associations; and providing members with a broad network of contacts. WITSA also hosts the World Congress on Information Technology and other worldwide events.

For more information, see www.witsa.org/.

World Resources Institute

The World Resources Institute is an independent center for policy research and technical assistance on global environmental and development issues. The institute provides—and helps other institutions provide—objective information and practical proposals for policy and institutional change that will foster environmentally sound, socially equitable development. The institute's current areas of work include trade, forests, energy, economics, technology, biodiversity, human health, climate change, sustainable agriculture, resource and environmental information, and national strategies for environmental and resource management.

For more information, see www.wri.org/.

USERS GUIDE

Tables

The tables are numbered by section and display the identifying icon of the section. Countries and economies are listed alphabetically (except for Hong Kong, China, which appears after China). Data are shown for 152 economies with populations of more than 1 million, as well as for Taiwan, China, in selected tables. Table 1.6 presents selected indicators for 56 other economies—small economies with populations between 30,000 and 1 million and smaller economies if they are members of the International Bank for Reconstruction and Development (IBRD) or, as it is commonly known, the World Bank. The term *country,* used interchangeably with *economy,* does not imply political independence, but refers to any territory for which authorities report separate social or economic statistics. When available, aggregate measures for income and regional groups appear at the end of each table.

Indicators are shown for the most recent year or period for which data are available and, in most tables, for an earlier year or period (usually 1990 in this edition). Time-series data are available on the *World Development Indicators* CD-ROM and in *WDI Online.*

Known deviations from standard definitions or breaks in comparability over time or across countries are either footnoted in the tables or noted in *About the data.* When available data are deemed to be too weak to provide reliable measures of levels and trends or do not adequately adhere to international standards, the data are not shown.

Aggregate measures for income groups

The aggregate measures for income groups include 208 economies (the economies listed in the main tables plus those in table 1.6) whenever data are available. To maintain consistency in the aggregate measures over time and between tables, missing data are imputed where possible. The aggregates are totals (designated by a *t* if the aggregates include gap-filled estimates for missing data and by an *s,* for simple totals, where they do not), median values (*m*), weighted averages (*w*), or simple averages (*u*). Gap filling of amounts not allocated to countries may result in discrepancies between subgroup aggregates and overall totals. For further discussion of aggregation methods, see *Statistical methods.*

Aggregate measures for regions

The aggregate measures for regions include only low- and middle-income economies (note that these measures include developing economies with populations of less than 1 million, including those listed in table 1.6).

The country composition of regions is based on the World Bank's analytical regions and may differ from common geographic usage. For regional classifications, see the map on the inside back cover and the list on the back cover flap. For further discussion of aggregation methods, see *Statistical methods.*

Statistics

Data are shown for economies as they were constituted in 2005, and historical data are revised to reflect current political arrangements. Exceptions are noted throughout the tables.

Additional information about the data is provided in *Primary data documentation.* That section summarizes national and international efforts to improve basic data collection and gives country-level information on primary sources, census years, fiscal years, statistical methods and concepts used, and other background information. *Statistical methods* provides technical information on some of the general calculations and formulas used throughout the book.

Data consistency, reliability, and comparability

Considerable effort has been made to standardize the data, but full comparability cannot be assured, and care must be taken in interpreting the indicators. Many factors affect data availability, comparability, and reliability: statistical systems in many developing economies are still weak; statistical methods, coverage, practices, and definitions differ widely; and cross-country and intertemporal comparisons involve complex technical and conceptual problems that cannot be resolved unequivocally. Data coverage may not be complete because of special circumstances affecting the collection and reporting of data, such as problems stemming from conflicts.

For these reasons, although data are drawn from the sources thought to be most authoritative, they should be construed only as indicating trends and characterizing major differences among economies rather than as offering precise quantitative measures of those differences. Discrepancies in data presented in different editions of *World Development Indicators* reflect updates by countries as well as revisions to historical series and changes in methodology. Thus readers are advised not to compare data series between editions of *World Development Indicators* or between different World Bank publications. Consistent time-series data for 1960–2005 are available on the *World Development Indicators* CD-ROM and in *WDI Online.*

Except where otherwise noted, growth rates are in real terms. (See *Statistical methods* for information on the methods used to calculate growth rates.) Data for some economic indicators for some economies are presented in fiscal years rather than calendar years; see *Primary data documentation.* All dollar figures are current U.S. dollars unless otherwise stated. The methods used for converting national currencies are described in *Statistical methods.*

Country notes

- Unless otherwise noted, data for China do not include data for Hong Kong, China; Macao, China; or Taiwan, China.
- Data for Indonesia include Timor-Leste through 1999 unless otherwise noted.
- Although Montenegro declared independence from Serbia and Montenegro on June 3, 2006, this edition of *World Development Indicators* continues to list and show data for Serbia and Montenegro together; any exceptions are noted. Data

from 1999 onward for Serbia and Montenegro for most indicators exclude data for Kosovo, a territory within Serbia that is currently under international administration pursuant to UN Security Council Resolution 1244 (1999); any exceptions are noted.

Classification of economies

For operational and analytical purposes the World Bank's main criterion for classifying economies is gross national income (GNI) per capita (calculated by the *World Bank Atlas* method). Every economy is classified as low income, middle income (subdivided into lower middle and upper middle), or high income. For income classifications see the map on the inside front cover and the list on the front cover flap. Low- and middle-income economies are sometimes referred to as developing economies. The term is used for convenience; it is not intended to imply that all economies in the group are experiencing similar development or that other economies have reached a preferred or final stage of development. Note that classification by income does not necessarily reflect development status. Because GNI per capita changes over time, the country composition of income groups may change from one edition of *World Development Indicators* to the next. Once the classification is fixed for an edition, based on GNI per capita in the most recent year for which data are available (2005 in this edition), all historical data presented are based on the same country grouping.

Low-income economies are those with a GNI per capita of $875 or less in 2005. Middle-income economies are those with a GNI per capita of more than $875 but less than $10,726. Lower middle-income and upper middle-income economies are separated at a GNI per capita of $3,465. High-income economies are those with a GNI per capita of $10,726 or more. The 13 participating member countries of the European Monetary Union (EMU) are presented as a subgroup under high-income economies. Note that Slovenia joined the EMU on January 1, 2007.

Symbols

..

means that data are not available or that aggregates cannot be calculated because of missing data in the years shown.

0 or 0.0

means zero or small enough that the number would round to zero at the displayed number of decimal places.

/

in dates, as in 2003/04, means that the period of time, usually 12 months, straddles two calendar years and refers to a crop year, a survey year, or a fiscal year.

$

means current U.S. dollars unless otherwise noted.

>

means more than.

<

means less than.

Data presentation conventions

- A blank means not applicable or, for an aggregate, not analytically meaningful.
- A billion is 1,000 million.
- A trillion is 1,000 billion.
- Figures in italics refer to years or periods other than those specified or to growth rates calculated for less than the full period specified.
- Data for years that are more than three years from the range shown are footnoted.

The cutoff date for data is February 1, 2007.

1 WORLD VIEW

Measuring development—in ways familiar and new

To achieve the Millennium Development Goals by 2015 many countries need to quickly improve their economic growth and their education and health systems, their management of environmental resources, and their infrastructure for water, sanitation, telecommunications, and transportation.

Over the last 10 years developing economies have grown faster than in any period since 1965—and even faster since 2000. While the global picture is dominated by the larger economies—Brazil, China, India, Russia, and South Africa, recently joined by the major oil exporters—more are now doing well and fewer have suffered severe recessions, raising average growth rates.

Economic growth is a clear marker of development, and countries that grow usually reduce poverty. But if the fruits of growth are not widely shared many poor people can be left behind even as average incomes rise. Nor does economic growth guarantee that access to water will improve or that more children will attend school. But failing to grow almost always makes matters worse.

In considering the recent progress of developing countries on many social, economic, and environmental indicators, the Millennium Development Goals set one standard for all countries. But country performance is influenced by many factors. One is the starting point. Countries starting from worse positions have the potential to make faster progress, as they may benefit from the experience and technologies of more advanced economies. But poor countries may also face unusual obstacles in reaching their development goals. In either case, comparing a country's progress over the last decade with the average progress of those starting from a similar position can help to identify countries that have made exceptional progress—and those whose progress has been unexpectedly slow.

This section compares the progress of developing countries measured by the rate of change of selected indicators after first taking into account countries' starting points. The difference between actual progress and the average progress of countries starting from a similar position is referred to as *country performance,* and countries are classified as follows:

- *Best performers* are significantly above the average of countries with similar starting points.
- *Good performers* are above average, yet not significantly so in a statistical sense.
- *Poor performers* are below the average, yet not significantly so in a statistical sense.
- *Worst performers* are significantly below the average of countries with similar starting points.

Those that perform well on one indicator may not perform well on another. The patterns are complex, but they begin to highlight more of the diversity—and sometimes the commonality—of outcomes in development.

Economic growth

Per capita GDP growth accelerated in low- and middle-income countries in the last decade (1995–2005), as more countries grew at a moderate pace and fewer experienced severe recessions (figure 1a). And it was systematically faster in developing countries than in high-income countries in the last five years—for the first time since the de-colonization period (figure 1b).

Current projections suggest that developing countries will continue to grow more rapidly than high-income ones in the next 25 years. Based on these scenarios, the developing country share of the global economy could rise from 23 percent of world GDP today to 31 percent in 2030, and developing country average incomes could increase from 16 percent to 24 percent of those of high-income countries (World Bank, *Global Economic Prospects 2007*). But the income gap between developing and high-income economies will remain substantial, and the absolute difference in per capita incomes will continue to widen.

Although developing economies as a whole are catching up with high-income economies, there is little evidence of convergence between low- and middle-income economies. For them, the relationship between per capita growth rates and initial levels of per capita GDP shows that lower initial per capita GDP was not systematically associated with higher per capita GDP growth (figure 1c). This tells us that countries start out with roughly the same potential for economic growth. Differences in performance are likely to be associated with policies and institutions that encourage productive investment in human, social, and physical capital. But luck also plays an important role, particularly in the small and poor countries, which are more sensitive to external shocks, good and bad: conflicts, terms of trade, and the like.

Globalization's intense pace in the last decade—in trade, finance, technology, ideas, and migration—has changed the external environment for countries. Most developing countries have further integrated into world markets, notably through a reduction in trade barriers and transport costs. Here, trade integration is measured by the ratio of imports and exports of goods and services to GDP. For countries starting from

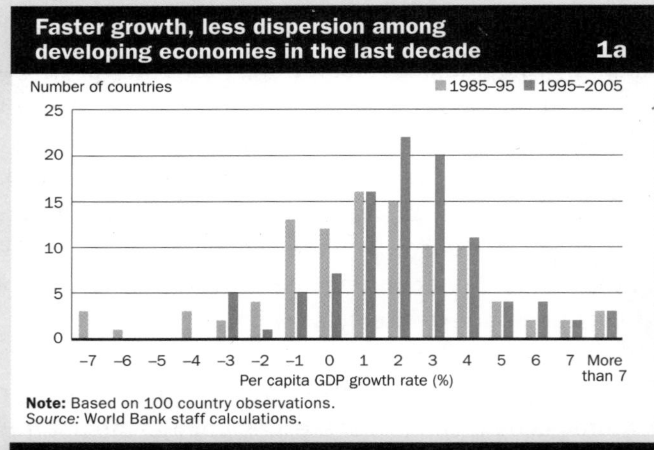

Faster growth, less dispersion among developing economies in the last decade 1a

Note: Based on 100 country observations.
Source: World Bank staff calculations.

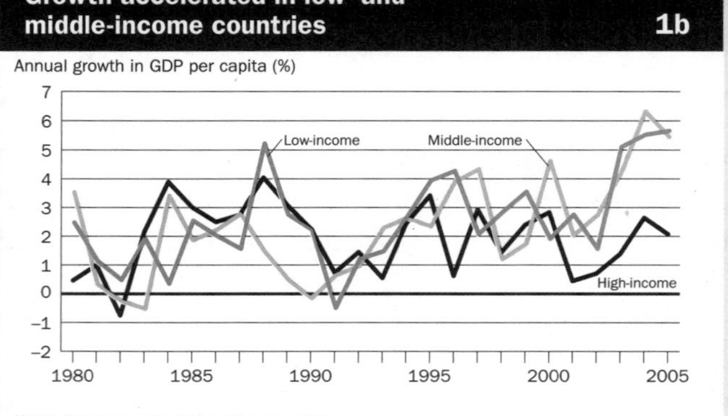

Growth accelerated in low- and middle-income countries 1b

Note: Based on market exchange rates.
Source: World Bank staff calculations.

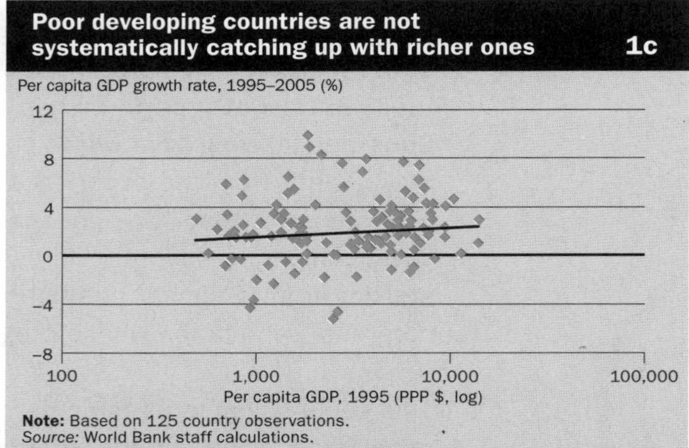

Poor developing countries are not systematically catching up with richer ones 1c

Note: Based on 125 country observations.
Source: World Bank staff calculations.

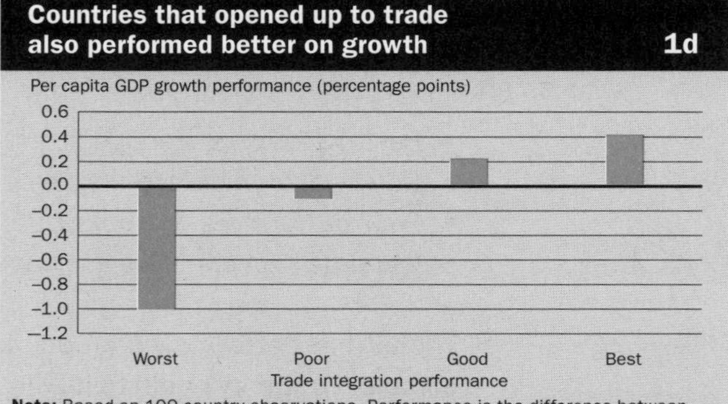

Countries that opened up to trade also performed better on growth 1d

Note: Based on 109 country observations. Performance is the difference between actual rate of change and average rate of change of countries starting from similar positions in trade integration or per capita GDP. Trade integration is measured by the ratio of imports and exports of goods and services to GDP.
Source: World Bank staff calculations.

similar positions, countries integrating less rapidly recorded much lower per capita GDP growth (figure 1d). But that does not mean that trade integration necessarily causes growth. Other factors, such as gains in competitiveness caused by domestic policies, can cause both faster growth and increased trade.

Macroeconomic management also improved in the developing world, reflected in the sharp drop in the number of countries with very high price inflation (figure 1e). The best growth performers recorded average annual inflation of 12 percent over the last decade—worst performers, 29 percent.

Cumbersome business environments also hamper growth. The cost of starting a private business, as a percentage of per capita income, is an indicator of the opportunity for entrepreneurs to develop new economic activities and to compete with existing businesses, an important force driving economic growth. That cost varies from less than 5 percent to a striking 1,440 percent—or 14 years of per capita income in 2005. Countries that performed worst on growth in the last decade also had much higher startup costs than other countries in 2005 (figure 1f).

Country growth performance is benchmarked against the average growth rate for countries that started with a similar per capita GDP in 1995 (in purchasing power parity terms). Because initial levels of per capita GDP had little influence on growth rates over the period, potential average growth is almost identical for all countries (figure 1g). The best and worst performers, which significantly deviated from averages in one direction or the other, are marked with an asterisk.

Among rapidly growing countries, many are in Eastern Europe or are oil exporters. One can also find some post-conflict countries. At the slow end of the spectrum are countries that experienced major conflicts or financial crises in the last decade, are landlocked, or are far from major trade routes. Most of them are located in Sub-Saharan Africa.

Price inflation dropped in most developing countries in the last decade **1e**

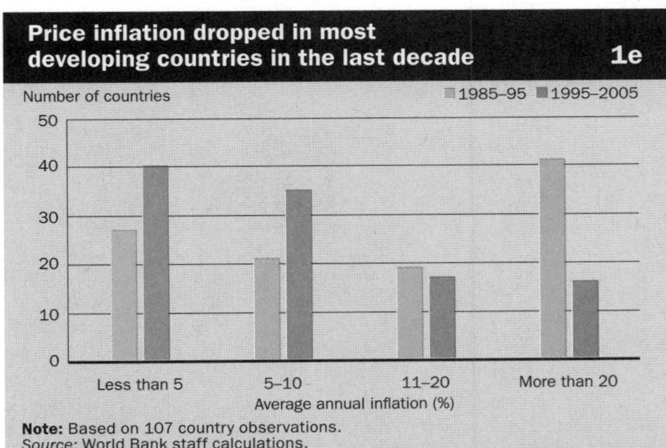

Note: Based on 107 country observations.
Source: World Bank staff calculations.

The worst growth performers have much higher costs to start a business **1f**

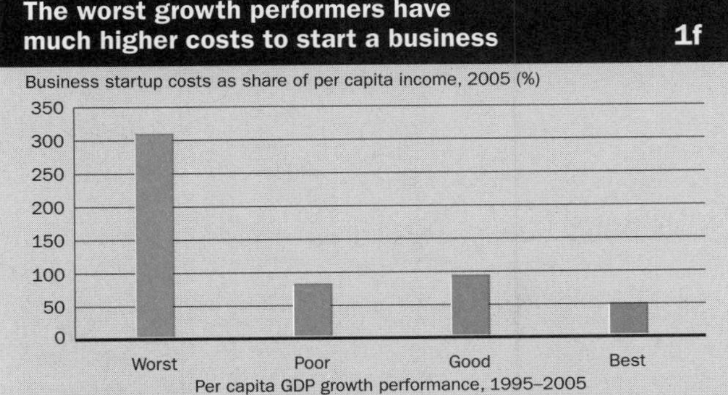

Note: Based on 109 country observations. Performance is the difference between actual growth and average growth of countries starting from similar positions in per capita GDP.
Source: World Bank staff calculations.

Best and worst growth performers in annual per capita GDP growth, 1995–2005 **1g**

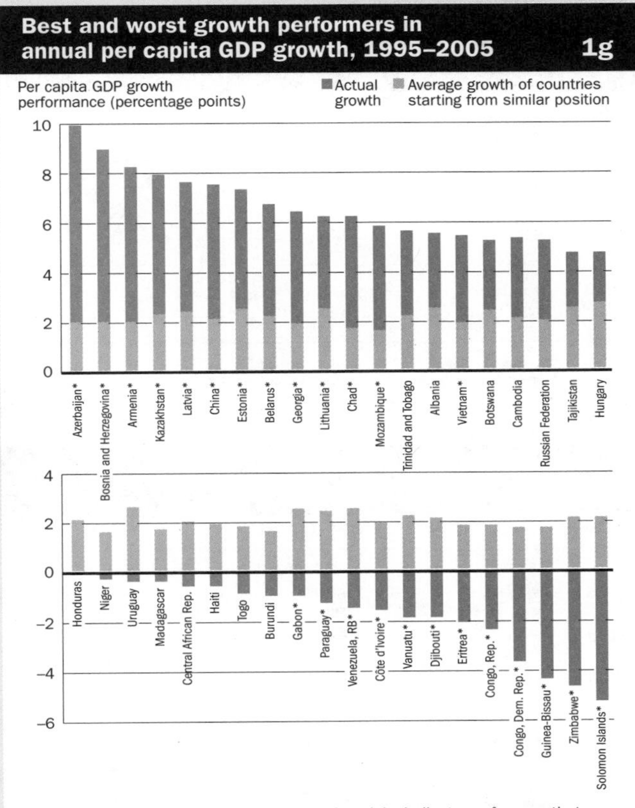

Note: Based on 125 country observations. Asterisks indicate performers that significantly deviated, positively or negatively, from average per capita GDP growth of countries with similar starting points.
Source: World Bank staff calculations.

Poverty reduction

The number of people living on less than $1 a day in developing countries fell by more than 260 million over 1990–2004, thanks in large part to massive poverty reduction in China. In contrast, the number of poor people continued to increase in Sub-Saharan Africa, rising by almost 60 million (figure 1h). In turn, the share of the population in Sub-Saharan Africa living on less than $1 a day dropped from 47 percent in 1990 to 41 percent in 2004 (figure 1i).

The Millennium Development Goal of halving the proportion of poor people is still within reach at the worldwide level—with a projected decline from 29 percent to 10 percent between 1990 and 2015. But many countries will most likely not reach it, particularly those in Sub-Saharan Africa, where average poverty rates remain above 40 percent, raising concerns of widening inequalities between regions.

The responsiveness of poverty to growth depends on the distribution of income (or consumption) and how it changes. Many factors influence how the benefits of growth are shared: health, education, infrastructure, gender parity, social safety nets, rule of law, political voice and participation, and access to markets, technology, information, and credit (World Bank 2005d). In the last decade poverty reduction was not always or everywhere commensurate with income growth. In some countries and regions, inequality worsened, as poor people did not reap the fruits of economic expansion, lacking opportunities to do so.

Fifty-nine countries with comparable $1 or $2 a day poverty data measured at two points in time (with a gap of at least 10 years) over the last two decades show that growth and changes in income distribution can reinforce or offset their effects on poverty reduction (figures 1j and 1k). In 26 cases income growth was accompanied by increased inequality, and in 20 more income distribution worsened as average incomes fell.

The number of poor people declined, mostly in East Asia and Pacific **1h**

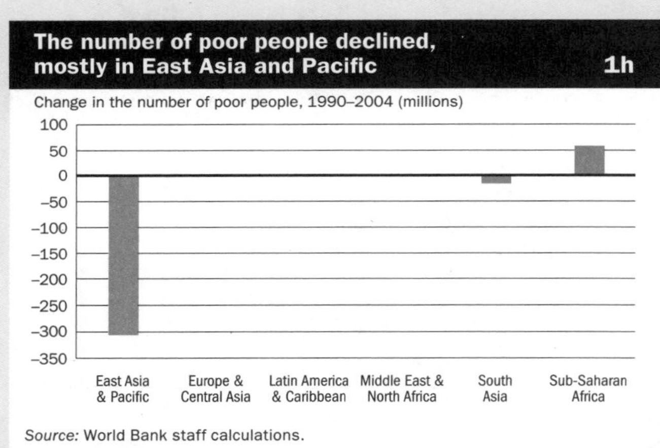

Source: World Bank staff calculations.

Inequality has increased in many countries, with or without growth **1j**

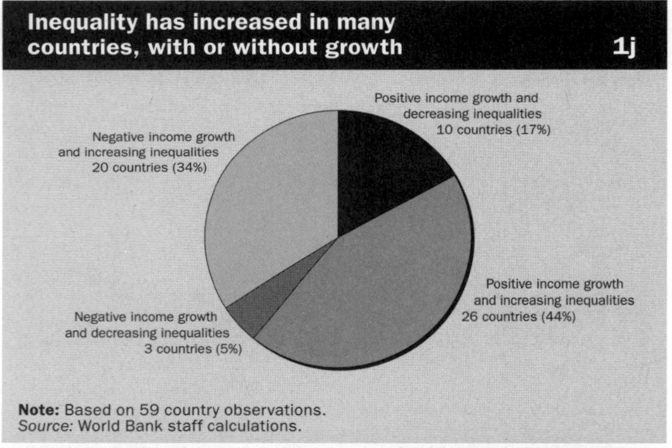

Note: Based on 59 country observations.
Source: World Bank staff calculations.

Poverty rates are on the decline in South and East Asia **1i**

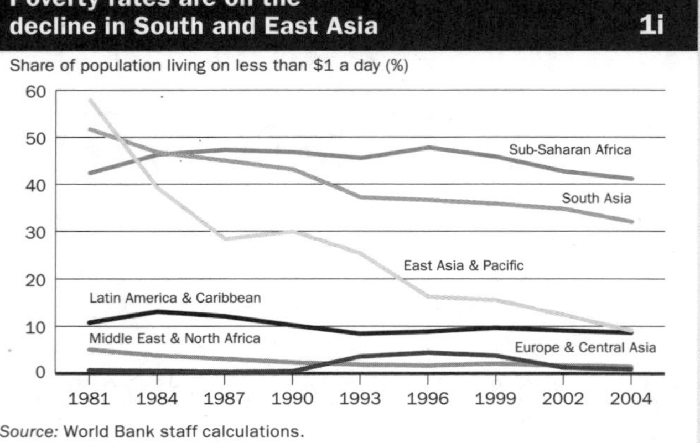

Source: World Bank staff calculations.

Changes in income growth and distribution both affect poverty reduction **1k**

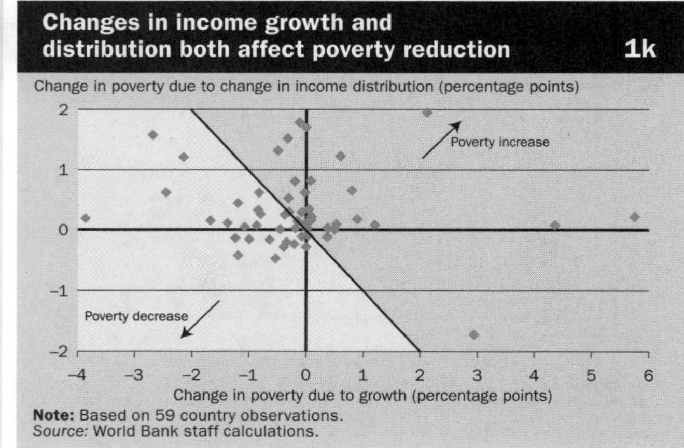

Note: Based on 59 country observations.
Source: World Bank staff calculations.

But this is not to say that growth is bad for poverty reduction. In 17 cases the contribution of growth to poverty reduction surpassed the negative impact of worsening inequality, and in another 11 cases reduction in inequality added to the poverty-reducing effect of positive growth. In only one case—out of 60—was poverty reduced despite negative income growth.

Looking at the relationship between countries' per capita income growth and performance in reducing $1 a day poverty (controlling for starting points) also suggests a positive and significant statistical relationship between the two (figure 1l).

The worst poverty reduction performers recorded particularly weak income growth performance (figure 1m). But the distinction among the three other groups of performers (poor, good, and best) is less pronounced. This suggests that the relationship between income growth and poverty reduction is more diverse when the economy is not in deep recession. In other words, income growth is necessary but may not be sufficient for sustained poverty reduction.

Countries are ranked here by poverty reduction in the most recent 10-year period with data (figure 1n; periods vary from country to country depending on the availability of poverty surveys). Also shown is the average poverty reduction of countries starting from a similar initial poverty rate. The best and worst performers, which significantly deviated from expectations in one direction or the other, are marked with an asterisk.

There is great diversity in the characteristics of good performers. Among them are low- and middle-income countries from most regions and with varying population sizes. Note too that the best and worst performers are not necessarily the countries that recorded the largest absolute changes in poverty rates. Mauritania, for example, recorded a substantial reduction but still fell short of the average performance of countries with similar initial poverty rates. Mexico experienced a smaller poverty reduction but significantly exceeded the average benchmark.

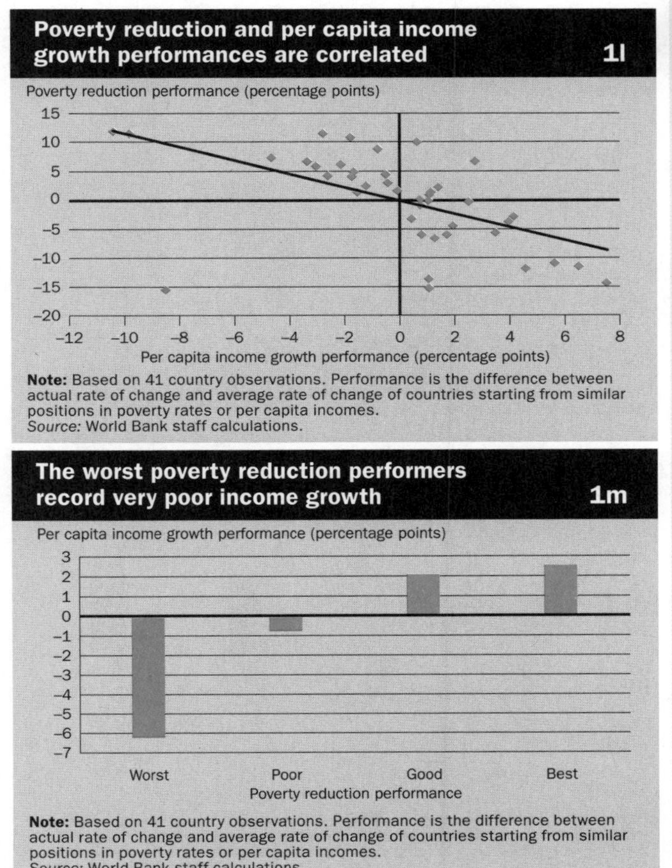

Poverty reduction and per capita income growth performances are correlated **1l**

Note: Based on 41 country observations. Performance is the difference between actual rate of change and average rate of change of countries starting from similar positions in poverty rates or per capita incomes.
Source: World Bank staff calculations.

The worst poverty reduction performers record very poor income growth **1m**

Note: Based on 41 country observations. Performance is the difference between actual rate of change and average rate of change of countries starting from similar positions in poverty rates or per capita incomes.
Source: World Bank staff calculations.

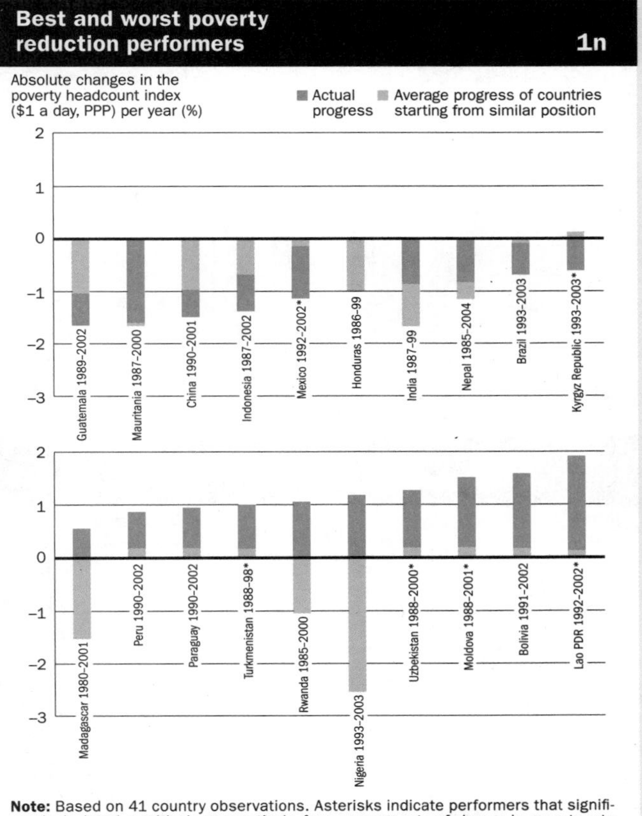

Best and worst poverty reduction performers **1n**

Note: Based on 41 country observations. Asterisks indicate performers that significantly deviated, positively or negatively, from average rate of change in poverty rate of countries with similar initial position over the period indicated.
Source: World Bank staff calculations.

Health

More than 10 million children in developing countries die before the age of five every year, mostly from preventable illnesses. Child mortality has declined in every region since 1990 (figure 1o), but progress is slow: only 35 countries are on track to meet the Millennium Development Goal of reducing under-five mortality by two-thirds between 1990 and 2015. Progress is particularly slow in Sub-Saharan Africa, where AIDS, malaria, and malnutrition are driving up mortality rates.

Improving maternal health, itself a goal, is a powerful instrument for reducing child mortality. More than 500,000 women in developing countries die in childbirth each year, and at least 10 million suffer injuries, infections, and disabilities. High mortality results from malnutrition, frequent pregnancies, and inadequate healthcare during pregnancy and delivery. Women are receiving better care during childbirth, with the proportion of births attended by skilled health staff going up from 60 percent to 70 percent between 1990 and 2004 (figure 1p). Countries in Africa and South Asia nevertheless lag behind, with much lower ratios.

Performance in reducing child mortality is measured by progress from a given starting position. Worrying—and unlike other development goals—countries with high initial mortality rates face greater difficulties in reducing them (in relative terms) than do countries starting from more favorable positions (figure 1q). HIV/AIDS and other communicable diseases are probably behind this, as countries with higher HIV prevalence rates record significantly lower reductions in child mortality. Countries with high under-five mortality rates are also often countries where malaria is prevalent and difficult to curb.

Economic growth is associated with improving mortality outcomes. On average, good and best performers in reducing under-five mortality had significantly higher growth performance than did poor and worst performers (figure 1r). Accordingly, country case studies emphasize the influence of poverty in determining child mortality. Because poor children are more likely to be malnourished and to receive less healthcare, they are more exposed to the risk of dying before the age of five.

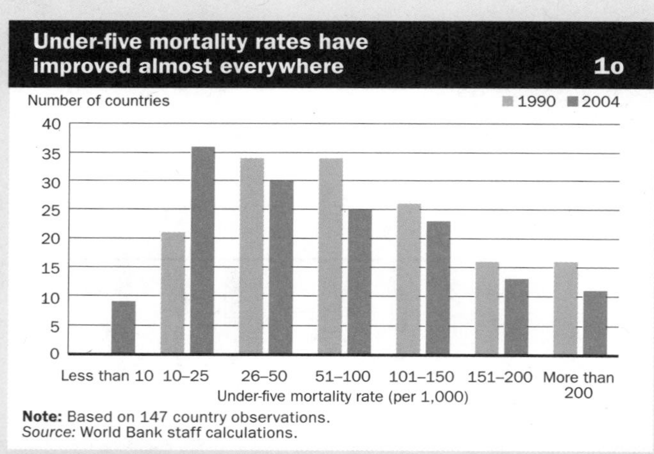

Under-five mortality rates have improved almost everywhere **1o**

Note: Based on 147 country observations.
Source: World Bank staff calculations.

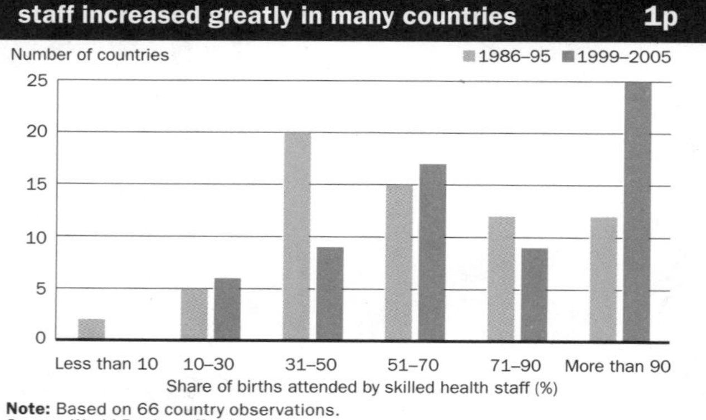

The proportion of births attended by skilled staff increased greatly in many countries **1p**

Note: Based on 66 country observations.
Source: World Bank staff calculations.

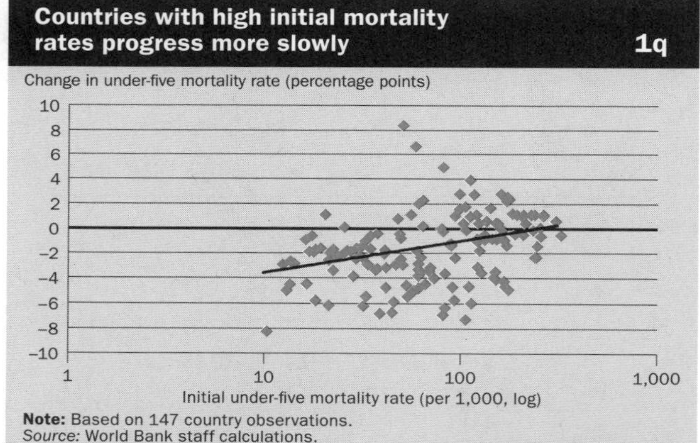

Countries with high initial mortality rates progress more slowly **1q**

Note: Based on 147 country observations.
Source: World Bank staff calculations.

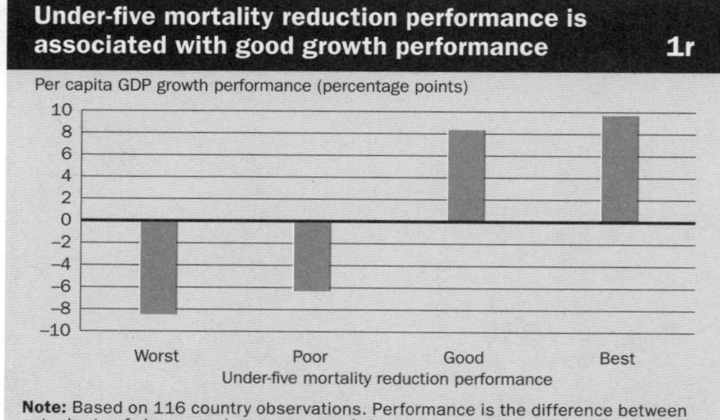

Under-five mortality reduction performance is associated with good growth performance **1r**

Note: Based on 116 country observations. Performance is the difference between actual rate of change and average rate of change of countries starting from similar positions in under-five mortality rates or per capita GDP.
Source: World Bank staff calculations.

Performance in reducing under-five mortality rates is significantly associated with education (primary school completion) and gender (equal access to schooling), suggesting that there are synergies among the Millennium Development Goals (figure 1s).

The relationship between per capita GDP growth performance and improvements in maternal healthcare performance (as measured by the proportion of births attended by skilled health staff) is not straightforward—no direct statistical relationship can be observed between the two. But performance in improving maternal healthcare is strongly associated with performance in reducing under-five mortality (figure 1t). This might not reflect any direct causal relationship between these two indicators. Rather, it could reflect the impact of health infrastructure and policies on these two indicators.

Countries are ranked here by their reduction in under-five mortality rates over 1990–2004 (figure 1u). Also shown is the average reduction of countries starting from a similar position. The best and worst performers, which far exceeded averages in one direction or the other, are marked with an asterisk.

Most of the worst performers are in Sub-Saharan Africa, where HIV is rampant, particularly in the east and south. But Sub-Saharan Africa also hosts some of the countries that recorded the largest drops in under-five mortality. In South Asia 4 of the 8 countries are among the 10 countries that recorded the largest improvements in mortality rates. Three of them are among the best performers, after accounting for their starting positions. Iraq, starting from a favorable initial position, saw its under-five mortality rate grow from 50 to 125 per 1,000 over the period 1990–2004.

Important synergies between health- and education-related Millennium Development Goals 1s

Performance in maternal health and under-five mortality are associated 1t

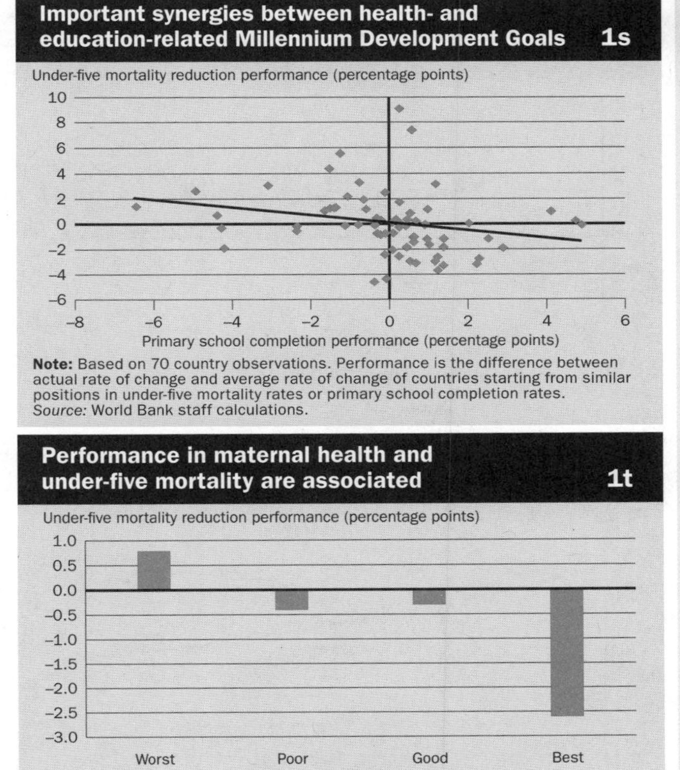

Note: Based on 70 country observations. Performance is the difference between actual rate of change and average rate of change of countries starting from similar positions in under-five mortality rates or primary school completion rates.
Source: World Bank staff calculations.

Note: Based on 66 country observations. Performance is the difference between actual rate of change and average rate of change of countries starting from similar positions in maternal healthcare or under-five mortality rates.
Source: World Bank staff calculations.

Best and worst performers in reducing child mortality 1u

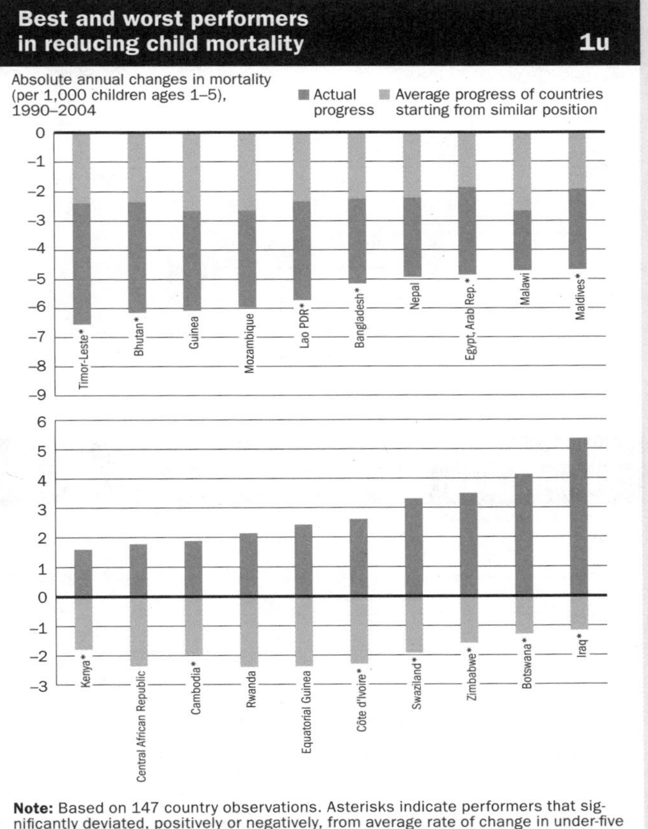

Note: Based on 147 country observations. Asterisks indicate performers that significantly deviated, positively or negatively, from average rate of change in under-five mortality rate of countries with similar initial position.
Source: World Bank staff calculations.

Education and gender

As a result of significant progress over the last decade, the average primary completion rate has risen from 62 percent to 72 percent (figure 1v). But even at this pace Sub-Saharan Africa and South Asia may not reach the Millennium Development Goals target of having all children of relevant age complete primary school by 2015. In 2001–02 it was estimated that about 100 million primary-school-age children were not attending school, three-quarters of them in these two regions.

Beyond the necessity of educating all children, eliminating discrimination against girls' participation in school is a powerful instrument for empowering half the world's people, improving the health of children, and reducing poverty. Progress in eliminating gender disparities in primary and secondary school has been remarkable in the last decade (figure 1w). On average the deviation from perfect parity (a gender parity index of 100 percent) shrank from 14 percent in 1991 to 8 percent in 2003–05.

The ability of countries to raise their primary school completion rates in the last decade was determined largely by their starting point. Countries with lower initial primary completion rates made faster progress (figure 1x), probably reflecting the fact that it becomes more difficult and costly to enroll and keep all children in school as the number of those left out falls. Country case studies suggest that girls, poor children, and children living in rural areas are less likely to complete schooling. These are the areas where faster progress must be made to achieve education for all.

Improvements in gender parity in school are also significantly associated with initial conditions. On average countries starting with greater initial gender disparity have made faster progress (figure 1y).

When all children are enrolled and complete school, there will be no gender disparity in school. Over the last decade the number of countries in which the number of boys in primary and secondary schools exceed that of girls by more than 40 percent (a gender parity index below 60 percent) fell—from

Most countries are progressing in primary school completion **1v**

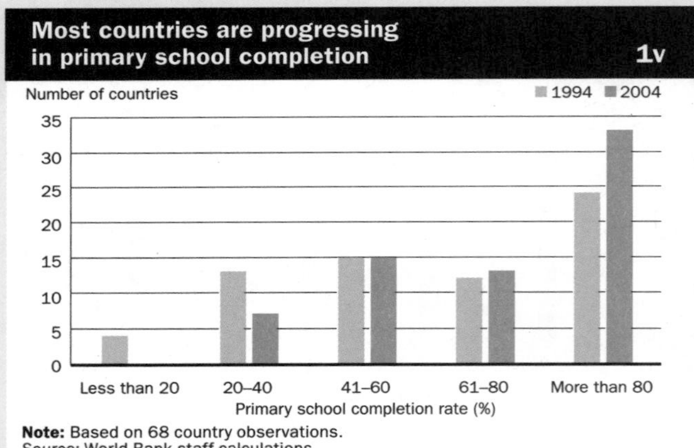

Note: Based on 68 country observations.
Source: World Bank staff calculations.

The number of countries with large gender disparity gaps in school is falling rapidly **1w**

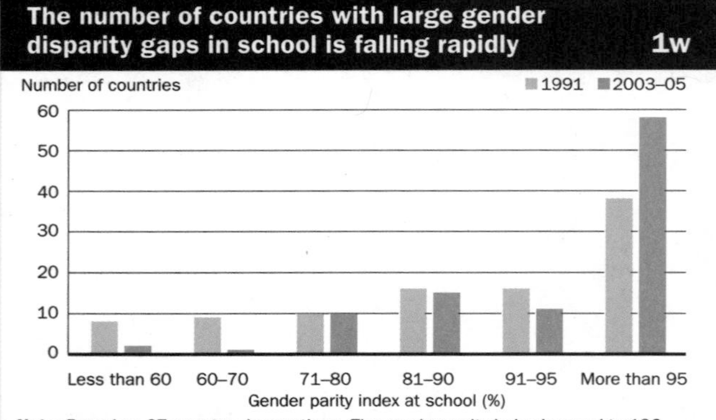

Note: Based on 97 country observations. The gender parity index is equal to 100 minus the relative excess or deficit of boys over girls in primary and secondary school.
Source: World Bank staff calculations.

Countries starting from low levels progress faster in primary school completion **1x**

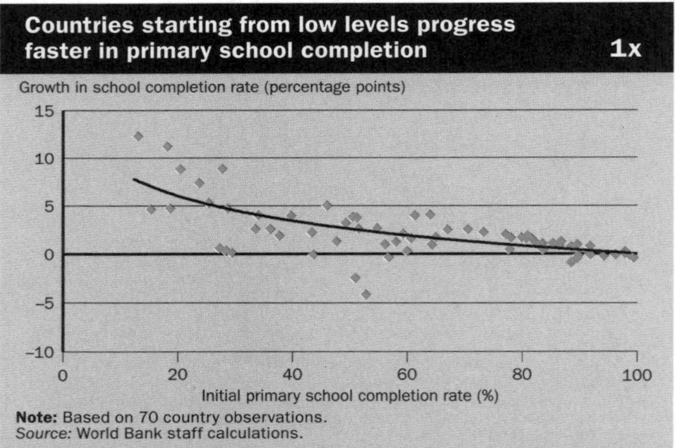

Note: Based on 70 country observations.
Source: World Bank staff calculations.

Countries starting from low levels improve gender parity more rapidly **1y**

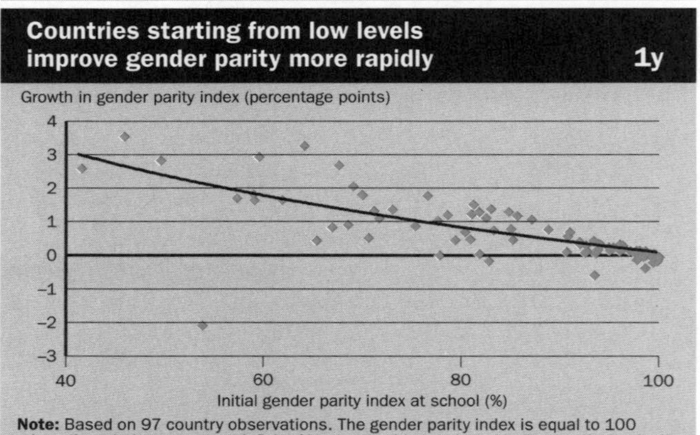

Note: Based on 97 country observations. The gender parity index is equal to 100 minus the relative excess or deficit of boys over girls in primary and secondary school.
Source: World Bank staff calculations.

17 (of 97) to 3. And the number of countries with gender parity index above 90 percent increased from 54 to 69. But the relationship between school completion and improvements in gender parity performance (accounting for initial conditions) appears to be more pronounced and uniform on the negative side than it is on the positive side (figure 1z). Countries that most improved their gender parity index did not record significantly higher school completion performances. But countries in which gender parity declined the most were countries where school completion performance was also particularly poor, possibly reflecting the fact that dropout rates are higher for girls than for boys during difficult periods.

There is not a statistically significant correlation between performance in per capita GDP growth and primary school completion. While the relationship shows up at the extremes—the best and worst school completion performers record very distinct growth performances—the growth performance of poor school completion performers cannot be clearly distinguished from that of good performers (figure 1aa).

Countries are ranked here by their primary school completion progress in the last decade (figure 1bb). Also shown is the average progress of countries starting from a similar position. The best and worst performers, which far exceeded averages in one direction or the other, are marked with an asterisk.

The two groups of performers, best and worst, both include a large number of Sub-Saharan African countries, illustrating the diversity of performance in the region. Developing countries improved their primary completion rates by 1 percentage point every year on average over the last decade or so. The best performers all recorded yearly increases exceeding 2.8 percentage points.

The worst gender parity performance is associated with poor school completion performance **1z**

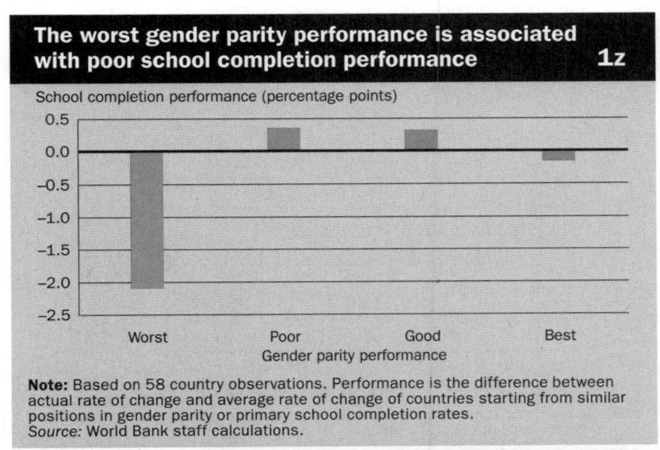

Note: Based on 58 country observations. Performance is the difference between actual rate of change and average rate of change of countries starting from similar positions in gender parity or primary school completion rates.
Source: World Bank staff calculations.

The worst performers on school completion were poor growth performers **1aa**

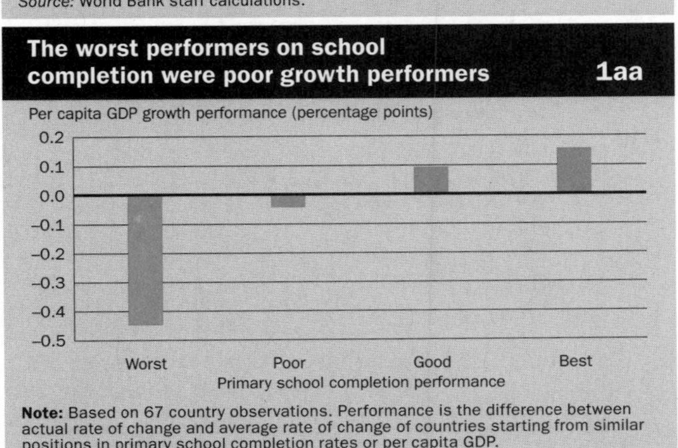

Note: Based on 67 country observations. Performance is the difference between actual rate of change and average rate of change of countries starting from similar positions in primary school completion rates or per capita GDP.
Source: World Bank staff calculations.

Best and worst primary school completion performers **1bb**

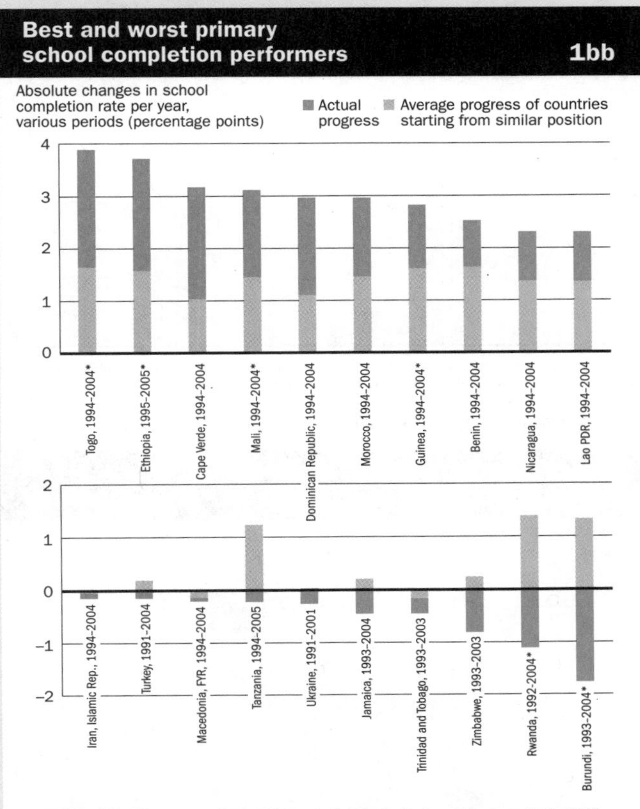

Note: Based on 70 country observations. Asterisks indicate performers that significantly deviated, positively or negatively, over the period indicated from the average rate of change in primary school completion rate of countries with similar initial position.
Source: World Bank staff calculations.

Environment

Access to improved water sources and emissions of carbon dioxide are among the indicators that the international community uses to monitor progress toward environmental sustainability.

Today, more than a billion people in developing countries lack access to an adequately protected source of water close to their dwellings (figure 1cc). Progress to improve access has been significant in the last decade, but probably insufficient in Africa to meet the 2015 Millennium Development Goal target of halving the proportion of people in 1990 without sustainable access to safe drinking water.

The role of carbon dioxide in climate change is now well documented, but the use of carbon-based energy has additional effects on human health through local air pollution. Yet emissions mount as countries grow economically, unless they reduce the carbon content of their economic activity through technological progress or shift away from carbon-intensive production and consumption (figure 1dd).

Between 1990 and 2004 the proportion of people in developing countries with access to an improved water source increased from 73 percent to 80 percent, and the number of countries with more than half the population lacking access fell from 24 to 11 (figure 1ee). Countries starting from lower positions advanced faster.

Economic activity, agriculture, and industry in particular compete with human needs for access to water sources. But greater wealth and urbanization allow more of the population to connect to safe drinking water networks. The data do not reveal a statistically significant correlation between water access and growth performance overall. But the worst growth performers distinctively record poor water access performance (figure 1ff). Such countries may also be those with degraded water infrastructure and poor management capacity.

More than a billion people still lack access to safe drinking water **1cc**

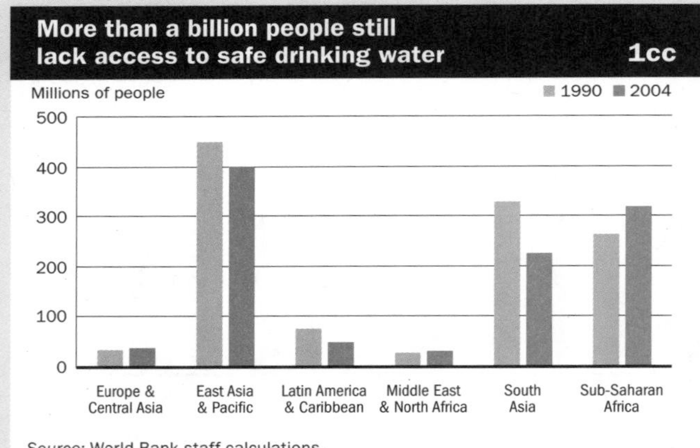

Source: World Bank staff calculations.

Carbon dioxide emissions are mounting and accumulating in the atmosphere **1dd**

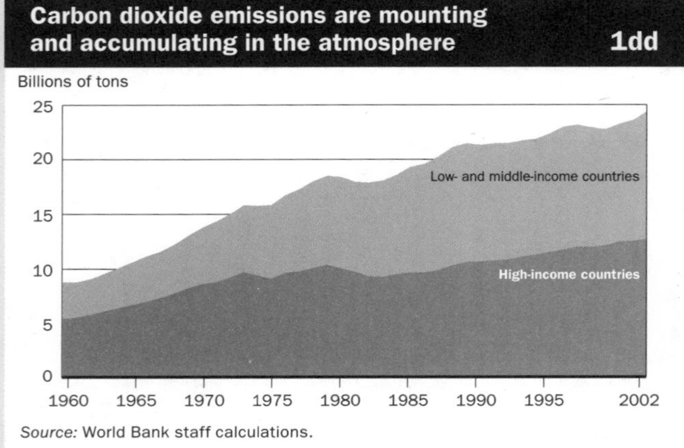

Source: World Bank staff calculations.

Access to water improved almost everywhere **1ee**

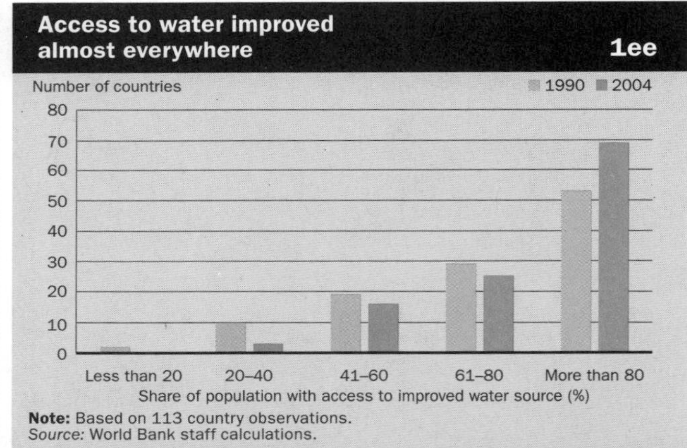

Note: Based on 113 country observations.
Source: World Bank staff calculations.

Growth and water access performance are not systematically associated **1ff**

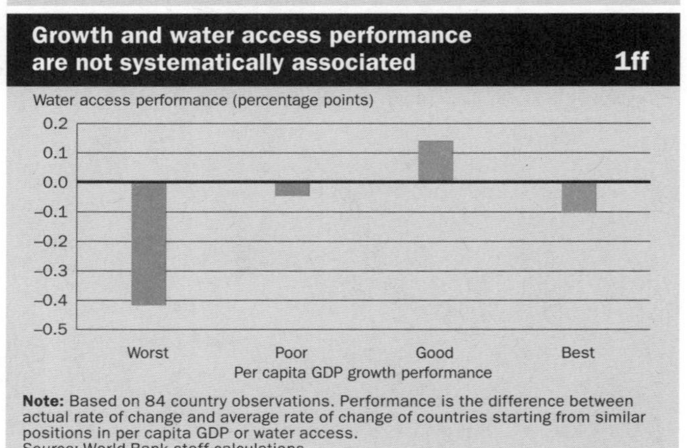

Note: Based on 84 country observations. Performance is the difference between actual rate of change and average rate of change of countries starting from similar positions in per capita GDP or water access.
Source: World Bank staff calculations.

In the next decades all countries need to make important efforts to reduce their carbon emissions. In developing economies such a commitment might be perceived as at odds with that of fostering growth. But recent history suggests that developing countries that have grown the fastest also made the greatest reductions in the carbon content of their economic activities (measured by carbon dioxide emissions per unit of GDP in PPP terms; figure 1gg). It is likely that growth was accompanied by more rapid adoption of new, more energy efficient technologies and a shift toward less carbon-intensive production and consumption.

This is not enough, however, to claim that growth is good for mitigating carbon dioxide emissions: the best growth performers recorded much higher growth in carbon dioxide emissions than other groups (figure 1hh). Technical efficiency gains were not sufficient to compensate for the growth in output.

Countries are ranked here by their progress in water access in 1990–2004. Also shown is the average progress of countries starting from a similar position (figure 1ii). The best and worst performers, which far exceeded averages in one direction or the other, are marked with an asterisk.

A number of poor performers suffered from particularly difficult geographical constraints—small Pacific island or desert countries with low rainfall, for instance. But others, also facing difficult geographical constraints, greatly improved access to safe water. The best and worst performers are not necessarily countries that registered the largest absolute changes. Indeed, the initial rate of access to improved water sources can alone explain almost half the differences in progress across countries. Accounting for starting points thus portrays a different picture of relative performances across countries.

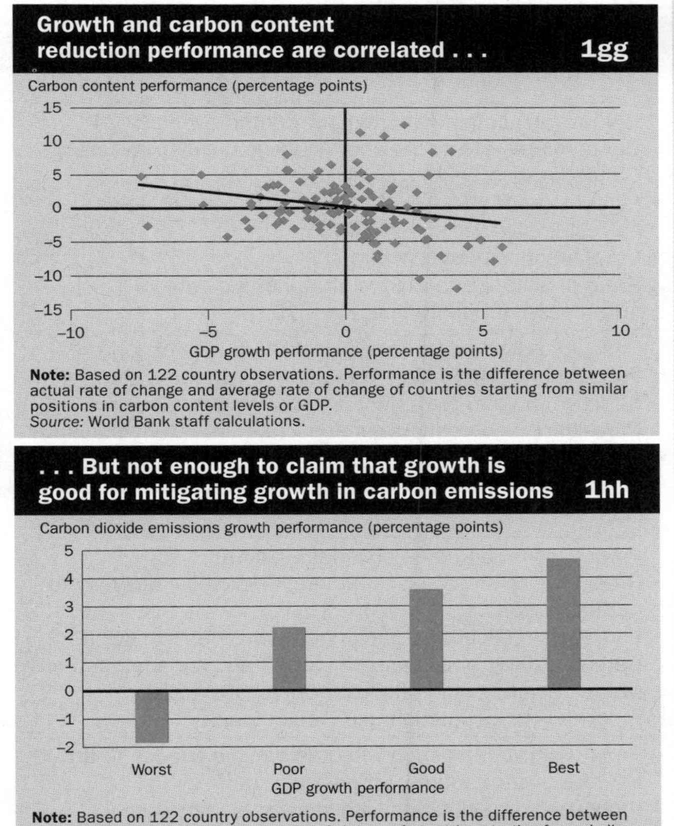

Note: Based on 122 country observations. Performance is the difference between actual rate of change and average rate of change of countries starting from similar positions in carbon content levels or GDP.
Source: World Bank staff calculations.

Note: Based on 122 country observations. Performance is the difference between actual rate of change and average rate of change of countries starting from similar positions in GDP or carbon dioxide emissions.
Source: World Bank staff calculations.

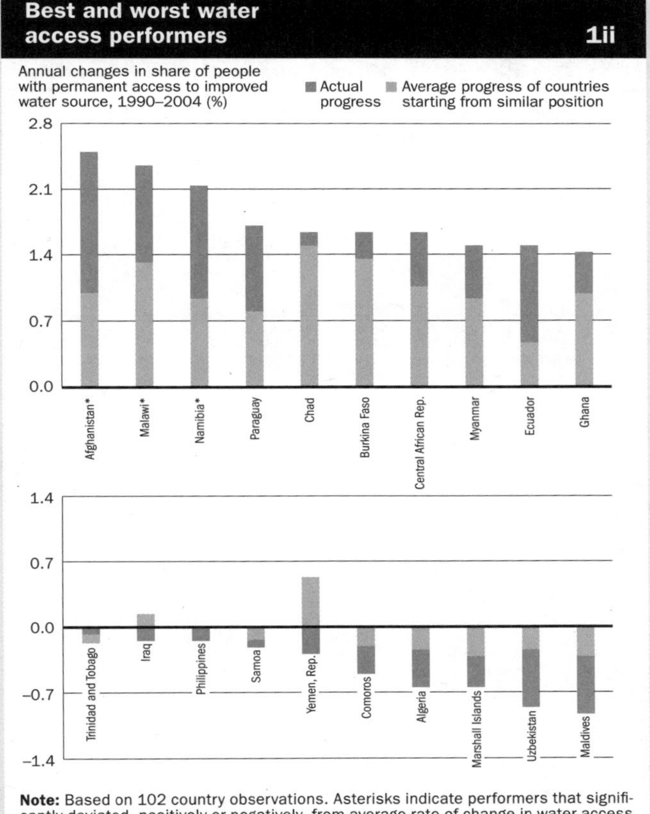

Note: Based on 102 country observations. Asterisks indicate performers that significantly deviated, positively or negatively, from average rate of change in water access of countries with similar initial position.
Source: World Bank staff calculations.

Goals, targets, and indicators

Goals and targets from the Millennium Declaration		Indicators for monitoring progress	
Goal 1	**Eradicate extreme poverty and hunger**		
Target 1	Halve, between 1990 and 2015, the proportion of people whose income is less than $1 a day	1	Proportion of population below $1 (PPP) a day[a]
		1a	Poverty headcount ratio (percentage of population below the national poverty line)
		2	Poverty gap ratio [incidence × depth of poverty]
		3	Share of poorest quintile in national consumption
Target 2	Halve, between 1990 and 2015, the proportion of people who suffer from hunger	4	Prevalence of underweight children under five years of age
		5	Proportion of population below minimum level of dietary energy consumption
Goal 2	**Achieve universal primary education**		
Target 3	Ensure that, by 2015, children everywhere, boys and girls alike, will be able to complete a full course of primary schooling	6	Net enrollment ratio in primary education
		7	Proportion of pupils starting grade 1 who reach grade 5[b]
		8	Literacy rate of 15- to 24-year-olds
Goal 3	**Promote gender equality and empower women**		
Target 3	Ensure that, by 2015, children everywhere, boys and girls alike, will be able to complete a full course of primary schooling	6	Net enrollment ratio in primary education
		7	Proportion of pupils starting grade 1 who reach grade 5[b]
		8	Literacy rate of 15- to 24-year-olds
Target 4	Eliminate gender disparity in primary and secondary education, preferably by 2005, and in all levels of education no later than 2015	9	Ratios of girls to boys in primary, secondary, and tertiary education
		10	Ratio of literate women to men ages 15–24
		11	Share of women in wage employment in the nonagricultural sector
		12	Proportion of seats held by women in national parliaments
Goal 4	**Reduce child mortality**		
Target 5	Reduce by two-thirds, between 1990 and 2015, the under-five mortality rate	13	Under-five mortality rate
		14	Infant mortality rate
		15	Proportion of one-year-old children immunized against measles
Goal 5	**Improve maternal health**		
Target 6	Reduce by three-quarters, between 1990 and 2015, the maternal mortality ratio	16	Maternal mortality ratio
		17	Proportion of births attended by skilled health personnel
Goal 6	**Combat HIV/AIDS, malaria, and other diseases**		
Target 7	Have halted by 2015 and begun to reverse the spread of HIV/AIDS	18	HIV prevalence among pregnant women ages 15–24
		19	Condom use rate of the contraceptive prevalence rate[c]
		19a	Condom use at last high-risk sex
		19b	Percentage of 15- to 24-year-olds with comprehensive correct knowledge of HIV/AIDS[d]
		19c	Contraceptive prevalence rate
		20	Ratio of school attendance of orphans to school attendance of nonorphans ages 10–14
Target 8	Have halted by 2015 and begun to reverse the incidence of malaria and other major diseases	21	Prevalence and death rates associated with malaria
		22	Proportion of population in malaria-risk areas using effective malaria prevention and treatment measures[e]
		23	Prevalence and death rates associated with tuberculosis
		24	Proportion of tuberculosis cases detected and cured under directly observed treatment, short course (DOTS)
Goal 7	**Ensure environmental sustainability**		
Target 9	Integrate the principles of sustainable development into country policies and programs and reverse the loss of environmental resources	25	Proportion of land area covered by forest
		26	Ratio of area protected to maintain biological diversity to surface area
		27	Energy use (kilograms of oil equivalent) per $1 GDP (PPP)
		28	Carbon dioxide emissions per capita and consumption of ozone-depleting chlorofluorocarbons (ODP tons)
		29	Proportion of population using solid fuels
Target 10	Halve, by 2015, the proportion of people without sustainable access to safe drinking water and basic sanitation	30	Proportion of population with sustainable access to an improved water source, urban and rural
		31	Proportion of population with access to improved sanitation, urban and rural

Goals and targets from the Millennium Declaration		Indicators for monitoring progress
Target 11	By 2020, to have achieved a significant improvement in the lives of at least 100 million slum dwellers	32 Proportion of households with access to secure tenure
Goal 8	**Develop a global partnership for development**	
Target 12	Develop further an open, rule-based, predictable, nondiscriminatory trading and financial system Includes a commitment to good governance, development and poverty reduction—both nationally and internationally	Some of the indicators listed below are monitored separately for the least developed countries (LDCs), Africa, landlocked countries and small island developing states. **Official development assistance (ODA)** 33 Net ODA, total and to the least developed countries, as a percentage of OECD/DAC donors' gross national income 34 Proportion of total bilateral, sector-allocable ODA of OECD/DAC donors to basic social services (basic education, primary healthcare, nutrition, safe water and sanitation) 35 Proportion of bilateral official development assistance of OECD/DAC donors that is untied 36 ODA received in landlocked countries as a proportion of their gross national incomes 37 ODA received in small island developing states as proportion of their gross national incomes **Market access** 38 Proportion of total developed country imports (by value and excluding arms) from developing countries and from the least developed countries, admitted free of duty 39 Average tariffs imposed by developed countries on agricultural products and textiles and clothing from developing countries 40 Agricultural support estimate for OECD countries as a percentage of their gross domestic product 41 Proportion of ODA provided to help build trade capacity **Debt sustainability** 42 Total number of countries that have reached their HIPC decision points and number that have reached their HIPC completion points (cumulative) 43 Debt relief committed under HIPC Debt Initiative 44 Debt service as a percentage of exports of goods and services
Target 13	Address the special needs of the least developed countries Includes tariff and quota free access for the least developed countries' exports; enhanced programme of debt relief for heavily indebted poor countries (HIPC) and cancellation of official bilateral debt; and more generous ODA for countries committed to poverty reduction	
Target 14	Address the special needs of landlocked countries and small island developing states (through the Programme of Action for the Sustainable Development of Small Island Developing States and the outcome of the 22nd special session of the General Assembly)	
Target 15	Deal comprehensively with the debt problems of developing countries through national and international measures in order to make debt sustainable in the long term	
Target 16	In cooperation with developing countries, develop and implement strategies for decent and productive work for youth	45 Unemployment rate of 15- to 24-year-olds, male and female and total[f]
Target 17	In cooperation with pharmaceutical companies, provide access to affordable essential drugs in developing countries	46 Proportion of population with access to affordable essential drugs on a sustainable basis
Target 18	In cooperation with the private sector, make available the benefits of new technologies, especially information and communications	47 Telephone lines and cellular subscribers per 100 people 48a Personal computers in use per 100 people 48b Internet users per 100 people

Note: Goals, targets, and indicators effective September 8, 2003.
a. For monitoring country poverty trends, indicators based on national poverty lines should be used, where available. b. An alternative indicator under development is "primary completion rate." c. Among contraceptive methods, only condoms are effective in preventing HIV transmission. Since the condom use rate is only measured among women in union, it is supplemented by an indicator on condom use in high-risk situations (indicator 19a) and an indicator on HIV/AIDS knowledge (indicator 19b). Indicator 19c (contraceptive prevalence rate) is also useful in tracking progress in other health, gender, and poverty goals. d. This indicator is defined as the percentage of 15- to 24-year-olds who correctly identify the two major ways of preventing the sexual transmission of HIV (using condoms and limiting sex to one faithful, uninfected partner), who reject the two most common local misconceptions about HIV transmission, and who know that a healthy-looking person can transmit HIV. However, since there are currently not a sufficient number of surveys to be able to calculate the indicator as defined above, UNICEF, in collaboration with UNAIDS and WHO, produced two proxy indicators that represent two components of the actual indicator. They are the percentage of women and men ages 15–24 who know that a person can protect herself from HIV infection by "consistent use of condom," and the percentage of women and men ages 15–24 who know a healthy-looking person can transmit HIV. e. Prevention to be measured by the percentage of children under age five sleeping under insecticide-treated bednets; treatment to be measured by percentage of children under age five who are appropriately treated. f. An improved measure of the target for future years is under development by the International Labour Organization.

1.1 Size of the economy

	Population	Surface area	Population density	Gross national income		Gross national income per capita		PPP gross national income[a]			Gross domestic product	
	millions	thousand sq. km	people per sq. km	$ billions	Rank	$	Rank	$ billions	Per capita $	Rank	% growth	Per capita % growth
	2005	2005	2005	2005[b]	2005	2005[b]	2005	2005	2005	2005	2004–05	2004–05
Afghanistan	..	652	..	7.0	114	..[c]	..	..	..	..	14.0	..
Albania	3	29	114	8.0	109	2,570	115	17.0	5,420	121	5.5	4.9
Algeria	33	2,382	14	89.6	49	2,730	108	222.4[d]	6,770[d]	103	5.3	3.7
Angola	16	1,247	13	22.5	80	1,410	134	35.2[d]	2,210[d]	160	20.6	17.2
Argentina	39	2,780	14	173.1	34	4,470	89	539.4	13,920	64	9.2	8.1
Armenia	3	30	107	4.4	137	1,470	132	15.3	5,060	127	14.0	14.4
Australia	20	7,741	3	673.2	13	33,120	20	622.3	30,610	21	2.8	1.6
Austria	8	84	100	306.2	21	37,190	16	272.9	33,140	12	1.8	1.1
Azerbaijan	8	87	101	10.4	102	1,240	142	41.0	4,890	130	26.2	25.0
Bangladesh	142	144	1,090	66.7	55	470	175	296.4	2,090	165	6.0	4.0
Belarus	10	208	47	27.0	69	2,760	107	77.1	7,890	95	9.2	9.8
Belgium	10	31	347	378.7	18	36,140	17	342.0	32,640	14	1.2	0.7
Benin	8	113	76	4.3	138	510	173	9.4	1,110	189	3.9	0.7
Bolivia	9	1,099	8	9.3	105	1,010	148	25.2	2,740	151	4.1	2.1
Bosnia and Herzegovina	4	51	76	10.5	101	2,700	111	30.4	7,790	96	5.0	5.1
Botswana	2	582	3	9.9	104	5,590	77	18.1	10,250	80	6.2	6.4
Brazil	186	8,515	22	662.0	14	3,550[e]	96	1,534.1	8,230	89	2.3	0.9
Bulgaria	8	111	71	26.7	70	3,450	98	66.8	8,630	86	5.5	6.1
Burkina Faso	13	274	48	5.2	131	400	183	16.1[d]	1,220[d]	186	4.8	1.6
Burundi	8	28	294	0.7	188	100	208	4.8[d]	640[d]	208	0.9	–2.6
Cambodia	14	181	80	6.1	121	430	180	35.0[d]	2,490[d]	154	13.4	11.2
Cameroon	16	475	35	16.4	86	1,000	150	35.1	2,150	162	2.0	0.3
Canada	32	9,985	4	1,052.6	9	32,590	21	1,040.7	32,220	16	2.9	1.9
Central African Republic	4	623	6	1.4	168	350	186	4.6[d]	1,140[d]	188	2.2	0.9
Chad	10	1,284	8	3.9	143	400	183	14.3[d]	1,470[d]	182	5.6	2.3
Chile	16	757	22	95.7	47	5,870	76	186.9	11,470	76	6.3	5.2
China	1,305	9,634[f]	140	2,269.7	5	1,740	128	8,609.7[g]	6,600[g]	107	10.2	9.5
Hong Kong, China	7	1	6,664	192.1	30	27,670	29	240.7	34,670	9	7.3	6.3
Colombia	46	1,139	41	104.5	45	2,290	123	338.4[d]	7,420[d]	98	5.1	3.5
Congo, Dem. Rep.	58	2,345	25	7.0	115	120	207	41.4[d]	720[d]	204	6.5	3.4
Congo, Rep.	4	342	12	3.8	144	950	151	3.2	810	200	9.2	6.0
Costa Rica	4	51	85	20.3	82	4,700	87	41.9[d]	9,680[d]	83	5.9	4.1
Côte d'Ivoire	18	322	57	15.7	87	870	156	27.0	1,490	181	1.8	0.2
Croatia	4	57	79	36.9	61	8,290	65	56.7	12,750	69	4.3	4.3
Cuba	11	111	103	..	..	..[h]	..	..	..	..	5.4	5.2
Czech Republic	10	79	132	114.8	41	11,220[i]	56	206.1	20,140	49	6.1	5.8
Denmark	5	43	128	261.8	26	48,330	6	181.8	33,570	11	3.1	2.8
Dominican Republic	9	49	184	21.9	81	2,460	117	63.6[d]	7,150[d]	101	9.3	7.7
Ecuador	13	284	48	34.7	63	2,620	113	53.8	4,070	138	4.7	3.3
Egypt, Arab Rep.	74	1,001	74	93.0	48	1,260	140	328.7	4,440	133	4.9	3.0
El Salvador	7	21	332	16.8	85	2,450	119	35.2[d]	5,120[d]	125	2.8	1.0
Eritrea	4	118	44	0.8	187	170	201	4.4[d]	1,010[d]	192	0.5	–3.4
Estonia	1	45	32	12.2	98	9,060	63	20.8	15,420	60	9.8	10.0
Ethiopia	71	1,104	71	11.1	99	160	202	71.3[d]	1,000[d]	193	8.7	6.8
Finland	5	338	17	196.9	29	37,530	14	163.5	31,170	20	2.1	1.7
France	61	552	111	2,169.2[j]	6	34,600[j]	19	1,859.1	30,540	22	1.2	0.6
Gabon	1	268	5	6.9	116	5,010	81	8.2	5,890	115	2.2	0.6
Gambia, The	2	11	152	0.4	192	290	192	2.9[d]	1,920[d]	172	5.0	2.3
Georgia	4	70	64	5.9	124	1,320	137	14.6	3,270	147	9.3	10.3
Germany	82	357	236	2,875.6	3	34,870	18	2,408.9	29,210	27	1.0	1.0
Ghana	22	239	97	10.0	103	450	176	52.4[d]	2,370[d]	155	5.9	3.8
Greece	11	132	86	220.3	28	19,840	38	262.3	23,620	41	3.7	3.3
Guatemala	13	109	116	30.3	66	2,400	120	55.6[d]	4,410[d]	134	3.2	0.8
Guinea	9	246	38	3.9	140	420	182	21.1	2,240	158	3.3	1.1
Guinea-Bissau	2	36	56	0.3	201	180	200	1.1[d]	700[d]	206	3.5	0.5
Haiti	9	28	309	3.9	142	450	176	15.7[d]	1,840[d]	175	2.0	0.5

Size of the economy 1.1

	Population millions 2005	Surface area thousand sq. km 2005	Population density people per sq. km 2005	Gross national income $ billions 2005[b]	Gross national income Rank 2005	Gross national income per capita $ 2005[b]	Gross national income per capita Rank 2005	PPP gross national income[a] $ billions 2005	PPP gross national income[a] Per capita $ 2005	PPP gross national income[a] Rank 2005	Gross domestic product % growth 2004–05	Gross domestic product Per capita % growth 2004–05
Honduras	7	112	64	8.0	110	1,120	145	20.9[d]	2,900[d]	150	4.0	1.8
Hungary	10	93	113	101.6	46	10,070	59	170.9	16,940	56	4.1	4.3
India	1,095	3,287	368	804.1	10	730	158	3,787.3[d]	3,460[d]	143	9.2	7.7
Indonesia	221	1,905	122	282.2	23	1,280	139	820.5	3,720	140	5.6	4.2
Iran, Islamic Rep.	68	1,648	42	177.3	32	2,600	114	549.4	8,050	91	4.4	2.9
Iraq	..	438	..	..	..	..[h]	..	..	..	..	*46.5*	..
Ireland	4	70	60	171.1	35	41,140	9	144.4	34,720	8	5.5	3.2
Israel	7	22	320	128.7	36	18,580	43	175.0	25,280	37	5.2	3.3
Italy	59	301	199	1,772.9	7	30,250	26	1,690.2	28,840	28	0.0	–0.8
Jamaica	3	11	245	9.0	106	3,390	99	10.9	4,110	137	1.8	1.3
Japan	128	378	351	4,976.5	2	38,950	12	4,013.4	31,410	18	2.6	2.6
Jordan	5	89	62	13.5	94	2,460	117	28.9	5,280	123	7.3	4.8
Kazakhstan	15	2,725	6	44.6	59	2,940	103	117.1	7,730	97	9.7	8.7
Kenya	34	580	60	18.4	83	540	171	40.1	1,170	187	5.8	3.4
Korea, Dem. Rep.	22	121	187	..	..	..[c]	..	..	..	..	..	..
Korea, Rep.	48	99	489	765.0	11	15,840	49	1,055.2	21,850	45	4.0	3.5
Kuwait	3	18	142	77.7	51	30,630	25	*59.1*[d]	*24,010*[d]	36	8.5	5.3
Kyrgyz Republic	5	200	27	2.3	157	450	176	9.6	1,870	174	–0.6	–1.6
Lao PDR	6	237	26	2.6	154	430	180	12.0	2,020	166	7.0	4.6
Latvia	2	65	37	15.6	88	6,770	74	31.0	13,480	67	10.2	10.8
Lebanon	4	10	350	22.6	79	6,320	75	20.5	5,740	118	1.0	0.0
Lesotho	2	30	59	1.7	165	950	151	6.1[d]	3,410[d]	144	1.2	1.4
Liberia	3	111	34	0.4	193	130	206	..	..	..	5.3	3.9
Libya	6	1,760	3	32.4	64	5,530	78	..	..	..	3.5	1.5
Lithuania	3	65	54	24.6	76	7,210	72	48.6	14,220	62	7.5	8.1
Macedonia, FYR	2	26	80	5.8	126	2,830	106	14.4	7,080	102	4.0	3.8
Madagascar	19	587	32	5.4	130	290	192	16.4	880	197	4.6	1.8
Malawi	13	118	137	2.1	161	160	202	8.4	650	207	2.6	0.4
Malaysia	25	330	77	125.9	38	4,970	82	261.6	10,320	79	5.2	3.3
Mali	14	1,240	11	5.2	132	380	185	13.5	1,000	193	6.1	3.0
Mauritania	3	1,026	3	1.8	163	580	169	6.6[d]	2,150[d]	162	5.4	2.4
Mauritius	1	2	612	6.5	118	5,250	79	15.5	12,450	71	4.6	3.7
Mexico	103	1,958	54	753.4	12	7,310	71	1,034.0	10,030	81	3.0	1.9
Moldova	4	34	128	3.2[k]	148	930[k]	154	9.0	2,150	162	7.1	7.4
Mongolia	3	1,567	2	1.8	164	690	160	5.6	2,190	161	6.2	4.6
Morocco	30	447	68	52.6	56	1,740	128	131.5	4,360	135	1.7	0.6
Mozambique	20	802	25	6.2	119	310	191	25.1[d]	1,270[d]	184	7.7	5.7
Myanmar	51	677	77	..	..	..[c]	..	..	..	..	5.0	3.9
Namibia	2	824	2	6.1	122	2,990	102	16.1[d]	7,910[d]	93	3.5	2.4
Nepal	27	147	190	7.3	113	270	195	41.5	1,530	179	2.7	0.7
Netherlands	16	42	482	642.0	15	39,340	11	530.1	32,480	15	1.1	0.9
New Zealand	4	271	15	106.3	44	25,920	32	94.4	23,030	42	1.9	1.0
Nicaragua	5	130	42	4.9	133	950	151	18.8[d]	3,650[d]	141	4.0	3.4
Niger	14	1,267	11	3.3	146	240	196	11.2[d]	800[d]	201	4.5	1.1
Nigeria	132	924	144	74.0	52	560	170	136.8	1,040	191	6.9	4.7
Norway	5	324	15	281.5	24	60,890	2	186.9	40,420	4	2.3	1.6
Oman	3	310	8	*23.0*	..	*9,070*	..	*37.2*	*14,680*	..	*3.1*	*2.2*
Pakistan	156	796	202	107.3	43	690	160	366.1	2,350	157	7.8	5.2
Panama	3	76	43	15.0	90	4,630	88	23.6	7,310	99	6.4	4.5
Papua New Guinea	6	463	13	*2.8*	141	*500*	162	14.0[d]	2,370[d]	155	3.3	1.3
Paraguay	6	407	15	6.1	120	1,040	146	29.3[d]	4,970[d]	129	2.9	1.0
Peru	28	1,285	22	74.0	53	2,650	112	163.1	5,830	117	6.4	4.9
Philippines	83	300	279	109.7	42	1,320	137	440.2	5,300	122	5.0	3.2
Poland	38	313	125	273.1	25	7,160	73	514.9	13,490	66	3.4	3.4
Portugal	11	92	115	181.3	31	17,190	47	208.1	19,730	50	0.4	–0.1
Puerto Rico	4	9	441	..	..	..[l]	..	..	..	..	..	..

1.1 Size of the economy

	Population	Surface area	Population density	Gross national income		Gross national income per capita		PPP gross national income[a]			Gross domestic product	
	millions	thousand sq. km	people per sq. km	$ billions	Rank	$	Rank	$ billions	Per capita $	Rank	% growth	Per capita % growth
	2005	2005	2005	2005[b]	2005	2005[b]	2005	2005	2005	2005	2004–05	2004–05
Romania	22	238	94	84.6	50	3,910	93	193.4	8,940	85	4.1	4.3
Russian Federation	143	17,098	9	638.1	16	4,460	90	1,522.7	10,640	78	6.4	6.9
Rwanda	9	26	366	2.1	160	230	197	11.9[d]	1,320[d]	183	6.0	4.2
Saudi Arabia	23	2,000[m]	12	289.2	22	12,510	55	340.8[d]	14,740[d]	61	6.6	3.8
Senegal	12	197	61	8.2	107	700	159	20.6	1,770	176	5.1	2.7
Serbia and Montenegro	8	102	79	26.3[n]	72	3,220[n]	100	..	..	..	4.7	5.0
Sierra Leone	6	72	77	1.2	174	220	199	4.3	780	202	7.5	3.8
Singapore	4	1	6,302	119.8	39	27,580	30	129.3	29,780	24	6.4	3.9
Slovak Republic	5	49	112	42.8	60	7,950	68	84.9	15,760	58	6.0	5.9
Slovenia	2	20	99	34.9	62	17,440	45	44.3	22,160	44	4.0	3.8
Somalia	8	638	13	..	..	..[c]	..	..	..	..	..	..
South Africa	47	1,219	39	223.5	27	4,770	85	568.3[d]	12,120[d]	73	4.9	3.7
Spain	43	505	87	1,095.9	8	25,250	34	1,120.5	25,820	33	3.4	1.7
Sri Lanka	20	66	304	22.8	78	1,160	144	88.7	4,520	132	5.3	4.4
Sudan	36	2,506	15	23.1	77	640	164	72.5[d]	2,000[d]	169	8.0	5.9
Swaziland	1	17	66	2.6	153	2,280	124	5.9	5,190	124	1.8	0.8
Sweden	9	450	22	369.1	19	40,910	10	283.5	31,420	17	2.7	2.3
Switzerland	7	41	186	411.4	17	55,320	3	275.8	37,080	5	1.9	1.2
Syrian Arab Republic	19	185	104	26.3	71	1,380	136	71.2	3,740	139	5.1	2.5
Tajikistan	7	143	46	2.2	158	330	190	8.2	1,260	185	7.5	6.2
Tanzania	38	945	43	12.7[o]	96	340[o]	189	28.0	730	203	7.0	5.0
Thailand	64	513	126	175.0	33	2,720	110	542.1	8,440	87	4.5	3.6
Togo	6	57	113	2.2	159	350	186	9.5[d]	1,550[d]	178	2.8	0.2
Trinidad and Tobago	1	5	254	13.4	95	10,300	58	17.2	13,170	68	7.0	6.7
Tunisia	10	164	65	28.8	68	2,880	105	79.2	7,900	94	4.2	3.2
Turkey	72	784	94	342.0	20	4,750	86	606.8	8,420	88	7.4	6.0
Turkmenistan	5	488	10	..	..	..[h]	..	..	..	..	..	..
Uganda	29	241	146	8.0	111	280	194	43.2[d]	1,500[d]	180	6.6	2.9
Ukraine	47	604	81	71.7	54	1,520	131	316.3	6,720	105	2.6	3.4
United Arab Emirates	5	84	54	*103.5*	..	*23,950*	..	*104.1*[d]	*24,090*[d]	..	8.5	3.4
United Kingdom	60	244	249	2,272.7	4	37,740	13	1,968.8	32,690	13	1.8	1.2
United States	296	9,629	32	12,912.9	1	43,560	7	12,434.4	41,950	3	3.2	2.2
Uruguay	3	176	20	15.1	89	4,360	91	34.0	9,810	82	6.6	5.8
Uzbekistan	26	447	62	13.6	93	520	172	52.9	2,020	166	7.0	5.8
Venezuela, RB	27	912	30	128.1	37	4,820	83	171.2	6,440	110	9.3	7.5
Vietnam	83	332	268	51.3	57	620	165	250.2	3,010	149	8.4	7.2
West Bank and Gaza	4	6	602	4.5	136	1,230	143	..	..	..	6.3	2.8
Yemen, Rep.	21	528	40	12.6	97	600	167	19.3	920	196	2.6	–0.6
Zambia	12	753	16	5.8	125	500	174	11.1	950	195	5.2	3.5
Zimbabwe	13	391	34	4.5	135	350	186	25.2	1,940	171	–6.5	–7.0
World	**6,438 s**	**133,841 s**	**50 w**	**45,135.2 t**		**7,011 w**		**60,669.6 t**	**9,424 w**		**3.5 w**	**2.3 w**
Low income	2,352	29,265	83	1,377.2		585		5,848.6	2,486		8.0	6.1
Middle income	3,074	70,081	45	8,137.8		2,647		22,133.7	7,199		6.4	5.5
Lower middle income	2,475	39,946	63	4,759.9		1,923		15,624.3	6,314		7.0	6.0
Upper middle income	600	30,135	21	3,379.3		5,634		6,557.0	10,931		5.5	4.9
Low & middle income	5,427	99,346	56	9,514.8		1,753		27,972.5	5,154		6.6	5.3
East Asia & Pacific	1,885	16,301	119	3,073.0		1,630		11,149.9	5,914		8.9	8.0
Europe & Central Asia	472	24,238	20	1,954.7		4,143		4,317.9	9,152		6.0	5.9
Latin America & Carib.	551	20,418	27	2,227.9		4,045		4,469.9	8,116		4.5	3.1
Middle East & N. Africa	306	8,984	34	672.7		2,198		1,861.9	6,084		4.3	2.4
South Asia	1,470	5,140	307	1,016.9		692		4,618.6	3,142		8.7	6.9
Sub-Saharan Africa	743	24,265	31	554.4		746		1,489.4	2,004		5.7	3.4
High income	1,011	34,595	31	35,643.4		35,264		32,899.9	32,550		2.7	1.9
Europe EMU	314	2,506	128	10,075.3		32,098		9,076.2	28,915		1.3	0.7

a. PPP is purchasing power parity; see *Definitions*. b. Calculated using the *World Bank Atlas* method. c. Estimated to be low-income ($875 or less). d. Based on regression; others are extrapolated from the latest International Comparison Program benchmark estimates. e. Included in the aggregates for lower middle-income economies based on earlier data. f. Includes Taiwan, China; Macao, China; and Hong Kong, China. g. Based on a 1986 bilateral comparison between China and the United States (Ruoen and Kai 1995) employing a different methodology than that used for other countries. This interim methodology will be revised in the next few years. h. Estimated to be lower middle-income ($876–$3,465). i. Included in the aggregates for upper middle-income economies based on earlier data. j. Includes the French overseas departments of French Guiana, Guadeloupe, Martinique, and Réunion. k. Excludes data for Transnistria. l. Estimated to be high-income ($10,726 or more). m. Provisional estimate. n. Excludes data for Kosovo. o. Data are for mainland Tanzania only.

About the data

Population, land area, income, output, and growth in output are basic measures of the size of an economy. They also provide a broad indication of actual and potential resources. Population, land area, income (as measured by gross national income, GNI) and output (as measured by gross domestic product, GDP) are therefore used throughout *World Development Indicators* to normalize other indicators.

Population estimates are generally based on extrapolations from the most recent national census. For further discussion of the measurement of population and population growth, see *About the data* for table 2.1 and *Statistical methods*.

The surface area of an economy includes inland bodies of water and some coastal waterways. Surface area thus differs from land area, which excludes bodies of water, and from gross area, which may include offshore territorial waters. Land area is particularly important for understanding an economy's agricultural capacity and the environmental effects of human activity. (For measures of land area and data on rural population density, land use, and agricultural productivity, see tables 3.1–3.3.) Innovations in satellite mapping and computer databases have resulted in more precise measurements of land and water areas.

Developing countries produce slightly less than half the world's output 1.1a

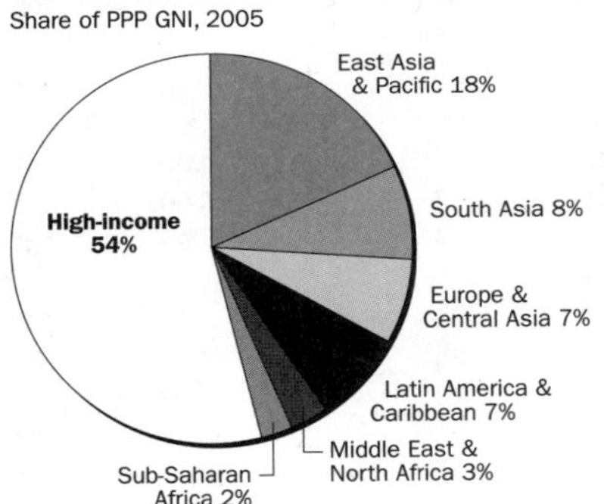

When measured by purchasing power parities (PPPs), which take into account national differences in the cost of living, developing countries produce a large part of the world's output. Much of this is in the form of nontradable goods and services, which are undervalued at market exchange rates. For this reason PPPs are used in international comparisons of well-being such as $1 and $2 a day measures of absolute poverty.

Source: World Bank staff estimates.

GNI measures the total domestic and foreign value added claimed by residents. GNI comprises GDP plus net receipts of primary income (compensation of employees and property income) from nonresident sources. The World Bank uses GNI per capita in U.S. dollars to classify countries for analytical purposes and to determine borrowing eligibility. For definitions of the income groups in *World Development Indicators*, see *Users guide*. For discussion of the usefulness of national income and output as measures of productivity or welfare, see *About the data* for tables 4.1 and 4.2.

When calculating GNI in U.S. dollars from GNI reported in national currencies, the World Bank follows its *Atlas* conversion method, using a three-year average of exchange rates to smooth the effects of transitory fluctuations in exchange rates. (For further discussion of the *Atlas* method, see *Statistical methods*.) GDP and GDP per capita growth rates are calculated from data in constant prices and national currency units.

Because exchange rates do not always reflect differences in price levels between countries, this table also converts GNI and GNI per capita estimates into international dollars using purchasing power parity (PPP) rates. PPP rates provide a standard measure allowing comparison of real levels of expenditure between countries, just as conventional price indexes allow comparison of real values over time. The PPP conversion factors used here are derived from price surveys covering 118 countries conducted by the International Comparison Program. For Organisation for Economic Co-operation and Development (OECD) countries data come from the most recent round of surveys, completed in 2002; the rest are from either the 1996 or the 1993 survey or earlier round and extrapolated to the 1996 benchmark. Estimates for countries not included in the surveys are derived from statistical models using available data.

All 208 economies shown in *World Development Indicators* are ranked by size, including those that appear in table 1.6. The ranks are shown only in table 1.1. No rank is shown for economies for which numerical estimates of GNI per capita are not published. Economies with missing data are included in the ranking at their approximate level, so that the relative order of other economies remains consistent.

Definitions

• **Population** is based on the de facto definition of population, which counts all residents regardless of legal status or citizenship—except for refugees not permanently settled in the country of asylum, who are generally considered part of the population of their country of origin. The values shown are midyear estimates for 2005. See also table 2.1. • **Surface area** is a country's total area, including areas under inland bodies of water and some coastal waterways. • **Population density** is midyear population divided by land area in square kilometers. • **Gross national income (GNI)** is the sum of value added by all resident producers plus any product taxes (less subsidies) not included in the valuation of output plus net receipts of primary income (compensation of employees and property income) from abroad. Data are in current U.S. dollars converted using the World Bank *Atlas* method (see *Statistical methods*). • **GNI per capita** is gross national income divided by midyear population. GNI per capita in U.S. dollars is converted using the *World Bank Atlas* method. • **PPP GNI** is gross national income converted to international dollars using purchasing power parity rates. An international dollar has the same purchasing power over GNI as a U.S. dollar has in the United States. • **Gross domestic product (GDP)** is the sum of value added by all resident producers plus any product taxes (less subsidies) not included in the valuation of output. Growth is calculated from constant price GDP data in local currency. • **GDP per capita** is gross domestic product divided by midyear population.

Data sources

Population estimates are prepared by World Bank staff from a variety of sources (see *Data sources* for table 2.1). Data on surface and land area are from the Food and Agriculture Organization (see *Data sources* for table 3.1). GNI, GNI per capita, GDP growth, and GDP per capita growth are estimated by World Bank staff based on national accounts data collected by World Bank staff during economic missions or reported by national statistical offices to other international organizations such as the OECD. Purchasing power parity conversion factors are estimates by World Bank staff based on data collected by the International Comparison Program.

1.2 Millennium Development Goals: eradicating poverty and improving lives

	Eradicate extreme poverty and hunger			Achieve universal primary education		Promote gender equality		Reduce child mortality		Improve maternal health		
	Share of poorest quintile in national consumption or income %	Prevalence of child malnutrition Underweight % of children under age 5		Primary completion rate[a] %		Ratio of female to male enrollments in primary and secondary school[a] %		Under-five mortality rate per 1,000		Maternal mortality ratio Modeled estimates per 100,000 live births	Births attended by skilled health staff % of total	
	1993–2005[b,c]	1990–95[b]	2000–05[b]	1991	2005[d]	1991	2005[d]	1990	2005[d]	2000	1990–95[b]	2000–05[b]
Afghanistan	..	..	39	*25*	32	..	55	..	..	1,900	..	14
Albania	8.2	..	14	..	*97*	96	*99*	45	18	55	..	98
Algeria	7.0	13	10	79	96	..	102	69	39	140	77	96
Angola	..	31	35	..	..	..	260	260	1,700	..	45	
Argentina	3.1[e]	2	4[f]	..	*100*	..	*111*	29	18	82	96	95
Armenia	8.5	..	3	*90*	91	..	108	54	29	55	..	98
Australia	5.9	..	..	..	..	103	*102*	10	6	8	100	99
Austria	8.6	..	..	..	..	94	*102*	10	5	4	100	..
Azerbaijan	7.4	..	7	..	94	96	98	105	89	94	..	88
Bangladesh	9.0	68	48	*49*	*77*	..	101	149	73	380	10	13
Belarus	8.5	..	..	95	100	..	105	19	12	35	..	100
Belgium	8.5	..	..	79	..	100	*103*	10	5	10	..	..
Benin	7.4	..	30	21	65	49	73	185	150	850	..	75
Bolivia	1.5	15	8	..	*101*	..	*93*	125	65	420	47	67
Bosnia and Herzegovina	9.5	..	4	..	..	..	..	22	15	31	97	100
Botswana	3.2	..	13	83	92	108	102	58	120	100	..	94
Brazil	2.8	..	..	*93*	*108*	..	*105*	60	33	260	72	97
Bulgaria	8.7	..	..	85	*98*	100	*100*	19	15	32	..	99
Burkina Faso	6.9	33	38	21	31	61	77	210	191	1,000	42	38
Burundi	5.1	..	45	46	36	81	83	190	190	1,000	..	25
Cambodia	6.8	..	36	..	92	..	87	115	87	450	..	44
Cameroon	5.6	15	18	56	62	..	83	139	149	730	58	62
Canada	7.2	..	..	..	..	106	*106*	8	6	6	98	98
Central African Republic	2.0	23	24	27	23	59	65	168	193	1,100	46	44
Chad	..	..	37	18	32	..	60	201	208	1,100	..	14
Chile	3.8	1	1	..	*95*	..	*98*	21	10	31	100	100
China	4.7	13	8	103	*98*	86	*98*	49	27	56	..	97
Hong Kong, China	5.3	..	..	102	110	..	93	..	..	..	..	100
Colombia	2.5	8	7	70	98	107	104	35	21	130	86	96
Congo, Dem. Rep.	..	34	31	46	*39*	..	73	205	205	990	..	61
Congo, Rep.	..	..	..	54	57	83	89	110	108	510	..	86
Costa Rica	3.5	2	..	79	92	..	*104*	18	12	43	98	99
Côte d'Ivoire	5.2	24	17	43	..	..	*67*	157	195	690	45	68
Croatia	8.3	1	..	*85*	*91*	..	*104*	12	7	8	100	100
Cuba	..	..	4	96	94	109	110	13	7	33	100	100
Czech Republic	10.3	1	..	..	*104*	97	*101*	13	4	9	99	100
Denmark	8.3	..	..	98	99	103	*109*	9	5	5	..	..
Dominican Republic	4.0	10	5	*61*	92	..	*111*	65	31	150	93	99
Ecuador	3.3	..	12	*91*	*101*	..	..	57	25	130	..	75
Egypt, Arab Rep.	8.6	17	9	..	*95*	79	..	104	33	84	46	74
El Salvador	2.7	11	10	41	87	..	100	60	27	150	51	92
Eritrea	..	44	40	*19*	51	..	70	147	78	630	21	28
Estonia	6.7	..	..	*93*	*101*	105	*114*	16	7	63	..	100
Ethiopia	9.1	48	38	*26*	55	68	76	204	127	850	..	6
Finland	9.6	..	..	97	*100*	110	*107*	7	4	6	100	100
France	7.2	..	..	104	..	104	*105*	9	5	17	99	..
Gabon	..	..	12	*58*	*66*	..	..	92	91	420	..	86
Gambia, The	4.8	..	17	*44*	..	..	*97*	151	137	540	44	55
Georgia	5.6	..	..	..	87	101	103	47	45	32	..	92
Germany	8.5	..	..	*100*	*96*	..	..	9	5	8	..	..
Ghana	5.6	27	22	63	72	78	91	122	112	540	44	47
Greece	6.7	..	..	*99*	*102*	98	*105*	11	5	9	..	..
Guatemala	2.9	27	23	..	74	..	91	82	43	240	34	41
Guinea	7.0	27	33	17	55	45	74	234	160	740	31	56
Guinea-Bissau	5.2	..	25	..	..	..	..	253	200	1,100	25	35
Haiti	2.4	28	17	27	..	..	..	150	120	680	20	24

Millennium Development Goals: eradicating poverty and improving lives

1.2

	Eradicate extreme poverty and hunger			Achieve universal primary education		Promote gender equality		Reduce child mortality		Improve maternal health		
	Share of poorest quintile in national consumption or income %	Prevalence of child malnutrition Underweight % of children under age 5		Primary completion rate[a] %		Ratio of female to male enrollments in primary and secondary school[a] %		Under-five mortality rate per 1,000		Maternal mortality ratio Modeled estimates per 100,000 live births	Births attended by skilled health staff % of total	
	1993–2005[b,c]	1990–95[b]	2000–05[b]	1991	2005[d]	1991	2005[d]	1990	2005[d]	2000	1990–95[b]	2000–05[b]
Honduras	3.4	18	17	65	*79*	106	*109*	59	40	110	45	56
Hungary	9.5	..	..	93	*95*	101	*107*	17	8	16	..	100
India	8.9	53	..	68	*89*	69	*87*	123	74	540	34	43
Indonesia	8.4	34	28	91	*101*	..	*97*	91	36	230	37	72
Iran, Islamic Rep.	5.1	16	..	91	96	83	99	72	36	76	..	90
Iraq	..	12	16	*58*	74	..	76	50	..	250	..	72
Ireland	7.4	..	..	..	*101*	103	*103*	9	6	5	..	100
Israel	5.7	..	..	..	*105*	104	*105*	12	6	17	..	..
Italy	6.5	..	..	104	*101*	98	*106*	9	4	5	..	..
Jamaica	5.3	5	4	90	*84*	100	*104*	20	20	87	..	97
Japan	10.6	..	..	101	..	96	*98*	6	4	10	100	..
Jordan	6.7	6	4	72	*97*	104	*102*	40	26	41	87	100
Kazakhstan	7.4	8	..	..	114	..	106	63	73	210	100	..
Kenya	6.0	23	20	..	95	..	*94*	97	120	1,000	45	42
Korea, Dem. Rep.	..	..	24	..	..	..	..	55	55	67	..	97
Korea, Rep.	7.9	..	..	98	104	89	87	9	5	20	98	100
Kuwait	..	..	..	..	100	..	110	16	11	5	..	100
Kyrgyz Republic	8.9	..	7	..	97	..	105	80	67	110	..	99
Lao PDR	8.1	40	40	*43*	76	..	84	163	79	650	..	19
Latvia	6.6	..	..	..	*92*	103	*115*	18	11	42	100	100
Lebanon	..	..	4	..	90	..	104	37	30	150	..	93
Lesotho	1.5	21	18	59	67	121	103	101	132	550	50	55
Liberia	..	..	27	..	..	..	..	235	235	760	..	51
Libya	..	5	..	..	..	..	*106*	41	19	97	94	..
Lithuania	6.8	..	..	*89*	*98*	..	*110*	13	9	13	..	100
Macedonia, FYR	6.1	..	..	*98*	*96*	99	*103*	38	17	23	..	99
Madagascar	4.9	34	42	33	58	97	96	168	119	550	57	51
Malawi	7.0	30	22	28	61	80	*98*	221	125	1,800	55	56
Malaysia	4.4	20	11	91	*94*	..	*109*	22	12	41	..	97
Mali	6.1	..	33	11	38	58	75	250	218	1,200	..	41
Mauritania	6.2	48	32	33	45	65	96	133	125	1,000	40	57
Mauritius	..	15	..	107	97	101	98	23	15	24	98	99
Mexico	4.3	..	..	86	*99*	95	*101*	46	27	83	..	83
Moldova	7.8	..	4	..	92	..	109	35	16	36	..	100
Mongolia	7.5	12	13	..	97	113	116	108	49	110	..	97
Morocco	6.5	10	10	47	80	69	88	89	40	220	40	63
Mozambique	5.4	27	24	27	42	..	*82*	235	145	1,000	..	48
Myanmar	..	43	32	..	79	..	104	130	105	360	..	57
Namibia	1.4	26	24	*78*	75	108	*101*	86	62	300	68	76
Nepal	6.0	49	45[g]	51	76[g]	58	88	145	74	740	7	15
Netherlands	7.6	..	..	..	*100*	95	99	9	5	16	..	..
New Zealand	6.4	..	..	100	..	102	*113*	11	6	7	100	..
Nicaragua	5.6	11	10	44	76	108	103	68	37	230	..	67
Niger	2.6	43	40	17	28	..	72	320	256	1,600	15	16
Nigeria	5.0	39	29	..	82	..	*82*	230	194	800	31	35
Norway	9.6	..	..	100	*101*	104	*109*	9	4	16	..	..
Oman	..	23	..	*74*	93	91	99	32	12	87	91	95
Pakistan	9.3	38	38	..	63	..	75	130	99	500	19	31
Panama	2.5	6	..	*86*	97	..	109	34	24	160	86	93
Papua New Guinea	4.5	..	..	47	*54*	..	*87*	94	74	300	..	41
Paraguay	2.4	4	5	71	*91*	..	*101*	41	23	170	67	77
Peru	3.7	11	7	..	*100*	..	*103*	78	27	410	..	73
Philippines	5.4	30	28	*86*	*97*	104	*106*	62	33	200	53	60
Poland	7.5	..	..	98	*100*	103	*109*	18	7	13	..	100
Portugal	5.8	..	..	95	*104*	105	*108*	14	5	5	..	100
Puerto Rico	..	..	..	..	..	..	..	..	..	25	..	100

1.2 Millennium Development Goals: eradicating poverty and improving lives

	Eradicate extreme poverty and hunger			Achieve universal primary education		Promote gender equality		Reduce child mortality		Improve maternal health		
	Share of poorest quintile in national consumption or income %	Prevalence of child malnutrition Underweight % of children under age 5		Primary completion rate[a] %		Ratio of female to male enrollments in primary and secondary school[a] %		Under-five mortality rate per 1,000		Maternal mortality ratio Modeled estimates per 100,000 live births	Births attended by skilled health staff % of total	
	1993–2005[b,c]	1990–95[b]	2000–05[b]	1991	2005[d]	1991	2005[d]	1990	2005[d]	2000	1990–95[b]	2000–05[b]
Romania	8.1	6	3	96	93	99	105	31	19	49	99	99
Russian Federation	6.1	3	6	93	94	108	110	27	18	67	..	99
Rwanda	5.3	29	23	33	39	..	99	173	203	1,400	26	39
Saudi Arabia	..	15	..	56	85	86	101	44	26	23	..	93
Senegal	6.6	22	23	39	52	..	90	149	119	690	47	58
Serbia and Montenegro	..	2	71	..	..	..	28	15	11	..	92	
Sierra Leone	1.1	29	27	..	..	..	71	302	282	2,000	..	42
Singapore	5.0	..	3	..	..	90	..	8	3	30	..	100
Slovak Republic	8.8	..	..	96	99	..	104	14	8	3	..	99
Slovenia	9.1	..	..	95	102	..	109	10	4	17	100	100
Somalia	..	..	33[g]	..	..	..	..	225	225	1,100	..	25
South Africa	3.5	9	..	75	99	103	101	60	68	230	82	92
Spain	7.0	..	..	..	109	104	107	9	5	4	..	..
Sri Lanka	7.0	33	29	97	..	101	102	32	14	92	94	96
Sudan	..	34	41	41	50	78	89	120	90	590	86	87
Swaziland	4.3	..	10	60	64	94	94	110	160	370	56	74
Sweden	9.1	..	..	96	..	105	112	7	4	2	..	..
Switzerland	7.6	..	..	53	97	92	94	9	5	7	..	..
Syrian Arab Republic	..	13	7	94	111	83	94	39	15	160	77	70
Tajikistan	7.9	..	..	..	102	..	84	115	71	100	..	71
Tanzania	7.3	29	22	61	54	96	95	161	122	1,500	44	43
Thailand	6.3	18	..	..	82	..	101	37	21	44	..	99
Togo	..	..	..	35	65	58	72	152	139	570	..	61
Trinidad and Tobago	..	..	6	100	99	101	104	33	19	160	..	96
Tunisia	6.0	9	4	74	97	84	105	52	24	120	81	90
Turkey	5.3	10	4	90	88	79	84	82	29	70	76	83
Turkmenistan	6.1	..	12	..	..	..	..	97	104	31	..	97
Uganda	5.7	26	23	..	57	81	96	160	136	880	38	39
Ukraine	9.2	..	1	94	114	..	102	26	17	35	..	100
United Arab Emirates	..	14	..	103	76	120	126	15	9	54	99	100
United Kingdom	6.1	..	..	..	..	96	107	10	6	13	..	..
United States	5.4	1	2	..	..	105	109	11	7	17	..	99
Uruguay	5.0[d]	5	..	94	91	..	114	23	15	27	..	99
Uzbekistan	7.2	..	8	..	97	..	96	79	68	24	..	96
Venezuela, RB	3.3	5	4	43	92	..	104	33	21	96	..	95
Vietnam	9.0	45	28	..	94	..	94	53	19	130	..	90
West Bank and Gaza	..	..	5	..	98	..	104	40	23	..	..	97
Yemen, Rep.	7.4	39	46	..	62	..	61	139	102	570	16	27
Zambia	3.6	25	23	..	78	..	92	180	182	750	51	43
Zimbabwe	4.6	16	..	99	80	91	95	80	132	1,100	69	..
World		30 w	.. w	.. w	85 w	.. w	94 w	95 w	75 w	410 w	.. w	63 w
Low income		46	..	60	74	..	87	147	114	684	33	41
Middle income		15	11	93	96	..	99	58	37	150	..	87
Lower middle income		17	12	94	97	90	99	62	39	163	..	86
Upper middle income		7	..	87	95	99	99	41	27	91	..	92
Low & middle income		32	22	79	84	..	93	103	82	450	..	61
East Asia & Pacific		20	15	100	98	..	99	59	33	117	..	87
Europe & Central Asia		..	5	91	92	98	96	48	32	58	..	94
Latin America & Carib.		..	..	83	98	99	102	54	31	194	..	87
Middle East & N. Africa		16	15	77	89	79	99	80	53	183	..	74
South Asia		53	..	76	82	69	87	129	83	564	30	37
Sub-Saharan Africa		32	30	50	58	..	86	185	163	921	..	45
High income		..	..	..	97	100	100	11	7	14	..	..

a. Because of the change from International Standard Classification of Education 1976 (ISCED76) to ISCED97 in 1998, data before 1998 are not fully comparable with data from 1998 onward. b. Data are for the most recent year available. c. See table 2.6 for survey year and whether share is based on income or consumption expenditure. d. Provisional data. e. Urban data. f. Data are for 2005–06. g. Data are for 2005.

Millennium Development Goals: eradicating poverty and improving lives 1.2

About the data

This table and the following two present indicators for 17 of the 18 targets specified by the Millennium Development Goals. Each of the eight goals comprises one or more targets, and each target has associated with it several indicators for monitoring progress toward the target. Most of the targets are set as a value of a specific indicator to be attained by a certain date. In some cases the target value is set relative to a level in 1990. In others it is set at an absolute level. Some of the targets for goals 7 and 8 have not yet been quantified

The indicators in this table relate to goals 1–5. Goal 1 has two targets between 1990 and 2015: to reduce by half the proportion of people whose income is less than $1 a day and to reduce by half the proportion of people who suffer from hunger. Estimates of poverty rates can be found in table 2.6. The indicator shown here, the share of the poorest quintile in national consumption, is a distributional measure. Countries with more unequal distributions of consumption (or income) will have a higher rate of poverty for a given average income. No single indicator captures the concept of suffering from hunger. Child malnutrition is a symptom of inadequate food supply, lack of essential nutrients, illnesses that deplete these nutrients, and undernourished mothers who give birth to underweight children.

Progress toward achieving universal primary education is measured by the primary school completion rate. Because many school systems do not record school completion on a consistent basis, it is estimated from the gross enrollment rate in the final grade of primary school, adjusted for repetition. Official enrollments sometimes differ significantly from actual attendance, and even school systems with high average enrollment ratios may have poor completion rates. Estimates of primary school completion rates are provided by the United Nations Educational, Scientific, and Cultural Organization Institute of Statistics and national sources.

Eliminating gender disparities in education would help to increase the status and capabilities of women. The ratio of girls' to boys' enrollments in primary and secondary school provides an imperfect measure of the relative accessibility of schooling for girls. With a target date of 2005, this is the first of the goals to fall due.

The targets for reducing under-five and maternal mortality are among the most challenging. Although estimates of under-five mortality rates are available at regular intervals for most countries, maternal mortality is difficult to measure, in part because it is relatively rare.

Most of the 48 indicators relating to the Millennium Development Goals can be found in *World Development Indicators*. Table 1.2a shows where to find the indicators for the first five goals. For more information about data collection methods and limitations, see *About the data* for the tables listed there. For information about the indicators for goals 6, 7, and 8, see *About the data* for tables 1.3 and 1.4.

Location of indicators for Millennium Development Goals 1–5 **1.2a**

	Table
Goal 1. Eradicate extreme poverty and hunger	
1. Proportion of population below $1 a day	2.6
2. Poverty gap ratio	2.6
3. Share of poorest quintile in national consumption	1.2, 2.7
4. Prevalence of underweight in children under age five	1.2, 2.17
5. Proportion of population below minimum level of dietary energy consumption	2.17
Goal 2. Achieve universal primary education	
6. Net enrollment ratio	2.10
7. Proportion of pupils starting grade 1 who reach grade 5	2.11
8. Literacy rate of 15- to 24-year-olds	2.12
Goal 3. Promote gender equality and empower women	
9. Ratio of girls to boys in primary, secondary, and tertiary education	1.2*
10. Ratio of literate females to males among 15- to 24-year-olds	2.12*
11. Share of women in wage employment in the nonagricultural sector	1.5, 2.2*
12. Proportion of seats held by women in national parliament	1.5
Goal 4. Reduce child mortality	
13. Under-five mortality rate	1.2, 2.20
14. Infant mortality rate	2.20
15. Proportion of one-year-old children immunized against measles	2.15
Goal 4. Improve maternal health	
16. Maternal mortality ratio	1.2, 2.16
17. Proportion of births attended by skilled health personnel	1.2, 2.16

* Table shows information on related indicators.

Definitions

• **Share of poorest quintile in national consumption or income** is the share of consumption or, in some cases, income that accrues to the poorest 20 percent of the population. • **Prevalence of child malnutrition** is the percentage of children under age five whose weight for age is more than two standard deviations below the median for the international reference population ages 0–59 months. The reference population, adopted by the World Health Organization in 1983, is based on children from the United States, who are assumed to be well nourished. • **Primary completion rate** is the percentage of students completing the last year of primary school. It is calculated as the total number of students in the last grade of primary school, minus the number of repeaters in that grade, divided by the total number of children of official graduation age. • **Ratio of female to male enrollments in primary and secondary school** is the ratio of female to male gross enrollment rate in primary and secondary school. • **Under-five mortality rate** is the probability that a newborn baby will die before reaching age five, if subject to current age-specific mortality rates. The probability is expressed as a rate per 1,000. • **Maternal mortality ratio** is the number of women who die from pregnancy-related causes during pregnancy and childbirth, per 100,000 live births. The data shown here have been collected in various years and adjusted to a common 2000 base year. The values are modeled estimates (see *About the data* for table 2.16). • **Births attended by skilled health staff** are the percentage of deliveries attended by personnel trained to give the necessary supervision, care, and advice to women during pregnancy, labor, and the postpartum period; to conduct deliveries on their own; and to care for newborns.

Data sources

The indicators here and throughout this book have been compiled by World Bank staff from primary and secondary sources. Efforts have been made to harmonize these data series with those published on the United Nations Millennium Development Goals Web site (www.un.org/millenniumgoals), but some differences in timing, sources, and definitions remain.

1.3 Millennium Development Goals: protecting our common environment

	Combat HIV/AIDS and other diseases		Ensure environmental sustainability						Develop a global partnership for development	
	HIV prevalence % of population ages 15–49	Incidence of tuberculosis per 100,000 people	Carbon dioxide emissions per capita metric tons		Access to an improved water source % of population		Access to improved sanitation facilities % of population		Youth unemployment % ages 15–24	Fixed-line and mobile phone subscribers per 1,000 people[a]
	2005	**2005**	**1990**	**2003**	**1990**	**2004**	**1990**	**2004**	**2005**	**2005**
Afghanistan	<0.1	168	0.2	0.0	4	39	3	34	..	44
Albania	..	20	2.2	1.0	96	96	..	91	..	*493*
Algeria	0.1	55	3.0	5.1	94	85	88	92	*43*	494
Angola	3.7	269	0.4	0.6	36	53	29	31	..	75
Argentina	0.6	41	3.4	3.4	94	96	81	91	24	797
Armenia	0.1	71	1.2	1.1	..	92	..	83	..	*260*
Australia	0.1	6	15.9	17.8	100	100	100	100	11	1,470
Austria	0.3	11	7.5	8.7	100	100	100	100	10	1,441
Azerbaijan	<0.1	76	7.5	3.5	68	77	..	54	..	397
Bangladesh	<0.1	227	0.1	0.3	72	74	20	39	*7*	71
Belarus	0.3	62	10.6	6.3	100	100	..	84	..	755
Belgium	0.3	13	10.1	9.9	100	100	100	100	*18*	*1,337*
Benin	1.8	88	0.1	0.3	63	67	12	33	..	98
Bolivia	0.1	211	0.8	0.9	72	85	33	46	..	334
Bosnia and Herzegovina	0.1	52	1.6	4.9	97	97	..	95	..	656
Botswana	24.1	654	1.5	2.3	93	95	38	42	..	541
Brazil	0.5	60	1.4	1.6	83	90	71	75	*18*	*587*
Bulgaria	0.1	39	8.6	5.6	99	99	99	99	22	1,128
Burkina Faso	2.0	223	0.1	0.1	38	61	7	13	..	51
Burundi	3.3	334	0.0	0.0	69	79	44	36	..	*18*
Cambodia	1.6	506	0.0	0.0	..	41	..	17	..	*40*
Cameroon	5.5[b]	174	0.1	0.2	50	66	48	51	..	*102*
Canada	0.3	5	15.0	17.9	100	100	100	100	12	1,080
Central African Republic	10.7	314	0.1	0.1	52	75	23	27	..	27
Chad	3.5	272	0.0	0.0	19	42	7	9	..	*14*
Chile	0.3	15	2.7	3.7	90	95	84	91	17	859
China	0.1[c]	100	2.1	3.2	70	77	23	44	..	570
Hong Kong, China	..	75	4.6	5.6	..	..	..	..	11	1,798
Colombia	0.6	45	1.6	1.3	92	93	82	86	*25*	648
Congo, Dem. Rep.	3.2	356	0.1	0.0	43	46	16	30	..	48
Congo, Rep.	5.3	367	0.5	0.4	..	58	..	27	..	*102*
Costa Rica	0.3	14	0.9	1.5	..	97	..	92	15	575
Côte d'Ivoire	7.1	382	0.4	0.3	69	84	21	37	..	*108*
Croatia	0.1	41	5.1	5.4	100	100	100	100	33	1,097
Cuba	0.1	9	3.0	2.3	..	91	98	98	..	87
Czech Republic	<0.1	10	15.6	11.4	100	100	99	98	19	1,465
Denmark	0.2	7	9.7	10.1	100	100	100	100	9	1,628
Dominican Republic	1.1	91	1.3	2.5	84	95	52	78	..	508
Ecuador	0.3	131	1.6	1.8	73	94	63	89	16	601
Egypt, Arab Rep.	<0.1	25	1.4	2.0	94	98	54	70	*27*	325
El Salvador	0.9	51	0.5	1.0	67	84	51	62	*12*	492
Eritrea	2.4	282	*0.0*	0.2	43	60	7	9	..	18
Estonia	1.3	43	18.1	13.5	100	100	97	97	16	1,402
Ethiopia	..	344	0.1	0.1	23	22	3	13	8	14
Finland	0.1	6	10.3	13.0	100	100	100	100	19	1,401
France	0.4	13	6.4	6.2	100	100	..	..	*23*	1,376
Gabon	7.9	308	6.3	0.9	..	88	..	36	..	498
Gambia, The	2.4	242	0.2	0.2	..	82	..	53	..	192
Georgia	0.2	83	3.2	0.8	80	82	97	94	28	*337*
Germany	0.1	7	12.3	9.8	100	100	100	100	15	1,628
Ghana	2.3	205	0.2	0.4	55	75	15	18	..	143
Greece	0.2	17	7.1	8.7	..	..	..	..	25	1,472
Guatemala	0.9	78	0.6	0.9	79	95	58	86	..	457
Guinea	1.5	236	0.2	0.1	44	50	14	18	..	*20*
Guinea-Bissau	3.8	206	0.2	0.2	..	59	..	35	..	*8*
Haiti	3.8	305	0.1	0.2	47	54	24	30	..	*64*

Millennium Development Goals: protecting our common environment

1.3

	Combat HIV/AIDS and other diseases		Ensure environmental sustainability						Develop a global partnership for development	
	HIV prevalence % of population ages 15–49	Incidence of tuberculosis per 100,000 people	Carbon dioxide emissions per capita metric tons		Access to an improved water source % of population		Access to improved sanitation facilities % of population		Youth unemployment % ages 15–24	Fixed-line and mobile phone subscribers per 1,000 people[a]
	2005	2005	1990	2003	1990	2004	1990	2004	2005	2005
Honduras	1.5	78	0.5	0.9	84	87	50	69	7	246
Hungary	0.1	22	5.8	5.7	99	99	..	95	19	1,257
India	0.9	168	0.8	1.2	70	86	14	33	*11*	128
Indonesia	0.1	239	0.8	1.4	72	77	46	55	..	271
Iran, Islamic Rep.	0.2	23	4.0	5.7	92	94	83	..	23	384
Iraq	..	56	2.6	2.7	83	81	81	79	..	*57*
Ireland	0.2	12	8.7	10.4	..	..	..	..	8	1,501
Israel	..	8	7.1	10.2	100	100	..	..	18	1,544
Italy	0.5	7	6.9	7.7	..	..	..	..	23	1,659
Jamaica	1.5	7	3.3	4.1	92	93	75	80	*28*	1,146
Japan	<0.1	28	8.7	9.6	100	100	100	100	9	1,202
Jordan	..	5	3.2	3.3	97	97	93	93	*30*	*423*
Kazakhstan	0.1	144	17.6	10.7	87	86	72	72	*14*	*350*
Kenya	6.1	641	0.2	0.3	45	61	40	43	..	143
Korea, Dem. Rep.	..	178	12.4	3.5	100	100	..	59	..	*41*
Korea, Rep.	<0.1	96	5.6	9.5	..	92	..	..	10	1,286
Kuwait	..	24	21.3	32.7	..	..	..	..	..	1,140
Kyrgyz Republic	<0.1	121	2.8	1.1	78	77	60	59	*20*	190
Lao PDR	0.1	155	0.1	0.2	..	51	..	30	..	120
Latvia	0.8	63	5.4	2.9	99	99	..	78	13	1,131
Lebanon	0.1	11	3.3	5.4	100	100	..	98	..	554
Lesotho	23.2	696	..	..	..	79	37	37	..	163
Liberia	..	301	0.2	0.1	55	61	39	27	..	..
Libya	..	18	8.7	8.9	71	..	97	97	..	*156*
Lithuania	0.2	63	6.6	3.7	..	..	..	..	16	1,510
Macedonia, FYR	<0.1	30	8.1	5.2	..	..	..	..	63	882
Madagascar	0.5	234	0.1	0.1	40	46	14	32	..	31
Malawi	14.1	409	0.1	0.1	40	73	47	61	..	41
Malaysia	0.5	102	3.1	6.4	98	99	..	94	..	943
Mali	1.7	278	0.0	0.0	34	50	36	46	..	70
Mauritania	0.7	298	1.3	0.9	38	53	31	34	..	256
Mauritius	0.6	62	1.4	2.6	100	100	..	94	26	862
Mexico	0.3	23	4.5	4.1	82	97	58	79	7	650
Moldova	1.1	138	5.5	1.7	..	92	..	68	19	480
Mongolia	<0.1	191	4.7	3.2	63	62	..	59	*20*	279
Morocco	0.1	89	1.0	1.3	75	81	56	73	*17*	455
Mozambique	16.1	447	0.1	0.1	36	43	20	32	..	*40*
Myanmar	1.3	171	0.1	0.2	57	78	24	77	..	13
Namibia	19.6	697	0.0	1.2	57	87	24	25	..	*206*
Nepal	0.5	180	0.0	0.1	70	90	11	35	..	26
Netherlands	0.2	7	9.3	8.7	100	100	100	100	10	1,436
New Zealand	0.1	9	6.8	8.7	97	..	..	..	9	1,283
Nicaragua	0.2	58	0.7	0.8	70	79	45	47	*13*	260
Niger	1.1	164	0.1	0.1	39	46	7	13	..	23
Nigeria	3.9	283	0.5	0.4	49	48	39	44	..	151
Norway	0.1	5	8.3	9.9	100	100	100	100	12	1,489
Oman	..	11	5.6	12.8	80	..	83	..	..	623
Pakistan	0.1	181	0.6	0.8	83	91	37	59	*12*	116
Panama	0.9	45	1.3	1.9	90	90	71	73	23	555
Papua New Guinea	1.8	250	0.6	0.4	39	39	44	44	..	*15*
Paraguay	0.4	68	0.5	0.7	62	86	58	80	..	374
Peru	0.6	172	1.0	1.0	74	83	52	63	21	280
Philippines	<0.1	291	0.7	1.0	87	85	57	72	16	459
Poland	0.1	26	9.1	8.0	..	..	..	..	38	1,073
Portugal	0.4	33	4.3	5.5	..	..	..	..	16	1,486
Puerto Rico	..	5	3.3	0.5	..	..	..	..	23	*974*

1.3 Millennium Development Goals: protecting our common environment

	Combat HIV/AIDS and other diseases		Ensure environmental sustainability						Develop a global partnership for development	
	HIV prevalence % of population ages 15–49	Incidence of tuberculosis per 100,000 people	Carbon dioxide emissions per capita metric tons		Access to an improved water source % of population		Access to improved sanitation facilities % of population		Youth unemployment % ages 15–24	Fixed-line and mobile phone subscribers per 1,000 people[a]
	2005	2005	1990	2003	1990	2004	1990	2004	2005	2005
Romania	0.1	134	6.7	4.2	..	57	..	..	20	820
Russian Federation	1.1	119	15.3	10.3	94	97	87	87	..	1,119
Rwanda	3.1	361	0.1	0.1	59	74	37	42	..	*18*
Saudi Arabia	..	41	12.0	13.7	90	..	..	..	..	740
Senegal	0.9	255	0.4	0.4	65	76	33	57	..	171
Serbia and Montenegro	0.2	*33*	6.2	6.2	93	93	87	87	..	*917*
Sierra Leone	1.6	475	0.1	0.1	..	57	..	39	..	*19*
Singapore	0.3	29	14.8	11.4	100	100	100	100	5	1,435
Slovak Republic	<0.1	17	9.7	7.0	100	100	99	99	30	1,065
Slovenia	<0.1	15	9.0	7.7	..	..	..	..	13	1,287
Somalia	0.9	224	0.0	..	..	29	..	26	..	73
South Africa	18.8	600	8.1	7.9	83	88	69	65	60	825
Spain	<0.1	27	5.5	7.4	100	100	100	100	20	1,374
Sri Lanka	0.1	60	0.2	0.5	68	79	69	91	26	235
Sudan	1.6	228	0.2	0.3	64	70	33	34	..	69
Swaziland	33.4	1,262	0.6	0.9	..	62	..	48	..	208
Sweden	0.2	6	5.8	5.9	100	100	100	100	14	*1,804*
Switzerland	0.4	7	6.4	5.5	100	100	100	100	9	1,609
Syrian Arab Republic	..	37	2.8	2.7	80	93	73	90	*26*	307
Tajikistan	<0.1	198	4.4	0.7	..	59	..	51	..	*46*
Tanzania	7.0[b]	342	0.1	0.1	46	62	47	47	..	*56*
Thailand	1.4	142	1.8	3.9	95	99	80	99	5	*537*
Togo	3.2	373	0.2	0.4	50	52	37	35	..	82
Trinidad and Tobago	2.6	9	13.9	22.1	92	91	100	100	*21*	861
Tunisia	0.1	24	1.6	2.1	81	93	75	85	31	692
Turkey	..	29	2.6	3.1	85	96	85	88	19	868
Turkmenistan	0.1	70	8.7	9.2	..	72	..	62	..	*82*
Uganda	6.4[d]	369	0.0	0.1	44	60	42	43	..	56
Ukraine	1.4	99	13.2	6.6	96	96	96	96	*17*	*545*
United Arab Emirates	..	16	30.8	33.4	100	100	97	98	..	1,273
United Kingdom	..	14	9.9	9.4	100	100	..	..	12	1,616
United States	0.6	5	19.3	19.9	100	100	100	100	11	*1,227*
Uruguay	0.5	28	1.3	1.3	100	100	100	100	30	624
Uzbekistan	0.2	113	6.3	4.8	94	82	51	67	..	*80*
Venezuela, RB	0.7	42	5.9	5.6	..	83	..	68	*28*	606
Vietnam	0.5[e]	175	0.3	0.9	65	85	36	61	*5*	306
West Bank and Gaza	..	21	..	..	..	92	..	73	*40*	398
Yemen, Rep.	..	82	0.8	0.9	71	67	32	43	..	*92*
Zambia	17.0	600	0.3	0.2	50	58	44	55	..	89
Zimbabwe	20.1	601	1.6	0.9	78	81	50	53	*25*	79
World	**1.0 w**	**136 w**	**4.3 w**	**4.3 w**	**77 w**	**83 w**	**45 w**	**57 w**	**.. w**	**523 w**
Low income	1.7	220	0.8	0.8	64	75	21	38	..	114
Middle income	0.6	111	3.5	3.6	78	84	48	62	..	590
Lower middle income	0.3	113	2.4	2.9	76	82	42	57	..	511
Upper middle income	2.2	104	8.1	6.4	90	94	79	84	*25*	901
Low & middle income	1.1	158	2.4	2.4	73	80	37	52	..	382
East Asia & Pacific	0.2	136	1.9	2.7	72	79	30	51	..	496
Europe & Central Asia	0.7	84	10.2	6.9	93	92	86	85	..	898
Latin America & Carib.	0.6	61	2.4	2.4	83	91	67	77	*17*	*496*
Middle East & N. Africa	0.1	43	2.5	3.4	88	89	70	76	..	389
South Asia	0.7	174	0.7	1.0	71	84	17	37	*11*	119
Sub-Saharan Africa	6.2	348	0.8	0.8	49	56	31	37	..	142
High income	0.4	17	11.8	12.8	100	100	100	100	13	1,338

a. Data are from the International Telecommunication Union's (ITU) World Telecommunication Development Report database. b. Survey data, 2004. c. Includes Hong Kong, China. d. Survey data, 2004–05. e. Survey data, 2005.

Millennium Development Goals: protecting our common environment 1.3

About the data

The Millennium Development Goals address issues of common concern to all nations. Diseases and environmental degradation do not respect national boundaries. Epidemic diseases, wherever they persist, pose a threat to people everywhere. And damage to the environment in one location may affect the well-being of plants, animals, and humans far away. The indicators in the table relate to goals 6 and 7 and the targets of goal 8 that address youth employment and access to new technologies. For the other targets of goal 8, see table 1.4.

Measuring the prevalence or incidence of a disease can be difficult. Much of the developing world lacks reporting systems for monitoring diseases. Estimates are often derived from surveys and reports from sentinel sites that must be extrapolated to the general population. Tracking diseases such as HIV/AIDS, which has a long latency between contraction of the virus and the appearance of symptoms, or malaria, which has periods of dormancy, can be particularly difficult. For some of the most serious illnesses international organizations have formed coalitions such as the Joint United Nations Programme on HIV/AIDS and the Roll Back Malaria campaign to gather information and coordinate global efforts to treat victims and prevent the spread of disease.

The models and data used to estimate HIV prevalence depend on the nature of the epidemic in each country. In early stages infections are usually concentrated in high-risk groups for which data are collected from sentinel sites or through targeted surveys. In older, generalized epidemics antenatal clinics are a key site for monitoring HIV and other sexually transmitted diseases. Recently, household surveys have been used to track the disease. The table shows the estimated prevalence among adults ages 15–49. Prevalence rates in the older population can be affected by life-prolonging treatment. The incidence of tuberculosis is based on data on case notifications and estimates of the proportion of cases detected in the population.

Carbon dioxide emissions are the primary source of greenhouse gases, which contribute to global warming.

Access to reliable supplies of safe drinking water and sanitary disposal of excreta are two of the most important means of improving human health and protecting the environment. There is no widespread program for testing the quality of water. The indicator shown here measures the proportion of households with access to an improved source, such as piped water or protected wells. Improved sanitation facilities prevent human, animal, and insect contact with excreta but do not include treatment to render sewage outflows innocuous.

The eighth goal—to develop a global partnership for development—takes note of the need for decent and productive work for youth. Labor market information, such as unemployment rates, is still generally unavailable for most low- and middle-income economies. Fixed telephone lines and mobile phones are among the telecommunications technologies that are changing the way the global economy works.

Location of indicators for Millennium Development Goals 6–7 — 1.3a

		Table
Goal 6. Combat HIV/AIDS, malaria, and other diseases		
18.	HIV prevalence among pregnant women ages 15–24	1.3*, 2.18*
19.	Condom use rate of the contraceptive prevalence rate	—
19a.	Condom use at last high-risk sex	—
19b.	Percentage of 15- to 24-year-olds with comprehensive correct knowledge of HIV/AIDS	—
19c.	Contraceptive prevalence rate	2.16
20.	Ratio of school attendance of orphans to school attendance of nonorphans ages 10–14	—
21.	Prevalence and death rates associated with malaria	—
22.	Proportion of population in malaria-risk areas using effective malaria prevention and treatment measures	2.15*
23.	Prevalence and death rates associated with tuberculosis	1.3*
24.	Proportion of tuberculosis cases detected and cured under DOTS	2.15
Goal 7. Ensure environmental sustainability		
25.	Proportion of land area covered by forest	3.4
26.	Ratio of area protected to maintain biological diversity to surface area	3.4
27.	Energy use (kilograms of oil equivalent) per $1 of GDP (PPP)	3.8
28.	Carbon dioxide emissions per capita and consumption of ozone-depleting chlorofluorocarbons	3.8*
29.	Proportion of population using solid fuels	3.7*
30.	Proportion of population with sustainable access to an improved water source, urban and rural	2.15, 3.5
31.	Proportion of population with access to improved sanitation, urban and rural	2.15, 3.10
32.	Proportion of population with access to secure tenure	3.11

— No data are available in the World Development Indicators database. * Table shows information on related indicators.

Definitions

• **HIV prevalence** is the percentage of people ages 15–49 who are infected with HIV. • **Incidence of tuberculosis** is the estimated number of new tuberculosis cases (pulmonary, smear positive, and extrapulmonary). • **Carbon dioxide emissions** are those stemming from the burning of fossil fuels and the manufacture of cement. They include carbon dioxide produced during consumption of solid, liquid, and gas fuels and gas flaring. • **Access to an improved water source** refers to the percentage of the population with reasonable access to an adequate amount of water from an improved source, such as piped water into a dwelling, plot, or yard; public tap or standpipe; tubewell or borehole; protected dug well or spring; and rainwater collection. Unimproved sources include unprotected dug well or spring, cart with small tank or drum, bottled water, and tanker trucks. Reasonable access is defined as the availability of at least 20 liters a person a day from a source within 1 kilometer of the dwelling. • **Access to improved sanitation facilities** refers to the percentage of the population with at least adequate access to excreta disposal facilities (private or shared, but not public) that can effectively prevent human, animal, and insect contact with excreta. Improved facilities range from simple but protected pit latrines to flush toilets with a sewerage connection. To be effective, facilities must be correctly constructed and properly maintained. • **Youth unemployment** refers to the share of the labor force ages 15–24 without work but available for and seeking employment. Definitions of labor force and unemployment differ by country. • **Fixed-line and mobile phone subscribers** are telephone mainlines connecting a customer's equipment to the public switched telephone network, and users of portable telephones subscribing to an automatic public mobile telephone service using cellular technology that provides access to the public switched telephone network.

Data sources

The indicators here and throughout this book have been compiled by World Bank staff from primary and secondary sources. Efforts have been made to harmonize these data series with those published on the United Nations Millennium Development Goals Web site (www.un.org/millenniumgoals), but some differences in timing, sources, and definitions remain.

1.4 Millennium Development Goals: overcoming obstacles

Development Assistance Committee members

	Official development assistance (ODA) by donor: Net % of donor GNI 2005	Official development assistance (ODA) by donor: For basic social services[a] % of total sector-allocable ODA 2004–05	Least developed countries' access to high-income markets: Goods (excluding arms) admitted free of tariffs % 1998	Goods (excluding arms) admitted free of tariffs % 2004	Average tariff on exports of least developed countries: Agricultural products % 1998	Agricultural products % 2004	Textiles % 1998	Textiles % 2004	Clothing % 1998	Clothing % 2004	Support to agriculture % of GDP 2005
Australia	0.25	10.7	95.4	97.3	0.2	0.4	8.9	0.9	25.4	0.0	0.29
Canada	0.34	30.4	62.9	98.9	0.5	0.2	9.8	0.3	20.5	1.4	0.75
European Union			97.5	96.0	3.4	2.8	0.0	0.2	0.0	1.0	1.14
Austria	0.52	13.9									
Belgium	0.53	16.5									
Denmark	0.81	17.6									
Finland	0.46	13.4									
France	0.47	6.3									
Germany	0.36	12.1									
Greece	0.17	18.8									
Ireland	0.42	32.0									
Italy	0.29	9.4									
Luxembourg	0.82	29.5									
Netherlands	0.82	22.0									
Portugal	0.21	2.7									
Spain	0.27	18.3									
Sweden	0.94	15.2									
United Kingdom	0.47	30.2									
Japan	0.28	4.6	58.0	33.7	7.0	6.7	3.8	1.7	0.5	0.1	1.28
New Zealand[b]	0.27	29.9	94.8	99.2	0.5	0.2	12.8	0.2	18.6	0.2	0.40
Norway[b]	0.94	14.3	90.7	99.1	17.2	3.5	15.6	0.0	16.3	0.0	1.11
Switzerland	0.44	7.2	99.9	99.4	4.1	6.7	0.0	0.0	0.0	0.0	1.68
United States	0.22	18.4	57.7	69.4	4.2	3.5	6.8	5.7	14.4	12.3	0.88

Heavily indebted poor countries (HIPCs)

	HIPC decision point[c]	HIPC completion point[d]	HIPC Inititaive assistance[e] $ millions	MDRI assistance[f] $ millions
Benin	Jul. 2000	Mar. 2003	328	571
Bolivia	Feb. 2000	Jun. 2001	1,663	1,004
Burkina Faso	Jul. 2000	Apr. 2002	672	573
Burundi	Aug. 2005	Floating	826	..
Cameroon	Oct. 2000	Apr. 2006	1,569	707
Chad	May 2001	Floating	202	..
Congo, Dem. Rep.	Jul. 2003	Floating	6,875	..
Congo, Rep.	Apr. 2006	Floating	1,679	..
Ethiopia	Nov. 2001	Apr. 2004	2,284	1,383
Gambia, The	Dec. 2000	Floating	83	..
Ghana	Feb. 2002	Jul. 2004	2,595	1,963
Guinea	Dec. 2000	Floating	676	..
Guinea-Bissau	Dec. 2000	Floating	515	..
Guyana	Nov. 2002	Dec. 2003	732	140
Haiti	Nov. 2006	Floating	..	..
Honduras	Jul. 2000	Apr. 2005	688	733
Madagascar	Dec. 2000	Oct. 2004	1,035	1,219
Malawi	Dec. 2000	Aug. 2006	1,211	618
Mali	Sep. 2000	Mar. 2003	667	985
Mauritania	Feb. 2000	Jun. 2002	770	424
Mozambique	Apr. 2000	Sep. 2001	2,599	1,004
Nicaragua	Dec. 2000	Jan. 2004	4,098	466
Niger	Dec. 2000	Apr.2004	798	489
Rwanda	Dec. 2000	Apr. 2005	814	206
São Tomé & Principe	Dec. 2000	Floating	120	..
Senegal	Jun. 2000	Apr. 2004	605	1,297
Sierra Leone	Mar. 2002	Dec. 2006	683	..
Tanzania	Apr. 2000	Nov. 2001	2,511	1,919
Uganda	Feb. 2000	May 2000	1,282	1,705
Zambia	Dec. 2000	Apr. 2005	3,096	1,522

a. Includes basic health, education, nutrition, and water and sanitation services. b. Estimates of market access to New Zealand and Norway for least developed countries are calculated by World Bank staff using the World Integrated Trade Solution based on the United Nations Conference on Trade and Development's Trade Analysis and Information System database. c. The date refers to the Enhanced Heavily Indebted Poor Countries (HIPC) initiative. The following countries reached their decision point under the original HIPC framework: Bolivia in September 1997, Burkina Faso in September 1997, Côte d'Ivoire in March 1998, Guyana in December 1997, Mali in September 1998, Mozambique in April 1998, and Uganda in April 1997. d. The date refers to the Enhanced HIPC framework. The following countries also reached completion points under the original framework: Bolivia in September 1998, Burkina Faso in July 2000, Guyana in May 1999, Mali in September 2000, Mozambique in July 1999, and Uganda in April 1998. e. HIPC debt relief is committed in net present value (NPV) terms as of the decision point (plus topping-up assistance at completion point in the cases of Burkina Faso, Ethiopia, Niger, and Rwanda) and is converted to end-2005 NPV terms. f. Multilateral Debt Relief Initiative (MDRI) assistance has been delivered in full to all post-completion point countries, shown in end-2005 NPV terms.

About the data

Achieving the Millennium Development Goals will require an open, rule-based global economy in which all countries, rich and poor, participate. Many poor countries, lacking the resources to finance their development, burdened by unsustainable levels of debt, and unable to compete in the global marketplace, need assistance from rich countries. For goal 8—develop a global partnership for development—many of the indicators therefore monitor the actions of members of the Development Assistance Committee (DAC) of the Organisation for Economic Co-operation and Development (OECD).

Official development assistance (ODA) has risen in recent years as a share of donor countries' gross national income (GNI), but the poorest countries will need additional assistance to achieve the Millennium Development Goals. Official aid rose to a record of $106 billion in 2005, and donor countries have pledged to increase ODA to more than $130 billion (in 2004 dollars) by 2010. However, this would still fall short of levels considered necessary to achieve the Millennium Development Goals.

One of the most important actions that high-income economies can take to help is to reduce barriers to the exports of low- and middle-income economies. The European Union has launched a program to eliminate tariffs on developing country exports of "everything but arms," and the United States offers special concessions to exports from Sub-Saharan Africa. However, there are still many restrictions built into these programs.

Average tariffs in the table reflect tariff schedules applied by high-income OECD members to exports of countries designated least developed countries by the United Nations. Agricultural commodities, textiles, and clothing are three of the most important exports of developing economies. Although average tariffs have been falling, averages may disguise high tariffs targeted at specific goods (see table 6.7 for estimates of the share of tariff lines with "international peaks" in each country's tariff schedule). The averages in the table include ad valorem duties and ad valorem equivalents of non-ad valorem duties. Subsidies to agricultural producers and exporters in OECD countries are another form of barrier to developing economies' exports. The table shows the value of total support to agriculture as a share of the economy's gross domestic product (GDP). Agricultural subsidies in OECD economies are estimated at $385 billion in 2005.

The Debt Initiative for Heavily Indebted Poor Countries (HIPCs) is the first comprehensive approach to reducing the external debt of the world's poorest, most heavily indebted countries. It represents an important step in placing debt relief within an overall framework of poverty reduction. A major review in 1999 led to an enhancement of the original framework. The Multilateral Debt Relief Initiative (MDRI), proposed by the Group of Eight countries, was launched in 2005 to further reduce the debt of HIPCs and provide additional resources to help them meet the Millennium Development Goals. Under the MDRI three multilateral institutions—the International Development Association (IDA), International Monetary Fund (IMF), and African Development Fund (AfDF)—provide 100 percent debt relief on eligible debts due to them from countries having completed the HIPC Initiative process. Debt relief under the two initiatives is expected to reduce the debt stocks of the 29 HIPCs that have reached the decision point by almost 90 percent. Debt service paid by these countries declined by about 2 percent of GDP between 1999 and 2005 and is expected to decline further in the medium term as a result of MDRI debt relief. Nineteen of these countries have reached the completion point and have received nearly $29 billion in HIPC Initiative assistance and have received or are expected to receive $18 billion in MDRI assistance.

Location of indicators for Millennium Development Goal 8 — 1.4a

Goal 8. Develop a global partnership for development		Table
33.	Net ODA as a percentage of DAC donors' gross national income	6.9
34.	Proportion of ODA for basic social services	1.4
35.	Proportion of ODA that is untied	6.10
36.	Proportion of ODA received in landlocked countries as a percentage of GNI	—
37.	Proportion of ODA received in small island developing states as a percentage of GNI	—
38.	Proportion of total developed country imports (by value, excluding arms) from developing countries admitted free of duty	1.4
39.	Average tariffs imposed by developed countries on agricultural products and textiles and clothing from developing countries	1.4, 6.7*
40.	Agricultural support estimate for OECD countries as a percentage of GDP	1.4
41.	Proportion of ODA provided to help build trade capacity	—
42.	Number of countries reaching HIPC decision and completion points	1.4
43.	Debt relief committed under new HIPC initiative	1.4
44.	Debt services as a percentage of exports of goods and services	4.17*
45.	Unemployment rate of 15- to 24-year-olds	1.3, 2.8
46.	Proportion of population with access to affordable, essential drugs on a sustainable basis	—
47.	Telephone lines and cellular subscribers per 100 people	1.3, 5.10
48a.	Personal computers in use per 100 people	5.11
48b.	Internet users per 100 people	5.11

— No data are available in the World Development Indicators database. * Table shows information on related indicators.

Definitions

• **Net official development assistance (ODA)** comprises grants and loans (net of repayments of principal) that meet the DAC definition of ODA and are made to countries and territories on the DAC list of recipient countries. • **ODA for basic social services** is aid reported by DAC donors for basic health, education, nutrition, and water and sanitation services. • **Goods admitted free of tariffs** refer to the value of exports of goods (excluding arms) from least developed countries admitted without tariff, as a share of total exports from least developed countries. • **Average tariff** is the simple mean tariff, the unweighted average of the effectively applied rates for all products subject to tariffs.• **Agricultural products** comprise plant and animal products, including tree crops but excluding timber and fish products. • **Textiles** and **clothing** include natural and synthetic fibers and fabrics and articles of clothing made from them. • **Support to agriculture** is the annual monetary value of all gross transfers from taxpayers and consumers arising from policy measures that support agriculture, net of the associated budgetary receipts, regardless of their objectives and impacts on farm production and income, or consumption of farm products. • **HIPC decision point** is the date at which a heavily indebted poor country with an established track record of good performance under adjustment programs supported by the International Monetary Fund and the World Bank commits to undertake additional reforms and to develop and implement a poverty reduction strategy.• **HIPC completion point** is the date at which the country successfully completes the key structural reforms agreed on at the decision point, including developing and implementing its poverty reduction strategy. The country then receives the bulk of debt relief under the HIPC Initiative without further policy conditions. • **HIPC Initiative assistance** is the present value of debt relief committed as of the decision point and measured in end-2005 terms.• **MDRI assistance** is the present value of debt relief under the Multilateral Debt Relief Initiative from IDA, IMF, and AfDB delivered to countries having reached the HIPC completion point and measured in end-2005 terms.

Data sources

The indicators here, and where they appear throughout the rest of the book, are compiled by World Bank staff from primary and secondary sources. Data on ODA and support to agriculture are from the OECD. The World Trade Organization, in collaboration with the United Nations Conference on Trade and Development and the International Trade Centre, provided the estimates of goods admitted free of tariffs and average tariffs. Data on the HIPC Initiative and MDRI are from the August 2006 report "Heavily Indebted Poor Countries (HIPC) Initiative and Multilateral Debt Relief Initiative (MDRI)—Status of Implementation."

1.5 Women in development

	Female population	Life expectancy at birth		Pregnant women receiving prenatal care	Teenage mothers	Women in nonagricultural sector	Unpaid family workers		Women in parliaments	
		years					Male	Female		
	% of total	Male	Female	%	% of women ages 15–19	% of total	% of male employment	% of female employment	% of total seats	
	2005	2005	2005	2000–05[a]	2000–05[a]	2004	2000–05[a]	2000–05[a]	1990	2006
Afghanistan	..	..	..	16	..	..	..	..	4	27
Albania	50.4	73	79	91	..	31.7	..	..	29	7
Algeria	49.5	70	73	81	..	17.0	7.1	13.6	2	6
Angola	50.7	40	43	66	..	..	..	..	15	15
Argentina	51.1	71	79	98	..	45.5	0.8	1.6	6	35
Armenia	53.4	70	76	93	6	46.5	1.1	0.8	36	5
Australia	50.6	78	83	..	..	48.6	0.2	0.4	6	25
Austria	51.1	77	82	..	..	46.2	0.6	1.6	12	32
Azerbaijan	51.5	70	75	70	..	48.8	..	..	..	11
Bangladesh	48.9	63	65	49	33[b]	23.1	9.9	48.0	10	15
Belarus	53.3	63	74	..	..	56.0	..	..	..	29
Belgium	50.9	77	82	..	..	44.8	..	..	9	35
Benin	49.6	54	56	81	22	..	..	..	3	7
Bolivia	50.2	63	67	79	16	36.5	5.2	11.1	9	17
Bosnia and Herzegovina	51.4	72	77	99	..	..	..	..	..	..
Botswana	50.9	35	34	97	..	43.0	1.4	1.2	5	11
Brazil	50.7	67	75	97	..	46.7	5.5	9.3	5	..
Bulgaria	51.6	69	76	..	..	53.0	1.2	2.6	21	22
Burkina Faso	49.7	48	49	73	23	14.6	..	..	..	12
Burundi	51.2	44	46	78	..	..	..	..	..	31
Cambodia	51.7	54	61	38	8	51.3	31.6	53.3	..	10
Cameroon	50.3	46	47	83	28	21.6	9.5	27.2	14	9
Canada	50.4	78	83	..	..	49.4	0.1	0.2	13	21
Central African Republic	51.2	39	40	62	..	..	..	..	4	11
Chad	50.5	43	45	39	37	12.8	..	..	..	7
Chile	50.5	75	81	..	..	38.1	1.4	3.2	..	15
China	48.6	70	74	90	..	40.9	..	..	21	20
Hong Kong, China	52.9	79	85	..	..	47.3	0.2	1.4	..	..
Colombia	50.6	70	76	94	21	48.3	3.5	7.7	5	..
Congo, Dem. Rep.	50.4	43	45	68	..	20.1	..	..	5	8
Congo, Rep.	50.4	52	54	88	..	..	..	..	14	9
Costa Rica	49.2	77	81	92	..	38.5	1.8	3.5	11	39
Côte d'Ivoire	49.2	45	47	88	..	..	..	..	6	9
Croatia	51.9	72	79	..	..	46.2	1.3	4.4	..	22
Cuba	50.0	75	79	100	..	37.7	..	..	34	36
Czech Republic	51.3	73	79	..	..	47.1	0.3	1.3	..	16
Denmark	50.5	76	80	..	..	48.8	0.2	1.3	31	37
Dominican Republic	49.5	65	72	99	23	38.2	..	..	8	20
Ecuador	49.9	72	78	84	..	42.7	3.7	11.0	5	..
Egypt, Arab Rep.	49.9	68	73	70	10	20.6	9.0	25.8	4	2
El Salvador	50.8	68	74	86	..	34.8	7.7	7.7	12	17
Eritrea	50.9	53	57	70	14	..	..	..	..	22
Estonia	54.0	67	78	..	..	52.2	0.5	0.5	..	19
Ethiopia	50.3	42	43	28	17	40.6	5.2	9.9	..	22
Finland	51.0	76	82	..	..	50.7	0.5	0.4	32	38
France	51.3	77	84	..	..	47.2	..	..	7	12
Gabon	50.2	53	54	94	33	..	..	..	13	9
Gambia, The	50.4	55	58	91	..	..	..	..	8	13
Georgia	52.7	68	75	95	..	50.3	19.0	39.0	..	9
Germany	51.2	76	82	..	..	46.6	0.5	1.9	..	32
Ghana	49.4	57	58	92	14	..	..	..	..	11
Greece	50.6	77	82	..	..	40.7	4.3	14.7	7	13
Guatemala	51.3	64	72	84	..	38.8	21.3	24.5	7	8
Guinea	48.8	54	54	82	..	..	..	..	..	19
Guinea-Bissau	50.6	44	47	62	..	..	..	..	20	14
Haiti	50.7	52	53	79	18	..	..	..	..	2

Women in development 1.5

	Female population	Life expectancy at birth		Pregnant women receiving prenatal care	Teenage mothers	Women in nonagricultural sector	Unpaid family workers		Women in parliaments	
		years					Male	Female		
	% of total	Male	Female	%	% of women ages 15–19	% of total	% of male employment	% of female employment	% of total seats	
	2005	2005	2005	2000–05[a]	2000–05[a]	2004	2000–05[a]	2000–05[a]	1990	2006
Honduras	49.6	67	71	83	..	46.8	12.1	8.3	10	23
Hungary	52.4	69	77	..	..	47.0	0.3	0.7	21	10
India	48.7	63	64	..	..	17.3	..	..	5	8
Indonesia	50.1	66	70	92	10	31.1	..	..	12	11
Iran, Islamic Rep.	49.3	70	73	..	..	13.7	..	..	2	4
Iraq	..	..	..	77	..	..	..	..	11	26
Ireland	50.3	77	82	..	..	47.6	0.6	0.9	8	13
Israel	50.5	78	82	..	..	49.6	0.2	0.5	7	14
Italy	51.5	78	83	..	..	41.3	3.0	5.8	13	17
Jamaica	50.6	69	73	98	..	47.0	0.4	2.5	5	12
Japan	51.1	79	86	..	..	41.2	1.5	8.6	1	9
Jordan	48.0	71	74	99	4	25.0	..	..	0	6
Kazakhstan	52.1	61	72	..	..	49.4	1.0	1.3	..	10
Kenya	49.9	50	48	88	23	38.7	..	..	1	7
Korea, Dem. Rep.	50.0	61	67	..	..	..	..	..	21	20
Korea, Rep.	49.9	74	81	..	..	41.6	1.3	14.8	2	13
Kuwait	40.0	75	80	..	..	25.2	..	..	..	2
Kyrgyz Republic	50.8	65	72	..	..	43.8	6.5	15.9	..	0
Lao PDR	50.0	54	57	27	..	..	..	..	6	25
Latvia	54.3	66	77	..	..	53.2	2.5	2.1	..	19
Lebanon	51.0	70	75	96	..	..	..	..	0	5
Lesotho	53.5	34	36	90	..	..	..	..	..	12
Liberia	50.1	42	43	85	..	..	..	..	..	13
Libya	48.4	72	77	..	..	..	..	..	..	8
Lithuania	53.4	65	77	..	..	52.2	2.6	4.4	..	22
Macedonia, FYR	50.1	71	76	81	..	42.3	6.4	12.0	..	28
Madagascar	50.3	55	57	80	34	..	29.7	51.9	7	7
Malawi	50.3	41	40	92	33	12.4	..	..	10	14
Malaysia	49.2	71	76	74	..	36.9	2.2	9.6	5	9
Mali	50.2	48	49	57	40	..	..	..	..	10
Mauritania	50.5	52	55	64	16	..	..	..	..	..
Mauritius	50.3	70	77	..	..	37.5	0.8	4.7	7	17
Mexico	51.1	73	78	..	..	37.4	5.5	11.0	12	..
Moldova	52.2	65	72	98	..	54.6	0.5	1.5	..	22
Mongolia	49.9	65	68	94	..	50.3	18.4	31.7	25	7
Morocco	50.3	68	73	68	7	21.8	21.6	52.5	0	11
Mozambique	51.6	41	42	85	41	..	..	..	16	35
Myanmar	50.3	58	64	76	..	..	..	..	..	..
Namibia	50.4	47	47	91	18	..	12.8	22.0	7	27
Nepal	50.4	62	63	28	21	..	..	..	6	6
Netherlands	50.4	77	82	..	..	45.4	0.2	1.0	21	37
New Zealand	50.9	78	82	..	..	50.5	0.4	0.9	14	32
Nicaragua	50.0	68	73	86	25	..	..	..	15	21
Niger	48.9	45	45	41	..	7.8	..	..	5	12
Nigeria	49.4	44	44	58	25	..	..	..	..	6
Norway	50.3	78	83	..	..	49.2	0.2	0.3	36	38
Oman	43.8	73	76	100	..	25.7	..	..	..	2
Pakistan	48.5	64	65	36	..	8.6	16.4	46.9	10	21
Panama	49.6	73	78	..	..	43.5	2.8	3.7	8	17
Papua New Guinea	48.5	56	57	..	..	35.4	..	..	0	1
Paraguay	49.6	69	74	94	..	43.9	..	..	6	10
Peru	49.7	68	73	92	13	34.6	2.6	7.4	6	29
Philippines	49.7	69	73	88	8	40.4	8.2	17.4	9	16
Poland	51.5	71	79	..	..	47.2	4.1	7.3	14	20
Portugal	51.7	75	81	..	..	46.6	1.0	2.3	8	21
Puerto Rico	52.0	74	82	..	..	39.3	0.1	0.9	..	..

1.5 Women in development

	Female population	Life expectancy at birth		Pregnant women receiving prenatal care	Teenage mothers	Women in nonagricultural sector	Unpaid family workers		Women in parliaments	
		years					Male	Female		
	% of total	Male	Female	%	% of women ages 15–19	% of total	% of male employment	% of female employment	% of total seats	
	2005	**2005**	**2005**	**2000–05[a]**	**2000–05[a]**	**2004**	**2000–05[a]**	**2000–05[a]**	**1990**	**2006**
Romania	51.3	68	75	94	..	46.5	7.7	21.2	34	11
Russian Federation	53.6	59	72	..	..	50.9	0.1	0.0	..	10
Rwanda	51.5	43	46	94	4	..	..	..	17	49
Saudi Arabia	46.0	71	75	..	..	13.5	..	..	..	0
Senegal	50.8	55	58	79	..	..	..	..	13	19
Serbia and Montenegro	50.2	70	76	..	..	45.4	..	..	..	..
Sierra Leone	50.7	40	43	68	..	..	..	..	..	15
Singapore	49.7	78	82	..	..	47.0	0.3	1.3	5	21
Slovak Republic	51.5	70	78	..	..	52.0	0.1	0.2	..	20
Slovenia	51.2	74	81	..	..	47.6	4.3	6.9	..	12
Somalia	50.4	47	49	..	..	..	..	..	4	8
South Africa	50.9	47	49	92	..	45.9	0.5	1.1	3	33
Spain	50.9	77	84	..	..	42.0	0.8	2.4	15	36
Sri Lanka	49.2	72	77	100	..	43.2	4.2	20.9	5	5
Sudan	49.7	55	58	60	..	16.8	..	..	..	15
Swaziland	51.8	42	41	90	..	29.9	..	..	4	11
Sweden	50.4	78	83	..	..	50.9	0.3	0.3	38	47
Switzerland	51.6	79	84	..	..	47.1	1.4	2.8	14	25
Syrian Arab Republic	49.7	72	76	71	..	18.2	..	..	9	12
Tajikistan	50.4	61	67	71	..	53.3	..	..	..	18
Tanzania	50.2	46	47	78	26	..	3.0	4.6	..	30
Thailand	50.9	68	74	92	..	46.4	14.7	31.4	3	..
Togo	50.6	53	57	85	..	..	..	..	5	9
Trinidad and Tobago	50.7	67	73	92	..	41.1	0.5	1.9	17	19
Tunisia	49.6	72	76	92	..	25.0	..	..	4	23
Turkey	49.6	69	74	81	..	19.9	8.9	49.8	1	4
Turkmenistan	50.8	59	67	98	4	..	..	..	26	16
Uganda	50.0	49	51	92	31	..	10.3	40.5	12	30
Ukraine	54.2	62	74	..	..	55.1	0.6	0.6	..	9
United Arab Emirates	31.9	77	82	..	..	14.5	..	..	0	0
United Kingdom	51.1	77	81	..	..	49.4	0.3	0.5	6	20
United States	50.8	75	81	..	..	48.5	0.1	0.1	7	15
Uruguay	51.5	72	79	..	..	46.8	0.9	2.0	6	11
Uzbekistan	50.3	64	71	97	..	39.5	..	..	..	18
Venezuela, RB	49.7	71	77	94	..	41.5	1.8	3.3	10	18
Vietnam	50.1	68	73	86	3	49.1	21.9	50.3	18	27
West Bank and Gaza	49.1	71	76	96	..	17.9	6.4	32.2	..	..
Yemen, Rep.	49.3	60	63	41	..	..	..	..	4	0[c]
Zambia	49.9	39	38	93	32	..	..	..	7	15
Zimbabwe	50.4	38	37	..	..	21.8	10.4	13.6	11	16
World	**49.7 w**	**66 w**	**70 w**	**..**		**38.1 w**	**.. w**	**.. w**	**13 w**	**17 w**
Low income	49.2	58	60	..		23.4	..	..	11	16
Middle income	49.8	68	73	..		40.9	..	..	14	16
Lower middle income	49.5	68	73	89		40.2	..	..	14	16
Upper middle income	51.4	66	74	..		44.2	3.5	7.5	..	15
Low & middle income	49.6	64	67	..		36.2	..	..	13	16
East Asia & Pacific	49.1	69	73	90		40.6	..	..	17	18
Europe & Central Asia	52.1	65	74	..		47.6	3.0	7.1	..	14
Latin America & Carib.	50.6	69	76	..		43.3	4.4	7.1	12	..
Middle East & N. Africa	49.5	68	72	..		17.7	..	..	4	8
South Asia	48.8	63	64	..		17.8	..	..	6	13
Sub-Saharan Africa	50.1	46	47	..		..	..	..	..	16
High income	50.7	76	82	..		46.0	0.6	2.7	12	22
Europe EMU	51.1	77	83	..		45.1	1.4	3.2	12	24

a. Data are for the most recent year available. b. Refers to women 15–49. c. Less than 0.5.

Women in development 1.5

About the data

Despite much progress in recent decades, gender inequalities remain pervasive in many dimensions of life—worldwide. But while disparities exist throughout the world, they are most prevalent in poor developing countries. Gender inequalities in the allocation of such resources as education, health care, nutrition, and political voice matter because of the strong association with well-being, productivity, and economic growth. This pattern of inequality begins at an early age, with boys routinely receiving a larger share of education and health spending than do girls, for example.

Because of biological differences girls are expected to experience lower infant and child mortality rates and to have a longer life expectancy than boys. This biological advantage, however, may be overshadowed by gender inequalities in nutrition and medical interventions, and by inadequate care during pregnancy and delivery, so that female rates of illness and death sometimes exceed male rates, particularly during early childhood and the reproductive years. In high-income countries women tend to outlive men by four to eight years on average, while in low-income countries the difference is narrower—about two to three years. The difference in child mortality rates (table 2.20) is another good indicator of female social disadvantage because nutrition and medical interventions are particularly important for the 1–5 age group. Female child mortality rates that are as high as or higher than male child mortality rates might be indicative of discrimination against girls.

Having a child during the teenage years limits girls' opportunities for better education, jobs, and income and increases the likelihood of divorce and separation. Pregnancy is more likely to be unintended during the teenage years, and births are more likely to be premature and are associated with greater risks of complications during delivery and of death. In many countries maternal mortality (tables 1.2 and 2.16) is a leading cause of death among women of reproductive age. Most maternal deaths result from preventable causes—hemorrhage, infection, and complications from unsafe abortions. Prenatal care is essential for recognizing, diagnosing, and promptly treating complications that arise during pregnancy. In high-income countries most women have access to health care during pregnancy, but in developing countries an estimated 8 million women suffer pregnancy- related complications every year, and over half a million die (WHO 2004). This is reflected in the differences in maternal mortality ratios between high- and low-income countries.

Women's wage work is important for economic growth and the well-being of families. But restricted access to education and vocational training, heavy workloads at home and in nonpaid domestic and market activities, and labor market discrimination often limit women's participation in paid economic activities, lower their productivity, and reduce their wages. When women are in salaried employment, they tend to be concentrated in the nonagricultural sector. However, in many developing countries women are a large part of agricultural employment, often as unpaid family workers. Among people who are unsalaried, women are more likely than men to be unpaid family workers, while men are more likely than women to be self-employed or employers. There are several reasons for this.

Few women have access to credit markets, capital, land, training, and education, which may be required to start up a business. Cultural norms may prevent women from working on their own or from supervising other workers. Also, women may face time constraints due to their traditional family responsibilities. Because of biases and misclassification substantial numbers of employed women may be underestimated or reported as unpaid family workers even when they work in association or equally with their husbands in the family enterprise.

Women are vastly underrepresented in decision-making positions in government, although there is some evidence of recent improvement. Gender parity in parliamentary representation is still far from being realized. In 2007 women represented 17 percent of parliamentarians worldwide, compared with 9 percent in 1987. Without representation at this level, it is difficult for women to influence policy.

For information on other aspects of gender, see tables 1.2 (Millennium Development Goals: eradicating poverty and improving lives), 2.3 (employment by economic activity), 2.4 (children at work), 2.5 (unemployment), 2.11 (education efficiency), 2.12 (education completion and outcomes), 2.16 (reproductive health), 2.18 (health risk factors and public health challenges), 2.19 (health gaps by income and gender), and 2.20 (mortality).

Definitions

• **Female population** is the percentage of the population that is female. • **Life expectancy at birth** is the number of years a newborn infant would live if prevailing patterns of mortality at the time of its birth were to stay the same throughout its life. • **Pregnant women receiving prenatal care** are the percentage of women attended at least once during pregnancy by skilled health personnel for reasons related to pregnancy. • **Teenage mothers** are the percentage of women ages 15–19 who already have children or are currently pregnant. • **Women in nonagricultural sector** refers to women wage employees in the nonagricultural sector as a percentage of total nonagricultural employment. • **Unpaid family workers** are those who work without pay in a market-oriented establishment or activity operated by a related person living in the same household.• **Women in parliaments** are the percentage of parliamentary seats in a single or lower chamber held by women.

Data sources

Data on female population and life expectancy are from the World Bank's population database. Data on pregnant women receiving prenatal care are from United Nations Children's Fund's *State of the World's Children 2007*. Data on teenage mothers are from Demographic and Health Surveys by Macro International. Data on labor force and employment are from the International Labour Organization's *Key Indicators of the Labour Market*, fourth edition. Data on women in parliaments are from the Inter-Parliamentary Union.

1.6 Key indicators for other economies

	Population	Surface area	Population density	Gross national income				Gross domestic product		Life expectancy at birth	Adult literacy rate	Carbon dioxide emissions
						PPP[a]						
	thousands 2005	thousand sq. km 2005	people per sq. km 2005	$ millions 2005[b]	Per capita $ 2005[b]	$ millions 2005	Per capita $ 2005	% growth 2004–05	Per capita % growth 2004–05	years 2005	% ages 15 and older 2006[c]	thousand metric tons 2003
American Samoa	58	0.2	292	..	..[d]	..	..	..	..	..	..	293
Andorra	66	0.5	141	..	..[e]	..	..	..	..	..	..	..
Antigua and Barbuda	83	0.4	188	*855*	*10,500*	969	11,700	*7.2*	*5.4*	..	..	399
Aruba	100	0.2	528	..	..[e]	..	..	*1.6*	..	..	97	2,154
Bahamas, The	323	13.9	32	..	..[e]	..	..	..	..	71	..	1,868
Bahrain	727	0.7	1,023	*10,288*	*14,370*	15,470	21,290	6.9	5.3	75	87	21,872
Barbados	270	0.4	627	..	..[d]	..	..	..	..	*75*	..	1,190
Belize	292	23.0	13	1,042	3,570	1,967	6,740	3.1	–0.2	72	..	780
Bermuda	63	0.1	1,265	..	..[e]	..	..	..	..	79	..	498
Bhutan	637	47.0	14	798	1,250[f]	..	..	6.1	2.6	64	60	385
Brunei Darussalam	374	5.8	71	..	..[e]	..	..	*1.7*	*–0.5*	77	93	4,549
Cape Verde	507	4.0	126	976	1,930	3,041[g]	6,000[g]	5.8	3.4	71	..	143
Cayman Islands	45	0.3	173	..	..[e]	..	..	..	..	..	..	304
Channel Islands	149	0.9	..	..	..[e]	..	..	..	..	*79*	..	..
Comoros	600	2.2	269	389	650	1,201[g]	2,000[g]	4.2	2.1	63	..	88
Cyprus	758	9.3	82	*13,633*	*18,430*	*16,446*	*22,230*	*3.7*	*1.3*	79	97	7,278
Djibouti	793	23.2	34	803	1,010	1,776[g]	2,240[g]	3.2	1.4	53	..	366
Dominica	72	0.8	96	*271*	*3,800*	400	5,560	*6.4*	*6.0*	..	..	139
Equatorial Guinea	504	28.1	18	..	..[d]	*3,731*[g]	*7,580*[g]	*10.0*	*7.5*	42	87	165
Faeroe Islands	48	1.4	35	..	..[e]	..	..	..	..	..	..	659
Fiji	848	18.3	46	2,684	3,170	5,052	5,960	0.7	–0.1	68	..	1,117
French Polynesia	257	4.0	70	..	..[e]	..	..	..	..	74	..	692
Greenland	57	410.5	0	..	..[e]	..	..	..	..	..	..	568
Grenada	107	0.3	313	*408*	*3,860*	773	7,260	*–4.1*	*–5.1*	..	..	220
Guam	170	0.6	308	..	..[e]	..	..	..	..	75	..	4,081
Guyana	751	215.0	4	770	1,020	3,178[g]	4,230[g]	–2.2	–2.4	64	..	1,630
Iceland	297	103.0	3	14,414	48,570	10,315	34,760	5.5	3.9	81	..	2,187
Isle of Man	78	0.6	136	*2,138*	*27,590*	..	..	*6.3*	*6.0*	..	..	..

About the data

This table shows data for 55 economies—small economies with populations between 30,000 and 1 million and smaller economies if they are members of the World Bank. Where data on gross national income (GNI) per capita are not available, the estimated range is given. For more information on the calculation of GNI (gross national product, or GNP, in the System of National Accounts 1968) and purchasing power parity (PPP) conversion factors, see *About the data* for table 1.1. Since 2000 this table has excluded France's overseas departments—French Guiana, Guadeloupe, Martinique, and Réunion—for which GNI and other economic measures are now included in the French national accounts.

Definitions

• **Population** is based on the de facto definition of population, which counts all residents regardless of legal status or citizenship—except for refugees not permanently settled in the country of asylum, who are generally considered part of the population of their country of origin. The values shown are midyear estimates for 2005. See also table 2.1. • **Surface area** is a country's total area, including areas under inland bodies of water and some coastal waterways. • **Population density** is midyear population divided by land area in square kilometers. • **Gross national income (GNI)** is the sum of value added by all resident producers plus any product taxes (less subsidies) not included in the valuation of output plus net receipts of primary income (compensation of employees and property income) from abroad. Data are in current U.S. dollars converted using the *World Bank Atlas* method (see *Statistical methods*). • **GNI per capita** is gross national income divided by midyear population. GNI per capita in U.S. dollars is converted using the *World Bank Atlas* method. • **PPP GNI** is gross national income converted to international dollars using purchasing power parity rates. An international dollar has the same purchasing power over GNI as a U.S. dollar has in the United States. • **Gross domestic product (GDP)** is the sum of value added by all resident producers plus any product taxes (less subsidies) not included in the valuation

Key indicators for other economies 1.6

	Population	Surface area	Population density	Gross national income				Gross domestic product		Life expectancy at birth	Adult literacy rate	Carbon dioxide emissions
						PPP[a]						
	thousands 2005	thousand sq. km 2005	people per sq. km 2005	$ millions 2005[b]	Per capita $ 2005[b]	$ millions 2005	Per capita $ 2005	% growth 2004–05	Per capita % growth 2004–05	years 2005	% ages 15 and older 2006[c]	thousand metric tons 2003
Kiribati	99	0.7	136	*119*	*1,210*	..	..	0.3	−0.9	..	..	29
Liechtenstein	35	0.2	217	..	..[e]	..	..	..	..	..	..	..
Luxembourg	457	2.6	176	*26,315*	*58,050*	29,841	65,340	4.0	3.3	79	..	9,927
Macao, China	460	0.0	16,318	..	..[e]	..	..	6.7	6.0	80	91	1,864
Maldives	329	0.3	1,097	762	2,320	..	..	−5.2	−7.5	68	96	443
Malta	404	0.3	1,261	5,491	13,610	7,650	18,960	2.5	1.9	80	88	2,462
Marshall Islands	63	0.2	351	185	2,930	..	..	3.5	0.1	..	..	..
Mayotte	180	0.4	481	..	..[d]	..	..	..	..	..	..	..
Micronesia, Fed. Sts.	110	0.7	158	254	2,300	..	..	0.3	−0.4	68	..	..
Monaco	33	0.0	17,128	..	..[e]	..	..	..	..	..	..	..
Netherlands Antilles	183	0.8	228	..	..[e]	..	..	..	..	76	..	4,051
New Caledonia	234	18.6	13	..	..[e]	..	..	..	..	75	96	1,868
Northern Mariana Islands	79	0.5	166	..	..[d]	..	..	..	..	..	..	..
Palau	20	0.5	44	154	7,670	..	..	5.5	5.0	..	..	242
Qatar	813	11.0	74	..	..[e]	..	..	6.1	1.4	74	89	46,172
Samoa	185	2.8	65	373	2,020	1,199[g]	6,480[g]	5.4	4.7	71	..	150
São Tomé and Principe	157	1.0	163	68	440	..	..	3.2	0.9	63	..	92
Seychelles	84	0.5	184	691	8,180	1,347[g]	15,940[g]	−2.3	−3.3	..	92	546
Solomon Islands	478	28.9	17	297	620	898[g]	1,880[g]	5.0	2.4	63	..	179
San Marino	28	0.1	470	..	..[e]	..	..	..	..	..	..	..
St. Kitts and Nevis	48	0.4	133	*369*	*7,840*	600	12,500	*8.8*	*8.2*	..	..	125
St. Lucia	165	0.6	270	*744*	*4,580*	985	5,980	*5.8*	*4.6*	74	..	326
St. Vincent & Grenadines	119	0.4	305	421	3,530	769	6,460	2.2	1.7	72	..	194
Suriname	449	163.3	3	1,141	2,540	..	..	5.1	4.5	70	90	2,238
Timor-Leste	976	14.9	66	588	600	..	..	2.5	−2.8	57	..	161
Tonga	102	0.8	142	*178*	*1,750*	823[g]	8,040[g]	2.3	2.0	73	99	114
Vanuatu	211	12.2	17	331	1,560	670[g]	3,170[g]	2.8	0.8	69	74	88
Virgin Islands (U.S.)	109	0.4	311	..	..[e]	..	..	..	..	79	..	13,524

a. PPP is purchasing power parity; see *Definitions*. b. Calculated using the *World Bank Atlas* method. c. Actual reference year varies by country; for more information see the original source. d. Estimated to be upper middle-income ($3,466–$10,725). e. Estimated to be high-income ($10,726 or more). f. Included in the aggregates for low-income economies based on earlier data. g. Based on regression; others are extrapolated from the latest International Comparison Program benchmark estimates.

of output. Growth is calculated from constant price GDP data in local currency. • **Life expectancy at birth** is the number of years a newborn infant would live if prevailing patterns of mortality at the time of its birth were to stay the same throughout its life. • **Adult literacy rate** is the percentage of adults ages 15 and older who can, with understanding, read and write a short, simple statement about their everyday life. • **Carbon dioxide emissions** are those stemming from the burning of fossil fuels and the manufacture of cement. They include carbon dioxide produced during consumption of solid, liquid, and gas fuels and gas flaring.

Data sources

The indicators here and throughout the rest of the book are compiled by World Bank Group staff from primary and secondary sources. More information about the indicators and their sources can be found in the *About the data*, *Definitions*, and *Data sources* entries that accompany each table in subsequent sections.

2 PEOPLE

The wide health divide

Advances in technology and knowledge for health and hygiene have transformed life over the past 50 years. In 1960 more than 20 percent of children in developing countries died before reaching their fifth birthday; by 2005 this had fallen to just over 8 percent. The declines are large, even for the poorest countries (figure 2a). But this reassuring picture, painted by rising global averages, obscures substantial disparities among the world's regions and among the poor within countries. For millions of people health services and modern medicines are still out of reach, and many die prematurely from diseases that are easily prevented or cured. More than 25 years after the Health for All declaration, improving the health of the poorest people in developing countries remains a challenge.

What can improve all this? There is no consensus on which determinants are most important across countries. But there is agreement on the need to reduce extreme income poverty, the major risk for poor health and premature death. The World Health Organization (WHO) concurs, noting that a poverty-oriented health strategy requires complementary policies in other sectors (WHO 2003). These include improving access to education, enhancing the position of women and other marginalized groups, shaping development policies in agriculture and rural development, and promoting open and participatory governance.

Priorities in healthcare are also clear: focus on health problems and diseases that affect the poor disproportionately. Health gains require directing program benefits toward the poor and increasing the quality and availability of health services, especially where they are least available. This section looks at the rich-poor health divide between and within countries—and at the factors behind that divide.

Child mortality has fallen in the past 25 years for countries at all incomes **2a**

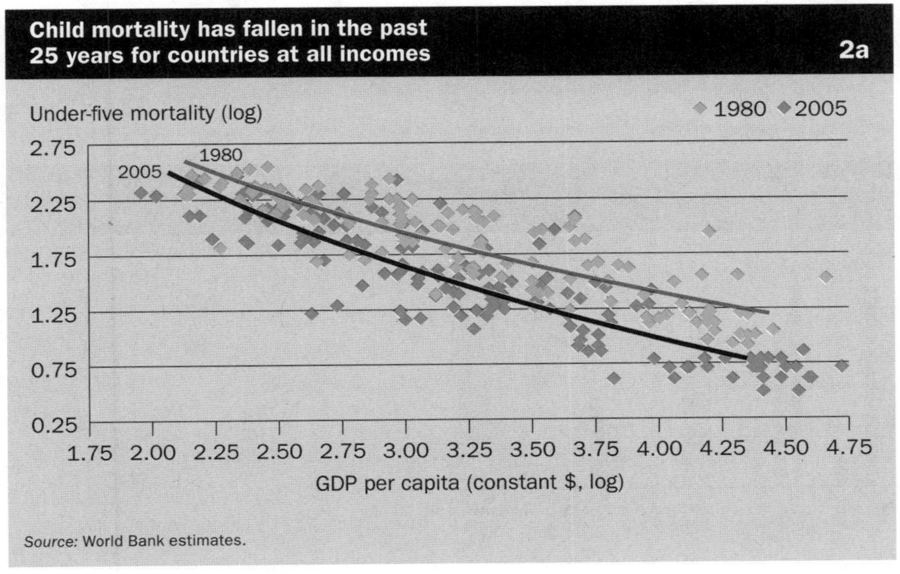

Source: World Bank estimates.

The divide between rich and poor countries

Differences in the health of rich and poor countries remain large and in some cases are increasing. Under-five mortality fell more than 36 percent in high-income countries from 1990 to 2005, but only 20 percent in developing countries, as preventable diseases continue to take a toll on the world's poorest people. But more important than the changes in proportions are the levels: under-five mortality is five times higher in middle-income countries than in high-income countries and 15 times higher in lower-income countries (figure 2b).

What accounts for these disparities? Child mortality from malaria doubled from 1990 to 2001, with the largest increase in Sub-Saharan Africa (Lopez and others 2006). Other increases in child mortality in developing countries came from HIV/AIDS, again with the largest increase in Sub-Saharan Africa, and problems in the first months of life, which depend strongly on the quality and availability of prenatal services. Child deaths from these causes are far less common in high-income countries, just as they are from acute respiratory infections, diarrheal diseases, and measles. But for developing countries, these diseases, along with malnutrition, remain significant causes of avoidable child deaths (figure 2c).

The differing patterns of mortality and well-being reflected in the age distributions of death for developing and high-income countries show their impact on life expectancies at birth (figures 2d, 2e, and 2f). In developing countries, where deaths of children under age five are still the major health issue, average life expectancy at birth is 65 years. But several countries—such as Lesotho, Zambia, and Zimbabwe, with high AIDS-related mortality—have life expectancies of less than 40 years. In high-income countries, by contrast, noncommunicable illnesses—such as cardiovascular diseases, diabetes, and related conditions of high blood pressure, high cholesterol, and excessive body weight—cluster deaths at older ages, and the average life expectancy at birth is 79 years. Indeed, in Canada, France, Japan, Norway, Sweden, and Switzerland life expectancies of 80 years and above are the norm. So any efforts to improve health and increase life expectancy in developing countries will have to focus on diseases that kill children.

Why are there health gaps between rich and poor countries? Poverty makes people in developing countries more vulnerable to disease. Nearly a third of the people in South Asia and half those in Sub-Saharan Africa lived on less than $1

Under-five mortality is 15 times higher in low-income countries than in high-income countries 2b

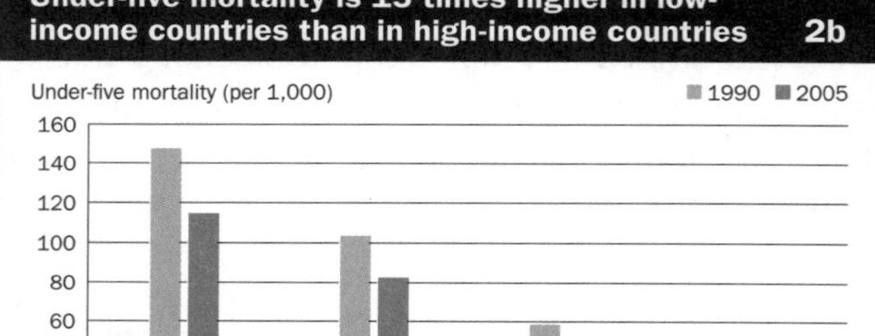

Source: Harmonized estimates from WHO, UNICEF, and World Bank.

Little reduction in risks for poor children 2c

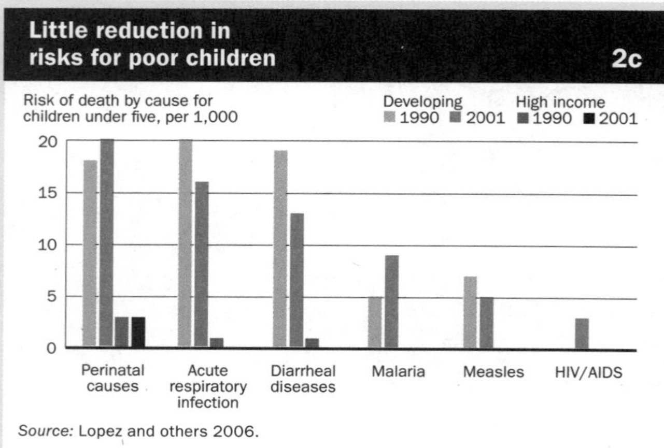

Source: Lopez and others 2006.

In Sierra Leone most deaths occur before age 5 2d

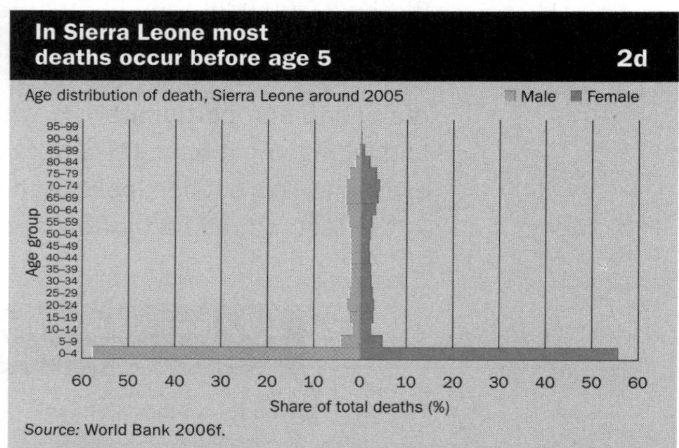

Source: World Bank 2006f.

A child born in Denmark can expect to live to be 78 2e

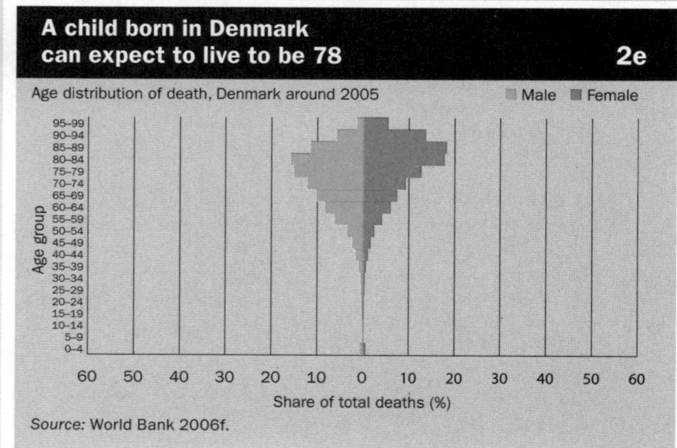

Source: World Bank 2006f.

a day in 2002. The majority of them typically lack access to safe drinking water and adequate sanitation, food, education, employment, health information, and professional healthcare. Almost half the people in Sub-Saharan Africa cannot obtain essential drugs (Jamison and others 2006). Many developing countries experienced little increase in immunization coverage between 1990 and 2005, and in 2005 only 75 percent of children ages 12–23 months were vaccinated against measles and diphtheria, pertussis, and whooping cough, compared with almost 95 percent for high-income countries.

Several barriers beyond low income exclude people in developing countries from getting appropriate care, and these can be related to services, clients, and institutions. Service factors include the high cost of care and transportation, poor quality and inappropriate care, and negative staff attitudes. Client factors include social and cultural constraints on women's movements and limited information about their health needs and availability of services. And institutional factors include men's control over decisionmaking and budgets, local perceptions about illness and treatment norms, and discrimination in health settings.

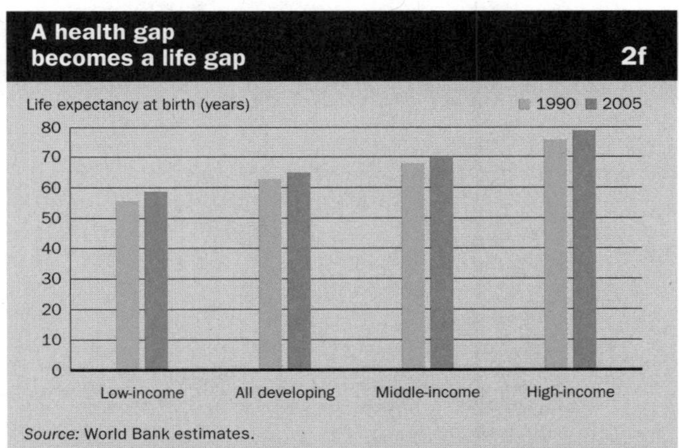

Source: World Bank estimates.

Health inequalities by social, cultural, and geographic factors — Box 2g

Inequalities in health go beyond income to such sociocultural, demographic, and geographic factors as sex, race, religion, ethnic group, language, and residence. In parts of India and China infant girls are more likely to die than infant boys because the cultural preference for male children puts girls at a disadvantage in nutrition and healthcare early in life. Women and girls also face discrimination in healthcare because cultural norms restrict them from traveling long distances, especially alone.

Poor communities—rural, remote, and in urban slums—typically face multiple health risks related to gaps in infrastructure, services, and trained personnel. For example, ethnic minorities, especially in isolated regions in Bangladesh, were less likely to be vaccinated for childhood diseases.

Source: Carr 2004; Ashford, Gwatkin, and Yazbeck 2006.

The health divide within countries: the rich-poor gap

Inequalities in health within countries are pervasive. Even in healthy countries such as Finland, the Netherlands, and the United Kingdom, the poor die 5–10 years before the rich (Carr 2004). But the inequalities are most apparent in poorer developing countries. Studies from many developing countries show that the poorest 20 percent of the population fares far worse than the richest 20 percent on a range of health outcomes, including child mortality and nutritional status (box 2g, figures 2h and 2i). On average a child in the poorest 20 percent is twice as likely to die before age 5 as a child in the richest 20 percent. The disparity is similar for maternal nutrition, with women in the poorest 20 percent almost twice as likely to be malnourished as those in the richest 20 percent.

Severe malnutrition among children reveals more pronounced inequality, with children in the poorest 20 percent more than three times as likely to be underweight as children in the richest 20 percent. The inequality is largest in South Asia, where 21 percent of children in the poorest 20 percent were underweight, compared with 6 percent in the richest.

Demographic and Health Surveys find that gaps in the use of health services are closely related to economic

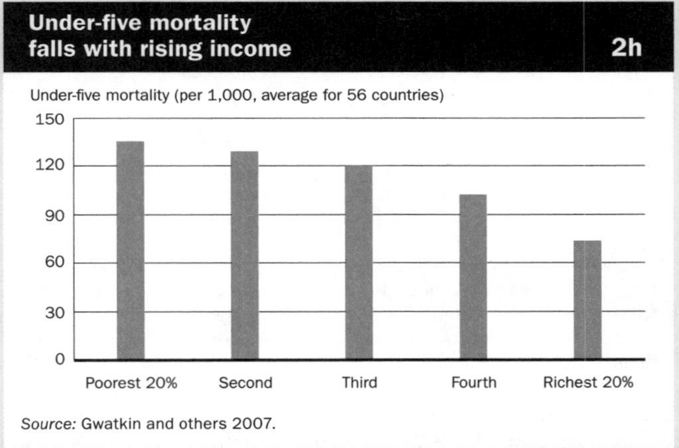

Source: Gwatkin and others 2007.

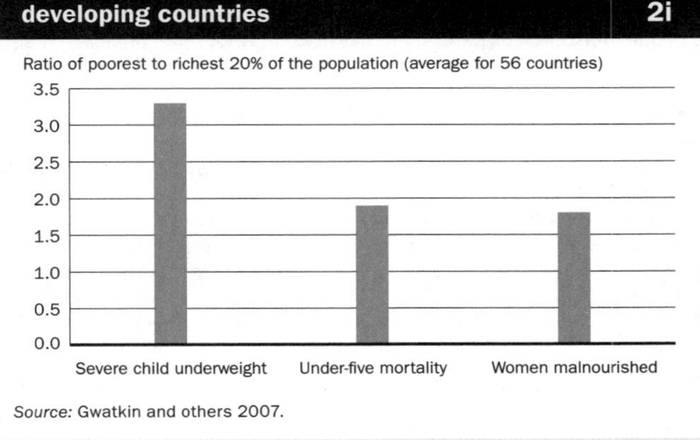

Source: Gwatkin and others 2007.

status (box 2j and figure 2k). On average, children ages 12–23 months in the richest 20 percent of the population are more than twice as likely as those in the poorest 20 percent to have received basic immunizations. Inequality in immunization is especially high in Sub-Saharan Africa: only 32 percent of children in the poorest 20 percent have been fully immunized, compared with 60 percent in the richest 20 percent.

Use of professional healthcare during childbirth also varies by income. Rich women are four times more likely to use modern methods of birth control than their poorer counterparts and nearly five times more likely to be attended by a skilled health professional during childbirth. Several countries, such as Benin, Morocco, Nicaragua, and Vietnam, have reduced inequalities and increased the coverage of trained medical staff attending childbirths for the poorest women (figure 2l). Childbirths attended by trained staff among the poorest 20 percent more than doubled in Nicaragua from 1997 to 2001, from 33 percent to 78 percent. In a few countries, such as Chad and Ghana, inequalities increased because of lack of progress in coverage among poor women.

Why do the poor receive and seek less health care than the rich? Box 2j

According to *World Development Report 2006: Equity and Development* (World Bank 2005d), inequities occur when some groups of people have less say and fewer opportunities to shape events and institutions around them, resulting in institutions that favor the privileged, who are often the rich. In health this translates into a lower likelihood of the poor taking preventive measures and seeking and using healthcare.

Government actions affect the health of poor people. Public spending on health can influence the type and quality of services available to the poor. Governments may allocate high proportions of their health budgets to urban hospitals, leaving rural residents without adequate health facilities. Income is another important constraint. In South Africa people in the poorest 20 percent have to travel an average of nearly two hours to obtain medical attention, compared with 34 minutes for those in the wealthiest 20 percent.

Additional barriers that lower demand for health services include a lack of knowledge about hygiene, nutrition, and the availability of treatment options, particularly among the uneducated. This can keep people from seeking care when they need it, even when price is not an issue. In India immunization rates are low, even though immunization is free: mothers cited lack of knowledge of the benefits of vaccination and of the clinic location as the main reasons why their children had not been immunized.

Lack of knowledge can also lead people to pay for inappropriate healthcare. Unqualified providers can overprescribe treatment to patients who do not know what is in their best interest. For example, instead of effective and inexpensive oral rehydration therapy, a poor child in Indonesia gets more than four (often useless) drugs per diarrhea episode.

Poorer members of a community often have less say in whether to seek care than wealthier members, and this can affect the level of resources used in their interest. Similarly, within a family, women and children have less voice than men and older family members.

Main determinant of health status: health spending

Differences in health spending contribute to global disparities in health outcomes (figure 2m). In rich countries, total health spending, at 6 percent of GDP, is almost twice that of developing countries, and childhood vaccinations, skilled attendants at birth, and access to effective health interventions are almost universal. In developing countries, where access to free health services is seen as a basic human right, public spending on health is less than 3 percent of GDP. In low-income countries the annual per capita spending on healthcare in 2004 was just $32, well below the $60 that the WHO deems sufficient for an adequately performing health system (WHO, *World Health Report 2000*). By contrast, annual per capita health spending in high-income countries was $3,724.

The most obvious barrier to expanding health coverage in developing countries is the current low level of spending. Expanding access to successful interventions will require more funds, a situation made more difficult as HIV/AIDS spreads and more spending is allocated to the treatment of AIDS and AIDS-related opportunistic infections, such as tuberculosis and pneumonia. As public funds for general health shrink, the

Rich people use health services more than poor people 2k

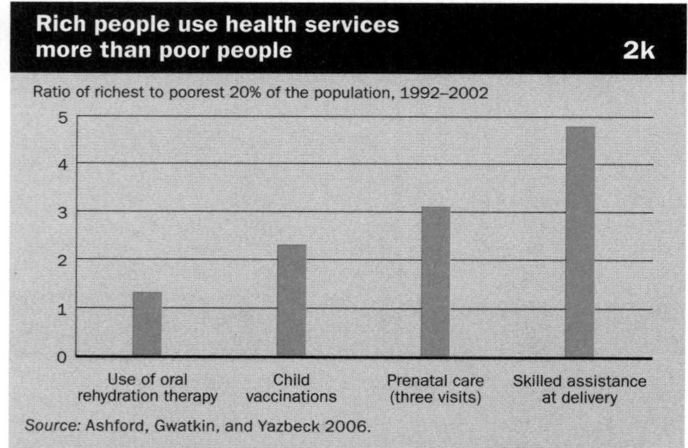

Source: Ashford, Gwatkin, and Yazbeck 2006.

Some countries have reduced inequalities in use of professional healthcare in childbirth 2l

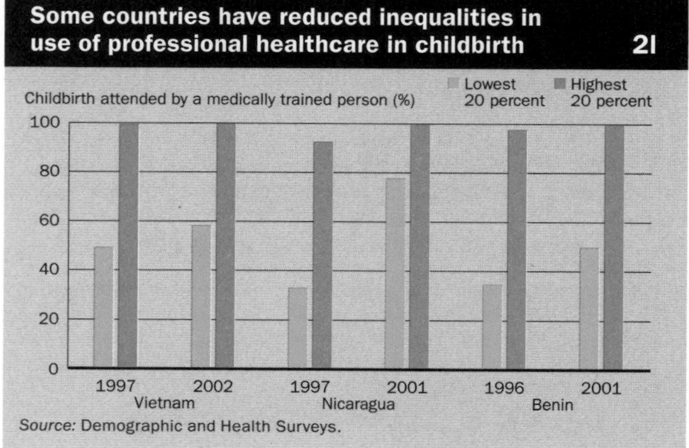

Source: Demographic and Health Surveys.

costs are borne more by households and the private sector. In 2004 more than 80 percent of the people in developing countries paid out of pocket for health services, compared with just 37 percent in high-income countries.

Greater public spending is not, however, always associated with better outcomes, and performance varies across countries based on the capabilities of government and health systems. In many countries staff ostensibly delivering services do not, and absenteeism is high (figure 2n). Corruption in the form of informal payments, coupled with the low technical quality of service providers and the poor attitudes of health staff, especially to the poorer population, often discourage a second visit. According to *World Development Report 2006: Equity and Development* (World Bank 2005d), more than 70 percent of patients in Azerbaijan, Poland, and the Russian Federation, and more than 90 percent in Armenia, made "informal payments" for services.

To improve health conditions among the poor and vulnerable in developing countries, governments support free or subsidized health services, often as part of a national policy to reduce poverty. Government spending on health is thus designed to give everyone equal access to care, and this rationale is typically invoked to justify direct government involvement in service provision. In reality, equal access is elusive, and research confirms that publicly financed healthcare benefits the rich more than the poor (figure 2o). In 21 countries the richest 20 percent received more than 26 percent of government health spending, compared with 16 percent for the poorest 20 percent. Even health programs that address illnesses affecting the poor tend to favor the rich. In Sub-Saharan Africa the rich benefited more (53 percent) from prophylactic treatment for malaria than did the poor (34 percent).

Primary healthcare is often free in the public health system, but treatment for major illnesses can be costly if payment is required for drugs and services on top of transport costs and time off from work. Indeed, health shocks can push a high proportion of households into poverty because of out-of-pocket health expenditures (figure 2p). This underscores the need for policymakers to maintain and improve the health status of the poor through effective interventions—and to protect households from falling into poverty.

Differences in healthcare spending contribute to global disparities **2m**

Health expenditure (% of GDP)
High income
Developing
12
10
8
6
4
2
0
Total
Public

Source: WHO and World Bank.

Where are healthcare workers hiding? **2n**

Country	Absence rates among healthcare workers in primary health facilities (%)
India (14 states)	43
Indonesia	42
Bangladesh	35
Uganda	35
Peru	26
Papua New Guinea	19

Source: World Bank 2003c.

Public health spending benefits the rich most **2o**

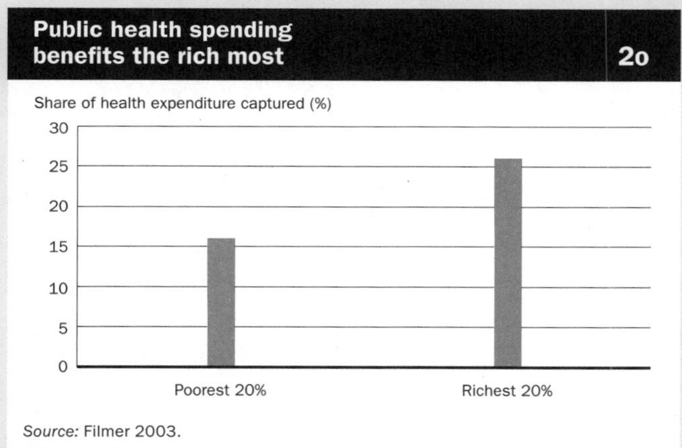

Source: Filmer 2003.

Health shocks can push households into poverty **2p**

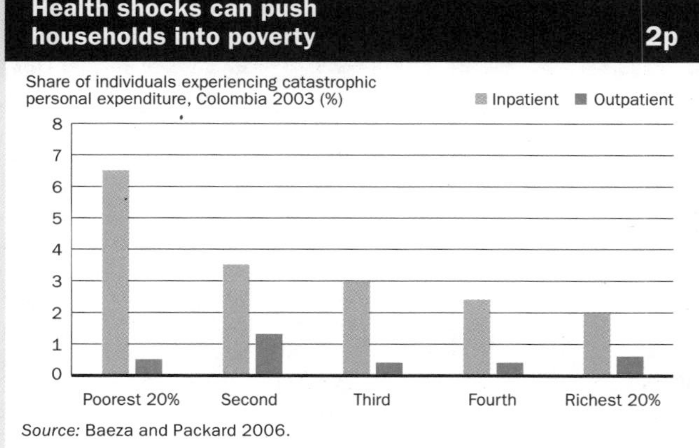

Source: Baeza and Packard 2006.

2.1 Population dynamics

	Total population			Average annual population growth rate		Population age composition			Dependency ratio		Crude death rate	Crude birth rate
						%			dependents as proportion of working-age population		per 1,000 people	per 1,000 people
		millions		%		Ages 0–14	Ages 15–64	Ages 65+	Young	Old		
	1990	2005	2015	1990–2005	2005–15	2005	2005	2005	2005	2005	2005	2005
Afghanistan	..	..	..	..	..	..	..	..	..	..	..	..
Albania	3.3	3.1	3.2	–0.3	0.4	27.0	64.7	8.3	0.4	0.1	6	13
Algeria	25.3	32.9	38.0	1.7	1.5	29.6	65.8	4.5	0.5	0.1	5	21
Angola	10.5	15.9	20.9	2.8	2.7	46.5	51.1	2.5	0.9	0.0[a]	22	48
Argentina	32.6	38.7	42.5	1.2	0.9	26.4	63.4	10.2	0.4	0.2	8	18
Armenia	3.5	3.0	3.0	–1.1	–0.2	20.8	67.1	12.1	0.3	0.2	8	12
Australia	17.1	20.3	22.3	1.2	0.9	19.6	67.7	12.7	0.3	0.2	6	13
Austria	7.7	8.2	8.3	0.4	0.1	15.5	67.8	16.7	0.2	0.2	9	10
Azerbaijan	7.2	8.4	9.2	1.1	0.9	25.8	67.1	7.1	0.4	0.1	6	17
Bangladesh	104.0	141.8	168.0	2.1	1.7	35.5	60.9	3.6	0.6	0.1	8	26
Belarus	10.2	9.8	9.2	–0.3	–0.6	15.2	70.2	14.7	0.2	0.2	15	9
Belgium	10.0	10.5	10.5	0.3	0.1	16.8	65.6	17.6	0.3	0.3	10	11
Benin	5.2	8.4	11.2	3.3	2.8	44.2	53.1	2.7	0.8	0.1	12	41
Bolivia	6.7	9.2	10.8	2.1	1.7	38.1	57.4	4.5	0.7	0.1	8	29
Bosnia and Herzegovina	4.3	3.9	3.9	–0.7	–0.1	16.5	69.5	14.0	0.2	0.2	9	9
Botswana	1.4	1.8	1.7	1.4	–0.4	37.6	59.0	3.3	0.6	0.1	27	26
Brazil	149.4	186.4	208.8	1.5	1.1	27.9	66.0	6.1	0.4	0.1	7	20
Bulgaria	8.7	7.7	7.1	–0.8	–0.8	13.8	69.4	16.8	0.2	0.2	15	9
Burkina Faso	8.5	13.2	17.3	2.9	2.7	47.2	50.1	2.7	0.9	0.1	16	46
Burundi	5.7	7.5	10.6	1.9	3.4	45.0	52.3	2.7	0.9	0.1	18	45
Cambodia	9.7	14.1	17.1	2.5	1.9	37.1	59.5	3.4	0.6	0.1	10	30
Cameroon	11.7	16.3	20.2	2.2	2.1	41.2	55.1	3.7	0.7	0.1	17	34
Canada	27.8	32.3	34.9	1.0	0.8	17.6	69.3	13.1	0.3	0.2	7	11
Central African Republic	3.0	4.0	4.6	2.0	1.4	43.0	53.0	4.1	0.8	0.1	22	37
Chad	6.1	9.7	12.5	3.2	2.5	47.3	49.7	3.0	1.0	0.1	20	49
Chile	13.2	16.3	17.9	1.4	0.9	24.9	67.0	8.1	0.4	0.1	5	16
China	1,135.2	1,304.5	1,378.1	0.9	0.5	21.4	71.0	7.6	0.3	0.1	6	12
Hong Kong, China	5.7	6.9	7.6	1.3	0.9	14.4	73.6	12.0	0.2	0.2	6	8
Colombia	35.0	45.6	51.5	1.8	1.2	31.0	63.9	5.1	0.5	0.1	5	21
Congo, Dem. Rep.	37.8	57.5	77.9	2.8	3.0	47.3	50.1	2.7	0.9	0.1	20	50
Congo, Rep.	2.5	4.0	5.2	3.2	2.7	47.1	49.9	2.9	0.9	0.1	13	44
Costa Rica	3.1	4.3	5.0	2.3	1.4	28.4	65.8	5.8	0.4	0.1	4	17
Côte d'Ivoire	12.7	18.2	21.6	2.4	1.7	41.9	54.9	3.3	0.8	0.1	17	36
Croatia	4.8	4.4	4.3	–0.5	–0.2	15.5	67.3	17.2	0.2	0.3	11	9
Cuba	10.5	11.3	11.4	0.4	0.1	19.1	70.1	10.8	0.3	0.2	7	11
Czech Republic	10.4	10.2	10.1	–0.1	–0.2	14.6	71.2	14.2	0.2	0.2	11	10
Denmark	5.1	5.4	5.5	0.3	0.2	18.8	66.2	15.0	0.3	0.2	10	12
Dominican Republic	7.1	8.9	10.1	1.5	1.3	32.7	63.1	4.1	0.5	0.1	6	24
Ecuador	10.3	13.2	15.1	1.7	1.3	32.4	61.8	5.8	0.5	0.1	5	22
Egypt, Arab Rep.	55.7	74.0	88.1	1.9	1.7	33.6	61.7	4.8	0.5	0.1	6	26
El Salvador	5.1	6.9	8.0	2.0	1.5	34.0	60.7	5.4	0.6	0.1	6	24
Eritrea	3.0	4.4	5.8	2.5	2.8	44.8	52.9	2.3	0.8	0.0[a]	11	39
Estonia	1.6	1.3	1.3	–1.0	–0.3	15.2	68.3	16.5	0.2	0.2	13	11
Ethiopia	51.2	71.3	86.8	2.2	2.0	44.5	52.5	2.9	0.8	0.1	19	39
Finland	5.0	5.2	5.3	0.3	0.2	17.3	66.8	15.9	0.3	0.2	9	11
France	56.7	60.9	62.4	0.5	0.2	18.2	65.2	16.6	0.3	0.3	9	13
Gabon	1.0	1.4	1.6	2.5	1.5	40.0	55.6	4.4	0.7	0.1	13	30
Gambia, The	0.9	1.5	1.9	3.2	2.2	40.1	56.1	3.7	0.7	0.1	11	34
Georgia	5.5	4.5	4.2	–1.3	–0.7	18.9	66.8	14.3	0.3	0.2	10	11
Germany	79.4	82.5	81.8	0.3	–0.1	14.3	66.9	18.8	0.2	0.3	10	8
Ghana	15.5	22.1	26.5	2.4	1.8	39.0	57.3	3.7	0.7	0.1	10	31
Greece	10.2	11.1	11.2	0.6	0.0	14.3	67.5	18.2	0.2	0.3	9	9
Guatemala	8.9	12.6	15.8	2.3	2.3	43.2	52.5	4.3	0.8	0.1	6	34
Guinea	6.2	9.4	11.8	2.8	2.3	43.7	52.7	3.5	0.8	0.1	13	41
Guinea-Bissau	1.0	1.6	2.1	3.0	2.9	47.5	49.4	3.1	1.0	0.1	19	50
Haiti	6.9	8.5	9.7	1.4	1.3	37.5	58.5	4.0	0.6	0.1	13	30

Population dynamics 2.1

	Total population			Average annual population growth rate		Population age composition			Dependency ratio		Crude death rate	Crude birth rate
		millions		%			%		dependents as proportion of working-age population		per 1,000 people	per 1,000 people
	1990	2005	2015	1990–2005	2005–15	Ages 0–14 2005	Ages 15–64 2005	Ages 65+ 2005	Young 2005	Old 2005	2005	2005
Honduras	4.9	7.2	8.8	2.6	2.0	39.2	56.9	3.9	0.7	0.1	6	28
Hungary	10.4	10.1	9.8	−0.2	−0.3	15.7	69.1	15.2	0.2	0.2	14	10
India	849.5	1,094.6	1,248.5	1.7	1.3	32.1	62.7	5.3	0.5	0.1	8	24
Indonesia	178.2	220.6	244.0	1.4	1.0	28.3	66.2	5.5	0.4	0.1	7	20
Iran, Islamic Rep.	54.4	68.3	78.4	1.5	1.4	28.7	66.8	4.5	0.4	0.1	4	15
Iraq	18.5	..	..	..	..	..	..	..	..	..	..	..
Ireland	3.5	4.2	4.7	1.1	1.1	20.2	68.9	10.9	0.3	0.2	7	15
Israel	4.7	6.9	8.1	2.6	1.5	27.8	62.1	10.1	0.4	0.2	6	21
Italy	56.7	58.6	58.0	0.2	−0.1	14.0	66.0	20.0	0.2	0.3	10	10
Jamaica	2.4	2.7	2.7	0.7	0.3	31.2	61.2	7.6	0.5	0.1	6	16
Japan	123.5	127.8	124.9	0.2	−0.2	14.0	66.3	19.7	0.2	0.3	9	8
Jordan	3.2	5.5	6.7	3.6	2.0	37.2	59.6	3.2	0.6	0.1	3	28
Kazakhstan	16.3	15.1	15.0	−0.5	−0.1	23.1	68.3	8.5	0.3	0.1	10	18
Kenya	23.4	34.3	44.1	2.5	2.5	42.8	54.4	2.8	0.8	0.1	14	39
Korea, Dem. Rep.	19.7	22.5	23.3	0.9	0.3	25.0	68.2	6.8	0.4	0.1	11	15
Korea, Rep.	42.9	48.3	49.2	0.8	0.2	18.6	72.0	9.4	0.3	0.1	5	9
Kuwait	2.1	2.5	3.4	1.2	2.8	24.3	73.9	1.8	0.3	0.0[a]	2	19
Kyrgyz Republic	4.4	5.1	5.7	1.0	1.0	31.5	62.4	6.1	0.5	0.1	7	21
Lao PDR	4.1	5.9	7.3	2.4	2.1	40.9	55.5	3.7	0.7	0.1	12	34
Latvia	2.7	2.3	2.2	−1.0	−0.6	14.7	68.4	16.9	0.2	0.2	14	9
Lebanon	2.7	3.6	4.0	1.8	1.0	28.6	64.0	7.3	0.4	0.1	7	18
Lesotho	1.6	1.8	1.7	0.8	−0.3	38.6	56.2	5.3	0.7	0.1	25	28
Liberia	2.1	3.3	4.4	2.9	2.9	47.1	50.7	2.2	0.9	0.0[a]	20	50
Libya	4.3	5.9	7.0	2.0	1.8	30.1	65.9	4.1	0.5	0.1	4	23
Lithuania	3.7	3.4	3.3	−0.5	−0.5	16.7	67.8	15.5	0.2	0.2	13	9
Macedonia, FYR	1.9	2.0	2.1	0.4	0.2	19.6	69.3	11.1	0.3	0.2	9	11
Madagascar	12.0	18.6	23.8	2.9	2.5	44.0	52.9	3.1	0.8	0.1	12	38
Malawi	9.5	12.9	16.0	2.1	2.2	47.3	49.6	3.0	1.0	0.1	21	43
Malaysia	17.8	25.3	29.5	2.3	1.5	32.4	63.0	4.6	0.5	0.1	5	21
Mali	8.9	13.5	18.0	2.8	2.9	48.2	49.1	2.7	1.0	0.1	17	49
Mauritania	2.0	3.1	4.0	2.8	2.6	43.0	53.6	3.4	0.8	0.1	13	40
Mauritius	1.1	1.2	1.3	1.1	0.7	24.6	68.8	6.6	0.4	0.1	7	15
Mexico	83.2	103.1	114.3	1.4	1.0	31.0	63.7	5.3	0.5	0.1	4	18
Moldova	4.4	4.2	4.1	−0.2	−0.3	18.3	71.6	10.1	0.3	0.1	12	11
Mongolia	2.1	2.6	2.9	1.3	1.2	30.5	65.8	3.8	0.5	0.1	6	18
Morocco	23.9	30.2	34.2	1.5	1.3	31.1	64.1	4.8	0.5	0.1	6	23
Mozambique	13.4	19.8	23.5	2.6	1.7	44.0	52.7	3.3	0.8	0.1	20	39
Myanmar	40.8	50.5	54.9	1.4	0.8	29.5	65.6	4.9	0.4	0.1	9	19
Namibia	1.4	2.0	2.2	2.5	1.0	41.5	55.0	3.5	0.8	0.1	6	22
Nepal	19.1	27.1	32.7	2.3	1.9	39.0	57.3	3.7	0.7	0.1	8	29
Netherlands	15.0	16.3	16.8	0.6	0.3	18.2	67.7	14.1	0.3	0.2	8	12
New Zealand	3.4	4.1	4.4	1.2	0.6	21.3	66.4	12.3	0.3	0.2	7	14
Nicaragua	4.0	5.1	6.2	1.8	1.8	38.9	57.8	3.3	0.7	0.1	5	28
Niger	8.5	14.0	19.2	3.3	3.2	49.0	49.0	2.0	1.0	0.0[a]	20	53
Nigeria	90.6	131.5	160.8	2.5	2.0	44.3	52.7	3.0	0.8	0.1	19	41
Norway	4.2	4.6	4.8	0.6	0.5	19.6	65.4	15.0	0.3	0.2	9	12
Oman	1.8	2.6	3.2	2.2	2.1	34.5	63.0	2.6	0.5	0.0[a]	3	25
Pakistan	108.0	155.8	190.5	2.4	2.0	38.3	57.9	3.8	0.7	0.1	7	26
Panama	2.4	3.2	3.8	2.0	1.5	30.4	63.6	6.0	0.5	0.1	5	22
Papua New Guinea	4.1	5.9	7.0	2.4	1.7	40.3	57.3	2.4	0.7	0.0[a]	10	29
Paraguay	4.2	5.9	7.1	2.2	1.8	37.6	58.7	3.7	0.6	0.1	5	29
Peru	21.8	28.0	32.1	1.7	1.4	32.2	62.5	5.3	0.5	0.1	6	22
Philippines	61.1	83.1	98.7	2.0	1.7	35.1	61.0	3.9	0.6	0.1	5	24
Poland	38.1	38.2	37.6	0.0[a]	−0.2	16.3	70.7	12.9	0.2	0.2	10	9
Portugal	9.9	10.5	10.9	0.4	0.3	15.9	67.0	17.1	0.2	0.3	10	11
Puerto Rico	3.5	3.9	4.1	0.7	0.4	22.3	65.7	12.1	0.3	0.2	8	13

2.1 Population dynamics

	Total population			Average annual population growth rate		Population age composition			Dependency ratio		Crude death rate	Crude birth rate
		millions		%			%		dependents as proportion of working-age population		per 1,000 people	per 1,000 people
						Ages 0–14	Ages 15–64	Ages 65+	Young	Old		
	1990	2005	2015	1990–2005	2005–15	2005	2005	2005	2005	2005	2005	2005
Romania	23.2	21.6	20.7	–0.5	–0.4	15.4	69.8	14.8	0.2	0.2	12	10
Russian Federation	148.3	143.1	136.0	–0.2	–0.5	15.3	70.9	13.8	0.2	0.2	16	10
Rwanda	7.1	9.0	11.3	1.6	2.2	43.5	54.0	2.5	0.8	0.0[a]	18	41
Saudi Arabia	16.4	23.1	28.9	2.3	2.2	37.3	59.8	2.9	0.6	0.0[a]	4	27
Senegal	8.0	11.7	14.5	2.5	2.2	42.6	54.3	3.1	0.8	0.1	11	36
Serbia and Montenegro	10.5[b]	8.1	8.0[c]	*0.1*[d]	–0.1[c]	18.3	67.6	14.1	0.3	0.2	14	11
Sierra Leone	4.1	5.5	6.9	2.0	2.2	42.8	53.8	3.3	0.8	0.1	23	46
Singapore	3.0	4.3	4.8	2.4	1.1	19.5	72.0	8.5	0.3	0.1	4	10
Slovak Republic	5.3	5.4	5.4	0.1	–0.1	16.7	71.5	11.8	0.2	0.2	10	10
Slovenia	2.0	2.0	2.0	0.0[a]	–0.2	13.9	70.5	15.6	0.2	0.2	9	9
Somalia	6.7	8.2	11.0	1.4	2.9	44.1	53.3	2.6	0.8	0.0[a]	17	44
South Africa	35.2	46.9	47.3	1.9	0.1	32.6	63.1	4.2	0.5	0.1	21	24
Spain	38.8	43.4	44.4	0.7	0.2	14.3	69.2	16.5	0.2	0.2	9	11
Sri Lanka	17.0	19.6	21.0	1.0	0.7	24.1	68.6	7.3	0.4	0.1	6	18
Sudan	26.1	36.2	44.1	2.2	2.0	39.2	57.2	3.6	0.7	0.1	11	32
Swaziland	0.8	1.1	1.1	2.6	–0.4	41.0	55.5	3.5	0.7	0.1	20	34
Sweden	8.6	9.0	9.3	0.4	0.3	17.5	65.3	17.2	0.3	0.3	10	10
Switzerland	6.7	7.4	7.5	0.7	0.0[a]	16.5	67.6	16.0	0.2	0.2	8	10
Syrian Arab Republic	12.8	19.0	23.8	2.6	2.2	36.9	60.0	3.1	0.6	0.1	3	28
Tajikistan	5.3	6.5	7.6	1.4	1.5	39.0	57.2	3.9	0.7	0.1	7	28
Tanzania	26.2	38.3	47.1	2.5	2.1	42.6	54.2	3.2	0.8	0.1	16	36
Thailand	54.6	64.2	69.0	1.1	0.7	23.8	69.1	7.1	0.3	0.1	7	16
Togo	4.0	6.1	7.8	2.9	2.4	43.5	53.4	3.1	0.8	0.1	12	38
Trinidad and Tobago	1.2	1.3	1.3	0.5	0.2	21.5	71.1	7.4	0.3	0.1	8	14
Tunisia	8.2	10.0	11.0	1.4	1.0	25.9	67.8	6.3	0.4	0.1	6	17
Turkey	56.2	72.1	80.7	1.7	1.1	28.4	65.7	5.9	0.4	0.1	6	19
Turkmenistan	3.7	4.8	5.5	1.8	1.3	31.8	63.6	4.7	0.5	0.1	8	22
Uganda	17.8	28.8	41.8	3.2	3.7	50.5	47.1	2.5	1.1	0.1	15	51
Ukraine	51.9	47.1	42.3	–0.6	–1.1	14.9	69.0	16.1	0.2	0.2	17	9
United Arab Emirates	1.8	4.5	5.6	6.3	2.2	22.0	76.9	1.1	0.3	0.0[a]	1	16
United Kingdom	57.6	60.2	61.7	0.3	0.2	17.9	66.1	16.0	0.3	0.2	10	12
United States	249.6	296.4	322.5	1.1	0.8	20.8	66.9	12.3	0.3	0.2	8	14
Uruguay	3.1	3.5	3.7	0.7	0.5	24.3	62.5	13.2	0.4	0.2	9	15
Uzbekistan	20.5	26.2	30.1	1.6	1.4	33.2	62.1	4.7	0.5	0.1	6	20
Venezuela, RB	19.8	26.6	31.1	2.0	1.6	31.2	63.7	5.1	0.5	0.1	5	22
Vietnam	66.2	83.1	92.1	1.5	1.0	29.5	65.0	5.4	0.5	0.1	6	18
West Bank and Gaza	2.0	3.6	4.9	4.1	3.0	45.5	51.4	3.1	0.9	0.1	4	33
Yemen, Rep.	12.1	21.0	28.4	3.7	3.0	46.4	51.4	2.3	0.9	0.0[a]	8	40
Zambia	8.4	11.7	13.8	2.2	1.7	45.8	51.2	3.0	0.9	0.1	22	40
Zimbabwe	10.6	13.0	13.8	1.4	0.6	40.0	56.4	3.6	0.7	0.1	23	29
World	**5,256.3 s**	**6,437.7 s**	**7,165.8 s**	**1.4 w**	**1.1 w**	**28.1 w**	**64.5 w**	**7.4 w**	**0.4 w**	**0.1 w**	**9 w**	**20 w**
Low income	1,739.4	2,352.4	2,787.8	2.0	1.7	36.4	59.3	4.3	0.6	0.1	10	29
Middle income	2,613.4	3,074.5	3,322.7	1.1	0.8	25.0	67.7	7.3	0.4	0.1	8	16
Lower middle income	2,083.6	2,474.6	2,694.1	1.1	0.8	25.3	67.9	6.9	0.4	0.1	7	16
Upper middle income	529.8	599.8	628.6	0.8	0.5	24.2	66.7	9.1	0.4	0.1	10	16
Low & middle income	4,352.8	5,426.9	6,110.5	1.5	1.2	30.0	64.0	6.0	0.5	0.1	9	22
East Asia & Pacific	1,596.1	1,885.5	2,027.8	1.1	0.7	23.9	69.2	6.9	0.3	0.1	7	15
Europe & Central Asia	466.1	471.8	471.5	0.1	0.0[a]	19.7	68.6	11.8	0.3	0.2	12	13
Latin America & Carib.	437.6	550.8	620.1	1.5	1.2	30.0	63.9	6.1	0.5	0.1	6	20
Middle East & N. Africa	225.5	306.0	365.1	2.0	1.8	33.5	62.3	4.2	0.5	0.1	6	24
South Asia	1,113.1	1,469.8	1,703.4	1.9	1.5	33.4	61.7	4.9	0.5	0.1	8	25
Sub-Saharan Africa	514.4	743.1	922.6	2.5	2.2	43.5	53.4	3.1	0.8	0.1	17	40
High income	903.5	1010.8	1055.3	0.7	0.4	18.2	67.0	14.8	0.3	0.2	8	12
Europe EMU	295.3	313.9	316.7	0.4	0.1	15.5	66.8	17.7	0.2	0.3	9	10

a. Less than 0.05. b. Includes population of Kosovo and Metahia until 1999. c. Projections are based on data for Serbia and Montenegro before it separated into two independent states in 2006. d. Data are for 1990–99.

Population dynamics 2.1

About the data

Population estimates are usually based on national population censuses, but the frequency and quality vary by country. Most countries conduct a complete enumeration no more than once a decade. Estimates for the years before and after the censuses are interpolations or extrapolations based on demographic models. Errors and undercounting occur even in high-income countries; in developing countries such errors may be substantial because of limits in the transport, communications, and other resources required to conduct and analyze a full census.

The quality and reliability of official demographic data are also affected by the public trust in the government, the government's commitment to full and accurate enumeration, the confidentiality and protection against misuse accorded to census data, and the independence of census agencies from undue political influence. Moreover, the international comparability of population indicators is limited by differences in the concepts, definitions, data collection procedures, and estimation methods used by national statistical agencies and other organizations that collect population data.

Of the 152 economies listed in the table, 130 (about 86 percent) conducted a census between 1995 and 2005. The currentness of a census, along with the availability of complementary data from surveys or registration systems, is one of many objective ways to judge the quality of demographic data. In some European countries registration systems offer complete information on population in the absence of a census. See *Primary data documentation* for the most recent census or survey year and for the completeness of registration.

Current population estimates for developing countries that lack recent census-based data, and pre- and post-census estimates for countries with census data, are provided by the United Nations Population Division and other agencies. The standard estimation method requires fertility, mortality, and net migration data, which are often collected from sample surveys, some of which may be small or limited in coverage. The population estimates are the product of demographic modeling and so are susceptible to biases and errors because of shortcomings in the model as well as in the data. Population projections are made using the cohort component method.

The growth rate of the total population conceals the fact that different age groups may grow at very different rates. In many developing countries the population under age 15 was previously growing rapidly but is now starting to shrink. Previously high fertility rates and declining mortality rates are now reflected in the larger share of the working-age population.

Dependency ratios take into account variations in the different age groups: the proportions of children, elderly people, and working-age people in the population. Separate calculations of young-age and old-age dependency suggest the burden of dependency that the working-age population must bear in relation to children and the elderly. But dependency ratios show only the age composition of a population, not economic dependency. Some children and elderly people are part of the labor force, and many working-age people are not.

The vital rates shown in the table are based on data derived from birth and death registration systems, censuses, and sample surveys conducted by national statistical offices and other organizations, or on demographic analysis. The estimates for 2005 for many countries are national projections based on extrapolations of levels and trends measured in earlier years.

Vital registers are the preferred source of these data, but in many developing countries systems for registering births and deaths do not exist or are incomplete because of deficiencies in the coverage of events or of geographic areas. Many developing countries carry out special household surveys that estimate vital rates by asking respondents about births and deaths in the recent past. Estimates derived in this way are subject to sampling errors as well as errors due to inaccurate recall by the respondents.

The United Nations Statistics Division monitors the completeness of vital registration systems. The share of countries with at least 90 percent complete vital registration increased from 45 percent in 1988 to 62 percent in 2005. Still, some of the most populous developing countries—China, India, Indonesia, Brazil, Pakistan, Bangladesh, Nigeria—do not have complete vital registration systems. Between 2003 and 2005, 51 percent of births and deaths and 48 percent of infant deaths worldwide were registered and reported.

International migration is the only other factor besides birth and death rates that directly determines a country's population growth. From 1990 to 2000 the number of migrants in high-income countries increased by 23 million. About 190 million people currently live outside their home country, accounting for about 3 percent of the world's population. Estimating international migration is difficult. At any time many people are located outside their home country as tourists, workers, or refugees or for other reasons. Standards relating to the duration and purpose of international moves that qualify as migration vary, and accurate estimates require information on flows into and out of countries that is difficult to collect.

Definitions

• **Total population** of an economy includes all residents regardless of legal status or citizenship—except for refugees not permanently settled in the country of asylum, who are generally considered part of the population of their country of origin. The values shown are midyear estimates for 1990 and 2005 and projections for 2015. • **Average annual population growth rate** is the exponential change for the period indicated. See *Statistical methods* for more information. • **Population age composition** refers to the percentage of the total population that is in specific age groups. • **Dependency ratio** is the ratio of dependents—people younger than 15 or older than 64—to the working-age population—those ages 15–64. • **Crude death rate** and **crude birth rate** are the number of deaths and the number of live births occurring during the year, per 1,000 population, estimated at midyear. Subtracting the crude death rate from the crude birth rate provides the rate of natural increase, which is equal to the population growth rate in the absence of migration.

Data sources

The World Bank's population estimates are compiled and produced by its Human Development Network and Development Data Group in consultation with its operational staff and country offices. Important inputs to the World Bank's demographic work come from the United Nations Population Division's *World Population Prospects: The 2004 Revision;* census reports and other statistical publications from national statistical offices; household surveys conducted by national agencies, Macro International, and the U.S. Centers for Disease Control and Prevention; Eurostat, *Demographic Statistics* (various years); Centro Latinoamericano de Demografía, *Boletín Demográfico* (various years); and U.S. Bureau of the Census, International Database.

2.2 Labor force structure

	Labor force participation rate				Labor force				
	% ages 15–64				Total millions		Ages 15 and older average annual % growth	Female % of labor force	
	Male		Female						
	1990	2005	1990	2005	1990	2005	1990–2005	1990	2005
Afghanistan	..	..	..	..	..	..	..	..	..
Albania	86.3	75.7	63.3	54.7	1.6	1.4	–0.9	40.2	42.1
Algeria	81.0	83.5	23.7	38.0	7.2	13.4	4.1	22.6	30.7
Angola	90.9	92.2	76.0	75.6	4.5	7.0	2.9	46.4	45.8
Argentina	84.7	82.4	43.5	61.1	13.0	18.4	2.3	34.4	42.9
Armenia	89.7	65.9	76.7	55.4	1.9	1.3	–2.8	47.7	49.2
Australia	84.4	80.8	61.5	67.4	8.4	10.3	1.3	41.3	45.5
Austria	80.1	77.4	55.3	63.8	3.5	4.0	0.8	40.8	44.6
Azerbaijan	80.6	78.1	68.5	66.2	3.3	4.1	1.5	47.4	47.7
Bangladesh	89.8	88.1	64.5	55.2	46.9	63.9	2.1	40.2	36.9
Belarus	82.2	72.3	72.4	66.4	5.3	4.8	–0.7	48.6	49.3
Belgium	71.3	72.5	46.2	57.3	3.9	4.5	0.9	39.0	43.5
Benin	90.0	86.5	59.2	54.8	2.0	3.3	3.3	40.8	38.3
Bolivia	80.9	84.3	49.9	64.5	2.5	4.2	3.4	39.2	43.6
Bosnia and Herzegovina	82.4	78.3	66.1	70.5	2.3	2.1	–0.7	44.7	48.1
Botswana	76.0	68.2	58.9	46.7	0.5	0.6	1.2	45.2	41.8
Brazil	88.8	83.6	47.6	61.0	62.4	91.3	2.5	35.0	42.9
Bulgaria	77.8	62.6	72.3	52.4	4.4	3.1	–2.4	48.0	46.0
Burkina Faso	92.1	90.2	79.3	79.5	3.8	5.8	2.9	46.3	46.6
Burundi	90.7	93.2	91.8	92.8	2.8	3.8	2.1	52.6	51.9
Cambodia	86.7	81.4	81.0	78.0	4.4	6.8	2.9	52.6	51.4
Cameroon	83.5	81.1	58.2	53.9	4.4	6.3	2.4	41.5	39.9
Canada	84.9	82.6	68.3	72.8	14.7	17.6	1.2	44.0	46.4
Central African Republic	89.4	89.4	71.7	70.8	1.4	1.8	2.0	47.0	46.1
Chad	79.0	77.0	64.7	66.0	2.3	3.7	3.0	46.0	46.9
Chile	80.9	76.0	35.2	40.9	5.0	6.5	1.8	30.5	35.1
China	88.9	87.8	79.1	75.8	650.1	776.0	1.2	44.8	44.5
Hong Kong, China	85.5	81.1	53.0	62.2	2.9	3.7	1.7	36.3	46.6
Colombia	85.0	85.2	48.5	65.9	14.1	22.3	3.1	36.9	44.3
Congo, Dem. Rep.	91.2	91.1	62.6	63.1	15.0	22.9	2.8	41.6	41.2
Congo, Rep.	86.3	86.6	57.7	56.1	1.0	1.5	3.0	41.5	40.3
Costa Rica	87.6	84.8	35.3	48.6	1.2	2.0	3.5	27.6	35.1
Côte d'Ivoire	90.3	89.1	44.5	40.1	4.6	6.8	2.6	30.2	29.3
Croatia	76.9	71.0	55.0	57.5	2.2	2.0	–0.8	42.1	45.0
Cuba	79.5	82.3	43.5	50.8	4.5	5.4	1.1	34.8	37.4
Czech Republic	82.2	77.4	74.1	64.0	5.5	5.2	–0.3	47.4	45.2
Denmark	87.1	82.6	77.6	74.2	2.9	2.8	–0.2	46.1	46.8
Dominican Republic	85.6	84.0	37.8	48.5	2.6	3.8	2.5	29.6	35.9
Ecuador	85.9	85.4	33.6	64.1	3.7	6.4	3.6	27.8	42.4
Egypt, Arab Rep.	76.7	76.9	27.6	21.6	16.6	22.9	2.1	26.3	21.7
El Salvador	81.9	78.7	53.5	50.4	2.0	2.8	2.3	41.2	40.2
Eritrea	92.6	90.7	63.1	59.8	1.2	1.8	2.5	42.4	41.1
Estonia	83.0	73.6	76.0	64.4	0.9	0.7	–1.7	49.9	49.4
Ethiopia	92.3	90.7	74.5	73.5	22.6	31.6	2.2	44.9	44.9
Finland	79.0	76.8	72.2	72.8	2.6	2.7	0.2	47.2	47.8
France	75.0	73.5	57.0	62.4	24.8	27.1	0.6	43.3	45.9
Gabon	85.5	83.9	65.5	64.1	0.4	0.6	2.7	43.9	43.3
Gambia, The	86.2	86.6	63.3	60.3	0.4	0.7	3.4	43.4	41.6
Georgia	78.2	76.1	79.1	52.4	2.9	2.3	–1.7	52.3	43.4
Germany	81.4	79.3	56.8	67.4	38.3	41.0	0.4	40.4	45.2
Ghana	80.5	75.7	77.5	71.8	6.7	9.8	2.5	48.9	48.0
Greece	76.7	78.8	43.1	56.0	4.2	5.1	1.4	36.2	40.9
Guatemala	90.7	84.7	30.2	35.2	2.9	4.1	2.3	24.7	31.2
Guinea	90.8	88.6	82.8	82.6	3.0	4.4	2.6	46.2	46.6
Guinea-Bissau	91.4	93.0	60.5	63.1	0.4	0.6	2.9	40.3	40.9
Haiti	82.7	83.3	59.1	57.9	2.6	3.7	2.2	43.3	41.7

Labor force structure 2.2

	Labor force participation rate				Labor force				
	% ages 15–64				Total millions		Ages 15 and older average annual % growth	Female % of labor force	
	Male		Female						
	1990	2005	1990	2005	1990	2005	1990–2005	1990	2005
Honduras	89.0	90.5	34.6	56.5	1.6	3.1	4.4	27.7	37.7
Hungary	74.4	66.8	57.3	53.5	4.5	4.2	–0.5	44.5	45.1
India	86.6	84.3	40.3	36.0	335.1	435.0	1.7	29.9	28.4
Indonesia	82.9	87.1	52.1	53.0	75.3	107.2	2.4	38.4	37.9
Iran, Islamic Rep.	82.3	75.5	22.5	40.5	15.6	27.5	3.8	20.2	33.8
Iraq	77.8	..	16.4	..	4.7	..	..	16.8	..
Ireland	77.9	80.4	42.3	62.2	1.3	2.1	3.0	34.3	43.0
Israel	68.1	65.6	46.8	58.7	1.6	2.7	3.4	40.5	47.0
Italy	76.7	74.3	44.6	50.1	23.9	24.4	0.1	37.1	40.1
Jamaica	83.0	78.0	71.3	59.3	1.1	1.2	0.3	46.8	43.6
Japan	83.1	84.8	57.1	60.5	63.9	66.6	0.3	40.6	41.1
Jordan	71.3	79.7	18.6	28.9	0.8	1.8	6.0	18.8	24.4
Kazakhstan	81.6	80.1	68.0	73.6	7.7	8.1	0.3	46.3	49.6
Kenya	90.6	89.6	76.2	71.3	9.8	15.5	3.0	46.0	43.8
Korea, Dem. Rep.	84.0	80.4	56.4	49.9	9.7	10.7	0.6	39.3	38.7
Korea, Rep.	75.3	77.3	49.7	54.2	19.1	24.4	1.6	39.3	40.8
Kuwait	83.1	86.4	35.6	50.4	0.9	1.4	3.2	21.8	25.4
Kyrgyz Republic	78.0	77.5	65.0	59.9	1.8	2.3	1.4	46.2	44.2
Lao PDR	81.6	82.3	56.3	56.4	1.5	2.4	2.8	41.3	40.6
Latvia	83.4	71.9	75.0	63.0	1.5	1.1	–1.9	49.5	48.7
Lebanon	81.5	83.9	34.4	35.7	0.9	1.4	2.7	31.8	30.4
Lesotho	86.8	73.8	59.4	48.7	0.6	0.6	0.3	46.5	44.5
Liberia	85.2	83.8	55.9	55.7	0.8	1.2	2.8	39.4	39.9
Libya	81.4	82.8	19.9	33.9	1.3	2.3	4.1	17.3	27.1
Lithuania	81.7	72.4	70.4	65.9	1.9	1.6	–1.1	48.1	49.2
Macedonia, FYR	77.5	73.2	52.8	47.9	0.9	0.9	0.1	40.0	39.2
Madagascar	83.6	86.3	79.5	79.8	5.4	8.6	3.1	49.2	48.4
Malawi	91.7	89.9	86.2	86.2	4.5	5.9	1.9	50.3	49.8
Malaysia	82.7	83.7	45.3	48.1	7.1	11.0	2.9	34.8	35.8
Mali	90.7	85.1	75.1	74.8	3.8	5.5	2.5	46.0	47.5
Mauritania	87.6	85.1	57.8	56.5	0.8	1.2	2.7	40.7	40.4
Mauritius	86.6	84.1	45.2	46.9	0.5	0.6	1.4	33.9	35.7
Mexico	85.4	83.0	36.2	42.6	29.5	42.3	2.4	30.6	35.2
Moldova	81.5	76.0	70.4	65.4	2.1	2.2	0.1	48.6	47.7
Mongolia	83.7	83.3	59.3	56.2	0.8	1.2	2.4	41.0	40.1
Morocco	83.9	83.8	25.6	28.7	7.5	11.1	2.6	23.7	25.5
Mozambique	88.0	82.7	88.1	84.9	6.3	9.3	2.6	54.0	53.5
Myanmar	89.2	87.7	71.2	70.0	20.0	27.4	2.1	44.6	45.0
Namibia	67.1	64.5	50.6	48.4	0.4	0.6	2.5	44.1	43.6
Nepal	82.5	80.6	50.4	52.5	7.1	10.5	2.6	37.9	40.5
Netherlands	80.0	84.5	53.1	69.5	6.9	8.6	1.4	39.1	44.2
New Zealand	83.0	83.3	63.2	71.2	1.7	2.2	1.7	43.1	46.6
Nicaragua	87.0	87.4	36.8	36.9	1.3	1.9	2.7	30.1	29.8
Niger	94.7	95.5	72.4	73.0	3.6	5.9	3.4	42.6	42.0
Nigeria	86.9	85.8	49.0	46.6	32.7	47.9	2.5	36.2	34.7
Norway	82.5	83.6	69.9	77.3	2.2	2.5	0.9	44.7	47.3
Oman	83.8	82.7	15.7	23.6	0.6	1.0	3.5	11.1	16.4
Pakistan	88.1	85.7	28.8	33.7	35.2	56.5	3.2	23.3	27.0
Panama	82.7	83.0	41.6	54.9	0.9	1.5	3.1	32.5	38.8
Papua New Guinea	75.9	75.2	72.3	72.8	1.8	2.6	2.5	46.4	47.6
Paraguay	85.7	86.9	54.4	68.6	1.6	2.8	3.4	38.3	43.5
Peru	82.0	83.5	48.6	61.2	8.5	13.3	3.0	37.0	42.0
Philippines	83.7	84.7	48.7	56.5	23.4	37.1	3.1	36.6	39.8
Poland	79.2	68.8	65.1	57.6	18.6	17.3	–0.5	45.8	45.7
Portugal	82.6	79.7	59.2	67.8	4.8	5.6	1.0	42.7	46.5
Puerto Rico	67.4	67.7	35.0	44.4	1.2	1.5	1.6	35.8	41.5

2.2 Labor force structure

	Labor force participation rate				Labor force				
	% ages 15–64				Total millions		Ages 15 and older average annual % growth	Female % of labor force	
	Male		Female						
	1990	2005	1990	2005	1990	2005	1990–2005	1990	2005
Romania	77.2	69.5	61.1	55.3	11.0	10.3	–0.4	44.3	46.2
Russian Federation	81.6	75.3	71.7	67.1	77.2	73.2	–0.4	48.3	49.0
Rwanda	88.3	84.9	87.4	82.0	3.1	4.2	2.1	51.0	51.2
Saudi Arabia	81.3	80.4	15.6	18.5	5.1	7.5	2.5	11.4	15.2
Senegal	87.8	83.4	63.4	58.4	3.1	4.6	2.6	43.4	42.5
Serbia and Montenegro	77.0	76.0	54.9	54.7	4.9[a]	3.9	0.0[b]	41.7	42.2
Sierra Leone	90.2	94.5	55.6	58.4	1.7	2.4	2.2	38.5	38.5
Singapore	83.9	82.8	54.2	56.7	1.6	2.2	2.4	38.8	39.9
Slovak Republic	82.5	76.4	70.6	62.4	2.6	2.7	0.1	46.3	45.1
Slovenia	76.9	75.5	63.3	66.6	1.0	1.0	0.4	45.5	46.2
Somalia	95.8	95.1	63.1	61.0	2.8	3.5	1.4	39.9	39.2
South Africa	81.6	81.9	57.4	49.3	14.4	19.6	2.1	41.6	38.2
Spain	80.3	80.7	41.9	57.2	16.0	20.9	1.8	34.3	41.0
Sri Lanka	82.9	81.9	48.2	38.5	7.3	8.4	1.0	34.8	30.4
Sudan	78.9	72.5	27.8	24.2	7.8	10.5	2.0	26.0	24.8
Swaziland	79.6	74.5	39.6	32.9	0.2	0.3	2.7	38.0	32.9
Sweden	86.0	79.0	81.9	74.9	4.7	4.7	–0.1	47.7	47.4
Switzerland	90.2	87.6	62.8	75.3	3.7	4.2	0.9	40.4	46.6
Syrian Arab Republic	83.7	89.2	29.7	39.9	3.7	7.6	4.8	26.2	30.6
Tajikistan	77.6	65.8	56.2	49.5	1.9	2.1	0.8	42.2	43.8
Tanzania	92.1	90.7	90.2	88.2	12.8	19.3	2.7	50.2	49.4
Thailand	90.6	84.5	79.2	71.0	30.4	35.7	1.1	46.6	46.2
Togo	90.8	90.4	55.2	51.7	1.5	2.4	3.1	38.5	36.9
Trinidad and Tobago	79.7	82.5	45.9	51.4	0.5	0.6	1.9	36.1	38.9
Tunisia	79.2	78.4	22.1	31.1	2.4	3.8	3.0	21.5	27.6
Turkey	84.5	76.0	36.2	27.2	21.0	26.6	1.6	29.4	26.4
Turkmenistan	80.0	76.5	69.1	65.1	1.5	2.2	2.4	46.9	46.7
Uganda	92.4	87.3	82.0	81.2	7.8	11.9	2.8	47.5	48.3
Ukraine	79.7	72.4	70.7	62.9	26.3	22.3	–1.1	49.2	49.1
United Arab Emirates	92.4	92.0	25.9	39.0	0.9	2.7	7.3	9.8	13.4
United Kingdom	87.9	81.9	67.2	69.3	29.4	30.6	0.3	44.0	46.0
United States	85.1	81.5	67.5	70.1	129.3	155.5	1.2	44.4	46.2
Uruguay	85.9	86.1	54.3	66.3	1.4	1.8	1.6	39.9	44.2
Uzbekistan	78.5	75.7	64.4	60.6	8.2	11.3	2.2	45.4	44.6
Venezuela, RB	82.4	85.7	39.8	61.9	7.3	12.9	3.8	31.8	40.9
Vietnam	85.5	82.4	79.4	77.4	31.3	44.0	2.3	48.3	48.5
West Bank and Gaza	67.0	68.8	9.5	10.9	0.4	0.8	4.5	11.9	13.1
Yemen, Rep.	76.1	77.5	28.6	30.8	3.0	5.9	4.6	27.3	27.9
Zambia	90.4	91.5	67.8	68.3	3.5	4.9	2.4	43.2	42.2
Zimbabwe	81.0	85.2	69.9	64.5	4.3	5.8	2.0	47.2	44.0
World	**85.5 w**	**83.8 w**	**58.9 w**	**57.9 w**	**2,390.7 t**	**3,027.5 t**	**1.6 w**	**39.9 w**	**40.1 w**
Low income	87.0	85.0	50.6	47.8	699.6	965.3	2.1	35.7	35.0
Middle income	85.8	84.0	63.9	62.7	1,263.5	1,569.4	1.4	41.8	42.1
Lower middle income	86.7	85.4	66.2	65.1	1,031.9	1,301.1	1.5	42.0	42.3
Upper middle income	82.2	77.9	55.0	52.6	231.6	268.3	1.0	40.6	40.9
Low & middle income	86.3	84.4	59.0	56.7	1,963.1	2,534.7	1.7	39.6	39.4
East Asia & Pacific	87.8	87.0	74.3	71.4	856.8	1,063.4	1.4	44.1	43.8
Europe & Central Asia	80.8	74.0	65.1	57.9	223.8	219.1	–0.1	45.6	44.9
Latin America & Carib.	85.9	83.5	43.8	56.0	171.0	252.9	2.6	34.0	40.7
Middle East & N. Africa	79.9	79.3	24.5	31.1	64.9	108.3	3.4	22.9	27.6
South Asia	86.9	84.8	41.7	38.1	437.0	585.0	1.9	30.6	29.4
Sub-Saharan Africa	87.8	86.3	65.1	62.6	209.7	306.0	2.5	43.0	42.1
High income	82.1	80.4	58.6	63.8	427.6	492.8	0.9	41.3	43.7
Europe EMU	78.5	77.4	51.7	61.1	131.5	147.2	0.8	39.6	43.7

a. Includes population of Kosovo and Metahia until 1999. b. Data are for 1990–99.

Labor force structure 2.2

About the data

The labor force is the supply of labor available for the production of goods and services in an economy. It includes people who are currently employed and people who are unemployed but seeking work as well as first-time job-seekers. Not everyone who works is included, however. Unpaid workers, family workers, and students are among those usually omitted, and in some countries members of the military are not counted. The size of the labor force tends to vary during the year as seasonal workers enter and leave it.

Data on the labor force are from labor force surveys, censuses, establishment censuses and surveys, and various types of administrative records such as employment exchange registers and unemployment insurance schemes. For some countries a combination of these sources is used. While the resulting statistics may provide rough estimates of the labor force, they are not comparable across countries or sometimes within countries because of the noncomparability of the original data, differences in concepts and methodologies, and the different ways the original sources may be combined.

Labor force surveys are the most comprehensive source for internationally comparable labor force data. They can be designed to cover all noninstitutionalized civilians, all branches and sectors of the economy, and all categories of workers, including people who hold multiple jobs. By contrast, labor force data obtained from population censuses are often based on a limited number of questions on the economic characteristics of individuals, with little scope to probe. The resulting data are often contrary to labor force survey data and often vary considerably from country to country, depending on the scope and coverage of the census. Establishment censuses and surveys provide data only on the employed population, leaving out unemployed workers, workers in small establishments, and workers in the informal sector (International Labour Organization, *Key Indicators of the Labour Market 2001–2002).*

The reference period of the census or survey is another important source of differences: in some countries data refer to people's status on the day of the census or survey or during a specific period before the inquiry date, while in others the data are recorded without reference to any period. In developing countries, where the household is often the basic unit of production and all members contribute to output, but some at low intensity or irregular intervals, the estimated labor force may be significantly smaller than the numbers actually working.

The labor force participation rates presented in the table are from the International Labour Organization's (ILO) *Estimates and Projections of the Economically Active Population,* 5th edition. These new estimates used stricter data selection criteria and enhanced methods to ensure comparability across countries and over time, including collection and tabulation methodologies as well as for country-specific factors such as military service requirements. The estimates are based mainly on labor force surveys. Some population census estimates are also included in the estimates, but only when no labor force survey data are available. Data from official government estimates are not included as these methodologies can differ significantly across countries and over time. Data with limited age group and geographic coverage are also excluded.

The labor force participation rate of the population ages 15–64 provides an indication of the relative size of the labor supply. But in many developing countries children under age 15 work full or part time. And in some high-income countries many workers postpone retirement past age 65. As a result, labor force participation rates calculated in this way may systematically over- or under-estimate actual rates. For further information on the labor force participation rate, consult the original source.

The labor force estimates in the table were calculated by World Bank staff by applying labor force participation rates from the ILO database to World Bank population estimates to create a series consistent with these population estimates. This procedure sometimes results in estimates of labor force size that differ slightly from those in the ILO's *Yearbook of Labour Statistics* and its database Key Indicators of the Labour Market. The labor force estimates in this year's *World Development Indicators,* as were last year's, are for the population ages 15 and older. In previous editions the labor force included children under age 15. For this reason, labor force estimates are not comparable across editions.

In general, estimates of women in the labor force are lower than those of men and are not comparable internationally, reflecting the fact that for women demographic, social, legal, and cultural trends and norms determine whether their activities are regarded as economic. In many countries large numbers of women work on farms or in other family enterprises without pay, while others work in or near their homes, mixing work and family activities during the day. Countries differ in the criteria used to determine the extent to which such workers are to be counted as part of the labor force. In most economies the gap between male and female labor force participation rates has been narrowing since 1980. This stems from both falling rates for men and rising rates for women. The largest gap between men and women in labor force participation is observed in the Middle East and North Africa, where low participation of women in the work force also brings down the overall labor force participation rate.

Definitions

• **Labor force participation rate** is the proportion of the population ages 15–64 that is economically active: all people who supply labor for the production of goods and services during a specified period. • **Total labor force** comprises people ages 15 and older who meet the ILO definition of the economically active population. It includes both the employed and the unemployed. • **Average annual growth rate of the labor force** is calculated using the exponential endpoint method (see *Statistical methods* for more information). • **Females as a percentage of the labor force** show the extent to which women are active in the labor force.

Data sources

The labor force participation rates are from the ILO database Estimates and Projections of the Economically Active Population, 1980–2020, 5th edition. The ILO publishes estimates of the economically active population in its *Yearbook of Labour Statistics.* Labor force numbers were calculated by World Bank staff, applying labor force participation rates from the ILO database to population estimates.

2.3 Employment by economic activity

	Agriculture				Industry				Services			
	Male % of male employment		Female % of female employment		Male % of male employment		Female % of female employment		Male % of male employment		Female % of female employment	
	1990–92[a]	2000–05[a]	1990–92[a]	2000–05[a]	1990–92[a]	2000–05[a]	1990–92[a]	2000–05[a]	1990–92[a]	2000–05[a]	1990–92[a]	2000–05[a]
Afghanistan	..	..	..	..	..	..	..	..	..	..	..	..
Albania	..	..	..	..	..	..	..	..	..	..	..	..
Algeria	..	20	..	22	..	26	..	28	..	54	..	49
Angola	..	..	..	..	..	..	..	..	..	..	..	..
Argentina	0[b, c]	2[c]	0[b, c]	1[b, c]	40[c]	33[c]	18[c]	11[c]	59[c]	66[c]	81[c]	88[c]
Armenia	..	..	..	..	..	..	..	..	..	..	..	..
Australia	6	5[c]	4	3[c]	32	31[c]	12	9[c]	61	65[c]	84	88[c]
Austria	6	6[c]	8	6[c]	47	40[c]	20	13[c]	46	55[c]	72	81[c]
Azerbaijan	..	41	..	37	..	15	..	9	..	44	..	54
Bangladesh	54	50	85	59	16	12	9	18	25	38	2	23
Belarus	..	..	..	..	..	..	..	..	..	..	..	..
Belgium	3[c]	3[c]	2[c]	1[c]	41[c]	35[c]	16[c]	11[c]	56[c]	62[c]	81[c]	82[c]
Benin	..	..	..	..	..	..	..	..	..	..	..	..
Bolivia	3[c]	6[c]	1[c]	3[c]	42[c]	39[c]	17[c]	14[c]	55[c]	55[c]	82[c]	82[c]
Bosnia and Herzegovina	..	..	..	..	..	..	..	..	..	..	..	..
Botswana	..	26	..	19	..	29	..	13	..	43	..	58
Brazil	31[c]	25[c]	25[c]	16[c]	27[c]	27[c]	10[c]	13[c]	43[c]	48[c]	65[c]	71[c]
Bulgaria	..	11	..	7	..	39	..	29	..	50	..	64
Burkina Faso	..	..	..	..	..	..	..	..	..	..	..	..
Burundi	..	..	..	..	..	..	..	..	..	..	..	..
Cambodia	..	61	..	59	..	12	..	13	..	27	..	27
Cameroon	53	..	68	..	14	..	4	..	26	..	23	..
Canada	6[c]	4[c]	2[c]	2[c]	31[c]	32[c]	11[c]	11[c]	64[c]	64[c]	87[c]	88[c]
Central African Republic	..	..	..	..	..	..	..	..	..	..	..	..
Chad	..	..	..	..	..	..	..	..	..	..	..	..
Chile	24	17	6	6	32	29	15	12	45	54	79	83
China	..	..	..	..	..	..	..	..	..	..	..	..
Hong Kong, China	1	0[b]	0[b]	0[b]	37	22	27	7	63	77	73	93
Colombia	2[c]	32	1[c]	8	35[c]	21	25[c]	16	63[c]	48	74[c]	76
Congo, Dem. Rep.	..	..	..	..	..	..	..	..	..	..	..	..
Congo, Rep.	..	..	..	..	..	..	..	..	..	..	..	..
Costa Rica	32	21	5	5	27	26	25	13	41	52	69	82
Côte d'Ivoire	..	..	..	..	..	..	..	..	..	..	..	..
Croatia	..	16	..	19	..	37	..	18	..	47	..	63
Cuba	..	28	..	10	..	23	..	14	..	50	..	76
Czech Republic	9	5	7	3	55	49	33	27	36	46	61	71
Denmark	7	4	3	2	37	34	16	12	56	62	81	86
Dominican Republic	26	23	3	2	23	24	21	15	52	53	76	83
Ecuador	10[c]	11[c]	2[c]	4[c]	29[c]	27[c]	17[c]	12[c]	62[c]	62[c]	81[c]	84[c]
Egypt, Arab Rep.	35	28	52	39	25	23	10	6	41	49	37	55
El Salvador	48	30	15	3	23	25	23	22	29	45	63	75
Eritrea	..	..	..	..	..	..	..	..	..	..	..	..
Estonia	23	7	13	4	42	44	30	24	36	49	57	72
Ethiopia	..	..	..	..	..	..	..	..	..	..	..	..
Finland	11	7	6	3	38	38	15	12	51	56	78	84
France	..	5	..	3	..	35	..	12	..	60	..	84
Gabon	..	..	..	..	..	..	..	..	..	..	..	..
Gambia, The	..	..	..	..	..	..	..	..	..	..	..	..
Georgia	..	52	..	57	..	14	..	4	..	34	..	38
Germany	4	3	4	2	50	41	24	16	47	56	72	82
Ghana	66	60	59	50	10	14	10	15	23	27	32	36
Greece	20[c]	12[c]	26[c]	14[c]	32[c]	30[c]	17[c]	10[c]	48[c]	58[c]	56[c]	76[c]
Guatemala	..	50	..	18	..	18	..	23	..	27	..	56
Guinea	..	..	..	..	..	..	..	..	..	..	..	..
Guinea-Bissau	..	..	..	..	..	..	..	..	..	..	..	..
Haiti	..	..	..	..	..	..	..	..	..	..	..	..

Employment by economic activity 2.3

	Agriculture				Industry				Services			
	Male % of male employment		Female % of female employment		Male % of male employment		Female % of female employment		Male % of male employment		Female % of female employment	
	1990–92[a]	2000–05[a]	1990–92[a]	2000–05[a]	1990–92[a]	2000–05[a]	1990–92[a]	2000–05[a]	1990–92[a]	2000–05[a]	1990–92[a]	2000–05[a]
Honduras	53[c]	51[c]	6[c]	13[c]	18[c]	20[c]	25[c]	23[c]	29[c]	29[c]	69[c]	63[c]
Hungary	..	7[c]	..	3[c]	..	42[c]	..	21[c]	..	51[c]	..	76[c]
India	..	..	..	..	..	..	..	..	..	..	..	..
Indonesia	54	43	57	45	15	20	13	15	31	37	31	40
Iran, Islamic Rep.	..	23	..	34	..	31	..	28	..	46	..	37
Iraq	..	..	..	..	..	..	..	..	..	..	..	..
Ireland	19	9	3	1	33	39	18	12	48	51	78	86
Israel	5	3	2	1	38	32	15	11	57	64	83	88
Italy	8	5	9	3	37	39	22	18	55	56	70	79
Jamaica	36	25	16	9	25	27	12	5	39	48	72	86
Japan	6	4	7	5	40	35	27	18	54	59	65	77
Jordan	..	4	..	2	..	23	..	13	..	73	..	83
Kazakhstan	..	35	..	32	..	24	..	10	..	41	..	58
Kenya	19[c]	..	20[c]	..	23[c]	..	9[c]	..	58[c]	..	71[c]	..
Korea, Dem. Rep.	..	..	..	..	..	..	..	..	..	..	..	..
Korea, Rep.	14	7	18	9	40	34	28	17	46	59	54	74
Kuwait	..	..	..	..	..	..	..	..	..	..	..	..
Kyrgyz Republic	..	51	..	55	..	13	..	7	..	36	..	38
Lao PDR	..	..	..	..	..	..	..	..	..	..	..	..
Latvia	..	15[c]	..	8[c]	..	35[c]	..	16[c]	..	49[c]	..	75[c]
Lebanon	..	..	..	..	..	..	..	..	..	..	..	..
Lesotho	..	..	..	..	..	..	..	..	..	..	..	..
Liberia	..	..	..	..	..	..	..	..	..	..	..	..
Libya	..	..	..	..	..	..	..	..	..	..	..	..
Lithuania	25	17	15	11	46	37	31	21	29	46	54	68
Macedonia, FYR	..	20	..	19	..	34	..	30	..	46	..	51
Madagascar	..	77	..	79	..	7	..	6	..	16	..	15
Malawi	..	..	..	..	..	..	..	..	..	..	..	..
Malaysia	23	16	20	11	31	35	32	27	46	49	48	62
Mali	..	..	..	..	..	..	..	..	..	..	..	..
Mauritania	..	..	..	..	..	..	..	..	..	..	..	..
Mauritius	15[c]	11	13[c]	9	36[c]	34	48[c]	29	48[c]	55	39[c]	62
Mexico	33	21	10	5	25	30	19	19	41	49	62	76
Moldova	..	41	..	40	..	21	..	12	..	38	..	48
Mongolia	..	43	..	38	..	19	..	14	..	39	..	49
Morocco	..	41	..	63	..	23	..	15	..	36	..	22
Mozambique	..	..	..	..	..	..	..	..	..	..	..	..
Myanmar	..	..	..	..	..	..	..	..	..	..	..	..
Namibia	45	33	52	29	21	17	8	7	32	49	29	63
Nepal	..	..	..	..	..	..	..	..	..	..	..	..
Netherlands	5	4	3	2	33	30	10	8	60	62	82	86
New Zealand	13	9	8	5	31	32	13	11	56	59	80	84
Nicaragua	..	43	..	10	..	19	..	17	..	32	..	52
Niger	..	..	..	..	..	..	..	..	..	..	..	..
Nigeria	..	..	..	..	..	..	..	..	..	..	..	..
Norway	7	5	3	2	34	32	10	8	58	63	86	90
Oman	..	7	..	5	..	11	..	14	..	82	..	80
Pakistan	45	38	69	65	20	22	15	16	35	40	16	20
Panama	35	22	3	4	20	22	11	9	45	56	85	86
Papua New Guinea	..	..	..	..	..	..	..	..	..	..	..	..
Paraguay	3[c]	39	0[b, c]	20	33[c]	19	19[c]	10	64[c]	42	80[c]	70
Peru	1[c]	1[c]	0[b, c]	0[c]	30[c]	31[c]	13[c]	13[c]	69[c]	68[c]	87[c]	86[c]
Philippines	53	45	32	25	17	17	14	12	29	39	55	64
Poland	..	18[c]	..	17[c]	..	39[c]	..	17[c]	..	43[c]	..	66[c]
Portugal	10	12	13	13	39	42	24	21	51	46	63	66
Puerto Rico	5	3	0[b]	0[b]	27	25	19	11	67	72	80	89

2.3 Employment by economic activity

	Agriculture				Industry				Services			
	Male % of male employment		Female % of female employment		Male % of male employment		Female % of female employment		Male % of male employment		Female % of female employment	
	1990–92[a]	2000–05[a]	1990–92[a]	2000–05[a]	1990–92[a]	2000–05[a]	1990–92[a]	2000–05[a]	1990–92[a]	2000–05[a]	1990–92[a]	2000–05[a]
Romania	29	31	38	33	44	35	30	25	28	34	33	42
Russian Federation	..	12	..	8	..	38	..	21	..	50	..	71
Rwanda	..	..	..	..	..	..	..	..	..	..	..	..
Saudi Arabia	..	5	..	1	..	24	..	1	..	71	..	98
Senegal	..	..	..	..	..	..	..	..	..	..	..	..
Serbia and Montenegro	..	..	..	..	..	..	..	..	..	..	..	..
Sierra Leone	..	..	..	..	..	..	..	..	..	..	..	..
Singapore	1	0[b]	0[b]	0[b]	36	36	32	21	63	63	68	79
Slovak Republic	..	6[c]	..	3[c]	..	50[c]	..	25[c]	..	44[c]	..	72[c]
Slovenia	..	9	..	9	..	47	..	25	..	43	..	65
Somalia	..	..	..	..	..	..	..	..	..	..	..	..
South Africa	..	13	..	7	..	33	..	14	..	54	..	79
Spain	11[c]	6[c]	8[c]	4[c]	41[c]	41[c]	16[c]	12[c]	49[c]	52[c]	76[c]	84[c]
Sri Lanka	..	32[c]	..	40[c]	..	40[c]	..	35[c]	..	29[c]	..	25[c]
Sudan	..	..	..	..	..	..	..	..	..	..	..	..
Swaziland	..	..	..	..	..	..	..	..	..	..	..	..
Sweden	5	3	2	1	40	34	12	9	55	63	86	90
Switzerland	4	5[c]	4	3[c]	37	32[c]	15	12[c]	59	63[c]	81	85[c]
Syrian Arab Republic	..	24	..	58	..	31	..	7	..	45	..	35
Tajikistan	..	..	..	..	..	..	..	..	..	..	..	..
Tanzania	78[c]	80[c]	90[c]	84[c]	7[c]	4[c]	1[c]	1[c]	15[c]	16[c]	8[c]	15[c]
Thailand	59	44	60	41	16	22	14	19	25	34	25	41
Togo	..	..	..	..	..	..	..	..	..	..	..	..
Trinidad and Tobago	15	10	6	2	34	37	14	14	51	53	80	84
Tunisia	..	..	..	..	..	..	..	..	..	..	..	..
Turkey	33	22	72	52	26	28	11	15	41	50	17	33
Turkmenistan	..	..	..	..	..	..	..	..	..	..	..	..
Uganda	91	60	91	77	4	11	6	5	5	28	3	17
Ukraine	..	21	..	17	..	38	..	21	..	41	..	62
United Arab Emirates	..	9	..	0[b]	..	36	..	14	..	55	..	86
United Kingdom	3	2	1	1	41	33	16	9	55	65	82	90
United States	4	2	1	1	34	30	14	10	62	68	85	90
Uruguay	7[c]	7[c]	1[c]	2[c]	36[c]	29[c]	21[c]	13[c]	57[c]	64[c]	78[c]	86[c]
Uzbekistan	..	..	..	..	..	..	..	..	..	..	..	..
Venezuela, RB	17	16[c]	2	2[c]	32	25[c]	16	11[c]	52	59[c]	82	86[c]
Vietnam	..	56	..	60	..	21	..	14	..	23	..	26
West Bank and Gaza	..	12	..	34	..	28	..	8	..	59	..	56
Yemen, Rep.	..	..	..	..	..	..	..	..	..	..	..	..
Zambia	..	..	..	..	..	..	..	..	..	..	..	..
Zimbabwe	..	..	..	..	..	..	..	..	..	..	..	..
World	.. w	.. w	.. w	.. w	.. w	.. w	.. w	.. w	.. w	.. w	.. w	.. w
Low income	..	..	..	..	..	..	..	..	..	..	..	..
Middle income	..	..	..	..	..	..	..	..	..	..	..	..
Lower middle income	..	..	..	..	..	..	..	..	..	..	..	..
Upper middle income	..	16	..	12	..	34	..	19	..	50	..	69
Low & middle income	..	..	..	..	..	..	..	..	..	..	..	..
East Asia & Pacific	..	..	..	..	..	..	..	..	..	..	..	..
Europe & Central Asia	..	17	..	17	..	35	..	20	..	47	..	63
Latin America & Carib.	20	21	14	10	30	27	14	14	50	52	72	76
Middle East & N. Africa	..	..	..	..	..	..	..	..	..	..	..	..
South Asia	..	..	..	..	..	..	..	..	..	..	..	..
Sub-Saharan Africa	..	..	..	..	..	..	..	..	..	..	..	..
High income	6	4	5	2	38	34	19	12	56	62	77	96
Europe EMU	7	5	7	3	42	39	20	15	50	56	72	82

Note: Data across sectors may not sum to 100 percent because of workers not classified by sectors.
a. Data are for the most recent year available. b. Less than 0.5. c. Limited coverage.

Employment by economic activity 2.3

About the data

The International Labour Organization (ILO) classifies economic activity using the International Standard Industrial Classification (ISIC) of All Economic Activities, revision 2 (1968) and revision 3 (1990). Because this classification is based on where work is performed (industry) rather than on what type of work is performed (occupation), all of an enterprise's employees are classified under the same industry, regardless of their trade or occupation. The categories should add up to 100 percent. Where they do not, the differences arise because of workers who cannot be classified by economic activity.

Data on employment are drawn from labor force surveys, household surveys, official estimates, censuses and administrative records of social insurance schemes, and establishment surveys when no other information is available. The concept of employment generally refers to people above a certain age who worked, or who held a job, during a reference period. Employment data include both full-time and part-time workers.

There are many differences in how countries define and measure employment status, particularly part-time workers, members of the armed forces, and household or contributing family workers. Where the armed forces are included, they are allocated to the service sector, causing that sector to be somewhat overstated relative to the service sector in economies where they are excluded. Where data are obtained from establishment surveys, they cover only employees; thus self-employed and contributing family workers are excluded. In such cases the employment share of the agricultural sector is severely underreported. Caution should be also used where the data refer only to urban areas, which record little or no agricultural work. Moreover, the age group and area covered could differ by country or change over time within a country. For detailed information on breaks in series, consult the original source.

Countries also take different approaches to the treatment of unemployed people. In most countries unemployed people with previous job experience are classified according to their last job. But in some countries the unemployed and people seeking their first job are not classifiable by economic activity. Because of these differences, the size and distribution of employment by economic activity may not be fully comparable across countries.

The ILO's *Yearbook of Labour Statistics* and its database Key Indicators of the Labour Market report data by major divisions of the ISIC revision 2 or revision 3. In this table the reported divisions or categories are aggregated into three broad groups: agriculture, industry, and services. Such broad classification may obscure fundamental shifts within countries' industrial patterns. A slight majority of countries report economic activity according to the ISIC revision 2 instead of ISIC revision 3. The use of one classification or another should not have a significant impact on the information for the three broad sectors presented in this table.

The distribution of economic wealth in the world remains strongly correlated with employment by economic activity. The wealthier economies are those with the largest share of total employment in services, whereas the poorer economies are largely agriculture based.

The distribution of economic activity by gender reveals some clear patterns. Men still make up the majority of people employed in all three sectors, but the gender gap is biggest in industry. Employment in agriculture is also male-dominated, although not as much as industry. Segregating one sex in a narrow range of occupations significantly reduces economic efficiency by reducing labor market flexibility and thus the economy's ability to adapt to change. This segregation is particularly harmful for women, who have a much narrower range of labor market choices and lower levels of pay than men (see box 2.3a). But it is also detrimental to men when job losses are concentrated in industries dominated by men and job growth is centered in service occupations, where women have better chances, as has been the recent experience in many countries.

There are several explanations for the rising importance of service jobs for women. Many service jobs—such as nursing and social and clerical work—are considered "feminine" because of a perceived similarity to women's traditional roles. Women often do not receive the training needed to take advantage of changing employment opportunities. And the greater availability of part-time work in service industries may lure more women, although it is unclear whether this is a cause or an effect.

Lower wages and less rewarding employment opportunities mean higher risk of poverty for women — Box 2.3a

Within any employment status, women's earnings in Egypt tend to be lower than men's (see table). A small- and micro-enterprise survey for Egypt found that while workers' wages increased with firm size, women accounted for a decreasing share of total employment. Taken together, less rewarding employment opportunities and lower wages mean that women face a higher risk of poverty.

Average wages per worker and women's share of employment by firm size in Egypt, 2003

Size of firm	Average wages (2002 Egyptian pounds)	Women as share of total employment (%)
1 worker	112.8	17.1
2–4 workers	172.1	9.4
5–9 workers	290.1	7.9
10–24 workers	1,073.4	5.9
Total (firms of all sizes)	160.1	14.3

Source: UNIFEM 2005.

Definitions

• **Agriculture** corresponds to division 1 (ISIC revision 2) or tabulation categories A and B (ISIC revision 3) and includes hunting, forestry, and fishing. • **Industry** corresponds to divisions 2–5 (ISIC revision 2) or tabulation categories C–F (ISIC revision 3) and includes mining and quarrying (including oil production), manufacturing, construction, and public utilities (electricity, gas, and water). • **Services** correspond to divisions 6–9 (ISIC revision 2) or tabulation categories G–P (ISIC revision 3) and include wholesale and retail trade and restaurants and hotels; transport, storage, and communications; financing, insurance, real estate, and business services; and community, social, and personal services.

Data sources

Data on employment are from the ILO database Key Indicators of the Labour Market, 4th edition.

2.4 Children at work

	Survey year	Economically active children					Employment by economic activity[a]					
			% of children ages 7–14		% of economically active children ages 7–14		% of economically active children ages 7–14					
							Agriculture		Manufacturing		Services	
		Total	Male	Female	Work only	Work and study	Male	Female	Male	Female	Male	Female
Afghanistan		..	..	..	..	..	..	..	..	..	..	
Albania	2000	36.6	41.1	31.8	43.1	56.9	..	..	..	..	..	..
Algeria		..	..	..	..	..	..	..	..	..	..	
Angola[b]	2001	30.1	30.0	30.3	26.6	73.4	..	..	..	..	..	..
Argentina	1997	20.7	25.4	16.0	8.6	91.4	..	..	..	..	..	..
Armenia		..	..	..	..	..	..	..	..	..	..	
Australia		..	..	..	..	..	..	..	..	..	..	
Austria		..	..	..	..	..	..	..	..	..	..	
Azerbaijan	2000	9.7	12.0	7.3	4.2	95.8	..	..	..	..	..	..
Bangladesh	2003	17.5	20.9	13.9	63.3	36.7	61.4	64.0	11.6	15.5	25.2	18.3
Belarus		..	..	..	..	..	..	..	..	..	..	
Belgium		..	..	..	..	..	..	..	..	..	..	
Benin		..	..	..	..	..	..	..	..	..	..	
Bolivia	2000	19.2	20.4	18.0	19.7	80.3	77.8	72.9	4.3	3.5	15.0	23.6
Bosnia and Herzegovina	2000	20.2	22.8	17.6	4.0	96.0	..	..	..	..	..	..
Botswana		..	..	..	..	..	..	..	..	..	..	
Brazil	2003	7.1	9.5	4.6	5.8	94.2	64.3	49.8	6.5	9.1	26.8	40.9
Bulgaria		..	..	..	..	..	..	..	..	..	..	
Burkina Faso[c]	1998	66.5	65.4	67.7	95.9	4.1	98.0	98.2	0.6	0.5	1.3	1.2
Burundi	2000	37.0	38.4	35.7	48.3	51.7	..	..	..	..	..	..
Cambodia	2001	52.3	52.4	52.1	16.5	83.5	78.5	73.6	4.7	5.4	15.7	20.4
Cameroon[c]	2001	15.9	14.5	17.4	52.5	47.5	90.4	86.3	1.9	2.3	5.1	8.8
Canada		..	..	..	..	..	..	..	..	..	..	
Central African Republic	2000	67.0	66.5	67.6	54.9	45.1	..	..	..	..	..	..
Chad	2000	69.9	73.5	66.5	44.6	55.4	..	..	..	..	..	..
Chile	2003	8.8	10.5	6.9	4.0	96.0	31.5	11.9	7.6	5.8	58.5	80.6
China		..	..	..	..	..	..	..	..	..	..	
Hong Kong, China		..	..	..	..	..	..	..	..	..	..	
Colombia	2001	12.2	16.6	7.7	23.0	77.0	..	..	..	..	..	..
Congo, Dem. Rep.	2000	39.8	39.9	39.8	35.7	64.3	..	..	..	..	..	..
Congo, Rep.		..	..	..	..	..	..	..	..	..	..	
Costa Rica	2002	6.7	9.7	3.5	20.8	79.2	56.5	55.2	8.7	2.7	28.0	42.1
Côte d'Ivoire	2000	40.7	40.9	40.5	46.4	53.6	..	..	..	..	..	..
Croatia		..	..	..	..	..	..	..	..	..	..	
Cuba		..	..	..	..	..	..	..	..	..	..	
Czech Republic		..	..	..	..	..	..	..	..	..	..	
Denmark		..	..	..	..	..	..	..	..	..	..	
Dominican Republic	2000	12.5	16.7	8.1	7.2	92.8	..	..	..	..	..	..
Ecuador	2001	17.9	22.1	13.6	25.0	75.0	65.1	69.2	10.7	8.6	21.2	22.1
Egypt, Arab Rep.	1998	6.4	4.0	8.9	60.9	39.1	..	..	..	..	..	..
El Salvador	2003	12.7	17.1	8.1	19.5	80.5	66.4	17.6	10.8	16.1	21.2	66.3
Eritrea		..	..	..	..	..	..	..	..	..	..	
Estonia		..	..	..	..	..	..	..	..	..	..	
Ethiopia	2001	57.1	67.9	45.9	63.5	36.5	96.5	88.7	0.5	2.8	2.5	6.2
Finland		..	..	..	..	..	..	..	..	..	..	
France		..	..	..	..	..	..	..	..	..	..	
Gabon		..	..	..	..	..	..	..	..	..	..	
Gambia, The	2000	25.3	25.4	25.3	41.6	58.4	..	..	..	..	..	..
Georgia		..	..	..	..	..	..	..	..	..	..	
Germany		..	..	..	..	..	..	..	..	..	..	
Ghana	2000	28.5	28.5	28.4	36.4	63.6	81.0	59.1	4.5	7.6	13.8	32.0
Greece		..	..	..	..	..	..	..	..	..	..	
Guatemala	2000	20.1	25.9	13.9	38.5	61.5	74.5	39.8	5.9	20.1	14.7	40.0
Guinea	1994	48.3	47.2	49.5	98.6	1.4	..	..	..	..	..	..
Guinea-Bissau	2000	67.5	67.4	67.5	63.7	36.3	..	..	..	..	..	..
Haiti		..	..	..	..	..	..	..	..	..	..	

	Survey year	Economically active children					Employment by economic activity[a]					
			% of children ages 7–14		% of economically active children ages 7–14		% of economically active children ages 7–14					
							Agriculture		Manufacturing		Services	
		Total	Male	Female	Work only	Work and study	Male	Female	Male	Female	Male	Female
Honduras	2002	11.4	16.5	6.1	41.9	58.1	73.6	19.8	5.9	24.4	18.6	55.7
Hungary		..	..	..	..	..	..	..	..	..	..	
India	2000	5.2	5.3	5.1	89.8	10.2	70.5	76.6	10.0	15.4	15.9	6.5
Indonesia		..	..	..	..	..	..	..	..	..	..	
Iran, Islamic Rep.		..	..	..	..	..	..	..	..	..	..	
Iraq	2000	13.7	17.4	9.7	51.7	48.3	..	..	..	..	..	..
Ireland		..	..	..	..	..	..	..	..	..	..	
Israel		..	..	..	..	..	..	..	..	..	..	
Italy		..	..	..	..	..	..	..	..	..	..	
Jamaica	2000	1.1	1.5	0.6	17.1	82.9	36.8	17.1	6.2	11.6	43.6	71.3
Japan		..	..	..	..	..	..	..	..	..	..	
Jordan		..	..	..	..	..	..	..	..	..	..	
Kazakhstan	1996	29.7	30.3	29.1	4.4	95.6	..	..	..	..	..	..
Kenya	1999	6.7	6.9	6.4	44.8	55.2	87.3	74.4	2.5	0.3	8.8	25.3
Korea, Dem. Rep.		..	..	..	..	..	..	..	..	..	..	
Korea, Rep.		..	..	..	..	..	..	..	..	..	..	
Kuwait		..	..	..	..	..	..	..	..	..	..	
Kyrgyz Republic	1998	8.6	9.7	7.6	7.0	93.0	93.0	96.3	0.0	0.0	7.0	2.7
Lao PDR		..	..	..	..	..	..	..	..	..	..	
Latvia		..	..	..	..	..	..	..	..	..	..	
Lebanon		..	..	..	..	..	..	..	..	..	..	
Lesotho	2000	30.8	34.2	27.5	17.6	82.4	..	..	..	..	..	..
Liberia		..	..	..	..	..	..	..	..	..	..	
Libya		..	..	..	..	..	..	..	..	..	..	
Lithuania		..	..	..	..	..	..	..	..	..	..	
Macedonia, FYR		..	..	..	..	..	..	..	..	..	..	
Madagascar	2001	25.6	26.1	25.1	85.1	14.9	94.1	93.9	0.6	1.4	2.0	2.9
Malawi	2000	10.6	9.4	11.6	17.1	82.9	..	..	..	..	..	..
Malaysia		..	..	..	..	..	..	..	..	..	..	
Mali	2001	25.3	32.3	18.6	68.7	31.3	..	..	..	..	..	..
Mauritania		..	..	..	..	..	..	..	..	..	..	
Mauritius		..	..	..	..	..	..	..	..	..	..	
Mexico[d]	1996	14.7	20.0	9.5	45.6	54.4	61.3	38.3	11.4	12.9	22.6	48.2
Moldova	2000	33.5	34.1	32.8	3.8	96.2	..	..	..	..	..	..
Mongolia	2000	22.0	23.5	20.6	28.2	71.8	..	..	..	..	..	..
Morocco	1998–99	13.2	13.5	12.8	93.2	6.8	60.8	60.3	8.1	8.5	13.5	6.4
Mozambique		..	..	..	..	..	..	..	..	..	..	
Myanmar		..	..	..	..	..	..	..	..	..	..	
Namibia	1999	15.4	16.2	14.7	9.5	90.5	91.5	91.7	0.4	0.4	8.1	8.0
Nepal	1999	47.2	42.2	52.4	35.6	64.4	89.0	86.1	1.2	1.5	9.7	12.3
Netherlands		..	..	..	..	..	..	..	..	..	..	
New Zealand		..	..	..	..	..	..	..	..	..	..	
Nicaragua	2001	12.1	17.5	6.5	33.3	66.7	73.2	32.0	3.0	10.2	23.3	57.8
Niger		..	..	..	..	..	..	..	..	..	..	
Nigeria		..	..	..	..	..	..	..	..	..	..	
Norway		..	..	..	..	..	..	..	..	..	..	
Oman		..	..	..	..	..	..	..	..	..	..	
Pakistan		..	..	..	..	..	..	..	..	..	..	
Panama	2000	4.0	6.4	1.4	37.5	62.5	71.1	38.4	1.4	8.0	27.2	49.5
Papua New Guinea		..	..	..	..	..	..	..	..	..	..	
Paraguay	1999	8.1	11.7	4.4	24.2	75.7	61.2	30.9	3.8	4.6	33.1	64.5
Peru	1994	17.7	20.4	15.2	7.3	92.7	78.9	76.3	3.6	3.4	17.5	20.3
Philippines	2001	13.3	16.3	10.0	14.8	85.2	72.6	53.6	3.6	5.3	22.1	41.0
Poland		..	..	..	..	..	..	..	..	..	..	
Portugal	2001	3.6	4.6	2.6	3.6	96.4	52.7	40.7	11.4	10.7	25.6	47.7
Puerto Rico		..	..	..	..	..	..	..	..	..	..	

2.4 Children at work

	Survey year	Economically active children					Employment by economic activity[a]					
			% of children ages 7–14		% of economically active children ages 7–14		% of economically active children ages 7–14					
							Agriculture		Manufacturing		Services	
		Total	Male	Female	Work only	Work and study	Male	Female	Male	Female	Male	Female
Romania	2000	1.4	1.7	1.1	20.7	79.3	96.4	98.1	0.0	0.0	2.6	1.9
Russian Federation		..	..	..	..	..	..	..	..	..	..	
Rwanda	2000	33.1	36.1	30.3	27.5	72.5	..	..	..	..	..	..
Saudi Arabia		..	..	..	..	..	..	..	..	..	..	
Senegal	2000	35.4	43.2	27.7	56.2	43.8	..	..	..	..	..	..
Serbia and Montenegro		..	..	..	..	..	..	..	..	..	..	
Sierra Leone	2000	74.0	24.7	72.7	53.8	46.2	..	..	..	..	..	..
Singapore		..	..	..	..	..	..	..	..	..	..	
Slovak Republic		..	..	..	..	..	..	..	..	..	..	
Slovenia		..	..	..	..	..	..	..	..	..	..	
Somalia		..	..	..	..	..	..	..	..	..	..	
South Africa	1999	27.7	29.0	26.4	5.1	94.9	..	..	..	..	..	..
Spain		..	..	..	..	..	..	..	..	..	..	
Sri Lanka	1998	17.0	20.4	13.4	5.4	94.6	71.1	71.4	12.0	15.0	15.8	13.5
Sudan	2000	19.1	21.5	16.8	55.9	44.1	..	..	..	..	..	..
Swaziland	2000	11.2	11.4	10.9	14.0	86.0	..	..	..	..	..	..
Sweden		..	..	..	..	..	..	..	..	..	..	
Switzerland		..	..	..	..	..	..	..	..	..	..	
Syrian Arab Republic		..	..	..	..	..	..	..	..	..	..	
Tajikistan		..	..	..	..	..	..	..	..	..	..	
Tanzania	2001	40.4	41.5	39.2	40.0	60.0	83.5	73.1	0.1	0.2	16.3	26.7
Thailand		..	..	..	..	..	..	..	..	..	..	
Togo	2000	72.5	73.4	71.6	28.4	71.6	..	..	..	..	..	..
Trinidad and Tobago	2000	3.9	5.2	2.8	12.8	87.2	..	..	..	..	..	..
Tunisia		..	..	..	..	..	..	..	..	..	..	
Turkey	1999	4.5	5.2	3.8	66.8	33.2	52.7	83.4	19.9	10.2	10.2	1.8
Turkmenistan		..	..	..	..	..	..	..	..	..	..	
Uganda	2002–03	13.1	15.0	11.3	18.3	81.7	94.3	92.3	1.5	1.3	3.2	6.0
Ukraine		..	..	..	..	..	..	..	..	..	..	
United Arab Emirates		..	..	..	..	..	..	..	..	..	..	
United Kingdom		..	..	..	..	..	..	..	..	..	..	
United States		..	..	..	..	..	..	..	..	..	..	
Uruguay		..	..	..	..	..	..	..	..	..	..	
Uzbekistan	2000	18.1	22.0	14.0	4.1	95.9	..	..	..	..	..	..
Venezuela, RB[c]	2003	9.1	11.4	6.6	17.6	82.4	35.2	9.2	7.3	9.5	53.9	81.0
Vietnam		..	..	..	..	..	..	..	..	..	..	
West Bank and Gaza		..	..	..	..	..	..	..	..	..	..	
Yemen, Rep.	1999	13.1	12.4	14.0	64.3	35.7	87.2	96.6	1.2	0.8	10.8	1.8
Zambia	1999	14.4	15.0	13.9	72.8	27.2	92.7	88.1	0.3	0.8	6.6	11.0
Zimbabwe	1999	14.3	13.3	15.3	12.0	88.0	..	..	..	..	..	..

a. Shares by major industrial category do not sum to 100 percent because of a residual category not included in the table. b. The totals (urban and rural combined) represent what can be described as Angola-Secured Territory but not the nation as a whole. c. Data are for children ages 10–14. d. Data are for children ages 12–14.

About the data

The data in the table refer to children's economic activity, a broader concept than child labor. According to a gradually emerging consensus, child labor is a subset of children's economic activity or children's work that is injurious and therefore targeted for elimination. There is also growing recognition that there are certain intolerable, or "unconditionally worst," forms of child labor that constitute especially serious violations of children's rights, and these should be targeted as a priority for immediate action.

In line with the international definition of employment, the threshold for classifying a child as economically active is spending one hour on economic activity during the reference week. Economic activity is as defined by the 1993 United Nations System of National Accounts (revision 3) and corresponds to the international definition of employment adopted by the Thirteenth International Conference of Labor Statisticians in 1982. Economic activity covers all market production and certain types of nonmarket production, including production of goods for own use. It excludes household chores performed by children in their own household. But some forms of economic activity are not captured by household surveys and so are not reflected in the estimates. These include unconditional forms of child labor, which require different data collection methodologies.

The data used to develop the indicators are from household surveys conducted by the International Labour Organization (ILO), the United Nations Children's Fund (UNICEF), the World Bank, and national statistical offices. These surveys yield a variety of data in education, employment, health, expenditure, and consumption that relate to child work. But they do not provide information on unconditional forms of children's work.

Household survey data generally include information on work type—for example, whether a child is working for pay in cash or in kind or is involved in unpaid work, whether a child is working for someone who is not a member of the household, whether a child is involved in any type of family work (on the farm or in a business), and the like. The ages used in country surveys to define child labor range from 5 to 14 years old. The data in the table have been recalculated to present statistics for children ages 7–14.

Although efforts are made to harmonize the definition of employment and the questions on employment used in survey questionnaires, some differences remain among the survey instruments used to collect the information on working children. Differences exist not only among different household surveys in the same country, but also within the same type of survey carried out in different countries.

Because of the differences in the underlying survey instruments and in survey dates, estimates of the economically active child population are not fully comparable across countries. Caution should be exercised in drawing conclusions concerning relative levels of child economic activity across countries or regions based on the published estimates.

The table aggregates the distribution of working children by the industrial categories of the International Standard Industrial Classification (ISIC): agriculture, industry, and services. The residual category, which includes mining and quarrying; electricity, gas, and water; construction; extraterritorial organization; and other inadequately defined activities, is not presented in the table, and so the broad groups do not add up to 100 percent. The use of either ISIC revision 2 or revision 3 is strictly related to the codification applied by each country in describing the economic activity. The use of two different classifications does not affect the definition of the groups presented in the table.

Child labor is an obstacle to education for all — Box 2.4a

There is broad consensus that the single most effective way to stem the flow of school-age children into work is to extend and improve access to school, so that families have the opportunity to invest in their children's education and it is worthwhile for them to do so. With no access to quality education, millions of children are left to work. More than one in five children ages 5–17 is economically active (see table).

Age group	Economically active children (% of age group)
5–17	20.3
5–14	15.8
15–17	35.2

Source: ILO 2006.

Definitions

• **Survey year** is the year in which the underlying data were collected. • **Economically active children** refer to children involved in economic activity for at least one hour in the reference week of the survey. • **Work only** refers to children involved in economic activity and not attending school. • **Work and study** refer to children attending school in combination with economic activity. • **Employment by economic activity** refers to the distribution of economically active children by the major industrial categories (ISIC revision 2 or revision 3). • **Agriculture** corresponds to division 1 (ISIC revision 2) or categories A and B (ISIC revision 3) and includes agriculture and hunting, forestry and logging, and fishing. • **Manufacturing** corresponds to division 3 (ISIC revision 2) or category D (ISIC revision 3). • **Services** correspond to divisions 6–9 (ISIC revision 2) or categories G–P (ISIC revision 3) and include wholesale and retail trade, hotels and restaurants, transport, financial intermediation, real estate, public administration, education, health and social work, other community services, and private household activity.

Data sources

Estimates are produced by the Understanding Children's Work project based on household survey datasets made available by the ILO's International Programme on the Elimination of Child Labour under its Statistical Monitoring Programme on Child Labour, UNICEF under its Multiple Indicator Cluster Survey program, the World Bank under its Living Standards Measurement Study program, and national statistical offices. Information on how the data were collected and some indication of their reliability can be found at www.ilo.org/public/english/standards/ipec/simpoc/, www.childinfo.org, and www.worldbank.org/lsms. Detailed country statistics can be found at www.ucw-project.org.

2.5 Unemployment

	Unemployment						Long-term unemployment			Unemployment by educational attainment		
	Male % of male labor force		Female % of female labor force		Total % of total labor force		% of total unemployment			% of total unemployment		
	1990–92[a]	2000–05[a]	1990–92[a]	2000–05[a]	1990–92[a]	2000–05[a]	Male 2000–03[a]	Female 2000–03[a]	Total 2000–03[a]	Primary 2000–04[a]	Secondary 2000–04[a]	Tertiary 2000–04[a]
Afghanistan	..	..	..	..	..	..	..	..	..	..	..	..
Albania	..	13.2	..	18.3	..	15.2	..	..	..	56.4	38.4	3.4
Algeria	..	19.8	..	21.3	..	20.1	..	..	..	..	..	..
Angola	..	..	..	..	..	..	..	..	..	..	..	..
Argentina	6.4[b]	16.3[b]	7.0[b]	14.7[b]	6.7[b]	15.6[b]	..	..	..	42.8[b]	38.5[b]	17.7[b]
Armenia	..	..	..	..	..	..	72.2	70.8	71.6	5.2	81.5	13.3
Australia	11.3	5.3[b]	9.5	5.5[b]	10.5	5.4[b]	27.1[b]	17.0[b]	22.5[b]	48.3	32.7	19.0
Austria	3.5	4.5	3.8	5.4	3.6	4.9	25.0	23.9	24.5	37.3	55.7	7.0
Azerbaijan	..	..	..	..	..	..	..	..	..	4.6	31.4	64.1
Bangladesh	2.0	4.2	1.9	4.9	1.9	4.3	..	..	..	54.3	22.7	8.4
Belarus	..	..	..	..	..	..	..	..	..	10.2	40.6	49.1
Belgium	4.8	6.6	9.5	8.3	6.7	7.4	44.8	48.2	46.3	43.7	38.1	18.2
Benin	..	..	..	..	..	..	..	..	..	..	..	..
Bolivia	5.5[b]	4.3	5.6[b]	6.9	5.5[b]	5.5	..	..	..	60.2[b]	32.5[b]	4.4[b]
Bosnia and Herzegovina	..	..	..	..	..	..	..	..	..	..	..	..
Botswana	11.7	15.7	17.3	22.3	13.9	18.6	..	..	..	63.8	23.8	..
Brazil	5.4[b]	7.8[b]	7.9[b]	12.3[b]	6.4[b]	9.7[b]	..	..	..	..	..	..
Bulgaria	..	12.5	..	11.5	..	12.1	..	..	..	37.8	50.9	11.4
Burkina Faso	..	..	..	..	..	..	..	..	..	46.8	19.3	5.6
Burundi	0.7	..	0.3	..	0.5	..	..	..	..	..	..	..
Cambodia	..	0.8	..	0.9	..	0.8	..	..	..	..	..	..
Cameroon	..	8.2	..	6.7	..	7.5	..	..	..	..	..	..
Canada	12.1[b]	7.5[b]	10.2[b]	6.8[b]	11.2[b]	7.2[b]	11.4	8.4	10.1	29.0[b]	30.8[b]	40.2[b]
Central African Republic	..	..	..	..	..	..	..	..	..	..	..	..
Chad	..	..	..	..	..	..	..	..	..	..	..	..
Chile	3.9	6.9	5.3	9.5	4.4	7.8	..	..	..	18.5	59.0	21.8
China	..	..	..	..	2.3[b]	4.2	..	..	..	..	..	..
Hong Kong, China	2.0	7.8	1.9	5.6	2.0	6.8	..	..	..	48.6	39.4	10.1
Colombia	6.7[b]	10.6	13.0[b]	17.8	9.4[b]	13.7	..	..	..	26.9	52.9	16.5
Congo, Dem. Rep.	..	..	..	..	..	..	..	..	..	..	..	..
Congo, Rep.	..	..	..	..	..	..	..	..	..	..	..	..
Costa Rica	3.4	5.4	5.4	8.5	4.0	6.4	8.9	13.3	10.9	62.2	24.1	9.9
Côte d'Ivoire	..	..	..	..	..	..	..	..	..	..	..	..
Croatia	..	11.7	..	14.0	..	12.7	52.9[c]	56.3[c]	54.6[c]	21.5	68.4	9.8
Cuba	..	..	..	..	4.6	3.3	..	..	..	..	..	..
Czech Republic	..	7.0	..	9.9	..	8.3	47.4	51.9	49.9	24.6	71.8	3.5
Denmark	8.3	5.0	9.9	5.4	9.0	5.2	21.8	17.9	19.9	25.9	46.6	25.5
Dominican Republic	11.7	10.5	34.9	30.7	20.3	18.4	2.2	1.3	1.6	..	..	..
Ecuador	6.0[b]	6.6[b]	13.2[b]	11.4[b]	8.9[b]	8.6[b]	..	..	..	28.8	47.7	21.9
Egypt, Arab Rep.	6.4	7.3	17.0	23.2	9.0	11.0	..	..	..	..	..	..
El Salvador	3.9[b]	8.7	4.9[b]	3.9	4.3[b]	6.8	..	..	..	..	..	..
Eritrea	..	..	..	..	..	..	..	..	..	..	..	..
Estonia	3.9	10.4	3.5	8.9	3.7	9.6	..	..	..	20.9	62.1	16.8
Ethiopia	..	15.8[b]	..	31.2[b]	..	23.1[b]	..	..	..	..	..	..
Finland	13.6	8.8	9.7	9.0	11.7	8.9	27.7	21.4	24.7	35.8	46.3	17.5
France	7.9[b]	9.0[b]	12.7[b]	11.1[b]	10.0[b]	9.9[b]	43.1[b]	42.8[b]	42.9[b]	40.6	39.9	17.7
Gabon	..	..	..	..	..	..	..	..	..	..	..	..
Gambia, The	..	..	..	..	..	..	..	..	..	..	..	..
Georgia	..	13.4[b]	..	11.8[b]	..	12.6[b]	..	..	..	5.8	57.6	36.5
Germany	5.3	10.2	8.4	9.3	6.6	9.8	48.3	52.3	50.0	27.1	60.5	12.4
Ghana	..	7.5	..	8.7	..	8.2	..	..	..	..	..	..
Greece	4.9	6.4	12.9	15.9	7.8	10.2	49.2	61.0	56.5	34.2	50.0	15.1
Guatemala	2.6[b]	2.2	4.6[b]	3.7	3.2[b]	2.8	..	..	..	..	..	..
Guinea	..	..	..	..	..	..	..	..	..	..	..	..
Guinea-Bissau	..	..	..	..	..	..	..	..	..	..	..	..
Haiti	11.2	..	13.6	..	12.2	..	..	..	..	..	..	..

	Unemployment						Long-term unemployment			Unemployment by educational attainment		
	Male % of male labor force		Female % of female labor force		Total % of total labor force		% of total unemployment			% of total unemployment		
	1990–92[a]	2000–05[a]	1990–92[a]	2000–05[a]	1990–92[a]	2000–05[a]	Male 2000–03[a]	Female 2000–03[a]	Total 2000–03[a]	Primary 2000–04[a]	Secondary 2000–04[a]	Tertiary 2000–04[a]
Honduras	3.3[b]	4.7[b]	3.0[b]	8.3[b]	3.2[b]	5.9[b]	..	..	..	..	..	..
Hungary	11.0	6.1	8.7	6.1	9.9	6.1	42.2	42.2	42.2	33.5	61.2	5.4
India	..	4.9[b]	..	5.3[b]	..	5.0[b]	..	..	..	27.0	41.1	31.9
Indonesia	2.7	8.1	3.1	12.9	2.9	9.9	..	..	..	46.0	36.6	6.7
Iran, Islamic Rep.	9.5	10.1	24.4	20.4	11.1	11.6	..	..	..	38.3	37.1	19.3
Iraq	..	29.4	..	15.0	..	26.8	..	..	..	..	..	..
Ireland	15.2	4.9	15.2	3.7	15.2	4.4	40.9	26.0	35.4	48.2	24.9	24.0
Israel	9.2	10.2	13.9	11.3	11.2	10.7	..	..	..	20.2	48.8	27.0
Italy	8.1	6.4	17.3	10.5	11.6	8.0	57.5	58.9	58.2	49.4	41.4	7.5
Jamaica	9.4	8.1	22.2	15.7	15.4	11.4	24.4	36.2	31.7	13.0	5.4	6.1
Japan	2.1[b]	4.9[b]	2.2[b]	4.4[b]	2.2[b]	4.7[b]	38.9	24.6	33.5	70.8	53.4	29.2
Jordan	..	11.8	..	16.5	..	12.4	..	..	..	..	..	..
Kazakhstan	..	7.0	..	9.8	..	8.4	..	..	..	7.9	53.2	38.9
Kenya	..	..	..	..	..	..	..	..	..	..	..	..
Korea, Dem. Rep.	..	..	..	..	..	..	..	..	..	..	..	..
Korea, Rep.	2.8	3.7	2.1	3.1	2.5	3.5	0.7	0.3	0.6	17.0	53.4	29.6
Kuwait	..	..	..	..	..	1.7	..	..	..	27.5	39.9	6.1
Kyrgyz Republic	..	11.2	..	14.3	..	12.5	..	..	..	13.7	67.8	18.5
Lao PDR	..	..	..	..	..	..	..	..	..	..	..	..
Latvia	..	9.0	..	8.4	..	8.7	..	..	..	22.4	68.5	8.8
Lebanon	..	..	..	..	..	..	..	..	..	..	..	..
Lesotho	..	..	..	..	..	..	..	..	..	..	..	..
Liberia	..	..	..	..	..	..	..	..	..	..	..	..
Libya	..	..	..	..	..	..	..	..	..	..	..	..
Lithuania	..	..	..	..	..	8.3	..	..	57.8	15.0	68.5	16.5
Macedonia, FYR	..	36.7	..	37.8	..	37.2	..	..	..	..	..	..
Madagascar	..	3.5	..	5.6	..	4.5	..	..	..	42.7	18.8	6.1
Malawi	..	..	..	..	..	..	..	..	..	..	..	..
Malaysia	..	3.6	..	3.6	3.7	3.5	..	..	..	32.0	48.8	15.6
Mali	..	7.2	..	10.9	..	8.8	..	..	..	..	..	..
Mauritania	..	..	..	..	..	..	..	..	..	..	..	..
Mauritius	3.2	5.8	3.1	13.5	3.1	8.5	..	..	..	71.5[b]	28.2[b]	..
Mexico	2.7	2.9	4.0	3.4	3.1	3.0	1.1	0.8	1.0	13.7	30.1	46.4
Moldova	..	10.0	..	6.3	..	8.1	..	..	..	..	..	..
Mongolia	..	14.3	..	14.1	..	14.2	..	..	..	35.0	45.8	18.4
Morocco	13.0[b]	11.0	25.3[b]	11.8	16.0[b]	11.2	..	..	..	51.5[c]	20.1[c]	19.8[c]
Mozambique	..	..	..	..	..	..	..	..	..	..	..	..
Myanmar	4.7	..	8.8	..	6.0	..	..	..	..	..	..	..
Namibia	20.0	26.8	19.0	35.9	19.0	31.1	..	..	..	..	..	..
Nepal	..	7.4	..	10.7	..	8.8	..	..	..	..	..	..
Netherlands	4.3	4.1	7.3	4.4	5.5	4.3	30.1	28.1	29.2	46.3	35.1	17.4
New Zealand	11.0[b]	3.5[b]	9.6[b]	4.4[b]	10.4[b]	3.9[b]	15.5	11.0	13.3	1.0	48.8	16.0
Nicaragua	11.3	7.6	19.4	8.0	14.4	7.8	..	..	..	50.8[b]	24.8[b]	19.7[b]
Niger	..	..	..	..	..	..	..	..	..	..	..	..
Nigeria	..	..	..	..	..	..	..	..	..	..	..	..
Norway	6.6	4.8	5.1	3.8	5.9	4.4	7.1	5.4	6.4	21.7	54.7	21.7
Oman	..	..	..	..	..	..	..	..	..	..	..	..
Pakistan	3.8	6.6	14.0	12.8	5.2	7.7	..	..	..	14.7	12.3	24.1
Panama	10.8	9.4	22.3	17.2	14.7	12.3	24.0	35.7	29.3	35.9	37.3	26.0
Papua New Guinea	9.0	4.3	5.9	1.3	7.7	2.8	..	..	..	..	..	..
Paraguay	6.4[b]	6.7	3.8[b]	10.1	5.3[b]	8.1	..	..	..	..	..	..
Peru	7.5[b]	9.4[b]	12.5[b]	12.0[b]	9.4[b]	10.5[b]	..	..	..	9.4[b]	61.4[b]	28.6[b]
Philippines	7.9	10.4	9.9	11.7	8.6	10.9	..	..	..	..	..	..
Poland	12.2	16.6	14.7	19.1	13.3	17.7	56.1[c]	59.3[c]	57.7[c]	18.0	75.4	6.7
Portugal	3.5[b]	5.8	5.0[b]	7.6	4.1[b]	6.7[b]	31.2	32.7	32.0	70.7	14.6	8.8
Puerto Rico	19.2	11.7	13.3	9.1	17.0	10.6	..	..	..	..	..	..

	Unemployment						Long-term unemployment			Unemployment by educational attainment		
	Male % of male labor force		Female % of female labor force		Total % of total labor force		% of total unemployment			% of total unemployment		
	1990–92[a]	2000–05[a]	1990–92[a]	2000–05[a]	1990–92[a]	2000–05[a]	Male 2000–03[a]	Female 2000–03[a]	Total 2000–03[a]	Primary 2000–04[a]	Secondary 2000–04[a]	Tertiary 2000–04[a]
Romania	..	9.0	..	6.9	..	8.0	..	..	..	26.0	66.9	5.4
Russian Federation	5.4	7.8	5.2	8.0	5.3	7.9	..	..	..	..	..	..
Rwanda	..	..	..	..	..	..	..	..	..	60.7	24.1	5.9
Saudi Arabia	7.4	4.7	4.9	14.7	..	..	..	..	..	12.0[c]	49.0[c]	40.0[c]
Senegal	..	..	..	..	..	..	..	..	..	..	..	..
Serbia and Montenegro	..	14.4	..	16.4	..	15.2	..	..	..	..	..	..
Sierra Leone	..	..	..	..	..	..	..	..	..	..	..	..
Singapore	2.7	5.5	2.6	5.3	2.7	5.4	..	..	..	22.4	25.0	38.8
Slovak Republic	..	17.3	..	19.1	..	18.1	60.2	62.1	61.1	24.1[b]	71.7[b]	4.3[b]
Slovenia	..	5.7	..	6.5	..	6.1	..	..	..	26.2	63.9	8.2
Somalia	..	..	..	..	..	..	..	..	..	..	..	..
South Africa	..	23.5[b]	..	31.6[b]	..	27.1[b]	..	..	..	50.2	41.0	5.1
Spain	13.9	8.2	25.8	15.0	18.1	11.0	34.3	43.9	39.8	56.0	20.4	22.7
Sri Lanka	10.1[b]	6.0[b]	19.8[b]	13.5[b]	13.3[b]	8.5[b]	..	..	..	47.2	..	52.8
Sudan	..	..	..	..	..	..	..	..	..	..	..	..
Swaziland	..	..	..	..	..	..	..	..	..	..	..	..
Sweden	6.8	6.9	4.6	6.2	5.7	6.5	19.6	15.3	17.8	23.2	58.1	17.5
Switzerland	2.3	3.9	3.5	4.8	2.8	4.3	21.6	32.6	27.0	28.7	54.5	16.9
Syrian Arab Republic	..	9.0	..	28.3	..	12.3	..	..	..	75.2	10.3	9.8
Tajikistan	..	..	..	..	..	..	..	..	..	..	..	..
Tanzania	2.7[b]	4.4	4.2[b]	5.8	3.5[b]	5.1[b]	..	..	..	..	..	..
Thailand	1.3	1.6	1.5	1.4	1.4	1.5	..	..	..	40.0	47.2	0.2
Togo	..	..	..	..	..	..	..	..	..	..	..	..
Trinidad and Tobago	17.0[b]	7.8[b]	23.9[b]	14.5[b]	19.6[b]	10.4[b]	20.3	34.7	27.6	55.5	40.5	1.8
Tunisia	..	..	..	..	..	14.7	..	..	..	43.4	37.4	10.0
Turkey	8.8	10.3	7.8	10.3	8.5	10.3	36.5[c]	46.9[c]	39.2[c]	55.7[c]	28.1[c]	11.4[c]
Turkmenistan	..	..	..	..	..	..	..	..	..	..	..	..
Uganda	..	2.5	..	3.9	..	3.2	..	..	..	..	..	..
Ukraine	..	8.9	..	8.3	..	8.6	..	..	..	13.5	54.3	32.2
United Arab Emirates	..	2.2	..	2.6	..	2.3	..	..	..	..	..	..
United Kingdom	11.5	5.0	7.3	4.2	9.7	4.6	26.5	17.1	23.0	30.3	44.4	14.6
United States	7.9	5.6	7.0	5.4	7.5	5.5	12.5	11.0	11.8	18.4	34.3	47.3
Uruguay	6.8[b]	13.5[b]	11.8[b]	20.8[b]	9.0[b]	16.8[b]	..	..	..	54.8[b]	31.3[b]	13.9[b]
Uzbekistan	..	..	..	..	..	..	..	..	..	..	..	..
Venezuela, RB	8.2	14.4[b]	6.8	20.3[b]	7.7	16.8[b]	..	..	..	..	..	..
Vietnam	..	1.9	..	2.4	..	2.1	..	..	..	..	..	..
West Bank and Gaza	..	28.1	..	20.1	..	26.8	..	..	..	57.5	14.5	17.6
Yemen, Rep.	..	..	..	..	..	..	..	..	..	..	..	..
Zambia	16.3	..	22.4	..	18.9	..	..	..	..	..	..	..
Zimbabwe	..	10.4	..	6.1	..	8.2	..	..	..	..	..	..
World	.. w	.. w	.. w	.. w	.. w	6.4 w	.. w	.. w	.. w	.. w	.. w	.. w
Low income	..	..	..	..	..	..	..	..	..	..	..	..
Middle income	..	..	..	..	3.9	6.6	..	..	..	..	..	..
Lower middle income	..	..	..	..	3.4	5.9	..	..	..	..	..	..
Upper middle income	6.3	9.6	6.8	10.8	6.4	9.8	..	..	..	37.7	48.2	11.3
Low & middle income	..	..	..	..	..	6.4	..	..	..	..	..	..
East Asia & Pacific	..	..	..	..	2.5	4.2	..	..	..	..	..	..
Europe & Central Asia	..	9.9	..	9.9	..	9.9	..	..	..	..	..	..
Latin America & Carib.	5.4	8.1	8.5	12.0	6.6	9.6	..	..	..	..	..	..
Middle East & N. Africa	..	13.4	..	21.3	..	14.8	..	..	..	..	..	..
South Asia	..	5.1	..	6.2	..	5.4	..	..	..	30.0	34.8	27.4
Sub-Saharan Africa	..	..	..	..	..	..	..	..	..	..	..	..
High income	7.0	6.2	7.9	6.6	7.4	6.4	27.3	23.9	26.0	34.8	39.3	29.7
Europe EMU	7.5	8.2	12.6	10.6	9.5	9.2	44.1	46.4	45.5	40.3	42.5	16.3

a. Data are for the most recent year available. b. Limited coverage. c. Data are for 2005.

Unemployment 2.5

About the data

Unemployment and total employment in an economy are the broadest indicators of economic activity as reflected by the labor market. The International Labour Organization (ILO) defines the unemployed as members of the economically active population who are without work but available for and seeking work, including people who have lost their jobs and those who have voluntarily left work. Some unemployment is unavoidable in all economies. At any time some workers are temporarily unemployed—between jobs as employers look for the right workers and workers search for better jobs. Such unemployment, often called frictional unemployment, results from the normal operation of labor markets.

Changes in unemployment over time may reflect changes in the demand for and supply of labor, but they may also reflect changes in reporting practices. Ironically, low unemployment rates can often disguise substantial poverty in a country, while high unemployment rates can occur in countries with a high level of economic development and low incidence of poverty. In countries without unemployment or welfare benefits, people eke out a living in the informal sector. In countries with well-developed safety nets, workers can afford to wait for suitable or desirable jobs. But high and sustained unemployment indicates serious inefficiencies in the allocation of resources.

The ILO definition of unemployment notwithstanding, reference periods, the criteria for those considered to be seeking work, and the treatment of people temporarily laid off and those seeking work for the first time vary across countries. In many developing countries it is especially difficult to measure employment and unemployment in agriculture. The timing of a survey, for example, can maximize the effects of seasonal unemployment in agriculture. And informal sector employment is difficult to quantify where informal activities are not registered and tracked.

Data on unemployment are drawn from labor force sample surveys and general household sample surveys, censuses, and official estimates, which are generally based on information from different sources and can be combined in many ways. Administrative records, such as social insurance statistics and employment office statistics, are not included in this table because of their limitations in coverage. Labor force surveys generally yield the most comprehensive data because they include groups not covered in other unemployment statistics, particularly people seeking work for the first time. These surveys generally use a definition of unemployment that follows the international recommendations more closely than that used by other sources and therefore generate statistics that are more comparable internationally. But the age group, geographic coverage, and collection methods could differ by country or change over time within a country. For detailed information on breaks in series, consult the original source.

Women tend to be excluded from the unemployment count for various reasons. Women suffer more from discrimination and from structural, social, and cultural barriers that impede them from actively seeking work. Also, women are often responsible for the care of children and the elderly or for other household affairs. They may not be available for work during the short reference period, as they need to make arrangements before starting work. Furthermore, women are considered to be employed when they are working part-time or in temporary jobs in the informal sector, despite the instability of these jobs or their active searching for more secure employment.

Long-term unemployment is measured by the length of time that an unemployed person has been without work and looking for a job. The data in this table are from labor force surveys. The underlying assumption is that shorter periods of joblessness are of less concern, especially when the unemployed are covered by unemployment benefits or similar forms of welfare support. The length of time that a person has been unemployed is difficult to measure, because the ability to recall that time diminishes as the period of joblessness extends. Women's long-term unemployment is likely to be lower in countries where women constitute a large share of the unpaid family workforce. Women in such countries have more access than men to nonmarket work and are more likely to drop out of the labor force and not be counted as unemployed.

Unemployment by level of educational attainment provides insights into the relationship between the educational attainment of workers and unemployment and may be used to draw inferences about changes in employment demand. Information on education attainment is the best available indicator of skill levels of the labor force.

Besides the limitations to comparability raised for measuring unemployment, the different ways of classifying the level of education across countries may also cause inconsistency. The level of education is supposed to be classified according to International Standard Classification of Education 1997 (ISCED97). For more information on ISCED97, see *About the data* for table 2.9.

Definitions

• **Unemployment** refers to the share of the labor force without work but available for and seeking employment. Definitions of labor force and unemployment may differ by country (see *About the data*). • **Long-term unemployment** refers to the number of people with continuous periods of unemployment extending for a year or longer, expressed as a percentage of the total unemployed. • **Unemployment by educational attainment** shows the unemployed by level of educational attainment as a percentage of the total unemployed. The levels of educational attainment accord with the ISCED97 of the United Nations Educational, Cultural, and Scientific Organization.

Data sources

Data on unemployment are from the ILO database Key Indicators of the Labour Market, 4th edition.

2.6 Poverty

	National poverty line								International poverty line				
		Population below the poverty line				Population below the poverty line							
	Survey year	Rural %	Urban %	National %	Survey year	Rural %	Urban %	National %	Survey year	Population below $1 a day %	Poverty gap at $1 a day %	Population below $2 a day %	Poverty gap at $2 a day %
Afganistan		..	..	..		..	..	..		..	..	..	..
Albania	2002	29.6	19.8	25.4		..	..	..	2004[a]	<2	<0.5	10.0	1.6
Algeria	1988	16.6	7.3	12.2	1995	30.3	14.7	22.6	1995[a]	<2	<0.5	15.1	3.8
Angola		..	..	..		..	..	..		..	..	..	..
Argentina	1995	..	28.4		1998		29.9		2004[b]	6.6	2.1	17.4	7.1
Armenia	1998–99	50.8	58.3	55.1	2001	48.7	51.9	50.9	2003[a]	<2	<0.5	31.1	7.1
Australia		..	..	..		..	..	..		..	..	..	..
Austria		..	..	..		..	..	..		..	..	..	..
Azerbaijan	1995	..	..	68.1	2001	42.0	55.0	49.6	2001[a]	3.7	0.6	33.4	9.1
Bangladesh	1995–96	55.2	29.4	51.0	2000	53.0	36.6	49.8	2000[a]	41.3	10.3	84.0	38.3
Belarus	2000	..	..	41.9					2002[a]	<2	<0.5	<2	<0.5
Belgium		..	..	..		..	..	..		..	..	..	..
Benin	1995	25.2	28.5	26.5	1999	33.0	23.3	29.0	2003[a]	30.9	8.2	73.7	31.7
Bolivia	1997	77.3	53.8	63.2	1999	81.7	50.6	62.7	2002[b]	23.2	13.6	42.2	23.2
Bosnia and Herzegovina	2001–02	19.9	13.8	19.5		..	..	..		..	..	..	..
Botswana									1993[a]	28.0	9.9	55.5	26.5
Brazil	1998	51.4	14.7	22.0	2002–03	41.0	17.5	21.5	2004[b]	7.5	3.4	21.2	8.5
Bulgaria	1997	..	..	36.0	2001	..	..	12.8	2003[a]	<2	<0.5	6.1	1.5
Burkina Faso	1998	61.1	22.4	54.6	2003	52.4	19.2	46.4	2003[a]	27.2	7.3	71.8	30.4
Burundi	1990	36.0	43.0	36.4		..	..	..	1998[a]	54.6	22.7	87.6	48.9
Cambodia	1997	40.1	21.1	36.1	2004	38.0	18.0	35.0	1997[a]	34.1	9.7	77.7	34.5
Cameroon	1996	59.6	41.4	53.3	2001	49.9	22.1	40.2	2001[a]	17.1	4.1	50.6	19.3
Canada		..	..	..		..	..	..		..	..	..	..
Central African Republic		..	..	..		..	..	..	1993[a]	66.6	38.1	84.0	58.4
Chad	1995–96	67.0	63.0	64.0		..	..	..		..	..	..	..
Chile	1996	..	..	19.9	1998	..	..	17.0	2003[b]	<2	<0.5	5.6	1.3
China	1996	7.9	<2	6.0	1998	4.6	<2	4.6	2004[a]	9.9	2.1	34.9	12.5
Hong Kong, China		..	..	..		..	..	..		..	..	..	..
Colombia	1995	79.0	48.0	60.0	1999	79.0	55.0	64.0	2003[b]	7.0	3.1	17.8	7.7
Congo, Dem. Rep.		..	..	..		..	..	..		..	..	..	..
Congo, Rep.		..	..	..		..	..	..		..	..	..	..
Costa Rica	1992	25.5	19.2	22.0		..	..	..	2003[b]	3.3	1.6	9.8	4.0
Côte d'Ivoire		..	..	..		..	..	..	2002[a]	14.8	4.1	48.8	18.4
Croatia		..	..	..		..	..	..	2001[a]	<2	<0.5	<2	<0.5
Cuba		..	..	..		..	..	..		..	..	..	..
Czech Republic		..	..	..		..	..	..	1996[b]	<2	<0.5	<2	<0.5
Denmark		..	..	..		..	..	..		..	..	..	..
Dominican Republic	2000	45.3	18.2	27.7	2004	55.7	34.7	42.2	2004[b]	2.8	0.5	16.2	4.9
Ecuador	1995	56.0	19.0	34.0	1998	69.0	30.0	46.0	1998[b]	17.7	7.1	40.8	17.7
Egypt, Arab Rep.	1995–96	23.3	22.5	22.9	1999–00	..	..	16.7	1999–2000[a]	3.1	<0.5	43.9	11.3
El Salvador	1995	64.8	38.9	50.6	2002	49.8	28.5	37.2	2002[b]	19.0	9.3	40.6	17.7
Eritrea	1993–94	..	..	53.0		..	..	..		..	..	..	..
Estonia	1995	14.7	6.8	8.9		..	..	..	2003[a]	<2	<0.5	7.5	1.9
Ethiopia	1995–96	47.0	33.3	45.5	1999–00	45.0	37.0	44.2	1999–2000[a]	23.0	4.8	77.8	29.6
Finland		..	..	..		..	..	..		..	..	..	..
France		..	..	..		..	..	..		..	..	..	..
Gabon		..	..	..		..	..	..		..	..	..	..
Gambia, The	1992	..	..	64.0	1998	61.0	48.0	57.6	1998[a]	59.3	28.8	82.9	51.1
Georgia	2002	55.4	48.5	52.1	2003	52.7	56.2	54.5	2003[a]	6.5	2.1	25.3	8.6
Germany		..	..	..		..	..	..		..	..	..	..
Ghana	1992	..	..	50.0	1998–99	49.9	18.6	39.5	1998–99[a]	44.8	17.3	78.5	40.8
Greece		..	..	..		..	..	..		..	..	..	..
Guatemala	1989	71.9	33.7	57.9	2000	74.5	27.1	56.2	2002[b]	13.5	5.5	31.9	13.8
Guinea	1994	..	..	40.0		..	..	..		..	..	..	..
Guinea Bissau		..	..	..		..	..	..		..	..	..	..
Haiti	1987	..	..	65.0	1995	66.0	..	..	2001[b]	53.9	26.6	78.0	47.4

	National poverty line								International poverty line				
		Population below the poverty line				Population below the poverty line							
	Survey year	Rural %	Urban %	National %	Survey year	Rural %	Urban %	National %	Survey year	Population below $1 a day %	Poverty gap at $1 a day %	Population below $2 a day %	Poverty gap at $2 a day %
Honduras	1998–99	71.2	28.6	52.5	2004	70.4	29.5	50.7	2003[b]	14.9	4.4	35.7	15.1
Hungary	1993	..	..	14.5	1997	..	..	17.3	2002[a]	<2	<0.5	<2	<0.5
India	1993–94	37.3	32.4	36.0	1999–00	30.2	24.7	28.6	2004–05[a]	33.5	7.6	80.0	34.6
Indonesia	1996	..	..	15.7	1999	34.4	16.1	27.1	2002[a]	7.5	0.9	52.4	15.7
Iran, Islamic Rep.		..	..	..		..	..	..	1998[a]	<2	<0.5	7.3	1.5
Iraq		..	..	..		..	..	..		..	..	..	..
Ireland		..	..	..		..	..	..		..	..	..	..
Israel		..	..	..		..	..	..		..	..	..	..
Italy		..	..	..		..	..	..		..	..	..	..
Jamaica	1995	37.0	18.7	27.5	2000	25.1	12.8	18.7	2004[a]	<2	<0.5	14.4	3.3
Japan		..	..	..		..	..	..		..	..	..	..
Jordan	1997	27.0	19.7	21.3	2002	18.7	12.9	14.2	2002–03[a]	<2	<0.5	7.0	1.5
Kazakhstan	1996	39.0	30.0	34.6		..	..	..	2003[a]	<2	<.5	16.0	3.8
Kenya	1994	47.0	29.0	40.0	1997	53.0	49.0	52.0	1997[a]	22.8	5.9	58.3	23.9
Korea, Dem. Rep.		..	..	..		..	..	..		..	..	..	..
Korea, Rep.		..	..	..		..	..	..	1998[b]	<2	<0.5	<2	<0.5
Kuwait		..	..	..		..	..	..		..	..	..	..
Kyrgyz Republic	2001	51.0	41.2	47.6	2003	..	..	41.0	2003[a]	<2	<0.5	21.4	4.4
Lao PDR	1993	48.7	33.1	45.0	1997–98	41.0	26.9	38.6	2002[a]	27.0	6.1	74.1	30.2
Latvia		..	..	..		..	..	..	2003[a]	<2	<0.5	4.7	1.2
Lebanon		..	..	..		..	..	..		..	..	..	..
Lesotho									1995[a]	36.4	19.0	56.1	33.1
Liberia		..	..	..		..	..	..		..	..	..	..
Libya		..	..	..		..	..	..		..	..	..	..
Lithuania		..	..	..		..	..	..	2003[a]	<2	<0.5	7.8	1.8
Macedonia, FYR	2002	25.3	..	21.4	2003	22.3	..	21.7	2003[a]	<2	<0.5	<2	<0.5
Madagascar	1997	76.0	63.2	73.3	1999	76.7	52.1	71.3	2001[a]	61.0	27.9	85.1	51.8
Malawi	1990–91	..	..	54.0	1997–98	66.5	54.9	65.3	2004–05[a]	20.8	4.7	62.9	24.3
Malaysia	1989	..	..	15.5		..	..	..	1997[b]	<2	<0.5	9.3	2.0
Mali	1998	75.9	30.1	63.8		..	..	..	2001[a]	36.1	12.2	72.1	34.2
Mauritania	1996	65.5	30.1	50.0	2000	61.2	25.4	46.3	2000[a]	25.9	7.6	63.1	26.8
Mauritius		..	..	..		..	..	..		..	..	..	..
Mexico	2000	42.4	12.6	24.2	2004	27.9	11.3	17.6	2004[a]	3.0	1.4	11.6	4.2
Moldova	2001	64.1	58.0	62.4	2002	67.2	42.6	48.5	2003[a]	<2	<0.5	20.8	4.7
Mongolia	1998	32.6	39.4	35.6	2002	43.4	30.3	36.1	2002[a]	10.8	2.2	44.6	15.1
Morocco	1990–91	18.0	7.6	13.1	1998–99	27.2	12.0	19.0	1998–99	<2	<0.5	14.3	3.1
Mozambique	1996–97	71.3	62.0	69.4		..	..	..	2002–03	36.2	11.6	74.1	34.9
Myanmar		..	..	..		..	..	..		..	..	..	..
Namibia		..	..	..		..	..	..	1993[b]	34.9	14.0	55.8	30.4
Nepal	1995–96	43.3	21.6	41.8	2003–04	34.6	9.6	30.9	2003–04[a]	24.1	5.4	68.53	26.79
Netherlands		..	..	..		..	..	..		..	..	..	..
New Zealand		..	..	..		..	..	..		..	..	..	..
Nicaragua	1993	76.1	31.9	50.3	1998	68.5	30.5	47.9	2001[a]	45.1	16.7	79.9	41.2
Niger	1989–93	66.0	52.0	63.0		..	..	..	1995[a]	60.6	34.0	85.8	54.6
Nigeria	1985	49.5	31.7	43.0	1992–93	36.4	30.4	34.1	2003[a]	70.8	34.5	92.4	59.5
Norway		..	..	..		..	..	..		..	..	..	..
Oman		..	..	..		..	..	..		..	..	..	..
Pakistan	1993	33.4	17.2	28.6	1998–99	35.9	24.2	32.6	2002[a]	17.0	3.1	73.6	26.1
Panama	1997	64.9	15.3	37.3		..	..	..	2003[b]	7.4	2.1	18.0	7.5
Papua New Guinea	1996	41.3	16.1	37.5		..	..	..		..	..	..	..
Paraguay	1991	28.5	19.7	21.8		..	..	..	2003[b]	13.6	5.6	29.8	13.8
Peru	2001	77.1	42.0	54.3	2004	72.1	42.9	53.1	2003[b]	10.5	2.9	30.6	11.9
Philippines	1994	53.1	28.0	40.6	1997	50.7	21.5	36.8	2002[a]	14.8	2.9	43.0	16.3
Poland	1993	..	..	23.8		..	..	..	2002[a]	<2	<0.5	<2	<0.5
Portugal		..	..	..		..	..	..		..	..	..	..
Puerto Rico		..	..	..		..	..	..		..	..	..	..

2.6 Poverty

	National poverty line								International poverty line				
		Population below the poverty line				Population below the poverty line							
	Survey year	Rural %	Urban %	National %	Survey year	Rural %	Urban %	National %	Survey year	Population below $1 a day %	Poverty gap at $1 a day %	Population below $2 a day %	Poverty gap at $2 a day %
Romania	1994	27.9	20.4	21.5		..	..	..	2003[a]	<2	0.5	12.9	3.0
Russian Federation	1994	..	..	30.9		..	..	..	2002[a]	<2	<0.5	12.1	3.1
Rwanda	1993	..	..	51.2	1999–00	65.7	14.3	60.3	2000[a]	60.3	25.6	87.8	51.5
Saudi Arabia		..	..	..		..	..	..		..	..	..	..
Senegal	1992	40.4	23.7	33.4		..	..	..	2001[a]	17.0	3.6	56.2	20.9
Serbia and Montenegro		..	..	..		..	..	..		..	..	..	..
Sierra Leone	1989	..	..	82.8	2003–04	79.0	56.4	70.2	1989[a]	57.0	39.5	74.5	51.8
Singapore		..	..	..		..	..	..		..	..	..	..
Slovak Republic		..	..	..		..	..	..	1996[b]	<2	<0.5	2.9	0.8
Slovenia		..	..	..		..	..	..	1998[a]	<2	<0.5	<2	<0.5
Somalia		..	..	..		..	..	..		..	..	..	..
South Africa		..	..	..		..	..	..	2000[a]	10.7	1.7	34.1	12.6
Spain		..	..	..		..	..	..		..	..	..	..
Sri Lanka	1990–91	22.0	15.0	20.0	1995–96	27.0	15.0	25.0	2002[a]	5.6	0.8	41.6	11.9
Sudan		..	..	..		..	..	..		..	..	..	..
Swaziland		..	..	..		..	..	..	2000–01[a]	47.7	19.4	77.8	42.4
Sweden		..	..	..		..	..	..		..	..	..	..
Switzerland		..	..	..		..	..	..		..	..	..	..
Syrian Arab Republic		..	..	..		..	..	..		..	..	..	..
Tajikistan		..	..	..		..	..	..	2003[a]	7.4	1.3	42.8	13.0
Tanzania	1991	40.8	31.2	38.6	2000–01	38.7	29.5	35.7	2000–01[a]	57.8	20.7	89.9	49.3
Thailand	1994	..	..	9.8	1998	..	..	13.6	2002[a]	<2	<0.5	25.2	6.2
Togo	1987–89	..	..	32.3		..	..	..		..	..	..	..
Trinidad and Tobago	1992	20.0	24.0	21.0		..	..	..	1992[b]	12.4	3.5	39.0	14.6
Tunisia	1990	13.1	3.5	7.4	1995	13.9	3.6	7.6	2000[a]	<2	<0.5	6.6	1.3
Turkey	1994	..	..	28.3	2002	34.5	22.0	27.0	2003[a]	3.4	0.8	18.7	5.7
Turkmenistan		..	..	..		..	..	..		..	..	..	..
Uganda	1999–2000	37.4	9.6	33.8	2002–03	41.7	12.2	37.7		..	..	..	..
Ukraine	2000	34.9	..	31.5	2003	28.4	..	19.5	2003[a]	<2	<0.5	4.9	0.9
United Arab Emirates		..	..	..		..	..	..		..	..	..	..
United Kingdom		..	..	..		..	..	..		..	..	..	..
United States		..	..	..		..	..	..		..	..	..	..
Uruguay	1994	..	20.2	..	1998	..	24.7	..	2003[b]	<2	<0.5	5.7	1.6
Uzbekistan	2000	30.5	22.5	27.5		..	..	..	2003[a]	<2	<0.5	<2	0.6
Venezuela, RB	1989	..	..	31.3		..	..	..	2003[b]	18.5	8.9	40.1	19.2
Vietnam	1998	45.5	9.2	37.4	2002	35.6	6.6	28.9		..	..	..	..
West Bank and Gaza		..	..	..		..	..	..		..	..	..	..
Yemen, Rep.	1998	45.0	30.8	41.8		..	..	..	1998[a]	15.7	4.5	45.2	15.0
Zambia	1998	83.1	56.0	72.9	2004	78.0	53.0	68.0	2004[a]	63.8	32.6	87.2	55.2
Zimbabwe	1990–91	35.8	3.4	25.8	1995–96	48.0	7.9	34.9	1995–96[a]	56.1	24.2	83.0	48.2

a. Expenditure base. b. Income base.

Regional poverty estimates 2.6a

Region	1981	1984	1987	1990	1993	1996	1999	2002	2004[a]
People living on less than $1 a day (millions)									
East Asia & Pacific	796	564	429	476	420	279	277	227	169
China	634	425	310	374	334	211	223	177	128
Europe & Central Asia	3	2	2	2	17	21	18	6	4
Latin America & Caribbean	39	51	50	45	39	43	49	48	47
Middle East & North Africa	9	7	6	5	5	4	6	5	4
South Asia	473	457	469	479	440	459	475	485	462
Sub-Saharan Africa	168	200	223	240	252	286	296	296	298
Total	**1,489**	**1,281**	**1,179**	**1,247**	**1,172**	**1,093**	**1,120**	**1,067**	**986**
Excluding China	855	856	868	873	838	881	897	890	857
Share of people living on less than $1 a day (%)									
East Asia & Pacific	57.7	39.0	28.2	29.8	25.2	16.1	15.5	12.3	9.0
China	63.8	41.0	28.6	33.0	28.4	17.4	17.8	13.8	9.9
Europe & Central Asia	0.7	0.5	0.4	0.5	3.6	4.4	3.8	1.3	0.9
Latin America & Caribbean	10.8	13.1	12.1	10.2	8.4	8.9	9.7	9.1	8.6
Middle East & North Africa	5.1	3.8	3.1	2.3	1.9	1.7	2.1	1.7	1.5
South Asia	51.6	46.6	44.9	43.0	37.1	36.6	35.8	34.7	32.0
Sub-Saharan Africa	42.3	46.2	47.2	46.7	45.5	47.7	45.8	42.6	41.1
Total	**40.6**	**33.0**	**28.7**	**28.7**	**25.6**	**22.7**	**22.3**	**20.4**	**18.4**
Excluding China	32.0	30.1	28.7	27.1	24.6	24.6	23.8	22.6	21.1
People living on less than $2 a day (millions)									
East Asia & Pacific	1,170	1,116	1,041	1,113	1,083	908	883	766	684
China	876	819	744	819	803	649	628	524	452
Europe & Central Asia	20	17	14	20	78	85	88	61	46
Latin America & Caribbean	104	126	122	115	111	122	128	131	121
Middle East & North Africa	51	49	50	49	52	55	64	61	59
South Asia	818	853	904	954	976	1,035	1,073	1,124	1,124
Sub-Saharan Africa	295	333	365	396	422	458	491	513	522
Total	**2,457**	**2,494**	**2,496**	**2,647**	**2,722**	**2,664**	**2,727**	**2,665**	**2,556**
Excluding China	1,581	1,675	1,752	1,828	1,919	2,014	2,099	2,131	2,104
Share of people living on less than $2 a day (%)									
East Asia & Pacific	84.8	77.2	68.5	69.7	65.0	52.5	49.3	41.7	36.6
China	88.1	79.0	68.6	72.2	68.1	53.3	50.1	40.9	34.9
Europe & Central Asia	4.6	3.9	3.1	4.3	16.5	18.0	18.6	12.9	9.8
Latin America & Caribbean	28.4	32.2	29.6	26.2	24.1	25.2	25.3	24.8	22.2
Middle East & North Africa	29.2	25.6	24.2	21.7	21.4	21.4	23.6	21.1	19.7
South Asia	89.1	87.1	86.6	85.7	82.4	82.4	80.8	80.3	77.7
Sub-Saharan Africa	74.5	77.0	77.4	77.1	76.1	76.4	75.8	73.8	72.0
Total	**67.1**	**64.3**	**60.7**	**60.8**	**59.4**	**55.5**	**54.4**	**50.8**	**47.7**
Excluding China	59.3	58.9	57.9	56.8	56.4	56.2	55.8	54.1	51.8

a. Preliminary estimate.

2.6 Poverty

About the data

The World Bank produced its first global poverty estimates for developing countries for *World Development Report 1990* using household survey data for 22 countries (Ravallion, Datt, and van de Walle 1991). Incorporating survey data collected during the last 17 years, the database has expanded considerably and now includes more than 550 surveys representing about 100 developing countries. Some 1.1 million randomly sampled households were interviewed in these surveys, representing 93 percent of the population of developing countries. The surveys asked detailed questions on sources of income and how it was spent and on other household characteristics such as the number of people sharing that income. Most interviews were conducted by staff of government statistics offices. Along with improvements in data coverage and quality, the underlying methodology has also improved, resulting in better and more comprehensive estimates.

Data availability

Since 1979 there has been considerable expansion in the number of countries that field such surveys, the frequency of the surveys, and the quality of their data. The number of data sets rose dramatically from a mere 10 between 1979 and 1981 to 162 between 2000 and 2004. The drop to 30 available surveys after 2002 reflects the lag between the time data are collected and the time they become available for analysis, not a reduction in data collection. Data coverage is improving in all regions, but the Middle East and North Africa continues to lag, with only three countries having at least one data set available since 2000. A complete overview of data availability by year and country can be obtained at http://iresearch.worldbank.org/povcalnet/.

Data quality

The problems of estimating poverty and comparing poverty rates do not end with data availability. Several other issues, some related to data quality, also arise in measuring household living standards from survey data. One relates to the choice of income or consumption as a welfare indicator. Income is generally more difficult to measure accurately, and consumption comes closer to the notion of standard of living. And income can vary over time even if the standard of living does not. But consumption data are not always available. Another issue is that household surveys can differ widely, for example, in the number of consumer goods they identify. And even similar surveys may not be strictly comparable because of differences in timing or the quality and training of survey enumerators.

Comparisons of countries at different levels of development also pose a potential problem because of differences in the relative importance of consumption of nonmarket goods. The local market value of all consumption in kind (including own production, particularly important in underdeveloped rural economies) should be included in total consumption expenditure. Similarly, imputed profit from the production of nonmarket goods should be included in income. This is not always done, though such omissions were a far bigger problem in surveys before the 1980s. Most survey data now include valuations for consumption or income from own production. Nonetheless, valuation methods vary. For example, some surveys use the price in the nearest market, while others use the average farmgate selling price.

Whenever possible, the table uses consumption data in deciding who is poor and income surveys only when consumption data are unavailable. In recent editions there has been a change in how income surveys are used. In the past, average household income was adjusted to accord with consumption and income data from national accounts. But when this approach was tested using data for some 20 countries for which income and consumption expenditure data were both available from the same surveys, income was found to yield a higher mean than consumption but also higher inequality. When poverty measures based on consumption and income were compared, these two effects roughly cancelled each other out: statistically, there was no significant difference. So recent editions use income data to estimate poverty directly, without adjusting average income measures.

International poverty lines

International comparisons of poverty estimates entail both conceptual and practical problems. Countries have different definitions of poverty, and consistent comparisons across countries can be difficult. Local poverty lines tend to have higher purchasing power in rich countries, where more generous standards are used, than in poor countries. Is it reasonable to treat two people with the same standard of living—in terms of their command over commodities—differently because one happens to live in a better-off country?

Poverty measures based on an international poverty line attempt to hold the real value of the poverty line constant across countries, as is done when making comparisons over time. The commonly used $1 a day standard, measured in 1985 international prices and adjusted to local currency using purchasing power parities (PPPs), was chosen for the World Bank's *World Development Report 1990: Poverty* because it is typical of the poverty lines in low-income countries. PPP exchange rates, such as those from the Penn World Tables or the World Bank, are used because they take into account the local prices of goods and services not traded internationally. But PPP rates were designed for comparing aggregates from national accounts, not for making international poverty comparisons. As a result, there is no certainty that an international poverty line measures the same degree of need or deprivation across countries.

Early editions of *World Development Indicators* used PPPs from the Penn World Tables. Recent editions use 1993 consumption PPP estimates produced by the World Bank. Recalculated in 1993 PPP terms, the original international poverty line of $1 a day in 1985 PPP terms is now about $1.08 a day. The 2005 round of the International Comparison Program will provide new consumption PPPs in the coming year. Any revisions in the PPP of a country to incorporate better price indexes can produce dramatically different poverty lines in local currency.

Issues also arise when comparing poverty measures within countries. For example, the cost of living is typically higher in urban than in rural areas. One reason is that food staples tend to be more expensive in urban areas. So the urban monetary poverty line should be higher than the rural poverty line. But it is not always clear that the difference between urban and rural poverty lines found in practice reflects only differences in the cost of living. In some countries the urban poverty line in common use has a higher real value—meaning that it allows the purchase of more commodities for consumption—than does the rural poverty line. Sometimes the difference has been so large as to imply that the incidence of poverty is greater in urban than in rural areas, even though the reverse is found when adjustments are made only for differences in the cost of living. As with international comparisons, when the real value of the poverty line varies it is not clear how meaningful such urban-rural comparisons are.

By combining all this information, a team in the World Bank's Development Research Group calculates the number of people living below various international poverty lines, as well as other poverty and inequality measures that are published in *World*

Development Indicators. The database is updated annually as new survey data become available, and a major reassessment of progress against poverty is made about every three years.

Do it yourself: PovcalNet

Recently, this research team developed *PovcalNet*, an interactive Web-based computational tool that allows users to replicate the calculations by the World Bank's researchers in estimating the extent of absolute poverty in the world. *PovcalNet* is self contained and powered by reliable built-in software that performs the relevant calculations from a primary database. The underlying software can also be downloaded from the site and used with distributional data of various formats. The *PovcalNet* primary database consists of distributional data calculated directly from household survey data. Detailed information for each of these is also available from the site.

Estimation from distributional data requires an interpolation method. The method chosen was Lorenz curves with flexible functional forms, which have proved reliable in past work. The Lorenz curve can be graphed as the cumulative percentages of total consumption or income against the cumulative number of people, starting with the poorest individual. The empirical Lorenz curves estimated by *PovcalNet* are weighted by household size, so they are based on percentiles of population, not households.

PovcalNet also allows users to calculate poverty measures under different assumptions. For example, instead of $1 a day, users can specify a different poverty line, say $1.50 or $3. Users can also specify different PPP rates and aggregate the estimates using alternative country groupings (for example, UN country groupings or groupings based on average incomes) or a selected set of individual countries. *PovcalNet* is available online at http://iresearch.worldbank.org/povcalnet/

Definitions

• **Survey year** is the year in which the underlying data were collected. • **Rural poverty rate** is the percentage of the rural population living below the national rural poverty line. • **Urban poverty rate** is the percentage of the urban population living below the national urban poverty line. • **National poverty rate** is the percentage of the population living below the national poverty line. National estimates are based on population-weighted subgroup estimates from household surveys. • **Population below $1 a day** and **population below $2 a day** are the percentages of the population living on less than $1.08 a day and $2.15 a day at 1993 international prices. As a result of revisions in PPP exchange rates, poverty rates for individual countries cannot be compared with poverty rates reported in earlier editions. • **Poverty gap** is the mean shortfall from the poverty line (counting the nonpoor as having zero shortfall), expressed as a percentage of the poverty line. This measure reflects the depth of poverty as well as its incidence.

Data sources

The poverty measures are prepared by the World Bank's Development Research Group. The national poverty lines are based on the World Bank's country poverty assessments. The international poverty lines are based on nationally representative primary household surveys conducted by national statistical offices or by private agencies under the supervision of government or international agencies and obtained from government statistical offices and World Bank Group country departments. The World Bank Group has prepared an annual review of its poverty work since 1993. For details on data sources and methods used in deriving the World Bank's latest estimates, see Chen and Ravallion's "How Have the World's Poorest Fared Since the Early 1980s?" (2004).

2.7 Distribution of income or consumption

	Survey year	Gini index	Percentage share of income or consumption						
			Lowest 10%	Lowest 20%	Second 20%	Third 20%	Fourth 20%	Highest 20%	Highest 10%
Afghanistan		..	..	..	..	..	..	..	..
Albania	2004[a]	31.1	3.4	8.2	12.6	17.0	22.6	39.5	24.4
Algeria	1995[a]	35.3	2.8	7.0	11.6	16.1	22.7	42.6	26.8
Angola		..	..	..	..	..	..	..	..
Argentina[b]	2004[c]	51.3	0.9	3.1	7.6	12.8	21.1	55.4	38.2
Armenia	2003[a]	33.8	3.6	8.5	12.3	15.7	20.6	42.8	29.0
Australia	1994[c]	35.2	2.0	5.9	12.0	17.2	23.6	41.3	25.4
Austria	2000[c]	29.1	3.3	8.6	13.3	17.4	22.9	37.8	23.0
Azerbaijan	2001[a]	36.5	3.1	7.4	11.5	15.3	21.2	44.5	29.5
Bangladesh	2000[a]	33.4	3.7	8.6	12.1	15.6	21.0	42.7	27.9
Belarus	2002[a]	29.7	3.4	8.5	13.2	17.3	22.7	38.3	23.5
Belgium	2000[c]	33.0	3.4	8.5	13.0	16.3	20.8	41.4	28.1
Benin	2003[a]	36.5	3.1	7.4	11.3	15.4	21.5	44.5	29.0
Bolivia	2002[c]	60.1	0.3	1.5	5.9	10.9	18.7	63.0	47.2
Bosnia and Herzegovina	2001[a]	26.2	3.9	9.5	14.2	17.9	22.6	35.8	21.4
Botswana	1993[a]	60.5	1.2	3.2	6.0	9.7	16.0	65.1	51.0
Brazil	2004[c]	57.0	0.9	2.8	6.4	11.0	18.7	61.1	44.8
Bulgaria	2003[a]	29.2	3.4	8.7	13.7	17.2	22.1	38.3	23.9
Burkina Faso	2003[a]	39.5	2.8	6.9	10.9	14.5	20.5	47.2	32.2
Burundi	1998[a]	42.4	1.7	5.1	10.3	15.1	21.5	48.0	32.8
Cambodia	2004[a]	41.7	2.9	6.8	10.2	13.7	19.6	49.6	34.8
Cameroon	2001[a]	44.6	2.3	5.6	9.3	13.7	20.4	50.9	35.4
Canada	2000[c]	32.6	2.6	7.2	12.7	17.2	23.0	39.9	24.8
Central African Republic	1993[a]	61.3	0.7	2.0	4.9	9.6	18.5	65.0	47.7
Chad		..	..	..	..	..	..	..	..
Chile	2003[c]	54.9	1.4	3.8	7.3	11.1	17.8	60.0	45.0
China	2004[c]	46.9	1.6	4.3	8.5	13.7	21.7	51.9	34.9
Hong Kong, China	1996[c]	43.4	2.0	5.3	9.4	13.9	20.7	50.7	34.9
Colombia	2003[c]	58.6	0.74	2.48	6.20	10.60	18.05	62.67	46.90
Congo, Dem. Rep.		..	..	..	..	..	..	..	..
Congo, Rep.		..	..	..	..	..	..	..	..
Costa Rica	2003[c]	49.8	1.0	3.5	8.2	13.1	21.2	54.1	37.4
Côte d'Ivoire	2002[a]	44.6	2.0	5.2	9.1	13.7	21.3	50.7	34.0
Croatia	2001[a]	29.0	3.4	8.3	12.8	16.8	22.6	39.6	24.5
Cuba		..	..	..	..	..	..	..	..
Czech Republic	1996[c]	25.4	4.3	10.3	14.5	17.7	21.7	35.9	22.4
Denmark	1997[c]	24.7	2.6	8.3	14.7	18.2	22.9	35.8	21.3
Dominican Republic	2004[c]	51.6	1.4	4.0	7.8	12.1	19.3	56.7	41.1
Ecuador	1998[c]	53.6	0.9	3.3	7.5	11.7	19.4	58.0	41.6
Egypt, Arab Rep.	1999–2000[a]	34.4	3.7	8.6	12.1	15.4	20.4	43.6	29.5
El Salvador	2002[c]	52.4	0.7	2.7	7.5	12.8	21.2	55.9	38.8
Eritrea		..	..	..	..	..	..	..	..
Estonia	2003[a]	35.8	2.5	6.7	11.8	16.3	22.4	42.8	27.6
Ethiopia	1999–2000[a]	30.0	3.9	9.1	13.2	16.8	21.5	39.4	25.5
Finland	2000[c]	26.9	4.0	9.6	14.1	17.5	22.1	36.7	22.6
France	1995[c]	32.7	2.8	7.2	12.6	17.2	22.8	40.2	25.1
Gabon		..	..	..	..	..	..	..	..
Gambia, The	1998[a]	50.2	1.8	4.8	8.7	12.8	20.3	53.4	37.0
Georgia	2003[a]	40.4	2.0	5.6	10.5	15.3	22.3	46.4	30.3
Germany	2000[c]	28.3	3.2	8.5	13.7	17.8	23.1	36.9	22.1
Ghana	1998–99[a]	40.8	2.1	5.6	10.1	14.9	22.9	46.6	30.0
Greece	2000[c]	34.3	2.5	6.7	11.9	16.8	23.0	41.5	26.0
Guatemala	2002[c]	55.1	0.9	2.9	7.0	11.6	19.0	59.5	43.4
Guinea	2003[a]	38.6	2.9	7.0	10.8	14.7	21.4	46.1	30.7
Guinea-Bissau	1993[a]	47.0	2.1	5.2	8.8	13.1	19.4	53.4	39.3
Haiti	2001[c]	59.2	0.7	2.4	6.2	10.4	17.7	63.4	47.7

Distribution of income or consumption 2.7

	Survey year	Gini index	Percentage share of income or consumption						
			Lowest 10%	Lowest 20%	Second 20%	Third 20%	Fourth 20%	Highest 20%	Highest 10%
Honduras	2003[c]	53.8	1.2	3.4	7.1	11.6	19.6	58.3	42.2
Hungary	2002[a]	26.9	4.0	9.5	13.9	17.6	22.4	36.5	22.2
India	2004–05[a]	36.8	3.6	8.1	11.3	14.9	20.4	45.3	31.1
Indonesia	2002[a]	34.3	3.6	8.4	11.9	15.4	21.0	43.3	28.5
Iran, Islamic Rep.	1998[a]	43.0	2.0	5.1	9.4	14.1	21.5	49.9	33.7
Iraq		..	..	..	..	..	..	..	..
Ireland	2000[c]	34.3	2.9	7.4	12.3	16.3	21.9	42.0	27.2
Israel	2001[c]	39.2	2.1	5.7	10.5	15.9	23.0	44.9	28.8
Italy	2000[c]	36.0	2.3	6.5	12.0	16.8	22.8	42.0	26.8
Jamaica	2004[a]	45.5	2.1	5.3	9.2	13.2	20.6	51.6	35.8
Japan	1993[c]	24.9	4.8	10.6	14.2	17.6	22.0	35.7	21.7
Jordan	2002–03[a]	38.8	2.7	6.7	10.8	14.9	21.3	46.3	30.6
Kazakhstan	2003[a]	33.9	3.0	7.4	11.9	16.4	22.8	41.5	25.9
Kenya	1997[a]	42.5	2.5	6.0	9.8	14.3	20.8	49.1	33.9
Korea, Dem. Rep.		..	..	..	..	..	..	..	..
Korea, Rep.	1998[c]	31.6	2.9	7.9	13.6	18.0	23.1	37.5	22.5
Kuwait		..	..	..	..	..	..	..	..
Kyrgyz Republic	2003[a]	30.3	3.8	8.9	12.8	16.4	22.5	39.4	24.3
Lao PDR	2002[a]	34.6	3.4	8.1	11.9	15.6	21.1	43.3	28.5
Latvia	2003[a]	37.7	2.5	6.6	11.2	15.5	22.0	44.7	29.1
Lebanon		..	..	..	..	..	..	..	..
Lesotho	1995[a]	63.2	0.5	1.5	4.3	8.9	18.8	66.5	48.3
Liberia		..	..	..	..	..	..	..	..
Libya		..	..	..	..	..	..	..	..
Lithuania	2003[a]	36.0	2.7	6.8	11.6	16.0	22.3	43.2	27.7
Macedonia, FYR	2003[a]	39.0	2.4	6.1	10.8	15.5	22.2	45.5	29.6
Madagascar	2001[a]	47.5	1.9	4.9	8.5	12.7	20.4	53.5	36.6
Malawi	2004–05[a]	39.0	2.9	7.0	10.8	14.8	20.7	46.6	31.8
Malaysia	1997[c]	49.2	1.7	4.4	8.1	12.9	20.3	54.3	38.4
Mali	2001[a]	40.1	2.4	6.1	10.2	14.7	22.2	46.6	30.2
Mauritania	2000[a]	39.0	2.5	6.2	10.6	15.2	22.3	45.7	29.5
Mauritius		..	..	..	..	..	..	..	..
Mexico	2004[a]	46.1	1.6	4.3	8.3	12.6	19.7	55.1	39.4
Moldova	2003[a]	33.2	3.2	7.8	12.2	16.5	22.1	41.4	26.4
Mongolia	2002[a]	32.8	3.0	7.5	12.2	16.8	23.1	40.5	24.6
Morocco	1998–99[a]	39.5	2.6	6.5	10.6	14.8	21.3	46.6	30.9
Mozambique	2002–03[a]	47.3	2.1	5.4	9.3	13.0	18.7	53.6	39.4
Myanmar		..	..	..	..	..	..	..	..
Namibia	1993[c]	74.3	0.5	1.4	3.0	5.4	11.5	78.7	64.5
Nepal	2003–04[a]	47.2	2.6	6.0	9.0	12.4	18.0	54.6	40.6
Netherlands	1999[c]	30.9	2.5	7.6	13.2	17.2	23.3	38.7	22.9
New Zealand	1997[c]	36.2	2.2	6.4	11.4	15.8	22.6	43.8	27.8
Nicaragua	2001[a]	43.1	2.2	5.6	9.8	14.2	21.1	49.3	33.8
Niger	1995[a]	50.5	0.8	2.6	7.1	13.9	23.1	53.3	35.4
Nigeria	2003[a]	43.7	1.9	5.0	9.6	14.5	21.7	49.2	33.2
Norway	2000[c]	25.8	3.9	9.6	14.0	17.2	22.0	37.2	23.4
Oman		..	..	..	..	..	..	..	..
Pakistan	2002[a]	30.6	4.0	9.3	13.0	16.3	21.1	40.3	26.3
Panama	2003[c]	56.1	0.7	2.5	6.6	11.4	19.6	59.9	43.0
Papua New Guinea	1996[a]	50.9	1.7	4.5	7.9	11.9	19.2	56.5	40.5
Paraguay	2003[c]	58.4	0.7	2.4	6.3	10.8	18.6	61.9	46.1
Peru	2003[c]	52.0	1.3	3.7	7.7	12.2	19.7	56.7	40.9
Philippines	2003[a]	44.5	2.2	5.4	9.1	13.6	21.3	50.6	34.2
Poland	2002[a]	34.5	3.1	7.5	11.9	16.1	22.2	42.2	27.0
Portugal	1997[c]	38.5	2.0	5.8	11.0	15.5	21.9	45.9	29.8
Puerto Rico		..	..	..	..	..	..	..	..

2.7 Distribution of income or consumption

	Survey year	Gini index	Percentage share of income or consumption						
			Lowest 10%	Lowest 20%	Second 20%	Third 20%	Fourth 20%	Highest 20%	Highest 10%
Romania	2003[a]	31.0	3.3	8.1	12.9	17.1	22.7	39.2	24.4
Russian Federation	2002[a]	39.9	2.4	6.1	10.5	14.9	21.8	46.6	30.6
Rwanda	2000[a]	46.8	2.1	5.3	9.1	13.2	19.4	53.0	38.2
Saudi Arabia		..	..	..	..	..	..	..	..
Senegal	2001[a]	41.3	2.7	6.6	10.3	14.2	20.6	48.4	33.4
Serbia and Montenegro	2003[a]	30.0	3.4	8.3	13.0	17.3	23.0	38.4	23.4
Sierra Leone	1989[a]	62.9	0.5	1.1	2.0	9.8	23.7	63.4	43.6
Singapore	1998[c]	42.5	1.9	5.0	9.4	14.6	22.0	49.0	32.8
Slovak Republic	1996[c]	25.8	3.1	8.8	14.9	18.7	22.8	34.8	20.9
Slovenia	1998[a]	28.4	3.6	9.1	14.2	18.1	22.9	35.7	21.4
Somalia		..	..	..	..	..	..	..	..
South Africa	2000[a]	57.8	1.4	3.5	6.3	10.0	18.0	62.2	44.7
Spain	2000[c]	34.7	2.6	7.0	12.1	16.4	22.5	42.0	26.6
Sri Lanka	2002[a]	40.2	3.0	7.0	10.5	14.2	20.4	48.0	32.7
Sudan		..	..	..	..	..	..	..	..
Swaziland	2000–01[c]	50.4	1.6	4.3	8.2	12.3	18.9	56.3	40.7
Sweden	2000[c]	25.0	3.6	9.1	14.0	17.6	22.7	36.6	22.2
Switzerland	2000[c]	33.7	2.9	7.6	12.2	16.3	22.6	41.3	25.9
Syrian Arab Republic		..	..	..	..	..	..	..	..
Tajikistan	2003[a]	32.6	3.3	7.9	12.3	16.5	22.4	40.8	25.6
Tanzania	2000–01[a]	34.6	2.9	7.3	12.0	16.1	22.3	42.4	26.9
Thailand	2002[a]	42.0	2.7	6.3	9.9	14.0	20.8	49.0	33.4
Togo		..	..	..	..	..	..	..	..
Trinidad and Tobago	1992[c]	38.9	2.2	5.9	10.8	15.3	23.1	44.9	28.8
Tunisia	2000[a]	39.8	2.3	6.0	10.3	14.8	21.7	47.3	31.5
Turkey	2003[a]	43.6	2.0	5.3	9.7	14.2	21.0	49.7	34.1
Turkmenistan	1998[a]	40.8	2.6	6.1	10.2	14.7	21.5	47.5	31.7
Uganda	2002[a]	45.7	2.3	5.7	9.4	13.2	19.1	52.5	37.7
Ukraine	2003[a]	28.1	3.9	9.2	13.6	17.3	22.4	37.5	23.0
United Arab Emirates		..	..	..	..	..	..	..	..
United Kingdom	1999[c]	36.0	2.1	6.1	11.4	16.0	22.5	44.0	28.5
United States	2000[c]	40.8	1.9	5.4	10.7	15.7	22.4	45.8	29.9
Uruguay[b]	2003[c]	44.9	1.9	5.0	9.1	14.0	21.5	50.5	34.0
Uzbekistan	2003[a]	36.8	2.8	7.2	11.7	15.4	21.0	44.7	29.6
Venezuela, RB	2003[c]	48.2	0.7	3.3	8.7	13.9	22.0	52.1	35.2
Vietnam	2004[a]	34.4	4.2	9.0	11.4	14.7	20.5	44.3	28.8
West Bank and Gaza		..	..	..	..	..	..	..	..
Yemen, Rep.	1998[a]	33.4	3.0	7.4	12.2	16.7	22.5	41.2	25.9
Zambia	2004[a]	50.8	1.2	3.6	7.9	12.6	20.8	55.1	38.8
Zimbabwe	1995–96[a]	50.1	1.8	4.6	8.1	12.2	19.3	55.7	40.3

a. Refers to expenditure shares by percentiles of population, ranked by per capita expenditure. b. Urban data. c. Refers to income shares by percentiles of population, ranked by per capita income.

Distribution of income or consumption 2.7

About the data

Inequality in the distribution of income is reflected in the percentage shares of income or consumption accruing to portions of the population ranked by income or consumption levels. The portions ranked lowest by personal income receive the smallest shares of total income. The Gini index provides a convenient summary measure of the degree of inequality. Data on the distribution of income or consumption come from nationally representative household surveys. Where the original data from the household survey were available, they have been used to directly calculate the income or consumption shares by quintile. Otherwise, shares have been estimated from the best available grouped data.

For most countries the income distribution indicators are based on the same data used to derive the $1 and $2 a day poverty estimates in table 2.6. This table contains additional countries for which poverty estimates are not provided in table 2.6, either because no reasonable purchasing power parity estimates are available or because the international poverty lines are not relevant for high-income economies.

The distribution data have been adjusted for household size, providing a more consistent measure of per capita income or consumption. No adjustment has been made for spatial differences in cost of living within countries, because the data needed for such calculations are generally unavailable. For further details on the estimation method for low- and middle-income economies, see Ravallion and Chen (1996).

Because the underlying household surveys differ in method and type of data collected, the distribution data are not strictly comparable across countries. These problems are diminishing as survey methods improve and become more standardized, but achieving strict comparability is still impossible (see *About the data* for table 2.6).

Two sources of noncomparability should be noted in particular. First, the surveys can differ in many respects, including whether they use income or consumption expenditure as the living standard indicator. The distribution of income is typically more unequal than the distribution of consumption. In addition, the definitions of income used differ more often among surveys. Consumption is usually a much better welfare indicator, particularly in developing countries. Second, households differ in size (number of members) and in the extent of income sharing among members. And individuals differ in age and consumption needs. Differences among countries in these respects may bias comparisons of distribution.

World Bank staff have made an effort to ensure that the data are as comparable as possible. Wherever possible, consumption has been used rather than income. Income distribution and Gini indexes for high-income countries are calculated directly from the Luxembourg Income Study database, using an estimation method consistent with that applied for developing countries.

Definitions

• **Survey year** is the year in which the underlying data were collected. • **Gini index** measures the extent to which the distribution of income (or consumption expenditure) among individuals or households within an economy deviates from a perfectly equal distribution. A Lorenz curve plots the cumulative percentages of total income received against the cumulative number of recipients, starting with the poorest individual. The Gini index measures the area between the Lorenz curve and a hypothetical line of absolute equality, expressed as a percentage of the maximum area under the line. Thus a Gini index of 0 represents perfect equality, while an index of 100 implies perfect inequality. • **Percentage share of income or consumption** is the share of total income or consumption that accrues to subgroups of population indicated by deciles or quintiles. Percentage shares by quintile may not sum to 100 because of rounding.

Data sources

Data on distribution are compiled by the World Bank's Development Research Group using primary household survey data obtained from government statistical agencies and World Bank country departments. Data for high-income economies are estimated from the Luxembourg Income Study database.

2.8 Assessing vulnerability and security

	Urban informal sector employment		Youth unemployment		Female-headed households	Pension contributors			Public expenditure on pensions			
	% of urban employment		Male	Female								
	Male	Female	% of male labor force ages 15–24	% of female labor force ages 15–24	% of total	Year	% of labor force	% of working-age population	Year	% of GDP	Year	Average pension % of per capita income
	1998–2001[a]	1998–2001[a]	2000–05[a]	2000–05[a]	2000–05[a]							
Afghanistan	..	..	..	..	..		..	..	2005	0.5		..
Albania	..	..	42	27	..	2004	48.8	33.0	2004	4.6		..
Algeria	..	..	43	46	..	2002	36.7	22.0	2002	3.2	2002	89.1
Angola	..	..	..	..	..		..	..		..		..
Argentina	..	..	22[b]	28[b]	..	2004	34.9	25.8	1994	6.2	2002	73.7
Armenia	..	..	..	..	29	2002	64.4	48.3	2004	3.4		..
Australia	..	..	11	10	..		..	..	2003	5.4	2002	52.4
Austria	..	..	11[b]	10[b]	..	2004	80.8	58.8	2003	11.6	2002	93.2
Azerbaijan	..	..	..	..	..	1996	52.0	46.0	1996	2.5		..
Bangladesh	..	..	7	6	10	2004	2.8	2.1	1992	0.0		..
Belarus	..	..	..	..	..	1992	97.0	94.0	1997	7.7		..
Belgium	..	..	16	20	..	1995	86.2	65.9	2003	8.5	2002	62.8
Benin	50	41	..	..	21	1996	4.8	..	1993	0.4		..
Bolivia	..	..	..	..	20	2002	10.1	7.8	2000	4.5		..
Bosnia and Herzegovina	..	..	..	..	..	2004	35.9	24.6	2004	8.8		..
Botswana	..	..	34	46	..		..	..		..		..
Brazil	..	..	14[b]	23[b]	..	2004	52.2	38.7	1997	9.8		..
Bulgaria	..	..	23	21	..	1994	64.0	63.0	2005	8.9	2002	75.2
Burkina Faso	..	..	..	..	9	1993	3.1	3.0	1992	0.3		..
Burundi	..	..	..	..	..	1993	3.3	3.0	1991	0.2		..
Cambodia	..	..	..	..	25		..	..		..		..
Cameroon	..	..	..	..	24	1993	13.7	11.5	2001	0.8		..
Canada	..	..	14[b]	11[b]	..	2003	57.0	63.0	2003	5.4	2002	57.1
Central African Republic	..	..	..	..	..		..	..	1990	0.3		..
Chad	..	..	..	..	20	1990	1.1	1.0	1997	0.1		..
Chile	..	..	15	21	..	2003	58.0	35.2	2001	2.9	2002	53.5
China	..	..	..	..	..	2005	20.5	17.2	1996	2.7		..
Hong Kong, China	..	..	14	8	..		..	..		..		..
Colombia	..	..	20	32	30	2000	19.0	14.0	1994	1.1	2002	54.4
Congo, Dem. Rep.	..	..	..	..	..		..	..		..		..
Congo, Rep.	..	..	..	..	..	1992	5.8	5.6	1992	0.9		..
Costa Rica	..	..	11	22	..	2004	55.2	37.6	1997	4.2	2002	103.1
Côte d'Ivoire	..	..	..	..	..	1997	9.3	9.1	1997	0.3		..
Croatia	..	..	30	36	..	2004	71.0	46.0	2005	12.3	2002	61.6
Cuba	..	..	..	..	..		..	..	1992	12.6		..
Czech Republic	..	..	19	19	..	2003	86.0	61.0	2003	10.5	2002	58.2
Denmark	..	..	9	9	..	2003	92.0	74.0	2003	9.6	2002	54.1
Dominican Republic	..	..	16	34	28	2005	27.2	18.6	2000	0.8	2002	55.9
Ecuador	..	..	12[b]	21[b]	..	2004	27.0	20.7	2002	2.5		..
Egypt, Arab Rep.	..	..	21	40	12	2004	55.4	27.7	2004	4.1	2002	119.8
El Salvador	..	..	13	9	..	2003	18.0	12.0	1997	1.3	2002	39.3
Eritrea	..	..	..	..	47		..	..	2001	0.3		..
Estonia	..	..	16	15	..	2000	91.0	66.0	2003	6.3	2002	60.9
Ethiopia	39	65	4	11	24		..	..	1993	0.9		..
Finland	..	..	18	19	..	2003	90.3	67.0	2003	9.0	2002	78.8
France	..	..	22[b]	24[b]	..	2003	90.0	62.0	2003	13.3	2002	65.0
Gabon	..	..	..	..	26	1995	15.0	14.0		..		..
Gambia, The	..	..	..	..	..		..	..		..		..
Georgia	21	7	27	31	..	2004	30.0	22.7	2004	3.0		..
Germany	..	..	16	14	..	2003	88.0	64.0	2003	13.2	2002	71.8
Ghana	..	..	13	19	34	2003	9.1	7.1	2002	1.3		..
Greece	..	..	18	35	..	2002	79.0	52.0	2003	12.8	2002	99.9
Guatemala	..	..	..	..	..	2000	19.0	11.7	1995	0.7		..
Guinea	..	..	..	..	..	1993	1.5	1.8		..		..
Guinea-Bissau	..	..	..	..	..		..	..		..		..
Haiti	..	..	..	..	43		..	..		..		..

Assessing vulnerability and security

	Urban informal sector employment		Youth unemployment		Female-headed households	Pension contributors			Public expenditure on pensions			
	% of urban employment		Male % of male labor force ages 15–24	Female % of female labor force ages 15–24	% of total		% of labor force	% of working-age population		% of GDP		Average pension % of per capita income
	Male **1998–2001[a]**	Female **1998–2001[a]**	**2000–05[a]**	**2000–05[a]**	**2000–05[a]**	Year			Year		Year	
Honduras	..	..	5[b]	11[b]	..	1999	20.6	17.7	1994	0.6		..
Hungary	..	..	20	19	..	1996	77.0	65.0	2003	11.0	2002	90.5
India	54	41	10[b]	11[b]	..	2004	9.1	5.7		..		..
Indonesia	..	..	..	..	12	1995	8.0	7.0		..		..
Iran, Islamic Rep.	..	..	20	32	..	2001	35.0	20.0	2000	1.1	2002	124.2
Iraq	..	..	..	..	..		..	..		..		..
Ireland	..	..	9	7	..	2002	93.0	64.7	2003	4.7	2002	36.6
Israel	..	..	17	19	..	1992	82.0	63.0	1996	5.9		..
Italy	..	..	21	27	..	2003	90.0	56.0	2003	15.5	2002	88.8
Jamaica	..	..	22	36	..		..	..		..		..
Japan	..	..	10	7	..	2003	94.0	73.0	2003	8.9	2002	59.1
Jordan	..	..	28	43	12	2003	30.3	17.4	2001	2.2	2002	76.1
Kazakhstan	..	..	13	16	..	2004	33.7	26.3	2004	4.9		..
Kenya	..	..	..	..	32	2005	8.0	6.2	1993	0.5		..
Korea, Dem. Rep.	..	..	..	..	..		..	..		..		..
Korea, Rep.	..	..	12	9	..	1996	58.0	43.0	2003	1.3	2002	43.3
Kuwait	..	..	..	..	..		..	..	1990	3.5		..
Kyrgyz Republic	33	25	19	21	..	2004	40.1	28.3	1997	6.4		..
Lao PDR	..	..	..	..	..		..	..		..		..
Latvia	..	..	12	14	..	2003	90.0	64.0	2002	8.2	2002	81.8
Lebanon	..	..	..	..	..	2003	32.1	19.6	2003	2.1		..
Lesotho	..	..	..	..	..		..	..		..		..
Liberia	..	..	..	..	..		..	..		..		..
Libya	..	..	..	..	..	2003	65.5	37.1	2001	2.1	2002	91.2
Lithuania	50	27	16	15	..	2004	79.7	58.9	2003	6.2	2002	71.3
Macedonia, FYR	..	..	63	62	..	2000	63.8	38.8	1998	8.7		..
Madagascar	..	..	..	..	22	1993	5.4	4.8	1990	0.2		..
Malawi	..	..	..	..	27		..	..		..		..
Malaysia	..	..	8	8	..	1993	48.7	37.8	1999	6.5		..
Mali	..	..	..	..	11	1990	2.5	2.0	1991	0.4		..
Mauritania	..	..	..	..	29	1995	5.0	4.0	1992	0.2		..
Mauritius	..	..	21	34	..	2000	51.3	33.6	1999	4.4		..
Mexico	18	22	6	7	..	2002	34.6	22.6	2003	1.3	2002	45.1
Moldova	..	..	19	18	..	2000	60.0	43.0	2003	8.0		..
Mongolia	..	..	20	21	..	2002	61.4	49.1	2002	5.8		..
Morocco	..	..	17	16	17	2003	22.4	12.3	2003	1.9	2002	74.1
Mozambique	..	..	..	..	26	1995	2.0	2.1	1996	0.0		..
Myanmar	..	..	..	..	..		..	..		..		..
Namibia	..	..	40	49	42		..	..		..		..
Nepal	60	76	..	..	16	2003	2.1	1.4	2003	0.3		..
Netherlands	..	..	10	10	..	2002	94.0	72.0	2003	9.0	2002	84.1
New Zealand	..	..	9	10	..		..	..	2003	7.4	2002	39.5
Nicaragua	..	..	11[b]	16[b]	31	2005	17.9	11.5	1996	2.5		..
Niger	..	..	..	..	..	1992	1.3	1.5	1992	0.1		..
Nigeria	..	..	..	..	17	2000	1.9	1.3	1991	0.1		..
Norway	..	..	13	12	..	2003	92.0	75.0	2003	10.7	2002	65.1
Oman	..	..	..	..	..		..	..		..		..
Pakistan	64	61	11	15	..	2004	6.4	4.0	1993	0.9		..
Panama	..	..	19	30	..	1998	51.6	40.7	1996	4.3		..
Papua New Guinea	..	..	..	5	..		..	..		..		..
Paraguay	..	..	12	17	..	2004	11.6	9.1	2001	1.2		..
Peru	..	..	21[b]	21[b]	20	2003	16.3	12.3	2000	2.6	2002	43.9
Philippines	..	..	15	19	15	2000	27.0	18.6	1993	1.0		..
Poland	..	..	37	39	..	2005	84.8	54.5	2003	15.8	2002	69.7
Portugal	..	..	14	19	..	2003	92.0	71.0	2003	11.9	2002	79.8
Puerto Rico	..	..	25[b]	21[b]	..		..	..		..		..

2.8 Assessing vulnerability and security

	Urban informal sector employment		Youth unemployment		Female-headed households	Pension contributors			Public expenditure on pensions			
	% of urban employment		Male	Female								Average pension
	Male 1998–2001[a]	Female 1998–2001[a]	% of male labor force ages 15–24 2000–05[a]	% of female labor force ages 15–24 2000–05[a]	% of total 2000–05[a]	Year	% of labor force	% of working-age population	Year	% of GDP	Year	% of per capita income
Romania	..	..	21	18	..	2005	57.5	39.1	2003	6.9		..
Russian Federation	10	9	..	..	..		..	..	2004	5.8		..
Rwanda	..	..	..	..	36		..	..		..		..
Saudi Arabia	..	..	..	..	..		..	..		..		..
Senegal	..	..	..	..	..	2003	5.2	3.8	2003	1.3		..
Serbia and Montenegro	..	..	..	..	..	2003	45.9	32.1	2003	12.4		..
Sierra Leone	..	..	..	..	..	2004	4.6	3.6		..		..
Singapore	..	..	4	6	..	1995	73.0	56.0	1996	1.4		..
Slovak Republic	..	..	30[b]	29[b]	..	2003	58.8	55.0	2003	8.5	2002	60.2
Slovenia	..	..	11	12	..	1995	86.0	68.7	2003	10.1		..
Somalia	..	..	..	..	..		..	..		..		..
South Africa	16	28	56	65	..		..	..		..		..
Spain	..	..	17	24	..	2003	92.0	63.0	2003	10.6	2002	88.3
Sri Lanka	..	..	20	37	..	2004	35.6	22.2	1996	2.4		..
Sudan	..	..	..	..	..	1995	12.1	12.0		..		..
Swaziland	..	..	..	..	..		..	..		..		..
Sweden	..	..	16	13	..	2003	90.0	72.0	2003	14.0	2002	68.2
Switzerland	..	..	9	9	..	2003	99.0	84.0	2003	12.1	2002	67.3
Syrian Arab Republic	..	..	21	39	..		..	..	1991	0.5		..
Tajikistan	..	..	..	..	..		..	..	1996	3.0		..
Tanzania	..	..	..	..	25	1996	2.0	2.0		..		..
Thailand	..	..	5	5	..	1999	18.0	17.0		..		..
Togo	..	..	..	..	..	1997	15.9	15.0	1997	0.6		..
Trinidad and Tobago	..	..	17[b]	26[b]	..		..	..	1996	0.6		..
Tunisia	..	..	31	29	..	2003	54.9	30.0	2003	4.3	2002	72.7
Turkey	10	6	19	19	..	2002	44.9	24.3	2002	7.1	2002	103.3
Turkmenistan	..	..	..	..	27		..	..	1996	2.3		..
Uganda	..	..	..	..	28	2004	1.8	1.6	2003	0.3		..
Ukraine	..	..	16	17	..	2005	76.0	52.0	2005	15.4		..
United Arab Emirates	..	..	..	..	..		..	..		..		..
United Kingdom	..	..	13	10	..	2003	94.0	73.0	2003	8.3	2002	47.6
United States	..	..	12	10	..	2003	91.0	71.0	2003	7.5	2002	51.0
Uruguay	..	..	25[b]	35[b]	..	2001	57.7	44.3	1996	15.0	2002	125.4
Uzbekistan	..	..	..	..	..		..	..	1995	5.3		..
Venezuela, RB	..	..	24[b]	35[b]	..	2001	20.8	14.6	2001	2.7		..
Vietnam	..	..	4	5	27	1998	8.4	10.0	1998	1.6		..
West Bank and Gaza	..	..	39	45	..	2000	19.0	6.4	2001	0.8		..
Yemen, Rep.	..	..	..	..	..	1999	15.0	7.0	1994	0.1	2002	106.3
Zambia	..	..	..	..	23	2000	5.9	4.9	1993	0.1		..
Zimbabwe	..	..	28	21	..	1995	12.0	10.0	2002	2.3		..
World			.. w	.. w								
Low income			..	..								
Middle income			..	..								
Lower middle income			..	..								
Upper middle income			24	27								
Low & middle income			..	..								
East Asia & Pacific			..	..								
Europe & Central Asia			..	..								
Latin America & Carib.			14	20								
Middle East & N. Africa			..	..								
South Asia			11	12								
Sub-Saharan Africa			..	..								
High income			13	12								
Europe EMU			16	19								

a. Data are for the most recent year available. b. Limited coverage.

Assessing vulnerability and security 2.8

About the data

As traditionally defined and measured, poverty is a static concept, and vulnerability a dynamic one. Vulnerability reflects a household's resilience in the face of shocks and the likelihood that a shock will lead to a decline in well-being. Thus, it depends primarily on the household's asset endowment and insurance mechanisms. Because poor people have fewer assets and less diversified sources of income than the better-off, fluctuations in income affect them more.

Enhancing security for poor people means reducing their vulnerability to such risks as ill health, providing them the means to manage risk themselves, and strengthening market or public institutions for managing risk. The tools include microfinance programs, old age assistance and pensions, and public provision of education and basic health care (see tables 2.9 and 2.14).

Poor households face many risks, and vulnerability is thus multidimensional. The indicators in the table focus on individual risks—informal sector employment, youth unemployment, female-headed households, income insecurity in old age, and the extent to which publicly provided services may be capable of mitigating some of these risks. Poor people face labor market risks, often having to take up precarious, low-quality jobs in the informal sector and to increase their household's labor market participation by sending their children to work (see table 2.4). Income security is a prime concern for the elderly.

For informal sector employment the data are from a variety of sources, including labor force and special informal sector surveys, household surveys, surveys of household industries or economic activities, surveys of small enterprises and micro enterprises, and official estimates. The international comparability of the data is affected by differences among countries in definitions and coverage and in treatment of domestic workers. The data in the table are based on national definitions of informal sector and urban areas established by countries and therefore data may not be comparable across countries. For details on these definitions, consult the original source.

Youth unemployment is an important policy issue for many economies. Experiencing unemployment may permanently impair a young person's productive potential and future employment opportunities. The table presents unemployment among youth ages 15–24, but the lower age limit for young people in a country could be determined by the minimum age for leaving school, so age groups could differ across countries. Also, since this age group is likely to include school leavers, the level of youth unemployment varies considerably over the year as a result of different school opening and closing dates. The youth unemployment rate shares similar limitations on comparability as the general unemployment rate. For further information, see *About the data* for table 2.5 and the original source.

The data on female-headed households are from recent Demographic and Health Surveys. The definition and concept of the female-headed household differ greatly across countries, making cross-country comparison difficult. In some cases it is assumed that a woman cannot be the head of any household in which an adult male is present, because of sex-biased stereotype. Users need to be cautious when interpreting the data.

The data on pension contributors come from national sources, the International Labour Organization (ILO), and International Monetary Fund country reports. Coverage by pension schemes may be broad or even universal where eligibility is determined by citizenship, residency, or income status. In contribution-related schemes, however, eligibility is usually restricted to individuals who have made contributions for a minimum number of years. Definitional issues—relating to the labor force, for example—may arise in comparing coverage by contribution-related schemes over time and across countries (for country-specific information, see Palacios and Pallares-Miralles 2000). The share of the labor force covered by a pension scheme may be overstated in countries that do not attempt to count informal sector workers as part of the labor force.

Public interventions and institutions can provide services directly to poor people, although whether these interventions and institutions work well for the poor is debated. State action is often ineffective, in part because governments can influence only a few of the many sources of well-being and in part because of difficulties in delivering good and services. The effectiveness of public provision is further constrained by the fiscal resources at governments' disposal and the fact that state institutions may not be responsive to the needs of poor people.

The data on public pension spending are from national sources and cover all government expenditures, including the administrative costs of pension programs. They cover noncontributory pensions or social assistance targeted to the elderly and disabled and spending by social insurance schemes for which contributions had previously been made. The pattern of spending in a country is correlated with its demographic structure—spending increases as the population ages.

Definitions

• **Urban informal sector employment** is all persons who, during a given reference period, were employed in at least one informal enterprise, irrespective of their status in employment and whether it was their main or secondary job. • **Youth unemployment** refers to the share of the labor force ages 15–24 without work but available for and seeking employment. • **Female-headed households** refer to the percentage of households with a female head. • **Pension contributors** refer to the share of the labor force or working-age population (here defined as ages 15–64) covered by a pension scheme. • **Public expenditure on pensions** includes all government expenditures on cash transfers to the elderly, the disabled, and survivors and the administrative costs of these programs. • **Average pension** is estimated by dividing total pension expenditure by the number of pensioners.

Data sources

Data on urban informal sector employment and youth unemployment are from the ILO database Key Indicators of the Labour Market, 4th edition. Data on female-headed household are from Demographic and Health Surveys by Macro International. Data on pension contributors and pension spending are from Robert Palacios and Montserrat Pallares-Miralles's "International Patterns of Pension Provision" (2000) and updates, Edward Whitehouse's *Pensions Panorama* (2007), and the Organisation for Economic Co-operation and Development's Social Expenditure database (forthcoming). Further updates, notes, and sources will be available in the World Bank's *Progress Report of Pensions Indicators* (forthcoming).

2.9 Education inputs

	Public expenditure per student[a]						Public expenditure on education		Trained teachers in primary education	Primary pupil-teacher ratio
	% of GDP per capita									
	Primary		Secondary		Tertiary		% of GDP	% of total government expenditure	% of total	pupils per teacher
	1991	2005[b]	1998	2005[b]	1998	2005[b]	2005[b]	2005[b]	2005[b]	2005[b]
Afghanistan	..	..	..	..	..	..	..	..	36.5	83
Albania	..	7.8	..	12.0	..	36.6	2.9	8.4	..	21
Algeria	26.5	11.3	..	17.1	..	..	..	..	98.5	25
Angola	..	..	..	..	..	..	..	..	..	..
Argentina	..	10.9	13.6	14.3	20.2	10.3	3.5	12.0	..	17
Armenia	..	..	..	..	..	..	..	..	77.5	21
Australia	..	16.4	14.5	14.4	27.0	22.5	4.8	..	..	..
Austria	18.2	23.2	29.9	28.6	51.6	45.7	5.5	10.8	..	13
Azerbaijan	..	6.3	15.4	10.2	19.1	10.4	2.5	19.6	100.0	13
Bangladesh	..	7.0	12.4	14.7	46.3	49.7	2.5	14.2	48.0	51
Belarus	..	14.1	..	25.3	..	28.3	6.0	11.3	99.8	16
Belgium	16.3	20.2	..	23.1	..	37.1	6.2	11.8	..	12
Benin	..	11.5	..	21.2	..	..	3.5	14.1	72.2	47
Bolivia	..	16.2	12.0	13.0	52.2	36.0	6.4	18.1	63.3	24
Bosnia and Herzegovina	..	..	..	..	..	..	..	..	..	..
Botswana	..	17.2	..	44.0	..	479.9	10.7	21.5	92.5	26
Brazil	..	10.8	10.4	11.2	85.7	48.9	4.1	10.9	..	22
Bulgaria	..	19.0	..	20.9	..	28.3	4.2	..	95.1	17
Burkina Faso	..	34.7	..	21.6	..	212.3	4.7	16.6	88.3	47
Burundi	13.4	19.1	..	73.3	1051.9	348.8	5.1	17.7	87.5	49
Cambodia	..	6.1	11.4	..	..	77.5	1.9	..	97.7	53
Cameroon	..	10.3	18.2	16.0	69.7	67.9	1.8	8.6	62.7	48
Canada	..	..	..	..	49.0	44.6	5.2	..	..	..
Central African Republic	11.9	11.8	..	..	..	..	..	..	..	..
Chad	8.0	7.3	27.5	30.1	..	359.9	2.1	10.1	26.8	63
Chile	..	12.8	13.8	14.2	21.0	15.5	3.7	18.5	96.4	27
China	..	..	11.5	..	90.1	..	..	..	84.7	21
Hong Kong, China	..	14.9	..	19.9	..	60.6	4.2	23.0	93.2	18
Colombia	..	19.5	14.9	18.4	35.6	24.6	4.8	11.1	..	29
Congo, Dem. Rep.	..	..	..	..	..	..	..	..	..	34
Congo, Rep.	..	4.0	..	18.3	404.9	245.9	2.2	8.1	62.2	83
Costa Rica	7.8	17.0	23.2	17.1	55.0	36.1	4.9	18.5	96.8	21
Côte d'Ivoire	..	..	54.5	..	212.8	..	..	21.6	100.0	42
Croatia	..	20.2	..	26.0	41.5	31.5	4.7	10.0	100.0	15
Cuba	..	37.6	38.3	41.1	115.9	59.0	9.8	16.6	100.0	10
Czech Republic	..	12.9	22.1	23.4	34.4	33.6	4.5	8.5	..	18
Denmark	..	25.5	38.3	35.0	66.2	67.2	8.4	15.1	..	..
Dominican Republic	..	8.1	..	5.5	..	..	1.8	9.7	88.3	24
Ecuador	..	..	..	..	..	..	..	..	70.9	23
Egypt, Arab Rep.	..	..	..	..	..	..	..	..	..	22
El Salvador	..	9.2	8.2	10.5	10.5	17.2	2.8	20.0	100.0	30
Eritrea	..	11.3	..	15.4	..	1,101.3	5.4	..	83.6	48
Estonia	..	20.1	27.9	27.7	32.6	23.2	5.7	15.4	..	14
Ethiopia	22.1	..	..	..	..	..	5.0	19.4	97.1	72
Finland	21.9	18.7	26.4	28.1	41.3	37.4	6.5	12.8	..	16
France	11.8	17.6	28.6	29.6	29.7	33.9	5.9	11.0	..	19
Gabon	..	..	..	..	..	..	..	..	100.0	36
Gambia, The	13.2	7.4	..	9.1	..	238.0	2.0	8.9	57.8	35
Georgia	..	..	..	..	..	..	2.9	13.1	89.7	14
Germany	..	16.6	20.5	22.3	..	..	4.7	9.7	..	14
Ghana	..	12.8	..	34.5	..	209.8	5.4	..	53.2[c]	35[c]
Greece	7.6	16.1	15.5	22.5	30.7	24.3	4.0	8.0	..	11
Guatemala	..	6.5	..	3.5	..	..	..	..	..	31
Guinea	..	..	..	..	..	244.1	2.0	..	68.1	45
Guinea-Bissau	..	..	..	..	..	..	..	..	..	..
Haiti	9.1	..	..	..	..	..	..	..	40.5	..

Education inputs 2.9

	Public expenditure per student[a]						Public expenditure on education		Trained teachers in primary education	Primary pupil-teacher ratio
	% of GDP per capita									
	Primary		Secondary		Tertiary		% of GDP	% of total government expenditure	% of total	pupils per teacher
	1991	2005[b]	1998	2005[b]	1998	2005[b]	2005[b]	2005[b]	2005[b]	2005[b]
Honduras	..	..	..	..	..	..	..	..	87.2	33
Hungary	21.2	21.9	18.6	26.8	36.0	31.9	5.9	10.3	..	10
India	..	11.1	21.2	19.8	74.5	68.6	3.7	10.7	..	40
Indonesia	..	2.6	..	4.9	..	13.3	0.9	9.0	92.9	20
Iran, Islamic Rep.	..	9.7	..	11.0	..	22.8	4.7	22.8	100.0	19
Iraq	..	..	..	..	..	..	..	..	100.0	21
Ireland	11.6	13.9	17.5	20.0	29.4	24.8	4.5	13.1	..	18
Israel	12.6	22.8	23.3	23.4	32.9	30.0	7.3	13.7	..	12
Italy	15.3	25.9	28.6	29.2	28.4	24.1	4.9	9.5	..	11
Jamaica	9.9	11.5	..	20.0	..	40.7	4.5	9.5	100.0	28
Japan	..	22.6	19.9	22.3	13.2	19.6	3.7	10.7	..	19
Jordan	..	14.0	15.7	16.9	..	..	..	..	..	20
Kazakhstan	..	10.0	..	7.9	..	5.7	2.3	..	97.2	17
Kenya	12.9	23.6	..	23.5	..	262.6	6.7	29.2	98.8	40
Korea, Dem. Rep.	..	..	..	..	..	..	..	..	..	..
Korea, Rep.	11.8	18.6	14.9	25.1	7.0	9.3	4.6	15.0	100.0	29
Kuwait	35.4	12.2	..	18.1	..	116.4	5.1	12.7	100.0	12
Kyrgyz Republic	..	7.6	11.9	14.3	27.7	20.8	4.4	..	58.0	24
Lao PDR	..	8.6	4.3	4.0	66.9	22.4	2.3	11.7	83.4	31
Latvia	..	20.6	24.0	24.5	34.3	14.4	5.3	15.4	..	13
Lebanon	..	7.2	..	7.6	12.8	15.9	2.6	11.0	14.4	14
Lesotho	..	24.2	68.4	49.0	1237.4	1104.8	13.4	29.8	63.7	42
Liberia	..	..	..	..	..	..	..	..	..	..
Libya	..	..	..	..	23.8	..	..	..	..	..
Lithuania	..	14.4	..	20.1	..	20.6	5.2	15.7	..	15
Macedonia, FYR	..	23.8	..	7.5	..	22.6	3.4	16.4	100.0	20
Madagascar	..	8.4	39.9	..	180.9	175.0	3.2	25.3	36.5	54
Malawi	7.2	13.5	..	28.6	..	..	5.8	..	85.8	64
Malaysia	10.1	18.6	..	26.3	..	93.7	8.0	28.0	..	18
Mali	..	..	61.6	..	265.0	..	4.3	14.8	..	54
Mauritania	..	9.8	38.7	24.7	85.0	39.9	2.3	8.3	100.0	40
Mauritius	10.1	11.8	..	19.8	..	37.1	4.5	14.3	100.0	22
Mexico	4.8	15.5	14.2	16.8	47.8	44.1	5.8	23.8	84.3	28
Moldova	..	16.6	..	24.1	..	12.9	4.3	21.1	..	18
Mongolia	..	14.3	..	13.2	..	22.8	5.3	..	96.4	34
Morocco	15.3	22.9	49.1	39.6	104.8	93.0	6.7	27.2	100.0	27
Mozambique	..	14.1	..	48.4	..	435.3	3.7	19.5	59.8	66
Myanmar	..	2.7	..	2.9	..	..	..	..	76.0	31
Namibia	..	20.1	36.4	24.1	157.6	106.6	6.9	..	16.7	33
Nepal	..	12.4	13.1	10.5	..	71.1	3.4	14.9	95.8	40[c]
Netherlands	12.6	18.7	21.8	23.6	44.2	43.0	5.3	10.8	..	..
New Zealand	17.3	19.4	24.5	22.7	42.0	34.1	6.8	20.9	..	16
Nicaragua	..	8.8	..	10.4	..	..	3.1	15.0	76.9	34
Niger	..	19.0	..	64.3	..	..	2.3	..	75.8	44
Nigeria	..	..	..	..	..	..	..	..	49.8	37
Norway	32.7	21.7	30.6	33.0	47.8	50.4	7.7	15.7	..	11
Oman	10.5	16.3	22.2	15.5	..	28.7	3.6	24.2	..	..
Pakistan	..	7.0	..	11.0	..	..	2.3	10.9	85.5	38
Panama	11.3	9.6	19.1	12.3	33.6	26.5	3.8	8.9	89.6	24
Papua New Guinea	..	..	..	..	..	..	..	..	100.0	35
Paraguay	..	12.6	..	14.1	..	30.1	4.3	10.8	67.0	28
Peru	..	6.7	10.8	8.9	..	12.3	2.4	13.7	..	22
Philippines	..	11.7	..	10.1	..	14.1	3.2	17.2	100.0	35
Poland	12.9	22.9	16.5	21.7	36.3	19.7	5.6	12.3	..	13
Portugal	17.2	24.4	29.1	33.0	29.7	27.8	5.9	12.4	..	12
Puerto Rico	..	..	..	..	..	..	..	..	..	..

2.9 Education inputs

	Public expenditure per student[a] (% of GDP per capita)						Public expenditure on education		Trained teachers in primary education	Primary pupil-teacher ratio
	Primary		Secondary		Tertiary		% of GDP	% of total government expenditure	% of total	pupils per teacher
	1991	2005[b]	1998	2005[b]	1998	2005[b]	2005[b]	2005[b]	2005[b]	2005[b]
Romania	..	..	..	..	..	..	3.6	..	25.9	17
Russian Federation	..	..	..	..	..	12.1	3.7	12.3	99.0	17
Rwanda	..	11.3	..	18.6	..	408.8	3.8	12.2	81.7	62
Saudi Arabia	..	..	..	..	..	..	6.8	27.6	..	..
Senegal	18.9	18.7	..	32.2	..	267.6	5.4	18.9	100.0	47
Serbia and Montenegro	..	..	..	..	..	..	..	..	..	..
Sierra Leone	..	..	..	..	..	..	3.8	..	61.5	67
Singapore	..	..	..	..	..	..	..	..	..	..
Slovak Republic	..	13.0	18.5	17.8	33.0	29.3	4.4	11.2	..	18
Slovenia	17.4	30.0	..	25.7	..	26.4	6.0	12.6	..	15
Somalia	..	..	..	..	..	..	..	..	..	..
South Africa	20.2	14.2	21.2	17.6	64.3	49.6	5.4	17.9	78.7	36
Spain	11.2	18.6	24.4	23.8	19.6	22.7	4.3	11.2	..	14
Sri Lanka	..	..	..	..	..	..	..	..	..	22
Sudan	..	..	..	..	..	..	..	..	55.1	28
Swaziland	6.5	12.4	26.1	30.9	388.4	341.5	6.2	..	90.5	32
Sweden	46.2	24.0	26.3	26.8	53.3	46.9	7.5	12.8	..	10
Switzerland	36.1	24.9	27.7	29.2	54.5	64.8	6.1	13.0	..	..
Syrian Arab Republic	..	14.2	22.1	26.3	..	..	..	..	88.4	25
Tajikistan	..	8.7	..	11.3	..	14.1	3.5	18.0	84.1	21
Tanzania	..	..	..	..	..	..	..	..	100.0	56
Thailand	11.6	13.9	..	13.1	..	23.0	4.2	27.5	79.3	21
Togo	..	6.7	30.9	..	317.9	..	2.6	13.6	36.8	34
Trinidad and Tobago	..	15.7	12.2	..	147.6	..	4.2	..	81.0	18
Tunisia	..	24.1	..	24.1	..	80.6	8.1	..	..	21
Turkey	10.7	11.8	..	14.8	..	44.7	4.0	13.6	..	..
Turkmenistan	..	..	..	..	..	..	..	..	..	..
Uganda	..	11.3	..	34.0	..	188.8	5.2	18.3	80.4	50
Ukraine	..	14.8	..	23.9	..	34.1	6.4	18.9	99.7	19
United Arab Emirates	..	7.1	11.5	9.3	..	28.9	1.3	27.4	60.0	15
United Kingdom	15.0	18.4	26.6	28.4	32.8	28.1	5.5	11.9	..	18
United States	..	21.5	22.5	25.8	27.5	26.7	5.9	15.2	..	14
Uruguay	7.8	6.5	..	7.2	..	19.5	2.2	7.9	100.0	21
Uzbekistan	..	..	..	..	..	..	..	..	..	..
Venezuela, RB	..	..	..	..	..	..	..	..	84.0	19
Vietnam	..	..	..	..	..	..	..	..	93.4	22
West Bank and Gaza	..	..	..	..	..	..	..	..	100.0	25
Yemen, Rep.	..	..	..	..	..	..	..	..	..	26
Zambia	..	5.4	..	8.2	..	..	2.0	14.8	100.0	51
Zimbabwe	20.7	..	..	..	..	..	..	..	..	39
World	.. m	15.4 m	.. m	20.3 m	.. m	32.6 m	4.7 m	.. m	.. m	29 m
Low income	..	..	..	..	..	..	..	..	..	42
Middle income	..	14.1	..	17.4	..	32.5	4.5	15.2	..	22
Lower middle income	..	11.7	..	16.5	..	36.6	4.3	..	..	22
Upper middle income	..	14.7	..	20.1	33.6	26.3	4.6	15.4	..	22
Low & middle income	..	..	..	..	..	..	4.3	..	..	31
East Asia & Pacific	..	6.3	..	..	..	..	2.7	..	95.7	22
Europe & Central Asia	..	16.7	..	20.5	..	23.2	4.4	13.9	..	17
Latin America & Carib.	..	12.3	..	14.9	..	31.3	4.3	15.0	..	24
Middle East & N. Africa	..	14.3	..	17.5	..	..	..	..	..	23
South Asia	..	9.7	13.1	12.1	..	68.6	2.9	12.8	..	41
Sub-Saharan Africa	..	..	..	..	..	..	4.3	..	..	48
High income	16.3	18.7	24.4	24.4	29.7	29.4	5.9	12.8	..	16
Europe EMU	15.3	18.7	25.4	24.7	29.7	27.8	5.4	11.1	..	14

a. Because of the change from International Standard Classification of Education (ISCED) 76 to ISCED 97 in 1998, data before 1998 are not fully comparable with data from 1998 onward. b. Provisional data. c. Data are for 2006.

About the data

Data on education are compiled by the United Nations Educational, Scientific, and Cultural Organization (UNESCO) Institute for Statistics from official responses to surveys and from reports provided by education authorities in each country. Such data are used for monitoring, policymaking, and resource allocation. For a variety of reasons, however, education statistics generally fail to provide a complete and accurate picture of a country's education system. Statistics often lag by one to two years, though an effort is being made to shorten the delay. Moreover, coverage and data collection methods vary across countries and over time within countries, so comparisons should be interpreted with caution.

The data on education spending in the table for the majority of the countries refer to public spending—government spending on public education plus subsidies for private education. The data generally exclude foreign aid for education. They may also exclude spending by religious schools, which play a significant role in many developing countries. Data for some countries and for some years refer to spending by the ministry of education only (excluding education expenditures by other ministries and departments and local authorities).

Many developing countries have sought to supplement public funds for education. Some countries have adopted tuition fees to recover part of the cost of providing education services or to encourage development of private schools. Charging fees raises difficult questions relating to equity, efficiency, access, and taxation, however, and some governments have used scholarships, vouchers, and other methods of public finance to counter criticism. For most countries, the data reflect only public spending. Data for a few countries include private spending, although national practices vary with respect to whether parents or schools pay for books, uniforms, and other supplies. For greater detail, see the country- and indicator-specific notes in the source.

The share of public expenditure devoted to education allows an assessment of the priority a government assigns to education relative to other public investments, as well as a government's commitment to investing in human capital development. It also reflects the development status of a country's education system relative to that of others. However, returns on investment to education, especially primary and lower secondary education, cannot be understood simply by comparing current education indicators with national income. It takes a long time before currently enrolled children can productively contribute to the national economy (Hanushek 2002).

The share of trained teachers in primary education measures the quality of the teaching staff. It does not take account of competencies acquired by teachers through their professional experience or self-instruction or of such factors as work experience, teaching methods and materials, or classroom conditions, which may affect the quality of teaching. Since the training teachers receive varies greatly (pre-service or in-service), care should be taken in comparing across countries.

The primary pupil-teacher ratio reflects the average numbers of pupils per teacher. It is different from the average class size because of the different practices countries employ, such as part-time teaching, school shifts, and multigrade classes. The comparability of pupil-teacher ratios across countries is affected by the definition of teachers and by differences in class size by grade and in the number of hours taught, as well as the different practices mentioned above. Moreover, the underlying enrollment levels are subject to a variety of reporting errors (for further discussion of enrollment data see *About the data* for table 2.10). While the pupil-teacher ratio is often used to compare the quality of schooling across countries, it is often weakly related to the value added of schooling systems.

In 1998 UNESCO introduced the new International Standard Classification of Education 1997. Thus the time-series data for the years through 1997 are not consistent with those for 1998 and later. Any time-series analysis should therefore be undertaken with extreme caution.

In 2006 the UNESCO Institute for Statistics also changed its convention for citing the reference year of education data and indicators to the calendar year in which the academic or financial year ends. Data that used to be listed for 2004/05, for example, are now listed for 2005. This change was implemented to present the most recent data available and to align the data reporting with that of other international organizations (in particular the Organisation for Economic Co-operation and Development and Eurostat).

Definitions

• **Public expenditure per student** is public current spending on education divided by the number of students by level, as a percentage of gross domestic product (GDP) per capita. • **Public expenditure on education** is current and capital public expenditure on education, as a percentage of GDP and as a percentage of total government expenditure. • **Trained teachers in primary education** are the percentage of primary school teachers who have received the minimum organized teacher training (pre-service or in-service) required for teaching in their country. • **Primary pupil-teacher ratio** is the number of pupils enrolled in primary school divided by the number of primary school teachers (regardless of their teaching assignment).

Data sources

Data on education inputs are from the UNESCO Institute for Statistics, which compiles international data on education in cooperation with national commissions and national statistical services. Data for latest years are provisional, as of January 2007.

2.10 Participation in education

	Gross enrollment ratio				Net enrollment ratio[a]				Children out of school	
	% of relevant age group				% of relevant age group				thousand primary-school-age children	
	Preprimary	Primary	Secondary	Tertiary	Primary		Secondary		Male	Female
	2005[b]	2005[b]	2005[b]	2005[b]	1991	2005[b]	1991	2005[b]	2005[b]	2005[b]
Afghanistan	1	87	16	1	..	..	..	..	..	..
Albania	49	106	78	19	95	94	..	74	7	7
Algeria	6	112	83	20	89	97	53	66	0	39
Angola	..	..	..	1	50	..	..	..	..	..
Argentina	62	112	86	64	..	99	..	79	3	19
Armenia	33	94	88	28	..	79	..	84	11	7
Australia	102	103	149	72	99	96	79	85	42	35
Austria	89	106	101	50	88	..	..	..	..	..
Azerbaijan	29	96	83	15	89	85	..	78	45	46
Bangladesh	11	109	46	6	..	93	..	43	..	..
Belarus	105	101	95	62	86	89	..	89	17	21
Belgium	116	104	109	63	96	99	87	97	4	3
Benin	5	96	33	..	41	78	..	..	..	..
Bolivia	50	113	88	41	..	94	..	73	28	19
Bosnia and Herzegovina	..	..	..	..	..	..	..	..	..	..
Botswana	..	105	75	5	83	83	35	55	26	25
Brazil	68	141	102	22	85	93	17	76	..	..
Bulgaria	78	105	102	41	86	95	63	88	5	5
Burkina Faso	2	58	14	2	29	45	..	11	553	649
Burundi	2	85	13	2	53	60	..	..	222	258
Cambodia	9	134	29	3	69	99	..	24	..	..
Cameroon	25	117	44	6	74	..	..	..	..	..
Canada	68	100	109	60	98	..	89	..	..	..
Central African Republic	2	56	12	2	52	..	..	..	..	..
Chad	1	77	16	1	35	61	..	11	..	..
Chile	52	104	89	43	89	..	55	..	..	..
China	36	118	73	19	97	..	..	..	..	..
Hong Kong, China	69	105	87	31	..	93	..	80	1	12
Colombia	39	113	79	28	69	87	34	55	276	257
Congo, Dem. Rep.	1	62	22	..	54	..	..	..	..	..
Congo, Rep.	6	88	39	4	79	44	..	..	203	173
Costa Rica	69	110	79	25	87	..	38	..	..	..
Côte d'Ivoire	3	72	25	..	45	56	..	20	519	705
Croatia	48	96	88	42	79	87	63	85	7	7
Cuba	113	102	94	61	93	97	70	87	5	14
Czech Republic	107	102	96	43	87	..	..	..	..	..
Denmark	91	101	124	74	98	98	87	92	5	2
Dominican Republic	34	113	71	33	57	88	..	53	67	53
Ecuador	77	117	61	..	98	98	..	52	11	0
Egypt, Arab Rep.	14	101	87	33	84	95	..	79	58	161
El Salvador	51	113	63	19	..	93	..	53	26	22
Eritrea	12	64	31	1	16	47	..	25	144	164
Estonia	114	100	98	65	99	94	..	90	2	1
Ethiopia	2	93	31	3	22	61	..	28	..	..
Finland	59	101	109	90	98	99	93	94	1	1
France	114	105	111	56	100	99	..	96	11	4
Gabon	14	130	50	..	85	..	..	..	..	..
Gambia, The	18	81	47	1	48	..	..	45	..	..
Georgia	51	94	83	46	97	87	..	72	26	22
Germany	97	100	100	..	84	..	..	..	..	..
Ghana	56[c]	94[c]	45[c]	5[c]	54	69[c]	..	38[c]	510[c]	480[c]
Greece	66	102	96	79	95	99	83	87	0	3
Guatemala	28	114	51	10	..	94	..	34	..	..
Guinea	7	81	30	3	27	66	..	24	..	..
Guinea-Bissau	..	..	..	..	38	..	..	..	..	..
Haiti	..	..	..	..	22	..	..	..	..	..

Participation in education

	Gross enrollment ratio				Net enrollment ratio[a]				Children out of school	
	% of relevant age group				% of relevant age group				thousand primary-school-age children	
	Preprimary	Primary	Secondary	Tertiary	Primary		Secondary		Male	Female
	2005[b]	2005[b]	2005[b]	2005[b]	1991	2005[b]	1991	2005[b]	2005[b]	2005[b]
Honduras	33	113	65	16	89	91	21	..	43	27
Hungary	81	98	97	60	91	89	75	91	10	9
India	36	116	54	12	..	90	..	..	..	..
Indonesia	22	117	64	17	97	94	39	57	0	246
Iran, Islamic Rep.	46	111	81	24	92	95	..	77	307	0
Iraq	6	98	45	15	94	88	..	38	..	..
Ireland	..	106	112	59	90	96	80	87	8	7
Israel	112	110	93	56	92	98	..	89	9	7
Italy	103	101	99	63	100	99	..	92	4	7
Jamaica	92	95	88	19	96	91	64	79	16	14
Japan	85	100	102	54	100	100	97	100	7	0
Jordan	30	98	87	39	94	91	..	81	26	17
Kazakhstan	34	109	99	53	89	91	..	92	4	6
Kenya	54	114	49	3	..	80	..	42	526	506
Korea, Dem. Rep.	..	..	..	..	..	..	..	..	..	..
Korea, Rep.	91	105	93	90	100	99	86	90	4	10
Kuwait	73	98	95	18	49	87	..	78	14	14
Kyrgyz Republic	13	98	86	41	92	87	..	80	13	11
Lao PDR	9	116	47	8	63	84	..	38	55	71
Latvia	79	93	97	74	92	..	..	..	..	..
Lebanon	74	106	89	51	73	92	..	..	12	12
Lesotho	34	132	39	3	71	87	15	25	25	16
Liberia	..	..	..	..	..	..	..	..	..	..
Libya	8	107	104	56	96	..	..	..	..	..
Lithuania	64	97	102	73	..	89	..	94	7	6
Macedonia, FYR	32	98	84	28	94	92	..	81	2	1
Madagascar	8	138	..	3	64	92	..	..	93	95
Malawi	..	122	28	0[b]	48	95	..	24	83	30
Malaysia	108	93	76	32	..	93	..	76	112	110
Mali	3	66	24	3	21	51	5	..	505	607
Mauritania	2	93	21	3	35	72	..	15	65	65
Mauritius	95	102	89	17	91	95	..	82	3	2
Mexico	84	109	80	23	98	98	44	64	22	7
Moldova	62	92	82	34	89	86	..	76	12	12
Mongolia	40	118	94	41	90	89	..	78	13	9
Morocco	54	105	50	11	56	86	..	35	216	309
Mozambique	..	105	14	1	43	79	..	7	331	468
Myanmar	..	100	40	11	98	90	..	37	267	221
Namibia	29	99	61	6	..	72	..	38	62	50
Nepal	64[c]	126[c]	43[c]	6	..	78	..	..	..	..
Netherlands	89	107	119	59	95	99	84	89	3	11
New Zealand	92	102	118	86	98	99	85	91	1	1
Nicaragua	37	112	66	18	73	87	..	43	27	27
Niger	1	47	9	1	22	40	5	8	634	737
Nigeria	15	103	34	10	58	91	..	27	..	..
Norway	85	99	116	80	100	99	88	96	2	2
Oman	7	84	87	15	69	76	..	75	41	38
Pakistan	50	87	27	5	33	68	..	21	2,328	3,975
Panama	62	111	70	44	..	98	..	64	1	2
Papua New Guinea	59	75	26	..	..	..	..	..	..	..
Paraguay	31	106	63	24	94	..	26	..	..	..
Peru	60	114	92	33	..	97	..	69	12	2
Philippines	40	112	86	29	96	94	..	61	392	255
Poland	53	99	97	61	97	97	76	90	41	33
Portugal	76	116	97	57	98	98	..	82	1	2
Puerto Rico	..	..	..	..	..	..	..	..	..	..

2.10 Participation in education

	Gross enrollment ratio				Net enrollment ratio[a]				Children out of school	
	% of relevant age group				% of relevant age group				thousand primary-school-age children	
	Preprimary	Primary	Secondary	Tertiary	Primary		Secondary		Male	Female
	2005[b]	2005[b]	2005[b]	2005[b]	1991	2005[b]	1991	2005[b]	2005[b]	2005[b]
Romania	76	107	85	40	81	92	..	81	23	24
Russian Federation	85	123	93	68	99	91	..	..	198	171
Rwanda	3	120	14	3	66	74	7	..	196	177
Saudi Arabia	10	91	88	28	59	78	31	66	426	367
Senegal	8	88	26	5	43	76	..	21	167	195
Serbia and Montenegro	..	..	..	..	..	..	..	..	..	..
Sierra Leone	4	155	30	2	43	..	..	..	..	..
Singapore	..	..	..	..	..	..	..	..	..	..
Slovak Republic	92	99	94	36	..	..	..	..	..	..
Slovenia	79	99	100	74	96	98	..	95	0[d]	0
Somalia	2[c]	17	..	..	9	19[c]	..	..	..	..
South Africa	37	104	93	16	90	87	45	..	321	248
Spain	111	108	119	66	100	99	..	97	3	10
Sri Lanka	..	98	83	..	..	97	..	..	9	13
Sudan	25	60	34	..	40	..	..	..	..	..
Swaziland	18	107	45	4	77	80	31	33	21	19
Sweden	85	99	103	84	100	99	85	98	4	5
Switzerland	95	102	93	47	84	94	80	83	5	4
Syrian Arab Republic	10	124	68	..	91	95	43	62	0	70
Tajikistan	9	101	82	17	77	97	..	80	2	15
Tanzania	29	106	..	1	49	91	..	..	273	331
Thailand	90	97	73	43	76	..	..	..	..	..
Togo	2	100	40	..	64	78	15	..	..	..
Trinidad and Tobago	86	106	88	12	91	95	..	75	0[d]	0
Tunisia	22	110	81	29	94	97	..	67	11	6
Turkey	8	93	79	29	89	89	42	..	354	546
Turkmenistan	..	..	..	..	..	..	..	..	..	..
Uganda	2	118	16	3	..	..	..	13	..	..
Ukraine	86	107	89	69	80	83	..	79	152	144
United Arab Emirates	64	83	64	22	99	71	60	57	37	39
United Kingdom	59	107	105	60	98	99	81	95	1	0[d]
United States	62	99	95	82	97	92	85	89	593	1,028
Uruguay	61	109	108	39	91	..	..	..	..	..
Uzbekistan	28	100	95	15	78	..	..	..	..	..
Venezuela, RB	58	105	74	41	87	91	18	63	130	106
Vietnam	60	95	76	16	90	88	..	69	..	..
West Bank and Gaza	30	89	99	38	..	80	..	95	35	35
Yemen, Rep.	1	87	48	9	51	75	..	..	..	..
Zambia	..	111	28	..	..	89	..	26	119	109
Zimbabwe	43	96	36	4	..	82	..	34	224	206
World	38 w	107 w	65 w	24 w	83 w	.. w	.. w	.. w		
Low income	27	102	45	9	..	78	..	37		
Middle income	39	113	77	26	92	..	..	69		
Lower middle income	35	115	76	22	92	93	..	65		
Upper middle income	59	105	86	43	93	94	..	75		
Low & middle income	33	107	61	18	81	..	..	..		
East Asia & Pacific	36	114	71	19	96	93	..	..		
Europe & Central Asia	50	102	90	49	90	91	..	84		
Latin America & Carib.	62	118	86	28	85	95	30	67		
Middle East & N. Africa	21	103	73	22	84	90	..	65		
South Asia	33	110	50	10	..	86	..	..		
Sub-Saharan Africa	16	92	30	5	50	66	..	24		
High income	76	100	100	67	95	94	..	90		
Europe EMU	101	104	106	62	95	99	..	94		

a. Because of the change from International Standard Classification of Education (ISCED) 76 to ISCED 97 in 1998, data before 1998 are not fully comparable with data from 1998 onward. b. Provisional data. c. Data are for 2006. d. Less than 0.5.

Participation in education 2.10

About the data

School enrollment data are reported to the United Nations Educational, Scientific, and Cultural Organization (UNESCO) Institute for Statistics by national education authorities and statistical offices. Enrollment ratios help to monitor two important issues for universal primary education: whether a country is on track to achieve the Millennium Development Goal of universal primary completion by 2015, which implies achieving a net primary enrollment ratio of 100 percent, and whether an education system has sufficient capacity to meet the needs of universal primary education, as indicated in part by its gross enrollment ratios.

Enrollment ratios, while a useful measure of participation in education, also have some limitations. They are based on data collected during annual school surveys, which are typically conducted at the beginning of the school year. They do not reflect actual rates of attendance or dropouts during the school year. And school administrators may report exaggerated enrollments, especially if there is a financial incentive to do so. Typically, the total number of teachers allocated to a given school is related to enrollment. This may create perverse incentives to inflate enrollment levels, particularly when enrollment is closely linked to government school funding formulas, such as student capitation grants.

Also as international indicators, the gross and net primary enrollment ratios have an inherent weakness: the length of primary education differs significantly across countries, although the International Standard Classification of Education tries to minimize the difference. A relatively short duration for primary education tends to increase the ratio, whereas a relatively long duration tends to decrease it (in part because there are more dropouts among older children).

Overage or underage enrollments frequently occur, particularly when parents prefer, for cultural or economic reasons, to have children start school at other than the official age. Children's age at enrollment may be inaccurately estimated or misstated, especially in communities where registration of births is not strictly enforced. Parents who want to enroll an underage child in primary school may do so by overstating the child's age. And in some education systems ages for children repeating a grade may be underreported.

Other problems affecting cross-country comparisons of enrollment data stem from errors in estimates of school-age populations. Age-sex structures from censuses or vital registration systems, the primary sources of data on school-age populations, are commonly subject to underenumeration (especially of young children) aimed at circumventing laws or regulations. Errors are also introduced when parents round up children's ages. While census data are often adjusted for age bias, adjustments are rarely made for inadequate vital registration systems. Compounding these problems, pre- and post-census estimates of school-age children are interpolations or projections based on models that may miss important demographic events (see the discussion of demographic data in *About the data* for table 2.1).

Thus gross enrollment ratios indicate the capacity of each level of the education system, but a high ratio does not necessarily mean a successful education system. The net enrollment ratio excludes overage and underage students in an attempt to capture more accurately the system's coverage and internal efficiency. It does not solve the problem completely, however, because some children fall outside the official school age because of late or early entry rather than because of grade repetition. The difference between gross and net enrollment ratios shows the incidence of overage and underage enrollments.

In using enrollment data, it is also important to consider repetition rates. These rates are quite high in some developing countries, leading to a substantial number of overage children enrolled in each grade and raising the gross enrollment ratio.

Children out of school are children in the primary school age group who are not enrolled in primary or secondary education. The data are calculated by the UNESCO Institute for Statistics using administrative data. Children out of school include dropouts and children who never enrolled as well as children of primary age enrolled in preprimary education. The large number of children out of school creates pressure for the education system to enroll children and to provide classrooms, teachers, and educational materials, a task made difficult in many developing countries by limited education budgets. However, getting these children into school is a high priority for countries and crucial for their prospects for achieving the Millennium Development Goal of universal primary education.

In 2006 the UNESCO Institute for Statistics changed its convention for citing the reference year. For more information, see *About the data* for table 2.9.

Definitions

• **Gross enrollment ratio** is the ratio of total enrollment, regardless of age, to the population of the age group that officially corresponds to the level of education shown. • **Preprimary education** refers to the initial stage of organized instruction, designed primarily to introduce very young children to a school-type environment. • **Primary education** provides children with basic reading, writing, and mathematics skills along with an elementary understanding of such subjects as history, geography, natural science, social science, art, and music. • **Secondary education** completes the provision of basic education that began at the primary level and aims at laying the foundations for lifelong learning and human development by offering more subject- or skill-oriented instruction using more specialized teachers. • **Tertiary education** refers to a wide range of post-secondary education institutions, including technical and vocational education, colleges, and universities, whether or not leading to an advanced research qualification, that normally require as a minimum condition of admission the successful completion of education at the secondary level. • **Net enrollment ratio** is the ratio of total enrollment of children of official school age based on the International Standard Classification of Education 1997 to the population of the age group that officially corresponds to the level of education shown. • **Children out of school** are the number of primary school age children not enrolled in primary or secondary school.

Data sources

Data on gross and net enrollment ratios and out of school children are from the UNESCO Institute for Statistics. Data for latest years are provisional, as of January 2007.

2.11 Education efficiency

	Gross intake rate in grade 1		Share of cohort reaching grade 5[a]				Repeaters in primary school		Transition to secondary education	
	% of relevant age group		% of grade 1 students				% of enrollment		% of enrollment in last year of primary	
	Male	Female	Male		Female		Male	Female	Male	Female
	2005[b]	2005[b]	1991	2004[b]	1991	2004[b]	2005[b]	2005[b]	2004[b]	2004[b]
Afghanistan	96	67	..	..	..	..	18	14	..	..
Albania	*99*	*99*	..	..	..	..	*3*	*2*	*100*	*99*
Algeria	102	99	95	94	94	97	14	8	76	83
Angola	..	..	..	..	..	..	..	..	..	..
Argentina	*110*	*110*	..	*84*	..	*85*	*8*	*5*	*92*	*94*
Armenia	98	102	..	..	..	..	0[c]	0[c]	93	93
Australia	*103*	*102*	98	..	99	..	..	..	*100*	*100*
Austria	*105*	*105*	..	..	..	..	..	..	..	..
Azerbaijan	94	93	..	..	..	..	0[c]	0[c]	99	99
Bangladesh	116	*131*	..	*63*	..	*67*	*7*	*7*	89[d]	96[d]
Belarus	105	103	..	..	..	..	0[c]	0[c]	99	100
Belgium	*103*	*104*	90	..	92	..	..	..	..	..
Benin	109	97	54	53	56	50	17	17	*51*	*51*
Bolivia	*119*	*119*	..	*85*	..	*85*	*2*	*1*	*90*	*90*
Bosnia and Herzegovina	..	..	..	..	..	..	..	..	..	..
Botswana	108	102	81	*89*	87	*92*	6	4	97	98
Brazil	*127*	*117*	..	..	..	..	..	..	..	..
Bulgaria	*107*	*104*	91	..	90	..	*3*	*2*	*96*	*96*
Burkina Faso	81	69	71	75	68	76	12	12	47	44
Burundi	92	84	65	66	58	68	30	30	35	30
Cambodia	137	128	..	62	..	65	15	12	84	80
Cameroon	120	104	..	*64*	..	*63*	26	25	43	47
Canada	*97*	*96*	95	..	98	..	..	..	..	..
Central African Republic	69	50	24	..	22	..	30	31	..	..
Chad	112	81	56	34	41	32	22	24	56	42
Chile	*99*	*97*	94	*99*	91	*99*	*3*	*2*	*95*	*98*
China	*95*	*93*	58	..	78	..	*0*[c]	*0*[c]	..	..
Hong Kong, China	93	87	..	99	..	100	1	1	100	100
Colombia	126	119	..	81	..	86	5	4	100	100
Congo, Dem. Rep.	*72*	*61*	58	..	50	..	*16*	*17*	..	..
Congo, Rep.	62	62	56	*65*	65	*67*	25	23	58	58
Costa Rica	103	103	83	84	85	90	8	6	*92*	*91*
Côte d'Ivoire	*75*	*68*	75	..	70	..	*17*	*18*	*42*	*36*
Croatia	*99*	*97*	..	..	..	..	*0*[c]	*0*[c]	*100*	*100*
Cuba	105	104	..	96	..	98	1	0[c]	98	99
Czech Republic	*97*	*96*	..	*98*	..	*99*	*1*	*1*	*99*	*99*
Denmark	*98*	*99*	94	..	94	..	..	..	*100*	*100*
Dominican Republic	118	108	..	..	..	..	10	6	83	92
Ecuador	*136*	*134*	..	*75*	..	*77*	*2*	*2*	76	71
Egypt, Arab Rep.	*99*	*99*	..	*98*	..	*99*	*5*	*3*	*83*	*89*
El Salvador	129	123	56	67	60	72	7	5	93	93
Eritrea	55	45	..	83	..	74	13	13	91	85
Estonia	*101*	*101*	..	*99*	..	*99*	*3*	*1*	*94*	*99*
Ethiopia	148	135	16	..	23	..	8	6	84	84
Finland	*98*	*97*	100	*100*	100	*100*	*1*	*0*[c]	*100*	*100*
France	..	..	69	..	95	..	..	..	..	..
Gabon	*94*	*94*	..	*68*	..	*71*	*35*	*34*	..	..
Gambia, The	*87*	*99*	..	..	..	..	*10*	*9*	..	..
Georgia	103	105	..	76	..	83	0[c]	0[c]	*98*	*99*
Germany	*105*	*105*	..	..	..	..	*2*	*1*	*99*	*99*
Ghana	107[e]	113[e]	81	*62*	79	*65*	6	6	*87*	*87*
Greece	*103*	*103*	100	..	100	..	*0*	*0*	..	..
Guatemala	125	122	..	70	..	66	13	12	*97*	*95*
Guinea	87	81	64	78	48	73	8	9	68	58
Guinea-Bissau	..	..	..	..	..	..	..	..	..	..
Haiti	..	..	..	..	..	..	..	..	..	..

Education efficiency

	Gross intake rate in grade 1		Share of cohort reaching grade 5[a]				Repeaters in primary school		Transition to secondary education	
	% of relevant age group		% of grade 1 students				% of enrollment		% of enrollment in last year of primary	
	Male	Female	Male		Female		Male	Female	Male	Female
	2005[b]	2005[b]	1991	2004[b]	1991	2004[b]	2005[b]	2005[b]	2004[b]	2004[b]
Honduras	129	127	..	..	..	..	9	7	..	..
Hungary	96	94	77	..	98	..	3	2	98	99
India	139	130	..	81	..	76	3	3	87	82
Indonesia	121	116	34	88	78	90	3	3	84	84
Iran, Islamic Rep.	107	139	91	88	89	87	3	1	95	86
Iraq	110	103	..	87	..	73	9	7	73	66
Ireland	102	101	99	100	100	100	1	1	..	..
Israel	99	102	..	100	..	100	2	1	74	74
Italy	103	103	..	96	..	97	0[c]	0[c]	100	99
Jamaica	93	92	..	86	..	92	3	2	..	..
Japan	98	98	100	..	100	..	..	..	..	..
Jordan	91	92	..	99	..	99	1	1	97	97
Kazakhstan	108	107	..	..	..	..	0[c]	0[c]	100	100
Kenya	120	116	75	81	78	85	6	6	..	..
Korea, Dem. Rep.	..	..	..	..	..	..	..	..	..	..
Korea, Rep.	105	107	99	98	100	98	0	0	99	98
Kuwait	93	92	..	..	..	..	2	2	93	97
Kyrgyz Republic	97	94	..	..	..	..	0[c]	0[c]	98	100
Lao PDR	121	111	..	64	..	62	20	18	80	75
Latvia	90	89	..	..	..	..	4	2	97	99
Lebanon	102	100	..	91	..	96	12	8	83	88
Lesotho	128	120	58	58	73	69	21	17	67	65
Liberia	..	..	..	..	..	..	..	..	..	..
Libya	..	..	..	..	..	..	..	..	..	..
Lithuania	101	102	..	..	..	..	1	0[c]	99	99
Macedonia, FYR	98	97	..	..	..	..	0[c]	0[c]	99	98
Madagascar	182	176	22	43	21	43	19	18	56	53
Malawi	177	188	71	40	57	37	9	8	77	72
Malaysia	94	94	97	99	97	98	..	..	..	..
Mali	70	59	71	78	67	70	18	19	53	48
Mauritania	112	113	76	51	75	55	10	10	48	43
Mauritius	102	102	97	97	98	97	5	4	60	69
Mexico	106	105	35	92	71	94	6	4	95	92
Moldova	93	91	..	..	..	..	0[c]	0[c]	99	98
Mongolia	148	149	..	..	..	..	0[c]	0[c]	96	99
Morocco	101	97	75	81	76	77	15	10	79	78
Mozambique	161	150	36	66	32	58	11	10	51	56
Myanmar	123	122	..	68	..	72	0[c]	0[c]	72	71
Namibia	93	94	60	84	65	85	15	12	90	93
Nepal	160[e]	160[e]	51	75[d]	51	83[d]	21[e]	20[e]	79	74
Netherlands	100	99	..	100	..	99	..	..	96	100
New Zealand	100	99	..	..	..	..	..	..	..	..
Nicaragua	147	137	11	51	37	56	11	9	..	..
Niger	65	51	61	66	65	64	5	6	63	53
Nigeria	124	107	..	71	..	75	2	3	..	..
Norway	98	98	99	99	100	100	..	..	100	100
Oman	73	74	97	98	96	98	1	1	98	99
Pakistan	128	103	..	68	..	72	3	3	67	72
Panama	110	109	..	85	..	86	7	5	64	65
Papua New Guinea	101	90	70	68	68	68	0	0	77	77
Paraguay	109	106	73	80	75	83	9	6	91	91
Peru	105	106	..	90	..	90	8	7	96	94
Philippines	138	129	..	71	..	80	3	1	97	96
Poland	97	97	89	..	96	..	1	0[c]	..	..
Portugal	105	106	..	..	..	..	13	7	..	..
Puerto Rico	..	..	..	..	..	..	..	..	..	..

2.11 Education efficiency

	Gross intake rate in grade 1		Share of cohort reaching grade 5[a]				Repeaters in primary school		Transition to secondary education	
	% of relevant age group		% of grade 1 students				% of enrollment		% of enrollment in last year of primary	
	Male	Female	Male		Female		Male	Female	Male	Female
	2005[b]	2005[b]	1991	2004[b]	1991	2004[b]	2005[b]	2005[b]	2004[b]	2004[b]
Romania	126	126	..	..	..	..	3	2	98	98
Russian Federation	98	97	..	..	..	..	..	..	..	..
Rwanda	178	177	61	43	59	49	19	19	..	..
Saudi Arabia	85	89	82	100	84	94	5	5	93	97
Senegal	101	105	..	79	..	77	13	13	63	59
Serbia and Montenegro	..	..	..	..	..	..	..	..	..	..
Sierra Leone	..	..	..	..	..	..	..	..	..	..
Singapore	..	..	..	..	..	..	..	..	..	..
Slovak Republic	97	96	..	..	..	..	3	2	98	99
Slovenia	145	144	..	..	..	..	1	0[c]	100	99
Somalia	..	..	..	66	..	52	..	..	..	..
South Africa	117	111	..	82	..	83	8	8	89	91
Spain	103	102	..	..	..	..	3	2	..	..
Sri Lanka	99	97	92	..	93	..	..	..	96	98
Sudan	72	62	90	78	99	79	1	2	88	91
Swaziland	122	114	74	74	80	80	18	14	91	89
Sweden	92	93	100	..	100	..	..	..	..	..
Switzerland	89	94	..	..	..	..	2	1	100	100
Syrian Arab Republic	123	119	97	93	95	92	8	6	94	95
Tajikistan	101	97	..	..	..	..	0[c]	0[c]	98	97
Tanzania	125	124	81	76	82	76	4	4	34	33
Thailand	..	..	..	..	..	..	..	..	..	..
Togo	94	88	52	79	42	70	23	23	70	63
Trinidad and Tobago	99	98	..	66	..	76	6	4	95	97
Tunisia	94	96	94	96	77	97	9	6	86	90
Turkey	93	88	98	95	97	94	3	4	93	89
Turkmenistan	..	..	..	..	..	..	..	..	..	..
Uganda	164	163	..	63	..	64	14	14	36	36
Ukraine	104	104	..	..	..	..	0[c]	0[c]	99	100
United Arab Emirates	89	89	80	96	80	97	2	2	97	98
United Kingdom	..	..	..	..	..	..	0	0	..	..
United States	100	99	..	..	..	..	..	..	..	..
Uruguay	105	106	96	87	98	90	10	7	76	87
Uzbekistan	102	102	..	..	..	..	0	0	100	99
Venezuela, RB	101	98	82	88	90	95	8	5	98	99
Vietnam	101	95	..	87	..	86	3	2	95	94
West Bank and Gaza	82	82	..	..	..	..	1[c]	1[c]	100	100
Yemen, Rep.	122	97	..	78	..	67	5	4	..	..
Zambia	126	123	..	..	..	..	7	6	54	57
Zimbabwe	122	118	72	68	81	71	..	..	69	70
World	138 w	140 w	.. w	.. w	.. w	.. w	5 w	4 w	.. w	.. w
Low income	138	140	..	77	..	75	6	6	81	77
Middle income	104	102	..	..	..	..	3	3	..	..
Lower middle income	104	102	59	..	79	..	3	2	..	..
Upper middle income	103	100	..	..	..	..	..	..	..	..
Low & middle income	138	140	..	..	..	..	5	4	..	..
East Asia & Pacific	104	101	55	..	78	..	1	1	..	..
Europe & Central Asia	99	97	..	..	..	..	..	..	..	..
Latin America & Carib.	120	115	..	..	..	..	..	..	..	..
Middle East & N. Africa	104	103	..	90	..	87	8	5	85	88
South Asia	160	160	..	79	..	75	4	4	85	82
Sub-Saharan Africa	120	110	..	..	..	..	9	9	..	..
High income	100	100	..	..	..	..	..	..	..	..
Europe EMU	104	104	..	..	..	..	2	1	..	..

a. Because of the change from International Standard Classification of Education (ISCED) 76 to ISCED 97 in 1998, data before 1998 are not fully comparable with data from 1998 onward.
b. Provisional data. c. Less than 0.5. d. Data are for 2005. e. Data are for 2006.

Education efficiency 2.11

About the data

Indicators of students' progress through school are estimated by the United Nations Educational, Scientific, and Cultural Organization (UNESCO) Institute for Statistics. These indicators measure an education system's success in extending coverage to all students, maintaining the flow of students efficiently from one grade to the next, and imparting a particular level of education.

Gross intake rate indicates the general level of access to primary education. It also indicates the capacity of the education system to provide access to primary education. Low gross intake rates in grade 1 reflect the fact that many children do not enter primary school even though school attendance, at least through the primary level, is mandatory in all countries. Because the gross intake rate includes all new entrants regardless of age, it can be more than 100 percent. Once enrolled, students drop out for a variety of reasons, including low quality of schooling, relevance of curriculum (whether real or perceived by parents or students), repetition and discouragement over poor performance, and the direct and indirect costs of schooling. Students' progress to higher grades may also be limited by the availability of teachers, classrooms, and educational materials.

The share of cohort reaching grade 5 (cohort survival rate) is estimated as the proportion of an entering cohort of grade 1 students that eventually reaches grade 5. It measures the holding power and internal efficiency of an education system. Cohort survival rates approaching 100 percent indicate a high level of retention and a low level of dropout.

Cohort survival rates are typically estimated from data on enrollment and repetition by grade for two consecutive years, in a procedure called the reconstructed cohort method. This method makes three simplifying assumptions: dropouts never return to school; promotion, repetition, and dropout rates remain constant over the entire period in which the cohort is enrolled in school; and the same rates apply to all pupils enrolled in a given grade, regardless of whether they previously repeated a grade (Fredricksen 1993). Given these assumptions, cross-country comparisons should be made with caution, because other flows—caused by new entrants, reentrants, grade skipping, migration, or school transfers during the school year—are not considered.

The UNESCO Institute for Statistics measures the share of cohort reaching grade 5 because research suggests that five to six years of schooling is a critical threshold for the achievement of sustainable basic literacy and numeracy skills. But the indicator only indirectly reflects the quality of schooling, and a high rate does not guarantee these learning outcomes. Measuring actual learning outcomes requires setting curriculum standards and measuring students' learning progress against those standards through standardized assessments or tests. Currently, many countries do not systematically measure learning progress and outcomes.

The data on repeaters are often used to indicate the internal efficiency of the education system. Repeaters not only increase the cost of education for the family and for the school system, but also use limited school resources. Countries have different policies on repetition and promotion; in some cases the number of repeaters is controlled because of limited capacity. Care should be taken in interpreting this indicator.

The transition rate from primary school to secondary school conveys the degree of access or transition between the two levels of education. As completing primary education is a prerequisite for participating in lower secondary school, growing numbers of primary completers will inevitably create pressures for expanding the number of places available at the secondary level. A low transition rate can signal problems such as an inadequate promotion and examination system or insufficient capacity in secondary schools. The quality of data on the transition rate is affected when new entrants and repeaters are not correctly distinguished in the first grade of secondary school. Students who interrupt their studies for one or more years after completing primary school could also affect the quality of the data.

In 2006 the UNESCO Institute for Statistics changed its convention for citing the reference year. For more information, see *About the data* for table 2.9.

Definitions

• **Gross intake rate in grade 1** is the number of new entrants in the first grade of primary education regardless of age, expressed as a percentage of the population of the official primary school entrance age. • **Share of cohort reaching grade 5** is the percentage of children enrolled in the first grade of primary school who eventually reach grade 5. The estimate is based on the reconstructed cohort method (see *About the data*). • **Repeaters in primary school** are the number of students enrolled in the same grade as in the previous year, as a percentage of all students enrolled in primary school. • **Transition to secondary education** refers to the number of new entrants to the first grade of secondary school in a given year, as a percentage of the number of students enrolled in the final grade of primary school in the previous year.

Data sources

Data on education efficiency are from the UNESCO Institute for Statistics. Data for latest years are provisional, as of January 2007.

2.12 Education completion and outcomes

	Primary completion rate						Youth literacy rate				Adult literacy rate	
	% of relevant age group						% ages 15–24				% ages 15 and older	
	Total[a]		Male[a]		Female[a]		Male		Female		Male	Female
	1991	2005[b]	1991	2005[b]	1991	2005[b]	1990	2006[c]	1990	2006[c]	2006[c]	2006[c]
Afghanistan	25	32	37	46	13	18	..	51	..	18	43	13
Albania	..	97	..	97	..	97	97	99	92	99	99	98
Algeria	79	96	86	96	73	95	86	94	68	86	80	60
Angola	35	..	..	..	..	..	..	84	..	63	83	54
Argentina	..	100	..	99	..	105	98	99	98	99	97	97
Armenia	90	91	..	89	..	92	100	100	99	100	100	99
Australia	..	..	..	..	..	..	..	..	..	..	..	..
Austria	..	..	..	..	..	..	..	..	..	..	..	..
Azerbaijan	..	94	..	95	..	93	..	100	..	100	99	98
Bangladesh	49	77	..	74	..	79	51	..	33	..	..	..
Belarus	95	100	95	102	96	97	100	100	100	100	100	99
Belgium	79	..	76	..	82	..	..	..	..	..	..	..
Benin	21	65	28	78	13	52	57	59	25	33	48	23
Bolivia	..	101	..	102	..	99	96	99	89	96	93	81
Bosnia and Herzegovina	..	..	..	..	..	..	..	100	..	100	99	94
Botswana	83	92	75	90	90	94	79	92	87	96	80	82
Brazil	93	108	..	..	..	..	91	96	93	98	88	89
Bulgaria	85	98	87	99	83	97	100	98	99	98	99	98
Burkina Faso	21	31	26	35	16	27	..	38	..	25	29	15
Burundi	46	36	49	40	43	31	58	77	45	70	67	52
Cambodia	..	92	..	94	..	90	81	88	66	79	85	64
Cameroon	56	62	60	68	52	57	86	..	76	..	77	60
Canada	..	..	..	..	..	..	..	..	..	..	..	..
Central African Republic	27	23	35	29	18	16	66	70	39	47	65	33
Chad	18	32	30	42	7	21	58	56	38	23	41	13
Chile	..	95	..	96	..	95	98	99	98	99	96	96
China	103	98	..	..	..	..	97	99	93	99	95	87
Hong Kong, China	102	110	..	112	..	107	..	..	..	..	..	..
Colombia	70	98	67	96	73	100	94	98	96	98	93	93
Congo, Dem. Rep.	46	39	58	47	34	31	80	78	58	63	81	54
Congo, Rep.	54	57	59	60	49	55	95	..	90	..	..	..
Costa Rica	79	92	77	91	81	93	97	97	98	98	95	95
Côte d'Ivoire	43	..	55	..	32	..	65	71	40	52	61	39
Croatia	85	91	..	92	..	91	100	100	100	100	99	97
Cuba	96	94	..	95	..	93	99	100	99	100	100	100
Czech Republic	..	104	..	104	..	104	..	..	..	..	..	..
Denmark	98	99	98	99	98	100	..	..	..	..	..	..
Dominican Republic	61	92	..	88	..	96	87	93	88	95	87	87
Ecuador	91	101	91	100	92	101	96	96	95	96	92	90
Egypt, Arab Rep.	..	95	..	96	..	93	71	90	51	79	83	59
El Salvador	41	87	38	86	43	87	85	..	83	..	..	..
Eritrea	19	51	22	58	17	44	73	..	49	..	..	..
Estonia	93	101	93	103	94	100	100	100	100	100	100	100
Ethiopia	26	55	32	61	19	49	52	..	34	..	..	..
Finland	97	100	98	99	97	100	..	..	..	..	..	..
France	104	..	..	..	..	..	..	..	..	..	..	..
Gabon	58	66	55	65	61	68	..	..	..	..	..	..
Gambia, The	44	..	55	..	33	..	50	..	34	..	..	..
Georgia	..	87	..	86	..	87	..	..	..	..	..	..
Germany	100	96	99	96	100	96	..	..	..	..	..	..
Ghana	63	72	70	75	55	69	88	76	75	65	66	50
Greece	99	102	99	103	98	101	99	99	100	99	98	94
Guatemala	..	74	..	79	..	69	80	86	66	78	75	63
Guinea	17	55	24	64	9	45	62	59	26	34	43	18
Guinea-Bissau	..	..	..	..	..	..	..	..	..	..	..	..
Haiti	27	..	29	..	26	..	56	..	54	..	..	..

Education completion and outcomes

	Primary completion rate						Youth literacy rate				Adult literacy rate	
	% of relevant age group						% ages 15–24				% ages 15 and older	
	Total[a]		Male[a]		Female[a]		Male		Female		Male	Female
	1991	2005[b]	1991	2005[b]	1991	2005[b]	1990	2006[c]	1990	2006[c]	2006[c]	2006[c]
Honduras	65	*79*	67	*77*	62	*82*	78	87	81	91	80	80
Hungary	93	*95*	*88*	*95*	*90*	*96*	100	..	100	..	..	..
India	68	*89*	81	*93*	55	*84*	73	84	54	68	73	48
Indonesia	91	*101*	..	*101*	..	*102*	97	99	93	99	94	87
Iran, Islamic Rep.	91	96	97	91	85	100	92	..	81	..	84	70
Iraq	*59*	74	*64*	85	*53*	63	56	89	25	80	84	64
Ireland	..	*101*	..	*100*	..	*102*	..	..	..	..	..	..
Israel	..	*105*	..	*104*	..	*105*	99	100	98	100	98	96
Italy	104	*101*	104	*101*	104	*101*	..	100	..	100	99	98
Jamaica	90	*84*	86	*83*	94	*86*	87	..	95	..	74	86
Japan	101	..	101	..	102	..	..	..	..	..	..	..
Jordan	72	*97*	69	*97*	77	*96*	98	99	95	99	95	85
Kazakhstan	..	114	..	115	..	113	100	100	100	100	100	99
Kenya	..	95	..	96	..	94	93	80	87	81	78	70
Korea, Dem. Rep.	..	..	..	..	..	..	..	..	..	..	..	..
Korea, Rep.	98	104	98	104	98	104	..	..	..	..	..	..
Kuwait	..	100	..	104	..	97	88	100	87	100	94	91
Kyrgyz Republic	..	97	..	97	..	98	..	100	..	100	99	98
Lao PDR	*43*	76	*48*	80	*38*	72	79	83	61	75	77	61
Latvia	..	*92*	..	*93*	..	*92*	..	100	..	100	100	100
Lebanon	..	90	..	88	..	91	95	..	89	..	..	..
Lesotho	59	67	42	55	76	79	77	..	97	..	74	90
Liberia	..	..	..	..	..	..	75	..	39	..	..	..
Libya	..	..	..	..	..	..	99	..	83	..	..	..
Lithuania	*89*	*98*	..	*99*	..	*97*	100	100	100	100	100	100
Macedonia, FYR	*98*	*96*	..	*96*	..	*97*	..	99	..	98	98	94
Madagascar	33	58	33	58	34	58	78	73	67	68	77	65
Malawi	28	61	36	62	21	59	76	82	51	71	75	54
Malaysia	91	*94*	91	*91*	91	*91*	95	97	94	97	92	85
Mali	11	38	13	45	9	31	..	32	..	17	27	12
Mauritania	33	45	40	46	26	43	56	68	36	55	60	43
Mauritius	107	97	107	97	107	98	91	94	91	95	88	81
Mexico	86	*99*	*89*	*98*	*90*	*100*	96	98	94	98	92	90
Moldova	..	92	..	93	..	91	100	99	100	100	99	98
Mongolia	..	97	..	94	..	99	..	97	..	98	98	98
Morocco	47	80	55	84	38	77	68	81	42	60	66	40
Mozambique	27	42	33	49	22	35	66	..	32	..	..	..
Myanmar	..	79	..	78	..	80	90	96	86	93	94	86
Namibia	*78*	75	*70*	71	*86*	80	86	91	89	93	87	83
Nepal	51	76[d]	*68*	80[d]	*40*	72[d]	67	81	27	60	63	35
Netherlands	..	*100*	..	*101*	..	*99*	..	..	..	..	..	..
New Zealand	100	..	101	..	99	..	..	..	..	..	..	..
Nicaragua	44	76	*43*	73	59	80	68	84	69	89	77	77
Niger	17	28	21	34	12	22	25	52	9	23	43	15
Nigeria	..	82	..	89	..	74	81	..	66	..	..	..
Norway	100	*101*	100	*101*	100	*101*	..	..	..	..	..	..
Oman	*74*	93	*78*	94	*70*	93	95	98	75	97	87	74
Pakistan	..	63	..	73	..	52	63	76	31	55	63	36
Panama	*86*	97	*86*	97	*86*	97	96	97	95	96	93	91
Papua New Guinea	47	*54*	52	*58*	42	*50*	74	69	62	64	63	51
Paraguay	71	*91*	70	*90*	71	*91*	96	..	95	..	..	..
Peru	..	*100*	..	*100*	..	*99*	97	98	92	96	93	82
Philippines	*86*	*97*	*84*	93	*84*	*100*	97	94	97	96	93	93
Poland	98	*100*	..	..	..	..	..	..	..	..	..	..
Portugal	95	*104*	94	*102*	95	*107*	..	..	..	..	..	..
Puerto Rico	..	..	..	..	..	..	..	..	..	..	..	..

2.12 Education completion and outcomes

	Primary completion rate						Youth literacy rate				Adult literacy rate	
	% of relevant age group						% ages 15–24				% ages 15 and older	
	Total[a]		Male[a]		Female[a]		Male		Female		Male	Female
	1991	2005[b]	1991	2005[b]	1991	2005[b]	1990	2006[c]	1990	2006[c]	2006[c]	2006[c]
Romania	96	93	96	94	96	93	99	98	99	98	98	96
Russian Federation	93	94	92	..	93	..	100	100	100	100	100	99
Rwanda	33	39	36	40	30	38	78	79	67	77	71	60
Saudi Arabia	56	85	60	85	51	86	91	98	79	94	87	69
Senegal	39	52	47	56	30	49	50	58	30	41	51	29
Serbia and Montenegro	71	..	..	..	..	..	..	99[e]	..	99[e]	99[e]	94[e]
Sierra Leone	..	..	..	..	..	..	..	59	..	37	47	24
Singapore	..	..	..	..	..	..	99	99	99	100	97	89
Slovak Republic	96	99	95	99	96	100	..	100	..	100	100	100
Slovenia	95	102	..	103	..	102	100	..	100	..	..	..
Somalia	..	..	..	..	..	..	..	..	..	..	..	..
South Africa	75	99	71	99	80	99	89	93	88	94	84	81
Spain	..	109	..	110	..	109	..	..	..	..	..	..
Sri Lanka	97	..	98	..	96	..	96	95	94	96	92	89
Sudan	41	50	46	53	37	46	76[f]	85[f]	54[f]	71[f]	71[f]	52[f]
Swaziland	60	64	57	62	63	66	85	87	85	90	81	78
Sweden	96	..	96	..	96	..	..	..	..	..	..	..
Switzerland	53	97	53	96	54	98	..	..	..	..	..	..
Syrian Arab Republic	89	111	94	112	84	109	92	94	67	90	86	74
Tajikistan	..	102	..	104	..	100	100	100	100	100	100	99
Tanzania	61	54	60	55	62	53	89	81	77	76	78	62
Thailand	..	82	..	83	..	81	..	98	..	98	95	91
Togo	35	65	48	76	22	54	79	84	48	64	69	38
Trinidad and Tobago	100	99	97	97	102	100	100	..	100	..	..	..
Tunisia	74	97	79	97	69	98	93	96	75	92	83	65
Turkey	90	88	93	93	86	82	97	98	88	93	95	80
Turkmenistan	..	..	..	..	..	..	..	100	..	100	99	98
Uganda	..	57	..	61	..	53	80	83	60	71	77	58
Ukraine	94	114	98	..	97	..	100	100	100	100	100	99
United Arab Emirates	103	76	104	78	103	75	82	..	89	..	..	..
United Kingdom	..	..	..	..	..	..	..	..	..	..	..	..
United States	..	..	..	..	..	..	..	..	..	..	..	..
Uruguay	94	91	91	89	96	93	98	..	99	..	..	..
Uzbekistan	..	97	..	97	..	96	100	..	100	..	..	..
Venezuela, RB	43	92	37	89	49	95	95	96	97	98	93	93
Vietnam	..	94	..	104	..	98	94	94	94	94	94	87
West Bank and Gaza	..	98	..	98	..	98	..	99	..	99	97	88
Yemen, Rep.	..	62	..	78	..	46	74	..	25	..	..	..
Zambia	..	78	..	89	..	66	86	73	76	66	76	60
Zimbabwe	99	80	100	82	97	79	97	..	91	..	..	..
World	.. w	85 w	.. w	87 w	.. w	83 w	.. w	90 w	.. w	84 w	87 w	77 w
Low income	60	74	70	79	49	69	73	80	55	67	71	50
Middle income	93	96	96	96	90	95	95	97	91	95	93	87
Lower middle income	94	97	99	97	91	96	95	97	90	95	93	85
Upper middle income	87	95	86	95	87	95	97	98	95	98	96	93
Low & middle income	79	84	85	86	73	81	86	89	77	82	85	72
East Asia & Pacific	100	98	105	98	96	98	97	98	93	97	95	87
Europe & Central Asia	91	92	93	93	92	91	99	99	97	99	99	96
Latin America & Carib.	83	98	82	98	84	99	93	96	93	96	91	89
Middle East & N. Africa	77	89	83	92	71	86	80	89	59	77	81	61
South Asia	76	82	86	86	65	77	70	80	50	63	70	45
Sub-Saharan Africa	50	58	55	63	46	53	76	78	61	68	70	53
High income	..	97	..	98	..	97	..	99	..	99	99	98
Europe EMU	..	..	..	..	..	..	..	..	..	..	..	..

a. Because of the change from International Standard Classification of Education (ISCED) 76 to ISCED 97 in 1998, data before 1998 are not fully comparable with data from 1998 onward. b. Provisional data. c. Actual reference year varies by country. For more information, see the original source. d. Data are for 2006. e. Data exclude Kosovo and Metohia. f. Data are for North Sudan only.

Education completion and outcomes 2.12

About the data

Many governments collect and publish statistics that indicate how their education systems are working and developing—statistics on enrollment and on such efficiency indicators as repetition rates, pupil-teacher ratios, and cohort progression through school. The World Bank and the United Nations Educational, Scientific, and Cultural Organization (UNESCO) Institute for Statistics worked jointly to develop the primary completion rate indicator. Increasingly used as a core indicator of an education system's performance, it reflects both the coverage of the education system and the educational attainment of students. The indicator is vital as a key measure of educational outcome at the primary level and of progress on the Millennium Development Goals and the Education for All initiative. However, because curricula and standards for school completion vary across countries, a high rate of primary completion does not necessarily mean high levels of student learning.

The primary completion rate reflects the primary cycle as defined by the International Standard Classification of Education, ranging from three or four years of primary education (in a very small number of countries) to five or six years (in most countries) and seven (in a small number of countries).

The data in the table are for the proxy primary completion rate, calculated by taking the total number of students in the last grade of primary school, minus the number of repeaters in that grade, divided by the total number of children of official graduation age. Data limitations preclude adjusting this number for students who drop out during the final year of primary school. Thus proxy rates should be taken as an upper-bound estimate of the actual primary completion rate.

There are many reasons why the primary completion rate can exceed 100 percent. The numerator may include late entrants and overage children who have repeated one or more grades of primary school but are now completing primary school as well as children who entered school early, while the denominator is the number of children of official completing age. There are other data limitations that contribute to completion rates exceeding 100 percent, such as the use of estimates for the population with varying reliability for some countries, the conduct of school and population surveys at different times of year, and other discrepancies in the numbers used in the calculation.

Basic student outcomes include achievements in reading and mathematics judged against established standards. In many countries national learning assessments are enabling ministries of education to monitor progress in these outcomes. Internationally, the UNESCO Institute for Statistics has established literacy as an outcome indicator based on an internationally agreed definition.

The literacy rate is defined as the percentage of people who can, with understanding, both read and write a short, simple statement about their everyday life. In practice, literacy is difficult to measure. To estimate literacy using such a definition requires census or survey measurements under controlled conditions. Many countries estimate the number of literate people from self-reported data. Some use educational attainment data as a proxy but apply different lengths of school attendance or levels of completion. Because definition and methodologies of data collection differ across countries, data need to be used with caution.

The reported literacy data are compiled by the UNESCO Institute for Statistics based on national censuses and household surveys during 1995–2005. The data for 1991 are based on model estimations. Therefore the data for 1991 and later years may not be comparable. The estimation methodology can be reviewed at www.uis.unesco.org.

Literacy statistics for most countries cover the population ages 15 and older, by five-year age groups, but some include younger ages or are confined to age ranges that tend to inflate literacy rates. The UNESCO Institute for Statistics has reported the narrower age range of 15–24, which is better in capturing the ability of participants in the formal education system and in reflecting recent progress in education. The youth literacy rate reported in the table measures the accumulated outcomes of primary education over the previous 10 years or so by indicating the proportion of people who have passed through the primary education system and acquired basic literacy and numeracy skills.

Definitions

• **Primary completion rate** is the percentage of students completing the last year of primary school. It is calculated by taking the total number of students in the last grade of primary school, minus the number of repeaters in that grade, divided by the total number of children of official completing age. • **Youth literacy rate** is the percentage of people ages 15–24 that can, with understanding, both read and write a short, simple statement about their everyday life. • **Adult literacy rate** is the literacy rate among people ages 15 and older.

Children from poorer families are less likely to complete their schooling **2.12a**

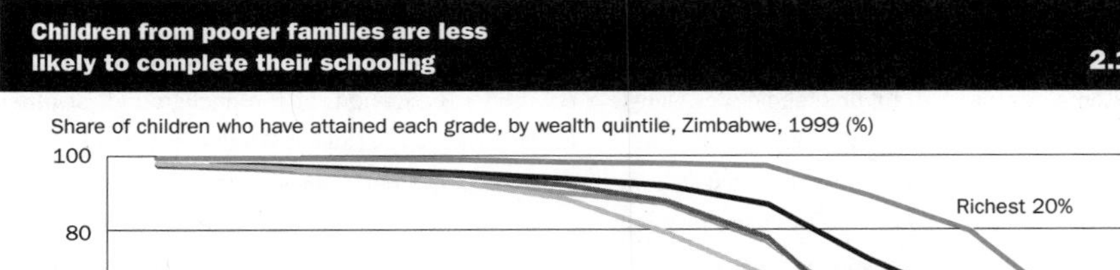

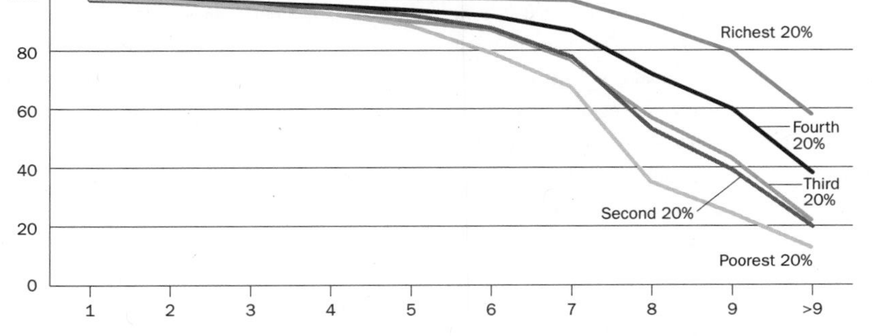

Source: Demographic and Health Survey.

Data sources

Data on the primary completion rate for 1991 and 2005 are primarily from the UNESCO Institute for Statistics. The data for the latest years are provisional, as of January 2007. Data on literacy rates are from the UNESCO Institute for Statistics.

2.13 Education gaps by income and gender

	Survey year	Gross intake rate in grade 1		Gross primary participation rate		Average years of schooling		Primary completion rate				Children out of school	
		% of relevant age group		% of relevant age group		ages 15–24		% of relevant age group				% of children ages 6–11	
		Poorest quintile	Richest quintile	Poorest quintile	Richest quintile	Poorest quintile	Richest quintile	Poorest quintile	Richest quintile	Male	Female	Poorest quintile	Richest quintile
Armenia	2000	105	93	177	181	9	11	96	98	96	98	14	13
Bangladesh	2004	193	156	107	120	3	8	26	70	47	58	25	10
Benin	2001	74	112	51	115	1	6	7	45	23	15	66	21
Bolivia	2003	98	95	92	98	6	11	48	90	75	75	24	5
Burkina Faso	2003	24	97	20	98	1	6	8	52	24	20	87	32
Cambodia	2000	146	187	78	134	2	7	4	45	18	17	50	12
Cameroon	2004	115	100	94	122	3	9	12	69	36	37	42	4
Central African Republic	1994–95	103	118	57	130	2	6	0[a]	18	8	6	65	21
Chad	2004	3	14	15	98	0[a]	5	1	36	15	8	91	36
Colombia	2005	157	85	126	99	6	11	50	90	70	77	8	1
Comoros	1996	84	119	56	147	2	6	4	29	12	12	72	26
Côte d'Ivoire	1994	26	39	41	103	2	6	6	41	25	17	70	23
Dominican Republic	2002	170	103	149	156	6	11	38	87	57	69	14	4
Egypt, Arab Rep.	2003	87	120	96	103	6	11	58	87	77	71	24	5
Eritrea	1995	55	117	42	154	1	7	3	65	21	24	84	10
Ethiopia	2000	87	257	61	186	1	5	4	44	15	12	87	42
Gabon	2000	..	..	155	140	5	8	12	60	35	40	8	3
Ghana	2003	90	90	71	108	4	9	15	66	38	41	57	20
Guatemala	1995	114	124	62	122	2	9	9	76	41	40	58	8
Guinea	1999	13	39	10	38	1	5	3	27	18	9	95	77
Haiti	2000	141	200	94	152	3	8	1	40	13	18	64	21
India	1999	99	72	87	122	3	10	31	87	64	55	35	2
Indonesia	2002–03	85	92	103	104	7	11	75	97	86	89	19	6
Jordan	2002	..	..	101	99	10	12	93	98	97	97	11	9

About the data

The data in the table describe basic information on school participation and attainment by individuals in different socioeconomic groups within countries. The data are from Demographic and Health Surveys conducted by Macro International with the support of the U.S. Agency for International Development. These large-scale household sample surveys, conducted periodically in developing countries, collect information on a large number of health, nutrition, and population measures as well as on respondents' social, demographic, and economic characteristics using a standard set of questionnaires. The data presented here draw on responses to individual and household questionnaires.

Typically, Demographic and Health Surveys collect basic information on educational attainment and enrollment levels from every household member ages 5 or 6 and older as background characteristics. As the surveys are intended for the collection of demographic and health information, the education section of the survey is not as robust and detailed as the health section; however, it still provides useful micro-level information on education that cannot be explained by aggregate national level data.

The table defines socioeconomic status in terms of a household's assets, including ownership of consumer items, features of the household's dwelling, and other characteristics related to wealth. Each household asset on which information was collected was assigned a weight generated through principal-component analysis. The resulting scores were standardized in relation to a standard normal distribution with a mean of zero and a standard deviation of one. The standardized scores were then used to create break-points defining wealth quintiles, expressed as quintiles of individuals in the population.

The choice of the asset index for defining socioeconomic status was based on pragmatic rather than conceptual considerations: Demographic and Health Surveys do not provide income or consumption data but do have detailed information on households' ownership of consumer goods and access to a variety of goods and services. Like income or consumption, the asset index defines disparities in primarily economic terms. It therefore excludes other possibilities of disparities among groups, such as those based on gender, education, ethnic background, or other facets of social exclusion. To that extent the index provides only a partial view of the multidimensional concepts of poverty, inequality, and inequity.

Creating one index that includes all asset indicators limits the types of analysis that can be performed. In particular, the use of a unified index does not permit a disaggregated analysis to examine which asset indicators have a more or less important association with health status or use of health services. In addition, some asset indicators may reflect household wealth better in some countries than in others—or reflect different degrees of wealth in different countries. Taking such information into

Education gaps by income and gender

	Survey year	Gross intake rate in grade 1		Gross primary participation rate		Average years of schooling		Primary completion rate				Children out of school	
		% of relevant age group		% of relevant age group		ages 15–24		% of relevant age group				% of children ages 6–11	
		Poorest quintile	Richest quintile	Poorest quintile	Richest quintile	Poorest quintile	Richest quintile	Poorest quintile	Richest quintile	Male	Female	Poorest quintile	Richest quintile
Kazakhstan	1999	..	..	125	130	10	11	98	100	98	99	24	18
Kenya	2003	128	123	104	118	5	9	14	57	30	36	24	4
Kyrgyz Republic	1997	..	..	133	138	10	10	86	88	85	87	21	18
Madagascar	1997	84	87	59	134	2	7	1	47	13	16	60	6
Malawi	2002	180	226	103	126	4	8	10	52	32	14	29	9
Mali	2001	45	89	36	101	1	5	3	37	16	11	75	29
Morocco	2003–04	109	85	98	116	2	9	17	78	47	46	26	2
Mozambique	2003	104	134	79	150	2	5	2	17	8	7	59	13
Namibia	1992	..	..	138	116	5	8	15	65	25	34	22	9
Nepal	2001	240	249	116	160	3	7	18	59	37	28	33	6
Nicaragua	2001	127	108	79	104	3	10	14	88	47	59	46	5
Niger	1998	11	69	15	77	1	4	8	46	22	13	90	44
Nigeria	2003	77	106	67	111	4	10	16	70	39	37	56	5
Pakistan	1990–91	68	173	45	127	2	8	11	55	32	22	72	13
Paraguay	1990	137	106	103	114	5	10	29	77	49	54	21	10
Peru	2000	114	94	112	109	6	11	41	93	72	72	9	1
Philippines	2003	131	102	103	102	6	11	46	88	67	79	17	2
Rwanda	2000	216	197	100	126	3	6	7	28	14	14	43	23
Tanzania	1999	95	231	63	119	4	7	27	55	34	34	74	27
Uganda	2000–01	145	127	106	120	4	8	7	43	19	21	28	6
Uzbekistan	1996	..	..	102	114	10	10	84	87	84	86	29	23
Vietnam	2002	121	105	139	127	5	10	58	97	84	84	8	2
Zambia	2001–02	83	119	74	112	4	9	16	79	38	43	61	18
Zimbabwe	1994	138	114	104	109	7	10	36	80	51	57	22	8

a. Less than 0.5.

account and creating country-specific asset indexes with country-specific choices of asset indicators might produce a more effective and accurate index for each country. The asset index used in the table does not have this flexibility.

The analysis was carried out for 48 countries. The table shows the estimates for the poorest and richest quintiles only; the full set of estimates for 32 indicators is available in the country reports (see *Data sources*). The data in this table will differ from data for similar indicators in preceding tables either because the indicator refers to a period a few years preceding the survey date or because the indicator definition or methodology is different. Findings should be interpreted with caution because of measurement error inherent in the use of survey data.

Definitions

• **Survey year** is the year in which the underlying data were collected. • **Gross intake rate in grade 1** is the number of students in the first grade of primary education, regardless of age, expressed as a percentage of the population of the official primary school entrance age. These data may differ from those in table 2.11. • **Gross primary participation rate** is the ratio of total students attending primary school, regardless of age, to the population of the age group that officially corresponds to primary education. • **Average years of schooling** are the years of formal schooling received, on average, by adults ages 15–24. • **Primary completion rate** is the percentage of children of the official primary school completing age to the official primary school completing age plus four, who have completed the last year of primary school or higher. These data differ from those in table 2.12 as the definition and methodology are different. • **Children out of school** are the percentage of children ages 6–11 who are not in school. These data differ from those in table 2.10 because the definition and methodology are different.

Data sources

Data on education gaps by income and gender are from an analysis of Demographic and Health Surveys by Macro International and the World Bank. Country reports are available at http://devdata.worldbank.org/edstats/td16.asp.

2.14 Health expenditure, services, and use

	Health expenditure						Physicians		Health worker density index	Hospital beds	
	Total	Public		Out of pocket	External resources[a]	Per capita			Physicians, nurses, and midwives		
	% of GDP	% of GDP	% of total	% of private	% of total	$	per 1,000 people		per 1,000 people	per 1,000 people	
	2004	2004	2004	2004	2004	2004	1990	2000–05[b]	2000–03[b]	1990	2000–05[b]
Afghanistan	4.4	0.7	16.9	97.7	6.1	14	0.1	0.2	0.4	0.2	0.4
Albania	6.7	3.0	44.1	99.8	2.4	157	1.4	1.3	5.4	4.0	3.1
Algeria	3.6	2.6	72.5	94.6	0.0	94	0.9	1.1	..	2.5	..
Angola	1.9	1.5	79.4	100.0	9.1	26	0.0[c]	0.1	..	1.3	..
Argentina	9.6	4.3	45.3	48.7	0.2	383	2.7	..	..	4.6	4.1
Armenia	5.4	1.4	26.2	89.2	7.2	63	3.9	3.6	8.8	9.1	4.4
Australia	9.6	6.5	67.5	61.6	0.0	3,123	2.2	2.5	10.8	*9.2*	7.4
Austria	10.3	7.8	75.6	67.9	0.0	3,683	2.2	3.4	9.3	10.2	8.3
Azerbaijan	3.6	0.9	25.0	93.6	1.6	37	3.9	3.5	12.0	10.1	8.3
Bangladesh	3.1	0.9	28.1	88.3	15.1	14	0.2	0.3	0.5	0.3	..
Belarus	6.2	4.6	74.9	72.7	*0.1*	147	3.6	4.6	17.5	13.2	11.3
Belgium	9.7	6.9	71.1	83.5	0.0	3,363	3.3	3.9	15.6	8.0	6.9
Benin	4.9	2.5	51.2	99.9	10.2	24	0.1	0.0[c]	..	0.8	..
Bolivia	6.8	4.1	60.7	82.5	9.1	66	0.4	1.2	1.1	1.3	1.0
Bosnia and Herzegovina	8.3	4.1	49.4	100.0	1.3	198	1.6	1.3	5.7	4.5	3.1
Botswana	6.4	4.0	62.9	27.9	2.5	329	*0.2*	0.4	..	1.6	..
Brazil	8.8	4.8	54.1	64.2	0.0	290	1.4	2.1	2.6	3.3	2.7
Bulgaria	8.0	4.6	57.6	98.0	1.0	251	3.2	3.6	8.3	9.8	6.3
Burkina Faso	6.1	3.3	54.8	97.9	26.8	24	*0.0*[c]	0.1	0.3	0.3	..
Burundi	3.2	0.8	26.2	100.0	17.6	3	0.1	0.0[c]	0.3	*0.7*	..
Cambodia	6.7	1.7	25.8	85.4	28.5	24	*0.1*	0.2	1.0	2.1	0.6
Cameroon	5.2	1.5	28.0	94.5	5.3	51	0.1	0.2	..	2.6	..
Canada	9.8	6.8	69.8	49.4	0.0	3,038	2.1	2.1	12.2	6.0	3.7
Central African Republic	4.1	1.5	36.8	95.4	47.7	13	0.0[c]	0.1	..	0.9	..
Chad	4.2	1.5	36.9	95.8	7.0	20	*0.0*[c]	0.0[c]	0.2	*0.7*	..
Chile	6.1	2.9	47.0	45.9	0.1	359	1.1	1.1	1.7	3.2	2.6
China	4.7	1.8	38.0	86.5	0.1	71	1.5	1.5	2.7	2.6	2.5
Hong Kong, China	..	..	..	..	..	..	..	..	..	..	..
Colombia	7.8	6.7	86.0	49.0	0.1	168	1.1	1.4	1.9	1.4	1.1
Congo, Dem. Rep.	4.0	1.1	28.1	100.0	19.1	5	0.1	0.1	..	1.4	..
Congo, Rep.	2.5	1.2	49.2	100.0	3.6	28	0.3	0.2	..	3.3	..
Costa Rica	6.6	5.1	77.0	88.7	0.8	290	1.3	1.3	2.4	2.5	1.4
Côte d'Ivoire	3.8	0.9	23.2[d]	88.7	5.0	33	0.1	0.1	..	0.8	..
Croatia	8.0[d]	6.1[d]	81.0	93.8	0.4	609	2.1	2.4	7.7	7.4	5.5
Cuba	6.3	5.5	87.8	74.5	0.3	230	3.6	5.9	13.4	5.4	4.9
Czech Republic	7.3	6.5	89.2	95.5	0.0	771	2.7	3.5	13.4	11.3	8.8
Denmark	8.6	7.1	82.3	81.3	0.0	3,897	2.5	2.9	13.6	5.6	4.0
Dominican Republic	6.0	1.9	31.6	73.1	1.5	148	1.5	1.9	3.7	1.9	2.1
Ecuador	5.5	2.2	40.7	85.4	0.8	127	1.5	1.5	3.1	1.6	1.5
Egypt, Arab Rep.	5.9	2.2	37.0	*99.0*	*0.8*	64	0.8	0.5	4.9	2.1	2.2
El Salvador	7.9	3.5	44.4	94.2	1.2	184	0.8	1.2	2.0	1.5	..
Eritrea	4.5	1.8	39.2	100.0	59.6	10	..	0.1	..	..	..
Estonia	5.3	4.0	76.0	88.8	0.5	463	3.5	3.2	9.8	11.6	6.0
Ethiopia	5.3	2.7	51.5	78.3	35.2	6	*0.0*[c]	0.0[c]	0.2	0.2	..
Finland	7.4	5.7	77.2	80.8	0.0	2,664	2.0	2.6	25.6	12.5	7.2
France	10.5	8.2	78.4	34.9	0.0	3,464	3.1	3.4	10.2	9.7	7.7
Gabon	4.5	3.1	68.8	100.0	1.3	231	*0.5*	0.3	..	3.2	..
Gambia, The	6.8	1.8	27.1	68.2	23.0	19	..	0.1	..	0.6	..
Georgia	5.3	1.5	27.4	87.2	9.8	60	4.9	4.1	7.9	9.8	4.2
Germany	10.6	8.2	76.9	57.5	0.0	3,521	*2.8*	3.4	13.2	10.4	8.9
Ghana	6.7	2.8	42.2	78.2	29.9	27	*0.0*[c]	0.2	0.9	1.5	..
Greece	7.9	4.2	52.8	95.7	..	1,879	3.4	4.4	7.5	5.1	4.7
Guatemala	5.7	2.3	41.0	90.5	2.3	127	0.8	..	..	1.1	0.5
Guinea	5.3	0.7	13.2	99.5	9.5	22	0.1	0.1	0.6	0.6	..
Guinea-Bissau	4.8	1.3	27.3	90.0	31.6	9	..	0.1	..	1.5	..
Haiti	7.6	2.9	38.5	69.6	14.2	33	0.1	..	..	0.8	0.8

Health expenditure, services, and use

	Health expenditure						Physicians		Health worker density index	Hospital beds	
	Total	Public		Out of pocket	External resources[a]	Per capita			Physicians, nurses, and midwives		
	% of GDP	% of GDP	% of total	% of private	% of total	$	per 1,000 people		per 1,000 people	per 1,000 people	
	2004	**2004**	**2004**	**2004**	**2004**	**2004**	**1990**	**2000–05[b]**	**2000–03[b]**	**1990**	**2000–05[b]**
Honduras	7.2	4.0	54.9	84.3	8.7	77	0.7	0.6	..	1.0	1.0
Hungary	7.9	5.7	71.6	88.0	0.4	800	2.8	3.2	11.9	..	7.8
India	5.0	0.9	17.3	93.8	0.5	31	*0.5*	0.6	..	*0.8*	0.9
Indonesia	2.8	1.0	34.2	74.7	1.3	33	0.1	0.1	0.7	0.7	..
Iran, Islamic Rep.	6.6	3.2	47.8	94.8	0.2	158	*0.3*	0.4	..	1.4	1.6
Iraq	5.3[e]	4.2[e]	78.5[e]	100.0[e]	2.5[e]	58[e]	0.6	0.7	3.6	1.7	1.3
Ireland	7.2	5.7	79.5	65.9	0.0	3,234	*2.0*	2.8	19.0	6.1	4.3
Israel	8.7	6.1	70.0	75.0	3.2	1,534	3.2	3.8	10.3	6.2	6.1
Italy	8.7	6.5	75.1	84.4	0.0	2,580	..	4.2	10.5	7.2	4.4
Jamaica	5.2	2.8	54.3	63.6	1.4	176	0.6	0.8	2.5	2.2	1.4
Japan	7.8	6.3	81.0	93.4	0.0	2,831	1.7	2.0	10.4	..	14.3
Jordan	9.8[f]	4.7[f]	48.4[f]	73.8	7.1[f]	200[f]	*1.3*	2.0	4.8	1.8	1.7
Kazakhstan	3.8	2.3	59.8	100.0	0.9	109	4.0	3.5	9.5	13.7	7.7
Kenya	4.1	1.8	42.7	81.9	18.3	20	0.0[c]	0.1	..	1.6	..
Korea, Dem. Rep.	3.5	3.0	85.6	100.0	53.6	0[g]	..	3.3	..	..	..
Korea, Rep.	5.6	2.9	51.4	76.0	0.0	787	0.8	1.6	5.4	3.1	7.1
Kuwait	2.8	2.2	77.6	90.4	0.0	633	0.2	1.5	5.4	*3*	2.2
Kyrgyz Republic	5.6	2.3	40.9	94.3	15.1	24	3.4	2.5	10.1	12.0	5.3
Lao PDR	3.9	0.8	20.5	90.3	10.2	17	0.2	..	..	2.6	1.2
Latvia	7.1	4.0	56.6	98.3	0.3	418	4.1	3.0	8.2	14.1	7.8
Lebanon	11.6	3.2	27.4	82.2	1.7	670	*1.3*	3.3	4.4	1.7	3.0
Lesotho	6.5	5.5	84.2	18.2	8.7	49	0.0[c]	0.0[c]	..	..	..
Liberia	5.6	3.6	63.9	98.5	37.8	9	..	0.0[c]	..	..	..
Libya	3.8	2.8	74.9	100.0	0.0	195	1.1	..	..	4.2	3.9
Lithuania	6.5	4.9	75.0	96.8	3.1	424	4.0	4.0	12.4	12.5	8.7
Macedonia, FYR	8.0	5.7	71.0	100.0	1.4	212	2.2	2.2	8.1	5.9	4.8
Madagascar	3.0	1.8	59.1	52.5	45.5	7	0.1	0.3	0.4	0.9	0.4
Malawi	12.9	9.6	74.7	35.2	59.4	19	0.0[c]	0.0[c]	0.3	1.6	..
Malaysia	3.8	2.2	58.8	74.1	0.1	180	0.4	0.7	2.4	2.1	1.9
Mali	6.6	3.2	49.2	99.5	13.8	24	0.1	0.1	0.2	..	..
Mauritania	2.9	2.0	69.4	100.0	20.2	15	0.1	0.1	..	0.7	..
Mauritius	4.3	2.4	54.7	80.8	1.4	222	0.8	1.1	..	2.9	..
Mexico	6.5	3.0	46.4	94.4	0.3	424	1.0	1.5	3.9	1.0	1.0
Moldova	7.4	4.2	56.8	96.0	4.8	46	3.6	2.6	9.2	13.1	6.7
Mongolia	6.0	4.0	66.6	92.3	4.6	37	2.5	2.6	6.0	*11.5*	..
Morocco	5.1	1.7	34.3	76.0	0.9	82	*0.2*	0.5	1.5	1.3	0.8
Mozambique	4.0	2.7	68.4	38.5	55.9	12	0.0[c]	0.0[c]	0.3	0.9	..
Myanmar	2.2	0.3	12.9	99.4	13.1	5	0.1	0.4	0.8	0.6	0.6
Namibia	6.8	4.7	69.0	18.1	16.9	190	*0.2*	0.3	..	..	..
Nepal	5.6	1.5	26.3	88.1	17.6	14	0.1	0.2	0.3	0.2	..
Netherlands	9.2	5.7	62.4	20.6	0.0	3,442	2.5	3.1	16.7	5.8	4.7
New Zealand	8.4	6.5	77.4	76.1	0.0	2,040	1.9	2.2	10.9	8.5	6.1
Nicaragua	8.2	3.9	47.1	95.9	11.3	67	0.7	0.4	1.8	1.8	0.9
Niger	4.2	2.2	52.5	85.1	21.3	9	0.0[c]	0.0[c]	0.3	..	..
Nigeria	4.6	1.4	30.4	90.4	5.6	23	*0.2*	0.3	1.5	1.7	..
Norway	9.7	8.1	83.5	95.2	0.0	5,405	*2.6*	3.1	24.9	4.6	3.8
Oman	3.0	2.4	81.4	57.1	0.0	295	0.6	1.3	4.2	2.1	2.0
Pakistan	2.2	0.4	19.6	98.0	2.5	14	0.5	0.7	1.1	0.6	0.7
Panama	7.7	5.2	66.9	82.5	0.2	343	1.6	1.5	3.2	2.5	2.5
Papua New Guinea	3.6	3.0	84.3	46.4	26.5	30	0.1	0.1	0.6	4.0	..
Paraguay	7.7	2.6	33.7	72.2	1.9	88	0.6	1.1	1.4	0.9	1.2
Peru	4.1	1.9	46.9	79.2	1.3	104	1.1	..	..	1.4	1.4
Philippines	3.4	1.4	39.8	77.9	3.6	36	0.1	1.2	7.4	1.4	1.0
Poland	6.2	4.3	68.6	89.6	0.1	411	2.1	2.5	7.7	5.7	5.6
Portugal	9.8	7.0	71.6	79.4	0.0	1,665	2.8	3.3	7.0	4.1	3.6
Puerto Rico	..	..	..	..	..	..	..	..	..	..	..

2.14 Health expenditure, services, and use

	Health expenditure						Physicians		Health worker density index	Hospital beds	
	Total	Public		Out of pocket	External resources[a]	Per capita			Physicians, nurses, and midwives		
	% of GDP	% of GDP	% of total	% of private	% of total	$	per 1,000 people		per 1,000 people	per 1,000 people	
	2004	2004	2004	2004	2004	2004	1990	2000–05[b]	2000–03[b]	1990	2000–05[b]
Romania	5.1	3.4	66.1	93.4	25.0	178	1.8	1.9	6.2	8.9	6.6
Russian Federation	6.0	3.7	61.3	76.7	0.1	245	4.1	4.3	12.5	13.1	10.5
Rwanda	7.5	4.3	56.8	36.9	37.1	16	*0.0*[c]	*0.0*[c]	0.2	1.7	..
Saudi Arabia	3.3	2.5	75.4	31.0	..	348	1.4	1.4	4.4	2.5	2.2
Senegal	5.9	2.4	40.3	94.5	12.8	39	0.1	0.1	..	0.7	..
Serbia and Montenegro	10.1[h]	7.3[h]	72.1[h]	88.2[h]	0.5[h]	219[h]	2.0	2.1	..	5.9	6.0
Sierra Leone	3.3	1.9	59.0	100.0	35.4	7	..	0.0[c]	..	..	..
Singapore	3.7	1.3	34.0	96.9	0.0	943	1.3	1.4	5.6	3.6	2.9
Slovak Republic	7.2	5.3	73.8	73.1	0.0	565	..	3.1	10.6	7.4	7.2
Slovenia	8.7	6.6	75.6	39.5	*0.1*	1,438	2.0	2.3	9.4	6.0	5.0
Somalia	..	..	..	..	..	..	..	..	..	0.8	..
South Africa	8.6	3.5	40.4	17.2	0.5	390	*0.6*	0.8	4.6	..	..
Spain	8.1	5.7	70.9	81.0	0.0	1,971	..	3.2	6.8	4.6	3.8
Sri Lanka	4.3	2.0	45.6	84.0	1.2	43	*0.1*	0.5	1.2	2.7	3.1
Sudan	4.1	1.5	35.4	98.1	5.1	25	..	0.2	1.0	1.1	0.7
Swaziland	6.3	4.0	63.8	40.2	9.5	146	0.1	0.2	3.4	..	..
Sweden	9.1	7.7	84.9	92.0	0.0	3,532	2.9	3.3	13.5	12.4	3.6
Switzerland	11.5	6.7	58.5	76.7	0.0	5,572	3.0	3.6	12.1	*19.9*	6.0
Syrian Arab Republic	4.7	2.2	47.4	100.0	0.2	58	0.8	1.4	3.3	1.1	1.5
Tajikistan	4.4	1.0	21.6	97.3	9.1	14	2.6	2.0	7.2	10.7	6.1
Tanzania	4.0	1.7	43.6	83.2	27.1	12	..	0.0[c]	0.4	1.0	..
Thailand	3.5	2.3	64.7	74.7	0.3	88	0.2	0.4	..	1.6	..
Togo	5.5	1.1	20.7	84.9	8.9	18	*0.1*	0.0[c]	0.3	1.5	..
Trinidad and Tobago	3.5	1.4	38.9	88.5	0.2	329	0.7	..	..	4.0	3.4
Tunisia	*5.6*	*2.8*	*50.0*	..	..	*126*	0.5	1.3	..	1.9	1.7
Turkey	7.7	5.2[e]	72.3	69.1	0.0	325	0.9	1.3	4.2	2.4	2.6
Turkmenistan	4.8	3.3	68.9	100.0	0.4	124	3.6	4.2	..	11.5	..
Uganda	7.6	2.5	32.7	51.3	25.2	19	*0.0*[c]	0.1	0.1	*0.9*	..
Ukraine	6.5	3.7	56.7	90.5	0.7	90	4.3	3.0	11.2	13.0	8.8
United Arab Emirates	2.9	2.0	69.9	71.0	0.0	711	0.8	2.0	6.2	2.6	2.2
United Kingdom	8.1	7.0	86.3	91.8	0.0	2,900	1.6	2.2	..	5.9	4.2
United States	15.4	6.9	44.7	23.8	0.0	6,096	1.8	2.3	13.2	4.9	3.3
Uruguay	8.2	3.6	43.5	31.1	0.3	315	3.7	3.7	4.5	4.5	1.9
Uzbekistan	5.1	2.4	46.6	96.2	3.9	23	3.4	2.7	13.7	12.5	5.5
Venezuela, RB	4.7	2.0	42.0	88.3	0.0	196	1.6	1.9	2.6	2.7	0.8
Vietnam	5.5	1.5	27.1	88.0	2.0	30	0.4	0.5	1.3	3.8	2.4
West Bank and Gaza	*13.0*	*7.8*	60.0	*100.0*	*42.0*	..	..	0.8	..	..	..
Yemen, Rep.	5.0	1.9	38.3	95.5	15.0	34	0.0[c]	0.3	0.7	0.8	0.6
Zambia	6.3	3.4	54.7	71.4	36.3	30	0.1	0.1	..	..	..
Zimbabwe	7.5	3.5	46.1	48.7	13.1	27	0.1	0.2	0.6	0.5	..
World	**10.1 w**	**5.9 w**	**59.1 w**	**44.4 w**	**0.1 w**	**649 w**	**1.4 w**	**.. w**	**.. w**	**3.7 w**	**.. w**
Low income	4.7	1.1	23.8	94.0	5.4	24	*0.5*	0.5	..	..	..
Middle income	5.9	3.1	52.6	77.0	0.6	141	1.6	1.5	..	3.6	..
Lower middle income	5.4	2.6	47.7	81.0	0.5	92	1.4	1.3	..	2.8	..
Upper middle income	6.6	3.8	57.8	71.7	0.7	342	2.3	2.7	7.5	6.7	5.7
Low & middle income	5.8	2.8	49.3	80.8	1.2	90	1.3	..	..	3.1	..
East Asia & Pacific	4.4	1.7	39.8	87.6	0.5	62	1.2	1.5	3.0	2.3	2.5
Europe & Central Asia	6.6	4.5	67.8	82.1	1.1	250	3.2	3.1	10.3	10.2	7.6
Latin America & Carib.	7.3	3.7	51.9	74.1	0.4	272	1.4	..	..	2.5	..
Middle East & N. Africa	5.6	2.7	48.9	89.7	1.3	103	..	..	..	1.8	..
South Asia	4.6	0.9	18.8	93.6	1.5	27	*0.5*	0.6	..	*0.7*	0.9
Sub-Saharan Africa	6.3	2.6	41.8	44.8	6.8	45	..	..	..	1.2	..
High income	11.2	6.7	60.4	37.8	0.0	3,727	1.9	2.6	..	6.2	6.4
Europe EMU	9.6	7.2	74.7	59.9	0.0	2,969	2.9	3.5	12.2	8.1	6.6

a. 0 for category not applicable or less than 0.05. b. Data are for the most recent year available. c. Less than 0.05. d. Data are for 2005. e. Excludes northern Iraq. f. Includes contributions from the United Nations Relief and Works Agency for Palestine Refugees in the Near East to Palestinian refugees. g. Less than 0.5. h. Excludes Kosovo and Metahia.

Health expenditure, services, and use 2.14

About the data

National health accounts track financial flows in the health sector, including public and private expenditures, by source of funding. In contrast with high-income countries, few developing countries have health accounts that are methodologically consistent with national accounting approaches. The difficulties in creating national health accounts go beyond data collection. To establish a national health accounting system, a country needs to define the boundaries of the health care system and to define a taxonomy of health care delivery institutions. The accounting system should be comprehensive and standardized, providing not only accurate measures of financial flows but also information on the equity and efficiency of health financing to inform health policy.

The absence of consistent national health accounting systems in most developing countries makes cross-country comparisons of health spending difficult. Compiling estimates of public health expenditures is complicated in countries where state or provincial and local governments are involved in financing and delivering health care, because the data on public spending often are not aggregated. There are a number of potential data sources related to external resources for health, including government expenditure accounts, government records on external assistance, routine surveys of external financing assistance, and special surveys. Survey data are the major source of information about out of pocket expenditure on health. The data in the table are the product of an effort by the World Health Organization (WHO), the Organisation for Economic Co-operation and Development (OECD), and the World Bank to collect all available information on health expenditures from national and local government budgets, national accounts, household surveys, insurance publications, international donors, and existing tabulations.

Indicators on health services (physicians, health worker density, and hospital beds per 1,000 people) come from a variety of sources (see *Data sources*). Data are lacking for many countries, and for others comparability is limited by differences in definitions. In estimates of health personnel, for example, some countries incorrectly include retired physicians (because deletions to physician rosters are made only periodically) or physicians working outside the health sector. There is no universally accepted definition of hospital beds. Moreover, figures on physicians and hospital beds are indicators of availability, not of quality or use. They do not show how well trained the physicians are or how well equipped the hospitals or medical centers are. And physicians and hospital beds tend to be concentrated in urban areas, so these indicators give only a partial view of health services available to the entire population.

The WHO receives data on health professionals from ministries of health through its six regional offices, often in cooperation with national statistical offices. The data are scrutinized using such additional resources as national and international employment surveys, records from professional associations, and other publications. Significant inconsistencies are returned to national authorities for validation and resubmission.

The health worker density index indicates the overall level of health workers (physicians, nurses, and midwives) in the country. Dentists and pharmacists are not included. Comparability of the index across countries is affected by differences in the definition of health workers. Many countries continue to use national definitions and classifications for data collection, and some countries provide information only for public sector workers.

Differences in healthcare expenditures contribute to global disparities in health outcomes 2.14a

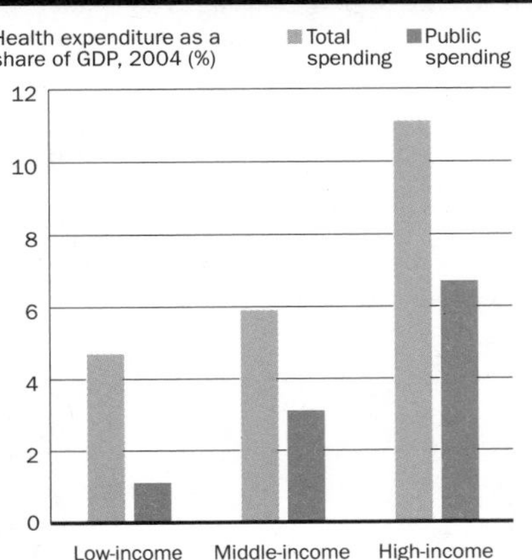

Source: World Health Organization, Organisation for Economic Co-operation and Development, and World Bank.

Definitions

• **Total health expenditure** is the sum of public and private health expenditure. It covers the provision of health services (preventive and curative), family planning activities, nutrition activities, and emergency aid designated for health but does not include provision of water and sanitation. • **Public health expenditure** consists of recurrent and capital spending from government (central and local) budgets, external borrowings and grants (including donations from international agencies and nongovernmental organizations), and social (or compulsory) health insurance funds. • **Out of pocket health expenditure** is any direct outlay by households, including gratuities and in-kind payments, to health practitioners and suppliers of pharmaceuticals, therapeutic appliances, and other goods and services whose primary intent is to contribute to the restoration or enhancement of the health status of individuals or population groups. It is a part of private health expenditure. • **External resources for health** are funds or services in kind that are provided by entities not part of the country in question. The resources may come from international organizations, other countries through bilateral arrangements, or foreign nongovernmental organizations. These resources are part of total health expenditure. • **Health expenditure per capita** is total health expenditure divided by number of people in the country. • **Physicians** are graduates of any faculty or school of medicine who are working in the country in any medical field (practice, teaching, or research). • **Health worker density index** reflects a combined density of physicians, nurses, and midwives per 1,000 people. • **Hospital beds** include inpatient beds available in public, private, general, and specialized hospitals and rehabilitation centers. In most cases beds for both acute and chronic care are included.

Data sources

Data on health expenditure come mostly from the WHO's National Health Account database (www.who.int/nha/en) and from the OECD for its member countries, supplemented by World Bank poverty assessments and country and sector studies. Data are also drawn from World Bank public expenditure reviews, the International Monetary Fund's Government Finance Statistics database, and other studies. Data on physicians are from the WHO's *World Health Report 2006* and Global Atlas of the Health Workforce database, OECD, and TransMONEE, supplemented by country data. Data for the health worker density index are from the Joint Learning Initiative's *Human Resources for Health*. Data on hospital beds are from the WHO's *World Health Statistics 2006*, OECD's *Health Data 2006*, and TransMONEE, supplemented by country data.

Disease prevention coverage and quality

	Access to an improved water source		Access to improved sanitation facilities		Child immunization rate		Children with acute respiratory infection taken to health provider	Children with diarrhea who received oral rehydration and continued feeding	Children sleeping under treated bednets[a]	Children with fever receiving antimalarial drugs	Tuberculosis treatment success rate	DOTS detection rate
	% of population		% of population		% of children ages 12–23 months[b]		% of children under age 5 with ARI	% of children under age 5 with diarrhea	% of children under age 5	% of children under age 5 with fever	% of registered cases	% of estimated cases
					Measles	DPT						
	1990	2004	1990	2004	2005	2005	2000–05[c]	1998–2005[c]	2000–05[c]	2000–05[c]	2004	2005
Afghanistan	4	39	3	34	64	76	28	48	..	..	89	44
Albania	96	96	..	91	97	98	83	51	..	..	78	25
Algeria	94	85	88	92	83	88	52	..	..	..	91	106
Angola	36	53	29	31	45	47	58	32	2	63	68	85
Argentina	94	96	81	91	99	92	..	..	..	..	58	67
Armenia	..	92	..	83	94	90	28	48	..	..	70	60
Australia	100	100	100	100	94	92	..	..	..	..	85	42
Austria	100	100	100	100	75	86	..	..	..	..	69	56
Azerbaijan	68	77	..	54	98	93	36	40	1	1	60	55
Bangladesh	72	74	20	39	81	88	20	53	..	..	90	59
Belarus	100	100	..	84	99	99	..	..	..	..	74	46
Belgium	100	100	100	100	88	97	..	..	..	..	72	64
Benin	63	67	12	33	85	93	35	42	7	60	83	83
Bolivia	72	85	33	46	64	81	52	54	..	..	80	72
Bosnia and Herzegovina	97	97	..	95	90	93	80	23	..	..	98	71
Botswana	93	95	38	42	90	97	14	7	..	..	65	69
Brazil	83	90	71	75	99	96	..	..	..	..	81	53
Bulgaria	99	99	99	99	96	96	..	..	..	..	80	90
Burkina Faso	38	61	7	13	84	96	36	47	2	50	67	18
Burundi	69	79	44	36	75	74	40	16	1	31	78	30
Cambodia	..	41	..	17	79	82	37	59	..	..	91	66
Cameroon	50	66	48	51	68	80	40	43	1	53	71	106
Canada	100	100	100	100	94	94	..	..	..	..	62	64
Central African Republic	52	75	23	27	35	40	32	47	2	69	91	40
Chad	19	42	7	9	23	20	12	27	1	44	69	22
Chile	90	95	84	91	90	91	..	..	..	..	83	112
China	70	77	23	44	86	87	..	..	..	..	94	80
Hong Kong, China	..	..	..	..	81	85	..	..	..	..	80	53
Colombia	92	93	82	86	89	87	57	39	1	..	85	26
Congo, Dem. Rep.	43	46	16	30	70	73	36	17	1	45	85	72
Congo, Rep.	..	58	..	27	56	65	38	..	..	..	63	57
Costa Rica	..	97	..	92	89	91	..	..	..	..	*94*	118
Côte d'Ivoire	69	84	21	37	51	56	38	34	4	58	71	38
Croatia	100	100	100	100	96	96	..	..	..	..	..	..
Cuba	..	91	98	98	98	99	..	..	..	..	93	98
Czech Republic	100	100	99	98	97	97	..	..	..	..	73	65
Denmark	100	100	100	100	95	93	..	..	..	..	88	71
Dominican Republic	84	95	52	78	99	77	63	42	..	..	80	76
Ecuador	73	94	63	89	93	94	..	..	..	..	85	28
Egypt, Arab Rep.	94	98	54	70	98	98	73	29	..	..	70	63
El Salvador	67	84	51	62	99	89	62	..	..	..	90	67
Eritrea	43	60	7	9	84	83	44	54	4	4	85	13
Estonia	100	100	97	97	96	96	..	..	..	..	71	64
Ethiopia	23	22	3	13	59	69	19	38	2	3	79	33
Finland	100	100	100	100	97	97	..	..	..	..	..	..
France	100	100	..	..	87	98	..	..	..	..	..	..
Gabon	..	88	..	36	55	38	48	44	..	..	40	57
Gambia, The	..	82	..	53	84	88	75	38	15	55	86	69
Georgia	80	82	97	94	92	84	99	..	..	..	68	91
Germany	100	100	100	100	93	90	..	..	..	..	68	52
Ghana	55	75	15	18	83	84	44	40	4	63	72	37
Greece	..	..	..	..	88	88	..	..	..	..	..	..
Guatemala	79	95	58	86	77	81	64	22	..	..	85	55
Guinea	44	50	14	18	59	69	33	44	4	56	72	56
Guinea-Bissau	..	59	..	35	80	80	64	23	7	58	75	79
Haiti	47	54	24	30	54	43	26	41	..	12	80	57

2.15 Disease prevention coverage and quality

	Access to an improved water source % of population 1990	2004	Access to improved sanitation facilities % of population 1990	2004	Child immunization rate % of children ages 12–23 months[b] Measles 2005	DPT 2005	Children with acute respiratory infection taken to health provider % of children under age 5 with ARI 2000–05[c]	Children with diarrhea who received oral rehydration and continued feeding % of children under age 5 with diarrhea 1998–2005[c]	Children sleeping under treated bednets[a] % of children under age 5 2000–05[c]	Children with fever receiving antimalarial drugs % of children under age 5 with fever 2000–05[c]	Tuberculosis treatment success rate % of registered cases 2004	DOTS detection rate % of estimated cases 2005
Honduras	84	87	50	69	92	91	..	..	..	..	85	82
Hungary	99	99	..	95	99	99	..	..	..	..	54	43
India	70	86	14	33	58	59	..	22	..	12	86	61
Indonesia	72	77	46	55	72	70	61	56	26	1	90	66
Iran, Islamic Rep.	92	94	83	..	94	95	93	..	..	..	84	64
Iraq	83	81	81	79	90	81	76	54	0[d]	1	85	43
Ireland	..	..	..	..	84	90	..	..	..	..	..	..
Israel	100	100	..	..	95	95	..	..	..	..	80	42
Italy	..	..	..	..	87	96	..	..	..	..	95	72
Jamaica	92	93	75	80	84	88	39	21	..	..	46	61
Japan	100	100	100	100	99	99	..	..	..	..	57	57
Jordan	97	97	93	93	95	95	78	44	..	..	85	63
Kazakhstan	87	86	72	72	99	98	..	22	..	..	72	72
Kenya	45	61	40	43	69	76	49	33	5	27	80	43
Korea, Dem. Rep.	100	100	..	59	96	79	93	..	..	..	89	99
Korea, Rep.	..	92	..	..	99	96	..	..	..	..	80	18
Kuwait	..	..	..	..	99	99	..	..	..	..	63	66
Kyrgyz Republic	78	77	60	59	99	98	..	..	..	..	85	67
Lao PDR	..	51	..	30	41	49	36	37	18	9	86	68
Latvia	99	99	..	78	95	99	..	..	..	..	73	83
Lebanon	100	100	..	98	96	92	74	..	..	..	90	74
Lesotho	..	79	37	37	85	83	54	53	..	..	69	85
Liberia	55	61	39	27	94	87	70	..	..	..	70	50
Libya	71	..	97	97	97	98	..	..	..	..	64	178
Lithuania	..	..	..	..	97	94	..	..	..	..	72	100
Macedonia, FYR	..	..	..	..	96	97	..	..	..	..	84	66
Madagascar	40	46	14	32	59	61	48	47	..	34	71	67
Malawi	40	73	47	61	82	93	27	51	15	28	71	39
Malaysia	98	99	..	94	90	90	..	..	..	..	56	73
Mali	34	50	36	46	86	85	36	45	8	38	71	21
Mauritania	38	53	31	34	61	71	41	28	2	33	22	28
Mauritius	100	100	..	94	98	97	..	..	..	..	89	32
Mexico	82	97	58	79	96	98	..	..	..	..	82	110
Moldova	..	92	..	68	97	98	54	52	..	..	62	65
Mongolia	63	62	..	59	99	99	78	66	..	..	88	82
Morocco	75	81	56	73	97	98	38	46	..	..	87	101
Mozambique	36	43	20	32	77	72	54	47	..	15	77	49
Myanmar	57	78	24	77	72	73	66	48	..	..	84	95
Namibia	57	87	24	25	73	86	53	39	3	14	68	90
Nepal	70	90	11	35	74	75	26	43	..	..	87	67
Netherlands	100	100	100	100	96	98	..	..	..	..	83	47
New Zealand	97	..	..	..	82	89	..	..	..	..	66	51
Nicaragua	70	79	45	47	96	86	57	49	..	2	87	88
Niger	39	46	7	13	83	89	27	43	6	48	61	50
Nigeria	49	48	39	44	35	25	33	28	1	34	73	22
Norway	100	100	100	100	90	91	..	..	..	..	89	44
Oman	80	..	83	..	98	99	..	..	..	..	90	108
Pakistan	83	91	37	59	78	72	..	..	..	..	82	37
Panama	90	90	71	73	99	85	..	..	..	..	78	131
Papua New Guinea	39	39	44	44	60	61	..	..	..	..	65	21
Paraguay	62	86	58	80	90	75	..	..	..	..	83	33
Peru	74	83	52	63	80	84	68	57	..	..	90	86
Philippines	87	85	57	72	80	79	55	76	..	..	87	75
Poland	..	..	..	..	98	99	..	..	..	..	79	62
Portugal	..	..	..	..	93	93	..	..	..	..	84	85
Puerto Rico	..	..	..	..	..	..	..	..	..	..	71	74

2.15 Disease prevention coverage and quality

	Access to an improved water source (% of population)		Access to improved sanitation facilities (% of population)		Child immunization rate (% of children ages 12–23 months[b])		Children with acute respiratory infection taken to health provider (% of children under age 5 with ARI)	Children with diarrhea who received oral rehydration and continued feeding (% of children under age 5 with diarrhea)	Children sleeping under treated bednets[a] (% of children under age 5)	Children with fever receiving antimalarial drugs (% of children under age 5 with fever)	Tuberculosis treatment success rate (% of registered cases)	DOTS detection rate (% of estimated cases)
	1990	2004	1990	2004	Measles 2005	DPT 2005	2000–05[c]	1998–2005[c]	2000–05[c]	2000–05[c]	2004	2005
Romania	..	57	..	..	97	97	..	..	31	..	82	82
Russian Federation	94	97	87	87	99	98	..	..	..	..	59	30
Rwanda	59	74	37	42	89	95	27	16	13	12	77	29
Saudi Arabia	90	..	..	..	96	96	..	..	..	..	82	38
Senegal	65	76	33	57	74	84	27	33	14	29	74	51
Serbia and Montenegro	93	93	87	87	96	98	97	..	..	..	89	31
Sierra Leone	..	57	..	39	67	64	50	39	2	61	82	37
Singapore	100	100	100	100	96	96	..	..	..	..	81	100
Slovak Republic	100	100	99	99	98	99	..	..	..	..	88	39
Slovenia	..	..	..	..	94	96	..	..	..	..	90	84
Somalia	..	29	..	26	35	35	..	..	9[e]	..	91	86
South Africa	83	88	69	65	82	94	..	37	..	..	70	103
Spain	100	100	100	100	97	96	..	..	..	..	..	..
Sri Lanka	68	79	69	91	99	99	..	..	..	..	85	86
Sudan	64	70	33	34	60	59	57	38	0[d]	50	77	35
Swaziland	..	62	..	48	60	71	60	24	0[d]	26	50	42
Sweden	100	100	100	100	94	99	..	..	..	..	64	56
Switzerland	100	100	100	100	82	93	..	..	..	..	..	..
Syrian Arab Republic	80	93	73	90	98	99	66	..	..	..	86	42
Tajikistan	..	59	..	51	84	81	51	29	2	69	84	22
Tanzania	46	62	47	47	91	90	57	53	16	58	81	45
Thailand	95	99	80	99	96	98	..	..	..	..	74	73
Togo	50	52	37	35	70	82	30	25	54	60	67	18
Trinidad and Tobago	92	91	100	100	93	95	74	31	..	..	..	..
Tunisia	81	93	75	85	96	98	43	..	..	..	90	82
Turkey	85	96	85	88	91	90	41	19	..	..	91	3
Turkmenistan	..	72	..	62	99	99	51	..	..	..	86	43
Uganda	44	60	42	43	86	84	67	28	0[d]	..	70	45
Ukraine	96	96	96	96	96	96	..	..	..	..	..	..
United Arab Emirates	100	100	97	98	92	94	..	..	..	..	70	19
United Kingdom	100	100	..	..	82	91	..	..	..	..	..	..
United States	100	100	100	100	93	96	..	..	..	..	61	85
Uruguay	100	100	100	100	95	96	..	..	..	..	86	83
Uzbekistan	94	82	51	67	99	99	57	33	..	..	78	39
Venezuela, RB	..	83	..	68	76	87	72	51	..	..	81	73
Vietnam	65	85	36	61	95	95	71	39	16	7	93	84
West Bank and Gaza	..	92	..	73	99	99	65	..	..	..	50	2
Yemen, Rep.	71	67	32	43	76	86	47	..	..	..	82	41
Zambia	50	58	44	55	84	80	69	48	7	52	83	52
Zimbabwe	78	81	50	53	85	90	..	80	..	..	54	41
World	**77 w**	**83 w**	**45 w**	**57 w**	**77 w**	**78 w**					**84 w**	**60 w**
Low income	64	75	21	38	65	66					83	52
Middle income	78	84	48	62	87	88					85	74
Lower middle income	76	82	42	57	86	86					88	74
Upper middle income	90	94	79	84	93	94					70	73
Low & middle income	73	80	37	52	75	76					84	61
East Asia & Pacific	72	79	30	51	83	84					90	76
Europe & Central Asia	93	92	86	85	96	95					73	42
Latin America & Carib.	83	91	67	77	92	91					82	64
Middle East & N. Africa	88	89	70	76	92	93					84	71
South Asia	71	84	17	37	64	65					86	58
Sub-Saharan Africa	49	56	31	37	64	65					74	49
High income	100	100	100	100	93	95					66	40
Europe EMU	100	100	..	..	90	95					..	35

a. For malaria prevention only. b. Refers to children who were immunized before age 12 months or, in some cases, ages 12–23 months. c. Data are for the most recent year available. d. Less than 0.5. e. Data are for 2006.

Disease prevention coverage and quality

About the data

People's health is influenced by the environment in which they live. Lack of clean water and basic sanitation is the main reason diseases transmitted by feces are so common in developing countries. The data on access to an improved water source measure the percentage of the population using improved drinking water sources or delivery points. Access to drinking water from an improved source and access to improved sanitation do not ensure safety or adequacy, as these characteristics are not tested at the time of the surveys. But improved drinking water technologies and improved sanitation facilities are more likely than those characterized as unimproved to provide safe drinking water and to prevent contact with human excreta. The data are derived by the Joint Monitoring Programme (JMP) of the WHO and United Nations Children's Fund (UNICEF) based on national censuses and nationally representative household surveys. The coverage rates for water and sanitation are based on information from service users on the facilities their households actually use rather than on information from service providers, who may include nonfunctioning systems. While the estimates are based on use, the JMP reports use as access, because access is the term used in the Millennium Development Goal target for drinking water and sanitation.

Governments in developing countries usually finance immunization against measles and diphtheria, pertussis (whooping cough), and tetanus (DPT) as part of the basic public health package. In many developing countries, lack of precise information on the size of the cohort of one-year-old children makes immunization coverage difficult to estimate from program statistics. The data shown here are based on an assessment of national immunization coverage rates by the WHO and UNICEF. The assessment considered both administrative data from service providers and household survey data on children's immunization histories. Based on the data available, consideration of potential biases, and contributions of local experts, the most likely true level of immunization coverage was determined for each year.

Acute respiratory infection continues to be a leading cause of death among young children, killing about 2 million children under age five in developing countries in 2000. An estimated 60 percent of these deaths can be prevented by the selective use of antibiotics by appropriate health care providers. Data are drawn mostly from household health surveys in which mothers report on number of episodes and treatment for acute respiratory infection.

Since 1990 diarrhea-related deaths among children have declined tremendously. Most diarrhea-related deaths are due to dehydration, and many of these deaths can be prevented with the use of oral rehydration salts at home. However, recommendations for the use of oral rehydration therapy have changed over time based on scientific progress, so it is difficult to accurately compare use rates among countries. Until the current recommended method for home management of diarrhea is adopted and applied in all countries, the data should be used with caution. Also, the prevalence of diarrhea may vary by season. Since country surveys are administered at different times, data comparability is further affected.

Malaria is endemic to the poorest countries in the world, mainly in tropical and subtropical regions of Africa, Asia, and the Americas. An estimated 300–500 million clinical malaria cases and more than 1 million malaria deaths occur each year—the vast majority in Sub-Saharan Africa and among children under age five. Insecticide-treated bednets, if properly used and maintained, are one of the most important malaria-preventive strategies to limit human-mosquito contact. Studies have emphasized that mortality rates could be reduced by about 25–30 percent if every child under age five in malaria-risk areas such as Africa slept under a treated bednet every night.

Prompt and effective treatment of malaria is a critical element of malaria control. It is vital that sufferers, especially children under age five, start treatment within 24 hours of the onset of symptoms, to prevent progression—often rapid—to severe malaria and death.

Data on the success rate of tuberculosis treatment are provided for countries that have implemented DOTS, the internationally recommended tuberculosis control strategy. Countries that have not adopted DOTS or have only recently done so are omitted because of lack of data or poor comparability or reliability of reported results. The treatment success rate for tuberculosis provides a useful indicator of the quality of health services. A low rate or no success suggests that infectious patients may not be receiving adequate treatment. An essential complement to the tuberculosis treatment success rate is the DOTS detection rate, which indicates whether there is adequate coverage by the recommended case detection and treatment strategy. A country with a high treatment success rate may still face big challenges if its DOTS detection rate remains low.

Definitions

• **Access to an improved water source** refers to the percentage of the population with reasonable access to an adequate amount of water from an improved source, such as piped water into a dwelling, plot, or yard; public tap or standpipe; tubewell or borehole; protected dug well or spring; and rainwater collection. Unimproved sources include unprotected dug well or spring, cart with small tank or drum, bottled water, and tanker trucks. Reasonable access is defined as the availability of at least 20 liters a person a day from a source within 1 kilometer of the dwelling. • **Access to improved sanitation facilities** refers to the percentage of the population with at least adequate access to excreta disposal facilities that can effectively prevent human, animal, and insect contact with excreta. Improved facilities range from simple but protected pit latrines to flush toilets with a sewerage connection. To be effective, facilities must be correctly constructed and properly maintained. • **Child immunization rate** is the percentage of children ages 12–23 months who received vaccinations before 12 months or at any time before the survey for four diseases—measles and diphtheria, pertussis (whooping cough), and tetanus (DPT). A child is considered adequately immunized against measles after receiving one dose of vaccine and against DPT after receiving three doses. • **Children with acute respiratory infection taken to a health provider** refer to the percentage of children under age five with acute respiratory infection in the two weeks prior to the survey who were taken to an appropriate health provider, including hospital, health center, dispensary, village health worker, clinic, and private physician • **Children with diarrhea who received oral rehydration and continued feeding** refer to the percentage of children under age five with diarrhea in the two weeks prior to the survey who received either oral rehydration therapy or increased fluids, with continued feeding. • **Children sleeping under treated bednets** refer to the percentage of children under age five who slept under an insecticide-treated bednet to prevent malaria. • **Children with fever receiving antimalarial drugs** refer to the percentage of children under age five who were ill with fever in the last two weeks and received any appropriate (locally defined) antimalarial drugs. • **Tuberculosis treatment success rate** is the percentage of new, registered smear-positive (infectious) cases that were cured or in which a full course of treatment was completed. • **DOTS detection rate** is the percentage of estimated new infectious tuberculosis cases detected under the directly observed treatment, short course case detection and treatment strategy.

Data sources

Data on water and sanitation are from the WHO and UNICEF's *Meeting the MDG Drinking Water and Sanitation Target* (www.who.int/water_sanitation_health/monitoring/jmp2006). Data on immunization are from WHO and UNICEF estimates of national immunization coverage (www.who.int/immunization_monitoring/en). Data on children with acute respiratory infection, children with diarrhea, children sleeping under treated bednets, and children receiving antimalarial drugs are from UNICEF's *State of the World's Children 2007*, Childinfo, and Demographic and Health Surveys by Macro International. Data on tuberculosis are from the WHO's *Global Tuberculosis Control Report 2007*.

2.16 Reproductive health

	Total fertility rate births per woman 1990	Total fertility rate births per woman 2005	Adolescent fertility rate births per 1,000 women ages 15–19 2005	Unmet need for contraception % of married women ages 15–49 2000–05[a]	Contraceptive prevalence rate % of married women ages 15–49 2000–05[a]	Tetanus vaccinations % of pregnant women 2005	Pregnant women receiving prenatal care % 2000–05[a]	Births attended by skilled health staff % of total 1990–92[a]	Births attended by skilled health staff % of total 2000–05[a]	Maternal mortality ratio per 100,000 live births National estimates 1990–2005[a]	Maternal mortality ratio per 100,000 live births Modeled estimates 2000
Afghanistan	..	..	..	..	10	55	16	..	14	1,600	1,900
Albania	2.9	1.8	16	..	75	..	91	..	98	16	55
Algeria	4.6	2.4	8	..	57	..	81	77	96	120	140
Angola	7.1	6.6	140	..	6	75	66	..	45	..	1,700
Argentina	3.0	2.3	58	..	..	..	98	96	95	39	82
Armenia	2.5	1.4	30	12	61	..	93	..	98	16	55
Australia	1.9	1.8	14	..	..	..	..	100	99	..	8
Austria	1.5	1.4	12	..	..	..	..	..	..	..	4
Azerbaijan	2.7	2.3	31	..	55	..	70	..	88	19	94
Bangladesh	4.3	3.0	118	11	58	89	49	..	13	320	380
Belarus	1.9	1.2	26	..	..	..	..	..	100	17	35
Belgium	1.6	1.7	8	..	..	..	..	..	..	..	10
Benin	6.7	5.6	127	27	19	69	81	..	75	500	850
Bolivia	4.9	3.7	81	23	58	..	79	..	67	30	420
Bosnia and Herzegovina	1.7	1.2	22	..	48	..	99	97	100	8	31
Botswana	4.4	3.0	74	..	48	..	97	..	94	330	100
Brazil	2.8	2.3	89	..	..	..	97	72	97	72	260
Bulgaria	1.8	1.3	43	..	..	..	..	..	99	6	32
Burkina Faso	6.9	5.9	156	29	14	75	73	..	38	480	1,000
Burundi	6.8	6.8	50	..	16	45	78	..	25	..	1,000
Cambodia	5.5	3.9	46	30	24	53	38	..	44	440	450
Cameroon	5.9	5.0	110	20	26	65	83	58	62	670	730
Canada	1.8	1.5	13	..	..	..	..	..	98	..	6
Central African Republic	5.6	4.7	122	..	28	56	62	..	44	1,100	1,100
Chad	6.7	6.3	191	21	3	39	39	..	14	1,100	1,100
Chile	2.6	2.0	60	..	..	..	..	..	100	17	31
China	2.1	1.8	5	..	87	..	90	..	97	51	56
Hong Kong, China	1.3	1.0	5	..	..	..	..	..	100	..	..
Colombia	3.1	2.4	75	6	78	86	94	82	96	84	130
Congo, Dem. Rep.	6.7	6.7	225	..	31	66	68	..	61	1,300	990
Congo, Rep.	6.3	5.6	144	..	44	65	88	..	86	..	510
Costa Rica	3.2	2.0	74	..	..	..	92	98	99	36	43
Côte d'Ivoire	6.5	4.7	117	..	..	73	88	..	68	600	690
Croatia	1.6	1.4	14	..	..	..	..	100	100	8	8
Cuba	1.7	1.5	50	..	73	..	100	..	100	37	33
Czech Republic	1.9	1.3	11	..	..	..	..	..	100	4	9
Denmark	1.7	1.8	7	..	..	..	..	..	..	10	5
Dominican Republic	3.3	2.7	91	11	70	..	99	93	99	180	150
Ecuador	3.6	2.7	83	..	73	..	84	..	75	80	130
Egypt, Arab Rep.	4.3	3.1	41	11	59	80	70	41	74	84	84
El Salvador	3.7	2.8	83	..	67	..	86	..	92	170	150
Eritrea	6.2	5.2	92	27	8	62	70	..	28	1,000	630
Estonia	2.0	1.5	23	..	..	..	..	..	100	8	63
Ethiopia	6.9	5.3	87	35	15	45	28	..	6	673	850
Finland	1.8	1.8	10	..	..	..	..	..	100	6	6
France	1.8	1.9	7	..	..	..	..	..	..	10	17
Gabon	5.3	3.7	102	28	33	60	94	..	86	520	420
Gambia, The	5.8	4.4	116	..	18	..	91	44	55	730	540
Georgia	2.1	1.4	32	..	47	..	95	..	92	52	32
Germany	1.5	1.4	10	..	..	..	..	..	..	8	8
Ghana	5.7	4.1	61	34	25	84	92	..	47	..	540
Greece	1.4	1.3	9	..	..	..	..	..	..	1	9
Guatemala	5.6	4.3	110	..	43	..	84	..	41	150	240
Guinea	6.5	5.6	186	..	7	76	82	31	56	530	740
Guinea-Bissau	7.1	7.1	192	..	8	54	62	..	35	910	1,100
Haiti	5.2	3.8	61	40	28	52	79	..	24	520	680

Reproductive health

	Total fertility rate		Adolescent fertility rate	Unmet need for contraception	Contraceptive prevalence rate	Tetanus vaccinations	Pregnant women receiving prenatal care	Births attended by skilled health staff		Maternal mortality ratio	
	births per woman		births per 1,000 women ages 15–19	% of married women ages 15–49	% of married women ages 15–49	% of pregnant women	%	% of total		per 100,000 live births	
										National estimates	Modeled estimates
	1990	2005	2005	2000–05[a]	2000–05[a]	2005	2000–05[a]	1990–92[a]	2000–05[a]	1990–2005[a]	2000
Honduras	5.1	3.5	97	..	62	..	83	45	56	110	110
Hungary	1.8	1.3	21	..	..	..	..	..	100	7	16
India	3.8	2.8	70	..	47	80	..	..	43	540	540
Indonesia	3.1	2.3	53	9	57	70	92	32	72	310	230
Iran, Islamic Rep.	4.8	2.1	19	..	74	..	..	..	90	37	76
Iraq	5.9	..	..	..	44	70	77	..	72	290	250
Ireland	2.1	1.9	13	..	..	..	..	..	100	6	5
Israel	2.8	2.8	14	..	..	..	..	..	..	5	17
Italy	1.3	1.3	7	..	..	..	..	..	..	7	5
Jamaica	2.9	2.4	78	..	69	..	98	..	97	110	87
Japan	1.5	1.3	4	..	56	..	..	100	..	8	10
Jordan	5.4	3.3	26	11	56	..	99	87	100	41	41
Kazakhstan	2.7	1.7	29	..	..	..	..	..	..	42	210
Kenya	5.8	5.0	95	25	..	72	88	..	42	410	1,000
Korea, Dem. Rep.	2.4	2.0	2	..	..	..	..	..	97	110	67
Korea, Rep.	1.6	1.1	4	..	..	..	..	98	100	20	20
Kuwait	3.5	2.4	23	..	..	..	..	..	100	5	5
Kyrgyz Republic	3.7	2.4	32	..	..	..	..	..	99	49	110
Lao PDR	6.0	4.5	88	..	32	30	27	..	19	410	650
Latvia	2.0	1.3	17	..	..	..	..	..	100	14	42
Lebanon	3.1	2.3	26	..	63	..	96	..	93	..	150
Lesotho	4.8	3.4	36	..	30	..	90	..	55	760	550
Liberia	6.9	6.8	222	..	10	72	85	..	51	..	760
Libya	4.7	2.8	7	..	..	..	..	..	..	77	97
Lithuania	2.0	1.3	21	..	..	..	..	..	100	3	13
Macedonia, FYR	2.1	1.6	23	..	..	..	81	..	99	21	23
Madagascar	6.2	5.0	121	24	27	45	80	57	51	470	550
Malawi	7.0	5.8	155	30	31	70	92	55	56	980	1,800
Malaysia	3.8	2.7	18	..	..	..	74	..	97	30	41
Mali	7.4	6.7	197	29	8	75	57	..	41	580	1,200
Mauritania	6.1	5.6	97	32	8	34	64	40	57	750	1,000
Mauritius	2.3	2.0	32	..	76	..	..	96	99	22	24
Mexico	3.3	2.1	66	..	73	..	..	..	83	63	83
Moldova	2.4	1.3	30	..	68	..	98	..	100	22	36
Mongolia	4.0	2.3	53	..	69	..	94	..	97	93	110
Morocco	4.0	2.4	42	10	63	..	68	31	63	230	220
Mozambique	6.2	5.3	101	18	26	70	85	..	48	410	1,000
Myanmar	4.0	2.2	18	..	34	85	76	..	57	230	360
Namibia	5.9	3.7	51	22	44	67	91	68	76	270	300
Nepal	5.1	3.5	110	28	38	42	28	7	15	540	740
Netherlands	1.6	1.7	5	..	..	..	..	..	..	7	16
New Zealand	2.2	2.0	23	..	..	..	..	..	..	15	7
Nicaragua	4.8	3.1	118	15	69	..	86	..	67	83	230
Niger	8.2	7.7	255	..	14	54	41	15	16	590	1,600
Nigeria	6.7	5.5	137	17	13	51	58	31	35	..	800
Norway	1.9	1.8	9	..	..	..	..	..	..	6	16
Oman	6.5	3.4	45	..	32	..	100	..	95	23	87
Pakistan	5.8	4.1	69	..	28	57	36	19	31	530	500
Panama	3.0	2.6	85	..	..	..	..	..	93	40	160
Papua New Guinea	5.1	3.8	57	..	..	10	..	..	41	..	300
Paraguay	4.7	3.7	63	..	73	..	94	67	77	180	170
Peru	3.9	2.7	53	10	69	..	92	..	73	190	410
Philippines	4.3	3.2	35	17	49	70	88	..	60	170	200
Poland	2.0	1.2	14	..	..	..	..	..	100	4	13
Portugal	1.4	1.4	18	..	..	..	..	..	100	8	5
Puerto Rico	2.2	1.8	53	..	..	..	..	..	100	..	25

2.16 Reproductive health

	Total fertility rate		Adolescent fertility rate	Unmet need for contraception	Contraceptive prevalence rate	Tetanus vaccinations	Pregnant women receiving prenatal care	Births attended by skilled health staff		Maternal mortality ratio per 100,000 live births	
	births per woman		births per 1,000 women ages 15–19	% of married women ages 15–49	% of married women ages 15–49	% of pregnant women	%	% of total		National estimates	Modeled estimates
	1990	2005	2005	2000–05[a]	2000–05[a]	2005	2000–05[a]	1990–92[a]	2000–05[a]	1990–2005[a]	2000
Romania	1.8	1.3	34	..	70	..	94	..	99	17	49
Russian Federation	1.9	1.3	29	..	..	..	..	..	99	..	67
Rwanda	7.4	5.8	46	36	17	*76*	94	26	39	750	1,400
Saudi Arabia	5.9	3.8	32	..	..	..	..	..	93	..	23
Senegal	6.4	4.9	80	..	11	85	79	..	58	430	690
Serbia and Montenegro	2.1	1.6	23	..	58	..	..	..	92	7	11
Sierra Leone	6.5	6.5	172	..	4	*76*	68	..	42	1,800	2,000
Singapore	1.9	1.2	5	..	..	..	..	..	100	6	30
Slovak Republic	2.1	1.3	20	..	..	..	..	..	99	4	3
Slovenia	1.5	1.2	6	..	..	..	..	100	100	17	17
Somalia	6.8	6.2	68	..	15[b]	25	..	..	33[b]	1,000	1,100
South Africa	3.3	2.8	65	..	60	*61*	92	..	92	150	230
Spain	1.3	1.3	9	..	..	..	..	..	..	6	4
Sri Lanka	2.5	1.9	18	..	70	76	100	..	96	43	92
Sudan	5.6	4.1	50	..	7	41	60	69	87	..	590
Swaziland	5.3	3.9	35	..	48	..	90	..	74	230	370
Sweden	2.1	1.8	7	..	..	..	..	..	..	5	2
Switzerland	1.6	1.4	4	..	..	..	..	..	..	5	7
Syrian Arab Republic	5.2	3.2	32	..	48	..	71	..	70	65	160
Tajikistan	5.1	3.5	29	..	34	..	71	..	71	37	100
Tanzania	6.1	5.2	106	22	26	90	78	44	43	578	1,500
Thailand	2.2	1.9	47	..	72	..	92	..	99	24	44
Togo	6.4	5.0	95	..	26	*61*	85	..	61	480	570
Trinidad and Tobago	2.4	1.6	35	..	38	..	92	..	96	45	160
Tunisia	3.5	2.0	7	..	66	..	92	..	90	69	120
Turkey	3.0	2.2	40	..	71	47	81	..	83	..	70
Turkmenistan	4.2	2.6	16	10	62	..	98	..	97	14	31
Uganda	7.2	7.1	207	35	23	56	92	..	39	510	880
Ukraine	1.8	1.2	28	..	89	..	..	..	100	13	35
United Arab Emirates	4.3	2.4	19	..	..	..	..	..	100	3	54
United Kingdom	1.8	1.8	25	..	84	..	..	..	..	7	13
United States	2.1	2.1	50	..	..	..	..	..	99	8	17
Uruguay	2.5	2.0	69	..	..	..	..	..	99	26	27
Uzbekistan	4.1	2.2	35	..	68	..	97	..	96	30	24
Venezuela, RB	3.4	2.7	91	..	..	..	94	..	95	58	96
Vietnam	3.6	1.8	19	5	77	*85*	86	..	90	170	130
West Bank and Gaza	*6.3*	4.6	..	..	51	..	96	..	97	..	..
Yemen, Rep.	7.9	5.9	91	..	23	24	41	16	27	370	570
Zambia	6.5	5.4	126	27	34	98	93	51	43	730	750
Zimbabwe	5.2	3.3	89	..	..	*70*	..	..	..	1,100	1,100
World	**3.1 w**	**2.6 w**	**57 w**		**60 w**	**.. w**	**.. w**	**.. w**	**63 w**		**410 w**
Low income	4.7	3.6	92		40	69	..	33	41		684
Middle income	2.6	2.1	32		76	..	89	..	87		150
Lower middle income	2.7	2.1	29		77	..	89	..	86		163
Upper middle income	2.6	1.9	46		..	..	..	..	92		91
Low & middle income	3.4	2.7	60		60	..	..	..	61		450
East Asia & Pacific	2.5	2.0	16		79	..	89	..	87		117
Europe & Central Asia	2.3	1.6	29		..	..	..	..	94		58
Latin America & Carib.	3.2	2.4	77		..	..	95	..	87		194
Middle East & N. Africa	4.8	3.0	32		59	..	..	..	74		183
South Asia	4.1	3.1	76		46	77	..	30	37		564
Sub-Saharan Africa	6.2	5.3	132		23	61	70	..	45		921
High income	1.8	1.7	24		..	..	..	..	..		14
Europe EMU	1.5	1.5	9		..	..	..	..	..		10

a. Data are for the most recent year available. b. Data are for 2006.

About the data

Reproductive health is a state of physical and mental well-being in relation to the reproductive system and its functions and processes. Means of achieving reproductive health include education and services during pregnancy and childbirth, provision of safe and effective contraception, and prevention and treatment of sexually transmitted diseases. Complications of pregnancy and childbirth are the leading cause of death and disability among women of reproductive age in developing countries. Reproductive health services will need to expand rapidly over the next two decades, when the number of women and men of reproductive age is projected to increase by about 500 million.

Total and adolescent fertility rates are based on data on registered live births from vital registration systems or, in the absence of such systems, from censuses or sample surveys. As long as the surveys are fairly recent, the estimated rates are generally considered reliable measures of fertility in the recent past. Where no empirical information on age-specific fertility rates is available, a model is used to estimate the share of births to adolescents. For countries without vital registration systems, fertility rates are generally based on extrapolations from trends observed in censuses or surveys from earlier years.

An increasing number of couples in the developing world want to limit or postpone childbearing but are not using effective contraceptive methods. These couples have an unmet need for contraception, shown in the table as the percentage of married women of reproductive age who do not want to become pregnant but are not using contraception (Bulatao 1998). Information on this indicator is collected through surveys and excludes women not exposed to the risk of unintended pregnancy because of menopause, infertility, or postpartum anovulation. Common reasons for not using contraception are lack of knowledge about contraceptive methods and concerns about possible health side-effects.

Contraceptive prevalence reflects all methods—ineffective traditional methods as well as highly effective modern methods. Contraceptive prevalence rates are obtained mainly from household surveys, including Demographic and Health Surveys, Multiple Indicator Cluster Surveys, and contraceptive prevalence surveys (see *Primary data documentation* for the most recent survey year). Unmarried women are often excluded from such surveys, which may bias the estimates.

Neonatal tetanus is an important cause of infant mortality in some developing countries. It can be prevented through immunization of the mother during pregnancy. Recommended doses for full protection are generally two tetanus shots during the first pregnancy and one booster shot during each subsequent pregnancy, with five doses considered adequate for lifetime protection. Information on tetanus shots during pregnancy is collected through surveys in which pregnant respondents are asked to show antenatal cards on which tetanus shots have been recorded. Because not all women have antenatal cards, respondents are also asked about their receipt of these injections. Poor recall may result in a downward bias in estimates of the share of births protected. But in settings where receiving injections is common, respondents may erroneously report having received tetanus shots.

The share of births attended by skilled health staff is an indicator of a health system's ability to provide adequate care for pregnant women. Good antenatal and postnatal care improve maternal health and reduce maternal and infant mortality. But data may not reflect such improvements because health information systems are often weak, maternal deaths are underreported, and rates of maternal mortality are difficult to measure.

Maternal mortality ratios are generally of unknown reliability, as are many other cause-specific mortality indicators. Household surveys such as the Demographic and Health Surveys attempt to measure maternal mortality by asking respondents about survivorship of sisters. The main disadvantage of this method is that the estimates of maternal mortality that it produces pertain to 12 years or so before the survey, making them unsuitable for monitoring recent changes or observing the impact of interventions. In addition, measurement of maternal mortality is subject to many types of errors. Even in high-income countries with vital registration systems, misclassification of maternal deaths has been found to lead to serious underestimation.

The maternal mortality ratios shown in the table as national estimates are based on national surveys, vital registration records, and surveillance data or are derived from community and hospital records. The ratios shown as modeled estimates are based on an exercise by the World Health Organization (WHO), United Nations Children's Fund (UNICEF), and the United Nations Population Fund (UNFPA). For countries with national data, reported maternal mortality was adjusted by a factor of under- or over-enumeration and misclassification. For countries with no national data, maternal mortality was estimated with a regression model using information on fertility, birth attendants, and GDP. Neither set of ratios can be assumed to provide an accurate estimate of maternal mortality for any of the countries in the table.

Definitions

• **Total fertility rate** is the number of children that would be born to a woman if she were to live to the end of her childbearing years and bear children in accordance with current age-specific fertility rates. • **Adolescent fertility rate** is the number of births per 1,000 women ages 15–19. • **Unmet need for contraception** is the percentage of fertile, married women of reproductive age who do not want to become pregnant and are not using contraception. • **Contraceptive prevalence rate** is the percentage of women married or in-union ages 15–49 who are practicing, or whose sexual partners are practicing, any form of contraception. • **Tetanus vaccinations** refer to the percentage of pregnant women who receive two tetanus toxoid injections during their first pregnancy and one booster shot during each subsequent pregnancy, with five doses considered adequate for a lifetime. • **Pregnant women receiving prenatal care** are the percentage of women attended at least once during pregnancy by skilled health personnel for reasons related to pregnancy. • **Births attended by skilled health staff** are the percentage of deliveries attended by personnel trained to give the necessary supervision, care, and advice to women during pregnancy, labor, and the postpartum period; to conduct deliveries on their own; and to care for newborns. • **Maternal mortality ratio** is the number of women who die from pregnancy-related causes during pregnancy and childbirth, per 100,000 live births.

Data sources

Data on fertility rates are compiled and estimated by the World Bank's Development Data Group. Important inputs come from the following sources: the United Nations Population Division's *World Population Prospects: The 2004 Revision;* census reports and other statistical publications from national statistical offices; and household surveys such as Demographic and Health Surveys. Data on women with unmet need for contraception and contraceptive prevalence rates are from household surveys, including Demographic and Health Surveys by Macro International and Multiple Indicator Cluster Surveys by UNICEF. Data on tetanus vaccinations, pregnant women receiving prenatal care, births attended by skilled health staff, and national estimates of maternal mortality ratios are from UNICEF's *State of the World's Children 2007* and Childinfo, and Demographic and Health Surveys by Macro International. Modeled estimates for maternal mortality ratios are from Carla AbouZahr and Tessa Wardlaw's "Maternal Mortality in 2000: Estimates Developed by WHO, UNICEF, and UNFPA" (2003).

2.17 Nutrition

	Prevalence of undernourishment		Prevalence of child malnutrition		Prevalence of overweight children	Low-birthweight babies	Exclusive breastfeeding	Consumption of iodized salt	Vitamin A supplementation
	% of population		% of children under age 5		% of children under age 5	% of births	% of children under 6 months	% of households	% of children 6–59 months
			Underweight	Stunting					
	1990–92	2002–04[a]	2000–05[b]	2000–05[b]	2000–05[b]	2000–05[b]	2000–05[b]	2000–05[b]	2004
Afghanistan	..	..	39.3	53.7	..	..	..	28	96
Albania	5[c]	6	14.0	35.1	22.4	5	6	62	..
Algeria	5	4	10.4	19.1	10.1	7	13	69	..
Angola	58	35	30.5	45.2	..	12	11	35	77
Argentina	<2.5	3	3.8[d]	4.2[d]	..	8	..	..	..
Armenia	52[c]	24	2.6	12.9	10.4	7	33	97	..
Australia	<2.5	<2.5	..	..	..	7	..	..	..
Austria	<2.5	<2.5	..	..	..	7	..	..	..
Azerbaijan	34[c]	7	6.8	13.3	2.6	12	7	26	14
Bangladesh	35	30	47.5	43.0	0.8	36	36	70	83
Belarus	<2.5[c]	4	..	..	..	5	..	55	..
Belgium	<2.5	<2.5	..	..	..	..	..	..	..
Benin	20	12	30.0	30.7	1.8	16	38	72	94
Bolivia	28	23	7.6	26.7	5.6	7	54	90	42
Bosnia and Herzegovina	9[c]	9	4.1	9.7	13.2	4	..	62	..
Botswana	23	32	12.5	23.1	6.9	10	34	66	62[e]
Brazil	12	7	..	..	..	8	..	88	..
Bulgaria	8[c]	8	..	..	..	10	..	98	..
Burkina Faso	21	15	37.7	38.7	2.9	19	19	45	95
Burundi	48	66	45.1	56.8	0.7	16	62	96	94
Cambodia	43	33	36.0	44.6	2.0	11	12	14	72
Cameroon	33	26	18.1	31.7	5.2	13	24	88	81
Canada	<2.5	<2.5	..	..	..	6	..	..	..
Central African Republic	50	44	24.3	38.9	..	14	17	86	79
Chad	58	35	36.7	40.9	1.5	22	2	56	84
Chile	8	4	0.7	1.4	8.1	6	63	..	..
China	16	12	7.8	14.2	2.6	4	51	93	..
Hong Kong, China	..	..	..	..	..	5	..	..	..
Colombia	17	13	7.0	12.0	3.7	6	47	..	..
Congo, Dem. Rep.	31	74	31.0	38.1	3.9	12	24	72	81
Congo, Rep.	54	33	..	..	..	..	19	..	94
Costa Rica	6	5	..	..	..	7	..	..	60
Côte d'Ivoire	18	13	17.2	..	..	17	5	84	..
Croatia	16[c]	7	..	..	..	6	..	..	..
Cuba	7	<2.5	3.9	4.6	..	5	41	88	..
Czech Republic	<2.5[c]	<2.5	..	..	..	7	..	..	..
Denmark	<2.5	<2.5	..	..	..	5	..	..	..
Dominican Republic	27	29	5.3	8.9	6.5	11	10	18	..
Ecuador	8	6	11.6	..	..	..	..	..	..
Egypt, Arab Rep.	4	4	8.6	15.6	6.7	12	38	78	..
El Salvador	12	11	10.3	18.9	3.6	7	24	62	..
Eritrea	70[c]	75	39.6	37.6	0.7	14	52	68	50
Estonia	9[c]	<2.5	..	..	..	4	..	..	..
Ethiopia	69[c]	46	38.4	46.5	1.2	14	49	28	52
Finland	<2.5	<2.5	..	..	..	4	..	..	..
France	<2.5	<2.5	..	..	..	..	..	..	..
Gabon	10	5	11.9	20.7	3.7	14	6	36	..
Gambia, The	22	29	17.2	19.2	1.5	17	26	8	27
Georgia	44[c]	9	..	..	..	7	..	68	..
Germany	<2.5	<2.5	..	..	..	..	..	..	..
Ghana	37	11	22.1	29.9	2.9	16	53	28	95
Greece	<2.5	<2.5	..	..	..	..	..	..	..
Guatemala	16	22	22.7	49.3	5.4	12	51	67	18[e]
Guinea	39	24	32.7	..	..	16	27	68	95
Guinea-Bissau	24	39	25.0	30.5	3.3	22	37	2	64
Haiti	65	46	17.2	22.7	2.0	21	24	11	..

	Prevalence of undernourishment		Prevalence of child malnutrition		Prevalence of overweight children	Low-birthweight babies	Exclusive breastfeeding	Consumption of iodized salt	Vitamin A supplementation
	% of population		% of children under age 5		% of children under age 5	% of births	% of children under 6 months	% of households	% of children 6–59 months
			Underweight	Stunting					
	1990–92	**2002–04[a]**	**2000–05[b]**	**2000–05[b]**	**2000–05[b]**	**2000–05[b]**	**2000–05[b]**	**2000–05[b]**	**2004**
Honduras	23	23	16.6	29.2	2.2	14	35	..	40
Hungary	<2.5[c]	<2.5	..	..	..	9	..	..	..
India	25	20	..	..	..	..	37[f]	57	51[e]
Indonesia	9	6	28.2	..	..	9	40	73	73[e]
Iran, Islamic Rep.	4	4	..	..	..	..	44	..	..
Iraq	..	..	15.9	22.1	3.0	15	12	40	..
Ireland	<2.5	<2.5	..	..	..	..	..	..	..
Israel	<2.5	<2.5	..	..	..	8	..	..	..
Italy	<2.5	<2.5	..	..	..	..	..	..	..
Jamaica	14	9	3.6	..	..	10	..	..	..
Japan	<2.5	<2.5	..	..	..	8	..	..	..
Jordan	4	6	4.4	8.5	3.5	12	27	88	..
Kazakhstan	<2.5[c]	6	..	..	..	..	..	83	..
Kenya	39	31	19.9	30.3	3.7	10	13	91	63
Korea, Dem. Rep.	18	33	23.9	38.6	0.6	7	65	40	95
Korea, Rep.	<2.5	<2.5	..	..	..	4	..	..	..
Kuwait	24	5	..	..	..	..	..	..	..
Kyrgyz Republic	21[c]	4	6.7	..	..	..	..	42	95
Lao PDR	29	19	40.4	42.4	1.2	14	23	75	48
Latvia	3[c]	3	..	..	..	5	..	..	..
Lebanon	<2.5	3	3.9	11.0	..	6	27[f]	92	..
Lesotho	17	13	18.0	46.1	12.1	13	36	91	71
Liberia	34	50	26.5	39.5	2.3	..	35	..	95
Libya	<2.5	<2.5	..	..	..	..	..	..	..
Lithuania	4[c]	<2.5	..	..	..	4	..	..	..
Macedonia, FYR	15[c]	5	..	..	..	6	99	94	..
Madagascar	35	38	41.9	47.7	..	17	67	75	89
Malawi	50	35	21.9	49.0	4.3	16	53	49	57
Malaysia	3	3	10.6	..	..	9	..	..	..
Mali	29	29	33.2	38.2	1.5	23	25	74	97
Mauritania	15	10	31.8	34.5	..	..	20	2	95
Mauritius	6	5	..	..	..	14	21[f]	..	..
Mexico	5	5	..	..	..	8	..	91	..
Moldova	5[c]	11	4.3	8.4	..	5	46	59	..
Mongolia	34	27	12.7	24.6	..	7	51	75	93
Morocco	6	6	10.2	18.1	9.2	15	31	59	..
Mozambique	66	44	23.7	41.0	3.0	15	30	54	26
Myanmar	10	5	31.8	32.2	1.6	15	15[f]	60	96
Namibia	34	24	24.0	23.6	2.2	14	19	63	..
Nepal	20	17	45.0[g]	43.0[g]	0.2	21	68[g]	63	97
Netherlands	<2.5	<2.5	..	..	..	..	..	..	..
New Zealand	<2.5	<2.5	..	..	..	6	..	..	..
Nicaragua	30	27	9.6	20.2	4.7	12	31	97	98
Niger	41	32	40.1	39.7	0.8	13	1	15	..
Nigeria	13	9	28.7	38.3	3.6	14	17	97	85
Norway	<2.5	<2.5	..	..	..	5	..	..	..
Oman	..	..	..	..	..	8	..	..	95
Pakistan	24	24	37.8	36.8	2.1	..	..	17	95
Panama	21	23	..	..	..	10	..	..	..
Papua New Guinea	..	..	..	..	..	..	..	..	32
Paraguay	18	15	4.6	..	..	9	22	88	..
Peru	42	12	7.1	25.4	7.6	11	64	91	..
Philippines	26	18	27.6	..	..	20	34	56	85
Poland	<2.5[c]	<2.5	..	..	..	6	..	..	..
Portugal	<2.5	<2.5	..	..	..	8	..	..	..
Puerto Rico	..	..	..	..	..	..	..	..	..

2.17 Nutrition

	Prevalence of undernourishment		Prevalence of child malnutrition		Prevalence of overweight children	Low-birthweight babies	Exclusive breastfeeding	Consumption of iodized salt	Vitamin A supplementation
	% of population		% of children under age 5		% of children under age 5	% of births	% of children under 6 months	% of households	% of children 6–59 months
	1990–92	2002–04[a]	Underweight 2000–05[b]	Stunting 2000–05[b]	2000–05[b]	2000–05[b]	2000–05[b]	2000–05[b]	2004
Romania	<2.5[c]	<2.5	3.2	10.1	5.5	8	16	53	..
Russian Federation	4[c]	3	5.5	10.6	..	6	..	35	..
Rwanda	43	33	22.5	45.3	4.0	9	88	90	95
Saudi Arabia	4	4	..	..	..	..	..	..	..
Senegal	23	20	22.7	25.4	2.2	18	34	41	95
Serbia and Montenegro	5[c]	9	1.9	5.1	..	4	11[f]	73	..
Sierra Leone	46	51	27.2	33.8	..	23	4	23	95
Singapore	..	..	3.4	2.2	2.2	8	..	..	..
Slovak Republic	4[c]	7	..	..	..	7	..	..	..
Slovenia	3[c]	3	..	..	..	6	..	..	..
Somalia	..	..	33.0[g]	23.3	..	..	..	..	6
South Africa	<2.5	<2.5	..	..	..	..	7	..	37
Spain	<2.5	<2.5	..	..	..	..	..	..	..
Sri Lanka	28	22	29.4	13.5	..	22	53	94	57[e]
Sudan	31	26	40.7	43.3	3.4	..	16	1	70
Swaziland	14	22	10.3	30.2	..	9	24	59	86
Sweden	<2.5	<2.5	..	..	..	..	..	..	..
Switzerland	<2.5	<2.5	..	..	..	..	..	..	..
Syrian Arab Republic	5	4	6.9	18.8	..	6	81[f]	79	..
Tajikistan	22[c]	56	..	36.2	..	15	50	28	98
Tanzania	37	44	21.8	37.7	..	10	41	43	94
Thailand	30	22	..	..	..	9	..	63	..
Togo	33	24	..	..	..	18	18	67	95
Trinidad and Tobago	13	10	5.9	3.6	..	23	2	1	..
Tunisia	<2.5	<2.5	4.0	12.3	..	7	47	97	..
Turkey	<2.5	3	3.9	..	..	..	21	64	..
Turkmenistan	12[c]	7	12.0	22.3	..	6	13	100	..
Uganda	24	19	22.9	39.1	2.6	12	63	95	68
Ukraine	<2.5[c]	<2.5	1.0	2.7	20.1	5	22	32	..
United Arab Emirates	4	3	..	..	..	..	..	..	..
United Kingdom	<2.5	<2.5	..	..	..	8	..	..	..
United States	<2.5	<2.5	1.6	1.1	5.6	8	..	..	..
Uruguay	7	<2.5	..	..	..	8	..	..	..
Uzbekistan	8[c]	25	7.9	21.1	..	7	19	57	86
Venezuela, RB	11	18	4.4	12.8	3.2	9	..	..	..
Vietnam	31	16	28.4	36.5	2.7	9	15	83	95[e]
West Bank and Gaza	..	16	4.9	9.9	..	9	29[f]	64	..
Yemen, Rep.	34	38	45.6	53.1	..	..	12	30	20
Zambia	48	46	23.0	46.8	3.0	12	40	77	50
Zimbabwe	45	47	..	..	..	..	..	..	20
World	**17 w**	**14 w**	**.. w**	**.. w**		**11 w**	**37 w**	**69 w**	**.. w**
Low income	27	24	..	..		..	33	56	68
Middle income	14	10	11.5	15.6		8	42	80	..
Lower middle income	16	11	12.5	16.4		8	44	83	..
Upper middle income	..	4	..	..		8	..	..	..
Low & middle income	20	16	21.7	..		11	37	69	..
East Asia & Pacific	17	12	14.9	17.7		7	44	85	..
Europe & Central Asia	6[c]	6	4.9	..		7	..	49	..
Latin America & Carib.	13	10	..	..		9	..	84	..
Middle East & N. Africa	6	7	14.6	22.2		11	34	66	..
South Asia	26	21	..	..		..	37	54	62
Sub-Saharan Africa	29	30	29.6	39.2		14	29	63	73
High income	3	3	..	..		..	..	..	..
Europe EMU	3	3	..	..		..	..	..	..

a. Preliminary data. b. Data are for the most recent year available. c. Data are for 1993–95. d. Data are for 2005–06. e. Country's vitamin A supplementation programs do not target children all the way up to 59 months of age. f. Refers to exclusive breastfeeding of children under four months. g. Data are for 2006.

About the data

Data on undernourishment are produced by the Food and Agriculture Organization (FAO) of the United Nations based on the calories available from local food production, trade, and stocks; the number of calories needed by different age and gender groups; the proportion of the population represented by each age group; and a coefficient of distribution to take account of inequality in access to food (FAO, *State of Food Insecurity in the World 2000*). From a policy and program standpoint, however, this measure has its limits. First, food insecurity exists even where food availability is not a problem because of inadequate access of poor households to food. Second, food insecurity is an individual or household phenomenon, and the average food available to each person, even corrected for possible effects of low income, is not a good predictor of food insecurity among the population. And third, nutrition security is determined not only by food security but also by the quality of care of mothers and children and the quality of the household's health environment (Smith and Haddad 2000).

Estimates of child malnutrition, based on weight for age (underweight) and height for age (stunting), are from national survey data. The proportion of children who are underweight is the most common indicator of malnutrition. Being underweight, even mildly, increases the risk of death and inhibits cognitive development in children. Moreover, it perpetuates the problem from one generation to the next, as malnourished women are more likely to have low-birthweight babies. Height for age reflects linear growth achieved pre- and postnatally, and a deficit indicates long-term, cumulative effects of inadequacies of health, diet, or care. It is often argued that stunting is a proxy for multifaceted deprivation and is a better indicator of long-term changes in malnutrition.

Estimates of children who are overweight are also from national survey data. Overweight in children has become a growing concern in developing countries. Researchers show an association between obesity in childhood and a high prevalence of diabetes, respiratory disease, high blood pressure, and psychosocial and orthopedic disorders (de Onis and Blössner 2000). The survey data were analyzed in a standardized way by the World Health Organization (WHO) to allow comparisons across countries.

New international child growth standards for infants and young children, called the Child Growth Standards, were released in 2006 by the WHO. The new standards confirm that children born anywhere in the world, raised in healthy environments, and following recommended feeding practice have the potential to develop to within the same range of height and weight. Naturally, there are individual differences among children, but the differences in children's growth to age five are influenced more by nutrition, feeding practices, environment, and healthcare than by genetics or ethnicity. The new standards are the result of a community-based, multicountry project involving more than 8,000 children from Brazil, Ghana, India, Norway, Oman, and the United States. The children were selected based on an optimal environment for growth, including breastfeeding, good healthcare, and mothers who did not smoke. Previously, the U.S. National Center for Health Statistics–WHO growth reference has been used to chart children's growth. This reference was based on data from a limited sample of a random mix of breastfed and artificially fed children from the United States only, and the growth reference describes only how children grow in a particular region and time. Thus it does not provide a sound basis for evaluation against international standards and norms.

Adoption of the new standards will have important implications for monitoring children's growth. A study based on the new standards shows that the underweight rates increased during the first six months and decreased thereafter and that stunting and overweight rates increased for all age groups (birth to five years). Differences are particularly important during infancy, likely due to the inclusion of only breast-fed infants in the new standards (de Onis and others 2006).

The new standards are expected to be widely used as a tool for monitoring the nutritional status of communities and alerting practitioners and policymakers to unhealthy trends in the population. They are also expected to play a key role in measuring and monitoring health targets for the Millennium Development Goals. Currently, national surveys are being reanalyzed with the new standards to update the global database, but the updated data are not yet available. The data on malnutrition and overweight presented in the table are still based on the old standard.

Low birthweight, which is associated with maternal malnutrition, raises the risk of infant mortality and stunts growth in infancy and childhood. There is also emerging evidence that low-birthweight babies are more prone to noncommunicable diseases such as diabetes and cardiovascular diseases. Estimates of low-birthweight infants are drawn mostly from hospital records and household surveys. Many births in developing countries take place at home, and these births are seldom recorded. A hospital birth may indicate higher income and therefore better nutrition, or it could indicate a higher-risk birth, possibly skewing the data on birthweights downward. The data should therefore be treated with caution.

It is estimated that improved breastfeeding practice can save some 1.3 million children a year. Breast milk alone contains all the nutrients, antibodies, hormones, and antioxidants an infant needs to thrive. It protects babies from diarrhea and acute respiratory infections, stimulates their immune systems and response to vaccination, and according to some studies confers cognitive benefits as well. The data on breastfeeding are derived from national surveys.

Iodine deficiency is the single most important cause of preventable mental retardation, and it contributes significantly to the risk of stillbirth and miscarriage. Iodized salt is the best source of iodine, and a global campaign to iodize edible salt is significantly reducing the risks (UNICEF, *State of the World's Children 1999*).

Vitamin A is essential for the functioning of the immune system. A child deficient in vitamin A faces a 23 percent greater risk of dying from a range of childhood ailments such as measles, malaria, and diarrhea. Improving the vitamin A status of pregnant women helps reduce anemia, improves their resistance to infection, and may reduce their risk of dying during pregnancy and childbirth. Giving vitamin A to new mothers who are breastfeeding helps to protect their children during the first months of life. Food fortification with vitamin A is being introduced in many developing countries.

Definitions

• **Prevalence of undernourishment** is the percentage of the population that is undernourished—whose dietary energy consumption is continuously below a minimum dietary energy requirement for maintaining a healthy life and carrying out light physical activity. • **Prevalence of child malnutrition** is the percentage of children under age five whose weight for age (underweight) or height for age (stunting) is more than two standard deviations below the median for the international reference population ages 0–59 months. For children up to two years old height is measured by recumbent length. For older children height is measured by stature while standing. The new Child Growth Standards were released by the WHO in 2006, but the data using these standards are not yet available • **Prevalence of overweight children** is the percentage of children under age five whose weight for height is more than two standard deviations above the median for the international reference population of the corresponding age, established by the U.S. National Center for Health Statistics and the WHO. The new Child Growth Standards were released by WHO in 2006, but the data using these standards are not yet available. • **Low-birthweight babies** are the percentage of newborns weighing less than 2,500 grams, with the measurement taken within the first hours of life, before significant postnatal weight loss has occurred. • **Exclusive breastfeeding** refers to the percentage of children less than six months old who are fed breast milk alone (no other liquids) in the past 24 hours. • **Consumption of iodized salt** refers to the percentage of households that use edible salt fortified with iodine. • **Vitamin A supplementation** refers to the percentage of children ages 6–59 months old who received at least one high-dose vitamin A capsule in the previous six months.

Data sources

Data on undernourishment are from www.fao.org/faostat/foodsecurity/index_en.htm. Data on malnutrition and overweight are from WHO's Global Database on Child Growth and Malnutrition. Data on low-birthweight babies, breastfeeding, iodized salt consumption, and vitamin A supplementation are from the WHO's *World Health Report 2006* and the United Nations Children's Fund's *State of the World's Children 2007*.

2.18 Health risk factors and public health challenges

	Prevalence of smoking		Incidence of tuberculosis	Prevalence of diabetes	Mortality caused by road traffic injury	Prevalence of HIV				Cause of death		
	% of adults									% of total deaths		
	Male	Female	per 100,000 people	% of population ages 20–79	per 100,000 people	Total % of population ages 15–49		Female % of population with HIV		Communicable diseases and maternal, perinatal, and nutrition conditions	Non-communicable diseases	Injuries
	2000–05[a]	2000–05[a]	2005	2007	1998–2003[a]	2003	2005	2003	2005	2002	2002	2002
Afghanistan	..	..	168	9.7	..	<0.1	<0.1	..	..	65	29	6
Albania	60	18	20	4.5	11.1	..	..	..	..	8	83	9
Algeria	32	0[b]	55	8.4	..	0.1	0.1	20.6	21.6	33	54	13
Angola	..	..	269	3.3	..	3.7	3.7	59.3	60.7	75	17	8
Argentina	32	25	41	5.6	..	0.6	0.6	26.7	27.7	13	80	7
Armenia	62	2	71	7.7	5.6	0.1	0.1	..	..	5	90	5
Australia	19	16	6	5.0	8.2	0.1	0.1	..	..	4	89	6
Austria	..	..	11	7.9	11.5	0.3	0.3	19.2	19.2	3	92	6
Azerbaijan	..	1	76	7.3	6.9	<0.1	<0.1	..	..	17	79	4
Bangladesh	55	27	227	5.3	..	<0.1	<0.1	..	12.7	46	44	10
Belarus	53	7	62	7.6	14.3	0.3	0.3	24.4	25.5	3	85	12
Belgium	30	25	13	5.2	13.1	0.2	0.3	45.5	38.6	7	88	6
Benin	..	..	88	4.4	..	2.0	1.8	59.3	58.4	69	23	7
Bolivia	..	..	211	5.8	..	0.1	0.1	27.0	27.9	38	54	8
Bosnia and Herzegovina	49	30	52	7.0	..	..	0.1	..	..	3	92	5
Botswana	..	..	654	5.2	..	24.0	24.1	56.0	53.8	87	10	2
Brazil	22	14	60	6.2	..	0.5	0.5	34.5	36.1	19	70	11
Bulgaria	44	23	39	7.6	10.2	..	0.1	..	..	3	94	4
Burkina Faso	..	..	223	3.7	..	1.8[c]	2.0	59.2	57.1	78	16	6
Burundi	..	..	334	1.7	..	3.3	3.3	60.8	60.8	71	17	12
Cambodia	..	..	506	5.0	..	2.0	1.6	46.4	45.4	61	34	5
Cameroon	..	..	174	3.7	..	5.5	5.5[d]	62.2	61.7	68	26	7
Canada	22	17	5	7.4	8.7	0.3	0.3	12.2	16.3	5	89	6
Central African Republic	..	..	314	4.4	..	10.8	10.7	59.1	56.5	73	21	6
Chad	..	..	272	3.6	..	3.4	3.5	54.7	56.3	74	19	6
Chile	48	37	15	5.6	10.7	0.3	0.3	26.4	27.1	12	79	9
China	67	4	100	4.1	19.0	0.1[e]	0.1[e]	24.5[e]	27.7[e]	12	77	11
Hong Kong, China	22	4	75	8.2	..	..	..	..	..	..	..	..
Colombia	..	..	45	5.0	24.2	0.5	0.6	26.4	28.1	16	60	24
Congo, Dem. Rep.	..	..	356	3.0	..	3.2	3.2	59.0	58.4	73	17	11
Congo, Rep.	..	..	367	5.0	..	5.4	5.3	58.6	61.0	67	23	9
Costa Rica	29	10	14	9.3	20.1	0.3	0.3	27.0	27.4	12	77	11
Côte d'Ivoire	..	..	382	4.6	..	7.0	7.1	57.8	58.8	67	23	9
Croatia	34	27	41	7.1	11.4	..	0.1	..	..	3	91	5
Cuba	..	..	9	9.3	13.9	0.1	0.1	54.8	55.3	11	80	9
Czech Republic	31	20	10	7.6	14.2	<0.1	<0.1	..	..	3	91	6
Denmark	31	25	7	5.5	8.0	0.2	0.2	24.0	23.6	4	90	6
Dominican Republic	16	11	91	8.7	41.1	1.0[f]	1.1	49.2	50.0	35	58	8
Ecuador	..	..	131	5.7	16.9	0.3	0.3	52.4	54.5	24	63	13
Egypt, Arab Rep.	40	18	25	11.0	7.5	<0.1	<0.1	..	..	18	78	4
El Salvador	42	15	51	9.0	41.7	0.9	0.9	27.1	28.3	29	57	14
Eritrea	..	..	282	2.3	..	2.4	2.4	59.2	58.5	70	22	7
Estonia	45	18	43	7.6	14.8	1.1	1.3	22.1	24.0	3	84	12
Ethiopia	6	0[b]	344	2.3	..	..	..	..	..	71	23	6
Finland	26	19	6	5.9	7.3	0.1	0.1	..	..	6	86	8
France	30	21	13	5.9	10.2	0.4	0.4	33.3	34.6	6	85	8
Gabon	..	..	308	4.9	..	7.7	7.9	59.6	58.9	53	39	7
Gambia, The	..	..	242	4.1	..	2.2	2.4	58.8	57.9	59	32	8
Georgia	53	6	83	7.4	6.2	0.1	0.2	..	..	4	93	2
Germany	37	28	7	7.9	8.0	0.1	0.1	29.5	30.6	4	92	4
Ghana	7	1	205	4.2	..	2.2[c]	2.3	60.7	60.0	59	33	8
Greece	47	29	17	5.9	19.3	0.2	0.2	20.7	21.5	4	92	4
Guatemala	21	2	78	8.6	..	0.9	0.9	26.4	27.1	50	40	10
Guinea	..	..	236	4.1	..	1.6	1.5	68.9	67.9	68	24	9
Guinea-Bissau	..	..	206	3.8	..	3.8	3.8	59.3	58.6	75	19	6
Haiti	15	6	305	9.0	..	3.8	3.8	52.9	53.3	69	29	2

Health risk factors and public health challenges 2.18

	Prevalence of smoking		Incidence of tuberculosis	Prevalence of diabetes	Mortality caused by road traffic injury	Prevalence of HIV				Cause of death		
										% of total deaths		
	% of adults		per 100,000 people	% of population ages 20–79	per 100,000 people	Total % of population ages 15–49		Female % of population with HIV		Communicable diseases and maternal, perinatal, and nutrition conditions	Non-communicable diseases	Injuries
	Male 2000–05[a]	Female 2000–05[a]	2005	2007	1998–2003[a]	2003	2005	2003	2005	2002	2002	2002
Honduras	..	..	78	9.1	..	1.5	1.5	25.0	26.2	32	59	9
Hungary	41	28	22	7.6	13.1	0.1	0.1	..	..	2	91	7
India	47	17	168	6.7	..	0.9	0.9	28.8	28.6	41	49	10
Indonesia	58	3	239	2.3	..	0.1	0.1	13.6	17.1	29	61	10
Iran, Islamic Rep.	22	2	23	7.8	..	0.1	0.2	13.0	16.7	12	70	18
Iraq	..	..	56	10.0	8.4	..	..	..	..	43	43	13
Ireland	28	26	12	5.1	10.1	0.2	0.2	32.0	36.0	10	85	5
Israel	32	18	8	6.9	5.9	..	..	..	..	6	88	6
Italy	31	17	7	5.8	10.5	0.5	0.5	33.6	33.3	4	92	4
Jamaica	..	..	7	10.3	..	1.5	1.5	27.1	27.6	14	84	2
Japan	47	15	28	4.9	7.0	<0.1	<0.1	56.5	58.2	12	81	8
Jordan	51	8	5	9.8	..	..	..	..	..	18	65	16
Kazakhstan	65	9	144	5.6	..	0.1	0.1	56.0	56.7	8	79	13
Kenya	21	1	641	3.3	..	6.7[c]	6.1	64.2	61.7	72	22	6
Korea, Dem. Rep.	..	..	178	5.2	..	..	..	..	..	32	61	7
Korea, Rep.	..	..	96	7.8	15.1	<0.1	<0.1	59.1	56.9	6	83	12
Kuwait	..	..	24	14.4	23.7	..	..	..	..	13	72	15
Kyrgyz Republic	51	5	121	5.1	12.9	<0.1	<0.1	..	..	17	74	9
Lao PDR	59	13	155	3.1	..	0.1	0.1	..	..	55	36	9
Latvia	51	19	63	7.6	22.7	0.6	0.8	20.3	22.0	4	86	11
Lebanon	42	31	11	7.7	..	0.1	0.1	..	..	10	77	13
Lesotho	..	..	696	3.8	..	23.7	23.2	56.0	60.0	81	16	3
Liberia	..	..	301	4.6	..	..	..	..	..	76	15	10
Libya	..	..	18	4.4	..	..	..	..	..	17	73	10
Lithuania	44	13	63	7.6	19.3	0.1	0.2	..	..	2	85	13
Macedonia, FYR	..	..	30	7.1	5.1	<0.1	<0.1	..	..	3	89	8
Madagascar	..	..	234	3.0	..	0.5	0.5	28.2	27.7	65	27	8
Malawi	21	5	409	2.1	..	14.2	14.1	59.3	58.8	79	17	4
Malaysia	43	2	102	10.7	..	0.4	0.5	25.0	25.4	20	71	9
Mali	..	..	278	4.1	..	1.8[g]	1.7	57.3	60.0	78	16	6
Mauritania	..	..	298	4.6	..	0.7	0.7	59.2	57.3	65	27	8
Mauritius	32	1	62	11.1	14.7	0.2	0.6	..	..	7	86	6
Mexico	13	5	23	10.6	11.8	0.3	0.3	20.0	23.3	16	72	11
Moldova	34	2	138	7.6	14.1	0.9	1.1	56.5	57.1	5	86	9
Mongolia	68	26	191	1.9	..	<0.1	<0.1	..	..	23	66	11
Morocco	29	0[b]	89	8.1	..	0.1	0.1	18.2	21.1	23	69	8
Mozambique	..	..	447	3.7	..	16.0	16.1	57.5	60.0	83	14	2
Myanmar	36	12	171	3.2	..	1.4	1.3	31.6	31.4	45	47	9
Namibia	23	10	697	4.2	..	19.5	19.6	60.0	61.9	71	24	5
Nepal	49	24	180	4.2	..	0.5	0.5	20.3	21.6	49	42	9
Netherlands	36	28	7	5.2	6.4	0.2	0.2	33.8	34.7	8	89	4
New Zealand	24	22	9	6.4	11.5	0.1	0.1	..	..	3	91	6
Nicaragua	..	5	58	10.1	20.1	0.2	0.2	22.4	23.6	30	58	12
Niger	..	..	164	3.7	..	1.1	1.1	59.7	59.2	80	14	6
Nigeria	..	1	283	4.5	..	3.7	3.9	58.3	61.5	71	22	7
Norway	27	25	5	3.6	6.1	0.1	0.1	..	..	8	87	5
Oman	..	..	11	13.1	..	..	..	..	..	13	75	12
Pakistan	..	..	181	9.6	..	0.1	0.1	13.3	16.7	53	39	8
Panama	..	..	45	9.7	16.4	0.9	0.9	26.0	25.3	21	69	10
Papua New Guinea	..	..	250	2.9	..	1.6	1.8	59.2	59.6	52	38	9
Paraguay	23	7	68	4.8	..	0.4	0.4	27.3	26.9	28	62	10
Peru	..	..	172	6.0	17.6	0.5	0.6	26.8	28.6	32	58	9
Philippines	41	8	291	7.6	..	<0.1	<0.1	20.2	28.3	35	56	9
Poland	40	25	26	7.6	14.8	0.1	0.1	30.0	30.0	3	90	7
Portugal	..	..	33	5.7	14.8	0.4	0.4	3.9	4.1	9	86	4
Puerto Rico	17	10	5	10.7	..	..	..	..	..	..	..	..

2.18 Health risk factors and public health challenges

	Prevalence of smoking		Incidence of tuberculosis	Prevalence of diabetes	Mortality caused by road traffic injury	Prevalence of HIV				Cause of death		
										% of total deaths		
	% of adults		per 100,000 people	% of population ages 20–79	per 100,000 people	Total % of population ages 15–49		Female % of population with HIV		Communicable diseases and maternal, perinatal, and nutrition conditions	Non-communicable diseases	Injuries
	Male 2000–05[a]	Female 2000–05[a]	2005	2007	1998–2003[a]	2003	2005	2003	2005	2002	2002	2002
Romania	32	10	134	7.6	16.8	..	0.1	..	..	5	90	5
Russian Federation	60	16	119	7.6	19.4	0.9	1.1	21.1	22.3	4	81	15
Rwanda	..	..	361	1.5	..	3.8	3.1	52.6	56.9	76	18	6
Saudi Arabia	19	8	41	16.7	..	..	..	..	..	15	69	16
Senegal	..	..	255	4.6	..	0.9	0.9	58.5	58.9	64	26	10
Serbia and Montenegro	48	34	33	7.1	..	0.2	0.2	22.2	20.0	3	93	4
Sierra Leone	..	..	475	4.3	..	1.6	1.6	60.0	60.5	78	14	8
Singapore	24	4	29	10.1	5.2	0.3	0.3	25.5	27.3	12	82	5
Slovak Republic	..	..	17	7.6	11.3	<0.1	<0.1	..	..	4	90	6
Slovenia	28	20	15	7.6	12.1	<0.1	<0.1	..	..	4	87	8
Somalia	..	..	224	2.8	..	0.9	0.9[h]	60.5	57.5	66	23	10
South Africa	23	8	600	4.4	..	15.6[f]	18.8	56.9	58.5	65	28	7
Spain	39	25	27	5.7	12.8	<0.1	<0.1	22.9	22.9	5	90	5
Sri Lanka	23	2	60	8.4	..	0.1	0.1	..	..	13	76	10
Sudan	..	..	228	4.0	..	1.6	1.6	56.7	56.3	45	41	14
Swaziland	11	3	1,262	4.0	..	32.4	33.4	63.2	57.1	84	13	3
Sweden	17	18	6	5.2	5.9	0.2	0.2	31.3	31.3	5	90	5
Switzerland	27	23	7	7.9	7.5	0.4	0.4	36.0	36.9	6	89	5
Syrian Arab Republic	..	..	37	10.6	..	..	..	..	..	17	73	9
Tajikistan	..	..	198	4.9	5.6	<0.1	<0.1	..	..	27	67	6
Tanzania	..	..	342	2.9	..	6.6	7.0[d]	52.3	54.6	77	17	6
Thailand	49	3	142	6.9	..	1.4	1.4	38.6	39.3	31	58	11
Togo	..	..	373	4.1	..	3.2	3.2	58.9	61.0	66	26	8
Trinidad and Tobago	..	..	9	11.5	..	2.6	2.6	56.0	57.7	23	71	6
Tunisia	50	2	24	5.2	..	0.1	0.1	..	22.1	9	80	11
Turkey	49	18	29	7.8	..	..	..	..	..	14	79	6
Turkmenistan	..	..	70	5.2	10.3	..	0.1	..	..	19	73	8
Uganda	25	3	369	2.0	..	6.8	6.4[i]	57.6	57.8	75	18	7
Ukraine	53	11	99	7.6	10.8	1.3	1.4	47.4	48.8	4	87	9
United Arab Emirates	17	1	16	19.5	..	..	..	..	..	12	67	21
United Kingdom	27	25	14	2.9	6.1	..	..	..	..	12	85	3
United States	24	19	5	7.8	14.7	0.6	0.6	25.5	25.0	6	88	6
Uruguay	35	24	28	5.6	10.0	0.4	0.5	55.6	55.8	7	86	7
Uzbekistan	24	1	113	5.1	9.8	0.1	0.2	..	13.2	14	80	7
Venezuela, RB	..	..	42	5.4	23.1	0.6	0.7	27.7	28.2	15	66	18
Vietnam	35	2	175	2.9	..	0.4	0.5[j]	30.5	33.6	24	66	9
West Bank and Gaza	..	..	21	8.4	..	..	..	..	..	..	..	..
Yemen, Rep.	..	..	82	2.9	..	..	..	..	..	48	43	10
Zambia	16	1	600	3.8	..	15.6[k]	17.0	56.3	57.0	86	12	2
Zimbabwe	20	2	601	4.0	..	22.1	20.1	58.1	59.3	83	14	3
World	.. w	.. w	136 w		.. w	0.9 w	1.0 w	30.3 w	31.3 w	32 w	59 w	9 w
Low income	..	15	220		..	1.7	1.7	35.6	34.2	54	37	9
Middle income	..	..	111		..	0.6	0.6	26.1	28.7	18	72	11
Lower middle income	..	..	113		..	0.3	0.3	25.9	28.7	18	71	11
Upper middle income	..	..	104		..	2.2	2.2	27.1	28.6	15	74	11
Low & middle income	..	..	158		..	1.1	1.1	29.8	31.0	36	54	10
East Asia & Pacific	67	4	136		19.0	0.2	0.2	24.3	27.4	19	71	10
Europe & Central Asia	..	..	84		..	0.6	0.7	..	..	6	84	11
Latin America & Carib.	..	..	61		..	0.5	0.6	30.3	32.0	22	67	11
Middle East & N. Africa	..	..	43		..	0.1	0.1	..	..	24	65	11
South Asia	47	18	174		..	0.7	0.7	26.9	25.6	43	47	10
Sub-Saharan Africa	..	..	348		..	6.4	5.8	57.6	58.4	72	21	7
High income	..	..	17		10.9	0.4	0.4	33.1	33.2	7	87	6
Europe EMU	..	..	13		10.0	0.4	0.3	29.3	29.7	5	90	5

a. Data are for the most recent year available. b. Less than 0.5. c. Survey data, 2003. d. Survey data, 2004. e. Includes Hong Kong, China. f. Survey data, 2002. g. Survey data, 2001. h. Survey data, 2006. i. Survey data, 2004–05. j. Survey data, 2005. k. Survey data, 2001/02.

About the data

The limited availability of data on health status is a major constraint in assessing the health situation in developing countries. Surveillance data are lacking for many major public health concerns. Estimates of prevalence and incidence are available for some diseases but are often unreliable and incomplete. National health authorities differ widely in their capacity and willingness to collect or report information. To compensate for the paucity of data and ensure reasonable reliability and international comparability, the World Health Organization (WHO) prepares estimates in accordance with epidemiological models and statistical standards.

Smoking is the most common form of tobacco use in many countries, and the prevalence of smoking is therefore a good measure of the extent of the tobacco epidemic (Corrao and others 2000). While the prevalence of smoking has been declining in some high-income countries, it has been increasing in many developing countries. Tobacco use causes heart and other vascular diseases and cancers of the lung and other organs. Given the long delay between starting to smoke and the onset of disease, the health impact of smoking in developing countries will increase rapidly in the next few decades. Because the data present a one-time estimate, with no information on the intensity or duration of smoking, and because the definition of adult varies across countries, the data should be interpreted with caution.

Tuberculosis is one of the main causes of death from a single infectious agent among adults in developing countries. In high-income countries tuberculosis has reemerged largely as a result of cases among immigrants. The estimates of tuberculosis incidence in the table are based on a new approach in which reported cases are adjusted using the ratio of case notifications to the estimated share of cases detected by panels of 80 epidemiologists convened by the WHO.

Diabetes, an important cause of ill health and a risk factor for other diseases in developed countries, is spreading rapidly in developing countries. While diabetes is most common among the elderly, prevalence rates are rising among younger and productive populations in developing countries. Economic development has led to the greater adoption of Western lifestyles and diet in developing countries, resulting in a substantial increase in diabetes. Without effective prevention and control programs, diabetes will likely continue to increase. Data are estimated based on sample surveys.

Data for mortality caused by road traffic injury are collected by the WHO based on vital registries. There is considerable difference in completeness of the vital registry data. In some countries the vital registry system covers only part of the country. In some, not all deaths are registered. In addition, mortality from different causes is difficult to measure. For countries with incomplete vital registry systems, the WHO has used demographic techniques to estimate deaths.

Adult HIV prevalence rates reflect the rate of HIV infection in each country's population. Low national prevalence rates can be very misleading, however. They often disguise serious epidemics that are initially concentrated in certain localities or among specific population groups and threaten to spill over into the wider population. In many parts of the developing world most new infections occur in young adults, with young women especially vulnerable.

Estimates from recent Demographic and Health Surveys that have collected data on HIV/AIDS differ from those of the Joint United Nations Programme on HIV/AIDS (UNAIDS) and the WHO, which are based on surveillance systems that focus on pregnant women who attend sentinel antenatal clinics. There are reasons to be cautious about comparing the two sets of estimates. Demographic and Health Surveys are household surveys that use a representative sample from the whole population, whereas surveillance data from antenatal clinics are limited to pregnant women. Representative household surveys also frequently provide better coverage of rural populations. However, the fact that some respondents refuse to participate or are absent from the household adds considerable uncertainty to survey-based HIV estimates, because the possible association of absence or refusal with higher HIV prevalence is unknown. UNAIDS and WHO estimates are generally based on surveillance systems that focus on pregnant women who attend sentinel antenatal clinics. UNAIDS and the WHO use a methodology to estimate HIV prevalence for the adult population (ages 15–49) that assumes that prevalence among pregnant women is a good approximation of prevalence among men and women. However, this assumption might not apply to all countries or over time. There are also other potential biases associated with the use of antenatal clinic data, such as differences among women who attend antenatal clinics and those who do not.

The data on cause of death are compiled by WHO, based mainly on data from national vital registry systems, as well as sample registration systems, population laboratories and epidemiological analyses of specific conditions. Data are classified based on the International Statistical Classification of Diseases and Related Health Problems, 10th revision. Cause of death data have been carefully analyzed to take into account incomplete coverage of vital registration and the likely differences in cause of death patterns that would be expected in the uncovered and often poorer subpopulations. Special attention has also been paid to problems of misattribution or miscoding of causes of death in cardiovascular diseases, cancer, injuries, and general ill-defined categories. For further information, consult the original source.

Definitions

• **Prevalence of smoking** is the percentage of men and women who smoke cigarettes. The age range varies, but in most countries is 18 and older or 15 and older. • **Incidence of tuberculosis** is the estimated number of new tuberculosis cases (pulmonary, smear positive, extrapulmonary). • **Prevalence of diabetes** refers to the percentage of people ages 20–79 who have type 1 or type 2 diabetes. • **Mortality caused by road traffic injury** refers to the number of deaths per 100,000 people caused by road traffic injury. • **Prevalence of HIV** is the percentage of people who are infected with HIV. • **Cause of death** refers to the share of all deaths by underlying causes. • **Communicable diseases and maternal, perinatal, and nutrition conditions** include infectious and parasitic diseases, respiratory infections, and nutritional deficiencies such as underweight and stunting. • **Noncommunicable diseases** include cancer, diabetes mellitus, cardiovascular diseases, digestive diseases, skin diseases, musculoskeletal diseases, and congenital anomalies. • **Injuries** include unintentional and intentional injuries.

Data sources

Data on smoking are from J. McCay, M. Erkson, and O. Shafey's *Tobacco Atlas*, 2nd edition (2006). Data on tuberculosis are from the WHO's *Global Tuberculosis Control Report 2007*. Data on diabetes are from the International Diabetes Federation's *Diabetes Atlas*, 3rd edition. Data on mortality caused by road traffic injury are from the WHO and the World Bank's *World Report on Road Traffic Injury Prevention* (2004) and the Organisation for Economic Co-operation and Development. Data on HIV are from UNAIDS and the WHO's *2006 Report on the Global AIDS Epidemic*. Data on cause of death are from the Disease Control Priorities Project's (2006) *Global Burden of Disease and Risk Factors* (www.dcp2.org/pubs/GBD).

2.19 Health gaps by income and gender

	Survey year	Prevalence of child malnutrition		Child immunization rate				Infant mortality rate		Under-five mortality rate	
		Underweight % of children under age 5		% of children ages 12–23 months[a]				per 1,000 live births		per 1,000	
				Measles		DPT					
		Poorest quintile	Richest quintile	Poorest quintile	Richest quintile	Poorest quintile	Richest quintile	Poorest quintile	Richest quintile	Poorest quintile	Richest quintile
Armenia	2000	3	1	68	74[b]	89	84[b]	52	27	61	30
Bangladesh	2004	41	24	60	91	71	91	90	65	121	71
Benin	2001	22	9	57	83	63	89	112	50	198	93
Bolivia	2003	10	1	62	74	64	85	87	32	119	37
Brazil	1996	10	3	78	90	66	82	83	29	99	33
Burkina Faso	2003	26	16	48	71	45	73	97	78	206	144
Cambodia	2000	35	28	44	82	39	75	110	50	155	64
Cameroon	2004	22	5	57	86	55	86	101	52	189	88
Central African Republic	1994–95	25	15	31	80	27	76	132	54	193	98
Chad	2004	27	19	8	38	5	42	109	101	176	187
Colombia	2005	11	3	70	91	73	91	32	14	39	16
Comoros	1996	22	14	51	86	58	92	87	65	129	87[b]
Côte d'Ivoire	1994	21	10	31	79	26	74	117	63	190	97
Dominican Republic	2002	9	1	83	94	46	66	50	20	66	22
Egypt, Arab Rep.	2000	5	2	95	99	94	93	76	30	98	34
Eritrea	1995	27	19	37	92	30	89	74	68	152	104
Ethiopia	2000	32	29	18	52	14	43	93	95	159	147
Gabon	2000	15	7	34	71	18	49	57	36	93	55
Ghana	2003	22	10	74	88	64	87	61	58	128	88
Guatemala	1998–99	26	10	80	91	74	76	58	39	78	39
Guinea	1999	22	13	33	73	30	69	119	70	230	133
Haiti	2000	18	6	43	63	31	58	100	97	164	109
India	1998–99	33	21	28	81	36	85	97	38	141	46
Indonesia	2002–03	..	..	59	85	42	72	61	17	77	22
Jordan	1997	7	3	90	93	98	93	35	23	42	25
Kazakhstan	1999	5	6	74	76[b]	90	82[b]	68	42	82	45
Kenya	2003	22	7	54	88	56	73	96	62	149	91
Kyrgyz Republic	1997	10	7	82	81	82	87	83	46	96	49
Madagascar	1997	29	24	32	79	32	81	119	58	195	101
Malawi	2000	24	11	80	90	79	93	132	86	231	149
Mali	2001	26	13	40	77	28	71	137	90	248	148
Mauritania	2000–01	23	15	42	86	18	61	61	62	98	79
Morocco	2003–04	13	3	83	98	89	98	62	24	78	26
Mozambique	2003	21	7	61	96	52	96	143	71	196	108
Namibia	2000	22	10	76	86	76	83	36	23	55	31
Nepal	2001	40	26	61	83	62	85	86	53	130	68
Nicaragua	2001	13	2	76	94	77	83	50	16	64	19
Niger	1998	30	26	23	66	9	68	131	86	282	184
Nigeria	2003	24	10	16	71	7	61	133	52	257	79
Pakistan	1990–91	33	19	28	75	24	64	89	63	125	74
Paraguay	1990	5	1	48	69	40	69	43	16	57	20
Peru	2000	13	1	81	92	76	93	64	14	93	18
Philippines	2003	..	..	70	89	64	92	42	19	66	21
Rwanda	2000	19	12	84	89	80	89	139	88	246	154
Senegal	1997	..	..	..	..	..	..	85	45	181	70
South Africa	1998	..	..	74	85	64	85	62	17	87	22
Tanzania	2004	20	11	65	91	34	36	88	64	137	93
Togo	1998	23	10	35	63	29	68	84	66	168	97
Turkey	1998	13	3	64	89	45	81	68	30	85	33
Turkmenistan	2000	12	10	91	80	97	86	89	58	106	70
Uganda	2000–01	21	10	49	65	35	55	106	60	192	106
Uzbekistan	1996	15	10	96	93	89	82	54	46	70	50
Vietnam	2002	..	..	64	98	53	94	39	14	53	16
Yemen, Rep.	1997	36	24	16	73	14	71	109	60	163	73
Zambia	2001–02	24	17	81	88	74	89	115	57	192	92
Zimbabwe	1999	16	6	80	86	81	86	59	44	100	62

Health gaps by income and gender

	Survey year	Prevalence of child malnutrition		Child immunization rate				Infant mortality rate		Under-five mortality rate	
		Underweight % of children under age 5		% of children ages 12–23 months[a] Measles		DPT		per 1,000 live births		per 1,000	
		Male	Female	Male	Female	Male	Female	Male	Female	Male	Female
Armenia	2000	2	3	71	79	90	89	46	42	51	45
Bangladesh	2004	34	35	76	76	81	81	80	64	102	91
Benin	2001	19	17	69	67	74	71	98	92	162	163
Bolivia	2003	6	6	65	63	70	73	71	64	94	91
Brazil	1996	6	5	87	87	82	80	52	44	60	53
Burkina Faso	2003	25	23	54	58	57	57	95	89	195	192
Cambodia	2000	32	33	57	54	50	47	103	82	133	110
Cameroon	2004	14	15	65	66	65	68	88	74	154	141
Central African Republic	1994–95	21	19	52	53	49	46	109	94	165	152
Chad	2004	23	23	23	23	20	21	122	108	207	198
Colombia	2005	6	6	83	82	84	81	26	18	30	21
Comoros	1996	19	17	63	64	68	69	93	75	122	103
Côte d'Ivoire	1994	19	16	54	52	49	45	99	83	163	137
Dominican Republic	2002	5	5	89	88	54	61	38	31	46	40
Egypt, Arab Rep.	2000	4	3	97	97	94	94	55	55	69	70
Eritrea	1995	26	27	52	50	49	49	82	69	163	141
Ethiopia	2000	32	31	28	26	22	19	124	101	197	178
Gabon	2000	10	9	55	55	40	33	74	49	103	80
Ghana	2003	17	17	82	83	81	77	70	59	111	108
Guatemala	1998–99	21	18	82	87	73	74	50	48	64	65
Guinea	1999	17	19	52	52	46	47	112	101	202	188
Haiti	2000	14	13	54	54	43	43	97	83	143	132
India	1998–99	28	30	52	50	56	54	75	71	98	105
Indonesia	2002–03	..	..	73	71	58	59	46	40	58	51
Jordan	1997	4	5	90	90	96	96	34	23	38	30
Kazakhstan	1999	4	4	79	78	89	88	62	47	72	53
Kenya	2003	18	14	73	72	71	74	84	67	122	103
Kyrgyz Republic	1997	11	8	84	85	83	81	72	60	81	70
Madagascar	1997	27	27	47	45	48	49	109	90	176	152
Malawi	2000	20	19	83	83	84	85	117	108	207	199
Mali	2001	24	21	49	48	41	38	136	116	250	226
Mauritania	2000–01	22	22	61	63	39	41	74	59	110	94
Morocco	2003–04	9	8	88	92	95	95	51	37	59	48
Mozambique	2003	18	17	77	76	73	71	127	120	181	176
Namibia	2000	19	18	79	82	78	81	45	34	67	54
Nepal	2001	35	36	73	69	74	70	79	75	105	112
Nicaragua	2001	9	7	87	86	84	81	39	32	48	41
Niger	1998	29	30	36	34	25	25	141	131	299	306
Nigeria	2003	19	20	34	38	19	24	116	102	222	212
Pakistan	1990–91	27	27	55	46	45	40	102	86	122	119
Paraguay	1990	3	4	56	61	50	57	39	33	49	45
Peru	2000	6	6	84	85	85	84	46	40	64	57
Philippines	2003	..	..	78	81	78	80	35	25	48	34
Rwanda	2000	19	19	86	88	85	87	123	112	215	198
Senegal	1997	..	..	..	..	..	..	74	65	144	134
South Africa	1998	..	..	84	81	74	78	49	35	66	48
Tanzania	2004	18	18	80	80	37	33	83	82	135	130
Togo	1998	19	18	45	40	43	41	89	71	156	132
Turkey	1998	7	7	79	78	60	57	51	46	61	58
Turkmenistan	2000	11	10	87	88	93	92	83	60	101	76
Uganda	2000–01	18	17	56	57	45	48	93	85	164	149
Uzbekistan	1996	15	13	91	92	87	90	50	37	65	46
Vietnam	2002	..	..	84	82	72	73	25	25	34	31
Yemen, Rep.	1997	33	30	45	40	41	39	98	80	128	114
Zambia	2001–02	21	21	83	86	78	82	95	93	176	160
Zimbabwe	1999	12	11	77	81	80	82	63	56	95	85

2.19 Health gaps by income and gender

	Survey year	Pregnant women receiving prenatal care %		Contraceptive prevalence % of married women ages 15–49		Births attended by skilled health staff[c] % of total		Total fertility rate[d] births per woman		Exclusive breastfeeding % of children under 4 months	
		Poorest quintile	Richest quintile	Poorest quintile	Richest quintile	Poorest quintile	Richest quintile	Poorest quintile	Richest quintile	Poorest quintile	Richest quintile
Armenia	2000	85	97	16	29	93	100	2.5	1.6	..	..
Bangladesh	2004	25	81	45	50	3	39	4.1	2.2	62	31
Benin	2001	73	100	4	15	50	99	7.2	3.5	50	42[b]
Bolivia	2003	62	98	23	49	27	98	6.7	2.0	79	31
Brazil	1996	72	98	56	77	72	99	4.8	1.7	33	60[b]
Burkina Faso	2003	56	96	2	27	19	84	6.6	3.6	17	28
Cambodia	2000	22	80	13	25	15	81	4.7	2.2	14	18
Cameroon	2004	65	97	2	27	29	95	6.5	3.2	33	30[b]
Central African Republic	1994–95	39	91	1	9	14	82	5.1	4.9	9	4
Chad	2004	9	77	0	7	1	51	5.1	6.0	1	2
Colombia	2005	84	99	60	72	72	99	4.1	1.4	60	64
Comoros	1996	67	95	7	19	26	85	6.4	3.0	3[b]	..
Côte d'Ivoire	1994	62	98	1	13	17	84	6.4	3.7	0	5
Dominican Republic	2002	97	99	59	70	94	100	4.5	2.1	18	6
Egypt, Arab Rep.	2000	31	84	43	61	31	94	4.0	2.9	72	57
Eritrea	1995	34	90	0[e]	19	5	74	8.0	3.7	64	73
Ethiopia	2000	15	60	3	23	1	25	6.3	3.6	63	46
Gabon	2000	85	98	6	18	67	97	6.3	3.0	6	5[b]
Ghana	2003	83	98	9	26	21	90	6.4	2.8	62[b]	..
Guatemala	1998–99	37	97	55	32	9	92	7.6	2.9	62	..
Guinea	1999	58	97	1	9	12	82	5.8	4.0	9	8
Haiti	2000	65	91	17	24	4	70	6.8	2.7	40	15[b]
India	1998–99	44	93	29	55	16	84	3.4	1.8	64	37
Indonesia	2002–03	78	99	49	58	40	94	3.0	2.2	58	35
Jordan	1997	93	97	28	47	91	99	5.2	3.1	14	14[b]
Kazakhstan	1999	97	91	49	55	99	99	3.4	1.2	..	..
Kenya	2003	75	94	12	44	17	75	7.6	3.1	22	17
Kyrgyz Republic	1997	96	99	44	54	96	100	4.6	2.0	18[b]	..
Madagascar	1997	67	96	2	24	30	89	8.1	3.4	57	65
Malawi	2000	89	98	20	40	43	83	7.1	4.8	53	72
Mali	2001	42	92	4	18	22	89	7.3	5.3	38	18
Mauritania	2000–01	33	89	0[e]	17	15	93	5.4	3.5	28	30
Morocco	2003–04	40	93	51	57	29	95	3.3	1.9	53	36
Mozambique	2003	67	98	14	37	25	89	6.3	3.8	47	27
Namibia	2000	81	96	29	64	55	97	6.0	2.7	100[b]	85[b]
Nepal	2001	30	80	24	55	4	45	5.3	2.3	76	67
Nicaragua	2001	69	97	50	71	78	99	5.6	2.1	53	15[b]
Niger	1998	24	85	1	18	4	63	8.4	5.7	1	3
Nigeria	2003	37	96	4	21	13	85	6.5	4.2	15	34
Pakistan	1990–91	8	72	1	23	5	55	5.1	4.0	36	9
Paraguay	1990	73	98	21	46	41	98	7.9	2.7	7	0
Peru	2000	41	74	37	58	13	88	5.5	1.6	88	59
Philippines	2003	72	97	24	35	25	92	5.9	2.0	60	20
Rwanda	2000	90	95	2	15	17	60	6.0	5.4	89	79
Senegal	1997	67	97	1	24	20	86	7.4	3.6	13	19
South Africa	1998	96	94	34	70	68	98	4.8	1.9	15	11[b]
Tanzania	2004	91	97	11	36	31	87	7.3	3.3	58	55
Togo	1998	69	97	3	13	25	91	7.3	2.9	7	34
Turkey	1998	38	96	24	48	53	98	3.9	1.7	10	4[b]
Turkmenistan	2000	98	97	51	50	97	98	3.4	2.1	11	28[b]
Uganda	2000–01	88	98	11	41	20	77	8.5	4.1	73	59
Uzbekistan	1996	93	96	46	52	92	100	4.4	2.2	..	..
Vietnam	2002	68	100	58	52	58	100	2.2	1.4	18[b]	..
Yemen, Rep.	1997	17	68	1	24	7	50	7.3	4.7	20	13
Zambia	2001–02	89	99	11	53	20	91	7.3	3.6	39	70[b]
Zimbabwe	1999	94	97	41	67	57	94	4.9	2.6	36	46[b]

a. Refers to children who were immunized at any time before the survey. b. Data contain large sampling errors because of the small number of cases. c. Based on births in the five years before the survey. d. Based on information in the three years before the survey. e. Less than 0.5.

Health gaps by income and gender 2.19

About the data

The data in the table describe the health status and use of health services by individuals in different socioeconomic groups within countries. The data are from Demographic and Health Surveys conducted by Macro International with the support of the U.S. Agency for International Development. These large-scale household sample surveys, conducted periodically in developing countries, collect information on a large number of health, nutrition, and population measures as well as on respondents' social, demographic, and economic characteristics using a standard set of questionnaires. The data presented here draw on responses to individual and household questionnaires.

The table defines socioeconomic status in terms of a household's assets, including ownership of consumer items, features of the household's dwelling, and other characteristics related to wealth. Each household asset on which information was collected was assigned a weight generated through principal-component analysis. The resulting scores were standardized in relation to a standard normal distribution with a mean of zero and a standard deviation of one. The standardized scores were then used to create break-points defining wealth quintiles, expressed as quintiles of individuals in the population rather than quintiles of individuals at risk with respect to any one health indicator.

The choice of the asset index for defining socioeconomic status was based on pragmatic rather than conceptual considerations: Demographic and Health Surveys do not provide income or consumption data but do have detailed information on households' ownership of consumer goods and access to a variety of goods and services. Like income or consumption, the asset index defines disparities in primarily economic terms. It therefore excludes other possibilities of disparities among groups, such as those based on gender, education, ethnic background, or other facets of social exclusion. To that extent the index provides only a partial view of the multidimensional concepts of poverty, inequality, and inequity.

Creating one index that includes all asset indicators limits the types of analysis that can be performed. In particular, the use of a unified index does not permit a disaggregated analysis to examine which asset indicators have a more or less important association with health status or use of health services. In addition, some asset indicators may reflect household wealth better in some countries than in others—or reflect different degrees of wealth in different countries. Taking such information into account and creating country-specific asset indexes with country-specific choices of asset indicators might produce a more effective and accurate index for each country. The asset index used in the table does not have this flexibility.

The analysis was carried out for 56 countries, with the results issued in country reports. The table shows the estimates for the poorest and richest quintiles and by sex only; the full set of estimates for up to 117 indicators is available in the country reports (see *Data sources*). The data in this table will differ from data for similar indicators in preceding tables either because the indicator refers to a period a few years preceding the survey date or because the indicator definition or methodology is different.

Definitions

• **Survey year** is the year in which the underlying data were collected. • **Prevalence of child malnutrition** is the percentage of children under age five whose weight for age is between two and three standard deviations below the median reference standard for their age as established by the World Health Organization, the U.S. Centers for Disease Control and Prevention, and the U.S. National Center for Health Statistics. These data may differ from those in table 2.17. • **Child immunization rate** is the percentage of children ages 12–23 months at the time of the survey who received vaccinations at any time before the survey for four diseases—measles and diphtheria, pertussis (whooping cough), and tetanus (DPT). These data may differ from those in table 2.15. • **Infant mortality rate** is the number of infants dying before reaching one year of age, per 1,000 live births in a given year. Data in the table are based on births in the 10 years preceding the survey and may therefore differ from the estimates in table 2.20. • **Under-five mortality rate** is the probability that a newborn baby will die before reaching age five, if subject to current age-specific mortality rates. The probability is expressed as a rate per 1,000. Data in the table are based on births in the 10 years preceding the survey and may therefore differ from the estimates in table 2.20. • **Pregnant women receiving prenatal care** are the percentage of women with one or more births during the five years preceding the survey, who were attended at least once during pregnancy by skilled health personnel for reasons related to pregnancy. These data may differ from those in table 2.16. • **Contraceptive prevalence** is the percentage of women married or in-union ages 15–49 who are practicing, or whose sexual partners are practicing, any modern method of contraception. These data may differ from those in table 2.16. • **Births attended by skilled health staff** are the percentage of deliveries attended by personnel trained to give the necessary supervision, care, and advice to women during pregnancy, labor, and the postpartum period; to conduct deliveries on their own; and to care for newborns. Skilled health staff include doctors, nurses, and trained midwives, but exclude trained or untrained traditional birth attendants. Data in the tables are based on births in the five years preceding the survey and may therefore differ from the estimates in table 2.16. • **Total fertility rate** is the number of children that would be born to a woman if she were to live to the end of her childbearing years and bear children in accordance with current age-specific fertility rates. Data in the table are based on the information in the three years preceding the survey and may therefore differ from the estimates in table 2.16. • **Exclusive breastfeeding** refers to the percentage of children ages 0–3 months who received only the breast milk in the 24 hours preceding the survey. These data differ from those in table 2.17 because the definition differs.

Data sources

Data on health gaps by income and gender are from an analysis of Demographic and Health Surveys by the World Bank and Macro International. Country reports are available at www.worldbank.org/povertyandhealth/countrydata.

2.20 Mortality

	Life expectancy at birth		Infant mortality rate		Under-five mortality rate		Child mortality rate		Adult mortality rate		Survival to age 65	
	years		per 1,000 live births		per 1,000		per 1,000		per 1,000		% of cohort	
							Male	Female	Male	Female	Male	Female
	1990	2005	1990	2005	1990	2005	1997–2005[a]	1997–2005[a]	2001–05[a]	2001–05[a]	2005	2005
Afghanistan	..	..	..	..	..	..	..	..	..	..	..	..
Albania	72	75	37	16	45	18	..	..	96	55	81	88
Algeria	67	72	54	34	69	39	..	..	132	112	76	80
Angola	40	41	154	154	260	260	..	..	505	461	29	34
Argentina	72	75	26	15	29	18	..	..	174	87	73	86
Armenia	68	73	46	26	54	29	5	3	204	92	67	82
Australia	77	81	8	5	10	6	..	..	89	50	86	92
Austria	76	79	8	4	10	5	..	..	120	59	83	91
Azerbaijan	71	72	84	74	105	89	..	..	226	104	61	77
Bangladesh	55	64	100	54	149	73	24	29	238	205	61	66
Belarus	71	68	16	10	19	12	..	..	357	128	52	80
Belgium	76	79	8	4	10	5	..	..	125	67	83	91
Benin	53	55	111	89	185	150	72	79	309	277	50	55
Bolivia	59	65	89	52	125	65	25	29	253	192	61	69
Bosnia and Herzegovina	72	74	18	13	22	15	..	..	152	78	75	86
Botswana	64	35	45	87	58	120	..	..	841	853	11	11
Brazil	66	71	50	31	60	33	..	..	252	132	65	79
Bulgaria	72	73	15	12	19	15	..	..	216	91	70	85
Burkina Faso	48	48	113	96	210	191	110	113	407	386	40	43
Burundi	44	45	114	114	190	190	..	..	512	492	32	35
Cambodia	54	57	80	68	115	87	34	30	372	208	47	63
Cameroon	52	46	85	87	139	149	73	72	508	499	34	36
Canada	77	80	7	5	8	6	..	..	97	60	86	91
Central African Republic	48	39	102	115	168	193	..	..	658	662	22	24
Chad	46	44	120	124	201	208	96	101	495	471	32	35
Chile	74	78	18	8	21	10	..	..	131	65	80	89
China	69	72	38	23	49	27	..	..	141	87	75	82
Hong Kong, China	77	82	..	..	..	..	..	..	79	34	87	94
Colombia	68	73	26	17	35	21	4	3	182	103	72	82
Congo, Dem. Rep.	46	44	129	129	205	205	..	..	486	460	32	36
Congo, Rep.	54	53	83	81	110	108	..	..	450	424	40	46
Costa Rica	77	79	16	11	18	12	..	..	117	66	82	89
Côte d'Ivoire	52	46	103	118	157	195	83	58	474	461	35	38
Croatia	72	76	11	6	12	7	..	..	164	67	74	89
Cuba	75	77	11	6	13	7	..	..	121	81	81	87
Czech Republic	71	76	11	3	13	4	..	..	161	69	76	89
Denmark	75	78	8	4	9	5	..	..	121	74	82	88
Dominican Republic	66	68	50	26	65	31	9	9	267	145	62	76
Ecuador	69	75	43	22	57	25	..	..	184	105	73	83
Egypt, Arab Rep.	63	71	76	28	104	33	15	16	171	104	71	81
El Salvador	66	71	47	23	60	27	..	..	221	137	68	79
Eritrea	48	55	88	50	147	78	55	50	455	384	39	48
Estonia	69	73	12	6	16	7	..	..	288	94	60	85
Ethiopia	45	43	122	80	204	127	83	86	451	425	37	41
Finland	75	79	6	3	7	4	..	..	136	61	82	92
France	77	80	7	4	9	5	..	..	135	60	82	92
Gabon	60	54	60	60	92	91	32	33	438	432	44	46
Gambia, The	50	57	103	97	151	137	..	..	320	281	51	56
Georgia	70	71	43	41	47	45	..	..	214	82	67	83
Germany	75	79	7	4	9	5	..	..	119	61	83	91
Ghana	56	57	75	68	122	112	44	52	344	330	51	54
Greece	77	79	10	4	11	5	..	..	112	49	83	92
Guatemala	62	68	60	32	82	43	15	18	296	172	61	74
Guinea	47	54	139	97	234	160	101	98	324	303	49	52
Guinea-Bissau	42	45	153	124	253	200	..	..	465	423	34	39
Haiti	49	53	102	84	150	120	52	54	454	447	41	43

	Life expectancy at birth		Infant mortality rate		Under-five mortality rate		Child mortality rate		Adult mortality rate		Survival to age 65	
	years		per 1,000 live births		per 1,000		per 1,000		per 1,000		% of cohort	
	1990	2005	1990	2005	1990	2005	Male 1997–2005[a]	Female 1997–2005[a]	Male 2001–05[a]	Female 2001–05[a]	Male 2005	Female 2005
Honduras	65	69	44	31	59	40	..	..	245	201	65	72
Hungary	69	73	15	7	17	8	..	..	261	111	67	85
India	59	64	80	56	123	74	25	37	235	154	61	69
Indonesia	62	68	60	28	91	36	13	11	205	155	66	74
Iran, Islamic Rep.	65	71	54	31	72	36	..	..	158	104	73	81
Iraq	62	..	40	..	50	..	..	..	..	..	..	..
Ireland	75	79	8	5	9	6	..	..	94	56	84	90
Israel	77	80	10	5	12	6	..	..	86	46	86	92
Italy	77	80	8	4	9	4	..	..	92	48	85	92
Jamaica	71	71	17	17	20	20	..	..	237	194	68	73
Japan	79	82	5	3	6	4	..	..	92	45	86	94
Jordan	68	72	33	22	40	26	5	5	165	123	73	79
Kazakhstan	68	66	53	63	63	73	11	6	343	152	49	73
Kenya	58	49	64	79	97	120	42	39	479	551	38	35
Korea, Dem. Rep.	65	64	42	42	55	55	..	..	305	208	53	67
Korea, Rep.	71	78	8	5	9	5	..	..	138	54	79	91
Kuwait	75	78	14	9	16	11	..	..	88	58	83	88
Kyrgyz Republic	68	68	68	58	80	67	10	11	264	124	60	77
Lao PDR	50	56	120	62	163	79	..	..	318	269	50	55
Latvia	69	71	14	9	18	11	..	..	300	116	62	83
Lebanon	69	73	32	27	37	30	..	..	151	99	74	83
Lesotho	57	35	81	102	101	132	..	..	853	817	10	14
Liberia	43	42	157	157	235	235	..	..	535	500	28	32
Libya	68	74	35	18	41	19	..	..	137	93	76	84
Lithuania	71	71	10	7	13	9	..	..	303	106	62	86
Macedonia, FYR	72	74	33	15	38	17	..	..	139	81	76	85
Madagascar	51	56	103	74	168	119	45	45	337	294	49	54
Malawi	46	41	131	79	221	125	101	102	635	653	25	25
Malaysia	70	74	16	10	22	12	..	..	154	89	75	84
Mali	46	49	140	120	250	218	132	125	358	323	42	46
Mauritania	49	54	85	78	133	125	38	38	341	284	46	52
Mauritius	69	73	20	13	23	15	..	..	207	110	68	82
Mexico	71	75	37	22	46	27	..	..	155	86	76	85
Moldova	68	68	29	14	35	16	..	..	276	137	60	77
Mongolia	63	67	78	39	108	49	..	..	237	168	60	69
Morocco	64	70	69	36	89	40	9	11	162	109	72	80
Mozambique	43	42	158	100	235	145	61	64	600	593	26	28
Myanmar	56	61	91	75	130	105	..	..	301	200	54	65
Namibia	62	47	60	46	86	62	22	20	620	625	30	31
Nepal	55	63	100	56	145	74	28	40	248	222	60	63
Netherlands	77	79	7	4	9	5	..	..	90	64	84	90
New Zealand	75	80	8	5	11	6	..	..	99	65	85	90
Nicaragua	64	70	52	30	68	37	10	9	219	146	68	76
Niger	40	45	191	150	320	256	184	202	368	339	39	41
Nigeria	46	44	120	100	230	194	120	123	499	495	32	33
Norway	77	80	7	3	9	4	..	..	92	57	86	91
Oman	70	75	25	10	32	12	..	..	114	85	80	85
Pakistan	59	65	100	79	130	99	..	..	180	152	64	67
Panama	72	75	27	19	34	24	..	..	152	83	77	86
Papua New Guinea	52	56	69	55	94	74	..	..	388	349	44	49
Paraguay	68	71	33	20	41	23	..	..	159	106	72	81
Peru	66	71	58	23	78	27	19	17	186	120	69	78
Philippines	66	71	41	25	62	33	14	9	169	116	72	80
Poland	71	75	19	6	18	7	..	..	189	75	71	87
Portugal	74	78	11	4	14	5	..	..	139	58	81	91
Puerto Rico	75	78	..	..	..	..	..	..	186	69	74	89

Mortality

	Life expectancy at birth		Infant mortality rate		Under-five mortality rate		Child mortality rate		Adult mortality rate		Survival to age 65	
	years		per 1,000 live births		per 1,000		per 1,000		per 1,000		% of cohort	
							Male	Female	Male	Female	Male	Female
	1990	2005	1990	2005	1990	2005	1997–2005[a]	1997–2005[a]	2001–05[a]	2001–05[a]	2005	2005
Romania	70	72	27	16	31	19	..	..	223	96	67	84
Russian Federation	69	65	21	14	27	18	..	..	467	173	45	76
Rwanda	31	44	103	118	173	203	105	97	505	455	31	36
Saudi Arabia	68	73	35	21	44	26	3	4	148	101	77	82
Senegal	53	56	72	61	149	119	76	74	311	262	51	56
Serbia and Montenegro	72	73	24	12	28	15	..	..	164	89	73	85
Sierra Leone	39	41	175	165	302	282	..	..	432	379	32	37
Singapore	74	80	7	3	8	3	..	..	85	50	85	91
Slovak Republic	71	74	12	7	14	8	..	..	202	78	71	87
Slovenia	73	78	8	3	10	4	..	..	141	63	78	89
Somalia	42	48	133	133	225	225	..	..	395	341	39	44
South Africa	62	48	45	55	60	68	18	13	658	638	25	30
Spain	77	81	8	4	9	5	..	..	113	46	83	93
Sri Lanka	71	75	26	12	32	14	..	..	130	77	78	87
Sudan	53	57	74	62	120	90	..	..	339	299	50	55
Swaziland	57	41	78	110	110	160	..	..	885	893	8	8
Sweden	78	81	6	3	7	4	..	..	82	51	87	92
Switzerland	77	81	7	4	9	5	..	..	87	47	86	92
Syrian Arab Republic	68	74	31	14	39	15	..	..	130	90	77	84
Tajikistan	63	64	91	59	115	71	..	..	219	146	60	70
Tanzania	53	46	102	76	161	122	56	52	507	511	34	36
Thailand	68	71	31	18	37	21	..	..	228	119	68	82
Togo	57	55	88	78	152	139	73	65	369	310	47	55
Trinidad and Tobago	71	70	28	17	33	19	..	..	260	186	65	75
Tunisia	70	73	41	20	52	24	..	..	134	77	77	86
Turkey	66	71	67	26	82	29	10	13	186	115	69	79
Turkmenistan	63	63	80	81	97	104	19	17	305	156	53	71
Uganda	46	50	93	79	160	136	78	70	459	447	39	41
Ukraine	70	68	19	13	26	17	..	..	404	150	47	76
United Arab Emirates	73	79	13	8	15	9	..	..	78	50	86	91
United Kingdom	76	79	8	5	10	6	..	..	101	63	84	90
United States	75	78	9	6	11	7	..	..	144	84	80	87
Uruguay	73	76	21	14	23	15	..	..	161	83	74	87
Uzbekistan	69	67	65	57	79	68	..	..	247	145	61	74
Venezuela, RB	71	74	27	18	33	21	..	..	184	93	73	84
Vietnam	65	71	38	16	53	19	10	7	173	121	73	80
West Bank and Gaza	69	73	34	21	40	23	..	..	138	101	76	83
Yemen, Rep.	55	62	98	76	139	102	33	36	267	222	57	63
Zambia	46	38	101	102	180	182	89	74	672	713	21	20
Zimbabwe	59	37	53	81	80	132	35	31	772	808	16	14
World	**65 w**	**68 w**	**64 w**	**51 w**	**95 w**	**75 w**			**232 w**	**164 w**	**67 w**	**75 w**
Low income	56	59	94	75	147	114			290	237	55	61
Middle income	68	70	44	30	58	37			196	120	70	79
Lower middle income	67	71	46	31	62	39			176	111	71	80
Upper middle income	69	70	33	22	41	27			289	159	62	78
Low & middle income	63	65	69	56	103	82			235	167	64	72
East Asia & Pacific	67	71	43	26	59	33			162	105	73	80
Europe & Central Asia	69	69	39	27	48	32			320	136	58	79
Latin America & Carib.	68	72	43	26	54	31			208	118	70	81
Middle East & N. Africa	64	70	60	43	80	53			171	119	71	79
South Asia	59	63	86	62	129	83			230	161	61	68
Sub-Saharan Africa	49	47	109	96	185	163			483	470	35	38
High income	76	79	9	6	11	7			122	65	82	90
Europe EMU	76	80	8	4	9	5			118	57	83	92

a. Data are for the most recent year available.

About the data

Mortality rates for different age groups (infants, children, and adults) and overall indicators of mortality (life expectancy at birth or survival to a given age) are important indicators of health status in a country. Because data on the incidence and prevalence of diseases (morbidity data) are frequently unavailable, mortality rates are often used to identify vulnerable populations. And they are among the indicators most frequently used to compare levels of socioeconomic development across countries.

The main sources of mortality data are vital registration systems and direct or indirect estimates based on sample surveys or censuses. A "complete" vital registration system—one covering at least 90 percent of vital events in the population—is the best source of age-specific mortality data. But such systems are fairly uncommon in developing countries. Thus estimates must be obtained from sample surveys or derived by applying indirect estimation techniques to registration, census, or survey data. Survey data are subject to recall error, and surveys estimating infant deaths require large samples because households in which a birth or an infant death has occurred during a given year cannot ordinarily be pre-selected for sampling. Indirect estimates rely on estimated actuarial "life" tables that may be inappropriate for the population concerned. Because life expectancy at birth is constructed using infant mortality data and model life tables, similar reliability issues arise for this indicator.

Life expectancy at birth and age-specific mortality rates are generally estimates based on vital registration or the most recent census or survey available (see *Primary data documentation*). Extrapolations based on outdated surveys may not be reliable for monitoring changes in health status or for comparative analytical work.

To produce harmonized estimates of infant and under-five mortality rates that use all available information in a transparent way, the United Nations Children's Fund (UNICEF) and the World Bank developed and adopted a methodology that fits a regression line to the relationship between mortality rates and their reference dates using weighted least squares. (For further discussion of methodology for childhood mortality estimates, see Hill and others 1999.)

Infant and child mortality rates are higher for boys than for girls in countries in which parental gender preferences are insignificant. Child mortality captures the effect of gender discrimination better than does infant mortality, as malnutrition and medical interventions are more important in this age group. Where female child mortality is higher, as in some countries in South Asia, girls probably have unequal access to resources.

Adult mortality rates have increased in many countries in Sub-Saharan Africa and Europe and Central Asia. In Sub-Saharan Africa the increase stems from AIDS-related mortality and affects both men and women. In Europe and Central Asia the causes are more diverse and affect men more. They include a high prevalence of smoking, a high-fat diet, excessive alcohol use, and stressful conditions related to the economic transition.

The percentage of a cohort surviving to age 65 reflects both child and adult mortality rates. Like life expectancy, it is a synthetic measure based on current age-specific mortality rates. It shows that even in countries where mortality is high, a certain share of the current birth cohort will live well beyond the life expectancy at birth, while in low-mortality countries close to 90 percent will reach at least age 65.

Under-five mortality rates improve as mothers' education levels rise **2.20a**

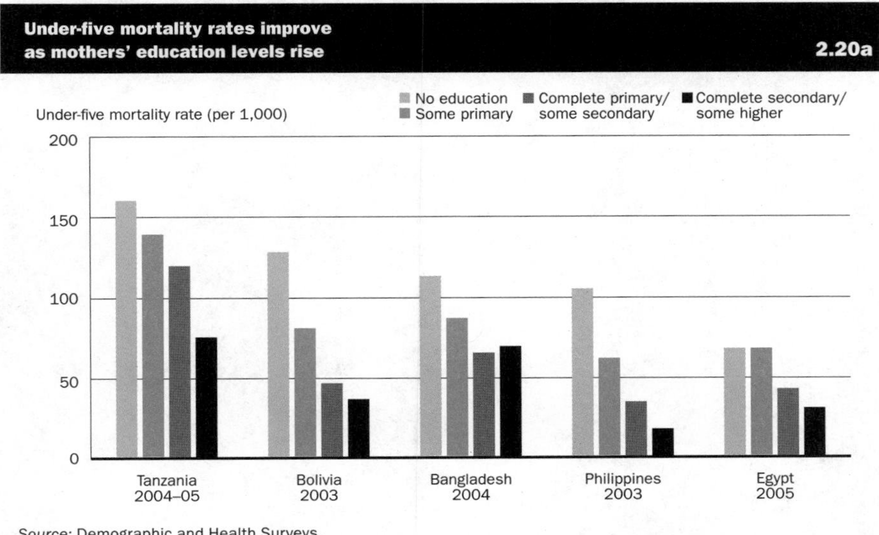

Source: Demographic and Health Surveys.

Definitions

• **Life expectancy at birth** is the number of years a newborn infant would live if prevailing patterns of mortality at the time of its birth were to stay the same throughout its life. • **Infant mortality rate** is the number of infants dying before reaching one year of age, per 1,000 live births in a given year. • **Under-five mortality rate** is the probability that a newborn baby will die before reaching age five, if subject to current age-specific mortality rates. The probability is expressed as a rate per 1,000. • **Child mortality rate** is the probability of dying between the ages of one and five, if subject to current age-specific mortality rates. The probability is expressed as a rate per 1,000. • **Adult mortality rate** is the probability of dying between the ages of 15 and 60—that is, the probability of a 15-year-old dying before reaching age 60—if subject to current age-specific mortality rates between those ages. • **Survival to age 65** refers to the percentage of a cohort of newborn infants that would survive to age 65, if subject to current age-specific mortality rates.

Data sources

Data on infant and under-five mortality are the harmonized estimates of the World Health Organization, UNICEF, and the World Bank, based mainly on household surveys, censuses, and vital registration data, supplemented by the World Bank's estimates based on household surveys and vital registration data. Other estimates are compiled and produced by the World Bank's Human Development Network and Development Data Group in consultation with its operational staff and country offices. Important inputs to the World Bank's demographic work come from the United Nations Population Division's *World Population Prospects: The 2004 Revision,* census reports and other statistical publications from national statistical offices, Demographic and Health Surveys by Macro International, and the Human Mortality Database by the University of California, Berkeley, and the Max Planck Institute for Demographic Research (www.mortality.org/).

3 ENVIRONMENT

Agriculture is environment

For the 70 percent of the world's poor in rural areas, agriculture is the major source of income and employment. It takes up more than one-third of the world's area and more than two-thirds of the world's water withdrawals. Competition for these resources is increasing with growth of population, cities, and demand for food. And climate change is altering the patterns of rainfall and temperature that agriculture depends on. The depletion and degradation of these resources thus pose serious challenges to the capacity of agriculture to produce enough food and other agricultural products to sustain the livelihoods of rural populations and accommodate the needs of urban populations.

In the agriculture-based economies of Sub-Saharan Africa agriculture contributed a third to economic growth in 1990–2005. In the transforming economies of Asia, mainly China, India, and Indonesia, it contributed 8 percent to economic growth, while making up a fifth of the economy and employing half the labor force. And in the urbanizing economies of Latin America and some countries of Eastern Europe and Central Asia, it contributed 10 percent to the economy and to growth. Agriculture is a way of life throughout the world, with 2.5 billion of 3 billion rural people tied to agricultural activities, particularly to producing food.

Producing food requires enormous amounts of water and cropland. In some parts of the world, the demand for water exceeds the supply. But in many places it appears that water scarcity is caused not by shortages of water but by its mismanagement. Not enough is known because data on the availability and productivity of water are limited. However, water is clearly central to the social, political, and economic affairs of a country and to cooperation or conflict across boundaries.

Agricultural intensification—producing more crops on the same or smaller amounts of land—along with irrigation and the conversion of forest lands to cropland have helped meet the increasing demand for food. Food production has thankfully outpaced population growth in most regions. But this has too often been at the expense of soil degradation, water pollution, and added pressure on water resources. Turning forests into agricultural lands reduces biodiversity and contributes to global warming. Rising sea levels, warming temperatures, and changes in weather patterns affect millions of people. The impact is especially severe for those in developing countries, threatening their potential to move out of poverty.

Agriculture, poverty reduction, and food security

With economic growth the share of agriculture in the global economy declines. Even so, agriculture remains important in many developing economies and the source of income for many poor people. In some African countries more than half the GDP is in agriculture—in Liberia 64 percent, in Guinea-Bissau 60 percent, and in Central African Republic 54 percent. On average agriculture contributes more than 20 percent to value added in low-income economies (figure 3a).

Globally, about 40 percent of the active labor force is in agriculture, but in Sub-Saharan Africa and Asia and the Pacific about 60 percent is in agriculture. Compare that with 18 percent in Latin America and 4 percent in high-income economies. Variations across countries are even greater, with agricultural employment's share ranging from less than 2 percent in the United Kingdom and the United States to 44 percent in China and 80 percent in Nepal. Agriculture is associated with natural wealth—particularly in developing economies. A recent World Bank study estimates that roughly two-thirds of the natural wealth in low-income countries is embodied in cropland and pastureland (World Bank 2006e).

Agriculture's changing role is underscored by rapid rural-urban migration. The United Nations estimates that in 2007, for the first time, the majority of the global population will be urban (United Nations Population Division 2005, *World Population Prospects 2004*). And this will continue. Urban population is expected to grow 1.8 percent a year through 2030, almost twice as fast as the global population. Productivity must continue to rise, so that the shrinking rural population can provide more agricultural products for a rising urban population with higher incomes.

In recent years the increases in demand for food have been met by higher productivity through agricultural intensification, technological advance, mechanization, and irrigation (figure 3b). However, continuing depletion and degradation of natural resources that constitute the agricultural sector's main inputs—water and land—could slow the growth of productivity and undermine food security.

Agriculture's share in GDP—declining, but still more than a fifth in low-income economies 3a

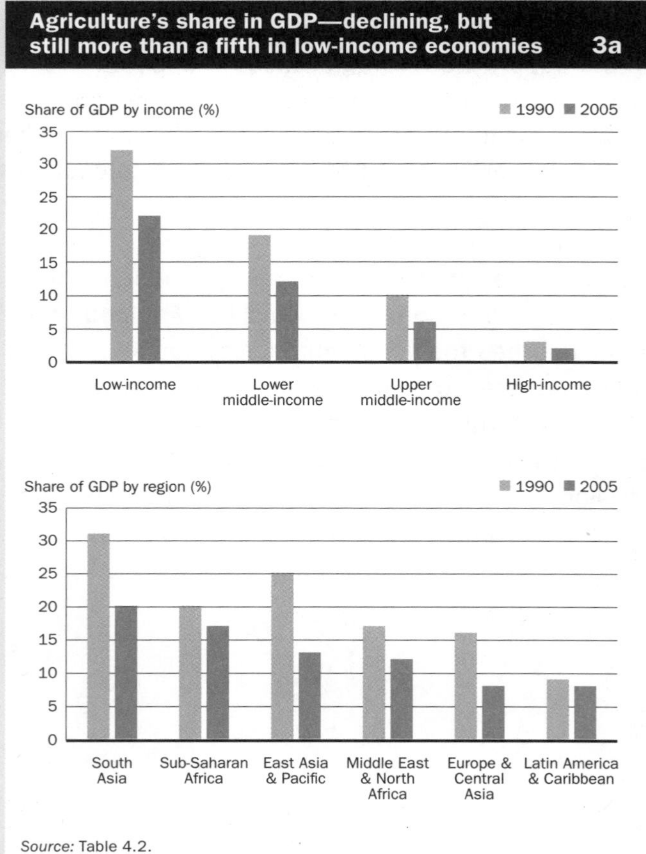

Source: Table 4.2.

Agricultural productivity has increased, yielding more output for all 3b

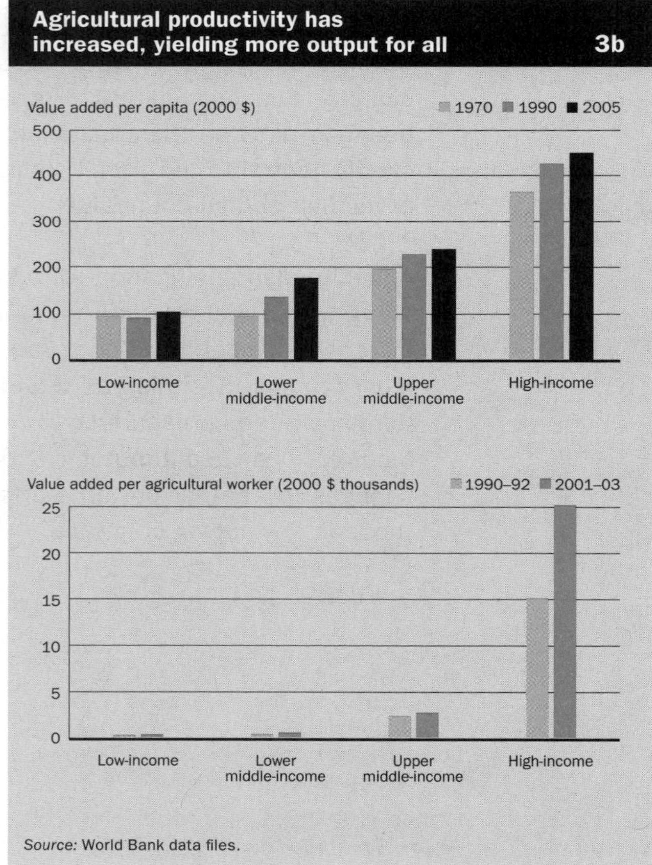

Source: World Bank data files.

Water . . . water . . .

Water is life. Water is health. Water is livelihood. But some 1.1 billion people in developing countries have inadequate access to water, and about 700 million people in 43 countries live below the water-stress threshold of 1,700 cubic meters per person per year (figure 3c). One billion people live in areas of *economic* water scarcity—where human, institutional, and financial capital limit access to water even though water in nature is available locally to meet human demands, a situation especially prevalent in much of Sub-Saharan Africa and South Asia (CAWMA 2007).

Water is needed for most economic activities, but agriculture is the most water-intensive sector (figure 3d), using 70 percent of global water withdrawals (indicator table 3.5). Each year some 7,100 cubic kilometers of water are consumed by crops to meet global food demand, the equivalent of 90 times the annual runoff of the Nile River, or more than 3,000 liters per person per day. Most of it (78 percent) comes directly from rainfall, the remainder from irrigation (CAWMA 2007). Competition between water for food production and for other sectors will intensify, but food production will remain the largest consumer of water worldwide. Water productivity is much lower in agriculture than it is in industry (figure 3e).

Globally, there is more than enough water for domestic purposes, for agriculture, and for industry. But access to water is very uneven across and within countries. Poor people have limited access, not so much because of physical water scarcity, but because of their lack of purchasing power and because of inappropriate policies that limit their access to infrastructure.

Techniques to control soil moisture and intensify agricultural production have been substantially improved in the last 50 years in many parts of the world. Irrigation is increasing globally, in all income groups and all regions (figure 3f). While the world's cultivated land increased by about 13 percent from 1961 to 2003, the irrigated area almost doubled, from 10 percent to 18 percent of cropland. About 70 percent of the world's irrigated land and 30 percent of cultivated land are in Asia. By contrast, there is very little irrigation in Sub-Saharan Africa, where agriculture is almost exclusively rainfed.

More people will experience water scarcity and water stress **3c**

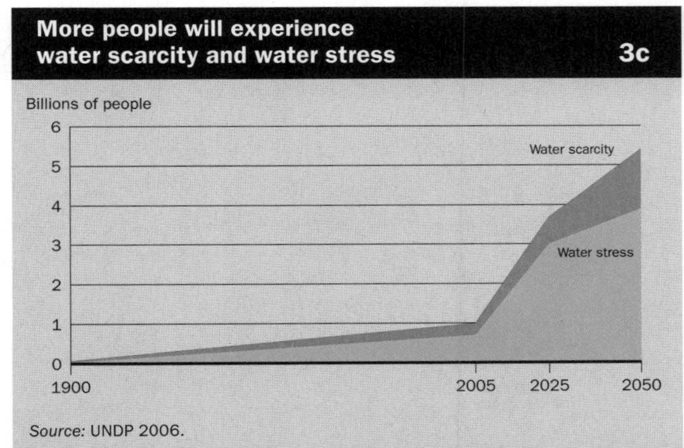

Source: UNDP 2006.

Agriculture is the biggest consumer of water . . . **3d**

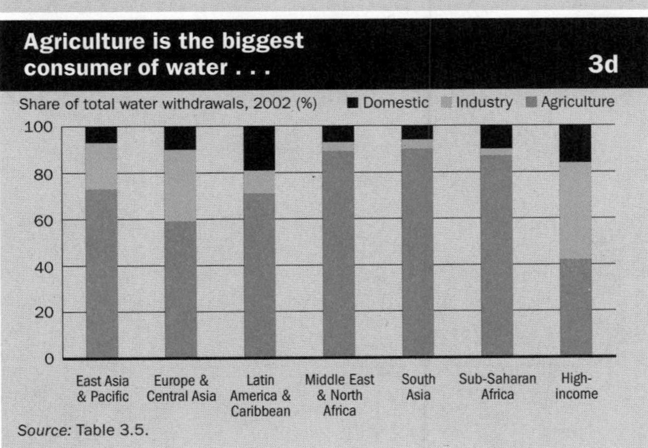

Source: Table 3.5.

. . . and the least productive user **3e**

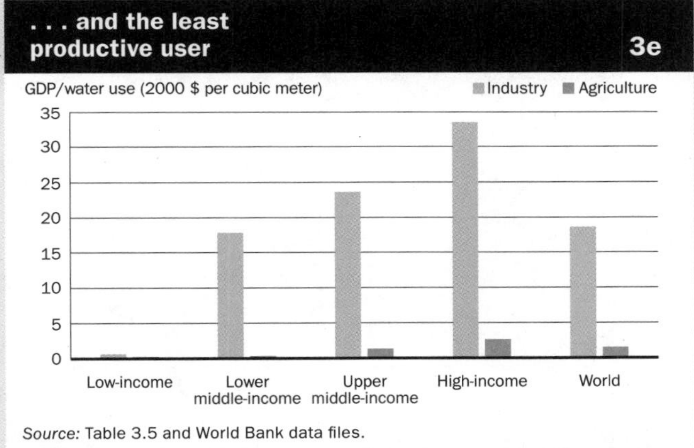

Source: Table 3.5 and World Bank data files.

Irrigation has increased, demanding more water **3f**

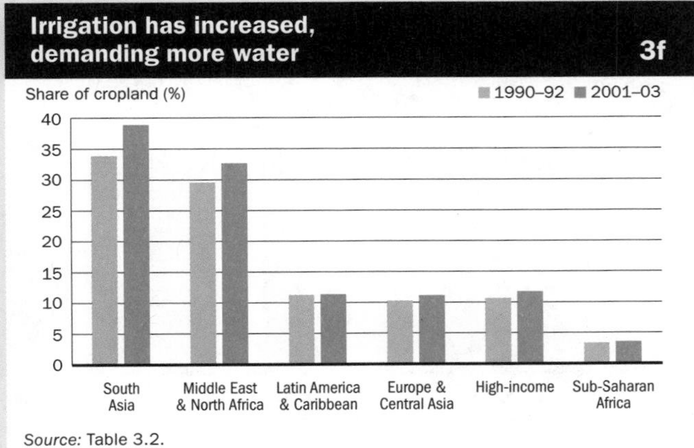

Source: Table 3.2.

Land use and land loss

Global demand for food is projected to double in the next 50 years, as urbanization proceeds and income rises (CAWMA 2007). But arable land per capita is shrinking. In the last 12 years it has fallen from 2,100 square meters per person to 1,700 in low-income countries, and from 2,300 to 2,100 in high-income economies.

Agricultural intensification has met global food demand. In Asia land under cereal production increased only 4 percent between 1970 and 1995, while cereal production doubled due to the green revolution (Rosengrant and Hazel 2000). More recently, the high-income economies, already the most intensified producers, realized an almost 20 percent increase—from 4,260 kilograms per hectare in 1990–92 to 5,040 in 2003–05 (figure 3g), substantially higher than their rate of population increase. In contrast, cereal yields in water-stressed Sub-Saharan Africa increased by 10 percent—far less than the region's population growth. The differences in productivity are even starker among countries, ranging from 296 kilograms per hectare in Eritrea to 8,710 in Belgium.

Perhaps more worrisome, productivity has declined substantially on approximately 16 percent of agricultural land in developing countries, especially in Africa and Central America. One study estimates that global cropland production is 12.7 percent lower and pastoral production 3.8 percent lower than would have been the case without soil degradation. This implies a total agricultural production loss of 4.8 percent. Another estimate puts the global loss at 8.9 percent (Scherr 1999, pp. 16–20).

In many countries soil degradation and the loss of agricultural land combined with population growth have created pressure that led to substantial deforestation. Global forested area in 2005 was about 4 billion hectares, covering 30 percent of total land area (figure 3h). But deforestation continues at about 13 million hectares a year. Reforestation reduced the net loss of forest areas to 7.3 million hectares a year in 2000–05—an improvement from losses of 8.9 million hectares a year in 1990–2000. Africa and Latin America continued to have the largest loss of forest after 1990.

Cereal yields have increased in most regions—East Asia has almost reached the high-income economies **3g**

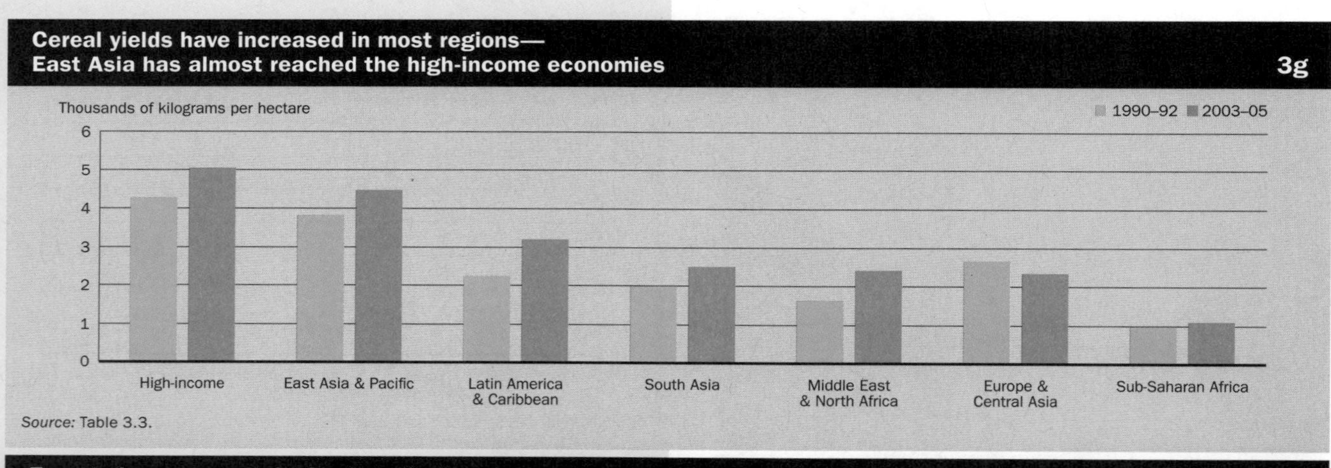

Source: Table 3.3.

Forested areas are shrinking in Latin America and Sub-Saharan Africa—recovering in East Asia **3h**

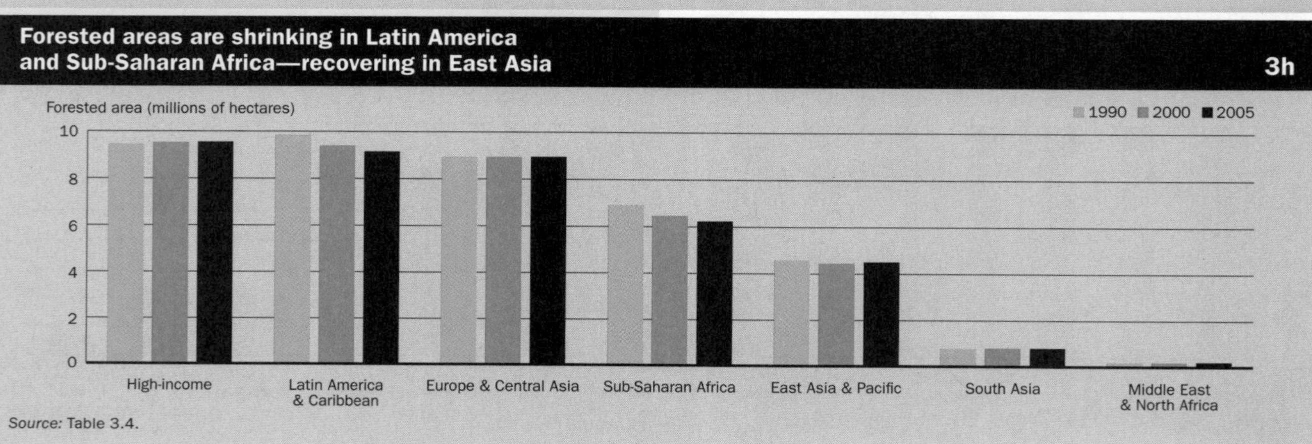

Source: Table 3.4.

Agriculture and climate change

Agriculture and deforestation are estimated to be responsible for one-third of greenhouse gas emissions, which are the main contributors to climate change (figure 3i). In turn, climate change affects agriculture more than any other sector, increasing risks of crop failures and livestock losses and threatening food security. The decline in crop yields, especially in Africa, could leave hundreds of millions without the ability to produce or purchase sufficient food. Warming may also induce sudden shifts in regional weather patterns that would have severe consequences for water availability and flooding in tropical regions. And the impact of sea level rise could be catastrophic for many developing countries (Dasgupta and others 2007).

Changes in climate patterns are already observed in some parts of the world. Average rainfall has fallen in the Sahel (figure 3j), with droughts in the 1970s and 1980s that resulted in more than 100,000 deaths (UNEP 2002, p. 219). Africa has had one major drought in each of the last three decades (box 3k). Ethiopia's 1984 drought affected 8.7 million people—one million died and millions more faced malnourishment and famine (UNEP 2002). The 1991–92 drought in South Africa reduced cereal harvests and exposed more than 17 million to the risk of starvation (UNEP 2002).

Delay in addressing climate change could prove tremendously costly, while efforts to mitigate may be less expensive than commonly feared. A recent cost assessment argues that tackling climate change is a pro-growth strategy—and that ignoring it will ultimately undermine economic growth (Stern 2006). If action does not start now, the world may face far higher costs later. Efforts to stabilize emissions must aim not only at the energy sector, but also at reducing deforestation, encouraging reforestation, and fostering more sustainable agricultural practices.

While all countries will be affected, the poorest countries and people will suffer earliest and most because they depend heavily on agriculture, the most climate-sensitive of all economic sectors. The developing regions are also at a geographic disadvantage. They are already warmer, on average, than developed regions. They suffer from high rainfall variability. And their low incomes and other vulnerabilities make their adaptation to climate change particularly difficult.

Agriculture accounts for a seventh of all greenhouse gas emissions **3i**

Greenhouse gas emissions by source, 2000

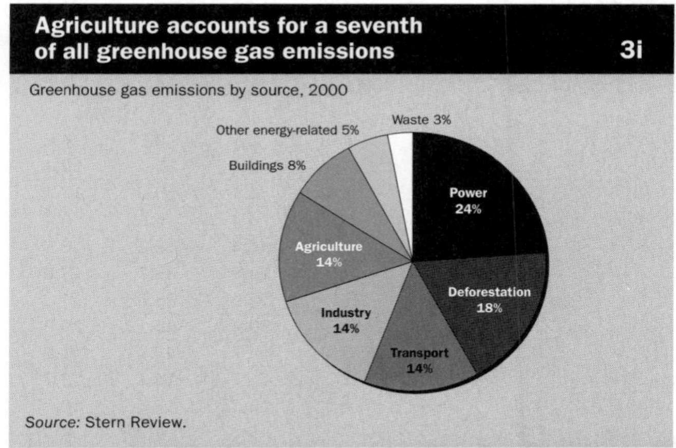

Source: Stern Review.

Horn of Africa suffers floods after parching drought **Box 3k**

In November 2006 thousands of Somalis trekked from flooded refugee camps to drier ground in northeast Kenya as UN agencies rushed emergency supplies to some 1.8 million people hit by the worst floods in the Horn of Africa in 50 years. The floods, which also affected Kenya and Ethiopia, began in late October. They worsened food insecurity caused by severe drought earlier this year. In some areas the soil was so parched that it was not able to absorb the rain, and the few crops that survived the drought were destroyed by floods.

The flood displaced more than 100,000 of the estimated 160,000 mainly Somali refugees in Dadaab, who had fled the increasing violence in their country. At least 80 people died in floods in southern Somalia. The rain also dislodged landmines seeded during Somalia's long-standing conflict, posing additional hazards.

Less rain is falling in the Sahel, with dire consequences **3j**

Mean normalized rainfall, 1950–2000, June–October

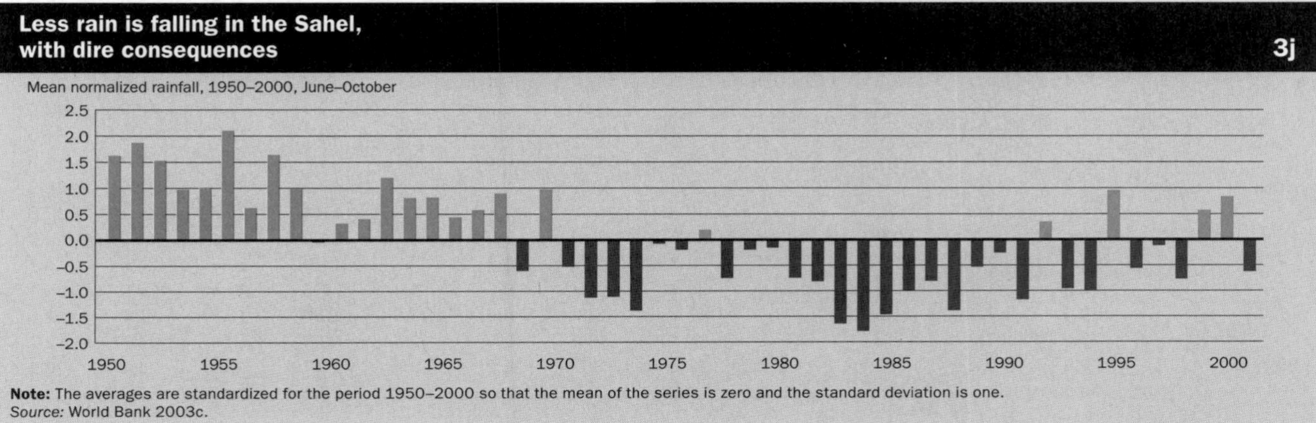

Note: The averages are standardized for the period 1950–2000 so that the mean of the series is zero and the standard deviation is one.
Source: World Bank 2003c.

3.1 Rural population and land use

	Rural population			Land area	Land use							
	% of total		average annual % growth	thousand sq. km	Forest area		% of land area Permanent cropland		Arable land		Arable land hectares per 100 people	
	1990	2005	1990–2005	2005	1990	2005	1990	2005	1990	2005	1990–92	2003–05
Afghanistan	..	..	..	652.1	2.0	1.3	0.2	0.2	12.1	12.1	..	..
Albania	63.6	54.6	–1.4	27.4	28.8	29.0	4.6	4.5	21.1	21.1	18.8	18.6
Algeria	47.9	36.7	–0.1	2,381.7	0.8	1.0	0.2	0.3	3.0	3.2	24.6	23.7
Angola	62.9	46.7	0.7	1,246.7	48.9	47.4	0.4	0.2	2.3	2.6	21.3	21.9
Argentina	13.0	9.9	–0.7	2,736.7	12.9	12.1	0.4	0.4	9.6	10.2	74.7	73.4
Armenia	32.5	35.9	–0.4	28.2	12.3	10.0	4.3	2.1	18.2	17.6	16.2	16.4
Australia	14.6	11.8	–0.3	7,682.3	21.9	21.3	0.0	0.0	6.2	6.4	249.0	241.1
Austria	34.2	34.0	0.3	82.5	45.8	46.8	1.0	0.8	17.3	16.8	17.3	17.0
Azerbaijan	46.3	48.5	1.4	82.7	11.2	11.3	6.0	2.7	21.1	22.3	22.6	22.2
Bangladesh	80.2	74.9	1.6	130.2	6.8	6.7	2.3	3.5	70.2	61.1	6.1	5.7
Belarus	33.6	27.8	–1.6	207.5	35.6	38.0	1.4	0.6	30.1	26.3	58.4	56.2
Belgium	3.6	2.8	–1.4	30.2	22.4	22.1	0.5	0.8	23.3	27.9	8.2	8.1
Benin	65.5	59.9	2.6	110.6	30.0	21.3	0.9	2.4	14.6	24.0	33.1	33.5
Bolivia	44.4	35.8	0.7	1,084.4	57.9	54.2	0.1	0.2	1.9	2.8	34.9	34.5
Bosnia and Herzegovina	60.8	54.3	–0.8	51.2	43.2	42.7	2.0	1.9	23.6	19.5	25.8	25.9
Botswana	58.1	42.6	–0.5	566.7	24.2	21.1	0.0	0.0	0.7	0.7	21.4	21.3
Brazil	25.2	15.8	–1.7	8,459.4	61.5	56.5	0.8	0.9	6.0	7.0	33.2	32.5
Bulgaria	33.6	30.0	–1.5	108.6	30.1	33.4	2.7	1.9	34.9	29.2	43.4	42.0
Burkina Faso	86.2	81.7	2.6	273.6	26.1	24.8	0.2	0.2	12.9	17.7	37.8	39.0
Burundi	93.7	90.0	1.4	25.7	11.3	5.9	14.0	14.2	36.2	38.6	14.7	14.1
Cambodia	87.4	80.3	1.8	176.5	73.3	59.2	0.6	0.9	20.9	21.0	28.5	26.8
Cameroon	59.3	45.4	0.5	465.4	52.7	45.6	2.6	2.6	12.8	12.8	39.3	37.8
Canada	23.4	19.9	–0.2	9,093.5	34.1	34.1	0.7	0.7	5.0	5.0	147.4	144.4
Central African Republic	63.2	62.0	1.9	623.0	37.2	36.5	0.1	0.2	3.1	3.1	50.4	49.0
Chad	79.2	74.7	2.8	1,259.2	10.4	9.5	0.0	0.0	2.6	2.9	42.0	39.4
Chile	16.7	12.4	–0.6	748.8	20.4	21.5	0.3	0.4	3.7	2.6	12.7	12.4
China	72.6	59.6	–0.4	9,598.1[a]	16.8	21.2	0.8	1.3	11.1	11.1	8.1	8.0
Hong Kong, China	0.5	0.0	..	1.0	..	..	..	..	..	..	..	..
Colombia	31.3	27.3	1.0	1,109.5	55.4	54.7	1.5	1.5	3.0	1.8	5.8	4.8
Congo, Dem. Rep.	72.2	67.9	2.3	2,267.1	62.0	58.9	0.5	0.5	2.9	3.0	13.1	12.4
Congo, Rep.	45.7	39.8	2.3	341.5	66.5	65.8	0.1	0.2	1.4	1.4	13.9	13.1
Costa Rica	49.3	38.3	0.7	51.1	50.2	46.8	4.9	5.9	5.1	4.4	5.6	5.4
Côte d'Ivoire	60.3	55.0	1.8	318.0	32.1	32.7	11.0	11.3	7.6	10.4	18.6	18.8
Croatia	46.0	43.5	–0.7	55.9	37.8	38.2	1.4	2.1	30.8	19.8	32.7	27.6
Cuba	26.6	24.5	–0.2	109.8	18.7	24.7	7.4	6.6	27.6	27.9	28.6	27.3
Czech Republic	24.8	26.5	0.3	77.3	34.0	34.3	3.1	3.1	41.1	39.4	30.1	29.9
Denmark	15.2	14.4	0.0	42.4	10.5	11.8	0.2	0.2	60.4	52.7	42.7	41.8
Dominican Republic	44.8	33.2	–0.5	48.4	28.4	28.4	9.3	10.3	21.7	22.7	13.1	12.7
Ecuador	44.9	37.2	0.4	276.8	49.9	39.2	4.8	4.4	5.8	4.9	12.0	10.0
Egypt, Arab Rep.	56.5	57.2	2.0	995.5	0.0	0.1	0.4	0.5	2.3	3.0	4.2	4.1
El Salvador	50.8	40.2	0.4	20.7	18.1	14.4	12.5	12.1	26.5	31.9	10.2	9.9
Eritrea	84.2	80.6	2.3	101.0	..	15.4	..	0.0	..	5.6	15.1	13.9
Estonia	28.9	30.9	–0.6	42.4	51.0	53.9	0.5	0.3	27.0	13.9	52.1	40.9
Ethiopia	87.4	84.0	2.0	1,000.0	13.7	13.0	0.6	0.7	9.8	11.1	15.5	16.1
Finland	38.6	38.9	0.4	304.6	72.9	73.9	0.0	0.0	7.4	7.3	42.2	42.5
France	25.9	23.3	–0.3	550.1	26.4	28.3	2.2	2.1	32.7	33.6	31.1	30.5
Gabon	30.9	16.4	–1.7	257.7	85.1	84.5	0.6	0.7	1.1	1.3	25.1	24.2
Gambia, The	61.7	46.1	1.3	10.0	44.2	47.1	0.5	0.5	18.2	31.5	22.5	21.9
Georgia	44.8	47.8	–0.9	69.5	39.7	39.7	7.8	3.8	11.8	11.5	17.1	17.8
Germany	26.6	24.8	–0.2	348.8	30.8	31.8	1.3	0.6	34.3	34.1	14.3	14.4
Ghana	63.5	52.2	1.1	227.5	32.7	24.2	6.6	9.7	11.9	18.4	20.0	19.7
Greece	41.2	41.0	0.6	128.9	25.6	29.1	8.3	8.8	22.5	20.4	24.9	24.1
Guatemala	58.9	52.8	1.6	108.4	43.8	36.3	4.5	5.6	12.0	13.3	12.3	12.0
Guinea	72.0	67.0	2.2	245.7	30.1	27.4	2.0	2.6	3.0	4.5	11.7	12.2
Guinea-Bissau	71.9	70.4	2.9	28.1	78.8	73.7	4.2	8.9	10.7	10.7	21.3	20.1
Haiti	70.5	61.2	0.5	27.6	4.2	3.8	11.6	11.6	28.3	28.3	9.7	9.4

Rural population and land use

	Rural population			Land area	Land use							
	% of total		average annual % growth	thousand sq. km	% of land area						Arable land hectares per 100 people	
					Forest area		Permanent cropland		Arable land			
	1990	**2005**	**1990–2005**	**2005**	**1990**	**2005**	**1990**	**2005**	**1990**	**2005**	**1990–92**	**2003–05**
Honduras	59.7	53.5	1.9	111.9	66.0	41.5	3.2	*3.2*	13.1	*9.5*	16.2	15.5
Hungary	34.2	33.7	–0.2	89.6	20.0	22.1	2.6	2.3	56.2	51.3	45.2	45.5
India	74.5	71.3	1.4	2,973.2	21.5	22.8	2.2	3.4	54.8	53.7	15.5	14.8
Indonesia	69.4	51.9	–0.6	1,811.6	64.3	48.8	6.5	7.5	11.2	12.7	10.3	10.6
Iran, Islamic Rep.	43.7	33.1	–0.4	1,636.2	6.8	6.8	0.8	0.9	9.3	9.8	23.3	24.4
Iraq	30.3	..	..	437.4	1.8	1.9	0.7	*0.6*	12.1	*13.1*	21.9	..
Ireland	43.1	39.5	0.5	68.9	6.4	9.7	0.0	0.0	15.1	17.6	29.7	29.5
Israel	9.6	8.4	1.6	21.6	7.1	7.9	4.1	3.5	15.9	14.6	5.3	4.8
Italy	33.3	32.4	0.0	294.1	28.5	33.9	10.1	8.6	30.6	26.3	14.7	13.6
Jamaica	50.6	46.9	0.2	10.8	31.9	31.3	9.2	*10.2*	11.0	*16.1*	6.7	6.6
Japan	36.9	34.2	–0.2	364.5	68.4	68.2	1.3	0.9	13.1	12.0	3.5	3.4
Jordan	27.8	17.7	0.4	88.2	0.9	0.9	0.8	1.0	2.0	2.1	3.9	3.5
Kazakhstan	43.7	42.7	–0.9	2,699.7	1.3	1.2	0.1	0.1	13.3	8.3	148.7	149.3
Kenya	81.8	79.3	2.3	569.1	6.5	6.2	0.9	*1.0*	7.4	*8.2*	14.6	14.2
Korea, Dem. Rep.	41.6	38.4	0.4	120.4	68.1	51.4	1.5	1.7	19.0	23.3	12.0	12.3
Korea, Rep.	26.2	19.2	–1.1	98.7	64.5	63.5	1.6	2.0	19.8	16.6	3.6	3.4
Kuwait	2.0	1.7	1.7	17.8	0.2	0.3	0.1	0.2	0.2	0.8	0.6	0.6
Kyrgyz Republic	62.2	64.2	1.3	191.8	4.4	4.5	0.6	0.4	7.1	6.7	27.2	25.9
Lao PDR	84.6	79.4	2.0	230.8	75.0	69.9	0.3	0.4	3.5	4.3	16.7	17.2
Latvia	30.7	32.2	–0.7	62.3	44.7	47.2	0.6	0.2	28.0	17.5	41.0	44.1
Lebanon	16.9	13.4	0.2	10.2	11.8	13.3	11.9	*14.0*	17.9	*16.6*	5.2	4.9
Lesotho	82.8	81.3	0.8	30.4	0.2	0.3	0.1	*0.1*	10.4	*10.9*	18.4	18.3
Liberia	54.7	41.9	2.1	96.3	42.1	32.7	2.2	*2.3*	4.2	*4.0*	12.1	11.9
Libya	21.4	15.2	–0.3	1,759.5	0.1	0.1	0.2	*0.2*	1.0	*1.0*	33.5	32.3
Lithuania	32.4	33.4	–0.4	62.7	31.0	33.5	1.1	0.6	47.3	30.4	58.8	49.0
Macedonia, FYR	42.2	31.1	–1.6	25.4	35.6	35.6	1.5	1.8	33.9	22.3	27.9	27.9
Madagascar	76.4	73.2	2.7	581.5	23.5	22.1	1.0	*1.0*	4.7	*5.1*	17.6	16.7
Malawi	88.4	82.8	1.7	94.1	41.4	36.2	1.2	*1.5*	19.3	*26.0*	18.7	19.9
Malaysia	50.2	32.7	–0.5	328.6	68.1	63.6	16.0	*17.6*	5.2	*5.5*	7.7	7.4
Mali	76.7	69.5	2.2	1,220.2	11.5	10.3	0.0	0.0	1.7	3.9	38.9	36.6
Mauritania	60.3	59.6	2.7	1,025.2	0.4	0.3	0.0	*0.0*	0.4	*0.5*	17.9	16.9
Mauritius	56.1	57.6	1.3	2.0	19.2	18.2	3.0	3.0	49.3	49.3	8.3	8.1
Mexico	27.5	24.0	0.5	1,908.7	36.2	33.7	1.0	*1.3*	12.6	*13.0*	25.1	24.6
Moldova	53.2	53.3	–0.3	32.9	9.7	10.0	22.9	9.1	54.3	56.2	43.3	43.9
Mongolia	43.0	43.3	1.3	1,566.5	7.3	6.5	0.0	*0.0*	0.9	*0.8*	49.1	48.3
Morocco	51.6	41.3	0.0	446.3	9.6	9.8	1.6	*2.0*	19.5	*19.0*	30.4	29.4
Mozambique	78.9	65.5	1.4	784.1	25.5	24.6	0.3	*0.3*	4.4	*5.5*	22.0	22.8
Myanmar	75.1	69.4	0.9	657.6	59.6	49.0	0.8	*1.4*	14.5	*15.3*	20.5	20.4
Namibia	72.3	64.9	1.8	823.3	10.6	9.3	0.0	*0.0*	0.8	*1.0*	42.3	41.0
Nepal	91.1	84.2	1.8	143.0	33.7	25.4	0.5	0.9	16.0	16.5	9.4	8.9
Netherlands	31.3	19.8	–2.4	33.9	10.2	10.8	0.9	1.0	25.9	26.8	5.7	5.6
New Zealand	15.3	13.8	0.5	268.0	28.8	31.0	5.1	*7.0*	9.4	*5.6*	38.5	37.4
Nicaragua	46.9	41.0	0.9	121.4	53.9	42.7	1.6	*1.9*	10.7	*15.9*	38.5	37.8
Niger	84.6	83.2	3.3	1,266.7	1.5	1.0	0.0	*0.0*	8.7	*11.4*	118.8	111.0
Nigeria	65.0	51.8	1.0	910.8	18.9	12.2	2.8	*3.2*	32.4	*33.5*	24.1	24.2
Norway	28.0	22.6	–0.9	304.3	30.0	30.8	..	..	2.8	2.8	19.6	18.9
Oman	34.6	28.5	1.1	309.5	0.0	0.0	0.1	*0.1*	0.1	*0.1*	1.5	1.5
Pakistan	69.4	65.1	2.0	770.9	3.3	2.5	0.6	1.0	26.6	27.6	15.2	14.1
Panama	46.1	29.2	–1.1	74.4	58.8	57.7	2.1	*2.0*	6.7	*7.4*	18.1	17.6
Papua New Guinea	86.9	86.6	2.4	452.9	69.6	65.0	1.3	*1.4*	0.4	*0.5*	3.9	4.0
Paraguay	51.3	41.5	0.8	397.3	53.3	46.5	0.2	*0.2*	5.3	*7.7*	54.3	53.6
Peru	31.1	27.4	0.9	1,280.0	54.8	53.7	0.3	*0.5*	2.7	*2.9*	14.0	13.6
Philippines	51.2	37.3	–0.1	298.2	35.5	24.0	14.8	*16.8*	18.4	*19.1*	7.4	7.1
Poland	38.7	37.9	–0.2	306.3	29.2	30.0	1.1	1.2	47.3	39.6	35.3	32.6
Portugal	52.1	42.4	–0.9	91.5	33.9	41.3	8.5	8.5	25.6	16.8	16.4	14.9
Puerto Rico	27.8	2.4	–14.6	8.9	45.5	46.0	5.6	4.7	7.3	8.0	1.7	1.8

3.1 Rural population and land use

	Rural population			Land area	Land use							
	% of total		average annual % growth	thousand sq. km	Forest area (% of land area)		Permanent cropland (% of land area)		Arable land (% of land area)		Arable land hectares per 100 people	
	1990	2005	1990–2005	2005	1990	2005	1990	2005	1990	2005	1990–92	2003–05
Romania	45.7	46.3	–0.4	230.0	27.8	27.7	2.6	2.3	41.2	40.4	42.4	43.2
Russian Federation	26.6	27.0	–0.2	16,381.4	49.4	49.4	0.2	0.1	8.3	7.4	85.0	84.9
Rwanda	94.6	80.7	1.8	24.7	12.9	19.5	12.4	10.9	35.7	48.6	12.0	13.7
Saudi Arabia	23.4	19.0	1.0	2,000.0[b]	1.4	1.4	0.0	0.1	1.7	1.8	17.0	16.3
Senegal	61.0	58.4	2.3	192.5	48.6	45.0	0.1	0.2	12.1	12.8	22.9	22.1
Serbia and Montenegro	49.1	47.8	–2.4	102.0	25.1	26.4	2.4	3.1	51.9	34.4	41.9	42.4
Sierra Leone	69.9	59.3	0.9	71.6	42.5	38.5	0.8	1.0	6.8	8.0	10.8	11.1
Singapore	0.0	0.0	..	0.7	3.0	2.9	1.5	0.3	1.5	0.9	0.0	0.0
Slovak Republic	43.5	43.8	0.2	48.1	40.0	40.1	1.0	0.5	32.5	28.9	27.1	26.0
Slovenia	49.6	49.0	–0.1	20.1	59.0	62.8	1.2	1.3	14.1	8.7	8.6	8.7
Somalia	70.3	64.8	1.0	627.3	13.2	11.4	0.0	0.0	1.6	1.7	14.5	13.6
South Africa	48.0	40.7	0.9	1,214.5	7.6	7.6	0.7	0.8	11.1	12.1	33.0	32.2
Spain	24.6	23.3	0.3	499.2	27.0	35.9	9.7	9.9	30.7	27.4	32.2	32.0
Sri Lanka	82.8	84.9	1.1	64.6	36.4	29.9	15.9	15.5	13.5	14.2	4.7	4.8
Sudan	73.4	59.2	0.8	2,376.0	32.1	28.4	0.1	0.2	5.5	7.2	48.4	48.8
Swaziland	77.1	75.9	2.6	17.2	27.4	31.5	0.7	0.8	10.5	10.3	16.7	16.1
Sweden	16.9	15.8	–0.1	410.3	66.7	67.1	0.0	0.0	6.9	6.6	30.3	29.8
Switzerland	31.6	24.8	–1.0	40.0	28.9	30.5	0.5	0.6	9.8	10.3	5.7	5.5
Syrian Arab Republic	51.1	49.4	2.4	183.8	2.0	2.5	4.0	4.7	26.6	26.5	26.6	25.6
Tajikistan	68.5	75.3	2.0	140.0	2.9	2.9	1.4	0.9	6.3	6.6	14.9	14.6
Tanzania	81.1	75.8	2.1	883.6	46.9	39.9	1.0	1.2	4.0	4.5	11.3	10.8
Thailand	70.6	67.7	0.8	510.9	31.2	28.4	6.1	7.0	34.2	27.7	25.6	22.4
Togo	69.9	59.9	2.0	54.4	12.6	7.1	1.7	2.2	38.6	46.1	45.5	43.0
Trinidad and Tobago	91.5	87.8	0.2	5.1	45.8	44.1	9.0	9.2	14.4	14.6	5.8	5.8
Tunisia	40.4	34.7	0.3	155.4	4.1	6.8	12.5	13.8	18.7	18.0	29.0	28.4
Turkey	40.8	32.7	0.2	769.6	12.6	13.2	3.9	3.6	32.0	31.0	34.8	33.2
Turkmenistan	54.9	53.8	1.6	469.9	8.8	8.8	0.2	0.1	3.0	4.7	40.5	46.8
Uganda	88.9	87.4	3.1	197.1	25.0	18.4	9.4	10.9	25.4	26.4	20.3	19.4
Ukraine	33.2	32.2	–0.9	579.4	16.0	16.5	3.1	1.6	59.2	56.0	66.9	68.5
United Arab Emirates	20.9	23.3	7.4	83.6	2.9	3.7	0.2	2.3	0.4	0.8	2.0	1.6
United Kingdom	11.3	10.3	–0.4	241.9	10.8	11.8	0.3	0.2	27.4	23.7	9.7	9.6
United States	24.7	19.2	–0.5	9,161.9	32.6	33.1	0.2	0.3	20.3	19.0	61.6	59.7
Uruguay	11.0	8.0	–1.3	175.0	5.2	8.6	0.3	0.2	7.2	7.8	40.7	40.1
Uzbekistan	59.9	63.3	2.0	425.4	7.2	7.7	0.6	0.8	10.8	11.0	18.0	18.4
Venezuela, RB	16.0	6.6	–3.9	882.1	59.0	54.1	0.9	0.9	3.2	2.9	10.5	10.1
Vietnam	79.7	73.6	1.0	310.1	28.8	41.7	3.2	7.6	16.4	21.3	8.2	8.0
West Bank and Gaza	32.1	28.4	3.4	6.0	1.5	1.5	19.1	19.1	18.4	17.8	3.4	3.1
Yemen, Rep.	79.1	72.7	3.1	528.0	1.0	1.0	0.2	0.3	2.9	2.9	8.2	7.8
Zambia	60.6	65.0	2.8	743.4	66.1	57.1	0.0	0.0	7.1	7.1	48.3	46.6
Zimbabwe	71.0	64.1	0.7	386.9	57.5	45.3	0.3	0.3	7.5	8.3	25.4	25.0
World	**57.0 w**	**51.2 w**	**0.6 w**	**129,606.2 s**	**31.5 w**	**30.5 w**	**1.0 w**	**1.1 w**	**10.7 w**	**10.6 w**	**22.3 w**	**21.9 w**
Low income	74.6	70.0	1.6	28,184.8	26.3	23.9	1.0	1.3	12.9	13.6	17.3	16.9
Middle income	55.6	46.1	–0.2	68,517.7	34.8	33.8	1.1	1.2	9.5	9.2	21.2	20.8
Lower middle income	61.7	50.5	–0.2	39,305.8	32.6	31.2	1.4	1.6	9.5	9.3	15.3	15.1
Upper middle income	31.7	28.0	0.0	29,211.9	37.7	37.2	0.6	0.6	9.5	8.9	45.1	43.9
Low & middle income	63.2	56.5	0.7	96,702.5	32.3	30.9	1.0	1.2	10.5	10.5	19.5	19.1
East Asia & Pacific	71.2	58.5	–0.2	15,869.9	28.8	28.4	2.2	2.8	10.8	11.0	9.5	9.4
Europe & Central Asia	36.9	36.3	–0.1	23,367.1	38.2	38.3	0.6	0.4	13.0	11.5	56.8	58.1
Latin America & Carib.	29.1	22.8	–0.1	20,126.9	48.9	45.5	0.9	1.0	6.5	7.1	27.3	26.6
Middle East & N. Africa	48.1	42.9	1.3	8,960.9	2.2	2.4	0.8	0.9	5.6	5.9	18.0	18.0
South Asia	75.1	71.5	1.5	4,781.3	16.5	16.8	1.8	2.8	42.6	47.1	14.6	13.8
Sub-Saharan Africa	72.1	64.8	1.8	23,596.5	29.2	26.5	0.8	0.9	6.4	7.5	25.1	24.8
High income	26.3	22.4	–0.3	32,903.7	29.1	29.4	0.7	0.7	11.5	11.0	37.5	36.9
Europe EMU	29.1	26.7	–0.2	2,455.3	33.5	37.3	4.7	4.4	27.0	25.6	20.5	20.2

a. Includes Taiwan, China; Macao, China; and Hong Kong, China. b. Provisional estimate.

Rural population and land use 3.1

About the data

Three billion people, including 70 percent of the world's poor people, live in rural areas. Therefore, adequate indicators to monitor progress in rural areas are essential However, indicators of rural development are sparse, as few indicators are disaggregated between rural and urban areas (for some that are, see tables 2.7, 3.5, and 3.10). This table shows indicators of rural population and land use. Rural population is approximated as the midyear nonurban population. While a practical means of identifying the rural population, it is not precise (see box 3a for more discussion of the issue).

The data in the table show that land use patterns are changing. They also indicate major differences in resource endowments and uses among countries. True comparability of the data is limited, however, by variations in definitions, statistical methods, and the quality of data collection. Countries use different definitions of rural and urban population and land use, for example. The Food and Agriculture Organization (FAO), the primary compiler of these data, occasionally adjusts its definitions of land use categories and sometimes revises earlier data. Because the data reflect changes in reporting procedures as well as actual changes in land use, apparent trends should be interpreted with caution.

Satellite images show land use that differs from that given by ground-based measures in both area under cultivation and type of land use. Moreover, land use data in countries such as India are based on reporting systems that were designed for the collection of tax revenue. Because taxes on land are no longer a major source of government revenue, the quality and coverage of land use data (except for cropland) have declined. Data on forest area may be particularly unreliable because of differences in definitions and irregular surveys (see *About the data* for table 3.4). FAO's *Global Forest Resources Assessment 2005* aims to address this limitation. FAO has been coordinating global forest resources assessments every 5–10 years since 1946. *Global Forest Resources Assessment 2005* was carried out between 2003 and 2005 and covered 229 countries and territories at three points in time: 1990, 2000, and 2005. It is the most comprehensive assessment of forests and forestry to date both in scope and in number of countries and people involved. It examines current status and recent trends for about 40 variables covering the extent, condition, uses, and values of forests and other wooded land with the aim of assessing all benefits from forest resources.

What is rural? Urban? — Box 3.1a

The rural population identified in table 3.1 is approximated as the difference between total population and the urban population, which is calculated on the basis of the urban share reported by the United Nations Population Division. However, there is no universal standard for distinguishing urban from rural areas, and any urban-rural dichotomy is an oversimplification (see *About the data* for table 3.10). The two distinct images—isolated farm, thriving metropolis—represent poles on a continuum. Life changes along a variety of dimensions, moving from the most remote forest outpost through fields and pastures, past tiny hamlets, through small towns with weekly farm markets, into intensively cultivated areas near large towns and small cities, eventually reaching the center of a cosmopolitan megacity. The changes may sometimes be abrupt, but more often they are gradual. Along the way access to infrastructure, social services, and nonfarm employment all increase, and with them population density and income. For policy purposes, therefore, one needs to go beyond the rural-urban dichotomy presented in tables 3.1 and 3.10, because rurality has many dimensions.

A recent World Bank Policy Research Paper proposes an operational definition of rurality based on two dimensions: population density and distance to large cities (population greater than 100,000; Chomitz, Buys, and Thomas 2005). The report argues that these criteria constitute important gradients along which economic behavior and appropriate development interventions vary substantially. Where population densities are low, markets of all kinds are thin, and the unit cost of delivering most social services and many types of infrastructure is high. Where large urban areas are distant, farm-gate (or factory-gate) prices of outputs will be low and prices of inputs will be high, and it will be difficult to recruit skilled people to public service or private enterprises. Thus, remoteness and low population density together define a set of rural areas that face special challenges in development.

Based on these criteria, and using the Gridded Population of the World (CIESIN 2005), the authors produced estimates of the rural population for Latin America and the Caribbean that differ substantially from those presented in table 3.1. The range of these estimates are from 13 percent of the total population, based on a population density of less than 20 people per square kilometer, to 64 percent, based on a population density of more than 500 people per square kilometer. Taking remoteness into account, the estimated rural population would be between 13 and 52 percent of the population. The estimate for Latin America and the Caribbean in table 3.1 is 23 percent.

Definitions

• **Rural population** is calculated as the difference between the total population and the urban population (see *Definitions* for tables 2.1 and 3.10). • **Land area** is a country's total area, excluding area under inland water bodies, national claims to the continental shelf, and exclusive economic zones. In most cases the definitions of inland water bodies includes major rivers and lakes. (See table 1.1 for the total surface area of countries.) • **Land use** can be broken into several categories, three of which are presented in this table (not shown are land used as permanent pasture and land under urban developments). • **Forest area** is land under natural or planted stands of trees, whether productive or not. • **Permanent cropland** is land cultivated with crops that occupy the land for long periods and need not be replanted after each harvest, such as cocoa, coffee, and rubber. This category includes land under flowering shrubs, fruit trees, nut trees, and vines, but excludes land under trees grown for wood or timber. • **Arable land** includes land defined by the FAO as under temporary crops (double-cropped areas are counted once), temporary meadows for mowing or for pasture, land under market or kitchen gardens, and land temporarily fallow. Land abandoned as a result of shifting cultivation is excluded.

Data sources

Data on urban population shares used to estimate rural population come from the United Nations Population Division's *World Urbanization Prospects: The 2005 Revision.* The total population figures are World Bank estimates. Data on land area and land use are from the FAO's electronic files. The FAO gathers these data from national agencies through annual questionnaires and by analyzing the results of national agricultural censuses. Data on forest area are from the FAO's *Global Forest Resources Assessment 2005.*

3.2 Agricultural inputs

	Agricultural land[a]		Irrigated land		Land under cereal production		Fertilizer consumption		Agricultural employment		Agricultural machinery	
	% of land area		% of cropland		thousand hectares		hundred grams per hectare of arable land		% of total employment		Tractors per 100 sq. km of arable land	
	1990–92	2003–05	1990–92	2001–03	1990–92	2003–05	1990–92	2000–02	1990–92	2001–03	1990–92	2001–03
Afghanistan	58.3	58.3	33.9	33.8	2,283	2,788	59	19	..	..	1	1
Albania	41.1	40.9	55.6	49.5	243	148	903	420	..	62.7	177	141
Algeria	16.3	16.8	6.4	6.9	3,105	2,751	144	130	..	21.1	128	129
Angola	46.1	46.2	2.3	2.3	893	1,306	29	5	..	..	35	33
Argentina	46.6	47.0	5.6	5.4	8,510	9,391	73	295	0.4	1.1	103	108
Armenia	43.1	49.3	49.9	51.2	163	198	493	157	..	45.7	277	289
Australia	60.5	57.5	4.2	5.2	12,814	19,905	275	479	5.5	4.4	67	65
Austria	42.5	40.0	0.3	0.3	903	810	1,995	1,540	7.5	5.6	2,367	2,380
Azerbaijan	51.5	57.5	68.0	70.5	628	788	432	61	32.5	40.1	184	164
Bangladesh	73.5	69.3	33.8	54.3	10,985	11,511	1,136	1,738	66.4	51.7	6	7
Belarus	43.6	42.7	2.1	2.3	2,581	2,148	2,251	1,325	21.7	..	195	111
Belgium	43.6	46.0	..	4.6	326	314	4,937	3,427	2.8	1.7	1,498	1,254
Benin	20.6	31.3	0.6	0.4	660	963	78	154	..	..	1	1
Bolivia	32.9	34.2	5.5	4.1	633	792	42	37	1.7	..	25	20
Bosnia and Herzegovina	15.0	42.1	0.2	0.3	333	326	..	356	..	..	235	289
Botswana	45.9	45.8	0.2	0.3	140	67	22	122	..	16.8	143	159
Brazil	28.9	31.2	4.6	4.4	19,633	19,806	656	1,201	25.6	20.6	142	137
Bulgaria	55.7	48.5	29.6	16.5	2,174	1,721	1,194	500	19.7	18.0	128	95
Burkina Faso	34.9	39.8	0.6	0.5	2,725	3,249	60	30	..	..	3	4
Burundi	82.9	91.3	1.2	1.6	219	210	34	33	..	..	2	2
Cambodia	30.2	30.3	6.6	7.0	1,801	2,332	19	..	..	70.2	3	7
Cameroon	19.7	19.7	0.3	0.4	816	1,077	34	75	60.6	..	1	1
Canada	7.5	7.4	1.4	1.5	20,864	17,272	476	549	4.2	2.8	162	160
Central African Republic	8.0	8.3	0.0	0.1	104	187	5	3	..	..	0	0
Chad	38.4	38.6	0.5	0.8	1,242	2,096	25	49	..	..	1	0
Chile	21.0	20.4	57.1	82.4	742	687	1,215	2,386	18.8	13.6	144	272
China	57.0	59.5	43.6	47.5	93,430	79,896	2,777	3,519	53.5	44.7	77	89
Hong Kong, China	..	..	..	..	..	..	..	..	0.8	0.2	..	..
Colombia	40.5	38.2	14.3	23.3	1,598	1,265	1,822	2,670	1.4	21.2	98	91
Congo, Dem. Rep.	10.1	10.1	0.1	0.1	1,868	1,974	8	7	..	..	4	4
Congo, Rep.	30.8	30.9	0.3	0.4	9	13	35	67	..	..	15	14
Costa Rica	55.7	56.1	15.2	20.6	83	58	4,522	6,455	25.2	15.5	259	311
Côte d'Ivoire	59.8	62.6	1.1	1.1	1,434	953	151	256	..	..	15	12
Croatia	15.0	50.8	0.2	0.4	647	646	1,514	1,303	..	15.8	35	25
Cuba	61.5	60.6	22.6	22.5	235	309	1,288	476	25.1	21.7	250	249
Czech Republic	55.4	55.2	..	0.7	..	1,563	..	1,186	10.1	4.7	..	305
Denmark	65.4	62.0	16.9	19.6	1,581	1,495	2,249	1,393	5.4	3.2	625	540
Dominican Republic	74.7	76.4	14.9	17.2	134	150	860	848	19.5	15.4	22	17
Ecuador	28.6	26.9	27.9	33.0	861	892	508	1,679	7.0	8.5	67	106
Egypt, Arab Rep.	2.7	3.5	100.0	100.0	2,410	2,851	3,977	4,464	36.2	28.6	251	309
El Salvador	71.1	82.2	4.9	4.9	453	330	1,336	1,054	17.9	19.9	60	52
Eritrea	..	74.6	..	3.7	..	370	..	119	..	..	..	8
Estonia	31.2	19.1	0.5	0.6	454	268	993	432	19.5	6.7	395	889
Ethiopia	51.0	31.8	1.4	2.6	4,586	9,039	..	145	..	..	..	3
Finland	7.9	7.4	2.8	2.9	1,050	1,200	1,647	1,353	8.8	5.3	1,040	882
France	55.3	53.9	11.0	13.3	9,212	9,160	2,918	2,221	..	4.3	784	685
Gabon	20.0	20.0	1.1	1.4	14	20	25	9	..	..	50	46
Gambia, The	63.2	77.9	0.9	0.6	90	186	44	26	..	..	2	1
Georgia	44.8	43.3	39.9	44.1	249	339	889	412	..	53.8	279	254
Germany	49.8	48.8	4.0	4.0	6,673	6,875	2,616	2,245	4.0	2.5	1,253	801
Ghana	55.7	64.8	0.7	0.5	1,078	1,376	38	60	62.2	..	15	9
Greece	71.3	65.2	31.1	37.4	1,455	1,272	2,289	1,580	22.7	15.6	774	939
Guatemala	39.5	42.9	6.8	6.4	768	666	1,072	1,427	..	38.7	33	30
Guinea	48.9	50.7	7.0	5.6	627	778	16	32	..	..	5	5
Guinea-Bissau	53.2	58.0	4.1	4.6	112	138	15	80	..	..	1	1
Haiti	57.9	57.7	8.0	8.4	406	458	35	181	..	..	2	2

Agricultural inputs 3.2

	Agricultural land[a]		Irrigated land		Land under cereal production		Fertilizer consumption		Agricultural employment		Agricultural machinery	
	% of land area		% of cropland		thousand hectares		hundred grams per hectare of arable land		% of total employment		Tractors per 100 sq. km of arable land	
	1990–92	2003–05	1990–92	2001–03	1990–92	2003–05	1990–92	2000–02	1990–92	2001–03	1990–92	2001–03
Honduras	29.8	26.2	3.8	5.6	502	391	203	1,193	42.1	35.1	31	49
Hungary	70.7	65.4	4.1	4.8	2,803	2,940	796	993	11.3	6.0	158	247
India	60.9	60.6	28.3	32.7	100,760	97,872	758	1,044	68.1	..	65	141
Indonesia	23.5	26.3	14.5	12.7	13,861	15,140	1,330	1,259	54.9	44.8	18	41
Iran, Islamic Rep.	37.7	37.9	39.7	42.7	9,612	8,983	750	890	25.6	..	136	161
Iraq	21.9	22.9	63.0	58.6	3,506	3,221	347	968	..	..	72	80
Ireland	70.2	62.4	..	..	298	294	6,591	5,172	14.1	6.8	1,667	1,324
Israel	26.7	24.4	44.4	45.4	108	92	2,836	2,575	3.7	2.0	763	714
Italy	55.4	50.7	22.9	24.9	4,347	4,142	2,195	1,819	8.4	5.0	1,619	2,031
Jamaica	44.0	47.4	11.0	5.9	3	1	1,737	1,258	27.3	20.4	242	177
Japan	15.5	12.9	54.3	54.7	2,439	2,008	3,779	3,066	6.8	4.7	4,297	4,588
Jordan	12.0	11.5	25.0	27.3	112	53	969	1,322	..	3.9	352	308
Kazakhstan	79.1	76.9	9.8	15.7	22,174	13,697	133	23	..	35.4	59	22
Kenya	45.7	..	1.3	1.8	1,766	2,017	255	320	19.0	..	24	28
Korea, Dem. Rep.	21.0	24.9	58.2	50.9	1,569	1,272	3,522	1,018	..	..	297	241
Korea, Rep.	21.9	19.2	47.1	47.1	1,368	1,093	4,932	4,317	16.7	9.4	275	1,239
Kuwait	7.9	8.6	60.0	77.0	0	1	2,000	711	..	..	215	69
Kyrgyz Republic	50.7	56.2	72.6	76.0	579	596	238	209	35.5	52.8	179	167
Lao PDR	7.2	8.5	16.2	17.2	630	758	31	94	..	..	11	12
Latvia	39.3	26.5	1.1	2.1	699	451	977	572	..	14.8	343	580
Lebanon	31.1	32.2	28.1	33.2	41	61	1,639	2,838	..	..	188	488
Lesotho	76.7	76.9	0.6	0.9	178	177	167	309	..	..	57	61
Liberia	27.1	27.0	0.5	0.5	135	120	8	..	..	..	8	9
Libya	8.8	8.8	21.8	21.9	355	341	458	349	..	..	187	219
Lithuania	52.1	42.5	0.5	0.4	1,135	899	531	903	18.8	17.7	242	641
Macedonia, FYR	17.9	48.8	12.1	9.0	257	195	..	502	..	23.0	730	954
Madagascar	47.0	47.4	30.7	30.6	1,321	1,457	34	31	..	78.0	11	12
Malawi	40.2	47.2	1.2	2.3	1,443	1,544	351	400	..	..	8	6
Malaysia	22.7	24.0	4.8	4.8	699	701	5,264	6,548	23.9	14.8	161	241
Mali	26.3	32.4	3.7	5.0	2,393	3,292	91	88	..	..	11	6
Mauritania	38.7	38.8	11.8	6.5	133	176	132	59	..	..	8	8
Mauritius	55.7	55.7	16.0	20.1	1	0	2,732	3,035	14.3	10.5	36	37
Mexico	54.5	56.2	22.4	23.2	10,075	10,126	696	727	24.2	17.2	129	131
Moldova	75.1	76.7	14.2	13.9	676	927	762	86	..	47.9	293	221
Mongolia	79.9	83.3	5.8	7.0	620	180	111	31	..	45.0	73	42
Morocco	68.2	68.1	13.2	15.5	5,374	5,565	353	440	..	44.8	46	58
Mozambique	60.9	62.0	2.8	2.7	1,509	2,071	12	53	..	..	16	14
Myanmar	15.8	17.2	10.1	17.9	5,283	7,215	79	146	69.4	..	12	10
Namibia	47.0	47.2	0.7	1.0	215	244	..	4	48.2	..	47	39
Nepal	29.0	29.5	43.0	47.2	2,957	3,346	340	333	82.3	..	23	24
Netherlands	58.9	56.8	61.0	60.0	185	217	6,298	4,286	4.3	2.8	2,056	1,645
New Zealand	65.0	64.3	7.6	8.5	153	121	1,892	5,704	10.7	8.7	322	507
Nicaragua	52.1	57.5	4.0	2.8	299	502	270	177	38.7	26.8	20	15
Niger	27.0	30.4	0.5	0.5	7,011	8,111	1	3	..	..	0	0
Nigeria	79.4	79.7	0.7	0.8	16,417	17,799	142	66	..	..	8	10
Norway	3.3	3.4	..	..	361	326	2,362	2,086	5.9	3.8	1,723	1,486
Oman	3.5	3.5	71.6	88.4	2	2	2,441	2,491	..	..	42	50
Pakistan	33.7	35.2	78.5	81.1	11,777	12,587	962	1,378	48.9	45.3	133	149
Panama	28.7	30.0	4.8	6.2	182	195	666	545	25.8	17.7	103	148
Papua New Guinea	2.0	2.3	..	..	2	3	622	556	..	..	59	53
Paraguay	59.6	62.5	2.9	2.1	455	782	92	319	1.7	32.2	72	55
Peru	17.1	16.6	29.9	27.9	683	1,116	246	759	1.0	3.5	36	36
Philippines	37.4	40.9	15.7	14.5	6,957	6,613	935	1,313	45.3	37.3	20	20
Poland	61.6	52.8	0.7	0.7	8,523	8,290	895	1,151	25.2	18.9	821	1,034
Portugal	42.8	41.7	20.5	27.2	780	435	1,123	1,258	15.6	12.5	569	1,044
Puerto Rico	47.5	25.1	36.8	37.1	0	0	..	..	3.5	2.0	..	..

3.2 Agricultural inputs

	Agricultural land[a]		Irrigated land		Land under cereal production		Fertilizer consumption		Agricultural employment		Agricultural machinery	
	% of land area		% of cropland		thousand hectares		hundred grams per hectare of arable land		% of total employment		Tractors per 100 sq. km of arable land	
	1990–92	2003–05	1990–92	2001–03	1990–92	2003–05	1990–92	2000–02	1990–92	2001–03	1990–92	2001–03
Romania	64.4	63.8	31.0	31.2	5,842	5,675	788	355	30.6	38.1	146	179
Russian Federation	13.0	13.2	4.2	3.7	59,600	39,471	410	121	14.5	11.4	92	52
Rwanda	75.6	78.4	0.3	0.7	258	332	20	48	..	..	1	1
Saudi Arabia	..	..	44.2	42.7	1,062	669	1,446	1,067	..	5.4	20	28
Senegal	41.9	42.4	3.3	4.6	1,154	1,202	65	140	..	..	2	3
Serbia and Montenegro	21.1	54.8	1.9	0.8	2,618	1,987	265	732	..	..	1,067	1,023
Sierra Leone	38.3	39.7	5.2	5.0	452	253	23	5	..	..	3	2
Singapore	2.2	1.2	..	..	..	..	54,333	25,920	0.3	0.3	637	794
Slovak Republic	50.9	42.3	..	12.6	1	802	..	..	..	6.0	..	..
Slovenia	9.8	25.0	0.8	1.5	130	99	3,168	4,239	..	9.3	..	..
Somalia	70.2	70.3	19.2	18.7	531	682	26	5	..	..	21	16
South Africa	80.2	82.0	8.3	9.5	5,736	4,429	549	558	..	10.7	101	46
Spain	60.8	58.3	16.9	20.7	7,588	6,573	1,186	1,653	10.7	6.1	494	712
Sri Lanka	36.2	36.5	28.0	34.4	834	882	2,016	2,862	44.3	34.7	71	113
Sudan	52.0	56.6	13.9	11.0	6,267	10,005	51	40	..	..	8	7
Swaziland	75.8	80.9	24.1	26.0	69	61	688	371	..	..	251	222
Sweden	8.2	7.8	4.1	4.3	1,184	1,098	1,112	1,010	3.3	2.2	604	615
Switzerland	46.9	38.1	6.0	5.8	207	164	4,032	2,272	4.2	4.2	2,870	2,649
Syrian Arab Republic	73.7	75.6	14.3	24.0	3,812	3,195	621	718	..	30.3	137	224
Tajikistan	30.9	30.4	72.9	68.2	266	393	1,461	175	..	..	392	233
Tanzania	53.7	54.4	3.2	3.5	3,003	3,340	136	31	84.2	82.1	19	19
Thailand	41.9	36.2	21.0	26.6	10,594	11,134	598	1,039	61.5	45.7	39	144
Togo	58.7	66.7	0.3	0.3	610	767	56	74	..	..	0	0
Trinidad and Tobago	25.7	25.9	3.3	3.3	6	2	1,111	631	11.8	7.4	354	360
Tunisia	58.4	63.0	7.3	8.0	1,525	1,450	330	372	..	..	88	126
Turkey	51.8	53.3	14.8	19.5	13,760	13,817	757	768	46.5	35.5	287	410
Turkmenistan	66.1	70.2	..	89.1	332	983	1,273	543	..	..	439	256
Uganda	61.0	..	0.1	0.1	1,098	1,550	1	14	91.5	69.1	9	9
Ukraine	69.8	71.4	7.6	6.8	12,555	13,082	792	154	..	19.5	145	124
United Arab Emirates	3.7	6.7	..	29.2	1	0	4,810	5,149	..	..	50	55
United Kingdom	75.0	70.2	2.5	3.0	3,549	3,040	3,323	3,141	2.2	1.4	762	878
United States	46.6	45.3	11.3	12.5	64,547	57,163	1,015	1,096	2.9	2.2	245	270
Uruguay	84.7	85.4	10.2	14.3	509	528	610	849	4.5	4.3	259	241
Uzbekistan	62.8	64.1	87.3	87.4	1,227	1,692	1,602	1,614	..	..	380	373
Venezuela, RB	24.7	24.5	13.9	16.9	799	1,042	1,388	1,132	12.6	10.0	176	189
Vietnam	21.0	30.8	44.6	33.9	6,726	8,392	1,299	3,172	73.8	61.9	60	247
West Bank and Gaza	..	..	..	..	..	..	..	..	..	14.1	..	..
Yemen, Rep.	33.4	33.6	24.3	31.4	738	635	127	95	..	..	40	43
Zambia	47.4	47.5	0.7	2.8	813	717	131	84	..	..	11	11
Zimbabwe	52.3	53.1	3.6	5.2	1,431	1,617	508	443	..	..	61	75
World	**37.7 w**	**38.3 w**	**17.7 w**	**18.4 w**	**704,675 s**	**677,585 s**	**925 w**	**1,020 w**	**41.8 w**	**.. w**	**186 w**	**200 w**
Low income	44.3	45.2	21.8	24.4	211,290	230,781	541	686	..	..	52	84
Middle income	34.6	35.5	20.1	18.5	350,107	310,863	970	1,110	44.2	35.8	127	137
Lower middle income	41.2	42.6	24.4	24.4	228,729	208,372	1,278	1,573	48.9	40.1	99	112
Upper middle income	25.7	25.9	11.8	9.5	121,378	102,492	553	471	20.8	15.5	164	173
Low & middle income	37.4	38.2	20.7	20.7	561,397	541,644	817	951	50.6	..	100	117
East Asia & Pacific	48.4	50.7	..	..	142,270	133,753	..	..	54.2	44.9	63	89
Europe & Central Asia	28.4	27.6	10.3	11.2	140,517	114,042	581	347	22.4	20.9	172	185
Latin America & Carib.	34.7	35.8	11.3	11.4	47,720	49,696	587	896	18.1	16.7	123	123
Middle East & N. Africa	22.6	23.2	29.6	32.7	30,593	29,108	643	833	..	..	115	142
South Asia	54.7	54.5	33.9	38.9	129,690	129,043	767	1,067	66.1	..	67	129
Sub-Saharan Africa	43.4	44.1	3.4	3.6	70,608	86,002	136	125	..	..	19	13
High income	38.5	38.6	10.7	11.8	143,278	135,941	1,213	1,212	5.7	3.8	417	431
Europe EMU	49.7	47.5	14.9	17.0	32,976	31,419	2,332	2,059	7.3	4.9	992	1,002

a. Agricultural land includes permanent pastures, arable land, and land under permanent crops.

Agricultural inputs 3.2

About the data

Agriculture is still a major sector in many economies, and agricultural activities provide developing countries with food and revenue. But they also can degrade natural resources. Poor farming practices can cause soil erosion and loss of soil fertility. Efforts to increase productivity through the use of chemical fertilizers, pesticides, and intensive irrigation have environmental costs and health impacts. Excessive use of chemical fertilizers can alter the chemistry of soil. Pesticide poisoning is common in developing countries. And salinization of irrigated land diminishes soil fertility. Thus inappropriate use of inputs for agricultural production has far-reaching effects.

This table provides indicators of major inputs to agricultural production: land, fertilizer, labor, and agricultural machinery. There is no single correct mix of inputs: appropriate levels and application rates vary by country and over time, depending on the type of crops, the climate and soils, and the production process used.

The data shown here and in table 3.3 are collected by the Food and Agriculture Organization (FAO) through annual questionnaires. The FAO tries to impose standard definitions and reporting methods, but exact consistency across countries and over time is not possible. For example, despite standard definitions, data on agricultural land in different climates may not be comparable. For example, permanent pastures are quite different in nature and intensity in African countries and dry Middle Eastern countries. Data on agricultural employment, in particular, should be used with caution. In many countries much agricultural employment is informal and unrecorded, including substantial work performed by women and children.

Fertilizer consumption measures the quantity of plant nutrients. Consumption is calculated as production plus imports minus exports. Because some chemical compounds used for fertilizers have other industrial applications, the consumption data may overstate the quantity available for crops.

To smooth annual fluctuations in agricultural activity, the indicators in the table have been averaged over three years.

Nearly 40 percent of land globally is used for agriculture **3.2a**

Total land: 130 million square kilometers

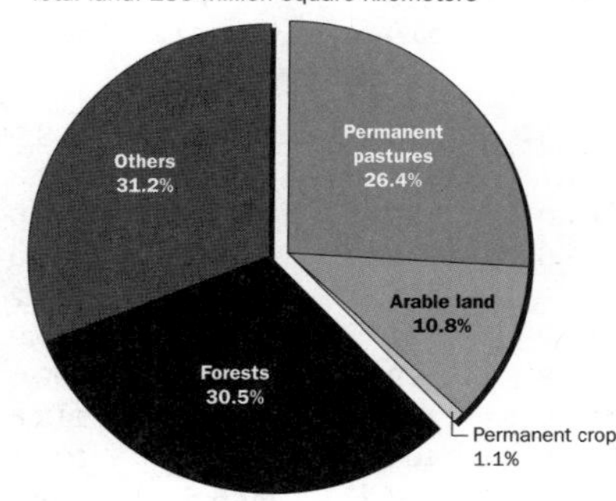

Note: Agricultural land includes permanent pastures, arable land, and land under permanent crops.
Source: Tables 3.1 and 3.2.

Definitions

• **Agricultural land** refers to the share of land area that is arable, under permanent crops, or under permanent pastures. Arable land includes land defined by the FAO as land under temporary crops (double-cropped areas are counted once), temporary meadows for mowing or for pasture, land under market or kitchen gardens, and land temporarily fallow. Land abandoned as a result of shifting cultivation is excluded. Land under permanent crops is land cultivated with crops that occupy the land for long periods and need not be replanted after each harvest, such as cocoa, coffee, and rubber. This category includes land under flowering shrubs, fruit trees, nut trees, and vines, but excludes land under trees grown for wood or timber. Permanent pasture is land used for five or more years for forage, including natural and cultivated crops. • **Irrigated land** refers to areas purposely provided with water, including land irrigated by controlled flooding. • **Cropland** refers to arable land and permanent cropland (see table 3.1). • **Land under cereal production** refers to harvested areas, although some countries report only sown or cultivated area. • **Fertilizer consumption** is the quantity of plant nutrients used per unit of arable land. Fertilizer products cover nitrogenous, potash, and phosphate fertilizers (including ground rock phosphate). Traditional nutrients—animal and plant manures—are not included. The time reference for fertilizer consumption is the crop year (July through June). • **Agricultural employment** refers to employment in agriculture, forestry, hunting, and fishing (see table 2.3 for more detail). • **Agricultural machinery** refers to wheel and crawler tractors (excluding garden tractors) in use in agriculture at the end of the calendar year specified or during the first quarter of the following year.

Data sources

Data on agricultural inputs are from electronic files that the FAO makes available to the World Bank.

3.3 Agricultural output and productivity

	Crop production index		Food production index		Livestock production index		Cereal yield		Agricultural productivity	
	1999–2001 = 100		1999–2001 = 100		1999–2001 = 100		kilograms per hectare		Agriculture value added per worker 2000 $	
	1990–92	**2002–04**	**1990–92**	**2002–04**	**1990–92**	**2002–04**	**1990–92**	**2003–05**	**1990–92**	**2001–03**
Afghanistan	..	..	..	..	..	..	..	..	..	..
Albania	86.2	100.6	74.2	105.9	66.6	108.9	2,372	3,491	773	1,314
Algeria	85.4	122.9	81.7	113.2	80.7	103.3	915	1,468	1,911	2,067
Angola	60.5	119.4	65.0	113.0	75.6	100.0	378	547	183	160
Argentina	67.2	106.4	73.6	101.4	89.2	92.0	2,652	3,771	6,764	9,272
Armenia	106.5	119.2	112.9	121.8	118.9	123.2	1,826	2,122	1,428	2,645
Australia	59.7	81.6	69.2	91.7	83.3	96.9	1,739	1,960	22,405	31,218
Austria	93.4	99.1	89.8	99.0	92.5	99.6	5,400	5,738	12,048	20,587
Azerbaijan	137.4	122.7	104.8	118.6	98.2	113.6	2,113	2,633	1,085	1,033
Bangladesh	75.4	104.7	73.8	104.6	73.8	103.2	2,567	3,533	246	308
Belarus	107.3	124.7	136.1	107.2	146.5	99.7	2,739	2,850	1,977	2,513
Belgium	77.6	106.0	91.3	101.3	94.3	99.7	6,122	8,710	21,356	36,043
Benin	57.7	125.4	62.7	126.3	89.1	109.2	880	1,147	368	578
Bolivia	63.6	116.4	70.0	111.6	77.2	107.9	1,385	1,857	670	746
Bosnia and Herzegovina	107.2	101.1	120.3	96.0	122.7	86.6	3,548	3,393	..	5,696
Botswana	96.2	111.5	114.8	104.8	118.8	103.4	312	514	571	410
Brazil	77.2	119.6	70.4	118.0	65.5	116.8	1,916	3,149	1,700	3,002
Bulgaria	149.2	110.9	137.5	101.7	147.1	96.2	3,639	3,157	2,493	6,313
Burkina Faso	67.0	126.6	68.7	116.2	70.7	108.1	783	959	143	163
Burundi	112.4	107.0	112.1	106.3	135.1	100.2	1,370	1,336	110	80
Cambodia	65.2	105.8	65.1	106.3	65.7	103.5	1,356	2,062	..	296
Cameroon	71.2	103.0	73.9	104.2	84.1	103.1	1,166	1,720	713	1,102
Canada	87.9	93.8	84.1	94.8	78.3	103.6	2,559	2,962	28,224	37,590
Central African Republic	74.4	97.7	69.9	106.9	68.1	113.5	884	1,046	290	407
Chad	69.0	110.9	72.5	110.2	84.5	105.4	636	711	179	225
Chile	78.2	110.5	74.0	108.6	68.0	107.0	3,949	5,621	3,618	4,795
China	69.6	110.6	60.1	113.2	49.4	116.1	4,307	5,057	254	368
Hong Kong, China	..	..	..	..	..	..	..	..	..	..
Colombia	98.4	107.4	83.9	106.8	80.6	107.1	2,492	3,567	3,406	2,951
Congo, Dem. Rep.	124.7	97.2	121.4	97.5	100.8	99.2	791	767	186	154
Congo, Rep.	80.2	105.1	79.0	107.0	76.0	114.5	688	806	314	329
Costa Rica	71.4	99.6	72.2	101.0	79.9	101.4	3,188	4,001	3,143	4,283
Côte d'Ivoire	73.0	96.2	72.9	100.0	74.9	110.9	869	1,266	605	798
Croatia	79.9	97.2	99.0	98.9	126.6	108.2	3,975	4,179	4,751	8,957
Cuba	112.1	112.6	111.5	108.1	130.0	92.7	2,092	3,076	..	..
Czech Republic	..	94.8	..	96.6	..	95.8	..	4,816	..	4,564
Denmark	103.5	97.7	97.6	100.6	89.0	102.8	5,448	6,080	15,157	35,696
Dominican Republic	119.1	110.0	104.0	106.1	79.5	103.7	4,078	4,177	2,254	4,108
Ecuador	80.1	95.9	72.4	106.5	65.1	115.3	1,724	2,485	1,686	1,486
Egypt, Arab Rep.	69.2	104.2	67.5	107.7	65.4	115.3	5,738	7,528	1,531	1,975
El Salvador	102.2	90.6	86.4	102.9	74.5	108.5	1,871	2,462	1,633	1,616
Eritrea	..	67.7	..	83.2	..	97.1	..	296	..	64
Estonia	121.4	89.9	181.3	100.4	193.3	101.7	1,304	2,274	3,002	3,168
Ethiopia	..	106.7	..	110.6	..	117.7	..	1,261	..	150
Finland	97.5	102.4	104.0	103.3	106.5	104.3	3,246	3,284	15,425	29,735
France	94.0	98.8	97.4	99.5	97.3	100.4	6,370	6,876	22,234	39,220
Gabon	87.2	101.9	89.1	101.6	86.5	100.5	1,712	1,641	1,566	1,696
Gambia, The	55.8	65.2	60.2	68.7	98.8	102.6	1,120	1,155	224	226
Georgia	120.6	91.9	102.7	100.9	78.9	110.3	1,998	2,152	2,388	1,404
Germany	83.7	95.1	98.0	97.5	107.5	101.0	5,578	6,497	14,025	23,475
Ghana	59.1	117.0	61.1	116.9	89.8	108.7	1,084	1,437	302	331
Greece	86.9	90.4	93.7	92.2	101.5	98.2	3,589	3,699	7,563	9,114
Guatemala	77.6	102.6	75.4	105.5	76.6	100.6	1,882	1,747	2,149	2,274
Guinea	73.7	107.5	72.9	110.7	60.5	111.8	1,064	1,476	172	225
Guinea-Bissau	71.1	104.9	73.1	105.1	81.2	106.6	1,529	1,149	205	225
Haiti	108.5	98.8	99.8	101.9	69.8	111.6	997	824	..	..

Agricultural output and productivity

	Crop production index		Food production index		Livestock production index		Cereal yield		Agricultural productivity	
									Agriculture value added per worker 2000 $	
	1999–2001 = 100		1999–2001 = 100		1999–2001 = 100		kilograms per hectare			
	1990–92	2002–04	1990–92	2002–04	1990–92	2002–04	1990–92	2003–05	1990–92	2001–03
Honduras	92.9	118.9	86.5	111.9	69.3	105.8	1,371	1,095	976	1,110
Hungary	114.0	99.7	117.0	100.9	125.5	101.9	4,551	4,718	3,268	4,120
India	79.6	100.0	75.9	102.5	69.4	110.5	1,947	2,391	332	381
Indonesia	82.8	112.7	83.8	113.1	85.8	127.3	3,826	4,278	483	556
Iran, Islamic Rep.	73.8	118.1	72.2	113.3	68.8	103.3	1,523	2,411	1,953	2,330
Iraq	..	..	..	..	..	..	..	..	..	2,256
Ireland	92.7	100.3	95.3	96.4	94.3	96.1	6,653	7,390	..	..
Israel	97.8	103.3	82.8	106.5	72.4	113.1	3,132	3,725	..	..
Italy	97.3	92.6	97.0	94.3	95.1	99.4	4,340	5,057	11,536	21,113
Jamaica	84.9	96.7	85.7	97.9	87.2	102.8	1,298	1,162	2,013	1,944
Japan	112.9	95.0	108.4	97.4	106.8	100.2	5,713	5,807	20,196	33,546
Jordan	100.1	136.6	85.4	124.1	71.2	94.1	1,167	1,354	1,892	1,099
Kazakhstan	163.8	108.4	163.0	106.4	178.5	111.6	1,338	994	1,745	1,389
Kenya	86.9	103.2	85.7	106.4	83.9	110.4	1,645	1,409	335	327
Korea, Dem. Rep.	126.2	108.4	119.6	109.1	145.1	114.2	5,073	3,408	..	..
Korea, Rep.	88.2	91.3	79.8	92.8	68.1	100.4	5,885	6,233	5,677	9,948
Kuwait	33.6	110.6	26.4	122.0	27.9	115.7	3,112	1,975	..	13,048
Kyrgyz Republic	68.5	102.9	74.0	101.0	106.9	98.4	2,772	2,984	676	929
Lao PDR	62.2	115.3	59.1	115.9	60.6	107.5	2,344	3,180	360	459
Latvia	128.7	119.4	222.3	111.0	273.8	101.1	1,641	2,225	1,790	2,442
Lebanon	109.7	94.1	100.4	100.4	65.6	120.4	2,001	2,377	..	24,436
Lesotho	67.5	100.8	87.8	100.4	115.0	100.0	703	906	476	503
Liberia	62.3	97.7	80.5	96.2	90.4	107.8	951	889	..	..
Libya	79.2	96.9	77.1	101.6	75.9	101.0	706	626	..	..
Lithuania	80.2	113.1	159.9	111.0	187.0	107.8	1,938	3,183	..	4,117
Macedonia, FYR	107.4	93.3	107.8	96.2	105.1	103.3	2,652	3,053	2,256	2,964
Madagascar	93.6	103.5	90.4	101.8	93.3	97.1	1,935	2,321	185	177
Malawi	57.5	84.3	49.6	87.1	85.4	101.8	871	1,150	72	130
Malaysia	74.4	114.0	70.5	113.7	81.3	115.1	2,827	3,293	3,803	4,570
Mali	73.8	107.4	78.6	105.8	81.3	112.9	840	872	204	227
Mauritania	63.2	97.2	84.2	107.6	87.4	109.3	802	1,075	574	385
Mauritius	110.7	101.6	101.1	104.9	71.1	116.8	4,117	3,436	3,942	5,065
Mexico	82.8	103.8	77.7	105.5	71.4	107.8	2,520	2,872	2,247	2,708
Moldova	136.6	112.2	153.3	112.6	198.7	103.2	2,928	2,572	1,286	725
Mongolia	246.9	107.3	98.3	96.4	93.9	95.9	967	808	703	684
Morocco	101.1	133.4	94.3	122.6	81.3	102.0	1,095	1,282	1,438	1,515
Mozambique	64.7	106.1	70.5	103.0	94.8	100.9	330	921	108	137
Myanmar	61.5	114.7	62.3	115.2	65.0	115.1	2,739	3,420	..	..
Namibia	71.9	111.4	99.5	109.8	104.1	109.3	381	441	811	1,057
Nepal	73.5	111.2	75.2	109.4	80.1	107.3	1,831	2,284	196	208
Netherlands	93.7	97.9	105.5	94.8	105.3	92.6	7,145	8,036	24,056	37,337
New Zealand	78.9	101.9	77.8	112.1	80.7	112.1	5,257	7,360	20,180	26,310
Nicaragua	76.6	115.3	64.0	119.4	57.5	119.9	1,529	1,778	..	1,901
Niger	71.4	119.5	75.4	116.3	82.0	104.7	323	394	170	172
Nigeria	68.9	103.4	69.1	103.7	76.9	106.6	1,135	1,057	592	843
Norway	120.7	103.4	104.1	98.6	98.2	97.3	3,744	4,121	20,055	32,649
Oman	62.8	87.3	60.2	89.9	65.7	94.0	2,145	2,332	1,005	1,128
Pakistan	80.6	102.5	70.6	106.0	67.6	109.1	1,818	2,438	589	690
Panama	110.9	104.2	94.8	101.8	76.3	101.1	1,862	1,958	2,363	3,557
Papua New Guinea	78.5	101.6	79.9	105.9	80.8	110.1	2,504	3,539	..	614
Paraguay	85.8	120.7	77.4	110.3	87.3	98.2	1,905	2,245	1,596	1,939
Peru	52.6	108.1	57.1	110.7	68.3	114.1	2,463	3,399	930	1,428
Philippines	84.2	109.6	77.9	112.2	62.1	120.7	2,070	2,946	899	1,010
Poland	109.1	91.6	110.0	103.6	114.8	105.0	2,958	3,191	1,502	1,967
Portugal	103.1	98.6	98.7	99.1	85.7	98.2	1,939	2,683	4,640	5,925
Puerto Rico	167.7	114.6	127.6	97.8	118.4	94.1	1,100	1,731	..	..

3.3 Agricultural output and productivity

	Crop production index		Food production index		Livestock production index		Cereal yield		Agricultural productivity	
	1999–2001 = 100		1999–2001 = 100		1999–2001 = 100		kilograms per hectare		Agriculture value added per worker 2000 $	
	1990–92	**2002–04**	**1990–92**	**2002–04**	**1990–92**	**2002–04**	**1990–92**	**2003–05**	**1990–92**	**2001–03**
Romania	92.2	112.2	97.7	110.7	114.5	107.6	2,777	3,255	2,196	3,477
Russian Federation	125.8	116.0	132.6	110.2	152.1	103.2	1,743	1,839	1,824	2,226
Rwanda	111.4	117.6	107.3	117.2	77.7	107.3	1,088	989	192	222
Saudi Arabia	120.7	114.8	105.2	116.0	67.8	104.9	4,212	4,430	7,867	13,964
Senegal	73.0	68.3	71.9	74.9	74.8	98.2	803	1,013	250	250
Serbia and Montenegro	97.6	110.0	109.2	106.0	103.8	94.9	2,926	4,056	..	1,562
Sierra Leone	128.1	113.5	118.9	112.3	86.1	105.2	1,223	1,223	..	..
Singapore	157.1	100.0	352.1	69.3	396.3	74.2	..	..	25,421	34,911
Slovak Republic	..	..	..	..	..	..	..	..	..	3,475
Slovenia	93.1	110.2	77.2	105.8	73.6	103.6	3,609	5,247	11,310	32,311
Somalia	..	..	..	..	..	..	..	..	..	..
South Africa	79.6	102.4	84.2	105.7	94.6	108.2	1,602	2,907	1,796	2,391
Spain	87.9	106.1	87.1	105.3	79.5	107.2	2,310	3,040	9,515	18,691
Sri Lanka	86.2	98.8	88.9	100.0	94.6	109.9	2,950	3,428	705	737
Sudan	68.9	110.8	66.7	107.6	67.6	106.3	596	481	346	707
Swaziland	106.6	100.1	108.9	105.3	130.3	111.9	1,299	1,114	1,239	1,149
Sweden	102.2	102.1	97.9	100.0	95.7	97.7	4,272	4,835	21,463	30,116
Switzerland	112.4	95.3	104.9	100.1	104.8	101.9	6,102	6,150	22,228	22,348
Syrian Arab Republic	73.6	117.1	75.1	122.2	75.0	115.6	947	1,786	2,247	3,248
Tajikistan	123.6	132.9	138.1	132.6	192.6	139.2	1,037	2,252	391	379
Tanzania	92.7	103.6	88.7	105.0	82.9	109.4	1,276	1,469	245	283
Thailand	82.0	106.1	84.1	106.0	86.8	105.5	2,186	2,725	501	586
Togo	73.4	110.3	74.1	104.2	87.9	106.7	791	1,040	354	404
Trinidad and Tobago	116.3	91.9	88.7	122.1	73.5	142.6	3,159	2,722	1,666	2,435
Tunisia	104.6	104.2	91.2	103.0	60.3	99.9	1,401	1,539	2,431	2,431
Turkey	88.0	104.0	89.5	103.2	92.2	101.6	2,192	2,399	1,788	1,764
Turkmenistan	111.4	116.5	57.1	125.2	64.0	121.7	2,210	3,011	1,222	..
Uganda	78.0	106.6	79.5	107.7	82.3	112.9	1,487	1,667	187	230
Ukraine	130.6	114.0	146.0	108.1	170.0	108.1	2,834	2,436	1,194	1,433
United Arab Emirates	23.4	56.0	26.5	62.2	57.5	116.9	2,042	3,119	9,390	34,155
United Kingdom	104.9	100.3	107.2	98.9	105.6	98.5	6,321	7,097	22,506	25,876
United States	88.4	101.5	84.8	102.7	83.4	102.6	4,875	6,444	20,797	36,216
Uruguay	70.4	112.7	76.7	104.3	84.2	98.3	2,445	4,279	5,714	6,743
Uzbekistan	107.8	109.0	91.3	107.9	99.7	104.7	1,777	3,461	1,274	1,524
Venezuela, RB	79.5	96.0	73.9	98.9	73.5	100.4	2,561	3,329	4,548	5,899
Vietnam	60.1	116.6	63.1	118.3	57.9	124.9	3,097	4,651	215	290
West Bank and Gaza	..	..	..	..	..	..	..	..	..	..
Yemen, Rep.	75.0	100.1	71.5	107.4	66.3	115.5	906	772	273	348
Zambia	80.7	102.4	84.3	104.1	80.1	99.2	1,251	1,584	161	205
Zimbabwe	69.2	69.3	77.3	85.7	90.1	100.1	1,123	676	244	266
World	**82.5 w**	**105.7 w**	**82.0 w**	**106.2 w**	**83.4 w**	**107.0 w**	**2,868 w**	**3,247 w**	**756 w**	**875 w**
Low income	78.5	103.5	76.1	105.2	73.5	109.6	1,753	2,086	315	364
Middle income	80.9	110.2	79.8	110.5	81.2	111.0	2,987	3,312	535	717
Lower middle income	77.5	111.7	72.8	112.5	67.9	114.1	3,206	3,629	424	576
Upper middle income	93.1	104.9	101.8	104.2	115.8	102.7	2,453	2,673	2,378	2,731
Low & middle income	80.1	108.1	78.7	108.9	79.3	110.6	2,452	2,791	448	562
East Asia & Pacific	71.8	110.8	64.5	112.4	52.4	116.6	3,816	4,460	303	412
Europe & Central Asia	113.2	107.1	127.1	106.1	149.3	104.1	2,657	2,324	1,817	1,946
Latin America & Carib.	78.2	111.5	74.4	110.4	72.9	108.9	2,234	3,204	2,223	2,924
Middle East & N. Africa	78.8	113.7	75.7	112.5	70.4	107.7	1,632	2,405	1,575	1,919
South Asia	79.9	101.0	75.5	103.5	69.1	109.8	1,992	2,497	340	393
Sub-Saharan Africa	75.9	103.9	77.6	105.1	84.5	107.1	986	1,102	314	337
High income	89.9	98.2	89.7	99.9	90.1	101.2	4,263	5,041	15,048	25,144
Europe EMU	91.5	97.8	94.6	98.8	97.9	99.7	4,656	5,426	12,644	21,414

Agricultural output and productivity 3.3

About the data

The agricultural production indexes in the table are prepared by the Food and Agriculture Organization (FAO). The FAO obtains data from official and semiofficial reports of crop yields, area under production, and livestock numbers. If data are not available, the FAO makes estimates. The indexes are calculated using the Laspeyres formula: production quantities of each commodity are weighted by average international commodity prices in the base period and summed for each year. Because the FAO's indexes are based on the concept of agriculture as a single enterprise, estimates of the amounts retained for seed and feed are subtracted from the production data to avoid double counting. The resulting aggregate represents production available for any use except as seed and feed. The FAO's indexes may differ from other sources because of differences in coverage, weights, concepts, time periods, calculation methods, and use of international prices.

To ease cross-country comparisons, the FAO uses international commodity prices to value production. These prices, expressed in international dollars (equivalent in purchasing power to the U.S. dollar), are derived using a Geary-Khamis formula applied to agricultural outputs (see Inter-Secretariat Working Group on National Accounts 1993, sections 16.93–96). This method assigns a single price to each commodity so that, for example, one metric ton of wheat has the same price regardless of where it was produced. The use of international prices eliminates fluctuations in the value of output due to transitory movements of nominal exchange rates unrelated to the purchasing power of the domestic currency.

Data on cereal yield may be affected by a variety of reporting and timing differences. Cereal crops harvested for hay or harvested green for food, feed, or silage, and those used for grazing, are generally excluded. But millet and sorghum, which are grown as feed for livestock and poultry in Europe and North America, are used as food in Africa, Asia, and countries of the former Soviet Union. So some cereal crops are excluded from the data for some countries and included elsewhere, depending on their use.

The five countries with the highest agricultural productivity 3.3a

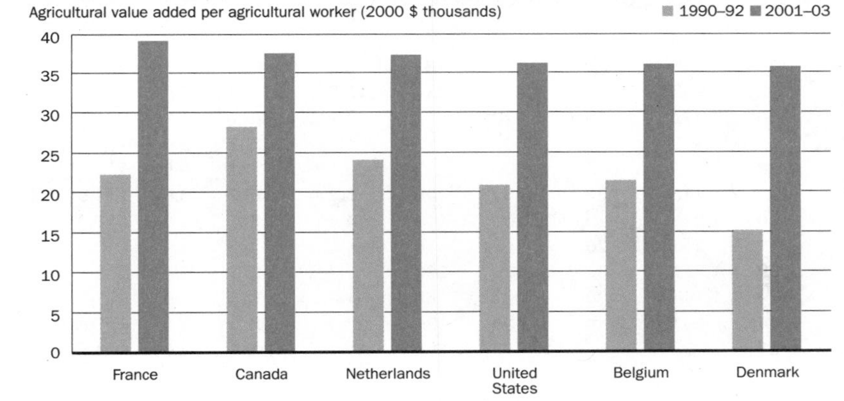

Source: Table 3.3.

The 10 countries with the highest cereal yield in 2003–05—and the 10 with the lowest 3.3b

Country	Kilograms per hectare
Belgium	8,710
Netherlands	8,036
Egypt, Arab Rep.	7,528
Ireland	7,390
New Zealand	7,360
United Kingdom	7,097
France	6,876
Germany	6,497
United States	6,444
Korea, Rep.	6,233

Country	Kilograms per hectare
Eritrea	296
Niger	394
Namibia	441
Sudan	481
Botswana	514
Angola	547
Libya	626
Zimbabwe	676
Chad	711
Congo, Dem. Rep.	767

Source: Table 3.3.

Definitions

• **Crop production index** shows agricultural production for each period relative to the base period 1999–2001. It includes all crops except fodder crops. The regional and income group aggregates for the FAO's production indexes are calculated from the underlying values in international dollars, normalized to the base period 1999–2001. The data in this table are three-year averages. • **Food production index** covers food crops that are considered edible and that contain nutrients. Coffee and tea are excluded because, although edible, they have no nutritive value. • **Livestock production index** includes meat and milk from all sources, dairy products such as cheese, and eggs, honey, raw silk, wool, and hides and skins. • **Cereal yield,** measured in kilograms per hectare of harvested land, includes wheat, rice, maize, barley, oats, rye, millet, sorghum, buckwheat, and mixed grains. Production data on cereals refer to crops harvested for dry grain only. Cereal crops harvested for hay or harvested green for food, feed, or silage, and those used for grazing, are excluded. The FAO allocates production data to the calendar year in which the bulk of the harvest took place. But most of a crop harvested near the end of a year will be used in the following year.• **Agricultural productivity** refers to the ratio of agricultural value added, measured in 2000 U.S. dollars, to the number of workers in agriculture. Agricultural productivity is measured by value added per unit of input. (For further discussion of the calculation of value added in national accounts, see *About the data* for tables 4.1 and 4.2.) Agricultural value added includes that from forestry and fishing. Thus interpretations of land productivity should be made with caution. To smooth annual fluctuations in agricultural activity, the indicators in the table have been averaged over three years.

Data sources

The agricultural production indexes are prepared by the FAO. The FAO makes these data and the data on cereal yield and agricultural employment available to the World Bank in electronic files that may contain more recent information than published versions. For sources of data on agricultural value added, see *Data sources* for table 4.2.

3.4 Deforestation and biodiversity

	Forest area	Average annual deforestation[a]	Mammals		Birds		Higher plants[b]		GEF benefits index for biodiversity	Nationally protected areas		Marine protected areas	
	thousand sq. km	%	Total known species	Threatened species	Total known species	Threatened species	Total known species	Threatened species		thousand sq. km	% of total land area	thousand sq. km	% of surface area
	2005	1990–2005	2004	2004	2004	2004	2002	2002	2005	2004[c]	2004[c]	2004[c]	2004[c]
Afghanistan	9	2.3	144	12	434	17	4,000	1	3.6	2.2	0.3	..	..
Albania	8	0.0	73	1	303	9	3,031	0	0.2	0.7	2.7	0.3	1.0
Algeria	23	–1.8	100	12	372	11	3,164	2	3.0	118.6	5.0	0.9	0.0
Angola	591	0.2	296	11	930	20	5,185	26	9.6	125.5	10.1	29.1	2.3
Argentina	330	0.4	375	32	1,038	55	9,372	42	18.5	174.5	6.4	7.8	0.3
Armenia	3	1.2	78	9	302	12	3,553	1	0.3	3.0	10.6	..	..
Australia	1,637	0.2	376	63	851	60	15,638	56	95.8	745.3	9.7	680.8	8.8
Austria	39	–0.2	101	5	412	8	3,100	3	0.3	23.5	28.5	..	..
Azerbaijan	9	0.0	82	11	364	11	4,300	0	0.9	4.0	4.8	1.2	1.4
Bangladesh	9	0.1	131	22	604	23	5,000	12	1.6	0.7	0.5	0.3	0.2
Belarus	79	–0.5	71	6	226	4	2,100	0	0.0	13.2	6.3	..	..
Belgium[d]	7	0.1	92	9	427	10	1,550	0	0.0	1.0	3.5	0.0	0.0
Benin	24	1.9	159	6	485	2	2,500	14	0.2	26.4	23.9	..	..
Bolivia	587	0.4	361	26	1,414	30	17,367	70	13.8	211.0	19.5	..	..
Bosnia and Herzegovina	22	0.1	78	8	312	8	..	1	0.4	0.3	0.5	..	..
Botswana	119	0.9	169	6	570	9	2,151	0	1.5	174.9	30.9	..	..
Brazil	4,777	0.5	578	74	1,712	120	56,215	381	100.0	1,532.6	18.1	47.4	0.6
Bulgaria	36	–0.6	106	12	379	11	3,572	0	0.9	11.2	10.3	0.0	0.0
Burkina Faso	68	0.3	129	6	452	2	1,100	2	0.3	42.1	15.4	..	..
Burundi	2	3.2	116	7	597	9	2,500	2	0.5	1.5	5.7	..	..
Cambodia	104	1.3	127	23	521	24	..	31	3.9	41.5	23.5	1.9	1.1
Cameroon	212	0.9	322	42	936	18	8,260	334	13.3	37.4	8.0	3.9	0.8
Canada	3,101	0.0	211	16	472	19	3,270	1	22.2	628.7	6.9	362.7	3.6
Central African Republic	228	0.1	187	11	663	3	3,602	15	1.7	103.3	16.6	..	..
Chad	119	0.6	104	12	531	5	1,600	2	2.1	119.8	9.5	..	..
Chile	161	–0.4	159	22	445	32	5,284	40	16.2	26.9	3.6	114.5	15.1
China	1,973	–1.7	580	80	1,221	82	32,200	443	64.8	1,100.7	11.8	16.0	0.2
Hong Kong, China	..	..	57	1	306	20	..	6	..	0.3	24.7	0.3	..
Colombia	607	0.1	467	39	1,821	86	51,220	222	57.3	825.3	74.4	8.1	0.7
Congo, Dem. Rep.	1,336	0.3	430	29	1,148	30	11,007	65	17.0	194.4	8.6	..	..
Congo, Rep.	225	0.1	166	14	597	4	6,000	35	3.4	61.3	18.0	..	..
Costa Rica	24	0.4	232	13	838	18	12,119	110	11.1	12.1	23.6	4.8	9.4
Côte d'Ivoire	104	–0.1	229	23	702	11	3,660	105	3.9	54.5	17.1	0.3	0.1
Croatia	21	–0.1	96	7	365	9	4,288	0	0.5	3.6	6.5	2.5	4.4
Cuba	27	–2.1	65	11	358	18	6,522	163	13.5	1.5	1.4	31.7	28.6
Czech Republic	26	0.0	88	6	386	9	1,900	4	0.1	14.4	18.7	..	..
Denmark	5	–0.8	81	4	427	10	1,450	3	0.2	10.9	25.7	5.1	11.8
Dominican Republic	14	0.0	36	5	224	16	5,657	30	6.8	11.9	24.6	8.6	17.6
Ecuador	109	1.4	341	34	1,515	69	19,362	1	30.0	67.2	24.3	141.0	49.7
Egypt, Arab Rep.	1	–3.5	118	6	481	17	2,076	2	3.2	56.0	5.6	76.7	7.7
El Salvador	3	1.4	137	2	434	3	2,911	25	0.8	0.4	1.9	0.1	0.4
Eritrea	16	0.3	70	9	537	7	..	3	0.9	5.0	5.0	..	..
Estonia	23	–0.4	67	4	267	3	1,630	0	0.0	8.9	21.1	..	..
Ethiopia	130	0.9	288	35	839	20	6,603	22	8.5	186.2	18.6	..	..
Finland	225	–0.1	80	3	421	10	1,102	1	0.2	29.5	9.7	1.1	0.3
France	156	–0.5	148	16	517	15	4,630	2	3.9	16.2	3.0	0.5	0.1
Gabon	218	0.0	166	11	632	5	6,651	107	3.4	8.8	3.4	1.0	0.4
Gambia, The	5	–0.4	133	3	535	2	974	4	0.1	0.3	3.5	0.2	1.9
Georgia	28	0.0	98	11	268	8	4,350	0	0.7	3.0	4.3	0.0	0.1
Germany	111	–0.2	126	9	487	14	2,682	12	0.7	111.5	32.0	9.1	2.6
Ghana	55	1.7	249	15	729	8	3,725	117	2.0	36.9	16.2	..	..
Greece	38	–0.9	118	11	412	14	4,992	2	3.0	4.3	3.3	2.5	1.9
Guatemala	39	1.1	193	7	684	10	8,681	85	8.9	25.4	23.4	0.1	0.1
Guinea	67	0.6	215	18	640	10	3,000	22	2.6	15.6	6.4	..	..
Guinea-Bissau	21	0.4	101	5	459	1	1,000	4	0.7	0.0	0.0	..	..
Haiti	1	0.6	41	4	271	15	5,242	28	5.8	0.1	0.3	..	..

Deforestation and biodiversity

	Forest area	Average annual deforestation[a]	Mammals		Birds		Higher plants[b]		GEF benefits index for biodiversity	Nationally protected areas		Marine protected areas	
	thousand sq. km	%	Total known species	Threatened species	Total known species	Threatened species	Total known species	Threatened species		thousand sq. km	% of total land area	thousand sq. km	% of surface area
	2005	1990–2005	2004	2004	2004	2004	2002	2002	2005	2004[c]	2004[c]	2004[c]	2004[c]
Honduras	46	2.5	201	10	699	6	5,680	111	7.9	23.4	21.0	1.9	1.7
Hungary	20	–0.6	88	7	367	9	2,214	1	0.2	8.3	9.3	..	..
India	677	–0.4	422	85	1,180	79	18,664	246	43.9	156.3	5.3	16.1	0.5
Indonesia	885	1.6	667	146	1,604	121	29,375	383	90.0	259.9	14.3	130.1	6.8
Iran, Islamic Rep.	111	0.0	158	21	498	18	8,000	1	7.9	105.5	6.5	6.2	0.4
Iraq	8	–0.1	102	9	396	18	..	0	1.7	0.0	0.0	..	..
Ireland	7	–3.4	63	4	408	8	950	1	0.7	0.8	1.1	0.0	0.0
Israel	2	–0.7	115	13	534	18	2,317	0	0.9	4.6	21.3	0.1	0.6
Italy	100	–1.3	132	12	478	15	5,599	3	4.4	32.4	11.0	1.5	0.5
Jamaica	3	0.1	35	5	298	12	3,308	208	4.9	1.8	16.2	8.2	74.5
Japan	249	0.0	171	37	592	53	5,565	12	41.4	52.2	14.3	10.6	2.8
Jordan	1	0.0	93	7	397	14	2,100	0	0.3	9.7	11.0	0.0	0.0
Kazakhstan	33	0.2	145	15	497	23	6,000	1	5.4	77.4	2.9	0.5	0.0
Kenya	35	0.3	407	33	1,103	28	6,506	103	9.9	71.9	12.6	3.1	0.5
Korea, Dem. Rep.	62	1.6	105	12	369	22	2,898	3	0.7	3.2	2.6	..	..
Korea, Rep.	63	0.1	89	12	423	34	2,898	0	1.8	3.5	3.6	3.5	3.5
Kuwait	0	–6.7	23	1	358	12	234	0	0.1	0.0	0.0	0.3	1.5
Kyrgyz Republic	9	–0.3	58	6	207	4	4,500	1	1.2	7.2	3.7	..	..
Lao PDR	161	0.5	215	30	704	21	8,286	19	5.4	37.4	16.2	..	..
Latvia	29	–0.4	68	4	325	8	1,153	0	0.0	9.7	15.6	0.2	0.2
Lebanon	1	–0.8	70	5	377	10	3,000	0	0.2	0.1	0.7	0.0	0.0
Lesotho	0	–4.0	59	3	311	7	1,591	1	0.3	0.1	0.2	..	..
Liberia	32	1.5	183	20	576	11	2,200	46	2.9	15.2	15.8	0.6	0.5
Libya	2	0.0	87	5	326	7	1,825	1	1.7	1.2	0.1	0.5	0.0
Lithuania	21	–0.5	71	5	227	4	1,796	0	0.0	5.9	9.5	0.5	0.8
Macedonia, FYR	9	0.0	89	9	291	9	3,500	0	0.2	2.0	7.9	..	..
Madagascar	128	0.4	165	49	262	34	9,505	276	31.4	18.3	3.1	0.2	0.0
Malawi	34	0.8	207	7	658	13	3,765	14	3.9	19.4	20.6	..	..
Malaysia	209	0.4	337	50	746	40	15,500	683	14.8	100.8	30.7	5.0	1.5
Mali	126	0.7	134	12	624	5	1,741	6	1.6	46.7	3.8	..	..
Mauritania	3	2.4	94	7	521	5	1,100	0	1.4	2.5	0.2	15.0	1.5
Mauritius	0	0.3	14	3	137	13	750	87	4.2	0.1	3.3	0.1	4.4
Mexico	642	0.5	544	72	1,026	57	26,071	261	75.8	99.0	5.2	82.1	4.2
Moldova	3	–0.2	50	4	203	8	1,752	0	0.0	0.5	1.4	..	..
Mongolia	103	0.7	140	13	387	22	2,823	0	4.4	217.9	13.9	..	..
Morocco	44	–0.1	129	12	430	13	3,675	2	4.0	4.7	1.1	0.5	0.1
Mozambique	193	0.2	228	12	685	23	5,692	46	8.2	45.3	5.8	22.5	2.8
Myanmar	322	1.2	288	39	1,047	41	7,000	38	10.6	35.3	5.4	0.2	0.0
Namibia	77	0.8	192	10	619	18	3,174	24	5.9	46.0	5.6	74.0	9.0
Nepal	36	1.6	203	29	*274*	31	6,973	7	2.2	26.6	18.6	..	..
Netherlands	4	–0.4	95	9	444	11	1,221	0	0.1	9.5	28.0	0.8	1.9
New Zealand	83	–0.5	73	8	351	74	2,382	21	22.3	64.7	24.1	22.7	8.4
Nicaragua	52	1.4	181	6	632	8	7,590	39	3.6	28.1	23.1	1.3	1.0
Niger	13	2.3	123	10	493	2	1,460	2	0.9	96.9	7.7	..	..
Nigeria	111	2.4	290	25	899	9	4,715	170	6.6	55.0	6.0	..	..
Norway	94	–0.2	83	9	442	6	1,715	2	1.6	19.7	6.5	1.3	0.4
Oman	0	0.0	74	12	483	14	1,204	6	4.4	0.2	0.1	29.6	9.6
Pakistan	19	1.6	195	17	625	30	4,950	2	5.1	73.1	9.5	2.2	0.3
Panama	43	0.1	241	17	904	20	9,915	195	11.7	13.1	17.6	10.0	13.3
Papua New Guinea	294	0.4	260	58	720	33	11,544	142	27.7	7.3	1.6	3.5	0.8
Paraguay	185	0.8	168	11	696	27	7,851	10	3.3	16.6	4.2	..	..
Peru	687	0.1	441	46	1,781	94	17,144	274	36.3	216.1	16.9	3.4	0.3
Philippines	72	2.2	222	50	590	70	8,931	212	33.7	24.3	8.2	16.6	5.5
Poland	92	–0.2	110	12	424	12	2,450	4	0.6	70.3	23.1	0.7	0.2
Portugal	38	–1.5	105	15	501	15	5,050	15	3.8	4.7	5.1	2.0	2.2
Puerto Rico	4	–0.1	38	2	310	12	2,493	52	3.8	0.3	3.5	1.7	19.1

3.4 Deforestation and biodiversity

	Forest area	Average annual deforestation[a]	Mammals		Birds		Higher plants[b]		GEF benefits index for biodiversity	Nationally protected areas		Marine protected areas	
	thousand sq. km	%	Total known species	Threatened species	Total known species	Threatened species	Total known species	Threatened species		thousand sq. km	% of total land area	thousand sq. km	% of surface area
	2005	1990–2005	2004	2004	2004	2004	2002	2002	2005	2004[c]	2004[c]	2004[c]	2004[c]
Romania	64	0.0	101	15	365	13	3,400	1	..	5.8	2.5	6.1	2.6
Russian Federation	8,088	0.0	296	43	645	47	11,400	7	37.1	1,287.0	7.9	301.8	1.8
Rwanda	5	–3.4	206	13	665	9	2,288	3	1.1	1.9	7.9	..	..
Saudi Arabia	27	0.0	94	9	433	17	2,028	3	3.4	819.1	41.0	5.2	0.2
Senegal	87	0.5	191	11	612	5	2,086	7	1.3	21.6	11.2	0.9	0.4
Serbia and Montenegro	27	–0.4	96	10	381	10	4,082	1	..	3.8	3.7	0.1	0.1
Sierra Leone	28	0.6	197	12	626	10	2,090	47	1.5	3.2	4.5	..	..
Singapore	0	0.0	73	3	400	10	2,282	54	0.1	0.0	4.2	0.0	0.1
Slovak Republic	19	0.0	87	7	332	11	3,124	2	0.1	11.0	22.8	..	..
Slovenia	13	–0.4	87	7	350	7	3,200	0	0.2	2.9	14.5	0.0	0.0
Somalia	71	0.9	182	15	642	13	3,028	17	6.7	1.9	0.3	3.3	0.5
South Africa	92	0.0	320	29	829	36	23,420	75	23.5	74.0	6.1	3.4	0.3
Spain	179	–2.2	132	20	515	20	5,050	14	6.6	46.2	9.3	1.8	0.4
Sri Lanka	19	1.2	123	21	381	16	3,314	280	6.6	17.7	27.3	2.3	3.5
Sudan	675	0.8	302	16	952	10	3,137	17	5.5	123.0	5.2	0.3	0.0
Swaziland	5	–1.0	124	6	490	6	2,715	11	0.1	0.6	3.5	..	..
Sweden	275	0.0	85	5	457	9	1,750	3	0.3	44.8	10.9	4.3	1.0
Switzerland	12	–0.4	93	4	382	8	3,030	2	0.2	11.9	29.6	..	..
Syrian Arab Republic	5	–1.6	82	3	350	11	3,000	0	0.9	2.7	1.5	..	..
Tajikistan	4	0.0	76	7	351	9	5,000	2	0.7	26.0	18.6	..	..
Tanzania	353	1.0	375	34	1,056	37	10,008	239	15.1	374.3	42.4	2.3	0.2
Thailand	145	0.6	300	36	971	42	11,625	84	8.0	80.3	15.7	5.8	1.1
Togo	4	2.9	175	7	565	2	3,085	10	0.4	6.5	11.9	..	..
Trinidad and Tobago	2	0.3	116	1	435	2	2,259	1	2.4	0.2	4.7	0.1	1.3
Tunisia	11	–4.3	78	10	360	9	2,196	0	0.5	2.3	1.5	0.2	0.1
Turkey	102	–0.3	145	15	436	14	8,650	3	6.0	20.3	2.6	4.5	0.6
Turkmenistan	41	0.0	103	12	318	13	..	0	2.0	19.8	4.2	..	..
Uganda	36	1.8	360	29	1,015	15	4,900	38	3.3	64.3	32.6	..	..
Ukraine	96	–0.2	120	14	325	13	5,100	1	0.4	19.4	3.3	3.1	0.5
United Arab Emirates	3	–1.8	30	5	268	11	..	0	0.2	0.2	0.2	..	..
United Kingdom	28	–0.6	103	10	557	10	1,623	13	2.1	60.5	25.0	22.5	9.2
United States	3,031	–0.1	468	40	888	71	19,473	240	90.3	1,490.1	16.3	909.5	9.4
Uruguay	15	–4.4	118	6	414	24	2,278	1	1.4	0.7	0.4	0.1	0.0
Uzbekistan	33	–0.5	91	7	343	16	4,800	1	1.2	20.5	4.8	..	..
Venezuela, RB	477	0.6	353	26	1,392	25	21,073	67	26.8	644.4	73.1	21.3	2.3
Vietnam	129	–2.5	279	41	837	41	10,500	145	11.7	13.6	4.4	0.7	0.2
West Bank and Gaza	0	..	..	*1*	..	*1*	..	..	..	..	..	..	..
Yemen, Rep.	5	0.0	74	6	385	14	1,650	159	3.4	0.0	0.0	..	..
Zambia	425	0.9	255	11	770	12	4,747	8	5.0	312.3	42.0	..	..
Zimbabwe	175	1.4	222	8	661	10	4,440	17	2.1	57.5	14.9	..	..
World	39,426 s	0.1 w								15,048.4 s	11.6 w	4,348.9 s	3.8 w
Low income	6,746	0.5								2,806.6	10.0	73.8	..
Middle income	23,132	0.1								7,988.4	11.7	1,233.1	1.9
Lower middle income	12,255	0.2								5,196.6	13.2	632.6	1.7
Upper middle income	10,878	0.1								2,791.8	9.6	600.6	2.1
Low & middle income	29,878	0.2								10,795.0	11.2	1,307.0	1.6
East Asia & Pacific	4,507	–0.2								1,924.7	12.1	192.1	1.3
Europe & Central Asia	8,946	0.0								1,657.2	7.1	321.6	1.4
Latin America & Carib.	9,150	0.4								3,966.3	19.7	495.7	2.7
Middle East & N. Africa	211	–0.5								301.1	3.4	114.7	1.5
South Asia	801	–0.2								288.6	6.0	20.9	0.5
Sub-Saharan Africa	6,263	0.6								2,657.1	11.3	162.0	..
High income	9,548	–0.1								4,253.5	12.9	3,042.0	8.8
Europe EMU	915	–0.8								283.1	11.5	19.5	0.8

a. Negative numbers indicate an increase in forest area. b. Flowering plants only. c. Data may refer to earlier years. They are the most recent reported by the World Conservation Monitoring Centre in 2004. d. Includes Luxembourg.

Deforestation and biodiversity 3.4

About the data

Biological diversity is defined in terms of the variability in genes, species, and ecosystems. Faced with mounting threats to biodiversity, the international community has increasingly focused on conserving this diversity. Deforestation is a major cause of loss of biodiversity, and habitat conservation is vital for stemming this loss. Conservation efforts traditionally have focused on protecting areas of high biodiversity.

The estimates of forest area are from the Food and Agriculture Organization's (FAO) *Global Forest Resources Assessment 2005,* which provides detailed information on forest cover in 2005 and adjusted estimates of forest cover in 1990 and 2000. The current survey is the latest global forest assessment and uses a uniform global definition of forest. No breakdown of forest cover between natural forest and plantation is shown in the table because of space limitations. (This breakdown is provided by the FAO only for developing countries.) For this reason the deforestation data in the table may underestimate the rate at which natural forest is disappearing in some countries.

Measures of species richness are among the most straightforward ways to indicate the importance of an area for biodiversity. The number of threatened species is also an important measure of the immediate need for conservation efforts in a geographic area. Global analyses of the status of threatened species have been carried out for few groups of organisms. Only for mammals, birds, and amphibians has the status of virtually all known species been assessed. Threatened species are defined according to the World Conservation Union's (IUCN) classification categories: endangered (in danger of extinction and unlikely to survive if causal factors continue operating), vulnerable (likely to move into the endangered category in the near future if causal factors continue operating), rare (not endangered or vulnerable but at risk), indeterminate (known to be endangered, vulnerable, or rare but not enough information is available to say which), out of danger (formerly included in one of the above categories but now considered relatively secure because appropriate conservation measures are in effect), and insufficiently known (suspected but not definitely known to belong to one of the above categories).

While the number of birds and mammals is fairly well known, it is difficult to make an accurate count of plants. The number of plant species is highly debated. The IUCN's *2003 IUCN Red List of Threatened Plants* provides the most comprehensive list of threatened species on a global scale, the result of more than 20 years' work by botanists from around the world. Only 5 percent of plant species have been evaluated, and 70 percent of these are threatened with extinction. Plant species data should be interpreted with caution since they are not necessarily comparable across countries because of differences in taxonomic concepts and coverage. However, they do identify countries that are major sources of global biodiversity and that show national commitments to habitat protection.

Setting priorities for conserving biodiversity requires a broader set of information than species richness. With the support of the World Bank's Development Research Group and in close collaboration with scientific nongovernmental organizations, the Global Environment Facility (GEF) developed the GEF benefits index for biodiversity, a comprehensive indicator of national biodiversity status, to guide its biodiversity priorities. This indicator incorporates information on individual species range maps available from the IUCN for virtually all mammals (4,612), amphibians (5,327), and endangered birds (1,098); country-level data from the World Resources Institute (WRI) for reptiles and vascular plants; country-level data from FishBase for 27,669 fish species; and the ecological characteristics of 867 terrestrial ecoregions of the world from WWF International. For each country the biodiversity indicator incorporates the best available and comparable information in four relevant dimensions: represented species, threatened species, represented ecoregions, and threatened ecoregions. To combine these dimensions into one measure, the indicator uses dimensional weights that reflect the consensus of conservation scientists in the GEF, IUCN, WWF International, and other nongovernmental organizations. The index shown in the table has been normalized so that values run from 0 (no biodiversity potential) to 100 (maximum biodiversity potential).

The table shows information on protected areas, numbers of certain species, and numbers of those species under threat. The World Conservation Monitoring Centre (WCMC) compiles these data from a variety of sources. Because of differences in definitions and reporting practices, cross-country comparability is limited. Compounding these problems, available data cover different periods.

Nationally protected areas are areas of at least 1,000 hectares that fall into one of six IUCN management categories:

- Scientific reserves and strict nature reserves with limited public access.
- National parks of national or international significance and not materially affected by human activity.
- Natural monuments and natural landscapes with unique aspects.
- Managed nature reserves and wildlife sanctuaries.
- Protected landscapes (which may include cultural landscapes).
- Areas managed mainly for the sustainable use of natural systems to ensure long-term protection and maintenance of biological diversity.

Designating land as a protected area does not necessarily mean that protection is in force. And for small countries that may only have protected areas smaller than 1,000 hectares, this size limit in the definition will result in an underestimate of the extent and number of protected areas.

Due to variations in consistency and methodology of collection, the quality of the data are highly variable across countries. Some countries update their information more frequently than others, some may have more accurate data on extent of coverage, and many underreport the number or extent of protected areas.

Definitions

• **Forest area** is land under natural or planted stands of trees, whether productive or not. • **Average annual deforestation** refers to the permanent conversion of natural forest area to other uses, including shifting cultivation, permanent agriculture, ranching, settlements, and infrastructure development. Deforested areas do not include areas logged but intended for regeneration or areas degraded by fuelwood gathering, acid precipitation, or forest fires. Negative numbers indicate an increase in forest area. • **Mammals** exclude whales and porpoises. • **Birds** are listed for countries included within their breeding or wintering ranges. • **Higher plants** refer to native vascular plant species. • **Threatened species** are the number of species classified by the IUCN as endangered, vulnerable, rare, indeterminate, out of danger, or insufficiently known. • **GEF benefits index for biodiversity** is a composite index of relative biodiversity potential for each country based on the species represented in each country, their threat status, and the diversity of habitat types in each country. The index shown in the table has been normalized so that values run from 0 (no biodiversity potential) to 100 (maximum biodiversity potential). • **Nationally protected areas** are totally or partially protected areas of at least 1,000 hectares that are designated as scientific reserves with limited public access, national parks, natural monuments, nature reserves or wildlife sanctuaries, and protected landscapes. Marine areas, unclassified areas, and littoral (intertidal) areas are not included. The data also do not include sites protected under local or provincial law. Total land area is used to calculate the percentage of total area protected (see table 3.1). • **Marine protected areas** are areas of intertidal or subtidal terrain—and overlying water and associated flora and fauna and historical and cultural features—that have been reserved by law or other effective means to protect part or all of the enclosed environment.

Data sources

Data on forest area and deforestation are from the FAO's *Global Forest Resources Assessment 2005.* Data on species are from the electronic files of the United Nations Environmental Program and WCMC and *2003 IUCN Red List of Threatened Plants.* For China the number of mammals is from Princeton University Press *Guide to the Mammals of China* (forthcoming). The GEF benefits index for biodiversity is from Kiran Dev Pandey, Piet Buys, Ken Chomitz, and David Wheeler's, "Biodiversity Conservation Indicators: New Tools for Priority Setting at the Global Environment Facility" (2006). Data on protected areas are from the United Nations Environment Programme and WCMC.

3.5 Freshwater

	Renewable internal freshwater resources[a]		Annual freshwater withdrawals					Water productivity	Access to an improved water source	
	Flows billion cu. m 2005	Per capita cu. m 2005	billion cu. m 2002[b]	% of internal resources 2002[b]	% for agriculture 2002[b]	% for industry 2002[b]	% for domestic 2002[b]	GDP/water use 2000 $ per cu. m 2002	% of urban population 2004	% of rural population 2004
Afghanistan	55	..	23.3	42.3	98	0	2	..	..	..
Albania	27	8,595	1.7	6.4	62	11	27	2.4	99	94
Algeria	11	341	6.1	54.2	65	13	22	9.7	88	80
Angola	148	9,284	0.4	0.2	60	17	23	30.8	75	40
Argentina	276	7,123	29.2	10.6	74	9	17	8.3	98	80
Armenia	9	3,017	3.0	32.4	66	4	30	0.8	99	80
Australia	492	24,202	23.9	4.9	75	10	15	17.9	100	100
Austria	55	6,680	2.1	3.8	1	64	35	93.5	100	100
Azerbaijan	8	966	17.3	213.0	68	28	5	0.4	95	59
Bangladesh	105	740	79.4	75.6	96	1	3	0.7	82	72
Belarus	37	3,805	2.8	7.5	30	47	23	5.0	100	100
Belgium	12	1,145	..	..	..	..	..	..	100	100
Benin	10	1,221	0.1	1.3	45	23	32	19.0	78	57
Bolivia	304	33,054	1.4	0.5	81	7	13	6.1	95	68
Bosnia and Herzegovina	36	9,086	..	..	..	..	..	..	99	96
Botswana	2	1,360	0.2	8.1	41	18	41	35.4	100	90
Brazil	5,418	29,066	59.3	1.1	62	18	20	10.5	96	57
Bulgaria	21	2,713	10.5	50.0	19	78	3	1.3	100	97
Burkina Faso	13	945	0.8	6.4	86	1	13	3.6	94	54
Burundi	10	1,338	0.3	2.9	77	6	17	2.6	92	77
Cambodia	121	8,571	4.1	3.4	98	0	1	1.0	64	35
Cameroon	273	16,726	1.0	0.4	74	8	18	11.1	86	44
Canada	2,850	88,238	46.0	1.6	12	69	20	16.3	100	99
Central African Republic	141	34,920	0.0	0.0	4	16	80	38.4	93	61
Chad	15	1,539	0.2	1.5	83	0	17	7.2	41	43
Chile	884	54,249	12.6	1.4	64	25	11	6.3	100	58
China	2,812	2,156	630.3	22.4	68	26	7	2.2	93	67
Hong Kong, China	..	..	..	..	..	..	..	..	..	..
Colombia	2,112	46,316	10.7	0.5	46	4	50	8.1	99	71
Congo, Dem. Rep.	900	15,639	0.4	0.0	31	17	53	12.1	82	29
Congo, Rep.	222	55,515	0.0	0.0	9	22	70	76.0	84	27
Costa Rica	112	25,975	2.7	2.4	53	17	29	6.2	100	92
Côte d'Ivoire	77	4,231	0.9	1.2	65	12	24	11.0	97	74
Croatia	38	8,485	..	..	..	..	..	..	100	100
Cuba	38	3,381	8.2	21.5	69	12	19	..	95	78
Czech Republic	13	1,290	2.6	19.5	2	57	41	23.0	100	100
Denmark	6	1,108	1.3	21.2	43	25	32	127.5	100	100
Dominican Republic	21	2,361	3.4	16.1	66	2	32	6.3	97	91
Ecuador	432	32,657	17.0	3.9	82	5	12	1.0	97	89
Egypt, Arab Rep.	2	24	68.3	3,794.4	86	6	8	1.6	99	97
El Salvador	18	2,587	1.3	7.2	59	16	25	10.7	94	70
Eritrea	3	636	0.3	10.7	97	0	3	2.3	74	57
Estonia	13	9,435	0.2	1.2	5	38	57	39.5	100	99
Ethiopia	122	1,712	5.6	4.6	94	0	6	1.5	81	11
Finland	107	20,396	2.5	2.3	3	84	14	50.3	100	100
France	179	2,932	40.0	22.4	10	74	16	34.2	100	100
Gabon	164	118,511	0.1	0.1	42	8	50	42.1	95	47
Gambia, The	3	1,977	0.0	1.0	65	12	23	14.1	95	77
Georgia	58	12,985	3.6	6.2	59	21	20	0.9	96	67
Germany	107	1,297	47.1	44.0	20	68	12	40.9	100	100
Ghana	30	1,370	1.0	3.2	66	10	24	5.5	88	64
Greece	58	5,223	7.8	13.4	80	3	16	16.1	..	..
Guatemala	109	8,667	2.0	1.8	80	13	6	10.0	99	92
Guinea	226	24,037	1.5	0.7	90	2	8	2.2	78	35
Guinea-Bissau	16	10,086	0.2	1.1	82	5	13	1.1	79	49
Haiti	13	1,524	1.0	7.6	94	1	5	3.8	52	56

Freshwater

	Renewable internal freshwater resources[a]		Annual freshwater withdrawals					Water productivity	Access to an improved water source	
	Flows billion cu. m 2005	Per capita cu. m 2005	billion cu. m 2002[b]	% of internal resources 2002[b]	% for agriculture 2002[b]	% for industry 2002[b]	% for domestic 2002[b]	GDP/water use 2000 $ per cu. m 2002	% of urban population 2004	% of rural population 2004
Honduras	96	13,311	0.9	0.9	80	12	8	7.3	95	81
Hungary	6	595	7.6	127.3	32	59	9	6.7	100	98
India	1,261	1,152	645.8	51.2	86	5	8	0.8	95	83
Indonesia	2,838	12,867	82.8	2.9	91	1	8	2.2	87	69
Iran, Islamic Rep.	129	1,883	72.9	56.7	91	2	7	1.5	99	84
Iraq	35	..	42.7	121.3	92	5	3	0.5	..	..
Ireland	49	11,781	1.1	2.3	0	77	23	95.9	100	..
Israel	1	116	2.1	256.3	62	7	31	55.5	100	100
Italy	183	3,114	44.4	24.3	45	37	18	25.3	100	..
Jamaica	9	3,541	0.4	4.4	49	17	34	20.2	98	88
Japan	430	3,365	88.4	20.6	62	18	20	52.9	100	100
Jordan	1	128	1.0	144.3	75	4	21	9.3	99	91
Kazakhstan	75	4,978	35.0	46.4	82	17	2	0.7	97	73
Kenya	21	604	1.6	7.6	64	6	30	8.4	83	46
Korea, Dem. Rep.	67	2,979	9.0	13.5	55	25	20	..	100	100
Korea, Rep.	65	1,344	18.6	28.6	48	16	36	30.6	97	71
Kuwait	0	0	0.4	..	52	2	45	90.8	..	..
Kyrgyz Republic	47	9,041	10.1	21.7	94	3	3	0.1	98	66
Lao PDR	190	32,140	3.0	1.6	90	6	4	0.6	79	43
Latvia	17	7,259	0.3	1.8	13	33	53	30.0	100	96
Lebanon	5	1,342	1.4	28.8	67	1	33	13.1	100	100
Lesotho	5	2,897	0.1	1.0	20	40	40	18.4	92	76
Liberia	200	60,915	0.1	0.1	55	18	27	5.4	72	52
Libya	1	103	4.3	711.3	83	3	14	8.7	..	..
Lithuania	16	4,569	0.3	1.7	7	15	78	48.2	..	..
Macedonia, FYR	5	2,655	..	..	..	..	..	..	..	..
Madagascar	337	18,113	15.0	4.4	96	2	3	0.2	77	35
Malawi	16	1,250	1.0	6.3	80	5	15	1.7	98	68
Malaysia	580	22,882	9.0	1.6	62	21	17	10.5	100	96
Mali	60	4,438	6.5	10.9	90	1	9	0.4	78	36
Mauritania	0	130	1.7	425.0	88	3	9	0.7	59	44
Mauritius	3	2,252	0.6	21.8	..	..	..	7.9	100	100
Mexico	409	3,967	78.2	19.1	77	5	17	7.5	100	87
Moldova	1	238	2.3	231.0	33	58	10	0.6	97	88
Mongolia	35	13,626	0.4	1.3	52	27	20	2.3	87	30
Morocco	29	961	12.6	43.4	87	3	10	2.9	99	56
Mozambique	100	5,068	0.6	0.6	87	2	11	7.3	72	26
Myanmar	881	17,431	33.2	3.8	98	1	1	..	80	77
Namibia	6	3,052	0.3	4.8	71	5	24	12.4	98	81
Nepal	198	7,305	10.2	5.1	96	1	3	0.6	96	89
Netherlands	11	674	7.9	72.2	34	60	6	49.4	100	100
New Zealand	327	79,778	2.1	0.6	42	9	48	27.2	100	..
Nicaragua	190	36,840	1.3	0.7	83	2	15	3.1	90	63
Niger	4	251	2.2	62.3	95	0	4	0.9	80	36
Nigeria	221	1,680	8.0	3.6	69	10	21	6.0	67	31
Norway	382	82,625	2.2	0.6	11	67	23	79.2	100	100
Oman	1	390	1.4	136.0	90	2	7	16.0	..	..
Pakistan	52	336	169.4	323.3	96	2	2	0.5	96	89
Panama	147	45,613	0.8	0.6	28	5	67	14.6	99	79
Papua New Guinea	801	136,059	..	..	..	..	..	..	88	32
Paraguay	94	15,936	0.5	0.5	71	8	20	14.7	99	68
Peru	1,616	57,780	20.1	1.2	82	10	8	2.8	89	65
Philippines	479	5,767	28.5	6.0	74	9	17	2.8	87	82
Poland	54	1,404	16.2	30.2	8	79	13	10.8	100	..
Portugal	38	3,602	11.3	29.6	78	12	10	10.3	..	..
Puerto Rico	7	1,815	..	..	..	..	..	..	..	..

3.5 Freshwater

	Renewable internal freshwater resources[a]		Annual freshwater withdrawals					Water productivity	Access to an improved water source	
	Flows billion cu. m 2005	Per capita cu. m 2005	billion cu. m 2002[b]	% of internal resources 2002[b]	% for agriculture 2002[b]	% for industry 2002[b]	% for domestic 2002[b]	GDP/water use 2000 $ per cu. m 2002	% of urban population 2004	% of rural population 2004
Romania	42	1,955	23.2	54.8	57	34	9	1.8	91	16
Russian Federation	4,313	30,135	76.7	1.8	18	63	19	3.7	100	88
Rwanda	10	1,051	0.2	1.6	68	8	24	14.1	92	69
Saudi Arabia	2	104	17.3	721.7	89	1	10	11.0	97	..
Senegal	26	2,213	2.2	8.6	93	3	4	2.1	92	60
Serbia and Montenegro	44	5,456	..	..	..	..	..	..	99	86
Sierra Leone	160	28,957	0.4	0.2	92	3	5	2.5	75	46
Singapore	1	138	..	..	..	..	..	..	100	..
Slovak Republic	13	2,339	..	..	..	..	..	..	100	99
Slovenia	19	9,348	..	..	..	..	..	..	..	..
Somalia	6	729	3.3	54.8	100	0	0	..	32	27
South Africa	45	955	12.5	27.9	63	6	31	11.3	99	73
Spain	111	2,562	35.6	32.0	68	19	13	17.3	100	100
Sri Lanka	50	2,548	12.6	25.2	95	2	2	1.3	98	74
Sudan	30	828	37.3	124.4	97	1	3	0.4	78	64
Swaziland	3	2,299	1.0	40.1	97	1	2	1.4	87	54
Sweden	171	18,949	3.0	1.7	9	54	37	84.3	100	100
Switzerland	40	5,432	2.6	6.4	2	74	24	97.0	100	100
Syrian Arab Republic	7	368	20.0	285.0	95	2	3	1.0	98	87
Tajikistan	66	10,189	12.0	18.0	92	5	4	0.1	92	48
Tanzania	84	2,192	5.2	6.2	89	0	10	2.0	85	49
Thailand	210	3,269	87.1	41.5	95	2	2	1.5	98	100
Togo	12	1,871	0.2	1.5	45	2	53	8.2	80	36
Trinidad and Tobago	4	2,911	0.3	8.2	6	26	68	29.6	92	88
Tunisia	4	419	2.6	62.9	82	4	14	7.9	99	82
Turkey	227	3,150	37.5	16.5	74	11	15	5.3	98	93
Turkmenistan	1	290	24.7	1,760.7	98	1	2	..	93	54
Uganda	39	1,353	0.3	0.8	40	17	43	22.0	87	56
Ukraine	53	1,128	37.5	70.7	52	35	12	1.0	99	91
United Arab Emirates	0	44	2.3	1,150.0	68	9	23	34.0	100	100
United Kingdom	145	2,408	9.5	6.6	3	75	22	157.7	100	100
United States	2,800	9,446	479.3	17.1	41	46	13	20.9	100	100
Uruguay	59	17,036	3.2	5.3	96	1	3	5.6	100	100
Uzbekistan	16	623	58.3	357.9	93	2	5	0.3	95	75
Venezuela, RB	723	27,185	8.4	1.2	47	7	46	13.2	85	70
Vietnam	367	4,409	71.4	19.5	68	24	8	0.5	99	80
West Bank and Gaza	0	0	..	..	..	..	..	..	94	88
Yemen, Rep.	4	195	6.6	161.7	95	1	4	1.5	71	65
Zambia	80	6,873	1.7	2.2	76	7	17	2.0	90	40
Zimbabwe	12	945	4.2	34.2	79	7	14	1.6	98	72
World	43,507 s	6,794 w	3,807.4 s	9.1 w	70 w	20 w	10 w	8.6 w	95 w	72 w
Low income	7,404	3,149	1,240.7	18.9	89	5	6	0.8	88	70
Middle income	26,662	8,677	1,667.0	6.3	71	19	10	3.3	95	92
Lower middle income	18,455	7,460	1,337.3	7.3	75	17	8	2.5	94	71
Upper middle income	8,207	13,701	329.6	4.0	54	29	18	6.8	98	82
Low & middle income	34,066	6,280	2,907.6	8.8	78	13	8	2.3	93	71
East Asia & Pacific	9,454	5,019	958.8	11.1	74	20	7	2.1	92	70
Europe & Central Asia	5,255	11,139	383.2	7.5	59	31	10	2.7	99	80
Latin America & Carib.	13,429	24,402	265.3	2.0	71	10	19	7.6	96	73
Middle East & N. Africa	228	746	239.8	105.0	89	4	7	2.0	96	81
South Asia	1,816	1,236	941.1	51.8	90	4	6	0.7	94	81
Sub-Saharan Africa	3,884	5,229	119.3	3.1	87	3	10	3.1	80	43
High income	9,441	9,640	899.7	10.2	42	42	15	28.2	100	99
Europe EMU	929	2,959	199.7	22.3	38	48	15	30.5	100	100

a. River flows from other countries are not included because of data unreliability. b. Data are for the most recent year available for 1987–2002 (see *Primary data documentation*).

About the data

The data on freshwater resources are based on estimates of runoff into rivers and recharge of groundwater. These estimates are based on different sources and refer to different years, so cross-country comparisons should be made with caution. Because the data are collected intermittently, they may hide significant variations in total renewable water resources from one year to the next. The data also fail to distinguish between seasonal and geographic variations in water availability within countries. Data for small countries and countries in arid and semiarid zones are less reliable than those for larger countries and countries with greater rainfall.

Caution is also needed in comparing data on annual freshwater withdrawals, which are subject to variations in collection and estimation methods. In addition, inflows and outflows are estimated at different times and at different levels of quality and precision, requiring caution in interpreting the data, particularly for water-short countries, notably in the Middle East.

The data on access to an improved water source measure the percentage of the population with ready access to water for domestic purposes. The data are based on surveys and estimates provided by governments to the Joint Monitoring Program of the World Health Organization (WHO) and the United Nations Children's Fund (UNICEF). The coverage rates are based on information from service users on what their households actually use rather than on information from service providers, which may include nonfunctioning systems. Access to drinking water from an improved source does not ensure that the water is safe or adequate, as these characteristics are not tested at the time of surveys. While information on access to an improved water source is widely used, it is extremely subjective, and such terms as *safe, improved, adequate,* and *reasonable* may have different meaning in different countries despite official WHO definitions (see *Definitions*). Even in high-income countries treated water may not always be safe to drink. While access to an improved water source is equated with connection to a supply system, this does not take into account variations in the quality and cost (broadly defined) of the service once connected.

Water productivity is an indication only of the efficiency by which each country uses its water resources. Given the different economic structure of each country, these indicators should be used with proper caution, taking into account the countries' sectoral activities and natural resource endowments.

The rural-urban divide in access to an improved water source 

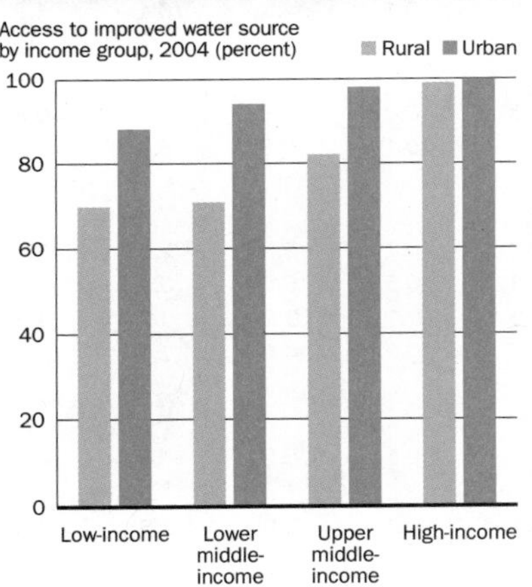

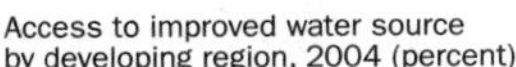

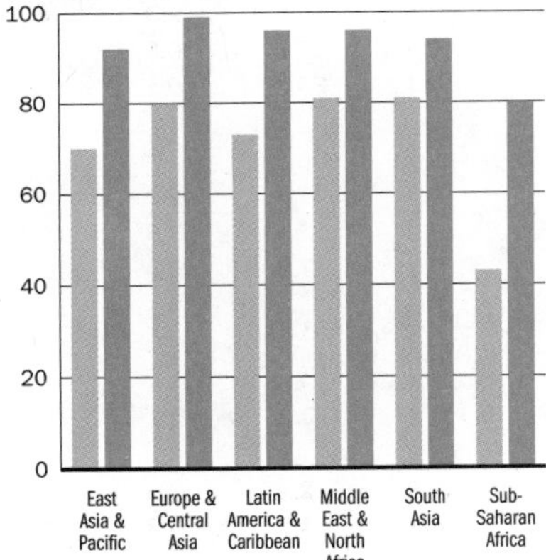

Source: Table 3.5.

Definitions

• **Renewable internal freshwater resources flows** refer to internal renewable resources (internal river flows and groundwater from rainfall) in the country. • **Renewable internal freshwater resources per capita** are calculated using the World Bank's population estimates (see table 2.1). • **Annual freshwater withdrawals** refer to total water withdrawals, not counting evaporation losses from storage basins. Withdrawals also include water from desalination plants in countries where they are a significant source. Withdrawals can exceed 100 percent of total renewable resources where extraction from nonrenewable aquifers or desalination plants is considerable or where there is significant water reuse. Withdrawals for agriculture and industry are total withdrawals for irrigation and livestock production and for direct industrial use (including withdrawals for cooling thermoelectric plants). Withdrawals for domestic uses include drinking water, municipal use or supply, and use for public services, commercial establishments, and homes. • **Water productivity** is calculated as GDP in constant prices divided by annual total water withdrawal. • **Access to an improved water source** refers to the percentage of the population with reasonable access to an adequate amount of water from an improved source, such as piped water into a dwelling, plot, or yard; public tap or standpipe; tubewell or borehole; protected dug well or spring; and rainwater collection. Unimproved sources include unprotected dug wells or springs, cart with small tank or drum, bottled water, and tanker trucks. Reasonable access is defined as the availability of at least 20 liters a person a day from a source within 1 kilometer of the dwelling.

Data sources

Data on freshwater resources and withdrawals are compiled by the World Resources Institute from various sources and published in *World Resources 2005* (produced in collaboration with the United Nations Environment Programme, United Nations Development Programme, and World Bank). These data are supplemented by the Food and Agriculture Organization's AQUASTAT data. Data on access to water are from WHO and UNICEF's *Meeting the MDG Drinking Water and Sanitation Target* (www.unicef.org/wes/mdgreport).

3.6 Water pollution

	Emissions of organic water pollutants				Industry shares of emissions of organic water pollutants							
	thousand kilograms per day		kilograms per day per worker		% of total							
					Primary metals	Paper and pulp	Chemicals	Food and beverages	Stone, ceramics, and glass	Textiles	Wood	Other
	1990	2003[a]	1990	2003[a]	2003[a]	2003[a]	2003[a]	2003[a]	2003[a]	2003[a]	2003[a]	2003[a]
Afghanistan	5.9	0.2	0.16	0.21	..	37.7	17.5	31.1	0.4	13.2	..	..
Albania	34.8	..	0.14	..	..	..	..	..	..	..	..	..
Algeria	107.0	..	0.25	..	..	..	..	..	..	..	..	..
Angola	4.5	..	0.19	..	..	..	..	..	..	..	..	..
Argentina	186.7	164.3	0.20	0.23	5.6	14.6	8.6	58.9	0.1	7.6	1.1	3.5
Armenia	37.9	7.1	0.11	0.28	..	..	..	77.6	..	22.4	..	..
Australia	186.1	111.7	0.18	0.18	..	..	5.6	77.1	0.2	5.1	5.3	..
Austria	94.1	36.9	0.15	0.08	14.6	14.8	15.4	34.9	0.6	0.9	12.3	3.5
Azerbaijan	53.3	15.5	0.15	0.16	20.2	5.5	15.9	39.2	0.3	11.0	0.9	6.9
Bangladesh	171.1	303.3	0.17	0.14	1.6	6.2	2.6	23.8	0.1	64.2	0.4	1.0
Belarus	..	..	..	..	..	..	..	..	..	..	..	..
Belgium	118.0	102.3	0.16	0.17	13.6	18.4	11.2	40.3	0.2	5.9	2.2	8.2
Benin	..	..	..	..	..	..	..	..	..	..	..	..
Bolivia	8.4	11.5	0.24	0.25	1.2	15.1	6.8	64.9	0.2	8.7	2.3	0.7
Bosnia and Herzegovina	50.7	..	0.14	..	..	..	..	..	..	..	..	..
Botswana	4.5	5.5	0.19	0.19	1.9	10.8	1.6	56.3	0.3	25.0	1.7	2.5
Brazil	780.4	..	0.19	..	..	..	..	..	..	..	..	..
Bulgaria	149.4	101.9	0.11	0.17	7.9	9.5	6.6	46.1	0.2	22.2	2.3	5.2
Burkina Faso	..	2.6	..	0.22	3.5	1.1	5.4	73.8	0.1	4.1	10.1	1.9
Burundi	1.6	..	0.24	..	..	..	..	..	..	..	..	..
Cambodia	11.8	..	0.14	..	..	..	..	..	..	..	..	..
Cameroon	14.0	10.0	0.28	0.19	0.4	5.2	36.1	48.8	0.0	3.8	5.0	0.8
Canada	321.5	312.5	0.17	0.16	9.6	22.1	8.6	39.5	0.1	5.8	5.4	8.9
Central African Republic	1.0	..	0.18	..	..	..	..	..	..	..	..	..
Chad	..	..	..	..	..	..	..	..	..	..	..	..
Chile	66.8	72.9	0.22	0.24	6.9	11.3	8.9	62.7	0.1	5.0	2.6	2.5
China	7,038.1	6,088.7	0.14	0.14	20.4	10.9	14.8	28.1	0.5	15.5	0.9	8.8
Hong Kong, China	86.1	34.3	0.12	0.20	1.2	43.5	3.9	30.5	0.1	16.2	0.2	4.6
Colombia	93.3	93.9	0.19	0.21	3.1	16.2	9.7	53.2	0.2	14.2	1.0	2.4
Congo, Dem. Rep.	..	..	..	..	..	..	..	..	..	..	..	..
Congo, Rep.	2.5	..	0.32	..	..	..	..	..	..	..	..	..
Costa Rica	27.2	31.2	0.20	0.22	1.6	10.0	8.2	65.7	0.1	10.2	1.3	2.9
Côte d'Ivoire	7.9	..	0.22	..	..	..	..	..	..	..	..	..
Croatia	80.0	42.9	0.15	0.17	6.1	15.9	7.5	48.4	0.2	12.0	3.6	6.3
Cuba	173.0	..	0.25	..	..	..	..	..	..	..	..	..
Czech Republic	205.1	158.5	0.13	0.14	15.6	7.0	7.9	43.6	0.3	10.4	3.9	11.4
Denmark	91.9	83.6	0.18	0.17	4.4	29.1	7.9	44.2	0.2	2.2	3.5	8.6
Dominican Republic	47.9	..	0.36	..	..	..	..	..	..	..	..	..
Ecuador	25.6	40.2	0.23	0.28	2.2	11.2	5.9	72.3	0.1	5.8	1.3	1.3
Egypt, Arab Rep.	211.5	186.1	0.20	0.20	10.8	8.2	9.0	50.7	0.3	17.7	0.6	2.8
El Salvador	5.5	22.8	0.22	0.18	2.1	10.2	8.1	43.5	0.1	34.1	0.5	1.4
Eritrea	..	..	..	..	..	..	..	..	..	..	..	..
Estonia	..	..	..	..	..	..	..	..	..	..	..	..
Ethiopia	18.6	22.1	0.23	0.23	2.3	11.0	5.5	61.0	0.3	17.3	2.0	0.7
Finland	79.5	67.4	0.18	0.16	8.7	40.1	7.6	26.6	0.2	2.4	3.9	10.6
France	653.5	564.6	0.15	0.15	7.2	13.8	12.9	49.5	0.2	2.9	2.3	11.1
Gabon	2.0	..	0.25	..	..	..	..	..	..	..	..	..
Gambia, The	0.8	..	0.34	..	..	..	..	..	..	..	..	..
Georgia	..	..	..	..	..	..	..	..	..	..	..	..
Germany	835.0	966.7	0.12	0.14	9.3	20.4	11.8	38.7	0.2	2.3	2.1	15.1
Ghana	16.5	..	0.20	..	..	..	..	..	..	..	..	..
Greece	63.5	43.7	0.18	0.19	8.1	9.7	9.0	55.0	0.3	12.4	1.6	4.0
Guatemala	21.6	19.3	0.23	0.28	4.9	7.2	6.1	72.8	0.1	6.9	0.8	1.0
Guinea	..	..	..	..	..	..	..	..	..	..	..	..
Guinea-Bissau	..	..	..	..	..	..	..	..	..	..	..	..
Haiti	5.4	..	0.20	..	..	..	..	..	..	..	..	..

Water pollution

	Emissions of organic water pollutants				Industry shares of emissions of organic water pollutants							
					% of total							
	thousand kilograms per day		kilograms per day per worker		Primary metals	Paper and pulp	Chemicals	Food and beverages	Stone, ceramics, and glass	Textiles	Wood	Other
	1990	2003[a]	1990	2003[a]	2003[a]	2003[a]	2003[a]	2003[a]	2003[a]	2003[a]	2003[a]	2003[a]
Honduras	17.8	..	0.23	..	..	..	..	..	..	..	..	..
Hungary	178.0	60.7	0.16	0.10	11.8	..	12.8	49.1	0.4	..	5.5	9.8
India	1,410.6	1,519.8	0.20	0.20	12.2	7.6	9.2	53.7	0.3	12.7	0.3	3.9
Indonesia	495.6	733.0	0.19	0.18	2.5	8.2	9.2	53.7	0.1	19.4	4.5	2.4
Iran, Islamic Rep.	102.7	164.8	0.16	0.15	15.6	8.0	10.7	46.7	0.7	9.5	0.9	8.1
Iraq	26.7	..	0.19	..	..	..	..	..	..	..	..	..
Ireland	34.6	11.6	0.18	0.21	1.9	..	10.4	22.9	0.7	3.1	7.5	9.3
Israel	46.4	54.0	0.16	0.16	3.6	22.3	10.5	45.5	0.1	6.0	1.9	10.1
Italy	358.1	488.9	0.13	0.12	9.4	16.6	10.7	30.8	0.3	15.0	3.9	13.3
Jamaica	18.7	..	0.29	..	..	..	..	..	..	..	..	..
Japan	1,556.6	1,184.7	0.14	0.15	7.1	19.0	9.4	45.7	0.2	4.8	1.6	12.3
Jordan	8.3	23.5	0.19	0.18	5.1	12.7	10.8	53.4	0.4	10.8	3.3	3.4
Kazakhstan	..	..	..	..	..	..	..	..	..	..	..	..
Kenya	42.6	56.1	0.23	0.24	..	11.5	5.4	66.8	0.1	12.8	1.7	..
Korea, Dem. Rep.	..	..	..	..	..	..	..	..	..	..	..	..
Korea, Rep.	369.2	315.2	0.12	0.12	11.4	18.9	13.0	25.8	0.2	13.6	1.5	15.7
Kuwait	9.1	11.9	0.16	0.17	2.1	16.6	11.1	50.2	0.4	11.6	2.8	5.2
Kyrgyz Republic	30.9	19.1	0.12	0.21	7.3	7.8	3.5	65.4	0.4	11.0	0.9	3.7
Lao PDR	..	..	..	..	..	..	..	..	..	..	..	..
Latvia	39.9	29.2	0.12	0.19	4.1	15.4	3.6	53.8	0.1	9.6	9.7	3.7
Lebanon	..	14.9	..	0.19	0.9	15.6	4.0	60.7	0.5	10.2	4.6	3.4
Lesotho	3.0	3.1	0.16	0.16	1.2	4.0	0.7	39.7	0.1	51.3	0.6	2.3
Liberia	0.6	..	0.30	..	..	..	..	..	..	..	..	..
Libya	..	..	..	..	..	..	..	..	..	..	..	..
Lithuania	53.8	45.3	0.13	0.17	0.8	10.6	4.9	54.0	0.2	18.1	7.1	4.3
Macedonia, FYR	32.4	..	0.18	..	..	..	..	..	..	..	..	..
Madagascar	11.0	..	0.27	..	..	..	..	..	..	..	..	..
Malawi	10.0	11.8	0.29	0.29	0.0	16.0	3.7	70.0	0.0	7.8	1.7	0.7
Malaysia	104.7	183.8	0.13	0.12	7.8	14.9	15.5	33.7	0.2	8.3	6.8	12.8
Mali	..	..	..	..	..	..	..	..	..	..	..	..
Mauritania	..	..	..	..	..	..	..	..	..	..	..	..
Mauritius	17.8	17.7	0.16	0.15	0.9	6.6	2.6	32.8	0.1	55.4	0.6	1.1
Mexico	174.3	296.1	0.18	0.20	7.8	12.5	10.4	55.6	0.2	7.5	0.9	5.1
Moldova	55.9	21.6	0.15	0.45	..	2.2	..	97.7	..	..	..	..
Mongolia	10.2	..	0.18	..	..	..	..	..	..	..	..	..
Morocco	41.7	72.1	0.14	0.16	2.1	8.0	6.8	43.0	0.3	35.3	1.1	3.4
Mozambique	20.4	10.2	0.27	0.31	1.1	7.1	2.7	81.2	0.1	5.8	1.4	0.7
Myanmar	7.7	6.2	0.17	0.18	56.5	4.6	13.2	14.9	0.4	2.9	1.7	5.8
Namibia	7.4	..	0.35	..	..	..	..	..	..	..	..	..
Nepal	20.9	26.9	0.13	0.16	3.5	9.7	5.9	55.1	1.4	21.7	1.7	1.0
Netherlands	136.7	..	0.18	..	..	..	..	..	..	..	..	..
New Zealand	50.2	46.1	0.22	0.22	3.2	21.7	5.2	57.3	0.1	4.6	3.6	4.2
Nicaragua	10.5	..	0.27	..	..	..	..	..	..	..	..	..
Niger	..	0.4	..	0.32	..	17.0	4.4	76.9	0.3	..	0.8	..
Nigeria	70.8	..	0.22	..	..	..	..	..	..	..	..	..
Norway	55.0	51.7	0.20	0.20	9.0	31.3	4.7	42.8	0.1	1.4	3.1	7.5
Oman	0.4	5.8	0.11	0.17	7.3	13.3	10.1	54.3	0.9	8.3	2.4	3.4
Pakistan	104.1	..	0.18	..	..	..	..	..	..	..	..	..
Panama	9.7	11.7	0.26	0.32	1.5	13.2	4.6	76.6	0.2	3.2	0.4	0.4
Papua New Guinea	5.7	..	0.25	..	..	..	..	..	..	..	..	..
Paraguay	3.3	..	0.28	..	..	..	..	..	..	..	..	..
Peru	56.1	..	0.20	..	..	..	..	..	..	..	..	..
Philippines	228.3	..	0.21	..	..	..	..	..	..	..	..	..
Poland	428.9	329.4	0.14	0.17	7.5	11.7	7.6	52.2	0.2	9.1	4.3	7.3
Portugal	147.9	127.5	0.15	0.15	3.1	16.4	4.9	37.8	0.4	26.1	5.3	6.0
Puerto Rico	19.0	9.2	0.15	0.18	1.9	14.9	36.4	..	0.2	9.8	2.4	9.7

3.6 Water pollution

	Emissions of organic water pollutants				Industry shares of emissions of organic water pollutants (% of total)							
	thousand kilograms per day		kilograms per day per worker		Primary metals	Paper and pulp	Chemicals	Food and beverages	Stone, ceramics, and glass	Textiles	Wood	Other
	1990	**2003[a]**	**1990**	**2003[a]**	**2003[a]**	**2003[a]**	**2003[a]**	**2003[a]**	**2003[a]**	**2003[a]**	**2003[a]**	**2003[a]**
Romania	413.9	38.4	0.12	0.07	..	17.6	..	5.1	..	28.7	12.5	..
Russian Federation	1,911.3	1,388.1	0.13	0.18	20.3	8.1	3.2	51.9	0.4	5.9	2.6	7.5
Rwanda	1.6	..	0.25	..	..	..	..	..	..	..	..	..
Saudi Arabia	18.5	..	0.15	..	..	..	..	..	..	..	..	..
Senegal	10.3	6.6	0.32	0.30	5.8	8.4	10.7	70.1	0.1	4.2	0.4	0.3
Serbia and Montenegro	137.8	98.7	0.15	0.16	9.9	11.8	8.2	47.4	0.3	12.7	2.2	7.6
Sierra Leone	4.2	..	0.32	..	..	..	..	..	..	..	..	..
Singapore	32.4	34.3	0.09	0.10	1.4	24.6	16.0	25.4	0.1	3.9	1.6	26.9
Slovak Republic	77.2	43.3	0.13	0.14	2.9	16.9	8.4	43.7	0.3	12.2	4.0	11.6
Slovenia	55.6	38.4	0.16	0.16	33.7	14.7	8.3	23.7	0.2	10.8	2.0	6.7
Somalia	6.2	..	0.38	..	..	..	..	..	..	..	..	..
South Africa	261.6	221.3	0.17	0.18	15.1	18.0	10.5	36.0	0.1	10.9	3.9	5.5
Spain	320.3	352.9	0.17	0.15	7.5	20.6	9.5	39.6	0.4	8.6	4.3	9.6
Sri Lanka	53.0	78.4	0.19	0.18	0.5	7.2	6.6	51.5	0.2	31.6	1.1	1.2
Sudan	..	38.6	..	0.29	0.7	2.5	3.1	88.6	0.4	3.2	0.6	1.1
Swaziland	6.6	..	0.33	..	..	..	..	..	..	..	..	..
Sweden	109.6	103.9	0.15	0.14	11.3	35.0	7.8	26.6	0.1	1.3	3.0	14.9
Switzerland	146.0	..	0.16	..	..	..	..	..	..	..	..	..
Syrian Arab Republic	21.7	15.1	0.22	0.20	4.1	1.5	3.9	69.8	0.9	19.4	0.2	0.2
Tajikistan	..	..	..	..	..	..	..	..	..	..	..	..
Tanzania	31.1	35.2	0.24	0.25	1.5	9.4	2.7	69.3	0.1	14.0	1.5	1.4
Thailand	291.6	..	0.17	..	..	..	..	..	..	..	..	..
Togo	..	..	..	..	..	..	..	..	..	..	..	..
Trinidad and Tobago	10.0	7.9	0.26	0.23	6.5	18.8	11.9	55.3	0.2	3.8	2.0	1.5
Tunisia	44.6	55.8	0.18	0.14	2.5	6.1	5.5	35.8	0.4	43.3	1.9	4.6
Turkey	177.3	172.2	0.18	0.16	11.4	4.8	8.0	43.7	0.3	26.4	0.4	5.0
Turkmenistan	..	..	..	..	..	..	..	..	..	..	..	..
Uganda	16.7	..	0.30	..	..	..	..	..	..	..	..	..
Ukraine	692.4	445.8	0.14	0.18	28.1	4.2	7.0	46.8	0.4	5.4	1.1	7.0
United Arab Emirates	5.6	..	0.14	..	..	..	..	..	..	..	..	..
United Kingdom	739.6	331.0	0.15	0.12	9.0	48.0	17.5	0.6	0.3	5.2	4.0	15.4
United States	2,565.2	1,805.9	0.15	0.13	9.6	10.6	14.0	42.1	0.2	5.4	4.2	13.9
Uruguay	38.7	15.8	0.23	0.28	1.2	3.7	6.6	79.2	0.1	7.4	0.6	1.2
Uzbekistan	..	..	..	..	..	..	..	..	..	..	..	..
Venezuela, RB	96.5	94.2	0.21	0.21	13.7	10.4	10.2	53.1	0.3	7.5	1.5	3.3
Vietnam	..	..	..	..	..	..	..	..	..	..	..	..
West Bank and Gaza	..	..	..	..	..	..	..	..	..	..	..	..
Yemen, Rep.	6.9	15.4	0.27	0.23	..	7.7	6.8	74.6	0.4	7.6	0.9	..
Zambia	15.9	..	0.23	..	..	..	..	..	..	..	..	..
Zimbabwe	37.1	..	0.20	..	..	..	..	..	..	..	..	..

Note: Industry shares may not sum to 100 percent because data may be for different years.
a. Data are for most recent year available for 1993–2003.

About the data

Emissions of organic pollutants from industrial activities are a major cause of degradation of water quality. Water quality and pollution levels are generally measured in terms of concentration or load—the rate of occurrence of a substance in an aqueous solution. Polluting substances include organic matter, metals, minerals, sediment, bacteria, and toxic chemicals. This table focuses on organic water pollution resulting from industrial activities. Because water pollution tends to be sensitive to local conditions, the national-level data in the table may not reflect the quality of water in specific locations.

The data in the table come from an international study of industrial emissions that may be the first to include data from developing countries (Hettige, Mani, and Wheeler 1998). These data were updated through 2003 by the World Bank's Development Research Group. Unlike estimates from earlier studies based on engineering or economic models, these estimates are based on actual measurements of plant-level water pollution. The focus is on organic water pollution caused by organic waste, measured in terms of biochemical oxygen demand (BOD), because the data for this indicator are the most plentiful and the most reliable for cross-country comparisons of emissions. BOD measures the strength of an organic waste by the amount of oxygen consumed in breaking it down. A sewage overload in natural waters exhausts the water's dissolved oxygen content. Wastewater treatment, by contrast, reduces BOD.

Data on water pollution are more readily available than other emissions data because most industrial pollution control programs start by regulating emissions of organic water pollutants. Such data are fairly reliable because sampling techniques for measuring water pollution are more widely understood and much less expensive than those for air pollution.

Hettige, Mani, and Wheeler (1998) used plant- and sector-level information on emissions and employment from 13 national environmental protection agencies and sector-level information on output and employment from the United Nations Industrial Development Organization (UNIDO). Their econometric analysis found that the ratio of BOD to employment in each industrial sector is about the same across countries. This finding allowed the authors to estimate BOD loads across countries and over time. The estimated BOD intensities per unit of employment were multiplied by sectoral employment numbers from UNIDO's industry database for 1980–98. The estimates of sectoral emissions were then totaled to get daily emissions of organic water pollutants in kilograms per day for each country and year. The data in the table were derived by updating these estimates through 2003.

Emissions of organic water pollutants declined in most countries from 1990 to 2003, even among the top emitters 3.6a

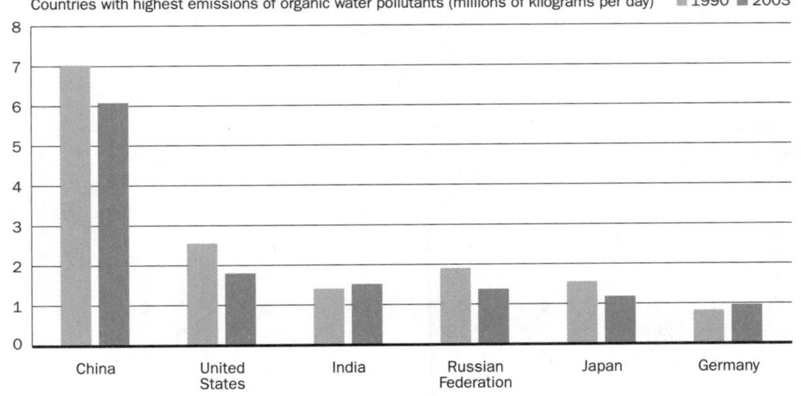

Source: Table 3.6.

Definitions

• **Emissions of organic water pollutants** are measured in terms of biochemical oxygen demand, which refers to the amount of oxygen that bacteria in water will consume in breaking down waste. This is a standard water treatment test for the presence of organic pollutants. Emissions per worker are total emissions divided by the number of industrial workers. • **Industry shares of emissions of organic water pollutants** refer to emissions from manufacturing activities as defined by two-digit divisions of the International Standard Industrial Classification (ISIC) revision 2: primary metals (ISIC division 37); paper and pulp (34); chemicals (35); food and beverages (31); stone, ceramics, and glass (36); textiles (32); wood (33); and other (38 and 39).

Data sources

Data on water pollution come from a 1998 study by Hemamala Hettige, Muthukumara Mani, and David Wheeler, "Industrial Pollution in Economic Development: Kuznets Revisited" (available at www.worldbank.org/nipr). The data were updated through 2003 by the World Bank's Development Research Group using the same methodology as the initial study. Sectoral employment numbers are from UNIDO's industry database.

3.7 Energy production and use

	Total energy production		Energy use								Net energy imports[a]	
			Total			Per capita			Combustible renewables and waste			
	million metric tons of oil equivalent		million metric tons of oil equivalent		average annual % growth	kilograms of oil equivalent		average annual % growth	% of total		% of energy use	
	1990	2004	1990	2004	1990–2004	1990	2004	1990–2004	1990	2004	1990	2004
Afghanistan	..	..	..	..	..	..	..	..	..	..	..	..
Albania	2.4	1.0	2.7	2.4	1.9	809	760	2.5	13.6	6.3	8	59
Algeria	104.4	165.7	23.9	32.9	2.2	943	1,017	0.5	0.1	0.2	–338	–404
Angola	28.7	57.4	6.3	9.5	2.9	597	613	0.2	68.8	64.7	–356	–505
Argentina	48.5	85.4	46.1	63.7	2.0	1,415	1,661	0.8	3.7	3.3	–5	–34
Armenia	*0.3*	0.7	*4.3*	2.1	–1.5	*1,246*	704	–0.5	*0.0*	0.0	*94*	65
Australia	157.5	261.8	87.5	115.8	2.2	5,130	5,762	1.1	4.5	4.3	–80	–126
Austria	8.1	9.9	25.0	33.2	1.9	3,246	4,060	1.6	9.9	11.3	68	70
Azerbaijan	*18.2*	20.1	*16.7*	12.9	–2.4	*2,259*	1,559	–3.3	*0.0*	0.0	*–9*	–55
Bangladesh	10.8	18.4	12.8	22.8	4.5	123	164	2.3	53.5	35.7	16	19
Belarus	*3.5*	3.6	*38.9*	26.8	–1.9	*3,810*	2,725	–1.5	*0.6*	4.2	*91*	86
Belgium	13.1	13.5	49.1	57.7	1.3	4,927	5,536	1.0	1.4	2.2	73	77
Benin	1.8	1.6	1.7	2.5	2.7	324	303	–0.5	93.2	65.6	–6	34
Bolivia	4.9	11.8	2.8	5.0	4.1	416	553	1.9	27.2	14.7	–77	–137
Bosnia and Herzegovina	*3.6*	3.2	*4.5*	4.7	5.8	*1,130*	1,203	5.0	*3.6*	3.9	*19*	31
Botswana	0.9	1.0	1.3	1.9	2.9	890	1,055	1.3	33.1	24.4	28	46
Brazil	98.1	176.3	134.0	204.8	3.2	897	1,114	1.7	31.1	26.5	27	14
Bulgaria	9.6	10.3	28.8	18.9	–2.0	3,306	2,434	–1.2	0.6	3.9	67	46
Burkina Faso	..	..	..	..	..	..	..	..	..	..	..	..
Burundi	..	..	..	..	..	..	..	..	..	..	..	..
Cambodia	..	..	..	..	..	..	..	..	..	..	..	..
Cameroon	12.1	12.5	5.0	6.9	2.5	432	433	0.2	75.9	77.8	–140	–80
Canada	273.7	397.5	209.4	269.0	1.7	7,534	8,411	0.7	3.9	4.4	–31	–48
Central African Republic	..	..	..	..	..	..	..	..	..	..	..	..
Chad	..	..	..	..	..	..	..	..	..	..	..	..
Chile	7.6	8.4	14.1	27.9	5.4	1,067	1,732	3.9	19.0	15.4	46	70
China	889.3	1,536.8	866.5	1,609.3	3.6	763	1,242	2.6	23.1	13.7	–3	5
Hong Kong, China	0.0	0.0	10.7	17.1	3.1	1,869	2,488	1.6	0.5	0.3	100	100
Colombia	48.5	76.2	25.0	27.7	0.5	716	616	–1.2	23.2	14.9	–94	–175
Congo, Dem. Rep.	12.0	17.0	11.9	16.6	2.4	315	297	–0.3	84.0	92.5	–1	–3
Congo, Rep.	9.0	12.6	1.1	1.1	–0.6	425	274	–3.8	69.4	61.7	–753	–1,084
Costa Rica	1.0	1.7	2.0	3.7	4.7	658	870	2.3	36.6	8.2	49	53
Côte d'Ivoire	3.4	7.2	4.4	6.9	3.6	348	388	1.0	72.1	64.9	23	–4
Croatia	*4.3*	3.9	*6.7*	8.8	2.2	*1,502*	1,985	2.5	*3.8*	4.3	*35*	56
Cuba	6.5	5.9	16.8	10.7	–1.6	1,594	950	–2.0	34.8	19.4	61	45
Czech Republic	40.1	34.2	49.0	45.5	–0.3	4,728	4,460	–0.2	*1.2*	3.3	18	25
Denmark	10.0	31.0	17.9	20.1	0.4	3,481	3,716	0.0	6.4	11.7	44	–55
Dominican Republic	1.0	1.6	4.1	7.7	5.1	584	873	3.6	24.2	19.3	75	79
Ecuador	16.5	29.3	6.1	10.1	3.9	597	773	2.2	13.5	5.7	–169	–191
Egypt, Arab Rep.	54.9	64.7	31.9	56.9	4.4	573	783	2.5	3.3	2.5	–72	–14
El Salvador	1.7	2.4	2.5	4.5	4.1	496	664	2.0	48.2	32.5	32	46
Eritrea	..	..	..	..	..	..	..	..	..	..	..	..
Estonia	*4.1*	3.6	*6.3*	5.2	–1.2	*4,091*	3,835	–0.2	*2.9*	11.7	*34*	31
Ethiopia	14.2	19.4	15.2	21.2	2.6	296	303	0.3	92.8	90.4	7	9
Finland	12.1	15.9	29.2	38.1	2.0	5,851	7,286	1.7	15.6	20.3	59	58
France	111.9	137.4	227.3	275.2	1.3	4,006	4,547	0.8	4.8	4.3	51	50
Gabon	14.6	12.1	1.2	1.7	2.2	1,298	1,243	–0.4	59.8	58.8	–1,077	–615
Gambia, The	..	..	..	..	..	..	..	..	..	..	..	..
Georgia	*1.5*	1.3	*8.8*	2.8	–7.9	*1,642*	626	–6.6	*7.7*	22.8	*83*	54
Germany	186.2	136.0	356.2	348.0	0.0	4,485	4,218	–0.2	1.3	3.0	48	61
Ghana	4.4	6.2	5.3	8.4	3.6	345	386	1.2	73.1	69.1	18	25
Greece	9.2	10.3	22.2	30.5	2.5	2,183	2,755	1.9	4.0	3.2	59	66
Guatemala	3.4	5.3	4.5	7.6	4.3	504	616	1.9	67.9	52.9	24	30
Guinea	..	..	..	..	..	..	..	..	..	..	..	..
Guinea-Bissau	..	..	..	..	..	..	..	..	..	..	..	..
Haiti	1.3	1.7	1.6	2.2	3.2	231	262	1.8	76.5	74.0	21	25

3.7 Energy production and use

	Total energy production		Energy use								Net energy imports[a]	
						Per capita						
	million metric tons of oil equivalent		Total million metric tons of oil equivalent		average annual % growth	kilograms of oil equivalent		average annual % growth	Combustible renewables and waste % of total		% of energy use	
	1990	2004	1990	2004	1990–2004	1990	2004	1990–2004	1990	2004	1990	2004
Honduras	1.7	1.7	2.4	3.9	3.0	496	548	0.3	62.0	40.0	30	55
Hungary	14.3	10.2	28.6	26.4	−0.2	2,753	2,608	0.0	1.3	3.3	50	61
India	333.4	466.9	361.6	572.9	3.3	426	531	1.5	48.6	37.4	8	19
Indonesia	164.7	258.0	97.6	174.0	4.0	548	800	2.6	40.4	27.1	−69	−48
Iran, Islamic Rep.	179.7	278.0	68.8	145.8	5.3	1,264	2,167	3.7	1.0	0.5	−161	−91
Iraq	104.9	103.4	19.1	29.7	3.5	1,029	..	..	0.1	0.1	−451	−248
Ireland	3.5	1.9	10.4	15.2	3.5	2,969	3,738	2.5	1.0	1.4	67	87
Israel	0.4	1.7	12.1	20.7	4.0	2,599	3,049	1.3	0.0	0.0	96	92
Italy	25.3	30.1	148.0	184.5	1.6	2,610	3,171	1.5	0.6	3.3	83	84
Jamaica	0.5	0.5	2.9	4.1	2.6	1,231	1,541	1.8	16.2	11.7	84	88
Japan	76.8	96.8	446.0	533.2	1.2	3,610	4,173	1.0	1.1	1.2	83	82
Jordan	0.2	0.3	3.5	6.5	3.7	1,104	1,219	0.3	0.1	0.0	95	96
Kazakhstan	*89.0*	118.6	*79.7*	54.8	−2.8	*4,846*	3,652	−2.0	*0.1*	0.1	*−12*	−116
Kenya	10.3	13.7	12.5	16.9	2.1	533	506	−0.4	78.4	74.1	18	19
Korea, Dem. Rep.	28.7	19.2	32.9	20.4	−3.4	1,670	910	−4.2	2.9	5.0	13	6
Korea, Rep.	21.9	38.0	92.7	213.0	6.0	2,161	4,431	5.1	*0.3*	0.8	76	82
Kuwait	50.4	132.8	8.5	25.1	8.4	3,985	10,212	6.4	0.1	..	−495	−429
Kyrgyz Republic	*1.8*	1.5	*5.1*	2.8	−3.5	*1,114*	546	−4.6	*0.1*	0.1	*64*	47
Lao PDR	..	..	..	..	..	..	..	..	..	..	..	..
Latvia	*0.8*	2.1	*5.9*	4.6	−1.8	*2,245*	1,988	−0.8	*8.2*	29.9	*87*	53
Lebanon	0.1	0.2	2.3	5.4	5.9	842	1,525	4.1	4.5	2.4	94	96
Lesotho	..	..	..	..	..	..	..	..	..	..	..	..
Liberia	..	..	..	..	..	..	..	..	..	..	..	..
Libya	73.2	85.4	11.5	18.2	2.9	2,663	3,169	0.9	1.1	0.8	−534	−369
Lithuania	*4.4*	5.2	*11.1*	9.2	−1.0	*3,002*	2,666	−0.4	*2.6*	7.6	*60*	43
Macedonia, FYR	*1.7*	1.5	*2.9*	2.7	−1.0	*1,515*	1,328	−1.4	*6.4*	6.3	*41*	43
Madagascar	..	..	..	..	..	..	..	..	..	..	..	..
Malawi	..	..	..	..	..	..	..	..	..	..	..	..
Malaysia	48.8	88.5	22.6	56.7	6.3	1,269	2,279	3.8	9.4	4.9	−115	−56
Mali	..	..	..	..	..	..	..	..	..	..	..	..
Mauritania	..	..	..	..	..	..	..	..	..	..	..	..
Mauritius	..	..	..	..	..	..	..	..	..	..	..	..
Mexico	194.8	253.9	124.3	165.5	1.9	1,494	1,622	0.4	5.9	5.0	−57	−53
Moldova	*0.1*	0.1	*6.9*	3.4	−6.0	*1,575*	802	−5.7	*0.5*	2.3	*99*	98
Mongolia	..	..	..	..	..	..	..	..	..	..	..	..
Morocco	0.8	0.7	6.7	11.5	3.8	281	384	2.3	4.7	3.9	89	94
Mozambique	6.8	8.2	7.2	8.6	1.1	536	441	−1.6	94.4	84.1	5	4
Myanmar	10.7	19.0	10.7	14.1	2.0	262	283	0.5	84.4	73.4	0	−34
Namibia	*0.2*	0.3	*0.7*	1.3	5.1	*449*	665	2.5	*16.0*	13.8	*67*	76
Nepal	5.5	8.1	5.8	9.1	3.3	304	341	0.9	93.4	86.8	5	11
Netherlands	60.5	67.9	66.7	82.1	1.3	4,464	5,045	0.6	1.4	2.6	9	17
New Zealand	12.0	13.0	13.8	17.6	1.9	3,990	4,344	0.7	4.0	5.0	13	26
Nicaragua	1.5	1.9	2.1	3.3	2.9	535	643	1.0	53.2	51.1	29	41
Niger	..	..	..	..	..	..	..	..	..	..	..	..
Nigeria	150.5	229.4	70.9	99.0	2.3	783	769	−0.3	79.8	80.2	−112	−132
Norway	120.3	238.6	21.5	27.7	1.6	5,067	6,024	1.0	4.8	4.9	−460	−763
Oman	38.3	58.1	4.6	11.8	6.8	2,475	4,667	4.4	..	..	−740	−391
Pakistan	34.4	59.0	43.4	74.4	3.7	402	489	1.2	43.2	35.6	21	21
Panama	0.6	0.8	1.5	2.5	4.2	618	801	2.2	28.3	16.8	59	70
Papua New Guinea	..	..	..	..	..	..	..	..	..	..	..	..
Paraguay	4.6	6.6	3.1	4.0	1.9	731	694	−0.3	72.3	53.8	−48	−65
Peru	10.6	9.5	10.0	13.2	2.1	458	479	0.3	26.9	17.7	−6	28
Philippines	13.7	23.4	26.2	44.3	4.3	428	542	2.1	29.2	23.9	48	47
Poland	99.4	78.8	99.9	91.7	−0.9	2,620	2,403	−0.8	2.2	5.0	1	14
Portugal	3.4	3.9	17.7	26.5	3.3	1,793	2,528	2.9	14.0	10.9	81	85
Puerto Rico	..	..	..	..	..	..	..	..	..	..	..	..

3.7 Energy production and use

	Total energy production		Energy use								Net energy imports[a]	
						Per capita			Combustible renewables and waste			
	million metric tons of oil equivalent		Total million metric tons of oil equivalent		average annual % growth	kilograms of oil equivalent		average annual % growth	% of total		% of energy use	
	1990	2004	1990	2004	1990–2004	1990	2004	1990–2004	1990	2004	1990	2004
Romania	40.8	28.1	62.4	38.6	–2.9	2,689	1,778	–2.4	1.0	8.4	35	27
Russian Federation	*1,118.7*	1,158.5	*774.8*	641.5	–1.2	*5,211*	4,460	–0.9	*1.6*	1.1	*–44*	–81
Rwanda	..	..	..	..	..	..	..	..	..	..	..	..
Saudi Arabia	376.9	556.2	67.4	140.4	4.3	4,114	6,233	1.9	0.0	0.0	–459	–296
Senegal	1.4	1.1	2.2	2.8	1.6	281	242	–0.9	60.6	38.9	39	60
Serbia and Montenegro	13.2	*11.5*	21.5	*16.2*	–1.1	2,044	*2,004*	1.1	1.8	*4.9*	38	*29*
Sierra Leone	..	..	..	..	..	..	..	..	..	..	..	..
Singapore	..	*0.1*	13.4	25.6	3.4	4,384	6,034	0.8	..	..	..	*99*
Slovak Republic	5.3	6.5	21.3	18.3	–0.3	4,035	3,407	–0.4	0.8	2.2	75	65
Slovenia	*2.8*	3.4	*5.0*	7.2	2.7	*2,508*	3,591	2.7	*5.3*	6.7	*45*	52
Somalia	..	..	..	..	..	..	..	..	..	..	..	..
South Africa	114.5	156.0	91.2	131.1	2.4	2,592	2,829	0.3	11.4	10.0	–26	–19
Spain	34.6	32.5	91.1	142.2	3.4	2,345	3,331	2.7	4.5	3.4	62	77
Sri Lanka	4.2	5.2	5.5	9.4	3.8	324	485	2.9	71.0	52.0	24	45
Sudan	8.8	29.3	10.6	17.6	3.7	408	497	1.4	81.7	79.2	18	–66
Swaziland	..	..	..	..	..	..	..	..	..	..	..	..
Sweden	29.8	35.1	47.6	53.9	0.7	5,557	5,998	0.4	11.6	16.7	37	35
Switzerland	9.7	11.8	25.0	27.1	0.7	3,724	3,672	0.1	3.7	6.3	61	56
Syrian Arab Republic	22.3	29.5	11.7	18.4	3.2	909	993	0.5	0.0	0.0	–91	–60
Tajikistan	*1.6*	1.5	*9.1*	3.3	–5.5	*1,647*	519	–6.7	..	..	*83*	55
Tanzania	9.1	17.5	9.8	18.7	4.6	374	498	1.9	91.0	91.6	8	7
Thailand	26.5	50.1	43.9	97.1	5.2	803	1,524	4.1	33.4	16.4	40	48
Togo	1.2	1.9	1.4	2.7	4.6	365	449	1.4	82.6	70.6	17	29
Trinidad and Tobago	12.6	29.4	6.0	11.3	5.4	4,968	8,675	4.9	0.8	0.2	–109	–160
Tunisia	6.1	6.8	5.5	8.7	3.4	679	876	2.0	18.7	12.4	–11	22
Turkey	25.8	24.1	53.0	81.9	3.4	943	1,151	1.6	13.6	6.8	51	71
Turkmenistan	*48.8*	58.2	*11.3*	15.6	3.1	*2,912*	3,265	1.4	..	..	*–332*	–274
Uganda	..	..	..	..	..	..	..	..	..	..	..	..
Ukraine	*101.3*	76.3	*210.0*	140.3	–3.0	*4,027*	2,958	–2.1	*0.1*	0.2	*52*	46
United Arab Emirates	109.4	164.0	22.5	43.8	4.6	12,716	10,142	–1.8	*0.1*	0.0	–385	–274
United Kingdom	208.0	225.2	212.2	233.7	0.6	3,686	3,906	0.3	0.3	1.3	2	4
United States	1,650.5	1,641.0	1,927.6	2,325.9	1.4	7,722	7,921	0.2	3.2	3.0	14	29
Uruguay	1.1	0.9	2.3	2.9	1.1	725	832	0.3	24.3	15.4	49	70
Uzbekistan	*40.5*	56.9	*45.0*	54.0	1.9	*2,098*	2,088	0.3	..	..	*10*	–5
Venezuela, RB	148.9	196.1	43.9	56.2	1.6	2,224	2,149	–0.5	1.2	1.0	–239	–249
Vietnam	24.7	65.3	24.3	50.2	5.1	367	611	3.5	77.7	47.2	–2	–30
West Bank and Gaza	..	..	..	..	..	..	..	..	..	..	..	..
Yemen, Rep.	9.4	20.6	2.6	6.4	6.2	212	313	2.4	3.0	1.2	–266	–224
Zambia	4.9	6.4	5.5	6.9	1.6	653	605	–0.7	73.4	79.1	10	8
Zimbabwe	8.6	8.6	9.4	9.3	–0.1	888	719	–1.5	50.4	63.8	9	8
World	**8,798.3 t**	**11,171.2 t**	**8,609.9 t**	**11,026.3 t**	**1.7 w**	**1,685 w**	**1,793 w**	**0.3 w**	**10.8 w**	**10.3 w**	**–2 w**	**–2 w**
Low income	791.6	1,173.8	773.3	1,136.6	2.8	464	513	0.7	55.6	47.8	–2	–3
Middle income	4,386.6	5,604.9	3,502.9	4,431.1	1.4	1,349	1,451	0.2	11.8	10.5	–25	–27
Lower middle income	2,160.0	3,257.8	1,923.6	2,889.6	2.5	953	1,175	1.1	18.4	13.9	–12	–13
Upper middle income	2,226.9	2,347.3	1,579.4	1,541.6	–0.2	2,980	2,583	–1.1	3.7	4.0	–41	–52
Low & middle income	5,175.0	6,767.1	4,267.1	5,548.9	1.6	1,008	1,068	0.2	19.0	17.5	–21	–22
East Asia & Pacific	1,218.4	2,079.8	1,135.3	2,085.8	3.7	722	1,124	2.5	26.1	16.1	–7	0
Europe & Central Asia	1,885.7	1,721.9	1,733.4	1,335.7	–1.9	3,726	2,847	–2.0	1.9	2.4	–9	–30
Latin America & Carib.	618.0	910.5	459.8	644.6	2.5	1,050	1,187	0.9	18.2	14.8	–34	–41
Middle East & N. Africa	601.9	823.7	194.4	356.7	4.3	861	1,189	2.3	1.8	1.2	–210	–131
South Asia	391.5	562.2	432.8	694.3	3.4	394	486	1.5	49.1	38.0	10	19
Sub-Saharan Africa	481.8	715.4	317.4	452.2	2.4	693	703	0.0	56.6	55.7	–52	–58
High income	3,657.9	4,450.0	4,369.4	5,512.8	1.7	4,842	5,511	0.9	2.9	3.1	16	19
Europe EMU	470.7	462.9	1,053.1	1,245.1	1.3	3,568	3,990	0.9	3.1	4.2	55	63

a. Negative value indicates that a country is a net exporter.

Energy production and use 3.7

About the data

In developing countries growth in energy use is closely related to growth in the modern sectors—industry, motorized transport, and urban areas—but energy use also reflects climatic, geographic, and economic factors (such as the relative price of energy). Energy use has been growing rapidly in low- and middle-income countries, but high-income countries still use more than five times as much energy on a per capita basis.

Energy data are compiled by the International Energy Agency (IEA). IEA data for countries that are not members of the Organisation for Economic Co-operation and Development (OECD) are based on national energy data adjusted to conform to annual questionnaires completed by OECD member governments.

Total energy use refers to the use of primary energy before transformation to other end-use fuels (such as electricity and refined petroleum products). It includes energy from combustible renewables and waste—solid biomass and animal products, gas and liquid from biomass, and industrial and municipal waste. Biomass is defined as any plant matter used directly as fuel or converted into fuel, heat, or electricity. (The data series published in *World Development Indicators 1998* and earlier editions did not include energy from combustible renewables and waste.) Data for combustible renewables and waste are often based on small surveys or other incomplete information. Thus the data give only a broad impression of developments and are not strictly comparable between countries. The IEA reports include country notes that explain some of these differences (see *Data sources*). All forms of energy—primary energy and primary electricity—are converted into oil equivalents. To convert nuclear electricity into oil equivalents, a notional thermal efficiency of 33 percent is assumed; for hydroelectric power 100 percent efficiency is assumed.

The IEA makes these estimates in consultation with national statistical offices, oil companies, electricity utilities, and national energy experts. The IEA occasionally revises its time series to reflect political changes. In addition, energy statistics for other countries have undergone continuous changes in coverage or methodology as more detailed energy accounts have become available in recent years. Breaks in series are therefore unavoidable.

Energy use per capita varies widely among the top energy users **3.7a**

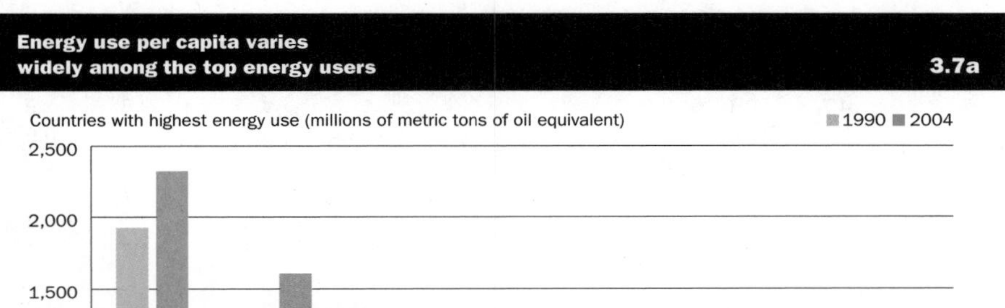

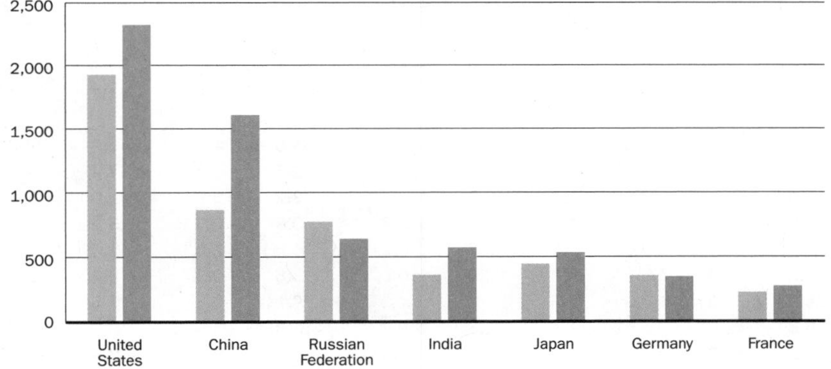

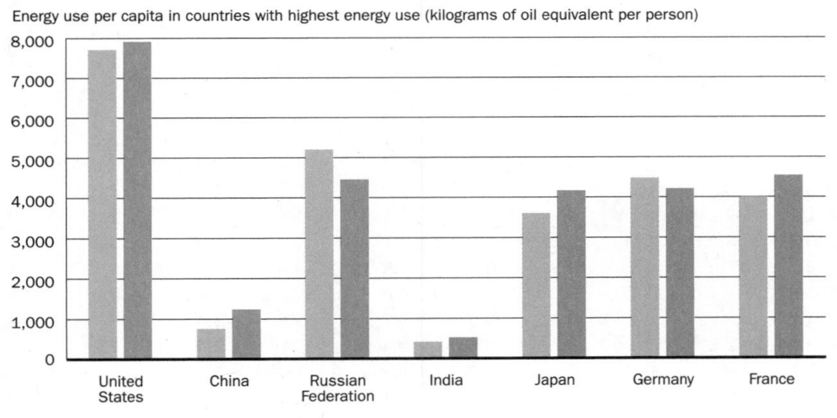

Source: Table 3.7.

Definitions

• **Total energy production** refers to forms of primary energy—petroleum (crude oil, natural gas liquids, and oil from non-conventional sources), natural gas, solid fuels (coal, lignite, and other derived fuels), and combustible renewables and waste—and primary electricity, all converted into oil equivalents (see *About the data*). • **Energy use** refers to use of primary energy before transformation to other end-use fuels, which is equal to indigenous production plus imports and stock changes, minus exports and fuels supplied to ships and aircraft engaged in international transport (see *About the data*). • **Combustible renewables and waste** comprise solid biomass, liquid biomass, biogas, industrial waste, and municipal waste, measured as a percentage of total energy use. • **Net energy imports** are estimated as energy use less production, both measured in oil equivalents. The deviations from zero of the world net imports are from statistical errors and changes in stock.

Data sources

Data on energy production and use come from IEA electronic files. The IEA's data are published in its annual publications, *Energy Statistics and Balances of Non-OECD Countries, Energy Statistics of OECD Countries,* and *Energy Balances of OECD Countries.*

3.8 Energy efficiency and emissions

	GDP per unit of energy use		Carbon dioxide emissions							Methane emissions		Nitrous oxide emissions	
	2000 PPP $ per kilogram of oil equivalent		Total million metric tons		average annual % change	Per capita metric tons		kilograms per 2000 PPP $ of GDP		million metric tons of carbon dioxide equivalent	average annual % change	million metric tons of carbon dioxide equivalent	average annual % change
	1990	2004	1990	2003	1990–2003	1990	2003	1990	2003	2000	1990–2000	2000	1990–2000
Afghanistan	..	..	2.6	0.7	–9.0	0.2	..	..	..	13.2	5.3	7.5	3.4
Albania	3.8	5.9	7.3	3.0	–3.7	2.2	1.0	0.9	0.2	0.5	–3.8	0.1	–0.5
Algeria	5.7	6.0	77.0	163.6	7.8	3.0	5.1	0.7	0.8	28.5	4.0	9.2	1.4
Angola	3.7	3.3	4.6	8.6	4.3	0.4	0.6	0.3	0.3	15.8	1.6	6.1	2.0
Argentina	6.4	7.4	109.7	127.5	1.2	3.4	3.4	0.5	0.3	86.7	0.7	63.4	1.2
Armenia	*1.6*	5.6	4.2	3.4	–0.9	1.2	1.1	0.5	0.3	2.8	–2.0	0.3	–4.1
Australia	4.0	4.8	272.2	354.1	2.7	15.9	17.8	1.0	0.6	113.2	0.1	27.0	3.4
Austria	7.1	7.3	57.7	70.3	1.2	7.5	8.7	0.4	0.3	9.7	–1.6	2.8	1.0
Azerbaijan	..	2.5	53.7	29.2	–5.1	7.5	3.5	1.9	1.0	11.9	–2.4	0.8	–4.2
Bangladesh	9.8	10.5	15.4	34.6	6.9	0.1	0.3	0.2	0.1	47.6	0.9	44.8	3.7
Belarus	*1.2*	2.4	107.8	62.5	–4.4	10.6	6.3	2.4	1.0	21.6	–1.1	8.3	–3.4
Belgium	4.7	5.2	100.6	102.8	–0.4	10.1	9.9	0.5	0.3	11.7	–0.4	13.3	0.1
Benin	2.6	3.3	0.7	2.0	7.4	0.1	0.3	0.2	0.2	3.3	2.2	2.7	2.7
Bolivia	5.1	4.5	5.5	7.9	4.4	0.8	0.9	0.5	0.3	21.3	1.2	5.8	–0.1
Bosnia and Herzegovina	..	5.3	6.9	19.1	15.3	1.6	4.9	..	..	1.4	–3.0	0.6	–5.1
Botswana	6.2	8.6	2.2	4.1	4.2	1.5	2.3	0.3	0.2	7.0	1.3	4.8	1.0
Brazil	7.2	6.8	202.6	298.3	3.7	1.4	1.6	0.3	0.2	297.2	0.9	207.7	1.1
Bulgaria	2.1	3.0	75.3	44.0	–3.6	8.6	5.6	1.6	0.7	10.0	–6.3	18.5	–2.2
Burkina Faso	..	..	1.0	1.0	1.2	0.1	0.1	0.2	0.1	8.8	2.1	11.7	2.3
Burundi	..	..	0.2	0.2	1.9	0.0	0.0	0.0	0.0	1.8	2.0	1.2	0.9
Cambodia	..	..	0.5	0.5	1.4	0.0	0.0	..	0.0	68.0	1.0	0.1	3.6
Cameroon	4.7	4.5	1.6	3.5	4.7	0.1	0.2	0.1	0.1	11.8	1.2	9.8	1.9
Canada	3.0	3.4	415.7	565.5	2.2	15.0	17.9	0.8	0.6	123.4	5.8	57.5	0.9
Central African Republic	..	..	0.2	0.3	2.3	0.1	0.1	0.1	0.1	6.6	1.6	5.1	1.8
Chad	..	..	0.1	0.1	2.8	0.0	0.0	0.0	0.0	9.6	1.6	8.7	2.2
Chile	5.5	6.1	35.3	58.5	5.2	2.7	3.7	0.6	0.4	14.5	1.5	7.5	3.6
China	2.1	4.4	2,398.2	4,143.5	2.5	2.1	3.2	1.6	0.6	802.9	1.8	644.7	2.4
Hong Kong, China	10.8	11.5	26.2	37.8	2.5	4.6	5.6	0.3	0.2	..	..	..	..
Colombia	8.4	10.9	56.8	55.5	–0.6	1.6	1.3	0.4	0.2	55.5	1.2	41.2	4.8
Congo, Dem. Rep.	5.0	2.2	4.0	1.8	–6.5	0.1	0.0	0.1	0.1	32.9	0.6	17.2	0.0
Congo, Rep.	2.3	3.3	1.2	1.4	–1.0	0.5	0.4	0.5	0.3	3.2	1.9	1.0	2.6
Costa Rica	9.7	10.0	2.9	6.3	5.1	0.9	1.5	0.2	0.2	3.6	–0.3	3.6	–1.0
Côte d'Ivoire	5.2	3.7	5.4	5.7	1.3	0.4	0.3	0.3	0.2	6.5	2.0	2.9	1.8
Croatia	*5.0*	5.6	24.6	23.8	1.6	5.1	5.4	0.6	0.5	3.8	–0.5	3.4	–1.2
Cuba	..	..	32.0	25.2	–1.8	3.0	2.3	..	..	9.1	–0.8	9.3	–3.3
Czech Republic	*3.1*	4.0	161.7	116.3	–2.2	15.6	11.4	1.3	0.6	10.8	–3.5	8.2	–4.8
Denmark	6.9	7.9	49.7	54.5	–1.2	9.7	10.1	0.5	0.3	6.0	–0.3	9.3	–1.5
Dominican Republic	7.1	7.6	9.6	21.3	6.8	1.3	2.5	0.4	0.3	5.9	1.1	4.3	0.4
Ecuador	5.8	4.8	16.6	23.2	2.4	1.6	1.8	0.6	0.5	16.2	1.8	2.9	–0.3
Egypt, Arab Rep.	5.1	4.9	75.4	139.6	5.6	1.4	2.0	0.6	0.5	34.3	4.1	16.0	3.9
El Salvador	7.3	7.0	2.6	6.5	6.4	0.5	1.0	0.2	0.2	3.2	1.9	2.2	0.7
Eritrea	..	..	..	0.7	..	..	0.2	..	0.2	0.0	..	..	..
Estonia	*1.6*	3.5	28.3	18.2	–3.9	18.1	13.5	2.5	1.1	2.4	–4.4	0.4	–5.8
Ethiopia	2.6	2.8	3.0	7.3	8.0	0.1	0.1	0.1	0.1	47.5	2.0	12.2	6.6
Finland	3.8	3.8	51.2	67.8	1.4	10.3	13.0	0.6	0.4	4.3	–3.4	7.3	–1.5
France	5.5	5.9	362.3	373.9	0.1	6.4	6.2	0.4	0.2	59.3	–1.1	72.3	–1.7
Gabon	4.8	4.9	6.0	1.2	–9.1	6.3	0.9	1.2	0.1	3.8	2.3	1.8	0.0
Gambia, The	..	..	0.2	0.3	3.4	0.2	0.2	0.2	0.1	0.7	1.7	0.5	0.3
Georgia	*1.2*	4.1	17.3	3.7	–11.3	3.2	0.8	0.8	0.3	4.4	–1.9	1.1	–4.4
Germany	4.7	6.2	980.3	805.0	–1.1	12.3	9.8	0.7	0.4	62.7	–4.4	60.5	–3.2
Ghana	4.6	5.4	3.8	7.7	5.7	0.2	0.4	0.2	0.2	7.1	3.4	7.4	6.4
Greece	6.7	7.4	72.2	96.2	2.6	7.1	8.7	0.6	0.4	10.9	2.4	11.2	0.2
Guatemala	6.7	6.4	5.1	10.7	6.7	0.6	0.9	0.2	0.2	6.2	0.5	5.2	0.8
Guinea	..	..	1.0	1.3	2.3	0.2	0.1	0.1	0.1	5.7	1.9	2.4	2.9
Guinea-Bissau	..	..	0.2	0.3	2.0	0.2	0.2	0.3	0.2	0.9	0.0	0.8	2.4
Haiti	10.4	6.2	1.0	1.7	7.2	0.1	0.2	0.1	0.1	3.4	1.7	2.6	0.7

Energy efficiency and emissions

	GDP per unit of energy use		Carbon dioxide emissions							Methane emissions		Nitrous oxide emissions	
	2000 PPP $ per kilogram of oil equivalent		Total million metric tons		average annual % change	Per capita metric tons		kilograms per 2000 PPP $ of GDP		million metric tons of carbon dioxide equivalent	average annual % change	million metric tons of carbon dioxide equivalent	average annual % change
	1990	2004	1990	2003	1990–2003	1990	2003	1990	2003	2000	1990–2000	2000	1990–2000
Honduras	5.0	4.8	2.6	6.5	7.5	0.5	0.9	0.2	0.3	4.9	–0.2	3.5	0.0
Hungary	4.2	5.9	60.1	58.2	–0.4	5.8	5.7	0.6	0.4	11.3	–2.5	12.9	13.6
India	4.0	5.5	677.7	1,273.2	4.9	0.8	1.2	0.6	0.4	445.3	1.6	399.0	2.6
Indonesia	4.1	4.1	149.3	295.0	4.6	0.8	1.4	0.5	0.4	169.2	1.4	38.7	1.0
Iran, Islamic Rep.	3.6	3.1	218.2	381.4	3.7	4.0	5.7	1.0	0.8	96.9	6.7	43.8	1.5
Iraq	..	..	48.5	72.9	3.8	2.6	..	..	..	14.4	0.7	6.5	0.1
Ireland	5.2	9.5	30.6	41.4	2.9	8.7	10.4	0.7	0.3	12.9	–0.1	9.8	0.6
Israel	7.0	7.3	33.1	68.3	5.8	7.1	10.2	0.5	0.4	11.4	3.3	1.7	2.0
Italy	8.4	8.2	389.5	445.5	1.0	6.9	7.7	0.4	0.3	37.0	–0.7	43.5	0.6
Jamaica	3.0	2.5	8.0	10.7	2.4	3.3	4.1	1.3	1.0	1.3	0.8	1.3	0.3
Japan	6.5	6.4	1,070.4	1,231.3	1.0	8.7	9.6	0.4	0.3	21.8	–1.7	37.0	–0.6
Jordan	3.5	3.6	10.2	17.1	3.8	3.2	3.3	1.0	0.7	7.9	1.0	0.2	9.2
Kazakhstan	*1.0*	1.9	288.1	159.2	–6.0	17.6	10.7	3.8	1.7	27.3	–4.5	7.8	–6.5
Kenya	2.2	2.1	5.8	8.8	5.0	0.2	0.3	0.3	0.2	21.5	1.1	22.6	0.3
Korea, Dem. Rep.	..	..	244.6	77.5	–11.9	12.4	3.5	..	..	33.5	0.3	6.5	–4.0
Korea, Rep.	4.5	4.2	241.1	455.9	4.6	5.6	9.5	0.7	0.5	25.0	–0.2	16.1	4.8
Kuwait	*1.2*	1.9	45.2	78.5	11.0	21.3	32.7	*1.5*	1.4	9.9	6.5	0.2	14.1
Kyrgyz Republic	*1.7*	3.3	12.6	5.3	–7.5	2.8	1.1	1.4	0.6	2.2	–2.4	0.1	1.2
Lao PDR	..	..	0.2	1.3	16.7	0.1	0.2	0.1	0.1	6.2	0.9	0.1	2.7
Latvia	*2.5*	5.6	14.5	6.7	–6.9	5.4	2.9	0.7	0.3	2.6	–4.0	1.2	–6.6
Lebanon	2.7	3.5	9.1	19.0	5.1	3.3	5.4	1.5	1.1	1.3	8.6	1.1	5.5
Lesotho	..	..	..	..	..	..	..	..	..	1.2	2.0	1.5	0.5
Liberia	..	..	0.5	0.5	3.1	0.2	0.1	..	..	1.2	–0.8	0.8	0.9
Libya	..	..	37.8	50.2	2.3	8.7	8.9	..	..	9.6	0.9	2.5	–1.1
Lithuania	*2.8*	4.5	24.3	12.7	–5.2	6.6	3.7	0.7	0.3	5.9	–4.2	3.5	16.8
Macedonia, FYR	*4.1*	4.6	15.5	10.5	–0.7	8.1	5.2	1.4	0.8	1.3	0.0	1.1	1.5
Madagascar	..	..	0.9	2.3	8.5	0.1	0.1	0.1	0.2	18.9	1.5	11.6	1.2
Malawi	..	..	0.6	0.9	2.8	0.1	0.1	0.2	0.1	3.6	1.6	2.3	1.3
Malaysia	4.4	4.1	55.3	156.4	6.8	3.1	6.4	0.7	0.7	30.4	4.3	13.3	1.5
Mali	..	..	0.4	0.6	2.3	0.0	0.0	0.1	0.0	12.0	0.9	13.8	2.4
Mauritania	..	..	2.6	2.5	–1.2	1.3	0.9	0.9	0.4	4.4	1.3	6.4	1.3
Mauritius	..	..	1.5	3.1	6.4	1.4	2.6	0.3	0.2	0.3	5.0	0.9	1.7
Mexico	5.1	5.5	375.1	415.9	0.7	4.5	4.1	0.7	0.4	111.7	0.0	10.0	1.1
Moldova	*1.4*	2.0	23.8	7.2	–10.1	5.5	1.7	1.9	1.0	2.6	–4.1	1.6	–6.0
Mongolia	..	..	10.0	8.0	–2.6	4.7	3.2	3.3	1.8	8.2	1.7	12.1	3.7
Morocco	11.9	10.3	23.5	37.9	3.7	1.0	1.3	0.4	0.3	10.0	1.0	15.7	0.6
Mozambique	1.3	2.6	1.0	1.6	3.2	0.1	0.1	0.1	0.1	11.1	1.8	3.2	1.0
Myanmar	..	..	4.3	9.5	6.5	0.1	0.2	..	..	61.1	2.4	12.5	3.2
Namibia	*12.3*	10.2	0.0	2.3	..	0.0	1.2	0.0	0.2	4.5	0.5	4.2	–0.2
Nepal	3.4	4.0	0.6	2.9	11.4	0.0	0.1	0.0	0.1	16.4	1.5	11.3	1.5
Netherlands	5.2	5.8	139.7	140.9	0.2	9.3	8.7	0.5	0.3	21.6	–2.3	17.2	0.3
New Zealand	4.1	5.1	23.6	34.8	3.3	6.8	8.7	0.5	0.4	36.2	–0.5	12.4	0.5
Nicaragua	5.3	5.5	2.6	3.9	5.0	0.7	0.8	0.3	0.2	5.3	1.3	4.0	0.8
Niger	..	..	1.0	1.2	1.1	0.1	0.1	0.2	0.1	6.5	2.5	5.0	2.8
Nigeria	1.1	1.4	45.3	52.2	–0.1	0.5	0.4	0.7	0.4	72.5	4.2	41.6	1.9
Norway	5.1	5.9	35.3	45.0	2.0	8.3	9.9	0.4	0.3	7.1	0.6	5.1	0.0
Oman	4.3	3.0	10.3	32.2	8.7	5.6	12.8	0.6	0.9	3.7	8.5	1.0	1.9
Pakistan	3.9	4.2	68.0	114.1	4.3	0.6	0.8	0.5	0.4	94.7	2.5	84.6	3.4
Panama	7.4	8.4	3.1	6.0	5.5	1.3	1.9	0.4	0.3	3.3	1.0	2.7	0.7
Papua New Guinea	..	..	2.4	2.5	–0.2	0.6	0.4	0.4	0.2	3.9	3.9	2.3	1.8
Paraguay	6.5	6.6	2.3	4.1	4.7	0.5	0.7	0.1	0.2	12.3	0.5	10.2	0.2
Peru	8.4	10.9	21.0	26.1	2.3	1.0	1.0	0.3	0.2	19.6	1.5	21.9	8.0
Philippines	9.1	7.9	43.9	76.9	5.0	0.7	1.0	0.2	0.2	34.2	0.7	20.8	3.3
Poland	2.9	5.1	347.5	304.5	–1.3	9.1	8.0	1.5	0.7	47.2	–2.2	23.9	–2.2
Portugal	7.9	7.1	42.3	57.5	3.0	4.3	5.5	0.4	0.3	14.3	0.3	8.1	0.3
Puerto Rico	..	..	11.8	2.1	–4.1	3.3	0.5	..	..	..	..	..	..

3.8 Energy efficiency and emissions

	GDP per unit of energy use		Carbon dioxide emissions							Methane emissions		Nitrous oxide emissions	
	2000 PPP $ per kilogram of oil equivalent		Total million metric tons		average annual % change	Per capita metric tons		kilograms per 2000 PPP $ of GDP		million metric tons of carbon dioxide equivalent	average annual % change	million metric tons of carbon dioxide equivalent	average annual % change
	1990	**2004**	**1990**	**2003**	**1990–2003**	**1990**	**2003**	**1990**	**2003**	**2000**	**1990–2000**	**2000**	**1990–2000**
Romania	2.5	4.5	155.0	91.1	–4.0	6.7	4.2	1.2	0.6	36.1	–1.7	7.2	–6.6
Russian Federation	*1.6*	2.0	2,261.7	1,493.0	–3.3	15.3	10.3	1.8	1.2	298.7	–4.6	51.5	–3.7
Rwanda	..	..	0.5	0.6	1.7	0.1	0.1	0.1	0.1	2.2	–1.5	1.2	–1.4
Saudi Arabia	2.8	2.2	197.4	302.3	0.5	12.1	13.7	1.1	0.9	54.4	5.7	8.7	1.5
Senegal	5.0	6.5	3.1	4.8	2.6	0.4	0.4	0.3	0.3	8.4	2.5	6.6	3.8
Serbia and Montenegro	..	..	65.4	49.9	–0.4	6.2	6.2	..	..	9.5	–2.6	6.1	–3.5
Sierra Leone	..	..	0.3	0.7	4.3	0.1	0.1	0.1	0.2	2.6	0.8	0.9	3.0
Singapore	3.4	4.4	45.1	47.8	1.2	14.8	11.4	1.2	0.5	1.2	7.1	0.9	46.1
Slovak Republic	2.7	3.9	51.4	37.5	–1.8	9.7	7.0	1.1	0.5	4.2	–3.1	3.2	–4.9
Slovenia	*4.9*	5.4	18.0	15.4	1.1	9.0	7.7	0.8	0.4	2.5	–0.7	2.0	2.3
Somalia	..	..	0.0	..	..	0.0	..	..	..	..	..	..	..
South Africa	3.9	3.7	285.4	364.2	1.7	8.1	7.9	1.1	0.8	37.4	0.7	25.8	0.1
Spain	7.3	6.9	211.8	309.2	3.2	5.5	7.4	0.4	0.3	39.6	2.3	30.1	1.5
Sri Lanka	7.3	8.3	3.8	10.3	8.8	0.2	0.5	0.1	0.1	13.3	2.9	2.9	2.0
Sudan	2.7	3.7	5.4	9.0	5.0	0.2	0.3	0.2	0.1	46.6	1.7	47.1	2.0
Swaziland	..	..	0.4	1.0	12.0	0.6	0.9	0.2	0.2	1.1	1.0	1.2	1.2
Sweden	4.0	4.5	49.4	52.7	0.0	5.8	5.9	0.3	0.2	7.1	–1.0	7.1	–0.4
Switzerland	8.2	8.3	42.7	40.4	–0.2	6.4	5.5	0.3	0.2	5.0	–1.1	3.7	0.3
Syrian Arab Republic	2.9	3.4	35.8	48.9	1.9	2.8	2.7	1.4	0.8	9.7	6.7	9.4	2.0
Tajikistan	*0.9*	2.1	23.4	4.7	–12.5	4.4	0.7	2.2	0.7	1.4	0.8	0.1	1.5
Tanzania	1.4	1.3	2.3	3.8	2.8	0.1	0.1	0.2	0.2	31.7	1.8	27.1	1.6
Thailand	5.7	4.9	95.7	245.9	6.4	1.8	3.9	0.5	0.5	75.9	0.4	13.1	0.7
Togo	4.3	3.1	0.8	2.2	7.8	0.2	0.4	0.2	0.3	2.1	1.7	2.3	1.5
Trinidad and Tobago	1.4	1.3	16.9	28.6	3.5	13.9	22.1	2.4	1.8	3.1	2.4	0.3	–1.6
Tunisia	6.7	8.2	13.3	20.9	3.2	1.6	2.1	0.4	0.3	4.8	3.0	5.2	1.4
Turkey	5.8	6.2	146.2	220.0	3.6	2.6	3.1	0.6	0.4	97.4	2.1	40.6	–1.2
Turkmenistan	*1.6*	..	32.0	43.3	2.6	8.7	9.2	1.9	..	27.1	1.7	0.6	–1.4
Uganda	..	..	0.8	1.7	7.2	0.0	0.1	0.1	0.0	12.4	2.5	12.9	2.7
Ukraine	*1.8*	2.0	684.0	314.4	–6.6	13.2	6.6	1.8	1.2	153.5	–2.2	19.9	–4.3
United Arab Emirates	1.9	2.2	54.7	135.0	7.4	30.8	33.4	1.5	1.5	35.2	7.1	0.1	3.2
United Kingdom	5.9	7.3	569.1	558.5	–0.4	9.9	9.4	0.6	0.3	51.1	–3.3	43.8	–3.5
United States	3.7	4.6	4,816.2	5,788.2	1.7	19.3	19.9	0.8	0.5	613.4	–0.5	430.0	0.8
Uruguay	9.9	10.4	3.9	4.4	0.7	1.3	1.3	0.2	0.2	18.3	2.0	0.7	3.0
Uzbekistan	*0.7*	0.8	129.2	123.6	0.1	6.3	4.8	4.2	2.8	46.2	1.5	13.5	1.9
Venezuela, RB	2.6	2.6	117.3	144.0	2.0	5.9	5.6	1.3	1.1	95.1	2.4	6.9	–0.5
Vietnam	3.3	4.2	21.4	76.1	11.5	0.3	0.9	0.3	0.4	68.1	1.5	12.9	5.2
West Bank and Gaza	..	..	..	..	..	..	..	..	..	..	..	..	..
Yemen, Rep.	3.0	2.8	9.6	17.1	4.2	0.8	0.9	1.4	1.0	8.7	8.9	5.6	0.9
Zambia	1.5	1.5	2.4	2.2	–2.0	0.3	0.2	0.4	0.2	11.2	1.4	5.5	1.3
Zimbabwe	3.0	2.6	16.6	11.5	–2.7	1.6	0.9	0.7	0.4	11.0	0.2	8.6	–0.5
World	3.9 w	4.8 w	22,501.8 t	26,750.9 t	1.2 w	4.3 w	4.3 w	0.7 w	0.5 w	5,893.6 t	–0.6 w	3,454.4 t	0.3 w
Low income	3.5	4.4	1,336.9	1,893.3	2.4	0.8	0.8	0.5	0.4	1,344.6	1.8	910.8	2.7
Middle income	3.0	4.2	9,319.6	10,753.5	0.5	3.5	3.6	1.1	0.6	3,033.6	0.8	1,545.4	1.0
Lower middle income	3.1	4.5	4,965.3	6,943.3	1.7	2.4	2.9	1.0	0.5	2,080.8	1.5	1,242.3	1.7
Upper middle income	2.8	3.7	4,353.8	3,811.5	–1.1	8.1	6.4	1.2	0.7	952.9	–0.1	303.4	0.0
Low & middle income	3.0	4.3	10,656.6	12,646.8	0.8	2.4	2.4	1.0	0.5	4,377.7	1.0	2,455.6	1.2
East Asia & Pacific	2.6	4.4	3,030.6	5,100.6	2.5	1.9	2.7	1.2	0.6	1,365.5	1.7	780.0	2.2
Europe & Central Asia	2.1	2.8	4,821.9	3,265.3	–3.1	10.2	6.9	1.6	0.9	844.1	–2.0	236.3	–1.9
Latin America & Carib.	6.0	6.2	1,037.3	1,299.9	2.0	2.4	2.4	0.5	0.3	800.9	0.8	418.8	1.4
Middle East & N. Africa	4.6	4.2	575.4	1,012.5	4.5	2.5	3.4	0.8	0.7	233.0	4.2	118.3	1.9
South Asia	4.2	5.5	768.4	1,436.7	4.9	0.7	1.0	0.5	0.4	631.7	1.7	550.3	2.8
Sub-Saharan Africa	2.8	2.8	418.3	531.9	1.6	0.8	0.8	0.6	0.4	504.6	1.5	353.8	1.2
High income	4.7	5.2	10,651.9	12,738.4	1.5	11.8	12.8	0.6	0.4	1,450.2	–0.9	961.9	0.1
Europe EMU	5.8	6.5	2,466.1	2,535.8	0.4	8.3	8.2	0.5	0.3	287.0	–1.8	278.2	–1.1

Energy efficiency and emissions 3.8

About the data

The ratio of GDP to energy use provides a measure of energy efficiency. To produce comparable and consistent estimates of real GDP across countries relative to physical inputs to GDP—that is, units of energy use—GDP is converted to 2000 constant international dollars using purchasing power parity (PPP) rates. Differences in this ratio over time and across countries reflect in part structural changes in the economy, changes in the energy efficiency of particular sectors, and differences in fuel mixes.

Because commercial energy is widely traded, it is necessary to distinguish between its production and its use. Net energy imports show the extent to which an economy's use exceeds its domestic production. High-income countries are net energy importers; middle-income countries have been their main suppliers.

Carbon dioxide emissions, largely byproducts of energy production and use (see table 3.7), account for the largest share of greenhouse gases, which are associated with global warming. Anthropogenic carbon dioxide emissions result primarily from fossil fuel combustion and cement manufacturing. In combustion, different fossil fuels release different amounts of carbon dioxide for the same level of energy use. Burning oil releases about 50 percent more carbon dioxide than burning natural gas, and burning coal releases about twice as much. Cement manufacturing releases about half a metric ton of carbon dioxide for each metric ton of cement produced.

Methane emissions, largely the result of agricultural activities and industrial production of methane, are expressed in carbon dioxide equivalents using global warming potential, which allows different gases to be compared on the basis of their effective contributions. A kilogram of methane is 23 times as effective at trapping heat in the earth's atmosphere as a kilogram of carbon dioxide within a time horizon of 100 years. The global warming potential of a kilogram of nitrous oxide is nearly 300 times that of a kilogram of carbon dioxide within the same time horizon.

The Carbon Dioxide Information Analysis Center (CDIAC), sponsored by the U.S. Department of Energy, calculates annual anthropogenic emissions of carbon dioxide. These calculations are based on data on fossil fuel consumption (from the World Energy Data Set maintained by the United Nations Statistics Division) and data on world cement manufacturing (from the Cement Manufacturing Data Set maintained by the U.S. Bureau of Mines). Emissions of carbon dioxide are often calculated and reported in terms of their content of elemental carbon. For this table these values were converted to the actual mass of carbon dioxide by multiplying the carbon mass by 3.664 (the ratio of the mass of carbon to that of carbon dioxide). Although the estimates of global carbon dioxide emissions are probably within 10 percent of actual emissions (as calculated from global average fuel chemistry and use), country estimates may have larger error bounds. The world totals shown in the table include the carbon dioxide emissions not allocated to specific countries. Trends estimated from a consistent time series tend to be more accurate than individual values. Each year the CDIAC recalculates the entire time series from 1950 to the present, incorporating its most recent findings and the latest corrections to its database. Estimates do not include fuels supplied to ships and aircraft engaged in international transport because of the difficulty of apportioning these fuels among the countries benefiting from that transport.

High-income countries contribute more than half of global carbon dioxide emissions **3.8a**

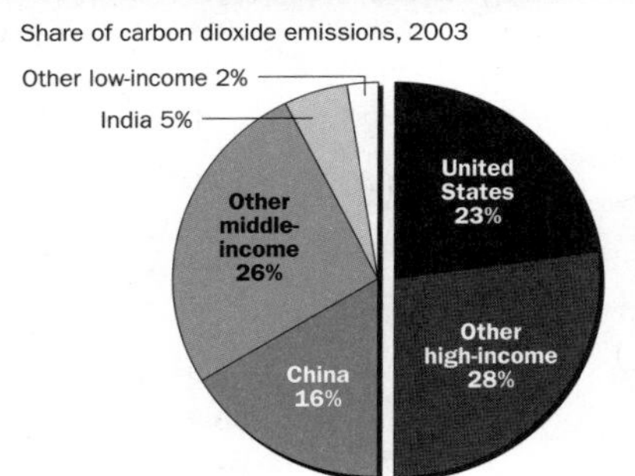

Source: Table 3.8.

The five largest contributors to carbon dioxide emissions differ considerably in per capita emissions **3.8b**

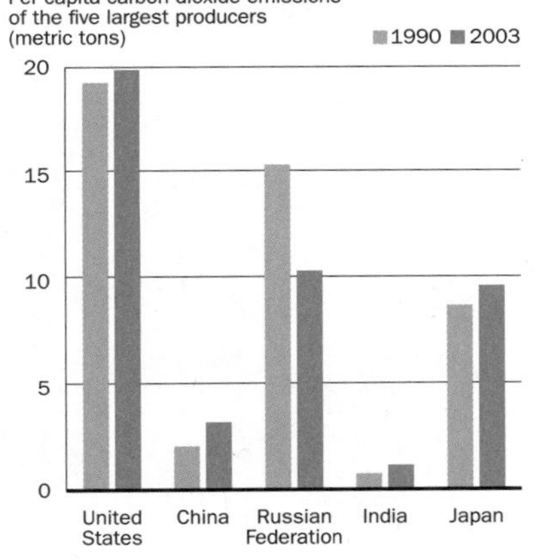

Source: Table 3.8.

Definitions

• **GDP per unit of energy use** is the PPP GDP per kilogram of oil equivalent of energy use. PPP GDP is gross domestic product converted to 2000 constant international dollars using purchasing power parity rates. An international dollar has the same purchasing power over GDP as a U.S. dollar has in the United States. • **Carbon dioxide emissions** are those stemming from the burning of fossil fuels and the manufacture of cement. They include carbon dioxide produced during consumption of solid, liquid, and gas fuels and gas flaring. • **Methane emissions** are those stemming from human activities such as agriculture and from industrial methane production. • **Nitrous oxide emissions** are those stemming from agriculture, biomass burning, industrial activities, and livestock management.

Data sources

The underlying data on energy use are from electronic files of the International Energy Agency. Data on carbon dioxide emissions are from the CDIAC, Environmental Sciences Division, Oak Ridge National Laboratory, in the U.S. state of Tennessee. Data on methane and nitrous oxide emissions are compiled by the World Resources Institute.

3.9 Sources of electricity

	Electricity production		Sources of electricity[a]									
			% of total									
	billion kilowatt hours		Coal		Gas		Oil		Hydropower		Nuclear power	
	1990	2004	1990	2004	1990	2004	1990	2004	1990	2004	1990	2004
Afghanistan	..	..	..	..	..	..	..	..	..	..	..	..
Albania	3.2	5.6	..	..	..	..	10.9	1.7	89.1	98.3	..	..
Algeria	16.1	31.3	..	..	93.7	97.0	5.4	2.2	0.8	0.8	..	..
Angola	0.8	2.2	..	..	..	..	13.8	33.5	86.2	66.5	..	..
Argentina	51.0	100.3	1.3	1.7	39.0	54.8	9.7	4.0	35.6	30.4	14.3	7.8
Armenia	*9.0*	6.0	..	..	*22.9*	30.4	*43.3*	..	*33.8*	33.1	..	36.5
Australia	154.3	239.3	77.1	79.3	10.6	12.3	2.7	0.7	9.2	6.8	..	..
Austria	49.3	61.6	14.2	14.8	15.7	17.8	3.8	3.0	63.9	59.1	..	..
Azerbaijan	*19.7*	21.6	..	..	*0.5*	58.9	*91.1*	28.4	*8.9*	12.7	..	..
Bangladesh	7.7	21.5	..	..	84.3	87.5	4.3	6.7	11.4	5.7	..	..
Belarus	*37.6*	31.2	..	0.0	*47.9*	87.3	*52.1*	12.6	*0.0*	0.1	..	..
Belgium	70.3	84.4	28.2	13.6	7.7	25.5	1.9	2.0	0.4	0.4	60.8	56.1
Benin	0.0	0.1	..	..	..	..	100.0	98.8	..	1.2	..	..
Bolivia	2.1	4.4	..	..	37.6	29.2	5.3	19.7	55.3	49.0	..	..
Bosnia and Herzegovina	*6.5*	12.6	*47.8*	52.1	..	..	..	1.1	*52.2*	46.8	..	..
Botswana	0.9	1.3	88.1	95.7	..	..	11.9	4.3	..	..	..	..
Brazil	222.8	387.5	2.0	2.7	0.0	5.0	2.2	3.2	92.8	82.8	1.0	3.0
Bulgaria	42.1	41.4	50.3	46.1	7.6	3.6	2.9	2.0	4.5	7.6	34.8	40.6
Burkina Faso	..	..	..	..	..	..	..	..	..	..	..	..
Burundi	..	..	..	..	..	..	..	..	..	..	..	..
Cambodia	..	0.8	..	..	..	..	..	49.3	..	1.8	..	..
Cameroon	2.7	4.1	..	..	..	..	1.5	4.6	98.5	95.4	..	..
Canada	481.9	598.4	17.1	17.2	2.0	5.4	3.4	3.6	61.6	57.0	15.1	15.1
Central African Republic	..	..	..	..	..	..	..	..	..	..	..	..
Chad	..	..	..	..	..	..	..	..	..	..	..	..
Chile	18.4	52.0	34.3	16.1	1.3	34.0	7.6	1.5	55.3	45.4	..	..
China	621.2	2,199.6	71.2	77.9	0.5	0.4	7.9	3.3	20.4	16.1	*0.2*	2.3
Hong Kong, China	28.9	37.1	98.3	68.5	..	30.9	1.7	0.6	..	..	..	..
Colombia	36.2	50.2	9.8	6.0	12.4	12.9	1.0	0.2	76.0	79.8	..	..
Congo, Dem. Rep.	5.7	6.9	..	..	..	..	0.4	0.3	99.6	99.7	..	..
Congo, Rep.	0.5	0.4	..	..	..	..	0.6	..	99.4	100.0	..	..
Costa Rica	3.5	8.2	..	..	..	..	2.5	1.8	97.5	79.0	..	..
Côte d'Ivoire	2.0	5.4	..	..	..	67.5	33.3	0.1	66.7	32.4	..	..
Croatia	*8.9*	13.2	..	16.2	*15.4*	18.6	*35.8*	12.4	*48.8*	52.7	..	..
Cuba	15.0	15.7	..	..	0.2	*0.0*	91.5	95.3	0.6	0.6	..	..
Czech Republic	62.3	83.8	76.4	60.3	0.6	2.6	0.9	0.4	1.9	2.4	20.2	31.4
Denmark	26.0	40.5	90.7	46.1	2.7	24.7	3.4	4.0	0.1	0.1	..	..
Dominican Republic	3.7	13.8	1.2	15.2	..	0.1	88.6	72.6	9.4	11.5	..	..
Ecuador	6.3	12.6	..	..	..	8.5	21.5	32.6	78.5	58.9	..	..
Egypt, Arab Rep.	42.3	101.3	..	..	39.6	70.8	36.9	16.2	23.5	12.5	..	..
El Salvador	2.2	4.4	..	..	..	..	6.9	45.6	73.5	31.2	..	..
Eritrea	..	..	..	..	..	..	..	..	..	..	..	..
Estonia	*11.8*	10.3	*90.0*	92.4	*5.5*	4.7	*4.5*	0.3	*0.0*	0.2	..	..
Ethiopia	1.2	2.5	..	..	..	..	11.6	0.7	88.4	99.3	..	..
Finland	54.4	85.8	33.0	27.5	8.6	14.9	3.1	0.7	20.0	17.6	35.3	26.5
France	417.2	567.1	8.5	5.0	0.7	3.2	2.1	1.0	12.9	10.5	75.3	79.0
Gabon	1.0	1.5	..	..	16.4	16.7	11.2	24.8	72.1	58.1	..	..
Gambia, The	..	..	..	..	..	..	..	..	..	..	..	..
Georgia	*11.2*	6.9	..	..	*36.6*	12.0	*5.0*	0.6	*58.3*	87.4	..	..
Germany	547.7	610.0	58.8	50.5	7.4	10.1	1.9	1.7	3.2	3.5	27.8	27.4
Ghana	5.7	6.0	..	..	..	..	..	12.6	100.0	87.4	..	..
Greece	34.8	58.8	72.4	60.2	0.3	15.3	22.3	14.3	5.1	7.9	..	..
Guatemala	2.3	7.0	..	17.1	..	..	9.0	35.7	76.0	34.7	..	..
Guinea	..	..	..	..	..	..	..	..	..	..	..	..
Guinea-Bissau	..	..	..	..	..	..	..	..	..	..	..	..
Haiti	0.6	0.5	..	..	..	..	20.6	52.5	76.5	47.5	..	..

3.9 Sources of electricity

	Electricity production		Sources of electricity[a]									
			% of total									
	billion kilowatt hours		Coal		Gas		Oil		Hydropower		Nuclear power	
	1990	**2004**	**1990**	**2004**	**1990**	**2004**	**1990**	**2004**	**1990**	**2004**	**1990**	**2004**
Honduras	2.3	4.9	..	..	..	..	1.7	51.5	98.3	48.1	..	..
Hungary	28.4	33.7	30.5	24.7	15.7	34.8	4.8	2.3	0.6	0.6	48.3	35.3
India	289.4	667.8	65.3	69.1	3.4	9.5	4.3	5.4	24.8	12.7	2.1	2.5
Indonesia	33.3	120.2	31.5	40.1	2.3	16.1	42.7	30.2	20.2	8.1	..	..
Iran, Islamic Rep.	59.1	164.5	..	..	52.5	76.2	37.3	17.3	10.3	6.5	..	..
Iraq	24.0	32.3	..	..	..	..	89.2	98.5	10.8	1.5	..	..
Ireland	14.2	25.2	57.4	30.6	27.7	51.1	10.0	12.7	4.9	2.5	..	..
Israel	20.9	49.1	50.1	75.3	..	8.8	49.9	15.8	0.0	0.1	..	..
Italy	213.1	293.0	16.8	17.4	18.6	44.3	48.2	15.7	14.8	13.5	*0.1*	..
Jamaica	2.5	7.2	..	..	..	..	92.4	96.5	3.6	1.9	..	..
Japan	838.2	1,071.0	13.9	27.5	19.8	22.8	18.4	9.2	10.7	8.8	24.1	26.4
Jordan	3.6	9.0	..	..	11.9	50.2	87.8	49.2	0.3	0.6	..	..
Kazakhstan	*82.7*	66.9	*72.3*	69.9	*10.6*	10.6	*8.8*	7.4	*8.3*	12.0	..	..
Kenya	3.0	5.6	..	..	..	..	7.6	24.1	81.6	51.5	..	..
Korea, Dem. Rep.	27.7	22.0	40.1	38.6	..	..	3.6	4.5	56.3	56.9	..	..
Korea, Rep.	105.4	366.6	16.8	38.8	9.1	16.2	17.9	7.6	6.0	1.2	50.2	35.7
Kuwait	18.5	41.3	..	..	45.7	20.5	54.3	79.5	..	..	..	..
Kyrgyz Republic	*11.9*	15.1	*9.1*	3.5	*13.6*	3.5	..	..	*77.4*	93.1	..	..
Lao PDR	..	..	..	..	..	..	..	..	..	..	..	..
Latvia	*4.0*	4.7	*3.8*	*0.6*	*25.4*	30.6	*7.6*	1.3	*63.3*	66.4	..	..
Lebanon	1.5	10.2	..	..	..	..	66.7	89.0	33.3	11.0	..	..
Lesotho	..	..	..	..	..	..	..	..	..	..	..	..
Liberia	..	..	..	..	..	..	..	..	..	..	..	..
Libya	10.2	20.2	..	..	..	19.3	100.0	80.7	..	..	..	..
Lithuania	*18.7*	18.8	..	..	*6.7*	14.4	*12.4*	1.9	*2.5*	2.2	*78.2*	80.5
Macedonia, FYR	*6.1*	6.7	*85.0*	77.6	..	..	*1.0*	0.2	*14.0*	22.2	..	..
Madagascar	..	..	..	..	..	..	..	..	..	..	..	..
Malawi	..	..	..	..	..	..	..	..	..	..	..	..
Malaysia	23.0	82.9	12.3	27.9	20.4	61.8	50.0	3.3	17.3	7.0	..	..
Mali	..	..	..	..	..	..	..	..	..	..	..	..
Mauritania	..	..	..	..	..	..	..	..	..	..	..	..
Mauritius	..	..	..	..	..	..	..	..	..	..	..	..
Mexico	124.1	224.1	6.3	10.7	11.6	38.8	56.7	31.1	18.9	11.2	2.4	4.1
Moldova	*11.2*	3.6	*34.4*	..	*36.9*	97.9	*26.4*	0.4	*2.3*	1.6	..	..
Mongolia	..	..	..	..	..	..	..	..	..	..	..	..
Morocco	9.6	19.3	23.0	67.4	..	..	64.4	23.2	12.7	8.4	..	..
Mozambique	0.5	11.7	13.9	..	*0.2*	0.1	23.6	0.2	62.6	99.7	..	..
Myanmar	2.5	6.4	1.6	..	39.3	57.0	10.9	6.8	48.1	36.2	..	..
Namibia	*1.4*	1.7	*1.5*	0.4	..	..	*3.3*	2.7	*95.2*	96.9	..	..
Nepal	0.9	2.3	..	..	..	..	0.1	0.2	99.9	99.8	..	..
Netherlands	71.9	100.8	38.3	26.0	50.9	60.5	4.3	2.8	0.1	0.1	4.9	3.8
New Zealand	32.1	41.8	1.5	9.9	17.7	16.7	0.0	0.1	72.6	64.6	..	..
Nicaragua	1.4	2.8	..	..	..	..	39.8	75.2	28.8	11.4	..	..
Niger	..	..	..	..	..	..	..	..	..	..	..	..
Nigeria	13.5	20.2	0.1	..	53.7	62.7	13.7	3.1	32.6	34.2	..	..
Norway	121.6	110.1	0.1	0.1	*0.0*	0.3	0.0	0.0	99.6	98.8	..	..
Oman	4.5	11.5	..	..	81.6	82.0	18.4	18.0	..	..	..	..
Pakistan	37.7	85.7	0.1	0.2	33.6	50.7	20.6	15.9	44.9	30.0	0.8	3.3
Panama	2.7	5.8	..	..	..	..	14.7	34.0	83.2	65.6	..	..
Papua New Guinea	..	..	..	..	..	..	..	..	..	..	..	..
Paraguay	27.2	51.9	..	..	..	..	0.0	..	99.9	100.0	..	..
Peru	13.8	24.3	..	3.8	1.7	8.2	21.5	15.1	75.8	72.3	..	..
Philippines	25.2	56.0	7.7	28.9	..	22.1	46.7	15.2	24.0	15.4	..	..
Poland	134.4	152.6	97.5	94.1	0.1	2.1	1.2	1.6	1.1	1.4	..	..
Portugal	28.4	44.8	32.1	33.1	..	26.1	33.1	12.7	32.3	22.0	..	..
Puerto Rico	..	..	..	..	..	..	..	..	..	..	..	..

3.9 Sources of electricity

	Electricity production		Sources of electricity[a]									
			% of total									
	billion kilowatt hours		Coal		Gas		Oil		Hydropower		Nuclear power	
	1990	**2004**	**1990**	**2004**	**1990**	**2004**	**1990**	**2004**	**1990**	**2004**	**1990**	**2004**
Romania	64.3	56.5	28.8	38.5	35.1	18.5	18.4	3.9	17.7	29.2	..	9.8
Russian Federation	*1,008.5*	929.9	*15.3*	17.3	*45.7*	45.3	*9.9*	2.7	*17.0*	18.9	*11.9*	15.6
Rwanda	..	..	..	..	..	..	..	..	..	..	..	..
Saudi Arabia	69.2	159.9	..	..	43.5	49.2	56.5	50.8	..	..	..	..
Senegal	0.9	2.4	..	..	2.0	1.8	98.0	75.0	..	12.5	..	..
Serbia and Montenegro	*36.5*	*35.4*	*65.6*	*69.9*	*1.6*	*1.5*	*1.7*	*0.8*	*31.1*	*27.9*	..	..
Sierra Leone	..	..	..	..	..	..	..	..	..	..	..	..
Singapore	15.7	36.8	..	..	*11.8*	68.8	100.0	31.2	..	..	..	..
Slovak Republic	25.5	30.5	31.9	20.0	7.1	7.9	6.4	2.4	7.4	13.5	47.2	55.9
Slovenia	*12.1*	15.3	*36.2*	34.0	*0.2*	2.3	*2.5*	0.3	*28.2*	26.8	*32.9*	35.7
Somalia	..	..	..	..	..	..	..	..	..	..	..	..
South Africa	165.4	242.2	94.3	93.2	..	0.0	*0.0*	..	0.6	0.9	5.1	5.5
Spain	151.2	277.1	40.1	29.0	1.0	20.0	5.7	8.6	16.8	11.4	35.9	23.0
Sri Lanka	3.2	8.0	..	..	..	..	0.2	63.2	99.8	36.8	..	..
Sudan	1.5	3.9	..	..	..	..	36.8	72.8	63.2	27.2	..	..
Swaziland	..	..	..	..	..	..	..	..	..	..	..	..
Sweden	146.0	151.7	1.1	1.7	0.3	0.5	0.9	1.3	49.7	39.6	46.7	51.1
Switzerland	54.9	63.6	0.1	..	0.6	1.5	0.7	0.3	54.3	53.1	43.1	42.4
Syrian Arab Republic	11.6	32.1	..	..	20.5	41.2	56.0	45.6	23.5	13.2	..	..
Tajikistan	*16.8*	17.3	..	..	*5.3*	2.3	..	..	*94.7*	97.7	..	..
Tanzania	1.6	2.5	..	3.5	..	..	4.9	1.5	95.1	95.1	..	..
Thailand	44.2	125.7	25.0	15.9	40.2	71.0	23.5	6.2	11.3	4.8	..	..
Togo	0.2	0.3	..	..	..	..	39.9	38.9	60.1	61.1	..	..
Trinidad and Tobago	3.6	6.4	..	..	99.0	99.5	0.1	0.1	..	..	..	..
Tunisia	5.8	13.1	..	..	63.7	90.2	35.5	8.3	0.8	1.2	..	..
Turkey	57.5	150.7	35.1	22.9	17.7	41.3	6.9	5.1	40.2	30.6	..	..
Turkmenistan	*13.2*	11.5	..	..	*100.0*	100.0	..	..	*0.0*	0.0	..	..
Uganda	..	..	..	..	..	..	..	..	..	..	..	..
Ukraine	*252.5*	182.0	*41.8*	24.7	*16.8*	20.7	*9.0*	0.3	*3.2*	6.5	*29.2*	47.8
United Arab Emirates	17.1	52.4	..	..	96.3	97.5	3.7	2.5	..	..	..	..
United Kingdom	317.8	393.2	65.0	34.1	1.6	40.6	10.9	1.3	1.6	1.3	20.7	20.3
United States	3,202.8	4,147.7	53.1	50.4	11.9	17.6	4.1	3.4	8.5	6.5	19.1	19.6
Uruguay	7.4	5.9	..	..	..	0.0	5.1	18.3	94.2	81.0	..	..
Uzbekistan	*50.9*	51.0	*4.9*	3.9	*75.9*	74.0	*6.9*	9.2	*12.3*	12.8	..	..
Venezuela, RB	59.3	98.5	..	..	26.2	16.9	11.5	12.1	62.3	71.0	..	..
Vietnam	8.7	46.0	23.1	15.3	0.1	42.7	15.0	3.7	61.8	38.4	..	..
West Bank and Gaza	..	..	..	..	..	..	..	..	..	..	..	..
Yemen, Rep.	1.7	4.3	..	..	..	..	100.0	100.0	..	..	..	..
Zambia	8.0	8.5	0.5	0.2	..	..	0.3	0.4	99.2	99.4	..	..
Zimbabwe	9.4	9.7	53.3	43.0	..	..	..	0.2	46.7	56.8	..	..
World	**11,787.7 s**	**17,372.6 s**	**38.1 w**	**39.8 w**	**13.8 w**	**19.7 w**	**10.3 w**	**6.4 w**	**18.1 w**	**16.0 w**	**17.1 w**	**15.8 w**
Low income	518.1	1,026.4	40.9	47.1	15.0	19.9	6.6	7.0	34.8	23.4	1.2	1.9
Middle income	3,842.9	6,258.9	35.8	42.7	19.5	20.6	14.7	7.6	21.6	21.5	7.4	6.7
Lower middle income	1,828.6	3,903.4	41.5	50.0	10.4	13.3	16.0	8.0	27.5	23.4	5.0	4.3
Upper middle income	2,014.3	2,355.4	30.6	30.6	27.6	32.6	13.5	6.9	16.2	18.3	9.6	10.7
Low & middle income	4,361.0	7,285.3	36.4	43.3	18.9	20.5	13.7	7.5	23.1	21.8	6.7	6.0
East Asia & Pacific	785.8	2,659.5	61.3	69.1	3.5	7.6	12.7	4.9	21.7	15.6	*0.2*	1.9
Europe & Central Asia	2,213.4	1,964.1	33.0	28.6	28.4	33.8	12.1	3.2	13.3	17.4	12.0	16.6
Latin America & Carib.	608.5	1,088.3	3.8	4.7	9.7	19.6	18.8	14.0	63.5	56.3	2.0	2.6
Middle East & N. Africa	190.0	449.0	1.2	2.9	38.4	60.2	48.2	29.8	12.2	7.0	..	..
South Asia	338.9	785.3	55.8	58.7	8.6	16.0	6.1	7.1	27.6	14.9	1.9	2.5
Sub-Saharan Africa	224.4	339.0	72.1	68.2	3.3	4.9	2.2	2.7	18.4	19.5	3.8	3.9
High income	7,426.7	10,087.3	39.1	37.3	10.8	19.1	8.4	5.6	15.2	11.9	23.2	22.8
Europe EMU	1,667.3	2,227.2	34.5	27.0	8.6	18.3	9.4	4.9	11.1	10.0	35.4	34.0

a. Shares may not sum to 100 percent because some sources of generated electricty are not shown.

Sources of electricity 3.9

About the data

Use of energy is important in improving people's standard of living. But electricity generation also can damage the environment. Whether such damage occurs depends largely on how electricity is generated. For example, burning coal releases twice as much carbon dioxide—a major contributor to global warming—as does burning an equivalent amount of natural gas (see *About the data* for table 3.8). Nuclear energy does not generate carbon dioxide emissions, but it produces other dangerous waste products. The table provides information on electricity production by source. Shares may not sum to 100 percent because some sources of generated electricity (such as wind, solar, and geothermal) are not shown.

The International Energy Agency (IEA) compiles data on energy inputs used to generate electricity. IEA data for countries that are not members of the Organisation for Economic Co-operation and Development (OECD) are based on national energy data adjusted to conform to annual questionnaires completed by OECD member governments. In addition, estimates are sometimes made to complete major aggregates from which key data are missing, and adjustments are made to compensate for differences in definitions. The IEA makes these estimates in consultation with national statistical offices, oil companies, electricity utilities, and national energy experts. It occasionally revises its time series to reflect political changes. Since 1990, for example, it has constructed energy statistics for countries of the former Soviet Union. In addition, energy statistics for other countries have undergone continuous changes in coverage or methodology as more detailed energy accounts have become available in recent years. Breaks in series are therefore unavoidable.

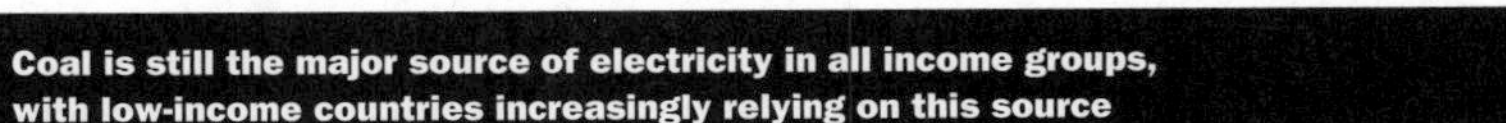

Coal is still the major source of electricity in all income groups, with low-income countries increasingly relying on this source 3.9a

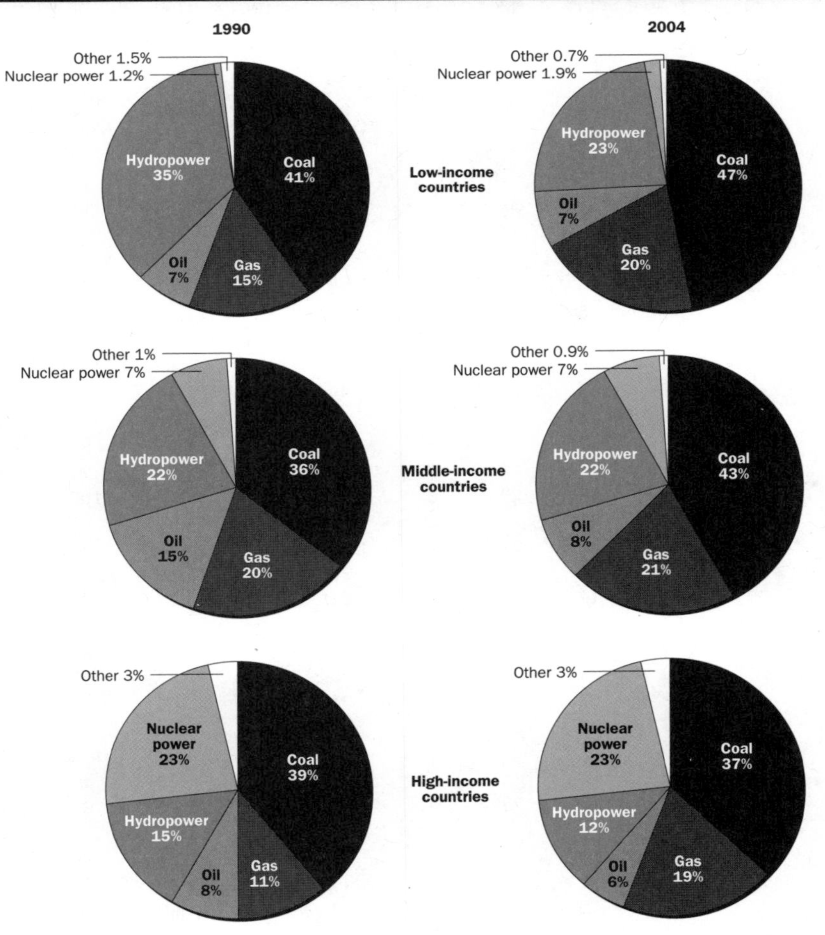

Note: Components may not sum to 100 percent because of rounding.
Source: Table 3.9.

Definitions

• **Electricity production** is measured at the terminals of all alternator sets in a station. In addition to hydropower, coal, oil, gas, and nuclear power generation, it covers generation by geothermal, solar, wind, and tide and wave energy as well as that from combustible renewables and waste. Production includes the output of electricity plants designed to produce electricity only, as well as that of combined heat and power plants. • **Sources of electricity** refer to the inputs used to generate electricity: coal, gas, oil, hydropower, and nuclear power. • **Coal** refers to all coal and brown coal, both primary (including hard coal and lignite-brown coal) and derived fuels (including patent fuel, coke oven coke, gas coke, coke oven gas, and blast furnace gas). Peat is also included in this category. • **Gas** refers to natural gas but not to natural gas liquids. • **Oil** refers to crude oil and petroleum products. • **Hydropower** refers to electricity produced by hydroelectric power plants.• **Nuclear power** refers to electricity produced by nuclear power plants.

Data sources

Data on electricity production are from the IEA's electronic files and its annual publications *Energy Statistics and Balances of Non-OECD Countries, Energy Statistics of OECD Countries,* and *Energy Balances of OECD Countries.*

Urbanization

	Urban population					Population in urban agglomerations of more than 1 million		Population in largest city		Access to improved sanitation facilities			
	millions		% of total population		average annual % growth	% of total population		% of urban population		% of urban population		% of rural population	
	1990	**2005**	**1990**	**2005**	**1990–2005**	**1990**	**2005**	**1990**	**2005**	**1990**	**2004**	**1990**	**2004**
Afghanistan	..	..	..	..	..	..	..	..	..	..	..	..	..
Albania	1.2	1.4	36	45	1.0	..	..	..	..	99	99	..	84
Algeria	13.2	20.8	52	63	3.0	8	10	14	15	99	99	77	82
Angola	3.9	8.5	37	53	5.2	15	17	40	33	61	56	18	16
Argentina	28.3	34.9	87	90	1.4	39	39	37	36	86	92	45	83
Armenia	2.4	1.9	68	64	–1.4	33	37	49	57	96	96	..	61
Australia	14.6	17.9	85	88	1.4	60	61	25	24	100	100	100	100
Austria	5.1	5.4	66	66	0.4	27	27	41	42	100	100	100	100
Azerbaijan	3.8	4.3	54	52	0.7	24	22	45	43	..	73	..	36
Bangladesh	20.6	35.6	20	25	3.7	9	13	32	35	55	51	12	35
Belarus	6.8	7.1	66	72	0.3	16	18	24	25	..	93	..	61
Belgium	9.6	10.2	96	97	0.4	10	10	10	10	100	100	100	100
Benin	1.8	3.4	35	40	4.3	..	..	..	..	32	59	2	11
Bolivia	3.7	5.9	56	64	3.1	25	31	29	26	49	60	14	22
Bosnia and Herzegovina	1.7	1.8	39	46	1.0	..	..	..	..	99	99	..	92
Botswana	0.6	1.0	42	57	3.5	..	..	..	..	61	57	21	25
Brazil	111.7	157.0	75	84	2.3	34	37	13	12	82	83	37	37
Bulgaria	5.8	5.4	66	70	–0.5	14	14	21	20	100	100	96	96
Burkina Faso	1.2	2.4	14	18	4.9	..	..	50	38	32	42	3	6
Burundi	0.4	0.8	6	10	4.9	..	..	..	..	42	47	44	35
Cambodia	1.2	2.8	13	20	5.6	6	10	48	49	..	53	..	8
Cameroon	4.7	8.9	41	55	4.3	14	20	20	20	59	58	40	43
Canada	21.3	25.9	77	80	1.3	40	44	18	21	100	100	99	99
Central African Republic	1.1	1.5	37	38	2.2	..	..	..	..	34	47	17	12
Chad	1.3	2.5	21	25	4.6	..	..	38	36	28	24	2	4
Chile	11.0	14.3	83	88	1.8	35	35	42	40	91	95	52	62
China	311.0	527.0	27	40	3.6	13	18	3	3	64	69	7	28
Hong Kong, China	5.7	6.9	100	100	1.4	100	100	100	100	..	..	..	..
Colombia	24.0	33.2	69	73	2.1	30	36	20	23	95	96	52	54
Congo, Dem. Rep.	10.5	18.5	28	32	3.7	15	17	35	33	53	42	1	25
Congo, Rep.	1.3	2.4	54	60	4.0	28	29	52	49	..	28	..	25
Costa Rica	1.6	2.7	51	62	3.7	24	28	47	46	..	89	97	97
Côte d'Ivoire	5.0	8.2	40	45	3.3	17	20	42	44	37	46	10	29
Croatia	2.6	2.5	54	57	0.0	..	..	..	..	100	100	100	100
Cuba	7.7	8.5	73	76	0.7	20	19	27	26	99	99	95	95
Czech Republic	7.8	7.5	75	74	–0.3	12	11	16	16	99	99	97	97
Denmark	4.4	4.6	85	86	0.4	26	20	31	23	100	100	100	100
Dominican Republic	3.9	5.9	55	67	2.9	21	23	39	34	60	81	43	73
Ecuador	5.7	8.3	55	63	2.5	26	29	28	29	77	94	45	82
Egypt, Arab Rep.	24.2	31.7	44	43	1.8	22	20	37	35	70	86	42	58
El Salvador	2.5	4.1	49	60	3.4	19	22	39	37	70	77	33	39
Eritrea	0.5	0.9	16	19	4.0	..	..	..	..	44	32	0	3
Estonia	1.1	0.9	71	69	–1.2	..	..	..	..	97	97	96	96
Ethiopia	6.4	11.4	13	16	3.9	3	4	28	25	13	44	2	7
Finland	3.1	3.2	61	61	0.3	17	21	28	34	100	100	100	100
France	42.0	46.7	74	77	0.7	23	22	22	21	..	..	..	..
Gabon	0.7	1.2	69	84	3.8	..	..	..	..	..	37	..	30
Gambia, The	0.4	0.8	38	54	5.7	..	..	..	..	..	72	..	46
Georgia	3.0	2.3	55	52	–1.7	22	23	41	45	99	96	94	91
Germany	58.3	62.0	73	75	0.4	8	8	6	5	100	100	100	100
Ghana	5.6	10.6	37	48	4.2	12	16	21	19	23	27	10	11
Greece	6.0	6.6	59	59	0.6	30	29	51	49	..	..	..	..
Guatemala	3.7	5.9	41	47	3.3	..	..	22	17	73	90	47	82
Guinea	1.7	3.1	28	33	3.8	14	15	51	46	27	31	10	11
Guinea-Bissau	0.3	0.5	28	30	3.3	..	..	..	..	..	57	..	23
Haiti	2.0	3.3	30	39	3.3	17	25	56	64	25	57	23	14

	Urban population					Population in urban agglomerations of more than 1 million		Population in largest city		Access to improved sanitation facilities			
	millions		% of total population		average annual % growth	% of total population		% of urban population		% of urban population		% of rural population	
	1990	2005	1990	2005	1990–2005	1990	2005	1990	2005	1990	2004	1990	2004
Honduras	2.0	3.4	40	47	3.6	..	..	29	28	77	87	31	54
Hungary	6.8	6.7	66	66	–0.2	19	17	29	25	100	100	..	85
India	216.6	314.1	26	29	2.5	10	12	6	6	45	59	3	22
Indonesia	54.5	106.1	31	48	4.6	9	12	14	12	65	73	37	40
Iran, Islamic Rep.	30.6	45.7	56	67	2.7	23	23	21	16	86	..	78	..
Iraq	12.9	..	70	..	..	26	..	32	..	95	..	48	..
Ireland	2.0	2.5	57	61	1.5	26	25	46	41	..	..	..	..
Israel	4.2	6.3	90	92	2.6	43	44	48	47	100	100	..	..
Italy	37.8	39.6	67	68	0.2	19	17	9	8	..	..	..	..
Jamaica	1.2	1.4	49	53	1.2	..	..	..	..	86	91	64	69
Japan	78.0	84.1	63	66	0.5	46	48	42	42	100	100	100	100
Jordan	2.3	4.5	72	82	4.1	27	24	37	29	97	94	82	87
Kazakhstan	9.2	8.7	56	57	–0.7	7	8	12	13	87	87	52	52
Kenya	4.3	7.1	18	21	3.4	6	8	32	39	48	46	37	41
Korea, Dem. Rep.	11.5	13.9	58	62	1.3	16	20	22	24	..	58	..	60
Korea, Rep.	31.6	39.0	74	81	1.4	51	51	33	25	..	..	..	..
Kuwait	2.1	2.5	98	98	2.9	65	71	67	73	..	..	..	..
Kyrgyz Republic	1.7	1.8	38	36	0.6	..	..	38	43	75	75	51	51
Lao PDR	0.6	1.2	15	21	4.4	..	..	..	..	..	67	..	20
Latvia	1.9	1.6	69	68	–1.2	..	..	..	..	..	82	..	71
Lebanon	2.3	3.1	83	87	2.0	47	50	57	57	100	100	..	87
Lesotho	0.3	0.3	17	19	1.4	..	..	..	..	61	61	32	32
Liberia	1.0	1.9	45	58	5.7	..	..	55	49	59	49	24	7
Libya	3.4	5.0	79	85	2.5	49	55	44	42	97	97	96	96
Lithuania	2.5	2.3	68	67	–0.7	..	..	..	..	..	..	..	..
Macedonia, FYR	1.1	1.4	58	69	1.6	..	..	..	..	..	..	..	..
Madagascar	2.8	5.0	24	27	3.8	8	9	33	32	27	48	10	26
Malawi	1.1	2.2	12	17	4.8	..	..	..	..	64	62	45	61
Malaysia	8.9	17.1	50	67	4.5	6	6	13	8	95	95	..	93
Mali	2.1	4.1	23	31	4.7	8	10	36	33	50	59	32	39
Mauritania	0.8	1.2	40	40	2.9	..	..	..	..	42	49	22	8
Mauritius	0.5	0.5	44	42	0.9	..	..	..	..	95	95	..	94
Mexico	60.3	78.3	73	76	1.8	32	35	25	25	75	91	13	41
Moldova	2.0	2.0	47	47	–0.3	..	..	..	..	..	86	..	52
Mongolia	1.2	1.4	57	57	1.2	..	..	48	60	..	75	..	37
Morocco	11.6	17.7	48	59	2.7	16	16	23	18	87	88	27	52
Mozambique	2.8	6.8	21	35	6.0	6	7	27	19	49	53	12	19
Myanmar	10.1	15.5	25	31	2.9	7	8	29	27	48	88	16	72
Namibia	0.4	0.7	28	35	4.2	..	..	..	..	70	50	8	13
Nepal	1.7	4.3	9	16	6.4	..	..	23	19	48	62	7	30
Netherlands	10.3	13.1	69	80	1.6	14	14	10	9	100	100	100	100
New Zealand	2.9	3.5	85	86	1.2	25	28	30	33	..	..	88	..
Nicaragua	2.1	3.0	53	59	2.6	19	23	35	38	64	56	24	34
Niger	1.3	2.3	15	17	4.0	..	..	33	36	35	43	2	4
Nigeria	31.7	63.4	35	48	4.7	11	14	15	17	51	53	33	36
Norway	3.1	3.6	72	77	1.1	..	..	22	22	100	100	100	100
Oman	1.2	1.8	65	72	2.7	..	..	..	..	97	97	61	..
Pakistan	33.0	54.4	31	35	3.4	16	18	22	21	82	92	17	41
Panama	1.3	2.3	54	71	3.9	35	38	65	53	89	89	51	51
Papua New Guinea	0.5	0.8	13	13	2.6	..	..	..	..	67	67	41	41
Paraguay	2.1	3.5	49	59	3.5	22	31	45	54	72	94	45	61
Peru	15.0	20.3	69	73	2.0	27	26	39	35	69	74	15	32
Philippines	29.8	52.1	49	63	3.8	14	14	27	21	66	80	48	59
Poland	23.4	23.7	61	62	0.1	4	4	7	7	..	..	..	..
Portugal	4.7	6.1	48	58	1.7	37	39	54	45	..	..	..	..
Puerto Rico	2.6	3.8	72	98	2.6	44	67	60	68	..	..	..	..

3.10 Urbanization

	Urban population					Population in urban agglomerations of more than 1 million		Population in largest city		Access to improved sanitation facilities			
	millions		% of total population		average annual % growth	% of total population		% of urban population		% of urban population		% of rural population	
	1990	**2005**	**1990**	**2005**	**1990–2005**	**1990**	**2005**	**1990**	**2005**	**1990**	**2004**	**1990**	**2004**
Romania	12.6	11.6	54	54	–0.5	8	9	14	17	..	89	..	..
Russian Federation	108.8	104.5	73	73	–0.3	18	19	8	10	93	93	70	70
Rwanda	0.4	1.7	5	19	12.4	..	..	57	45	49	56	36	38
Saudi Arabia	12.5	18.7	77	81	2.7	30	36	19	22	100	100	..	..
Senegal	3.1	4.8	39	42	3.0	17	19	44	45	53	79	19	34
Serbia and Montenegro	5.4	4.2	51	52	–2.1	11	14	22	26	97	97	77	77
Sierra Leone	1.2	2.2	30	41	4.0	..	..	43	36	..	53	..	30
Singapore	3.0	4.3	100	100	2.4	99	100	99	100	100	100	..	..
Slovak Republic	3.0	3.0	57	56	0.1	..	..	..	..	100	100	98	98
Slovenia	1.0	1.0	50	51	0.1	..	..	..	..	..	..	..	..
Somalia	2.0	2.9	30	35	2.7	14	16	48	46	..	48	..	14
South Africa	18.3	27.8	52	59	2.9	25	30	10	12	85	79	53	46
Spain	29.3	33.3	75	77	0.8	22	24	15	17	100	100	100	100
Sri Lanka	2.9	3.0	17	15	0.0	..	..	..	..	89	98	64	89
Sudan	6.9	14.8	27	41	5.2	9	12	34	31	53	50	26	24
Swaziland	0.2	0.3	23	24	3.1	..	..	..	..	..	59	..	44
Sweden	7.1	7.6	83	84	0.4	17	19	21	22	100	100	100	100
Switzerland	4.6	5.6	68	75	1.2	14	15	20	20	100	100	100	100
Syrian Arab Republic	6.3	9.6	49	51	2.9	25	25	25	26	97	99	50	81
Tajikistan	1.7	1.6	32	25	–0.3	..	..	..	..	..	70	..	45
Tanzania	5.0	9.3	19	24	4.2	5	7	27	29	52	53	45	43
Thailand	16.1	20.7	29	32	1.7	11	10	37	32	95	98	74	99
Togo	1.2	2.5	30	40	5.1	16	22	52	54	71	71	24	15
Trinidad and Tobago	0.1	0.2	9	12	2.9	..	..	..	..	100	100	100	100
Tunisia	4.9	6.5	60	65	2.0	..	..	..	..	95	96	47	65
Turkey	33.2	48.5	59	67	2.6	22	26	20	20	96	96	70	72
Turkmenistan	1.7	2.2	45	46	1.9	..	..	..	..	..	77	..	50
Uganda	2.0	3.6	11	13	4.1	4	5	38	36	54	54	41	41
Ukraine	34.7	31.9	67	68	–0.7	12	13	7	8	98	98	92	93
United Arab Emirates	1.4	3.5	79	77	6.3	27	29	34	38	98	98	95	95
United Kingdom	51.1	54.0	89	90	0.4	26	26	15	16	..	..	..	..
United States	188.0	239.5	75	81	1.6	41	43	9	8	100	100	100	100
Uruguay	2.8	3.2	89	92	1.0	41	36	46	40	100	100	99	99
Uzbekistan	8.2	9.6	40	37	1.0	10	8	25	23	69	78	39	61
Venezuela, RB	16.6	24.8	84	93	2.7	34	37	17	12	..	71	..	48
Vietnam	13.4	21.9	20	26	3.3	13	13	30	23	58	92	30	50
West Bank and Gaza	1.3	2.6	68	72	4.6	..	..	..	..	..	78	..	61
Yemen, Rep.	2.5	5.7	21	27	5.4	5	9	26	31	82	86	19	28
Zambia	3.3	4.1	39	35	1.3	9	11	23	31	63	59	31	52
Zimbabwe	3.1	4.7	29	36	2.8	10	12	34	32	69	63	42	47
World	**2,253.0 s**	**3,128.3 s**	**43 w**	**49 w**	**2.2 w**	**18 w**	**20 w**	**17 w**	**16 w**	**77 w**	**80 w**	**23 w**	**38 w**
Low income	442.0	704.7	25	30	3.2	10	12	17	18	50	61	12	28
Middle income	1,160.1	1,657.4	44	54	2.4	17	20	15	14	79	81	25	42
Lower middle income	798.0	1,225.8	38	50	2.9	16	19	14	12	75	77	22	39
Upper middle income	362.0	431.6	68	72	1.2	..	..	18	19	89	91	58	66
Low & middle income	1,602.1	2,362.1	37	44	2.6	14	17	16	15	71	75	19	35
East Asia & Pacific	459.7	781.5	29	41	3.6	..	..	9	8	65	72	15	36
Europe & Central Asia	294.0	300.5	63	64	0.1	15	16	13	15	94	93	72	71
Latin America & Carib.	310.1	425.4	71	77	2.1	32	34	24	22	81	86	36	49
Middle East & N. Africa	117.1	174.7	52	57	2.7	20	20	27	25	87	92	52	58
South Asia	277.7	418.4	25	28	2.8	10	12	10	11	50	63	6	27
Sub-Saharan Africa	143.5	261.7	28	35	4.1	..	..	26	26	52	53	24	28
High income	650.9	766.2	74	78	1.1	..	..	20	19	100	100	100	100
Europe EMU	209.5	230.1	71	73	0.6	18	18	15	15	..	..	..	..

About the data

There is no consistent and universally accepted standard for making the distinction between urban and rural. The wide variety of situations across countries makes it difficult to adopt uniform criteria for distinguishing urban and rural areas. Most countries have adopted an urban classification related to the size or characteristics of settlements. Other countries have defined urban areas based on the presence of certain infrastructure and services. And some countries have designated urban areas based on administrative arrangements. The population of a city or metropolitan area depends on the boundaries chosen. For example, in 1990 Beijing, China, contained 2.3 million people in 87 square kilometers of "inner city" and 5.4 million in 158 square kilometers of "core city." The population of "inner city and inner suburban districts" was 6.3 million, and that of "inner city, inner and outer suburban districts, and inner and outer counties" was 10.8 million. (For most countries the last definition is used.) For further discussion of urban-rural issues see box 3.1a in *About the data* for table 3.1.

Estimates of the world's urban population would change significantly if China, India, and a few other populous nations were to change their definition of urban centers. According to China's State Statistical Bureau, by the end of 1996 urban residents accounted for about 43 percent of China's population, while in 1994 only 20 percent of the population was considered urban. In addition to the continuous migration of people from rural to urban areas, one of the main reasons for this shift was the rapid growth in the hundreds of towns reclassified as cities in recent years. Because the estimates in the table are based on national definitions of what constitutes a city or metropolitan area, cross-country comparisons should be made with caution. To estimate urban populations, UN ratios of urban to total population were applied to the World Bank's estimates of total population (see table 2.1).

The urban population with access to improved sanitation facilities is defined as people with access to at least adequate excreta disposal facilities that can effectively prevent human, animal, and insect contact with excreta. The rural population with access is included to allow comparison of rural and urban access. This definition and the definition of urban areas vary, however, so comparisons between countries can be misleading.

Population of the world's largest metropolitan areas in 1000, 1900, 2000, and 2015 (millions) — 3.10a

1000 City	Population	1900 City	Population
Cordova	0.45	London	6.5
Kaifeng	0.40	New York	4.2
Constantinopole	0.30	Paris	3.3
Angkor	0.20	Berlin	2.7
Kyoto	0.18	Chicago	1.7
Cairo	0.14	Vienna	1.7
Baghdad	0.13	Tokyo	1.5
Nishapur	0.13	St. Petersburg	1.4
Hasa	0.11	Manchester	1.4
Anhivada	0.10	Philadelphia	1.4

2000 City	Population	2015 City	Population
Tokyo	34.5	Tokyo	35.5
Mexico City	18.1	Mumbai	21.9
New York–Newark	17.9	Mexico City	21.6
São Paulo	17.1	São Paulo	20.5
Mumbai	16.1	New York–Newark	19.9
Shanghai	13.2	Delhi	18.6
Kolkata	13.1	Shanghai	17.2
Delhi	12.4	Kolkata	17.0
Buenos Aires	11.9	Dhaka	16.8
Los Angeles–Long Beach–Santa Ana	11.8	Jakarta	16.8

Source: O'Meara 1999; United Nations Population Division, 2005, *World Urbanization Prospects: The 2005 Revision.*

Definitions

• **Urban population** is the midyear population of areas defined as urban in each country and reported to the United Nations (see *About the data*). • **Population in urban agglomerations of more than 1 million** is the percentage of a country's population living in metropolitan areas that in 2005 had a population of more than 1 million. • **Population in largest city** is the percentage of a country's urban population living in that country's largest metropolitan area. • **Access to improved sanitation facilities** refers to the percentage of the urban or rural population with access to at least adequate excreta disposal facilities (private or shared but not public) that can effectively prevent human, animal, and insect contact with excreta. Improved facilities range from simple but protected pit latrines to flush toilets with a sewerage connection. To be effective, facilities must be correctly constructed and properly maintained.

Data sources

Data on urban population and the population in urban agglomerations and in the largest city are from the United Nations Population Division's *World Urbanization Prospects: The 2005 Revision.* The total population figures are World Bank estimates. Data on access to sanitation in urban and rural areas are from the World Health Organization.

3.11 Urban housing conditions

	Census year	Household size		Overcrowding		Durable dwelling units		Home ownership		Multiunit dwellings		Vacancy rate	
		number of people		People living in overcrowded dwellings[a] % of total		Buildings with durable structure % of total		Privately owned dwellings % of total		% of total		Unoccupied dwellings % of total	
		National	Urban	National	Urban	National	Urban	National	Urban	National	Urban	National	Urban
Afghanistan		..	..	..	..	..	..	..	..	..	..	..	..
Albania	2001	4.2	3.9	..	..	..	..	65[b]	30[b]	..	..	12	13
Algeria	1998	4.9	..	..	..	..	..	67	..	..	..	19	..
Angola		..	..	..	..	..	..	..	..	..	..	..	..
Argentina	2001	3.6	..	19	..	97	..	..	..	4	..	16[b]	..
Armenia	2001	4.1	4.0	4	6	93	93	95	90	1	1	..	..
Australia	2001	3.8	..	1	..	..	..	..	..	..	..	..	..
Austria	1991	2.6	..	2	..	..	..	..	..	50	..	13	..
Azerbaijan	1999	4.7	4.4	..	..	..	..	74	62	4	5	..	..
Bangladesh	2001	4.8	4.8	..	..	21[b]	42[b]	88[b]	61[b]	..	..	..	..
Belarus	1999	..	..	..	..	..	..	..	..	..	..	..	..
Belgium	2001	2.6	..	0[b]	..	..	..	67	..	32[b]	..	..	..
Benin	1992	5.9	..	..	..	26	..	59	..	..	..	..	..
Bolivia	2001	4.2	4.3	40	..	43	58	70	59	3[b]	5[b]	6	4
Bosnia and Herzegovina		..	..	..	..	..	..	..	..	..	..	..	..
Botswana	2001	4.2	3.9	27	47	88	90[b]	61	47	1	..	..	..
Brazil	2000	3.8	3.7	..	..	..	..	74	75	..	..	..	..
Bulgaria	2001	2.7	2.7	..	..	79	89	98	98	..	..	23	17
Burkina Faso	1996	6.2	5.8	30	53	..	..	..	..	..	..	..	..
Burundi	1990	4.7	..	..	..	..	..	..	..	..	..	..	..
Cambodia	1998	5.2	..	..	..	..	..	..	..	..	..	..	..
Cameroon	1987	5.2	5.1	67	77	77	..	73	48	27	42	..	..
Canada	2001	2.6	..	..	..	..	..	64	..	32	..	8	..
Central African Republic	2003	5.2	5.8	32	36[b]	78	92	85	74	..	..	..	..
Chad	1993	5.1	5.1	..	..	..	..	..	..	..	..	..	..
Chile	2002	3.4	3.5	..	..	91	92	66	65	13	15	11	10
China	2000	3.4	3.2	..	..	82	..	88	74	..	..	1	..
Hong Kong, China		..	..	..	..	..	..	..	..	..	..	..	..
Colombia	1993	4.8	..	27[b]	..	83[b]	..	68[b]	..	13	..	10[b]	..
Congo Dem Rep	1984	5.4	..	55	..	..	..	..	..	..	..	..	..
Congo Rep	1984	10.5	..	..	..	..	..	76	..	..	..	..	..
Costa Rica	2000	4.0	..	22	..	88	..	72	..	2	3	9	6
Côte d'Ivoire	1998	5.4	..	..	..	..	..	..	..	..	..	..	..
Croatia	2001	3.0	..	..	..	..	..	..	..	..	..	12	..
Cuba	1981	4.2	4.2	..	..	..	..	..	..	15	21	0	0
Czech Republic	2001	2.4	..	..	..	..	..	52	..	49	..	12	..
Denmark	2001	2.2	..	..	..	..	..	..	..	..	..	..	..
Dominican Republic	2002	3.9	..	..	..	97	..	..	..	8	..	11	..
Ecuador	2001	3.5	3.7	30	..	81	88	68[b]	58[b]	9	14	12	7
Egypt	1996	4.7	..	..	..	..	..	..	..	75	..	..	..
El Salvador	1992	..	..	63	..	67	83	70	68	3	6	11	11
Eritrea		..	..	..	..	..	..	..	..	..	..	..	..
Estonia	2000	2.4	2.3	3	..	..	..	..	..	72	..	13	..
Ethiopia	1994	4.8	4.7	..	..	..	23	..	54	..	..	..	..
Finland	2000	2.2	..	..	..	..	..	64	..	44	..	..	..
France	1999	2.5	..	..	..	..	..	55	..	..	..	7	..
Gabon	2003	5.2	..	..	..	..	..	..	..	..	..	..	..
Gambia	1993	8.9	..	..	..	18	..	68	..	..	..	..	..
Georgia	2002	3.5	3.5	..	..	..	..	..	..	..	..	..	..
Germany	2001	2.3	..	..	..	..	..	43	..	..	..	7	..
Ghana	2000	5.1	5.1	..	..	45	..	57	..	53	..	5	..
Greece	2001	3.0	..	1	..	..	..	..	..	..	..	..	..
Guatemala	2002	4.4	4.7	..	..	67	80	81	74	2	4	13	11
Guinea		..	..	..	..	..	..	..	..	..	..	..	..
Guinea-Bissau		..	..	..	..	..	..	..	..	..	..	..	..
Haiti	1982	4.2	..	26	..	..	..	92	68	..	..	9	19

Urban housing conditions

	Census year	Household size		Overcrowding		Durable dwelling units		Home ownership		Multiunit dwellings		Vacancy rate	
		number of people		People living in overcrowded dwellings[a] % of total		Buildings with durable structure % of total		Privately owned dwellings % of total		% of total		Unoccupied dwellings % of total	
		National	Urban	National	Urban	National	Urban	National	Urban	National	Urban	National	Urban
Honduras	2001	4.4	..	..	..	69	85	..	..	..	..	14	..
Hungary	1990	2.7	..	..	..	..	..	..	..	..	..	4	..
India	2001	5.3	5.3	77	71	83	81	87	67	..	..	6	9
Indonesia	2000	4.0	..	..	..	..	..	..	..	..	..	..	..
Iran, Islamic Rep.	1996	4.8	4.6	33[b]	26[b]	72	76	73	67	..	..	..	..
Iraq	1997	7.7	7.2	..	..	88	96	70	66	4	5	13	15
Ireland	2002	3.0	..	..	..	..	..	..	..	8[b]	..	..	..
Israel	1995	3.5	..	..	..	..	..	..	..	..	..	..	..
Italy	2001	2.8	..	..	..	..	..	..	..	..	..	21	..
Jamaica	2001	3.5	..	..	..	98[b]	..	58[b]	..	2[b]	..	..	..
Japan	2000	2.7	..	..	..	..	..	61	..	37	..	..	..
Jordan	1994	6.2	6.0	1	..	97	97	69	64	57	67	..	..
Kazakhstan		..	..	..	..	..	..	..	..	..	..	..	..
Kenya	1999	4.6	3.4	..	..	35	72	72	25	..	..	39	17
Korea, Dem Rep	2000	3.8	..	23	..	..	..	50	..	15	..	..	..
Korea, Rep.	1993	4.4	..	..	..	..	..	..	..	..	..	..	..
Kuwait	1995	6.4	..	..	..	..	..	..	..	9[b]	..	11	..
Kyrgyz Republic	1999	4.4	3.6	..	..	..	..	..	..	..	..	..	..
Laos	1995	6.1	6.1	..	..	49	77	96	86	..	..	..	..
Latvia	2000	3.0	2.6	4	..	88	..	58	..	74	..	0	..
Lebanon		..	..	..	..	..	..	..	..	..	..	..	..
Lesotho	2001	5.0	..	10[b]	..	..	..	84	..	0	..	..	..
Liberia	1974	4.8	..	31	..	20	..	1	..	..	..	..	..
Libya		6.4	..	..	..	..	..	..	..	..	..	7	..
Lithuania	2001	2.6	..	7	..	..	..	..	..	..	..	..	..
Macedonia, FYR	2002	3.6	3.6[b]	8[b]	..	95[b]	95[b]	48[b]	..	..	..	7[b]	3[b]
Madagascar	1993	4.9	4.8	64	57	..	..	81	59	..	..	..	..
Malawi	1998	4.4	4.4	30	..	48	84	86	47	..	..	..	..
Malaysia	2000	4.5	4.4	..	..	..	..	..	..	10[b]	16[b]	..	..
Mali	1998	5.6	..	..	..	..	..	..	..	..	..	..	..
Mauritania	1988	..	..	..	..	..	..	..	..	..	..	..	..
Mauritius	2000	3.9	3.8	6	7	91	94	87	81	..	..	7	6
Mexico	2000	4.4	..	27[b]	..	87	..	78	..	6	..	..	..
Moldova	2003	..	..	..	..	..	..	..	..	..	..	..	..
Mongolia	2000	4.4	4.5	..	..	..	..	..	..	48	56	..	..
Morocco	1982	5.9	5.3	..	..	..	..	..	..	..	..	..	..
Mozambique	1997	4.4	4.9	37	28	7	20	92	83	1	1	0	..
Myanmar		..	..	..	..	..	..	..	..	..	..	..	..
Namibia	2001	5.3	..	..	..	..	..	..	..	..	..	..	..
Nepal	2001	5.4	4.9	..	..	..	..	88	..	..	..	0	..
Netherlands		..	..	..	..	..	..	..	..	..	..	..	..
New Zealand	2001	2.8	..	1[b]	..	..	..	65	..	17	..	10	..
Nicaragua	1995	5.3	..	..	..	79	87	84	86	0	0	8	..
Niger	2001	6.4	6.0	..	..	..	..	77	40	..	..	..	..
Nigeria	1991	5.0	4.7	..	..	..	..	..	..	..	..	..	..
Norway	1980	2.7	..	1	..	..	..	67	..	38	..	..	..
Oman	2003	7.1	..	..	..	..	..	..	..	..	..	..	..
Pakistan	1998	6.8	6.8	..	..	58	86	81	..	..	..	..	..
Panama	2000	4.1	..	28[b]	..	88	98[b]	80	66[b]	10[b]	10[b]	14	..
Papua New Guinea	1990	4.5[b]	6.5	..	..	..	..	..	44	..	8	..	..
Paraguay	2002	4.6	4.5	38[b]	..	95[b]	98[b]	79	75	1[b]	2[b]	6[b]	6[b]
Peru	1993	..	..	..	..	49	64	..	..	..	..	7	3
Philippines	1990	5.3	5.3	..	..	62	..	83	76	6	11	4	4
Poland	1988	3.2	..	..	..	..	..	..	..	..	..	1	..
Portugal	2001	2.8	..	..	..	..	..	76	..	86	..	..	..
Puerto Rico	1990	3.3	..	..	..	..	..	72	..	..	..	11	..

3.11 Urban housing conditions

	Census year	Household size		Overcrowding		Durable dwelling units		Home ownership		Multiunit dwellings		Vacancy rate	
		number of people		People living in overcrowded dwellings[a] % of total		Buildings with durable structure % of total		Privately owned dwellings % of total		% of total		Unoccupied dwellings % of total	
		National	Urban	National	Urban	National	Urban	National	Urban	National	Urban	National	Urban
Romania	1992	3.1	3.1	..	..	58	..	87	77	39	71	6	4
Russia	2002	2.8	2.7	7	5	..	..	..	..	73	86	..	..
Rwanda	1991	4.7	..	..	..	79	78	92	73	19	25	..	..
Saudi Arabia	1992	6.1	..	..	..	92	..	42	..	..	..	..	..
Senegal		..	..	..	..	..	..	..	..	..	..	..	..
Serbia	2001	2.9	2.2	..	..	..	..	..	..	..	..	..	..
Sierra Leone	1985	6.8	..	..	..	34	..	68	..	..	..	..	..
Singapore	2000	4.4	..	..	..	..	..	..	..	..	..	..	..
Slovak Republic		..	..	..	..	..	..	..	..	..	..	..	..
Slovenia	1991	3.1	..	..	..	..	..	69	..	37	..	9	..
Somalia	1975	..	..	..	..	..	..	..	..	..	..	..	..
South Africa	2001	4.0	..	..	..	..	..	..	..	7	..	..	..
Spain	1991	3.3	..	0	..	..	..	78	..	..	..	..	..
Sri Lanka	2001	3.8	..	..	..	93[b]	92[b]	70[b]	58[b]	1	14[b]	13	1[b]
Sudan	1993	5.8	6.0	..	..	..	..	86[b]	58[b]	0[b]	1[b]	..	..
Swaziland	1997	5.4	3.7	..	..	..	..	..	..	..	..	..	..
Sweden	1990	2.0	..	..	..	..	..	..	..	54	..	1	..
Switzerland	1990	2.4	2.1	..	..	..	..	31	24	28	32	11	7
Syrian Arab Republic	1981	6.3	6.0	..	..	..	..	..	..	..	..	..	..
Tajikistan	2000	..	..	..	..	..	..	..	..	..	..	..	..
Tanzania	2002	4.9	4.5[b]	33[b]	7[b]	..	..	82[b]	43[b]	..	..	..	..
Thailand	2000	3.8	..	..	..	93	93	81	62	3	..	3	..
Togo		..	..	..	..	..	..	..	..	..	..	..	..
Trinidad and Tobago	2000	3.7	..	9[b]	..	98[b]	..	74[b]	..	17[b]	..	..	..
Tunisia	1994	8.0	..	..	..	99	..	71	89[b]	6	10[b]	15	12[b]
Turkey	1990	5.0	..	..	..	..	..	70	..	..	..	..	..
Turkmenistan		..	..	..	..	..	..	..	..	..	..	..	..
Uganda	1991	4.9	4.0[b]	..	..	21[b]	..	80[b]	24[b]	0[b]	2[b]	..	..
Ukraine	2003	..	..	..	..	..	..	..	..	..	..	..	..
United Arab Emirates		..	..	..	..	..	..	..	..	..	..	..	..
United Kingdom	2001	..	2.4	..	..	..	..	..	69	..	19	..	..
United States	2000	2.7	..	..	..	..	..	66	..	..	..	9	7
Uruguay	1996	3.3	3.4[b]	22[b]	..	..	..	57[b]	57[b]	..	..	13[b]	13[b]
Uzbekistan		..	..	..	..	..	..	..	..	..	..	..	..
Venezuela. RB	2001	4.4	..	..	..	..	..	78	..	14	..	16	..
Vietnam	1999	4.6	4.5	..	..	77	89	95	86	..	..	..	..
West Bank and Gaza	1997	7.1	..	..	..	..	..	78	..	45	..	..	..
Yemen	1994	6.7	6.8	54[b]	6[b]	..	..	88[b]	68[b]	3[b]	11[b]	..	..
Zambia	2000	5.3	5.9	..	..	..	..	94	30	..	..	..	..
Zimbabwe	1992	4.8	4.2	..	..	..	..	94	30	6	..	..	..

a. More than two people per room. b. Data are from a previous census.

About the data

Urbanization can yield important social benefits, improving access to public services and the job market. At the same time it also leads to significant demands for services. Inadequate living quarters and demand for housing and shelter are major concerns for policymakers. The unmet demand for affordable housing, along with urban poverty, has led to the emergence of slums in many poor countries. Improving the shelter situation requires a better understanding of the mechanisms governing housing markets and the processes governing housing availability. That requires good data and adequate policy-oriented analysis so that housing policy can be formulated in a global comparative perspective and drawn from the lessons learned in other countries. Housing policies and outcomes affect such broad socioeconomic conditions as the infant mortality rate, performance in school, household saving, productivity levels, capital formation, and government budget deficits. A good understanding of housing conditions thus requires an extensive set of indicators within a reasonable framework.

There is a strong demand for quantitative indicators that can measure housing conditions on a regular basis to monitor progress. However, data deficiencies and lack of rigorous quantitative analysis hamper informed decision-making on desirable policies to improve housing conditions. The data in the table are from housing and population censuses, collected using similar definitions. The table will incorporate household survey data in future editions. The table focuses attention on urban areas, where housing conditions are typically most severe. Not all the compiled indicators are presented in the table because of space limitations. Additional indicators for more countries will be available in the World Bank's central database.

Selected housing indicators for smaller economies — 3.11a

	Census year	Household size	Overcrowding	Durable dwelling units	Home ownership	Multiunit dwellings	Vacancy rate
		number of people	People living in overcrowded dwellings[a] % of total	Buildings with durable structure % of total	Privately owned dwellings % of total	% of total	Unoccupied dwellings % of total
Antigua and Barbuda	2001	3.0	..	99[b]	65[b]	3[b]	22
Bahamas	1990	3.8	12	99	55	13	14
Bahrain	2001	5.9	..	94[b]	51	28	6
Barbados	1990	3.5	3	100	76	9	9
Belize	2000	4.6	..	93	63	4	..
Cape Verde	1990	5.1	28	78	72	2	..
Cayman Islands	1999	3.1	..	100	53	38	19
Equatorial Guinea	1993	7.5	14	56[b]	75	14	..
Fiji	1996	5.4	..	60	65	7	..
Guam	2000	4.0	2[b]	93	48	29	19
Isle of Man	2001	2.4	0	..	68	16	..
Maldives	2000	6.6	..	93	..	1	15
Marshall Islands	1999	7.8	..	95	72	12	8
Netherlands Antilles	2001	2.9	24[b]	99	60	16	12
New Caledonia	1989	4.1	..	77	53	9	13
Northern Mariana Islands	1995	4.9	9[b]	99	33	27	17
Palau	2000	5.7	8	76	79	11	3
Seychelles	1997	4.2	15[b]	97	78	..	0
Solomon Islands	1999	6.3	51	23	85	1	..
St. Vincent & Grenadines	1991	3.9	..	98	71	7	..
Turks and Caicos	1990	3.3	4	96	66	11	..
Virgin Islands (UK)	1991	3.0	2	99	40	46	..
Western Samoa	1991	7.3	..	42	90	47	30

a. More than two people per room. b. Data are from a previous census.
Source: National population and housing censuses.

Definitions

• **Census year** is the year in which the underlying data were collected. • **Household size** refers to the average number of people within a household. It is calculated by dividing total population by the number of households in the country and in urban areas. • **Overcrowding** refers to the number of households living in dwellings with two or more people per room as a percentage of the total number of households in the country and in urban areas. • **Durable dwelling units** refer to the number of housing units in structures made of durable building materials (concrete, stone, cement, brick, asbestos, zinc, and stucco) expected to maintain their stability for 20 years or longer under local conditions with normal maintenance and repair, taking into account location and environmental hazards such as floods, mudslides, and earthquakes as a percentage of total dwellings. • **Home ownership** refers to the number of privately owned dwellings as a percentage of total dwellings or the number of households that own housing units as a percentage of total households. This category includes privately owned and owner-occupied units, depending on the definition used in the census data. State- and community-owned units, rented, squatted, and rent-free units are not included. • **Multiunit dwellings** refer to the number of multiunit dwellings, such as apartments, flats, condominiums, barracks, boarding houses, orphanages, retirement houses, hostels, hotels, and collective dwellings, as a percentage of total occupied dwellings. • **Vacancy rate** refers to the percentage of completed dwelling units that are currently unoccupied. It includes all vacant units, whether on the market or not (such as second homes).

Data sources

Data on urban housing conditions are from national population and housing censuses.

3.12 Traffic and congestion

	Motor vehicles				Passenger cars		Road density	Fuel prices		Particulate matter concentrations	
	per 1,000 people		per kilometer of road		per 1,000 people		km. of road per 100 sq. km. of land	$ per liter		Urban-population-weighted PM10 micrograms per cubic meter	
								Super gasoline	Diesel fuel		
	1990	2004[a]	1990	2004[a]	1990	2004[a]	2004[a]	2006	2006	1990	2004
Afghanistan	3	..	3	..	2	9	5	0.68	0.65	75	46
Albania	11	70	3	12	2	47	66	1.44	1.29	92	56
Algeria	55	..	15	..	26	..	5	0.32	0.19	115	88
Angola	19	..	3	..	14	..	4	0.50	0.36	142	91
Argentina	181	181	27	37	134	140	15	0.62	0.48	105	78
Armenia	5	..	2	..	1	..	27	0.96	0.77	..	69
Australia	530	..	11	..	450	..	11	0.93	0.94	22	16
Austria	421	599	30	33	387	503	162	1.32	1.26	38	35
Azerbaijan	52	66	7	9	36	53	72	0.46	0.41	105	59
Bangladesh	1	1	0	1	0	0	184	0.79	0.45	223	140
Belarus	61	168	13	18	59	174	45	0.79	0.55	7	7
Belgium	423	529	30	37	385	468	498	1.63	1.34	32	25
Benin	3	..	2	..	2	..	17	0.81	0.81	75	43
Bolivia	41	49	6	7	25	15	6	0.54	0.47	120	86
Bosnia and Herzegovina	114	..	24	..	101	..	43	1.34	1.24	42	19
Botswana	18	105	3	8	10	42	4	0.78	0.74	119	69
Brazil	88	170	8	18	84	136	21	1.26	0.84	40	28
Bulgaria	163	360	39	63	146	314	40	1.05	1.08	111	55
Burkina Faso	4	..	3	..	2	..	6	1.15	1.12	149	94
Burundi	..	..	3	..	3	..	48	1.20	1.22	56	39
Cambodia	..	30	0	31	..	25	22	1.01	0.78	116	64
Cameroon	10	..	3	..	6	..	11	1.14	1.07	119	64
Canada	605	577	20	34	468	561	15	0.84	0.78	25	19
Central African Republic	1	..	0	..	1	..	4	1.37	1.27	61	48
Chad	2	..	0	..	1	..	3	1.31	1.20	214	127
Chile	81	136	13	26	52	89	11	1.09	0.86	88	54
China	5	15	4	11	1	10	20	0.69	0.61	113[b]	72[b]
Hong Kong, China	66	72	253	254	42	53	186	1.69	1.06	..	..
Colombia	39	51	13	19	21	43	10	0.98	0.57	38	23
Congo, Dem. Rep.	..	..	9	..	17	..	7	0.94	1.00	73	52
Congo, Rep.	18	..	3	..	12	..	5	0.96	0.67	130	85
Costa Rica	87	198	7	24	55	146	69	0.98	0.67	45	39
Côte d'Ivoire	24	..	6	..	15	..	25	1.20	1.06	94	38
Croatia	..	370	34	58	185	302	51	1.34	1.22	60	31
Cuba	37	..	16	..	18	..	55	1.10	0.91	44	19
Czech Republic	246	391	46	31	228	358	165	1.30	1.29	73	23
Denmark	368	424	27	32	320	360	169	1.58	1.45	30	20
Dominican Republic	75	..	48	..	21	..	26	1.03	0.75	44	30
Ecuador	35	55	8	17	31	32	16	0.47	0.39	38	25
Egypt, Arab Rep.	29	..	33	..	21	..	9	0.30	0.12	221	135
El Salvador	33	..	14	..	17	..	48	0.82	0.80	46	35
Eritrea	1	..	1	..	1	..	4	1.90	0.81	122	85
Estonia	211	459	22	11	154	349	134	1.23	1.22	19	16
Ethiopia	1	2	2	4	1	1	4	0.93	0.62	134	76
Finland	441	515	29	34	386	446	26	1.55	1.26	24	19
France	494	597	32	38	405	495	173	1.48	1.33	18	14
Gabon	32	..	4	..	19	..	4	0.64	0.39	9	6
Gambia, The	13	7	5	3	6	5	37	1.08	1.01	141	95
Georgia	107	63	27	16	89	50	29	0.86	0.89	..	45
Germany	405	580	53	207	386	546	..	1.55	1.38	27	19
Ghana	8	..	4	..	5	..	21	0.86	0.84	39	35
Greece	248	476	22	46	171	368	89	1.16	1.19	69	41
Guatemala	21	57	16	45	11	52	13	0.78	0.64	63	67
Guinea	4	..	1	..	2	..	18	0.79	0.82	105	71
Guinea-Bissau	7	..	2	..	4	..	12	..	..	117	78
Haiti	8	..	14	..	5	..	15	0.88	0.60	70	42

Traffic and congestion

	Motor vehicles				Passenger cars		Road density	Fuel prices		Particulate matter concentrations	
	per 1,000 people		per kilometer of road		per 1,000 people		km. of road per 100 sq. km. of land	$ per liter		Urban-population-weighted PM10 micrograms per cubic meter	
								Super gasoline	Diesel fuel		
	1990	2004[a]	1990	2004[a]	1990	2004[a]	2004[a]	2006	2006	1990	2004
Honduras	22	61	10	28	5	52	12	0.89	0.73	45	47
Hungary	212	313	21	19	188	274	178	1.30	1.31	36	18
India	4	9	2	3	2	6	114	1.01	0.75	110	72
Indonesia	16	..	10	..	7	..	20	0.57	0.44	139	102
Iran, Islamic Rep.	34	..	14	..	25	..	11	0.09	0.03	86	58
Iraq	14	..	6	..	1	..	10	..	..	146	138
Ireland	270	447	10	11	227	382	140	1.34	1.35	26	19
Israel	210	288	74	112	174	234	81	1.47	1.27	71	38
Italy	529	610	99	73	476	590	165	1.56	1.49	42	27
Jamaica	52	..	7	..	43	135	194	0.82	0.75	58	42
Japan	469	586	52	63	283	441	323	1.09	0.90	43	31
Jordan	60	106	26	77	44	71	8	0.86	0.45	110	50
Kazakhstan	76	100	8	17	50	80	3	0.70	0.45	12	19
Kenya	12	18	5	10	10	9	11	1.12	0.98	66	39
Korea, Dem. Rep.	..	..	..	..	..	..	26	0.71	0.79	184	79
Korea, Rep.	79	302	60	145	48	218	102	1.65	1.33	82	38
Kuwait	474	422	165	181	368	349	32	0.22	0.21	82	108
Kyrgyz Republic	44	38	10	10	44	39	10	0.64	0.54	65	24
Lao PDR	9	..	3	..	6	..	14	0.86	0.73	73	47
Latvia	135	348	6	12	106	297	112	1.20	1.15	40	16
Lebanon	321	..	183	..	300	..	71	0.74	0.62	45	42
Lesotho	11	..	4	..	3	..	20	0.89	0.88	85	54
Liberia	14	..	4	..	7	..	11	0.79	0.85	59	44
Libya	165	..	10	..	96	..	5	0.13	0.13	107	98
Lithuania	160	421	12	18	133	383	127	1.08	1.09	30	10
Macedonia, FYR	132	..	30	..	121	..	34	1.23	1.09	38	20
Madagascar	6	..	2	..	4	..	9	1.15	1.00	77	45
Malawi	4	..	4	..	2	..	16	1.17	1.12	74	46
Malaysia	124	254	26	75	101	222	30	0.53	0.40	37	29
Mali	3	..	2	..	2	..	2	1.22	1.04	264	165
Mauritania	10	..	3	..	7	..	1	0.97	0.84	146	103
Mauritius	59	130	35	79	44	96	99	0.74	0.56	26	16
Mexico	119	211	41	93	82	142	18	0.74	0.52	69	39
Moldova	53	87	17	29	48	65	39	0.45	0.31	110	39
Mongolia	21	41	1	2	6	26	3	0.88	0.87	65	68
Morocco	37	45	15	23	28	45	13	1.22	0.87	32	20
Mozambique	4	..	2	..	3	..	4	1.15	1.06	110	39
Myanmar	2	..	3	..	1	..	4	0.66	0.75	116	69
Namibia	71	82	1	4	39	42	5	0.87	0.87	74	43
Nepal	..	..	..	..	..	..	12	0.94	0.73	67	39
Netherlands	405	427	58	58	368	429	372	1.70	1.32	45	34
New Zealand	524	701	19	31	436	592	35	0.98	0.70	16	15
Nicaragua	19	46	5	13	10	18	15	0.67	0.58	49	31
Niger	6	..	4	..	5	..	1	1.14	1.11	216	144
Nigeria	30	..	21	..	12	17	21	0.51	0.66	179	67
Norway	458	527	22	26	380	424	30	1.80	1.66	24	12
Oman	130	..	9	..	83	..	11	0.31	0.39	148	120
Pakistan	6	14	4	8	4	10	34	1.01	0.64	224	128
Panama	75	107	18	27	60	76	16	0.70	0.60	58	37
Papua New Guinea	27	..	6	..	7	..	4	0.94	0.64	34	19
Paraguay	27	88	4	15	16	52	7	0.97	0.77	105	101
Peru	128	47	43	16	62	30	6	1.22	0.86	98	65
Philippines	10	34	4	13	7	9	67	0.76	0.67	55	32
Poland	168	354	18	33	138	294	138	1.30	1.30	59	38
Portugal	222	463	34	278	162	429	86	1.56	1.10	52	26
Puerto Rico	295	..	79	..	242	..	289	0.65	0.78	27	20

3.12 Traffic and congestion

	Motor vehicles				Passenger cars		Road density	Fuel prices		Particulate matter concentrations	
	per 1,000 people		per kilometer of road		per 1,000 people		km. of road per 100 sq. km. of land	$ per liter Super gasoline	$ per liter Diesel fuel	Urban-population-weighted PM10 micrograms per cubic meter	
	1990	2004[a]	1990	2004[a]	1990	2004[a]	2004[a]	2006	2006	1990	2004
Romania	72	185	11	20	56	149	86	1.26	1.24	36	16
Russian Federation	*87*	*174*	*14*	*48*	*65*	*140*	*3*	0.77	0.66	13	20
Rwanda	2	..	1	..	1	..	57	1.11	1.08	49	37
Saudi Arabia	165	..	19	..	98	..	*8*	0.16	0.07	163	133
Senegal	11	*14*	6	*9*	8	*11*	*7*	1.31	1.09	95	76
Serbia and Montenegro	137	199	31	102	133	181	*44*	1.48	1.31	28	13
Sierra Leone	10	*4*	4	*2*	7	*2*	*16*	0.98	0.98	91	56
Singapore	130	134	142	179	89	99	463	0.92	0.63	106	44
Slovak Republic	194	256	57	32	163	222	89	1.35	1.43	40	16
Slovenia	306	505	42	26	289	456	191	1.23	1.21	*40*	30
Somalia	2	..	1	..	1	..	*4*	0.74	0.67	78	41
South Africa	139	*144*	26	*24*	97	*92*	*30*	0.85	0.84	34	26
Spain	360	*558*	43	*34*	309	*455*	*133*	1.15	1.10	41	33
Sri Lanka	21	*34*	4	..	7	*13*	*151*	0.88	0.55	95	104
Sudan	9	..	22	..	8	..	*1*	0.72	0.49	288	182
Swaziland	66	*83*	18	*24*	35	*40*	*21*	0.80	0.85	60	34
Sweden	464	*504*	29	*11*	426	457	104	1.46	1.44	15	12
Switzerland	491	559	46	58	449	516	178	1.27	1.36	37	24
Syrian Arab Republic	26	36	10	7	10	12	52	0.60	0.13	158	86
Tajikistan	3	..	1	..	0	..	*20*	0.80	0.74	*148*	55
Tanzania	5	..	2	..	1	..	*9*	1.04	0.99	57	28
Thailand	46	..	36	..	14	..	*11*	0.70	0.65	88	73
Togo	24	..	11	..	16	..	*14*	1.03	1.01	49	43
Trinidad and Tobago	*117*	..	*19*	..	*98*	..	*162*	0.43	0.24	142	114
Tunisia	48	95	19	49	23	83	12	0.83	0.57	71	33
Turkey	50	108	8	18	34	75	55	1.88	1.62	75	48
Turkmenistan	..	..	..	..	..	..	*5*	..	..	*185*	62
Uganda	2	*5*	..	*4*	1	*2*	*36*	1.17	1.01	27	17
Ukraine	63	138	20	39	63	115	29	0.81	0.87	47	27
United Arab Emirates	121	..	52	..	97	..	*1*	0.37	0.53	264	126
United Kingdom	400	510	64	79	341	451	160	1.63	1.73	25	15
United States	758	808	30	37	573	465	70	0.63	0.69	30	23
Uruguay	138	..	45	..	122	..	34	1.23	0.94	237	134
Uzbekistan	..	..	..	..	..	..	*19*	0.85	0.54	79	76
Venezuela, RB	*93*	..	*25*	..	*73*	..	*11*	0.03	0.02	22	7
Vietnam	..	..	..	..	..	..	72	0.67	0.53	124	65
West Bank and Gaza	..	35	..	24	..	27	83	1.29	0.98	..	..
Yemen, Rep.	34	..	8	..	14	..	*12*	0.30	0.28	*142*	91
Zambia	14	..	3	..	8	..	*12*	1.31	1.22	95	58
Zimbabwe	*32*	*50*	*4*	*7*	*29*	*44*	*25*	*0.61*	*0.65*	35	28
World	**118 w**	***141 w***	**..**	**..**	**91 w**	***100 w***	***22 w***	**0.97 m**	**0.84 m**	**77 w**	**54 w**
Low income	5	*8*	..	..	3	*5*	*19*	0.98	0.84	129	77
Middle income	37	*69*	..	..	24	*51*	*15*	0.86	0.74	79	56
Lower middle income	22	*38*	..	..	10	*27*	16	0.85	0.70	93	64
Upper middle income	*119*	*186*	..	..	*90*	*142*	*12*	0.92	0.79	50	36
Low & middle income	25	*47*	..	..	16	*35*	*15*	0.89	0.79	93	63
East Asia & Pacific	9	*20*	..	..	4	*14*	*18*	*0.53*	*0.40*	112	72
Europe & Central Asia	*97*	*170*	..	..	*79*	*142*	*12*	1.14	1.09	38	30
Latin America & Carib.	100	*153*	..	..	*72*	*108*	17	0.82	0.67	59	38
Middle East & N. Africa	36	..	..	..	24	..	*7*	0.46	0.34	124	84
South Asia	4	*10*	..	..	2	*6*	..	0.91	0.65	131	84
Sub-Saharan Africa	21	..	..	..	14	..	*6*	1.03	0.98	114	64
High income	499	636	..	..	390	457	*41*	1.33	1.24	38	28
Europe EMU	428	*569*	..	..	379	522	*139*	1.52	1.29	33	24

a. Data are for 2004 or most recent year available. b. Includes Taiwan, China; Macao, China; and Hong Kong, China.

Traffic and congestion

About the data

Traffic congestion in urban areas constrains economic productivity, damages people's health, and degrades the quality of their lives. The particulate air pollution emitted by motor vehicles—the dust and soot in exhaust—is proving to be far more damaging to human health than was once believed. (For information on particulate matter and other air pollutants, see table 3.13.)

In recent years ownership of passenger cars has increased, and the expansion of economic activity has led to the transport by road of more goods and services over greater distances (see table 5.9). These developments have increased demand for roads and vehicles, adding to urban congestion, air pollution, health hazards, and traffic accidents and injuries. Congestion, the most visible cost of expanding vehicle ownership, is reflected in the indicators in the table. Other relevant indicators—such as average vehicle speed in major cities or the cost of traffic congestion, which takes a heavy toll on economic productivity—are not included because data are incomplete or difficult to compare.

The data in the table—except those on fuel prices and particulate matter—are compiled by the International Road Federation (IRF) through questionnaires sent to national organizations. The IRF uses a hierarchy of sources to gather as much information as possible. The primary sources are national road associations. Where such an association lacks data or does not respond, other agencies are contacted, including road directorates, ministries of transport or public works, and central statistical offices. As a result, the compiled data are of uneven quality. The coverage of each indicator may differ across countries because of differences in definitions. Comparability also is limited when time series data are reported. The IRF recently took steps to improve the quality of the data published in its 2006 *World Road Statistics*. However, this effort covers data only for 1999–2004. Therefore, the data shown in this table for 1990 and 2004 may not be comparable. Moreover, the data do not capture the quality or age of vehicles. Road density is a very rough indicator of accessibility and does not capture the condition, type, or width of roads. Thus comparisons over time and between countries should be made with caution.

The data on fuel prices are compiled by the German Agency for Technical Cooperation (GTZ) from its global network of regional offices and representatives and other sources, including the Allgemeiner Deutscher Automobile Club (for Europe) and a project of the Latin American Energy Organization for Latin America. Local prices are converted to U.S. dollars using the exchange rate on the survey date listed in the international monetary table of the *Financial Times*. For countries with multiple exchange rates the market, parallel, or black market rate is used rather than the official exchange rate.

Significant uncertainties exist around estimates of particulate matter concentrations, and caution should be used in interpreting them. But they do allow for cross-country comparisons of the relative risk of particulate matter pollution that urban residents face. Major sources of urban outdoor particulate matter pollution are emissions from traffic and industrial sources, but nonanthropogenic sources such as dust storms may also be a significant contributor for some cities. Data on particulate matter for selected cities are in table 3.13. Estimates of economic damages from death and illness due to particulate matter pollution are shown in table 3.15.

The 15 economies with the most expensive gasoline—and the 15 with the cheapest, 2006 — **3.12a**

Economy	$ per liter	Economy	$ per liter
Eritrea	1.90	Venezuela, RB	0.03
Turkey	1.88	Iran, Islamic Rep.	0.09
Norway	1.80	Libya	0.13
Netherlands	1.70	Saudi Arabia	0.16
Hong Kong, China	1.69	Kuwait	0.22
Korea, Rep.	1.65	Egypt, Arab Rep.	0.30
Belgium	1.63	Yemen, Rep.	0.30
United Kingdom	1.63	Oman	0.31
Denmark	1.58	Algeria	0.32
Italy	1.56	United Arab Emirates	0.37
Portugal	1.56	Trinidad and Tobago	0.43
Finland	1.55	Azerbaijan	0.46
Germany	1.55	Ecuador	0.47
France	1.48	Angola	0.50
Serbia and Montenegro	1.48	Nigeria	0.51

Source: Table 3.12.

Definitions

• **Motor vehicles** include cars, buses, and freight vehicles but not two-wheelers. Population figures refer to the midyear population in the year for which data are available. Roads refer to motorways, highways, main or national roads, and secondary or regional roads. A motorway is a road specially designed and built for motor traffic that separates the traffic flowing in opposite directions. • **Passenger cars** refer to road motor vehicles, other than two-wheelers, intended for the carriage of passengers and designed to seat no more than nine people (including the driver). • **Road density** refers to the ratio of the length of the country's total road network to the country's land area. The road network includes all roads in the country—motorways, highways, main or national roads, secondary or regional roads, and other urban and rural roads. • **Fuel prices** refer to the pump prices of the most widely sold grade of gasoline and of diesel fuel. Prices are converted from the local currency to U.S. dollars (see *About the data*). • **Particulate matter concentrations** refer to fine suspended particulates less than 10 microns in diameter (PM10) that are capable of penetrating deep into the respiratory tract and causing significant health damage. Data for countries and aggregates for regions and income groups are urban-population-weighted PM10 levels in residential areas of cities with more than 100,000 residents. The estimates represent the average annual exposure level of the average urban resident to outdoor particulate matter. The state of a country's technology and pollution controls is an important determinant of particulate matter concentrations.

Data sources

Data on vehicles and traffic are from the IRF's electronic files and its annual *World Road Statistics*. The data on fuel prices are from the GTZ's electronic files. Data on particulate matter concentrations are from Kiran Dev Pandey, David Wheeler, Bart Ostro, Uwe Deichmann, Kirk Hamilton, and Katie Bolt's "Ambient Particulate Matter Concentrations in Residential and Pollution Hotspot Areas of World Cities: New Estimates Based on the Global Model of Ambient Particulates (GMAPS)" (2006).

3.13 Air pollution

	City	City population	Particulate matter	Sulfur dioxide	Nitrogen dioxide
		thousands	micrograms per cubic meter	micrograms per cubic meter	micrograms per cubic meter
		2005	2004	1995–2001[a]	1995–2001[a]
Argentina	Córdoba	1,423	58	..	97
	Melbourne	3,626	12	..	30
	Perth	1,474	12	5	19
	Sydney	4,331	20	28	81
Austria	Vienna	2,260	41	14	42
Belgium	Brussels	1,012	28	20	48
Brazil	Rio de Janeiro	11,469	35	129	..
	São Paulo	18,333	40	43	83
Bulgaria	Sofia	1,093	61	39	122
Canada	Montréal	3,640	19	10	42
	Toronto	5,312	22	17	43
	Vancouver	2,188	13	14	37
Chile	Santiago	5,683	61	29	81
China	Anshan	1,611	82	115	88
	Beijing	10,717	89	90	122
	Changchun	3,046	74	21	64
	Chengdu	4,065	86	77	74
	Chongqing	6,363	123	340	70
	Dalian	3,073	50	61	100
	Guangzhou	8,425	63	57	136
	Guiyang	3,447	70	424	53
	Harbin	3,695	77	23	30
	Jinan	2,743	94	132	45
	Kunming	2,837	70	19	33
	Lanzhou	2,411	91	102	104
	Liupanshui	1,149	59	102	..
	Nanchang	2,188	78	69	29
	Pingxiang	905	67	75	..
	Quingdao	2,817	68	190	64
	Shanghai	14,503	73	53	73
	Shenyang	4,720	101	99	73
	Taiyuan	2,794	88	211	55
	Tianjin	7,040	125	82	50
	Wulumqi	2,025	57	60	70
	Wuhan	7,093	79	40	43
	Zhengzhou	2,590	97	63	95
	Zibo	2,982	74	198	43
Colombia	Bogotá	7,747	31	..	..
Croatia	Zagreb	908[b]	33	31	..
Cuba	Havana	2,189	21	1	5
Czech Republic	Prague	1,171	23	14	33
Denmark	Copenhagen	1,088	21	7	54
Ecuador	Guayaquil	2,387	23	15	..
	Quito	1,514	30	22	..
Egypt, Arab Rep.	Cairo	11,128	169	69	..
Finland	Helsinki	1,091	21	4	35
France	Paris	9,820	11	14	57
Germany	Berlin	3,389	22	18	26
	Frankfurt	668[b]	19	11	45
	Munich	1,263	20	8	53
Ghana	Accra	1,981	33	..	..
Greece	Athens	3,230	43	34	64
Hungary	Budapest	1,693	19	39	51
Iceland	Reykjavik	164[b]	18	5	42
India	Ahmadabad	5,120	83	30	21
	Bangalore	6,462	45	..	..

About the data

Indoor and outdoor air pollution place a major burden on world health. More than half of the world's population rely on dung, wood, crop waste, or coal to meet their basic energy needs. Cooking and heating with such solid fuels on open fires or stoves without chimneys leads to indoor air pollution. Every year indoor air pollution is responsible for the deaths of 1.6 million people—one death every 20 seconds. In many urban areas exposure to air pollution is the main environmental threat to human health. Long-term exposure to high levels of soot and small particles in the air contributes to a wide range of health effects, including respiratory diseases, lung cancer, and heart disease. Particulate pollution, on its own or in combination with sulfur dioxide, leads to an enormous burden of ill health.

Emissions of sulfur dioxide and nitrogen oxides lead to the deposition of acid rain and other acidic compounds over long distances. Acid deposition changes the chemical balance of soils and can lead to the leaching of trace minerals and nutrients critical to trees and plants.

Where coal is the primary fuel for power plants, steel mills, industrial boilers, and domestic heating, the result is usually high levels of urban air pollution—especially particulates and sometimes sulfur dioxide—and, if the sulfur content of the coal is high, widespread acid deposition. Where coal is not an important primary fuel or is used in plants with effective dust control, the worst emissions of air pollutants stem from the combustion of petroleum products.

The data on sulfur dioxide and nitrogen dioxide concentrations are based on reports from urban monitoring sites. Annual means (measured in micrograms per cubic meter) are average concentrations observed at these sites. Coverage is not comprehensive because not all cities have monitoring systems.

The data on concentrations of particulate matter are estimates, for selected cities, of average annual concentrations in residential areas away from air pollution "hotspots," such as industrial districts and transport corridors. The data are extracted from a complete set of estimates by the World Bank's Development Research Group and Environment Department in a study of annual ambient concentrations of particulate matter in world cities with populations exceeding 100,000 (Pandey and others 2006).

Pollutant concentrations are sensitive to local conditions, and even in the same city different monitoring sites may register different concentrations. Thus these data should be considered only a general

Air pollution 3.13

	City	City population	Particulate matter	Sulfur dioxide	Nitrogen dioxide
		thousands	micrograms per cubic meter	micrograms per cubic meter	micrograms per cubic meter
		2005	2004	1995–2001[a]	1995–2001[a]
India	Kolkata	14,277	128	49	34
	Madras	6,916	37	15	17
	Delhi	15,048	150	24	41
	Hyderabad	6,115	41	12	17
	Kanpur	3,018	109	15	14
	Lucknow	2,566	109	26	25
	Mumbai	18,196	63	33	39
	Nagpur	2,350	56	6	13
	Pune	4,409	47	..	..
Indonesia	Jakarta	13,215	104	..	..
Iran, Islamic Rep.	Tehran	7,314	58	209	..
Ireland	Dublin	1,037	19	20	..
Italy	Milan	2,953	30	31	248
	Rome	3,348	29	..	..
	Turin	1,660	44	..	..
Japan	Osaka-Kobe	11,268	35	19	63
	Tokyo	35,197	40	18	68
	Yokohama	3,366[b]	31	100	13
Kenya	Nairobi	2,773	43	..	..
Korea, Rep	Pusan	3,554	*44*	60	51
	Seoul	9,645	41	44	60
	Taegu	2,511	*50*	81	62
Malaysia	Kuala Lumpur	1,405	29	24	..
Mexico	Mexico City	19,411	51	74	130
Netherlands	Amsterdam	1,147	34	10	58
New Zealand	Auckland	1,148	14	3	20
Norway	Oslo	802	14	8	43
Philippines	Manila	10,686	39	33	..
Poland	Katowice	2,914[b]	39	83	79
	Lódz	776	39	21	43
	Warsaw	1,680	43	16	32
Portugal	Lisbon	2,761	23	8	52
Romania	Bucharest	1,934	18	10	71
Russian Federation	Moscow	10,654	21	109	..
	Omsk	1,132	22	20	34
Singapore	Singapore	4,326	44	20	30
Slovak Republic	Bratislava	456[b]	15	21	27
South Africa	Cape Town	3,083	16	21	72
	Durban	2,631	32	31	..
	Johannesburg	3,254	33	19	31
Spain	Barcelona	4,795	35	11	43
	Madrid	5,608	30	24	66
Sweden	Stockholm	1,708	11	3	20
Switzerland	Zurich	1,144	23	11	39
Thailand	Bangkok	6,593	79	11	23
Turkey	Ankara	3,573	46	55	46
	Istanbul	9,712	55	120	..
Ukraine	Kiev	2,672	35	14	51
United Kingdom	Birmingham	2,280	25	9	45
	London	8,505	21	25	77
	Manchester	2,228	15	26	49
United States	Chicago	8,814	25	14	57
	Los Angeles	12,298	34	9	74
	New York–Newark	18,718	21	26	79
Venezuela, RB	Caracas	2,913	10	33	57

a. Data are for the most recent year available. b. Data are for 2000.

indication of air quality in each city, and cross-country comparisons should be made with caution. The current World Health Organization (WHO) air quality guidelines are annual mean concentrations of 20 micrograms per cubic meter for particulate matter less than 10 microns in diameter (PM10) and 40 micrograms for nitrogen dioxide and daily mean concentrations of 20 micrograms per cubic meter for sulfur dioxide.

Definitions

• **City population** is the number of residents of the city or metropolitan area as defined by national authorities and reported to the United Nations. • **Particulate matter** refers to fine suspended particulates less than 10 microns in diameter (PM10) that are capable of penetrating deep into the respiratory tract and causing significant health damage. Data are extracted from a larger study of urban-population-weighted PM10 levels in residential areas of cities with more than 100,000 residents. The estimates represent the average annual exposure level of the average urban resident to outdoor particulate matter. The state of a country's technology and pollution controls is an important determinant of particulate matter concentrations. • **Sulfur dioxide** is an air pollutant produced when fossil fuels containing sulfur are burned. It contributes to acid rain and can damage human health, particularly that of the young and the elderly. • **Nitrogen dioxide** is a poisonous, pungent gas formed when nitric oxide combines with hydrocarbons and sunlight, producing a photochemical reaction. These conditions occur in both natural and anthropogenic activities. Nitrogen dioxide is emitted by bacteria, motor vehicles, industrial activities, nitrogenous fertilizers, combustion of fuels and biomass, and aerobic decomposition of organic matter in soils and oceans.

Data sources

Data on city population are from the United Nations Population Division. Data on particulate matter concentrations are from a recent World Bank study by Kiran D. Pandey, David Wheeler, Bart Ostro, Uwe Deichman, Kirk Hamilton, and Kathrine Bolt, "Ambient Particulate Matter Concentration in Residential and Pollution Hotspot Areas of World Cities: New Estimates Based on the Global Model of Ambient Particulates (GMAPS)" (2006). Data on sulfur dioxide and nitrogen dioxide concentrations are from the WHO's Healthy Cities Air Management Information System and the World Resources Institute.

3.14 Government commitment

	Environmental strategies or action plans	Biodiversity assessments, strategies, or action plans	Participation in treaties[a]								
			Climate change[b]	Ozone layer	CFC control	Law of the Sea[c]	Biological diversity[b]	Kyoto Protocol	CITES	CCD	Stockholm Convention
Afghanistan	..	..	2002	2004[f]	2004[f]	..	2002	1985[f]	1995[f]	..	
Albania	1993	..	1995	1999[f]	1999[f]	2003[f]	1994[f]	2005[f]	2003[f]	2000[f]	2004
Algeria	2001	..	1994	1992[f]	1992[f]	1996	1995	2005[f]	1983[f]	1996	2006
Angola	..	..	2000	2000[f]	2000[f]	1994	1998	..	..	1997	2006
Argentina	1992	..	1994	1990	1990	1995	1994	2001	1981	1997	2005
Armenia	..	..	1994	1999[f]	1999[f]	2002[f]	1993[d]	2003[f]	..	1997	2003
Australia	1992	1994	1994	1987[f]	1989	1994	1993	..	1976	2000	2004
Austria	..	..	1994	1987	1989	1995	1994	2002	1982[f]	1997[f]	2002
Azerbaijan	1998	..	1995	1996[f]	1996[f]	..	2000[e]	2000[f]	1998[f]	1998[f]	2004[f]
Bangladesh	1991	1990	1994	1990[f]	1990[f]	2001	1994	2001[f]	1981	1996	..
Belarus	..	..	2000	1986[d]	1988[d]	2006[f]	1993	..	1995[f]	2001[f]	2004[f]
Belgium	..	..	1996	1988	1988	1998	1996	2002	1983	1997[f]	2006
Benin	1993	..	1994	1993[f]	1993[f]	1997	1994	2002[f]	1984[f]	1996	2004
Bolivia	1994	1988	1995	1994[f]	1994[f]	1995	1994	1999	1979	1996	2003
Bosnia and Herzegovina	..	..	2000	1992[g]	1992[g]	1994[g]	2002[f]	..	2002	2002[f]	..
Botswana	1990	1991	1994	1991[f]	1991[f]	1994	1995	2003[f]	1977[f]	1996	2002[f]
Brazil	..	1988	1994	1990[f]	1990[f]	1994	1994	2002	1975	1997	2004
Bulgaria	..	1994	1995	1990[f]	1990[f]	1996	1996	2002	1991[f]	2001[f]	2004
Burkina Faso	1993	..	1994	1989	1989	2005	1993	2005[f]	1989[f]	1996	2004
Burundi	1994	1989	1997	1997[f]	1997[f]	..	1997	2001[f]	1988[f]	1997	2005
Cambodia	1999	..	1996	2001[f]	2001[f]	..	1995[f]	2002[f]	1997	1997	2006
Cameroon	..	1989	1995	1989[f]	1989[f]	1994	1994	2002[f]	1981[f]	1997	..
Canada	1990	1994	1994	1986	1988	2003	1992	2002	1975	1995	2001
Central African Republic	..	..	1995	1993[f]	1993[f]	..	1995	..	1980[f]	1996	..
Chad	1990	..	1994	1989[f]	1994	..	1994	..	1989[f]	1996	2004
Chile	..	1993	1995	1990	1990	1997	1994	2002	1975	1997	2005
China	1994	1994	1994	1989[f]	1991[f]	1996	1993	2002[e]	1981[f]	1997	2004
Hong Kong, China	..	..	..	..	..	..	..	..	..	..	..
Colombia	1998	1988	1995	1990[f]	1993[f]	1994	2001[f]	1981	1999	..	
Congo, Dem. Rep.	..	1990	1995	1994[f]	1994[f]	1995	1996	2005[f]	1976[f]	1997	2005[f]
Congo, Rep.	..	1990	1997	1994[f]	1994[f]	..	1994	..	1983[f]	1999	..
Costa Rica	1990	1992	1994	1991[f]	1991[f]	1994	1994	2002	1975	1998	..
Côte d'Ivoire	1994	1991	1995	1993[f]	1993[f]	1994	1994	..	1994[f]	1997	2004
Croatia	2001	2000	1996	1991[d]	1991[d]	1994[g]	1996	..	2000[f]	2000[d]	..
Cuba	..	..	1994	1992[f]	1992[f]	1994	1994	2002	1990[f]	1997	..
Czech Republic	1994	..	1994	1993[d]	1993[d]	1996	1993[e]	2001[e]	993[g]	2000[f]	2002
Denmark	1994	..	1994	1988	1988	2004	1993	2002	1977	1995[f]	2003
Dominican Republic	..	1995	1999	1993[f]	1993[f]	..	1996	2002[f]	1986[f]	1997[f]	..
Ecuador	1993	1995	1994	1990[f]	1990[f]	..	1993	2000	1975	1995	2004
Egypt, Arab Rep.	1992	1988	1995	1988	1988	1994	1994	2005[f]	1978	1995	2003
El Salvador	1994	1988	1996	1992	1992	..	1994	1998	1987[f]	1997[f]	..
Eritrea	1995	..	1995	2005[f]	2005[f]	..	1996[f]	2005[f]	1994[f]	1996	2005[f]
Estonia	1998	..	1994	1996[f]	1996[f]	2005[f]	1994	2002	1992[f]	..	..
Ethiopia	1994	1991	1994	1994[f]	1994[f]	..	1994	2005[f]	1989[f]	1997	2003
Finland	1995	..	1994	1986	1988	1996	1994[d]	2002	1976[f]	1995[d]	2002[d]
France	1990	..	1994	1987[e]	1988[e]	1996	1994	2002[e]	1978	1997	2004[e]
Gabon	..	1990	1998	1994[f]	1994[f]	1998	1997	..	1989[f]	1996[f]	..
Gambia, The	1992	1989	1994	1990[f]	1990[f]	1994	1994	2001[f]	1977[f]	1996	2006
Georgia	1998	..	1994	1996[f]	1996[f]	1996[f]	1994[f]	1999[f]	1996[f]	1999	2006
Germany	..	..	1994	1988	1988	1994[f]	1993	2002	1976	1996	2002
Ghana	1992	1988	1995	1989[f]	1989	1994	1994	2003[f]	1975	1996	2003
Greece	..	..	1994	1988	1988	1995	1994	2002	1992[f]	1997	2006
Guatemala	1994	1988	1996	1987[f]	1989[f]	1997	1995	1999	1979	1998[f]	..
Guinea	1994	1988	1994	1992[f]	1992[f]	1994	1993	2000[f]	1981[f]	1997	..
Guinea-Bissau	1993	1991	1996	2002[f]	2002[f]	1994	1995	..	1990[f]	1995	..
Haiti	1999	..	1996	2000[f]	2000[f]	1996	1996	2005[f]	..	1996	..

Government commitment

	Environmental strategies or action plans	Biodiversity assessments, strategies, or action plans	Participation in treaties[a]								
			Climate change[b]	Ozone layer	CFC control	Law of the Sea[c]	Biological diversity[b]	Kyoto Protocol	CITES	CCD	Stockholm Convention
Honduras	1993	..	1996	1993[f]	1993[f]	1994	1995	2000	1985[f]	1997	2005
Hungary	1995	..	1994	1988[f]	1989[f]	2002	1994	2002[f]	1985[f]	1999[f]	..
India	1993	1994	1994	1991[f]	1992[f]	1995	1994	2002[f]	1976	1996	2006
Indonesia	1993	1993	1994	1992[f]	1992	1994	1994	2004	1978[f]	1998	..
Iran, Islamic Rep.	..	..	1996	1990[f]	1990[f]	..	1996	2005[f]	1976	1997	2006
Iraq	..	..	..	..	..	1994	..	..	..	..	..
Ireland	..	..	1994	1988[f]	1988	1996	1996	2002	2002	1997	..
Israel	..	..	1996	1992[f]	1992	..	1995	2004	1979	1996	..
Italy	..	..	1994	1988	1988	1995	1994	2002	1979	1997	..
Jamaica	1994	..	1995	1993[f]	1993[f]	1994	1995	1999[f]	1997[f]	1997[f]	..
Japan	..	..	1994	1988[f]	1988	1996	1993[d]	2002[d]	1980	1998[d]	2002[f]
Jordan	1991	..	1994	1989[f]	1989[f]	1995[f]	1993	2003[f]	1978[f]	1996	2004
Kazakhstan	..	..	1995	1998[f]	1998[f]	..	1994	..	2000[f]	1997	..
Kenya	1994	1992	1994	1988[f]	1988	1994	1994	2005[f]	1978	1997	2004
Korea, Dem. Rep.	..	..	1995	1995[f]	1995[f]	..	1994[e]	2005[f]	..	2003[f]	2002[f]
Korea, Rep.	..	..	1994	1992	1992	1996	1994	2002	1993[f]	1999	2007
Kuwait	..	..	1995	1992[f]	1992[f]	1994	2002	2005[f]	2002	1997	2006
Kyrgyz Republic	1995	..	2000	2000[f]	2000[f]	..	1996[e]	2003[f]	..	1997[f]	2006
Lao PDR	1995	..	1995	1998[f]	1998[f]	1998	1996[e]	2003[f]	2004[f]	1996[d]	2006
Latvia	..	..	1995	1995[f]	1995[f]	2004[f]	1995	2002	1997[f]	2002[f]	2004
Lebanon	..	..	1995	1993[f]	1993[f]	1995	1994	..	..	1996	2003
Lesotho	1989	..	1995	1994[f]	1994[f]	..	1995	2000[f]	2003	1995	2002
Liberia	2003	1996[f]	1996[f]	..	2000	2002[f]	2005[f]	1998[f]	2002[f]		
Libya	..	..	1999	1990[f]	1990[f]	..	2001	..	2003[f]	1996	2005[f]
Lithuania	..	..	1995	1995[f]	1995[f]	2003[f]	1996	2003	2001[f]	2003[f]	2006
Macedonia, FYR	..	..	1998	1994[g]	1994[g]	1994[g]	1997[f]	2004[f]	2000[f]	2002[f]	2004
Madagascar	1988	1991	1999	1996[f]	1996[f]	2001	1996	2003[f]	1975	1997	..
Malawi	1994	..	1994	1991[f]	1991[f]	..	1994	2001[f]	1982[f]	1996	..
Malaysia	1991	1988	1994	1989[f]	1989[f]	1996	1994	2002	1977[f]	1997	..
Mali	..	1989	1995	1994[f]	1994[f]	1994	1995	2002	1994[f]	1995	2003
Mauritania	1988	..	1994	1994[f]	1994[f]	1996	1996	2005[f]	1998[f]	1996	2005
Mauritius	1990	..	1994	1992[f]	1992[f]	1994	1992	2001[f]	1975	1996	2004
Mexico	..	1988	1994	1987	1988	1994	1993	2000	1991[f]	1995	2003
Moldova	2002	..	1995	1996[f]	1996[f]	..	1995	2003[f]	2001[f]	1999[f]	2004
Mongolia	1995	..	1994	1996[f]	1996[f]	1996	1993	1999[f]	1996[f]	1996	2004
Morocco	..	1988	1996	1995	1995	..	1995	2002[f]	1975	1996	2004
Mozambique	1994	..	1995	1994[f]	1994[f]	1997	1995	2005[f]	1981[f]	1997	2005
Myanmar	..	1989	1995	1993[f]	1993[f]	1996	1995	2003[f]	1997[f]	1997[f]	2004[f]
Namibia	1992	..	1995	1993[f]	1993[f]	1994	1997	2003[f]	1990[f]	1997	2005[f]
Nepal	1993	..	1994	1994[f]	1994[f]	1998	1993	2005[f]	1975[f]	1996	..
Netherlands	1994	..	1994	1988[f]	1988[d]	1996	1994[d]	2002[f]	1984	1995[d]	2002[d]
New Zealand	1994	..	1994	1987	1988	1996	1993	2002	1989[f]	2000[f]	2004
Nicaragua	1994	..	1996	1993[f]	1993[f]	2000	1995	1999	1977[f]	1998	..
Niger	..	1991	1995	1992[f]	1992[f]	..	1995	2004	1975	1996	2006
Nigeria	1990	1992	1994	1988[f]	1988[f]	1994	1994	2004[f]	1974	1997	2004
Norway	..	1994	1994	1986	1988	1996	1993	2002	1976	1996	2002
Oman	..	..	1995	1999[f]	1999[f]	1994	1995	2005[f]	..	1996[f]	2005
Pakistan	1994	1991	1994	1992[f]	1992[f]	1997	1994	2005[f]	1976[f]	1997	..
Panama	1990	..	1995	1989[f]	1989	1996	1995	1999	1978	1996	2003
Papua New Guinea	1992	1993	1994	1992[f]	1992[f]	1997	1993	2002	1975[f]	2000[f]	2003
Paraguay	..	..	1994	1992[f]	1992[f]	1994	1994	1999	1976	1997	2004
Peru	..	1988	1994	1989	1993[f]	..	1993	2002	1975	1995	2005
Philippines	1989	1989	1994	1991[f]	1991	1994	1993	2003	1981	2000	2004
Poland	1993	1991	1994	1990[f]	1990[f]	1998	1996	2002	1989	2001[f]	..
Portugal	1995	..	1994	1988[f]	1988	1997	1993	2002[e]	1980	1996	2004[d]
Puerto Rico	..	..	..	..	..	..	..	..	..	..	..

3.14 Government commitment

	Environmental strategies or action plans	Biodiversity assessments, strategies, or action plans	Participation in treaties[a]								
			Climate change[b]	Ozone layer	CFC control	Law of the Sea[c]	Biological diversity[b]	Kyoto Protocol	CITES	CCD	Stockholm Convention
Romania	1995	..	1994	1993[f]	1993[f]	1996	1994	2001	1994[f]	1998[f]	2004
Russian Federation	1999	1994	1995	1986[d]	1988[d]	1997	1995	2004	1992	2003[f]	..
Rwanda	1991	..	1998	2001[f]	2001[f]	..	1996	2004[f]	1980[f]	1998	2002[f]
Saudi Arabia	..	..	1995	1993[f]	1993[f]	1996	2001[e]	2005[f]	1996[f]	1997[f]	..
Senegal	1984	1991	1995	1993[f]	1993	1994	1994	2001[f]	1977[f]	1995	2003
Serbia and Montenegro	2001	2001[g]	2001[g]	2001[g]	2002	..	2002	..	2002		
Sierra Leone	1994	..	1995	2001[f]	2001[f]	1994	1994[e]	2006[f]	1994[f]	1997	2003[f]
Singapore	1993	1995	1997	1989[f]	1989[f]	1994	1995	2006[f]	1986[f]	1999[f]	2005
Slovak Republic	..	..	1994	1993[g]	1993[g]	1996	1994[e]	2002	1993	2001[f]	2002
Slovenia	1994	..	1996	1992[g]	1992[g]	1995[g]	1996	2002	2000[f]	2001[f]	2004
Somalia	..	2001[f]	2001[f]	1994	..	..	1985[f]	2002[f]	..		
South Africa	1993	..	1997	1990[f]	1990[f]	1997	1995	2002[f]	1975	1997	2002
Spain	..	..	1994	1988[f]	1988	1997	1995	2002	1986[f]	1996	2004
Sri Lanka	1994	1991	1994	1989[f]	1989[f]	1994	1994	2002[f]	1979[f]	1998[f]	..
Sudan	..	..	1994	1993[f]	1993[f]	1994	1995	2004[f]	1982	1995	2006
Swaziland	1997	1992[f]	1992[f]	..	1994	..	1997[f]	1996	2006		
Sweden	..	..	1994	1986	1988	1996	1993	2002	1974	1995	2002
Switzerland	..	..	1994	1987	1988	..	1994	2006[f]	1974	1996	2003
Syrian Arab Republic	1999	..	1996	1989[f]	1989[f]	..	1996	2006[f]	2003[f]	1997	2005
Tajikistan	..	..	1998	1996[f]	1998[f]	..	1997[e]	..	..	1997[f]	..
Tanzania	1994	1988	1996	1993[f]	1993[f]	1994	1996	2002[f]	1979	1997	2004
Thailand	..	..	1995	1989[f]	1989	..	2004	2002	1983	2001[f]	2005
Togo	1991	..	1995	1991[f]	1991	1994	1995[d]	2004[f]	1978	1995[d]	2004
Trinidad and Tobago	..	..	1994	1989[f]	1989[f]	1994	1996	1999	1984[f]	2000[f]	2002[f]
Tunisia	1994	1988	1994	1989[f]	1989[f]	1994	1993	2003[f]	1974	1995	2004
Turkey	1998	..	2004	1991[f]	1991[f]	..	1997	..	1996[f]	1998	..
Turkmenistan	..	..	1995	1993[f]	1993[f]	..	1996[e]	1999	..	1996	..
Uganda	1994	1988	1994	1988[f]	1988	1994	1993	2002[f]	1991[f]	1997	2004[f]
Ukraine	1999	..	1997	1986[d]	1988[d]	1999	1995	2004	1999[f]	2002[f]	..
United Arab Emirates	..	..	1996	1989[f]	1989[f]	..	2000	2005[f]	1990[f]	1998[f]	2002
United Kingdom	1995	1994	1994	1987	1988	1997[f]	1994	2002	1976	1996	2005
United States	1995	1995	1994	1986	1988	..	..	..	1974	2000	..
Uruguay	..	..	1994	1989[f]	1991[f]	1994	1993	2001	1975	1999[f]	2004
Uzbekistan	..	..	1994	1993[f]	1993[f]	..	1995[e]	1999	1997[f]	1995	..
Venezuela	..	..	1995	1988[f]	1989	..	1994	..	1977	1998[f]	2005
Vietnam	..	1993	1995	1994[f]	1994[f]	2006[f]	1994	2002	1994[f]	1998[f]	2002
West Bank and Gaza	..	..	..	..	..	..	..	..	..	..	
Yemen, Rep.	1996	1992	1996	1996[f]	1996[f]	1994	1996	2004[f]	1997[f]	1997[f]	2004
Zambia	1994	..	1994	1990[f]	1990[f]	1994	1993	2006[f]	1980[f]	1996	2006
Zimbabwe	1987	..	1994	1992[f]	1992[f]	1994	1994	..	1981[f]	1997	..

a. Ratification of the treaty. b. Years shown refer to the year the treaty entered into force in that country. c. Convention became effective November 16, 1994. d. Acceptance. e. Approval. f. Accession. g. Succession.

About the data

National environmental strategies and participation in international treaties on environmental issues provide some evidence of government commitment to sound environmental management. But the signing of these treaties does not always imply ratification, nor does it guarantee that governments will comply with treaty obligations.

In many countries efforts to halt environmental degradation have failed, primarily because governments have neglected to make this issue a priority, a reflection of competing claims on scarce resources. To address this problem, many countries are preparing national environmental strategies—some focusing narrowly on environmental issues, and others integrating environmental, economic, and social concerns. Among such initiatives are conservation strategies and environmental action plans. Some countries have also prepared country environmental profiles and biodiversity strategies and profiles.

National conservation strategies—promoted by the World Conservation Union (IUCN)—provide a comprehensive, cross-sectoral analysis of conservation and resource management issues to help integrate environmental concerns with the development process. Such strategies discuss current and future needs, institutional capabilities, prevailing technical conditions, and the status of natural resources in a country.

National environmental action plans, supported by the World Bank and other development agencies, describe a country's main environmental concerns, identify the principal causes of environmental problems, and formulate policies and actions to deal with them. These plans are a continuing process in which governments develop comprehensive environmental policies, recommend specific actions, and outline the investment strategies, legislation, and institutional arrangements required to implement them.

Biodiversity profiles—prepared by the World Conservation Monitoring Centre and the IUCN—provide basic background on species diversity, protected areas, major ecosystems and habitat types, and legislative and administrative support. In an effort to establish a scientific baseline for measuring progress in biodiversity conservation, the United Nations Environment Programme (UNEP) coordinates global biodiversity assessments.

To address global issues, many governments have also signed international treaties and agreements launched in the wake of the 1972 United Nations Conference on Human Environment in Stockholm and the 1992 United Nations Conference on Environment and Development (the Earth Summit) in Rio de Janeiro, which produced Agenda 21—an array of actions to address environmental challenges:

- The Framework Convention on Climate Change aims to stabilize atmospheric concentrations of greenhouse gases at levels that will prevent human activities from interfering dangerously with the global climate.
- The Vienna Convention for the Protection of the Ozone Layer aims to protect human health and the environment by promoting research on the effects of changes in the ozone layer and on alternative substances (such as substitutes for chlorofluorocarbon) and technologies, monitoring the ozone layer, and taking measures to control the activities that produce adverse effects.
- The Montreal Protocol for Chlorofluorocarbon Control requires that countries help protect the earth from excessive ultraviolet radiation by cutting chlorofluorocarbon consumption by 20 percent over their 1986 level by 1994 and by 50 percent over their 1986 level by 1999, with allowances for increases in consumption by developing countries.
- The United Nations Convention on the Law of the Sea, which became effective in November 1994, establishes a comprehensive legal regime for seas and oceans, establishes rules for environmental standards and enforcement provisions, and develops international rules and national legislation to prevent and control marine pollution.
- The Convention on Biological Diversity promotes conservation of biodiversity through scientific and technological cooperation among countries, access to financial and genetic resources, and transfer of ecologically sound technologies.

But 10 years after Rio the World Summit on Sustainable Development in Johannesburg recognized that many of the proposed actions have yet to materialize. To help developing countries comply with their obligations under these agreements, the Global Environment Facility (GEF) was created to focus on global improvement in biodiversity, climate change, international waters, and ozone layer depletion. The UNEP, United Nations Development Programme, and the World Bank manage the GEF according to the policies of its governing body of country representatives. The World Bank is responsible for the GEF Trust Fund and is chair of the GEF.

Definitions

• **Environmental strategies or action plans** provide a comprehensive, cross-sectoral analysis of conservation and resource management issues to help integrate environmental concerns with the development process. They include national conservation strategies, national environmental action plans, national environmental management strategies, and national sustainable development strategies. The year shown for a country refers to the year in which a strategy or action plan was adopted. • **Biodiversity assessments, strategies, or action plans** include biodiversity profiles (see *About the data*). • **Participation in treaties** covers nine international treaties (see *About the data*). • **Climate change** refers to the Framework Convention on Climate Change (signed in New York in 1992). • **Ozone layer** refers to the Vienna Convention for the Protection of the Ozone Layer (signed in 1985). • **CFC control** refers to the Montreal Protocol for Chlorofluorocarbon Control (formally, the Protocol on Substances That Deplete the Ozone Layer, signed in 1987). • **Law of the Sea** refers to the United Nations Convention on the Law of the Sea (signed in Montego Bay, Jamaica, in 1982). • **Biological diversity** refers to the Convention on Biological Diversity (signed at the Earth Summit in Rio de Janeiro in 1992). • **Kyoto Protocol** refers to the protocol on climate change adopted at the third conference of the parties to the United Nations Framework Convention on Climate Change, held in Kyoto, Japan, in December 1997. • **CITES** refers to the Convention on International Trade in Endangered Species of Wild Fauna and Flora, an agreement among governments to ensure that the survival of wild animals and plants is not threatened by uncontrolled exploitation. • **CCD** refers to the United Nations Convention to Combat Desertification, an international convention dedicated to addressing the problems of land degradation in the world's drylands. Adopted in Paris on June 17, 1994, it entered into force on December 26, 1996. • **Stockholm Convention** is an international legally binding instrument designed to protect human health and the environment from persistent organic pollutants. It was adopted on May 22, 2001, and entered into force May 17, 2004.

Data sources

Data on environmental strategies and participation in international environmental treaties are from the Secretariat of the United Nations Framework Convention on Climate Change, the Ozone Secretariat of the UNEP, the World Resources Institute, the UNEP, the Center for International Earth Science Information Network, and the United Nations Treaty Series.

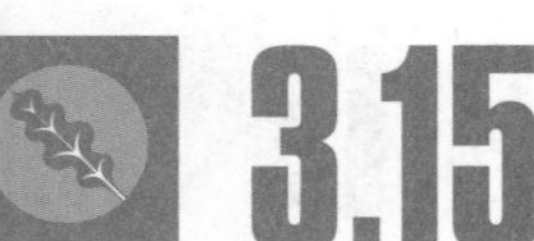

3.15 Toward a broader measure of savings

	Gross savings % of GNI 2005	Consumption of fixed capital % of GNI 2005	Net savings % of GNI 2005	Education expenditure % of GNI 2005	Energy depletion % of GNI 2005	Mineral depletion % of GNI 2005	Net forest depletion % of GNI 2005	Carbon dioxide damage % of GNI 2005	Particulate emission damage % of GNI 2005	Adjusted net savings % of GNI 2005
Afghanistan	23.8	7.6	16.2	..	0.0	..	1.0	0.1	0.7	..
Albania	15.6	10.7	4.9	2.8	1.9	0.0	0.0	0.2	0.2	5.4
Algeria	53.8	11.6	42.2	4.5	46.9	0.1	0.1	1.3	0.3	–2.1
Angola	23.4	12.0	11.3	3.0	51.3	0.0	0.0	0.3	1.8	–39.1
Argentina	24.8	12.1	12.8	4.1	10.4	0.4	0.0	0.6	1.6	3.9
Armenia	25.7	10.1	15.6	3.0	0.0	0.8	0.0	0.7	1.8	15.3
Australia	20.7[a]	15.0	5.8	4.8	3.1	3.1	0.0	0.4	0.1	3.9
Austria	24.6	14.3	10.3	5.6	0.2	0.0	0.0	0.2	0.3	15.2
Azerbaijan	34.5	11.6	22.9	3.5	60.4	0.0	0.0	2.8	1.1	–37.9
Bangladesh	28.8	8.2	20.7	1.7	3.8	0.0	0.7	0.4	0.5	17.0
Belarus	30.9	11.0	19.9	5.5	2.4	0.0	0.0	1.8	..	21.2[b]
Belgium	23.4	15.4	8.0	3.0	0.0	0.0	0.0	0.2	0.2	10.6
Benin	10.7	8.7	2.0	2.4	0.0	0.0	0.9	0.3	0.4	2.7
Bolivia	20.4	10.0	10.4	6.3	33.7	1.0	0.0	0.7	1.3	–20.0
Bosnia and Herzegovina	–1.9	10.3	–12.2	..	1.2	0.0	..	1.5	0.1	..
Botswana	49.2	12.9	36.3	5.6	0.4	2.1	0.0	0.3	..	39.1[b]
Brazil	23.0	11.9	11.1	4.1	4.1	2.4	0.0	0.3	0.3	8.0
Bulgaria	17.0	11.1	5.9	3.5	1.2	1.0	0.0	1.3	1.4	4.7
Burkina Faso	..	8.3	..	2.4	0.0	0.0	1.2	0.2	1.4	..
Burundi	8.7	6.7	2.0	3.9	0.0	0.1	11.3	0.2	0.1	–5.8
Cambodia	15.0	8.8	6.2	1.8	0.0	0.0	0.3	0.1	0.4	7.3
Cameroon	18.1	9.9	8.2	3.2	13.8	0.0	0.0	0.2	0.8	–3.4
Canada	21.7[a]	14.6	7.1	5.2	6.8	0.4	0.0	0.3	0.2	4.6
Central African Republic	14.0	8.1	5.9	1.6	0.0	0.0	0.0	0.1	0.4	6.9
Chad	25.4	10.8	14.6	1.4	73.3	0.0	0.0	0.0	1.1	–58.4
Chile	19.1	13.4	5.6	3.9	0.4	13.6	0.0	0.4	0.6	–5.5
China	50.4	10.2	40.2	2.0	6.8	0.8	0.0	1.4	1.4	31.8
Hong Kong, China	31.9	13.9	18.0	3.7	0.0	0.0	0.0	0.2	..	21.6[b]
Colombia	19.0	11.4	7.6	4.9	10.2	0.7	0.0	0.4	0.1	1.1
Congo, Dem. Rep.	14.1	7.0	7.1	0.9	4.3	1.6	0.0	0.2	0.6	1.2
Congo, Rep.	37.6	12.8	24.8	3.8	74.9	0.0	0.0	0.2	0.8	–47.3
Costa Rica	19.2	6.1	13.0	4.0	0.0	0.0	0.2	0.2	0.3	16.3
Côte d'Ivoire	13.3	9.9	3.5	4.6	5.4	0.0	0.0	0.3	0.3	2.1
Croatia	24.0	12.9	11.1	4.1	1.6	0.0	0.2	0.5	0.4	12.5
Cuba	..	..	..	8.1	..	..	..	..	..	..
Czech Republic	25.6	13.6	12.0	4.2	0.7	0.0	0.0	0.8	0.1	14.6
Denmark	23.7	15.1	8.6	8.1	2.3	0.0	0.0	0.1	0.1	14.2
Dominican Republic	20.5	11.9	8.6	1.2	0.0	1.5	0.0	0.6	0.3	7.5
Ecuador	24.9	11.5	13.3	1.4	28.1	0.1	0.0	0.5	0.1	–14.2
Egypt, Arab Rep.	21.4	9.8	11.6	4.4	17.5	0.2	0.2	1.2	0.9	–4.0
El Salvador	11.2	11.1	0.0	2.8	0.0	0.0	0.5	0.3	0.2	1.8
Eritrea	10.3	7.6	2.8	2.7	0.0	0.0	1.2	0.5	0.7	3.2
Estonia	22.4[a]	13.5	8.9	5.1	1.7	0.0	0.2	1.2	0.0	11.0
Ethiopia	17.3	7.1	10.2	3.0	0.0	0.0	0.0	0.5	0.3	12.3
Finland	22.6	16.1	6.5	6.0	0.0	0.0	0.0	0.2	0.1	12.2
France	18.0	12.5	5.5	5.2	0.0	0.0	0.0	0.1	0.0	10.5
Gabon	35.5	13.2	22.2	3.3	37.8	0.0	0.0	0.2	..	–12.5[b]
Gambia, The	15.6	8.2	7.4	2.0	0.0	0.0	0.6	0.5	0.8	7.5
Georgia	20.0	9.9	10.1	2.9	0.6	0.0	0.0	0.5	1.1	10.7
Germany	21.1	14.8	6.3	4.3	0.2	0.0	0.0	0.2	0.1	10.1
Ghana	22.2	8.7	13.6	2.8	0.1	0.5	1.8	0.5	0.1	13.3
Greece	14.9	8.7	6.2	3.1	0.3	0.1	0.0	0.3	0.9	7.7
Guatemala	14.8	10.9	3.8	1.6	1.5	0.0	0.7	0.2	0.5	2.5
Guinea	6.6	8.3	–1.7	2.0	0.0	3.5	2.0	0.3	0.3	–5.8
Guinea-Bissau	7.8	7.6	0.2	2.3	0.0	0.0	0.0	0.6	1.0	0.8
Haiti	..	8.6	..	1.5	0.0	0.0	0.8	0.2	0.5	..

Toward a broader measure of savings

	Gross savings	Consumption of fixed capital	Net savings	Education expenditure	Energy depletion	Mineral depletion	Net forest depletion	Carbon dioxide damage	Particulate emission damage	Adjusted net savings
	% of GNI 2005	% of GNI 2005	% of GNI 2005	% of GNI 2005	% of GNI 2005	% of GNI 2005	% of GNI 2005	% of GNI 2005	% of GNI 2005	% of GNI 2005
Honduras	30.8	10.1	20.6	3.5	0.0	0.3	0.0	0.6	0.4	22.9
Hungary	16.5	13.6	2.9	5.8	0.8	0.0	0.0	0.4	0.1	7.4
India	32.2	9.2	23.0	4.0	4.8	1.0	0.6	1.3	0.7	18.6
Indonesia	24.7	10.2	14.4	0.9	13.7	2.0	0.0	0.8	1.1	–2.3
Iran, Islamic Rep.	41.6	11.1	30.5	4.4	48.1	0.5	0.0	1.4	0.8	–16.0
Iraq	..	..	..	..	..	..	..	..	..	..
Ireland	27.6[a]	10.9	16.7	4.8	0.0	0.1	0.0	0.2	0.1	21.1
Israel	..	17.6	..	7.3	0.2	0.0	0.0	0.4	0.5	..
Italy	19.9	13.4	6.5	4.6	0.2	0.0	0.0	0.2	0.2	10.5
Jamaica	19.6[a]	7.6	12.0	5.0	0.0	1.7	0.0	0.8	0.3	14.3
Japan	26.2[a]	14.0	12.2	3.1	0.0	0.0	0.0	0.2	0.5	14.6
Jordan	6.5	10.4	–3.9	5.6	0.5	0.1	0.0	1.0	0.7	–0.5
Kazakhstan	28.5	12.5	16.0	4.4	53.6	1.7	0.0	2.5	0.3	–37.6
Kenya	12.2	8.8	3.4	6.6	0.0	0.0	1.1	0.4	0.1	8.3
Korea, Dem. Rep.	..	..	..	..	..	..	..	..	..	..
Korea, Rep.	32.2	13.4	18.9	3.7	0.0	0.0	0.0	0.4	0.6	21.5
Kuwait	..	12.8	..	6.9	52.1	0.0	0.0	0.7	1.3	..
Kyrgyz Republic	5.7	8.8	–3.1	4.4	1.5	0.0	0.0	1.5	0.3	–1.9
Lao PDR	1.7	9.5	–7.8	1.4	0.0	0.0	0.0	0.4	0.7	–7.5
Latvia	22.7	17.8	4.9	5.6	0.0	0.0	0.8	0.4	0.1	9.2
Lebanon	–0.9	12.3	–13.2	2.4	0.0	0.0	0.0	0.6	1.1	–12.5
Lesotho	21.7	7.6	14.1	6.7	0.0	0.0	1.4	0.0	0.3	19.1
Liberia	23.0	9.0	14.0	..	0.0	0.0	6.1	0.6	0.5	..
Libya	..	12.4	..	..	76.9	0.0	0.0	1.0	..	..
Lithuania	18.5	12.4	6.1	5.7	0.5	0.0	0.1	0.4	0.2	10.7
Macedonia, FYR	20.3	11.1	9.2	4.9	0.0	0.0	0.2	1.4	0.1	12.4
Madagascar	11.6	7.9	3.7	2.5	0.0	0.0	0.0	0.3	0.2	5.6
Malawi	–7.6	7.2	–14.8	5.1	0.0	0.0	0.9	0.3	0.3	–11.3
Malaysia	37.6	12.4	25.2	5.8	20.9	0.0	0.0	0.9	0.2	9.0
Mali	12.0	8.7	3.3	2.7	0.0	0.0	0.0	0.1	1.1	4.8
Mauritania	–5.2	8.6	–13.8	3.2	0.0	28.1	0.6	1.0	2.5	–42.7
Mauritius	19.8	11.8	8.0	3.9	0.0	0.0	0.0	0.4	..	11.6[b]
Mexico	21.5	12.5	9.0	5.3	9.6	0.2	0.0	0.4	0.4	3.6
Moldova	20.8	8.1	12.7	4.2	0.0	0.0	0.0	1.8	0.7	14.4
Mongolia	38.2	8.9	29.3	5.4	0.0	13.0	0.0	3.6	1.2	16.9
Morocco	29.1	10.3	18.8	6.0	0.0	0.3	0.0	0.5	0.1	23.9
Mozambique	4.7	8.6	–3.9	1.8	0.1	0.0	0.5	0.2	0.3	–3.2
Myanmar	..	..	..	0.8	..	..	..	..	..	..
Namibia	39.2	10.9	28.3	7.3	0.0	1.2	0.0	0.3	0.1	34.1
Nepal	31.0	7.8	23.2	2.6	0.0	0.0	2.5	0.3	0.1	23.0
Netherlands	26.5	15.0	11.5	4.9	1.6	0.0	0.0	0.2	0.6	14.1
New Zealand	23.0[a]	13.7	9.3	7.2	1.0	0.1	0.0	0.2	0.1	15.1
Nicaragua	12.9	9.6	3.3	2.9	0.0	0.1	0.0	0.6	0.1	5.4
Niger	10.3	7.7	2.7	2.3	0.0	0.0	2.6	0.3	0.8	1.3
Nigeria	34.1	10.5	23.6	0.9	54.4	0.0	0.1	0.5	0.8	–31.4
Norway	37.1	13.4	23.7	7.0	16.0	0.0	0.0	0.1	0.1	14.6
Oman	..	..	..	4.2	..	..	..	..	..	..
Pakistan	18.4	8.9	9.5	1.6	7.5	0.0	0.4	0.8	1.5	0.9
Panama	10.5	12.6	–2.1	4.4	0.0	0.0	0.0	0.3	0.2	1.8
Papua New Guinea	..	..	..	..	..	..	..	..	..	..
Paraguay	16.4	9.8	6.6	4.2	0.0	0.0	0.0	0.4	0.7	9.7
Peru	19.9	11.7	8.2	2.9	2.2	3.4	0.0	0.3	0.7	4.5
Philippines	28.2	8.1	20.1	2.8	0.5	0.4	0.2	0.6	0.4	20.8
Poland	18.2	12.8	5.4	5.6	1.7	0.4	0.0	0.8	0.4	7.7
Portugal	13.1	17.1	–4.1	5.7	0.0	0.0	0.0	0.2	0.4	1.0
Puerto Rico	..	..	..	..	..	..	..	..	..	..

3.15 Toward a broader measure of savings

	Gross savings	Consumption of fixed capital	Net savings	Education expenditure	Energy depletion	Mineral depletion	Net forest depletion	Carbon dioxide damage	Particulate emission damage	Adjusted net savings
	% of GNI 2005	% of GNI 2005	% of GNI 2005	% of GNI 2005	% of GNI 2005	% of GNI 2005	% of GNI 2005	% of GNI 2005	% of GNI 2005	% of GNI 2005
Romania	14.2	11.7	2.4	3.2	4.2	0.1	0.0	0.7	0.1	0.6
Russian Federation	32.7	7.0	25.7	3.5	36.8	0.8	0.0	1.6	0.4	–10.4
Rwanda	19.5	7.7	11.8	3.5	0.0	0.0	2.6	0.2	0.1	12.3
Saudi Arabia	..	13.0	..	7.2	61.4	0.0	0.0	0.7	1.2	..
Senegal	15.8	9.3	6.5	3.7	0.0	0.0	0.0	0.4	0.9	8.8
Serbia and Montenegro	9.8	11.3	–1.5	..	2.4	0.0	..	1.4	0.0	..
Sierra Leone	7.0	7.7	–0.6	1.0	0.0	0.0	1.9	0.5	1.1	–3.1
Singapore	..	14.6	..	2.7	0.0	0.0	0.0	0.4	0.9	..
Slovak Republic	21.2	22.5	–1.3	4.1	0.1	0.0	0.5	0.7	0.0	1.5
Slovenia	25.2	13.5	11.7	5.4	0.1	0.0	0.2	0.3	0.2	16.3
Somalia	..	..	..	..	..	..	..	..	..	..
South Africa	14.4	12.0	2.4	5.3	4.8	1.2	0.2	1.1	0.1	0.3
Spain	22.6	14.6	8.1	4.1	0.0	0.0	0.0	0.2	0.4	11.6
Sri Lanka	20.5	9.9	10.6	2.6	0.0	0.0	0.3	0.3	0.4	12.1
Sudan	18.5	9.9	8.6	0.9	18.9	0.0	0.0	0.2	0.4	–10.1
Swaziland	16.6	10.6	6.0	6.3	0.0	0.0	0.0	0.3	0.1	11.9
Sweden	23.1	12.1	11.0	8.0	0.0	0.2	0.1	0.1	0.0	18.6
Switzerland	..	13.7	..	5.0	0.0	0.0	0.0	0.1	0.2	..
Syrian Arab Republic	14.6	10.3	4.3	2.6	43.8	0.1	0.0	1.4	0.9	–39.4
Tajikistan	7.3	8.5	–1.2	2.6	0.8	0.0	0.0	1.8	0.4	–1.6
Tanzania	9.3	8.0	1.3	2.4	0.0	0.4	0.0	0.2	0.2	2.8
Thailand	30.1	11.2	18.9	4.7	3.8	0.0	0.3	1.0	0.4	18.2
Togo	9.9	8.3	1.6	2.6	0.0	0.1	2.8	0.6	0.3	0.4
Trinidad and Tobago	..	12.4	..	4.0	57.9	0.0	0.0	1.7	0.2	..
Tunisia	21.9	11.6	10.3	5.9	6.3	0.2	0.1	0.6	0.3	8.7
Turkey	18.5	11.8	6.7	3.5	0.4	0.1	0.0	0.5	1.3	7.9
Turkmenistan	36.4	11.0	25.4	..	..	0.0	..	3.7	1.1	..
Uganda	10.1	8.1	2.0	4.0	0.0	0.0	4.6	0.2	0.0	1.1
Ukraine	22.7	10.4	12.2	4.4	9.0	0.0	0.0	3.2	0.7	3.7
United Arab Emirates	..	..	..	..	..	..	..	..	..	..
United Kingdom	13.9	10.3	3.6	5.3	1.6	0.0	0.0	0.2	0.0	7.1
United States	13.0[a]	12.2	0.8	4.8	1.9	0.0	0.0	0.3	0.3	3.0
Uruguay	13.1	12.1	1.0	2.6	0.0	0.0	0.3	0.2	1.8	1.3
Uzbekistan	35.1	8.7	26.4	9.4	75.4	0.0	0.0	7.1	1.1	–47.9
Venezuela, RB	40.5	12.0	28.5	4.4	37.9	1.0	0.0	0.8	0.0	–6.9
Vietnam	34.4	9.2	25.3	2.8	17.5	0.0	0.5	1.1	0.6	8.5
West Bank and Gaza	11.6	8.8	2.8	..	0.0	0.0	..	..	..	..
Yemen, Rep.	35.4	10.2	25.2	..	52.3	0.0	0.0	0.9	0.8	..
Zambia	10.9	9.5	1.4	2.9	0.1	7.9	0.0	0.2	1.0	–4.9
Zimbabwe	2.9	8.1	–5.2	6.9	5.2	2.7	0.0	2.2	0.1	–8.6
World	**20.8 w**	**12.6 w**	**8.2 w**	**4.4 w**	**4.1 w**	**0.3 w**	**0.0 w**	**0.4 w**	**0.4 w**	**7.4 w**
Low income	28.1	9.1	19.0	3.3	9.8	0.7	0.6	1.1	0.7	9.5
Middle income	30.0	11.0	19.0	3.6	12.1	0.9	0.0	1.0	0.7	7.8
Lower middle income	35.0	10.7	24.3	2.9	10.4	1.0	0.0	1.1	0.9	13.7
Upper middle income	23.4	11.4	12.0	4.5	14.4	0.8	0.0	0.8	0.5	–0.1
Low & middle income	29.7	10.7	19.0	3.5	11.8	0.9	0.1	1.0	0.7	8.0
East Asia & Pacific	44.4	10.3	34.1	2.2	7.8	0.8	0.0	1.2	1.2	25.3
Europe & Central Asia	23.2	10.6	12.6	4.1	16.6	0.4	0.0	1.2	0.5	–2.0
Latin America & Carib.	22.9	12.0	10.9	4.4	8.9	1.7	0.0	0.4	0.5	3.7
Middle East & N. Africa	30.9	11.0	19.9	4.5	35.2	0.2	0.1	1.2	0.6	–13.0
South Asia	30.1	9.1	21.0	3.6	4.9	0.8	0.6	1.1	0.8	16.4
Sub-Saharan Africa	17.4	10.7	6.7	3.8	15.5	0.8	0.3	0.7	0.5	–7.3
High income	18.7	13.1	5.7	4.6	2.0	0.1	0.0	0.3	0.3	7.7
Europe EMU	20.7	13.9	6.8	4.6	0.2	0.0	0.0	0.2	0.2	10.8

a. World Bank estimate based on preliminary data. b. Adjusted net savings do not include particulate emission damage.

Toward a broader measure of savings

About the data

Adjusted net savings measure the change in value of a specified set of assets, excluding capital gains. If a country's net savings are positive and the accounting includes a sufficiently broad range of assets, economic theory suggests that the present value of social welfare is increasing. Conversely, persistently negative adjusted net savings indicate that an economy is on an unsustainable path.

The table provides a test to check the extent to which today's rents from a number of natural resources and changes in human capital are balanced by net savings, that is, this generation's bequest to future generations.

Adjusted net savings are derived from standard national accounting measures of gross savings by making four adjustments. First, estimates of capital consumption of produced assets are deducted to obtain net savings. Second, current public expenditures on education are added to net savings (in standard national accounting these expenditures are treated as consumption). Third, estimates of the depletion of a variety of natural resources are deducted to reflect the decline in asset values associated with their extraction and harvest. And fourth, deductions are made for damages from carbon dioxide and particulate emissions.

The exercise treats public education expenditures as an addition to savings effort. However, because of the wide variability in the effectiveness of government education expenditures, these figures cannot be construed as the value of investments in human capital. The reader should bear in mind that current expenditure of $1 on education does not necessarily yield $1 of human capital. The calculation should also consider private education expenditure, but data are not available for a large number of countries.

While extensive, the accounting of natural resource depletion and pollution costs still has some gaps. Key estimates missing on the resource side include the value of fossil water extracted from aquifers, net depletion of fish stocks, and depletion and degradation of soils. Important pollutants affecting human health and economic assets are excluded because no internationally comparable data are widely available on damage from ground-level ozone or from sulfur oxides.

Estimates of resource depletion are based on the calculation of unit resource rents. An economic rent represents an excess return to a given factor of production—in this case the returns from resource extraction or harvest are higher than the normal rate of return on capital. Natural resources give rise to rents because they are not produced; in contrast, for produced goods and services competitive forces will expand supply until economic profits are driven to zero. For each type of resource and each country, unit resource rents are derived by taking the difference between world prices and the average unit extraction or harvest costs (including a "normal" return on capital). Unit rents are then multiplied by the physical quantity extracted or harvested in order to arrive at a depletion figure. This figure is one of a range of depletion estimates that are possible, depending on the assumptions made about future quantities, prices, and costs, and there is reason to believe that it is at the high end of the range. World prices are used in order to reflect the social opportunity cost of depleting minerals and energy.

A positive net depletion figure for forest resources implies that the harvest rate exceeds the rate of natural growth; this is not the same as deforestation, which represents a change in land use (see *Definitions* for table 3.4). In principle, there should be an addition to savings in countries where growth exceeds harvest, but empirical estimates suggest that most of this net growth is in forested areas that cannot be exploited economically at present. Because the depletion estimates reflect only timber values, they ignore all the external and nontimber benefits associated with standing forests.

Pollution damage from emissions of carbon dioxide is calculated as the marginal social cost per unit multiplied by the increase in the stock of carbon dioxide. The unit damage figure represents the present value of global damage to economic assets and to human welfare over the time the unit of pollution remains in the atmosphere.

Pollution damage from particulate emissions is estimated by valuing the human health effects from exposure to particulate matter pollution in urban areas. The estimates are calculated as willingness to pay to avoid mortality and morbidity from cardiopulmonary disease and lung cancer in adults and acute respiratory infections in children that is attributable to particulate emissions.

For a detailed note on methodology, see www.worldbank.org/data.

Definitions

• **Gross savings** are the difference between gross national income and public and private consumption, plus net current transfers. • **Consumption of fixed capital** represents the replacement value of capital used up in the process of production. • **Net savings** are gross savings minus the value of consumption of fixed capital. • **Education expenditure** refers to public current operating expenditures in education, including wages and salaries and excluding capital investments in buildings and equipment. • **Energy depletion** is the product of unit resource rents and the physical quantities of energy extracted. It covers coal, crude oil, and natural gas. • **Mineral depletion** is the product of unit resource rents and the physical quantities of minerals extracted. It refers to tin, gold, lead, zinc, iron, copper, nickel, silver, bauxite, and phosphate. • **Net forest depletion** is the product of unit resource rents and the excess of roundwood harvest over natural growth. • **Carbon dioxide damage** is estimated to be $20 per ton of carbon (the unit damage in 1995 U.S. dollars) times the number of tons of carbon emitted. • **Particulate emission damage** is the willingness to pay to avoid mortality and morbidity attributable to particulate emissions.• **Adjusted net savings** are net savings plus education expenditure and minus energy depletion, mineral depletion, net forest depletion, and carbon dioxide and particulate emissions damage.

Data sources

Gross savings are derived from the World Bank's national accounts data files, described in the Economy section. Consumption of fixed capital is from the United Nations Statistics Division's *National Accounts Statistics: Main Aggregates and Detailed Tables, 1997,* extrapolated to 2005. Data on education expenditure are from the United Nations Statistics Division's *Statistical Yearbook 1997* and from the United Nations Educational, Scientific, and Cultural Organization Institute for Statistics online database. Missing data are estimated. The wide range of data sources and estimation methods used to arrive at resource depletion estimates are described in Kunte and others' "Estimating National Wealth" (1998). The unit damage figure for carbon dioxide emissions is from Frankhauser's "Fractales, tissues urbains et reseaux de transport" (1994). The estimates of damage from particulate emissions are from Pandey and others' "The Human Costs of Air Pollution: New Estimates for Developing Countries" (2006). The conceptual underpinnings of the savings measure appear in Hamilton and Clemens' "Genuine Savings Rates in Developing Countries" (1999).

4 ECONOMY

A portrait of the global economy

A portrait of the global economy and the activity of more than 200 countries and territories that produce, trade, and consume the world's output—that is what the data in this section provide. Timely and reliable macroeconomic statistics are important for three reasons. First, they provide a measure of the wealth of economies, reflecting the welfare of their residents and prospects for future growth. Second, because the design of sound macroeconomic policies requires an understanding of historical patterns and trends, they provide guidance in shaping development policies. Third, they inform consumers, workers, investors, taxpayers, voters, and citizens on how their economy is managed so that they can make appropriate choices and exert control over their governments.

Developing economies grew faster over the last decade (1995–2005) than in the two previous decades and faster than high-income countries. World output in 2005 amounted to about $61 trillion, measured in purchasing power parities. This was a 45 percent increase over 1995, when the world output was $42.3 trillion (figure 4a). The share of developing economies in global output increased from 39 percent to 46 percent. The developing economies in the East Asia and the Pacific region grew the most, doubling their output and increasing their share of global output from 13 percent to 19 percent.

Further integration into world markets, better functioning internal markets, and rising demand for many commodities all contributed to the acceleration of growth in developing countries. Past periods of growth were often interrupted by financial or balance of payments crises. Indeed, from 1997 to 1998 some of the fastest growing economies experienced a major financial crisis, which started in Asia and spread to the transition economies of Europe and Central Asia. But recovery from this crisis has been widespread and durable. Developing economies are running lower fiscal and external deficits, accumulating larger reserves, and adopting more cautious monetary and financial policies. These policies make economies less vulnerable to shocks and less volatile, increasing the confidence of investors. The financial shocks of the period also revealed the importance of reliable, publicly available data for monitoring the actions of governments and private agents.

Developing economies increase their share of global output 4a

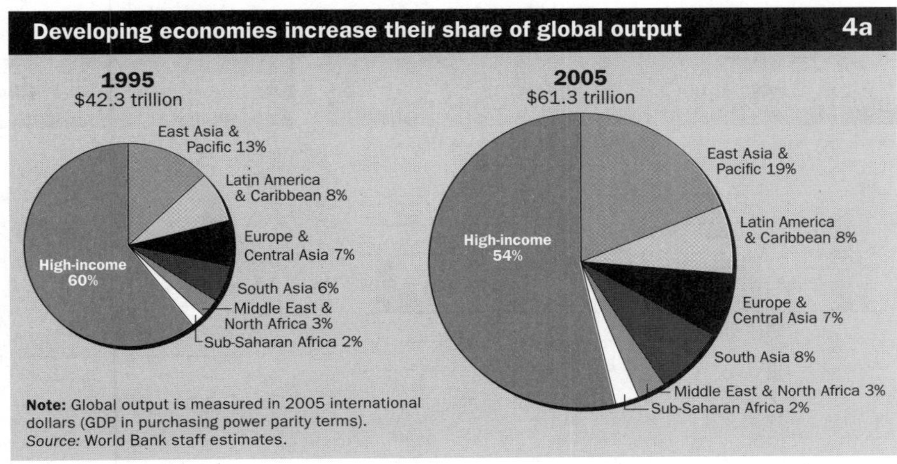

Note: Global output is measured in 2005 international dollars (GDP in purchasing power parity terms).
Source: World Bank staff estimates.

Long-term trends

Developing economies are expected to grow faster than high-income economies. The surprise is that they often don't. Labor surpluses and higher returns to physical capital in developing countries, along with ready access to technology already developed and amortized in high-income countries, are among the reasons that developing economies are expected to grow faster and, in the long run, close the gap with richer economies. But until recently only a few developing economies enjoyed sustained periods of high growth. And even fewer have reached the average growth of the high-income economies. Poverty traps, exclusion from global markets, and government and market failures are some of the reasons put forward to explain the failure to converge.

The last decade brought a change, however. The average growth of low- and middle-income economies surpassed that of high-income economies (figure 4b). The most successful are no longer counted as "developing." During this period 13 countries graduated from the World Bank's classification of low- and middle-income economies: Antigua and Barbuda, Bahrain, Greece, Guam, Isle of Man, Republic of Korea, Malta, New Caledonia, Northern Mariana Islands, Puerto Rico, Saudi Arabia, San Marino, and Slovenia. But these are only a few, and they account for less than 2 percent of the world's population. Growth is still uneven (figure 4c). Global and regional averages are driven by a few large countries, which carry large weights in the aggregate measures.

Better policies to achieve macroeconomic stability

The high growth experienced in the developing world was due in part to expanding trade (section 6) and a better investment climate (section 5). The very rapid industrialization of large countries such as China and India also benefited the exporters of primary commodities—oil, metals and minerals, and agricultural produce.

Macroeconomic stability also helped. Since the high inflation and the debt crises of the 1970s and 1980s, better fiscal, monetary, and exchange rate policies have brought inflation rates down in most developing countries. And the very rapid inflation in European and Central Asian countries after the collapse of the Soviet Union came back to earth after their transition from central planning to market economies (figure 4d).

Macroeconomic stability, one factor in a favorable investment climate, promotes economic growth (figure 4e). But low inflation does not always lead to high economic growth. In general, developed economies have lower inflation and economic growth rates. The median inflation rate was below 10 percent in all developing regions, well below the median of around 15 percent or higher in 1990 in three regions.

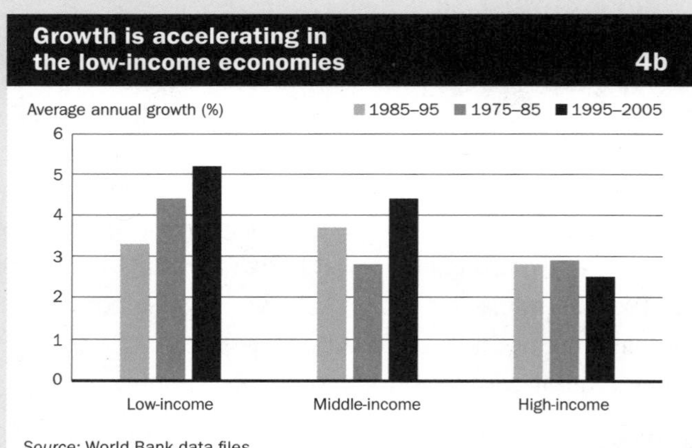

Growth is accelerating in the low-income economies **4b**

Source: World Bank data files.

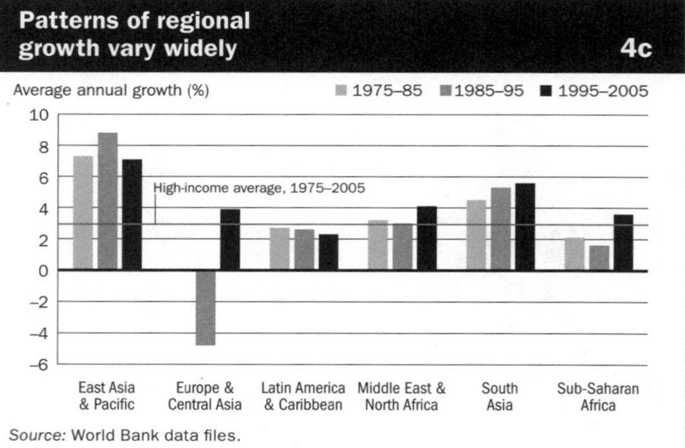

Patterns of regional growth vary widely **4c**

Source: World Bank data files.

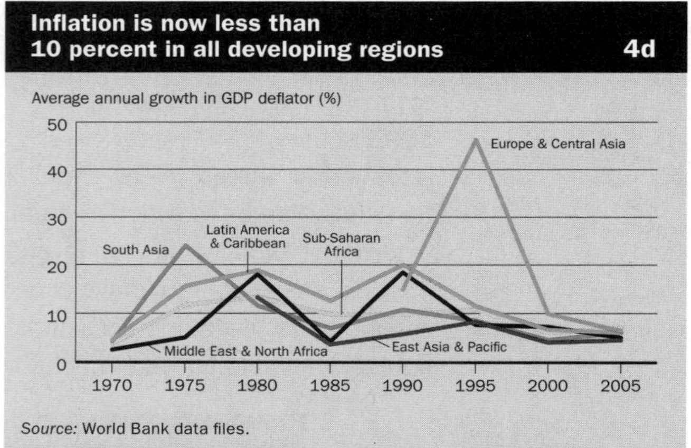

Inflation is now less than 10 percent in all developing regions **4d**

Source: World Bank data files.

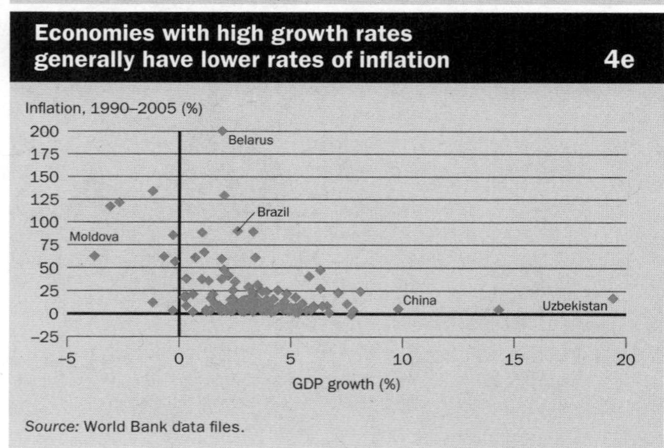

Economies with high growth rates generally have lower rates of inflation **4e**

Source: World Bank data files.

Rising reserves

Trade surpluses and growing workers' remittances have allowed many developing countries to accumulate large holdings of reserve assets over the past five years. One motive may be the desire to maintain larger precautionary reserves to protect against financial and balance of payments crises. Indeed, the globalization of financial transactions may have made countries with open capital accounts more vulnerable.

China, India, and the Russian Federation are now among the top 10 economies with the largest reserves holdings (table 4f). Together they accounted for 25 percent of the world reserves in 2005. In contrast, the United States holds only 4 percent of the world reserves. With one exception in 1991, the current account deficit of the United States increased steadily from around $12 billion in 1982 to $792 billion in 2005. The U.S. current account deficit is financed largely by China's current account surplus and growing investments by major oil exporters.

Large reserve holdings also make economies less vulnerable to debt crises, reassuring lenders and lowering interest rates. Economies with large reserves are less likely to require assistance from lenders of last resort, such as the World Bank or International Monetary Fund (IMF). Since 1995 the ratio of reserves to external debt has increased for many economies (figure 4g).

Top 10 economies with largest reserves **4f**

Economy	International reserves $ billions 2004	2005	Share of world total (%)	Increase over 2004 (%)	Reserves (months of import coverage)
Japan	844.7	846.9	18	0.3	16
China	622.9	831.4	18	33.5	14
Taiwan, China	247.7	260.3	6	5.1	14
Korea, Rep.	199.2	210.6	5	5.7	8
United States	190.5	188.3	4	–1.2	1
Russian Federation	126.3	182.3	4	44.4	11
India	131.6	137.8	3	4.7	12
Hong Kong, China	123.6	124.3	3	0.6	4
Singapore	112.2	115.8	3	3.2	5
Germany	97.2	101.7	2	4.6	1

Source: International Monetary Fund and World Bank data files.

More reserves to cover debt **4g**

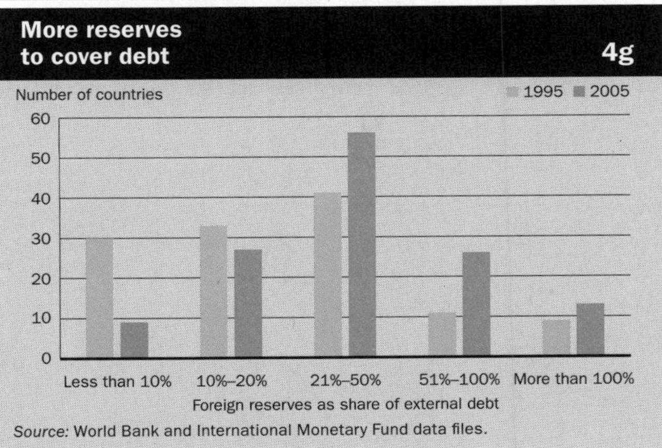

Source: World Bank and International Monetary Fund data files.

External public debt relief

Improvements in macroeconomic management of the poorest countries have also paved the way for more extensive debt relief.

Since 1996 developing countries have benefited from debt writeoffs by official donors and will continue to do so. It makes sense to relieve debt when the causes of excessive indebtedness are being tackled at their roots and when the benefits of debt reduction are directed toward more effective poverty reduction programs.

Making debt sustainable for poor countries is one of the Millennium Development Goals. Debt can bridge financing gaps and meet investment needs for projects with high social returns. But when unsustainable, it obliges countries to undertake policies that might be disruptive and harmful for growth and welfare, such as default, large fiscal adjustments, and devaluation.

In 2005 the external debt of developing countries amounted to $2,730 billion, and related debt service (principal and interest) to $513 billion. The debt stock has been declining in most regions and, accordingly, debt service declined. The ratio of debt service to exports in 2005 was 13.8 percent, the lowest in the last 20 years. The ratio of total external debt to GDP declined from nearly 6.6 percent in 1999 to 5.4 percent in 2005.

The debt crises of the 1980s and 1990s were the result of excessive borrowing with overly optimistic expectations. But cyclical global recessions, declining agricultural commodity prices, and conflicts also left many poor countries unable to service their debt. Traditional debt relief, based on rescheduling and restructuring of payments, proved ineffective for them.

Special programs to address the problems of the poor countries with predominantly official creditors were started in 1996, when the World Bank and the IMF launched the Heavily Indebted Poor Countries (HIPC) Initiative. The initiative aims to provide permanent relief from unsustainable debt by redirecting the resources for debt service toward social expenditures aimed at poverty reduction. The initiative relieved $61 billion in total nominal debt service for 29 countries, and another 11 countries are eligible for additional debt relief.

The debt stock of the 29 HIPCs was reduced by 90 percent and their debt service by 2 percent between 1999 and 2005. And as a direct result of debt relief, public expenditures in education and health have increased by 3 percent in these countries.

The International Development Association (IDA), the IMF, and the African Development Fund have committed to cancel an additional debt stock of $49 billion for all HIPCs under the new Multilateral Debt Relief Initiative in 2006. IDA has since canceled $27 billion and the IMF $3 billion for 19 countries that have made progress in their economic and social reforms.

4.a

Recent economic performance

	Gross domestic product		Exports of goods and services		Imports of goods and services		GDP deflator		Current account balance		Total reserves[a]	
	average annual % growth		average annual % growth		average annual % growth		% growth		% of GDP		$ millions	months of import coverage
	2004	2005	2004	2005	2004	2005	2004	2005	2004	2005	2005	2005
Algeria	5.3	5.2	5.8	5.1	7.8	23.1	16.1	17.8	..	21.2	..	..
Argentina	9.2	8.0	13.5	11.6	20.1	12.3	8.8	9.3	3.2	3.0	..	..
Armenia	14.0	9.5	15.9	4.5	11.7	12.5	3.2	4.0	–3.9	–4.7	841	3.8
Azerbaijan	26.2	22.7	58.5	48.0	–0.6	20.1	10.3	17.7	1.3	–3.3	1,028	1.9
Bangladesh	6.0	6.7	15.6	15.7	19.1	14.1	5.1	5.2	–0.2	0.9	3,488	2.5
Bolivia	4.1	4.1	9.6	4.5	13.5	15.2	4.7	4.6	5.3	..	2,545	7.7
Bosnia and Herzegovina	5.0	5.7	20.8	12.0	13.2	3.9	1.6	–5.5	–21.7	–15.4	2,457	5.0
Botswana	6.2	4.2	22.0	4.6	5.2	2.4	8.8	8.4	14.2	10.8	6,335	13.5
Brazil	2.3	3.5	11.6	–3.1	9.5	–1.8	7.2	5.3	1.8	1.3	60,357	5.0
Bulgaria	5.5	5.6	7.2	11.8	14.6	8.9	3.8	5.2	–11.3	–12.5	10,253	4.6
Cameroon	2.0	3.5	–3.9	1.7	23.1	9.3	4.7	5.1	..	–1.2	131	0.3
Chile	6.3	5.0	6.1	4.8	20.4	8.9	4.8	3.7	0.6	3.9	..	..
China	10.2	10.4	24.3	14.6	11.4	16.5	3.9	3.6	7.2	5.6	1,046,465	13.6
Colombia	5.1	4.7	4.6	4.4	25.2	2.4	6.2	5.8	–1.6	–1.3	13,659	5.0
Congo, Dem. Rep.	5.9	6.5	14.3	2.4	20.0	5.3	21.5	7.9	0.0	–9.7	470	1.5
Congo, Rep.	9.2	5.7	14.9	4.2	16.4	6.5	7.2	–5.6	17.7	1.4	..	..
Costa Rica	5.9	6.5	12.6	5.6	11.7	6.2	11.1	11.5	–4.8	–4.9	2,682	2.5
Côte d'Ivoire	1.8	1.9	1.5	9.0	7.3	2.9	3.6	3.3	–0.1	1.8	..	..
Croatia	4.3	4.6	4.6	5.2	3.5	5.0	3.2	2.9	–6.7	–6.8	10,101	4.8
Dominican Republic	9.3	9.0	6.1	–8.2	14.2	11.3	4.2	8.6	–1.7	–2.2	2,325	1.9
Ecuador	4.7	4.5	7.4	8.5	13.5	17.6	6.7	7.0	–0.2	0.8	3,923	2.9
Egypt, Arab Rep.	4.9	5.8	22.5	14.9	23.8	21.2	5.4	4.5	2.4	1.7	26,660	8.4
El Salvador	2.8	3.8	0.4	4.4	0.8	8.4	4.4	3.9	–4.6	–4.6	1,922	2.5
Gabon	2.2	2.7	–5.8	–8.0	1.8	0.2	8.9	2.3	..	1.8	..	..
Ghana	5.9	6.0	9.3	10.3	6.7	13.7	15.0	14.8	–7.6	–5.1	2,084	3.0
Honduras	4.0	5.1	6.0	8.9	9.3	15.7	10.3	5.5	–1.0	–0.6	2,776	4.9
India	9.2	8.3	21.9	5.2	22.1	1.1	4.4	4.4	..	–0.9	172,635	8.2
Indonesia	5.6	5.5	8.6	8.9	12.3	8.6	13.7	14.5	0.3	..	53,223	5.2
Iran, Islamic Rep.	4.4	5.8	–13.2	0.8	–13.2	13.7	16.0	23.5	..	5.6	47,130	9.0
Jamaica	1.8	2.7	..	..	..	..	9.6	13.0	–11.3	–9.6	1,728	2.7
Jordan	7.3	6.3	5.8	0.7	21.2	4.9	4.0	5.8	–18.2	–22.8	6,192	5.3
Kazakhstan	9.7	9.0	1.4	10.3	13.3	2.9	17.9	7.0	–1.3	7.0	11,800	4.2
Kenya	5.8	5.7	4.7	6.4	14.3	1.5	4.2	4.0	–2.6	–7.6	2,654	4.3
Lesotho	1.2	2.8	–2.6	2.4	–1.5	7.8	3.2	5.0	–3.0	1.7	455	3.9

	Gross domestic product		Exports of goods and services		Imports of goods and services		GDP deflator		Current account balance		Total reserves[a]	
	average annual % growth		average annual % growth		average annual % growth		% growth		% of GDP		$ millions	months of import coverage
	2004	2005	2004	2005	2004	2005	2004	2005	2004	2005	2005	2005
Macedonia, FYR	4.0	3.2	8.5	13.7	2.4	18.2	3.0	3.4	–1.4	–1.2	1,725	4.6
Malawi	2.6	9.2	20.2	2.1	11.0	–1.5	15.5	10.8	..	–16.1	..	..
Malaysia	5.2	5.5	8.6	5.5	8.0	5.0	4.6	1.4	15.3	15.6	86,827	6.6
Mauritius	4.6	3.5	5.7	7.0	4.8	7.7	4.8	4.1	–5.4	–5.2	1,244	3.3
Mexico	3.0	4.5	6.9	5.7	8.7	8.5	5.4	5.3	–0.6	–0.3	73,465	3.1
Moldova	7.1	3.0	20.2	–0.1	21.2	–2.0	7.3	11.9	–8.3	–21.2	603	2.1
Morocco	1.7	7.0	9.8	5.9	5.7	4.8	1.4	2.7	2.2	1.2	18,226	8.1
Nicaragua	4.0	3.7	5.3	13.9	6.2	9.8	10.3	10.7	–16.3	–15.6	899	2.8
Nigeria	6.9	6.3	–1.8	4.4	21.3	16.0	26.9	12.8	24.5	18.1	..	..
Pakistan	7.8	6.3	7.6	13.4	44.1	20.0	9.8	8.2	–3.1	–3.9	11,374	3.8
Panama	6.4	7.0	13.8	7.3	14.2	7.0	2.4	2.4	–5.1	–4.6	1,358	1.2
Paraguay	2.9	3.5	2.7	14.2	4.6	33.3	5.9	6.0	–0.3	–4.5	1,370	2.7
Peru	6.4	6.6	14.9	5.4	10.6	9.9	3.3	8.6	1.3	1.1	17,627	8.1
Philippines	5.0	5.4	4.2	8.5	2.4	6.1	6.2	6.0	2.4	2.3	21,800	4.1
Poland	3.4	5.0	8.1	5.7	4.9	6.9	2.8	2.0	–1.7	–1.5	39,656	3.5
Romania	4.1	5.8	4.2	10.3	3.7	8.6	12.0	8.5	–8.6	–11.4	20,730	4.9
Russian Federation	6.4	6.5	6.3	4.3	17.3	20.2	19.7	14.5	10.9	10.8	276,803	14.0
Senegal	5.1	5.1	3.1	–15.5	1.9	–21.2	2.6	2.3	..	–7.4	1,188	3.7
Serbia and Montenegro	4.7	6.1	10.0	41.7	–4.0	28.9	17.3	5.4	..	–9.6	6,149	4.5
Slovak Republic	6.0	6.7	10.9	10.2	11.2	11.6	2.4	6.3	..	–7.2	18,750	4.7
South Africa	4.9	4.2	6.7	5.2	10.1	9.4	4.7	5.8	–3.8	–4.8	22,218	3.0
Sri Lanka	5.3	6.0	7.5	5.4	8.7	5.4	10.4	7.8	–2.8	–5.7	2,731	2.9
Swaziland	1.8	2.3	6.0	6.0	6.3	5.5	4.9	4.0	1.7	–11.5	382	1.6
Syrian Arab Republic	5.1	4.0	3.9	–1.5	17.9	1.9	5.8	4.0	–4.0	–2.5	3,064	2.8
Thailand	4.5	4.5	4.3	8.4	9.4	0.6	4.6	5.5	–2.1	1.4	56,681	4.6
Tunisia	4.2	5.3	3.2	3.9	1.1	1.4	1.9	2.4	–1.1	–1.2	6,824	4.5
Turkey	7.4	5.0	8.6	14.3	11.6	5.5	5.4	9.6	–6.4	–6.8	..	..
Ukraine	2.6	5.2	–11.2	–1.3	2.1	8.4	20.0	12.3	3.1	0.3	16,934	4.2
Uruguay	6.6	5.0	16.8	8.5	8.8	15.0	1.7	5.1	..	–3.5	3,329	5.7
Uzbekistan	7.0	6.0	7.1	2.0	7.3	1.2	15.9	22.0	..	5.2	2,460	6.2
Venezuela, RB	9.3	8.5	5.2	8.5	30.0	28.2	29.1	15.0	18.1	17.2	31,033	8.3
Zambia	5.2	6.0	12.3	6.3	20.6	11.0	19.0	14.3	..	–10.4	350	0.9
Zimbabwe	–6.5	–5.1	–4.3	3.5	–3.1	3.6	237.7	1,216.0	..	–8.0	..	..

Note: Data for 2006 are the latest preliminary estimates and may differ from those in earlier World Bank publications.
a. International reserves including gold valued at the London gold price.
Source: World Bank staff estimates.

4.1 Growth of output

	Gross domestic product		Agriculture		Industry		Manufacturing		Services	
	average annual % growth		average annual % growth		average annual % growth		average annual % growth		average annual % growth	
	1990–2000	2000–05	1990–2000	2000–05	1990–2000	2000–05	1990–2000	2000–05	1990–2000	2000–05
Afghanistan	..	12.0	..	0.4	..	21.1	..	13.8	..	21.9
Albania	3.5	5.3	4.3	1.4	–0.5	3.4	..	–0.2	6.9	8.3
Algeria	1.9	5.2	3.6	7.3	1.8	4.4	–2.1	2.4	1.8	5.2
Angola[a]	1.6	9.9	–1.4	14.1	4.4	10.5	–0.3	13.4	–2.2	6.7
Argentina	4.3	2.2	3.5	2.5	3.8	3.8	2.7	3.7	4.5	0.9
Armenia	–1.9	12.4	0.5	8.4	–7.8	16.8	–4.3	9.2	6.4	12.2
Australia	4.0	3.2	3.8	–0.5	2.8	3.0	2.1	1.6	4.5	3.6
Austria	2.4	1.5	1.6	–0.2	2.7	2.1	2.7	1.4	2.3	1.4
Azerbaijan	–6.3	12.7	–2.1	6.6	–0.8	16.7	–12.0	9.1	–2.3	8.8
Bangladesh	4.8	5.4	2.9	2.5	7.3	7.3	7.2	6.7	4.5	5.6
Belarus	–1.7	7.5	–4.0	6.0	–1.8	11.1	–0.7	11.5	–0.4	5.3
Belgium	2.1	1.5	2.9	–0.1	1.6	0.4	2.5	0.4	1.9	1.9
Benin[a]	4.8	4.0	5.8	4.6	4.1	3.8	5.8	2.7	4.2	3.5
Bolivia	4.0	3.0	2.9	3.6	4.1	3.2	3.8	3.2	4.3	2.1
Bosnia and Herzegovina	..	5.0	..	1.5	..	4.9	..	5.6	..	5.2
Botswana	6.0	5.9	–1.2	2.1	5.8	5.7	4.4	0.8	7.8	5.4
Brazil	2.9	2.2	3.3	4.5	2.6	2.3	1.6	1.8	3.0	1.7
Bulgaria	–1.8	5.0	3.0	0.4	–5.0	5.7	..	8.7	–5.2	5.1
Burkina Faso[a]	4.0	5.1	4.2	5.8	2.3	2.7	1.6	2.2	4.5	12.0
Burundi	–2.9	2.2	–1.9	–1.5	–4.3	–6.2	–8.7	..	–2.8	10.4
Cambodia	7.1	8.9	3.9	5.7	14.3	14.2	18.6	14.1	7.1	8.2
Cameroon	1.7	3.7	5.5	3.9	–0.9	3.9	1.4	5.3	0.2	7.5
Canada	3.1	2.5	1.1	0.9	3.2	1.6	4.5	0.2	3.0	3.0
Central African Republic	2.0	–1.4	3.8	2.6	0.7	4.2	–0.2	4.0	–0.3	–12.9
Chad	2.2	14.5	4.9	2.2	0.6	45.9	..	..	0.9	8.4
Chile	6.6	4.3	2.2	6.0	5.6	3.8	4.4	3.7	6.9	4.0
China[a,b]	10.6	9.6	4.1	3.9	13.7	10.9	12.7	11.1	10.2	10.0
Hong Kong, China	4.1	4.3	..	–0.2	..	–3.4	..	–5.7	..	5.7
Colombia	2.8	3.5	–2.2	1.9	1.8	4.9	–2.2	4.1	4.2	2.8
Congo, Dem. Rep.	–4.9	4.4	1.4	0.4	–8.0	9.0	–8.7	4.8	–12.3	5.5
Congo, Rep.[a]	1.2	3.9	1.0	5.6	3.2	1.4	–3.0	12.7	–0.6	4.2
Costa Rica	5.3	4.2	4.1	1.7	6.2	3.6	6.8	3.3	4.7	5.4
Côte d'Ivoire[a]	3.2	–0.1	3.5	0.9	6.3	–1.8	5.5	–3.3	2.0	0.2
Croatia	0.6	4.7	–2.6	–0.2	–2.4	5.3	–3.5	4.5	1.9	5.1
Cuba[a]	4.2	3.4	..	..	..	..	..	..	..	..
Czech Republic	1.1	3.5	0.0	4.4	0.2	3.6	4.3	4.7	1.2	3.6
Denmark	2.7	1.2	4.6	–0.1	2.5	–0.9	2.2	–2.5	2.7	1.8
Dominican Republic[a]	6.0	2.8	3.9	2.8	7.0	–0.6	4.9	0.7	6.0	4.6
Ecuador[a]	1.9	5.1	–1.7	4.4	2.6	6.2	1.5	4.5	2.4	4.6
Egypt, Arab Rep.	4.4	3.7	3.1	3.4	5.1	4.3	6.4	2.8	4.0	3.4
El Salvador	4.8	2.2	1.2	1.4	5.1	2.1	5.2	2.2	4.0	2.4
Eritrea	5.7	3.5	1.5	0.8	15.0	4.1	10.6	6.6	5.7	3.5
Estonia	0.2	7.5	–3.4	–1.7	–3.3	10.5	5.9	11.5	3.1	6.6
Ethiopia	3.5	4.2	2.2	3.1	4.0	5.8	3.8	2.4	4.5	3.9
Finland	2.5	2.4	1.8	–0.2	3.9	1.7	7.6	1.9	2.2	2.6
France	1.9	1.5	2.0	–0.9	1.0	1.4	..	1.2	2.2	1.6
Gabon[a]	2.8	1.7	–1.4	4.9	2.5	2.8	0.6	..	3.9	0.0
Gambia, The	3.0	3.7	3.3	1.4	1.0	5.9	0.9	4.2	3.7	5.4
Georgia	–7.1	7.4	–11.0	3.1	–8.1	12.6	–7.0	6.3	–0.3	7.8
Germany	1.8	0.7	–0.1	1.6	–0.1	0.6	0.2	1.0	2.9	1.0
Ghana[a]	4.3	5.1	3.4	5.0	2.6	4.6	–3.2	1.4	5.7	5.3
Greece	2.2	4.4	0.5	–2.0	1.0	3.3	2.0	2.2	2.6	4.7
Guatemala[a]	4.2	2.5	2.8	2.6	4.3	1.5	2.8	1.5	4.7	2.8
Guinea	4.4	2.9	4.6	4.0	4.7	3.1	4.1	1.9	3.6	1.9
Guinea-Bissau	1.2	–0.5	3.9	4.0	–3.1	3.6	–2.0	3.5	–0.6	0.7
Haiti	–1.5	–0.5	..	..	..	..	..	..	..	..

4.1 Growth of output

	Gross domestic product		Agriculture		Industry		Manufacturing		Services	
	average annual % growth		average annual % growth		average annual % growth		average annual % growth		average annual % growth	
	1990–2000	2000–05	1990–2000	2000–05	1990–2000	2000–05	1990–2000	2000–05	1990–2000	2000–05
Honduras	3.2	3.6	2.2	3.4	3.6	3.6	4.0	4.2	3.8	4.3
Hungary	1.6	4.1	–2.4	7.2	3.5	3.8	*8.2*	4.7	1.2	3.6
India	6.0	7.0	3.0	2.5	6.3	7.5	7.0	6.9	8.0	8.5
Indonesia[a]	4.2	4.7	2.0	3.4	5.2	3.9	6.7	5.2	4.0	6.2
Iran, Islamic Rep.	3.1	5.8	3.2	5.5	2.6	7.0	5.1	10.2	3.8	5.1
Iraq	..	*–11.4*	..	*–3.6*	..	*–17.0*	..	*–12.8*	..	*5.9*
Ireland	7.5	5.2	..	..	..	..	..	..	..	..
Israel	5.3	1.9	..	..	..	..	..	..	..	..
Italy	1.5	0.6	2.1	0.2	0.8	–0.2	1.4	–1.2	1.7	0.9
Jamaica	1.8	1.8	–0.3	–2.7	–1.0	2.0	–2.2	0.1	2.3	1.7
Japan	1.1	1.4	–1.6	*–0.9*	–0.3	*0.0*	..	*0.8*	1.9	*1.7*
Jordan	5.0	6.1	–3.0	12.2	5.2	9.3	5.6	11.6	5.0	4.9
Kazakhstan	–4.1	10.1	–8.0	4.6	*0.6*	11.3	*2.7*	9.2	*0.3*	10.8
Kenya	2.2	3.4	1.9	2.8	1.2	4.5	1.3	3.3	3.2	3.1
Korea, Dem. Rep.	..	..	..	..	..	..	..	..	..	..
Korea, Rep.	5.8	4.6	1.6	–0.1	6.0	6.3	7.3	7.0	5.6	3.7
Kuwait[a]	*4.9*	7.3	*1.0*	*15.1*	*0.3*	*1.9*	*–0.1*	*2.5*	*3.5*	*10.2*
Kyrgyz Republic	–4.1	4.0	1.5	2.8	–10.3	0.6	–7.5	0.9	–4.9	7.3
Lao PDR	6.5	6.2	4.8	2.8	11.1	12.1	11.7	10.4	6.6	6.7
Latvia	–1.5	7.9	–5.5	2.8	–8.5	8.4	–7.6	7.4	2.7	8.1
Lebanon	6.0	4.0	*2.3*	1.8	*–0.9*	4.5	*–5.0*	5.1	*3.2*	4.3
Lesotho	3.9	2.9	2.0	–1.1	5.0	3.7	6.6	4.1	4.4	3.4
Liberia[a]	4.1	–6.8	..	..	..	..	..	..	..	..
Libya	..	5.3	..	..	..	..	..	..	..	..
Lithuania	–2.7	7.8	*–0.8*	3.0	*3.3*	10.5	*5.7*	10.2	5.5	7.0
Macedonia, FYR	–0.8	1.7	0.2	0.9	–2.3	1.3	–5.3	1.2	0.5	2.2
Madagascar	2.0	2.0	1.9	1.7	2.4	1.1	2.0	2.7	2.3	1.7
Malawi	3.7	3.4	8.6	0.5	2.0	3.8	0.5	1.7	1.6	3.2
Malaysia[a]	7.0	4.8	0.3	3.4	8.6	4.6	9.5	5.2	7.3	5.3
Mali	4.1	5.9	2.6	4.9	6.4	5.1	–1.4	5.7	3.0	6.2
Mauritania	2.9	4.0	–0.2	–2.4	3.4	3.1	5.8	–4.1	4.9	6.8
Mauritius	5.2	4.0	–0.5	2.0	5.5	1.9	5.3	0.6	6.4	5.9
Mexico	3.1	1.9	1.5	1.9	3.8	0.6	4.3	0.0	2.9	2.4
Moldova	–9.6	7.1	*–11.2*	1.4	*–13.6*	8.9	*–7.1*	7.7	*0.7*	6.4
Mongolia	2.7	5.8	3.7	0.1	2.3	7.5	*–9.7*	5.5	0.2	7.8
Morocco[a]	2.3	4.3	–0.8	6.9	3.2	4.0	2.7	3.4	2.8	3.8
Mozambique	5.9	8.6	4.9	8.3	12.8	10.3	*10.2*	14.5	3.6	7.8
Myanmar[a]	6.9	9.2	5.7	..	10.5	..	7.9	..	7.2	..
Namibia	4.0	4.6	3.8	1.4	2.4	7.3	2.6	6.2	4.5	4.3
Nepal	4.9	2.8	2.4	3.2	7.2	1.1	8.9	–0.6	6.4	2.8
Netherlands	2.9	0.7	2.0	1.3	1.5	–0.1	..	..	3.3	1.1
New Zealand	3.2	3.7	2.9	*0.3*	2.4	*4.0*	2.2	*3.1*	3.5	*4.3*
Nicaragua	3.7	3.0	*4.7*	2.3	*5.5*	3.9	*5.3*	4.5	*5.2*	3.7
Niger[a]	2.4	3.7	3.0	*6.4*	2.0	*3.1*	2.6	*3.9*	1.9	*4.3*
Nigeria	2.5	5.9	3.4	5.8	1.0	5.5	1.1	8.8	3.3	6.3
Norway	4.0	2.0	2.6	2.1	3.8	0.7	1.6	*0.7*	4.0	2.5
Oman[a]	4.5	*3.0*	5.0	*2.2*	3.9	*–0.5*	6.0	*9.3*	5.0	5.9
Pakistan	3.8	4.8	4.4	2.3	4.1	6.5	3.8	9.1	4.4	5.4
Panama	4.7	4.3	3.1	4.8	6.0	1.6	2.7	–1.4	4.5	4.8
Papua New Guinea	4.3	1.6	..	*2.2*	..	*–3.6*	..	*–1.1*	..	*1.4*
Paraguay[a]	2.2	2.6	3.3	5.5	0.6	1.3	1.4	0.9	2.5	1.9
Peru	4.7	4.3	5.5	3.1	5.4	5.3	3.8	4.9	4.0	3.9
Philippines[a]	3.3	4.7	1.7	3.9	3.5	3.3	3.0	4.3	4.0	6.0
Poland	4.7	3.2	*0.5*	3.3	*7.1*	3.2	*9.9*	6.7	*5.1*	3.0
Portugal	2.8	0.5	–0.3	–1.8	3.1	–1.1	*3.6*	*0.0*	2.4	1.4
Puerto Rico[a]	4.2	..	..	..	..	..	..	..	..	..

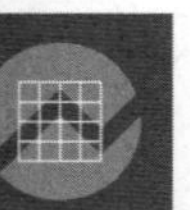

4.1 Growth of output

	Gross domestic product		Agriculture		Industry		Manufacturing		Services	
	average annual % growth		average annual % growth		average annual % growth		average annual % growth		average annual % growth	
	1990–2000	2000–05	1990–2000	2000–05	1990–2000	2000–05	1990–2000	2000–05	1990–2000	2000–05
Romania	–0.6	5.8	–1.9	8.8	–1.2	5.6	..	..	0.9	5.5
Russian Federation	–4.7	6.2	–4.9	4.5	–7.1	6.1	..	..	–1.7	6.4
Rwanda[a]	–0.3	5.1	2.6	4.3	–3.7	5.6	–6.0	1.4	–1.2	5.8
Saudi Arabia[a]	2.1	4.2	1.6	*1.1*	2.2	*3.6*	5.6	*5.5*	2.2	*3.6*
Senegal[a]	3.2	4.7	2.9	1.8	4.1	6.5	3.1	5.2	3.0	5.1
Serbia and Montenegro	*1.4*	5.1	..	–2.9	..	1.9	..	..	..	7.3
Sierra Leone	–5.1	13.7	–13.0	..	–4.5	..	6.1	..	–2.9	..
Singapore	7.6	4.2	–1.8	0.9	7.7	3.2	7.0	5.2	7.8	4.8
Slovak Republic[a]	1.9	4.9	*2.7*	4.7	*2.4*	6.4	*6.6*	6.7	*5.7*	4.1
Slovenia	2.7	3.4	0.0	0.7	1.3	3.6	1.1	4.2	3.4	3.8
Somalia	..	..	..	..	..	..	..	..	..	..
South Africa	2.1	3.7	1.0	0.8	1.1	2.7	1.6	2.3	2.7	4.4
Spain	2.7	3.1	3.1	–0.5	2.3	2.6	..	*1.0*	2.7	3.3
Sri Lanka	5.3	4.2	1.8	0.7	6.9	3.3	8.1	2.9	5.7	5.8
Sudan	5.4	6.1	9.2	..	5.8	..	4.4	..	2.7	..
Swaziland	3.3	2.3	1.2	0.3	3.7	1.9	2.8	1.8	3.6	3.1
Sweden	2.1	2.3	–1.1	0.2	4.2	3.7	*8.6*	*2.7*	1.9	1.7
Switzerland	1.0	0.9	–2.0	*–5.3*	0.4	*1.1*	1.2	*0.9*	1.2	*0.2*
Syrian Arab Republic	5.1	3.7	6.0	3.7	9.2	–0.7	..	29.6	1.5	5.9
Tajikistan	–10.4	9.6	–6.8	10.3	–10.8	11.6	–10.0	10.3	–12.7	7.0
Tanzania[c]	2.9	6.9	3.2	5.1	3.1	9.7	2.7	8.0	2.7	6.0
Thailand[a]	4.2	5.4	1.0	1.9	5.7	6.9	6.9	7.2	3.7	4.5
Togo[a]	3.5	2.7	4.0	2.8	1.8	8.1	1.8	7.5	3.9	–0.1
Trinidad and Tobago	3.1	8.3	2.7	–7.3	3.2	12.7	4.9	6.7	3.2	3.8
Tunisia[a]	4.7	4.5	2.3	3.6	4.6	3.1	5.5	3.0	5.3	5.4
Turkey	3.8	5.2	1.4	1.4	4.1	4.6	4.9	5.9	4.0	5.1
Turkmenistan	–4.8	..	–5.7	..	–3.4	..	..	..	–5.4	..
Uganda	7.1	5.6	3.7	4.1	12.2	7.3	14.1	5.7	8.2	7.4
Ukraine	–9.3	8.0	–5.6	3.3	–12.9	9.4	–11.2	*14.0*	–8.1	7.7
United Arab Emirates	4.8	8.2	13.2	2.9	3.0	5.6	11.9	8.5	7.2	9.3
United Kingdom	2.7	2.4	–0.2	0.7	1.5	–0.1	..	*–0.9*	3.4	3.1
United States	3.5	2.6	3.7	*0.2*	3.7	*0.7*	..	*1.3*	3.4	*2.7*
Uruguay	3.4	0.9	2.8	5.6	1.1	0.7	–0.1	2.3	3.7	–0.5
Uzbekistan	–0.2	5.3	0.5	6.9	–3.4	3.9	*0.7*	1.8	0.4	5.1
Venezuela, RB	1.6	1.3	1.2	4.7	1.2	–0.2	4.5	0.8	–0.1	3.1
Vietnam[a]	7.9	7.5	4.3	3.8	11.9	10.2	11.2	11.5	7.5	6.9
West Bank and Gaza[a]	*7.3*	–0.9	..	..	..	..	..	..	..	..
Yemen, Rep.	6.0	3.3	5.6	0.6	8.2	0.0	5.7	2.8	5.0	6.5
Zambia	0.5	4.7	4.2	1.4	–4.2	9.6	0.8	5.3	2.5	4.0
Zimbabwe	2.1	–5.9	4.3	–8.5	0.4	–10.0	0.4	–12.0	2.9	–8.7
World	2.9 w	2.8 w	2.0 w	2.2 w	2.4 w	*2.0* w	.. w	*2.3* w	3.1 w	*2.7* w
Low income	4.8	6.1	3.2	3.0	4.9	6.9	5.9	6.9	6.0	7.2
Middle income	3.8	5.2	2.0	3.6	4.5	6.1	6.9	7.2	3.9	4.9
Lower middle income	5.3	6.3	2.7	3.8	7.1	7.7	8.5	9.4	5.0	6.2
Upper middle income	2.1	3.5	0.3	3.1	1.4	3.2	4.4	3.1	2.8	3.5
Low & middle income	3.9	5.3	2.4	3.4	4.6	6.2	6.8	7.2	4.1	5.2
East Asia & Pacific	8.5	8.4	3.4	3.7	11.0	9.4	10.8	9.8	8.1	8.7
Europe & Central Asia	–0.7	5.4	–1.7	3.5	–2.9	5.6	..	..	0.9	5.2
Latin America & Carib.	3.3	2.3	2.0	3.3	3.2	2.2	3.4	1.7	3.3	2.2
Middle East & N. Africa	3.8	4.1	2.9	4.5	4.1	2.6	3.8	6.4	3.4	4.5
South Asia	5.6	6.5	3.1	2.4	6.1	7.2	6.6	7.0	7.1	7.8
Sub-Saharan Africa	2.5	4.3	3.3	3.8	1.9	4.7	1.9	2.6	2.5	4.3
High income	2.7	2.2	1.3	*–0.1*	1.8	*0.9*	..	*1.1*	2.9	*2.3*
Europe EMU	2.1	1.3	1.7	–0.1	0.9	0.9	*2.0*	*0.6*	2.4	1.5

a. Components are at producer prices. b. China has revised its national accounts data from 1993 onwards. Data before 1993 are linked to the revised data on the basis of earlier growth rates. c. Data cover mainland Tanzania only.

Growth of output 4.1

About the data

An economy's growth is measured by the change in the volume of its output or in the real incomes of its residents. The 1993 United Nations System of National Accounts (1993 SNA) offers three plausible indicators for calculating growth: the volume of gross domestic product (GDP), real gross domestic income, and real gross national income. The volume of GDP is the sum of value added, measured at constant prices, by households, government, and industries operating in the economy.

Each industry's contribution to growth in the economy's output is measured by growth in the industry's value added. In principle, value added in constant prices can be estimated by measuring the quantity of goods and services produced in a period, valuing them at an agreed set of base year prices, and subtracting the cost of intermediate inputs, also in constant prices. This double-deflation method, recommended by the 1993 SNA and its predecessors, requires detailed information on the structure of prices of inputs and outputs.

In many industries, however, value added is extrapolated from the base year using single volume indexes of outputs or, more rarely, inputs. Particularly in the services industries, including most of government, value added in constant prices is often imputed from labor inputs, such as real wages or number of employees. In the absence of well-defined measures of output, measuring the growth of services remains difficult.

Moreover, technical progress can lead to improvements in production processes and in the quality of goods and services that, if not properly accounted for, can distort measures of value added and thus of growth. When inputs are used to estimate output, as is the case for nonmarket services, unmeasured technical progress leads to underestimates of the volume of output. Similarly, unmeasured improvements in the quality of goods and services produced lead to underestimates of the value of output and value added. The result can be underestimates of growth and productivity improvement and overestimates of inflation. These issues are highly complex, and only a few high-income countries have attempted to introduce any GDP adjustments for these factors.

Informal economic activities pose a particular measurement problem, especially in developing countries, where much economic activity may go unrecorded. Obtaining a complete picture of the economy requires estimating household outputs produced for home use, sales in informal markets, barter exchanges, and illicit or deliberately unreported activities. The consistency and completeness of such estimates depend on the skill and methods of the compiling statisticians and the resources available to them.

Rebasing national accounts

When countries rebase their national accounts, they update the weights assigned to various components to better reflect the current pattern of production or uses of output. The new base year should represent normal operation of the economy—that is, it should be a year without major shocks or distortions. Some developing countries have not rebased their national accounts for many years. Using an old base year can be misleading because implicit price and volume weights become progressively less relevant and useful.

To obtain comparable series of constant price data, the World Bank rescales GDP and value added by industrial origin to a common reference year. This year's *World Development Indicators* continues to use 2000 as the reference year. Because rescaling changes the implicit weights used in forming regional and income group aggregates, aggregate growth rates in this year's *World Development Indicators* are not comparable with those from earlier publications with different base years.

Rescaling may result in a discrepancy between the rescaled GDP and the sum of the rescaled components. Because allocating the discrepancy would cause distortions in the growth rates, the discrepancy is left unallocated. As a result, the weighted average of the growth rates of the components generally will not equal the GDP growth rate.

Computing growth rates

Growth rates of GDP and its components are calculated using the least squares method and constant price data in the local currency. Constant price U.S. dollar series are used to calculate regional and income group growth rates. Local currency series are converted to constant price U.S. dollars using an exchange rate in the common reference year. The growth rates in the table are average annual compound growth rates. Methods of computing growth rates and the alternative conversion factor are described in *Statistical methods.*

Changes in the System of National Accounts

World Development Indicators adopted the terminology of the 1993 SNA in 2001. Although many countries continue to compile their national accounts according to the SNA version 3 (referred to as the 1968 SNA), more and more are adopting the 1993 SNA. Some low-income countries still use concepts from the even older 1953 SNA guidelines, including valuations such as factor cost, in describing major economic aggregates. Countries that use the 1993 SNA are identified in *Primary data documentation.*

Definitions

• **Gross domestic product (GDP)** at purchaser prices is the sum of gross value added by all resident producers in the economy plus any product taxes (less subsidies) not included in the valuation of output. It is calculated without deducting for depreciation of fabricated capital assets or for depletion and degradation of natural resources. Value added is the net output of an industry after adding up all outputs and subtracting intermediate inputs. The industrial origin of value added is determined by the International Standard Industrial Classification (ISIC) revision 3. • **Agriculture** corresponds to ISIC divisions 1–5 and includes forestry and fishing. • **Industry** covers mining, manufacturing (also reported separately), construction, electricity, water, and gas (ISIC divisions 10–45). • **Manufacturing** corresponds to industries belonging to ISIC divisions 15–37. • **Services** correspond to ISIC divisions 50–99. This sector is derived as a residual (from GDP less agriculture and industry) and may not properly reflect the sum of services output, including banking and financial services. For some countries it includes product taxes (minus subsidies) and may also include statistical discrepancies.

Data sources

National accounts data for most developing countries are collected from national statistical organizations and central banks by visiting and resident World Bank missions. Data for high-income economies come from data files of the Organisation for Economic Co-operation and Development (for information on the OECD's national accounts series, see its *Annual National Accounts for OECD Member Countries: Data from 1970 Onwards*). The World Bank rescales constant price data to a common reference year. The complete national accounts time series is available on the *World Development Indicators 2007* CD-ROM. The United Nations Statistics Division publishes detailed national accounts for UN member countries in *National Accounts Statistics: Main Aggregates and Detailed Tables* and publishes updates in the *Monthly Bulletin of Statistics.*

4.2 Structure of output

	Gross domestic product $ millions		Agriculture % of GDP		Industry % of GDP		Manufacturing % of GDP		Services % of GDP	
	1990	2005	1990	2005	1990	2005	1990	2005	1990	2005
Afghanistan	..	7,308	..	36	..	25	..	15	..	39
Albania	2,102	8,380	36	23	48	22	..	*12*	16	56
Algeria	62,045	102,256	11	9	48	62	11	6	41	30
Angola[a]	10,260	32,811	18	7	41	74	5	4	41	19
Argentina	141,352	183,193	8	9	36	36	27	23	56	55
Armenia	2,257	4,903	17	21	52	44	33	21	31	35
Australia	319,265	732,499	4	*3*	30	*27*	15	*12*	66	*70*
Austria	164,984	306,073	4	2	32	31	21	*20*	64	68
Azerbaijan	8,858	12,561	29	10	33	62	19	8	38	28
Bangladesh	30,129	60,034	30	20	22	27	13	17	48	53
Belarus	17,370	29,566	24	10	47	41	39	33	29	49
Belgium	202,691	370,824	2	1	31	24	..	*17*	67	75
Benin[a]	1,845	4,287	36	32	13	13	8	8	51	54
Bolivia	4,868	9,334	17	15	35	32	19	14	49	53
Bosnia and Herzegovina	..	9,949	..	10	..	25	..	12	..	65
Botswana	3,792	10,317	5	2	61	53	5	4	34	44
Brazil	461,952	796,055	8	8	39	38	..	..	53	54
Bulgaria	20,726	26,648	17	10	49	32	..	20	34	59
Burkina Faso[a]	3,120	5,171	28	31	20	20	15	14	52	50
Burundi	1,132	800	56	35	19	20	13	9	25	45
Cambodia	1,115	6,187	..	34	..	27	..	19	..	39
Cameroon	11,152	16,875	25	41	30	14	15	7	46	45
Canada	574,192	1,113,810	3	..	32	..	17	..	65	..
Central African Republic	1,488	1,369	48	54	20	21	11	..	33	25
Chad	1,739	5,469	29	23	18	51	14	5	53	26
Chile	31,559	115,248	9	6	42	47	20	18	50	48
China[a,b]	354,644	2,234,297	27	13	42	48	33	34	31	40
Hong Kong, China	76,887	177,703	0	*0*	24	*10*	17	*4*	75	*90*
Colombia	40,274	122,309	17	13	38	34	21	15	45	53
Congo, Dem. Rep.	9,350	7,103	31	46	29	25	11	6	40	29
Congo, Rep.[a]	2,799	5,091	13	6	41	46	8	6	47	48
Costa Rica	7,403	20,021	12	9	30	30	23	22	58	62
Côte d'Ivoire[a]	10,796	16,344	33	23	23	26	21	19	44	51
Croatia	*18,156*	38,506	11	7	36	31	29	20	53	62
Cuba[a]	..	..	..	..	..	..	..	..	..	..
Czech Republic	34,880	124,365	6	3	49	37	..	25	45	60
Denmark	135,838	258,714	4	2	26	25	17	*14*	70	74
Dominican Republic[a]	7,074	29,502	13	12	31	26	18	15	55	62
Ecuador[a]	10,356	36,489	13	7	38	46	19	9	49	48
Egypt, Arab Rep.	43,130	89,369	19	15	29	36	18	17	52	49
El Salvador	4,801	16,974	17	10	27	30	22	23	55	60
Eritrea	*477*	970	*31*	23	*12*	23	*8*	8	*57*	55
Estonia	5,010	13,101	17	4	50	29	42	19	34	67
Ethiopia	12,083	11,174	52	48	12	13	5	5	36	39
Finland	138,231	193,160	6	3	33	30	..	*22*	61	68
France	1,239,256	2,126,630	4	2	27	21	..	13	70	77
Gabon[a]	5,952	8,055	7	8	43	58	6	5	50	35
Gambia, The	317	461	29	33	13	13	7	5	58	54
Georgia	7,738	6,395	32	17	34	27	24	18	35	56
Germany	1,707,383	2,794,926	2	1	38	30	*28*	*23*	61	69
Ghana[a]	5,886	10,720	45	38	17	23	10	8	38	39
Greece	85,929	225,206	10	5	26	21	..	*11*	63	74
Guatemala[a]	7,650	31,717	26	23	20	19	15	13	54	58
Guinea	2,818	3,289	24	25	33	36	5	5	43	39
Guinea-Bissau	244	301	61	60	19	12	8	9	21	28
Haiti	2,864	4,268	..	*28*	..	*17*	..	*8*	..	*55*

Structure of output 4.2

	Gross domestic product $ millions		Agriculture % of GDP		Industry % of GDP		Manufacturing % of GDP		Services % of GDP	
	1990	2005	1990	2005	1990	2005	1990	2005	1990	2005
Honduras	3,049	8,291	22	14	26	31	16	20	51	55
Hungary	33,056	109,239	15	4	39	31	23	23	46	65
India	316,937	805,714	31	18	28	27	17	16	41	54
Indonesia[a]	114,426	287,217	19	13	39	46	21	28	42	41
Iran, Islamic Rep.	116,035	189,784	19	10	29	45	12	12	52	45
Iraq	48,422	12,602	..	9	..	70	..	2	..	21
Ireland	47,854	201,817	9	3	35	37	..	27	57	60
Israel	52,490	123,434	..	..	..	..	..	..	..	..
Italy	1,133,407	1,762,519	4	2	32	27	23	18	64	71
Jamaica	4,592	9,574	..	6	..	33	..	14	..	61
Japan	3,018,112	4,533,965	3	2	40	30	..	21	58	68
Jordan	4,020	12,712	8	3	28	30	15	19	64	68
Kazakhstan	26,933	57,124	27	7	45	40	9	15	29	54
Kenya	8,591	18,730	30	27	19	19	12	12	51	54
Korea, Dem. Rep.	..	..	..	..	..	..	..	..	..	..
Korea, Rep.	263,777	787,624	9	3	42	40	27	28	50	56
Kuwait[a]	18,428	80,781	1	1	52	51	12	2	47	49
Kyrgyz Republic	2,674	2,441	34	34	36	21	28	14	30	45
Lao PDR	866	2,875	61	45	15	30	10	21	24	26
Latvia	7,447	15,826	22	4	46	22	35	13	32	74
Lebanon	2,838	21,944	..	7	..	22	..	14	..	71
Lesotho	615	1,450	24	17	33	41	14	19	44	41
Liberia[a]	384	548	54	64	17	15	..	12	29	21
Libya	28,905	38,756	..	..	..	..	..	..	..	..
Lithuania	10,507	25,625	27	6	31	34	21	22	42	61
Macedonia, FYR	4,472	5,766	9	13	45	29	36	18	47	58
Madagascar	3,081	5,040	29	28	13	16	11	14	59	56
Malawi	1,881	2,072	45	35	29	19	20	13	26	46
Malaysia[a]	44,024	130,326	15	9	42	52	24	31	43	40
Mali	2,421	5,305	46	37	16	24	9	3	39	39
Mauritania	1,020	1,850	30	24	29	29	10	5	42	47
Mauritius	2,383	6,290	13	6	33	28	25	20	54	66
Mexico	262,710	768,438	8	4	28	26	21	18	64	70
Moldova	3,593	2,917	36	17	37	25	..	17	27	59
Mongolia	2,093	1,880	15	22	41	29	36	3	44	49
Morocco[a]	25,821	51,621	18	14	32	30	18	17	50	56
Mozambique	2,463	6,636	37	22	18	30	10	14	45	48
Myanmar[a]	..	..	57	..	11	..	8	..	32	..
Namibia	2,350	6,126	12	10	38	32	14	14	50	58
Nepal	3,628	7,391	51	38	16	21	6	8	34	41
Netherlands	307,384	624,202	4	2	28	24	..	14	67	74
New Zealand	43,898	109,291	7	..	28	..	19	..	65	..
Nicaragua	1,009	4,911	..	19	..	28	..	18	..	53
Niger[a]	2,481	3,405	35	40	16	17	7	7	49	43
Nigeria	28,472	98,951	33	23	41	57	6	4	26	20
Norway	116,108	295,513	4	2	36	43	13	11	61	55
Oman[a]	11,685	24,284	3	2	54	56	3	8	43	42
Pakistan	40,010	110,732	26	22	25	25	17	18	49	53
Panama	5,313	15,467	10	8	15	16	10	8	75	76
Papua New Guinea	3,221	4,945	..	42	..	39	..	6	..	19
Paraguay[a]	5,265	7,328	28	22	25	19	17	12	47	59
Peru	26,294	79,379	9	7	27	35	18	16	64	58
Philippines[a]	44,312	99,029	22	14	35	32	25	23	44	53
Poland	58,976	303,229	8	5	50	31	..	18	42	65
Portugal	75,274	183,305	9	3	29	25	..	16	62	73
Puerto Rico[a]	30,604	..	1	..	42	..	40	..	57	..

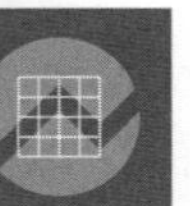

4.2 Structure of output

	Gross domestic product $ millions		Agriculture % of GDP		Industry % of GDP		Manufacturing % of GDP		Services % of GDP	
	1990	2005	1990	2005	1990	2005	1990	2005	1990	2005
Romania	38,299	98,565	24	10	50	35	*34*	24	26	55
Russian Federation	516,814	763,720	17	6	48	38	..	18	35	56
Rwanda[a]	2,584	2,153	33	42	25	21	18	8	43	37
Saudi Arabia[a]	116,778	309,778	6	*4*	49	*59*	9	*10*	46	*37*
Senegal[a]	5,699	8,238	20	18	19	19	13	11	61	63
Serbia and Montenegro	..	26,215	..	16	..	33	..	20	..	51
Sierra Leone	650	1,193	47	46	19	24	5	*4*	34	30
Singapore	36,842	116,764	0	0	35	34	27	28	65	66
Slovak Republic[a]	15,485	46,412	7	4	59	29	..	19	34	67
Slovenia	17,382	34,354	6	3	42	34	34	25	52	63
Somalia	917	..	66	..	..	..	5	..	..	..
South Africa	112,014	239,543	5	3	40	30	24	19	55	67
Spain	520,969	1,124,640	6	3	34	30	..	*16*	61	67
Sri Lanka	8,032	23,479	26	17	26	26	15	15	48	57
Sudan	13,167	27,542	..	34	..	30	..	7	..	37
Swaziland	882	2,731	13	12	42	48	35	37	45	41
Sweden	242,178	357,683	3	1	31	28	..	*20*	66	71
Switzerland	235,808	367,029	3	*1*	33	*28*	22	*20*	64	*70*
Syrian Arab Republic	12,309	26,320	30	23	25	35	21	30	45	41
Tajikistan	2,629	2,312	33	24	38	32	25	24	29	44
Tanzania[c]	4,259	12,111	46	45	18	18	9	8	36	38
Thailand[a]	85,345	176,634	13	10	37	44	27	35	50	46
Togo[a]	1,628	2,203	34	42	23	23	10	10	44	35
Trinidad and Tobago	5,068	14,358	3	1	47	60	14	6	50	40
Tunisia[a]	12,291	28,683	16	12	30	29	17	18	55	60
Turkey	150,642	362,502	18	12	30	24	20	14	52	65
Turkmenistan	3,232	8,067	32	*20*	30	*41*	..	*22*	38	*39*
Uganda	4,304	8,724	57	33	11	25	6	9	32	43
Ukraine	81,456	82,876	26	11	45	34	*39*	21	30	55
United Arab Emirates	33,653	129,702	2	2	64	56	8	14	35	42
United Kingdom	989,524	2,198,789	2	1	35	26	23	*15*	63	73
United States	5,757,200	12,416,505	2	*1*	28	*22*	19	*14*	70	*77*
Uruguay	9,287	16,791	9	9	33	31	27	22	58	60
Uzbekistan	13,361	13,951	33	28	33	29	*22*	11	34	43
Venezuela, RB	47,028	140,192	6	*5*	61	*52*	15	*18*	34	*44*
Vietnam[a]	6,472	52,408	39	21	23	41	12	21	39	38
West Bank and Gaza[a]	..	4,014	..	..	..	..	..	..	..	..
Yemen, Rep.	4,828	15,066	24	13	27	*41*	9	*5*	49	*45*
Zambia	3,288	7,270	21	19	51	25	36	12	28	56
Zimbabwe	8,784	3,372	17	18	33	23	23	13	50	59
World	21,784,509 t	44,645,437 t	5 w	*4* w	33 w	*28* w	*21* w	*18* w	61 w	*69* w
Low income	595,576	1,416,212	32	22	26	28	15	15	41	50
Middle income	3,253,159	8,553,721	16	9	39	38	24	23	46	53
Lower middle income	1,636,824	4,879,773	19	12	38	42	27	27	43	47
Upper middle income	1,615,064	3,673,796	11	6	39	32	22	19	50	62
Low & middle income	3,849,735	9,969,591	18	11	37	37	23	22	45	52
East Asia & Pacific	667,503	3,039,976	25	13	40	46	30	32	35	41
Europe & Central Asia	1,101,711	2,201,159	16	8	43	32	..	18	41	60
Latin America & Carib.	1,103,860	2,460,991	9	8	36	34	..	*12*	55	59
Middle East & N. Africa	276,910	625,311	17	12	33	40	14	14	50	48
South Asia	401,938	1,016,267	31	19	27	27	17	16	43	54
Sub-Saharan Africa	302,890	621,879	20	17	34	32	17	14	47	52
High income	17,935,976	34,687,058	3	*2*	32	*26*	*21*	*17*	65	*72*
Europe EMU	5,653,415	9,984,125	4	2	32	26	..	*19*	64	72

a. Components are at producer prices. b. China has revised its national accounts data from 1993 onwards. Data before 1993 are not comparable with the later revised data. c. Data cover mainland Tanzania only.

About the data

An economy's gross domestic product (GDP) represents the sum of value added by all producers in that economy. Value added is the value of the gross output of producers less the value of intermediate goods and services consumed in production, before taking account of the consumption of fixed capital in the production process. The United Nations System of National Accounts calls for estimates of value added to be valued at either basic prices (excluding net taxes on products) or producer prices (including net taxes on products paid by producers but excluding sales or value added taxes). Both valuations exclude transport charges that are invoiced separately by producers. Total GDP shown in the table and elsewhere in this book is measured at purchaser prices. Value added by industry is normally measured at basic prices. When value added is measured at producer prices, this is noted in *Primary data documentation*.

While GDP estimates based on the production approach are generally more reliable than estimates compiled from the income or expenditure side, different countries use different definitions, methods, and reporting standards. World Bank staff review the quality of national accounts data and sometimes make adjustments to improve consistency with international guidelines. Nevertheless, significant discrepancies remain between international standards and actual practice. Many statistical offices, especially those in developing countries, face severe limitations in the resources, time, training, and budgets required to produce reliable and comprehensive series of national accounts statistics.

Data problems in measuring output

Among the difficulties faced by compilers of national accounts is the extent of unreported economic activity in the informal or secondary economy. In developing countries a large share of agricultural output is either not exchanged (because it is consumed within the household) or not exchanged for money.

Agricultural production often must be estimated indirectly, using a combination of methods involving estimates of inputs, yields, and area under cultivation. This approach sometimes leads to crude approximations that can differ from the true values over time and across crops for reasons other than climatic conditions or farming techniques. Similarly, agricultural inputs that cannot easily be allocated to specific outputs are frequently "netted out" using equally crude and ad hoc approximations. For further discussion of the measurement of agricultural production, see *About the data* for table 3.3.

Ideally, industrial output should be measured through regular censuses and surveys of firms. But in most developing countries such surveys are infrequent, so earlier survey results must be extrapolated using an appropriate indicator. The choice of sampling unit, which may be the enterprise (where responses may be based on financial records) or the establishment (where production units may be recorded separately), also affects the quality of the data. Moreover, much industrial production is organized in unincorporated or owner-operated ventures that are not captured by surveys aimed at the formal sector. Even in large industries, where regular surveys are more likely, evasion of excise and other taxes and nondisclosure of income lower the estimates of value added. Such problems become more acute as countries move from state control of industry to private enterprise, because new firms enter business and growing numbers of established firms fail to report. In accordance with the System of National Accounts, output should include all such unreported activity as well as the value of illegal activities and other unrecorded, informal, or small-scale operations. Data on these activities need to be collected using techniques other than conventional surveys of firms.

In industries dominated by large organizations and enterprises, such as public utilities, data on output, employment, and wages are usually readily available and reasonably reliable. But in the services industry the many self-employed workers and one-person businesses are sometimes difficult to locate, and they have little incentive to respond to surveys, let alone to report their full earnings. Compounding these problems are the many forms of economic activity that go unrecorded, including the work that women and children do for little or no pay. For further discussion of the problems of using national accounts data, see Srinivasan (1994) and Heston (1994).

Dollar conversion

To produce national accounts aggregates that are measured in the same standard monetary units, the value of output must be converted to a single common currency. The World Bank conventionally uses the U.S. dollar and applies the average official exchange rate reported by the International Monetary Fund for the year shown. An alternative conversion factor is applied if the official exchange rate is judged to diverge by an exceptionally large margin from the rate effectively applied to transactions in foreign currencies and traded products.

Definitions

• **Gross domestic product (GDP)** at purchaser prices is the sum of gross value added by all resident producers in the economy plus any product taxes (less subsidies) not included in the valuation of output. It is calculated without deducting for depreciation of fabricated assets or for depletion and degradation of natural resources. Value added is the net output of an industry after adding up all outputs and subtracting intermediate inputs. The industrial origin of value added is determined by the International Standard Industrial Classification (ISIC) revision 3. • **Agriculture** corresponds to ISIC divisions 1–5 and includes forestry and fishing. • **Industry** covers mining, manufacturing (also reported separately), construction, electricity, water, and gas (ISIC divisions 10–45). • **Manufacturing** corresponds to industries belonging to ISIC divisions 15–37. • **Services** correspond to ISIC divisions 50–99. This sector is derived as a residual (from GDP less agriculture and industry) and may not properly reflect the sum of services output, including banking and financial services. For some countries it includes product taxes (minus subsidies) and may also include statistical discrepancies.

Data sources

National accounts data for most developing countries are collected from national statistical organizations and central banks by visiting and resident World Bank missions. Data for high-income economies come from data files of the Organisation for Economic Co-operation and Development (for information on the OECD's national accounts series, see its *Annual National Accounts for OECD Member Countries: Data from 1970 Onwards*). The complete national accounts time series is available on the *World Development Indicators 2007* CD-ROM. The United Nations Statistics Division publishes detailed national accounts for UN member countries in *National Accounts Statistics: Main Aggregates and Detailed Tables* and publishes updates in the *Monthly Bulletin of Statistics*.

4.3 Structure of manufacturing

	Manufacturing value added		Food, beverages, and tobacco		Textiles and clothing		Machinery and transport equipment		Chemicals		Other manufacturing[a]	
	$ millions		% of total		% of total		% of total		% of total		% of total	
	1990	2003	1990	2003	1990	2003	1990	2003	1990	2003	1990	2003
Afghanistan	..	679	..	..	..	..	..	..	..	..	..	..
Albania	..	610	24	..	33	..	..	..	..	..	44	..
Algeria	6,452	4,458	13	10	17	19	..	3	..	4	70	64
Angola	513	542	..	..	..	..	..	..	..	..	..	..
Argentina	37,868	29,142	20	*30*	10	*7*	13	*10*	12	*16*	46	*37*
Armenia	681	541	..	..	..	..	..	..	..	..	..	..
Australia	42,564	62,976	18	14	6	4	20	19	7	7	49	56
Austria	31,439	44,672	15	..	7	..	28	..	8	..	43	..
Azerbaijan	1,561	628	..	..	..	..	..	..	..	..	..	..
Bangladesh	3,839	7,899	24	39	38	1	7	1	17	10	15	49
Belarus	6,630	4,751	..	..	..	..	..	..	..	..	..	..
Belgium	..	48,185	17	18	7	15	..	23	13	7	62	37
Benin	145	301	..	..	..	..	..	..	..	..	..	..
Bolivia	826	1,036	28	*39*	5	*4*	1	*1*	3	*5*	63	*52*
Bosnia and Herzegovina	..	727	12	..	15	..	18	..	7	..	49	..
Botswana	181	323	*51*	20	*12*	5	..	..	..	..	*37*	75
Brazil	..	..	14	..	12	..	27	..	..	..	48	..
Bulgaria	..	3,184	..	19	..	20	..	19	..	10	..	32
Burkina Faso	460	539	*46*	46	*3*	4	*1*	2	*1*	1	*49*	48
Burundi	134	45	83	16	9	5	..	..	2	6	7	73
Cambodia	58	854	..	..	..	..	..	..	..	..	..	..
Cameroon	1,581	1,061	61	*37*	-13	*6*	1	*1*	5	*10*	46	*46*
Canada	91,671	*119,900*	15	17	6	9	26	21	10	7	44	46
Central African Republic	154	..	58	*6*	6	*53*	2	*0*	6	*2*	28	*39*
Chad	239	211	..	..	..	..	..	..	..	..	..	..
Chile	5,613	13,268	25	21	8	14	5	12	10	9	52	45
China[b]	116,573	539,026	15	13	15	10	24	32	13	11	34	33
Hong Kong, China	12,357	5,702	8	11	36	23	21	21	2	4	33	41
Colombia	8,034	11,606	31	21	15	18	9	5	14	11	31	45
Congo, Dem. Rep.	1,029	302	..	..	..	..	..	..	..	..	..	..
Congo, Rep.	234	227	*58*	..	*4*	..	*3*	..	..	..	*35*	..
Costa Rica	1,514	3,361	47	45	8	5	7	6	9	11	30	34
Côte d'Ivoire	2,257	2,452	*38*	..	*7*	..	*8*	..	..	..	*47*	..
Croatia	*4,770*	4,850	22	..	15	..	20	..	8	..	36	..
Cuba	..	..	*67*	..	*5*	..	*1*	..	..	..	*27*	..
Czech Republic	..	20,466	..	..	..	..	..	..	..	..	..	..
Denmark	20,364	27,476	22	20	4	6	24	27	12	4	39	43
Dominican Republic	1,270	2,550	*78*	109	*7*	11	*0*	1	*4*	5	*11*	-25
Ecuador	1,988	2,735	22	27	10	4	5	3	8	4	56	61
Egypt, Arab Rep.	7,296	14,466	19	..	16	..	9	..	14	..	43	..
El Salvador	1,043	3,391	*36*	43	*14*	26	*4*	4	*24*	9	*23*	18
Eritrea	*35*	61	*53*	50	*18*	9	*2*	2	*18*	8	*9*	31
Estonia	1,985	1,458	..	15	..	13	..	13	..	4	..	55
Ethiopia	601	410	12	*4*	5	*3*	0	*0*	0	*1*	82	*93*
Finland	..	31,856	13	17	4	12	24	18	8	6	52	48
France	..	227,906	13	15	6	3	31	32	9	14	41	37
Gabon	332	297	*45*	..	*2*	..	*1*	..	*7*	..	*45*	..
Gambia, The	18	18	..	..	..	..	..	..	..	..	..	..
Georgia	1,773	706	..	..	..	..	..	..	..	..	..	..
Germany	*451,915*	489,786	..	9	..	2	..	43	..	..	..	47
Ghana	575	684	..	22	..	3	..	1	..	4	..	70
Greece	..	17,716	22	20	20	22	12	13	10	9	36	36
Guatemala	1,151	3,157	*38*	32	*11*	4	*4*	3	*18*	4	*29*	58
Guinea	126	159	..	..	..	..	..	..	..	..	..	..
Guinea-Bissau	19	23	..	..	..	..	..	..	..	..	..	..
Haiti	..	216	*51*	..	*9*	..	..	..	..	..	*40*	..

Structure of manufacturing

	Manufacturing value added		Food, beverages, and tobacco		Textiles and clothing		Machinery and transport equipment		Chemicals		Other manufacturing[a]	
	$ millions		% of total		% of total		% of total		% of total		% of total	
	1990	2003	1990	2003	1990	2003	1990	2003	1990	2003	1990	2003
Honduras	443	1,253	45	57	10	9	3	1	6	4	36	30
Hungary	*6,613*	15,887	14	12	9	15	26	19	12	3	39	51
India	48,808	84,971	12	12	15	0	26	4	14	5	34	79
Indonesia	23,643	68,794	28	23	15	13	12	18	9	10	37	36
Iran, Islamic Rep.	13,357	15,034	12	10	20	5	20	28	8	13	40	44
Iraq	..	263	*20*	22	*16*	17	*4*	8	*11*	3	*49*	51
Ireland	..	39,819	27	*37*	4	*21*	29	*13*	17	6	24	*24*
Israel	..	..	14	16	9	14	32	12	9	4	37	55
Italy	240,462	258,746	8	9	13	11	35	27	7	8	37	45
Jamaica	853	1,017	41	15	5	7	..	..	..	..	54	78
Japan	..	886,172	9	8	5	2	40	19	10	7	37	65
Jordan	520	1,527	28	26	7	11	4	5	15	16	47	42
Kazakhstan	*1,941*	4,384	..	..	..	..	..	..	..	..	..	..
Kenya	864	1,448	39	39	10	7	10	17	9	8	33	29
Korea, Dem. Rep.	..	..	..	..	..	..	..	..	..	..	..	..
Korea, Rep.	64,605	141,947	11	32	12	20	32	8	9	10	36	31
Kuwait	2,142	1,087	4	*10*	3	*5*	2	*5*	3	*3*	88	*76*
Kyrgyz Republic	706	255	..	..	..	..	..	..	..	..	..	..
Lao PDR	85	405	..	..	..	..	..	..	..	..	..	..
Latvia	2,474	1,330	..	24	..	10	..	11	..	4	..	51
Lebanon	..	2,328	..	..	..	..	..	..	..	..	..	..
Lesotho	71	189	..	..	..	..	..	..	..	..	..	..
Liberia	..	30	..	..	..	..	..	..	..	..	..	..
Libya	..	..	48	73	5	4	..	4	1	15	47	5
Lithuania	2,164	3,211	..	23	..	15	..	15	..	4	..	43
Macedonia, FYR	1,411	730	20	..	26	..	14	..	9	..	31	..
Madagascar	314	688	*39*	3	*36*	6	*3*	6	*8*	1	*14*	84
Malawi	313	175	38	*262*	10	*9*	1	*6*	18	*50*	33	*-227*
Malaysia	10,665	32,355	13	*9*	7	*3*	31	*39*	11	*9*	39	*40*
Mali	200	114	..	..	..	..	..	..	..	..	..	..
Mauritania	94	70	..	..	..	..	..	..	..	..	..	..
Mauritius	491	1,010	30	*78*	46	*5*	2	*4*	4	*3*	17	*9*
Mexico	49,992	104,107	22	..	5	..	24	..	18	..	32	..
Moldova	..	308	..	57	..	11	..	7	..	..	..	25
Mongolia	745	62	33	..	37	..	1	..	1	..	27	..
Morocco	4,753	7,319	22	*33*	17	*18*	8	*8*	12	*13*	41	*28*
Mozambique	230	605	..	75	..	19	..	8	..	4	..	-6
Myanmar	..	..	..	..	..	..	..	..	..	..	..	..
Namibia	292	512	..	..	..	..	..	..	..	..	..	..
Nepal	209	441	37	*45*	31	*19*	1	*2*	5	*10*	26	*23*
Netherlands	..	67,292	21	3	3	1	25	3	17	2	35	92
New Zealand	7,613	*8,097*	28	19	8	7	13	12	7	4	44	58
Nicaragua	..	692	40	31	3	9	0	2	3	9	54	50
Niger	163	179	37	*32*	29	..	..	..	..	*25*	34	*43*
Nigeria	1,562	2,268	*15*	..	*46*	..	*13*	..	*4*	..	*22*	..
Norway	13,450	21,702	18	3	2	11	25	24	9	8	46	55
Oman	343	1,782	..	9	..	2	..	2	..	4	..	84
Pakistan	6,184	12,387	24	*35*	28	*92*	9	*14*	15	*15*	25	*-56*
Panama	502	924	51	48	8	7	2	2	8	3	31	39
Papua New Guinea	..	215	6	19	..	..	7	10	..	4	87	68
Paraguay	883	691	*56*	54	*16*	15	..	1	..	4	*29*	27
Peru	3,926	8,811	23	..	11	..	8	..	9	..	49	..
Philippines	11,003	18,824	39	38	11	10	13	8	12	12	26	33
Poland	..	33,786	21	9	9	3	26	7	7	4	37	78
Portugal	..	21,352	15	14	21	18	13	17	6	6	45	45
Puerto Rico	12,126	*27,099*	16	..	5	..	18	..	44	..	17	..

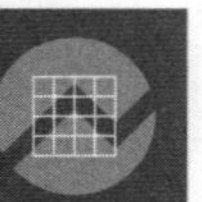

4.3 Structure of manufacturing

	Manufacturing value added		Food, beverages, and tobacco		Textiles and clothing		Machinery and transport equipment		Chemicals		Other manufacturing[a]	
	$ millions		% of total		% of total		% of total		% of total		% of total	
	1990	2003	1990	2003	1990	2003	1990	2003	1990	2003	1990	2003
Romania	9,152	16,141	19	..	18	..	14	..	4	..	45	..
Russian Federation	..	64,391	..	..	..	..	..	..	..	..	..	..
Rwanda	473	149	..	93	..	..	..	..	..	..	..	7
Saudi Arabia	10,049	23,005	7	..	1	..	4	..	39	..	50	..
Senegal	747	752	60	..	3	..	5	..	9	..	23	..
Serbia and Montenegro	..	3,305	..	36	..	6	..	14	..	11	..	33
Sierra Leone	28	34	..	..	..	..	..	..	..	..	..	..
Singapore	9,562	22,207	4	3	3	1	53	50	10	24	29	22
Slovak Republic	..	6,255	..	..	..	..	..	..	..	..	..	..
Slovenia	5,190	6,433	12	10	15	8	16	17	9	15	48	50
Somalia	41	..	2	31	3	16	..	..	..	..	95	54
South Africa	24,043	29,301	15	16	8	13	18	17	9	9	50	45
Spain	..	134,438	18	13	8	19	25	16	10	11	39	41
Sri Lanka	1,077	2,524	51	37	24	33	4	5	4	6	17	20
Sudan	..	1,205	..	66	..	4	..	4	..	4	..	21
Swaziland	250	432	69	37	8	2	1	..	..	..	22	60
Sweden	..	52,365	10	10	2	4	33	24	9	3	47	59
Switzerland	49,484	60,215	10	..	4	..	34	..	..	..	53	..
Syrian Arab Republic	2,508	1,737	35	36	29	41	..	2	..	2	36	19
Tajikistan	653	436	..	..	..	..	..	..	..	..	..	..
Tanzania[c]	361	685	51	39	3	23	7	3	11	5	29	29
Thailand	23,217	49,735	24	23	30	14	19	4	2	25	26	34
Togo	162	163	..	..	..	7	..	..	..	9	..	84
Trinidad and Tobago	681	747	31	16	3	1	3	4	19	1	44	78
Tunisia	2,075	4,480	19	35	20	12	5	5	4	20	52	29
Turkey	26,882	26,753	16	29	15	22	16	6	10	2	43	42
Turkmenistan	..	1,045	..	..	..	..	..	..	..	..	..	..
Uganda	230	538	61	10	14	28	3	1	6	..	16	62
Ukraine	31,517	9,320	..	..	..	..	..	..	..	..	..	..
United Arab Emirates	2,643	11,495	..	..	..	2	..	..	..	3	..	95
United Kingdom	206,719	238,575	13	12	5	11	32	32	11	10	38	36
United States	1,040,600	1,488,100	12	12	5	8	31	30	12	10	40	39
Uruguay	2,597	2,078	31	..	18	..	9	..	10	..	32	..
Uzbekistan	..	807	..	..	..	..	..	..	..	..	..	..
Venezuela, RB	6,921	14,289	17	25	5	8	5	14	9	9	64	44
Vietnam	793	8,115	..	..	..	..	..	..	..	..	..	..
West Bank and Gaza	..	..	..	..	..	..	..	..	..	..	..	..
Yemen, Rep.	449	517	..	48	..	7	..	0	..	..	..	44
Zambia	1,048	473	44	63	12	8	7	6	9	12	29	12
Zimbabwe	1,799	911	28	26	19	16	10	10	6	11	38	37
World	4,401,339 t	6,163,496 t										
Low income	81,598	136,860										
Middle income	577,839	1,358,768										
Lower middle income	312,003	913,666										
Upper middle income	271,707	440,727										
Low & middle income	665,884	1,495,945										
East Asia & Pacific	188,030	722,097										
Europe & Central Asia	..	..										
Latin America & Carib.	174,072	281,559										
Middle East & N. Africa	32,128	56,299										
South Asia	60,477	108,845										
Sub-Saharan Africa	43,592	50,518										
High income	..	4,693,358										
Europe EMU	..	1,390,728										

a. Includes unallocated data. b. China has revised its national accounts data from 1993 onwards. Data before 1993 are not comparable with the later revised data. c. Data cover mainland Tanzania only.

Structure of manufacturing 4.3

About the data

The data on the distribution of manufacturing value added by industry are provided by the United Nations Industrial Development Organization (UNIDO). UNIDO obtains data on manufacturing value added from a variety of national and international sources, including the United Nations Statistics Division, the World Bank, the Organisation for Economic Co-operation and Development, and the International Monetary Fund. To improve comparability over time and across countries, UNIDO supplements these data with information from industrial censuses, statistics supplied by national and international organizations, unpublished data that it collects in the field, and estimates by the UNIDO Secretariat. Nevertheless, coverage may be less than complete, particularly for the informal sector. To the extent that direct information on inputs and outputs is not available, estimates may be used, which may result in errors in industry totals. Moreover, countries use different reference periods (calendar or fiscal year) and valuation methods (basic or producer prices) to estimate value added. (See also *About the data* for table 4.2.)

The data on manufacturing value added in U.S. dollars are from the World Bank's national accounts files. These figures may differ from those used by UNIDO to calculate the shares of value added by industry, in part because of differences in exchange rates. Thus estimates of value added in a particular industry calculated by applying the shares to total manufacturing value added will not match those from UNIDO sources. The classification of manufacturing industries in the table accords with the United Nations International Standard Industrial Classification (ISIC) revision 2. First published in 1948, the ISIC has its roots in the work of the League of Nations Committee of Statistical Experts. The committee's efforts, interrupted by the Second World War, were taken up by the United Nations Statistical Commission, which at its first session appointed a committee on industrial classification. The latest revision, ISIC revision 3, was completed in 1989, and many countries have now switched to it. But revision 2 is still widely used for compiling cross-country data. Concordances matching ISIC categories to national systems of classification and to related systems such as the Standard International Trade Classification are readily available.

In establishing a classification system, compilers must define both the types of activities to be described and the organizational units whose activities are to be reported. There are many possibilities, and the choices made affect how the resulting statistics can be interpreted and how useful they are in analyzing economic behavior. The ISIC emphasizes commonalities in the production process and is explicitly not intended to measure outputs (for which there is a newly developed Central Product Classification). Nevertheless, the ISIC views an activity as defined by "a process resulting in a homogeneous set of products" (United Nations 1990 [ISIC, series M, no. 4, rev. 3], p. 9).

Firms typically use a multitude of processes to produce a final product. For example, an automobile manufacturer engages in forging, welding, and painting as well as advertising, accounting, and many other service activities. In some cases the processes may be carried out by different technical units within the larger enterprise, but collecting data at such a detailed level is not practical, nor would it be useful to record production data at the very highest level of a large, multiplant, multiproduct firm. The ISIC has therefore adopted as the definition of an establishment "an enterprise or part of an enterprise which independently engages in one, or predominantly one, kind of economic activity at or from one location . . . for which data are available . . ." (United Nations 1990, p. 25). By design, this definition matches the reporting unit required for the production accounts of the UN System of National Accounts.

Definitions

• **Manufacturing value added** is the sum of gross output less the value of intermediate inputs used in production for industries classified in ISIC major division 3. • **Food, beverages, and tobacco** correspond to ISIC division 31. • **Textiles and clothing** correspond to ISIC division 32. • **Machinery and transport equipment** correspond to ISIC groups 382–84. • **Chemicals** correspond to ISIC groups 351 and 352. • **Other manufacturing** covers wood and related products (ISIC division 33), paper and related products (ISIC division 34), petroleum and related products (ISIC groups 353–56), basic metals and mineral products (ISIC divisions 36 and 37), fabricated metal products and professional goods (ISIC groups 381 and 385), and other industries (ISIC group 390). When data for textiles and clothing, machinery and transport equipment, or chemicals are shown in the table as not available, they are included in "other manufacturing."

Manufacturing continues to show strong growth in East Asia **4.3a**

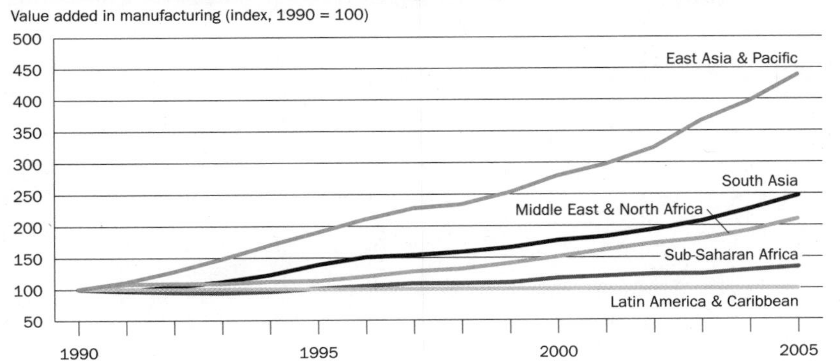

Manufacturing continues to be the dominant sector in the East Asia and Pacific region, growing by an average of about 10 percent a year between 1990 and 2005.

Source: World Bank data files.

Data sources

Data on value added in manufacturing in U.S. dollars are from the World Bank's national accounts files. Data used to calculate shares of value added by industry are provided to the World Bank in electronic files by UNIDO. The most recent published source is UNIDO's *International Yearbook of Industrial Statistics 2006*. The ISIC system is described in the United Nations' *International Standard Industrial Classification of All Economic Activities, Third Revision* (1990). The discussion of the ISIC draws on Jacob Ryten's "Fifty Years of ISIC: Historical Origins and Future Perspectives" (1998).

4.4 Structure of merchandise exports

	Merchandise exports		Food		Agricultural raw materials		Fuels		Ores and metals		Manufactures	
	$ millions		% of total		% of total		% of total		% of total		% of total	
	1990	2005	1990	2005	1990	2005	1990	2005	1990	2005	1990	2005
Afghanistan	235	560	..	..	..	..	..	..	..	..	..	..
Albania	230	658	..	6	..	4	..	3	..	7	..	80
Algeria	12,930	46,001	0	*0*	..	..	96	*97*	0	*0*	3	*2*
Angola	3,910	23,400	0	..	0	..	93	..	6	..	0	..
Argentina	12,353	40,044	56	47	4	1	8	16	2	3	29	31
Armenia	..	950	..	12	..	1	..	2	..	13	..	71
Australia	39,752	105,825	22	17	10	3	21	27	20	20	27	25
Austria	41,265	123,987	3	6	4	2	1	5	3	3	88	80
Azerbaijan	..	7,649	..	7	..	1	..	77	..	1	..	13
Bangladesh	1,671	9,294	14	*8*	7	*2*	1	*0*	..	*0*	77	*90*
Belarus	..	15,977	..	8	..	3	..	35	..	1	..	52
Belgium	117,703[a]	334,298	9[a]	8	2[a]	1	3[a]	7	4[a]	3	77[a]	79
Benin	288	561	*15*	25	*56*	61	*15*	1	*0*	1	*13*	13
Bolivia	926	2,671	19	21	8	2	25	49	44	17	5	11
Bosnia and Herzegovina	*276*	2,402	..	..	..	..	..	..	..	..	..	..
Botswana	1,784	4,425	..	*2*	..	*0*	..	*0*	..	*11*	..	*86*
Brazil	31,414	118,308	28	26	3	4	2	6	14	10	52	54
Bulgaria	5,030	11,725	..	11	..	2	..	10	..	14	..	59
Burkina Faso	152	493	..	*16*	..	*72*	..	*3*	..	*1*	..	*8*
Burundi	75	111	..	87	..	4	..	0	..	2	..	6
Cambodia	86	3,100	..	*1*	..	*2*	..	..	..	*0*	..	*97*
Cameroon	2,002	2,829	20	17	14	13	50	50	7	6	9	3
Canada	127,629	359,399	9	7	9	5	10	20	9	6	59	58
Central African Republic	120	128	*31*	1	*24*	41	..	..	*1*	17	*44*	36
Chad	188	3,065	..	..	..	..	..	..	..	..	..	..
Chile	8,372	40,574	24	19	9	7	1	2	55	56	11	14
China†	62,091	761,954	13	3	3	1	8	2	2	2	72	92
Hong Kong, China[b]	82,390	292,119	4	1	1	1	1	0	1	1	92	96
Colombia	6,766	21,146	33	18	4	5	37	40	0	1	25	36
Congo, Dem. Rep.	2,326	2,050	..	..	..	..	..	..	..	..	..	..
Congo, Rep.	981	5,000	..	..	..	..	..	..	..	..	..	..
Costa Rica	1,448	7,039	58	30	5	3	1	0	1	1	27	66
Côte d'Ivoire	3,072	7,610	..	*56*	..	*9*	..	*13*	..	*0*	..	*20*
Croatia	*4,597*	8,809	*13*	10	*6*	3	*9*	14	*5*	4	*68*	68
Cuba	5,100	2,682	..	*40*	..	*0*	..	*2*	..	*39*	..	*19*
Czech Republic	*12,170*	78,246	..	4	..	1	..	3	..	2	..	88
Denmark	36,870	85,137	27	18	3	3	3	9	1	1	60	65
Dominican Republic	2,170	6,133	*21*	..	*0*	..	*0*	..	*0*	..	*78*	..
Ecuador	2,714	10,100	44	28	1	4	52	58	0	0	2	9
Egypt, Arab Rep.	3,477	10,654	10	*10*	10	*7*	29	*43*	9	*4*	42	*31*
El Salvador	582	3,390	57	*32*	1	*1*	2	*4*	3	*3*	38	*60*
Eritrea	*16*	10	..	..	..	..	..	..	..	..	..	..
Estonia	..	7,667	..	7	..	6	..	7	..	2	..	69
Ethiopia	298	883	..	*62*	..	*26*	..	*0*	..	*1*	..	*11*
Finland	26,571	66,016	2	2	10	5	1	4	4	3	83	84
France	216,588	460,157	16	11	2	1	2	4	3	2	77	80
Gabon	2,204	4,920	..	*1*	..	*10*	..	*76*	..	*6*	..	*7*
Gambia, The	31	8	..	78	..	4	..	*1*	..	0	..	17
Georgia	..	867	..	36	..	2	..	3	..	18	..	40
Germany	421,100	969,858	5	4	1	1	1	2	3	2	89	83
Ghana	897	2,490	*51*	*77*	*15*	*5*	*9*	*3*	*17*	*2*	*8*	*12*
Greece	8,105	17,044	30	22	3	2	7	9	7	8	54	56
Guatemala	1,163	5,381	67	34	6	3	2	6	0	1	24	57
Guinea	671	890	..	..	..	..	..	..	..	..	..	..
Guinea-Bissau	19	101	..	..	..	..	..	..	..	..	..	..
Haiti	160	470	14	..	1	..	0	..	0	..	85	..
†Data for Taiwan, China	67,245	197,776	4	1	2	1	1	5	1	2	93	91

Structure of merchandise exports

	Merchandise exports		Food		Agricultural raw materials		Fuels		Ores and metals		Manufactures	
	$ millions		% of total		% of total		% of total		% of total		% of total	
	1990	2005	1990	2005	1990	2005	1990	2005	1990	2005	1990	2005
Honduras	831	1,695	82	55	4	3	1	0	4	5	9	36
Hungary	10,000	62,109	23	6	3	1	3	3	6	2	63	84
India	17,969	95,096	16	9	4	2	3	11	5	7	70	70
Indonesia	25,675	86,226	11	12	5	5	44	28	4	8	35	47
Iran, Islamic Rep.	19,305	56,252	..	4	..	0	..	83	..	1	..	9
Iraq	12,380	24,096	..	..	..	..	..	..	..	..	..	..
Ireland	23,743	109,853	22	8	2	0	1	1	1	1	70	86
Israel	12,080	42,659	8	2	3	1	1	0	2	1	87	83
Italy	170,304	367,200	6	6	1	1	2	3	1	1	88	85
Jamaica	1,158	1,500	19	*22*	0	*0*	1	*2*	9	*9*	70	*66*
Japan	287,581	594,905	1	1	1	1	0	1	1	2	96	92
Jordan	1,064	4,302	10	15	1	0	0	0	33	12	56	72
Kazakhstan	..	27,849	..	*4*	..	*1*	..	*65*	..	*14*	..	*16*
Kenya	1,031	3,293	49	*40*	6	*12*	13	*23*	3	*4*	30	*21*
Korea, Dem. Rep.	1,857	1,338	..	..	..	..	..	..	..	..	..	..
Korea, Rep.	65,016	284,419	3	1	1	1	1	5	1	2	94	91
Kuwait	7,042	45,011	1	..	0	..	93	..	0	..	6	..
Kyrgyz Republic	..	672	..	11	..	8	..	12	..	4	..	27
Lao PDR	79	510	..	..	..	..	..	..	..	..	..	..
Latvia	..	5,161	..	11	..	16	..	9	..	4	..	57
Lebanon	494	2,337	..	*16*	..	*1*	..	*0*	..	*12*	..	*70*
Lesotho	62	649	..	..	..	..	..	..	..	..	..	..
Liberia	868	200	..	..	..	..	..	..	..	..	..	..
Libya	13,225	30,110	*1*	..	*0*	..	*95*	..	..	..	*4*	..
Lithuania	..	11,813	*24*	12	*6*	3	*8*	27	*1*	2	*59*	56
Macedonia, FYR	*1,199*	2,041	..	16	..	1	..	8	..	3	..	72
Madagascar	319	760	73	*61*	4	*6*	1	*4*	8	*5*	14	*22*
Malawi	417	520	91	80	2	4	0	0	0	0	7	16
Malaysia	29,452	140,949	12	7	14	3	18	13	2	1	54	75
Mali	359	1,109	36	..	62	..	..	..	0	..	2	..
Mauritania	469	565	..	..	..	..	..	..	..	..	..	..
Mauritius	1,194	2,144	32	28	1	0	1	0	0	1	66	70
Mexico	40,711	213,711	12	5	2	1	38	15	6	2	43	77
Moldova	..	1,091	..	53	..	6	..	0	..	2	..	39
Mongolia	661	1,054	..	2	..	14	..	5	..	58	..	21
Morocco	4,265	10,641	26	21	3	2	4	2	15	9	52	65
Mozambique	126	1,745	..	12	..	4	..	15	..	58	..	7
Myanmar	325	2,925	*51*	..	*36*	..	*0*	..	*2*	..	*11*	..
Namibia	1,085	2,070	..	*48*	..	*1*	..	*1*	..	*7*	..	*41*
Nepal	204	850	13	*21*	3	*1*	..	..	..	*4*	83	*74*
Netherlands	131,775	402,407	20	14	4	3	10	12	3	3	59	68
New Zealand	9,394	21,729	45	50	18	10	4	2	5	4	26	31
Nicaragua	330	858	77	85	14	2	0	1	1	1	8	11
Niger	282	502	..	*30*	..	*4*	..	*2*	..	*55*	..	*8*
Nigeria	13,596	42,277	*1*	*0*	*1*	*0*	*97*	*98*	*0*	..	*1*	*2*
Norway	34,047	103,780	7	5	2	0	48	68	10	6	32	17
Oman	5,508	18,692	1	2	0	0	92	86	1	1	5	6
Pakistan	5,615	15,917	9	12	10	1	1	4	0	0	79	82
Panama	340	1,010	75	85	1	1	0	1	1	4	21	9
Papua New Guinea	1,177	3,192	22	*21*	9	*3*	0	*22*	58	*49*	10	*6*
Paraguay	959	1,688	52	*75*	38	*12*	*0*	*0*	0	*1*	10	*13*
Peru	3,230	17,206	21	21	3	2	10	11	47	49	18	17
Philippines	8,117	41,255	19	6	2	1	2	2	8	2	38	89
Poland	14,320	89,288	12	9	3	1	12	5	10	4	58	78
Portugal	16,417	38,133	7	8	6	2	3	4	3	3	80	75
Puerto Rico	..	..	..	..	..	..	..	..	..	..	..	..

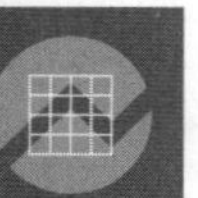

4.4 Structure of merchandise exports

	Merchandise exports		Food		Agricultural raw materials		Fuels		Ores and metals		Manufactures	
	$ millions		% of total		% of total		% of total		% of total		% of total	
	1990	2005	1990	2005	1990	2005	1990	2005	1990	2005	1990	2005
Romania	4,960	27,730	1	3	3	2	18	11	4	4	73	80
Russian Federation	..	243,569	..	2	..	3	..	49	..	7	..	19
Rwanda	110	125	..	52	..	7	..	7	..	23	..	10
Saudi Arabia	44,417	181,440	1	1	0	0	90	89	1	0	8	9
Senegal	761	1,641	53	29	3	2	12	21	9	3	23	43
Serbia and Montenegro	2,539	5,065	19	21	3	4	6	2	10	11	62	61
Sierra Leone	138	158	..	..	..	..	..	..	..	..	..	..
Singapore[b]	52,730	229,649	5	2	3	0	18	12	2	1	72	81
Slovak Republic	6,355	31,956	..	4	..	2	..	7	..	3	..	84
Slovenia	6,681	18,633	7	3	2	2	3	2	3	4	86	88
Somalia	..	..	..	..	..	..	..	..	..	..	..	..
South Africa	23,549	51,876	8[c]	9	4[c]	2	7[c]	10	10[c]	22	29[c]	57
Spain	55,642	187,182	15	14	2	1	4	4	2	2	75	77
Sri Lanka	1,912	6,347	34	22	6	2	1	0	2	4	54	70
Sudan	374	4,824	60	7	38	5	..	87	0	0	2	0
Swaziland	556	2,020	..	..	..	..	..	..	..	..	..	..
Sweden	57,540	130,104	2	3	7	4	3	5	3	3	83	79
Switzerland	63,784	130,898	3	3	1	0	0	0	3	3	94	93
Syrian Arab Republic	4,212	5,760	14	15	5	4	45	68	1	1	36	11
Tajikistan	..	909	..	..	..	..	..	..	..	..	..	..
Tanzania	331	1,481	..	57	..	17	..	0	..	12	..	14
Thailand	23,068	110,110	29	12	5	5	1	4	1	1	63	77
Togo	268	569	23	21	21	9	0	1	45	10	9	58
Trinidad and Tobago	1,960	9,035	5	3	0	0	67	70	1	0	27	26
Tunisia	3,526	10,494	11	11	1	1	17	10	2	1	69	78
Turkey	12,959	73,414	22	10	3	1	2	4	4	2	68	82
Turkmenistan	..	4,935	..	..	..	..	..	..	..	..	..	..
Uganda	152	853	..	64	..	12	..	5	..	2	..	17
Ukraine	..	34,287	..	12	..	1	..	10	..	6	..	69
United Arab Emirates	23,544	115,453	2	..	0	..	7	..	78	..	12	..
United Kingdom	185,172	382,761	7	5	1	1	8	9	3	3	79	77
United States	393,592	904,383	11	7	4	2	3	3	3	3	75	82
Uruguay	1,693	3,405	40	55	21	7	0	5	0	1	39	32
Uzbekistan	..	4,749	..	..	..	..	..	..	..	..	..	..
Venezuela, RB	17,497	55,487	2	0	0	0	80	89	7	2	10	9
Vietnam	2,404	31,625	..	23	..	2	..	21	..	1	..	53
West Bank and Gaza	..	..	..	..	..	..	..	..	..	..	..	..
Yemen, Rep.	692	6,380	8	4	1	0	74	92	1	0	15	4
Zambia	1,309	1,720	..	13	..	5	..	1	..	72	..	9
Zimbabwe	1,726	1,820	44	31	7	16	1	2	16	23	31	28
World	3,474,778 t	10,433,971 t	10 w	7 w	3 w	2 w	9 w	10 w	4 w	3 w	73 w	75 w
Low income	67,127	261,853	15	15	4	3	27	28	5	3	49	50
Middle income	552,565	2,795,181	17	9	4	2	21	17	6	5	50	65
Lower middle income	272,538	1,520,827	18	10	4	2	16	12	5	4	54	71
Upper middle income	281,789	1,274,355	16	8	5	2	28	22	7	5	44	58
Low & middle income	620,808	3,057,040	17	9	4	2	20	17	6	5	51	64
East Asia & Pacific	155,928	1,185,572	15	6	6	2	13	8	3	3	60	81
Europe & Central Asia	..	761,588	..	6	..	2	..	23	..	5	..	56
Latin America & Carib.	143,275	565,896	21	15	3	2	30	22	10	7	36	54
Middle East & N. Africa	81,103	225,759	..	6	..	1	..	69	..	2	..	20
South Asia	27,754	128,475	16	11	5	2	2	9	4	6	71	72
Sub-Saharan Africa	68,368	189,745	..	15	..	5	..	36	..	10	..	33
High income	2,850,034	7,376,990	8	6	3	2	6	8	3	3	77	78
Europe EMU	1,241,084	3,113,158	11	8	2	1	3	5	3	2	80	80

Note: Components may not sum to 100 percent because of unclassified trade. Exports of gold are excluded.
a. Includes Luxembourg. b. Includes re-exports. c. Refers to the South African Customs Union (Botswana, Lesotho, Namibia, South Africa, and Swaziland).

Structure of merchandise exports 4.4

About the data

Data on merchandise trade are from customs reports of goods movement into or out of an economy or from reports of the financial transactions related to merchandise trade recorded in the balance of payments. Because of differences in timing and definitions, estimates of trade flows from customs reports are likely to differ from those based on the balance of payments. Moreover, several international agencies process trade data, each correcting unreported or misreported data, and this leads to other differences in the available data.

The most detailed source of data on international trade in goods is the Commodity Trade (Comtrade) database maintained by the United Nations Statistics Division. In addition, the International Monetary Fund (IMF) collects customs-based data on exports and imports of goods. The value of exports is recorded as the cost of the goods delivered to the frontier of the exporting country for shipment—the free on board (f.o.b.) value. Many countries report trade data in U.S. dollars. When countries report in local currency, the United Nations Statistics Division applies the average official exchange rate for the period shown.

Countries may report trade according to the general or special system of trade (see *Primary data documentation*). Under the general system, exports comprise outward-moving goods that are (a) goods wholly or partly produced in the country; (b) foreign goods, neither transformed nor declared for domestic consumption in the country, that move outward from customs storage; and (c) goods previously included as imports for domestic consumption but subsequently exported without transformation. Under the special system exports comprise categories a and c. In some compilations categories b and c are classified as re-exports. Because of differences in reporting practices, data on exports may not be fully comparable across economies.

The data on total exports of goods (merchandise) in this table come from the World Trade Organization (WTO). The WTO uses two main sources, national statistical offices and the IMF's *International Financial Statistics*. It supplements these with the Comtrade database and publications or databases of regional organizations, specialized agencies, economic groups, and private sources (such as Eurostat, the Food and Agriculture Organization, and country reports of the Economist Intelligence Unit). In recent years country websites and direct contacts through email have helped to improve the collection of up-to-date statistics for many countries, reducing the proportion of estimated figures. The WTO database now covers most of the major traders in Africa, Asia, and Latin America, which together with the high-income countries account for nearly 95 percent of total world trade. There has also been a remarkable improvement in the availability of reliable figures for countries in Europe and Central Asia.

The shares of exports by major commodity group are from Comtrade. The values of total exports reported here have not been fully reconciled with the estimates of exports of goods and services from the national accounts or those from the balance of payments.

The classification of commodity groups is based on the Standard International Trade Classification (SITC) revision 1. Most countries now report using later revisions of the SITC or the Harmonized System. Concordance tables are used to convert data reported in one system of nomenclature to another. The conversion process may introduce some errors of classification, but conversions from later to earlier systems are generally reliable.

Developing economies' share of world merchandise exports continues to expand — 4.4a

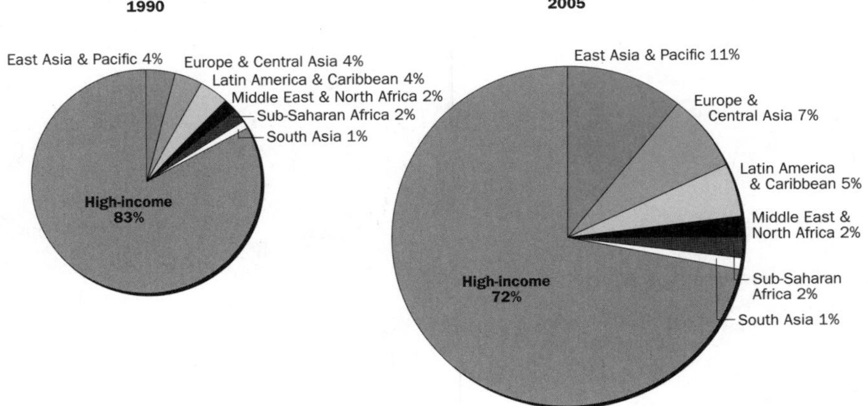

Developing economies' share of world merchandise exports increased by 11 percentage points from 1990 to 2005. East Asia and Pacific was the biggest gainer, capturing an additional 7 percentage points.

Source: World Bank data files.

Definitions

• **Merchandise exports** are the f.o.b. value of goods provided to the rest of the world, valued in U.S. dollars. • **Food** corresponds to the commodities in SITC sections 0 (food and live animals), 1 (beverages and tobacco), and 4 (animal and vegetable oils and fats) and SITC division 22 (oil seeds, oil nuts, and oil kernels). • **Agricultural raw materials** correspond to SITC section 2 (crude materials except fuels) excluding divisions 22, 27 (crude fertilizers and minerals excluding coal, petroleum, and precious stones), and 28 (metalliferous ores and scrap). • **Fuels** correspond to SITC section 3 (mineral fuels). • **Ores and metals** correspond to the commodities in SITC divisions 27, 28, and 68 (nonferrous metals). • **Manufactures** correspond to the commodities in SITC sections 5 (chemicals), 6 (basic manufactures), 7 (machinery and transport equipment), and 8 (miscellaneous manufactured goods), excluding division 68.

Data sources

The WTO publishes data on world trade in its *Annual Report*. The IMF publishes estimates of total exports of goods in its *International Financial Statistics* and *Direction of Trade Statistics*, as does the United Nations Statistics Division in its *Monthly Bulletin of Statistics*. And the United Nations Conference on Trade and Development publishes data on the structure of exports and imports in its *Handbook of International Trade and Development Statistics*. Tariff line records of exports and imports are compiled in the United Nations Statistics Division's Comtrade database.

4.5 Structure of merchandise imports

	Merchandise imports $ millions		Food % of total		Agricultural raw materials % of total		Fuels % of total		Ores and metals % of total		Manufactures % of total	
	1990	2005	1990	2005	1990	2005	1990	2005	1990	2005	1990	2005
Afghanistan	936	3,200	..	..	..	..	..	..	..	..	..	..
Albania	380	2,614	..	17	..	1	..	9	..	2	..	71
Algeria	9,780	20,357	24	22	5	2	1	1	2	1	68	74
Angola	1,578	8,150	..	..	..	..	..	..	..	..	..	..
Argentina	4,076	28,692	4	3	4	2	8	5	6	3	78	87
Armenia	..	1,768	..	18	..	1	..	16	..	3	..	62
Australia	41,985	125,280	5	5	2	1	6	11	1	1	85	81
Austria	49,146	126,179	5	6	3	2	6	13	4	4	81	74
Azerbaijan	..	4,200	..	10	..	1	..	12	..	2	..	74
Bangladesh	3,618	13,839	19	19	5	9	16	8	3	2	56	62
Belarus	..	16,699	..	9	..	2	..	33	..	3	..	46
Belgium	119,702[a]	318,658	10[a]	8	2[a]	1	8[a]	12	6[a]	4	68[a]	75
Benin	265	894	38	30	4	4	1	20	1	1	56	44
Bolivia	687	2,341	12	10	2	1	1	10	1	1	85	77
Bosnia and Herzegovina	360	7,097	..	..	..	..	..	..	..	..	..	..
Botswana	1,946	3,272	..	14	..	1	..	4	..	1	..	75
Brazil	22,524	77,585	9	5	3	2	27	19	5	4	56	71
Bulgaria	5,100	18,181	8	5	3	1	36	5	4	7	49	65
Burkina Faso	536	1,305	..	12	..	1	..	24	..	1	..	62
Burundi	231	267	..	6	..	1	..	8	..	1	..	82
Cambodia	164	3,700	..	8	..	2	..	10	..	0	..	79
Cameroon	1,400	2,885	19	18	0	2	2	26	1	1	78	53
Canada	123,244	319,686	6	6	2	1	6	9	3	3	81	80
Central African Republic	154	151	19	17	1	27	7	17	2	2	71	37
Chad	285	770	..	..	..	..	..	..	..	..	..	..
Chile	7,742	32,542	4	6	2	1	16	22	1	4	75	67
China†	53,345	660,003	9	3	6	4	2	10	3	8	80	75
Hong Kong, China	84,725	300,160	8	3	2	1	2	3	2	2	85	92
Colombia	5,590	21,204	7	9	4	2	6	3	3	3	77	83
Congo, Dem. Rep.	1,739	2,175	..	..	..	..	..	..	..	..	..	..
Congo, Rep.	621	1,415	..	..	..	..	..	..	..	..	..	..
Costa Rica	1,990	9,798	8	6	2	1	10	11	2	1	66	80
Côte d'Ivoire	2,097	5,350	..	22	..	1	..	17	..	1	..	48
Croatia	4,500	18,547	13	8	4	1	10	15	4	2	70	73
Cuba	4,600	7,125	12	22	3	1	32	22	1	1	46	54
Czech Republic	12,880	76,707	..	5	..	2	..	7	..	4	..	79
Denmark	33,333	76,018	12	11	3	2	7	7	2	2	73	76
Dominican Republic	3,006	9,614	..	..	..	..	..	..	..	..	..	..
Ecuador	1,861	10,309	9	8	3	1	2	8	3	1	84	82
Egypt, Arab Rep.	12,412	19,819	32	22	7	5	3	8	2	4	56	50
El Salvador	1,263	6,766	14	18	3	2	16	14	4	1	63	65
Eritrea	351	495	..	..	..	..	..	..	..	..	..	..
Estonia	..	10,033	..	8	..	3	..	9	..	1	..	71
Ethiopia	1,081	4,127	..	21	..	1	..	12	..	2	..	64
Finland	27,001	58,999	5	5	2	3	12	14	4	6	76	70
France	234,436	497,853	10	8	3	1	10	13	4	3	74	75
Gabon	918	1,393	..	24	..	1	..	3	..	1	..	70
Gambia, The	188	235	..	38	..	1	..	16	..	1	..	43
Georgia	..	2,491	..	17	..	0	..	20	..	1	..	61
Germany	355,686	773,804	10	7	3	1	8	11	4	4	72	68
Ghana	1,205	5,005	11	21	1	1	17	2	0	2	70	74
Greece	19,777	53,965	15	11	3	1	8	18	3	3	70	66
Guatemala	1,649	10,493	10	11	2	1	17	16	2	1	69	71
Guinea	723	820	..	..	..	..	..	..	..	..	..	..
Guinea-Bissau	86	119	..	..	..	..	..	..	..	..	..	..
Haiti	332	1,454	..	..	..	..	..	..	..	..	..	..
†Data for Taiwan, China	54,782	182,569	7	4	5	2	11	16	6	6	69	72

Structure of merchandise imports

	Merchandise imports $ millions		Food % of total		Agricultural raw materials % of total		Fuels % of total		Ores and metals % of total		Manufactures % of total	
	1990	2005	1990	2005	1990	2005	1990	2005	1990	2005	1990	2005
Honduras	935	4,484	10	16	1	1	16	20	1	1	71	63
Hungary	10,340	66,045	8	4	4	1	14	7	4	2	70	77
India	23,580	134,831	3	3	4	2	27	36	8	5	51	52
Indonesia	21,837	69,498	5	8	5	3	9	31	4	3	77	55
Iran, Islamic Rep.	20,322	35,859	..	8	..	2	..	10	..	2	..	70
Iraq	7,660	23,430	..	..	..	..	..	..	..	..	..	..
Ireland	20,669	68,007	11	8	2	1	6	7	2	1	76	77
Israel	16,793	47,142	8	5	2	1	9	15	3	2	77	76
Italy	181,968	379,772	12	9	6	3	11	12	5	4	64	66
Jamaica	1,928	4,460	15	*16*	1	*2*	20	*23*	1	*1*	61	*57*
Japan	235,368	514,922	15	10	7	2	24	26	9	6	44	54
Jordan	2,600	10,506	26	14	1	1	18	23	1	2	52	58
Kazakhstan	..	17,353	..	*7*	..	*1*	..	*13*	..	*2*	..	*77*
Kenya	2,223	6,149	9	*10*	3	*2*	20	*24*	2	*2*	66	*61*
Korea, Dem. Rep.	2,930	2,718	..	..	..	..	..	..	..	..	..	..
Korea, Rep.	69,844	261,238	6	4	8	2	16	25	7	7	63	61
Kuwait	3,972	16,275	17	..	1	..	1	..	2	..	79	..
Kyrgyz Republic	..	1,108	..	15	..	2	..	29	..	2	..	52
Lao PDR	185	745	..	..	..	..	..	..	..	..	..	..
Latvia	..	8,696	..	11	..	3	..	15	..	1	..	66
Lebanon	2,529	9,633	..	*16*	..	*1*	..	*22*	..	*2*	..	*58*
Lesotho	672	1,390	..	..	..	..	..	..	..	..	..	..
Liberia	570	1,190	..	..	..	..	..	..	..	..	..	..
Libya	5,336	7,000	*24*	*17*	*2*	*1*	*0*	*1*	*1*	*1*	*73*	*81*
Lithuania	..	15,453	*12*	8	*5*	2	*44*	24	*2*	2	*35*	62
Macedonia, FYR	*1,206*	3,228	..	13	..	1	..	19	..	3	..	64
Madagascar	651	1,550	11	*14*	1	*0*	17	*23*	1	*0*	69	*62*
Malawi	575	1,165	9	18	1	1	11	11	1	1	78	68
Malaysia	29,258	114,602	7	5	1	1	5	8	4	4	82	80
Mali	602	1,612	26	..	1	..	19	..	1	..	53	..
Mauritania	388	750	..	..	..	..	..	..	..	..	..	..
Mauritius	1,618	3,160	12	17	3	2	8	17	1	1	76	64
Mexico	43,548	231,670	15	6	4	1	4	6	3	3	64	83
Moldova	..	2,312	..	12	..	4	..	21	..	1	..	62
Mongolia	924	1,149	..	13	..	0	..	27	..	0	..	59
Morocco	6,922	20,332	10	11	6	3	17	22	6	3	61	62
Mozambique	878	2,408	..	14	..	1	..	2	..	0	..	49
Myanmar	270	2,250	*13*	..	*1*	..	*5*	..	*0*	..	*81*	..
Namibia	1,163	2,520	..	*15*	..	*1*	..	*10*	..	*4*	..	*69*
Nepal	672	1,820	15	*17*	7	*5*	9	*16*	2	*4*	67	*59*
Netherlands	126,098	359,055	13	10	2	2	10	15	3	3	71	70
New Zealand	9,501	26,239	7	8	1	1	8	12	3	2	81	77
Nicaragua	638	2,595	19	13	1	1	19	18	1	0	59	65
Niger	388	871	..	*34*	..	*4*	..	*17*	..	*1*	..	*44*
Nigeria	5,627	17,265	*6*	*16*	*1*	*1*	*0*	*16*	*2*	*2*	*67*	*66*
Norway	27,231	55,495	6	7	2	2	4	4	6	6	82	80
Oman	2,798	8,971	19	12	1	1	4	4	1	4	69	77
Pakistan	7,411	25,331	17	11	4	4	21	22	4	3	54	60
Panama	1,539	4,155	12	12	1	1	16	18	1	1	70	68
Papua New Guinea	1,193	1,729	18	*16*	0	*1*	7	*13*	1	*0*	73	*69*
Paraguay	1,352	3,700	8	*9*	0	*1*	14	*16*	1	*1*	77	*74*
Peru	2,634	12,502	24	11	2	2	12	20	1	1	61	66
Philippines	13,042	47,418	10	7	2	1	15	14	3	2	53	75
Poland	11,570	100,951	8	6	3	2	24	11	5	3	60	75
Portugal	25,263	61,126	12	11	4	2	11	14	2	3	71	65
Puerto Rico	..	..	..	..	..	..	..	..	..	..	..	..

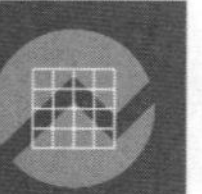

4.5 Structure of merchandise imports

	Merchandise imports $ millions		Food % of total		Agricultural raw materials % of total		Fuels % of total		Ores and metals % of total		Manufactures % of total	
	1990	2005	1990	2005	1990	2005	1990	2005	1990	2005	1990	2005
Romania	7,600	40,463	12	6	4	1	38	14	6	3	39	76
Russian Federation	..	125,303	..	16	..	1	..	2	..	2	..	73
Rwanda	288	403	..	12	..	4	..	16	..	2	..	67
Saudi Arabia	24,069	59,409	15	15	1	1	0	0	3	4	81	80
Senegal	1,219	3,190	29	28	2	2	16	23	2	2	51	45
Serbia and Montenegro	3,859	11,635	9	8	3	1	23	15	3	4	62	71
Sierra Leone	149	345	..	..	..	..	..	..	..	..	..	..
Singapore	60,774	200,047	6	3	2	0	16	18	2	2	73	77
Slovak Republic	6,670	35,337	..	6	..	1	..	14	..	3	..	75
Slovenia	6,142	20,090	9	6	4	3	11	10	4	5	67	75
Somalia	..	..	..	..	..	..	..	..	..	..	..	..
South Africa	18,399	62,304	8[b]	4	2[b]	1	1[b]	14	1[b]	2	75[b]	70
Spain	87,715	278,825	11	9	3	1	12	14	4	3	71	72
Sri Lanka	2,688	8,834	19	12	2	1	13	13	2	3	65	69
Sudan	618	6,757	13	13	1	1	20	1	0	1	66	83
Swaziland	663	2,080	..	..	..	..	..	..	..	..	..	..
Sweden	54,264	111,228	6	7	2	2	9	12	3	3	79	73
Switzerland	69,681	126,524	6	6	2	1	5	6	3	4	84	83
Syrian Arab Republic	2,400	8,106	31	17	2	4	3	7	1	3	62	64
Tajikistan	..	1,330	..	..	..	..	..	..	..	..	..	..
Tanzania	1,027	2,659	..	12	..	1	..	10	..	1	..	76
Thailand	33,045	118,191	5	4	5	2	9	18	4	4	75	70
Togo	581	895	22	16	1	1	8	29	1	2	67	53
Trinidad and Tobago	1,109	5,674	19	9	1	1	11	35	6	4	62	51
Tunisia	5,513	13,177	11	9	4	3	9	10	4	3	72	76
Turkey	22,302	116,553	8	3	4	3	21	14	5	6	61	69
Turkmenistan	..	3,588	..	..	..	..	..	..	..	..	..	..
Uganda	288	1,779	..	15	..	2	..	17	..	1	..	65
Ukraine	..	36,141	..	7	..	1	..	30	..	4	..	57
United Arab Emirates	11,199	80,744	17	..	0	..	6	..	4	..	72	..
United Kingdom	222,977	510,237	10	9	3	1	6	8	4	2	75	72
United States	516,987	1,732,348	6	4	2	1	13	17	3	2	73	72
Uruguay	1,343	3,879	7	8	4	3	18	24	2	2	69	63
Uzbekistan	..	3,666	..	..	..	..	..	..	..	..	..	..
Venezuela, RB	7,335	24,249	11	10	4	1	3	1	4	1	77	87
Vietnam	2,752	36,476	..	6	..	3	..	11	..	3	..	77
West Bank and Gaza	..	..	..	..	..	..	..	..	..	..	..	..
Yemen, Rep.	1,571	4,260	27	24	1	1	40	21	1	1	31	53
Zambia	1,220	2,750	..	6	..	1	..	12	..	3	..	78
Zimbabwe	1,847	2,330	4	19	3	2	16	14	2	10	73	54
World	3,549,585 t	10,684,930 t	9 w	6 w	3 w	2 w	11 w	14 w	4 w	3 w	71 w	72 w
Low income	78,024	316,559	7	11	3	3	22	22	5	3	56	61
Middle income	512,919	2,552,089	10	6	4	2	10	11	3	4	70	74
Lower middle income	273,099	1,380,029	10	6	5	3	9	15	3	5	72	71
Upper middle income	237,015	1,172,061	10	6	3	1	10	9	4	3	68	78
Low & middle income	592,618	2,868,603	10	6	4	2	11	13	4	4	69	73
East Asia & Pacific	160,502	1,061,614	8	4	5	3	5	13	3	6	77	74
Europe & Central Asia	163,450	747,497	..	7	..	2	..	11	..	3	..	72
Latin America & Carib.	120,119	520,640	12	6	3	1	10	10	3	3	66	79
Middle East & N. Africa	80,058	181,770	..	15	..	3	..	10	..	3	..	66
South Asia	39,124	188,994	8	5	4	2	24	32	6	5	54	55
Sub-Saharan Africa	57,641	168,092	..	12	..	1	..	14	..	2	..	67
High income	2,943,620	7,816,297	9	7	3	1	11	14	4	3	71	72
Europe EMU	1,261,194	3,018,041	11	8	3	2	9	13	4	3	71	71

Note: Components may not sum to 100 percent because of unclassified trade.
a. Includes Luxembourg. b. Refers to the South African Customs Union (Botswana, Lesotho, Namibia, South Africa, and Swaziland).

Structure of merchandise imports 4.5

About the data

Data on imports of goods are derived from the same sources as data on exports. In principle, world exports and imports should be identical. Similarly, exports from an economy should equal the sum of imports by the rest of the world from that economy. But differences in timing and definitions result in discrepancies in reported values at all levels. For further discussion of indicators of merchandise trade, see *About the data* for tables 4.4 and 6.2.

The value of imports is generally recorded as the cost of the goods when purchased by the importer plus the cost of transport and insurance to the frontier of the importing country—the cost, insurance, and freight (c.i.f.) value, corresponding to the landed cost at the point of entry of foreign goods into the country. A few countries, including Australia, Canada, and the United States, collect import data on a free on board (f.o.b.) basis and adjust them for freight and insurance costs. Many countries collect and report trade data in U.S. dollars. When countries report in local currency, the United Nations Statistics Division applies the average official exchange rate for the period shown.

Countries may report trade according to the general or special system of trade (see *Primary data documentation*). Under the general system imports include goods imported for domestic consumption and imports into bonded warehouses and free trade zones. Under the special system imports comprise goods imported for domestic consumption (including transformation and repair) and withdrawals for domestic consumption from bonded warehouses and free trade zones. Goods transported through a country en route to another are excluded.

The data on total imports of goods (merchandise) in this table come from the World Trade Organization (WTO). For further discussion of the WTO's sources and methodology, see *About the data* for table 4.4. The shares of imports by major commodity group are from the United Nations Statistics Division's Commodity Trade (Comtrade) database. The values of total imports reported here have not been fully reconciled with the estimates of imports of goods and services from the national accounts (shown in table 4.8) or those from the balance of payments (table 4.15).

The classification of commodity groups is based on the Standard International Trade Classification (SITC) revision 1. Most countries now report using later revisions of the SITC or the Harmonized System. Concordance tables are used to convert data reported in one system of nomenclature to another. The conversion process may introduce some errors of classification, but conversions from later to earlier systems are generally reliable. Shares may not sum to 100 percent because of unclassified trade.

Top 10 developing country exporters of merchandise in 2005 **4.5a**

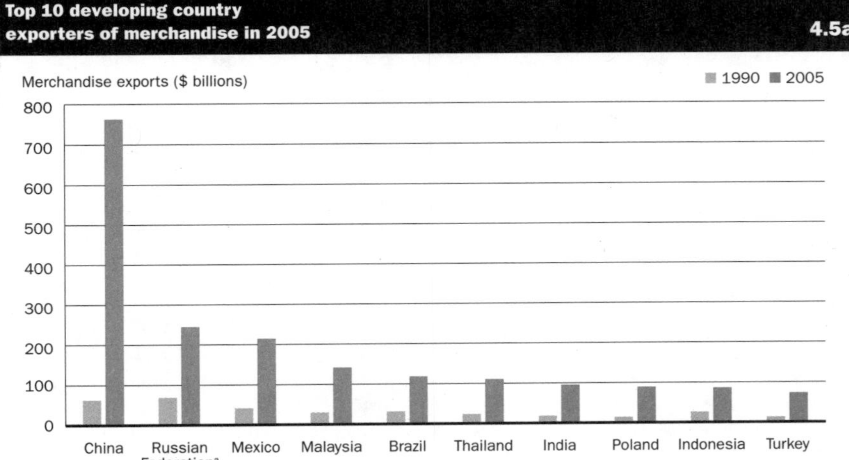

China continues to be the top developing country exporter. The Russian Federation has surpassed Mexico.

a. Data are for 1994 and 2005.
Source: World Trade Organization data files.

Definitions

• **Merchandise imports** are the c.i.f. value of goods purchased from the rest of the world valued in U.S. dollars. • **Food** corresponds to the commodities in SITC sections 0 (food and live animals), 1 (beverages and tobacco), and 4 (animal and vegetable oils and fats) and SITC division 22 (oil seeds, oil nuts, and oil kernels). • **Agricultural raw materials** correspond to SITC section 2 (crude materials except fuels) excluding divisions 22, 27 (crude fertilizers and minerals excluding coal, petroleum, and precious stones), and 28 (metalliferous ores and scrap). • **Fuels** correspond to SITC section 3 (mineral fuels). • **Ores and metals** correspond to the commodities in SITC divisions 27, 28, and 68 (nonferrous metals). • **Manufactures** correspond to the commodities in SITC sections 5 (chemicals), 6 (basic manufactures), 7 (machinery and transport equipment), and 8 (miscellaneous manufactured goods), excluding division 68.

Data sources

The WTO publishes data on world trade in its *Annual Report.* The International Monetary Fund publishes estimates of total imports of goods in its *International Financial Statistics* and *Direction of Trade Statistics,* as does the United Nations Statistics Division in its *Monthly Bulletin of Statistics.* And the United Nations Conference on Trade and Development publishes data on the structure of exports and imports in its *Handbook of International Trade and Development Statistics.* Tariff line records of exports and imports are compiled in the United Nations Statistics Division's Comtrade database.

4.6 Structure of service exports

	Commercial service exports		Transport		Travel		Insurance and financial services		Computer, information, communications, and other commercial services	
	$ millions		% of commercial services		% of commercial services		% of commercial services		% of commercial services	
	1990	2005	1990	2005	1990	2005	1990	2005	1990	2005
Afghanistan	*1*	..	..	..	..	..	..	..	..	..
Albania	32	1,154	20.0	10.9	11.1	74.0	2.2	1.9	66.7	13.2
Algeria	479	..	41.7	..	13.4	..	5.9	..	39.0	..
Angola	65	177	48.8	10.2	20.6	49.9	4.6	..	26.1	39.9
Argentina	2,264	6,121	51.1	21.2	39.9	45.0	..	0.1	9.0	33.8
Armenia	*17*	323	..	28.5	..	43.5	..	4.7	..	23.3
Australia	9,835	27,767	35.4	22.4	43.2	53.9	4.2	4.7	17.2	19.1
Austria	22,755	53,104	6.4	20.1	59.0	29.4	2.9	6.6	31.7	44.0
Azerbaijan	..	625	..	38.3	..	12.4	..	1.3	..	48.0
Bangladesh	296	472	13.0	23.8	6.4	14.8	0.1	4.8	80.6	56.6
Belarus	*185*	1,942	*54.1*	63.0	*13.3*	13.0	*1.0*	0.2	*31.6*	23.7
Belgium	26,646[a]	53,536	27.5[a]	26.0	14.0[a]	18.4	18.2[a]	7.9	40.3[a]	47.8
Benin	109	*204*	33.4	*16.5*	50.2	*58.1*	6.9	*1.5*	9.5	*23.9*
Bolivia	133	473	35.8	30.3	43.6	50.5	10.0	9.0	10.6	10.2
Bosnia and Herzegovina	..	1,010	..	6.9	..	56.0	..	3.5	..	33.6
Botswana	183	844	20.4	10.1	64.1	66.6	8.2	9.0	7.3	14.4
Brazil	3,706	14,901	36.4	21.4	37.3	25.9	3.1	4.3	23.2	48.4
Bulgaria	837	4,288	27.5	26.1	38.2	56.2	3.1	1.1	31.2	16.6
Burkina Faso	34	..	37.1	..	34.1	..	..	..	28.9	..
Burundi	7	7	38.7	25.6	51.4	22.2	1.6	0.7	8.3	51.5
Cambodia	*50*	1,052	..	12.0	..	79.8	..	0.1	..	8.1
Cameroon	369	*393*	42.6	*30.5*	14.4	*28.9*	9.4	*9.8*	33.6	*30.8*
Canada	18,350	52,193	23.0	18.4	34.7	26.0	..	9.3	42.3	46.3
Central African Republic	17	..	50.9	..	16.0	..	18.8	..	14.3	..
Chad	23	..	18.4	..	34.1	..	0.2	..	47.3	..
Chile	1,786	7,077	40.0	59.3	29.8	17.8	4.9	2.6	25.3	20.4
China	5,748	73,909	47.1	20.9	30.2	39.6	4.0	0.9	18.7	38.6
Hong Kong, China	..	62,175	..	*31.5*	..	*16.3*	..	*9.0*	..	*43.2*
Colombia	1,548	2,590	31.3	30.1	26.2	47.0	17.1	1.2	25.5	21.7
Congo, Dem. Rep.	..	..	..	..	..	..	..	..	..	..
Congo, Rep.	65	223	53.9	34.3	12.9	15.1	..	*15.9*	33.2	50.6
Costa Rica	583	2,579	16.3	10.9	48.9	64.6	..	0.4	34.8	24.1
Côte d'Ivoire	425	658	62.4	22.0	12.1	12.7	8.3	*14.9*	17.2	65.3
Croatia	*2,216*	9,920	*29.2*	11.0	*59.1*	74.3	*1.4*	0.6	*10.3*	14.1
Cuba	..	..	..	..	..	..	..	..	..	..
Czech Republic	*4,679*	10,729	*26.5*	30.6	*33.3*	43.1	*9.6*	4.1	*30.6*	22.3
Denmark	12,731	42,383	32.5	*47.1*	26.2	*15.6*	2.3	..	39.0	*37.4*
Dominican Republic	1,086	3,840	5.6	3.4	66.9	91.4	0.2	0.4	27.3	4.9
Ecuador	508	940	47.6	35.6	37.0	51.7	9.3	0.1	6.1	12.6
Egypt, Arab Rep.	4,813	14,449	50.1	32.8	22.9	47.4	1.0	1.4	26.1	18.4
El Salvador	301	1,116	26.2	32.5	25.3	48.6	7.5	3.6	41.1	15.3
Eritrea	*73*	..	*85.7*	..	*1.0*	..	..	..	*13.3*	..
Estonia	*200*	3,117	*74.7*	40.0	*13.7*	30.4	*0.1*	1.8	*11.5*	27.8
Ethiopia	261	789	80.7	59.0	2.1	21.3	0.7	4.0	16.6	15.7
Finland	4,562	16,895	38.4	14.4	25.8	12.9	0.1	0.9	35.6	71.8
France	74,948	114,955	21.7	23.6	27.1	36.7	14.8	2.7	36.4	37.0
Gabon	214	*136*	33.4	*59.8*	1.4	*7.2*	5.8	*17.1*	59.4	*15.9*
Gambia, The	53	80	8.8	19.4	87.9	70.8	0.1	0.5	3.3	9.4
Georgia	..	631	..	49.9	..	38.3	..	5.0	..	6.8
Germany	50,562	148,540	29.2	25.6	28.3	19.6	1.0	5.6	41.5	49.2
Ghana	79	1,043	49.2	14.0	5.6	76.3	2.7	0.8	42.6	8.9
Greece	6,514	34,051	4.9	50.8	39.7	39.9	0.1	1.1	55.2	8.3
Guatemala	313	1,138	7.4	8.6	37.6	74.3	2.0	6.3	53.1	10.8
Guinea	91	*31*	14.2	*21.8*	32.6	..	0.1	*0.4*	53.2	*77.8*
Guinea-Bissau	4	6	5.4	*22.9*	..	*16.6*	..	*19.5*	94.6	*41.0*
Haiti	43	112	19.8	..	78.9	98.0	1.3	..	..	2.0

Structure of service exports 4.6

	Commercial service exports		Transport		Travel		Insurance and financial services		Computer, information, communications, and other commercial services	
	$ millions		% of commercial services		% of commercial services		% of commercial services		% of commercial services	
	1990	2005	1990	2005	1990	2005	1990	2005	1990	2005
Honduras	121	716	35.1	10.2	24.0	65.9	12.9	2.4	28.0	21.4
Hungary	2,677	12,294	1.6	14.9	36.8	34.8	0.2	2.8	61.4	47.5
India	4,610	56,094[b]	20.8	13.3	33.8	16.8	2.7	3.5	42.7	66.4
Indonesia	2,488	12,570	2.8	22.6	86.5	36.0	..	3.0	10.7	38.4
Iran, Islamic Rep.	343	..	10.5	..	8.2	..	6.4	..	74.9	..
Iraq	..	..	..	..	..	..	..	..	..	..
Ireland	3,286	56,768	31.1	4.7	44.4	8.3	..	25.2	24.5	61.9
Israel	4,546	17,731	30.8	20.8	30.7	16.1	–0.3	0.1	38.8	63.0
Italy	48,579	88,820	21.0	17.6	33.9	39.8	5.5	3.1	39.6	39.6
Jamaica	976	2,296	18.0	19.7	77.0	67.3	1.4	2.8	3.6	10.2
Japan	41,384	107,876	40.4	33.1	7.9	11.5	–0.4	5.5	52.1	49.9
Jordan	1,430	2,188	26.0	21.5	35.8	65.8	..	..	38.3	12.7
Kazakhstan	..	2,019	..	51.6	..	34.7	..	1.1	..	12.6
Kenya	774	1,523	32.1	48.4	60.2	38.0	0.7	0.7	7.1	12.9
Korea, Dem. Rep.	..	..	..	..	..	..	..	..	..	..
Korea, Rep.	9,155	43,927	34.7	54.4	34.5	12.9	0.1	4.6	30.7	28.2
Kuwait	1,054	3,790	87.5	58.4	12.5	4.4	..	3.1	..	34.2
Kyrgyz Republic	9	234	25.1	25.9	3.8	31.3	..	1.7	71.1	41.1
Lao PDR	11	..	74.8	..	24.3	..	0.9	..	..	..
Latvia	290	2,137	94.9	57.2	2.5	16.0	..	6.5	2.6	20.3
Lebanon	..	10,740	..	4.1	..	50.6	..	2.3	..	43.0
Lesotho	34	47	14.1	1.3	51.2	64.9	..	–4.9	34.7	38.7
Liberia	32	..	84.6	..	15.4	..	..	..	..	..
Libya	83	419	83.8	27.7	7.7	59.7	..	10.3	8.5	2.4
Lithuania	198	3,075	83.6	51.6	10.9	30.0	..	0.5	5.5	17.9
Macedonia, FYR	..	445	..	30.0	..	18.8	..	1.9	..	49.3
Madagascar	129	142	32.1	28.2	31.3	43.6	0.3	0.1	36.4	28.1
Malawi	37	49	46.1	32.7	42.6	67.3	0.1	..	11.2	..
Malaysia	3,769	19,463	31.8	20.8	44.7	45.5	0.1	1.7	23.5	32.0
Mali	71	227	31.0	13.5	54.3	61.9	4.9	2.3	9.8	22.2
Mauritania	14	..	35.3	..	64.7	..	..	..	..	..
Mauritius	478	1,604	33.0	23.9	51.1	54.3	0.1	1.3	15.8	20.5
Mexico	7,222	16,098	12.4	10.9	76.5	73.3	4.6	9.6	6.5	6.2
Moldova	..	409	..	41.5	..	31.3	..	0.9	..	26.3
Mongolia	48	329	41.8	32.7	10.4	56.2	4.6	1.2	43.2	9.9
Morocco	1,871	7,570	9.6	17.2	68.4	60.9	0.8	1.0	21.2	21.0
Mozambique	103	316	61.3	28.3	..	41.1	..	0.4	38.7	30.2
Myanmar	94	232	10.3	36.8	20.9	36.2	0.5	..	68.3	27.0
Namibia	106	463	..	7.1	81.0	87.5	5.9	..	13.1	5.5
Nepal	166	271	3.6	12.0	65.6	48.4	..	1.4	30.8	38.2
Netherlands	28,478	78,183	45.4	27.4	14.6	13.4	0.8	1.7	39.2	57.5
New Zealand	2,415	8,408	43.4	19.5	42.7	59.3	–0.3	1.4	14.2	19.9
Nicaragua	34	272	19.2	12.4	35.5	76.2	..	1.0	45.4	10.4
Niger	22	88	5.2	8.5	59.5	35.6	13.5	1.4	21.8	54.4
Nigeria	965	4,164	3.9	17.5	2.5	0.4	0.3	0.2	93.3	81.8
Norway	12,452	28,457	68.7	54.7	12.6	11.5	0.4	1.6	18.3	32.2
Oman	68	822	15.3	36.4	84.7	58.5	..	0.6	..	4.4
Pakistan	1,218	2,042	59.3	52.7	12.0	8.9	1.4	3.9	27.3	34.6
Panama	907	3,106	64.9	57.2	18.9	25.1	3.8	7.5	12.4	10.3
Papua New Guinea	198	285	11.2	10.9	12.0	1.3	0.5	5.4	76.3	82.4
Paraguay	404	615	18.3	14.6	21.1	12.6	..	4.6	60.5	68.2
Peru	714	2,057	43.4	21.8	30.4	60.3	11.2	5.8	15.0	12.1
Philippines	2,897	4,462	8.5	23.3	16.1	47.7	0.5	1.5	74.9	27.5
Poland	3,200	16,181	57.3	33.7	11.2	38.8	4.0	1.8	27.6	25.8
Portugal	5,054	14,940	15.6	21.4	70.4	52.8	0.7	2.1	13.3	23.7
Puerto Rico	..	..	..	..	..	..	..	..	..	..

4.6 Structure of service exports

	Commercial service exports		Transport		Travel		Insurance and financial services		Computer, information, communications, and other commercial services	
	$ millions		% of commercial services		% of commercial services		% of commercial services		% of commercial services	
	1990	2005	1990	2005	1990	2005	1990	2005	1990	2005
Romania	610	5,056	50.5	29.1	17.4	20.8	5.6	2.6	26.6	47.5
Russian Federation	..	24,337	..	37.4	..	22.5	..	2.9	..	37.2
Rwanda	31	83	56.1	36.1	32.8	58.6	1.0	0.1	10.0	5.1
Saudi Arabia	3,027	5,916	..	..	..	..	..	..	..	..
Senegal	356	*598*	19.2	*16.1*	42.8	*35.4*	0.5	*1.6*	37.6	*47.0*
Serbia and Montenegro	..	..	..	..	..	..	..	..	..	..
Sierra Leone	45	78	9.7	14.9	76.2	82.1	..	3.0	14.1	0.1
Singapore	12,719	51,200	17.5	35.0	36.6	11.2	0.7	9.4	45.3	44.4
Slovak Republic	*1,939*	*3,270*	*23.7*	*43.2*	*19.8*	*26.4*	..	*2.3*	*56.5*	*28.1*
Slovenia	*1,219*	3,969	*22.6*	28.9	*55.0*	45.2	*1.2*	0.9	*21.2*	25.0
Somalia	..	..	..	..	..	..	..	..	..	..
South Africa	3,291	10,898	21.6	14.1	55.8	67.3	10.8	6.1	11.9	12.6
Spain	27,649	92,730	17.2	16.6	67.2	51.4	4.3	3.8	11.3	28.2
Sri Lanka	425	1,519	39.7	44.3	30.2	28.3	4.2	4.8	25.9	22.6
Sudan	134	101	14.1	3.4	15.7	88.7	0.5	4.1	69.7	3.9
Swaziland	102	272	24.5	10.3	29.2	25.5	..	56.0	46.3	8.2
Sweden	13,453	42,761	35.8	20.5	21.7	17.2	9.1	5.4	33.5	56.9
Switzerland	18,325	45,794	16.3	9.5	40.4	24.2	23.7	32.6	19.6	33.8
Syrian Arab Republic	740	2,827	29.8	8.6	43.3	76.9	..	1.0	27.0	13.4
Tajikistan	..	103	..	54.4	..	1.5	..	8.1	..	36.0
Tanzania	131	1,181	19.9	17.2	36.4	69.7	0.5	3.4	43.1	9.7
Thailand	6,292	20,495	21.1	22.6	68.7	49.3	0.2	1.4	10.0	26.8
Togo	114	*122*	26.9	*38.2*	50.8	*15.7*	13.7	*1.5*	8.6	*44.6*
Trinidad and Tobago	322	*838*	50.7	*35.2*	29.4	*40.8*	..	*13.5*	19.9	*10.5*
Tunisia	1,575	3,884	23.0	29.3	64.8	54.7	1.5	2.5	10.7	13.5
Turkey	7,882	25,552	11.7	15.8	40.9	71.0	..	2.6	47.4	10.6
Turkmenistan	..	..	..	..	..	..	..	..	..	..
Uganda	..	466	..	2.3	..	76.2	..	4.6	..	16.9
Ukraine	..	8,913	..	50.3	..	35.1	..	0.7	..	14.0
United Arab Emirates	..	..	..	..	..	..	..	..	..	..
United Kingdom	53,830	199,454	25.2	16.5	29.0	15.3	16.4	22.7	29.4	45.4
United States	132,880	354,020	28.1	17.9	37.9	28.8	3.5	10.2	30.5	43.1
Uruguay	460	1,304	36.9	33.8	51.8	45.5	1.0	5.3	10.3	15.4
Uzbekistan	..	..	..	..	..	..	..	..	..	..
Venezuela, RB	1,121	1,240	40.9	31.1	44.3	51.7	0.2	0.1	14.7	17.1
Vietnam	..	4,176	..	..	..	..	..	..	..	..
West Bank and Gaza	..	..	..	..	..	..	..	..	..	..
Yemen, Rep.	82	285	27.2	16.1	48.8	63.3	..	..	24.0	20.6
Zambia	95	..	68.9	..	13.5	..	4.1	..	13.4	..
Zimbabwe	253	..	44.3	..	25.3	..	1.2	..	29.2	..
World	**815,799 t**	**2,459,852 t**	**28.4 w**	**24.1 w**	**34.9 w**	**28.4 w**	**4.7 w**	**6.8 w**	**38.5 w**	***41.5 w***
Low income	13,307	84,840	23.8	*19.5*	23.3	*18.8*	1.9	*3.1*	51.2	*58.9*
Middle income	97,390	412,960	29.7	23.6	44.9	45.7	3.1	3.2	22.4	27.5
Lower middle income	46,586	217,782	32.1	23.5	39.5	41.3	3.3	1.8	25.2	33.4
Upper middle income	51,500	195,671	26.9	23.7	51.4	49.8	2.8	4.4	19.0	22.1
Low & middle income	110,583	495,951	29.2	23.7	43.0	44.6	3.0	3.1	24.9	28.7
East Asia & Pacific	22,788	137,881	32.3	21.4	43.5	42.1	2.0	1.5	22.2	35.0
Europe & Central Asia	*41,109*	142,205	..	33.1	..	34.5	..	2.5	..	29.8
Latin America & Carib.	25,840	72,823	25.8	19.5	56.2	56.5	4.1	5.8	13.9	18.2
Middle East & N. Africa	..	..	31.1	..	29.3	..	3.4	..	36.4	..
South Asia	6,847	60,989	26.8	*22.1*	28.2	*17.4*	2.3	*3.7*	42.7	*56.8*
Sub-Saharan Africa	9,580	29,946	25.7	16.7	31.6	42.1	5.4	3.8	37.9	37.7
High income	701,445	1,962,711	28.1	24.3	32.3	23.5	5.2	7.8	42.2	45.3
Europe EMU	312,162	796,772	27.1	22.8	30.3	26.5	5.9	5.1	36.7	45.7

a. Includes Luxembourg. b. World Trade Organization estimate.

Structure of service exports 4.6

About the data

Balance of payments statistics, the main source of information on international trade in services, have many weaknesses. Some large economies—such as the former Soviet Union—did not report data on trade in services until recently. Disaggregation of important components may be limited, and it varies significantly across countries. There are inconsistencies in the methods used to report items. And the recording of major flows as net items is common (for example, insurance transactions are often recorded as premiums less claims). These factors contribute to a downward bias in the value of the service trade reported in the balance of payments.

Efforts are being made to improve the coverage, quality, and consistency of these data. Eurostat and the Organisation for Economic Co-operation and Development, for example, are working together to improve the collection of statistics on trade in services in member countries. In addition, the International Monetary Fund (IMF) has implemented the new classification of trade in services introduced in the fifth edition of its *Balance of Payments Manual* (1993).

Still, difficulties in capturing all the dimensions of international trade in services mean that the record is likely to remain incomplete. Cross-border intrafirm service transactions, which are usually not captured in the balance of payments, have increased in recent years. One example of such transactions is transnational corporations' use of mainframe computers around the clock for data processing, exploiting time zone differences between their home country and the host countries of their affiliates. Another important dimension of service trade not captured by conventional balance of payments statistics is establishment trade—sales in the host country by foreign affiliates. By contrast, cross-border intrafirm transactions in merchandise may be reported as exports or imports in the balance of payments.

The data on exports of services in this table and on imports of services in table 4.7, unlike those in editions before 2000, include only commercial services and exclude the category "government services not included elsewhere." The data are compiled by the IMF based on returns from national sources. Data on total trade in goods and services from the IMF's Balance of Payments database are shown in table 4.15.

Top 10 developing country exporters of commercial services in 2005 — 4.6a

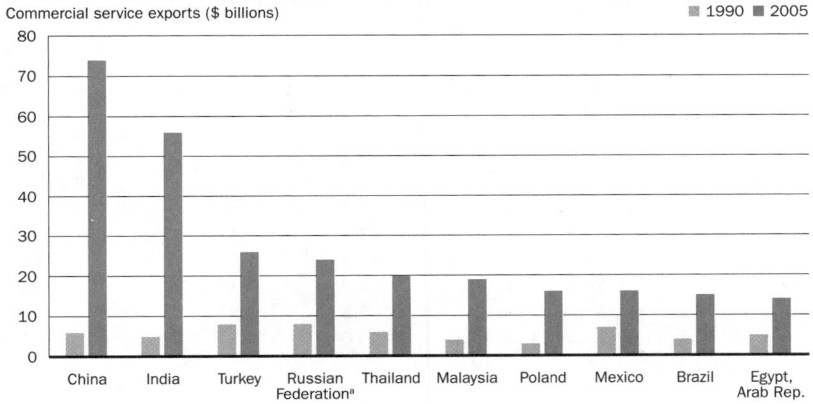

Commercial service exports ($ billions)

The top 10 developing country exporters of commercial services accounted for 60 percent of developing country commercial service exports and almost 12 percent of world commercial service exports.

a. Data are for 1994 and 2005.
Source: International Monetary Fund and World Trade Organization data files.

Definitions

• **Commercial service exports** are total service exports minus exports of government services not included elsewhere. International transactions in services are defined by the IMF's *Balance of Payments Manual* (1993) as the economic output of intangible commodities that may be produced, transferred, and consumed at the same time. Definitions may vary among reporting economies. • **Transport** covers all transport services (sea, air, land, internal waterway, space, and pipeline) performed by residents of one economy for those of another and involving the carriage of passengers, movement of goods (freight), rental of carriers with crew, and related support and auxiliary services. Excluded are freight insurance, which is included in insurance services; goods procured in ports by nonresident carriers and repairs of transport equipment, which are included in goods; repairs of harbors, railway facilities, and airfield facilities, which are included in construction services; and rental of carriers without crew, which is included in other services. • **Travel** covers goods and services acquired from an economy by travelers in that economy for their own use during visits of less than one year for business or personal purposes. Travel services include the goods and services consumed by travelers, such as meals, lodging, and transport (within the economy visited), including car rental. • **Insurance and financial services** cover freight insurance on goods exported and other direct insurance such as life insurance, financial intermediation services such as commissions, foreign exchange transactions, and brokerage services; and auxiliary services such as financial market operational and regulatory services. • **Computer, information, communications, and other commercial services** include such activities as international telecommunications and postal and courier services; computer data; news-related service transactions between residents and nonresidents; construction services; royalties and license fees; miscellaneous business, professional, and technical services; and personal, cultural, and recreational services.

Data sources

Data on exports of commercial services are from the IMF. The IMF publishes balance of payments data in its *International Financial Statistics* and *Balance of Payments Statistics Yearbook.*

4.7 Structure of service imports

	Commercial service imports		Transport		Travel		Insurance and financial services		Computer, information, communications, and other commercial services	
	$ millions		% of commercial services		% of commercial services		% of commercial services		% of commercial services	
	1990	2005	1990	2005	1990	2005	1990	2005	1990	2005
Afghanistan	*97*	..	*85.9*	..	..	..	*9.5*	..	*4.6*	..
Albania	29	1,318	26.3	17.2	..	59.7	2.9	3.6	70.8	19.5
Algeria	1,155	..	58.1	..	12.9	..	9.8	..	19.2	..
Angola	1,288	6,191	38.3	21.3	3.0	1.2	2.6	1.9	56.1	75.6
Argentina	2,876	7,353	32.6	26.8	40.7	38.3	...	6.1	26.7	28.7
Armenia	*40*	377	*89.2*	50.6	*0.9*	31.1	*9.9*	6.8	*0.0*	11.5
Australia	13,388	28,753	33.9	35.5	31.5	39.2	4.8	3.9	29.8	21.3
Austria	14,104	49,002	8.4	14.9	54.9	22.4	4.6	6.7	32.1	56.1
Azerbaijan	..	2,625	..	14.4	..	6.3	..	1.9	..	77.4
Bangladesh	554	1,983	71.1	76.9	14.1	6.6	6.6	8.1	8.3	8.4
Belarus	*125*	1,213	*34.0*	25.5	*44.6*	49.8	*12.3*	2.0	*9.2*	22.8
Belgium	25,924[a]	50,518	23.3[a]	24.4	21.1[a]	29.3	14.8[a]	8.0	40.8[a]	38.3
Benin	113	*273*	46.9	*63.4*	12.8	*10.6*	5.7	*11.3*	34.6	*14.7*
Bolivia	291	664	61.7	35.2	20.6	28.1	10.0	18.5	7.6	18.3
Bosnia and Herzegovina	..	449	..	44.7	..	27.3	..	12.8	..	15.3
Botswana	371	840	57.5	40.5	15.0	33.6	5.5	3.7	22.0	22.2
Brazil	6,733	22,296	44.4	22.3	22.4	21.2	2.7	6.5	30.5	50.1
Bulgaria	600	3,457	40.5	34.7	31.5	37.4	4.5	3.6	23.5	24.3
Burkina Faso	196	..	64.7	..	16.6	..	5.1	..	13.6	..
Burundi	59	104	62.6	21.1	29.0	58.1	6.3	4.2	2.2	16.7
Cambodia	*64*	620	*24.5*	57.9	..	15.6	..	4.7	*75.5*	21.8
Cameroon	1,018	*1,053*	45.3	*31.7*	27.5	*20.1*	7.2	*8.3*	20.1	*40.0*
Canada	27,479	64,170	21.1	22.6	39.8	28.6	..	10.9	39.2	37.9
Central African Republic	166	..	49.7	..	30.6	..	8.9	..	10.7	..
Chad	223	..	45.1	..	31.2	..	4.4	..	19.2	..
Chile	1,982	7,591	47.4	54.2	21.5	13.9	3.3	9.6	27.9	22.3
China	4,113	83,173	78.9	34.2	11.4	26.2	2.3	8.9	7.4	30.8
Hong Kong, China	..	32,384	..	*28.0*	..	*42.8*	..	*5.7*	..	*23.4*
Colombia	1,683	4,701	34.9	44.8	27.0	24.0	13.7	9.2	24.4	22.0
Congo, Dem. Rep.	..	..	..	..	..	..	..	..	..	..
Congo, Rep.	748	1,550	18.4	19.9	15.2	6.6	1.6	..	64.9	73.5
Costa Rica	540	1,496	41.2	42.3	28.8	31.5	6.0	6.0	24.0	20.3
Côte d'Ivoire	1,518	1,942	32.1	51.7	11.1	17.8	4.7	..	52.0	30.5
Croatia	*1,088*	3,349	*30.5*	18.7	*34.4*	22.5	*3.7*	4.1	*31.4*	54.8
Cuba	..	..	..	..	..	..	..	..	..	..
Czech Republic	*3,701*	9,870	*19.8*	18.2	*14.2*	24.4	*14.0*	11.9	*52.0*	45.5
Denmark	10,106	37,841	38.3	*43.4*	36.5	*21.8*	1.6	..	23.6	*34.8*
Dominican Republic	435	1,409	40.0	61.0	33.1	25.0	4.1	7.3	22.9	6.6
Ecuador	755	2,049	41.6	50.8	23.2	19.6	8.1	7.1	27.2	22.6
Egypt, Arab Rep.	3,327	9,507	44.0	39.3	3.9	17.1	4.6	10.3	47.5	33.3
El Salvador	296	1,194	45.9	44.1	20.6	29.0	12.1	9.3	21.5	17.6
Eritrea	*1*	..	..	..	..	..	..	..	..	..
Estonia	*123*	2,132	*76.3*	44.4	*15.4*	21.0	*0.3*	1.9	*8.0*	32.7
Ethiopia	348	1,178	76.5	64.9	3.3	6.5	3.4	5.1	16.9	23.5
Finland	7,432	15,061	26.1	26.8	37.2	20.3	1.1	1.6	35.5	51.3
France	59,560	104,897	29.4	27.3	20.7	29.7	19.2	5.1	30.7	37.9
Gabon	984	*921*	23.2	*33.5*	13.9	*23.2*	5.3	*5.8*	57.6	*37.5*
Gambia, The	35	45	65.1	75.4	23.1	11.7	9.0	10.8	2.8	2.2
Georgia	..	578	..	49.0	..	29.2	..	10.4	..	11.4
Germany	83,264	200,944	20.5	21.7	46.9	36.1	1.0	4.5	31.6	37.7
Ghana	226	1,131	55.1	51.3	5.9	26.8	11.2	5.1	27.8	16.8
Greece	2,756	14,292	34.0	54.2	39.5	21.3	5.4	5.7	21.0	18.9
Guatemala	363	1,423	41.0	51.3	27.4	31.2	3.4	11.8	28.2	5.7
Guinea	243	*195*	57.5	*47.3*	12.2	*12.8*	5.5	*12.7*	24.9	*27.2*
Guinea-Bissau	17	*42*	54.5	*53.5*	19.8	*30.9*	5.6	*0.4*	20.0	*15.1*
Haiti	71	431	47.9	50.4	52.1	12.6	..	..	..	37.0

Structure of service imports

	Commercial service imports		Transport		Travel		Insurance and financial services		Computer, information, communications, and other commercial services	
	$ millions		% of commercial services		% of commercial services		% of commercial services		% of commercial services	
	1990	2005	1990	2005	1990	2005	1990	2005	1990	2005
Honduras	213	831	45.4	49.8	17.6	29.9	15.0	..	22.0	20.4
Hungary	2,264	11,626	8.8	15.3	25.9	25.2	1.0	5.4	64.4	54.1
India	5,943	52,211[b]	57.5	*36.7*	6.6	*13.8*	5.8	*6.5*	30.1	*43.1*
Indonesia	5,898	23,516	47.4	29.9	14.2	15.2	4.0	3.7	34.5	51.1
Iran, Islamic Rep.	3,703	..	47.3	..	9.2	..	10.8	..	32.8	..
Iraq	..	..	..	..	..	..	..	..	..	..
Ireland	5,145	69,759	24.3	3.5	22.6	8.7	1.9	14.9	51.2	73.0
Israel	4,825	13,439	39.6	35.1	29.7	21.5	4.4	3.1	26.3	40.3
Italy	46,602	88,889	23.7	24.8	22.1	25.2	10.4	3.6	43.9	46.5
Jamaica	667	1,683	47.9	43.1	17.0	14.8	6.7	10.0	28.4	32.1
Japan	84,281	132,601	*30.8*	30.5	*27.9*	28.3	*2.1*	3.5	*39.3*	37.8
Jordan	1,118	2,465	52.0	54.4	30.1	23.7	5.2	8.5	12.7	13.3
Kazakhstan	..	7,404	..	15.8	..	10.2	..	3.1	..	71.0
Kenya	598	950	66.2	44.0	6.4	13.0	8.9	13.7	18.5	29.2
Korea, Dem. Rep.	..	..	..	..	..	..	..	..	..	..
Korea, Rep.	10,050	57,746	39.8	34.6	27.5	26.5	-0.1	1.4	32.8	37.5
Kuwait	2,805	7,571	31.9	39.8	65.5	56.5	1.2	1.9	1.4	1.8
Kyrgyz Republic	*51*	287	*74.1*	41.4	*0.8*	20.3	*7.6*	6.8	*17.6*	31.5
Lao PDR	25	..	73.0	..	*13.3*	..	6.4	..	20.6	..
Latvia	*120*	1,541	*82.3*	32.5	*10.9*	37.9	*4.8*	3.8	*2.1*	25.8
Lebanon	..	7,838	..	17.0	..	36.7	..	3.1	..	43.2
Lesotho	48	79	67.9	65.9	24.7	34.1	5.6	..	1.7	..
Liberia	*74*	..	*60.8*	..	*33.7*	..	*5.6*	..	..	..
Libya	926	2,128	41.9	47.7	45.8	32.0	4.1	8.5	8.3	11.8
Lithuania	*177*	1,989	*90.7*	45.1	*6.9*	37.4	..	1.7	*2.4*	15.9
Macedonia, FYR	..	483	..	41.2	..	12.3	..	4.3	..	42.2
Madagascar	172	157	43.5	48.5	23.4	15.8	3.5	1.0	29.5	34.7
Malawi	268	*222*	81.8	*50.1*	5.9	*35.2*	8.7	*0.0*	3.7	*14.7*
Malaysia	5,394	21,750	46.9	38.6	26.9	17.1	..	2.9	26.2	41.4
Mali	352	*528*	57.4	*64.9*	15.8	*12.6*	1.9	*6.5*	24.9	*16.0*
Mauritania	126	..	76.9	..	18.3	..	3.1	..	1.7	..
Mauritius	407	1,211	51.6	43.1	23.0	22.7	5.5	5.3	19.9	28.9
Mexico	10,063	20,915	25.0	13.0	54.9	36.3	6.2	44.3	14.0	6.4
Moldova	..	418	..	35.2	..	40.4	..	1.6	..	22.8
Mongolia	155	*496*	56.2	*40.2*	0.8	*38.8*	6.3	*8.2*	36.8	*12.8*
Morocco	940	3,103	58.3	50.9	19.9	19.7	6.0	2.6	15.9	26.8
Mozambique	206	627	57.7	36.6	..	28.1	4.3	3.1	38.1	32.2
Myanmar	73	*444*	35.4	*51.2*	22.6	*6.5*	2.5	..	39.5	*42.4*
Namibia	341	*376*	46.9	*36.1*	17.9	*23.3*	6.8	*5.5*	28.5	*35.1*
Nepal	159	424	40.8	38.0	28.5	38.5	3.2	6.2	27.5	17.3
Netherlands	28,995	72,414	37.7	20.7	25.4	22.3	0.6	2.5	36.3	54.6
New Zealand	3,251	8,135	40.6	33.8	29.5	32.7	2.5	4.0	27.5	29.5
Nicaragua	73	402	70.7	57.9	20.1	22.5	7.9	3.8	1.4	15.9
Niger	209	*250*	68.3	*65.3*	10.4	*8.9*	4.3	*3.0*	17.1	*22.8*
Nigeria	1,901	7,321	33.6	20.7	30.3	15.2	3.1	..	32.9	64.2
Norway	12,247	27,209	44.6	33.7	30.0	35.9	1.7	2.9	23.7	27.6
Oman	719	3,052	36.6	34.4	6.5	21.1	4.1	9.8	52.8	34.7
Pakistan	1,863	7,179	67.0	36.2	23.1	17.8	1.4	3.4	8.6	42.6
Panama	666	1,673	66.6	56.3	14.8	16.2	10.2	12.6	8.4	14.9
Papua New Guinea	393	1,151	35.6	24.2	12.8	4.8	4.0	10.3	47.6	60.7
Paraguay	361	325	61.6	55.6	19.8	24.2	11.4	17.2	7.3	3.1
Peru	1,070	2,959	43.5	44.4	27.6	23.0	10.9	8.7	18.0	24.0
Philippines	1,721	5,790	56.9	54.0	6.5	22.1	3.4	5.1	33.2	18.8
Poland	2,847	14,104	52.4	23.5	14.9	30.8	1.0	5.6	31.8	40.1
Portugal	3,772	9,891	48.5	30.8	23.0	31.1	5.1	4.6	23.5	33.5
Puerto Rico	..	..	..	..	..	..	..	..	..	..

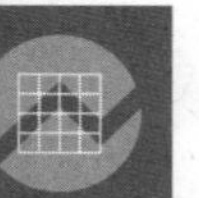

4.7 Structure of service imports

	Commercial service imports		Transport		Travel		Insurance and financial services		Computer, information, communications, and other commercial services	
	$ millions		% of commercial services		% of commercial services		% of commercial services		% of commercial services	
	1990	2005	1990	2005	1990	2005	1990	2005	1990	2005
Romania	787	5,425	65.5	36.2	13.1	17.1	7.3	5.4	14.1	41.3
Russian Federation	..	38,465	..	13.4	..	46.3	..	5.4	..	35.0
Rwanda	94	176	69.0	76.6	23.7	20.8	0.0	..	7.3	2.5
Saudi Arabia	12,677	14,239	18.1	29.2	..	..	2.2	3.2	79.7	67.6
Senegal	368	*681*	60.1	*55.8*	12.4	*8.4*	8.8	*10.2*	18.7	*25.6*
Serbia and Montenegro	..	..	..	..	..	..	..	..	..	..
Sierra Leone	67	85	29.5	50.0	32.7	37.8	4.8	9.7	33.0	2.5
Singapore	8,575	54,076	41.0	36.8	21.0	18.2	9.1	5.6	29.0	39.4
Slovak Republic	*1,666*	*3,012*	*17.3*	*29.8*	*13.1*	*19.0*	..	*8.7*	*69.6*	*42.4*
Slovenia	*1,034*	2,890	*42.5*	22.5	*27.3*	32.9	*2.5*	2.2	*27.8*	42.4
Somalia	*122*	..	*38.2*	..	..	..	*4.2*	..	*57.6*	..
South Africa	3,594	11,863	40.2	44.9	31.5	28.4	11.6	5.6	16.7	21.1
Spain	15,197	65,159	30.9	27.1	28.0	23.1	6.3	5.4	34.9	44.4
Sri Lanka	620	2,051	64.2	61.8	11.9	15.3	6.8	6.0	17.1	16.9
Sudan	202	1,801	31.9	59.9	25.4	37.1	4.9	0.7	37.8	2.3
Swaziland	171	431	6.1	20.4	20.6	3.5	..	30.8	73.4	45.3
Sweden	16,959	35,023	23.2	16.3	37.1	30.8	7.9	3.3	31.7	49.6
Switzerland	11,093	26,089	33.7	21.3	53.0	35.5	1.4	5.8	12.0	37.4
Syrian Arab Republic	702	2,136	54.5	64.6	35.5	25.8	4.4	3.4	5.7	6.3
Tajikistan	..	250	..	71.3	..	1.5	..	7.2	..	20.0
Tanzania	288	1,088	58.0	25.4	7.9	50.9	6.2	4.5	27.9	19.2
Thailand	6,160	27,458	58.1	51.0	23.3	18.2	5.5	6.0	13.3	24.8
Togo	217	*237*	56.9	*72.7*	18.4	*3.6*	9.1	*11.4*	15.6	*12.4*
Trinidad and Tobago	460	*314*	51.7	*51.7*	26.6	*30.5*	9.9	*0.1*	11.9	*17.7*
Tunisia	682	2,066	51.4	53.6	26.2	17.7	7.4	8.7	15.0	20.1
Turkey	2,794	10,697	32.2	49.8	18.6	26.9	..	11.9	49.2	11.4
Turkmenistan	..	..	..	..	..	..	..	..	..	..
Uganda	195	783	58.3	41.4	..	17.0	6.5	6.4	35.2	35.2
Ukraine	..	6,962	..	29.5	..	40.3	..	5.4	..	24.9
United Arab Emirates	..	..	..	..	..	..	..	..	..	..
United Kingdom	44,713	155,861	33.2	23.5	41.0	38.2	2.4	6.7	23.4	31.5
United States	97,950	281,168	36.3	31.4	38.9	26.2	4.5	12.5	20.4	30.0
Uruguay	363	857	48.2	48.6	30.7	29.4	1.5	3.1	19.6	18.9
Uzbekistan	..	..	..	..	..	..	..	..	..	..
Venezuela, RB	2,390	5,250	33.5	44.6	42.8	24.4	4.3	9.3	19.4	21.7
Vietnam	..	5,282	..	..	..	..	..	..	..	..
West Bank and Gaza	..	..	..	..	..	..	..	..	..	..
Yemen, Rep.	639	1,103	27.6	47.7	9.9	15.2	5.4	8.5	57.1	28.6
Zambia	370	..	76.8	..	14.6	..	5.3	..	3.3	..
Zimbabwe	460	..	51.8	..	14.4	..	3.4	..	30.4	..
World	**834,571 t**	**2,346,205 t**	**34.9 w**	**28.5 w**	**32.5 w**	**28.1 w**	**5.0 w**	**8.2 w**	**32.3 w**	**35.4 w**
Low income	21,190	101,435	55.6	*44.0*	13.0	*17.6*	5.2	*6.0*	26.6	*32.8*
Middle income	107,026	449,275	48.7	32.5	25.3	26.8	4.1	12.6	22.1	28.0
Lower middle income	51,519	254,719	61.6	38.3	15.9	23.6	4.3	7.3	18.3	30.9
Upper middle income	56,695	196,106	35.2	27.3	35.1	29.8	3.9	17.5	26.1	25.5
Low & middle income	128,521	548,077	49.3	33.1	24.1	26.4	4.2	12.4	22.5	28.2
East Asia & Pacific	25,122	171,206	65.5	38.8	15.8	22.1	2.6	6.6	16.2	32.5
Europe & Central Asia	..	132,848	*30.9*	27.7	*19.2*	30.9	*6.2*	7.1	*44.2*	34.3
Latin America & Carib.	33,527	88,781	34.0	25.6	40.9	30.2	5.9	25.7	19.6	18.5
Middle East & N. Africa	18,677	43,583	49.2	..	16.3	..	6.9	..	27.7	..
South Asia	9,262	64,639	60.5	*44.9*	10.7	*16.3*	5.3	*6.3*	23.5	*32.5*
Sub-Saharan Africa	18,237	50,365	45.1	40.8	22.6	23.4	7.6	5.9	25.5	31.0
High income	701,461	1,800,743	31.0	27.3	34.8	28.5	5.1	7.1	34.8	37.3
Europe EMU	301,701	768,538	26.3	23.8	31.1	28.2	7.6	5.0	35.0	43.0

a. Includes Luxembourg. b. World Trade Organization estimate.

Structure of service imports 4.7

About the data

Trade in services differs from trade in goods because services are produced and consumed at the same time. Thus services to a traveler may be consumed in the producing country (for example, use of a hotel room) but are classified as imports of the traveler's country. In other cases services may be supplied from a remote location; for example, insurance services may be supplied from one location and consumed in another. For further discussion of the problems of measuring trade in services, see *About the data* for table 4.6.

The data on exports of services in table 4.6 and on imports of services in this table, unlike those in editions before 2000, include only commercial services and exclude the category "government services not included elsewhere." The data are compiled by the International Monetary Fund (IMF) based on returns from national sources.

The mix of commercial service imports by developing countries is changing **4.7a**

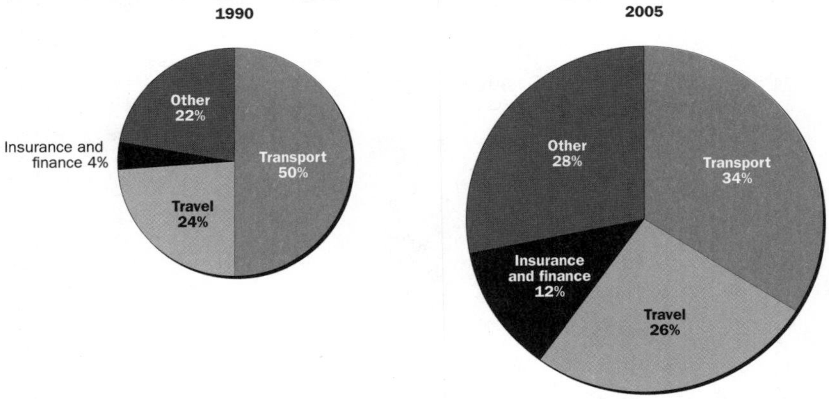

Between 1990 and 2005 transport was displaced by travel and insurance and other services as the most important services imported by developing economies.

Source: International Monetary Fund data files.

Definitions

• **Commercial service imports** are total service imports minus imports of government services not included elsewhere. International transactions in services are defined by the IMF's *Balance of Payments Manual* (1993) as the economic output of intangible commodities that may be produced, transferred, and consumed at the same time. Definitions may vary among reporting economies. • **Transport** covers all transport services (sea, air, land, internal waterway, space, and pipeline) performed by residents of one economy for those of another and involving the carriage of passengers, movement of goods (freight), rental of carriers with crew, and related support and auxiliary services. Excluded are freight insurance, which is included in insurance services; goods procured in ports by nonresident carriers and repairs of transport equipment, which are included in goods; repairs of harbors, railway facilities, and airfield facilities, which are included in construction services; and rental of carriers without crew, which is included in other services. • **Travel** covers goods and services acquired from an economy by travelers in that economy for their own use during visits of less than one year for business or personal purposes. Travel services include the goods and services consumed by travelers, such as meals, lodging, and transport (within the economy visited), including car rental. • **Insurance and financial services** cover freight insurance on goods imported and other direct insurance such as life insurance, financial intermediation services such as commissions, foreign exchange transactions, and brokerage services; and auxiliary services such as financial market operational and regulatory services. • **Computer, information, communications, and other commercial services** include such activities as international telecommunications, and postal and courier services; computer data; news-related service transactions between residents and nonresidents; construction services; royalties and license fees; miscellaneous business, professional, and technical services; and personal, cultural, and recreational services.

Data sources

Data on imports of commercial services are from the IMF. The IMF publishes balance of payments data in its *International Financial Statistics* and *Balance of Payments Statistics Yearbook.*

4.8 Structure of demand

	Household final consumption expenditure		General government final consumption expenditure		Gross capital formation		Exports of goods and services		Imports of goods and services		Gross savings	
	% of GDP		% of GDP		% of GDP		% of GDP		% of GDP		% of GDP	
	1990	**2005**	**1990**	**2005**	**1990**	**2005**	**1990**	**2005**	**1990**	**2005**	**1990**	**2005**
Afghanistan	..	110	..	9	..	25	..	12	..	56	..	24
Albania	61	91	19	9	29	24	15	22	23	46	21	16
Algeria	57	34	16	12	29	30	23	48	25	24	26	51
Angola	36	67	35	..[a]	12	8	39	74	21	48	9	21
Argentina	77	61	3	12	14	22	10	25	5	19	*13*	24
Armenia	46	73	18	11	47	30	35	27	46	40	..	26
Australia	59	*59*	19	*18*	23	*26*	16	*18*	16	*21*	19	*20*
Austria	57	56	19	18	24	21	38	53	37	48	24	24
Azerbaijan	51	48	18	11	27	38	44	57	39	54	..	30
Bangladesh	86	76	4	6	17	25	6	17	14	23	14	30
Belarus	47	50	24	20	27	30	46	61	44	60	29	31
Belgium	56	53	20	23	22	21	70	87	68	85	23	24
Benin	87	78	11	15	14	20	14	14	26	26	10	11
Bolivia	77	68	12	14	13	14	23	36	24	33	10	20
Bosnia and Herzegovina	..	99	..	26	..	19	..	36	..	81	..	–2
Botswana	33	28	24	25	37	32	55	51	50	35	43	46
Brazil	59	56	19	20	20	21	8	17	7	12	19	22
Bulgaria	60	70	18	19	26	28	33	61	37	77	16	17
Burkina Faso	82	80	13	13	18	21	11	9	24	22	13	*7*
Burundi	95	87	11	28	15	12	8	9	28	36	*–5*	9
Cambodia	91	85	7	4	8	20	6	65	13	74	6	14
Cameroon	67	71	13	10	18	21	20	23	17	25	16	18
Canada	56	*55*	23	*20*	21	*21*	26	*39*	26	*34*	18	*23*
Central African Republic	86	..	15	..	12	..	15	..	28	..	0	14
Chad	98	58	10	5	7	17	14	59	28	39	–3	21
Chile	61	57	10	12	25	23	34	42	31	34	24	17
China[b]	46[c]	37[c]	14	14	36	44	19	38	16	32	40	51
Hong Kong, China	57	58	7	9	27	21	131	198	122	185	33	32
Colombia	66	61	9	19	19	19	21	22	15	21	22	18
Congo, Dem. Rep.	79	85	12	8	9	14	30	32	29	39	1	14
Congo, Rep.	62	34	14	14	16	24	54	82	46	55	7	29
Costa Rica	73	66	15	14	19	26	30	49	36	54	10	19
Côte d'Ivoire	72	74	17	8	7	11	32	50	27	42	–4	13
Croatia	*75*	58	*24*	20	*11*	31	*78*	47	*86*	56	–16	23
Cuba	..	..	..	..	..	..	..	..	..	..	..	..
Czech Republic	49	49	23	22	25	27	45	72	43	70	*28*	24
Denmark	50	49	25	26	20	21	37	49	33	44	20	24
Dominican Republic	80	74	4	10	25	20	34	34	44	38	22	19
Ecuador	68	66	11	11	21	24	33	31	32	32	11	24
Egypt, Arab Rep.	73	71	11	13	29	18	20	31	33	33	21	21
El Salvador	89	93	10	10	14	15	19	27	31	45	6	11
Eritrea	*101*	82	*22*	45	*11*	20	*11*	9	*45*	56	*13*	10
Estonia	62	56	16	18	30	32	*60*	84	*54*	90	*41*	21
Ethiopia	77	82	13	14	13	26	6	16	9	39	12	17
Finland	52	54	22	23	29	20	22	39	24	35	24	23
France	57	57	22	24	22	20	21	26	23	27	21	18
Gabon	50	52	13	7	22	21	46	59	31	39	24	32
Gambia, The	76	96	14	..[a]	22	25	60	45	72	65	5	15
Georgia	65	68	10	18	31	26	40	42	46	55	..	20
Germany	57	59	20	19	24	17	25	40	25	35	24	21
Ghana	85	81	9	15	14	29	17	36	26	62	7	22
Greece	73	67	15	16	23	24	18	21	28	28	18	15
Guatemala	84	90	7	6	14	19	21	16	25	30	10	15
Guinea	73	86	9	5	18	12	31	26	31	30	11	7
Guinea-Bissau	87	85	10	18	30	15	10	38	37	55	15	8
Haiti	81	*92*	8	*8*	13	*30*	18	*16*	20	*45*	*6*	*28*

4.8 Structure of demand

	Household final consumption expenditure % of GDP		General government final consumption expenditure % of GDP		Gross capital formation % of GDP		Exports of goods and services % of GDP		Imports of goods and services % of GDP		Gross savings % of GDP	
	1990	2005	1990	2005	1990	2005	1990	2005	1990	2005	1990	2005
Honduras	67	77	13	14	23	30	37	41	40	61	22	30
Hungary	61	68	11	10	25	24	31	66	29	69	26	16
India	66	59	12	11	24	33	7	21	9	24	22	32
Indonesia	59	65	9	8	31	22	25	34	24	29	28	24
Iran, Islamic Rep.	59	46	12	12	37	33	15	39	23	30	*35*	41
Iraq	..	..	..	..	..	..	..	..	..	..	..	..
Ireland	58	*44*	16	*16*	21	*25*	57	*83*	52	*68*	19	*24*
Israel	56	59	30	28	25	19	35	46	45	51	22	..
Italy	57	59	20	20	22	21	19	26	19	26	21	20
Jamaica	65	73	13	15	26	32	48	41	52	61	19	*20*
Japan	53	*57*	13	*18*	33	*23*	11	*13*	10	*11*	34	*26*
Jordan	74	103	25	15	32	24	62	52	93	93	22	7
Kazakhstan	*52*	53	*18*	11	*32*	27	*74*	54	*75*	45	..	26
Kenya	63	74	19	17	24	17	26	27	31	35	19	12
Korea, Dem. Rep.	..	..	..	..	..	..	..	..	..	..	..	..
Korea, Rep.	52	53	12	14	38	30	28	43	29	40	37	32
Kuwait	57	28	39	15	18	20	45	68	58	30	..	..
Kyrgyz Republic	71	86	25	19	24	14	29	39	50	58	4	6
Lao PDR	..	72	..	..[a]	..	32	12	27	25	31	*–4*	2
Latvia	53	62	9	18	40	34	48	48	49	62	*56*	23
Lebanon	140	89	25	16	18	20	18	19	100	44	22	–1
Lesotho	139	84	14	15	53	41	17	48	122	88	60	27
Liberia	..	87	..	11	..	16	..	37	..	50	..	18
Libya	48	..	24	..	19	..	40	..	31	..	..	..
Lithuania	57	65	19	17	33	25	52	58	61	65	..	18
Macedonia, FYR	72	78	19	19	19	20	26	45	36	63	9	20
Madagascar	86	84	8	8	17	22	17	26	28	40	9	11
Malawi	72	95	15	17	23	15	24	27	33	53	14	–7
Malaysia	52	44	14	13	32	20	75	123	72	100	30	36
Mali	80	79	14	10	23	23	17	26	34	37	15	11
Mauritania	69	92	26	23	20	45	46	36	61	95	18	–5
Mauritius	64	67	13	14	31	23	64	57	71	61	26	20
Mexico	70	68	8	12	23	22	19	30	20	32	20	21
Moldova	77	93	..[a]	16	25	30	48	53	51	91	58	23
Mongolia	62	57	30	15	36	36	22	76	49	84	6	37
Morocco	65	58	16	23	25	26	27	36	32	43	25	29
Mozambique	92	79	14	10	22	20	8	33	36	42	2	4
Myanmar	89	..	..[a]	..	13	..	3	..	5	..	12	..
Namibia	51	50	31	23	34	26	52	46	67	45	35	40
Nepal	84	77	9	10	18	29	11	16	21	33	11	31
Netherlands	50	49	23	24	23	19	56	71	52	63	28	27
New Zealand	61	*59*	19	*18*	20	*25*	27	*29*	27	*30*	17	*17*
Nicaragua	59	89	44	11	19	29	25	28	46	58	–4	13
Niger	84	79	15	12	8	19	15	15	22	24	–2	10
Nigeria	56	40	15	21	15	21	43	53	29	35	19	30
Norway	49	42	21	20	23	21	40	45	34	28	26	37
Oman	46	*45*	22	*23*	12	*18*	47	*57*	28	*43*	..	..
Pakistan	74	80	15	8	19	17	16	15	23	20	22	18
Panama	57	73	18	12	17	19	87	69	79	73	24	10
Papua New Guinea	59	..	25	..	24	..	41	..	49	..	9	..
Paraguay	77	75	6	10	23	22	33	47	40	54	20	16
Peru	74	66	8	10	17	19	16	25	14	19	..	19
Philippines	72	80	10	10	24	15	28	47	33	52	20	31
Poland	48	62	19	19	26	19	29	37	22	37	27	18
Portugal	64	66	16	21	27	22	31	29	38	37	25	13
Puerto Rico	65	..	15	..	17	..	..	..	..	..	..	..

4.8 Structure of demand

	Household final consumption expenditure % of GDP		General government final consumption expenditure % of GDP		Gross capital formation % of GDP		Exports of goods and services % of GDP		Imports of goods and services % of GDP		Gross savings % of GDP	
	1990	2005	1990	2005	1990	2005	1990	2005	1990	2005	1990	2005
Romania	66	78	13	10	30	23	17	33	26	43	22	14
Russian Federation	49	49	21	17	30	21	18	35	18	22	*36*	32
Rwanda	84	85	10	13	15	22	6	11	14	31	11	19
Saudi Arabia	47	26	29	23	15	16	41	61	32	26	18	..
Senegal	76	77	15	14	14	23	25	27	30	42	6	16
Serbia and Montenegro	..	86	..	18	..	18	..	27	..	50	..	10
Sierra Leone	84	90	8	13	10	15	22	24	24	43	3	7
Singapore	46	41	10	11	37	19	..	243	..	213	46	..
Slovak Republic	54	56	22	20	33	29	27	79	36	83	..	20
Slovenia	53	55	17	20	17	26	91	65	79	65	*24*	25
Somalia	..	..	..	..	16	..	10	..	38	..	*17*	..
South Africa	57	63	20	20	18	18	24	27	19	29	20	14
Spain	60	58	17	18	26	30	16	25	19	31	23	22
Sri Lanka	77	77	10	9	23	26	29	34	38	46	17	20
Sudan	..	70	..	17	..	23	..	18	..	28	..	17
Swaziland	75	61	18	28	19	19	75	88	87	95	25	17
Sweden	49	48	27	27	23	17	30	49	30	41	21	23
Switzerland	57	*60*	11	*12*	31	*20*	36	*46*	34	*39*	34	*33*
Syrian Arab Republic	69	70	14	14	17	20	28	37	28	40	15	14
Tajikistan	74	95	9	9	25	14	28	54	35	73	*24*	7
Tanzania[d]	81	77	18	14	26	19	13	17	38	26	8	9
Thailand	57	58	9	12	41	32	34	74	42	75	33	29
Togo	71	86	14	10	27	18	34	34	45	47	20	10
Trinidad and Tobago	59	*58*	12	9	13	*20*	45	*58*	29	*46*	21	*29*
Tunisia	64	64	16	16	27	23	44	48	51	51	22	21
Turkey	69	69	11	13	24	25	13	27	18	34	24	18
Turkmenistan	49	46	23	13	40	23	..	65	..	48	..	34
Uganda	92	79	8	14	13	21	7	13	19	27	1	10
Ukraine	57	61	17	19	28	19	28	54	29	53	36	22
United Arab Emirates	38	46	16	11	21	24	66	94	41	76	..	..
United Kingdom	63	65	20	22	20	17	24	26	27	30	16	14
United States	67	*70*	17	*16*	18	*19*	10	*10*	11	*15*	15	*13*
Uruguay	70	74	12	11	12	13	24	30	18	28	14	13
Uzbekistan	61	51	25	16	32	23	29	40	48	30	*3*	35
Venezuela, RB	62	47	8	11	10	22	40	41	20	21	27	40
Vietnam	84	64	12	6	13	35	36	70	45	75	–2	34
West Bank and Gaza	..	96	..	33	..	26	..	14	..	68	..	13
Yemen, Rep.	74	50	18	16	15	27	14	46	20	38	28	32
Zambia	64	70	19	13	17	26	36	16	37	25	7	10
Zimbabwe	63	70	19	27	17	14	23	43	23	53	16	3
World	60 w	61 w	17 w	*17* w	23 w	22 w	19 w	26 w	19 w	*26* w	22 w	*21* w
Low income	70	64	12	11	21	29	13	25	16	29	18	28
Middle income	59	56	14	15	26	27	22	36	21	33	27	30
Lower middle income	56	51	15	15	29	31	19	34	19	31	30	35
Upper middle income	63	61	13	14	23	22	25	38	23	35	22	23
Low & middle income	61	57	14	14	26	27	20	34	20	32	26	29
East Asia & Pacific	50	44	13	13	35	38	24	46	23	41	36	45
Europe & Central Asia	56	60	17	16	27	23	24	41	24	41	*25*	23
Latin America & Carib.	67	62	12	15	19	21	17	26	15	23	20	22
Middle East & N. Africa	66	59	15	14	28	26	24	37	34	36	*26*	30
South Asia	69	64	11	10	23	31	9	20	12	25	21	30
Sub-Saharan Africa	64	65	17	18	18	19	27	33	26	35	16	17
High income	60	*62*	18	*18*	23	*20*	19	*25*	19	*25*	22	*19*
Europe EMU	57	58	20	21	23	20	27	37	28	36	23	21

a. Data on general government final consumption expenditure are not available separately; they are included in household final consumption expenditure. b. China has revised its national accounts data from 1993 onwards. However, data by expenditure are not available. Data shown here are based on earlier series. c. Includes the difference between the old and the new GDP series. d. Data cover mainland Tanzania only.

Structure of demand 4.8

About the data

Gross domestic product (GDP) from the expenditure side is made up of household final consumption expenditure, general government final consumption expenditure, gross capital formation (private and public investment in fixed assets, changes in inventories, and net acquisitions of valuables), and net exports (exports minus imports) of goods and services. Such expenditures are recorded in purchaser prices and include net taxes on products.

Because policymakers have tended to focus on fostering the growth of output, and because data on production are easier to collect than data on spending, many countries generate their primary estimate of GDP using the production approach. Moreover, many countries do not estimate all the separate components of national expenditures but instead derive some of the main aggregates indirectly using GDP (based on the production approach) as the control total. Household final consumption expenditure (private consumption in the 1968 System of National Accounts, or SNA) is often estimated as a residual, by subtracting from GDP all other known expenditures. The resulting aggregate may incorporate fairly large discrepancies. When household consumption is calculated separately, many of the estimates are based on household surveys, which tend to be one-year studies with limited coverage. Thus the estimates quickly become outdated and must be supplemented by estimates using price- and quantity-based statistical procedures. Complicating the issue, in many developing countries the distinction between cash outlays for personal business and those for household use may be blurred. *World Development Indicators* includes in household consumption the expenditures of nonprofit institutions serving households.

General government final consumption expenditure (general government consumption in the 1968 SNA) includes expenditures on goods and services for individual consumption as well as those on services for collective consumption. Defense expenditures, including those on capital outlays (with certain exceptions), are treated as current spending.

Gross capital formation (gross domestic investment in the 1968 SNA) consists of outlays on additions to the economy's fixed assets plus net changes in the level of inventories. It is generally obtained from reports by industry of acquisition and distinguishes only the broad categories of capital formation. The 1993 SNA recognizes a third category of capital formation: net acquisitions of valuables. Included in gross capital formation under the 1993 SNA guidelines are capital outlays on defense establishments that may be used by the general public, such as schools, airfields, and hospitals, and intangibles such as computer software and mineral exploration outlays. Data on capital formation may be estimated from direct surveys of enterprises and administrative records or based on the commodity flow method using data from production, trade, and construction activities. The quality of data on fixed capital formation by government depends on the quality of government accounting systems (which tend to be weak in developing countries). Measures of fixed capital formation by households and corporations—particularly capital outlays by small, unincorporated enterprises—are usually unreliable.

Estimates of changes in inventories are rarely complete but usually include the most important activities or commodities. In some countries these estimates are derived as a composite residual along with household final consumption expenditure. According to national accounts conventions, adjustments should be made for appreciation of the value of inventory holdings due to price changes, but this is not always done. In highly inflationary economies this element can be substantial.

Data on exports and imports are compiled from customs reports and balance of payments data. Although the data from the payments side provide reasonably reliable records of cross-border transactions, they may not adhere strictly to the appropriate definitions of valuation and timing used in the balance of payments or correspond to the change-of-ownership criterion. This issue has assumed greater significance with the increasing globalization of international business. Neither customs nor balance of payments data usually capture the illegal transactions that occur in many countries. Goods carried by travelers across borders in legal but unreported shuttle trade may further distort trade statistics.

Gross savings represent the difference between disposable income and consumption and replace gross domestic savings, a concept used by the World Bank and included in *World Development Indicators* editions before 2006. The change was made to conform to the SNA concepts and definitions. For further discussion of the problems in compiling national accounts, see Srinivasan (1994), Heston (1994), and Ruggles (1994). For an analysis of the reliability of foreign trade and national income statistics, see Morgenstern (1963).

Definitions

• **Household final consumption expenditure** is the market value of all goods and services, including durable products (such as cars, washing machines, and home computers), purchased by households. It excludes purchases of dwellings but includes imputed rent for owner-occupied dwellings. It also includes payments and fees to governments to obtain permits and licenses. Expenditures of nonprofit institutions serving households are included, even when reported separately by the country. In practice, household consumption expenditure may include any statistical discrepancy in the use of resources relative to the supply of resources. • **General government final consumption expenditure** includes all government current expenditures for purchases of goods and services (including compensation of employees). It also includes most expenditures on national defense and security but excludes government military expenditures that potentially have wider public use and are part of government capital formation. • **Gross capital formation** consists of outlays on additions to the fixed assets of the economy, net changes in the level of inventories, and net acquisitions of valuables. Fixed assets include land improvements (fences, ditches, drains, and so on); plant, machinery, and equipment purchases; and the construction of roads, railways, and the like, including schools, offices, hospitals, private residential dwellings, and commercial and industrial buildings. Inventories are stocks of goods held by firms to meet temporary or unexpected fluctuations in production or sales, and "work in progress." • **Exports** and **imports of goods and services** are the value of all goods and other market services provided to, or received from, the rest of the world. They include the value of merchandise, freight, insurance, transport, travel, royalties, license fees, and other services, such as communication, construction, financial, information, business, personal, and government services. They exclude compensation of employees and investment income (factor services in the 1968 SNA) as well as transfer payments. • **Gross savings** are calculated as gross national income less total consumption, plus net transfers.

Data sources

National accounts indicators for most developing countries are collected from national statistical organizations and central banks by World Bank missions. Data for high-income economies come from Organisation for Economic Co-operation and Development data files (see the OECD's *Annual National Accounts for OECD Member Countries: Data from 1970 Onwards*). The United Nations Statistics Division publishes detailed national accounts for UN member countries in *National Accounts Statistics: Main Aggregates and Detailed Tables* and updates in the *Monthly Bulletin of Statistics.*

4.9 Growth of consumption investment, and trade

	Household final consumption expenditure				General government final consumption expenditure		Gross capital formation		Goods and services			
	average annual % growth		Per capita average annual % growth		average annual % growth		average annual % growth		average annual % growth			
									Exports		Imports	
	1990–2000	2000–05	1990–2000	2000–05	1990–2000	2000–05	1990–2000	2000–05	1990–2000	2000–05	1990–2000	2000–05
Afghanistan	..	12.6	..	..	..	13.1	..	5.6	..	–17.6	..	1.9
Albania	4.3	3.5	5.2	3.0	2.4	1.1	25.8	3.3	*17.9*	15.6	*15.8*	15.0
Algeria	–0.1	5.7	–1.9	4.1	3.6	5.1	–0.6	10.6	3.2	4.4	–1.0	9.2
Angola	..	..	..	..	..	..	..	..	..	..	..	..
Argentina	*2.7*	0.6	*1.5*	–0.4	*2.2*	0.4	7.4	5.3	8.7	6.4	15.6	0.5
Armenia	–0.5	8.4	1.1	8.8	–1.6	8.7	–1.9	22.9	–18.4	20.6	–12.7	12.5
Australia	3.6	*4.2*	2.4	*2.9*	3.0	*3.4*	5.7	*9.7*	7.4	*0.6*	8.1	*10.4*
Austria	1.9	1.0	1.5	0.5	2.5	1.0	..	..	5.5	5.4	5.0	4.3
Azerbaijan	*1.5*	12.2	*0.4*	11.2	*–1.7*	4.7	*42.9*	39.0	*6.8*	16.2	*15.5*	27.3
Bangladesh	2.6	4.0	0.4	2.0	4.7	11.9	9.2	8.3	13.1	8.3	9.7	5.6
Belarus	–0.5	11.0	–0.3	11.5	–1.9	0.3	–7.5	15.5	–4.8	8.8	–8.7	11.7
Belgium	1.8	1.1	1.5	0.6	1.5	2.4	2.6	1.4	4.7	2.8	4.5	2.8
Benin	2.6	2.3	–0.7	–0.9	4.4	8.3	12.2	4.8	1.8	2.7	2.1	1.8
Bolivia	3.6	2.3	1.4	0.3	3.6	2.6	8.5	–2.7	4.5	10.8	6.0	5.4
Bosnia and Herzegovina	..	–1.3	..	..	..	7.0	..	3.0	..	12.7	..	4.5
Botswana	2.5	4.9	0.4	4.8	7.1	..	6.7	–0.7	4.7	2.2	3.8	3.3
Brazil[a]	4.8	0.5	3.3	–0.9	–0.4	1.0	3.4	–0.1	6.1	11.4	11.1	1.1
Bulgaria	–3.7	5.5	–3.0	6.3	–8.4	4.5	–5.0	15.1	3.9	9.1	2.7	12.4
Burkina Faso	4.2	*3.6*	1.3	*0.3*	–0.5	*2.6*	7.0	8.2	0.0	6.6	1.4	11.3
Burundi	–4.9	..	..	..	–2.6	..	–0.5	..	–1.2	..	–1.6	..
Cambodia[a]	*6.0*	8.3	*3.4*	6.2	*7.2*	4.0	*10.9*	12.1	*21.7*	17.0	*14.8*	15.3
Cameroon	3.1	4.2	0.7	2.3	0.7	4.6	0.4	8.1	3.2	1.0	5.1	6.8
Canada	2.6	*3.2*	1.6	*2.2*	0.3	*3.0*	4.5	*4.6*	8.7	*0.0*	7.2	*2.2*
Central African Republic[a]	..	..	..	..	..	..	..	..	..	..	..	..
Chad[a]	1.5	*5.0*	–1.6	*1.4*	–8.3	3.8	4.0	5.0	2.3	55.6	–1.7	*16.8*
Chile	7.3	4.6	5.6	3.4	3.7	3.8	9.3	8.8	9.5	6.6	11.7	10.4
China[b]	8.9	6.9	7.8	6.2	9.7	8.1	11.5	13.5	13.0	24.8	14.3	20.8
Hong Kong, China	3.9	1.9	2.1	1.1	3.3	1.6	5.6	0.3	8.1	10.2	8.4	8.7
Colombia	2.2	3.3	0.3	1.7	10.5	1.4	2.0	13.6	5.3	3.8	9.0	9.7
Congo, Dem. Rep.[a]	*–4.5*	..	*–7.1*	..	*–17.4*	..	*–0.7*	..	–0.5	7.8	–2.4	25.2
Congo, Rep.[a]	–1.7	18.5	–4.8	15.0	–2.0	9.8	0.4	22.4	5.1	5.5	2.9	26.1
Costa Rica[a]	5.1	3.0	2.5	1.1	2.0	1.4	5.1	8.9	10.9	6.0	9.2	5.7
Côte d'Ivoire	4.3	–0.5	1.4	–2.1	0.8	3.2	8.3	–9.7	1.5	3.5	6.8	3.5
Croatia	*2.8*	4.8	*3.2*	5.0	*1.3*	0.8	*5.6*	14.5	*5.9*	6.2	*4.6*	8.8
Cuba	..	..	..	..	..	..	..	..	..	..	..	..
Czech Republic	3.0	3.3	3.0	3.3	–0.9	3.2	4.8	3.9	8.7	10.1	12.0	9.8
Denmark	2.2	2.1	1.8	1.8	2.4	1.4	..	..	5.1	2.8	6.1	4.5
Dominican Republic[a]	5.3	0.7	3.7	–0.7	5.3	5.6	10.4	–2.9	9.1	2.7	9.4	–3.1
Ecuador[a]	2.1	5.8	0.3	4.3	–1.5	2.6	–0.7	10.1	5.3	6.6	2.8	10.4
Egypt, Arab Rep.	3.7	3.0	1.8	1.0	4.4	3.1	5.8	1.3	3.3	10.5	3.1	5.6
El Salvador	5.3	2.3	3.1	0.5	2.8	1.3	7.1	1.3	13.4	4.1	11.6	3.3
Eritrea	*–5.0*	*1.8*	*–6.7*	*–2.5*	*22.6*	*5.0*	*19.1*	–8.0	*–2.5*	–7.6	*7.5*	–4.1
Estonia	0.6	7.0	2.2	7.4	4.9	5.8	0.2	11.6	*11.2*	8.1	*12.0*	9.6
Ethiopia	2.8	6.7	0.6	4.5	9.6	–0.1	5.9	6.6	7.1	15.0	5.8	11.0
Finland	1.7	2.9	1.3	2.7	0.9	2.3	1.3	1.4	9.9	3.7	6.2	4.0
France	1.6	2.2	1.3	1.5	1.4	1.8	1.8	1.1	6.9	1.7	5.7	3.4
Gabon[a]	1.2	4.5	–1.7	2.8	5.4	0.2	3.8	1.4	1.5	1.7	0.7	2.9
Gambia, The	3.6	*1.8*	0.1	*–1.1*	–2.2	*4.2*	1.9	11.9	0.1	4.0	0.1	2.5
Georgia	*6.1*	7.1	*7.6*	8.3	*12.0*	1.0	–12.5	18.8	*12.2*	4.1	*11.2*	4.9
Germany	1.9	0.3	1.6	0.3	1.8	0.1	..	..	6.0	5.5	5.8	3.5
Ghana	4.4	*7.6*	1.9	*5.3*	4.8	*–7.0*	1.3	*10.7*	10.1	4.1	10.4	5.0
Greece	2.2	4.1	1.4	3.7	2.1	2.1	..	..	7.6	1.2	7.4	1.9
Guatemala[a]	4.2	3.7	1.9	1.2	5.1	–2.5	6.2	6.9	6.2	–1.0	9.2	5.6
Guinea	3.7	5.2	0.5	2.9	5.0	0.3	2.8	–3.6	4.6	0.7	1.3	–2.4
Guinea-Bissau	2.6	7.3	–0.4	4.1	1.9	–3.7	–6.5	–4.5	15.4	4.1	–0.5	–3.5
Haiti	..	..	..	..	..	..	..	..	..	..	..	..

Growth of consumption, investment, and trade 4.9

	Household final consumption expenditure				General government final consumption expenditure		Gross capital formation		Goods and services			
	average annual % growth		Per capita average annual % growth		average annual % growth		average annual % growth		average annual % growth			
									Exports		Imports	
	1990–2000	2000–05	1990–2000	2000–05	1990–2000	2000–05	1990–2000	2000–05	1990–2000	2000–05	1990–2000	2000–05
Honduras[a]	3.0	5.1	0.2	2.7	2.0	4.1	6.9	2.2	1.6	6.0	3.8	7.5
Hungary	−0.2	6.0	0.0	6.3	0.9	3.6	10.6	0.1	9.9	8.7	11.4	8.6
India	4.9	5.4	3.0	3.8	5.9	4.1	6.3	14.9	11.0	15.4	12.8	18.4
Indonesia	6.6	4.1	5.0	2.7	0.1	8.7	−0.6	4.9	5.9	5.5	5.7	7.4
Iran, Islamic Rep.	3.2	7.5	1.6	6.1	1.6	2.1	−0.1	9.3	1.2	2.1	−6.8	14.5
Iraq	..	..	..	..	..	..	..	..	..	..	..	..
Ireland	5.3	3.9	4.5	*2.2*	4.0	*5.6*	..	..	15.7	*4.7*	14.5	*3.0*
Israel	*4.5*	2.6	*1.9*	0.7	*3.0*	0.8	*1.5*	−3.9	*10.6*	4.1	*7.4*	1.6
Italy	1.5	0.5	1.5	−0.1	−0.4	1.8	..	..	5.1	−0.8	3.8	0.8
Jamaica	..	..	..	..	..	..	..	..	..	..	..	..
Japan	1.5	*1.2*	1.3	*1.0*	2.9	*2.4*	−1.8	*−2.2*	4.2	*6.2*	4.2	*3.3*
Jordan	5.9	8.4	1.9	5.8	1.7	4.5	1.1	10.2	2.5	11.5	2.0	13.0
Kazakhstan[a]	−8.1	9.6	−7.0	9.3	−7.1	7.1	−18.3	13.6	−2.6	8.0	−11.2	3.5
Kenya	3.6	3.0	0.8	0.8	6.9	2.2	6.1	2.0	1.1	7.4	9.4	5.2
Korea, Dem. Rep.	..	..	..	..	..	..	..	..	..	..	..	..
Korea, Rep.	4.9	2.5	3.9	2.0	4.7	4.5	3.4	3.2	16.0	12.1	10.0	9.4
Kuwait	*4.5*	*5.9*	*0.6*	*2.9*	*−2.4*	6.6	*1.0*	*13.7*	*−1.6*	*5.4*	*0.8*	*9.4*
Kyrgyz Republic	−6.5	10.6	*−7.4*	9.6	−8.8	1.0	−3.9	−5.3	*−1.6*	4.5	*−8.2*	10.1
Lao PDR	..	..	..	..	..	..	..	17.9	..	7.5	..	14.8
Latvia	−3.9	8.6	−2.7	9.3	1.8	2.2	−3.9	16.7	*4.3*	8.6	*7.6*	12.1
Lebanon	4.2	4.1	1.9	3.0	6.2	0.9	7.3	4.8	14.0	11.9	3.3	6.5
Lesotho	0.5	3.8	−0.7	3.7	6.0	−2.5	1.5	−2.3	11.1	10.2	0.9	4.7
Liberia	..	..	..	..	..	..	..	..	..	..	..	..
Libya	..	..	..	..	..	..	..	..	..	..	..	..
Lithuania[a]	*5.2*	8.8	*6.0*	9.3	*1.9*	3.9	*11.1*	17.0	*4.9*	12.1	*7.5*	14.8
Macedonia, FYR	2.2	2.6	1.7	2.4	−0.4	−2.0	3.6	2.2	4.2	−1.2	7.6	−0.6
Madagascar	2.3	5.3	−0.7	2.4	0.0	3.6	3.4	13.3	3.9	−2.5	4.3	10.3
Malawi	5.4	4.1	3.5	1.8	−4.4	8.5	−8.4	2.5	4.0	2.7	−1.1	6.2
Malaysia	5.3	6.8	2.6	4.7	4.8	9.9	5.3	1.5	12.0	6.1	10.3	6.8
Mali	3.0	*1.9*	0.2	−1.1	3.2	*21.1*	0.4	6.7	10.0	6.7	3.5	4.5
Mauritania	..	7.4	..	4.3	..	3.1	..	23.8	−1.4	−2.1	0.6	14.1
Mauritius	5.1	4.6	3.9	3.7	4.8	4.6	4.7	4.2	5.4	1.7	5.2	1.3
Mexico	2.4	3.0	0.7	1.9	1.8	−0.2	4.7	−0.4	14.6	4.0	12.3	4.1
Moldova[a]	*9.9*	9.6	*10.2*	9.9	*−12.4*	7.0	*−15.5*	8.4	*0.7*	16.3	*5.6*	15.8
Mongolia[a]	*5.4*	*3.3*	*4.3*	*2.1*	*11.8*	*2.2*	*7.6*	*4.0*	*30.9*	*8.4*	*29.3*	*7.8*
Morocco	1.6	3.4	0.1	1.7	3.8	4.7	2.9	5.5	5.4	5.0	4.8	4.6
Mozambique[a]	4.7	6.6	1.6	4.5	3.1	8.5	11.5	5.1	11.0	20.0	6.3	10.1
Myanmar	3.9	..	..	..	..	..	15.3	..	10.0	..	5.8	..
Namibia	4.8	−0.5	1.7	−1.8	3.3	0.9	6.9	9.6	3.8	7.2	5.4	1.4
Nepal	..	..	..	..	..	..	..	..	..	..	..	..
Netherlands	2.8	0.3	2.2	−0.2	2.0	2.1	3.2	−1.5	6.8	3.7	6.6	3.4
New Zealand	3.2	*5.0*	2.0	*3.6*	2.5	*3.5*	6.1	*9.3*	5.2	*4.2*	6.2	*9.5*
Nicaragua[a]	6.1	3.5	3.9	2.6	−1.5	1.1	11.3	−0.9	9.3	6.8	12.2	3.7
Niger	1.8	..	..	..	0.8	..	4.0	..	3.1	..	−2.1	..
Nigeria	0.2	4.0	..	..	−1.8	3.3	5.4	15.0	5.0	4.4	4.0	11.9
Norway	3.5	3.3	2.9	2.7	2.8	2.7	6.0	2.8	5.6	0.8	5.8	3.6
Oman	5.4	*1.3*	2.4	*0.4*	2.4	*6.1*	4.0	*17.0*	6.2	*7.0*	5.9	*12.8*
Pakistan	4.9	4.6	2.3	2.1	0.7	5.1	1.8	1.6	1.7	11.6	2.5	7.1
Panama[a]	6.4	8.0	4.2	6.0	1.7	3.4	10.4	3.2	−0.4	1.0	1.2	3.7
Papua New Guinea	5.6	..	..	..	2.7	..	0.5	..	4.3	..	2.8	..
Paraguay	2.6	1.0	0.2	−1.0	2.5	−0.2	0.7	2.9	3.1	3.9	2.9	0.6
Peru[a]	4.0	3.5	2.2	2.0	5.2	3.2	7.4	4.1	8.6	9.7	9.0	5.8
Philippines	3.7	4.8	1.5	2.9	3.8	−0.1	4.1	−0.6	7.8	5.4	7.8	6.2
Poland[a]	5.2	2.8	5.1	3.0	3.7	3.3	10.6	0.3	11.3	9.5	16.7	6.2
Portugal	3.0	1.4	2.7	0.7	2.8	2.0	5.6	−3.6	5.3	2.7	7.3	1.6
Puerto Rico	..	..	..	..	..	..	..	..	*1.6*	..	*4.5*	..

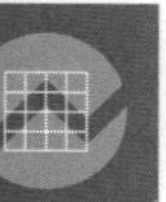

4.9 Growth of consumption, investment, and trade

	Household final consumption expenditure				General government final consumption expenditure		Gross capital formation		Goods and services			
	average annual % growth		Per capita average annual % growth		average annual % growth		average annual % growth		average annual % growth			
									Exports		Imports	
	1990–2000	2000–05	1990–2000	2000–05	1990–2000	2000–05	1990–2000	2000–05	1990–2000	2000–05	1990–2000	2000–05
Romania[a]	1.4	7.1	1.7	7.9	0.8	4.0	–5.1	9.4	8.1	11.4	6.0	13.4
Russian Federation	–0.9	9.3	–0.8	9.8	–2.2	1.8	–19.1	9.2	0.8	9.7	–6.1	18.0
Rwanda[a]	1.1	3.5	–0.1	1.3	–1.7	10.4	1.4	5.1	–3.8	11.4	5.0	4.6
Saudi Arabia	..	*1.9*	..	*–0.3*	..	*0.6*	..	*6.2*	..	*2.2*	..	*2.2*
Senegal	2.4	5.4	–0.2	2.9	2.1	7.5	7.9	10.4	6.3	3.3	3.5	5.9
Serbia and Montenegro	..	7.8	..	14.8	..	5.7	..	14.5	..	15.3	..	19.4
Sierra Leone	–4.4	..	..	..	10.4	..	–5.6	..	–11.2	..	–0.2	..
Singapore	..	3.3	..	..	..	1.2	..	0.3	..	..	..	..
Slovak Republic	*4.7*	3.4	*4.5*	3.4	*2.9*	3.1	*7.9*	5.2	*9.0*	11.9	11.7	10.8
Slovenia	3.9	2.6	3.9	2.5	2.2	2.8	10.9	5.2	1.7	7.5	5.2	7.3
Somalia	..	..	..	..	..	..	..	..	..	..	..	..
South Africa	2.9	4.6	0.7	3.3	0.3	5.5	5.0	7.5	5.6	1.9	7.1	8.0
Spain	2.4	3.4	2.0	1.8	2.7	4.8	..	..	10.5	2.8	9.4	6.1
Sri Lanka[a]	5.7	..	..	..	7.5	..	6.9	6.7	7.5	4.8	8.6	7.0
Sudan	*6.2*	..	*3.7*	..	*0.2*	..	*11.3*	*19.5*	*14.2*	9.1	*8.8*	*4.5*
Swaziland[a]	3.8	1.9	0.6	0.3	5.5	–1.1	2.7	4.3	3.8	2.1	4.5	1.4
Sweden	1.3	1.6	0.9	1.3	0.6	1.0	1.8	1.2	8.6	4.8	6.3	2.9
Switzerland	1.1	0.9	0.5	*0.2*	0.8	*2.3*	..	..	4.0	*1.4*	4.2	*1.7*
Syrian Arab Republic	3.0	6.2	0.2	3.6	2.0	6.5	3.3	10.6	12.0	0.2	4.4	10.1
Tajikistan	*–4.2*	..	*–5.5*	..	*–19.2*	..	–17.6	*18.2*	*–1.4*	13.8	*–3.9*	*1.7*
Tanzania[c]	2.1	1.7	–0.8	–0.2	3.4	19.1	–1.6	9.4	7.1	2.5	0.3	5.2
Thailand	3.7	5.5	2.5	4.5	5.1	3.9	–4.0	10.1	9.5	6.6	4.6	8.8
Togo	5.0	0.5	1.8	–2.2	0.0	1.3	–0.1	5.9	1.2	6.0	1.1	3.1
Trinidad and Tobago	0.7	13.3	0.1	12.9	0.3	4.3	12.5	4.2	6.9	5.9	9.9	9.5
Tunisia	4.3	5.0	2.6	4.0	4.1	4.5	3.6	0.9	5.1	2.9	3.8	1.8
Turkey	3.5	4.2	1.7	2.9	4.9	–0.2	5.0	11.6	11.7	11.8	11.0	12.8
Turkmenistan	..	..	..	..	..	..	*2.2*	..	*–6.1*	13.9	*0.6*	12.3
Uganda	6.7	4.1	3.4	0.6	7.1	5.1	8.9	8.8	14.7	8.7	10.0	8.0
Ukraine	–6.9	12.1	–6.4	13.1	–4.1	5.1	–18.5	5.8	–3.6	6.4	–6.6	7.5
United Arab Emirates	*7.1*	*12.9*	*0.7*	*5.1*	*6.9*	*0.8*	*5.5*	*5.5*	*5.5*	*12.2*	*6.4*	*13.6*
United Kingdom	2.9	2.9	2.6	2.8	1.1	3.5	4.6	2.3	6.6	2.6	6.8	4.5
United States	3.6	*3.0*	2.4	*2.0*	0.7	*3.5*	7.4	*1.2*	7.3	*0.3*	9.8	*3.9*
Uruguay[a]	5.0	–1.1	4.2	–1.8	2.3	–3.0	6.3	–0.9	6.0	5.1	9.9	–0.5
Uzbekistan	..	..	..	..	..	..	–2.6	4.7	*2.4*	5.3	*–1.2*	4.9
Venezuela, RB	0.6	3.7	–1.5	1.9	3.7	6.0	11.0	–1.0	1.0	–0.8	8.2	4.2
Vietnam	*5.4*	7.2	*3.8*	5.9	*3.2*	6.9	19.8	11.5	24.1	16.6	28.2	19.9
West Bank and Gaza	*5.3*	–1.5	*0.9*	–5.4	*12.8*	1.3	*9.2*	–3.0	*8.7*	–3.1	*7.5*	–2.3
Yemen, Rep.	3.2	*4.9*	–0.8	*1.7*	1.7	*8.7*	11.4	11.8	16.6	–0.3	8.3	7.1
Zambia	–3.6	3.2	–5.9	1.4	–8.1	7.2	5.4	4.9	2.8	12.7	1.5	8.4
Zimbabwe	0.0	–4.4	–1.7	–5.0	–2.2	–3.2	–2.5	–10.7	10.5	–7.6	9.4	–4.2
World	**3.0 w**	**2.6 w**	**1.5 w**	***1.4 w***	**1.7 w**	**2.9 w**	**3.2 w**	**2.5 w**	**6.9 w**	**5.9 w**	**6.9 w**	**5.2 w**
Low income	4.2	5.0	2.1	3.1	4.4	4.6	5.9	12.4	8.5	11.5	9.2	13.9
Middle income	3.9	4.4	2.6	3.4	2.9	3.9	2.6	7.8	7.3	10.9	6.6	10.4
Lower middle income	5.1	4.7	3.8	3.7	3.9	5.0	4.8	9.8	6.9	14.7	5.8	12.5
Upper middle income	2.6	4.0	1.6	3.4	1.6	2.3	–0.4	4.1	7.7	6.9	7.4	8.2
Low & middle income	3.9	4.5	2.3	3.1	3.0	4.0	2.9	8.4	7.4	11.0	6.9	10.8
East Asia & Pacific	7.5	6.3	6.1	5.4	8.1	7.6	8.2	12.0	11.0	16.5	10.4	15.0
Europe & Central Asia	1.1	6.1	0.9	6.2	0.1	2.4	–7.2	7.6	3.6	9.8	2.0	11.5
Latin America & Carib.	3.5	2.1	1.8	0.7	1.4	1.1	5.1	1.6	8.5	5.4	10.7	4.0
Middle East & N. Africa	3.1	4.8	0.9	2.8	3.2	3.8	1.9	7.3	4.1	5.2	0.6	8.4
South Asia	4.6	5.2	2.6	3.4	5.3	4.4	6.0	13.2	9.5	13.8	10.6	15.4
Sub-Saharan Africa	2.8	4.1	0.3	1.7	0.5	5.1	4.1	6.8	5.0	3.7	5.4	7.8
High income	2.8	*2.3*	2.0	*1.6*	1.5	*2.7*	3.3	0.6	6.8	*3.4*	7.0	*3.9*
Europe EMU	1.9	1.3	1.6	0.7	1.4	1.7	..	..	6.6	3.3	6.0	3.3

a. Household final consumption expenditure includes statistical discrepancy. b. China has revised its national accounts data from 1993 onwards. However, data by expenditure are not availble. Data shown here are based on earlier series. c. Data cover mainland Tanzania only.

About the data

Measures of growth in consumption and capital formation are subject to two kinds of inaccuracy. The first stems from the difficulty of measuring expenditures at current price levels, as described in *About the data* for table 4.8. The second arises in deflating current price data to measure volume growth, where results depend on the relevance and reliability of the price indexes and weights used. Measuring price changes is more difficult for investment goods than for consumption goods because of the one-time nature of many investments and because the rate of technological progress in capital goods makes capturing change in quality difficult. (An example is computers—prices have fallen as quality has improved.) Several countries estimate capital formation from the supply side, identifying capital goods entering an economy directly from detailed production and international trade statistics. This means that the price indexes used in deflating production and international trade, reflecting delivered or offered prices, will determine the deflator for capital formation expenditures on the demand side.

Growth rates of household final consumption expenditure, household final consumption expenditure per capita, general government final consumption expenditure, gross capital formation, and exports and imports of goods and services are estimated using constant price data. (Consumption, capital formation, and exports and imports of goods and services as shares of GDP are shown in table 4.8.)

To obtain government consumption in constant prices, countries may deflate current values by applying a wage (price) index or extrapolate from the change in government employment. Neither technique captures improvements in productivity or changes in the quality of government services. Deflators for household consumption are usually calculated on the basis of the consumer price index. Many countries estimate household consumption as a residual that includes statistical discrepancies associated with the estimation of other expenditure items, including changes in inventories; thus these estimates lack detailed breakdowns of household consumption expenditures.

Definitions

• **Household final consumption expenditure** is the market value of all goods and services, including durable products (such as cars, washing machines, and home computers), purchased by households. It excludes purchases of dwellings but includes imputed rent for owner-occupied dwellings. It also includes payments and fees to governments to obtain permits and licenses. *World Development Indicators* includes in household consumption expenditure the expenditures of nonprofit institutions serving households, even when reported separately by the country. In practice, household consumption expenditure may include any statistical discrepancy in the use of resources relative to the supply of resources. • **General government final consumption expenditure** includes all government current expenditures for purchases of goods and services (including compensation of employees). It also includes most expenditures on national defense and security but excludes government military expenditures that potentially have wider public use and are part of government capital formation. • **Gross capital formation** consists of outlays on additions to the fixed assets of the economy, net changes in the level of inventories, and net acquisitions of valuables. Fixed assets include land improvements (fences, ditches, drains, and so on); plant, machinery, and equipment purchases; and the construction of roads, railways, and the like, including schools, offices, hospitals, private residential dwellings, and commercial and industrial buildings. Inventories are stocks of goods held by firms to meet temporary or unexpected fluctuations in production or sales, and "work in progress." • **Exports and imports of goods and services** represent the value of all goods and other market services provided to, or received from, the rest of the world. They include the value of merchandise, freight, insurance, transport, travel, royalties, license fees, and other services, such as communication, construction, financial, information, business, personal, and government services. They exclude compensation of employees and investment income (factor services in the 1968 SNA) as well as transfer payments.

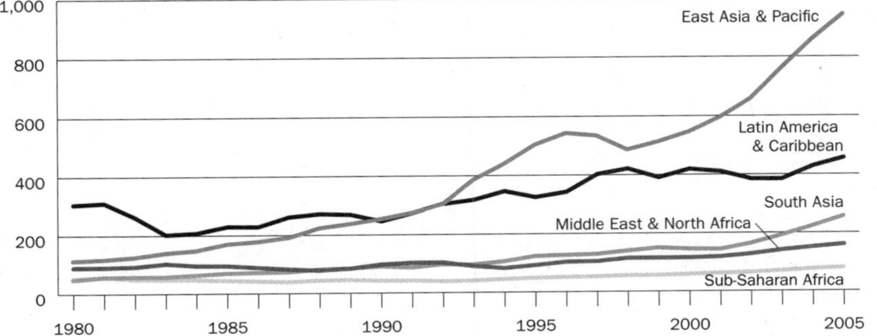

Between 1980 and 2005 investment increased eightfold in East Asia & Pacific and fivefold in South Asia.

Source: World Bank data files.

Data sources

National accounts indicators for most developing countries are collected from national statistical organizations and central banks by visiting and resident World Bank missions. Data for high-income economies come from data files of the Organisation for Economic Co-operation and Development (see the OECD's *Annual National Accounts for OECD Member Countries: Data from 1970 Onwards*). The United Nations Statistics Division publishes detailed national accounts for UN member countries in *National Accounts Statistics: Main Aggregates and Detailed Tables* and updates in the *Monthly Bulletin of Statistics*.

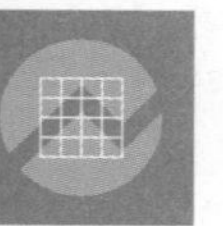

Central government finances

	Revenue[a] % of GDP		Expense % of GDP		Cash surplus or deficit % of GDP		Net incurrence of liabilities % of GDP Domestic		Net incurrence of liabilities % of GDP Foreign		Debt and interest payments	
	1995	2005	1995	2005	1995	2005	1995	2005	1995	2005	Total debt % of GDP 2005	Interest payments % of revenue 2005
Afghanistan[b]	..	6.2	..	11.9	..	0.9	..	0.1	..	1.4	9.4	0.3
Albania[b]	21.2	*23.6*	25.6	*21.9*	–8.9	*–3.0*	7.4	*1.9*	2.1	*1.0*	..	*15.5*
Algeria[b]	30.2	*35.3*	24.2	*24.1*	–1.3	*1.2*	–7.4	*1.8*	8.6	*–1.6*	*47.1*	8.6
Angola	..	..	..	..	..	..	..	..	..	..	..	..
Argentina	..	*18.1*	..	*18.3*	..	*–0.5*	..	*0.5*	..	*1.5*	..	*26.5*
Armenia[b]	..	19.3	..	18.1	..	–1.0	..	0.3	..	0.6	..	2.2
Australia	..	26.0	..	24.8	..	1.1	..	..	..	..	21.4	3.7
Austria	38.9	39.9	44.2	42.1	–5.4	–2.0	..	..	..	..	66.6	7.1
Azerbaijan[b]	18.0	..	19.8	..	–3.1	..	..	..	..	..	..	..
Bangladesh[b]	..	*10.0*	..	*8.8*	..	*–0.7*	..	*2.3*	..	*0.9*	*36.2*	*16.4*
Belarus[b]	30.0	33.3	28.7	29.8	–2.7	0.2	2.2	1.3	0.4	0.3	*12.3*	1.1
Belgium	41.5	42.1	45.6	42.3	–3.8	–0.1	..	..	..	..	88.7	9.5
Benin[b]	..	15.5	..	24.7	..	–10.3	..	2.7	..	3.0	..	1.5
Bolivia	..	23.5	..	26.6	..	–3.8	..	2.1	..	1.7	..	10.0
Bosnia and Herzegovina	..	39.1	..	36.2	..	2.3	..	–0.1	..	0.6	..	1.5
Botswana[b]	40.5	..	30.4	..	4.9	..	0.2	..	–0.4	..	..	..
Brazil[b]	*26.9*	..	*32.9*	..	*–2.7*	..	..	..	..	..	..	..
Bulgaria[b]	35.5	39.0	39.4	34.3	–5.1	3.5	7.4	–1.4	–0.8	–5.8	..	4.0
Burkina Faso	..	13.2	..	11.7	..	–4.1	..	–3.3	..	6.4	..	3.7
Burundi[b]	19.3	..	23.6	..	–4.7	..	*3.1*	..	4.0	..	..	..
Cambodia	..	9.8	..	7.7	..	0.0	..	–1.1	..	1.6	..	1.8
Cameroon[b]	13.0	..	11.7	..	0.3	..	–0.3	..	0.4	..	..	..
Canada[b]	20.6	20.0	24.6	18.1	–4.4	1.7	5.0	*–1.0*	0.0	*0.3*	*48.7*	7.5
Central African Republic[b]	..	*8.1*	..	*9.4*	..	*–0.5*	..	*1.2*	..	*0.1*	..	*8.0*
Chad	..	..	..	..	..	..	..	..	..	..	..	..
Chile	..	24.4	..	18.7	..	4.7	..	–2.0	..	–0.8	..	3.5
China[b]	5.4	*9.5*	..	*11.1*	..	*–2.1*	*1.6*	..	..	..	..	*4.7*
Hong Kong, China	..	..	..	..	..	..	..	..	..	..	..	..
Colombia	..	27.6	..	31.4	..	3.9	..	*5.2*	..	*–1.7*	56.7	21.6
Congo, Dem. Rep.[b]	5.3	*7.9*	8.2	..	0.0	..	0.0	..	*0.2*	..	..	..
Congo, Rep.	..	*30.9*	..	*19.9*	..	*6.4*	..	..	..	..	*0.2*	*18.1*
Costa Rica[b]	20.3	22.8	21.3	22.7	–2.1	–0.8	..	..	–0.8	..	..	18.0
Côte d'Ivoire[b]	20.1	17.1	..	16.9	..	–1.5	–1.2	–0.1	3.8	1.2	107.9	11.3
Croatia[b]	43.1	40.4	42.5	40.3	–1.3	–2.8	–2.7	5.3	0.8	–1.8	..	5.4
Cuba	..	..	..	..	..	..	..	..	..	..	..	..
Czech Republic[b]	33.2	31.6	32.6	35.8	–0.9	–3.5	–0.5	1.2	–0.4	2.1	23.1	2.4
Denmark	*39.1*	*36.0*	*38.2*	*34.7*	*1.5*	*1.8*	..	..	..	..	*42.2*	*8.4*
Dominican Republic[b]	16.0	*16.7*	10.2	*16.2*	0.8	*–0.7*	0.0	*1.0*	–1.0	*2.3*	..	*9.1*
Ecuador[b]	*14.1*	..	*12.0*	..	*0.0*	..	..	..	..	..	..	..
Egypt, Arab Rep.[b]	25.9	*19.5*	23.8	*22.6*	–1.1	*–5.7*	..	..	..	..	..	*29.4*
El Salvador	..	16.0	..	17.7	..	–4.4	..	3.6	..	2.9	48.7	13.6
Eritrea	..	..	..	..	..	..	..	..	..	..	..	..
Estonia	..	*32.6*	..	*29.5*	..	*2.7*	..	..	..	..	*9.6*	*0.4*
Ethiopia[b]	..	*15.2*	..	*22.0*	..	*–8.0*	..	*1.0*	..	*7.6*	..	*7.6*
Finland	*39.8*	39.2	*38.5*	36.6	*1.9*	3.2	*0.3*	*–1.0*	*–1.3*	2.3	45.6	4.0
France	*43.3*	43.1	*47.3*	46.1	*–4.1*	–2.8	..	..	..	..	71.9	5.8
Gabon	..	..	..	..	..	..	..	..	..	..	..	..
Gambia, The[b]	*23.7*	..	..	..	..	..	..	..	..	..	..	..
Georgia[b]	*12.2*	18.2	*15.4*	17.4	*–4.3*	1.5	2.2	–0.3	*2.4*	–0.3	35.2	5.4
Germany	29.9	28.7	38.6	31.2	–8.3	–2.3	..	1.7	..	0.3	44.2	5.8
Ghana[b]	*17.0*	*23.8*	..	*20.9*	..	*–2.9*	..	..	..	*3.3*	..	*14.4*
Greece	38.6	41.7	47.9	44.2	–10.0	–5.1	..	..	..	..	137.8	11.2
Guatemala[b]	8.4	10.1	7.6	11.0	–0.5	–1.5	..	1.5	0.4	0.7	18.3	11.6
Guinea[b]	*11.2*	..	*12.1*	..	*–4.3*	..	*–0.1*	..	*4.5*	..	..	..
Guinea-Bissau	..	..	..	..	..	..	..	..	..	..	..	..
Haiti	..	..	..	..	..	..	..	..	..	..	..	..

Central government finances

	Revenue[a]		Expense		Cash surplus or deficit		Net incurrence of liabilities				Debt and interest payments	
	% of GDP		% of GDP		% of GDP		% of GDP Domestic		Foreign		Total debt % of GDP	Interest payments % of revenue
	1995	2005	1995	2005	1995	2005	1995	2005	1995	2005	2005	2005
Honduras	..	..	..	..	..	..	..	..	..	..	..	..
Hungary	..	35.9	..	43.0	..	–7.4	..	1.3	..	4.2	67.2	11.3
India[b]	12.3	*12.5*	14.5	*15.8*	–2.2	*–3.6*	5.2	*3.6*	0.0	*0.3*	*65.4*	*31.9*
Indonesia[b]	17.7	*18.5*	9.7	*17.0*	3.0	*–1.1*	*–0.6*	*0.0*	–0.4	*–0.4*	*29.0*	*14.8*
Iran, Islamic Rep.[b]	24.2	35.6	15.8	20.5	1.1	7.4	..	–0.6	0.1	–0.9	..	0.7
Iraq	..	..	..	..	..	..	..	..	..	..	..	..
Ireland	33.6	31.8	37.4	30.3	–2.1	1.0	..	..	..	..	29.6	3.1
Israel	..	41.8	..	46.7	..	–2.6	..	..	..	..	..	12.1
Italy	40.3	35.7	48.0	39.4	–7.5	–3.5	..	..	..	..	114.4	12.7
Jamaica[b]	..	35.1	33.3	33.8	..	–1.2	..	..	..	..	139.6	41.3
Japan	*20.7*	..	..	..	..	..	*1.5*	..	..	..	..	..
Jordan[b]	28.2	28.4	26.1	35.3	0.9	–4.7	–2.5	*3.1*	6.1	*–3.0*	*89.1*	6.8
Kazakhstan[b]	*14.0*	21.3	*18.7*	18.2	*–1.8*	2.6	*0.8*	0.9	*2.8*	–1.5	7.1	1.7
Kenya[b]	21.6	*19.9*	25.9	*20.7*	–5.1	*–1.5*	3.9	*0.7*	–1.3	*0.7*	..	*10.2*
Korea, Dem. Rep.	..	..	..	..	..	..	..	..	..	..	..	..
Korea, Rep.[b]	17.8	23.4	14.3	21.4	2.4	0.8	–0.3	–0.1	–0.1	–0.3	..	5.4
Kuwait	..	37.2	..	26.2	..	8.2	..	..	..	..	..	0.1
Kyrgyz Republic[b]	16.7	..	25.6	..	–10.8	..	..	..	..	..	..	..
Lao PDR	..	..	..	..	..	..	..	..	..	..	..	..
Latvia[b]	25.8	26.6	28.3	29.4	–2.7	–0.9	2.4	0.5	1.5	–0.2	..	1.9
Lebanon	..	*21.4*	..	*26.2*	..	*–8.4*	..	*–1.3*	..	*12.3*	..	*56.0*
Lesotho[b]	49.8	*47.7*	34.4	*36.5*	5.1	*5.1*	*0.0*	..	6.2	..	..	*3.8*
Liberia	..	..	..	..	..	..	..	..	..	..	..	..
Libya	..	..	..	..	..	..	..	..	..	..	..	..
Lithuania	..	28.8	..	28.3	..	–0.4	..	–0.1	..	1.0	21.4	2.8
Macedonia, FYR	..	..	..	..	..	..	..	..	..	..	..	..
Madagascar	..	*60.4*	..	*63.0*	..	*–22.5*	..	*–3.6*	..	*31.8*	..	*14.5*
Malawi	..	..	..	..	..	..	..	..	..	..	..	..
Malaysia[b]	24.4	*23.7*	17.2	*20.1*	2.4	*–4.3*	..	..	–0.8	..	..	*10.5*
Mali	..	..	..	..	..	..	..	..	..	..	..	..
Mauritania	..	..	..	..	..	..	..	..	..	..	..	..
Mauritius[b]	21.6	21.1	19.9	20.9	–1.3	–2.1	3.1	2.9	–0.6	0.3	43.8	12.0
Mexico[b]	15.3	..	15.0	..	–0.6	..	..	..	5.5	..	..	..
Moldova[b]	28.4	32.5	*38.4*	30.0	*–6.3*	1.9	*3.0*	0.2	*2.7*	–0.1	33.2	3.8
Mongolia	..	*37.9*	..	*30.8*	..	*–0.5*	..	*11.3*	..	*–6.8*	*119.8*	*3.1*
Morocco[b]	..	28.8	..	31.3	..	–5.6	..	7.6	..	–0.7	*63.2*	13.0
Mozambique	..	..	..	..	..	..	..	..	..	..	..	..
Myanmar	6.4	*5.0*	..	..	..	..	..	..	..	..	..	..
Namibia[b]	31.7	*28.1*	*35.7*	*31.1*	–5.0	*–6.8*	..	*–20.0*	..	*–0.1*	..	*9.1*
Nepal[b]	10.5	12.8	..	16.6	..	–1.2	*0.6*	0.3	*2.5*	0.6	57.2	7.5
Netherlands	40.3	40.2	49.2	40.0	–8.9	0.0	..	..	..	..	55.5	5.1
New Zealand	..	38.0	..	32.5	..	4.6	..	–1.8	..	2.8	46.4	4.5
Nicaragua[b]	15.0	22.4	16.3	21.0	0.6	–0.7	..	..	*3.4*	..	..	7.4
Niger	..	..	..	..	..	..	..	..	..	..	..	..
Nigeria	..	..	..	..	..	..	..	..	..	..	..	..
Norway	..	50.7	..	34.1	..	16.3	..	0.0	..	1.1	37.0	1.7
Oman[b]	27.8	..	32.4	..	–8.9	..	–0.1	..	0.0	..	..	..
Pakistan[b]	17.2	12.9	19.1	14.5	–5.3	–3.2	..	..	..	..	..	31.8
Panama[b]	26.1	..	22.0	..	1.5	..	..	..	..	..	..	..
Papua New Guinea[b]	23.9	*22.5*	25.8	*22.1*	–0.5	*–2.3*	1.5	*4.9*	–0.7	*–2.2*	*69.7*	*19.9*
Paraguay[b]	..	21.2	..	16.7	..	1.1	..	0.1	..	–0.7	..	5.6
Peru[b]	17.4	17.6	17.4	17.3	–1.3	–0.8	..	1.9	3.9	–1.2	..	10.6
Philippines[b]	17.7	15.1	*15.9*	18.0	*–0.8*	–3.0	–0.5	1.4	–0.7	1.9	69.9	38.7
Poland	..	33.6	..	36.3	..	–2.3	..	–0.3	..	3.6	41.5	7.1
Portugal	*35.3*	37.9	*37.8*	42.4	*–3.0*	–5.8	*–3.5*	0.3	*4.1*	6.3	73.7	6.8
Puerto Rico	..	..	..	..	..	..	..	..	..	..	..	..

4.10 Central government finances

	Revenue[a]		Expense		Cash surplus or deficit		Net incurrence of liabilities				Debt and interest payments	
	% of GDP		% of GDP		% of GDP		% of GDP Domestic		Foreign		Total debt % of GDP	Interest payments % of revenue
	1995	2005	1995	2005	1995	2005	1995	2005	1995	2005	2005	2005
Romania	..	25.8	..	25.9	..	–2.0	..	0.4	..	1.7	..	8.4
Russian Federation	..	30.7	..	20.0	..	9.9	..	0.3	..	–4.2	41.4	3.1
Rwanda[b]	10.6	..	15.0	..	–5.6	..	2.9	..	..	..	..	..
Saudi Arabia	..	..	..	..	..	..	..	..	..	..	..	..
Senegal[b]	16.6	..	..	..	..	..	..	..	..	..	..	..
Serbia and Montenegro[b]	..	35.8	..	39.9	..	–3.0	..	..	..	..	..	2.6
Sierra Leone[b]	9.4	12.3	..	23.8	..	–2.5	0.3	..	..	..	..	21.0
Singapore[b]	26.7	20.1	12.4	15.4	19.8	4.1	10.3	9.2	0.0	..	108.9	0.8
Slovak Republic	..	31.4	..	34.9	..	–3.4	..	–0.6	..	–4.3	37.2	5.4
Slovenia[b]	36.7	40.3	35.2	41.3	–0.2	–1.5	–0.4	2.0	0.3	–1.9	..	4.0
Somalia	..	..	..	..	..	..	..	..	..	..	..	..
South Africa	..	30.2	..	29.6	..	0.2	..	1.8	..	0.1	..	11.1
Spain	32.0	26.9	37.1	24.9	–5.8	1.5	..	..	..	..	44.4	5.5
Sri Lanka[b]	20.4	16.1	26.0	21.0	–7.6	–7.3	5.2	5.6	3.2	2.0	94.2	29.1
Sudan[b]	7.2	..	6.8	..	–0.4	..	0.3	..	..	..	..	..
Swaziland[b]	..	26.6	..	24.4	..	–2.6	..	..	..	..	..	4.5
Sweden	40.4	38.9	39.0	36.1	2.2	2.1	..	–1.3	..	..	54.3	4.4
Switzerland[b]	22.7	19.4	25.8	19.2	–0.6	0.6	–0.5	–0.6	..	..	28.6	4.5
Syrian Arab Republic[b]	22.9	..	..	..	..	..	..	..	..	..	..	..
Tajikistan[b]	9.3	13.5	11.4	13.7	–3.3	–6.6	0.1	..	2.3	..	..	5.1
Tanzania	..	..	..	..	..	..	..	..	..	..	..	..
Thailand	..	21.0	..	16.3	..	2.5	..	–3.3	..	–0.9	27.3	6.1
Togo[b]	..	14.1	..	15.4	..	–5.5	..	..	..	..	..	7.1
Trinidad and Tobago[b]	27.2	28.5	25.3	24.6	–0.1	2.1	2.8	..	2.6	..	..	11.0
Tunisia[b]	30.0	29.7	28.4	29.5	–2.5	–3.0	0.9	–0.3	2.9	0.9	59.0	9.6
Turkey[b]	17.7	..	19.1	..	–1.8	..	..	..	..	..	..	..
Turkmenistan	..	..	..	..	..	..	..	..	..	..	..	..
Uganda[b]	10.6	12.1	..	22.8	..	–3.8	..	0.5	..	4.2	..	6.5
Ukraine[b]	..	36.5	..	37.5	..	–1.4	..	4.5	..	0.2	..	2.1
United Arab Emirates[b]	10.1	..	9.3	..	0.5	..	..	..	..	..	..	..
United Kingdom	37.2	38.0	37.1	41.1	0.3	–2.9	–0.3	3.6	0.0	0.0	..	5.6
United States	..	18.4	..	21.2	..	–2.9	..	1.7	..	1.2	47.2	11.1
Uruguay[b]	27.6	27.2	27.1	27.5	–1.2	–1.6	7.9	2.4	1.1	1.7	78.7	16.0
Uzbekistan	..	..	..	..	..	..	..	..	..	..	..	..
Venezuela, RB[b]	16.9	29.3	18.5	26.0	–2.3	2.3	1.1	1.3	0.1	3.4	..	10.4
Vietnam	..	..	..	..	..	..	..	..	..	..	..	..
West Bank and Gaza	..	..	..	..	..	..	..	..	..	..	..	..
Yemen, Rep.[b]	17.3	..	19.1	..	–3.9	..	..	..	..	..	..	..
Zambia[b]	20.0	..	21.4	..	–3.1	..	28.0	..	16.2	..	..	..
Zimbabwe[b]	26.7	..	32.1	..	–5.4	..	–1.4	..	1.6	..	..	..
World	.. w	26.6 w	.. w	28.2 w	.. w	–1.7 w	.. m	.. m	.. m	.. m	.. m	7.9 m
Low income	13.3	13.0	15.5	15.5	–2.7	–3.2	..	..	..	..	..	..
Middle income	17.2	..	..	..	..	..	..	1.1	..	0.6	..	6.8
Lower middle income	16.2	15.0	..	15.6	..	–1.7	..	1.1	..	1.1	..	6.8
Upper middle income	..	..	..	..	..	..	..	0.5	..	1.7	..	6.2
Low & middle income	16.6	..	..	..	..	..	..	..	..	..	..	10.2
East Asia & Pacific	8.4	11.4	..	12.5	..	–1.9	..	..	..	..	..	7.6
Europe & Central Asia	..	32.3	..	29.7	..	2.2	..	0.3	..	0.0	..	2.9
Latin America & Carib.	21.0	..	23.1	..	–1.5	..	..	..	..	..	..	11.1
Middle East & N. Africa	26.1	25.6	..	23.2	..	–2.8	..	..	..	..	..	10.1
South Asia	13.2	12.5	15.4	15.2	–2.7	–3.2	3.8	0.3	1.1	1.4	57.2	18.3
Sub-Saharan Africa	..	..	..	..	..	..	..	..	..	..	..	..
High income	..	26.5	..	28.4	..	–2.0	..	..	..	..	48.7	5.6
Europe EMU	34.8	35.2	42.3	37.2	–7.4	–2.0	..	..	..	..	69.2	5.8

a. Excluding grants. b. Data were reported on a cash basis and have been adjusted to the accrual framework.

Central government finances 4.10

About the data

Tables 4.10–4.12 present an overview of the size and role of central governments relative to national economies. The data in these tables are based on the concepts and recommendations of the second edition of the International Monetary Fund's (IMF) *Government Finance Statistics Manual 2001*. Before 2005, *World Development Indicators* reported data derived on the basis of the 1986 manual. The 2001 manual, which is harmonized with the 1993 System of National Accounts, recommends an accrual accounting method instead of the cash-based method of the 1986 manual. The new manual focuses on all economic events affecting assets, liabilities, revenues, and expenses, instead of only those represented by cash transactions. The new manual takes all stocks into account, so that the stock data at the end of an accounting period is equal to the stock data at the beginning of the period plus the flows during the period. The 1986 manual considered only the debt stock data. Further, the new manual does not distinguish between current and capital revenue or expenditures, unlike the 1986 manual. The new manual also introduces the concepts of nonfinancial and financial assets. Most countries still follow the previous manual, however. The IMF has reclassified historical *Government Finance Statistics Yearbook* data to conform to the format of the 2001 manual. Because of differences in reporting, the reclassified data understate both revenue and expense.

Government Finance Statistics Manual 2001 describes the economic functions of a government as the provision of goods and services to the community on a nonmarket basis for collective or individual consumption, and the redistribution of income and wealth through transfer payments. The activities of government are financed mainly by taxation and other transfers of income, though other forms of financing such as borrowing for temporary periods can also be used. The definition of government excludes public corporations and quasi corporations (such as the central bank).

Units of government meeting this definition exist at many levels, from local administrative units to the highest level of national government, but inadequate statistical coverage precludes the presentation of subnational data. Although data for general government are available for a few countries under the 2001 manual, only data for the central government are shown to minimize disparities. However, cross-country comparisons are potentially misleading due to different accounting concepts of central government.

Central government can refer to one of two accounting concepts: consolidated or budgetary. For most countries central government finance data have been consolidated into one account, but for others only budgetary central government accounts are available. Countries reporting budgetary data are noted in *Primary data documentation*. Because budgetary accounts do not necessarily include all central government units (such as extrabudgetary accounts and social security funds), the picture they provide of central government activities is usually incomplete.

Data on government revenues and expenditures are collected by the IMF through questionnaires distributed to member governments and by the Organisation for Economic Co-operation and Development. Despite the IMF's efforts to systematize and standardize the collection of public finance data, statistics on public finance are often incomplete, untimely, and not comparable across countries.

Government finance statistics are reported in local currency. The indicators here are shown as percentages of GDP. Many countries report government finance data by fiscal year; see *Primary data documentation* for information on fiscal year end by country.

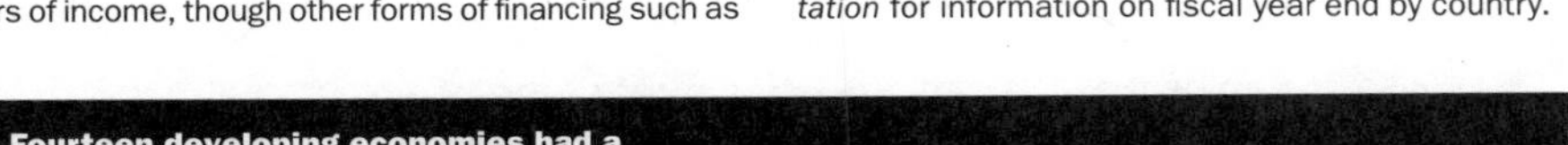

Fourteen developing economies had a cash deficit greater than 4 percent of GDP **4.10a**

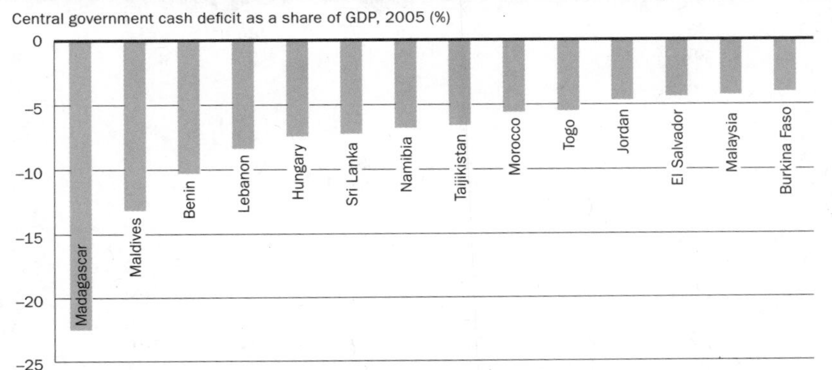

Note: Data are for the most recent year available for 2003–05.
Source: International Monetary Fund, *Government Finance Statistics* data files, and World Bank data files.

Definitions

• **Revenue** is cash receipts from taxes, social contributions, and other revenues such as fines, fees, rent, and income from property or sales. Grants are also considered as revenue but are excluded here. • **Expense** is cash payments for operating activities of the government in providing goods and services. It includes compensation of employees (such as wages and salaries), interest and subsidies, grants, social benefits, and other expenses such as rent and dividends. • **Cash surplus or deficit** is revenue (including grants) minus expense, minus net acquisition of nonfinancial assets. In the earlier version nonfinancial assets were included under revenue and expenditure in gross terms. This cash surplus or deficit is closest to the earlier overall budget balance (still missing is lending minus repayments, which are brought in below as a financing item under net acquisition of financial assets). • **Net incurrence of government liabilities** includes domestic financing (obtained from residents) and foreign financing (obtained from nonresidents), or the means by which a government provides financial resources to cover a budget deficit or allocates financial resources arising from a budget surplus. The net incurrence of liabilities should be offset by the net acquisition of financial assets (a third financing item). The difference between the cash surplus or deficit and the three financing items is the net change in the stock of cash. • **Total debt** is the entire stock of direct government fixed-term contractual obligations to others outstanding on a particular date. It includes domestic and foreign liabilities such as currency and money deposits, securities other than shares, and loans. It is the gross amount of government liabilities reduced by the amount of equity and financial derivatives held by the government. Because debt is a stock rather than a flow, it is measured as of a given date, usually the last day of the fiscal year. • **Interest payments** include interest payments on government debt—including long-term bonds, long-term loans, and other debt instruments —to domestic and foreign residents.

Data sources

Data on central government finances are from the IMF's *Government Finance Statistics Yearbook 2006* and IMF data files. Each country's accounts are reported using the system of common definitions and classifications in the IMF's *Government Finance Statistics Manual 2001*. See these sources for complete and authoritative explanations of concepts, definitions, and data sources.

4.11 Central government expenses

	Goods and services		Compensation of employees		Interest payments		Subsidies and other transfers		Other expense	
	% of expense		% of expense		% of expense		% of expense		% of expense	
	1995	2005	1995	2005	1995	2005	1995	2005	1995	2005
Afghanistan[a]	..	45	..	47	..	0	..	5	..	2
Albania[a]	18	*12*	14	*30*	9	*17*	59	*42*	0	*0*
Algeria[a]	6	*6*	39	*32*	13	*12*	34	*50*	8	..
Angola	..	..	..	..	..	..	..	..	..	..
Argentina	..	*5*	..	*12*	..	*26*	..	*50*	..	*7*
Armenia[a]	..	40	..	20	..	2	..	36	..	1
Australia	..	10	..	10	..	4	..	71	..	6
Austria	5	5	13	12	8	7	55	52	2	1
Azerbaijan[a]	49	..	10	..	0	..	41	..	0	..
Bangladesh[a]	..	*17*	..	*25*	..	*20*	..	*29*	..	*9*
Belarus[a]	39	11	5	13	1	1	55	67	*0*	8
Belgium	3	3	7	7	18	9	71	51	3	1
Benin[a]	..	72	..	25	..	1	..	1	..	..
Bolivia	..	14	..	23	..	10	..	47	..	5
Bosnia and Herzegovina	..	23	..	28	..	2	..	43	..	4
Botswana[a]	32	..	30	..	2	..	36	..	*2*	..
Brazil[a]	*5*	..	*8*	..	*45*	..	*45*	..	*1*	..
Bulgaria[a]	18	22	7	11	37	5	38	59	*2*	3
Burkina Faso	..	21	..	41	..	6	..	32	..	0
Burundi[a]	20	..	30	..	6	..	*14*	..	*10*	..
Cambodia	..	40	..	36	..	3	..	19	..	2
Cameroon[a]	17	..	40	..	26	..	14	..	..	..
Canada[a]	8	7	10	12	18	8	64	66	..	6
Central African Republic[a]	..	*27*	..	*53*	..	*9*	..	..	..	*11*
Chad	..	..	..	..	..	..	..	..	..	..
Chile	..	10	..	21	..	5	..	57	..	12
China[a]	..	..	..	..	..	*4*	..	*64*	..	*4*
Hong Kong, China	..	..	..	..	..	..	..	..	..	..
Colombia	..	10	..	20	..	19	..	42	..	9
Congo, Dem. Rep.[a]	37	..	58	..	1	..	2	..	..	..
Congo, Rep.	..	*29*	..	*37*	..	*29*	..	*5*	..	*0*
Costa Rica[a]	12	11	38	41	20	18	26	28	4	2
Côte d'Ivoire[a]	..	32	..	39	..	12	..	17	..	*2*
Croatia[a]	35	8	27	26	3	5	32	54	3	6
Cuba	..	..	..	..	..	..	..	..	..	..
Czech Republic[a]	7	6	9	9	3	2	75	68	5	15
Denmark	*8*	*10*	*13*	*13*	*13*	*9*	*64*	*66*	*4*	*4*
Dominican Republic[a]	16	*11*	41	*28*	9	*10*	19	*40*	*6*	*11*
Ecuador[a]	*6*	..	*49*	..	*26*	..	..	..	..	..
Egypt, Arab Rep.[a]	21	*10*	26	*33*	31	*27*	7	*18*	..	*12*
El Salvador	..	18	..	39	..	12	..	25	..	5
Eritrea	..	..	..	..	..	..	..	..	..	..
Estonia	..	*17*	..	*21*	..	*0*	..	*45*	..	*3*
Ethiopia[a]	..	*24*	..	*14*	..	*7*	..	*42*	..	*14*
Finland	*10*	10	*10*	10	*9*	4	68	71	*7*	7
France	*8*	6	*23*	22	*6*	5	*51*	53	*2*	2
Gabon	..	..	..	..	..	..	..	..	..	..
Gambia, The[a]	..	..	..	..	..	..	..	..	..	..
Georgia[a]	*52*	21	*11*	17	*10*	6	*26*	53	..	3
Germany	4	5	5	5	6	5	67	82	20	3
Ghana[a]	..	..	..	*45*	..	*21*	..	*5*	..	..
Greece	10	10	22	25	26	11	33	40	10	0
Guatemala[a]	15	12	50	25	12	11	18	24	6	28
Guinea[a]	*17*	..	*34*	..	*28*	..	*9*	..	*1*	..
Guinea-Bissau	..	..	..	..	..	..	..	..	..	..
Haiti	..	..	..	..	..	..	..	..	..	..

Central government expenses

	Goods and services		Compensation of employees		Interest payments		Subsidies and other transfers		Other expense	
	% of expense		% of expense		% of expense		% of expense		% of expense	
	1995	2005	1995	2005	1995	2005	1995	2005	1995	2005
Honduras	..	..	..	..	..	..	..	..	..	..
Hungary	..	8	..	14	..	10	..	61	..	11
India[a]	14	*15*	10	*10*	27	*26*	33	..	0	..
Indonesia[a]	21	*8*	20	*13*	16	*16*	41	*63*	2	*0*
Iran, Islamic Rep.[a]	21	13	56	47	0	1	..	34	..	5
Iraq	..	..	..	..	..	..	..	..	..	..
Ireland	5	14	15	24	14	3	33	36	1	1
Israel	..	27	..	24	..	11	..	31	..	8
Italy	4	4	14	16	24	12	54	46	6	2
Jamaica[a]	22	20	24	32	32	43	1	2	21	3
Japan	..	..	..	..	..	..	..	..	..	..
Jordan[a]	7	5	67	*58*	11	7	12	3	4	11
Kazakhstan[a]	..	18	..	7	*3*	2	*58*	44	..	28
Kenya[a]	15	*29*	28	*50*	46	*10*	..	*9*	2	*2*
Korea, Dem. Rep.	..	..	..	..	..	..	..	..	..	..
Korea, Rep.[a]	16	10	15	11	3	6	63	52	3	21
Kuwait	..	23	..	31	..	0	..	32	..	13
Kyrgyz Republic[a]	32	..	36	..	5	..	27	..	..	..
Lao PDR	..	..	..	..	..	..	..	..	..	..
Latvia[a]	20	13	20	16	3	2	56	39	0	31
Lebanon	..	*3*	..	*33*	..	*46*	..	*16*	..	*2*
Lesotho[a]	32	*31*	45	*38*	5	*5*	*8*	*26*	*3*	..
Liberia	..	..	..	..	..	..	..	..	..	..
Libya	..	..	..	..	..	..	..	..	..	..
Lithuania	..	13	..	20	..	3	..	58	..	8
Macedonia, FYR	..	..	..	..	..	..	..	..	..	..
Madagascar	..	*14*	..	*39*	..	*23*	..	*11*	..	*13*
Malawi	..	..	..	..	..	..	..	..	..	..
Malaysia[a]	23	*26*	34	*30*	17	*12*	27	*31*	1	*1*
Mali	..	..	..	..	..	..	..	..	..	..
Mauritania	..	..	..	..	..	..	..	..	..	..
Mauritius[a]	12	13	45	39	12	12	28	33	2	3
Mexico[a]	9	..	19	..	19	..	..	..	..	..
Moldova[a]	*10*	18	*8*	14	*11*	4	*71*	53	*1*	11
Mongolia	..	*36*	..	*30*	..	*4*	..	*31*	..	*0*
Morocco[a]	..	16	..	43	..	12	..	24	..	5
Mozambique	..	..	..	..	..	..	..	..	..	..
Myanmar	..	..	..	..	..	..	..	..	..	..
Namibia[a]	*28*	*28*	*53*	49	*1*	*8*	..	*14*	*4*	*2*
Nepal[a]	..	..	..	..	..	7	..	..	..	..
Netherlands	5	7	8	8	9	5	42	48	2	2
New Zealand	..	28	..	26	..	5	..	39	..	6
Nicaragua[a]	16	16	23	30	15	9	34	41	13	4
Niger	..	..	..	..	..	..	..	..	..	..
Nigeria	..	..	..	..	..	..	..	..	..	..
Norway	..	11	..	16	..	3	..	67	..	6
Oman[a]	55	..	30	..	7	..	8	..	0	..
Pakistan[a]	..	36	..	4	28	29	2	30	..	..
Panama[a]	16	..	45	..	8	..	30	..	1	..
Papua New Guinea[a]	19	*35*	36	*28*	20	*21*	26	*16*	*1*	..
Paraguay[a]	..	11	..	52	..	7	..	26	..	3
Peru[a]	20	20	19	20	19	11	33	45	8	4
Philippines[a]	*15*	18	*34*	30	*33*	32	*15*	17	..	2
Poland	..	7	..	12	..	7	..	69	..	7
Portugal	*7*	6	*30*	30	*10*	6	*43*	47	*11*	1
Puerto Rico	..	..	..	..	..	..	..	..	..	..

4.11 Central government expenses

	Goods and services		Compensation of employees		Interest payments		Subsidies and other transfers		Other expense	
	% of expense		% of expense		% of expense		% of expense		% of expense	
	1995	2005	1995	2005	1995	2005	1995	2005	1995	2005
Romania	..	*22*	..	*16*	..	*8*	..	*43*	..	*12*
Russian Federation	..	15	..	19	..	5	..	53	..	9
Rwanda[a]	*52*	..	*36*	..	*12*	..	*5*	..	..	..
Saudi Arabia	..	..	..	..	..	..	..	..	..	..
Senegal[a]	..	..	..	..	..	..	..	..	..	..
Serbia and Montenegro[a]	..	*10*	..	*14*	..	*2*	..	68	..	6
Sierra Leone[a]	..	*28*	..	*26*	..	*19*	..	*9*	..	*18*
Singapore[a]	38	*35*	39	*31*	8	*1*	15	*33*	..	..
Slovak Republic	..	10	..	13	..	5	..	63	..	9
Slovenia[a]	19	12	21	19	3	4	55	63	3	3
Somalia	..	..	..	..	..	..	..	..	..	..
South Africa	..	12	..	15	..	11	..	56	..	5
Spain	5	4	14	9	11	6	42	51	2	2
Sri Lanka[a]	23	11	20	28	22	24	24	28	10	8
Sudan[a]	*44*	..	*38*	..	*8*	..	*10*	..	..	..
Swaziland[a]	..	*29*	..	*42*	..	*5*	..	*21*	..	*2*
Sweden	*11*	12	*9*	10	*13*	5	*64*	68	*5*	8
Switzerland[a]	24	*9*	6	*7*	4	*5*	66	*74*	0	*5*
Syrian Arab Republic[a]	..	..	..	..	..	..	..	..	..	..
Tajikistan[a]	*47*	*29*	*8*	*9*	*12*	*5*	*33*	*27*	..	*30*
Tanzania	..	..	..	..	..	..	..	..	..	..
Thailand	..	22	..	35	..	8	..	33	..	5
Togo[a]	..	48	..	31	..	6	..	2	..	13
Trinidad and Tobago[a]	20	*18*	36	*33*	20	*13*	24	*35*	*1*	*1*
Tunisia[a]	7	7	37	39	13	10	36	34	*7*	10
Turkey[a]	8	..	28	..	14	..	*33*	..	*4*	..
Turkmenistan	..	..	..	..	..	..	..	..	..	..
Uganda[a]	..	*36*	..	*11*	..	*6*	..	*47*	..	..
Ukraine[a]	..	12	..	13	..	2	..	68	..	4
United Arab Emirates[a]	*50*	..	*37*	..	..	..	..	..	..	..
United Kingdom	*22*	18	*7*	15	*9*	5	*54*	54	*9*	10
United States	..	15	..	13	..	10	..	61	..	2
Uruguay[a]	13	14	17	22	6	16	64	47	0	..
Uzbekistan	..	..	..	..	..	..	..	..	..	..
Venezuela, RB[a]	6	6	22	16	27	12	*61*	64	2	3
Vietnam	..	..	..	..	..	..	..	..	..	..
West Bank and Gaza	..	..	..	..	..	..	..	..	..	..
Yemen, Rep.[a]	8	..	67	..	16	..	8	..	*0*	..
Zambia[a]	*32*	..	*35*	..	*16*	..	*19*	..	*0*	..
Zimbabwe[a]	16	..	34	..	31	..	19	..	..	..
World	.. m	*12* m	.. m	*21* m	.. m	*8* m	.. m	*44* m	.. m	*5* m
Low income	..	..	..	..	..	..	..	..	..	..
Middle income	..	13	..	*21*	..	7	..	44	..	5
Lower middle income	..	16	..	*28*	..	8	..	36	..	5
Upper middle income	14	10	29	18	10	6	..	57	..	*5*
Low & middle income	..	..	..	*27*	..	*11*	..	..	..	..
East Asia & Pacific	..	*27*	..	*31*	..	*7*	..	*31*	..	*0*
Europe & Central Asia	..	13	..	14	..	4	..	56	..	8
Latin America & Carib.	16	13	24	24	19	11	..	42	..	4
Middle East & N. Africa	8	*8*	39	*41*	13	*12*	..	..	..	..
South Asia	..	36	..	28	27	16	24	28	..	*9*
Sub-Saharan Africa	..	..	..	..	..	..	..	..	..	..
High income	*7*	10	*15*	14	*9*	5	*54*	52	*4*	3
Europe EMU	5	6	14	14	11	6	54	51	3	2

Note: Components may not sum to 100 percent because of rounding or missing data.
a. Data were reported on a cash basis and have been adjusted to the accrual framework.

Central government expenses 4.11

About the data

The term *expense* has replaced *expenditure* in this table since the 2005 edition of *World Development Indicators* in accordance with use in the International Monetary Fund's (IMF) *Government Finance Statistics Manual 2001*. Government expenses include all nonrepayable payments, whether current or capital, requited or unrequited. Total central government expense as presented in the IMF's *Government Finance Statistics Yearbook* is comparable to the concept used in the 1993 System of National Accounts.

Expenses can be measured either by function (health, defense, education) or by economic type (interest payments, wages and salaries, purchases of goods and services). Functional data are often incomplete, and coverage varies by country because functional responsibilities stretch across levels of government for which no data are available. Defense expenses, usually the central government's responsibility, are shown in table 5.7. For more information on education expenses, see table 2.9; for more on health expenses, see table 2.14.

The classification of expenses by economic type in this table shows whether the government produces goods and services and distributes them, purchases the goods and services from a third party and distributes them, or transfers cash to households to make the purchases directly. When the government produces and provides goods and services, the cost is reflected in compensation of employees, use of goods and services, and consumption of fixed capital. Purchases from a third party and cash transfers to households are shown as subsidies and other transfers, and other expenses. The economic classification can be problematic. For example, the distinction between current and capital expense may be arbitrary, and subsidies to public corporations or banks may be disguised as capital financing. Subsidies may also be hidden in special contractual pricing for goods and services. For further discussion of government finance statistics, see *About the data* for tables 4.10 and 4.12.

Interest payments are a large part of government expenses for some developing countries 4.11a

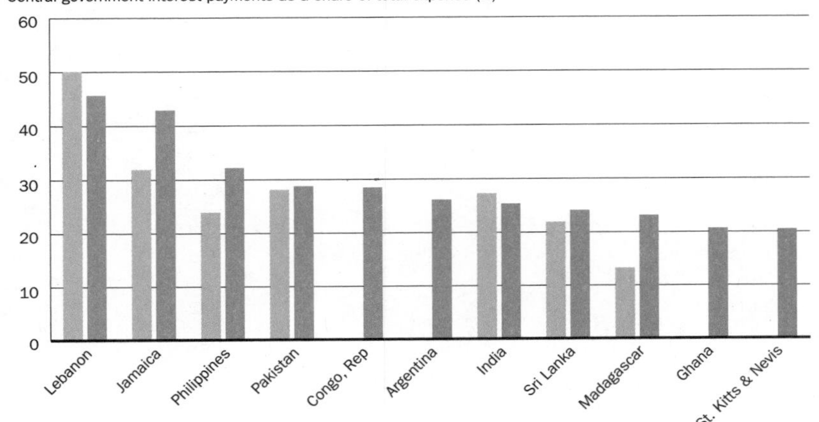

Interest payments accounted for more than 20 percent of total expenses in 2005 for 11 countries.

Note: Data are for the most recent year for 2003–05. For Lebanon, Madagascar, and Philippines, data for 1995 refer to 2000. No data for 1995 are available for Argentina, Republic of Congo, Ghana, and St. Kitts and Nevis.
Source: International Monetary Fund, *Government Finance Statistics* data files.

Definitions

• **Goods and services** include all government payments in exchange for goods and services used for the production of market and nonmarket goods and services. Own-account capital formation is excluded. • **Compensation of employees** consists of all payments in cash, as well as in kind (such as food and housing), to employees in return for services rendered, and government contributions to social insurance schemes such as social security and pensions that provide benefits to employees. • **Interest payments** are payments made to nonresidents, to residents, and to other general government units for the use of borrowed money. (Repayment of principal is shown as a financing item, and commission charges are shown as purchases of services.) • **Subsidies and other transfers** include all unrequited, nonrepayable transfers on current account to private and public enterprises; grants to foreign governments, international organizations, and other government units; and social security, social assistance benefits, and employer social benefits in cash and in kind. • **Other expense** is spending on dividends, rent, and other miscellaneous expenses, including provision for consumption of fixed capital.

Data sources

Data on central government expenses are from the IMF's *Government Finance Statistics Yearbook 2006* and IMF data files. Each country's accounts are reported using the system of common definitions and classifications in the IMF's *Government Finance Statistics Manual 2001*. See these sources for complete and authoritative explanations of concepts, definitions, and data sources.

4.12 Central government revenues

	Taxes on income, profits, and capital gains		Taxes on goods and services		Taxes on international trade		Other taxes		Social contributions		Grants and other revenue	
	% of revenue		% of revenue		% of revenue		% of revenue		% of revenue		% of revenue	
	1995	2005	1995	2005	1995	2005	1995	2005	1995	2005	1995	2005
Afghanistan[a]	..	2	..	3	..	20	..	1	..	0	..	74
Albania[a]	8	15	39	49	14	8	1	1	15	18	22	10
Algeria[a]	65	66	10	9	18	13	1	1	..	..	5	11
Angola	..	..	..	..	..	..	..	..	..	..	..	..
Argentina	..	19	..	29	..	16	..	14	..	17	..	5
Armenia[a]	..	16	..	32	..	3	..	20	..	14	..	14
Australia	..	65	..	24	..	2	..	0	..	..	..	8
Austria	20	23	21	23	0	0	5	4	41	38	..	..
Azerbaijan[a]	31	..	34	..	33	..	2	..	23	..	0	..
Bangladesh[a]	..	12	..	29	..	33	..	4	..	..	..	22
Belarus[a]	16	8	33	35	6	8	11	11	31	35	3	4
Belgium	36	37	23	25	..	..	2	1	36	34	3	2
Benin[a]	..	13	..	39	..	23	..	7	..	..	..	18
Bolivia	..	9	..	41	..	3	..	9	..	8	..	30
Bosnia and Herzegovina	..	2	..	19	..	29	..	5	..	34	..	11
Botswana[a]	21	..	4	..	15	..	0	..	..	..	59	..
Brazil[a]	14	..	24	..	2	..	4	..	31	..	26	..
Bulgaria[a]	17	13	28	43	8	2	3	0	21	26	23	16
Burkina Faso	..	16	..	38	..	11	..	3	..	..	..	33
Burundi[a]	14	..	30	..	20	..	1	..	5	..	30	..
Cambodia	..	7	..	37	..	21	..	0	..	..	..	35
Cameroon[a]	17	..	25	..	28	..	3	..	2	..	25	..
Canada[a]	50	53	17	17	2	1	..	..	22	23	10	6
Central African Republic[a]	..	14	..	23	..	19	..	4	..	6	..	34
Chad	..	..	..	..	..	..	..	..	..	..	..	..
Chile	..	30	..	41	..	2	..	6	..	6	..	15
China[a]	9	22	61	79	7	-12	0	1	..	..	22	10
Hong Kong, China	..	..	..	..	..	..	..	..	..	..	..	..
Colombia	..	21	..	29	..	3	..	1	..	7	..	39
Congo, Dem. Rep.[a]	21	25	12	24	21	27	5	1	1	..	41	23
Congo, Rep.	..	4	..	16	..	7	..	1	..	4	..	69
Costa Rica[a]	11	15	32	38	15	5	1	2	28	32	12	8
Côte d'Ivoire[a]	15	21	14	16	58	41	3	2	5	7	5	13
Croatia[a]	11	8	42	48	9	2	1	1	33	34	4	9
Cuba	..	..	..	..	..	..	..	..	..	..	..	..
Czech Republic[a]	15	20	32	27	4	0	1	1	40	46	8	7
Denmark	34	38	40	44	..	..	7	2	5	4	14	12
Dominican Republic[a]	16	19	34	41	36	28	1	2	4	2	9	9
Ecuador[a]	50	..	26	..	11	..	1	..	..	..	12	..
Egypt, Arab Rep.[a]	22	25	17	26	13	12	13	3	..	..	35	33
El Salvador	..	24	..	44	..	7	..	3	..	13	..	10
Eritrea	..	..	..	..	..	..	..	..	..	..	..	..
Estonia	..	14	..	38	..	0	..	0	..	34	..	..
Ethiopia[a]	..	15	..	12	..	27	..	0	..	5	..	41
Finland	21	21	34	35	0	..	2	2	32	31	12	12
France	17	24	25	24	0	0	3	4	47	42	7	6
Gabon	..	..	..	..	..	..	..	..	..	..	..	..
Gambia, The[a]	14	..	32	..	42	..	0	..	0	..	7	..
Georgia[a]	7	2	48	58	10	6	..	0	13	19	22	17
Germany	16	16	20	22	..	..	0	..	58	58	6	4
Ghana[a]	15	22	31	22	24	29	..	2	..	..	9	26
Greece	17	21	31	28	0	0	3	3	31	35	18	14
Guatemala[a]	19	26	46	52	23	15	3	1	2	2	6	4
Guinea[a]	8	..	4	..	62	..	2	..	1	..	23	..
Guinea-Bissau	..	..	..	..	..	..	..	..	..	..	..	..
Haiti	..	..	..	..	..	..	..	..	..	..	..	..

Central government revenues

	Taxes on income, profits, and capital gains		Taxes on goods and services		Taxes on international trade		Other taxes		Social contributions		Grants and other revenue	
	% of revenue		% of revenue		% of revenue		% of revenue		% of revenue		% of revenue	
	1995	2005	1995	2005	1995	2005	1995	2005	1995	2005	1995	2005
Honduras	..	..	..	..	..	..	..	..	..	..	..	..
Hungary	..	19	..	36	..	0	..	2	..	35	..	9
India[a]	23	*35*	28	*31*	24	*14*	0	*0*	0	*0*	25	*19*
Indonesia[a]	46	*28*	33	*32*	4	*3*	1	*4*	6	*3*	9	*30*
Iran, Islamic Rep.[a]	12	13	5	2	9	6	1	1	6	11	66	67
Iraq	..	..	..	..	..	..	..	..	..	..	..	..
Ireland	37	37	35	36	0	0	2	5	17	17	9	5
Israel	..	31	..	29	..	1	..	6	..	17	..	17
Italy	32	33	21	22	..	..	5	5	35	36	6	*5*
Jamaica[a]	..	15	..	33	..	10	..	20	..	7	..	15
Japan	*35*	..	*14*	..	*1*	..	*5*	..	*26*	..	*18*	..
Jordan[a]	10	9	23	36	22	11	9	14	..	1	36	28
Kazakhstan[a]	*11*	49	*28*	38	*3*	4	*5*	0	*48*	..	*6*	9
Kenya[a]	35	*29*	40	*40*	14	*11*	1	*0*	*0*	*0*	10	*20*
Korea, Dem. Rep.	..	..	..	..	..	..	..	..	..	..	..	..
Korea, Rep.[a]	31	29	32	28	7	3	10	7	8	16	12	16
Kuwait	..	1	..	..	..	2	..	0	..	..	..	97
Kyrgyz Republic[a]	26	..	56	..	5	..	1	..	..	..	11	..
Lao PDR	..	..	..	..	..	..	..	..	..	..	..	..
Latvia[a]	7	12	41	39	3	1	0	0	35	29	13	20
Lebanon	..	*11*	..	*45*	..	*8*	..	*12*	..	*1*	..	*24*
Lesotho[a]	15	*20*	12	*17*	49	*45*	1	*0*	..	..	24	*17*
Liberia	..	..	..	..	..	..	..	..	..	..	..	..
Libya	..	..	..	..	..	..	..	..	..	..	..	..
Lithuania	..	23	..	36	..	*0*	..	0	..	30	..	11
Macedonia, FYR	..	..	..	..	..	..	..	..	..	..	..	..
Madagascar	..	*6*	..	*16*	..	*27*	..	*4*	..	..	..	*46*
Malawi	..	..	..	..	..	..	..	..	..	..	..	..
Malaysia[a]	37	*47*	26	*21*	12	*6*	5	*0*	1	..	19	*26*
Mali	..	..	..	..	..	..	..	..	..	..	..	..
Mauritania	..	..	..	..	..	..	..	..	..	..	..	..
Mauritius[a]	12	15	25	45	34	20	6	5	6	4	16	11
Mexico[a]	27	..	54	..	4	..	2	..	14	..	16	..
Moldova[a]	*6*	2	*38*	47	*5*	6	*1*	1	*38*	24	2	20
Mongolia	..	*16*	..	*35*	..	*6*	..	*0*	..	*16*	..	*27*
Morocco[a]	..	32	..	36	..	11	..	5	..	..	..	15
Mozambique	..	..	..	..	..	..	..	..	..	..	..	..
Myanmar	20	*16*	26	*22*	12	*2*	..	..	..	..	42	*60*
Namibia[a]	27	*38*	32	*20*	28	*32*	2	*2*	..	*1*	11	*8*
Nepal[a]	10	11	33	32	26	19	4	4	..	..	27	34
Netherlands	26	25	24	28	..	1	2	3	40	34	..	..
New Zealand	..	55	..	27	..	2	..	0	..	0	..	16
Nicaragua[a]	8	19	46	42	6	4	0	0	10	16	29	19
Niger	..	..	..	..	..	..	..	..	..	..	..	..
Nigeria	..	..	..	..	..	..	..	..	..	..	..	..
Norway	..	34	..	25	..	0	..	1	..	18	..	22
Oman[a]	21	..	1	..	3	..	2	..	..	..	74	..
Pakistan[a]	18	20	27	34	24	14	7	4	..	..	24	28
Panama[a]	20	..	*17*	..	*11*	..	3	..	16	..	34	..
Papua New Guinea[a]	40	*50*	8	*13*	27	*26*	2	*3*	0	*0*	23	*8*
Paraguay[a]	..	10	..	35	..	8	..	3	..	15	..	28
Peru[a]	15	24	46	40	10	6	8	6	10	9	11	15
Philippines[a]	33	40	26	23	29	18	4	6	..	..	8	13
Poland	..	12	..	36	..	0	..	0	..	40	..	12
Portugal	*23*	*20*	*32*	*32*	*0*	*0*	*2*	*2*	29	33	*14*	*14*
Puerto Rico	..	..	..	..	..	..	..	..	..	..	..	..

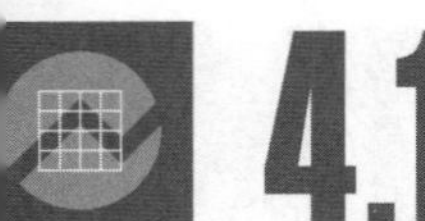

4.12 Central government revenues

	Taxes on income, profits, and capital gains % of revenue		Taxes on goods and services % of revenue		Taxes on international trade % of revenue		Other taxes % of revenue		Social contributions % of revenue		Grants and other revenue % of revenue	
	1995	2005	1995	2005	1995	2005	1995	2005	1995	2005	1995	2005
Romania	..	9	..	33	..	3	..	1	..	42	..	13
Russian Federation	..	6	..	24	..	24	..	0	..	18	..	29
Rwanda[a]	11	..	25	..	23	..	3	..	2	..	36	..
Saudi Arabia	..	..	..	..	..	..	..	..	..	..	..	..
Senegal[a]	17	..	19	..	36	..	2	..	..	..	26	..
Serbia and Montenegro[a]	..	13	..	39	..	7	..	4	..	29	..	9
Sierra Leone[a]	15	16	34	9	39	27	0	..	..	..	12	48
Singapore[a]	26	28	20	24	1	0	15	11	..	..	38	38
Slovak Republic	..	9	..	37	..	0	..	0	..	40	..	13
Slovenia[a]	13	15	33	33	9	0	0	4	42	38	3	10
Somalia	..	..	..	..	..	..	..	..	..	..	..	..
South Africa	..	50	..	33	..	4	..	4	..	2	..	7
Spain	28	27	21	18	0	..	0	0	40	48	..	..
Sri Lanka[a]	12	13	49	55	17	14	4	0	1	1	18	17
Sudan[a]	17	..	41	..	27	..	1	..	..	..	14	..
Swaziland[a]	..	28	..	19	..	48	..	0	..	..	..	5
Sweden	15	9	26	34	..	..	12	11	35	37	13	10
Switzerland[a]	11	16	21	30	1	1	2	3	49	39	17	11
Syrian Arab Republic[a]	23	..	37	..	13	..	8	..	0	..	19	..
Tajikistan[a]	6	3	63	54	12	11	0	1	13	12	5	18
Tanzania	..	..	..	..	..	..	..	..	..	..	..	..
Thailand	..	33	..	40	..	7	..	1	..	5	..	14
Togo[a]	..	19	..	48	..	22	..	6	..	..	..	5
Trinidad and Tobago[a]	50	42	26	21	6	6	1	16	2	5	15	11
Tunisia[a]	16	26	20	34	28	7	4	4	15	18	17	10
Turkey[a]	32	..	40	..	4	..	3	..	..	..	21	..
Turkmenistan	..	..	..	..	..	..	..	..	..	..	..	..
Uganda[a]	10	12	45	24	7	16	2	0	..	..	37	48
Ukraine[a]	..	15	..	28	..	5	..	0	..	35	..	16
United Arab Emirates[a]	..	..	15	..	..	..	..	..	1	..	84	..
United Kingdom	39	37	31	31	..	..	6	6	19	22	5	4
United States	..	55	..	3	..	1	..	1	..	37	..	2
Uruguay[a]	10	11	32	49	4	5	10	3	31	20	8	12
Uzbekistan	..	..	..	..	..	..	..	..	..	..	..	..
Venezuela, RB[a]	38	21	33	25	9	5	0	4	4	2	19	43
Vietnam	..	..	..	..	..	..	..	..	..	..	..	..
West Bank and Gaza	..	..	..	..	..	..	..	..	..	..	..	..
Yemen, Rep.[a]	17	..	10	..	18	..	3	..	..	..	51	..
Zambia[a]	27	..	22	..	36	..	0	..	0	..	15	..
Zimbabwe[a]	36	..	22	..	17	..	3	..	2	..	19	..
World	.. m	19 m	.. m	33 m	.. m	6 m	.. m	2 m	.. m	.. m	.. m	15 m
Low income	..	..	..	..	..	..	..	..	..	..	..	..
Middle income	17	15	29	36	12	5	3	1	..	16	17	14
Lower middle income	17	17	31	36	12	7	3	1	..	12	15	15
Upper middle income	20	15	29	37	8	3	2	1	..	30	16	11
Low & middle income	..	16	..	33	..	8	..	1	..	..	..	16
East Asia & Pacific	35	29	26	32	12	6	..	1	..	..	20	25
Europe & Central Asia	..	12	..	36	..	3	..	0	..	34	..	13
Latin America & Carib.	15	20	31	41	10	5	4	3	10	8	13	15
Middle East & N. Africa	19	22	14	29	16	12	4	3	..	..	35	21
South Asia	15	12	31	33	24	16	4	4	..	1	25	31
Sub-Saharan Africa	..	..	..	..	..	..	..	..	..	..	..	..
High income	25	30	24	27	..	1	4	4	32	34	12	9
Europe EMU	26	24	23	27	0	0	2	4	40	35	6	5

Note: Components may not sum to 100 percent because of missing data or adjustment to tax revenue.
a. Data were reported on a cash basis and have been adjusted to the accrual framework.

Central government revenues

About the data

The International Monetary Fund (IMF) classifies government revenues as taxes, grants, and property income. Taxes are classified by the base on which the tax is levied, grants by the source, and property income by type (for example, interest, dividends, or rent). The most important source of revenue is taxes. Grants are unrequited, nonrepayable, noncompulsory receipts from other government units and foreign governments or from international organizations. Transactions are generally recorded on an accrual basis.

The IMF's *Government Finance Statistics Manual 2001* describes taxes as compulsory, unrequited payments made to governments by individuals, businesses, or institutions. Taxes are classified in six major groups by the base on which the tax is levied: income, profits, and capital gains; payroll and workforce; property; goods and services; international trade and transactions; and other taxes. However, the distinctions are not always clear. Taxes levied on the income and profits of individuals and corporations are classified as direct taxes, and taxes and duties levied on goods and services are classified as indirect taxes. This distinction may be a useful simplification, but it has no particular analytical significance except with respect to the capacity to fix tax rates. Direct taxes tend to be progressive, whereas indirect taxes are proportional.

Social security taxes do not reflect compulsory payments made by employers to provident funds or other agencies with a like purpose. Similarly, expenditures from such funds are not reflected in government expenses (see table 4.11). For further discussion of taxes and tax policies, see *About the data* for table 5.6. For further discussion of government revenues and expenditures, see *About the data* for tables 4.10 and 4.11.

Rich countries rely more on direct taxes 4.12a

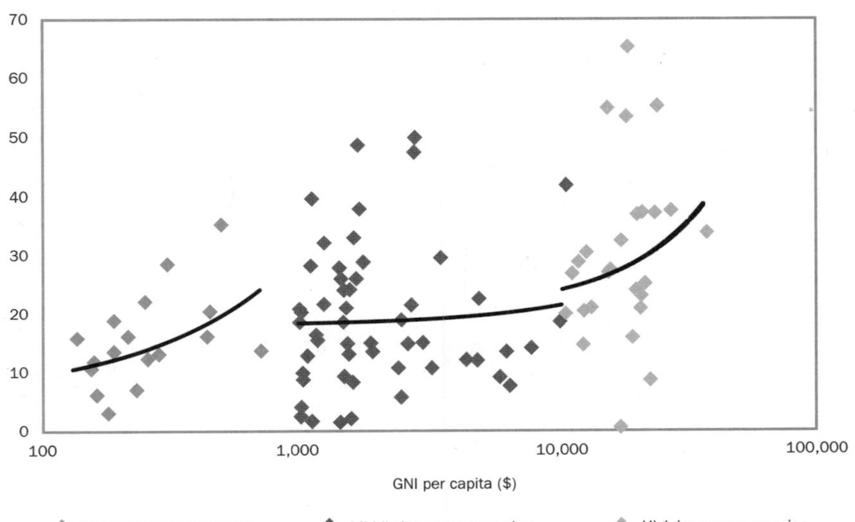

High-income economies prefer to tax income and property. Low-income economies tend to rely on indirect taxes on international trade and goods and services. But in all groups there are exceptions.

Source: International Monetary Fund, *Government Finance Statistics* data files, and World Bank data files.

Definitions

• **Taxes on income, profits, and capital gains** are levied on the actual or presumptive net income of individuals, on the profits of corporations and enterprises, and on capital gains, whether realized or not, on land, securities, and other assets. Intragovernmental payments are eliminated in consolidation. • **Taxes on goods and services** include general sales and turnover or value added taxes, selective excises on goods, selective taxes on services, taxes on the use of goods or property, taxes on extraction and production of minerals, and profits of fiscal monopolies. • **Taxes on international trade** include import duties, export duties, profits of export or import monopolies, exchange profits, and exchange taxes. • **Other taxes** include employer payroll or labor taxes, taxes on property, and taxes not allocable to other categories, such as penalties for late payment or nonpayment of taxes. • **Social contributions** include social security contributions by employees, employers, and self-employed individuals, and other contributions whose source cannot be determined. They also include actual or imputed contributions to social insurance schemes operated by governments. • **Grants and other revenue** include grants from other foreign governments, international organizations, and other government units; interest; dividends; rent; requited, nonrepayable receipts for public purposes (such as fines, administrative fees, and entrepreneurial income from government ownership of property); and voluntary, unrequited, nonrepayable receipts other than grants.

Data sources

Data on central government revenues are from the IMF's *Government Finance Statistics Yearbook 2006* and IMF data files. Each country's accounts are reported using the system of common definitions and classifications in the IMF's *Government Finance Statistics Manual 2001*. The IMF receives additional information from the Organisation for Economic Co-operation and Development on the tax revenues of some of its members. See the IMF sources for complete and authoritative explanations of concepts, definitions, and data sources.

4.13 Monetary indicators

	Money and quasi money		Claims on private sector		Claims on governments and other public entities		Interest rate					
	annual % growth		Annual growth % of M2		Annual growth % of M2		% Deposit		% Lending		% Real	
	1990	2005	1990	2005	1990	2005	1990	2005	1990	2005	1990	2005
Afghanistan	..	..	..	..	..	..	..	..	..	..	..	..
Albania	..	14.1	..	10.5	..	1.1	18.5	5.1	20.6	13.1	-65.5	9.3
Algeria	11.4	10.3	12.2	5.7	3.2	-25.0	8.0	1.8	..	8.0	..	-7.0
Angola	..	60.5	..	20.0	..	-27.1	..	13.4	..	67.7	..	16.9
Argentina	1,113.3	21.5	1,444.7	10.6	1,573.2	-10.5	1,517.9	3.8	..	6.2	..	-2.5
Armenia	1,076.8	27.8	92.0	16.5	583.8	8.0	..	5.8	..	18.0	..	14.4
Australia	12.8	7.7	13.8	17.2	-3.6	-2.0	13.5	3.7	17.9	9.1	14.0	4.2
Austria[a]	..	..	..	..	..	..	3.4	..	..	..	..	..
Azerbaijan	825.8	23.2	134.1	27.3	150.5	-3.0	..	8.5	..	17.0	..	6.1
Bangladesh	10.4	17.2	9.2	11.6	-0.6	3.4	12.0	8.1	16.0	14.0	9.1	8.5
Belarus	..	42.5	..	38.6	..	0.3	65.1	9.2	71.6	11.4	-85.1	-4.5
Belgium[a]	..	..	..	..	..	..	6.1	1.6	13.0	6.7	9.9	4.4
Benin	28.6	26.3	-1.3	12.5	12.4	4.6	7.0	3.5	16.0	..	14.2	..
Bolivia	52.9	16.8	43.7	2.9	-8.8	-0.3	23.8	4.9	41.8	16.6	22.0	11.5
Bosnia and Herzegovina	..	18.7	..	22.4	..	0.1	..	3.6	..	9.6	..	7.8
Botswana	-14.0	10.6	12.6	6.1	-53.1	-27.5	6.1	9.3	7.9	15.7	1.5	6.4
Brazil	1,251.8	19.6	2,100.5	10.8	2,400.8	7.9	9,394.3	17.6	..	55.4	..	44.9
Bulgaria	51.7	24.5	37.5	22.0	43.1	-0.1	39.5	3.0	52.5	7.9	-53.3	3.8
Burkina Faso	-0.5	-4.8	3.6	15.8	-1.5	0.7	7.0	3.5	16.0	..	14.4	..
Burundi	9.6	19.0	15.4	-0.6	-10.1	6.0	4.0	..	12.3	19.1	6.0	2.1
Cambodia	..	8.9	..	9.2	..	-5.5	..	1.9	..	17.3	..	11.0
Cameroon	-1.7	4.9	0.9	5.3	-1.9	-8.5	7.5	4.9	18.5	17.7	16.6	12.4
Canada	8.1	9.7	8.4	9.9	0.9	0.8	9.9	0.8	14.1	4.4	10.5	1.2
Central African Republic	-3.7	16.5	-1.6	-1.1	-5.0	11.9	7.5	4.9	18.5	17.7	15.9	15.0
Chad	-2.4	31.3	1.3	8.0	-6.0	0.8	7.5	4.9	18.5	17.7	9.7	-2.0
Chile	24.2	19.3	21.7	21.3	9.0	-7.9	40.4	3.9	48.9	6.7	21.6	1.8
China	28.9	17.9	26.5	6.9	1.5	-0.2	8.6	2.3	9.4	5.6	3.5	1.6
Hong Kong, China	8.5	3.5	7.9	3.3	-1.0	-1.0	6.7	1.3	10.0	7.8	0.3	8.0
Colombia	33.0	19.2	8.7	14.0	-0.7	5.9	36.4	7.0	45.2	14.6	15.2	7.9
Congo, Dem. Rep.	195.4	25.5	18.0	11.9	421.6	16.2	..	..	..	66.8	..	26.4
Congo, Rep.	18.4	37.1	5.3	1.2	-9.4	-70.2	7.5	4.9	18.5	17.7	19.7	9.8
Costa Rica	27.5	24.7	7.3	21.6	5.0	-2.4	21.2	10.1	32.6	24.7	13.2	12.2
Côte d'Ivoire	-2.6	7.7	-3.9	0.8	-3.0	1.9	7.0	3.5	16.0	..	21.5	..
Croatia	..	10.6	..	14.4	..	3.8	658.5	1.7	1,157.8	11.2	80.9	7.8
Cuba	..	..	..	..	..	..	..	..	..	..	..	..
Czech Republic	..	8.4	..	9.6	..	-7.5	7.0	1.2	14.1	5.8	-3.6	4.8
Denmark	6.5	16.1	3.0	40.9	-3.1	0.4	7.9	2.4	14.1	7.1	10.1	4.7
Dominican Republic	42.5	14.3	19.1	6.5	0.6	18.1	20.0	13.9	35.3	24.1	-14.5	19.1
Ecuador	50.3	20.9	9.3	21.4	-28.9	-10.9	43.5	3.5	37.5	9.3	29.9	2.4
Egypt, Arab Rep.	28.7	11.5	6.3	2.8	15.2	-1.6	12.0	7.2	19.0	13.1	0.5	7.4
El Salvador	-17.3	2.7	-30.1	8.7	15.9	-0.3	18.0	..	21.2	..	15.7	..
Eritrea	..	10.7	..	2.7	..	10.9	..	..	..	..	..	..
Estonia	76.5	41.9	27.6	66.9	1.7	-2.9	..	2.1	30.5	4.9	-86.6	-1.2
Ethiopia	19.9	18.6	0.3	14.7	23.1	12.8	3.6	3.5	6.0	7.0	2.0	1.0
Finland[a]	..	..	..	..	..	..	7.5	1.0	11.6	3.7	4.9	3.2
France[a]	..	..	..	..	..	..	4.5	2.1	10.6	6.6	8.2	4.9
Gabon	3.7	27.5	1.1	7.5	-21.0	-13.2	7.5	4.9	18.5	17.7	2.7	8.1
Gambia, The	8.4	13.1	7.8	4.9	-35.4	7.1	11.3	17.3	26.5	34.9	13.0	29.4
Georgia	..	26.5	..	49.5	..	-8.0	..	7.6	..	21.6	..	12.7
Germany[a]	..	..	..	..	..	..	7.1	2.7	11.6	9.7	8.1	8.1
Ghana	13.3	9.3	4.9	18.2	14.6	-2.0	21.3	10.2	25.6	..	-5.9	..
Greece[a]	..	..	..	..	..	..	19.5	2.2	27.6	6.8	5.7	3.2
Guatemala	22.2	14.1	19.8	15.2	13.5	3.7	18.2	4.3	23.3	13.0	-12.3	4.9
Guinea	-17.4	33.4	13.1	19.8	3.0	18.1	21.0	14.4	21.2	..	-2.2	..
Guinea-Bissau	574.6	21.3	90.5	2.5	460.7	3.4	32.7	3.5	45.8	..	11.9	..
Haiti	2.5	17.9	-0.6	7.9	2.2	2.2	..	3.4	..	27.4	..	10.3

Monetary indicators

	Money and quasi money		Claims on private sector		Claims on governments and other public entities		Interest rate					
	annual % growth		Annual growth % of M2		Annual growth % of M2		% Deposit		Lending		Real	
	1990	2005	1990	2005	1990	2005	1990	2005	1990	2005	1990	2005
Honduras	21.4	20.4	13.0	14.4	−10.9	−1.8	8.8	10.9	17.1	18.8	−3.4	7.7
Hungary	29.2	13.3	23.0	18.4	69.4	−1.3	24.7	5.2	28.8	8.5	2.5	5.9
India	15.1	15.6	5.9	14.7	10.5	−0.6	..	..	16.5	10.8	5.4	6.0
Indonesia	44.6	16.4	66.5	12.3	−5.6	0.5	17.5	8.1	20.8	14.1	12.2	0.3
Iran, Islamic Rep.	18.0	22.8	14.7	21.1	5.8	−4.1	..	11.8	..	16.0	..	0.1
Iraq	..	..	..	..	..	..	..	..	..	..	..	..
Ireland[a]	..	..	..	..	..	..	6.3	0.0	11.3	2.6	12.1	−0.9
Israel	19.4	11.2	18.5	10.8	4.9	−4.5	14.4	3.2	26.4	6.4	9.1	5.8
Italy[a]	..	..	..	..	..	..	6.8	*0.9*	14.9	5.3	6.0	3.2
Jamaica	21.6	10.1	8.3	6.4	−2.3	2.2	23.9	7.5	30.5	17.4	4.3	7.0
Japan	6.9	0.2	8.5	2.7	0.7	0.9	3.6	0.3	7.0	1.7	4.4	3.6
Jordan	8.3	21.4	4.7	17.8	1.0	4.9	8.2	2.9	10.3	7.6	−1.0	3.5
Kazakhstan	..	26.3	..	70.6	..	−23.8	..	..	..	..	..	..
Kenya	20.1	10.0	8.0	5.5	20.5	0.0	13.7	5.1	18.8	12.9	7.3	8.2
Korea, Dem. Rep.	..	..	..	..	..	..	..	..	..	..	..	..
Korea, Rep.	17.2	3.1	36.1	9.4	−1.2	2.9	10.0	3.7	10.0	5.6	−0.5	6.1
Kuwait	*4.8*	12.3	*0.4*	16.8	*−1.6*	−1.8	*7.4*	3.5	*8.4*	7.5	*10.3*	−13.6
Kyrgyz Republic	..	10.0	..	7.1	..	0.9	..	5.8	..	26.6	..	18.6
Lao PDR	7.8	7.9	3.6	9.0	−0.5	0.4	30.0	4.8	*26.0*	26.8	*11.4*	17.4
Latvia	..	38.3	..	70.5	..	3.3	*34.8*	2.8	*86.4*	6.1	*21.3*	−2.9
Lebanon	55.1	4.5	27.6	0.5	−35.2	3.1	16.9	8.1	39.9	10.6	21.2	10.3
Lesotho	9.7	9.1	8.4	11.0	−16.7	−8.3	13.0	4.0	20.4	11.7	10.8	8.3
Liberia	*21.1*	34.1	*19.0*	8.7	*33.2*	−11.1	*6.8*	3.4	*13.8*	17.0	*10.2*	7.4
Libya	19.0	29.0	2.0	0.9	9.4	−128.9	5.5	2.1	7.0	6.1	*0.4*	−14.7
Lithuania	..	32.9	..	40.4	..	1.2	*88.3*	*1.2*	*91.8*	*5.7*	*−52.8*	*2.9*
Macedonia, FYR	..	15.2	..	12.9	..	−12.0	..	6.6	..	12.2	..	8.8
Madagascar	4.5	2.2	23.8	9.2	−14.8	−5.6	20.5	18.8	25.8	27.0	12.9	7.3
Malawi	11.1	16.2	15.5	7.7	−14.0	2.3	12.1	10.9	21.0	33.1	9.3	15.3
Malaysia	−43.7	6.3	−13.2	8.1	−28.5	−1.0	5.7	3.0	8.8	6.0	4.8	1.3
Mali	−4.9	9.8	0.1	0.1	−13.4	4.3	7.0	3.5	16.0	..	10.6	..
Mauritania	11.5	*10.5*	20.2	*18.7*	1.5	*−15.8*	5.0	8.0	10.0	23.1	7.2	3.6
Mauritius	21.0	19.5	9.9	5.0	0.7	1.4	12.6	7.3	18.0	21.0	6.6	15.5
Mexico	83.8	10.0	48.4	9.3	10.6	−3.8	30.4	3.5	*17.7*	9.7	*7.5*	4.0
Moldova	*358.0*	34.4	*53.3*	17.8	*300.3*	−9.1	..	13.2	..	19.3	..	11.2
Mongolia	*31.6*	37.1	*40.2*	28.0	*6.8*	−10.0	300.0	13.0	*300.0*	23.6	*−5.8*	10.7
Morocco	21.5	14.0	*12.4*	7.9	−4.9	0.1	8.5	3.5	9.0	*11.5*	3.3	*9.9*
Mozambique	37.2	31.0	22.0	15.9	−8.0	−9.4	..	7.8	..	19.5	..	12.2
Myanmar	37.7	27.3	12.8	6.8	23.7	23.5	5.9	9.5	8.0	15.0	−8.9	−2.2
Namibia	*30.3*	9.8	*15.4*	25.3	*−7.8*	3.4	*12.8*	6.2	*23.4*	10.6	*17.9*	8.4
Nepal	18.5	9.8	5.7	..	6.0	2.6	11.9	2.3	14.4	8.1	3.2	3.4
Netherlands[a]	..	..	..	..	..	..	3.3	2.3	11.8	2.8	9.3	1.2
New Zealand	12.5	12.2	4.2	20.6	−1.6	−0.8	11.7	6.7	16.0	11.5	13.2	8.8
Nicaragua	7,677.8	9.8	4,932.9	19.1	3,222.5	−1.8	9.5	4.0	22.0	12.1	−97.6	1.7
Niger	−4.1	7.0	−5.1	8.5	1.4	−5.8	7.0	3.5	16.0	..	17.9	..
Nigeria	32.7	16.2	7.8	19.5	26.3	−23.6	19.8	10.5	25.3	17.9	16.9	−7.0
Norway	5.6	*3.4*	5.0	*10.4*	0.4	*−5.3*	9.7	1.8	14.2	4.0	10.0	−4.1
Oman	10.0	21.3	9.6	13.7	−11.2	−12.7	8.3	3.3	9.7	7.0	−12.1	*−1.4*
Pakistan	11.6	16.5	5.0	8.8	7.5	4.1	..	..	..	..	..	..
Panama	36.6	8.3	0.8	15.6	−25.7	−4.6	8.4	2.7	12.0	8.7	11.4	6.2
Papua New Guinea	4.3	29.5	−1.1	10.5	6.4	−4.6	8.7	0.9	15.5	11.5	10.9	−5.0
Paraguay	53.9	9.8	37.4	10.3	−5.2	−2.4	22.9	1.7	31.0	29.9	−3.9	22.7
Peru	6,384.9	16.8	2,123.7	10.9	2,127.1	−2.6	2,439.6	3.4	4,774.5	15.0	−29.7	11.2
Philippines	22.4	6.4	15.6	−1.2	1.8	−4.1	19.5	5.6	24.1	10.2	9.9	3.7
Poland	160.1	12.2	158.7	6.4	−20.6	−2.7	41.7	2.8	504.2	6.8	*−0.4*	3.9
Portugal[a]	..	..	..	..	..	..	14.0	..	21.8	..	7.6	..
Puerto Rico	..	..	..	..	..	..	..	..	..	..	..	..

4.13 Monetary indicators

	Money and quasi money		Claims on private sector		Claims on governments and other public entities		Interest rate					
	annual % growth		Annual growth % of M2		Annual growth % of M2		% Deposit		Lending		Real	
	1990	**2005**	**1990**	**2005**	**1990**	**2005**	**1990**	**2005**	**1990**	**2005**	**1990**	**2005**
Romania	30.1	20.2	..	24.3	..	–0.9	..	..	..	..	..	..
Russian Federation	..	36.3	..	27.3	..	–26.2	..	4.0	..	10.7	..	–7.5
Rwanda	5.6	18.0	–10.0	14.5	26.8	–13.8	6.9	7.9	13.2	..	–0.3	..
Saudi Arabia	4.6	13.2	–4.5	25.1	4.2	–33.2	8.0	3.8	..	..	..	..
Senegal	–4.8	8.2	–8.4	12.7	–5.3	–4.1	7.0	3.5	16.0	..	14.6	..
Serbia and Montenegro	..	..	..	..	..	..	..	..	..	..	..	..
Sierra Leone	74.0	31.3	4.9	4.4	228.6	–5.7	40.5	11.1	52.5	24.6	–10.6	10.2
Singapore	20.0	6.2	13.7	1.8	–4.9	–5.7	4.7	0.4	7.4	5.3	3.1	4.7
Slovak Republic	..	3.6	..	13.1	..	2.8	*8.0*	2.4	*14.4*	6.7	*–11.0*	4.1
Slovenia	*123.0*	7.5	*96.1*	19.7	*–10.4*	2.9	*682.5*	3.2	*824.6*	7.8	*374.3*	6.2
Somalia	..	..	..	..	..	..	..	..	..	..	..	..
South Africa	11.9	19.9	13.7	21.1	2.2	–6.1	18.9	6.0	21.0	10.6	4.7	5.6
Spain[a]	..	..	..	..	..	..	10.7	*2.5*	16.0	*4.3*	8.1	*–0.1*
Sri Lanka	19.9	19.0	16.2	15.9	4.4	3.1	19.4	10.2	13.0	7.0	–5.9	–3.1
Sudan	48.8	43.5	12.6	25.9	27.9	–4.5	..	..	..	..	..	..
Swaziland	0.6	9.7	20.5	22.9	–5.5	–25.1	8.7	4.0	14.5	10.6	–0.4	5.5
Sweden	*10.7*	11.2	13.6	23.7	–12.2	4.6	9.9	0.8	16.7	3.3	7.3	2.1
Switzerland	0.8	6.8	11.7	7.0	1.0	–1.0	8.3	0.8	7.4	3.1	2.9	2.5
Syrian Arab Republic	26.1	*15.3*	3.4	*4.4*	11.4	*3.3*	4.0	1.0	9.0	8.0	–8.7	2.1
Tajikistan	..	25.9	..	38.8	..	–8.2	..	9.7	..	23.3	..	13.4
Tanzania	41.9	38.2	22.6	12.8	80.6	16.2	*17.0*	4.7	*31.0*	15.1	*8.6*	11.0
Thailand	25.5	5.9	36.6	6.5	–4.4	–0.4	12.3	1.9	14.4	5.8	8.2	1.2
Togo	9.5	2.2	1.8	6.9	6.9	–0.8	7.0	3.5	16.0	..	12.6	..
Trinidad and Tobago	6.2	29.4	2.7	19.6	0.9	–21.6	6.0	2.2	12.9	9.1	–2.3	–0.8
Tunisia	7.6	11.0	5.9	8.8	1.8	1.0	*7.4*	..	*4.8*	..	*–3.7*	..
Turkey	53.2	25.3	43.0	20.2	–6.4	–0.2	47.5	20.4	..	..	..	..
Turkmenistan	..	..	..	..	..	..	..	..	..	..	..	..
Uganda	60.2	16.5	*23.3*	4.3	*0.8*	–6.1	31.3	8.8	38.7	19.6	–4.0	11.0
Ukraine	*1,809.2*	53.9	*78.3*	44.1	*109.3*	–16.1	*148.6*	8.6	*184.3*	16.2	*–91.7*	–3.2
United Arab Emirates	–8.2	30.5	1.3	34.4	–4.8	–1.9	..	..	..	..	..	..
United Kingdom	10.5	13.8	13.1	13.2	1.9	–0.1	12.5	..	14.8	4.6	6.6	2.6
United States	2.7	7.5	–0.5	8.1	0.7	0.4	..	..	10.0	6.2	5.9	3.1
Uruguay	118.5	0.3	56.2	–2.1	3.0	–14.7	147.5	2.8	163.8	13.6	27.5	11.7
Uzbekistan	..	..	..	..	..	..	..	..	..	..	..	..
Venezuela, RB	64.9	54.1	17.6	35.7	44.3	–1.4	27.8	11.6	35.5	16.8	–4.4	–9.5
Vietnam	*12.3*	30.9	*19.6*	26.8	*23.7*	6.9	*22.0*	7.1	*32.2*	11.0	*12.6*	2.4
West Bank and Gaza	..	..	..	..	..	..	..	..	..	..	..	..
Yemen, Rep.	*11.3*	14.4	*1.4*	4.3	*8.3*	–3.1	..	13.0	..	18.0	..	0.7
Zambia	47.9	1.9	22.8	6.7	185.8	–43.2	25.7	11.2	35.1	28.2	–34.5	7.7
Zimbabwe	15.1	532.7	13.5	154.0	7.4	421.5	8.8	91.1	11.7	235.7	–2.6	–0.6

a. As members of the European Monetary Union, these countries share a single currency, the euro.

About the data

Money and the financial accounts that record the supply of money lie at the heart of a country's financial system. There are several commonly used definitions of the money supply. The narrowest, M1, encompasses currency held by the public and demand deposits with banks. M2 includes M1 plus time and savings deposits with banks that require a notice for withdrawal. M3 includes M2 as well as various money market instruments, such as certificates of deposit issued by banks, bank deposits denominated in foreign currency, and deposits with financial institutions other than banks. However defined, money is a liability of the banking system, distinguished from other bank liabilities by the special role it plays as a medium of exchange, a unit of account, and a store of value.

The banking system's assets include its net foreign assets and net domestic credit. Net domestic credit includes credit extended to the private sector and general government and credit extended to the nonfinancial public sector in the form of investments in short- and long-term government securities and loans to state enterprises; liabilities to the public and private sectors in the form of deposits with the banking system are netted out. Net domestic credit also includes credit to banking and nonbank financial institutions.

Domestic credit is the main vehicle through which changes in the money supply are regulated, with central bank lending to the government often playing the most important role. The central bank can regulate lending to the private sector in several ways—for example, by adjusting the cost of the refinancing facilities it provides to banks, by changing market interest rates through open market operations, or by controlling the availability of credit through changes in the reserve requirements imposed on banks and ceilings on the credit provided by banks to the private sector.

Monetary accounts are derived from the balance sheets of financial institutions—the central bank, commercial banks, and nonbank financial intermediaries. Although these balance sheets are usually reliable, they are subject to errors of classification, valuation, and timing and to differences in accounting practices. For example, whether interest income is recorded on an accrual or a cash basis can make a substantial difference, as can the treatment of nonperforming assets. Valuation errors typically arise with respect to foreign exchange transactions, particularly in countries with flexible exchange rates or in those that have undergone a currency devaluation during the reporting period. The valuation of financial derivatives and the net liabilities of the banking system can also be difficult. The quality of commercial bank reporting also may be adversely affected by delays in reports from bank branches, especially in countries where branch accounts are not computerized. Thus the data in the balance sheets of commercial banks may be based on preliminary estimates subject to constant revision. This problem is likely to be even more serious for nonbank financial intermediaries.

Many interest rates coexist in an economy, reflecting competitive conditions, the terms governing loans and deposits, and differences in the position and status of creditors and debtors. In some economies interest rates are set by regulation or administrative fiat. In economies with imperfect markets, or where reported nominal rates are not indicative of effective rates, it may be difficult to obtain data on interest rates that reflect actual market transactions. Deposit and lending rates are collected by the International Monetary Fund (IMF) as representative interest rates offered by banks to resident customers. The terms and conditions attached to these rates differ by country, however, limiting their comparability. Real interest rates are calculated by adjusting nominal rates by an estimate of the inflation rate in the economy. A negative real interest rate indicates a loss in the purchasing power of the principal. The real interest rates in the table are calculated as $(i - P) / (1 + P)$, where i is the nominal lending interest rate and P is the inflation rate (as measured by the GDP deflator).

Definitions

• **Money and quasi money** comprise the sum of currency outside banks, demand deposits other than those of the central government, and the time, savings, and foreign currency deposits of resident sectors other than the central government. This definition of the money supply, often called M2, corresponds to lines 34 and 35 in the IMF's *International Financial Statistics* (IFS). The change in money supply is measured as the difference in end-of-year totals relative to M2 in the preceding year. • **Claims on private sector** (IFS line 32d) include gross credit from the financial system to individuals, enterprises, nonfinancial public entities not included under net domestic credit, and financial institutions not included elsewhere. • **Claims on governments and other public entities** (IFS line 32an + 32b + 32bx + 32c) usually comprise direct credit for specific purposes, such as financing the government budget deficit; loans to state enterprises; advances against future credit authorizations; and purchases of treasury bills and bonds, net of deposits by the public sector. Public sector deposits with the banking system also include sinking funds for the service of debt and temporary deposits of government revenues. • **Deposit interest rate** is the rate paid by commercial or similar banks for demand, time, or savings deposits. • **Lending interest rate** is the rate charged by banks on loans to prime customers. • **Real interest rate** is the lending interest rate adjusted for inflation as measured by the GDP deflator.

Data sources

Monetary and financial data are published by the IMF in its monthly *International Financial Statistics* and annual *International Financial Statistics Yearbook*. The IMF collects data on the financial systems of its member countries. The World Bank receives data from the IMF in electronic files that may contain more recent revisions than the published sources. The discussion of monetary indicators draws from an IMF publication by Marcello Caiola, *A Manual for Country Economists* (1995). Also see the IMF's *Monetary and Financial Statistics Manual* (2000) for guidelines for the presentation of monetary and financial statistics. World Bank data on the GDP deflator are used to derive real interest rates.

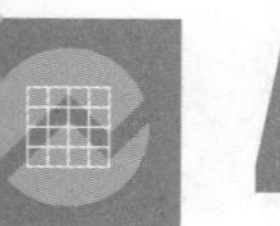

Exchange rates and prices

	Official exchange rate		Purchasing power parity (PPP) conversion factor		Ratio of PPP conversion factor to official exchange rate	Real effective exchange rate	GDP implicit deflator		Consumer price index		Wholesale price index	
	local currency units to $		local currency units to international $			Index 2000 = 100	average annual % growth		average annual % growth		average annual % growth	
	2005	2006	1990	2005	2005	2005	1990–2000	2000–05	1990–2000	2000–05	1990–2000	2000–05
Afghanistan	49.50	..	..	..	..	..	..	*12.2*	..	..	..	..
Albania	99.87	*122.20*[a]	2.1	50.3	0.5	..	38.0	4.0	*27.8*	3.2	..	5.4
Algeria	73.28	72.65	5.0	32.3	0.4	83.3	18.5	7.3	17.3	2.6	..	3.8
Angola	87.16	80.37	..	76.8	0.9	..	739.4	82.2	711.0	79.2	..	..
Argentina	2.90	3.05	0.3	1.0	0.3	..	5.2	12.4	8.9	11.2	*0.1*	22.6
Armenia	457.69	416.04	0.0	150.4	0.3	97.7	212.5	4.2	*72.8*	3.6	..	0.9
Australia	1.31	1.33	1.5	1.5	1.1	125.9	1.5	3.4	2.1	2.9	1.1	2.3
Austria[b]	0.80	0.80	0.9	0.9	1.1	105.7	1.7	1.6	2.2	1.9	0.3	2.0
Azerbaijan	0.95	0.89	..	0.3	0.3	..	203.0	6.0	*170.9*	4.3	..	..
Bangladesh	64.33	68.93	9.9	12.7	0.2	..	4.0	3.8	5.5	5.6	..	..
Belarus	2,153.82	*2,140.43*[a]	..	822.7	0.4	..	355.1	35.8	*271.3*	30.4	*267.8*	35.3
Belgium[b]	0.80	0.80	0.9	0.9	1.1	109.4	1.8	1.9	1.9	2.0	1.2	1.4
Benin	527.47	522.89	140.2	235.0	0.4	..	8.7	2.9	*8.7*	2.5	..	..
Bolivia	8.07	*7.99*[a]	1.4	2.9	0.4	79.8	8.6	4.8	8.7	3.1	..	..
Bosnia and Herzegovina	1.57	1.56	..	..	..	..	*3.4*	2.5	..	..	..	..
Botswana	5.11	*6.05*[a]	1.1	2.4	0.5	..	9.7	4.2	10.4	2.1	..	..
Brazil	2.43	2.18	..	1.2	0.5	..	208.0	10.1	199.5	9.1	204.9	15.6
Bulgaria	1.57	1.56	0.0	0.6	0.4	120.5	103.3	4.0	117.5	5.1	85.7	4.4
Burkina Faso	527.47	522.89	138.9	170.0	0.3	..	5.0	2.7	5.5	2.5	..	..
Burundi	1,081.58	*1,051.61*[a]	46.2	163.2	0.2	71.1	13.4	8.3	16.1	7.4	..	..
Cambodia	4,092.50	*4,122.00*[a]	..	660.6	0.2	88.0	*4.4*	2.8	*6.3*	2.7	..	..
Cameroon	527.47	522.89	168.8	237.3	0.5	109.6	*6.1*	2.1	6.5	1.8	..	..
Canada	1.21	1.13	1.3	1.3	1.0	119.7	1.5	2.4	1.7	2.3	2.7	0.7
Central African Republic	527.47	522.89	128.0	146.1	0.3	122.3	4.5	1.9	5.3	2.1	*6.0*	4.4
Chad	527.47	522.89	110.9	207.0	0.4	..	7.1	7.6	6.9	2.2	..	..
Chile	560.09	530.29	155.8	329.4	0.6	92.3	7.9	5.3	8.9	2.5	7.0	5.7
China	8.19	7.97	1.2[c]	2.1[c]	0.3[c]	92.5	7.9	3.2	8.6	1.3	..	..
Hong Kong, China	7.78	7.77	6.5	5.7	0.7	..	4.0	–3.6	5.9	–1.6	0.6	–0.3
Colombia	2,320.83	2,361.14	126.9	852.3	0.4	105.3	21.7	6.6	20.3	6.5	16.4	6.5
Congo, Dem. Rep.	473.91	*448.30*[a]	..	81.9	0.2	27.8	965.0	43.6	932.8	41.1	..	..
Congo, Rep.	527.47	522.89	299.8	532.0	1.0	..	8.9	–0.6	*9.3*	2.4	..	..
Costa Rica	477.79	511.30	43.1	217.1	0.5	91.9	15.9	9.7	15.6	10.9	14.1	11.3
Côte d'Ivoire	527.47	522.89	170.7	288.2	0.5	116.4	9.2	2.7	7.2	3.1	..	..
Croatia	5.95	5.84	0.0	4.0	0.7	109.7	86.0	3.6	86.2	2.4	83.9	1.7
Cuba	..	..	..	..	..	..	*3.0*	*2.6*	..	..	..	..
Czech Republic	23.96	22.60	5.0	14.2	0.6	125.2	12.8	2.5	*7.8*	2.0	8.2	1.9
Denmark	6.00	5.95	8.7	8.4	1.4	108.4	1.6	2.3	2.1	2.0	1.1	1.4
Dominican Republic	30.41	33.37	2.4	12.1	0.4	104.6	9.4	20.6	8.7	20.6	..	..
Ecuador	1.00	1.00	0.4	0.6	0.6	147.9	4.3	11.5	37.1	10.7	..	7.5
Egypt, Arab Rep.	5.78	*5.71*[a]	0.8	1.7	0.3	..	8.7	5.9	8.8	5.3	6.1	9.8
El Salvador	8.75	8.75	0.3	0.5	0.5	..	6.2	2.9	8.5	3.2	..	3.1
Eritrea	15.37	15.38	*1.0*	3.1	0.2	..	*7.9*	15.7	..	..	..	..
Estonia	12.58	12.47	0.1	7.9	0.6	..	53.6	3.9	*21.6*	3.3	*8.1*	1.7
Ethiopia	8.67	*8.75*[a]	0.7	1.3	0.1	..	6.3	4.2	5.5	5.8	..	..
Finland[b]	0.80	0.80	1.0	0.9	1.1	104.8	2.1	0.9	1.5	1.1	1.0	0.5
France[b]	0.80	0.80	1.0	0.9	1.2	107.9	1.4	2.0	1.6	2.1	..	1.3
Gabon	527.47	522.89	319.3	441.5	0.8	102.6	6.2	2.7	4.6	1.0	..	..
Gambia, The	28.58	*28.04*[a]	2.0	4.5	0.2	53.5	4.2	16.5	4.1	10.6	..	..
Georgia	1.81	1.78	..	0.8	0.4	..	356.7	6.0	*24.7*	5.6	..	..
Germany[b]	0.80	0.80	1.0	0.9	1.2	106.9	1.7	1.0	*2.0*	1.5	*0.4*	1.8
Ghana	9,072.54	*9,225.15*[a]	94.0	1,773.9	0.2	109.5	26.7	22.8	28.4	19.8	..	..
Greece[b]	0.80	0.80	0.3	0.7	0.9	113.7	9.2	3.3	9.0	3.4	*3.6*	3.3
Guatemala	7.63	7.60	1.4	4.2	0.6	..	10.4	7.2	10.1	7.2	..	..
Guinea	3,644.33	*5,597.00*[a]	201.7	550.6	0.2	..	5.6	13.2	..	..	..	..
Guinea-Bissau	527.47	522.89	9.9	121.1	0.2	..	32.5	0.7	34.0	1.0	..	..
Haiti	40.45	*39.58*[a]	1.2	12.2	0.3	..	22.7	18.0	21.9	21.3	..	..

Exchange rates and prices

	Official exchange rate		Purchasing power parity (PPP) conversion factor		Ratio of PPP conversion factor to official exchange rate	Real effective exchange rate	GDP implicit deflator		Consumer price index		Wholesale price index	
	local currency units to $		local currency units to international $			Index 2000 = 100	average annual % growth		average annual % growth		average annual % growth	
	2005	2006	1990	2005	2005	2005	1990–2000	2000–05	1990–2000	2000–05	1990–2000	2000–05
Honduras	18.83	*18.90*[a]	1.2	6.4	0.3	..	18.9	8.0	18.8	8.2	..	..
Hungary	199.58	210.39	21.3	120.8	0.6	132.6	19.4	6.1	20.3	5.8	16.8	2.3
India	44.10	45.31	5.0	9.4	0.2	..	8.0	3.9	9.1	4.0	7.4	4.8
Indonesia	9,704.74	9,159.32	652.2	3,220.5	0.3	..	15.8	8.2	13.7	8.9	15.4	7.5
Iran, Islamic Rep.	8,963.96	9,170.94	168.8	3,128.3	0.3	129.5	27.7	18.0	26.0	14.4	28.4	10.1
Iraq	1,472.00	..	..	..	..	..	..	*0.3*	..	..	..	..
Ireland[b]	0.80	0.80	0.8	1.0	1.3	123.5	3.5	3.5	2.3	3.5	1.6	–0.3
Israel	4.49	4.46	1.5	3.1	0.7	78.0	10.2	1.3	9.7	1.7	8.1	4.1
Italy[b]	0.80	0.80	0.7	0.8	1.1	111.0	3.8	2.9	3.7	2.4	2.9	1.8
Jamaica	62.28	*66.14*[a]	5.3	53.3	0.8	..	23.0	10.5	23.5	10.5	..	..
Japan	110.22	116.30	183.0	125.1	1.1	79.4	0.0	–1.5	0.8	–0.4	–1.0	–0.5
Jordan	0.71	0.71	0.3	0.3	0.4	..	3.2	2.1	3.5	2.4	..	*6.0*
Kazakhstan	132.88	126.09	0.0	63.8	0.5	..	204.7	12.0	*67.8*	6.8	*16.3*	9.4
Kenya	75.55	72.10	9.1	33.3	0.4	..	16.6	4.4	15.6	7.9	..	..
Korea, Dem. Rep.	..	..	..	..	..	..	..	..	..	..	..	..
Korea, Rep.	1,024.12	954.85	543.8	758.2	0.7	..	5.7	2.4	5.1	3.3	3.6	2.1
Kuwait	0.29	0.29	*0.3*	0.4	1.2	..	*1.5*	8.3	2.0	1.5	1.4	2.2
Kyrgyz Republic	41.01	40.15	0.0	10.1	0.2	..	110.6	4.6	*23.3*	3.8	*35.6*	6.4
Lao PDR	10,655.17	*10,184.00*[a]	173.9	2,539.9	0.2	..	27.0	11.2	28.2	10.9	..	..
Latvia	0.57	0.56	0.0	0.3	0.5	..	48.0	4.8	*29.2*	3.9	*12.0*	4.3
Lebanon	1,507.50	1,507.50	328.5	1,656.2	1.1	..	17.9	2.0	..	..	..	..
Lesotho	6.36	6.77	0.6	1.5	0.2	132.8	10.0	6.3	*9.8*	8.8	..	..
Liberia	57.10	*58.26*[a]	..	..	..	..	51.8	11.6	..	..	..	..
Libya	1.31	1.31	..	..	..	..	..	18.7	5.6	*–5.9*	..	..
Lithuania	2.77	2.75	0.0	1.4	0.5	..	75.0	1.2	*32.6*	0.6	*24.7*	2.0
Macedonia, FYR	49.28	*47.47*[a]	0.0	19.4	0.4	99.8	79.3	2.1	*10.8*	1.7	*8.4*	0.7
Madagascar	2,003.03	2,142.30	98.1	587.6	0.3	..	19.1	11.0	18.7	9.9	..	..
Malawi	118.42	*137.00*[a]	1.3	28.5	0.2	75.2	33.6	14.7	33.8	13.8	..	..
Malaysia	3.79	*3.63*[a]	1.5	1.8	0.5	95.2	3.9	3.4	3.6	1.6	3.4	3.6
Mali	527.47	522.89	131.4	200.4	0.4	..	7.0	4.0	5.2	1.7	..	..
Mauritania	265.53	*268.60*[a]	26.7	72.5	0.3	..	8.7	8.7	6.1	6.9	..	..
Mauritius	29.50	31.71	6.5	11.5	0.4	..	6.4	5.6	6.9	4.2	..	..
Mexico	10.90	10.90	1.4	7.6	0.7	..	19.0	7.1	19.4	4.9	18.4	6.5
Moldova	12.60	*13.17*[a]	0.0	4.2	0.3	109.1	119.6	10.6	*19.2*	10.3	..	..
Mongolia	1,205.22	*1,164.10*[a]	3.5	421.1	0.3	..	54.2	11.5	*36.7*	5.5	..	..
Morocco	8.87	8.80	3.3	3.3	0.4	91.8	2.9	0.9	3.8	1.5	2.9	*–0.6*
Mozambique	23.06	25.40	331.2	6,224.4	0.3	..	32.4	11.4	31.8	12.5	..	..
Myanmar	5.76	5.78	..	..	..	..	25.5	21.1	25.9	26.3	..	..
Namibia	6.36	6.77	1.0	2.5	0.4	..	10.4	5.3	..	*4.5*	..	..
Nepal	71.37	72.76	6.4	12.7	0.2	..	8.2	4.1	8.7	4.2	..	..
Netherlands[b]	0.80	0.80	0.9	0.9	1.2	113.3	2.0	2.7	2.4	2.4	1.3	2.3
New Zealand	1.42	1.54	1.6	1.5	1.1	114.4	1.7	2.3	1.7	2.4	1.4	1.8
Nicaragua	16.73	17.57	0.0	4.1	0.2	87.7	42.4	6.9	30.8	6.5	..	..
Niger	527.47	522.89	123.7	164.8	0.3	..	6.0	2.4	6.1	1.9	..	..
Nigeria	131.27	*127.02*[a]	4.2	87.6	0.7	123.8	29.5	15.9	32.4	15.6	..	..
Norway	6.44	6.41	8.3	9.9	1.5	111.1	2.7	2.9	2.2	1.7	1.6	3.7
Oman	0.39	0.39	0.3	*0.2*	*0.6*	..	0.1	*1.8*	0.6	–0.2	..	..
Pakistan	59.51	60.27	5.9	17.7	0.3	94.0	11.1	6.0	9.7	4.9	10.4	6.2
Panama	1.00	1.00	0.6	0.6	0.6	..	3.6	1.6	1.1	0.9	1.0	1.0
Papua New Guinea	3.10	*3.02*[a]	0.5	1.0	0.3	101.0	7.1	7.1	9.3	8.4	..	..
Paraguay	6,177.96	*5,411.40*[a]	422.6	1,583.6	0.3	78.0	11.5	11.1	13.1	9.0	..	14.5
Peru	3.30	3.27	0.1	1.5	0.5	..	26.7	2.8	27.3	2.0	23.7	1.9
Philippines	55.09	51.31	5.8	12.7	0.2	92.3	8.3	5.2	7.7	5.0	*6.3*	8.4
Poland	3.24	3.10	0.2	1.9	0.6	107.4	24.7	2.4	25.3	2.5	19.8	2.9
Portugal[b]	0.80	0.80	0.5	0.7	0.9	110.7	5.2	3.1	4.5	3.1	..	1.9
Puerto Rico	1.00	1.00	..	..	..	..	3.0	..	..	..	..	..

4.14 Exchange rates and prices

	Official exchange rate		Purchasing power parity (PPP) conversion factor		Ratio of PPP conversion factor to official exchange rate	Real effective exchange rate	GDP implicit deflator		Consumer price index		Wholesale price index	
	local currency units to $		local currency units to international $			Index 2000 = 100	average annual % growth		average annual % growth		average annual % growth	
	2005	2006	1990	2005	2005	2005	1990–2000	2000–05	1990–2000	2000–05	1990–2000	2000–05
Romania	2.91	2.81	0.0	1.5	0.5	119.9	98.0	21.8	100.5	17.7	93.8	21.4
Russian Federation	28.28	*26.59*[a]	0.0	13.9	0.5	149.2	161.5	16.8	*99.1*	14.4	*99.8*	17.4
Rwanda	557.82	*549.94*[a]	35.6	109.8	0.2	..	14.6	5.9	*16.2*	6.8	..	..
Saudi Arabia	3.75	3.75	2.5	3.0	0.8	82.3	1.6	6.2	1.0	0.2	1.3	1.3
Senegal	527.47	522.89	172.1	208.0	0.4	..	5.0	2.0	5.4	1.3	..	..
Serbia and Montenegro	72.44	*59.64*[a]	..	..	..	..	*55.0*	25.2	..	..	..	..
Sierra Leone	2,889.59	2,961.91	35.9	790.0	0.3	70.9	32.1	6.8	29.3	6.3	..	..
Singapore	1.66	1.59	1.8	1.5	0.9	92.1	1.3	0.2	1.7	0.6	–1.0	2.4
Slovak Republic	31.02	29.70	5.9	16.8	0.5	134.4	11.3	4.1	*8.4*	6.1	9.5	5.0
Slovenia	192.71	191.03	8.6	148.6	0.8	..	28.7	5.5	*12.0*	5.5	*9.1*	4.5
Somalia	..	..	..	..	..	..	..	..	..	..	..	..
South Africa	6.36	6.77	1.1	2.9	0.5	108.5	9.9	6.6	8.7	5.2	7.4	5.3
Spain[b]	0.80	0.80	0.6	0.8	1.0	112.9	3.9	4.2	3.8	3.2	2.4	2.2
Sri Lanka	100.50	103.91	9.8	26.2	0.3	..	9.1	8.7	9.9	9.2	8.1	9.3
Sudan	243.61	217.15	0.7	88.9	0.4	124.0	66.6	9.6	71.8	7.8	..	..
Swaziland	6.36	6.77	0.9	3.2	0.5	..	12.5	10.6	9.4	6.9	..	..
Sweden	7.47	7.38	9.1	9.1	1.2	96.9	2.2	1.5	1.9	1.5	2.4	1.6
Switzerland	1.25	1.25	2.0	1.7	1.4	104.0	1.0	1.0	1.6	0.8	–0.4	0.4
Syrian Arab Republic	11.23	11.23	10.2	19.2	0.4	..	7.9	4.2	6.4	..	4.7	..
Tajikistan	3.12	3.30	..	0.8	0.3	..	235.0	21.2	..	..	..	..
Tanzania	1,128.93	1,251.90	74.6	479.2	0.4	..	21.6	6.3	20.9	3.1	..	..
Thailand	40.22	37.88	10.7	12.7	0.3	..	4.2	2.3	4.9	2.1	3.8	4.6
Togo	527.47	522.89	92.6	125.6	0.2	113.6	7.0	1.2	8.5	2.0	..	..
Trinidad and Tobago	6.30	6.31	3.1	4.7	0.8	107.8	5.4	3.5	5.7	4.5	2.8	1.6
Tunisia	1.30	1.33	0.4	0.4	0.3	85.3	4.4	2.3	4.4	2.7	3.6	3.0
Turkey	1.34[d]	1.43[d]	1,569.1	804,128.7	0.6	..	76.1	25.5	79.9	26.5	..	..
Turkmenistan	..	..	0.0	..	..	..	407.5	..	..	..	..	..
Uganda	1,780.67	*1.81*[a]	114.5	361.9	0.2	88.8	11.8	5.0	10.5	4.1	..	..
Ukraine	5.13	5.05	..	1.3	0.3	106.0	271.0	10.9	*155.7*	7.1	*161.6*	10.8
United Arab Emirates	3.67	3.67	3.3	4.1	1.1	..	2.2	4.9	..	..	..	..
United Kingdom	0.55	0.54	0.5	0.6	1.1	101.3	2.8	2.5	2.9	2.5	2.4	1.3
United States	1.00	1.00	1.0	1.0	1.0	92.8	2.0	2.3	2.7	2.4	1.2	3.4
Uruguay	24.48	*24.48*	0.6	11.9	0.5	76.6	31.1	11.5	33.9	11.4	27.2	20.3
Uzbekistan	..	..	0.0	281.8	0.3	..	245.8	29.0	..	..	..	..
Venezuela, RB	2,089.75	2,147.00	23.8	1,662.2	0.8	69.0	45.3	28.6	49.0	22.0	44.1	32.9
Vietnam	15,858.92	*15,921.00*[a]	674.1	3,282.4	0.2	..	15.2	5.9	*4.1*	4.5	..	..
West Bank and Gaza	..	..	..	..	..	..	*5.7*	3.4	..	..	..	..
Yemen, Rep.	191.51	*198.08*[a]	18.0	147.9	0.8	..	22.4	10.3	26.3	*11.7*	..	..
Zambia	4,463.50	3,603.07	17.7	2,719.3	0.6	134.8	52.1	20.4	57.0	20.4	*101.4*	..
Zimbabwe	22.36	*250.00*[a]	0.9	2,844.9	0.1	..	26.7	232.6	29.0	..	*25.9*	..

Note: The inconsistencies in the growth rates of the GDP deflator and the consumer and wholesale price indexes are due mainly to uneven coverage of the time period.

a. Latest quarterly or monthly data available. b. As members of the European Monetary Union, these countries share a single currency, the euro. c. Based on a 1986 bilateral comparison of China and the United States (Rouen and Kai 1995), employing a different methodology than that used for other countries. This interim methodology will be revised when the next round of PPP estimates are completed in 2007. d. New liras per dollar.

Exchange rates and prices 4.14

About the data

In a market-based economy the choices that households, producers, and governments make about the allocation of resources are influenced by relative prices, including the real exchange rate, real wages, real interest rates, and a host of other prices in the economy. Relative prices also reflect, to a large extent, the choices of these agents. Thus relative prices convey vital information about the interaction of economic agents in an economy and with the rest of the world.

The exchange rate is the price of one currency in terms of another. Official exchange rates and exchange rate arrangements are established by governments. (Other exchange rates fully recognized by governments include market rates, which are determined largely by legal market forces, and for countries maintaining multiple exchange arrangements, principal rates, secondary rates, and tertiary rates.) Also see *Statistical methods* for information on alternative conversion factors used in the *World Bank Atlas* method of calculating gross national income (GNI) per capita in U.S. dollars.

The official or market exchange rate is often used to compare prices in different currencies. Since exchange rates reflect at best the relative prices of tradable goods, the volume of goods and services that a U.S. dollar buys in the United States may not correspond to what a U.S. dollar converted to another country's currency at the official exchange rate would buy in that country. Since identical volumes of goods and services in different countries correspond to different values (and vice versa) when official exchange rates are used, an alternative method of comparing prices across countries has been developed. In this method national currency estimates of GNI are converted to a common unit of account by using conversion factors that reflect equivalent purchasing power. Purchasing power parity (PPP) conversion factors are based on price and expenditure surveys conducted by the International Comparison Program and represent the conversion factors applied to equalize price levels across countries. See *About the data* for table 1.1 for further discussion of the PPP conversion factor.

The ratio of the PPP conversion factor to the official exchange rate (also referred to as the national price level) makes it possible to compare the cost of the bundle of goods that make up gross domestic product (GDP) across countries. These national price levels vary systematically, rising with GNI per capita. Real effective exchange rates represent a nominal effective exchange rate index adjusted for relative movements in national price or cost indicators of the home country, selected countries, and the euro area. A nominal effective exchange rate index represents the ratio (expressed on the base 2000 = 100) of an index of a currency's period-average exchange rate to a weighted geometric average of exchange rates for currencies of selected countries and the euro area. For most high-income countries, weights are derived from trade in manufactured goods among industrial countries. The data are compiled from the nominal effective exchange rate index and a cost indicator of relative normalized unit labor costs in manufacturing. For selected other countries the nominal effective exchange rate index is based on each country's trade in both manufactured goods and primary products with its partner or competitor countries. For these countries the real effective exchange rate index is derived from the nominal index adjusted for relative changes in consumer prices. An increase in the real effective exchange rate represents an appreciation of the local currency. Because of conceptual and data limitations, changes in real effective exchange rates should be interpreted with caution.

Controlling inflation is one of the primary goals of monetary policy and is intimately linked to the growth in money supply. Inflation is measured by the rate of increase in a price index, but actual price change can be negative. Which index is used depends on which set of prices in the economy is being examined. The GDP deflator reflects changes in prices for total gross domestic product. The most general measure of the overall price level, it takes into account changes in government consumption, capital formation (including inventory appreciation), international trade, and the main component, household final consumption expenditure. The GDP deflator is usually derived implicitly as the ratio of current to constant price GDP, resulting in a Paasche index. It is defective as a general measure of inflation for use in policy because of the long lags in deriving estimates and because it is often only an annual measure.

Consumer price indexes are produced more frequently and so are more current. They are also constructed explicitly, based on surveys of the cost of a defined basket of consumer goods and services. Nevertheless, consumer price indexes should be interpreted with caution. The definition of a household, the basket of goods chosen, and the geographic (urban or rural) and income group coverage of consumer price surveys can all vary widely across countries. In addition, the weights are derived from household expenditure surveys, which, for budgetary reasons, tend to be conducted infrequently in developing countries, leading to poor comparability over time. Although useful for measuring consumer price inflation within a country, consumer price indexes are of less value in making comparisons across countries. Food price indexes, like consumer price indexes, should be interpreted with caution because of the high variability across countries in the items covered.

Wholesale price indexes are based on the prices of commodities that have some significance in the output or consumption of the country at the first commercial transaction. The prices are farm gate prices for agricultural commodities and ex-factory prices for industrial goods. Preference should be given to indexes that provide the broadest coverage of the economy.

The least-squares method is used to calculate the growth rates of the GDP implicit deflator, consumer price index, and wholesale price index.

Definitions

• **Official exchange rate** is the exchange rate determined by national authorities or the rate determined in the legally sanctioned exchange market. It is calculated as an annual average based on monthly averages (local currency units relative to the U.S. dollar). • **Purchasing power parity (PPP) conversion factor** is the number of units of a country's currency required to buy the same amount of goods and services in the domestic market as a U.S. dollar would buy in the United States. • **Ratio of PPP conversion factor to official exchange rate** is the result obtained by dividing the PPP conversion factor by the official exchange rate. • **Real effective exchange rate** is the nominal effective exchange rate (a measure of the value of a currency against a weighted average of several foreign currencies) divided by a price deflator or index of costs. • **GDP implicit deflator** measures the average annual rate of price change in the economy as a whole for the periods shown. • **Consumer price index** reflects changes in the cost to the average consumer of acquiring a basket of goods and services that may be fixed or may change at specified intervals, such as yearly. The Laspeyres formula is generally used. • **Wholesale price index** refers to a mix of agricultural and industrial goods at various stages of production and distribution, including import duties. The Laspeyres formula is generally used.

Data sources

Data on official and real effective exchange rates and consumer and wholesale price indexes are from the International Monetary Fund's *International Financial Statistics*. PPP conversion factors and GDP deflators are from the World Bank's data files.

4.15 Balance of payments current account

	Goods and services				Net income		Net current transfers		Current account balance		Total reserves[a]	
	$ millions				$ millions		$ millions		$ millions		$ millions	
	Exports		Imports									
	1990	2005	1990	2005	1990	2005	1990	2005	1990	2005	1990	2005
Afghanistan	*261*	..	*727*	..	*12*	..	*311*	..	*–143*	..	638	..
Albania	354	1,821	485	3,860	–2	174	15	1,294	–118	–571	..	1,440
Algeria	13,462	..	10,106	..	–2,268	..	333	..	1,420	..	2,703	59,167
Angola	3,992	24,286	3,386	15,144	–765	–4,031	–77	27	–236	5,138	..	3,197
Argentina	14,800	46,343	6,846	34,916	–4,400	–6,207	998	570	4,552	5,789	6,222	28,082
Armenia	..	1,337	..	1,984	..	45	..	409	..	–193	*1*	669
Australia	49,846	135,505	53,056	149,738	–13,176	–27,690	439	–363	–15,948	–42,286	19,319	43,257
Austria	63,694	171,154	61,580	162,913	–942	–1,337	–6	–2,652	1,166	4,252	17,228	11,828
Azerbaijan	..	8,332	..	7,003	..	–1,646	..	484	..	167	..	1,178
Bangladesh	2,064	10,432	3,960	14,456	–116	–798	1,613	4,691	–398	–132	660	2,825
Belarus	..	18,068	..	17,859	..	56	..	169	..	434	..	1,342
Belgium	138,605[b]	318,775	135,098[b]	308,430	2,316[b]	5,394	–2,197[b]	–6,411	3,627[b]	9,328	23,789	11,996
Benin	364	*784*	454	*1,129*	–25	*–37*	97	*93*	–18	*–288*	69	657
Bolivia	977	3,160	1,086	2,872	–249	–373	159	584	–199	498	511	1,795
Bosnia and Herzegovina	..	3,602	..	8,004	..	405	..	1,841	..	–2,156	..	2,531
Botswana	2,005	5,285	1,987	3,683	–106	–812	69	678	–19	1,469	3,331	6,309
Brazil	35,170	134,403	28,184	97,794	–11,608	–25,967	799	3,558	–3,823	14,199	9,200	53,799
Bulgaria	6,950	16,057	8,027	20,600	–758	310	125	1,229	–1,710	–3,004	*670*	8,697
Burkina Faso	349	..	758	..	..	..	332	..	–77	..	305	438
Burundi	89	92	318	353	–15	–18	174	23	–69	–256	112	101
Cambodia	*314*	4,017	*507*	4,559	*–21*	–254	*120*	440	*–93*	–356	..	1,158
Cameroon	2,508	*2,894*	2,475	*3,239*	–558	*–445*	–26	*116*	–551	*–675*	37	965
Canada	149,538	427,955	149,118	385,473	–19,388	–15,508	–796	–419	–19,764	26,555	23,530	33,018
Central African Republic	220	..	410	..	–22	..	123	..	–89	..	123	145
Chad	271	..	488	..	–21	..	192	..	–46	..	132	231
Chile	10,221	47,746	9,166	38,154	–1,737	–10,624	198	1,735	–485	703	6,784	16,933
China[†]	57,374	836,888	46,706	712,090	1,055	10,635	274	25,385	11,997	160,818	34,476	831,410
Hong Kong, China	..	351,754	..	329,590	..	312	..	–2,192	..	20,284	24,656	124,278
Colombia	8,679	24,393	6,858	24,901	–2,305	–5,563	1,026	4,089	542	–1,981	4,869	14,955
Congo, Dem. Rep.	..	..	..	..	..	..	..	..	..	..	261	..
Congo, Rep.	1,488	4,964	1,282	2,917	–460	–1,122	3	–22	–251	903	10	738
Costa Rica	1,963	9,716	2,346	10,730	–233	–215	192	270	–424	–959	525	2,314
Côte d'Ivoire	3,503	8,289	3,445	7,174	–1,091	–662	–181	–465	–1,214	–12	21	1,322
Croatia	..	18,876	..	21,702	..	–1,235	..	1,475	..	–2,585	*167*	8,800
Cuba	..	..	..	..	..	..	..	..	..	..	..	..
Czech Republic	..	89,007	..	86,461	..	–5,929	..	888	..	–2,495	..	29,554
Denmark	48,902	125,046	41,415	112,482	–5,708	275	–408	–4,223	1,372	8,616	11,226	34,028
Dominican Republic	1,832	10,056	2,233	11,333	–249	–1,957	371	2,734	–280	–500	69	1,853
Ecuador	3,262	11,439	2,519	11,826	–1,210	–1,938	107	2,267	–360	–59	1,009	2,148
Egypt, Arab Rep.	9,895	30,716	14,091	34,326	–1,022	–35	7,545	5,748	2,327	2,103	3,620	21,857
El Salvador	973	4,573	1,624	7,652	–132	–571	631	2,865	–152	–786	595	1,890
Eritrea	..	..	..	..	..	..	..	..	..	..	..	28
Estonia	*664*	10,939	*711*	11,784	*–13*	–700	*97*	100	*36*	–1,445	*198*	1,947
Ethiopia	597	1,929	1,271	4,895	–69	–5	449	1,402	–294	–1,568	55	1,121
Finland	31,180	82,457	33,456	71,091	–3,735	–278	–952	–1,572	–6,962	9,517	10,415	11,332
France	285,389	555,204	283,238	577,463	–3,896	16,314	–8,199	–27,344	–9,944	–33,289	68,291	74,360
Gabon	2,730	*4,228*	1,812	*2,155*	–617	*–965*	–134	*–184*	168	*924*	279	675
Gambia, The	168	181	192	261	–11	–32	59	69	23	–44	55	98
Georgia	..	2,171	..	3,312	..	92	..	359	..	–690	..	479
Germany	473,672	1,127,020	427,547	985,673	22,574	10,676	–21,954	–35,989	46,745	116,035	104,547	101,676
Ghana	983	3,869	1,506	6,610	–111	–187	411	2,117	–223	–812	309	1,897
Greece	13,018	51,790	19,564	66,626	–1,709	–7,030	4,718	3,987	–3,537	–17,879	4,721	2,287
Guatemala	1,568	4,939	1,812	9,547	–196	–337	227	3,558	–213	–1,387	362	3,777
Guinea	829	*811*	953	*964*	–149	*–27*	70	*18*	–203	*–162*	*145*	97
Guinea-Bissau	26	*83*	88	*127*	–22	*–10*	39	*67*	–45	*14*	18	80
Haiti	318	593	515	1,756	–18	–37	193	1,254	–22	54	10	134
[†]Data for Taiwan, China	74,172	221,604	67,015	210,224	4,362	9,053	–596	–4,271	10,923	16,162	77,653	260,272

Balance of payments current account

	Goods and services				Net income		Net current transfers		Current account balance		Total reserves[a]	
	$ millions				$ millions		$ millions		$ millions		$ millions	
	Exports		Imports									
	1990	2005	1990	2005	1990	2005	1990	2005	1990	2005	1990	2005
Honduras	1,033	3,427	1,127	5,035	–237	–331	280	1,854	–51	–86	47	2,338
Hungary	12,035	74,168	11,017	75,596	–1,427	–6,915	787	237	379	–8,106	1,185	18,590
India	22,911	*82,735*	29,527	*93,918*	–3,257	*–4,451*	2,837	*22,488*	–7,036	*6,853*	5,637	137,825
Indonesia	29,295	99,104	27,511	87,584	–5,190	–11,849	418	1,258	–2,988	929	8,657	34,579
Iran, Islamic Rep.	19,741	..	22,292	..	378	..	2,500	..	327	..	..	..
Iraq	..	..	..	..	..	..	..	..	..	..	8,340	12,201
Ireland	26,786	161,366	24,576	137,081	–4,955	–30,307	2,384	691	–361	–5,331	5,362	869
Israel	17,312	57,874	20,228	57,525	–1,981	–2,622	5,061	6,029	163	3,756	6,598	28,059
Italy	219,971	462,709	218,573	463,295	–14,712	–17,078	–3,164	–10,061	–16,479	–27,724	88,595	65,954
Jamaica	2,217	3,994	2,390	5,975	–430	–676	291	1,578	–312	–1,079	168	2,170
Japan	323,692	677,782	297,306	607,869	22,492	103,444	–4,800	–7,573	44,078	165,783	87,828	846,896
Jordan	2,511	6,584	3,569	11,859	–214	376	1,045	2,588	–227	–2,311	1,139	5,461
Kazakhstan	..	30,548	..	25,503	..	–5,357	..	–412	..	–724	..	7,070
Kenya	2,228	5,126	2,705	6,540	–418	–108	368	1,028	–527	–495	236	1,799
Korea, Dem. Rep.	..	..	..	..	..	..	..	..	..	..	..	..
Korea, Rep.	73,297	334,370	76,373	313,989	–88	–1,320	1,150	–2,502	–2,014	16,559	14,916	210,552
Kuwait	8,268	51,574	7,169	24,513	7,738	8,834	–4,951	–3,261	3,886	32,634	2,929	10,165
Kyrgyz Republic	..	942	..	1,397	..	–81	..	332	..	–203	..	612
Lao PDR	102	..	212	..	–1	..	56	..	–55	..	8	309
Latvia	*1,090*	7,526	*997*	9,936	*2*	–188	*96*	596	*191*	–2,002	..	2,360
Lebanon	..	13,037	..	16,222	..	247	..	1,057	..	–1,881	4,210	16,618
Lesotho	100	705	754	1,354	433	305	286	301	65	–44	72	519
Liberia	..	..	..	..	..	..	..	..	..	..	*1*	25
Libya	11,468	29,383	8,960	13,523	174	–281	–481	–634	2,201	14,945	7,225	41,880
Lithuania	..	14,879	..	16,745	..	–627	..	662	..	–1,831	*107*	3,816
Macedonia, FYR	..	2,511	..	3,602	..	–55	..	1,065	..	–81	..	1,340
Madagascar	471	450	809	691	–161	–27	234	80	–265	–188	92	481
Malawi	443	..	549	..	–80	..	99	..	–86	..	142	165
Malaysia	32,665	161,384	31,765	130,609	–1,872	–6,318	102	–4,477	–870	19,980	10,659	70,450
Mali	420	*1,218*	830	*1,625*	–37	*–195*	225	*193*	–221	*–409*	198	855
Mauritania	471	..	520	..	–46	..	86	..	–10	..	59	*420*
Mauritius	1,722	3,762	1,916	4,154	–23	–8	97	61	–119	–340	761	1,372
Mexico	48,805	230,369	51,915	243,259	–8,316	–12,242	3,975	20,484	–7,451	–4,647	10,217	74,110
Moldova	..	1,528	..	2,743	..	403	..	570	..	–242	*2*	597
Mongolia	493	*1,211*	1,096	*1,405*	–44	*–11*	7	*269*	–640	*63*	*23*	430
Morocco	6,239	18,788	7,783	22,739	–988	–314	2,336	5,375	–196	1,110	2,338	16,551
Mozambique	229	2,087	996	2,891	–97	–360	448	403	–415	–761	232	1,103
Myanmar	319	*3,181*	603	*2,458*	–192	*–745*	39	*134*	–436	*112*	410	889
Namibia	1,220	*2,310*	1,584	*2,495*	37	*151*	354	*669*	28	*634*	*50*	312
Nepal	422	1,283	834	2,711	14	48	109	1,533	–289	153	354	1,565
Netherlands	159,304	427,949	147,652	374,710	–620	6,194	–2,943	–10,497	8,089	48,936	34,401	20,448
New Zealand	11,683	30,467	11,699	32,921	–1,576	–7,626	138	459	–1,453	–9,622	4,129	8,893
Nicaragua	392	1,861	682	3,292	–217	–119	202	750	–305	–800	166	728
Niger	533	*530*	728	*852*	–54	*–13*	14	*104*	–236	*–231*	226	250
Nigeria	14,550	52,233	6,909	24,609	–2,738	–6,732	85	3,310	4,988	24,202	4,129	28,632
Norway	47,078	133,032	38,910	81,545	–2,700	1,045	–1,476	–3,045	3,992	49,488	15,788	46,986
Oman	5,577	19,514	3,342	11,080	–254	–1,459	–874	–2,257	1,106	4,717	1,784	4,358
Pakistan	6,835	19,059	10,205	29,042	–1,084	–2,516	2,794	9,036	–1,661	–3,463	1,046	11,109
Panama	4,438	10,736	4,193	10,636	–255	–1,124	219	243	209	–782	344	1,211
Papua New Guinea	1,381	3,580	1,509	2,692	–103	–538	156	291	–76	640	427	750
Paraguay	2,514	3,927	2,169	4,098	2	–74	43	223	390	–22	675	1,297
Peru	4,120	19,426	4,087	15,176	–1,733	–5,011	281	1,791	–1,419	1,030	1,891	14,171
Philippines	11,430	44,693	13,967	53,635	–872	–123	714	11,403	–2,695	2,338	2,036	18,474
Poland	19,037	112,622	15,095	113,476	–3,386	–11,186	2,511	6,935	3,067	–5,105	4,674	42,561
Portugal	21,554	53,272	27,146	69,078	–96	–3,932	5,507	2,731	–181	–17,007	20,579	10,364
Puerto Rico	..	..	..	..	..	..	..	..	..	..	..	..

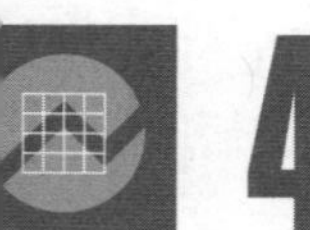

4.15 Balance of payments current account

	Goods and services ($ millions) Exports 1990	Exports 2005	Imports 1990	Imports 2005	Net income ($ millions) 1990	2005	Net current transfers ($ millions) 1990	2005	Current account balance ($ millions) 1990	2005	Total reserves[a] ($ millions) 1990	2005
Romania	6,380	32,813	9,901	42,866	161	–2,900	106	4,449	–3,254	–8,504	1,374	21,601
Russian Federation	..	268,136	..	164,718	..	–19,111	..	–1,122	..	83,184	..	182,272
Rwanda	143	257	354	659	–16	–16	143	366	–85	–52	44	406
Saudi Arabia	47,381	180,551	43,880	79,274	7,968	272	–15,616	–14,418	–4,147	87,131	13,437	28,888
Senegal	1,453	*2,180*	1,840	*3,194*	–129	*–131*	153	*632*	–363	*–513*	22	1,191
Serbia and Montenegro	..	..	..	..	..	..	..	..	..	..	..	..
Sierra Leone	210	263	215	452	–71	–51	7	137	–69	–103	5	171
Singapore	67,489	283,565	64,953	248,627	1,006	–541	–421	–1,184	3,122	33,212	27,748	115,794
Slovak Republic	..	*25,241*	..	*25,649*	..	*–119*	..	*245*	..	*–282*	..	15,480
Slovenia	*7,900*	22,121	*6,930*	22,319	*–38*	–363	*46*	–120	*978*	–682	*112*	8,160
Somalia	*68*	..	*468*	..	*–84*	..	*328*	..	*–157*	..	*23*	..
South Africa	27,160	66,437	21,017	68,639	–4,271	–4,929	–321	–2,011	1,552	–9,142	2,583	20,624
Spain	83,595	288,042	100,870	345,642	–3,533	–21,452	2,799	–4,084	–18,009	–83,136	57,238	17,227
Sri Lanka	2,293	7,887	2,965	10,066	–167	–297	541	1,828	–298	–647	447	2,736
Sudan	499	4,938	877	7,790	–136	–1,362	141	1,446	–372	–2,768	11	1,869
Swaziland	658	2,110	768	2,212	59	20	102	128	51	46	216	244
Sweden	70,560	178,072	70,490	150,358	–4,473	545	–1,936	–4,616	–6,339	23,643	20,324	24,868
Switzerland	97,033	197,159	96,389	171,456	7,878	37,132	–2,398	–8,977	6,124	53,859	61,284	57,575
Syrian Arab Republic	5,030	9,769	2,955	10,718	–401	–863	88	751	1,762	–1,061	*535*	..
Tajikistan	..	1,254	..	1,682	..	–41	..	450	..	–19	..	189
Tanzania	538	2,890	1,474	3,825	–185	–204	562	603	–559	–536	193	2,049
Thailand	29,229	129,847	35,870	133,599	–853	–2,921	213	3,004	–7,281	–3,670	14,258	52,076
Togo	663	*751*	847	*1,093*	–32	*–33*	132	*169*	–84	*–206*	358	195
Trinidad and Tobago	2,289	*7,254*	1,427	*5,266*	–397	*–597*	–6	*56*	459	*1,447*	513	4,888
Tunisia	5,203	14,492	6,039	14,638	–455	–1,659	828	1,501	–463	–303	867	4,548
Turkey	21,042	102,806	25,524	121,766	–2,508	–5,663	4,365	1,468	–2,625	–23,155	7,626	52,494
Turkmenistan	..	..	..	..	..	..	..	..	..	..	..	..
Uganda	178	1,343	686	2,584	–48	–157	293	1,139	–263	–259	44	1,344
Ukraine	..	44,378	..	43,707	..	–985	..	2,845	..	2,531	*469*	19,388
United Arab Emirates	..	..	..	..	..	..	..	..	..	..	4,891	21,010
United Kingdom	239,226	587,541	264,089	669,823	–5,154	54,814	–8,794	–21,990	–38,811	–49,459	43,146	43,593
United States	535,260	1,275,245	616,120	1,991,975	28,560	11,294	–26,660	–86,073	–78,960	–791,509	173,094	188,259
Uruguay	2,158	5,087	1,659	4,626	–321	–585	8	121	186	–2	1,446	3,078
Uzbekistan	..	..	..	..	..	..	..	..	..	..	..	..
Venezuela, RB	18,806	56,821	9,451	29,371	–774	–1,984	–302	–107	8,279	25,359	12,733	29,803
Vietnam	..	36,618	..	38,562	..	–1,219	..	3,380	..	217	..	9,051
West Bank and Gaza	..	..	..	..	..	..	..	..	..	..	..	..
Yemen, Rep.	1,490	6,752	2,170	5,285	–372	–1,657	1,790	1,406	739	1,215	441	6,141
Zambia	1,360	..	1,897	..	–437	..	380	..	–594	..	201	560
Zimbabwe	2,012	..	2,001	..	–263	..	112	..	–140	..	295	..
World	4,324,290 t	12,691,551 t	4,306,213 t	12,539,143 t								
Low income	79,141	*217,936*	97,905	*245,934*								
Middle income	635,146	3,261,414	591,292	2,905,260								
Lower middle income	302,331	1,793,100	300,012	1,586,704								
Upper middle income	336,906	1,483,562	291,782	1,328,253								
Low & middle income	714,951	3,596,835	689,821	3,263,799								
East Asia & Pacific	167,506	1,327,062	166,319	1,178,084								
Europe & Central Asia	..	926,132	..	865,611								
Latin America & Carib.	170,445	650,474	147,430	593,769								
Middle East & N. Africa	..	..	105,814	222,757								
South Asia	34,864	*114,362*	48,099	*131,775*								
Sub-Saharan Africa	78,020	228,841	72,772	209,500								
High income	3,594,026	9,151,976	3,592,287	9,318,222								
Europe EMU	1,530,521	3,731,193	1,491,055	3,590,256								

a. International reserves including gold valued at London gold price. b. Includes Luxembourg.

Balance of payments current account 4.15

About the data

The balance of payments records an economy's transactions with the rest of the world. Balance of payments accounts are divided into two groups: the current account, which records transactions in goods, services, income, and current transfers, and the capital and financial account, which records capital transfers, acquisition or disposal of nonproduced, nonfinancial assets, and transactions in financial assets and liabilities. The table presents data from the current account with the addition of gross international reserves.

The balance of payments is a double-entry accounting system that shows all flows of goods and services into and out of an economy; all transfers that are the counterpart of real resources or financial claims provided to or by the rest of the world without a quid pro quo, such as donations and grants; and all changes in residents' claims on and liabilities to nonresidents that arise from economic transactions. All transactions are recorded twice—once as a credit and once as a debit. In principle the net balance should be zero, but in practice the accounts often do not balance. In these cases a balancing item, net errors and omissions, is included.

Discrepancies may arise in the balance of payments because there is no single source for balance of payments data and therefore no way to ensure that the data are fully consistent. Sources include customs data, monetary accounts of the banking system, external debt records, information provided by enterprises, surveys to estimate service transactions, and foreign exchange records. Differences in collection methods—such as in timing, definitions of residence and ownership, and the exchange rate used to value transactions—contribute to net errors and omissions. In addition, smuggling and other illegal or quasi-legal transactions may be unrecorded or misrecorded. For further discussion of issues relating to the recording of data on trade in goods and services, see *About the data* for tables 4.4–4.7.

The concepts and definitions underlying the data in the table are based on the fifth edition of the International Monetary Fund's (IMF) *Balance of Payments Manual* (1993). That edition redefined as capital transfers some transactions previously included in the current account, such as debt forgiveness, migrants' capital transfers, and foreign aid to acquire capital goods. Thus the current account balance now reflects more accurately net current transfer receipts in addition to transactions in goods, services (previously nonfactor services), and income (previously factor income). Many countries maintain their data collection systems according to the fourth edition. Where necessary, the IMF converts such reported data to conform to the fifth edition (see *Primary data documentation*). Values are in U.S. dollars converted at market exchange rates.

The data in this table come from the IMF's Balance of Payments and International Financial Statistics databases.

Top 15 economies with the largest current account surplus—and top 15 economies with the largest current account deficit in 2005 **4.15a**

Economy	Surplus ($ billions)	Share of GDP (%)	Economy	Deficit ($ billions)	Share of GDP (%)
Japan	165.8	3.7	United States	–791.5	–6.4
China	160.8	7.2	Spain	–83.1	–7.4
Germany	116.0	4.2	United Kingdom	–49.5	–2.2
Saudi Arabia	87.1	28.1	Australia	–42.3	–5.8
Russian Federation	83.2	10.9	France	–33.3	–1.6
Switzerland	53.9	14.7	Italy	–27.7	–1.6
Norway	49.5	16.7	Turkey	–23.2	–6.4
Netherlands	48.9	7.8	Grece	–17.9	–7.9
Singapore	33.2	28.4	Portugal	–17.0	–9.3
Kuwait	32.6	40.4	New Zealand	–9.6	–8.8
Canada	26.6	2.4	South Africa	–9.1	–3.8
Venezuela, RB	25.4	18.1	Romania	–8.5	–8.6
Nigeria	24.2	24.5	Hungary	–8.1	–7.4
Sweden	23.6	6.6	Ireland	–5.3	–2.6
Hong Kong, China	20.3	11.4	Poland	–5.1	–1.7

Source: International Monetary Fund, balance of payments data files.

Definitions

• **Exports and imports of goods and services** comprise all transactions between residents of an economy and the rest of the world involving a change in ownership of general merchandise, goods sent for processing and repairs, nonmonetary gold, and services. • **Net income** refers to receipts and payments of employee compensation for nonresident workers, and investment income (receipts and payments on direct investment, portfolio investment, and other investments and receipts on reserve assets). Income derived from the use of intangible assets is recorded under business services. • **Net current transfers** are recorded in the balance of payments whenever an economy provides or receives goods, services, income, or financial items without a quid pro quo. All transfers not considered to be capital are current. • **Current account balance** is the sum of net exports of goods and services, net income, and net current transfers. • **Total reserves** comprise holdings of monetary gold, special drawing rights, reserves of IMF members held by the IMF, and holdings of foreign exchange under the control of monetary authorities. The gold component of these reserves is valued at year-end (31 December) London prices ($385.00 an ounce in 1990, and $438.00 an ounce in 2004).

Data sources

Data on the balance of payments are published in the IMF's *Balance of Payments Statistics Yearbook* and *International Financial Statistics*. The World Bank exchanges data with the IMF through electronic files that in most cases are more timely and cover a longer period than the published sources. More information about the design and compilation of the balance of payments can be found in the IMF's *Balance of Payments Manual*, fifth edition (1993), *Balance of Payments Textbook* (1996), and *Balance of Payments Compilation Guide* (1995). The IMF's International Financial Statistics and Balance of Payments databases are available on CD-ROM.

External debt

	Total external debt		Long-term debt		Public and publicly guaranteed debt				Private nonguaranteed external debt		Use of IMF credit	
	$ millions		$ millions		$ millions				$ millions		$ millions	
					Total		IBRD loans and IDA credits					
	1990	2005	1990	2005	1990	2005	1990	2005	1990	2005	1990	2005
Afghanistan	..	..	..	..	..	..	..	..	..	..	..	..
Albania	..	1,839	..	1,459	..	1,375	..	..	..	84	..	92
Algeria	28,149	16,879	26,688	16,363	26,688	15,476	1,208	..	..	887	670	0
Angola	8,592	11,755	7,603	9,428	7,603	9,428	..	..	0	..	0	..
Argentina	62,233	114,335	48,676	85,477	46,876	61,952	2,609	..	1,800	23,525	3,083	9,513
Armenia	..	1,861	..	1,386	..	923	..	752	..	464	..	176
Australia	..	..	..	..	..	..	..	..	..	..	..	..
Austria	..	..	..	..	..	..	..	..	..	..	..	..
Azerbaijan	..	1,881	..	1,531	..	1,344	..	501	..	187	..	164
Bangladesh	12,439	18,935	11,658	17,938	11,658	17,938	4,159	8,688	0	..	626	308
Belarus	..	4,734	..	1,231	..	783	..	..	..	448	..	0
Belgium	..	..	..	..	..	..	..	..	..	..	..	..
Benin	1,292	1,855	1,218	1,762	1,218	1,762	326	..	0	..	18	53
Bolivia	4,275	6,390	3,864	5,965	3,687	4,564	587	1,673	177	1,401	257	244
Bosnia and Herzegovina	..	5,564	..	4,400	..	2,560	..	1,403	..	1,840	..	62
Botswana	553	473	547	438	547	438	169	9	0	..	0	..
Brazil	119,964	187,994	94,427	164,001	87,756	94,497	8,427	..	6,671	69,505	1,821	0
Bulgaria	..	16,786	..	11,922	..	4,587	..	..	..	7,335	..	660
Burkina Faso	832	2,045	748	1,920	748	1,920	282	..	0	..	0	104
Burundi	907	1,322	851	1,228	851	1,228	..	..	0	..	43	58
Cambodia	1,845	3,515	1,683	3,155	1,683	3,155	..	..	0	..	27	81
Cameroon	6,431	7,151	5,373	6,114	5,144	5,521	871	1,115	230	592	121	272
Canada	..	..	..	..	..	..	..	..	..	..	..	..
Central African Republic	699	1,016	624	871	624	871	265	..	0	..	37	36
Chad	529	1,633	469	1,537	469	1,537	..	899	0	..	30	79
Chile	19,226	45,154	14,687	38,281	10,425	9,096	1,874	293	4,263	29,184	1,156	..
China	55,301	281,612	45,515	133,345	45,515	82,853	5,881	20,880	..	50,492	469	..
Hong Kong, China	..	..	..	..	..	..	..	..	..	..	..	..
Colombia	17,222	37,656	15,784	31,480	14,671	22,491	3,874	3,900	1,113	8,989	..	..
Congo, Dem. Rep.	10,259	10,600	8,994	9,412	8,994	9,412	1,161	..	0	..	521	791
Congo, Rep.	4,934	5,936	4,187	5,161	4,187	5,161	239	280	0	..	11	26
Costa Rica	3,756	6,223	3,367	4,118	3,063	3,470	412	60	304	648	11	..
Côte d'Ivoire	17,251	10,735	13,223	9,854	10,665	9,007	1,920	2,185	2,558	847	431	198
Croatia	..	30,169	..	25,848	..	9,782	..	..	..	16,066	..	..
Cuba	..	..	..	..	..	..	..	..	..	..	..	..
Czech Republic	..	..	..	..	..	..	..	..	..	..	..	..
Denmark	..	..	..	..	..	..	..	..	..	..	..	..
Dominican Republic	4,372	7,398	3,518	6,094	3,419	6,093	258	416	99	2	72	400
Ecuador	12,107	17,129	10,029	15,332	9,865	10,662	848	815	164	4,670	265	78
Egypt, Arab Rep.	33,017	34,114	28,439	28,132	27,439	24,892	2,401	1,912	1,000	3,240	125	..
El Salvador	2,149	7,088	1,938	5,513	1,913	4,760	164	448	26	754	0	..
Eritrea	..	736	..	723	..	723	..	..	..	..	..	..
Estonia	..	11,255	..	7,256	..	435	..	..	..	6,821	..	..
Ethiopia	8,630	6,259	8,479	5,897	8,479	5,897	851	..	0	..	6	160
Finland	..	..	..	..	..	..	..	..	..	..	..	..
France	..	..	..	..	..	..	..	..	..	..	..	..
Gabon	3,983	3,902	3,150	3,582	3,150	3,582	69	..	0	..	140	68
Gambia, The	369	672	308	626	308	626	102	..	0	..	45	21
Georgia	..	1,911	..	1,626	..	1,494	..	..	..	132	..	232
Germany	..	..	..	..	..	..	..	..	..	..	..	..
Ghana	3,734	6,739	2,670	5,734	2,637	5,734	1,423	4,234	33	0	745	417
Greece	..	..	..	..	..	..	..	..	..	..	..	..
Guatemala	2,849	5,349	2,368	3,793	2,241	3,688	293	..	127	105	67	..
Guinea	2,476	3,247	2,253	2,931	2,253	2,931	419	..	0	..	51	87
Guinea-Bissau	692	693	630	671	630	671	145	..	0	..	5	12
Haiti	917	1,323	778	1,276	778	1,276	324	..	0	..	38	21

External debt

	Total external debt		Long-term debt		Public and publicly guaranteed debt				Private nonguaranteed external debt		Use of IMF credit	
	$ millions		$ millions		$ millions				$ millions		$ millions	
					Total		IBRD loans and IDA credits					
	1990	2005	1990	2005	1990	2005	1990	2005	1990	2005	1990	2005
Honduras	3,718	5,242	3,487	4,660	3,420	4,152	635	1,353	66	509	32	168
Hungary	21,201	66,119	17,931	53,725	17,931	21,216	1,512	..	..	32,509	330	0
India	83,628	123,123	72,462	114,335	70,974	80,281	20,996	28,919	1,488	34,054	2,623	..
Indonesia	69,872	138,300	58,242	105,993	47,982	72,335	10,385	9,132	10,261	33,658	494	7,807
Iran, Islamic Rep.	9,020	21,260	1,797	10,574	1,797	10,493	86	..	..	81	0	..
Iraq	..	..	..	..	..	..	..	..	..	..	..	..
Ireland	..	..	..	..	..	..	..	..	..	..	..	..
Israel	..	..	..	..	..	..	..	..	..	..	..	..
Italy	..	..	..	..	..	..	..	..	..	..	..	..
Jamaica	4,752	6,511	4,049	5,897	4,015	5,508	672	..	34	390	357	0
Japan	..	..	..	..	..	..	..	..	..	..	..	..
Jordan	8,333	7,696	7,202	6,878	7,202	6,878	593	970	0	..	94	236
Kazakhstan	..	43,354	..	35,334	..	2,184	..	..	..	33,150	..	..
Kenya	7,055	6,169	5,639	5,520	4,759	5,520	2,056	2,663	880	0	482	159
Korea, Dem. Rep.	..	..	..	..	..	..	..	..	..	..	..	..
Korea, Rep.	..	..	..	..	..	..	..	..	..	..	..	..
Kuwait	..	..	..	..	..	..	..	..	..	..	..	..
Kyrgyz Republic	..	2,032	..	1,830	..	1,670	..	..	..	161	..	178
Lao PDR	1,768	2,690	1,757	2,656	1,757	1,971	131	..	..	685	8	29
Latvia	..	14,283	..	6,791	..	1,318	..	..	..	5,473	..	0
Lebanon	1,779	22,373	358	18,923	358	17,912	34	..	..	1,011	0	..
Lesotho	396	690	378	647	378	647	..	271	0	..	15	35
Liberia	1,849	2,581	1,116	1,115	1,116	1,115	248	251	0	..	322	320
Libya	..	..	..	..	..	..	..	..	..	..	..	..
Lithuania	..	11,201	..	5,876	..	1,511	..	..	..	4,365	..	0
Macedonia, FYR	..	2,243	..	2,084	..	1,613	..	608	..	471	..	62
Madagascar	3,689	3,465	3,320	3,178	3,320	3,178	797	..	0	..	144	212
Malawi	1,558	3,155	1,385	3,040	1,382	3,040	854	1,940	2	..	115	75
Malaysia	15,328	50,981	13,422	38,805	11,592	22,449	1,102	..	1,830	16,356	..	..
Mali	2,468	2,969	2,337	2,843	2,337	2,843	498	..	0	..	69	109
Mauritania	2,113	2,281	1,806	2,043	1,806	2,043	264	..	0	..	70	69
Mauritius	984	2,160	910	797	762	731	195	79	147	66	22	..
Mexico	104,442	167,228	81,809	160,649	75,974	108,786	11,030	..	5,835	51,863	6,551	0
Moldova	..	2,053	..	1,240	..	700	..	371	..	540	..	95
Mongolia	..	1,327	..	1,267	..	1,267	..	..	..	..	..	35
Morocco	25,004	16,846	23,847	16,164	23,647	13,113	3,138	2,278	200	3,051	750	0
Mozambique	4,650	5,121	4,231	4,419	4,211	3,727	..	1,575	19	692	74	157
Myanmar	4,695	6,645	4,466	5,196	4,466	5,196	..	..	0	..	0	..
Namibia	..	..	..	..	..	..	..	..	..	..	..	..
Nepal	1,640	3,285	1,572	3,217	1,572	3,217	667	..	0	..	44	20
Netherlands	..	..	..	..	..	..	..	..	..	..	..	..
New Zealand	..	..	..	..	..	..	..	..	..	..	..	..
Nicaragua	10,745	5,144	8,313	4,405	8,313	4,113	299	..	..	292	0	201
Niger	1,726	1,972	1,487	1,803	1,226	1,771	461	..	261	33	85	128
Nigeria	33,439	22,178	31,935	20,342	31,545	20,342	3,321	1,859	391	..	0	..
Norway	..	..	..	..	..	..	..	..	..	..	..	..
Oman	..	3,472	..	1,805	..	842	..	..	..	963	0	..
Pakistan	20,663	33,675	16,643	30,953	16,506	29,490	3,922	9,104	138	1,463	835	1,492
Panama	6,493	9,765	3,842	9,256	3,842	7,514	462	..	..	1,742	272	24
Papua New Guinea	2,594	1,849	2,461	1,654	1,523	1,266	349	327	938	387	61	0
Paraguay	2,105	3,120	1,732	2,607	1,713	2,264	320	244	19	343	0	..
Peru	20,044	28,653	13,959	25,387	13,629	22,222	1,188	..	330	3,165	755	57
Philippines	30,580	61,527	25,241	54,743	24,040	35,233	4,044	3,082	1,201	19,510	912	389
Poland	49,364	98,821	39,261	81,118	39,261	35,094	55	..	..	46,024	509	..
Portugal	..	..	..	..	..	..	..	..	..	..	..	..
Puerto Rico	..	..	..	..	..	..	..	..	..	..	..	..

4.16 External debt

	Total external debt		Long-term debt		Public and publicly guaranteed debt				Private nonguaranteed external debt		Use of IMF credit	
	$ millions		$ millions		$ millions				$ millions		$ millions	
					Total		IBRD loans and IDA credits					
	1990	2005	1990	2005	1990	2005	1990	2005	1990	2005	1990	2005
Romania	1,140	38,694	230	31,199	223	13,341	0	..	7	17,858	0	261
Russian Federation	..	229,042	..	204,911	..	75,359	..	..	..	129,552	..	0
Rwanda	712	1,518	664	1,420	664	1,420	340	..	0	..	0	77
Saudi Arabia	..	..	..	..	..	..	..	..	..	..	..	..
Senegal	3,744	3,793	3,008	3,609	2,948	3,467	835	..	60	141	314	148
Serbia and Montenegro	..	16,295	..	13,186	..	7,972	..	2,984	..	5,214	..	866
Sierra Leone	1,197	1,682	940	1,420	940	1,420	92	..	0	..	108	192
Singapore	..	..	..	..	..	..	..	..	..	..	..	..
Slovak Republic	..	23,654	..	8,493	..	3,340	..	..	..	5,153	..	..
Slovenia	..	..	..	..	..	..	..	..	..	..	..	..
Somalia	2,370	2,750	1,926	1,882	1,926	1,882	419	..	0	..	159	160
South Africa	..	30,632	..	20,922	..	11,662	..	..	..	9,260	..	..
Spain	..	..	..	..	..	..	..	..	..	..	..	..
Sri Lanka	5,863	11,444	5,049	10,055	4,947	9,812	946	2,095	102	243	410	381
Sudan	14,762	18,455	9,651	11,659	9,155	11,163	1,048	..	496	496	956	518
Swaziland	298	532	294	451	294	451	44	27	0	..	0	..
Sweden	..	..	..	..	..	..	..	..	..	..	..	..
Switzerland	..	..	..	..	..	..	..	..	..	..	..	..
Syrian Arab Republic	17,259	6,508	15,108	5,640	15,108	5,640	523	22	0	..	..	..
Tajikistan	..	1,022	..	811	..	785	..	..	..	26	..	127
Tanzania	6,454	7,763	5,794	6,192	5,782	6,183	1,493	3,861	12	9	140	342
Thailand	28,094	52,266	19,771	36,252	12,460	13,483	2,530	459	7,311	22,769	1	..
Togo	1,281	1,708	1,081	1,469	1,081	1,469	398	..	0	..	87	14
Trinidad and Tobago	2,511	2,652	2,055	1,310	1,782	1,197	41	..	273	113	329	..
Tunisia	7,688	17,789	6,878	14,723	6,660	12,982	1,406	1,594	218	1,741	176	0
Turkey	49,424	171,059	39,924	118,195	38,870	62,580	6,429	5,901	1,054	55,614	0	14,646
Turkmenistan	..	1,092	..	945	..	912	..	..	..	33	..	..
Uganda	2,584	4,463	2,162	4,250	2,162	4,250	969	..	0	..	282	131
Ukraine	..	33,297	..	20,047	..	10,458	..	..	..	9,588	..	1,188
United Arab Emirates	..	..	..	..	..	..	..	..	..	..	..	..
United Kingdom	..	..	..	..	..	..	..	..	..	..	..	..
United States	..	..	..	..	..	..	..	..	..	..	..	..
Uruguay	4,415	14,551	3,114	8,286	3,045	7,866	359	..	69	421	101	2,304
Uzbekistan	..	4,226	..	4,189	..	3,639	..	310	..	551	..	0
Venezuela, RB	33,171	44,201	28,159	33,984	24,509	29,317	974	..	3,650	4,667	3,012	..
Vietnam	23,270	19,287	21,378	16,513	21,378	16,513	59	..	0	..	112	203
West Bank and Gaza	..	..	..	..	..	..	..	..	..	..	..	..
Yemen, Rep.	6,352	5,363	5,160	4,717	5,160	4,717	602	..	0	..	0	292
Zambia	6,905	5,668	4,543	4,887	4,541	4,085	813	2,488	2	802	949	591
Zimbabwe	3,279	4,257	2,681	3,253	2,496	3,222	449	915	185	32	7	111
World	.. s	.. s	.. s	.. s	.. s	.. s	.. s	.. s	.. s	.. s	.. s	.. s
Low income	309,885	379,239	266,712	338,595	259,250	298,209	55,118	105,286	7,462	40,385	10,671	8,322
Middle income	1,020,176	2,363,139	827,982	1,808,585	775,449	1,063,425	82,201	116,307	52,533	745,160	23,981	40,857
Lower middle income	575,126	1,146,475	474,426	834,842	441,124	548,961	54,704	80,600	33,302	285,881	8,452	14,021
Upper middle income	445,050	1,216,664	353,557	973,742	334,325	514,464	27,497	35,708	19,232	459,278	15,529	26,836
Low & middle income	1,330,061	2,742,378	1,094,694	2,147,179	1,034,699	1,361,634	137,319	221,593	59,996	785,545	34,652	49,179
East Asia & Pacific	234,079	621,223	194,620	400,185	172,984	256,316	25,306	39,829	21,635	143,869	2,085	8,545
Europe & Central Asia	210,841	834,484	172,395	646,633	167,474	266,975	10,429	30,447	4,921	379,658	1,305	18,810
Latin America & Carib.	444,637	727,628	352,724	621,868	327,705	419,555	35,877	40,379	25,018	202,313	18,298	13,122
Middle East & N. Africa	139,541	152,724	118,031	124,308	116,613	113,334	10,074	10,102	1,418	10,974	1,815	547
South Asia	124,396	191,479	107,527	177,441	105,800	141,681	30,717	50,329	1,727	35,760	4,537	2,208
Sub-Saharan Africa	176,568	214,841	149,398	176,743	144,122	163,773	24,916	50,507	5,276	12,970	6,612	5,947
High income												
Europe EMU												

About the data

Data on the external debt of developing countries are gathered by the World Bank through its Debtor Reporting System. World Bank staff calculate the indebtedness of these countries using loan-by-loan reports submitted by them on long-term public and publicly guaranteed borrowing, along with information on short-term debt collected by the countries or collected from creditors through the reporting systems of the Bank for International Settlements and the Organisation for Economic Co-operation and Development. These data are supplemented by information on loans and credits from major multilateral banks, loan statements from official lending agencies in major creditor countries, and estimates by World Bank and International Monetary Fund (IMF) staff. In addition, the table includes data on private nonguaranteed debt for 77 countries either reported to the World Bank or estimated by its staff.

The coverage, quality, and timeliness of debt data vary across countries. Coverage varies for both debt instruments and borrowers. With the widening spectrum of debt instruments and investors and the expansion of private nonguaranteed borrowing, comprehensive coverage of long-term external debt becomes more complex. Reporting countries differ in their capacity to monitor debt, especially private nonguaranteed debt. Even data on public and publicly guaranteed debt are affected by coverage and accuracy in reporting—again because of monitoring capacity and sometimes because of an unwillingness to provide information. A key part often underreported is military debt.

Because debt data are normally reported in the currency of repayment, they have to be converted into U.S. dollars to produce summary tables. Stock figures (amount of debt outstanding) are converted using end-of-period exchange rates, as published in the IMF's *International Financial Statistics* (line ae). Flow figures are converted at annual average exchange rates (line rf). Projected debt service is converted using end-of-period exchange rates. Debt repayable in multiple currencies, goods, or services and debt with a provision for maintenance of the value of the currency of repayment are shown at book value.

Because flow data are converted at annual average exchange rates and stock data at end-of-period exchange rates, year-to-year changes in debt outstanding and disbursed are sometimes not equal to net flows (disbursements less principal repayments); similarly, changes in debt outstanding, including undisbursed debt, differ from commitments less repayments. Discrepancies are particularly significant when exchange rates have moved sharply during the year. Cancellations and reschedulings of other liabilities into long-term public debt also contribute to the differences.

Variations in reporting rescheduled debt also affect cross-country comparability. For example, rescheduling under the auspices of the Paris Club of official creditors may be subject to lags between the completion of the general rescheduling agreement and the completion of the specific bilateral agreements that define the terms of the rescheduled debt. Other areas of inconsistency include country treatment of arrears and of nonresident national deposits denominated in foreign currency.

External debt started to decline in the Sub-Saharan African economies in 2005 **4.16a**

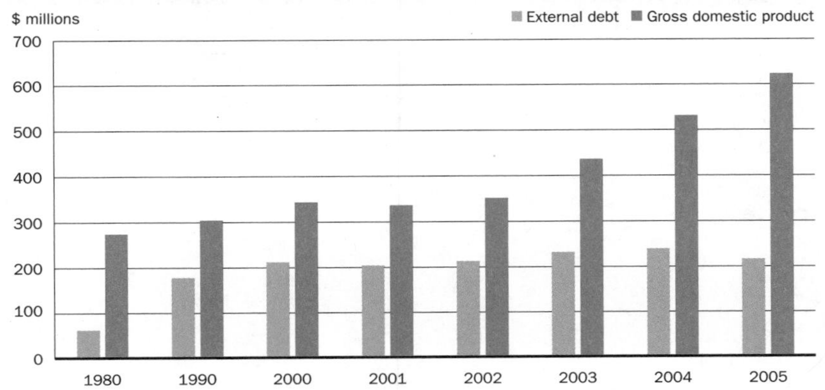

Because GDP has risen, the ratio of external debt to gross domestic product has declined for the last five years.

Source: World Bank data files.

Definitions

• **Total external debt** is debt owed to nonresidents repayable in foreign currency, goods, or services. It is the sum of public, publicly guaranteed, and private nonguaranteed long-term debt, use of IMF credit, and short-term debt. Short-term debt includes all debt having an original maturity of one year or less and interest in arrears on long-term debt. • **Long-term debt** is debt that has an original or extended maturity of more than one year. It has three components: public, publicly guaranteed, and private nonguaranteed debt. • **Public and publicly guaranteed debt** comprises the long-term external obligations of public debtors, including the national government and political subdivisions (or an agency of either) and autonomous public bodies, and the external obligations of private debtors that are guaranteed for repayment by a public entity. • **IBRD loans and IDA credits** are extended by the World Bank. The International Bank for Reconstruction and Development (IBRD) lends at market rates. The International Development Association (IDA) provides credits at concessional rates. • **Private nonguaranteed external debt** consists of the long-term external obligations of private debtors that are not guaranteed for repayment by a public entity. • **Use of IMF credit** denotes repurchase obligations to the IMF for all uses of IMF resources (excluding those resulting from drawings on the reserve tranche). These obligations, shown for the end of the year specified, comprise purchases outstanding under the credit tranches (including enlarged access resources) and all special facilities (the buffer stock, compensatory financing, extended fund, and oil facilities), trust fund loans, and operations under the structural adjustment and enhanced structural adjustment facilities.

Data sources

The main sources of external debt information are reports to the World Bank through its Debtor Reporting System from member countries that have received IBRD loans or IDA credits. Additional information is from the files of the World Bank and the IMF. Summary tables of the external debt of developing countries are published annually in the World Bank's *Global Development Finance* and on its *Global Development Finance* CD-ROM.

4.17 Debt ratios

	Present value of debt		Total debt service				Multilateral debt service		Short-term debt			
	% of GNI	% of exports of goods, sevices, and income[a]	% of GNI		% of exports of goods, sevices, and income[a]		% of public and publicly guaranteed debt		% of total debt		% of exports of goods, sevices, and income	
	2005[b]	2005[b]	1990	2005	1990	2005	1990	2005	1990	2005	1990	2005
Afghanistan	..	..	..	..	..	..	..	..	..	..	..	..
Albania	19	51	..	1.0	..	2.5	..	50.4	..	15.7	..	9.0
Algeria	21	45	14.7	6.1	63.4	..	5.0	26.6	2.8	3.1	5.7	..
Angola	59	72	4.0	7.8	8.1	9.2	2.2	0.6	11.5	19.8	24.7	9.6
Argentina	73	245	4.6	6.0	37.0	20.8	16.2	68.3	16.8	16.9	62.9	38.1
Armenia	36	100	..	2.8	..	7.9	..	87.0	..	16.0	..	17.0
Australia	..	..	..	..	..	..	..	..	..	..	..	..
Austria	..	..	..	..	..	..	..	..	..	..	..	..
Azerbaijan	18	27	..	2.2	..	2.6	..	37.0	..	9.9	..	2.1
Bangladesh	22	102	2.4	1.3	25.8	5.4	22.8	56.2	1.3	3.6	5.4	4.7
Belarus	20	31	..	2.3	..	3.7	..	21.8	..	74.0	..	19.1
Belgium	..	..	..	..	..	..	..	..	..	..	..	..
Benin	23[c]	112[c]	2.1	1.6	8.2	..	95.7	58.8	4.3	2.1	11.9	..
Bolivia	38[c]	112[c]	8.3	5.9	38.6	14.8	67.6	92.8	3.6	2.8	15.5	5.1
Bosnia and Herzegovina	52	102	..	2.6	..	4.9	..	73.6	..	19.8	..	19.9
Botswana	5	8	2.9	0.5	4.4	0.9	61.3	67.9	1.0	7.4	0.2	0.6
Brazil	34	183	1.8	8.1	22.2	44.8	43.5	15.9	19.8	12.8	64.4	17.1
Bulgaria	68	105	..	21.5	..	31.5	..	13.8	..	25.1	..	22.7
Burkina Faso	22[c]	196[c]	1.1	0.9	6.8	..	73.1	77.0	10.1	1.0	16.6	..
Burundi	110[c]	1,072[c]	3.8	5.0	43.4	41.4	51.1	87.1	1.5	2.7	13.7	37.4
Cambodia	58	84	2.7	0.5	..	0.7	..	74.6	7.4	8.0	..	6.6
Cameroon	14[c]	61[c]	4.8	4.9	20.4	..	43.9	21.8	14.6	10.7	36.9	..
Canada	..	..	..	..	..	..	..	..	..	..	..	..
Central African Republic	67[c]	715[c]	2.0	0.4	13.2	..	50.3	99.8	5.4	10.7	17.1	..
Chad	31[c]	51[c]	0.7	1.4	4.4	..	73.1	74.5	5.6	1.0	10.9	..
Chile	52	114	9.3	7.3	25.9	15.4	35.7	20.1	17.6	15.2	31.6	13.8
China	14	40	2.0	1.2	11.7	3.1	7.6	21.4	16.9	52.7	15.4	16.8
Hong Kong, China	..	..	..	..	..	..	..	..	..	..	..	..
Colombia	43	171	10.2	8.7	40.9	35.3	32.2	39.5	8.4	16.4	15.1	21.5
Congo, Dem. Rep.	123[c]	383[c]	4.1	3.1	..	..	49.7	30.6	7.3	3.8	..	..
Congo, Rep.	124[c]	106[c]	22.9	3.0	35.4	2.4	12.7	73.4	14.9	12.6	49.0	15.0
Costa Rica	36	69	7.0	3.1	23.9	5.9	36.1	67.7	10.1	33.8	18.0	20.3
Côte d'Ivoire	69[c]	131[c]	13.7	3.0	35.4	5.5	77.5	12.3	20.9	6.4	101.0	8.1
Croatia	89	159	..	13.2	..	24.0	..	9.8	..	14.3	..	21.0
Cuba	..	..	..	..	..	..	..	..	..	..	..	..
Czech Republic	..	..	..	..	..	..	..	..	..	..	..	..
Denmark	..	..	..	..	..	..	..	..	..	..	..	..
Dominican Republic	37	61	3.4	3.2	10.4	6.9	50.3	23.1	17.9	12.2	35.0	7.0
Ecuador	60	166	11.9	12.0	32.5	30.6	34.8	36.5	15.0	10.0	54.4	12.7
Egypt, Arab Rep.	36	99	7.3	2.9	20.4	6.8	18.7	23.8	13.5	17.5	29.6	16.1
El Salvador	48	105	4.4	4.0	15.3	8.6	60.2	49.7	9.8	22.2	15.5	20.8
Eritrea	57[c]	213[c]	..	2.1	..	..	..	61.6	..	1.7	..	..
Estonia	102	115	..	12.8	..	13.7	..	14.6	..	35.5	..	34.4
Ethiopia	21[c]	111[c]	2.0	0.8	39.0	4.1	14.5	53.6	1.7	3.2	24.0	9.4
Finland	..	..	..	..	..	..	..	..	..	..	..	..
France	..	..	..	..	..	..	..	..	..	..	..	..
Gabon	63	92	3.3	1.5	6.4	..	32.6	77.5	17.4	6.5	25.2	..
Gambia, The	99[c]	162[c]	13.0	6.5	22.2	12.1	25.3	62.0	4.3	3.7	9.3	10.2
Georgia	28	72	..	2.9	..	7.4	..	20.1	..	2.7	..	2.1
Germany	..	..	..	..	..	..	..	..	..	..	..	..
Ghana	26[c]	64[c]	6.3	2.7	38.1	7.1	31.2	36.5	8.6	8.7	33.5	14.6
Greece	..	..	..	..	..	..	..	..	..	..	..	..
Guatemala	20	77	3.1	1.5	13.6	5.8	33.4	57.6	14.5	29.1	24.4	19.0
Guinea	35[c]	146[c]	6.3	5.0	20.1	..	22.1	50.2	6.9	7.1	20.4	..
Guinea-Bissau	290[c]	660[c]	3.6	11.3	31.1	..	70.4	12.2	8.2	1.4	208.3	..
Haiti	24[c]	63[c]	1.3	1.4	11.1	3.7	70.5	81.3	11.0	1.9	31.0	1.6

Debt ratios

	Present value of debt		Total debt service				Multilateral debt service		Short-term debt			
	% of GNI	% of exports of goods, sevices, and income[a]	% of GNI		% of exports of goods, sevices, and income[a]		% of public and publicly guaranteed debt		% of total debt		% of exports of goods, sevices, and income	
	2005[b]	2005[b]	1990	2005	1990	2005	1990	2005	1990	2005	1990	2005
Honduras	37[c]	60[c]	13.9	4.8	35.3	7.2	90.8	86.0	5.4	7.9	18.1	7.8
Hungary	69	96	13.4	22.9	34.3	31.0	8.0	6.8	13.9	18.8	23.9	16.3
India	16	73	2.6	3.0	31.9	..	22.5	9.1	10.2	7.1	33.3	..
Indonesia	55	159	9.1	6.5	33.3	..	22.5	39.2	15.9	17.7	37.3	23.7
Iran, Islamic Rep.	13	39	0.6	1.4	3.2	..	30.5	9.1	80.1	50.3	35.8	..
Iraq	..	..	..	..	..	..	..	..	..	..	..	..
Ireland	..	..	..	..	..	..	..	..	..	..	..	..
Israel	..	..	..	..	..	..	..	..	..	..	..	..
Italy	..	..	..	..	..	..	..	..	..	..	..	..
Jamaica	93	141	15.9	10.8	26.9	16.3	38.6	20.1	7.3	9.4	14.1	10.3
Japan	..	..	..	..	..	..	..	..	..	..	..	..
Jordan	65	89	16.5	4.7	20.4	6.5	26.8	49.0	12.4	7.6	33.7	6.1
Kazakhstan	106	185	..	25.5	..	42.1	..	80.4	..	18.5	..	25.6
Kenya	28	103	9.6	1.3	35.4	4.4	44.7	60.7	13.2	8.0	41.8	9.1
Korea, Dem. Rep.	..	..	..	..	..	..	..	..	..	..	..	..
Korea, Rep.	..	..	..	..	..	..	..	..	..	..	..	..
Kuwait	..	..	..	..	..	..	..	..	..	..	..	..
Kyrgyz Republic	54[c]	106[c]	..	5.4	..	10.0	..	97.7	..	1.2	..	1.9
Lao PDR	63[c]	200[c]	1.1	6.6	8.7	..	54.3	72.2	0.1	0.2	2.1	..
Latvia	104	211	..	19.8	..	37.4	..	59.1	..	52.5	..	90.3
Lebanon	114	127	2.9	16.5	..	17.7	27.8	3.1	79.9	15.4	..	17.3
Lesotho	32	50	2.3	3.1	4.2	5.0	44.5	46.5	0.7	1.2	0.5	0.7
Liberia	1,087[c]	3,514[c]	..	0.2	..	..	99.8	100.0	22.2	44.4	..	..
Libya	..	..	..	..	..	..	..	..	..	..	..	..
Lithuania	52	90	..	10.3	..	16.5	..	19.4	..	47.5	..	34.1
Macedonia, FYR	40	89	..	4.2	..	8.6	..	41.7	..	4.3	..	3.5
Madagascar	37[c]	323[c]	7.5	1.6	45.5	17.0	23.7	66.4	6.1	2.2	46.0	16.4
Malawi	58[c]	162[c]	7.2	4.7	29.3	..	38.3	63.4	3.8	1.3	12.9	..
Malaysia	46	35	10.3	7.6	12.6	5.6	9.9	3.4	12.4	23.9	5.5	7.3
Mali	30[c]	100[c]	2.8	1.7	12.4	..	54.3	77.8	2.5	0.6	11.3	..
Mauritania	117[c]	289[c]	13.5	3.5	29.8	..	73.7	63.6	11.2	7.4	48.7	..
Mauritius	37	60	6.6	4.5	8.8	7.2	51.6	18.4	5.3	63.1	2.9	34.9
Mexico	26	79	4.5	5.8	20.7	17.2	26.0	12.8	15.4	3.9	29.5	2.6
Moldova	70	97	..	7.7	..	10.2	..	70.2	..	35.0	..	29.1
Mongolia	63	73	..	2.5	..	..	..	38.2	..	1.9	..	..
Morocco	34	77	7.2	5.3	21.6	11.3	39.8	38.8	1.6	4.1	4.9	2.8
Mozambique	28[c]	85[c]	3.4	1.5	26.2	4.3	30.6	63.0	7.4	10.6	115.2	24.9
Myanmar	..	148	..	..	18.4	..	43.6	2.7	4.9	21.8	69.8	..
Namibia	..	..	..	..	..	..	..	..	..	..	..	..
Nepal	34[c]	104[c]	1.9	1.6	15.7	4.6	36.9	75.5	1.5	1.4	5.4	1.8
Netherlands	..	..	..	..	..	..	..	..	..	..	..	..
New Zealand	..	..	..	..	..	..	..	..	..	..	..	..
Nicaragua	46[c]	94[c]	1.6	3.6	3.9	6.9	21.4	45.0	22.6	10.5	602.0	21.7
Niger	25[c]	142[c]	4.1	1.1	17.4	..	70.9	98.2	8.9	2.1	27.1	..
Nigeria	34	53	13.0	10.2	22.6	15.8	15.5	5.5	4.5	8.3	10.2	3.3
Norway	..	..	..	..	..	..	..	..	..	..	..	..
Oman	14	22	..	..	..	7.5	..	45.9	..	48.0	..	8.4
Pakistan	30	134	4.6	2.3	21.3	10.2	40.3	58.5	15.4	3.7	35.6	5.1
Panama	90	118	6.8	14.5	6.2	17.5	90.6	10.6	36.6	5.0	42.5	4.1
Papua New Guinea	55	60	17.9	..	37.2	10.8	23.0	46.3	2.8	10.6	4.8	5.4
Paraguay	54	84	6.0	6.7	12.4	11.4	35.9	49.6	17.7	16.4	14.2	12.0
Peru	49	198	1.9	7.5	10.8	26.0	28.8	21.6	26.6	11.2	121.1	14.9
Philippines	67	120	8.2	9.2	27.0	16.7	28.7	15.9	14.5	10.4	33.3	10.8
Poland	39	98	1.7	11.6	4.9	28.8	9.2	2.6	19.4	17.9	48.9	15.0
Portugal	..	..	..	..	..	..	..	..	..	..	..	..
Puerto Rico	..	..	..	..	..	..	..	..	..	..	..	..

4.17 Debt ratios

	Present value of debt		Total debt service				Multilateral debt service		Short-term debt			
	% of GNI	% of exports of goods, sevices, and income[a]	% of GNI		% of exports of goods, sevices, and income[a]		% of public and publicly guaranteed debt		% of total debt		% of exports of goods, sevices, and income	
	2005[b]	**2005[b]**	**1990**	**2005**	**1990**	**2005**	**1990**	**2005**	**1990**	**2005**	**1990**	**2005**
Romania	51	137	0.1	7.1	0.3	18.3	..	24.6	79.8	18.7	13.9	19.0
Russian Federation	40	104	..	5.6	..	14.6	..	3.6	..	10.5	..	8.4
Rwanda	18[c]	154[c]	0.8	1.1	14.2	8.1	60.6	77.5	6.6	1.4	31.9	7.4
Saudi Arabia	..	..	..	..	..	..	..	..	..	..	..	..
Senegal	34[c]	89[c]	5.9	2.4	19.9	..	40.0	60.2	11.3	0.9	25.9	..
Serbia and Montenegro	69	202	..	4.9	..	..	..	60.2	..	13.8	..	..
Sierra Leone	40[c]	178[c]	3.7	2.2	10.1	9.2	26.0	37.5	12.4	4.1	70.5	25.6
Singapore	..	..	..	..	..	..	..	..	..	..	..	..
Slovak Republic	61	73	..	13.2	..	..	..	11.6	..	64.1	..	..
Slovenia	..	..	..	..	..	..	..	..	..	..	..	..
Somalia	..	1,137	1.3	..	..	..	100.0	..	12.0	25.8	..	..
South Africa	14	47	..	2.0	..	6.9	..	3.7	..	31.7	..	13.7
Spain	..	..	..	..	..	..	..	..	..	..	..	..
Sri Lanka	48	109	4.9	1.9	13.8	4.5	13.8	45.6	6.9	8.8	14.5	10.2
Sudan	88[c]	358[c]	0.4	1.5	8.7	6.5	100.0	15.0	28.2	34.0	724.8	104.7
Swaziland	24	26	4.9	1.6	5.7	1.9	73.0	57.7	1.5	15.3	0.6	3.6
Sweden	..	..	..	..	..	..	..	..	..	..	..	..
Switzerland	..	..	..	..	..	..	..	..	..	..	..	..
Syrian Arab Republic	27	69	10.0	0.8	21.8	1.9	3.5	31.2	12.5	13.3	39.4	7.9
Tajikistan	41	53	..	3.5	..	4.5	..	37.1	..	8.2	..	4.9
Tanzania	22[c, d]	95[c, d]	4.4[d]	1.1[d]	32.9[d]	4.3[d]	52.7	97.0	8.1	15.8	95.5[d]	41.3[d]
Thailand	32	44	6.3	11.3	16.9	14.6	22.1	18.5	29.6	30.6	26.6	12.0
Togo	74[c]	162[c]	5.4	0.8	11.9	..	40.8	72.6	8.8	13.2	15.6	..
Trinidad and Tobago	24	36	9.6	2.8	19.3	..	4.7	35.3	5.1	50.6	5.5	..
Tunisia	69	125	12.1	7.7	24.5	13.0	26.0	45.8	8.3	17.2	10.8	19.2
Turkey	59	195	4.9	11.6	29.4	39.1	23.3	10.6	19.2	22.3	37.7	35.6
Turkmenistan	16	23	..	4.1	..	..	..	3.2	..	13.5	..	..
Uganda	29[c]	137[c]	3.4	2.0	81.4	9.2	37.4	49.7	5.4	1.8	78.8	4.4
Ukraine	53	89	..	7.2	..	13.0	..	21.3	..	36.2	..	26.6
United Arab Emirates	..	..	..	..	..	..	..	..	..	..	..	..
United Kingdom	..	..	..	..	..	..	..	..	..	..	..	..
United States	..	..	..	..	..	..	..	..	..	..	..	..
Uruguay	116	332	11.0	13.7	40.8	38.9	16.2	32.2	27.2	27.2	49.7	69.1
Uzbekistan	34	88	..	5.7	..	..	..	15.8	..	0.9	..	..
Venezuela, RB	48	118	10.8	4.0	23.3	9.1	1.6	16.0	6.0	23.1	9.3	16.7
Vietnam	38	56	2.9	1.9	..	2.6	3.4	10.7	7.7	13.3	..	7.0
West Bank and Gaza	..	..	..	..	..	..	..	..	..	..	..	..
Yemen, Rep.	32	56	3.5	1.6	5.6	2.6	50.9	57.4	18.8	6.6	39.4	4.3
Zambia	29[c]	80[c]	6.7	3.5	14.7	..	41.0	40.6	20.5	3.4	103.8	..
Zimbabwe	85	228	5.5	7.0	23.2	..	24.0	30.9	18.0	21.0	29.0	..
World			.. w	.. w	.. w	.. w	.. w	.. w	.. w	.. w	.. w	.. w
Low income			3.8	3.2	23.9	..	27.8	15.7	10.5	8.5	37.2	9.3
Middle income			4.7	5.8	19.6	14.2	18.3	17.6	16.5	21.8	29.8	15.5
Lower middle income			4.2	4.4	21.6	11.3	22.3	26.1	16.0	26.1	31.4	16.5
Upper middle income			..	7.5	17.5	17.8	13.7	11.2	17.1	17.8	27.7	14.3
Low & middle income			4.5	5.4	20.1	13.8	19.5	17.3	15.1	20.0	30.8	15.1
East Asia & Pacific			4.8	2.9	17.6	6.1	17.7	20.7	16.0	34.2	20.5	15.2
Europe & Central Asia			..	9.4	..	22.0	10.2	9.4	17.6	20.3	36.0	18.3
Latin America & Carib.			4.2	6.8	23.8	22.5	27.6	22.9	16.6	12.8	39.7	12.9
Middle East & N. Africa			6.4	3.9	20.6	8.9	13.1	25.2	14.1	19.2	23.9	11.4
South Asia			2.9	2.8	27.6	..	25.3	16.0	9.9	6.2	30.1	5.9
Sub-Saharan Africa			..	3.7	13.6	8.8	30.0	13.2	11.6	15.0	..	13.0
High income												
Europe EMU												

a. Includes workers' remittances. b. The numerator refers to 2005, whereas the denominator is a three-year average of 2003–05 data. c. Data are from debt sustainability analyses undertaken as part of the Heavily Indebted Poor Countries (HIPC) Initiative. Present value estimates for these countries are for public and publicly guaranteed debt only. d. GNP and export data refer to mainland Tanzania only.

About the data

The indicators in the table measure the relative burden on developing countries of servicing external debt. The present value of external debt provides a measure of future debt service obligations that can be compared with the current value of such indicators as gross national income (GNI) and exports of goods and services. The table shows the present value of total debt service both as a percentage of GNI in 2005 and as a percentage of exports in 2005. The ratios compare total debt service obligations with the size of the economy and its ability to obtain foreign exchange through exports. The ratios shown here may differ from those published elsewhere because estimates of exports and GNI have been revised to incorporate data available as of February 1, 2007. Exports refer to exports of goods, services, income, and workers' remittances.

The present value of external debt is calculated by discounting the debt service (interest plus amortization) due on long-term external debt over the life of existing loans. Short-term debt is included at its face value. The data on debt are in U.S. dollars converted at official exchange rates (see *About the data* for table 4.16). The discount rate applied to long-term debt is determined by the currency of repayment of the loan and is based on reference rates for commercial interest established by the Organisation for Economic Co-operation and Development. Loans from the International Bank for Reconstruction and Development (IBRD) and credits from the International Development Association (IDA) are discounted using a special drawing rights reference rate, as are obligations to the International Monetary Fund (IMF). When the discount rate is greater than the interest rate of the loan, the present value is less than the nominal sum of future debt service obligations.

The ratios in the table are used to assess the sustainability of a country's debt service obligations, but there are no absolute rules to determine what values are too high. Empirical analysis of the experience of developing countries and their debt service performance has shown that debt service difficulties become increasingly likely when the ratio of the present value of debt to exports reaches 200 percent. Still, what constitutes a sustainable debt burden varies from one country to another. Countries with fast-growing economies and exports are likely to be able to sustain higher debt levels.

The most indebted low-income countries may be eligible for debt relief under special programs, such as the Heavily Indebted Poor Countries Debt Initiative and Multilateral Debt Relief Initiative. Indebted countries may also apply to the Paris and London Clubs for renegotiation of obligations to public and private creditors. The World Bank no longer classifies countries by their level of indebtedness for the purposes of developing debt management strategies.

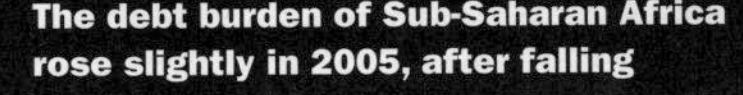

The debt burden of Sub-Saharan Africa rose slightly in 2005, after falling 4.17a

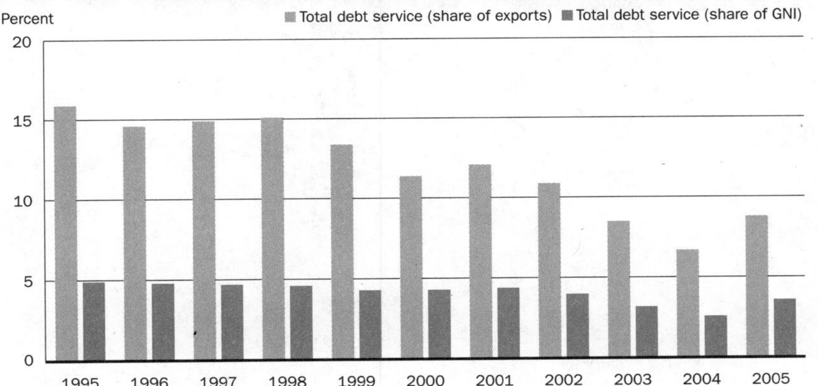

The debt burden of Sub-Saharan economies rose slightly in 2005 after falling to less than half its 1995 level.

a. Includes goods, services, income, and workers' remittances.
Source: World Bank data files.

Definitions

• **Present value of debt** is the sum of short-term external debt plus the discounted sum of total debt service payments due on public, publicly guaranteed, and private nonguaranteed long-term external debt over the life of existing loans. • **Exports of goods, services, and income** refer to international transactions involving a change in ownership of general merchandise, goods sent for processing and repairs, nonmonetary gold, services, receipts of employee compensation for nonresident workers, investment income, and workers' remittances. • **Total debt service** is the sum of principal repayments and interest actually paid on total long-term debt (public and publicly guaranteed and private nonguaranteed), use of IMF credit, and interest on short-term debt. • **Multilateral debt service** is the repayment of principal and interest to the World Bank, regional development banks, and other multilateral and intergovernmental agencies. • **Short-term debt** includes all debt having an original maturity of one year or less and interest in arrears on long-term debt.

Data sources

The main sources of external debt information are reports to the World Bank through its Debtor Reporting System from member countries that have received IBRD loans or IDA credits. Additional information is from the files of the World Bank and the IMF. Data on GNI and exports of goods and services are from the World Bank's national accounts files and the IMF's Balance of Payments database. Summary tables of the external debt of developing countries are published annually in the World Bank's *Global Development Finance* and on its *Global Development Finance* CD-ROM.

5 STATES & MARKETS

Country policies and governance matter for development

Governance matters for economic development. Capable governments and high-quality institutions promote growth, raise incomes, and reduce poverty. Governance indicators are tools for assessing the performance of governments and the strengths and weaknesses of public institutions. Donors and governments use them to identify weaknesses and improve the management of development programs. And by providing feedback to policymakers and citizens, governance indicators can help to improve the quality of governance over time. This section—on states and markets—includes a broad range of indicators showing how effective and accountable government, together with energetic private initiative, help to create opportunities for growth and development.

The World Bank defines governance as the way public officials and public institutions acquire and exercise authority to provide public goods and services, including basic services, infrastructure, and a sound investment climate. Measuring governance and measuring corruption are not the same thing. While governance encompasses all of the state institutions and arrangements that shape the relations between the state and society, corruption is one aspect of poor governance—an outcome and a consequence of the failure of public accountability. Measuring the quality of policies, institutions, and governance—and corruption—is difficult and often subject to margins of error, whether based on objective or subjective information.

The World Bank has used assessments of government performance in allocating concessional resources since the mid-1970s. Focusing at first on macroeconomic management, the assessment criteria have expanded to include trade and financial policies, business regulation, social sector policies, the effectiveness of the public sector, and transparency, accountability, and corruption. Now called the Country Performance and Institutional Assessment (CPIA), the criteria are assessed annually for all World Bank borrowers.

This edition of *World Development Indicators* includes a new indicator table—Table 5.8, Public policies and institutions—showing the most recent CPIA data for 76 countries eligible to receive grants or credits from the International Development Association (IDA), the World Bank's concessional lending arm. Indicator tables 5.2 and 5.3 continue to report on government policies and regulations affecting the investment climate. Improved infrastructure such as roads, ports, and rails (indicator table 5.9), power and telecommunications (indicator tables 5.10 and 5.11), and water supply and sanitation (indicator table 2.15) are crucial for citizens' health, economic growth, and competitiveness. And effective, accountable governments are needed to complement an energetic private sector to deliver these services.

Governance and growth

The first major World Bank discussion of the role of governance was the 1991 World Bank Discussion Paper *Managing Development: The Governance Dimension* (World Bank 1991). A few years later *World Development Report 1997: The State in a Changing World* (World Bank 1997d) argued that a determining factor in development was the effectiveness of the state. The report noted that "an effective state is vital for the provision of the goods and services—and the rules and institutions—that allow markets to flourish and people to lead healthier, happier lives. . . ." The 1997 report presented systematic assessments of the reliability of governmental institutions (predictability of rulemaking, perceptions of political stability, crime against persons and property, and reliability of judicial enforcement) and of corruption from a 1996 World Bank–sponsored survey. Subsequent research suggests that the causality between growth and governance is two-way—that improvements in either income or governance can give momentum to development—but that causation is stronger from governance to growth in income.

Although the links are complex, there is ample evidence of the connection between governance and long-term growth. Figure 5a shows the statistical relationship (controlling for initial income and schooling levels) between the quality of governance measured by an International Country Risk Guide (ICRG) index in 1982 and the growth of per capita income through 2002. The ICRG index comprises five elements of governance: corruption in government, rule of law, risk of expropriation, repudiation of contracts by government, and quality of the bureaucracy in 71 developing countries.

Governance and growth go together **5a**

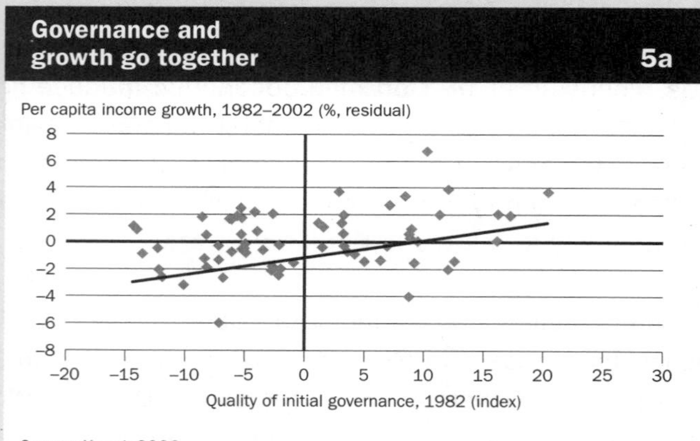

Source: Knack 2006.

Country Policy and Institutional Assessment

The CPIA indicators measure the extent to which a country's policy and institutional framework supports sustainable growth and poverty reduction and, consequently, the effective use of development assistance. Country performance is assessed against 16 criteria grouped in four clusters: economic management, structural policies, policies for social inclusion and equity, and public sector management and institutions (box 5b).

The overall score for each country, known as the IDA Resource Allocation Index (IRAI), is a key element of a country's IDA country performance rating. IDA resources are allocated in per capita terms on the basis of the country performance rating and, to a limited extent, per capita gross national income. This ensures that good performers receive a higher IDA allocation, in per capita terms. The individual CPIA criteria are also used to inform the World Bank's country policy dialogue with member governments and for other operational and research purposes. Reflecting the IDA14 funding agreement, the numerical IRAI scores and separate CPIA criteria were first publicly disclosed for IDA recipient countries in June 2006 to enhance transparency and external scrutiny of these scores (see indicator table 5.8 and figure 5c).

The scores depend on actual policies and performance, rather than on promises or intentions. In some cases the passage of specific legislation can represent an important action that deserves consideration. But it is implementation of legislation that determines its impact. The average

Criteria for measuring economic and sector policies and governance system **Box 5b**

Cluster A: Economic management
Macroeconomic management
Fiscal policy
Debt policy

Cluster B: Structural policies
Trade
Financial sector
Business regulatory environment

Cluster C: Policies for social inclusion and equity
Gender equality
Equity of public resource use
Building human resources
Social protection and labor
Policies and institutions for environmental sustainability

Cluster D: Public sector management and institutions
Property rights and rule-based governance
Quality of budgetary and financial management
Efficiency of revenue mobilization
Quality of public administration
Transparency, accountability, and corruption in the public sector

The IDA Resource Allocation Index is a key element of a country's IDA performance rating 5c

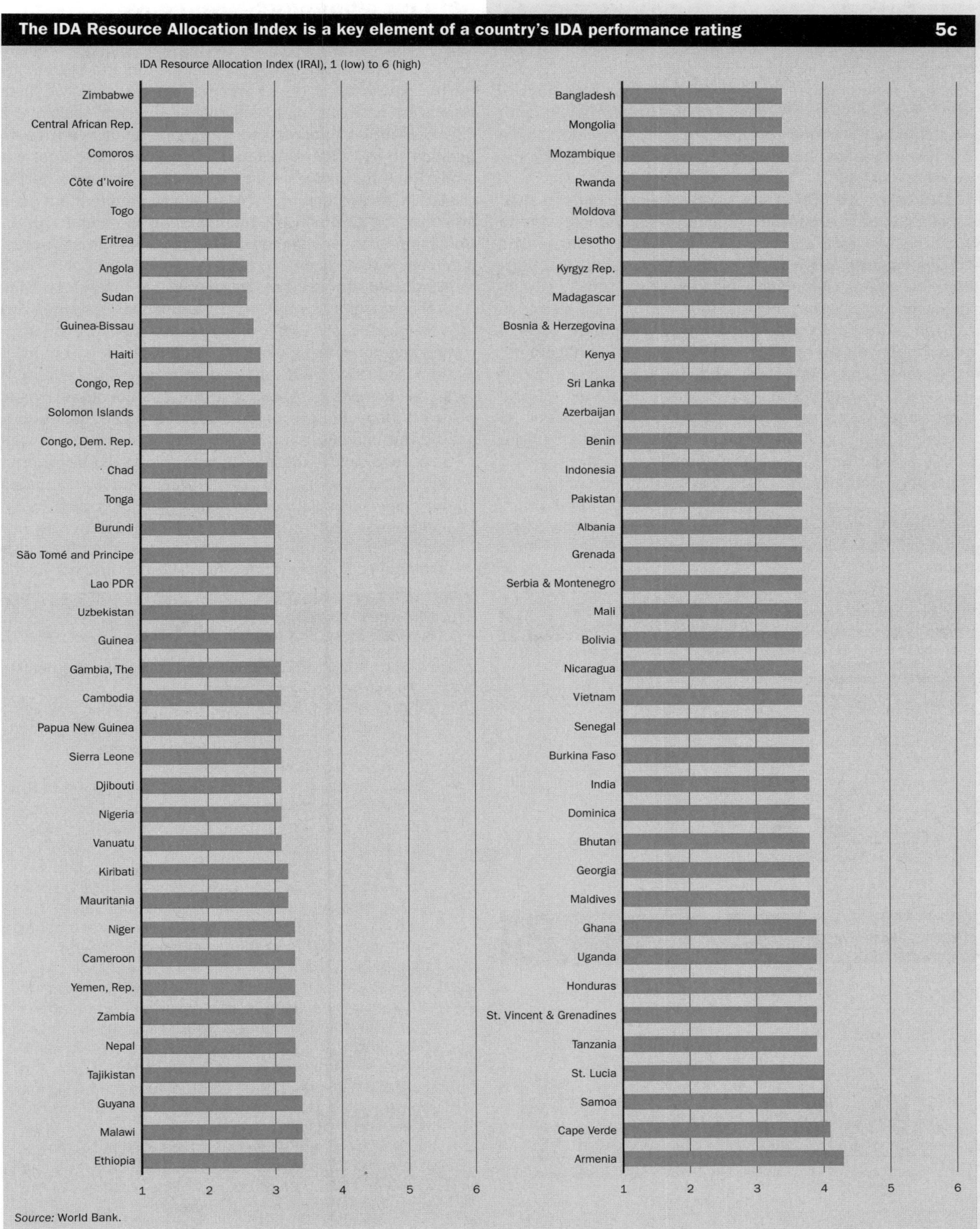

Source: World Bank.

score on public sector management and institutions can be used as an aggregate indicator of the country's governance system (focused primarily on economic governance). It is a part of the "governance factor" that is given extra weight in the IDA country performance rating for determining IDA resource allocations. (For more information see www.worldbank.org/ida.)

Scores on the CPIA public sector management and institutions cluster are bunched around the mid-range, with no countries scoring in either the lowest or highest ranges, and only one country in the 4.0–4.9 range (figure 5d). Although these measures give some indication of the quality of public sector management and institutions, for some countries they do not always match the strong performance on economic management policies (macroeconomic management, fiscal policy, and debt policy). Armenia, Bangladesh, Kyrgyz Republic, Tajikistan, and Uganda score relatively well on CPIA cluster A, economic management, but not so well on cluster D, public sector management and institutions (figure 5e). These patterns reveal the complexity of the relationships between measures of the quality of public sector management and institutions and economic outcomes, requiring better diagnostics and understanding of each country's situation to develop workable approaches to governance reform.

On public sector management, countries bunch around the middle 5d

Distribution of IDA recipient scores for CPIA cluster D, public sector management and institutions, 2005

Number of IDA recipient countries

30
25
20
15
10
5
0

1.0–2.0 2.0–2.4 2.5–2.9 3.0–3.4 3.5–3.9 4.0–4.9 5.0–6.0

CPIA score, 1 (low) to 6 (high)

Source: World Bank.

Strong performance on economic management, weaker on public sector management 5e

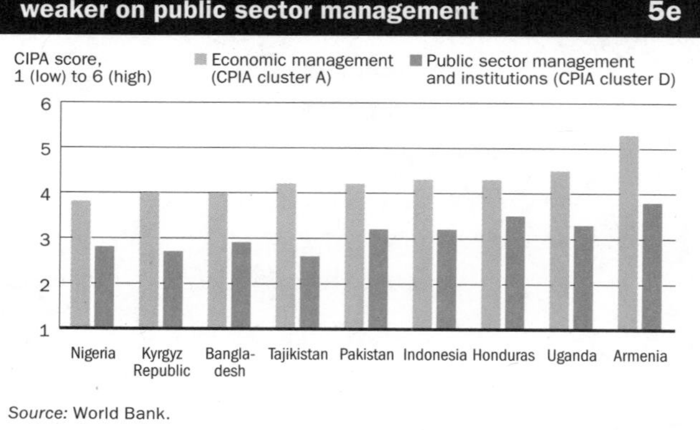

Source: World Bank.

Other World Bank sources of data for monitoring governance

The growing recognition of the link between good governance and successful development has stimulated efforts to monitor the performance of governments and other public institutions by private commercial rating agencies, multilateral development institutions, and nongovernmental agencies. In addition to the CPIA policy and governance measures, the World Bank has several other governance and governance-related measurement programs and indicators that are used in monitoring governance. (See box 5g at the end of this introduction for other selected organizations' governance measurement initiatives.)

- **Worldwide Governance Indicators** are the most comprehensive publicly available governance indicators and among the most widely used by the media, academia, and international organizations for assessing governance. Compiled since 1996, these data measure the quality of six dimensions of governance for 213 countries, based on 31 data sources produced by 25 organizations (box 5f). The underlying data are based on hundreds of variables and reflect the perceptions and views of experts, firm survey respondents, and citizens worldwide on various dimensions of governance. The measures, also known as Kaufmann-Kraay, include the margins of error associated with each estimate, allowing users to identify a range of statistically likely ratings for each country, not just a

Worldwide Governance Indicators— Six key dimensions of governance Box 5f

The Worldwide Governance Indicators measure the quality of six dimensions of governance:

- *Voice and accountability,* the extent to which a country's citizens are able to participate in selecting their government, as well as freedom of expression, freedom of association, and free media
- *Political stability and absence of violence,* perceptions of the likelihood that the government will be destabilized or overthrown by unconstitutional or violent means, including political violence and terrorism
- *Government effectiveness,* the quality of public services, the quality of the civil service and the degree of its independence from political pressures, the quality of policy formulation and implementation, and the credibility of the government's commitment to such policies
- *Regulatory quality,* the ability of the government to formulate and implement sound policies and regulations that permit and promote private sector development
- *Rule of law,* the extent to which agents have confidence in and abide by the rules of society, and in particular the quality of contract enforcement, the police, and the courts, as well as the likelihood of crime and violence
- *Control of corruption,* the extent to which public power is exercised for private gain, including both petty and grand forms of corruption, as well as "capture" of the state by elites and private interests.

single rating. Margins of error are present in all efforts to measure governance; some sources explicitly report them, while others do not. See www.govindicators.org.

- **Enterprise Surveys and the Business Environment and Enterprise Performance Surveys** capture business perceptions of the biggest obstacles to enterprise growth, the relative importance of various constraints to increasing employment and productivity, and the effects of a country's investment climate on its international competitiveness. Surveys cover almost 58,000 firms in 97 countries. Although designed to monitor the investment climate, which is a product of a number of governance-related factors, these surveys include measures, such as a business managers' perception of corruption as a constraint to doing business, that can be directly linked to governance and are therefore useful for governance monitoring at the country level. See indicator table 5.2 and www.enterprisesurveys.org and http://info.worldbank.org/governance/beeps.
- **Doing Business** surveys cover key indicators on the environment for doing business for 175 economies. The indicators identify regulations that enhance or constrain business investment, productivity, and growth. Some indicators, such as enforcing contracts, are useful in monitoring governance. See indicator table 5.3 and www.doingbusiness.org.
- **Anticorruption Diagnostic Surveys** are designed to facilitate governance monitoring by providing inputs to policymakers and civil society. The World Bank Institute's Governance Diagnostic Capacity Building program aims to strengthen the capacity of countries to conduct governance diagnostic surveys through technical assistance for the design of surveys and governance action plans, training, and partnerships between the government and civil society organizations. Agencies in several countries have undertaken governance and anticorruption diagnostic surveys. See www.worldbank.org/wbi/governance and click on Diagnostics.
- **HIPC (Highly Indebted Poor Countries) Public Expenditure Management Assessment and Action Plans** use expenditure tracking tools developed by the World Bank and the International Monetary Fund to monitor poverty-reducing public expenditures in HIPCs. Data are collected on 15 indicators on budget formulation, execution, and reporting, and 1 indicator on government procurement. A new program to measure public expenditure and management has been developed and will be used for monitoring in HIPCs. See www.worldbank.org/hipc.
- **Public Expenditure and Financial Accountability Program**, started by the World Bank in 2001, is now a partnership with several multilateral and bilateral development institutions that support an integrated and harmonized approach to assessment and reform in public expenditure, procurement, and financial accountability. The public expenditure and financial accountability framework includes 28 indicators on budget credibility, transparency, auditing, and procurement, and three indicators on donor practices that affect the country public financial management system. The program is being implemented in 70 countries; 8 countries have completed reviews and made them available publicly (in addition, one country has published data for the indicators). See www.pefa.org.
- **The Joint Venture on Procurement of the World Bank and the Organisation for Economic Co-operation and Development's Development Assistance Committee** has selected 22 pilot developing countries to test the Common Benchmarking and Assessment Tool for Public Procurement, which developing countries and donors can use to assess the quality and effectiveness of national procurement systems. See www.oecd.org and search for Joint Venture on Procurement.

For an overview of the World Bank's framework for global monitoring of governance and in-depth discussion of the uses and limitations of governance measures, see the World Bank and International Monetary Fund's (2006a) *Global Monitoring Report 2006*.

Other selected sources of data for monitoring governance — **Box 5g**

- **Freedom House,** a private nonprofit advocacy organization founded in 1941, was among the earliest to systematically measure and publish governance ratings. Freedom House has published *Freedom in the World* since 1972; it now includes ratings of political rights and civil liberties in 192 countries and territories. See www.freedomhouse.org.
- **International Country Risk Guide** is privately owned and has been assessing financial, economic, and political risks since 1980 for about 140 countries. See www.prsgroup.com.
- **Transparency International (TI),** a newer entrant, has attracted media attention since 1995 with its Corruption Perceptions Index. The index is a compilation of surveys of perceptions of resident and nonresident business people and expert assessments of the degree of corruption in a country. See www.transparency.org.
- **Global Integrity,** a Washington, D.C.–based nonprofit organization funded by private foundations and the World Bank, assesses the existence and effectiveness of anticorruption mechanisms that promote public integrity. More than 290 indicators are used to generate the Global Integrity Index for more than 40 countries. See www.globalintegrity.org.
- **The Open Budget Initiative,** sponsored by the International Budget Project, tracks 122 indicators of budget transparency for almost 60 countries. The country reports give citizens, legislators, and civil society advocates comprehensive and practical information that can be used to assess a government's commitment to budget transparency and accountability. The initiative is funded by private foundations and bilateral aid agencies such as the U.K. Department for International Development and the Swedish International Development Cooperation Agency. See www.openbudgetindex.org.

5.1 Private sector in the economy

	Investment in infrastructure projects with private participation[a]								Domestic credit to private sector		New businesses registered	Micro, small, and medium-size enterprises	
	$ millions												
	Telecommunications		Energy		Transport		Water and sanitation		% of GDP		% of total businesses registered	Total	per 1,000 people
	1995–99	2000–05	1995–99	2000–05	1995–99	2000–05	1995–99	2000–05	1990	2005	2003	2000–05[b]	2000–05[b]
Afghanistan	..	284.1	..	..	..	..	..	..	..	..	..	..	..
Albania	..	443.2	0.0	789.0	..	308.0	..	8.0	..	14.9	6	38,331	12.3
Algeria	..	3,422.5	..	962.0	..	..	..	510.0	44.4	11.8	15	580,000	18.8
Angola	..	278.7	..	45.0	..	55.0	..	..	..	4.8	..	..	..
Argentina	10,498.6	5,925.6	12,931.9	3,830.0	6,892.1	200.2	3,307.1	791.6	15.6	11.7	11	..	..
Armenia	1,680.5	243.4	0.0	47.0	..	50.0	..	0.0	*40.4*	8.0	7	99,805	33.1
Australia	..	..	..	..	..	..	..	..	59.9	104.6	11	1,269,000	63.2
Austria	..	..	..	..	..	..	..	..	89.7	112.9	7	252,399	30.9
Azerbaijan	122.0	355.6	..	375.2	..	..	..	0.0	*10.8*	10.0	7	49,527	6.0
Bangladesh	438.1	1,527.3	554.9	501.5	0.0	0.0	..	..	16.7	31.5	..	177,000	1.3
Belarus	20.0	735.4	500.0	..	..	..	..	..	..	16.2	..	25,108	2.5
Belgium	..	..	..	..	..	..	..	..	35.9	75.1	7	686,533	66.2
Benin	..	116.9	..	..	..	..	..	..	20.3	16.6	..	..	..
Bolivia	528.0	520.5	2,777.3	886.0	168.7	16.6	682.0	..	24.0	40.7	8	..	..
Bosnia and Herzegovina	0.0	0.0	..	277.9	..	..	..	..	..	47.9	6	14,986	3.8
Botswana	97.0	104.0	..	..	..	..	..	..	9.4	19.0	..	13,137	7.4
Brazil	45,135.2	41,018.7	34,196.8	28,204.0	17,195.0	4,271.3	2,137.0	1,587.6	39.0	34.8	..	4,903,268	27.4
Bulgaria	202.5	2,179.1	..	2,646.0	..	..	..	152.0	*82.8*	44.5	..	216,489	27.7
Burkina Faso	..	41.9	5.6	..	63.3	..	..	..	16.8	17.3	..	..	..
Burundi	..	53.6	..	..	..	..	..	..	13.7	20.8	..	..	..
Cambodia	102.4	148.1	143.0	88.1	120.0	125.3	..	..	..	9.4	..	..	..
Cameroon	12.7	394.4	..	91.9	90.0	0.0	..	..	26.7	9.4	..	..	..
Canada	..	..	..	..	..	..	..	..	92.2	181.4	*14*	2,245,245	69.5
Central African Republic	1.1	..	..	..	..	..	..	..	7.2	6.7	..	..	..
Chad	2.0	11.0	..	0.0	..	..	..	..	7.3	3.1	..	..	..
Chile	3,489.0	3,714.6	6,808.6	1,528.3	3,104.1	4,768.6	4,190.3	1,495.2	50.6	82.3	..	700,000	43.4
China	5,970.0	8,548.0	17,166.6	6,365.7	10,852.5	7,948.0	985.9	3,131.5	87.7	114.4	9	8,000,000	6.3
Hong Kong, China	..	..	..	..	..	..	..	..	160.6	146.2	13	263,959	38.4
Colombia	1,384.3	1,570.9	6,964.8	4,483.2	995.5	1,331.4	233.0	250.0	30.8	23.9	..	664,000	15.0
Congo, Dem. Rep.	68.0	453.4	..	..	0.0	..	..	..	1.8	1.9	10	..	..
Congo, Rep.	12.2	61.8	325.0	..	..	..	..	..	15.7	2.9	..	..	..
Costa Rica	..	..	301.2	80.0	..	465.2	..	..	12.2	35.8	..	40,921	9.6
Côte d'Ivoire	752.3	134.9	260.6	0.0	241.3	140.0	..	..	36.5	13.8	..	..	..
Croatia	978.0	1,181.9	368.5	7.1	672.2	451.0	..	298.7	..	61.2	..	94,088	21.2
Cuba	..	60.0	165.0	..	..	0.0	..	600.0	..	..	..	..	..
Czech Republic	6,178.5	8,348.0	944.1	3,865.3	283.7	106.7	135.5	263.7	..	37.0	4	..	..
Denmark	..	..	..	..	..	..	..	..	51.2	171.1	10	257,950	47.8
Dominican Republic	163.0	393.0	979.0	1,306.6	..	898.9	..	..	27.5	27.7	..	..	..
Ecuador	696.4	357.8	30.0	302.0	686.8	685.0	..	550.0	13.6	23.0	14	1,043,440	83.6
Egypt, Arab Rep.	1,914.5	3,360.9	700.0	678.0	123.9	821.5	..	..	30.6	52.4	..	..	..
El Salvador	610.5	821.2	900.2	85.0	..	..	..	..	16.9	43.4	7	461,642	72.1
Eritrea	..	40.0	..	..	..	..	..	..	..	31.0	..	..	..
Estonia	628.2	287.1	26.5	..	1.0	298.4	..	115.0	*20.2*	60.0	10	65,194	48.4
Ethiopia	..	..	..	300.0	..	..	..	..	13.9	25.3	..	..	..
Finland	..	..	..	..	..	..	..	..	85.8	76.1	10	221,000	42.4
France	..	..	..	..	..	..	..	..	94.3	93.1	8	2,612,960	43.2
Gabon	8.4	26.6	294.0	0.0	46.7	177.4	..	..	12.9	8.9	..	..	..
Gambia, The	..	6.6	..	..	..	..	..	..	11.0	13.0	..	..	..
Georgia	61.0	168.8	159.0	13.0	..	..	..	..	..	14.8	10	33,860	7.6
Germany	..	..	..	..	..	..	..	..	88.7	111.4	23	3,162,111	38.3
Ghana	491.1	156.5	376.0	184.0	..	10.0	..	0.0	4.9	15.5	..	25,679	1.2
Greece	..	..	..	..	..	..	..	..	35.5	84.8	*7*	771,000	69.9
Guatemala	1,366.3	560.1	1,223.2	110.0	33.8	..	..	..	14.2	25.2	..	..	..
Guinea	120.3	18.0	36.4	..	..	..	0.0	..	*3.5*	5.1	..	..	..
Guinea-Bissau	..	21.9	..	..	..	..	..	..	22.0	2.1	..	..	..
Haiti	1.5	18.0	4.7	..	..	..	..	..	12.6	15.4	..	..	..

Private sector in the economy 5.1

	Investment in infrastructure projects with private participation[a] $ millions								Domestic credit to private sector % of GDP		New businesses registered % of total businesses registered	Micro, small, and medium-size enterprises	
	Telecommunications		Energy		Transport		Water and sanitation					Total	per 1,000 people
	1995–99	2000–05	1995–99	2000–05	1995–99	2000–05	1995–99	2000–05	1990	2005	2003	2000–05[b]	2000–05[b]
Honduras	51.3	135.0	112.1	358.8	10.5	120.0	..	220.0	31.1	42.7	..	257,953	40.2
Hungary	6,430.2	5,234.8	3,812.1	260.6	135.0	3,297.5	205.8	0.0	46.6	51.7	8	..	..
India	7,456.8	20,642.0	7,182.7	8,882.1	1,275.1	3,941.1	..	2.1	25.2	40.8	..	..	..
Indonesia	8,852.5	6,494.6	9,942.1	1,575.6	1,530.8	3.7	955.2	36.7	48.1	26.9	..	41,362,315	195.3
Iran, Islamic Rep.	28.0	695.0	..	650.0	..	..	..	..	33.8	40.9	..	..	..
Iraq	..	984.0	..	..	..	..	..	..	..	..	..	..	..
Ireland	..	..	..	..	..	..	..	..	47.1	160.7	10	97,000	24.3
Israel	..	..	..	..	..	..	..	..	57.6	97.5	..	468,338	67.6
Italy	..	..	..	..	..	..	..	..	54.9	90.2	7	4,486,000	77.9
Jamaica	235.5	700.3	43.0	201.0	0.0	565.0	..	..	31.6	17.9	4	..	..
Japan	..	..	..	..	..	..	..	..	197.4	186.9	..	5,712,191	44.7
Jordan	39.9	1,589.0	..	..	182.0	0.0	0.0	169.0	72.3	87.2	..	141,327	26.4
Kazakhstan	1,633.5	1,078.2	1,825.0	300.0	..	..	..	100.0	..	35.7	12	..	..
Kenya	193.0	1,434.0	189.0	..	53.4	..	..	..	32.7	25.9	..	2,800,000	87.4
Korea, Dem. Rep.	..	..	..	..	..	..	..	..	..	..	..	..	..
Korea, Rep.	..	..	..	..	..	..	..	..	62.8	102.1	..	2,998,223	62.4
Kuwait	..	..	..	..	..	..	..	..	*52.1*	63.1	..	..	..
Kyrgyz Republic	100.0	9.1	..	..	..	..	..	..	..	8.0	..	142,475	28.3
Lao PDR	157.1	87.8	535.5	1,250.0	0.0	0.0	..	..	1.0	7.0	..	..	..
Latvia	600.9	708.9	106.0	71.1	75.0	..	..	..	..	59.9	6	32,571	13.8
Lebanon	485.7	138.1	..	..	..	153.0	..	0.0	79.4	76.3	..	..	..
Lesotho	15.7	88.4	..	0.0	..	..	..	..	15.1	8.4	..	..	..
Liberia	..	61.3	..	..	..	..	..	..	*30.9*	6.6	..	..	..
Libya	..	..	..	..	..	..	..	..	31.0	9.0	..	..	..
Lithuania	832.7	993.0	10.0	399.3	..	..	..	..	..	34.9	3	56,428	16.5
Macedonia, FYR	..	706.6	..	..	..	..	..	..	..	25.9	7	55,742	27.5
Madagascar	30.0	12.6	..	0.0	..	48.5	..	..	16.9	9.9	4	..	..
Malawi	23.1	36.3	..	0.0	6.0	..	..	..	10.9	10.5	13	747,396	64.9
Malaysia	4,187.6	3,756.9	1,610.2	6,637.6	8,200.1	4,276.4	10.0	6,502.2	69.4	128.3	..	518,996	20.5
Mali	..	82.6	..	365.9	..	55.4	..	..	12.8	18.4	..	..	..
Mauritania	..	92.1	..	..	..	..	..	..	43.5	*27.0*	..	..	..
Mauritius	..	413.0	109.3	0.0	42.6	..	..	..	35.6	76.7	..	75,267	62.2
Mexico	10,757.5	18,131.4	2,095.8	6,614.3	4,706.1	3,135.4	276.5	520.7	17.5	18.2	..	2,891,300	28.3
Moldova	84.6	46.1	60.0	25.3	..	..	..	..	*5.9*	24.2	5	25,667	6.1
Mongolia	21.9	22.1	..	..	..	..	..	..	*17.7*	37.5	18	..	..
Morocco	1,240.0	5,993.5	5,978.0	1,049.0	..	..	1,000.0	..	34.0	62.2	46	450,000	15.8
Mozambique	29.0	123.0	..	1,205.8	441.0	334.6	25.5	0.0	18.3	*11.2*	7	..	..
Myanmar	4.0	..	394.0	..	50.0	..	..	..	4.7	5.6	..	..	..
Namibia	55.2	35.2	4.0	1.0	..	450.0	..	0.0	22.6	61.4	..	..	..
Nepal	..	97.3	98.2	39.0	..	..	..	..	12.8	..	..	3,040	0.1
Netherlands	..	..	..	..	..	..	..	..	76.6	173.4	6	735,160	45.0
New Zealand	..	..	..	..	..	..	..	..	75.5	133.8	*18*	334,031	82.2
Nicaragua	24.5	278.5	232.4	115.0	..	104.0	..	..	112.6	29.1	..	..	..
Niger	..	85.5	..	..	..	..	..	3.4	12.3	6.8	..	..	..
Nigeria	69.0	6,950.7	..	1,248.0	..	22.8	..	..	9.4	14.9	8	..	..
Norway	..	..	..	..	..	..	..	..	81.7	9.0	7	316,243	68.4
Oman	..	1,047.0	183.0	1,364.3	77.5	473.8	..	..	20.6	*34.9*	5	7,373	2.9
Pakistan	75.5	5,572.2	4,298.3	598.6	421.3	71.0	..	..	24.2	28.4	4	2,956,704	19.0
Panama	1,429.2	183.4	669.2	445.7	994.6	51.4	25.0	..	46.7	91.7	..	..	..
Papua New Guinea	..	..	65.0	..	..	..	71.0	..	28.6	13.9	..	..	..
Paraguay	259.3	194.6	..	..	58.0	..	..	..	15.8	18.0	..	548,000	95.5
Peru	4,774.5	2,238.0	3,004.9	2,478.3	86.3	561.5	..	128.0	11.8	19.4	1	658,837	23.9
Philippines	5,358.3	4,570.9	6,998.0	3,783.4	1,364.0	1,060.5	7,567.2	0.0	22.3	30.5	..	808,634	10.1
Poland	6,403.1	16,800.0	628.1	2,341.5	169.4	1,672.0	6.1	64.3	21.1	27.4	7	1,654,822	43.3
Portugal	..	..	..	..	..	..	..	..	46.6	147.3	3	693,000	66.4
Puerto Rico	..	..	..	..	..	..	..	..	..	..	..	2,069	0.5

5.1 Private sector in the economy

	Investment in infrastructure projects with private participation[a]								Domestic credit to private sector		New businesses registered	Micro, small, and medium-size enterprises	
	$ millions												
	Telecommunications		Energy		Transport		Water and sanitation		% of GDP		% of total businesses registered	Total	per 1,000 people
	1995–99	2000–05	1995–99	2000–05	1995–99	2000–05	1995–99	2000–05	1990	2005	2003	2000–05[b]	2000–05[b]
Romania	2,072.8	3,073.9	100.0	1,240.8	23.4	..	..	1,022.0	..	20.0	11	392,544	18.1
Russian Federation	5,643.1	19,583.8	2,281.3	1,714.0	406.0	109.4	108.0	660.5	..	25.7	..	6,891,300	48.2
Rwanda	8.0	52.3	..	0.0	..	..	..	..	6.9	13.5	..	..	..
Saudi Arabia	..	8,537.0	..	..	55.0	190.0	..	52.0	54.7	53.9	..	..	..
Senegal	273.9	345.1	124.0	87.0	..	55.4	20.0	..	26.5	23.8	..	..	..
Serbia and Montenegro	1,590.0	830.6	..	..	..	..	..	0.0	..	..	9	68,220	8.4
Sierra Leone	7.0	48.8	..	..	..	..	..	..	3.2	4.5	29	..	..
Singapore	..	..	..	..	..	..	..	..	97.0	101.7	13	136,363	32.2
Slovak Republic	488.5	2,709.9	..	4,459.6	..	..	0.0	..	..	36.2	14	70,553	13.1
Slovenia	..	..	..	..	..	..	..	..	*34.9*	53.3	7	91,066	45.6
Somalia	0.0	13.4	..	..	..	..	..	..	..	..	..	..	..
South Africa	2,975.3	5,499.5	3.0	1,251.3	1,386.4	504.7	56.9	31.3	81.0	143.5	8	..	..
Spain	..	..	..	..	..	..	..	..	78.5	146.1	10	3,168,735	73.0
Sri Lanka	601.9	679.9	192.3	254.0	240.0	..	..	..	19.6	32.9	8	121,426	6.3
Sudan	18.3	621.2	..	..	..	..	..	..	4.8	10.0	..	22,460	0.7
Swaziland	21.2	27.7	..	..	..	..	..	..	20.7	20.0	..	..	..
Sweden	..	..	..	..	..	..	..	..	126.4	111.7	5	898,454	99.6
Switzerland	..	..	..	..	..	..	..	..	162.6	166.8	7	344,000	46.9
Syrian Arab Republic	..	583.2	..	..	..	..	..	..	7.5	*11.8*	..	..	..
Tajikistan	1.2	8.5	..	16.0	..	..	..	..	..	17.2	..	92,964	14.8
Tanzania	100.2	487.3	150.0	372.0	16.5	6.5	..	8.5	13.9	10.4	..	2,700,000	74.6
Thailand	2,735.2	5,470.7	6,550.4	4,693.3	2,001.1	939.0	246.3	245.6	83.4	93.1	10	842,360	13.5
Togo	5.0	0.0	0.0	67.7	0.0	..	..	..	22.6	16.8	6	..	..
Trinidad and Tobago	146.7	..	207.0	..	..	..	0.0	120.0	44.7	38.5	..	19,150	14.7
Tunisia	..	751.0	265.0	30.0	..	..	..	..	55.1	65.6	..	..	..
Turkey	3,269.7	12,515.9	2,992.2	6,569.8	610.0	3,943.6	942.0	..	16.7	26.1	..	210,134	3.1
Turkmenistan	..	..	..	..	..	..	..	..	..	..	..	..	..
Uganda	119.3	387.6	..	142.1	..	..	0.0	0.0	*4.0*	6.7	..	160,453	6.2
Ukraine	1,094.6	3,162.8	..	160.0	..	..	..	..	*2.6*	33.5	..	343,786	7.3
United Arab Emirates	..	..	..	..	..	..	..	..	38.0	60.9	..	..	..
United Kingdom	..	..	..	..	..	..	..	..	115.8	165.5	19	4,415,260	73.8
United States	..	..	..	..	..	..	..	..	118.9	194.8	..	5,868,737	20.0
Uruguay	63.7	114.2	86.0	330.0	20.0	196.1	..	351.0	32.4	27.0	..	143,035	42.8
Uzbekistan	513.8	277.6	..	..	..	..	..	0.0	..	..	..	212,424	8.3
Venezuela, RB	4,877.9	3,337.0	103.0	30.0	268.0	34.0	29.0	15.0	26.2	13.6	..	11,314	0.5
Vietnam	256.0	430.0	435.5	2,279.0	85.0	30.0	38.8	174.0	*2.5*	66.0	..	90,935	1.1
West Bank and Gaza	265.0	279.8	..	150.0	..	..	0.0	0.0	..	..	..	97,194	27.7
Yemen, Rep.	..	376.8	..	..	190.0	..	..	..	6.1	7.7	7	310,000	16.2
Zambia	64.2	208.3	277.0	12.4	..	15.6	..	..	8.9	7.6	10	..	..
Zimbabwe	46.0	59.0	600.0	..	85.0	..	..	..	23.0	26.9	0	..	..
World	.. s	.. s	.. s	.. s	.. s	.. s	.. s	.. s	104.3 w	133.8 w	9 u	139,432,731 s	
Low income	11,549.1	41,659.1	15,730.4	17,689.2	3,047.9	4,856.7	155.3	188.0	21.3	33.8	10	4,222,837	
Middle income	161,868.2	217,654.4	138,174.3	106,539.8	63,732.8	44,614.8	23,098.8	20,026.7	43.1	58.3	9	94,515,052	
Lower middle income	88,980.5	103,357.9	101,392.0	63,499.2	35,618.9	20,239.4	13,806.6	7,688.4	51.3	73.1	10	78,159,635	
Upper middle income	72,887.7	114,296.5	36,782.3	43,040.6	28,113.9	24,375.4	9,292.2	12,338.3	*38.4*	38.8	8	16,355,417	
Low & middle income	173,417.3	259,313.5	153,904.7	124,229.0	66,780.7	49,471.5	23,254.1	20,214.7	39.2	54.9	9	98,737,889	
East Asia & Pacific	27,681.5	29,637.6	43,840.3	26,679.7	24,203.5	14,382.9	9,874.4	10,090.0	73.9	101.1	12	68,387,110	
Europe & Central Asia	40,629.4	81,682.2	13,812.8	25,578.5	2,375.7	10,236.6	1,397.4	2,684.2	..	29.7	8	13,753,937	
Latin America & Carib.	86,847.8	80,778.2	73,997.4	51,388.2	35,219.5	17,442.2	10,879.9	6,716.2	28.6	27.8	7	9,077,990	
Middle East & N. Africa	3,973.1	19,220.8	7,126.0	4,883.3	573.4	1,498.3	1,000.0	679.0	35.0	39.9	18	3,669,844	
South Asia	8,604.5	28,856.1	12,326.4	10,275.2	1,936.4	4,012.1	..	2.1	24.2	38.7	6	177,000	
Sub-Saharan Africa	5,681.0	19,138.6	2,801.8	5,424.1	2,472.2	1,899.4	102.4	43.2	41.0	64.8	10	3,672,008	
High income	..	..	..	..	..	..	..	..	115.4	156.3	10	40,694,842	
Europe EMU	..	..	..	..	..	..	..	..	77.9	110.5	9	16,589,542	

a. Data refer to total for the period shown. Includes projects that became privatized during financial closure years 1990–2005. b. Data are for the most recent year available.

Private sector in the economy 5.1

About the data

Private sector development and investment—that is, tapping private sector initiative and investment for socially useful purposes—are critical for poverty reduction. In parallel with public sector efforts, private investment, especially in competitive markets, has tremendous potential to contribute to growth. Private markets are the engine of productivity growth, creating productive jobs and higher incomes. And with government playing a complementary role of regulation, funding, and service provision, private initiative and investment can help provide the basic services and conditions that empower poor people—by improving health, education, and infrastructure.

Investment in infrastructure projects with private participation has made important contributions to easing fiscal constraints, improving the efficiency of infrastructure services, and extending delivery to poor people. The privatization trend in infrastructure that began in the 1970s and 1980s took off in the 1990s, peaking in 1997. Developing countries have been at the head of this wave, pioneering better approaches to providing infrastructure services and reaping the benefits of greater competition and customer focus. Between 1990 and 2005 more than 3,200 projects in more than 139 developing countries introduced private participation in at least one infrastructure sector, with $964 billion in investments.

In 2005, investments in 160 new infrastructure projects with private participation valued at $40 billion were implemented. In addition, $56 billion in investment projects reached financial closure between 1990 and 2005. Telecommunications attracted $59 billion in investment in 2005, mostly in standalone mobile operations. Transport also saw an increase, from $7 billion in 2004 to $16 billion in 2005. Energy experienced some recovery, from $16 billion to $19 billion. Water, down from about $4.8 billion in 2004 to about $1.5 billion in 2005, was the only sector in which investment in infrastructure projects with private participation declined.

The data on investment in infrastructure projects with private participation refer to all investment (public and private) in projects in which a private company assumes operating risk during the operating period or assumes development and operating risk during the contract period. Investment refers to commitments not disbursements. Foreign state-owned companies are considered private entities for the purposes of this measure. The data are from the World Bank's Private Participation in Infrastructure (PPI) Project Database, which tracks more than 3,300 projects, newly owned or managed by private companies, that reached financial closure in low- and middle-income economies in 1990–2005. Aggregates for geographic regions and income groups are calculated by the World Bank's Development Data Group. For more information, see http://ppi.worldbank.org/.

Credit is an important link in the money transmission process; it finances production, consumption, and capital formation, which in turn affect the level of economic activity. The data on domestic credit to the private sector are taken from the banking survey of the International Monetary Fund's (IMF) *International Financial Statistics* or, when data are unavailable, from its monetary survey. The monetary survey includes monetary authorities (the central bank), deposit money banks, and other banking institutions, such as finance companies, development banks, and savings and loan institutions. In some cases credit to the private sector may include credit to state-owned or partially state-owned enterprises.

Entrepreneurship, the effort by individuals or groups to makes to initiate economic activity in the formal sector under a legal form of business, lends dynamism to an economy. Greater entry of new firms can foster competition and economic growth. This edition of *World Development Indicators* introduces a new indicator measuring entrepreneurship, new businesses registered as a percentage of total businesses.

Formal and informal micro, small, and medium-size enterprises employ more than half the working population in many market economies and account for about 90 percent of all firms. And they contribute significantly to innovation. If small businesses are allowed to compete on an equal playing field, the good ones can become larger, workers can earn higher wages, and productivity will increase. A good investment climate—one that provides opportunities and incentives for firms, reduces legal and regulatory costs, lowers the costs of financial institutions in providing financial services, and facilitates the transfer of technology and knowledge and the upgrading of capabilities in small and medium-size firms—is important for economic progress, better jobs, and a more inclusive society.

Data on the business registration of micro, small, and medium-size enterprises are collected by governments, international organizations, foundations, and small business organizations. These data have been collated by the International Finance Corporation (IFC) and are available in two databases: Entrepreneurship Data and Micro, Small, and Medium Enterprises: A Collection of Published Data. This IFC initiative is a work in progress, improved and updated as new data become available. Because the concepts and definitions of micro, small, and medium-size enterprises vary by source, using these data for precise country rankings may be inappropriate. See www.ifc.org/ifcext/sme.nsf/Content/Resources for additional information on sources and precise firm size.

Definitions

• **Investment in infrastructure projects with private participation** refers to infrastructure projects in telecommunications, energy (electricity and natural gas transmission and distribution), transport, and water and sanitation that have reached financial closure and directly or indirectly serve the public. Incinerators, movable assets, stand-alone solid waste projects, and small projects such as windmills are excluded. Included are operation and management contracts, operation and management contracts with major capital expenditure, greenfield projects (in which a private entity or a public-private joint venture builds and operates a new facility), and divestitures. Investment commitments are the sum of investments in facilities and investments in government assets. Investments in facilities are the resources the project company commits to invest during the contract period either in new facilities or in expansion and modernization of existing facilities. Investments in government assets are the resources the project company spends on acquiring government assets such as state-owned enterprises, rights to provide services in a specific area, or the use of specific radio spectrums. • **Domestic credit to private sector** refers to financial resources provided to the private sector—such as through loans, purchases of nonequity securities, and trade credits and other accounts receivable—that establish a claim for repayment. For some countries these claims include credit to public enterprises. •**New businesses registered** are the number of new firms, defined as firms registered in the current year of reporting, expressed as a percentage of total registered firms. Data are collected on firm entry and exit and total firms. Because of underreporting of firms that have closed or exited, especially in developing countries, the data on total registered firms may be biased upward. • **Micro, small, and medium-size enterprises** are business that may be defined by the number of employees. There is no international standard definition of firm size; however, many institutions that collect information use the following size categories: micro enterprises have 0–9 employees, small enterprises have 10–49 employees, and medium-size enterprises have 50–249 employees.

Data sources

Data on investment in infrastructure projects with private participation are from the World Bank's PPI Project database (http://ppi.worldbank. org). Data on domestic credit are from the IMF's *International Financial Statistics*. Data on business registration and micro, small, and medium-size enterprises are from the IFC's Micro, Small, and Medium Enterprises database (www.ifc.org/ifcext/sme.nsf/Content/Resources).

5.2 Investment climate: enterprise surveys

	Survey year	Policy uncertainty	Corruption	Courts		Crime	Regulation and tax administration			Finance	Electricity	Labor	
		Major constraint %	Major constraint %	Major constraint %	Lack confidence courts uphold property rights %	Major constraint %	Tax rates as major constraint %	Time dealing with officials % of management time	Average time to clear customs days	Major constraint %	Major constraint %	Major constraint % Skills	Major constraint % Regulation
Afghanistan		..	..	..	..	..	..	..	..	..	..	..	..
Albania	2005	18.7	31.0	23.2	43.6	8.4	40.9	10.4	1.4	27.1	34.5	10.3	2.5
Algeria	2002	38.8	34.3	..	27.3	..	44.6	..	8.6	62.3	11.4	25.4	12.7
Angola	2006	1.6	12.5	..	51.0	6.2	3.0	7.1	16.5	11.6	34.5	1.1	..
Argentina	2006	16.5	4.3	2.8	64.0	1.6	14.5	12.3	4.5	15.7	2.5	6.0	15.4
Armenia	2005	14.0	14.5	9.0	46.2	5.5	21.0	2.3	5.5	28.0	3.0	2.0	1.5
Australia		..	..	..	..	..	..	..	..	..	..	..	..
Austria		..	..	..	..	..	..	..	..	..	..	..	..
Azerbaijan	2005	2.5	19.5	6.5	34.7	4.0	24.5	5.2	1.7	12.5	6.0	1.0	1.5
Bangladesh	2002	44.3	57.6	..	83.0	39.1	35.3	3.7	8.3	56.7	72.9	19.2	8.3
Belarus	2005	23.3	6.2	2.5	33.4	2.8	20.2	3.6	2.8	29.5	0.9	6.5	3.4
Belgium		..	..	..	..	..	..	..	..	..	..	..	..
Benin	2004	61.4	81.7	48.7	65.3	47.2	86.8	6.5	6.3	82.7	68.5	25.4	35.0
Bolivia	2006	30.3	8.0	0.1	63.8	2.3	3.6	12.8	10.4	7.3	4.5	2.0	3.2
Bosnia and Herzegovina	2005	33.3	23.1	20.5	41.6	19.0	15.4	4.3	2.0	34.9	8.2	3.6	3.1
Botswana	2006	0.7	7.9	1.4	31.4	10.9	7.3	5.0	1.2	24.3	1.7	9.4	1.5
Brazil	2003	75.8	66.9	32.5	39.6	52.0	84.5	7.2	7.8	84.0	20.3	39.6	56.7
Bulgaria	2005	27.4	18.4	16.7	56.7	11.4	20.4	2.8	1.7	31.1	6.4	10.4	7.7
Burkina Faso	2006	..	5.1	0.7	29.9	1.4	18.8	9.5	3.1	37.0	19.6	..	..
Burundi	2006	14.3	2.2	0.2	36.9	2.9	3.7	5.7	4.4	16.0	40.7	0.1	..
Cambodia	2003	37.9	55.1	28.9	61.0	41.3	17.8	8.6	6.2	12.2	12.6	6.4	5.6
Cameroon	2006	..	5.2	1.2	37.3	2.9	32.6	12.8	4.3	13.4	15.1	..	1.2
Canada		..	..	..	..	..	..	..	..	..	..	..	..
Central African Republic		..	..	..	..	..	..	..	..	..	..	..	..
Chad		..	..	..	..	..	..	..	..	..	..	..	..
Chile	2004	15.3	12.9	11.9	22.9	14.7	22.8	5.8	4.0	27.1	17.8	23.8	25.4
China	2003	32.9	27.3	24.9	17.5	20.0	36.8	18.5	6.2	29.1	29.7	30.7	20.7
Hong Kong, China		..	..	..	..	..	..	..	..	..	..	..	..
Colombia	2006	3.3	2.6	1.6	37.8	13.0	12.5	14.2	6.5	7.6	4.3	9.3	1.8
Congo, Dem. Rep.	2006	5.3	0.5	..	56.5	1.8	9.6	6.3	3.6	14.5	45.5	1.0	..
Congo, Rep.		..	..	..	..	..	..	..	..	..	..	..	..
Costa Rica	2005	28.3	39.9	21.9	28.1	28.0	38.2	9.6	2.8	60.1	16.6	13.4	24.2
Côte d'Ivoire		..	..	..	..	..	..	..	..	..	..	..	..
Croatia	2005	17.4	17.4	28.9	26.0	3.8	11.9	2.7	2.0	17.9	2.1	7.2	3.0
Cuba		..	..	..	..	..	..	..	..	..	..	..	..
Czech Republic	2005	21.7	20.2	24.9	53.1	15.5	58.9	2.1	2.7	25.2	15.5	12.3	15.5
Denmark		..	..	..	..	..	..	..	..	..	..	..	..
Dominican Republic		..	..	..	..	..	..	..	..	..	..	..	..
Ecuador	2003	60.7	49.2	34.0	70.8	27.8	38.0	13.4	5.9	46.8	28.3	22.3	14.1
Egypt, Arab Rep.	2004	63.8	50.3	24.7	..	9.4	80.0	2.1	4.8	36.7	26.5	29.7	28.1
El Salvador	2003	28.4	35.1	16.3	46.6	49.0	22.6	7.2	1.5	37.6	21.5	20.0	3.9
Eritrea	2002	29.1	2.5	11.6	29.0	1.3	29.1	3.8	3.2	57.0	36.7	40.5	5.1
Estonia	2005	5.1	4.2	1.9	29.6	1.9	2.8	2.3	1.7	8.8	3.3	7.0	18.6
Ethiopia	2002	38.2	38.4	4.6	18.2	9.4	72.2	2.1	4.2	50.0	42.5	17.7	4.5
Finland		..	..	..	..	..	..	..	..	..	..	..	..
France		..	..	..	..	..	..	..	..	..	..	..	..
Gabon		..	..	..	..	..	..	..	..	..	..	..	..
Gambia, The	2006	2.1	0.6	2.3	28.4	2.3	6.5	7.3	5.0	11.6	53.7	1.7	..
Georgia	2005	44.7	19.6	11.6	29.0	23.6	35.7	3.0	3.4	31.2	33.2	14.1	7.0
Germany	2005	5.8	3.8	2.3	10.3	1.9	29.4	4.5	4.0	23.2	1.0	6.9	9.5
Ghana		..	..	..	..	..	..	..	..	..	..	..	..
Greece	2005	9.1	9.8	4.6	18.2	5.2	27.5	3.7	4.9	23.3	4.6	8.5	7.6
Guatemala	2003	66.4	80.9	31.2	71.3	80.4	56.5	12.4	1.9	47.5	26.6	31.4	16.7
Guinea	2006	1.4	2.7	0.4	59.0	1.7	3.1	2.6	4.1	8.3	61.0	..	..
Guinea-Bissau	2006	5.0	6.1	1.4	70.3	0.7	5.3	2.9	5.6	19.6	41.4	..	..
Haiti		..	..	..	..	..	..	..	..	..	..	..	..

Investment climate: enterprise surveys

	Survey year	Policy uncertainty	Corruption	Courts		Crime	Regulation and tax administration			Finance	Electricity	Labor	
		Major constraint %	Major constraint %	Major constraint %	Lack confidence courts uphold property rights %	Major constraint %	Tax rates as major constraint %	Time dealing with officials % of management time	Average time to clear customs days	Major constraint %	Major constraint %	Major constraint % Skills	Major constraint % Regulation
Honduras	2003	46.7	62.7	21.6	56.1	60.9	34.4	10.2	1.6	62.4	36.4	26.4	14.2
Hungary	2005	25.5	10.3	24.5	49.7	7.1	49.7	5.3	3.3	32.9	2.3	13.5	9.7
India	2006	9.2	25.0	2.7	25.3	11.8	27.5	6.7	13.6	19.4	32.0	7.9	8.6
Indonesia	2003	48.2	41.5	24.7	40.8	22.0	29.5	4.0	3.4	30.7	22.3	18.9	25.9
Iran, Islamic Rep.		..	..	..	..	..	..	..	..	..	..	..	..
Iraq		..	..	..	..	..	..	..	..	..	..	..	..
Ireland	2005	5.6	3.0	2.8	28.3	4.8	17.4	2.3	2.6	13.8	6.4	15.6	9.6
Israel		..	..	..	..	..	..	..	..	..	..	..	..
Italy		..	..	..	..	..	..	..	..	..	..	..	..
Jamaica	2005	41.1	45.6	20.0	26.7	54.4	60.0	6.3	4.3	72.2	45.6	41.1	18.9
Japan		..	..	..	..	..	..	..	..	..	..	..	..
Jordan		..	..	..	..	..	..	..	..	..	..	..	..
Kazakhstan	2005	9.7	11.3	14.3	42.0	6.7	16.0	3.2	6.0	20.0	3.7	7.7	2.3
Kenya	2003	49.6	72.5	..	51.3	69.6	67.8	11.7	4.3	72.5	47.1	27.5	22.5
Korea, Dem. Rep.		..	..	..	..	..	..	..	..	..	..	..	..
Korea, Rep.	2005	40.4	8.3	3.4	37.2	3.4	14.9	3.2	6.0	15.7	8.3	6.8	4.1
Kuwait		..	..	..	..	..	..	..	..	..	..	..	..
Kyrgyz Republic	2005	32.2	32.2	16.3	50.8	19.3	31.2	6.1	4.1	32.7	4.0	18.8	2.5
Lao PDR		..	..	..	..	..	..	..	..	..	..	..	..
Latvia	2005	21.8	8.9	5.4	51.3	3.0	29.2	2.9	1.7	9.9	4.5	17.8	3.5
Lebanon	2006	54.1	64.9	56.1	69.8	22.9	61.2	12.0	6.4	65.4	61.2	38.0	38.2
Lesotho	2003	31.1	35.1	24.3	38.2	45.9	41.9	19.8	2.3	54.1	35.1	29.7	17.6
Liberia		..	..	..	..	..	..	..	..	..	..	..	..
Libya		..	..	..	..	..	..	..	..	..	..	..	..
Lithuania	2005	22.1	13.2	14.2	49.7	9.3	40.7	5.1	1.8	15.2	3.9	15.2	8.8
Macedonia, FYR	2005	25.5	32.4	28.7	55.4	12.2	19.7	8.2	1.9	41.0	11.7	5.9	8.5
Madagascar	2005	41.0	46.1	33.4	44.6	37.2	44.7	20.8	2.9	68.3	41.3	30.4	14.7
Malawi	2005	5.8	3.2	1.3	28.9	5.1	9.6	5.8	3.5	27.6	19.2	5.8	0.6
Malaysia		..	..	..	..	..	..	..	..	..	..	..	..
Mali	2003	20.8	48.7	16.9	33.1	22.1	36.4	7.5	5.8	63.6	24.0	20.8	3.9
Mauritania	2006	0.7	1.5	0.8	35.6	1.2	12.8	5.8	3.9	21.6	13.0	3.8	0.4
Mauritius	2005	23.9	36.1	22.9	29.4	25.4	27.8	9.6	3.3	52.7	12.7	42.9	27.8
Mexico	2006	8.5	17.8	0.1	63.6	7.3	10.6	20.2	4.5	8.7	8.2	3.1	1.1
Moldova	2005	32.2	19.6	23.6	64.7	17.6	44.2	3.5	2.6	40.7	3.5	12.1	9.5
Mongolia	2004	39.2	48.5	24.7	37.1	27.8	64.9	5.7	3.5	64.4	25.8	28.9	10.3
Morocco	2004	39.2	16.9	29.1	23.5	7.6	62.6	7.5	2.0	84.4	8.9	21.1	16.2
Mozambique		..	..	..	..	..	..	..	..	..	..	..	..
Myanmar		..	..	..	..	..	..	..	..	..	..	..	..
Namibia	2006	0.8	9.3	0.6	24.9	20.6	17.2	2.9	1.3	11.8	3.1	9.4	4.4
Nepal		..	..	..	..	..	..	..	..	..	..	..	..
Netherlands		..	..	..	..	..	..	..	..	..	..	..	..
New Zealand		..	..	..	..	..	..	..	..	..	..	..	..
Nicaragua	2003	58.2	65.7	33.2	60.4	39.2	34.7	13.0	1.5	65.9	34.7	17.0	6.9
Niger	2005	..	11.2	1.6	50.0	..	32.8	11.5	4.0	12.0	1.6	..	0.8
Nigeria		..	..	..	..	..	..	..	..	..	..	..	..
Norway		..	..	..	..	..	..	..	..	..	..	..	..
Oman	2003	20.5	11.9	14.8	12.9	8.6	20.5	6.9	3.4	38.0	10.1	34.4	34.7
Pakistan	2002	40.1	40.3	20.0	62.6	21.5	45.6	8.7	8.9	47.5	39.2	12.7	15.0
Panama	2006	4.2	10.8	1.1	51.6	7.3	14.6	10.2	5.0	6.6	30.6	3.8	4.4
Papua New Guinea		..	..	..	..	..	..	..	..	..	..	..	..
Paraguay	2006	11.5	14.8	3.0	74.1	3.1	1.4	10.4	4.4	21.0	1.9	6.2	5.4
Peru	2006	17.0	4.3	0.6	75.2	5.5	7.7	8.2	4.1	9.3	2.2	2.4	4.0
Philippines	2003	29.5	35.2	13.0	33.8	26.5	30.4	6.9	5.4	25.0	33.4	11.9	24.7
Poland	2005	39.9	15.0	30.6	45.4	15.4	55.4	3.8	3.1	46.3	4.0	13.8	16.9
Portugal	2005	21.5	14.3	17.0	47.7	14.9	19.6	3.2	6.6	25.6	7.8	12.1	17.6
Puerto Rico		..	..	..	..	..	..	..	..	..	..	..	..

5.2 Investment climate: enterprise surveys

	Survey year	Policy uncertainty	Corruption	Courts		Crime	Regulation and tax administration			Finance	Electricity	Labor	
		Major constraint %	Major constraint %	Major constraint %	Lack confidence courts uphold property rights %	Major constraint %	Tax rates as major constraint %	Time dealing with officials % of management time	Average time to clear customs days	Major constraint %	Major constraint %	Major constraint % Skills	Major constraint % Regulation
Romania	2005	35.3	27.6	31.1	44.0	15.1	34.0	1.5	2.6	31.7	6.4	12.5	15.1
Russian Federation	2005	25.8	15.4	8.6	63.9	9.0	21.6	6.3	7.2	21.8	5.1	12.8	3.0
Rwanda	2006	0.9	0.8	..	34.6	..	26.9	5.9	6.7	13.6	31.8	2.8	..
Saudi Arabia		..	..	..	..	..	..	..	..	..	..	..	..
Senegal	2003	30.5	39.3	13.0	40.5	14.9	50.0	3.2	5.9	71.0	30.5	18.3	16.0
Serbia and Montenegro		..	..	..	..	..	..	..	..	..	..	..	..
Sierra Leone		..	..	..	..	..	..	..	..	..	..	..	..
Singapore		..	..	..	..	..	..	..	..	..	..	..	..
Slovak Republic	2005	12.7	10.0	12.3	44.4	5.0	8.2	3.0	5.8	10.9	2.7	8.2	4.5
Slovenia	2005	11.3	3.6	8.1	34.4	0.9	12.6	3.7	2.9	14.9	2.7	5.4	4.5
Somalia		..	..	..	..	..	..	..	..	..	..	..	..
South Africa	2003	17.9	16.1	8.8	20.8	29.0	18.6	9.2	4.3	22.6	9.0	35.5	32.8
Spain	2005	10.1	7.6	7.8	16.6	9.6	18.7	0.8	3.7	19.7	8.3	13.8	11.8
Sri Lanka	2004	34.0	16.9	..	31.2	14.0	19.1	3.5	3.1	28.0	41.3	21.3	25.6
Sudan		..	..	..	..	..	..	..	..	..	..	..	..
Swaziland	2006	0.6	5.2	1.0	56.7	18.5	15.4	4.4	1.9	10.3	6.8	2.3	0.4
Sweden		..	..	..	..	..	..	..	..	..	..	..	..
Switzerland		..	..	..	..	..	..	..	..	..	..	..	..
Syrian Arab Republic	2003	26.4	57.1	8.6	..	29.6	62.3	10.3	5.6	30.0	57.5	36.1	33.0
Tajikistan	2005	5.5	14.5	4.5	35.9	4.0	22.0	3.3	4.8	10.0	10.0	4.5	1.5
Tanzania	2006	0.5	0.5	..	35.4	1.9	3.9	4.0	4.8	9.3	72.9	1.4	..
Thailand	2004	29.1	18.3	38.6	25.8	10.3	24.4	1.3	1.3	20.6	25.6	30.0	11.4
Togo		..	..	..	..	..	..	..	..	..	..	..	..
Trinidad and Tobago		..	..	..	..	..	..	..	..	..	..	..	..
Tunisia		..	..	..	..	..	..	..	..	..	..	..	..
Turkey	2005	31.1	16.7	25.5	28.5	18.2	37.6	..	4.5	25.0	9.2	9.7	12.1
Turkmenistan		..	..	..	..	..	..	..	..	..	..	..	..
Uganda	2006	0.3	2.4	0.1	35.6	0.2	11.0	5.2	2.9	6.7	63.3	0.4	..
Ukraine	2005	31.0	21.2	13.7	48.2	11.9	45.6	8.1	3.9	40.5	4.9	19.8	6.4
United Arab Emirates		..	..	..	..	..	..	..	..	..	..	..	..
United Kingdom		..	..	..	..	..	..	..	..	..	..	..	..
United States		..	..	..	..	..	..	..	..	..	..	..	..
Uruguay	2006	5.8	2.4	1.5	37.9	5.3	20.8	6.8	1.7	11.8	5.2	1.8	7.2
Uzbekistan	2005	10.6	6.5	5.1	41.7	6.8	18.1	2.5	4.7	16.0	7.2	4.1	2.7
Venezuela, RB		..	..	..	..	..	..	..	..	..	..	..	..
Vietnam	2005	14.0	11.2	4.9	23.1	3.7	13.6	5.8	2.5	40.5	15.7	22.2	10.8
West Bank and Gaza		..	..	..	..	..	..	..	..	..	..	..	..
Yemen, Rep.		..	..	..	..	..	..	..	..	..	..	..	..
Zambia	2002	56.5	45.9	38.6	36.1	48.8	57.5	13.0	1.6	84.5	39.6	35.7	16.9
Zimbabwe		..	..	..	..	..	..	..	..	..	..	..	..

Note: Data are based on enterprise surveys conducted by the World Bank and its partners during 2002–06. While averages are reported, there are significant variations across firms. Surveys of Eastern Europe and Central Asia were conducted under the joint World Bank–European Bank for Reconstruction and Development Business Environment and Enterprise Performance Surveys Initiative.

Investment climate: enterprise surveys 5.2

About the data

The World Bank Group's Enterprise Surveys capture business perceptions on the biggest obstacles to enterprise growth, the relative importance of constraints to increasing employment and productivity, and the effects of a country's investment climate on its international competitiveness. These surveys cover almost 58,000 firms in 97 countries for 2002–06. In addition to these surveys, data from the Doing Business project, which benchmarks regulatory regimes in 175 countries, are presented in table 5.3.

Improving government policies and behaviors is key to shaping the investment climate because they are influential in driving growth and poverty reduction. Firms evaluating alternative investment options, governments interested in improving their investment climate, and economists seeking to understand the role of different factors in explaining economic performance have all grappled with defining and measuring the investment climate.

The indicators in the table cover eight dimensions of the investment climate: policy uncertainty, corruption, courts, crime, regulation and tax administration, finance, infrastructure (electricity), and labor.

Firms in developing countries rate access to and cost of finance as their dominant concern among investment climate constraints. Another highly ranked constraint is policy uncertainty, which measures the credibility of governments and their policies and the ability to deliver on promises. Corruption—the exploitation of public office for private gain—can harm the investment climate in several ways. It can distort policymaking, undermine government credibility, tax entrepreneurial activities, and divert resources from public coffers. Better courts reduce the risks firms face, so that firms are willing to invest more. And the importance of courts grows as the number of large and complex long-term transactions increases. Robbery, fraud, and other crimes against property and against the person undermine the investment climate.

Most countries have room to improve regulation and taxation without compromising broader social interests. The investment climate is harmed when governments impose unnecessary costs, by increasing uncertainty and risk and by erecting unjustified barriers to competition. Improvements in the tax system may include broadening the tax base, simplifying tax structures, increasing the autonomy of tax agencies, and improving compliance through computerization. When financial markets work well, they connect firms to lenders and investors, which allow firms to seize business opportunities and grow their businesses. But too often government distortions introduced by state ownership or directed credit undermine financial sector development, productivity, and economic growth. Firms that have access to modern infrastructure—telecommunications, reliable electricity supplies, and efficient transportation—are more productive, and improvements in infrastructure services also benefit households. Ill-considered labor regulations can discourage firms from creating more jobs, and while some employees may benefit, the unemployed, the low skilled, and those working in the informal economy will not.

Data in this table for 27 countries in the Europe and Central Asia region plus 7 comparators in Europe and Asia (Germany, Greece, Ireland, Republic of Korea, Portugal, Spain, and Vietnam) are based on the joint European Bank for Reconstruction and Development–World Bank Business Environment and Enterprise Performance Surveys (BEEPS). All other data are from the World Bank Group's Enterprise Surveys. Both surveys sample the universe of registered businesses and follow either a simple random sample or a stratified random sample methodology, drawing from registered establishments. BEEPS use a simple random sample methodology based on population proportions and can be compared across countries. In the Enterprise Surveys a random sample across sectors is supplemented by an emphasis on firms from the same few selected manufacturing industries plus the retail sector as a means of providing measures of productivity that can be compared across economies. Because the distribution of establishments in most countries is overwhelmingly populated by small and medium-size enterprises, Enterprise Surveys generally oversample large establishments. Other differences include the question related to "problems doing business," which offers a similar but slightly different response scale between the two surveys. As a result, the data are not strictly comparable. In the two countries where the two surveys overlapped (Turkey and Vietnam), BEEPS survey data were used for Turkey and Enterprise Survey data were used for Vietnam (a BEEPS comparator country). Sample sizes for recent surveys range from 200 to 1,500 businesses.

For the 2006 Enterprise Surveys in Africa and Latin America and for the 2005 surveys for Malawi and Niger the indicators for severity of constraints reflect the percentage of managers who identified a particular constraint as their biggest. In any given country some constraints may not be identified by any firms as the biggest constraint even if they would be considered major or severe. The 2006 Enterprise Surveys in Latin America and Africa, except those for Burkina Faso, Cameroon, and Cape Verde, have weights for the estimates of the aggregate indicators in order to account for the random stratified sample design.

For more information on the investment climate and Enterprise Surveys, see www.worldbank.org/eca/econ and www.enterprisesurveys.org/.

Definitions

• **Survey year** is the year in which the underlying data were collected. • **Policy uncertainty** measures the percentage of senior managers who ranked economic and regulatory policy uncertainty as a major or very severe constraint. • **Corruption** measures the percentage of senior managers who ranked corruption as a major or very severe constraint. • **Courts** measure the percentage of senior managers who ranked courts and dispute resolution systems as a major or very severe constraint. • **Lack confidence courts uphold property rights** measures the percentage of managers who do not agree with the statement: "I am confident that the judicial system will enforce my contractual and property rights in business disputes." • **Crime** measures the percentage of senior managers who ranked crime, theft, and disorder as a major or very severe constraint. • **Tax rates as major constraint** measure the percentage of senior managers who ranked tax rates as a major or very severe constraint. • **Time dealing with officials** is the percentage of management time in a given week spent on requirements imposed by government regulations (taxes, customs, labor regulations, licensing, and registration). • **Average time to clear customs** is the number of days to clear an imported good through customs. • **Finance** measures percentage of senior managers who ranked access to finance or cost of finance as a major or very severe constraint. • **Electricity** measures the percentage of senior managers who ranked electricity as a major or severe constraint. • **Labor skills** measure the percentage of senior managers who ranked skills of available workers as a major or severe constraint. • **Labor regulations** measure the percentage of senior managers who ranked labor regulations as a major or severe constraint.

Data sources

Data on the investment climate are from the World Bank Group's Enterprise Surveys website (www.enterprisesurveys.org/), which compiles data from surveys undertaken by the World Bank and other development partners.

5.3 Business environment: Doing Business indicators

	Starting a business			Registering property		Dealing with licenses		Employing workers	Enforcing contracts		Protecting investors	Closing a business
	Number of procedures April 2006	Time required days April 2006	Cost % of per capita income April 2006	Number of procedures April 2006	Time required days April 2006	Number of procedures to build a warehouse April 2006	Time required to build a warehouse days April 2006	Rigidity of employment index 0 (less rigid) to 100 (more rigid) April 2006	Number of procedures April 2006	Time required days April 2006	Disclosure index 0 (less disclosure) to 10 (more disclosure) April 2006	Time to resolve insolvency years April 2006
Afghanistan	3	8	67.4	11	252	..	..	46	..	1,642	0	..
Albania	11	39	22.4	7	47	22	344	38	39	390	0	4.0
Algeria	14	24	21.5	15	51	25	244	45	49	397	6	2.5
Angola	13	124	486.7	7	334	15	326	64	47	1,011	5	6.2
Argentina	15	32	12.1	5	44	23	288	41	33	520	6	2.8
Armenia	9	24	5.1	3	4	18	112	31	24	185	5	1.9
Australia	2	2	1.8	5	5	17	140	3	19	181	8	1.0
Austria	9	29	5.6	3	32	14	195	37	23	342	2	1.1
Azerbaijan	15	53	9.5	7	61	28	212	38	27	267	4	2.7
Bangladesh	8	37	87.6	8	425	13	185	30	50	1,442	6	4.0
Belarus	16	69	26.1	7	231	18	354	27	28	225	1	5.8
Belgium	4	27	5.8	7	132	15	184	20	27	328	8	0.9
Benin	7	31	173.3	3	50	16	333	46	49	720	5	4.0
Bolivia	15	50	140.6	7	92	14	183	74	47	591	1	1.8
Bosnia and Herzegovina	12	54	37.0	7	331	16	467	42	36	595	3	3.3
Botswana	11	108	10.6	4	30	24	169	20	26	501	8	1.3
Brazil	17	152	9.9	14	47	19	460	42	42	616	5	4.0
Bulgaria	9	32	7.9	9	19	22	226	47	34	440	10	3.3
Burkina Faso	8	34	120.8	8	107	32	226	64	41	446	6	4.0
Burundi	11	43	222.4	5	94	18	302	59	47	403	..	4.0
Cambodia	10	86	236.4	7	56	28	181	49	31	401	5	..
Cameroon	12	37	152.2	5	93	15	444	56	58	800	8	3.2
Canada	2	3	0.9	6	10	15	77	4	17	346	8	0.8
Central African Republic	10	14	209.3	3	69	21	245	73	45	660	4	4.8
Chad	19	75	226.1	6	44	16	199	60	52	743	3	10.0
Chile	9	27	9.8	6	31	12	171	24	33	480	8	5.6
China	13	35	9.3	3	32	29	367	24	31	292	10	2.4
Hong Kong, China	5	11	3.3	5	54	22	160	0	16	211	10	1.1
Colombia	13	44	19.8	7	23	12	150	27	37	1,346	7	3.0
Congo, Dem. Rep.	13	155	481.1	8	57	14	306	78	51	685	3	5.2
Congo, Rep.	8	71	214.8	7	137	15	175	69	47	560	4	3.0
Costa Rica	11	77	23.5	6	21	19	119	32	34	615	2	3.5
Côte d'Ivoire	11	45	134.1	6	32	22	569	45	25	525	6	2.2
Croatia	10	45	12.2	5	399	28	278	50	22	561	2	3.1
Cuba	..	..	..	..	..	..	..	..	..	..	..	..
Czech Republic	10	24	8.9	4	123	31	271	28	21	820	2	9.2
Denmark	3	5	0.0	6	42	7	70	17	15	190	7	3.0
Dominican Republic	10	73	30.2	7	107	17	165	42	29	460	5	3.5
Ecuador	14	65	31.8	10	20	19	149	51	41	498	1	8.0
Egypt, Arab Rep.	10	19	68.8	7	193	30	263	53	55	1,010	5	4.2
El Salvador	10	26	75.6	6	33	22	144	24	41	626	6	4.0
Eritrea	13	76	115.9	12	101	..	..	20	35	305	4	1.7
Estonia	6	35	5.1	3	51	13	117	58	25	275	8	3.0
Ethiopia	7	16	45.9	13	43	12	133	34	30	690	4	2.4
Finland	3	14	1.1	3	14	17	56	48	27	228	6	0.9
France	7	8	1.1	9	183	10	155	56	21	331	10	1.9
Gabon	10	60	162.8	8	60	13	268	59	32	880	5	5.0
Gambia, The	8	27	292.1	5	371	17	145	27	26	247	2	3.0
Georgia	7	16	10.9	6	9	17	137	7	24	285	4	3.3
Germany	9	24	5.1	4	40	11	133	44	30	394	5	1.2
Ghana	12	81	49.6	7	382	16	127	34	29	552	7	1.9
Greece	15	38	24.2	12	23	17	176	58	22	730	1	2.0
Guatemala	13	30	52.1	5	37	23	390	34	36	1,459	3	3.0
Guinea	13	49	186.5	6	104	29	278	41	44	276	5	3.8
Guinea-Bissau	17	233	261.2	9	211	11	161	77	40	1,140	0	..
Haiti	12	203	127.7	5	683	12	141	24	35	368	4	5.7

Business environment: Doing Business indicators 5.3

	Starting a business			Registering property		Dealing with licenses		Employing workers	Enforcing contracts		Protecting investors	Closing a business
	Number of procedures April 2006	Time required days April 2006	Cost % of per capita income April 2006	Number of procedures April 2006	Time required days April 2006	Number of procedures to build a warehouse April 2006	Time required to build a warehouse days April 2006	Rigidity of employment index 0 (less rigid) to 100 (more rigid) April 2006	Number of procedures April 2006	Time required days April 2006	Disclosure index 0 (less disclosure) to 10 (more disclosure) April 2006	Time to resolve insolvency years April 2006
Honduras	13	44	60.6	7	36	14	199	36	36	480	1	3.8
Hungary	6	38	20.9	4	78	25	212	34	21	335	2	2.0
India	11	35	73.7	6	62	20	270	41	56	1,420	7	10.0
Indonesia	12	97	86.7	7	42	19	224	44	34	570	8	5.5
Iran, Islamic Rep.	8	47	5.4	9	36	21	668	49	23	520	5	4.5
Iraq	11	77	67.6	5	8	14	216	59	65	520	4	..
Ireland	4	19	0.3	5	38	10	181	33	18	217	10	0.4
Israel	5	34	5.1	7	144	21	215	27	31	585	7	4.0
Italy	9	13	15.2	8	27	17	284	54	40	1,210	7	1.2
Jamaica	6	8	9.4	5	54	14	242	4	18	415	4	1.1
Japan	8	23	7.5	6	14	11	96	29	20	242	7	0.6
Jordan	11	18	73.0	8	22	16	122	27	43	342	5	4.3
Kazakhstan	7	20	7.0	8	52	32	248	23	37	183	7	3.3
Kenya	13	54	46.3	8	73	11	170	28	25	360	4	4.5
Korea, Dem. Rep.	..	..	..	..	..	..	..	..	..	..	..	..
Korea, Rep.	12	22	15.2	7	11	14	52	34	29	230	7	1.5
Kuwait	13	35	1.6	8	55	26	149	13	52	390	7	4.2
Kyrgyz Republic	8	21	9.8	7	8	20	218	38	44	140	8	4.0
Lao PDR	8	163	17.3	9	135	24	192	37	53	443	0	5.0
Latvia	5	16	3.5	8	54	22	152	59	21	240	5	3.0
Lebanon	6	46	105.4	8	25	16	275	24	39	721	9	4.0
Lesotho	8	73	39.9	6	101	14	265	35	58	695	2	2.6
Liberia	..	..	..	..	..	..	..	..	..	..	..	..
Libya	..	..	..	..	..	..	..	..	..	..	..	..
Lithuania	7	26	2.8	3	3	14	151	48	24	166	6	1.7
Macedonia, FYR	10	18	7.4	6	98	18	222	54	27	385	5	3.7
Madagascar	10	21	35.0	8	134	19	297	57	29	591	5	..
Malawi	10	37	134.7	6	118	22	185	21	40	337	4	2.6
Malaysia	9	30	19.7	5	144	25	281	10	31	450	10	2.3
Mali	13	42	201.9	5	33	15	209	51	28	860	6	3.6
Mauritania	11	82	121.6	4	49	19	152	59	40	400	0	8.0
Mauritius	6	46	8.0	6	210	21	145	30	37	630	6	1.7
Mexico	8	27	14.2	5	74	12	142	38	37	415	8	1.8
Moldova	10	30	13.3	6	48	34	158	54	37	310	7	2.8
Mongolia	8	20	5.1	5	11	18	96	34	29	314	5	4.0
Morocco	6	12	12.7	4	46	21	217	63	42	615	6	1.8
Mozambique	13	113	85.7	8	42	13	364	54	38	1,010	7	5.0
Myanmar	..	..	..	..	..	..	..	..	..	..	..	..
Namibia	10	95	18.0	9	23	11	105	27	31	270	5	1.5
Nepal	7	31	78.5	3	5	15	424	52	28	590	6	5.0
Netherlands	6	10	7.2	2	5	18	184	42	22	408	4	1.7
New Zealand	2	12	0.2	2	2	7	184	7	28	109	10	2.0
Nicaragua	6	39	131.6	8	124	12	192	24	20	486	4	2.2
Niger	11	24	416.8	5	49	19	148	77	33	360	4	5.0
Nigeria	9	43	54.4	16	80	16	465	21	23	457	6	1.5
Norway	4	13	2.5	1	1	13	104	54	14	277	7	0.9
Oman	9	34	4.5	2	16	16	242	35	41	598	8	4.0
Pakistan	11	24	21.3	6	50	12	218	43	55	880	6	2.8
Panama	7	19	23.9	7	44	22	121	56	45	686	3	2.5
Papua New Guinea	8	56	28.2	4	72	20	218	10	22	440	5	3.0
Paraguay	17	74	136.8	6	46	15	273	59	46	478	6	3.9
Peru	10	72	32.5	5	33	19	201	61	35	300	8	3.1
Philippines	11	48	18.7	8	33	23	197	39	25	600	1	5.7
Poland	10	31	21.4	6	197	25	322	33	41	980	7	3.0
Portugal	8	8	4.3	5	81	20	327	51	24	495	6	2.0
Puerto Rico	7	7	0.8	8	15	20	212	32	43	620	7	3.8

5.3 Business environment: Doing Business indicators

	Starting a business			Registering property		Dealing with licenses		Employing workers	Enforcing contracts		Protecting investors	Closing a business
	Number of procedures **April 2006**	Time required days **April 2006**	Cost % of per capita income **April 2006**	Number of procedures **April 2006**	Time required days **April 2006**	Number of procedures to build a warehouse **April 2006**	Time required to build a warehouse days **April 2006**	Rigidity of employment index 0 (less rigid) to 100 (more rigid) **April 2006**	Number of procedures **April 2006**	Time required days **April 2006**	Disclosure index 0 (less disclosure) to 10 (more disclosure) **April 2006**	Time to resolve insolvency years **April 2006**
Romania	5	11	4.4	8	150	17	242	51	43	335	9	4.6
Russian Federation	7	28	2.7	6	52	22	531	44	31	178	7	3.8
Rwanda	9	16	188.3	5	371	17	252	49	27	310	2	..
Saudi Arabia	13	39	58.6	4	4	18	125	7	44	360	8	2.8
Senegal	10	58	112.6	6	114	15	185	61	33	780	4	3.0
Serbia and Montenegro[a]	10	18	10.2	6	111	20	211	38	33	635	7	2.7
Sierra Leone	9	26	1,194.5	8	235	48	236	63	58	515	3	2.6
Singapore	6	6	0.8	3	9	11	129	0	29	120	10	0.8
Slovak Republic	9	25	4.8	3	17	13	272	39	27	565	2	4.0
Slovenia	9	60	9.4	6	391	14	207	57	25	1,350	3	2.0
Somalia	..	..	..	..	..	..	..	..	..	..	..	..
South Africa	9	35	6.9	6	23	17	174	41	26	600	8	2.0
Spain	10	47	16.2	3	17	11	277	63	23	515	5	1.0
Sri Lanka	8	50	9.2	8	63	17	167	27	20	837	4	2.2
Sudan	10	39	58.6	6	9	17	172	55	67	770	0	..
Swaziland	13	61	41.1	11	46	11	114	17	31	972	1	2.0
Sweden	3	16	0.7	1	2	8	116	43	19	208	6	2.0
Switzerland	6	20	2.2	4	16	15	152	23	22	215	0	3.0
Syrian Arab Republic	12	43	21.1	4	34	20	134	30	47	872	6	4.1
Tajikistan	14	67	75.1	6	37	18	187	31	46	257	0	3.0
Tanzania	13	30	91.6	10	123	26	313	67	21	393	3	3.0
Thailand	8	33	5.8	2	2	9	127	18	26	425	10	2.7
Togo	13	53	252.7	7	242	14	273	58	37	535	4	3.0
Trinidad and Tobago	9	43	1.1	8	162	19	292	7	37	1,340	4	..
Tunisia	10	11	9.3	5	57	24	79	46	21	481	0	1.3
Turkey	8	9	26.8	8	9	32	232	49	34	420	8	5.9
Turkmenistan	..	..	..	..	..	..	..	..	..	..	..	..
Uganda	17	30	114.0	13	227	19	156	7	19	484	7	2.2
Ukraine	10	33	9.2	10	93	18	242	55	28	183	1	2.9
United Arab Emirates	12	63	36.4	3	6	21	125	20	34	607	4	5.1
United Kingdom	6	18	0.7	2	21	19	115	14	19	229	10	1.0
United States	5	5	0.7	4	12	18	69	0	17	300	7	1.5
Uruguay	10	43	44.2	8	66	17	156	31	39	655	3	2.1
Uzbekistan	8	29	14.1	12	97	19	287	34	35	195	4	4.0
Venezuela, RB	16	141	25.4	8	47	13	276	76	41	435	3	4.0
Vietnam	11	50	44.5	4	67	14	133	37	37	295	4	5.0
West Bank and Gaza	12	93	324.7	10	72	21	134	31	26	700	7	..
Yemen, Rep.	12	63	228.0	6	21	13	107	33	37	360	6	3.0
Zambia	6	35	29.9	6	70	16	196	23	21	404	3	3.1
Zimbabwe	10	96	35.6	4	30	21	481	34	33	410	8	3.3
World	**9 u**	**48 u**	**69.0 u**	**6 u**	**86 u**	**18 u**	**205 u**	**37 u**	**35 u**	**540 u**	**5 u**	**2.9 u**
Low income	10	59	146.3	7	125	18	231	44	39	572	4	3.1
Middle income	10	51	48.6	6	80	18	210	35	35	575	5	3.2
Lower middle income	10	57	62.9	7	85	18	215	35	35	576	4	3.2
Upper middle income	9	42	26.0	6	72	18	201	35	36	573	5	3.2
Low & middle income	10	54	83.5	7	96	18	217	38	37	574	5	3.2
East Asia & Pacific	9	50	48.8	5	112	18	152	24	33	507	5	2.6
Europe & Central Asia	9	31	14.7	6	91	22	248	40	31	357	5	3.7
Latin America & Carib.	10	77	51.0	7	81	15	200	32	39	655	4	3.3
Middle East & N. Africa	10	40	89.5	7	48	19	223	42	42	643	6	2.8
South Asia	8	33	46.6	7	136	16	227	35	39	969	4	3.6
Sub-Saharan Africa	11	62	162.9	7	110	18	236	47	38	581	4	3.0
High income	7	21	7.7	5	44	16	155	30	26	398	6	1.8
Europe EMU	8	22	7.8	6	54	15	196	46	25	473	6	1.3

a. Data are for Serbia only.

Business environment: Doing Business indicators 5.3

About the data

The table presents key indicators on the environment for doing business. The indicators identify regulations that enhance or constrain business investment, productivity, and growth. The data are from the World Bank's Doing Business database, which now includes data on 175 economies.

A vibrant private sector is central to promoting growth and expanding opportunities for poor people. But encouraging firms to invest, improve productivity, and create jobs requires a legal and regulatory environment that fosters access to credit, protects property rights, and supports efficient judicial, taxation, and customs systems. The indicators in the table point to the administrative and regulatory reforms and institutions needed to create a favorable environment for doing business.

When entrepreneurs start a business, the first obstacles they face are the administrative and legal procedures required to register the new firm. Countries differ widely in how they regulate the entry of new businesses. In some countries the process is straightforward and affordable. But in others the procedures are so burdensome that entrepreneurs may opt to run their business informally. The data on starting a business cover the number of start-up procedures, the time required, and cost to complete them.

Property registries were first developed to help raise tax revenue, but they have benefited entrepreneurs as well. Securing rights to land and buildings, a major source of wealth in most countries, strengthens incentives to invest and facilitates trade. More complex procedures to register property are associated with less perceived security of property rights, more informality, and more corruption. The data cover the number procedures required and time required to secure rights to property.

Lack of access to credit is one of the biggest barriers entrepreneurs face in starting and operating a business. Indicators covering access to credit and financial information are presented in table 5.5.

There are many types of business licenses required, and striking the right balance between the ease of doing business and consumer safety requires continuous reform. Since construction is a large sector in most economies, the procedures required for a business in the construction industry to build a standardized warehouse are recorded. These include obtaining all necessary licenses and permits, completing all required notifications and inspections, and submitting the relevant documents to the authorities. The data cover the number of procedures and time needed by the construction firm to complete all procedures.

Every economy has a complex system of laws and institutions to protect the interests of workers and guarantee a minimum standard of living for its population. The rigidity of employment index focuses on the regulation of employment, specifically employing workers and the rigidity of working hours. This index is the average of three subindexes: a difficulty of hiring index, a rigidity of hours index, and a difficulty of firing index. All subindexes have several components and take values between 0 and 100, with higher values indicating more rigid regulation.

Contract enforcement is critical to enable businesses to engage with new borrowers or customers. Without good contract enforcement, trade and credit will be restricted to a small community of people who have developed relationships through repeated dealings or the security of assets. The institution that enforces contracts between debtors and creditors, and suppliers and customers, is the court. The efficiency of contract enforcement is reflected in two indicators: the number of judicial procedures to resolve a dispute and the time it takes to enforce a commercial contract.

What companies disclose to the public has a large impact on investor protection. Both investors and entrepreneurs benefit greatly from such legal protection. The disclosure index is based on several measures that cover ownership disclosure measures that reduce expropriation, and disclosures to help investors.

Unviable businesses prevent assets and human capital from being allocated to more productive uses in new companies or in viable companies that are financially distressed. The time to close a business (resolve an insolvency) captures the average time to complete a procedure, as estimated by insolvency lawyers. Information is collected on the sequence of bankruptcy procedures, and on whether any procedures can be carried out simultaneously. Delays due to legal derailment tactics that parties to the insolvency may use, in particular extension of response periods or appeals, are taken into account.

To ensure cross-country comparability, several standard characteristics of a company are defined in all surveys, such as size, ownership, location, legal status, and type of activities undertaken. For example, for the starting a business data, these standard characteristics include that the business is a limited liability company; operates in the country's most populous city; is 100 percent domestically owned and has five owners, none of whom is a legal entity; has start-up capital of 10 times income per capita at the end of 2005, has paid in cash; performs general industrial or commercial activities, such as production or sale of products or services to the public; does not perform foreign trade activities or handle products subject to a special tax regime; does not use heavily polluting production processes; leases the commercial plant and offices and is not a proprietor of real estate; does not qualify for investment incentives or any special benefits; has up to 50 employees within one month of commencement of operations, all of them nationals; has turnover at least 100 times income per capita; and has a company deed at least 10 pages long. The data were collected through a study of laws and regulations in each country, surveys of regulators or private sector professionals on each topic, and cooperative arrangements with private consulting firms and business and law associations.

For more information on the methodology, see www.doingbusiness.org/.

Definitions

• **Number of procedures for starting a business** is the number of procedures required to start a business, including interactions required to obtain necessary permits and licenses and to complete all inscriptions, verifications, and notifications to start operations. Data are for businesses with specific characteristics of ownership, size, and type of production. • **Time required for starting a business** is the number of calendar days needed to complete the required procedures for legally operating a business. If a procedure can be speeded up at additional cost, the fastest procedure, independent of cost, is chosen. • **Cost for starting a business** is normalized by presenting it as a percentage of gross national income (GNI) per capita. • **Number of procedures for registering property** is the number of procedures required for a business to secure rights to property • **Time required for registering property** is the number of calendar days needed for a business to secure rights to property • **Number of procedures to build a warehouse** is the number of interactions of a company's employees or managers with external parties, including government agency staff, public inspectors, notaries, land registry and cadastre staff, and technical experts apart from architects and engineers • **Time required to build a warehouse** is the number of calendar days needed to complete the required procedures for building a warehouse. If a procedure can be speeded up at additional cost, the fastest procedure, independent of cost, is chosen. • **Rigidity of employment index** measures the regulation of employment, specifically the employing of workers and the rigidity of working hours. This index is the average of three subindexes: a difficulty of hiring index, a rigidity of hours index, and a difficulty of firing index. The index ranges from 0 and 100, with higher values indicating more rigid regulations. • **Number of procedures for enforcing contracts** is the number of independent actions, mandated by law or court regulation, that demand interaction between the parties to a contract or between them and the judge or court officer. • **Time required for enforcing contracts** is the number of calendar days from the time of the filing of the lawsuit in court to the final determination and payment. • **Disclosure index** measures the degree to which investors are protected through disclosure of ownership and financial information. The index ranges from 0 to 10, with higher values indicating more disclosure. • **Time to resolve insolvency** is the number of years from the time of filing for insolvency in court until resolution of distressed assets.

Data sources

Data on the business environment are from the World Bank's Doing Business project (www.doingbusiness.org).

5.4 Stock markets

	Market capitalization				Market liquidity		Turnover ratio		Listed domestic companies		S&P/EMDB indexes	
	$ millions		% of GDP		Value traded % of GDP		Value of shares traded % of market capitalization		number		% change	
	2000	2006	2000	2005	2000	2005	2000	2006	2000	2006	2005	2006
Afghanistan	..	..	..	..	..	..	..	..	..	..	..	..
Albania	..	..	..	..	..	..	..	..	..	..	..	..
Algeria	..	..	..	..	..	..	..	..	..	..	..	..
Angola	..	..	..	..	..	..	..	..	..	..	..	..
Argentina	166,068	79,730	58.4	33.6	2.1	9.0	4.8	6.6	127	103	45.4[a]	57.6[a]
Armenia	*2*	*43*	*0.1*	0.9	*0.0*	0.0	*4.6*	*3.7*	*105*	*198*	..	..
Australia	372,794	*804,074*	93.3	109.8	56.6	84.1	56.5	*78.0*	1,330	*1,643*	..	..
Austria	29,935	*126,324*	15.4	41.3	4.8	15.0	29.8	*43.3*	97	*92*	..	..
Azerbaijan	*4*	..	*0.1*	..	..	..	..	..	*2*	..	..	..
Bangladesh	1,186	3,610	2.5	5.1	1.6	1.7	74.4	31.7	221	269	–27.7[b]	12.9[b]
Belarus	..	..	..	..	..	..	..	..	..	..	..	..
Belgium	182,481	*327,065*	78.7	88.2	16.4	30.7	20.7	*20.8*	174	*145*	..	..
Benin	..	..	..	..	..	..	..	..	..	..	..	..
Bolivia	1,742	*2,200*	20.7	23.6	0.8	0.0	*0.1*	*0.1*	26	*36*	..	..
Bosnia and Herzegovina	..	..	..	..	..	..	..	..	..	..	..	..
Botswana	978	3,947	15.8	23.6	0.8	0.4	4.8	2.4	16	18	–3.2[b]	53.0[b]
Brazil	226,152	711,100	37.6	59.6	16.8	19.4	43.5	42.5	459	392	47.6[a]	43.1[a]
Bulgaria	617	10,325	4.9	19.1	0.5	5.2	9.2	25.0	503	347	16.4[b]	31.4[b]
Burkina Faso	..	..	..	..	..	..	..	..	..	..	..	..
Burundi	..	..	..	..	..	..	..	..	..	..	..	..
Cambodia	..	..	..	..	..	..	..	..	..	..	..	..
Cameroon	..	..	..	..	..	..	..	..	..	..	..	..
Canada	841,385	*1,480,891*	117.8	133.0	88.8	75.9	77.3	*63.6*	1,418	*3,721*	..	..
Central African Republic	..	..	..	..	..	..	..	..	..	..	..	..
Chad	..	..	..	..	..	..	..	..	..	..	..	..
Chile	60,401	174,556	80.3	118.4	8.1	16.4	9.4	19.2	258	244	14.7[a]	28.6[a]
China	580,991	2,426,326	48.5	34.9	60.2	26.2	158.3	136.4	1,086	1,440	13.3[a]	80.7[a]
Hong Kong, China	623,398	*1,006,228*	369.4	566.2	223.9	258.9	61.3	*49.3*	779	*1,126*	..	..
Colombia	9,560	56,204	11.4	37.6	0.5	5.2	3.8	22.3	126	114	108.1[b]	12.7[b]
Congo, Dem. Rep.	..	..	..	..	..	..	..	..	..	..	..	..
Congo, Rep.	..	..	..	..	..	..	..	..	..	..	..	..
Costa Rica	2,924	*1,478*	18.3	7.4	*0.7*	0.8	*12.0*	*7.7*	21	*19*	..	..
Côte d'Ivoire	1,185	4,155	11.4	14.2	0.3	0.2	2.6	3.7	41	40	16.9[b]	35.6[b]
Croatia	2,742	29,006	14.9	33.5	1.0	2.1	7.4	9.8	64	183	7.4[b]	85.2[b]
Cuba	..	..	..	..	..	..	..	..	..	..	..	..
Czech Republic	11,002	48,604	19.4	30.8	11.6	33.0	60.3	77.5	131	29	43.5[a]	30.9[a]
Denmark	107,666	*178,038*	67.3	68.8	57.2	58.8	86.0	*92.3*	225	*168*	..	..
Dominican Republic	*141*	..	*0.8*	..	..	..	..	..	*6*	..	..	..
Ecuador	704	4,040	4.4	8.8	0.1	0.4	5.5	9.0	30	34	26.0[b]	32.0[b]
Egypt, Arab Rep.	28,741	93,477	28.8	89.1	11.1	28.4	34.7	55.2	1,076	603	158.0[a]	10.2[a]
El Salvador	2,041	*3,623*	15.5	21.3	0.2	0.4	*1.3*	*2.3*	40	*35*	..	..
Eritrea	..	..	..	..	..	..	..	..	..	..	..	..
Estonia	1,846	5,963	33.7	26.7	6.0	18.9	18.9	27.5	23	16	22.8[b]	30.3[b]
Ethiopia	..	..	..	..	..	..	..	..	..	..	..	..
Finland	293,635	*209,504*	243.6	108.5	171.4	141.6	64.3	*139.1*	154	*134*	..	..
France	1,446,634	*1,710,029*	108.9	80.4	81.6	69.4	74.1	*82.7*	808	*664*	..	..
Gabon	..	..	..	..	..	..	..	..	..	..	..	..
Gambia, The	..	..	..	..	..	..	..	..	..	..	..	..
Georgia	24	*355*	0.8	5.5	0.1	0.6	..	*13.6*	269	*257*	..	..
Germany	1,270,243	*1,221,250*	66.8	43.7	56.3	63.1	79.1	*146.0*	1,022	*648*	..	..
Ghana	502	1,729	10.1	12.8	0.2	0.4	1.5	3.4	22	32	–33.9[b]	9.7[b]
Greece	110,839	*145,013*	96.7	64.4	83.0	29.0	63.7	*48.3*	329	*307*	..	..
Guatemala	240	..	1.2	..	0.0	..	*0.0*	..	44	..	..	..
Guinea	..	..	..	..	..	..	..	..	..	..	..	..
Guinea-Bissau	..	..	..	..	..	..	..	..	..	..	..	..
Haiti	..	..	..	..	..	..	..	..	..	..	..	..

Stock markets 5.4

	Market capitalization				Market liquidity		Turnover ratio		Listed domestic companies		S&P/EMDB indexes	
	$ millions		% of GDP		Value traded % of GDP		Value of shares traded % of market capitalization		number		% change	
	2000	2006	2000	2005	2000	2005	2000	2006	2000	2006	2005	2006
Honduras	*458*	..	*8.8*	..	..	..	..	..	46	..	..	..
Hungary	12,021	41,935	25.6	29.8	25.8	21.9	90.7	88.2	60	41	16.1[a]	31.4[a]
India	148,064	818,879	32.2	68.6	110.8	55.0	133.6	96.4	5,937	4,796	33.6[a]	46.7[a]
Indonesia	26,834	138,886	16.3	28.4	8.7	14.6	32.9	45.5	290	344	9.1[a]	67.9[a]
Iran, Islamic Rep.	7,350	*38,724*	7.3	20.4	1.1	4.3	*12.7*	*19.1*	304	*420*	..	..
Iraq	..	..	..	..	..	..	..	..	..	..	..	..
Ireland	81,882	*114,134*	85.1	56.6	15.0	32.1	19.2	*56.7*	76	*53*	..	..
Israel	64,081	173,306	55.5	97.3	20.3	48.5	36.3	60.7	654	612	24.1[a]	–6.3[a]
Italy	768,364	*798,167*	70.0	45.3	70.9	63.3	104.0	*140.5*	291	*275*	..	..
Jamaica	3,582	12,277	44.6	136.1	0.9	4.5	2.5	3.0	46	41	–14.1[b]	–1.5[b]
Japan	3,157,222	*4,736,513*	67.9	104.5	57.9	110.2	69.9	*118.8*	2,561	*3,279*	21.7[c]	5.9[c]
Jordan	4,943	29,729	58.4	296.1	4.9	187.3	7.7	59.0	163	227	117.8[b]	–36.0[b]
Kazakhstan	1,342	*10,521*	7.3	18.4	0.5	1.9	*25.1*	*14.9*	23	*83*	..	..
Kenya	1,283	11,378	10.1	34.1	0.4	2.7	3.6	15.8	57	51	60.0[b]	60.3[b]
Korea, Dem. Rep.	..	..	..	..	..	..	..	..	..	..	..	..
Korea, Rep.	171,587	835,188	33.5	91.2	208.7	152.7	233.2	173.7	1,308	1,694	58.8[a]	13.3[a]
Kuwait	20,772	128,940	55.1	161.0	11.2	116.4	21.3	45.1	77	163	..	–4.6[b]
Kyrgyz Republic	4	*42*	0.3	1.7	1.7	0.5	..	*34.1*	80	*8*	..	..
Lao PDR	..	..	..	..	..	..	..	..	..	..	..	..
Latvia	563	2,705	7.2	16.0	2.9	0.6	48.6	4.9	64	40	32.8[b]	1.5[b]
Lebanon	1,583	8,279	9.4	22.5	0.7	4.2	6.7	38.1	12	11	111.8[b]	–9.2[b]
Lesotho	..	..	..	..	..	..	..	..	..	..	..	..
Liberia	..	..	..	..	..	..	..	..	..	..	..	..
Libya	..	..	..	..	..	..	..	..	..	..	..	..
Lithuania	1,588	10,191	13.9	31.9	1.8	2.9	14.8	23.5	54	44	6.2[b]	9.7[b]
Macedonia, FYR	7	*646*	0.2	11.2	3.3	1.7	*6.6*	*18.3*	1	*57*	..	..
Madagascar	..	..	..	..	..	..	..	..	..	..	..	..
Malawi	126	..	7.2	..	0.5	..	*13.8*	..	7	..	..	..
Malaysia	116,935	235,356	129.5	139.1	64.8	38.3	44.6	33.2	795	1,027	–2.9[a]	34.6[a]
Mali	..	..	..	..	..	..	..	..	..	..	..	..
Mauritania	*1,090*	..	*97.2*	..	..	..	..	..	*40*	..	..	..
Mauritius	1,331	3,598	29.8	41.6	1.7	2.4	5.0	6.0	40	41	10.5[b]	44.3[b]
Mexico	125,204	348,345	21.5	31.1	7.8	6.9	32.3	29.7	179	131	43.9[a]	41.1[a]
Moldova	392	*574*	30.4	*22.1*	1.9	0.6	*5.8*	*5.9*	36	*23*	..	..
Mongolia	37	*46*	3.9	2.4	0.8	0.1	*7.3*	*6.1*	410	*392*	..	..
Morocco	10,899	49,360	32.7	52.7	3.3	8.0	9.2	32.9	53	65	8.4[a]	78.5[a]
Mozambique	..	..	..	..	..	..	..	..	..	..	..	..
Myanmar	..	..	..	..	..	..	..	..	..	..	..	..
Namibia	311	542	9.1	6.8	0.6	0.1	4.5	4.6	13	9	–1.1[b]	12.8[b]
Nepal	790	*963*	14.4	13.0	0.6	0.3	*6.9*	*2.4*	110	*105*	..	..
Netherlands	640,456	*727,515*	165.7	116.6	175.2	121.3	101.4	*112.2*	234	*170*	..	..
New Zealand	18,866	*40,620*	35.8	37.2	20.5	15.9	45.9	*41.3*	142	*154*	..	..
Nicaragua	..	..	..	..	..	..	..	..	..	..	..	..
Niger	..	..	..	..	..	..	..	..	..	..	..	..
Nigeria	4,237	32,819	9.2	19.6	0.6	2.0	7.3	13.8	195	202	20.7[b]	34.0[b]
Norway	65,034	*190,952*	39.0	64.6	36.0	65.9	93.4	*117.2*	191	*202*	..	..
Oman	3,463	16,158	17.4	*26.0*	2.8	*7.4*	14.2	22.1	131	124	38.0[b]	7.9[b]
Pakistan	6,581	45,518	9.0	41.5	45.0	127.3	475.5	251.4	762	652	58.5[b]	1.3[b]
Panama	2,794	*5,074*	24.0	32.8	1.3	0.5	*1.7*	*1.8*	29	*24*	..	..
Papua New Guinea	*1,520*	*4,863*	*49.6*	98.3	*0.0*	0.3	..	*0.4*	*7*	*9*	..	..
Paraguay	*224*	*234*	*3.5*	3.2	*0.1*	0.0	*3.5*	*0.7*	56	54	..	..
Peru	10,562	59,658	19.8	45.3	2.9	2.5	12.6	9.2	230	193	29.8[a]	82.5[a]
Philippines	25,957	68,382	34.4	40.5	10.9	7.0	15.8	22.1	228	238	21.3[a]	50.3[a]
Poland	31,279	149,054	18.3	31.0	8.5	9.9	49.9	46.8	225	267	20.8[a]	38.1[a]
Portugal	60,681	*66,981*	53.9	36.5	48.3	21.2	85.5	*55.4*	109	*52*	..	..
Puerto Rico	..	..	..	..	..	..	..	..	..	..	..	..

5.4 Stock markets

	Market capitalization				Market liquidity		Turnover ratio		Listed domestic companies		S&P/EMDB indexes	
	$ millions		% of GDP		Value traded % of GDP		Value of shares traded % of market capitalization		number		% change	
	2000	2006	2000	2005	2000	2005	2000	2006	2000	2006	2005	2006
Romania	1,069	32,784	2.9	20.9	0.6	3.4	23.1	16.9	5,555	2,478	58.7[b]	54.2[b]
Russian Federation	38,922	1,321,833	15.0	71.8	7.8	20.9	36.9	65.7	249	309	64.9[a]	62.0[a]
Rwanda	..	..	..	..	..	..	..	..	..	..	..	..
Saudi Arabia	67,171	326,869	35.6	208.6	9.2	356.2	27.1	269.1	75	86	111.0[b]	–48.9[b]
Senegal	..	..	..	..	..	..	..	..	..	..	..	..
Serbia and Montenegro	*734*	*5,409*	*4.7*	20.6	0.1	2.5	*0.0*	*15.3*	6	*864*	..	..
Sierra Leone	..	..	..	..	..	..	..	..	..	..	..	..
Singapore	152,827	*208,300*	164.8	178.4	98.7	102.6	52.1	*63.1*	418	*557*	..	..
Slovak Republic	1,217	5,574	6.0	9.5	4.4	0.1	129.8	1.9	493	173	16.6[b]	24.0[b]
Slovenia	2,547	15,182	13.2	23.0	2.4	2.3	20.7	10.3	38	100	–6.9[b]	74.3[b]
Somalia	..	..	..	..	..	..	..	..	..	..	..	..
South Africa	204,952	715,025	154.2	236.0	58.3	83.8	33.9	49.5	616	401	24.8[a]	17.2[a]
Spain	504,219	*960,024*	86.8	85.4	169.8	138.5	210.7	*163.9*	1,019	*3,300*	..	..
Sri Lanka	1,074	7,769	6.6	24.4	0.9	4.8	11.0	14.8	239	237	29.3[b]	45.3[b]
Sudan	..	..	..	..	..	..	..	..	..	..	..	..
Swaziland	73	*197*	5.3	7.2	0.0	0.0	*9.8*	*0.0*	6	*6*	..	..
Sweden	328,339	*403,948*	135.7	112.9	161.2	129.7	111.2	*118.9*	292	*252*	..	..
Switzerland	792,316	*938,624*	322.0	255.7	247.6	240.7	82.0	*100.1*	252	*263*	..	..
Syrian Arab Republic	..	..	..	..	..	..	..	..	..	..	..	..
Tajikistan	..	..	..	..	..	..	..	..	..	..	..	..
Tanzania	233	*588*	2.6	4.9	0.4	0.1	*2.4*	*2.3*	4	*6*	..	..
Thailand	29,489	139,564	24.0	69.9	19.0	50.6	53.2	67.6	381	476	3.8[a]	6.2[a]
Togo	..	..	..	..	..	..	..	..	..	..	..	..
Trinidad and Tobago	4,330	15,571	53.1	118.2	1.7	4.4	3.1	3.0	27	37	–1.3[b]	–6.5[b]
Tunisia	2,828	4,446	14.5	10.0	3.2	1.6	23.3	15.2	44	48	11.1[b]	47.9[b]
Turkey	69,659	162,399	35.0	44.6	89.9	55.5	206.2	143.0	315	314	49.5[a]	–4.0[a]
Turkmenistan	..	..	..	..	..	..	..	..	..	..	..	..
Uganda	*35*	*103*	*0.6*	1.2	*0.0*	0.0	..	*3.1*	*2*	*5*	..	..
Ukraine	1,881	42,870	6.0	30.1	0.9	0.8	19.6	4.6	139	249	52.8[b]	48.6[b]
United Arab Emirates	5,727	138,531	8.1	173.9	0.2	110.4	*3.9*	65.9	54	81	..	–44.6[b]
United Kingdom	2,576,992	*3,058,182*	178.6	139.1	127.2	189.5	66.6	*141.9*	1,904	*2,759*	4.4[d]	26.2[d]
United States	15,104,037	*16,997,982*	154.7	136.9	326.3	173.2	200.8	*129.1*	7,524	*5,143*	3.0[e]	13.6[e]
Uruguay	161	*354*	0.8	2.1	*0.0*	0.0	*0.5*	*0.0*	16	*11*	..	..
Uzbekistan	32	*37*	0.2	0.3	0.1	0.3	..	*184.7*	5	*114*	..	..
Venezuela, RB	8,128	8,251	6.9	3.6	0.6	0.2	8.9	9.4	85	53	–22.0[b]	79.0[b]
Vietnam	..	..	..	..	..	..	..	..	..	..	..	..
West Bank and Gaza	765	*4,461*	18.6	111.1	4.6	61.7	*10.0*	*89.1*	24	*28*	..	..
Yemen, Rep.	..	..	..	..	..	..	..	..	..	..	..	..
Zambia	236	*989*	7.3	13.6	0.2	0.2	*20.8*	*2.0*	9	*12*	..	..
Zimbabwe	2,432	26,557	32.9	71.2	3.8	9.8	10.8	7.9	69	80	36.6[b]	912.3[b]
World	32,187,882 s	*43,642,048* s	103.0 w	99.6 w	153.4 w	108.1 w	122.4 w	78.2 w	47,884 s	49,946 s	..	..
Low income	166,928	944,645	23.9	54.2	78.0	49.7	151.6	96.6	7,929	6,122	..	..
Middle income	1,852,197	7,273,817	37.4	49.5	26.8	21.8	71.5	75.3	15,533	11,141	..	..
Lower middle income	979,347	3,854,955	35.9	41.1	32.4	21.3	92.3	95.2	5,931	5,057	..	..
Upper middle income	872,850	3,418,862	39.3	60.1	19.7	22.4	47.0	50.4	9,602	6,084	..	..
Low & middle income	2,019,125	8,218,463	35.8	50.1	33.1	25.3	81.3	78.2	23,462	17,263	..	..
East Asia & Pacific	780,487	3,008,514	47.2	41.3	50.0	26.4	125.2	123.1	3,190	3,525	..	..
Europe & Central Asia	176,208	1,863,241	19.2	45.8	25.4	21.9	81.9	68.5	8,295	4,490	..	..
Latin America & Carib.	626,283	1,469,731	32.6	44.6	8.6	10.7	26.9	29.2	1,806	1,342	..	..
Middle East & N. Africa	60,573	201,450	20.0	49.1	5.0	16.4	*12.6*	*27.0*	1,807	1,078	..	..
South Asia	157,695	875,775	26.2	60.4	90.3	58.2	167.6	108.7	7,269	5,954	..	..
Sub-Saharan Africa	217,880	799,751	89.3	137.0	32.1	46.2	22.2	32.6	1,095	874	..	..
High income	30,168,757	*38,980,586*	117.9	112.9	179.7	130.3	131.0	*122.2*	24,422	*28,733*	..	..
Europe EMU	5,425,933	*6,465,158*	87.5	64.8	80.8	72.8	90.6	*116.8*	4,405	*5,995*	..	..

a. Data refer to the S&P/IFC Investable index. b. Data refer to the S&P/IFC Global index. c. Data refer to the Nikkei 225 index. d. Data refer to the FT 100 index. e. Data refer to the S&P 500 index.

About the data

The development of an economy's financial markets is closely related to its overall development. Well functioning financial systems provide good and easily accessible information. That lowers transaction costs, which in turn improves resource allocation and boosts economic growth. Both banking systems and stock markets enhance growth, the main factor in poverty reduction. At low levels of economic development commercial banks tend to dominate the financial system, while at higher levels domestic stock markets tend to become more active and efficient relative to domestic banks.

Open economies with sound macroeconomic policies, good legal systems, and shareholder protection attract capital and therefore have larger financial markets. Recent research on stock market development shows that new communications technology and increased financial integration have resulted in more cross-border capital flows, a stronger presence of financial firms around the world, and the migration of stock exchange activities to international exchanges. Many firms in emerging markets now cross-list on international exchanges, which provides them with lower cost capital and more liquidity-traded shares. However, this also means that exchanges in emerging markets may not have enough financial activity to sustain them, putting pressure on them to rethink their operations.

The stock market indicators in the table include measures of size (market capitalization, number of listed domestic companies) and liquidity (value traded as a percentage of gross domestic product, value of shares traded as a percentage of market capitalization). The comparability of such indicators between countries may be limited by conceptual and statistical weaknesses, such as inaccurate reporting and differences in accounting standards. The percentage change in stock market prices in U.S. dollars, from the Standard & Poor's Emerging Markets Data Base (S&P/EMDB) indexes, is an important measure of overall performance. Regulatory and institutional factors that can affect investor confidence, such as entry and exit restrictions, the existence of a securities and exchange commission, and the quality of laws to protect investors, may influence the functioning of stock markets but are not included in the table.

Stock market size can be measured in a number of ways, and each may produce a different ranking of countries. Market capitalization shows the overall size of the stock market in U.S. dollars and as a percentage of GDP. The number of listed domestic companies is another measure of market size. Market size is positively correlated with the ability to mobilize capital and diversify risk.

Market liquidity, the ability to easily buy and sell securities, is measured by dividing the total value traded by GDP. The turnover ratio—the value of shares traded as a percentage of market capitalization—is also a measure of liquidity as well as of transaction costs. (High turnover indicates low transaction costs.) The turnover ratio complements the ratio of value traded to GDP, because the turnover ratio is related to the size of the market and the value traded ratio to the size of the economy. A small, liquid market will have a high turnover ratio but a low value traded ratio. Liquidity is an important attribute of stock markets because, in theory, liquid markets improve the allocation of capital and enhance prospects for long-term economic growth. A more comprehensive measure of liquidity would include trading costs and the time and uncertainty in finding a counterpart in settling trades.

The S&P/EMDB, the source for all the data in the table, provides regular updates on 56 emerging stock markets encompassing more than 2,200 stocks. Standard & Poor's maintains a series of indexes for investors interested in investing in stock markets in developing countries. At the core of the S&P/EMDB indexes, the Global (S&P/IFCG) index is intended to represent the most active stocks in the markets it covers and to be the broadest possible indicator of market movements. The Investable (S&P/IFCI) index, which applies the same calculation methodology as the S&P/IFCG index, is designed to measure the returns that foreign portfolio investors might receive from investing in emerging market stocks that are legally and practically open to foreign portfolio investment. These indexes are widely used benchmarks for international portfolio management. See Standard & Poor's (2000) for further information on the indexes.

Because markets included in Standard & Poor's emerging markets category vary widely in level of development, it is best to look at the entire category to identify the most significant market trends. And it is useful to remember that stock market trends may be distorted by currency conversions, especially when a currency has registered a significant devaluation.

About the data is based on Demirgüç-Kunt and Levine (1996), Beck and Levine (2001), and Claessens, Klingebiel, and Schmukler (2002).

Definitions

• **Market capitalization** (also known as market value) is the share price times the number of shares outstanding. • **Market liquidity** is the total value traded divided by GDP. Value traded is the total value of shares traded during the period. This indicator complements the market capitalization ratio by showing whether market size is matched by trading. • **Turnover ratio** is the total value of shares traded during the period divided by the average market capitalization for the period. Average market capitalization is calculated as the average of the end-of-period values for the current period and the previous period. • **Listed domestic companies** are the domestically incorporated companies listed on the country's stock exchanges at the end of the year. This indicator does not include investment companies, mutual funds, or other collective investment vehicles. • **S&P/EMDB indexes** measure the U.S. dollar price change in the stock markets covered by the S&P/IFCI country index and S&P/IFCG indexes.

Data sources

Data on stock markets are from Standard & Poor's *Global Stock Markets Factbook 2006*, which draws on the Emerging Markets Data Base, supplemented by other data from Standard & Poor's. The firm collects data through an annual survey of the world's stock exchanges, supplemented by information provided by its network of correspondents and by Reuters. Data on GDP are from the World Bank's national accounts data files.

5.5 Financial access, stability, and efficiency

	Getting credit				Bank capital to asset ratio	Bank nonperforming loans to total gross loans	Domestic credit provided by banking sector	Interest rate spread	Risk premium on lending
	Legal rights index 0 (weaker) to 10 (stronger)	Credit information index 0 (less) to 10 (more)	% of adults: Public credit registry coverage	% of adults: Private credit bureau coverage	%	%	% of GDP	Lending rate minus deposit rate percentage points	Prime lending rate minus treasury bill rate percentage points
	April 2006	April 2006	April 2006	April 2006	2005	2005	2005	2005	2005
Afghanistan	0	0	0.0	0.0	..	..	..	..	..
Albania	9	0	0.0	0.0	..	..	48.6	8.0	7.6
Algeria	3	2	0.2	0.0	..	..	11.1	6.3	6.7
Angola	3	4	2.9	0.0	*11.3*	*13.3*	2.1	54.3	..
Argentina	3	6	25.4	100.0	13.0	5.2	38.3	2.4	..
Armenia	5	3	1.5	0.0	21.5	*6.9*	8.8	12.2	13.9
Australia	9	5	0.0	100.0	5.9	0.2	109.8	5.4	..
Austria	5	6	1.2	39.9	7.4	*2.2*	127.6	..	..
Azerbaijan	7	4	1.1	0.0	14.2	7.2	11.8	8.5	9.5
Bangladesh	7	2	0.6	0.0	3.8	15.3	43.9	5.9	..
Belarus	2	3	0.0	0.0	19.8	1.9	22.2	2.1	..
Belgium	5	4	56.2	0.0	2.7	2.0	105.2	*5.2*	4.7
Benin	4	1	10.3	0.0	..	..	13.2	..	..
Bolivia	3	5	11.5	32.3	11.3	11.2	50.1	11.7	11.7
Bosnia and Herzegovina	8	5	0.0	22.9	15.0	5.3	47.7	6.0	..
Botswana	7	5	0.0	43.2	*9.7*	*2.8*	–5.3	6.5	..
Brazil	2	5	9.2	43.0	9.2	4.4	82.5	37.8	36.6
Bulgaria	6	4	20.7	..	10.5	1.7	43.6	4.8	*6.1*
Burkina Faso	4	1	2.4	0.0	..	..	16.2	..	..
Burundi	2	1	0.1	0.0	..	..	35.1	..	..
Cambodia	0	0	0.0	0.0	..	..	7.6	15.4	..
Cameroon	3	2	3.4	0.0	..	..	12.4	12.8	..
Canada	7	6	0.0	100.0	4.5	0.5	206.1	3.6	1.7
Central African Republic	3	2	1.1	0.0	..	..	17.5	12.8	..
Chad	4	1	0.2	0.0	..	..	7.5	12.8	..
Chile	4	6	31.3	19.3	6.8	0.9	85.8	2.7	..
China	2	4	10.2	0.0	3.8	10.5	135.7	3.3	..
Hong Kong, China	10	5	0.0	64.5	12.2	1.5	142.8	6.5	4.1
Colombia	3	4	0.0	28.3	12.3	2.7	35.1	7.5	..
Congo, Dem. Rep.	3	0	0.0	0.0	..	..	2.7	..	..
Congo, Rep.	3	2	1.4	0.0	..	..	1.5	12.8	..
Costa Rica	4	6	2.5	39.2	12.2	1.5	43.4	14.5	..
Côte d'Ivoire	3	1	3.1	0.0	..	..	18.2	..	..
Croatia	5	0	0.0	0.0	8.7	4.0	74.1	9.5	..
Cuba	..	..	..	..	..	..	..	..	..
Czech Republic	6	5	3.5	51.0	5.8	4.3	43.6	4.6	3.8
Denmark	8	4	0.0	11.5	5.7	*0.7*	177.5	..	..
Dominican Republic	4	6	11.9	57.1	9.4	5.9	40.4	10.2	..
Ecuador	3	5	15.2	43.7	9.6	4.9	16.8	5.8	..
Egypt, Arab Rep.	1	2	1.5	0.0	..	25.0	105.5	5.9	4.6
El Salvador	4	6	30.5	79.6	7.6	12.0	47.5	..	..
Eritrea	3	0	0.0	0.0	..	..	141.2	..	..
Estonia	4	5	0.0	18.2	8.6	0.2	71.3	2.8	..
Ethiopia	5	2	0.1	0.0	..	..	54.9	3.5	6.8
Finland	6	5	0.0	14.9	8.8	0.3	78.5	*2.7*	..
France	5	4	12.3	0.0	4.4	3.5	109.5	*4.4*	*4.3*
Gabon	4	2	2.6	0.0	..	*15.8*	10.4	12.8	..
Gambia, The	4	0	0.0	0.0	..	..	23.8	17.6	..
Georgia	6	3	0.0	0.0	18.8	3.8	21.7	14.1	*12.1*
Germany	8	6	0.5	93.9	4.4	4.8	135.8	..	..
Ghana	5	0	0.0	0.0	12.0	13.9	29.7	..	..
Greece	3	4	0.0	37.5	5.0	5.5	110.9	*4.3*	*4.4*
Guatemala	4	5	16.1	9.2	..	..	31.4	8.7	..
Guinea	4	1	0.0	0.0	..	..	15.8	..	..
Guinea-Bissau	3	1	1.0	0.0	..	..	9.1	..	..
Haiti	3	2	0.7	0.0	..	..	29.3	24.0	19.1

Financial access, stability, and efficiency

	Getting credit				Bank capital to asset ratio	Bank non-performing loans to total gross loans	Domestic credit provided by banking sector	Interest rate spread	Risk premium on lending
	Legal rights index 0 (weaker) to 10 (stronger)	Credit information index 0 (less) to 10 (more)	% of adults Public credit registry coverage	% of adults Private credit bureau coverage	%	%	% of GDP	Lending rate minus deposit rate percentage points	Prime lending rate minus treasury bill rate percentage points
	April 2006	**April 2006**	**April 2006**	**April 2006**	**2005**	**2005**	**2005**	**2005**	**2005**
Honduras	6	5	8.3	18.7	8.4	6.6	34.2	7.9	..
Hungary	6	5	0.0	5.9	9.1	2.1	62.9	3.4	1.6
India	5	3	0.0	6.1	6.3	5.2	60.4	..	..
Indonesia	5	2	8.4	0.2	10.5	15.6	47.0	6.0	..
Iran, Islamic Rep.	5	3	13.7	0.0	..	..	46.2	4.2	..
Iraq	4	0	0.0	0.0	..	..	..	..	..
Ireland	8	5	0.0	100.0	4.7	0.7	160.2	2.6	..
Israel	8	5	0.0	100.0	6.7	10.3	84.8	3.2	2.1
Italy	3	5	7.0	67.8	7.3	6.3	108.9	*4.9*	3.1
Jamaica	6	0	0.0	0.0	8.7	2.9	53.2	9.9	4.0
Japan	6	6	0.0	..	*4.2*	1.8	318.7	1.4	..
Jordan	5	2	0.7	0.0	*7.2*	*13.6*	111.6	4.7	..
Kazakhstan	5	4	0.0	5.5	8.7	9.6	24.7	..	..
Kenya	8	2	0.0	0.1	..	5.2	38.4	7.8	4.5
Korea, Dem. Rep.	..	..	..	..	..	..	..	..	..
Korea, Rep.	6	5	0.0	76.6	5.8	1.2	106.6	1.9	..
Kuwait	4	3	0.0	16.1	12.6	4.5	71.7	4.0	..
Kyrgyz Republic	5	3	0.0	0.4	..	..	9.5	20.8	22.2
Lao PDR	2	0	0.0	0.0	..	..	8.8	22.1	8.2
Latvia	8	4	1.9	0.0	7.6	0.7	72.8	3.3	*2.1*
Lebanon	4	5	4.3	0.0	..	15.8	184.0	2.5	5.4
Lesotho	5	0	0.0	0.0	..	..	–1.1	7.8	4.5
Liberia	..	..	..	..	..	..	188.9	13.6	..
Libya	..	..	..	..	..	..	–50.7	4.0	*0.6*
Lithuania	4	6	4.2	7.2	7.3	2.5	42.3	*4.5*	*3.2*
Macedonia, FYR	6	3	2.1	0.0	..	..	20.9	5.6	..
Madagascar	2	1	0.3	0.0	6.2	10.1	12.9	8.3	8.2
Malawi	8	0	0.0	0.0	..	..	22.1	22.2	8.7
Malaysia	8	6	42.2	..	7.9	9.9	143.7	3.0	3.5
Mali	3	1	2.9	0.0	..	..	17.5	..	..
Mauritania	5	1	0.2	0.0	..	..	*–6.1*	15.1	11.2
Mauritius	6	1	10.2	0.0	..	..	108.8	13.8	..
Mexico	2	6	0.0	69.5	12.0	1.8	35.3	6.2	0.5
Moldova	6	0	0.0	0.0	17.0	4.3	32.3	6.0	15.6
Mongolia	5	3	10.2	0.0	..	..	37.1	10.6	..
Morocco	3	1	2.3	0.0	7.7	15.7	88.0	*7.9*	..
Mozambique	4	3	0.7	0.0	6.5	4.6	8.8	11.7	10.4
Myanmar	..	..	..	..	..	..	28.1	5.5	..
Namibia	5	5	0.0	35.2	7.8	2.0	65.9	4.4	3.5
Nepal	4	2	0.0	0.1	..	..	..	5.9	5.9
Netherlands	7	5	0.0	68.9	4.0	1.2	184.8	0.4	..
New Zealand	9	5	0.0	100.0	..	..	132.8	4.9	5.0
Nicaragua	4	5	12.5	3.4	8.8	8.0	79.4	8.1	..
Niger	3	1	1.2	0.0	..	..	10.7	..	..
Nigeria	7	0	0.0	0.0	*9.9*	21.9	9.0	7.4	10.3
Norway	6	4	0.0	100.0	5.1	0.7	10.0	2.2	..
Oman	3	1	17.5	0.0	..	..	*34.9*	3.7	..
Pakistan	4	4	0.3	1.1	7.7	10.6	43.6	..	..
Panama	6	6	0.0	59.8	12.8	1.8	88.2	6.0	..
Papua New Guinea	6	0	0.0	0.0	..	..	21.9	10.6	7.7
Paraguay	3	6	10.6	52.2	11.0	3.2	20.1	28.2	..
Peru	4	6	19.2	28.6	7.7	2.1	17.6	11.5	..
Philippines	3	3	0.0	4.8	12.3	20.0	50.9	4.6	4.1
Poland	4	4	0.0	38.1	7.8	7.7	32.6	4.0	..
Portugal	4	4	72.0	9.1	5.2	1.6	150.7	..	..
Puerto Rico	6	5	0.0	63.6	..	..	..	..	..

5.5 Financial access, stability, and efficiency

	Getting credit				Bank capital to asset ratio	Bank non-performing loans to total gross loans	Domestic credit provided by banking sector	Interest rate spread	Risk premium on lending
	Legal rights index 0 (weaker) to 10 (stronger)	Credit information index 0 (less) to 10 (more)	% of adults Public credit registry coverage	% of adults Private credit bureau coverage	%	%	% of GDP	Lending rate minus deposit rate percentage points	Prime lending rate minus treasury bill rate percentage points
	April 2006	April 2006	April 2006	April 2006	2005	2005	2005	2005	2005
Romania	4	5	2.6	5.5	8.8	8.3	20.8	..	..
Russian Federation	3	0	0.0	0.0	13.5	3.2	20.7	6.7	*7.6*
Rwanda	1	2	0.2	0.0	..	34.1	9.7	..	..
Saudi Arabia	3	5	0.2	12.5	8.8	*3.0*	46.9	..	..
Senegal	3	1	4.7	0.0	*8.4*	*14.2*	23.1	..	..
Serbia and Montenegro	5[a]	5[a]	0.1[a]	43.4[a]	17.2	*19.8*	..	..	..
Sierra Leone	5	0	0.0	0.0	*11.6*	*14.8*	24.9	13.5	1.6
Singapore	9	4	0.0	38.6	10.5	3.8	70.8	4.9	3.3
Slovak Republic	9	3	1.0	45.3	7.6	2.0	49.6	4.2	..
Slovenia	6	3	2.9	0.0	7.4	4.9	64.8	4.6	4.1
Somalia	..	..	..	..	..	..	..	..	..
South Africa	5	5	0.0	53.0	8.3	1.5	184.6	4.6	3.7
Spain	5	6	44.9	7.4	4.9	0.6	159.7	..	..
Sri Lanka	3	3	0.0	3.1	*6.7*	9.6	44.3	–3.2	–2.0
Sudan	4	0	0.0	0.0	..	..	12.7	..	..
Swaziland	6	5	0.0	39.0	..	..	16.3	6.6	3.6
Sweden	6	4	0.0	100.0	5.8	1.1	120.7	2.5	1.6
Switzerland	6	5	0.0	24.5	5.1	0.5	179.9	2.4	2.4
Syrian Arab Republic	5	0	0.0	0.0	..	..	*31.3*	7.0	..
Tajikistan	4	0	0.0	0.0	..	..	16.4	13.5	..
Tanzania	5	0	0.0	0.0	..	..	14.0	10.4	4.4
Thailand	5	5	0.0	21.7	9.8	11.1	111.1	3.9	..
Togo	3	1	3.6	0.0	..	..	17.2	..	..
Trinidad and Tobago	6	3	0.0	31.5	..	..	25.7	6.9	4.2
Tunisia	3	3	11.6	0.0	7.7	20.9	71.5	..	..
Turkey	3	5	6.7	..	13.5	4.8	56.6	..	..
Turkmenistan	..	..	..	..	..	..	..	..	..
Uganda	3	0	0.0	0.0	*10.3*	*2.2*	9.9	10.9	11.1
Ukraine	8	0	0.0	0.0	11.5	19.6	34.6	7.6	..
United Arab Emirates	3	2	1.7	0.0	8.3	8.3	*59.5*	..	..
United Kingdom	10	6	0.0	86.1	*8.5*	1.0	168.0	..	0.1
United States	7	6	0.0	100.0	10.3	0.7	224.3	..	3.0
Uruguay	4	6	13.2	85.3	8.6	2.7	40.5	10.8	9.5
Uzbekistan	3	0	0.0	0.0	..	..	..	..	..
Venezuela, RB	4	0	0.0	0.0	11.1	1.2	13.1	5.2	..
Vietnam	4	3	2.7	0.0	..	..	69.6	3.9	4.9
West Bank and Gaza	5	3	0.7	0.0	..	..	..	..	..
Yemen, Rep.	3	2	0.1	0.0	..	..	4.7	5.0	3.1
Zambia	7	0	0.0	0.0	..	10.8	22.0	17.0	11.9
Zimbabwe	6	0	0.0	0.0	*12.1*	*23.2*	94.0	144.6	50.6
World	**4.8 w**	**2.6 w**	**3.8 m**	**17.4 m**	**8.6 m**	**4.4 m**	**164.6 w**	**6.5 m**	**..**
Low income	3.9	1.0	0.9	0.2	..	..	48.1	11.7	..
Middle income	4.7	2.8	4.6	14.2	9.3	4.6	76.0	6.5	..
Lower middle income	4.6	2.7	4.4	10.4	10.2	7.2	95.5	7.5	..
Upper middle income	5.0	3.1	4.9	20.4	8.7	2.5	50.6	6.0	..
Low & middle income	4.5	2.2	3.3	9.1	*9.7*	*7.3*	72.2	7.4	..
East Asia & Pacific	4.7	1.5	3.7	3.2	..	..	121.4	5.5	..
Europe & Central Asia	5.4	3.0	1.8	8.7	10.5	4.2	35.5	6.0	..
Latin America & Carib.	4.4	3.4	7.5	27.6	9.5	3.1	52.0	7.8	..
Middle East & N. Africa	3.7	1.9	4.1	0.0	..	..	53.6	4.8	..
South Asia	3.8	1.8	0.1	1.3	6.3	10.1	57.2	5.9	..
Sub-Saharan Africa	4.2	1.3	1.5	3.8	..	..	81.8	12.2	..
High income	6.2	4.6	6.0	52.9	5.8	1.5	191.0	*4.3*	..
European Monetary Union	5.4	4.9	17.6	39.9	5.0	2.0	128.6	*4.3*	..

a. Data are for Serbia only.

Financial access, stability, and efficiency 5.5

About the data

This year's table has been revised to include data on getting credit from the World Bank Group's Doing Business database.

Financial sector development has positive impacts on economic growth and poverty. The size of the sector determines the amount of resources mobilized for investment. Access to finance can expand opportunities for all—not just the rich and well connected—with higher levels of access and use of banking services associated with lower financing obstacles for people and businesses. A stable financial system that promotes efficient savings and investment is also crucial for a thriving democracy and market economy. The banking system is the largest sector in the financial system in most countries, so most indicators in the table cover the banking system.

There are several aspects of access to financial services: availability, cost, and quality of services. The development and growth of credit markets depend on access to timely, reliable, and accurate data on borrowers' credit experiences. For secured transactions, such as mortgages or vehicle loans, having rapid access to information in property registries is also vital, and for small business loans, corporate registry data are needed. An effective way to improve access to credit is to increase information about potential borrowers' creditworthiness and make it easy to create and enforce collateral agreements. Lenders look at the borrower's credit history and collateral when extending loans. Where credit registries and effective collateral laws are absent—as in many developing countries—banks make fewer loans. Indicators that cover financial access, or getting credit, include legal rights index, credit information index, public registry coverage, and private bureau coverage. Other measures of access and use, such as number of bank branches per capita and number of bank deposits per capita are not presented in the table this year since they are not collected or updated regularly.

The size and mobility of international capital flows have made it increasingly important to monitor the strength of financial systems. Robust financial systems help to increase economic activity and welfare, but instability in the financial system can disrupt financial activity and impose huge and widespread costs on the economy. The ratio of bank capital to assets, a measure of bank solvency and resiliency, provides a measure of the extent to which banks can deal with unexpected losses. Capital includes tier 1 capital (paid-up shares and common stock), which is a common feature in all countries' banking systems, and total regulatory capital, which includes several specified types of subordinated debt instruments that need not be repaid if the funds are required to maintain minimum capital levels (these comprise tier 2 and tier 3 capital). Total assets include all nonfinancial and financial assets. Data are from internally consistent financial statements to enhance the quality and analytical usefulness of the indicators.

The ratio of bank nonperforming loans to total gross loans is a measure of bank health and efficiency. It helps to identify problems with asset quality in the loan portfolio. A high ratio may signal deterioration in the quality of the credit portfolio. International guidelines recommend that loans be classified as nonperforming when payments of principal and interest are past due by 90 days or more or when future payments are not expected to be received in full. See the International Monetary Fund's (IMF) *Global Financial Stability Report* for detailed background information.

Domestic credit provided by the banking sector as a share of GDP is a measure of banking sector depth and financial sector development in terms of size. In a few countries governments may hold international reserves as deposits in the banking system rather than in the central bank. Since the claims on the central government are a net item (claims on the central government minus central government deposits), this net figure may be negative, resulting in a negative figure of domestic credit provided by the banking sector.

The interest rate spread—the margin between the cost of mobilizing liabilities and the earnings on assets—is a measure of the efficiency by which the financial sector intermediates funds. A narrow interest rate spread means low transaction costs, which lowers the overall cost of funds for investment, crucial to economic growth. The risk premium on lending is the spread between the lending rate to the private sector and the "risk-free" government rate. A small spread indicates that the market considers its best corporate customers to be low risk. Interest rate spreads are expressed as annual averages. In some countries this spread may be negative, indicating that the market considers its best corporate clients to be lower risk than the government.

Definitions

• **Legal rights index** measures the degree to which collateral and bankruptcy laws protect the rights of borrowers and lenders and thus facilitate lending. The index ranges from 0 to 10, with higher scores indicating that these laws are better designed to expand access to credit. • **Credit information index** measures rules affecting the scope, accessibility, and quality of credit information available through public or private credit registries. The index ranges from 0 to 6, with higher values indicating the availability of more credit information, from either a public registry or a private bureau, to facilitate lending decisions. • **Public credit registry coverage** reports the number of individuals and firms listed in a public credit registry with current information on repayment history, unpaid debts, or credit outstanding. The number is expressed as a percentage of the adult population • **Private credit bureau coverage** reports the number of individuals or firms listed by a private credit bureau with current information on repayment history, unpaid debts, or credit outstanding. The number is expressed as a percentage of the adult population. • **Bank capital to asset ratio** is the ratio of bank capital and reserves to total assets. Capital and reserves include funds contributed by owners, retained earnings, general and special reserves, provisions, and valuation adjustments. • **Bank nonperforming loans to total gross loans** are the value of nonperforming loans divided by the total value of the loan portfolio (including nonperforming loans before the deduction of specific loan loss provisions). The loan amount recorded as nonperforming should be the gross value of the loan as recorded on the balance sheet, not just the amount that is overdue. • **Domestic credit provided by banking sector** includes all credit to various sectors on a gross basis, except credit to the central government, which is net. The banking sector includes monetary authorities, deposit money banks, and other banking institutions for which data are available (including institutions that do not accept transferable deposits but do incur such liabilities as time and savings deposits). • **Interest rate spread** is the interest rate charged by banks on loans to prime customers minus the interest rate paid by commercial or similar banks for demand, time, or savings deposits. • **Risk premium on lending** is the interest rate charged by banks on loans to prime private sector customers minus the "risk free" treasury bill interest rate at which short-term government securities are issued or traded in the market.

Data sources

Data on getting credit are from the World Bank's Doing Business project (www.doingbusiness.org). Data on bank capital and nonperforming loans are from the IMF's *Global Financial Stability Report*. Data on credit and interest rates are from the IMF's *International Financial Statistics*.

5.6 Tax policies

	Tax revenue collected by central government		Taxes payable by businesses			Highest marginal tax rate[a]		
						Individual		
	% of GDP		Number of payments Fiscal year	Time to prepare, file, and pay taxes hours Fiscal year	Total tax rate % of profit Fiscal year	%	On income over $	Corporate %
	2000	2005	2006	2006	2006	2006	2006	2006
Afghanistan[b]	..	3.9	2	275	36.3	..	..	..
Albania[b]	*16.1*	17.3	42	240	55.8	20	2,003	20
Algeria[b]	36.9	..	61	504	76.4	..	..	..
Angola	..	..	42	272	64.4	..	..	..
Argentina	*9.8*	*14.2*	34	615	116.8	35	41,379	35
Armenia[b]	..	14.3	50	1,120	42.5	..	..	..
Australia	22.1	23.9	11	107	52.2	47	72,519	30
Austria	19.6	20.0	20	272	56.1	50	63,750	25
Azerbaijan[b]	*12.7*	..	36	1,000	44.9	35	12,632	22
Bangladesh[b]	*7.6*	*8.1*	17	400	40.3	..	..	..
Belarus[b]	16.6	20.6	125	1,188	186.1	..	..	..
Belgium	27.4	26.5	10	160	70.1	50	39,625	34
Benin[b]	..	14.6	72	270	68.5	35[c]	..	38[c]
Bolivia	*13.2*	16.6	41	1,080	80.3	..	..	25
Bosnia and Herzegovina	..	21.8	73	100	50.4	15	..	30
Botswana[b]	..	..	24	140	53.3	25	19,569	15
Brazil[b]	*12.2*	..	23	2,600	71.7	28	11,486	15
Bulgaria[b]	18.3	23.4	27	616	40.7	24	4,586	15
Burkina Faso	..	12.1	45	270	51.1	..	..	..
Burundi[b]	*13.6*	..	40	140	286.7	..	..	..
Cambodia	*8.2*	8.0	27	121	22.3	20	36,652	20
Cameroon[b]	12.3	..	39	1,300	46.2	..	..	..
Canada[b]	15.3	14.4	10	119	43.0	29	97,756	22
Central African Republic[b]	..	6.0	54	504	209.5	..	..	..
Chad	..	..	65	122	68.2	..	..	..
Chile	*16.6*	19.2	10	432	26.3	*40*	*6,127*	*17*
China[b]	6.8	8.8[c]	48	872	77.1	45	8,637	..
Hong Kong, China	..	..	4	80	28.8	20	11,568	18
Colombia	..	15.1	68	456	82.8	22	43,154	39
Congo, Dem. Rep.[b]	0.0	..	34	312	235.4	50	4,920	40
Congo, Rep.	*9.2*	*8.5*	94	576	57.3	..	..	..
Costa Rica[b]	12.1	13.7	41	402	83.0	25	19,414	30
Côte d'Ivoire[b]	14.6	14.5	71	270	45.7	10	4,550	35
Croatia[b]	26.2	23.3	39	196	37.1	45	3,765	20
Cuba	..	..	..	..	..	..	..	..
Czech Republic[b]	15.4	15.6	14	930	49.0	32	13,823	24
Denmark	31.0	*30.6*	18	135	31.5	59	53,117	28
Dominican Republic[b]	14.7	*15.1*	87	178	67.9	30	29,596	30
Ecuador[b]	..	..	8	600	34.9	25	61,440	25
Egypt, Arab Rep.[b]	14.6	..	41	536	50.4	20	6,920	..
El Salvador	*10.7*	12.6	66	224	27.4	..	..	..
Eritrea	..	..	18	216	86.3	..	..	..
Estonia	16.8	17.0	11	104	50.2	23	1,908	23
Ethiopia[b]	*10.8*	12.7[c]	20	212	32.8	35[c]	..	30[c]
Finland	24.9	22.9	19	264	47.9	33	72,750	26
France	23.4	22.7	33	128	68.2	*48*	*60,673*	33
Gabon	..	..	27	272	48.3	..	..	..
Gambia, The[b]	..	..	47	376	291.4	..	..	..
Georgia[b]	7.7	12.1	35	423	37.8	12	..	20
Germany	11.9	11.0	32	105	57.1	42	65,190	25
Ghana[b]	*17.2*	*22.4*	35	304	32.3	25	10,581	25
Greece	25.5	21.8	33	204	60.2	40	28,750	29
Guatemala[b]	10.1	9.6	50	294	40.9	31	38,663	31
Guinea[b]	11.1	..	55	416	49.4	..	..	..
Guinea-Bissau	..	..	47	208	47.5	..	..	..
Haiti	..	..	53	160	40.5	..	..	..

Tax policies

	Tax revenue collected by central government		Taxes payable by businesses			Highest marginal tax rate[a]		
	% of GDP		Number of payments	Time to prepare, file, and pay taxes hours	Total tax rate % of profit	Individual		Corporate
						%	On income over $	%
	2000	2005	Fiscal year 2006	Fiscal year 2006	Fiscal year 2006	2006	2006	2006
Honduras	..	..	48	424	51.4	25	26,553	*25*
Hungary	22.5	20.5	24	304	59.3	36	7,766	16
India[b]	9.0	*10.2*	59	264	81.1	30	5,669	34
Indonesia[b]	*11.3*	*12.5*	52	576	37.2	35	20,608	30
Iran, Islamic Rep.[b]	6.3	7.9	28	292	46.4	35	114,101	25
Iraq	..	..	13	312	38.7	..	..	..
Ireland	26.1	25.0	8	76	25.8	42	40,000	13
Israel	31.0	29.3	33	225	39.1	49	94,530	31
Italy	23.2	21.3	15	360	76.0	43	125,000	33
Jamaica[b]	24.7	27.3	72	414	52.3	*25*	*1,993*	*33*
Japan[b]	..	..	15	350	52.8	37	163,310	30
Jordan[b]	19.0	24.2	26	101	31.9	..	..	..
Kazakhstan[b]	10.2	20.6	34	156	45.0	20	55,810	30
Kenya[b]	16.8	16.9	17	432	74.2	*30*	*5,841*	*30*
Korea, Dem. Rep.	..	..	..	..	..	..	..	..
Korea, Rep.[b]	16.1	15.8	27	290	30.9	35	78,116	25
Kuwait	*1.0*	*1.0*	14	118	55.7	0	..	0
Kyrgyz Republic[b]	11.7	..	89	204	67.4	..	..	..
Lao PDR	..	..	31	180	32.5	..	..	..
Latvia[b]	14.2	15.3	8	320	42.6	25	..	15
Lebanon	12.2	*16.1*	21	208	37.3	..	..	..
Lesotho[b]	32.4	*41.7*	21	352	25.6	..	..	..
Liberia	..	..	..	..	..	..	..	..
Libya	..	..	..	..	..	..	..	..
Lithuania	14.5	17.5	13	162	48.4	33	..	15
Macedonia, FYR[b]	..	..	54	96	43.5	24	14,610	15
Madagascar	56.6	*54.4*	25	304	43.2	..	..	..
Malawi	..	..	29	878	32.6	..	..	..
Malaysia[b]	14.3	*17.6*	35	190	35.2	28	65,963	28
Mali	..	..	60	270	50.0	..	..	..
Mauritania	..	..	61	696	104.3	..	..	..
Mauritius[b]	18.2	18.1	7	158	24.8	30	16,949	25
Mexico[b]	11.7	..	49	552	37.1	29	9,470	29
Moldova[b]	14.7	18.9	44	250	48.8	20	1,667	15
Mongolia	..	*22.6*	42	204	32.2	..	..	..
Morocco	*22.3*	22.6	28	468	52.7	..	..	..
Mozambique	..	..	36	230	39.2	32	43,710	32
Myanmar[b]	3.0	..	..	..	..	..	..	..
Namibia[b]	30.0	*25.9*	34	..	25.6	35	31,447	35
Nepal[b]	8.7	10.1	35	408	32.8	..	..	..
Netherlands	22.2	23.2	22	250	48.1	52	65,285	30
New Zealand	*29.4*	31.8	9	70	36.5	39	42,254	33
Nicaragua[b]	13.8	16.6	64	240	66.4	30	29,886	30
Niger	..	..	44	270	46.0	..	..	..
Nigeria	..	..	35	1,120	31.4	..	..	..
Norway	27.7	30.4	3	87	46.1	..	..	28
Oman[b]	7.2	..	14	52	20.2	*0*	..	*12*
Pakistan[b]	10.2	9.5	47	560	43.4	35	11,763	37
Panama[b]	10.2	..	59	560	52.4	*30*	*200,000*	*30*
Papua New Guinea[b]	19.0	..	44	198	44.3	..	..	..
Paraguay[b]	..	12.1	33	328	43.2	10	..	..
Peru[b]	12.2	13.5	53	424	40.8	30	..	30
Philippines[b]	13.7	13.0	59	94	53.0	32	9,076	35
Poland	*16.0*	16.5	43	175	38.4	40	22,854	19
Portugal	21.5	21.6	7	328	47.0	42	75,000	25
Puerto Rico	..	..	17	140	40.9	*33*	*50,000*	*20*

5.6 Tax policies

	Tax revenue collected by central government		Taxes payable by businesses			Highest marginal tax rate[a]		
	% of GDP		Number of payments	Time to prepare, file, and pay taxes hours	Total tax rate % of profit	Individual		Corporate
						%	On income over $	%
	2000	2005	Fiscal year 2006	Fiscal year 2006	Fiscal year 2006	2006	2006	2006
Romania	*11.7*	..	89	198	48.9	16	..	16
Russian Federation	*13.6*	16.6	70	256	54.2	13	..	24
Rwanda[b]	..	..	43	168	41.1	..	..	..
Saudi Arabia	..	..	14	75	14.9	0	..	*0*
Senegal[b]	17.3	..	59	696	47.7	*0*	..	..
Serbia and Montenegro[b]	*23.0*	..	41[d]	168[d]	38.9[d]	10	..	10
Sierra Leone[b]	10.2	11.0	20	399	277	..	..	..
Singapore[b]	15.4	*12.4*	16	30	28.8	21	192,771	20
Slovak Republic	..	15.1	30	344	48.9	19	..	19
Slovenia[b]	21.2	21.4	34	272	39.4	50	..	25
Somalia	..	..	..	..	..	..	..	..
South Africa	24.0	27.5	23	350	38.3	40	47,170	29
Spain	16.2	12.6	7	602	59.1	29	58,524	35
Sri Lanka[b]	14.5	14.3	61	256	74.9	35	4,975	35
Sudan[b]	*6.4*	7.0[c]	66	180	37.1	..	..	..
Swaziland[b]	..	*26.0*	34	104	39.5	33	11,792	30
Sweden	19.7	20.8	5	122	57.0	25	61,673	28
Switzerland[b]	11.3	..	13	68	24.9	..	..	9
Syrian Arab Republic[b]	*17.4*	..	21	336	35.5	..	..	..
Tajikistan[b]	7.7	*9.8*	55	224	87.0	..	..	..
Tanzania	..	..	48	248	45.0	30	5,740	30
Thailand	..	17.1	46	104	40.2	37	99,453	30
Togo[b]	..	13.3	51	270	48.3	..	..	..
Trinidad and Tobago[b]	22.1	24.0	28	114	37.2	25	..	25
Tunisia[b]	21.3	21.3	45	268	58.8	..	..	..
Turkey[b]	*22.1*	..	18	254	46.3	35	..	30
Turkmenistan	..	..	..	..	..	..	..	..
Uganda[b]	10.9	*11.9*	31	237	32.2	30	2,763	30
Ukraine[b]	14.1	17.8	98	2,185	60.3	13	..	25
United Arab Emirates[b]	*1.7*	..	15	12	15.0	0	..	..
United Kingdom	29.0	28.3	7	105	35.4	40	60,545	30
United States	*12.7*	11.2	10	325	46.0	35	326,450	35
Uruguay[b]	16.7	18.5	41	300	27.6	0	..	30
Uzbekistan	..	..	130	152	122.3	29	960	12
Venezuela, RB[b]	13.3	16.1	68	864	51.9	34	93,767	34
Vietnam[b]	..	..	32	1,050	41.6	40	5,044	28
West Bank and Gaza	..	..	50	154	31.5	..	..	..
Yemen, Rep.[b]	*9.4*	..	32	248	48.0	..	..	..
Zambia[b]	*18.4*	..	37	131	22.2	*30*	*368*	*35*
Zimbabwe[b]	..	..	59	216	37.0	45	*26,249*	*30*
World	**15.8 w**	**16.1 w**	**35 u**	**334 u**	**54.0 u**			
Low income	9.8	*10.6*	43	331	70.5			
Middle income	*12.5*	*12.8*	38	378	48.6			
Lower middle income	*9.7*	*10.7*	43	442	50.0			
Upper middle income	..	..	30	280	46.5			
Low & middle income	*12.0*	*12.4*	40	361	56.4			
East Asia & Pacific	7.7	*9.8*	32	273	43.9			
Europe & Central Asia	*15.5*	17.3	48	448	58.2			
Latin America & Carib.	*11.8*	..	42	437	49.4			
Middle East & N. Africa	15.7	..	33	276	43.8			
South Asia	9.3	*10.1*	30	305	45.1			
Sub-Saharan Africa	..	..	41	336	71.2			
High income	*16.6*	16.0	17	220	43.8			
Europe EMU	19.2	18.1	19	250	56.0			

a. These data are from PriceWaterhouseCoopers' *Worldwide Tax Summaries* online b. Data on central government taxes were reported on a cash basis and have been adjusted to the accrual framework of the *Government Finance Statistics Manual 2001*. c. World Bank staff estimate. d. Data are for Serbia only.

About the data

Taxes are the main source of revenue for most governments. The sources of tax revenue and their relative contributions are determined by government policy choices about where and how to impose taxes and by changes in the structure of the economy. Tax policy may reflect concerns about distributional effects, economic efficiency (including corrections for externalities), and the practical problems of administering a tax system. There is no ideal level of taxation. But taxes influence incentives and thus the behavior of economic actors and the economy's competitiveness.

Taxes are compulsory transfers to governments from individuals, businesses, or institutions. Certain compulsory transfers, such as fines, penalties, and most social security contributions are excluded from tax revenue.

The level of taxation is typically measured by tax revenue as a share of gross domestic product (GDP). Comparing levels of taxation across countries provides a quick overview of the fiscal obligations and incentives facing the private sector. The table shows only central government data, which may significantly understate the total tax burden, particularly in countries where provincial and municipal governments are large or have considerable tax authority.

Low ratios of tax revenue to GDP may reflect weak administration and large-scale tax avoidance or evasion. Low ratios may also reflect a sizable parallel economy with unrecorded and undisclosed incomes. Tax revenue ratios tend to rise with income, with higher income countries relying on taxes to finance a much broader range of social services and social security than lower income countries are able to.

The new indicators covering taxes payable by businesses go beyond the usual measures of tax rates, which capture only part of the taxpayer burden. In some countries tax systems are so complex that businesses must make more than 100 payments and spend up to 2,600 hours a year to prepare and pay taxes.

Taxes are measured at all levels of government and include corporate income tax, personal income tax withheld by businesses, value-added or sales taxes, property transfer taxes, financial transactions taxes, dividend taxes, waste collection taxes, and vehicle and road taxes. To make the data comparable across countries, several assumptions are made about the business. The main assumptions are that they are limited liability companies, they operate in the country's most populous city, they are domestically owned, they perform general industrial or commercial activities, and they have a certain level of start-up capital, employees, and turnover. For details about the assumptions, see *Doing Business 2007.*

A potentially important influence on both domestic and international investors is a tax system's progressivity, as reflected in the highest marginal tax rate levied at the national level on individual and corporate income. Figures for individual marginal tax rates generally refer to employment income. In some countries the highest marginal tax rate is also the basic or flat rate, and other surtaxes, deductions, and the like may apply. And in many countries several different corporate tax rates may be levied, depending on the type of business (mining, banking, insurance, agriculture, manufacturing), ownership (domestic or foreign), volume of sales, or whether surtaxes or exemptions are included. The corporate tax rates in the table are mainly general rates applied to domestic companies. For more detailed information, see the country's laws, regulations, and tax treaties.

Definitions

• **Tax revenue collected by central government** refers to compulsory transfers to the central government for public purposes. Certain compulsory transfers such as fines, penalties, and most social security contributions are excluded. Refunds and corrections of erroneously collected tax revenue are treated as negative revenue. The analytic framework of the International Monetary Fund's (IMF) *Government Finance Statistics Manual 2001* (GFSM 2001) is based on accrual accounting and balance sheets. For countries still reporting government finance data on a cash basis, the IMF adjusts reported data to the GFSM 2001 accrual framework. These countries are footnoted in the table. • **Number of tax payments by businesses** is the total number of taxes paid by businesses during one year. When electronic filing is available, the tax is counted as paid once a year even if payments are more frequent. • **Time to prepare, file, and pay taxes** is the time, in hours per year, it takes to prepare, file, and pay (or withhold) three major types of taxes: the corporate income tax, the value-added or sales tax, and labor taxes, including payroll taxes and social security contributions. • **Total tax rate** is the total amount of taxes payable by businesses (except for labor taxes) after accounting for deductions and exemptions as a percentage of profit. For further details on the method used for assessing the total tax payable, see *Doing Business 2007.* • **Highest marginal tax rate** is the highest rate shown on the national level schedule of tax rates applied to the annual taxable income of individuals and corporations. Also presented are the income levels for individuals above which the highest marginal tax rates levied at the national level apply.

Data sources

Data on central government tax revenues are from print and electronic editions of the IMF's *Government Finance Statistics Yearbook.* Data on taxes payable by businesses are from *Doing Business 2007* (www.doingbusiness.org). Data on individual and corporate tax rates are from PricewaterhouseCoopers's *Worldwide Tax Summaries* online (www.pwc.com).

5.7 Defense expenditures and arms transfers

	Military expenditures				Armed forces personnel				Arms transfers			
	% of GDP		% of central government expenditure		thousands		% of labor force		$ millions 1990 prices Exports		Imports	
	1995	2005	1995	2005	1995	2005	1995	2005	1995	2005	1995	2005
Afghanistan	..	..	..	..	383	27	5.5	0.3	*0*	..	0	22
Albania	2.1	1.4	8.2	5.7	87	23	6.0	1.7	..	..	24	31
Algeria	3.0	2.8	12.2	..	163	319	1.8	2.4	..	..	346	149
Angola	8.1	5.0	..	..	122	118	2.3	1.7	0	0	1	22
Argentina	1.6	1.0	..	*5.9*	99	102	0.7	0.6	3	0	70	67
Armenia	4.1	2.7	..	15.0	61	49	4.2	3.8	..	..	49	0
Australia	1.9	1.8	..	7.2	57	53	0.6	0.5	28	50	147	396
Austria	0.9	0.7	2.0	1.7	56	40	1.4	1.0	0	3	23	21
Azerbaijan	2.3	2.1	11.7	..	127	82	3.8	2.0	..	..	0	0
Bangladesh	1.4	1.1	..	*13.6*	171	252	0.3	0.4	..	..	121	27
Belarus	1.6	1.2	5.5	4.2	106	183	2.1	3.8	8	0	0	0
Belgium	1.6	1.2	3.4	2.9	47	37	1.1	0.8	299	173	16	0
Benin	..	..	..	..	7	8	0.3	0.2	..	..	0	0
Bolivia	1.9	1.9	..	7.1	64	70	2.2	1.7	..	..	1	9
Bosnia and Herzegovina	..	1.8	..	4.8	92	12	5.2	0.6	0	0	0	0
Botswana	3.5	2.5	11.4	..	9	11	1.4	1.8	..	..	7	0
Brazil	2.1	1.6	*4.8*	..	681	673	0.9	0.7	28	62	237	142
Bulgaria	2.6	2.4	6.6	7.0	136	85	3.5	2.7	2	0	0	158
Burkina Faso	1.5	1.5	..	12.6	10	11	0.2	0.2	..	..	0	19
Burundi	4.2	0.0	17.8	..	15	82	0.5	2.1	..	..	0	0
Cambodia	5.4	1.8	..	23.1	309	191	6.2	2.8	0	0	0	0
Cameroon	1.4	1.3	11.8	..	24	23	0.5	0.4	..	..	0	0
Canada	1.6	1.1	6.4	6.3	76	71	0.5	0.4	369	365	339	112
CentralAfrican Republic	1.2	1.1	..	12.3	5	3	0.3	0.2	..	..	0	0
Chad	1.4	0.9	..	..	35	35	1.3	1.0	0	0	1	0
Chile	3.1	3.8	..	20.2	130	116	2.3	1.8	0	0	468	456
China	1.7[a]	2.0[a]	..[a]	*18.2*[a]	4,130	3,755	0.6	0.5	962	129	523	2,697
Hong Kong, China	..	..	..	..	..	..	..	..	..	..	..	..
Colombia	2.6	3.7	..	11.9	233	336	1.4	1.5	..	..	37	11
Congo, Dem. Rep.	*1.5*	2.1	*13.5*	..	65	65	0.4	0.3	..	..	0	14
Congo, Rep.	..	*1.4*	..	*6.9*	17	12	1.4	0.8	..	..	0	0
Costa Rica	..	..	..	..	16	0	1.2	0.0	..	..	0	0
Côte d'Ivoire	*0.8*	*1.6*	..	*8.9*	15	19	0.3	0.3	..	..	2	0
Croatia	9.4	1.6	22.2	4.0	150	31	7.2	1.6	0	0	22	0
Cuba	..	..	..	..	124	76	2.5	1.4	..	..	0	0
Czech Republic	1.7	1.8	5.2	5.0	92	28	1.8	0.5	122	10	0	630
Denmark	1.7	1.4	..	*4.2*	33	21	1.2	0.7	8	2	127	78
Dominican Republic	0.6	0.6	5.6	*3.3*	40	40	1.3	1.0	..	..	0	0
Ecuador	2.4	2.4	*9.2*	..	57	47	1.3	0.7	..	..	10	33
Egypt, Arab Rep.	3.5	2.8	14.7	..	610	799	3.5	3.5	7	0	1,700	596
El Salvador	1.0	0.6	..	3.5	39	16	1.8	0.6	*0*	..	3	0
Eritrea	20.8	*19.3*	..	..	55	202	4.4	11.3	0	0	3	276
Estonia	1.0	1.6	..	6.2	6	8	0.8	1.2	0	0	18	10
Ethiopia	1.6	3.1	..	..	120	183	0.5	0.6	0	0	0	0
Finland	1.5	1.2	..	3.3	35	31	1.4	1.2	20	22	159	77
France	3.0	2.5	6.2	5.4	502	359	2.0	1.3	681	2,399	43	3
Gabon	..	1.4	..	..	10	7	2.0	1.2	..	..	0	0
Gambia, The	0.8	0.3	..	..	1	1	0.2	0.1	..	..	0	0
Georgia	*2.2*	3.1	*8.2*	18.1	14	23	0.5	1.0	0	0	0	0
Germany	1.6	1.4	4.2	4.3	365	285	0.9	0.7	1,430	1,855	252	216
Ghana	0.8	0.7	..	*3.8*	13	7	0.2	0.1	..	..	0	0
Greece	4.2	4.5	8.8	10.1	202	168	4.5	3.3	0	0	870	1,114
Guatemala	1.0	0.4	13.1	3.8	57	48	1.8	1.2	..	..	3	0
Guinea	*1.4*	..	..	..	19	13	0.5	0.3	..	..	0	0
Guinea-Bissau	0.9	..	..	..	9	9	1.9	1.4	..	..	0	0
Haiti	0.1	..	..	..	7	0	0.2	0.0	..	..	..	..

Defense expenditures and arms transfers

	Military expenditures				Armed forces personnel				Arms transfers			
									$ millions 1990 prices			
	% of GDP		% of central government expenditure		thousands		% of labor force		Exports		Imports	
	1995	2005	1995	2005	1995	2005	1995	2005	1995	2005	1995	2005
Honduras	..	0.6	..	..	24	20	1.2	0.6	..	..	0	0
Hungary	1.6	1.3	..	3.1	73	44	1.7	1.0	6	70	24	12
India	2.7	2.9	18.4	*18.6*	2,150	3,047	0.6	0.7	2	0	943	1,471
Indonesia	1.6	0.9	16.2	*6.5*	461	582	0.5	0.5	25	8	339	19
Iran, Islamic Rep.	2.4	4.5	15.2	21.7	763	585	4.4	2.1	1	0	373	403
Iraq	..	..	..	..	407	227	7.0	2.7	0	0	0	290
Ireland	1.0	0.6	2.7	1.9	13	10	0.9	0.5	*0*	..	0	4
Israel	9.0	7.9	..	17.0	178	176	8.5	6.4	110	160	265	1,422
Italy	1.7	1.8	3.6	4.5	585	445	2.6	1.8	340	827	315	224
Jamaica	0.6	0.7	1.7	2.1	4	3	0.3	0.3	..	..	0	0
Japan	1.0	1.0	..	..	252	272	0.4	0.4	16	0	877	250
Jordan	12.4	7.7	47.5	21.7	129	111	10.2	6.0	0	15	19	23
Kazakhstan	1.1	1.1	*5.7*	5.8	75	101	1.0	1.2	24	0	99	68
Kenya	1.6	1.5	6.4	7.6	29	29	0.2	0.2	..	..	0	25
Korea, Dem. Rep.	..	..	..	..	1,243	1,295	12.4	12.1	52	0	68	2
Korea, Rep.	2.8	2.6	19.4	12.1	641	693	3.0	2.8	21	38	1,674	544
Kuwait	13.6	5.7	..	21.9	22	23	2.5	1.7	0	0	631	55
Kyrgyz Republic	1.6	*2.8*	6.1	..	7	18	0.4	0.8	61	0	0	3
Lao PDR	*2.9*	..	..	..	137	129	7.7	5.5	..	..	0	0
Latvia	0.9	1.7	3.1	5.8	11	5	0.9	0.5	0	0	16	7
Lebanon	6.4	*3.8*	..	*14.4*	63	85	5.5	6.0	0	0	34	1
Lesotho	3.7	2.4	10.7	*6.8*	2	2	0.3	0.3	..	..	0	0
Liberia	*31.2*	..	..	..	21	15	2.7	1.3	..	..	0	0
Libya	*4.1*	*1.9*	..	..	81	76	5.2	3.3	0	0	0	0
Lithuania	0.5	1.8	..	6.4	9	29	0.5	1.8	0	0	4	9
Macedonia, FYR	*3.0*	2.2	..	..	18	19	2.2	2.2	0	29	0	0
Madagascar	0.9	..	..	..	29	22	0.5	0.3	..	..	0	0
Malawi	0.8	*0.7*	..	..	10	7	0.2	0.1	0	0	0	0
Malaysia	2.8	1.9	16.0	*13.8*	140	135	1.7	1.2	0	0	898	467
Mali	2.2	1.9	..	..	15	12	0.4	0.2	..	..	0	0
Mauritania	2.0	1.0	..	..	21	21	2.3	1.7	..	..	1	0
Mauritius	0.4	0.2	1.8	1.0	2	2	0.4	0.4	..	..	0	0
Mexico	0.6	0.4	3.8	..	189	204	0.5	0.5	..	..	45	35
Moldova	0.9	0.3	*2.4*	1.0	15	10	0.8	0.5	0	4	6	0
Mongolia	1.7	*1.7*	..	*6.2*	31	16	3.3	1.3	..	..	0	0
Morocco	4.6	4.3	..	13.7	238	251	2.7	2.3	..	..	30	32
Mozambique	1.5	1.4	..	..	12	11	0.2	0.1	..	..	0	0
Myanmar	3.7	..	..	..	371	483	1.7	1.8	..	..	216	20
Namibia	1.9	3.0	..	*8.5*	8	15	1.5	2.3	..	..	4	0
Nepal	0.9	2.0	..	11.8	63	131	0.8	1.2	..	..	1	0
Netherlands	1.9	1.6	3.8	4.0	78	60	1.0	0.7	383	840	46	129
New Zealand	1.4	1.0	..	3.1	10	9	0.6	0.4	0	0	7	8
Nicaragua	1.1	0.7	6.8	3.3	12	14	0.8	0.7	5	0	0	0
Niger	1.0	*1.1*	..	..	11	10	0.3	0.2	..	..	0	0
Nigeria	0.7	0.9	..	..	89	161	0.2	0.3	0	0	2	0
Norway	2.4	1.6	..	4.8	31	47	1.4	1.9	22	13	83	9
Oman	14.6	*12.2*	45.2	..	48	46	6.2	4.8	0	0	157	98
Pakistan	6.0	3.4	31.4	23.1	846	921	2.2	1.6	0	9	..	..
Panama	1.2	..	5.6	..	12	12	1.1	0.8	..	..	0	0
Papua New Guinea	1.0	0.5	3.9	..	4	3	0.2	0.1	..	..	0	0
Paraguay	1.4	0.8	..	4.5	28	25	1.4	0.9	..	..	0	1
Peru	1.9	1.2	10.7	7.2	178	157	1.8	1.2	0	0	32	368
Philippines	1.4	0.8	*8.5*	4.5	149	147	0.5	0.4	..	..	36	38
Poland	2.0	1.8	..	4.9	302	162	1.7	0.9	176	124	125	96
Portugal	2.4	2.1	*5.7*	5.1	104	93	2.1	1.7	0	0	18	406
Puerto Rico	..	..	..	..	..	..	..	..	..	..	..	..

5.7 Defense expenditures and arms transfers

	Military expenditures				Armed forces personnel				Arms transfers			
	% of GDP		% of central government expenditure		thousands		% of labor force		$ millions 1990 prices Exports		Imports	
	1995	2005	1995	2005	1995	2005	1995	2005	1995	2005	1995	2005
Romania	2.8	2.1	..	..	297	177	2.4	1.7	6	17	0	579
Russian Federation	4.4	3.7	..	18.8	1,800	1,452	2.5	2.0	3,273	5,771	40	0
Rwanda	4.4	2.2	..	..	47	53	2.0	1.3	..	..	0	0
Saudi Arabia	9.3	8.2	..	..	178	216	3.0	2.7	0	36	975	470
Senegal	1.8	1.5	..	..	17	19	0.5	0.4	..	..	2	0
Serbia and Montenegro	*5.3*	2.7	..	..	165	*110*	3.5	*2.8*	0	*0*	18	*0*
Sierra Leone	2.9	1.1	..	5.1	7	13	0.4	0.6	..	..	15	0
Singapore	4.4	4.7	35.1	*30.5*	66	167	3.7	7.5	0	3	237	423
Slovak Republic	3.2	1.8	..	5.1	51	20	2.1	0.7	91	0	220	0
Slovenia	1.6	1.7	4.7	4.0	13	12	1.3	1.2	..	..	19	2
Somalia	..	..	..	..	225	0	8.3	0.0	..	..	0	0
South Africa	2.2	1.4	..	4.8	277	56	1.7	0.3	15	39	38	606
Spain	1.4	1.0	3.9	4.2	282	220	1.7	1.1	82	113	363	281
Sri Lanka	5.3	2.7	20.3	12.7	236	200	3.3	2.4	..	..	49	8
Sudan	2.7	*2.3*	..	..	134	123	1.6	1.2	..	..	3	0
Swaziland	2.4	..	..	..	3	..	1.1	..	..	..	0	0
Sweden	2.3	1.6	..	4.3	100	29	2.2	0.6	184	592	95	104
Switzerland	1.3	1.0	5.2	..	31	109	0.8	2.6	38	74	93	144
Syrian Arab Republic	7.1	*6.2*	..	..	531	416	11.2	5.5	0	0	43	0
Tajikistan	1.0	*2.2*	..	*15.8*	18	13	0.9	0.6	..	..	0	0
Tanzania	1.5	1.1	..	..	36	28	0.2	0.1	..	..	0	0
Thailand	2.3	1.1	..	7.0	421	421	1.3	1.2	0	0	558	98
Togo	2.4	1.5	..	9.8	8	10	0.4	0.4	..	..	3	0
Trinidad and Tobago	0.5	..	1.8	..	7	3	1.3	0.5	..	..	0	0
Tunisia	1.9	1.5	6.7	5.1	59	47	2.1	1.2	..	..	42	156
Turkey	3.9	3.2	20.4	..	690	617	3.0	2.3	0	28	1,562	746
Turkmenistan	2.3	..	..	..	11	26	0.7	1.2	..	..	0	0
Uganda	2.2	*2.5*	..	*11.1*	52	47	0.6	0.4	..	..	38	0
Ukraine	2.8	2.4	..	6.5	519	273	2.0	1.2	242	188	0	*29*
United Arab Emirates	5.2	1.9	*49.2*	..	71	51	5.5	1.9	27	10	426	2,381
United Kingdom	3.0	2.6	..	6.3	233	217	0.8	0.7	1,206	791	633	94
United States	3.8	4.1	..	19.3	1,636	1,546	1.2	1.0	10,689	7,101	415	387
Uruguay	2.1	1.4	7.9	5.0	27	25	1.8	1.4	0	0	8	18
Uzbekistan	1.1	*0.5*	..	..	42	91	0.5	0.8	0	0	0	0
Venezuela, RB	1.6	1.1	8.7	4.4	80	82	0.9	0.6	0	0	0	7
Vietnam	*2.6*	..	..	..	622	495	1.8	1.1	..	..	270	291
West Bank and Gaza	..	..	..	..	..	56	..	7.3	..	..	1	0
Yemen, Rep.	6.4	5.6	33.4	..	70	138	1.8	2.3	..	..	124	289
Zambia	2.2	..	..	..	23	16	0.6	0.3	0	0	0	0
Zimbabwe	3.6	*3.4*	11.2	..	68	51	1.4	0.9	..	..	0	0
World	**2.5 w**	**2.5 w**	**.. w**	***11.1* w**	**30,182 s**	**30,898 s**	**1.2 w**	**0.9 w**	**21,064 s**	**21,941 s**	**20,951 s**	**21,804 s**
Low income	2.7	2.6	19.6	*18.5*	7,698	8,536	1.0	0.9	115	9	1,813	2,459
Middle income	2.3	2.0	..	*13.2*	16,128	16,527	1.2	0.9	4,996	6,465	8,354	9,196
Lower middle income	2.1	2.0	..	*15.4*	11,456	12,989	1.0	0.8	1,304	406	4,598	5,352
Upper middle income	2.7	2.0	..	..	4,672	3,538	1.9	1.3	3,692	6,059	3,756	3,844
Low & middle income	2.4	2.1	..	*13.8*	23,826	25,063	1.1	0.9	5,111	6,474	10,167	11,655
East Asia & Pacific	1.8	1.8	..	*16.5*	8,021	10,125	0.9	0.7	1,039	137	2,920	3,632
Europe & Central Asia	3.4	2.7	..	11.2	4,971	3,581	2.3	1.7	4,011	6,212	2,227	2,349
Latin America & Carib.	1.7	1.3	*5.1*	..	2,112	2,076	1.1	0.8	36	62	914	1,147
Middle East & N. Africa	4.1	3.7	18.1	..	3,172	3,169	4.2	2.9	8	15	2,872	2,037
South Asia	3.0	2.8	20.4	*19.0*	3,852	4,578	0.8	0.8	2	9	1,114	1,528
Sub-Saharan Africa	2.1	1.6	..	..	1,698	1,534	0.7	0.5	15	39	120	962
High income	2.5	2.6	..	*10.6*	6,356	5,836	1.3	1.1	15,953	15,467	10,584	10,149
Europe EMU	2.0	1.7	3.9	4.5	2,270	1,750	1.7	1.2	3,235	6,232	2,105	2,475

Note: For some countries data are partial or uncertain or based on rough estimates; see SIPRI (2006).

a. Estimates differ from official statistics of the govenment of China, which has published the following estimates: military expenditure as 1.1 percent of GDP in 1995 and 1.6 percent in 2004 and 9.3 percent of central government expenditure in 1995 and 7.7 percent in 2004 (see National Bureau of Statistics of China, www.stats.gov.cn).

Defense expenditures and arms transfers 5.7

About the data

Although national defense is an important function of government and security from external threats contributes to economic development, high levels of defense spending burden the economy and may impede growth. Data on military expenditures as a share of gross domestic product (GDP) are a rough indicator of the portion of national resources used for military activities and of the burden on the national economy. Comparisons of defense spending between countries should take into account the many factors that influence perceptions of vulnerability and risk, including historical and cultural traditions, the length of borders that need defending, the quality of relations with neighbors, and the role of the armed forces in the body politic. As an "input" measure, military spending is not directly related to the "output" of military activities, capabilities, or military security.

Data on defense spending reported by governments are not compiled using standard definitions. They are often incomplete and unreliable. Even in countries where the parliament vigilantly reviews budgets and spending, defense spending and arms transfers rarely receive close scrutiny and full, public disclosure (see Ball 1984 and Happe and Wakeman-Linn 1994). The data on military expenditures as a share of GDP and a share of central government expenditure are estimated by the Stockholm International Peace Research Institute (SIPRI). Central government expenditures are from the International Monetary Fund (IMF). Therefore the data shown in the table may differ from comparable data published by national governments.

SIPRI's primary source of military expenditure data is official data provided by national governments. These data are derived from national budget documents, defense white papers, and other public documents from official government agencies, including governments' responses to questionnaires sent by SIPRI, the United Nations, or the Organization for Security and Co-operation in Europe. Secondary sources include international statistics, such as those of the North Atlantic Treaty Organization (NATO) and the IMF's *Government Finance Statistics Yearbook*. Other secondary sources include country reports of the Economist Intelligence Unit, country reports by IMF staff, and specialist journals and newspapers.

Lack of sufficiently detailed data makes it difficult to apply a common definition of military expenditure globally, so SIPRI has adopted a definition (derived from the NATO definition) as a guideline (see *Definitions*). This definition cannot be applied for all countries, however, since that would require much more detailed information than is available about what is included in military budgets and off-budget military expenditure items. In the many cases where SIPRI cannot make independent estimates, it uses the national data provided. Because of the differences in definitions and the difficulty in verifying the accuracy and completeness of data, the data on military spending are not strictly comparable across countries.

The data on armed forces are from the International Institute for Strategic Studies' *The Military Balance 2007*. These data refer to military personnel on active duty, including paramilitary forces. Reserve forces, which are units that are not fully staffed or operational in peace time, are not included. These data also exclude civilians in the defense establishment and so are not consistent with the data on military spending on personnel. Moreover, because data exclude personnel not on active duty, they underestimate the share of the labor force working for the defense establishment. Because governments rarely report the size of their armed forces, such data typically come from intelligence sources.

The data on arms transfers are from SIPRI's Arms Transfers Project, which reports on international flows of conventional weapons. Data are collected from open sources, and since publicly available information is inadequate for tracking all weapons and other military equipment, SIPRI covers only what it terms *major conventional weapons*.

SIPRI's data on arms transfers cover sales of weapons, manufacturing licenses, aid, and gifts; therefore the term *arms transfers* rather than *arms trade* is used. The transferred weapons must be transferred voluntarily by the supplier, must have a military purpose, and must be destined for the armed forces, paramilitary forces, or intelligence agencies of another country. SIPRI data also cover weapons supplied to or from rebel forces in an armed conflict as well as arms deliveries for which neither the supplier nor the recipient can be identified with an acceptable degree of certainty; these data are available in SIPRI's database.

SIPRI's estimates of arms transfers, presented in 1990 constant price U.S. dollars, are designed as a trend-measuring device in which similar weapons have similar values, reflecting both the value and quality of weapons transferred. The trends presented in the tables are based on actual deliveries only. SIPRI cautions that these estimated values do not reflect financial value (payments for weapons transferred) for three reasons: reliable data on the value of the transfer are not available; even when the value of a transfer is known, it usually includes more than the actual conventional weapons such as spares, support systems, and training; and even when the value of the transfer is known, details of the financial arrangements such as credit and loan conditions and discounts are usually not known.

Given these measurement issues, SIPRI's method of estimating the transfer of military resources includes an evaluation of the technical parameters of the weapons. Weapons for which a price is not known are compared with the same weapons for which actual acquisition prices are available ("core weapons") or for the closest match. These weapons are assigned a value in an index that reflects their military resource value in relation to the core weapons. These matches are based on such characteristics as size, performance, and type of electronics, and adjustments are made for second-hand weapons. More information on SIPRI's arms transfers project is available at www.sipri.org/contents/armstrad/.

Definitions

• **Military expenditures** data from SIPRI are derived from the NATO definition, which includes all current and capital expenditures on the armed forces, including peacekeeping forces; defense ministries and other government agencies engaged in defense projects; paramilitary forces, if these are judged to be trained and equipped for military operations; and military space activities. Such expenditures include military and civil personnel, including retirement pensions of military personnel and social services for personnel; operation and maintenance; procurement; military research and development; and military aid (in the military expenditures of the donor country). Excluded are civil defense and current expenditures for previous military activities, such as for veterans' benefits, demobilization, conversion, and destruction of weapons. This definition cannot be applied for all countries, however, since that would require much more detailed information than is available about what is included in military budgets and off-budget military expenditure items. (For example, military budgets might or might not cover civil defense, reserves and auxiliary forces, police and paramilitary forces, dual-purpose forces such as military and civilian police, military grants in kind, pensions for military personnel, and social security contributions paid by one part of government to another.) • **Armed forces personnel** are active duty military personnel, including paramilitary forces if the training, organization, equipment, and control suggest they may be used to support or replace regular military forces. • **Arms transfers** cover the supply of military weapons through sales, aid, gifts, and those made through manufacturing licenses. Data cover major conventional weapons such as aircraft, armored vehicles, artillery, radar systems, missiles, and ships designed for military use. Excluded are transfers of other military equipment such as small arms and light weapons, trucks, small artillery, ammunition, support equipment, technology transfers, and other services. See *About the data* for more detail.

Data sources

Data on military expenditures and arms transfers are from SIPRI's *Yearbook 2006: Armaments, Disarmament, and International Security.* Data on armed forces personnel are from the International Institute for Strategic Studies' *The Military Balance 2007.*

5.8 Public policies and institutions

	IDA Resource Allocation Index 1 (low) to 6 (high)	Economic management 1 (low) to 6 (high)				Structural policies 1 (low) to 6 (high)			
		Macroeconomic management	Fiscal policy	Debt policy	Average	Trade	Financial sector	Business regulatory environment	Average
	2005	2005	2005	2005	2005	2005	2005	2005	2005
Albania	3.7	4.5	3.5	4.0	4.0	4.5	4.0	3.5	4.0
Angola	2.6	3.0	2.5	2.0	2.5	4.0	2.5	2.0	2.8
Armenia	4.3	5.5	5.0	5.5	5.3	4.5	3.5	4.0	4.0
Azerbaijan	3.7	4.5	4.5	4.5	4.5	4.0	3.0	3.5	3.5
Bangladesh	3.4	4.0	3.5	4.5	4.0	3.0	3.0	3.5	3.2
Benin	3.7	4.5	4.0	3.5	4.0	4.5	3.5	4.0	4.0
Bhutan	3.8	4.0	4.0	4.0	4.0	3.0	3.0	3.5	3.2
Bolivia	3.7	4.0	4.0	4.0	4.0	5.0	3.5	3.0	3.8
Bosnia and Herzegovina	3.6	4.0	3.5	4.0	3.8	4.0	4.0	3.5	3.8
Burkina Faso	3.8	4.5	4.5	4.5	4.5	4.0	3.0	3.0	3.3
Burundi	3.0	3.5	3.5	3.0	3.3	3.0	3.0	2.5	2.8
Cambodia	3.1	4.0	3.5	3.5	3.7	3.5	2.0	3.5	3.0
Cameroon	3.3	4.0	3.5	2.5	3.3	3.5	3.0	3.5	3.3
Cape Verde	4.1	4.5	4.0	4.0	4.2	4.0	4.0	4.0	4.0
Central African Republic	2.4	3.0	3.0	1.5	2.5	3.5	2.5	2.0	2.7
Chad	2.9	4.0	3.0	3.0	3.3	3.0	3.0	3.0	3.0
Comoros	2.4	3.0	2.5	1.5	2.3	2.0	2.5	2.5	2.3
Congo, Dem. Rep.	2.8	3.5	3.5	2.5	3.2	4.0	2.0	3.0	3.0
Congo, Rep.	2.8	3.5	3.0	2.5	3.0	3.0	2.5	2.5	2.7
Côte d'Ivoire	2.5	2.5	2.0	1.5	2.0	3.5	3.0	3.0	3.2
Djibouti	3.1	3.5	3.0	3.0	3.2	4.0	3.5	3.0	3.5
Dominica	3.8	4.0	4.0	3.0	3.7	4.0	4.0	4.5	4.2
Eritrea	2.5	2.0	2.0	2.5	2.2	1.5	2.0	2.0	1.8
Ethiopia	3.4	3.5	4.0	3.5	3.7	3.0	3.0	3.5	3.2
Gambia, The	3.1	3.5	3.0	2.5	3.0	4.0	3.0	3.0	3.3
Georgia	3.8	4.5	4.0	4.0	4.2	3.5	3.5	4.0	3.7
Ghana	3.9	4.0	4.5	4.0	4.2	4.0	3.5	4.0	3.8
Grenada	3.7	4.0	3.0	2.5	3.2	4.0	3.5	4.5	4.0
Guinea	3.0	2.5	3.0	2.5	2.7	4.5	3.0	3.0	3.5
Guinea-Bissau	2.7	2.5	2.5	2.0	2.3	3.5	2.5	3.0	3.0
Guyana	3.4	3.5	3.5	3.5	3.5	4.0	3.5	3.0	3.5
Haiti	2.8	3.5	3.0	2.5	3.0	4.0	3.0	2.5	3.2
Honduras	3.9	4.5	4.5	4.0	4.3	4.5	3.5	4.0	4.0
India	3.8	4.5	3.0	4.5	4.0	3.5	4.0	3.5	3.7
Indonesia	3.7	4.5	4.0	4.5	4.3	4.5	3.5	3.0	3.7
Kenya	3.6	4.5	4.0	4.0	4.2	4.0	3.5	4.0	3.8
Kiribati	3.2	2.5	2.5	5.0	3.3	3.0	3.0	3.0	3.0
Kyrgyz Republic	3.5	4.5	3.5	4.0	4.0	4.5	3.5	3.5	3.8

About the data

The International Development Association (IDA) is the part of the World Bank Group that helps the poorest countries reduce poverty by providing concessional loans and grants for programs aimed at boosting economic growth and improving living conditions. IDA funding helps these countries deal with the complex challenges they face in striving to meet the Millennium Development Goals.

The World Bank's IDA Resource Allocation Index (IRAI), which is presented in the table, is based on the results of the annual Country Policy and Institutional Assessment (CPIA) exercise, which covers the IDA-eligible countries. Country assessments have been carried out annually by World Bank staff since the mid-1970s. Over time the criteria have been revised from a largely macroeconomic focus to include governance aspects and a broader coverage of social and structural dimensions. Country performance is assessed against a set of 16 criteria grouped into four clusters: economic management, structural policies, policies for social inclusion and equity, and public sector management and institutions. IDA resources are allocated to a county on per capita terms on the basis of its IDA country performance rating and, to a limited extent, on the basis of its per capita gross national income. This ensures that good performers receive a higher IDA allocation in per capita terms. The IRAI is a key element in the country performance rating.

The CPIA exercise is intended to capture the quality of a country's policies and institutional arrangements, focusing on key elements that are within the country's control, rather than on outcomes (such as economic growth rates) that are influenced by events beyond the country's control. More specifically, the CPIA measures the extent to which a country's policy and institutional framework supports sustainable growth and poverty reduction and, consequently, the effective use of development assistance.

All criteria within each cluster receive equal weight, and each cluster has a 25 percent weight in the overall score, which is obtained by averaging the

	IDA Resource Allocation Index 1 (low) to 6 (high)	Economic management 1 (low) to 6 (high)				Structural policies 1 (low) to 6 (high)			
		Macroeconomic management	Fiscal policy	Debt policy	Average	Trade	Financial sector	Business regulatory environment	Average
	2005	2005	2005	2005	2005	2005	2005	2005	2005
Lao PDR	3.0	4.0	3.5	3.5	3.7	3.5	1.5	3.0	2.7
Lesotho	3.5	4.0	4.0	4.0	4.0	3.5	3.5	3.0	3.3
Madagascar	3.5	3.5	3.0	3.5	3.3	4.0	3.5	4.0	3.8
Malawi	3.4	3.0	3.0	3.0	3.0	4.0	3.0	3.5	3.5
Maldives	3.8	3.5	3.5	4.5	3.8	4.0	4.0	4.0	4.0
Mali	3.7	4.5	4.0	4.5	4.3	4.0	3.0	3.5	3.5
Mauritania	3.2	2.0	2.5	4.0	2.8	4.5	2.5	3.5	3.5
Moldova	3.5	3.5	3.5	3.0	3.3	3.5	3.5	4.0	3.7
Mongolia	3.4	4.0	3.5	3.0	3.5	4.5	3.0	3.5	3.7
Mozambique	3.5	4.0	4.0	4.5	4.2	4.0	2.5	3.0	3.2
Nepal	3.3	4.5	3.5	3.5	3.8	4.0	3.0	3.0	3.3
Nicaragua	3.7	3.5	4.0	4.5	4.0	4.5	3.0	3.5	3.7
Niger	3.3	3.5	3.0	3.5	3.3	4.0	3.0	3.5	3.5
Nigeria	3.1	4.0	4.0	3.5	3.8	2.5	3.0	3.0	2.8
Pakistan	3.7	4.5	3.5	4.5	4.2	4.0	4.5	4.0	4.2
Papua New Guinea	3.1	4.0	3.0	3.5	3.5	4.0	3.0	3.0	3.3
Rwanda	3.5	4.0	3.5	3.0	3.5	3.5	3.5	3.5	3.5
Samoa	4.0	4.0	3.5	4.0	3.8	4.5	4.0	4.0	4.2
São Tomé and Principe	3.0	3.0	3.0	2.5	2.8	4.0	2.5	3.0	3.2
Senegal	3.8	4.5	4.0	4.0	4.2	4.5	3.5	3.5	3.8
Serbia and Montenegro	3.7	3.5	4.5	3.5	3.8	4.5	3.0	3.5	3.7
Sierra Leone	3.1	4.0	3.5	3.5	3.7	3.5	3.0	2.5	3.0
Solomon Islands	2.8	3.5	3.5	2.5	3.2	3.0	3.0	2.5	2.8
Sri Lanka	3.6	3.5	3.0	3.5	3.3	3.5	4.0	4.0	3.8
St. Lucia	4.0	4.5	3.5	4.0	4.0	4.0	4.0	4.5	4.2
St. Vincent & Grenadines	3.9	4.0	4.0	4.0	4.0	4.0	4.0	4.5	4.2
Sudan	2.6	3.5	3.5	1.5	2.8	3.0	2.5	3.0	2.8
Tajikistan	3.3	4.5	4.0	4.0	4.2	4.0	3.0	3.5	3.5
Tanzania	3.9	5.0	4.5	4.0	4.5	4.0	3.5	3.5	3.7
Togo	2.5	2.5	2.0	1.5	2.0	4.0	2.5	3.0	3.2
Tonga	2.9	3.0	2.0	3.5	2.8	3.0	3.0	3.0	3.0
Uganda	3.9	4.5	4.5	4.5	4.5	4.0	3.5	4.0	3.8
Uzbekistan	3.0	3.0	3.5	4.0	3.5	2.5	2.5	2.5	2.5
Vanuatu	3.1	3.0	3.0	4.0	3.3	4.0	3.0	3.0	3.3
Vietnam	3.7	5.0	4.0	4.0	4.3	3.5	3.0	3.5	3.3
Yemen, Rep.	3.3	4.0	3.0	4.5	3.8	4.5	2.5	3.0	3.3
Zambia	3.3	3.5	3.5	3.0	3.3	4.0	3.0	3.0	3.3
Zimbabwe	1.8	1.0	1.0	1.0	1.0	2.0	2.5	2.0	2.2

average scores of the four clusters. For each of the 16 criteria countries are rated on a scale of 1 (low) to 6 (high). The scores depend on the level of performance in a given year assessed against the criteria, rather than on changes in performance compared with the previous year. All 16 CPIA criteria contain a detailed description of each rating level. In assessing country performance World Bank staff evaluate the country's actual performance on each of the criteria and assign a rating. The ratings reflect a variety of indicators, observations, and judgments based on country knowledge and on relevant publicly available indicators. In interpreting the assessment scores, it should be noted that the criteria are designed in a developmentally neutral manner. Accordingly, higher scores can be attained by a country that, given its stage of development, has a policy and institutional framework that more strongly fosters growth and poverty reduction.

The country teams that prepare the ratings are very familiar with the country, and their assessments are based on country diagnostic studies prepared by the World Bank or other development organizations and on their own professional judgment. An early consultation is conducted with country authorities to make sure that the assessments are informed by up-to-date information. To ensure that scores are consistent across countries, the process involves two key phases. In the benchmarking phase a small representative sample of countries drawn from all regions is rated. Country teams prepare proposals that are reviewed first at the regional level and then in a Bankwide review process. A similar process is then followed to assess the performance of the remaining countries, using the benchmark countries' scores as guideposts. The final ratings are determined following a Bankwide review. The numerical IRAI overall score and the separate criteria scores were first publicly disclosed in June 2006.

See IDA's website at www.worldbank.org/ida for more information.

5.8 Public policies and institutions

	Policies for social inclusion and equity 1 (low) to 6 (high)						Public sector management and institutions 1 (low) to 6 (high)					
	Gender equality 2005	Equity of public resource use 2005	Building human resources 2005	Social protection and labor 2005	Policies and institutions for environmental sustainability 2005	Average 2005	Property rights and rule-based governance 2005	Quality of budgetary and financial manage-ment 2005	Efficiency of revenue mobilization 2005	Quality of public administration 2005	Transparency, accountability, and corruption in the public sector 2005	Average 2005
Albania	4.0	3.5	3.0	3.5	3.0	3.4	3.0	4.0	3.5	3.0	3.0	3.3
Angola	3.0	2.5	2.5	2.5	2.5	2.6	2.0	2.5	2.5	2.5	2.5	2.4
Armenia	4.5	4.5	4.0	4.5	3.5	4.2	3.5	4.0	4.0	4.0	3.5	3.8
Azerbaijan	4.0	3.5	3.0	3.5	3.0	3.4	3.0	4.0	3.5	3.0	2.5	3.2
Bangladesh	4.0	3.5	4.0	3.5	3.0	3.6	3.0	3.0	3.0	3.0	2.5	2.9
Benin	3.0	3.0	3.5	3.0	3.5	3.2	3.0	4.0	3.5	3.0	3.5	3.4
Bhutan	4.5	4.0	4.5	3.5	4.5	4.2	3.5	3.5	4.0	4.0	4.0	3.8
Bolivia	3.5	4.0	4.0	3.5	3.5	3.7	2.5	3.5	4.0	3.5	3.0	3.3
Bosnia and Herzegovina	4.0	3.0	3.5	3.5	3.0	3.4	3.0	3.5	4.0	3.0	3.0	3.3
Burkina Faso	3.5	4.0	3.5	3.5	3.5	3.6	3.5	4.0	3.5	3.5	3.5	3.6
Burundi	3.5	3.0	3.0	3.0	2.5	3.0	2.5	2.5	3.0	2.5	3.0	2.7
Cambodia	3.5	3.0	3.5	3.0	2.5	3.1	2.5	2.5	3.0	2.5	2.5	2.6
Cameroon	3.5	3.0	3.5	3.0	4.0	3.4	2.5	3.5	4.0	3.0	2.5	3.1
Cape Verde	4.5	4.5	4.0	4.5	4.0	4.3	4.0	3.5	3.5	4.0	4.5	3.9
Central African Republic	2.5	2.0	2.0	2.0	2.5	2.2	2.0	2.0	2.5	2.0	2.5	2.2
Chad	2.5	3.0	3.0	3.0	2.5	2.8	2.0	3.0	2.5	2.5	2.0	2.4
Comoros	3.0	3.0	3.0	2.5	2.0	2.7	2.5	2.0	2.5	2.0	2.5	2.3
Congo, Dem. Rep.	3.0	3.0	3.0	3.0	2.5	2.9	2.0	2.5	2.5	2.5	2.0	2.3
Congo, Rep.	3.0	3.0	3.0	2.5	3.0	2.9	2.0	3.0	3.0	2.5	2.5	2.6
Côte d'Ivoire	2.5	1.5	2.0	2.5	3.0	2.3	2.0	2.5	4.0	2.0	2.0	2.5
Djibouti	3.0	3.0	3.5	3.0	3.0	3.1	2.5	3.0	3.5	2.5	2.5	2.8
Dominica	4.5	3.5	4.0	3.5	3.0	3.7	4.0	3.0	3.5	3.5	4.0	3.6
Eritrea	3.5	3.0	3.5	3.0	3.0	3.2	2.5	2.5	3.5	3.0	2.5	2.8
Ethiopia	3.0	4.5	3.5	3.5	3.5	3.6	2.5	3.5	4.0	3.0	2.5	3.1
Gambia, The	3.5	3.0	3.5	2.5	3.0	3.1	3.5	2.5	3.5	3.0	2.0	2.9
Georgia	4.5	4.0	4.0	3.5	3.5	3.9	3.5	3.5	4.0	3.5	3.5	3.6
Ghana	4.0	4.0	3.5	3.5	3.5	3.7	3.5	3.5	4.5	3.5	3.5	3.7
Grenada	4.5	3.5	4.0	3.5	4.0	3.9	4.0	3.5	3.5	3.5	4.0	3.7
Guinea	4.0	3.0	3.0	3.5	2.5	3.2	2.0	3.0	3.0	3.0	2.5	2.7
Guinea-Bissau	3.0	3.0	2.5	2.5	3.0	2.8	2.5	2.5	3.0	2.5	2.5	2.6
Guyana	3.5	3.5	3.5	3.0	3.0	3.3	3.0	3.5	3.5	2.5	3.0	3.1
Haiti	3.0	2.5	2.5	2.5	2.5	2.6	2.0	2.5	2.5	2.5	2.0	2.3
Honduras	4.0	4.0	4.0	4.0	3.0	3.8	3.5	4.0	4.0	3.0	3.0	3.5
India	3.5	4.0	4.0	3.5	3.5	3.7	3.5	4.0	4.0	3.5	3.5	3.7
Indonesia	3.5	4.0	3.5	3.5	2.5	3.4	2.5	3.5	3.5	3.5	3.0	3.2
Kenya	3.0	3.0	3.5	3.0	3.0	3.1	3.0	3.5	4.0	3.0	3.0	3.3
Kiribati	3.0	3.5	2.5	3.0	3.0	3.0	3.5	3.5	3.0	3.0	3.5	3.3
Kyrgyz Republic	4.0	3.5	3.5	3.5	3.0	3.5	2.5	3.0	3.0	2.5	2.5	2.7

Definitions

• **IDA Resource Allocation Index** is obtained by calculating the average score for each cluster and then by averaging those scores. For each of 16 criteria countries are rated on a scale of 1 (low) to 6 (high) • **Economic management** cluster: **Macroeconomic management** assesses the monetary, exchange rate, and aggregate demand policy framework. • **Fiscal policy** assesses the short- and medium-term sustainability of fiscal policy (taking into account monetary and exchange rate policy and the sustainability of the public debt) and its impact on growth. • **Debt policy** assesses whether the debt management strategy is conducive to minimizing budgetary risks and ensuring long-term debt sustainability. • **Structural policies** cluster: **Trade** assesses how the policy framework fosters trade in goods. • **Financial sector** assesses the structure of the financial sector and the policies and regulations that affect it. • **Business regulatory environment** assesses the extent to which the legal, regulatory, and policy environments help or hinder private businesses in investing, creating jobs, and becoming more productive. • **Policies for social inclusion and equity** cluster: **Gender equality** assesses the extent to which the country has installed institutions and programs to enforce laws and policies that promote equal access for men and women in education, health, the economy, and protection under law. • **Equity of public resource use** assesses the extent to which the pattern of public expenditures and revenue collection affects the poor and is consistent with national poverty reduction priorities. • **Building human resources** assesses the national policies and public and private sector service delivery that affect the access to and quality of health and education services, including prevention and treatment of HIV/AIDS, tuberculosis, and malaria. • **Social protection and labor** assess government policies in social protection and labor market regulations that reduce the risk of becoming poor, assist those who are poor to better manage further risks, and ensure a minimal level of welfare to all people. • **Policies**

Public policies and institutions 5.8

	Policies for social inclusion and equity 1 (low) to 6 (high)						Public sector management and institutions 1 (low) to 6 (high)					
	Gender equality	Equity of public resource use	Building human resources	Social protection and labor	Policies and institutions for environmental sustainability	Average	Property rights and rule-based governance	Quality of budgetary and financial manage-ment	Efficiency of revenue mobilization	Quality of public administration	Transparency, accountability, and corruption in the public sector	Average
	2005	2005	2005	2005	2005	2005	2005	2005	2005	2005	2005	2005
Lao PDR	3.5	3.5	3.0	2.0	3.5	3.1	3.0	2.5	2.5	2.5	2.0	2.5
Lesotho	4.0	3.0	3.5	3.0	3.0	3.3	3.5	3.0	4.0	3.0	3.5	3.4
Madagascar	3.5	3.5	3.5	3.5	4.0	3.6	3.5	3.0	3.5	3.5	3.5	3.4
Malawi	3.5	3.5	3.5	3.5	3.5	3.5	3.5	3.0	4.0	3.5	3.0	3.4
Maldives	4.0	4.0	4.0	3.5	4.0	3.9	4.0	3.0	4.0	4.0	3.0	3.6
Mali	3.5	3.5	3.5	3.5	3.0	3.4	3.5	4.0	4.0	3.0	3.5	3.6
Mauritania	3.5	3.0	3.5	3.5	3.5	3.4	3.0	2.0	4.0	3.0	2.5	2.9
Moldova	4.5	3.5	4.0	3.5	3.5	3.8	3.5	3.5	3.0	3.0	3.0	3.2
Mongolia	3.5	3.5	3.5	3.5	2.5	3.3	3.0	4.0	3.5	3.5	2.5	3.3
Mozambique	3.5	3.5	3.5	3.0	3.0	3.3	3.0	3.5	3.5	3.0	3.0	3.2
Nepal	3.0	3.5	3.5	3.0	3.0	3.2	2.5	3.5	3.5	3.0	2.5	3.0
Nicaragua	4.0	4.0	3.5	3.5	3.5	3.7	3.0	3.5	4.0	3.5	3.5	3.5
Niger	2.5	3.5	3.0	3.0	3.0	3.0	3.0	3.5	3.5	3.0	3.0	3.2
Nigeria	3.0	3.5	3.0	3.0	3.0	3.1	2.5	3.0	3.0	2.5	3.0	2.8
Pakistan	2.0	3.5	3.5	3.0	3.5	3.1	3.0	3.5	3.5	3.5	2.5	3.2
Papua New Guinea	2.5	3.0	2.5	3.0	1.5	2.5	2.5	3.5	3.5	3.0	3.0	3.1
Rwanda	3.5	4.0	4.0	3.5	3.0	3.6	3.0	3.5	3.5	3.5	3.0	3.3
Samoa	4.0	4.0	4.0	3.5	4.0	3.9	4.0	4.0	4.0	4.0	4.0	4.0
São Tomé and Principe	3.0	3.5	2.5	2.5	2.5	2.8	2.5	3.0	3.5	3.0	3.5	3.1
Senegal	3.5	3.5	3.5	3.0	3.5	3.4	3.5	3.5	4.5	3.5	3.0	3.6
Serbia and Montenegro	4.5	4.0	3.5	4.0	3.5	3.9	3.0	3.5	3.5	4.0	3.0	3.4
Sierra Leone	3.0	3.0	3.0	3.0	2.5	2.9	2.5	3.5	3.0	3.0	2.5	2.9
Solomon Islands	3.0	3.0	3.0	2.5	2.0	2.7	2.5	3.0	2.5	2.0	3.0	2.6
Sri Lanka	4.0	3.5	4.5	3.5	3.5	3.8	3.5	4.0	3.5	3.0	3.5	3.5
St. Lucia	4.5	3.5	4.0	3.5	3.5	3.8	4.0	4.0	3.5	3.5	4.5	3.9
St. Vincent & Grenadines	4.5	3.5	4.0	3.5	3.5	3.8	4.0	3.5	3.5	3.5	4.0	3.7
Sudan	2.0	2.5	2.5	2.0	2.5	2.3	2.0	2.5	3.0	2.5	2.0	2.4
Tajikistan	3.5	3.0	3.0	3.5	2.5	3.1	2.5	3.0	3.0	2.5	2.0	2.6
Tanzania	4.0	4.0	4.0	3.5	3.5	3.8	3.5	4.5	4.0	3.5	3.5	3.8
Togo	3.0	2.0	3.0	2.5	2.5	2.6	2.5	2.0	2.5	2.0	2.0	2.2
Tonga	2.5	3.5	4.0	3.0	3.0	3.2	3.5	2.5	3.0	2.5	2.0	2.7
Uganda	3.5	4.5	4.0	3.5	4.0	3.9	3.5	4.0	3.0	3.0	3.0	3.3
Uzbekistan	3.5	3.5	4.0	3.5	3.5	3.6	2.0	3.0	3.0	2.5	1.5	2.4
Vanuatu	3.0	3.5	2.5	2.0	3.0	2.8	3.0	3.5	3.5	2.5	3.0	3.1
Vietnam	4.5	4.0	4.0	3.0	3.5	3.8	3.5	4.0	3.5	3.5	3.0	3.5
Yemen, Rep.	2.5	3.5	3.0	3.5	3.0	3.1	2.5	3.0	3.0	3.0	3.0	2.9
Zambia	3.5	3.5	3.5	3.0	3.5	3.4	3.0	3.0	4.0	3.0	3.0	3.2
Zimbabwe	2.5	1.5	2.0	1.5	2.5	2.0	1.0	2.5	3.5	2.0	1.5	2.1

and institutions for environmental sustainability assess the extent to which environmental policies foster the protection and sustainable use of natural resources and the management of pollution. • **Public sector management and institutions** cluster: **Property rights and rule-based governance** assess the extent to which private economic activity is facilitated by an effective legal system and rule-based governance structure in which property and contract rights are reliably respected and enforced. • **Quality of budgetary and financial management** assesses the extent to which there is a comprehensive and credible budget linked to policy priorities, effective financial management systems, and timely and accurate accounting and fiscal reporting, including timely and audited public accounts. • **Efficiency of revenue mobilization** assesses the overall pattern of revenue mobilization—not only the de facto tax structure, but also revenue from all sources as actually collected. • **Quality of public administration** assesses the extent to which civilian central government staff is structured to design and implement government policy and deliver services effectively. • **Transparency, accountability, and corruption in the public sector** assess the extent to which the executive can be held accountable for its use of funds and for the results of its actions by the electorate and by the legislature and judiciary, and the extent to which public employees within the executive are required to account for administrative decisions, use of resources, and results obtained. The three main dimensions assessed here are the accountability of the executive to oversight institutions and of public employees for their performance, access of civil society to information on public affairs, and state capture by narrow vested interests.

Data sources

Data on public policies and institutions are from the World Bank Group's CPIA database available at www.worldbank.org/ida.

5.9 Transport services

	Roads				Railways			Ports	Air		
	Total road network km	Paved roads %	Passengers carried million passenger-km	Goods hauled million ton-km	Rail lines total route-km	Passengers carried million passenger-km	Goods hauled million ton-km	Port container traffic thousand TEU	Registered carrier departures worldwide thousands	Passengers carried thousands	Air freight million ton-km
	2000–04[a]	2000–04[a]	2000–04[a]	2000–04[a]	2000–05[a]	2000–05[a]	2000–05[a]	2005	2005	2005	2005
Afghanistan	34,782	23.7	..	..	..	..	..	..	..	..	..
Albania	18,000	39.0	197	..	447	73	26	..	4	196	0
Algeria	108,302	70.2	..	..	3,572	929	1,471	..	46	3,037	32
Angola	51,429	10.4	166,045	4,709	2,761	..	..	..	5	240	68
Argentina	400,000	30.0	..	..	35,753	6,979	..	1,196	81	6,938	133
Armenia	7,633	100.0	1,867	280	732	30	678	..	6	556	7
Australia	810,200	..	..	152,777	9,528	1,290	46,164	4,830	343	44,657	2,445
Austria	133,928	100.0	69,000	26,411	5,781	8,586	17,060	..	142	8,038	537
Azerbaijan	59,141	49.4	10,279	6,965	2,122	789	7,551	..	12	1,134	12
Bangladesh	239,226	9.5	..	..	2,855	4,340	896	901	7	1,634	183
Belarus	93,310	87.0	9,382	13,969	5,498	13,568	43,559	..	5	282	1
Belgium	150,567	78.0	126,680	54,856	3,542	9,150	8,130	7,890	152	3,341	705
Benin	19,000	9.5	..	..	578	66	86	..	..	..	..
Bolivia	62,479	7.0	..	..	3,698	286	1,057	..	26	1,892	25
Bosnia and Herzegovina	..	..	..	..	1,000	53	1,173	..	*5*	*73*	*1*
Botswana	24,455	36.5	..	..	888	171	842	..	8	230	0
Brazil	1,751,868	5.5	..	..	29,314	..	221,600	5,598	515	37,662	1,531
Bulgaria	44,033	99.0	14,401	6,840	4,163	2,389	5,166	..	10	654	3
Burkina Faso	15,272	31.2	..	..	622	..	..	..	1	66	..
Burundi	12,322	10.4	..	..	..	..	..	..	..	..	..
Cambodia	38,257	6.3	..	..	650	45	92	..	3	169	1
Cameroon	50,000	10.0	..	..	974	324	1,119	..	11	384	24
Canada	1,408,900	..	..	184,774	57,671	2,790	338,661	4,163	1,018	45,230	1,527
Central African Republic	..	..	..	..	..	..	..	..	..	..	..
Chad	..	..	..	..	..	..	..	..	..	..	..
Chile	79,604	20.2	..	..	2,030	1,571	3,848	1,813	93	5,939	1,054
China	1,870,661	81.0	769,560	784,090	62,200	583,320	1,934,612	88,549[b]	1,349	136,722	7,579
Hong Kong, China	1,943	100.0	..	..	..	..	..	..	123	20,230	7,764
Colombia	..	..	..	..	2,137	..	7,751	1,165	162	9,984	1,092
Congo, Dem. Rep.	153,497	1.8	..	..	3,641	140	444	..	..	..	..
Congo, Rep.	17,289	5.0	..	..	795	135	231	..	*5*	*52*	..
Costa Rica	35,330	24.4	..	..	950	..	..	779	36	953	10
Côte d'Ivoire	80,000	8.1	..	..	639	10	675	710	..	..	..
Croatia	28,344	84.7	3,716	4,373	2,726	1,266	2,835	..	22	1,361	2
Cuba	..	..	..	..	4,382	..	..	..	11	813	31
Czech Republic	127,672	100.0	90,055	475	9,513	6,631	14,385	..	75	4,706	39
Denmark	71,847	100.0	61,258	17,766	2,212	5,459	1,888	1,321	160	10,340	190
Dominican Republic	..	..	..	..	1,743	..	..	*537*	..	..	..
Ecuador	43,197	15.0	10,641	5,453	966	..	..	633	30	2,011	5
Egypt, Arab Rep.	92,370	81.0	..	..	5,150	40,837	3,917	3,691	45	4,888	287
El Salvador	..	..	..	..	283	..	..	..	24	2,541	21
Eritrea	..	..	..	..	306	..	..	..	..	..	..
Estonia	56,856	23.5	2,465	6,722	959	248	10,311	..	8	578	1
Ethiopia	36,469	19.1	219,113	2,456	..	..	..	..	31	1,667	133
Finland	78,158	64.7	69,400	28,100	5,732	3,478	9,706	1,313	107	7,075	354
France	951,220	100.0	781,000	197,000	29,286	77,219	41,263	3,840	728	52,477	5,802
Gabon	9,170	10.2	..	..	810	95	2,219	..	9	465	66
Gambia, The	3,742	19.3	16	..	..	..	..	..	..	..	..
Georgia	20,247	39.4	5,200	570	1,336	720	6,127	..	5	249	3
Germany	..	100.0	1,062,700	232,296	34,228	72,568	88,022	13,507	1,024	90,789	7,722
Ghana	47,787	17.9	..	..	977	85	242	..	*1*	*96*	*7*
Greece	114,931	..	..	18,360	2,576	1,854	613	1,779	131	9,452	64
Guatemala	..	..	..	..	886	..	..	776	..	..	..
Guinea	44,348	9.8	..	..	1,115	..	..	..	..	..	..
Guinea-Bissau	3,455	27.9	..	..	..	..	..	..	..	..	..
Haiti	..	..	..	..	..	..	..	..	..	..	..

Transport services 5.9

	Roads				Railways			Ports	Air		
	Total road network km	Paved roads %	Passengers carried million passenger-km	Goods hauled million ton-km	Rail lines total route-km	Passengers carried million passenger-km	Goods hauled million ton-km	Port container traffic thousand TEU	Registered carrier departures worldwide thousands	Passengers carried thousands	Air freight million ton-km
	2000–04[a]	**2000–04[a]**	**2000–04[a]**	**2000–04[a]**	**2000–05[a]**	**2000–05[a]**	**2000–05[a]**	**2005**	**2005**	**2005**	**2005**
Honduras	..	..	..	..	699	..	..	553	..	..	..
Hungary	159,568	43.9	13,300	12,505	7,950	7,135	9,005	..	47	2,735	21
India	3,383,344	47.4	..	..	63,465	575,702	407,398	4,938	327	27,528	773
Indonesia	368,360	58.0	..	..	..	25,535	4,698	5,503	321	26,836	440
Iran, Islamic Rep.	179,388	67.4	..	..	7,131	11,149	19,127	1,326	121	12,708	98
Iraq	..	..	..	..	1,963	570	1,682	..	..	..	..
Ireland	96,602	100.0	..	6,500	1,919	1,781	303	980	304	42,873	107
Israel	17,446	100.0	..	..	899	1,618	1,149	1,525	34	4,392	1,213
Italy	484,688	100.0	..	184,756	16,751	47,368	21,045	9,856	446	36,116	1,365
Jamaica	20,996	73.3	..	..	272	..	..	1,671	22	1,574	16
Japan	1,177,278	77.7	947,562	327,632	20,052	145,957	22,632	16,777	652	102,279	8,549
Jordan	7,500	100.0	..	..	293	..	1,024	..	20	1,737	224
Kazakhstan	90,018	93.4	85,240	43,910	14,204	12,129	171,855	..	17	1,160	16
Kenya	63,265	14.1	..	22	1,917	226	1,399	..	28	2,424	253
Korea, Dem. Rep.	..	..	..	..	5,214	..	..	..	2	101	2
Korea, Rep.	100,279	86.8	9,169	518	3,392	31,004	10,108	15,113	221	33,888	7,433
Kuwait	5,749	85.0	..	..	..	..	..	..	19	2,433	242
Kyrgyz Republic	*18,840*	..	5,624	847	424	50	561	..	5	226	2
Lao PDR	31,210	14.4	..	..	..	..	..	..	9	293	2
Latvia	69,532	100.0	2,779	2,330	2,375	894	17,921	..	23	1,032	2
Lebanon	..	..	..	..	401	..	..	..	12	1,076	87
Lesotho	..	..	..	..	..	..	..	..	..	..	..
Liberia	..	..	..	..	490	..	..	..	..	..	..
Libya	..	..	..	..	2,757	..	..	..	8	918	0
Lithuania	79,331	91.3	23,184	12,279	1,772	428	12,457	..	12	505	1
Macedonia, FYR	..	..	..	..	699	94	530	..	2	192	0
Madagascar	..	..	..	..	732	10	12	..	18	575	15
Malawi	15,451	45.0	..	..	710	25	88	..	5	132	1
Malaysia	98,721	81.3	..	..	1,667	1,181	1,178	12,027	176	20,369	2,578
Mali	18,709	18.0	..	..	733	196	189	..	..	..	..
Mauritania	..	..	..	..	717	..	..	..	2	139	0
Mauritius	2,015	100.0	..	..	..	..	..	*382*	15	1,146	212
Mexico	337,192	49.5	410,000	199,800	26,662	74	..	2,145	331	21,858	390
Moldova	12,733	86.2	1,640	1,577	1,075	355	2,980	..	4	232	1
Mongolia	49,250	3.5	381	1,889	1,810	1,128	8,857	..	5	295	6
Morocco	57,493	56.9	..	1,251	1,907	2,987	5,919	*561*	49	3,493	61
Mozambique	..	..	..	..	3,070	172	768	..	10	347	5
Myanmar	..	..	..	..	..	..	..	..	26	1,504	3
Namibia	42,237	12.8	47	591	..	..	..	..	6	306	60
Nepal	17,380	30.3	..	..	59	..	..	..	6	480	7
Netherlands	126,100	..	..	45,700	2,813	14,730	4,026	9,521	241	26,133	4,894
New Zealand	92,931	64.3	..	..	3,898	..	3,853	1,614	209	11,952	781
Nicaragua	18,669	11.4	..	..	6	..	..	..	..	..	..
Niger	14,565	25.0	..	..	..	..	..	..	..	..	..
Nigeria	193,200	15.0	..	..	3,528	174	77	*513*	8	584	10
Norway	91,916	77.5	56,573	13,614	4,087	2,440	9,568	..	234	11,568	182
Oman	34,965	27.7	..	..	..	..	..	2,727	31	3,369	237
Pakistan	258,340	64.7	209,959	..	7,791	23,045	4,796	1,391	49	5,364	408
Panama	11,643	..	..	..	355	..	..	3,068	30	1,796	37
Papua New Guinea	..	..	..	..	..	..	..	..	20	819	21
Paraguay	..	..	..	..	441	..	..	..	10	446	..
Peru	78,829	14.4	..	..	2,177	119	1,159	992	61	4,332	139
Philippines	200,037	21.6	..	..	..	..	..	3,634	59	8,057	323
Poland	423,997	69.7	29,996	85,989	19,599	16,742	46,060	*428*	79	3,554	71
Portugal	78,470	..	..	20,470	2,839	3,412	2,422	905	149	10,140	235
Puerto Rico	25,645	95.0	..	10	96	..	..	1,727	..	..	..

5.9 Transport services

	Roads				Railways			Ports	Air		
	Total road network km	Paved roads %	Passengers carried million passenger-km	Goods hauled million ton-km	Rail lines total route-km	Passengers carried million passenger-km	Goods hauled million ton-km	Port container traffic thousand TEU	Registered carrier departures worldwide thousands	Passengers carried thousands	Air freight million ton-km
	2000–04[a]	**2000–04[a]**	**2000–04[a]**	**2000–04[a]**	**2000–05[a]**	**2000–05[a]**	**2000–05[a]**	**2005**	**2005**	**2005**	**2005**
Romania	198,817	50.7	5,283	267	10,781	7,960	16,032	771	39	1,708	5
Russian Federation	537,289	..	164	5,702	85,542	164,262	1,801,601	1,803	391	26,522	1,541
Rwanda	14,008	19.0	..	..	..	..	..	..	..	..	..
Saudi Arabia	152,044	29.9	..	..	1,020	393	1,192	897	116	15,933	1,021
Senegal	13,576	29.3	..	..	906	138	371	..	6	450	..
Serbia and Montenegro	45,290	62.0	..	452	3,809	..	..	..	*25*	*1,414*	6
Sierra Leone	11,300	8.0	..	..	..	..	..	..	0	17	8
Singapore	3,188	100.0	..	..	..	..	..	23,192	77	17,744	7,571
Slovak Republic	43,000	87.3	32,214	18,517	3,659	2,166	9,326	..	14	712	0
Slovenia	38,451	100.0	980	9,007	1,228	777	3,245	..	18	758	3
Somalia	..	..	..	..	..	..	..	..	..	..	..
South Africa	364,131	17.3	..	..	20,047	991	108,513	2,868	148	11,845	923
Spain	666,292	99.0	397,117	132,868	14,484	21,047	11,586	9,170	586	49,855	1,022
Sri Lanka	97,286	81.0	21,067	..	..	4,682	138	2,455	20	2,818	310
Sudan	..	..	..	..	5,478	40	766	..	9	511	43
Swaziland	3,594	..	..	..	301	..	11,394	..	..	..	..
Sweden	424,947	..	106,868	37,677	9,867	5,673	13,120	1,217	146	9,019	264
Switzerland	71,214	100.0	96,845	15,000	3,252	14,277	9,313	..	135	9,663	1,110
Syrian Arab Republic	94,890	20.1	..	..	2,702	571	2,075	..	17	1,240	22
Tajikistan	27,767	..	..	..	616	50	1,117	..	7	479	6
Tanzania	78,891	8.6	..	..	2,600[c]	628[c]	1,196[c]	..	7	263	2
Thailand	57,403	98.5	..	..	4,044	9,195	4,037	5,115	124	18,903	2,002
Togo	..	..	..	..	568	..	..	..	..	..	..
Trinidad and Tobago	..	..	..	..	..	..	..	*440*	14	1,055	48
Tunisia	19,232	65.8	..	16,611	1,909	1,294	2,082	..	21	1,997	18
Turkey	426,906	41.6	174,312	156,853	8,697	5,036	8,939	3,170	146	16,944	383
Turkmenistan	..	..	..	..	2,529	1,286	8,670	..	14	1,654	10
Uganda	70,746	23.0	..	..	259	..	218	..	0	49	29
Ukraine	169,447	97.2	58,308	28,847	22,001	52,655	223,980	580	42	2,513	39
United Arab Emirates	..	..	..	..	..	..	..	9,846	96	16,210	4,417
United Kingdom	387,674	100.0	736,000	160,000	16,208	44,036	22,110	8,599	1,018	93,603	5,998
United States	6,433,272	64.5	7,780,158	2,034,915	228,999	8,869	2,717,513[d]	38,519	9,970[e]	720,548[e]	37,358[e]
Uruguay	60,000	..	..	..	2,993	..	..	..	9	586	4
Uzbekistan	..	..	..	..	4,014	2,012	18,007	..	22	1,639	72
Venezuela, RB	..	..	..	..	682	..	32	1,121	136	5,043	2
Vietnam	222,179	..	..	..	2,671	4,558	2,928	2,694	54	5,454	230
West Bank and Gaza	4,996	100.0	..	..	..	..	..	..	..	..	..
Yemen, Rep.	..	..	..	..	..	..	..	..	17	1,083	67
Zambia	91,440	22.0	..	..	1,273	186	554	..	6	54	0
Zimbabwe	97,267	19.0	..	..	..	..	..	..	4	243	22
World		.. m	.. m	.. m	.. s	2,278 m	5,543 m	369,847 s	24,878 s	2,020,604 s	142,571 s
Low income		..	..	..	..	..	..	*9,772*	714	54,774	2,307
Middle income		..	..	..	..	1,290	5,919	155,727	5,297	440,245	22,500
Lower middle income		..	..	..	..	1,286	3,977	122,240	3,283	295,803	14,626
Upper middle income		50.5	..	..	..	1,571	10,311	33,487	2,014	144,442	7,875
Low & middle income		..	..	..	..	..	..	166,361	6,011	495,019	24,807
East Asia & Pacific		..	..	..	..	4,558	4,037	117,522	2,220	220,887	13,285
Europe & Central Asia		..	9,815	6,602	207,077	1,649	9,005	*5,530*	1,014	71,522	2,240
Latin America & Carib.		..	..	..	..	..	..	21,509	1,596	105,739	4,566
Middle East & N. Africa		..	..	..	..	1,265	2,082	..	387	35,547	1,132
South Asia		30.3	..	..	..	13,864	2,846	9,685	417	37,955	1,682
Sub-Saharan Africa		..	..	..	..	..	..	..	379	23,368	1,903
High income		100.0	..	29,960	..	8,586	10,847	203,486	18,866	1,525,585	117,763
Europe EMU		100.0	126,680	51,147	119,711	8,868	9,706	58,759	4,070	337,896	27,960

a. Data are for the latest year available in the period shown. b. Includes Hong Kong, China. c. Excludes Tazara railway. d. Refers to Class 1 railways only. e. Data cover only carriers designated by the U.S. Department of Transportation as major and national air carriers.

About the data

Transport infrastructure—highways, railways, ports and waterways, and airports and air traffic control systems—and the services that flow from it are crucial to the activities of households, producers, and governments. Because performance indicators vary significantly by transport mode and focus (whether physical infrastructure or the services flowing from that infrastructure), highly specialized and carefully specified indicators are required. The table provides selected indicators of the size, extent, and productivity of roads, railways, and air transport systems and of the volume of traffic in these modes as well as in ports.

Data for transport sectors are not always internationally comparable. Unlike for demographic statistics, national income accounts, and international trade data, the collection of infrastructure data has not been "internationalized." But data on roads are collected by the International Road Federation (IRF), and data on air transport by the International Civil Aviation Organization (ICAO).

National road associations are the primary source of IRF data. In countries where such an association is lacking or does not respond, other agencies are contacted, such as road directorates, ministries of transport or public works, or central statistical offices. As a result, due to differing definitions and data collections methods and quality, the compiled data are of uneven quality. Moreover, the quality of transport service (reliability, transit time, and condition of goods delivered) is rarely measured, though it may be as important as quantity in assessing an economy's transport system. Several new initiatives are under way to improve data availability and consistency. The IRF is collaborating with national and international development agencies to improve the quality and coverage of road statistics. To improve measures of progress and performance, the World Bank is also working on better measures of access, affordability, efficiency, quality, and fiscal and institutional aspects of infrastructure.

Unlike the road sector, where numerous qualified motor vehicle operators can operate anywhere on the road network, railways are a restricted transport system with vehicles confined to a fixed guideway. Considering their cost and service characteristics, railways generally are best suited to carry—and can effectively compete for—bulk commodities and containerized freight for distances of 500–5,000 kilometers, and passengers for distances of 50–1,000 kilometers. Below these limits road transport tends to be more competitive, while above these limits either air transport for passengers and freight or sea transport for freight tend to be more competitive. The railways indicators in the table focus on scale and output measures: total route-kilometers, passenger-kilometers, and goods (freight) hauled in ton-kilometers.

Measures of port container traffic, much of it commodities of medium to high value added, give some indication of economic growth in a country. But when traffic is merely transshipment, much of the economic benefit goes to the terminal operator and ancillary services for ships and containers rather than to the country more broadly. In transshipment centers empty containers may account for as much as 40 percent of traffic.

The air transport data represent the total (international and domestic) scheduled traffic carried by the air carriers registered in a country. Countries submit air transport data to ICAO on the basis of standard instructions and definitions issued by ICAO. In many cases, however, the data include estimates by ICAO for nonreporting carriers. Where possible, these estimates are based on previous submissions supplemented by information published by the air carriers, such as flight schedules.

The data cover the air traffic carried on scheduled services, but changes in air transport regulations in Europe have made it more difficult to classify traffic as scheduled or nonscheduled. Thus recent increases shown for some European countries may be due to changes in the classification of air traffic rather than actual growth. For countries with few air carriers or only one, the addition or discontinuation of a home-based air carrier may cause significant changes in air traffic.

Definitions

• **Total road network** covers motorways, highways, main or national roads, secondary or regional roads, and all other roads in a country. • **Paved roads** are roads surfaced with crushed stone (macadam) and hydrocarbon binder or bituminized agents, with concrete, or with cobblestones. • **Passengers carried by road** are the number of passengers transported by road times kilometers traveled. • **Goods hauled by road** are the volume of goods transported by road vehicles, measured in millions of metric tons times kilometers traveled. • **Rail lines** are the length of railway route available for train service, irrespective of the number of parallel tracks. • **Passengers carried by railway** are the number of passengers transported by rail times kilometers traveled. • **Goods hauled by railway** are the volume of goods transported by railway, measured in metric tons times kilometers traveled. • **Port container traffic** measures the flow of containers from land to sea transport modes and vice versa in twenty-foot-equivalent units (TEUs), a standard-size container. Data cover coastal shipping as well as international journeys. Transshipment traffic is counted as two lifts at the intermediate port (once to off-load and again as an outbound lift) and includes empty units. • **Registered carrier departures worldwide** are domestic takeoffs and takeoffs abroad of air carriers registered in the country.• **Passengers carried by air** include both domestic and international passengers of air carriers registered in the country. • **Air freight** is the volume of freight, express, and diplomatic bags carried on each flight stage (operation of an aircraft from takeoff to its next landing), measured in metric tons times kilometers traveled.

Data sources

Data on roads are from the IRF's *World Road Statistics,* supplemented by World Bank staff estimates. Data on railways are from a database maintained by the World Bank's Transport and Urban Development Department, Transport Division, based on data from the International Union of Railways. Data on port container traffic are from Containerisation International's *Containerisation International Yearbook.* Data on air transport are from the ICAO's *Civil Aviation Statistics of the World* and ICAO staff estimates.

5.10 Power and communications

	Electric power		Telephones									
			Access				Quality	Affordability and efficiency				
								$ per month				
	Consumption per capita kWh	Transmission and distribution losses % of output	per 1,000 people Fixed mainlines[a]	per 1,000 people Mobile subscribers[a]	Population covered by mobile telephony[a] %	International voice traffic minutes per person[a]	Faults per 100 mainlines[a]	Price basket for residential fixed line[b]	Price basket for mobile[a]	Cost of call to U.S. $ per 3 minutes[a]	Total telecommunications revenue[a] % of GDP	Total telephone subscribers per employee[a]
	2004	2004	2005	2005	2005	2005	2005	2005	2005	2005	2005	2005
Afghanistan	..	..	3	40	..	..	25.0	11.3	10.8	0.39	5.1	1,576
Albania	1,200	36	88	405	90	..	..	5.1	22.7	1.34	6.0	414
Algeria	812	16	78	416	75	52	0.8	6.3	7.5	2.08	3.4	302
Angola	124	14	6	69	..	..	..	..	11.9	3.23	..	..
Argentina	2,301	15	227	570	..	..	..	6.8	7.8	..	3.1	969
Armenia	1,428	16	192	106	88	29	52.9	2.4	8.3	2.42	3.0	146
Australia	11,193	6	564	906	96	..	11.2	30.5	18.3	..	5.7	506
Austria	7,850	5	450	991	99	293	5.0	29.0	23.7	0.71	2.4	592
Azerbaijan	2,437	13	130	267	99	33	45.2	8.5	15.1	4.18	1.7	139
Bangladesh	140	9	8	63	80	5	..	6.9	2.5	2.02	1.5	..
Belarus	3,144	11	336	419	88	64	23.1	2.4	11.8	1.90	1.3	203
Belgium	8,576	5	461	903	99	..	5.9	33.1	18.9	0.75	2.1	586
Benin	67	..	9	89	43	7	5.8	16.1	13.2	4.80	1.6	364
Bolivia	435	12	70	264	..	49	..	8.5	5.6	..	5.8	680
Bosnia and Herzegovina	2,180	16	248	408	95	190	..	4.9	6.5	3.62	7.1	337
Botswana	1,325	10	75	466	99	76	..	10.4	8.6	2.88	3.0	665
Brazil	1,955	17	230	462	88	..	1.6	15.6	26.5	0.71	3.7	..
Bulgaria	3,939	12	321	807	100	37	4.2	8.9	16.6	0.57	6.7	364
Burkina Faso	..	..	7	43	72	7	18.4	16.9	13.1	1.14	3.1	383
Burundi	..	..	4	20	..	..	6.0	4.5	12.4	2.45	..	234
Cambodia	..	..	3	75	88	2	..	5.2	5.1	2.94	0.4	539
Cameroon	207	19	6	138	73	..	..	9.3	16.5	..	5.3	420
Canada	17,156	7	566	514	95	..	..	..	6.9	..	2.7	456
Central African Republic	..	..	2	25	..	..	56.0	..	12.6	1.99	1.1	134
Chad	..	..	1	22	..	2	..	16.9	13.3	..	..	127
Chile	3,084	8	211	649	100	48	..	9.7	11.4	..	..	..
China	1,585	6	269	302	..	5	..	..	2.9	2.90	3.2	928
Hong Kong, China	5,699	13	546	1,252	100	1,049	1.1	12.6	2.2	0.77	3.8	623
Colombia	866	19	168	479	80	52	30.6	8.0	10.2	..	5.2	..
Congo, Dem. Rep.	93	3	0	48	..	..	..	..	11.0	..	6.6	513
Congo, Rep.	131	74	4	123	80	..	..	..	11.0	5.39	2.9	..
Costa Rica	1,667	11	321	254	..	82	4.0	6.0	1.9	..	2.5	388
Côte d'Ivoire	176	16	14	121	55	17	81.0	28.2	22.2	2.25	4.3	678
Croatia	3,316	17	425	672	98	170	14.0	13.1	14.9	..	2.6	407
Cuba	1,177	15	75	12	61	29	7.6	13.1	22.6	7.49	2.6	..
Czech Republic	6,224	6	314	1,151	100	73	6.5	24.1	17.7	1.06	4.1	699
Denmark	6,631	4	619	1,010	..	338	9.0	30.7	6.1	0.89	2.6	439
Dominican Republic	1,071	32	101	407	..	..	..	23.3	8.6	0.22	0.5	..
Ecuador	687	42	129	472	..	..	..	9.0	18.9	..	2.2	667
Egypt, Arab Rep.	1,215	12	140	184	98	23	0.1	4.0	5.8	1.45	3.5	312
El Salvador	629	13	141	350	95	397	1.7	12.8	8.5	2.40	36.1	1,182
Eritrea	..	..	9	9	0	10	54.3	6.2	..	3.59	2.6	71
Estonia	5,484	11	328	1,074	99	109	..	15.6	8.8	0.90	5.8	486
Ethiopia	33	10	9	6	..	2	100.0	2.9	3.0	4.01	1.7	81
Finland	16,780	3	404	997	99	..	..	28.7	6.8	1.80	3.0	420
France	7,900	6	586	789	99	177	..	29.0	30.0	0.84	2.4	585
Gabon	928	18	28	470	78	61	45.0	32.4	14.7	2.77	1.8	244
Gambia, The	..	..	29	163	..	..	..	..	..	1.81	..	..
Georgia	1,577	16	151	326	95	57	..	4.7	44.1	..	5.8	..
Germany	7,029	6	667	960	99	..	..	26.5	17.3	0.43	3.0	559
Ghana	247	15	15	129	69	15	5.6	14.8	6.9	0.39	..	557
Greece	5,148	9	568	904	100	..	13.8	21.1	23.6	1.09	4.4	612
Guatemala	514	4	99	358	..	129	..	15.4	6.1	1.21	..	..
Guinea	..	..	3	20	..	..	..	..	7.7	..	..	..
Guinea-Bissau	..	..	7	42	..	..	..	..	21.9	..	..	..
Haiti	30	53	17	48	..	..	..	..	4.6	2.15	..	92

Power and communications

	Electric power		Telephones									
			Access				Quality	Affordability and efficiency				
	Consumption per capita kWh	Transmission and distribution losses % of output	per 1,000 people Fixed mainlines[a]	per 1,000 people Mobile subscribers[a]	Population covered by mobile telephony[a] %	International voice traffic minutes per person[a]	Faults per 100 mainlines[a]	$ per month Price basket for residential fixed line[b]	$ per month Price basket for mobile[a]	Cost of call to U.S. $ per 3 minutes[a]	Total telecommunications revenue[a] % of GDP	Total telephone subscribers per employee[a]
	2004	2004	2005	2005	2005	2005	2005	2005	2005	2005	2005	2005
Honduras	586	23	69	178	..	82	..	5.9	10.8	2.52	5.9	186
Hungary	3,680	12	333	924	99	45	8.2	28.5	11.7	1.01	4.7	670
India	457	26	45	82	..	..	..	3.3	2.4	1.19	1.9	..
Indonesia	478	13	58	213	90	5	..	5.8	4.3	2.79	2.2	1,084
Iran, Islamic Rep.	2,036	17	278	106	90	8	..	2.4	2.6	0.55	1.3	407
Iraq	1,126	6	37	20	..	..	..	..	2.6	..	..	..
Ireland	6,169	8	489	1,012	99	..	5.6	39.5	19.7	0.71	2.5	401
Israel	6,803	3	424	1,120	99	..	..	10.5	9.3	0.59	4.5	692
Italy	5,640	7	427	1,232	100	236	..	26.6	14.4	0.79	3.0	948
Jamaica	2,455	10	129	1,017	95	233	31.0	9.1	7.5	0.87	4.1	686
Japan	8,072	5	460	742	99	43	..	26.1	20.5	1.63	3.9	1,283
Jordan	1,602	13	119	304	99	128	10.0	10.0	6.7	1.44	8.3	444
Kazakhstan	3,621	16	167	327	..	..	..	..	11.5	..	..	108
Kenya	140	17	8	135	..	5	130.4	13.9	16.5	3.00	4.1	141
Korea, Dem. Rep.	827	16	44	..	..	..	..	..	..	..	..	..
Korea, Rep.	7,391	3	492	794	99	81	1.0	8.3	14.2	0.76	4.8	567
Kuwait	14,955	11	201	939	100	..	4.0	10.5	75.2	1.51	3.4	338
Kyrgyz Republic	1,421	30	85	105	90	17	..	5.9	6.4	5.40	4.5	91
Lao PDR	..	..	13	108	..	3	..	5.6	3.8	1.11	1.7	130
Latvia	2,549	19	318	814	98	52	20.3	13.3	9.5	1.63	1.5	587
Lebanon	2,499	15	277	277	100	..	..	15.0	20.1	2.19	7.2	..
Lesotho	..	..	27	137	80	..	75.0	18.4	14.2	3.28	..	..
Liberia	..	..	..	49	16	..	..	..	..	..	..	..
Libya	2,519	28	133	41	..	..	..	..	6.3	..	..	..
Lithuania	3,145	7	235	1,275	100	37	3.8	17.7	9.1	1.55	3.5	..
Macedonia, FYR	3,183	21	262	620	99	..	..	11.4	14.8	..	5.7	..
Madagascar	..	..	4	27	30	1	59.6	18.5	7.9	0.59	12.8	148
Malawi	..	..	8	33	..	..	..	5.8	10.2	..	4.5	..
Malaysia	3,166	5	172	771	..	..	7.3	8.7	5.0	0.71	4.8	770
Mali	..	..	6	64	..	..	..	16.1	13.8	..	7.6	..
Mauritania	..	..	13	243	..	20	..	11.6	..	..	19.5	533
Mauritius	..	..	289	574	100	92	..	7.9	4.2	1.59	3.2	451
Mexico	1,838	16	189	460	100	119	1.8	16.1	14.0	0.83	2.7	617
Moldova	1,228	38	221	259	97	92	5.1	4.5	17.1	1.46	9.9	220
Mongolia	..	..	61	218	..	4	20.6	2.4	5.5	..	4.4	116
Morocco	595	16	44	411	98	55	25.0	23.0	16.3	1.69	5.4	821
Mozambique	367	10	4	62	95	17	66.0	17.6	10.3	1.17	1.8	392
Myanmar	104	20	9	4	..	3	125.0	..	..	0.17	0.6	66
Namibia	1,389	18	64	244	88	..	40.4	12.3	14.0	..	4.8	..
Nepal	69	19	17	9	..	6	68.0	3.1	2.0	2.04	1.2	110
Netherlands	6,920	4	466	970	100	..	..	..	23.4	0.32	..	..
New Zealand	8,937	13	422	861	98	363	..	28.6	19.1	1.30	3.9	962
Nicaragua	417	24	43	217	60	65	4.8	9.2	15.1	3.15	3.7	334
Niger	..	..	2	21	15	..	..	10.5	16.9	..	2.2	..
Nigeria	104	34	9	141	58	..	20.6	..	10.6	1.49	3.5	256
Norway	24,645	8	460	1,028	..	260	..	37.9	20.2	..	3.3	445
Oman	3,836	15	103	519	..	185	89.7	12.1	5.5	1.87	2.3	583
Pakistan	425	25	34	82	..	..	..	5.1	2.4	1.03	2.5	213
Panama	1,466	17	136	418	89	..	13.9	10.3	16.7	..	3.9	273
Papua New Guinea	..	..	11	4	..	..	..	7.3	14.8	..	..	..
Paraguay	816	4	54	320	..	28	8.2	6.4	3.3	0.90	4.2	..
Peru	794	10	80	200	..	64	..	19.6	22.9	1.80	0.8	472
Philippines	597	13	41	419	92	29	..	11.6	5.3	1.20	3.9	1,555
Poland	3,418	9	309	764	99	61	..	14.3	7.8	1.35	3.8	184
Portugal	4,526	9	401	1,085	100	137	9.7	31.8	23.6	1.04	5.1	988
Puerto Rico	..	..	285	689	100	..	..	33.5	..	..	..	..

5.10 Power and communications

	Electric power		Telephones									
			Access				Quality	Affordability and efficiency				
	Consumption per capita kWh	Transmission and distribution losses % of output	per 1,000 people Fixed mainlines[a]	per 1,000 people Mobile subscribers[a]	Population covered by mobile telephony[a] %	International voice traffic minutes per person[a]	Faults per 100 mainlines[a]	$ per month Price basket for residential fixed line[b]	$ per month Price basket for mobile[a]	Cost of call to U.S. $ per 3 minutes[a]	Total tele-communications revenue[a] % of GDP	Total tele-phone sub-scribers per employee[a]
	2004	2004	2005	2005	2005	2005	2005	2005	2005	2005	2005	2005
Romania	2,271	11	203	617	98	..	10.4	10.1	10.5	0.82	3.8	263
Russian Federation	5,642	12	280	838	..	..	..	..	6.0	2.03	2.9	334
Rwanda	..	..	3	32	75	..	..	6.6	12.3	2.43	2.7	..
Saudi Arabia	6,571	7	164	575	..	..	..	11.7	9.7	..	3.2	..
Senegal	176	15	23	148	85	55	..	15.4	9.6	1.02	6.9	408
Serbia and Montenegro	4,029	16	332	585	95	113	25.0	2.7	6.4	2.27	2.9	..
Sierra Leone	..	..	..	22	..	..	..	..	71.9	..	..	..
Singapore	8,170	6	425	1,010	100	..	0.3	6.7	6.1	0.69	3.4	..
Slovak Republic	5,088	4	222	843	99	88	9.5	19.8	12.3	1.06	3.8	508
Slovenia	6,835	6	408	879	99	..	13.6	17.6	10.3	0.65	3.2	1,228
Somalia	..	..	12	61	..	..	..	..	5.1	..	..	..
South Africa	4,885	6	101	724	96	..	..	22.7	13.3	0.79	5.7	725
Spain	5,924	9	422	952	99	117	14.2	25.8	22.1	0.60	3.0	643
Sri Lanka	344	17	63	171	85	..	8.1	8.2	1.2	2.11	2.2	313
Sudan	92	16	18	50	..	11	..	6.3	4.0	..	3.8	651
Swaziland	..	..	31	177	..	47	70.0	8.3	13.3	2.97	2.0	279
Sweden	15,424	7	717	935	99	..	..	26.7	6.2	0.41	2.8	858
Switzerland	8,204	6	689	921	100	..	..	29.5	28.4	0.32	3.5	525
Syrian Arab Republic	1,317	24	152	155	99	44	50.0	2.7	9.9	..	2.8	221
Tajikistan	2,240	15	39	41	..	10	144.0	0.8	23.3	7.84	0.6	57
Tanzania	53	23	4	52	25	..	..	14.0	9.5	3.17	..	..
Thailand	1,865	8	110	430	..	12	2.5	8.3	4.4	0.67	3.2	1,271
Togo	87	34	10	72	85	21	..	15.4	12.3	3.98	5.7	363
Trinidad and Tobago	4,658	6	248	613	..	381	..	7.0	6.7	2.19	2.7	..
Tunisia	1,157	12	125	566	98	84	30.0	3.7	5.4	..	4.4	740
Turkey	1,782	15	263	605	96	31	30.4	14.7	12.6	2.40	3.6	883
Turkmenistan	1,740	13	80	11	..	..	..	..	17.2	..	..	..
Uganda	..	..	3	53	85	2	..	16.8	9.3	3.21	4.2	750
Ukraine	3,152	15	256	366	96	36	..	..	9.3	1.65	5.9	..
United Arab Emirates	11,331	7	273	1,000	100	..	0.3	17.4	4.1	1.73	2.7	485
United Kingdom	6,206	8	528	1,088	99	..	..	31.3	14.0	0.77	3.1	..
United States	13,351	6	606	680	99	279	13.2	25.0	5.2	..	2.7	346
Uruguay	1,867	31	290	333	100	..	..	10.7	16.1	0.52	..	..
Uzbekistan	1,796	9	67	28	..	..	..	1.0	1.8	..	..	..
Venezuela, RB	2,760	27	136	470	..	..	..	..	1.2	0.84	3.5	..
Vietnam	501	10	191	115	..	..	..	3.7	6.2	1.95	0.0	79
West Bank and Gaza	..	..	96	302	95	66	69.4	7.5	9.8	1.17	0.7	871
Yemen, Rep.	165	23	39	95	68	..	..	2.8	4.3	2.39	1.3	..
Zambia	692	4	8	81	51	7	108.0	6.0	14.2	1.41	2.7	175
Zimbabwe	795	15	25	54	..	24	7.7	4.3	3.4	..	4.4	243
World	**2,606 w**	**9 w**	**180 w**	**342 w**	**.. w**	**.. w**	**.. m**	**11.7 m**	**10.5 m**	**1.44 m**	**3.6 w**	**479 m**
Low income	375	23	37	77	..	..	..	8.7	9.6	1.99	0.7	141
Middle income	1,840	11	211	379	..	22	..	9.7	10.1	1.65	3.6	497
Lower middle income	1,448	10	205	306	..	14	25.0	8.5	10.2	2.08	1.9	444
Upper middle income	3,454	12	230	671	..	..	..	12.1	9.5	1.06	3.6	583
Low & middle income	1,243	13	135	247	..	..	..	10.1	9.9	1.81	3.6	279
East Asia & Pacific	1,343	7	214	282	..	6	..	5.9	5.0	1.16	2.7	1,006
Europe & Central Asia	3,637	12	273	624	..	..	15.7	9.5	11.8	1.51	3.6	364
Latin America & Carib.	1,674	17	177	439	90	..	..	10.0	9.4	1.80	4.3	390
Middle East & N. Africa	1,289	16	160	229	90	30	25.0	7.3	6.3	1.66	1.3	501
South Asia	414	26	39	79	..	..	..	5.1	2.4	2.02	2.0	125
Sub-Saharan Africa	550	9	17	125	..	..	..	14.0	12.3	2.43	3.3	248
High income	9,609	6	503	835	99	171	5.8	27.6	17.8	0.76	4.5	586
European Monetary Union	6,869	6	531	980	99	..	7.8	29.0	20.9	0.73	3.0	592

a. Data are from the International Telecommunication Union's (ITU) World Telecommunication Development Report database. Please cite the ITU for third-party use of these data.
b. Calculated by the World Bank based on ITU data.

Power and communications 5.10

About the data

The quality of an economy's infrastructure, including power and communications, is an important element in investment decisions for both domestic and foreign investors. Government effort alone is not enough to meet the need for investments in modern infrastructure; public-private partnerships, especially those involving local providers and financiers, are critical for lowering costs and delivering value for money. In telecommunications, competition in the marketplace, along with sound regulation, is lowering costs and improving the quality of and access to services around the globe.

An economy's production and consumption of electricity is a basic indicator of its size and level of development. Although a few countries export electric power, most production is for domestic consumption. Expanding the supply of electricity to meet the growing demand of increasingly urbanized and industrialized economies without incurring unacceptable social, economic, and environmental costs is one of the great challenges facing developing countries.

Data on electric power production and consumption are collected from national energy agencies by the International Energy Agency (IEA) and adjusted by the IEA to meet international definitions (for data on electricity production, see table 3.9). Electricity consumption is equivalent to production less power plants' own use and transmission, distribution, and transformation losses less exports plus imports. It includes consumption by auxiliary stations, losses in transformers that are considered integral parts of those stations, and electricity produced by pumping installations. Where data are available, it covers electricity generated by primary sources of energy—coal, oil, gas, nuclear, hydro, geo-thermal, wind, tide and wave, and combustible renewables. Neither production nor consumption data capture the reliability of supplies, including breakdowns, load factors, and frequency of outages.

Over the past decade new financing and technology, along with privatization and liberalization, have spurred dramatic growth in telecommunications in many countries. With the rapid development of mobile telephony and the global expansion of the Internet, information and communication technologies are increasingly recognized as essential tools of development, contributing to global integration and enhancing public sector effectiveness, efficiency, and transparency. The table presents telecommunications indicators covering access, quality, and affordability and efficiency.

Operators are the main source of telecommunications data, so information on subscribers is widely available for most countries. This gives a general idea of access, but a more precise measure is the penetration rate—the share of households with access to telecommunications. Also important are data on actual use of the telecommunications equipment. Ideally, statistics on telecommunications (and other information and communications technologies) should be compiled for all three measures: subscription and possession, access, and use. The quality of data varies among reporting countries as a result of differences in regulations covering the provision of data.

Globally, there have been huge improvements in access to telecommunications, driven mainly by mobile telephony. By 2002 access to mobiles outpaced access to fixed-line telephones in developing countries, and rural areas are catching up with urban areas (although gaps are still large). By 2004 approximately 98 percent of the population in high income countries and about 64 percent of the population in developing countries were covered by mobile telephony (within range of a mobile cellular signal).

Telephone mainline faults are a measure of telecommunications quality. The definition varies among countries: some operators define faults as including malfunctioning customer equipment while others include only technical faults.

Although access is the key to delivering telecommunications services to people, if that service is not affordable to most people, then goals of universal usage will not be met. Three indicators of telecommunications affordability are presented in the table (price basket for fixed-line telephone service, price basket for mobile service, and the cost of an international call). Telecommunications efficiency is measured by total telecommunications revenue as percent of GDP and by total telephone subscribers per employee.

Definitions

• **Electric power consumption** measures the production of power plants and combined heat and power plants less transmission, distribution, and transformation losses and own use by heat and power plants. • **Electric power transmission and distribution losses** are losses in transmission between sources of supply and points of distribution and in distribution to consumers, including pilferage.• **Fixed telephone mainlines** are telephone lines connecting a subscriber to the telephone exchange equipment. • **Mobile telephone subscribers** are subscribers to a public mobile telephone service using cellular technology. • **Population covered by mobile telephony** is the percentage of people within range of a mobile cellular signal regardless of whether they are subscribers. • **International voice traffic** is the sum of international incoming and outgoing telephone traffic (in minutes) divided by total population. • **Telephone mainline faults** are the number of reported faults for the year divided by the number of telephone mainlines and multiplied by 100. • **Price basket for residential fixed line** is calculated as one-fifth of the installation charge, the monthly subscription charge, and the cost of local calls (15 peak and 15 off-peak calls of three minutes each). • **Price basket for mobile** is calculated as the pre-paid price for 25 calls per month spread over the same mobile network, other mobile networks, and mobile to fixed calls and during peak, off-peak, and weekend times. It also includes 30 text messages per month. • **Cost of call to U.S.** is the cost of a three-minute, peak rate, fixed-line call from the country to the United States. • **Total telecommunications revenue** is the revenue from the provision of telecommunications services such as fixed-line, mobile, and data divided by GDP. • **Total telephone subscribers per employee** are telephone subscribers (fixed-line plus mobile) divided by the total number of telecommunications employees.

Data sources

Data on electricity consumption and losses are from the IEA's *Energy Statistics and Balances of Non-OECD Countries 2003–2004*, the IEA's *Energy Statistics of OECD Countries 2003–2004*, and the United Nations Statistics Division's *Energy Statistics Yearbook*. Data on telecommunications are from the International Telecommunication Union's World Telecommunication Development Report database and World Bank estimates.

5.11 The information age

	Daily newspapers	Households with television[a]	Personal computers and the Internet								Information and communications technology expenditures	
			Access			Quality		Application	Affordability			
	per 1,000 people	%	per 1,000 people Personal computers[a]	per 1,000 people Internet users[a]	Schools connected to the Internet %	Broadband subscribers per 1,000 people[a]	International Internet bandwidth bits per capita[a]	Secure Internet servers per million people	Price basket for Internet $ per month[a]	% of GDP	Per capita $
	2000	2005	2005	2005	2005	2005	2005	October 2006	2005	2005	2005
Afghanistan	..	..	..	1	..	0.0	0	0	..	..	..
Albania	..	90	..	60	..	*0.0*	*4*	2	16.3	..	..
Algeria	*27*	88	11	58	*53*	5.9	..	0	9.4	2.4	76
Angola	*11*	9	..	11	..	..	..	0	34.3	..	..
Argentina	40	..	*83*	177	..	21.7	316	12	14.4	7.1	337
Armenia	..	91	*66*	53	..	*0.3*	*12*	3	52.5	..	..
Australia	161	96	*683*	698	*97*	103.4	5,903	581	22.8	6.2	2,247
Austria	309	95	607	486	..	142.8	*6,681*	284	15.5	5.5	2,059
Azerbaijan	*10*	..	23	81	..	0.3	29	0	10.0	..	..
Bangladesh	..	23	*12*	3	..	*0.0*	*0*	0	24.0	2.4	10
Belarus	..	97	..	347	..	0.2	48	1	10.5	..	..
Belgium	153	98	*348*	458	..	191.3	*11,279*	146	37.2	5.8	2,061
Benin	*5*	20	4	50	..	0.0	5	0	20.7	..	..
Bolivia	*99*	..	*23*	52	..	1.2	*44*	3	12.3	5.5	56
Bosnia and Herzegovina	..	87	..	206	..	3.5	40	4	7.8	..	..
Botswana	*25*	..	*45*	34	4	..	..	1	21.3	..	..
Brazil	46	91	*105*	195	*50*	17.7	*149*	16	26.0	7.8	333
Bulgaria	173	97	*59*	206	*60*	*0.2*	318	11	7.3	3.8	130
Burkina Faso	*1*	7	2	5	..	0.0	6	0	90.6	..	..
Burundi	*2*	14	*5*	5	..	*0.0*	..	0	52.0	..	..
Cambodia	..	43	*3*	*3*	..	*0.0*	*1*	0	33.1	..	..
Cameroon	*6*	18	*10*	15	..	..	..	0	44.6	5.0	52
Canada	168	99	*700*	520	*98*	207.6	*6,800*	645	8.9	5.9	2,034
Central African Republic	*2*	2	3	3	..	0.0	0	0	147.8	..	..
Chad	*0*	2	*2*	4	..	..	*0*	..	86.3	..	..
Chile	..	87	141	172	*62*	43.5	*788*	22	25.6	6.1	430
China	59	89	*41*	85	..	28.7	104	0	9.8	5.3	90
Hong Kong, China	218	99	601	508	100	238.9	9,451	191	3.9	8.9	2,280
Colombia	*26*	92	41	104	..	7.0	488	6	7.8	8.5	227
Congo, Dem. Rep.	*3*	2	..	2	..	0.0	0	0	93.2	..	..
Congo, Rep.	*6*	6	*4*	13	..	*0.0*	*0*	0	84.5	..	..
Costa Rica	70	93	*219*	254	*15*	*6.6*	241	67	28.1	7.7	358
Côte d'Ivoire	*16*	35	*15*	11	..	*0.0*	*3*	0	67.1	..	..
Croatia	134	94	*190*	327	100	20.2	1,074	48	16.1	..	..
Cuba	54	..	33	17	..	*0.0*	8	0	30.0	..	..
Czech Republic	..	..	*240*	269	*95*	43.7	..	64	18.8	7.1	866
Denmark	283	97	*656*	527	100	249.3	*34,891*	614	23.2	6.0	2,849
Dominican Republic	28	76	..	169	..	7.4	..	6	18.8	..	..
Ecuador	98	89	39	47	..	2.0	48	5	37.0	3.2	87
Egypt, Arab Rep.	*31*	89	38	68	*66*	1.5	49	1	5.0	1.5	18
El Salvador	*29*	..	51	93	..	6.1	23	6	22.6	..	..
Eritrea	..	14	8	16	..	0.0	2	..	28.6	..	..
Estonia	192	93	483	513	*75*	133.1	3,566	163	10.8	..	..
Ethiopia	*0*	2	*3*	2	*1*	*0.0*	..	0	23.3	..	..
Finland	445	94	*481*	534	..	223.8	*4,326*	380	22.2	6.9	2,527
France	142	95	575	430	94	155.5	3,286	96	12.4	6.3	2,213
Gabon	*29*	54	33	48	..	1.1	145	5	40.1	..	..
Gambia, The	*2*	12	*16*	*33*	13	0.0	6	1	17.8	..	..
Georgia	5	89	*42*	*39*	..	*0.3*	..	5	9.9	..	..
Germany	291	95	*545*	455	..	129.7	*6,860*	349	7.4	6.1	2,059
Ghana	*14*	26	*5*	18	*1*	0.1	8	0	23.6	..	..
Greece	..	100	*89*	180	..	14.4	*589*	40	16.4	4.1	822
Guatemala	..	..	*19*	79	..	2.2	*57*	6	54.3	..	..
Guinea	..	9	*5*	5	..	*0.0*	..	..	24.7	..	..
Guinea-Bissau	*5*	26	..	20	..	..	..	..	75.0	..	..
Haiti	..	27	..	70	..	..	..	1	71.0	..	..

The information age

	Daily newspapers	Households with television[a]	Personal computers and the Internet							Information and communications technology expenditures	
			Access			Quality		Application	Affordability		
	per 1,000 people	%	per 1,000 people Personal computers[a]	per 1,000 people Internet users[a]	Schools connected to the Internet %	Broadband subscribers per 1,000 people[a]	International Internet bandwidth bits per capita[a]	Secure Internet servers per million people	Price basket for Internet $ per month[a]	% of GDP	Per capita $
	2000	2005	2005	2005	2005	2005	2005	October 2006	2005	2005	2005
Honduras	..	58	16	36	..	0.0	..	4	33.4	4.6	53
Hungary	162	96	146	297	85	64.6	991	36	11.0	5.8	632
India	60	32	16	55	..	1.2	18	1	6.8	5.8	42
Indonesia	23	65	14	73	..	..	7	1	17.3	3.4	44
Iran, Islamic Rep.	..	77	109	103	..	0.3	15	0	2.3	2.5	69
Iraq	..	..	..	1	..	..	..	0	..	..	..
Ireland	148	95	494	276	..	65.1	6,043	416	31.1	4.4	2,127
Israel	..	93	740	470	95	177.6	2,499	182	22.0	8.3	1,475
Italy	109	96	367	478	..	115.7	2,080	53	24.8	4.3	1,308
Jamaica	..	70	63	404	..	..	..	17	34.3	10.6	381
Japan	566	99	542	668	99	175.0	1,038	331	13.8	7.5	2,678
Jordan	74	96	56	118	18	1.9	58	4	11.1	8.4	195
Kazakhstan	..	..	..	27	..	0.1	..	1	15.8	..	..
Kenya	8	17	9	32	..	0.0	3	0	75.9	2.8	15
Korea, Dem. Rep.	..	..	..	..	..	..	..	..	..	..	..
Korea, Rep.	..	..	545	684	100	252.4	1,030	22	32.6	6.9	1,127
Kuwait	..	95	237	276	..	8.1	348	35	22.2	1.4	437
Kyrgyz Republic	..	..	19	54	..	0.5	15	1	12.0	..	..
Lao PDR	..	30	17	4	..	0.0	3	0	27.6	..	..
Latvia	138	98	217	448	97	113.4	972	46	12.5	..	..
Lebanon	63	93	114	196	20	36.3	81	11	10.0	..	..
Lesotho	9	12	..	24	..	0.0	4	..	38.6	..	..
Liberia	14	..	..	..	..	0.0	..	..	..	..	..
Libya	14	..	..	36	..	..	..	0	22.0	..	..
Lithuania	31	98	155	358	56	68.6	1,460	26	7.2	..	..
Macedonia, FYR	54	95	222	79	100	6.1	17	2	25.3	..	..
Madagascar	5	8	5	5	..	0.0	2	0	45.9	..	..
Malawi	2	3	2	4	1	0.0	2	0	41.9	..	..
Malaysia	95	89	197	435	..	19.4	128	17	7.4	7.0	360
Mali	1	15	3	4	..	0.0	2	0	28.4	..	..
Mauritania	..	21	14	7	..	0.1	15	1	54.3	..	..
Mauritius	116	93	162	146	..	2.2	50	18	17.5	..	..
Mexico	94	93	136	181	60	22.4	110	10	20.0	3.3	246
Moldova	153	..	27	96	50	2.5	97	4	24.1	..	..
Mongolia	18	30	133	105	19	0.7	16	4	10.7	..	..
Morocco	29	76	25	152	..	8.3	235	1	26.8	6.3	108
Mozambique	3	6	6	7	0	..	1	0	32.9	..	..
Myanmar	9	3	8	2	..	0.0	2	0	48.9	..	..
Namibia	17	39	109	37	13	0.0	4	8	48.7	..	..
Nepal	..	..	4	4	..	..	2	1	8.1	..	..
Netherlands	279	99	682	739	..	251.2	20,549	413	12.4	6.3	2,402
New Zealand	202	98	474	672	100	80.8	1,126	594	11.9	9.8	2,611
Nicaragua	..	..	40	26	..	1.9	1	3	28.1	..	..
Niger	0	5	1	2	..	0.0	2	0	101.8	..	..
Nigeria	25	26	7	38	..	0.0	1	0	50.4	3.5	27
Norway	569	100	573	735	..	214.4	9,368	389	29.8	5.1	3,252
Oman	..	79	47	111	..	3.3	194	3	14.5	..	..
Pakistan	39	47	..	67	..	0.3	5	0	9.5	6.9	49
Panama	..	77	46	64	..	5.4	292	57	38.4	8.4	403
Papua New Guinea	..	9	64	23	..	..	..	1	25.0	..	..
Paraguay	..	76	75	32	..	0.9	42	1	11.7	..	..
Peru	23	69	100	164	..	12.5	358	6	23.6	6.6	187
Philippines	..	63	45	54	..	0.7	39	3	1.8	7.0	83
Poland	102	91	193	262	90	32.6	560	38	11.3	4.2	331
Portugal	102	99	133	279	..	114.9	833	65	37.8	4.4	758
Puerto Rico	..	97	..	221	..	..	..	33	..	..	..

5.11 The information age

	Daily newspapers	Households with television[a]	Personal computers and the Internet: Access			Quality		Application	Affordability	Information and communications technology expenditures	
			per 1,000 people		Schools connected to the Internet	Broadband subscribers per 1,000 people[a]	International Internet bandwidth bits per capita[a]	Secure Internet servers per million people	Price basket for Internet $ per month[a]		
	per 1,000 people	%	Personal computers[a]	Internet users[a]	%			October		% of GDP	Per capita $
	2000	2005	2005	2005	2005	2005	2005	2006	2005	2005	2005
Romania	..	94	*113*	*208*	*57*	34.7	623	7	17.0	3.6	164
Russian Federation	..	98	122	152	*43*	11.1	*100*	3	12.7	3.6	191
Rwanda	*0*	2	..	6	..	..	..	..	30.1	..	..
Saudi Arabia	..	99	*354*	66	..	*0.8*	*31*	4	21.3	2.3	285
Senegal	..	29	21	46	..	1.6	66	0	25.6	8.3	59
Serbia and Montenegro	..	92	*48*	*148*	*70*	..	*87*	*2*	*13.2*	..	..
Sierra Leone	..	7	..	*2*	..	..	..	0	10.6	..	..
Singapore	273	99	..	*571*	*100*	153.3	*5,826*	291	20.5	9.4	2,537
Slovak Republic	131	99	358	464	*65*	25.7	2,636	28	18.9	5.6	486
Slovenia	168	96	404	545	96	85.0	*1,258*	95	18.6	3.1	532
Somalia	..	8	*6*	11	..	*0.0*	*0*	..	..	..	..
South Africa	25	59	85	109	..	3.5	*19*	23	63.2	9.9	504
Spain	98	99	277	348	..	115.1	*2,822*	100	31.7	3.7	959
Sri Lanka	29	32	*27*	*14*	..	0.7	25	2	4.6	5.5	66
Sudan	..	49	90	77	..	0.0	6	..	65.5	..	..
Swaziland	..	18	*32*	*32*	..	*0.0*	..	4	51.7	..	..
Sweden	410	94	*763*	764	..	214.0	*17,531*	405	19.2	7.4	2,941
Switzerland	372	100	865	498	..	232.0	*9,671*	577	7.9	7.5	3,691
Syrian Arab Republic	..	80	42	58	..	*0.0*	..	0	14.0	..	..
Tajikistan	..	..	..	*1*	..	*0.0*	*0*	..	12.3	..	..
Tanzania	..	6	*7*	9	..	*0.0*	..	0	93.6	..	..
Thailand	*197*	92	58	110	..	*0.7*	106	6	6.9	4.1	112
Togo	2	51	30	49	..	0.0	7	0	44.7	..	..
Trinidad and Tobago	..	88	*79*	*123*	*15*	8.3	375	28	13.4	..	..
Tunisia	19	92	57	95	*25*	1.6	75	2	12.4	5.8	167
Turkey	..	92	*52*	222	*40*	22.1	405	25	11.6	7.9	396
Turkmenistan	7	..	..	*8*	..	..	..	..	69.5	..	..
Uganda	3	5	9	17	*1*	..	3	0	99.6	..	..
Ukraine	175	97	38	97	..	..	*17*	2	7.7	8.0	141
United Arab Emirates	..	86	*197*	308	..	28.3	923	54	13.1	3.6	1,027
United Kingdom	326	..	*600*	473	99	163.8	*13,062*	560	27.3	7.3	2,683
United States	196	98	*762*	*630*	100	166.6	*3,306*	870	15.0	8.8	3,690
Uruguay	..	93	*125*	193	*50*	17.7	462	29	23.9	7.9	385
Uzbekistan	..	..	..	*34*	..	*0.1*	*1*	0	5.7	..	..
Venezuela, RB	..	83	*82*	125	..	13.4	*51*	5	42.6	3.9	205
Vietnam	*6*	83	*13*	129	..	2.5	43	0	10.7	15.1	95
West Bank and Gaza	..	93	*48*	67	..	2.1	66	*1*	15.6	..	..
Yemen, Rep.	..	43	*15*	*9*	..	..	..	0	10.9	..	..
Zambia	22	26	*10*	*20*	..	0.0	2	0	68.4	..	..
Zimbabwe	..	26	92	77	..	0.8	4	0	24.6	7.7	33
World	90 w	79 m	130 w	137 w	.. m	41.6 w	*816 w*	74 w	22.0 m	6.8 w	538 w
Low income	*45*	15	*11*	44	..	0.9	15	0	30.1	5.9	41
Middle income	*55*	88	*58*	115	..	22.6	*92*	5	17.0	5.4	149
Lower middle income	61	84	*45*	95	..	23.1	116	2	16.8	5.5	108
Upper middle income	..	91	*113*	196	*60*	21.0	*218*	17	17.0	5.2	312
Low & middle income	*49*	48	*40*	84	..	13.4	*59*	3	23.4	5.4	109
East Asia & Pacific	60	36	*38*	89	..	25.9	97	1	10.7	5.3	89
Europe & Central Asia	..	92	*98*	190	..	20.9	*211*	13	12.2	5.1	274
Latin America & Carib.	61	87	*88*	156	..	16.4	*161*	12	25.8	5.9	278
Middle East & N. Africa	..	84	*48*	89	..	*0.5*	..	1	11.8	3.1	66
South Asia	*59*	32	16	49	..	1.0	18	1	8.1	5.7	40
Sub-Saharan Africa	*12*	14	*15*	29	..	..	..	2	45.3	*7.4*	..
High income	263	97	*579*	527	..	163.2	*4,530*	443	19.9	7.2	2,466
European Monetary Union	188	96	*421*	439	..	134.7	*5,784*	184	20.4	5.4	1,726

a. Data are from the International Telecommunication Union's (ITU) World Telecommunication Development Report database. Please cite the ITU for third-party use of these data.

The information age 5.11

About the data

The digital and information revolution has changed the way the world learns, communicates, does business, and treats illnesses. New information and communications technologies offer vast opportunities for progress in all walks of life in all countries—opportunities for economic growth, improved health, better service delivery, learning through distance education, and social and cultural advances. The table presents indicators of the penetration of the information economy (newspapers, televisions, personal computers, and Internet use), quality (broadband subscribers, international Internet bandwidth, and secure Internet servers), and some of the economics of the information age (Internet access charges and spending on information and communications technology).

The data on the number of daily newspapers in circulation are from surveys by the United Nations Educational, Scientific, and Cultural Organization (UNESCO) Institute for Statistics. In some countries definitions, classifications, and methods of enumeration do not entirely conform to UNESCO standards. For example, newspaper circulation data should refer to the number of copies distributed, but in some cases the figures reported are the number of copies printed. The data for other electronic communications and information technology are from the International Telecommunication Union (ITU), the Internet Software Consortium, Netcraft, the World Information Technology and Services Alliance (WITSA), Global Insights, and World Bank staff estimates. Estimates of households with television are derived from household surveys; data presented in the table are from the ITU and World Bank staff estimates.

The estimates of personal computers are derived from an annual ITU questionnaire, supplemented by other sources. In many countries mainframe computers are used extensively. Since thousands of users can be connected to a single mainframe computer, the number of personal computers understates the total use of computers.

The data on Internet users and related Internet indicators are based on nationally reported data. Some countries derive these data from Internet surveys, but since survey questions and definitions differ across countries, the estimates may not be strictly comparable. For example, questions on the age of Internet users and frequency of use vary by country. Countries that do not have surveys generally derive their estimates from reported Internet service provider subscriber counts, calculated by multiplying the number of subscribers by a selected multiplier. This method may undercount the actual number of people using the Internet, particularly in developing countries, where many commercial subscribers rent out computers connected to the Internet or prepaid cards are used to access the Internet.

The number of secure Internet servers, from the Netcraft Secure Server Survey, gives an indication of how many companies are conducting encrypted transactions over the Internet.

The data on information and communications technology expenditures cover the world's 75 largest buyers of such technology among countries and regions.

Ensuring universal access to information and communication technology is a goal of many countries, but not all countries regularly track accessibility. There is no common set of information and communications technology indicators and definitions, and data are often drawn from administrative records rather than from specific surveys. Access needs to be accurately measured in three major areas: individual, household, and community access.

Definitions

• **Daily newspapers** refer to those published at least four times a week and calculated as average circulation (or copies printed) per 1,000 people. • **Households with television** are the percentage of households with a television set. Some countries report only the number of households with a color television set, and therefore the true number may be higher than reported. • **Personal computers** are self-contained computers designed for use by a single individual. • **Internet users** are people with access to the worldwide network. • **Schools connected to the Internet** are the share of primary and secondary schools in the country that have access to the Internet. • **Broadband subscribers** are the number of broadband subscribers with a digital subscriber line, cable modem, or other high-speed technologies. Reporting countries may have different definitions of broadband, so data are not strictly comparable across countries. • **International Internet bandwidth** is the contracted capacity of international connections between countries for transmitting Internet traffic. • **Secure Internet servers** are servers using encryption technology in Internet transactions.• **Price basket for Internet** is calculated based on the cheapest available tariff for accessing the Internet 20 hours a month (10 hours peak and 10 hours off-peak). The basket does not include the telephone line rental but does include telephone use charges if applicable. Data are compiled in the national currency and converted to U.S. dollars using the annual average exchange rate. • **Information and communications technology expenditures** include computer hardware (computers, storage devices, printers, and other peripherals); computer software (operating systems, programming tools, utilities, applications, and internal software development); computer services (information technology consulting, computer and network systems integration, Web hosting, data processing services, and other services); and communications services (voice and data communications services) and wired and wireless communications equipment.

Data sources

Data on newspapers are compiled by the UNESCO Institute for Statistics. Data on televisions, personal computers, Internet users, broadband subscribers, international Internet bandwidth, and price basket for Internet are from the ITU's World Telecommunication Development Report database. Data on schools connected to the Internet are World Bank staff estimates. Data on secure Internet servers are from Netcraft (www.netcraft.com/). Data on information and communications technology expenditures are from WITSA's *Digital Planet 2006: The Global Information Economy* and from Global Insight, Inc.

5.12 Science and technology

	Researchers in R&D	Technicians in R&D	Scientific and technical journal articles	Expenditures for R&D	High-technology exports		Royalty and license fees		Patent applications filed[a]		Trademark applications filed[b]	
	per million people	per million people		% of GDP	$ millions	% of manufactured exports	Receipts $ millions	Payments $ millions	Residents	Non-residents	Residents	Non-residents
	2000–04[c]	2000–04[c]	2003	2000–04[c]	2005	2005	2005	2005	2004	2004	2004	2004
Afghanistan	..	..	..	..	..	..	..	..	..	..	..	..
Albania	..	..	..	..	5	1	1	4	*0*	..	..	..
Algeria	..	..	285	..	*7*	*1*	..	..	58	334	*1,488*	*871*
Angola	..	..	..	..	..	..	49	3	..	..	..	..
Argentina	720	316	3,086	0.41	809	7	54	635	786	3,816	*61,953*	*19,139*
Armenia	..	..	175	0.25	5	1	..	..	*151*	6	1,598	256
Australia	3,759	..	15,809	1.70	3,276	13	508	1,645	8,555	21,651	37,202	16,007
Austria	2,968	1,254	4,906	2.26	11,623	13	177	1,334	1,965	549	7,336	1,049
Azerbaijan	..	..	107	0.30	5	1	0	0	..	..	*144*	*339*
Bangladesh	..	..	204	0.62	*3*	*0*	0	3	..	..	..	..
Belarus	..	..	532	0.62	216	3	3	20	1,065	382	2,410	1,027
Belgium	3,065	1,473	6,604	1.90	22,809	9	1,107	1,107	*519*	*188*	*21,010*[d]	*10,695*[d]
Benin	..	..	..	..	0	0	*0*	*2*	..	..	..	..
Bolivia	120	6	..	0.28	*28*	*9*	2	11	..	..	..	..
Bosnia and Herzegovina	..	..	..	..	..	..	..	..	47	349	267	700
Botswana	..	..	76	..	..	..	0	12	*0*	..	..	..
Brazil	344	332	8,684	0.98	8,007	13	102	1,404	3,892	14,800	*81,036*	*13,218*
Bulgaria	1,263	477	829	0.51	326	5	5	79	263	133	5,978	1,086
Burkina Faso	..	..	..	..	*3*	*10*	..	..	..	..	..	..
Burundi	..	..	..	..	*0*	*6*	0	0	..	..	*20*	*132*
Cambodia	..	..	..	..	*4*	*0*	0	7	..	..	409	1,638
Cameroon	..	..	123	..	2	2	0	2	..	..	..	..
Canada	3,597	770	24,803	1.93	29,777	14	3,471	6,649	*3,929*	*33,298*	17,719	22,169
Central African Republic	..	..	..	..	0	0	..	..	..	..	..	..
Chad	..	..	..	..	..	..	..	..	..	..	..	..
Chile	444	303	1,500	0.61	*195*	*5*	54	322	..	..	..	..
China	708	..	29,186	1.44	214,246	31	157	5,321	65,586	64,798	527,591	52,788
Hong Kong, China	1,564	225	..	0.60	94,808	34	*218*	*1,111*	127	9,878	*7,374*	*11,208*
Colombia	109	77	337	0.17	362	5	10	118	*52*	*198*	..	..
Congo, Dem. Rep.	..	..	..	..	..	..	..	..	..	..	..	..
Congo, Rep.	30	32	..	..	..	..	..	..	..	..	..	..
Costa Rica	..	..	84	0.39	1,775	38	0	57	..	..	..	..
Côte d'Ivoire	..	..	..	..	*93*	*8*	*0*	*22*	..	..	..	..
Croatia	1,296	455	845	1.14	689	12	73	193	383	841	1,283	767
Cuba	..	..	264	0.65	..	..	..	..	..	..	379	1,937
Czech Republic	1,594	923	2,950	1.28	*7,662*	*13*	63	216	619	633	9,365	1,042
Denmark	5,016	2,713	5,291	2.63	11,733	22	..	..	1,843	172	4,185	944
Dominican Republic	..	..	..	..	..	..	0	31	..	..	..	..
Ecuador	50	..	..	0.07	64	8	*0*	42	*13*	489	5,571	4,822
Egypt, Arab Rep.	..	..	1,720	0.19	*15*	*1*	136	182	157	537	..	..
El Salvador	47	..	..	..	*37*	*4*	2	30	..	..	..	..
Eritrea	..	..	..	..	..	..	..	..	..	..	..	..
Estonia	2,523	427	368	0.91	931	18	5	25	27	97	1,241	583
Ethiopia	..	..	99	..	*0*	*0*	0	1	..	..	..	..
Finland	7,832	..	5,202	3.51	13,835	25	1,207	1,123	2,004	216	2,598	722
France	3,213	..	31,971	2.16	69,673	20	5,924	3,230	14,230	3,060	*57,784*	*2,935*
Gabon	..	..	..	..	*28*	*15*	..	..	..	..	..	..
Gambia, The	..	..	..	..	0	6	..	..	*0*	..	..	..
Georgia	..	..	117	0.29	76	23	9	5	248	210	148	132
Germany	3,261	1,089	44,305	2.49	137,547	17	6,828	6,589	48,329	10,905	62,576	3,342
Ghana	..	..	83	..	*19*	*9*	0	0	..	..	..	..
Greece	1,413	895	3,770	0.58	994	10	60	442	487	27	*5,290*	*1,143*
Guatemala	..	..	..	..	98	3	*0*	*0*	..	..	..	..
Guinea	..	..	..	..	..	..	*0*	*0*	..	..	..	..
Guinea-Bissau	..	..	..	..	..	..	..	*0*	..	..	..	..
Haiti	..	..	..	..	..	..	0	0	..	..	..	..

Science and technology

	Researchers in R&D	Technicians in R&D	Scientific and technical journal articles	Expenditures for R&D	High-technology exports		Royalty and license fees		Patent applications filed[a]		Trademark applications filed[b]	
	per million people	per million people		% of GDP	$ millions	% of manufactured exports	Receipts $ millions	Payments $ millions	Residents	Non-residents	Residents	Non-residents
	2000–04[c]	2000–04[c]	2003	2000–04[c]	2005	2005	2005	2005	2004	2004	2004	2004
Honduras	..	..	..	0.05	*6*	*2*	0	22	*7*	*161*	*1,149*	*3,388*
Hungary	1,472	466	2,503	0.88	13,045	25	834	1,068	738	1,919	4,293	1,047
India	..	..	12,774	0.85	*2,840*	5	*25*	*421*	6,795	10,671	..	..
Indonesia	207	..	178	0.05	6,571	16	263	961	226	3,441	..	..
Iran, Islamic Rep.	1,279	..	1,806	0.67	*98*	*3*	..	..	..	..	..	..
Iraq	..	..	..	..	..	..	..	..	..	..	..	..
Ireland	2,674	621	1,758	1.21	..	..	589	19,426	787	58	*1,285*	*1,142*
Israel	..	..	6,941	4.46	4,937	14	610	537	*1,329*	*8,929*	215	5,022
Italy	1,213	..	24,696	1.14	24,616	8	1,131	1,942	..	..	..	..
Jamaica	..	..	..	0.07	..	..	13	11	*15*	*54*	*663*	*1,433*
Japan	5,287	528	60,067	3.15	122,680	22	17,655	14,653	362,342	60,739	110,270	18,573
Jordan	..	..	263	..	160	5	..	..	..	..	..	..
Kazakhstan	629	92	128	0.22	*72*	*2*	0	31	*1,696*	*102*	2,908	1,070
Kenya	..	..	258	..	*18*	*3*	18	37	..	..	..	..
Korea, Dem. Rep.	..	..	..	..	..	..	..	..	..	..	..	..
Korea, Rep.	3,187	567	13,746	2.64	83,527	32	1,827	4,398	105,027	35,088	91,935	16,529
Kuwait	..	..	244	0.20	..	..	0	0	..	..	..	..
Kyrgyz Republic	..	..	..	0.20	4	2	2	2	*179*	*1*	133	345
Lao PDR	..	..	..	..	..	..	..	..	..	..	*25*	*656*
Latvia	1,434	318	153	0.42	159	5	10	14	107	44	1,290	595
Lebanon	..	..	223	..	*26*	*2*	*0*	*0*	..	..	..	..
Lesotho	..	0	..	0.01	..	..	18	..	..	..	..	..
Liberia	..	..	..	..	..	..	..	..	..	..	..	..
Libya	361	493	..	..	..	..	*0*	*0*	..	..	..	..
Lithuania	2,136	427	322	0.76	410	6	2	21	69	45	1,929	570
Macedonia, FYR	504	69	*74*	0.26	16	1	3	10	37	415	*478*	*515*
Madagascar	15	45	..	0.12	*1*	*1*	1	3	16	22	411	321
Malawi	..	..	..	..	6	7	..	..	..	..	*138*	*440*
Malaysia	299	58	520	0.69	57,376	55	27	1,370	..	..	..	..
Mali	..	..	..	..	..	..	*0*	*1*	..	..	..	..
Mauritania	..	..	..	..	..	..	..	..	..	..	..	..
Mauritius	..	..	..	0.35	298	21	0	5	..	..	..	..
Mexico	268	96	3,747	0.40	32,262	20	70	111	531	12,667	41,813	20,775
Moldova	..	..	78	..	11	3	2	2	297	9	1,574	372
Mongolia	..	..	..	0.28	0	0	..	..	143	86	423	1,321
Morocco	..	..	428	0.62	702	10	13	45	..	..	..	..
Mozambique	..	..	..	0.59	9	8	2	5	..	..	..	..
Myanmar	17	133	..	0.07	..	..	*0*	*0*	..	..	..	..
Namibia	..	..	..	..	*15*	*3*	*0*	*3*	..	..	..	..
Nepal	59	137	..	0.66	*1*	*0*	..	..	..	..	..	..
Netherlands	2,482	1,725	13,475	1.85	65,758	30	3,866	3,692	2,187	556	..	..
New Zealand	3,945	833	3,034	1.16	943	14	101	555	1,579	4,952	8,426	7,864
Nicaragua	..	..	..	0.05	4	5	0	0	..	..	..	..
Niger	..	..	..	..	*1*	*3*	..	*0*	..	..	..	..
Nigeria	..	..	384	..	*9*	*2*	..	45	..	..	..	..
Norway	4,587	1,754	3,339	1.75	3,010	17	364	546	..	..	..	*6,981*
Oman	..	..	114	..	25	2	..	..	*0*	..	..	..
Pakistan	..	..	368	0.22	211	2	15	110	..	1,081	8,319	4,455
Panama	97	387	..	0.34	1	1	0	42	..	..	..	..
Papua New Guinea	..	..	..	..	*47*	*39*	..	..	..	..	..	..
Paraguay	79	113	..	0.10	*14*	*7*	196	1	12	173	..	..
Peru	..	..	129	0.10	64	3	2	69	38	785	*8,227*	*5,661*
Philippines	48	8	179	0.11	26,077	71	6	265	157	2,539	6,861	5,253
Poland	1,581	282	6,770	0.58	2,688	4	61	1,036	2,381	5,359	13,776	1,153
Portugal	1,949	307	2,625	0.78	*2,639*	9	60	328	121	66	8,123	1,012
Puerto Rico	..	..	..	..	..	..	..	..	..	..	..	..

5.12 Science and technology

	Researchers in R&D	Technicians in R&D	Scientific and technical journal articles	Expenditures for R&D	High-technology exports		Royalty and license fees		Patent applications filed[a]		Trademark applications filed[b]	
	per million people	per million people		% of GDP	$ millions	% of manufactured exports	Receipts $ millions	Payments $ millions	Residents	Non-residents	Residents	Non-residents
	2000–04[c]	2000–04[c]	2003	2000–04[c]	2005	2005	2005	2005	2004	2004	2004	2004
Romania	976	249	988	0.40	758	3	48	173	937	163	10,298	1,193
Russian Federation	3,319	557	15,782	1.17	3,690	8	260	1,593	22,944	7,246	23,571	7,088
Rwanda	..	..	..	..	*1*	*25*	0	0	..	..	..	..
Saudi Arabia	..	..	573	..	215	1	0	0	*61*	*552*	..	..
Senegal	..	..	79	..	75	12	*0*	*7*	..	..	..	..
Serbia and Montenegro	..	..	600	1.17	..	..	..	..	*381*	..	*1,085*	*647*
Sierra Leone	..	..	..	..	..	..	*1*	0	..	..	..	..
Singapore	4,999	381	3,122	2.25	105,078	57	544	8,647	509	8,076	4,839	18,409
Slovak Republic	1,984	445	943	0.53	1,960	7	*50*	*91*	214	239	2,912	1,148
Slovenia	2,543	1,600	969	1.61	786	5	16	113	327	42	1,615	550
Somalia	..	..	..	..	..	..	..	..	..	..	..	..
South Africa	307	73	2,364	0.76	1,739	7	45	1,071	..	..	..	..
Spain	2,195	861	16,826	1.11	10,409	7	561	2,639	2,864	320	52,718	2,059
Sri Lanka	128	..	141	0.14	*60*	*1*	..	..	*95*	*189*	*3,989*	*1,773*
Sudan	..	..	..	0.34	*0*	*0*	0	0	..	..	..	..
Swaziland	..	..	..	..	..	..	0	88	..	..	..	..
Sweden	5,416	..	10,237	3.74	17,070	17	3,324	1,498	2,752	478	..	..
Switzerland	3,601	2,319	8,542	2.57	25,544	22	..	..	*1,827*	*466*	..	..
Syrian Arab Republic	..	..	67	..	*6*	*1*	..	12	..	..	..	..
Tajikistan	..	..	..	..	..	..	1	0	32	2	65	253
Tanzania	..	..	86	..	1	1	0	0	..	..	..	..
Thailand	287	208	1,072	0.26	22,480	27	17	1,674	*681*	*4,329*	*22,612*	*9,241*
Togo	..	..	..	..	0	0	*0*	*2*	..	..	..	..
Trinidad and Tobago	..	..	..	0.12	34	1	..	..	*2*	*205*	*340*	*1,317*
Tunisia	1,013	34	452	0.63	*370*	*5*	14	8	..	..	..	..
Turkey	341	37	6,224	0.66	906	2	*0*	439	*465*	*383*	*30,136*	*2,101*
Turkmenistan	..	..	..	..	..	..	..	..	..	..	..	..
Uganda	..	..	90	0.81	18	14	7	1	..	..	..	..
Ukraine	..	..	2,089	1.16	869	4	22	421	4,086	1,692	11,516	2,434
United Arab Emirates	..	..	193	..	..	..	..	..	..	..	..	..
United Kingdom	..	..	48,288	1.89	82,841	28	13,303	9,069	18,816	11,138	23,186	4,653
United States	4,605	..	211,233	2.68	233,079	32	57,410	24,501	185,008	171,935	213,495	26,988
Uruguay	366	50	194	0.26	*22*	*2*	0	4	37	514	*4,589*	*6,732*
Uzbekistan	..	..	192	..	..	..	..	..	273	205	438	494
Venezuela, RB	..	..	563	0.28	*118*	*3*	0	239	..	..	..	..
Vietnam	115	..	216	0.19	*594*	*6*	..	..	..	..	..	..
West Bank and Gaza	..	..	..	..	..	..	..	..	..	..	..	..
Yemen, Rep.	..	..	..	..	11	5	..	9	..	..	..	..
Zambia	..	..	..	..	2	1	..	..	..	..	..	..
Zimbabwe	..	..	96	..	*5*	*1*	..	..	..	..	..	..
World	.. w	.. w	697,397 s	2.28 w	*1,243,114* s	22 w	123,690 s	134,689 s	872,278 s	473,770 s	1,337,033 s	267,528 s
Low income	..	..	14,929	0.73	..	*4*	47	224	7,259	12,067	10,198	8,827
Middle income	725	..	100,288	0.85	*332,483*	21	2,693	19,573	105,144	120,688	678,572	107,953
Lower middle income	504	..	49,969	1.12	..	26	1,083	10,892	76,157	90,921	566,801	71,992
Upper middle income	1,453	308	50,319	0.67	*120,551*	17	1,610	8,681	28,987	29,767	111,771	35,961
Low & middle income	..	..	115,217	0.83	*270,664*	21	2,740	19,797	112,403	132,755	688,770	116,780
East Asia & Pacific	708	..	31,351	1.44	..	34	471	9,599	66,112	70,866	535,284	61,115
Europe & Central Asia	1,993	384	42,695	0.94	26,767	8	1,405	5,353	34,767	19,989	96,993	23,355
Latin America & Carib.	256	..	18,588	0.56	*40,879*	15	542	3,204	4,498	29,255	47,763	27,534
Middle East & N. Africa	..	..	5,358	..	*1,405*	*3*	163	256	215	871	*1,488*	*871*
South Asia	..	..	13,487	0.73	..	*4*	18	113	6,795	11,752	8,319	4,455
Sub-Saharan Africa	..	..	3,738	..	..	*4*	141	1,272	16	22	411	321
High income	3,781	..	582,180	2.45	*1,156,714*	22	120,950	114,892	759,875	341,015	648,263	150,748
Europe EMU	2,607	..	156,184	1.92	358,491	16	21,814	42,096	72,974	15,757	133,351	8,184

Note: The original information on patent and trademark application was provided by the World Intellectual Property Organization (WIPO). The International Bureau of WIPO assumes no responsibility with respect to the transformation of these data.

a. Excludes applications filed under the auspices of the European Patent Office (32,178 by residents, 91,523 by nonresidents) and the Eurasian Patent Organization (1,630 by nonresidents). b. Excludes applications filed under the auspices of the EU Office for Harmonization in the Internal Market (40,305 by residents, 18,540 by nonresidents). c. Data are for the most recent year available. d. Includes Luxembourg and the Netherlands.

About the data

Technological innovation, often fueled by government-led research and development (R&D), has been the driving force for industrial growth around the world. The best opportunities to improve living standards, including new ways of reducing poverty, will come from science and technology. Science, advancing rapidly in virtually all fields—particularly in biotechnology—is playing a growing economic role: countries able to access, generate, and apply relevant scientific knowledge will have a competitive edge over those that cannot. And there is greater appreciation of the need for high-quality scientific input into public policy issues such as regional and global environmental concerns.

Science and technology cover a range of issues too complex and too broad to be quantified by any single set of indicators, but those in the table shed light on countries' "technology base"—the availability of skilled human resources, the number of scientific and technical articles published, the competitive edge countries enjoy in high-technology exports, sales and purchases of technology through royalties and licenses, and the number of patent and trademark applications filed.

The United Nations Educational, Scientific, and Cultural Organization (UNESCO) Institute for Statistics (UIS) collects data on researchers, technicians and expenditure in R&D from countries and territories around the World, through questionnaires and special surveys as well as from other international sources. Data on researchers and technicians are normally calculated in terms of full-time equivalents.

R&D expenditures include all expenditures for R&D performed within a country, including both capital expenditures and current costs (annual wages and salaries and all associated costs of researchers, technicians and supporting staff, and other current costs, such as noncapital purchases of materials, supplies and R&D equipment such as utilities, books, journals, reference materials, subscriptions to libraries and scientific societies, and materials for laboratories).

The information does not reflect the quality of training and education, which varies widely. Similarly, R&D expenditures are no guarantee of progress; governments need to pay close attention to the practices that make R&D expenditures effective.

Article counts are from a set of journals classified and covered by the Institute for Scientific Information's Science Citation Index (SCI) and Social Sciences Citation Index (SSCI). Article counts are based on fractional assignments; for example, an article with two authors from different countries is counted as one-half of an article for each country (see *Definitions* for the fields covered). The SCI and SSCI databases cover the core set of scientific journals but may exclude some of regional or local importance. They may also reflect some bias toward English-language journals.

The method used for determining a country's high technology exports was developed by the Organisation for Economic Co-operation and Development in collaboration with Eurostat. Termed the "product approach" to distinguish it from a "sectoral approach," the method is based on the calculation of R&D intensity (R&D expenditure divided by total sales) for groups of products from six countries (Germany, Italy, Japan, the Netherlands, Sweden, and the United States). Because industrial sectors characterized by a few high-technology products may also produce many low-technology products, the product approach is more appropriate for analyzing international trade than is the sectoral approach. To construct a list of high-technology manufactured products (services are excluded), the R&D intensity was calculated for products classified at the three-digit level of the Standard International Trade Classification revision 3. The final list was determined at the four- and five-digit levels. At these levels, since no R&D data were available, final selection was based on patent data and expert opinion. This method takes only R&D intensity into account. Other characteristics of high technology are also important, such as know-how, scientific and technical personnel, and technology embodied in patents; considering these characteristics would result in a different list. (See Hatzichronoglou 1997 for further details.) Moreover, the R&D for high-technology exports may not have occurred in the reporting country.

Most countries have adopted systems that protect patentable inventions. The Patent Cooperation Treaty provides an international system for filing patent applications. The procedure consists of an international phase followed by a national or regional phase. In the international phase an applicant files an international application and designates the countries in which patent protection is eventually to be sought (since 2004 all eligible countries are automatically designated in every application under the treaty). The application is searched, published, and, optionally, an international preliminary examination is conducted. In the national (or regional) phase the applicant requests national processing of the application, pays additional fees, and initiates the national search, examination, and granting procedure. International applications under the treaty provide only for a national patent grant—there is no international patent. The national phase filing represents an action on the part of the applicant to actively seek patent protection for a given territory, whereas international filings and designations, while they represent a legal right, do not accurately reflect where patent protection is eventually sought. Resident filings are those from applicants who are a resident of the country or region concerned. Nonresident filings are from applicants outside the relevant country or region. In the case of regional offices such as the European Patent Office, an application from a resident of any member state of the regional patent convention is considered a resident filing. Some offices (notably the U.S. Patent and Trademark Office) use the residence of the inventor rather than the applicant to classify resident and nonresident filings.

A trademark provides protection to its owner by ensuring the exclusive right to use it to identify goods or services or to authorize another to use it in return for payment. The period of protection varies, but a trademark can be renewed indefinitely by paying additional fees. The trademark system helps consumers identify and purchase a product or service whose nature and quality, indicated by its unique trademark, meet their needs.

Definitions

• **Researchers in R&D** are professionals engaged in conceiving of or creating new knowledge, products, processes, methods, and systems, and also in managing the projects concerned. Postgraduate students at the PhD level (International Standard Classification of Education 1997 level 6) engaged in R&D are considered researchers. • **Technicians in R&D** and equivalent staff are people whose main tasks require technical knowledge and experience in fields of engineering, physical and life sciences (technicians), and social sciences and humanities (equivalent staff). They participate in R&D by performing scientific and technical tasks involving the application of concepts and operational methods, normally under the supervision of researchers. • **Scientific and technical journal articles** refer to published scientific and engineering articles in physics, biology, chemistry, mathematics, clinical medicine, biomedical research, engineering and technology, and earth and space sciences. • **Expenditures for R&D** are current and capital expenditures on creative work undertaken systematically to increase the stock of knowledge, including knowledge of humanity, culture, and society, and the use of this knowledge to devise new applications. The term *R&D* covers basic research, applied research, and experimental development. • **High-technology exports** are products with high R&D intensity, such as in aerospace, computers, pharmaceuticals, scientific instruments, and electrical machinery. • **Royalty and license fees** are payments and receipts between residents and nonresidents for the authorized use of intangible, nonproduced, nonfinancial assets, and proprietary rights (such as patents, copyrights, trademarks, franchises, and industrial processes) and for the use, through licensing agreements, of produced originals of prototypes (such as films and manuscripts). • **Patent applications filed** are worldwide patent applications filed through the Patent Cooperation Treaty procedure or with a national patent office. A patent is an exclusive right to an invention (a product or process that provides a new way of doing something or offers a new technical solution to a problem). It must be of practical use and display a new characteristic unknown in the body of existing knowledge in its technical field. A patent grants protection to the owner of the patent for a specified period, generally 20 years. • **Trademark applications filed** are applications to register a trademark with a national or regional trademark office. Trademarks are distinctive signs identifying goods or services as produced or provided by a specific person or enterprise. Trademarks protect owners of the mark by ensuring exclusive right to use it to identify goods or services or to authorize its use in return for payment.

Data sources

Data on R&D are provided by UIS. Data on scientific and technical journal articles are from the U.S. National Science Foundation's *Science and Engineering Indicators 2006*. Data on high-technology exports are from the United Nations Statistics Division's Commodity Trade (Comtrade) database. Data on royalty and license fees are from the International Monetary Fund's *Balance of Payments Statistics Yearbook*. Data on patents and trademarks are from the World Intellectual Property Organization's *WIPO Patent Report: Statistics on Worldwide Patent Activity* (2006 edition).

6 GLOBAL LINKS

Globalization and global links

Globalization—the integration of the world economy—has been a persistent theme of the past quarter century. The growth of cross-border economic activity has changed the structure of economies and the political and social organization of countries. Not all effects of globalization can be measured directly. But the scope and pace of change can be monitored along four important channels: trade in goods and services, financial flows, the movement of people, and the diffusion of technology and knowledge.

- Exports and imports of goods and services exceeded $26 trillion in 2005, or 58 percent of total global output, up from 44 percent in 1980. Developing economies still account for less than one-third of global trade, but their share has been increasing steadily.
- Gross private capital flows across national borders exceeded 32 percent of global output in 2005, up from 9 percent in 1980. Foreign direct investment and cross-border portfolio investment flows to developing economies have soared despite occasional setbacks.
- People have become more mobile. More than 800 million people traveled to foreign destinations in 2005, nearly triple the number in 1980. Some 190 million people are estimated to reside outside their land of birth, nearly double the 1980 level.
- Technology and knowledge are diffusing at unprecedented speed across countries. International phone traffic, measured in minutes, increased more than fourfold between 1995 and 2005 (see section 5).

Many factors have accelerated the pace of globalization. Barriers to international trade and investment are coming down. Technological progress has dramatically cut transportation and communications costs, enabling production processes and distribution networks to move from local to global. Some previously nontradable services can now be traded easily around the world. Efficiency gains due to resource allocation at global scale have made globalization an increasingly powerful source of growth.

Globalization has created opportunities and challenges for developing countries. While the experiences of China, India, Indonesia, Thailand, and some other countries have demonstrated that integration into the global economy is necessary for long-term growth and poverty reduction, concerns have emerged over equality of opportunity and the unequal distribution of benefits. Many poor countries and poor people in many countries have not been able to take full advantage of the opportunities brought by globalization or to participate in its benefits.

Removing the obstacles to full participation by poor countries and poor people is essential to making globalization more inclusive. For example, subsidies to domestic farmers in high-income economies have created formidable barriers for developing economies trying to reach global markets for agricultural products. But there is much that developing countries need to do to make their economies more competitive. Scaling up and increasing the flexibility of official development assistance could assist low-income countries' efforts to attract investment and improve their trade-facilitating infrastructure, whose limitations now constrict poor countries' capacity to take advantage of growing global opportunities.

Expanding trade

International trade is the hallmark of an integrated global economy. Between 1990 and 2005 growth in trade outpaced growth in the overall economy across the board (figure 6a). Low- and middle-income economies gained market share in world merchandise exports—from about 16 percent in 1990 to almost 30 percent in 2005 (indicator table 6.3)—but the Sub-Saharan share lagged at around 1.5 percent.

Trade between developing economies has expanded considerably and now makes up about 8 percent of world merchandise exports. Between 1990 and 2005 merchandise exports between developing economies grew at an impressive average annual rate of 13 percent, compared with less than 6 percent for exports between high-income economies (figure 6b). But tariff barriers affecting exports to developing economies are still much higher than those affecting exports to high-income economies. The simple mean tariff rate averages 9 percent in developing economies but less than 4 percent in high-income economies (indicator table 6.7).

Expanding flows of private financial resources

International private financial flows have increased rapidly in both gross and net terms. Between 1990 and 2005 total gross capital flows recorded in the balance of payments tripled as a share of world GDP, and high-income economies still account for the lion's share (indicator table 6.1). All types of external financial flows to developing economies have soared during this period, but foreign direct investment (FDI) remains the largest (figure 6c). From a low initial level of less than $25 billion in 1990, net inflows of FDI to developing countries increased tenfold by 2005 (indicator table 6.8).

Large differences in external financial inflows exist among developing economies. The top 10 receivers of FDI net inflows accounted for about two-thirds of total FDI inflows among developing economies in 2005. FDI inflows are dominant in Latin America and Caribbean and East Asia and Pacific; portfolio investments are more important in South Asia (figure 6d). Meanwhile, some developing economies are increasingly investing overseas to expand their global operations.

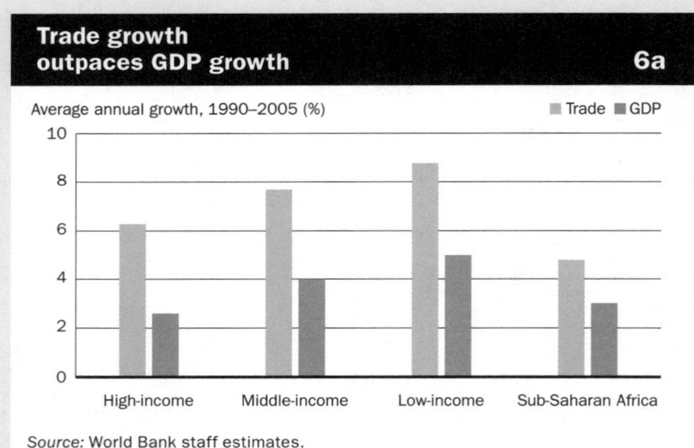

Trade growth outpaces GDP growth 6a

Source: World Bank staff estimates.

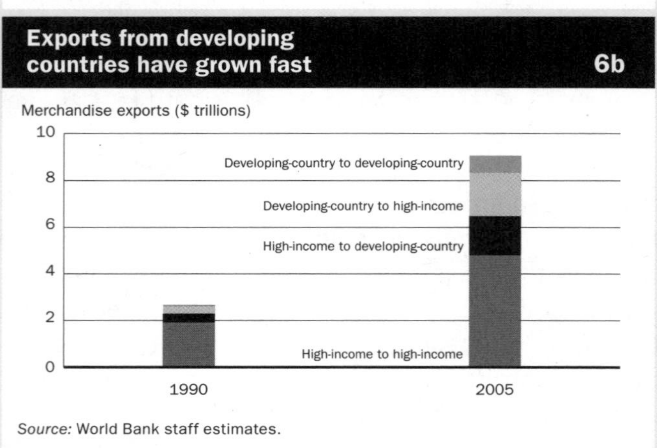

Exports from developing countries have grown fast 6b

Source: World Bank staff estimates.

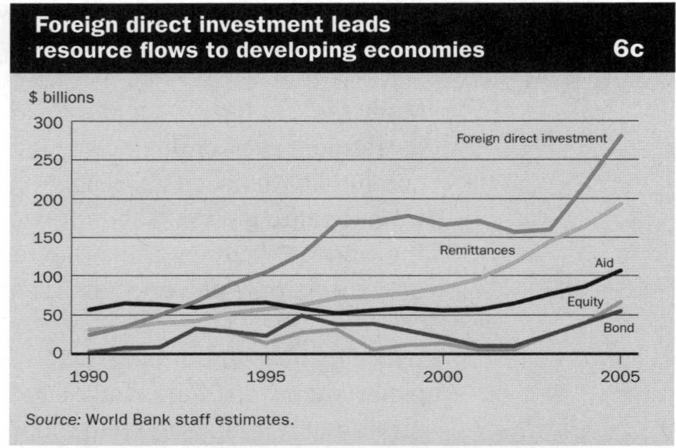

Foreign direct investment leads resource flows to developing economies 6c

Source: World Bank staff estimates.

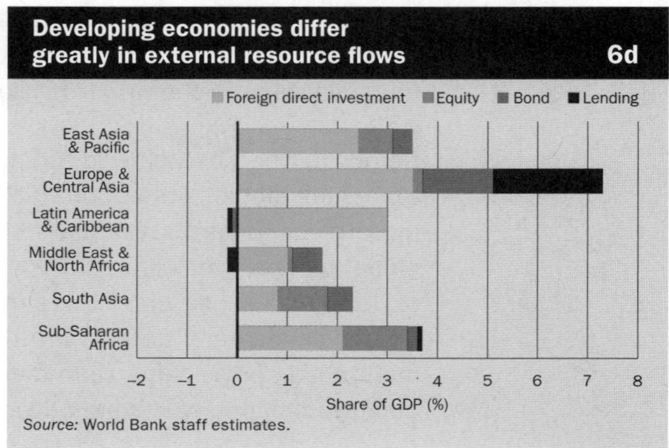

Developing economies differ greatly in external resource flows 6d

Source: World Bank staff estimates.

Expanding aid and increasing emphasis on effective aid

Developed economies have committed to providing more and better aid, especially to the poorest economies that commit themselves to poverty reduction and good governance. After a period of decline and stagnation, aid flows began to rise, particularly after the Financing for Development conference in Monterrey, Mexico, in 2002. Total official development assistance (ODA) rose to a record high of $106.8 billion in 2005 (indicator table 6.9). However, many donor economies still need to scale up aid significantly to fulfill commitments made at the Monterrey conference and at the Gleneagles Group of Eight summit in 2005 (figure 6e).

A large amount of aid is earmarked for special purposes. In 2005 more than half of ODA was used for special purposes such as debt relief, technical cooperation and administrative costs, and emergency relief and food aid (indicator table 6.10). Excluding these "special purpose" items and setting aside aid to Afghanistan and Iraq, only 41 percent of ODA in 2005 was available to finance development projects and budget support for general financing needs (figure 6f).

Expanding movements of people

The flow of people across national borders is another mark of integration. Important for many developing economies, international tourism has increased rapidly since its downturn in 2001. In 2005 international tourist arrivals worldwide exceeded 800 million, nearly double the 1990 level. Receipts reached $680 billion (excluding air tickets), accounting for 6.5 percent of global exports of goods and services (indicator table 6.15). Developing economies, accounting for a third of international tourist arrivals, are attracting new tourists at a faster rate than the world as whole (figure 6g).

International migration is a major global development issue, posing opportunities and challenges to both developed and developing economies. In 2005 recorded remittance flows repatriated by developing economy migrants were $188 billion, close to 2 percent of GDP (indicator table 6.14). While high-income economies are the most popular destinations, migration between developing economies accounts for nearly half the migrants from developing economies (figure 6h). Migration between developing economies occurs primarily between neighbors, particularly in Europe and Central Asia and Sub-Saharan Africa.

Aid flows are rising **6e**

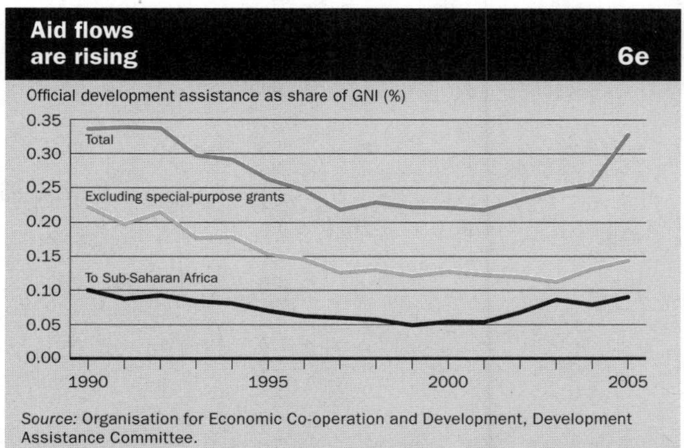

Source: Organisation for Economic Co-operation and Development, Development Assistance Committee.

Only 41 percent of aid finances development projects and general budget support **6f**

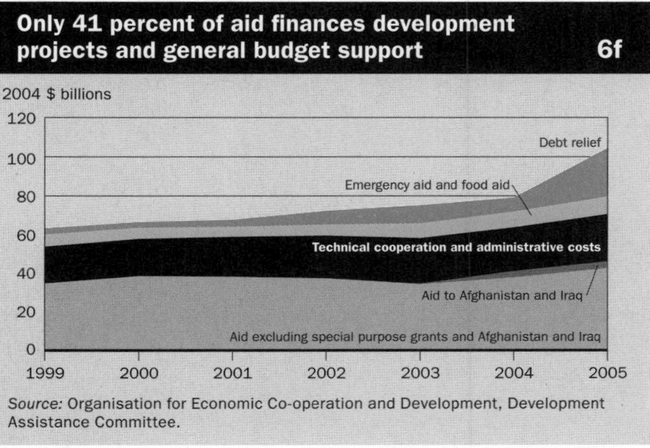

Source: Organisation for Economic Co-operation and Development, Development Assistance Committee.

Fast growth in tourism, especially for low-income countries **6g**

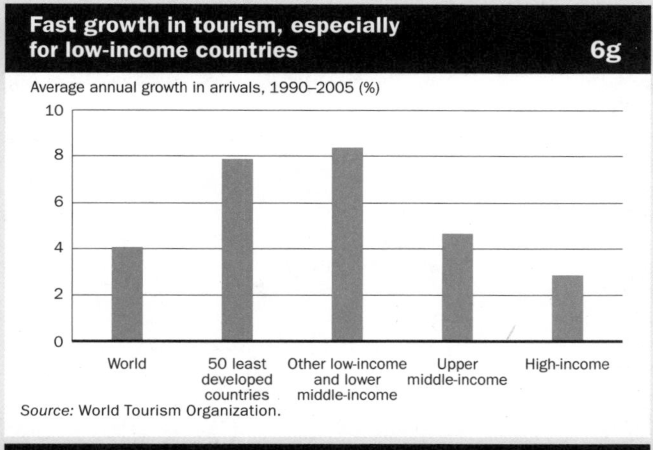

Source: World Tourism Organization.

Migration to developing economies accounts for almost half of all migrants **6h**

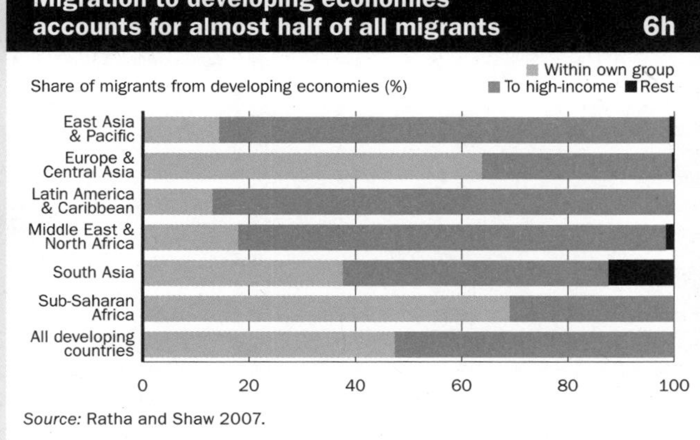

Source: Ratha and Shaw 2007.

6.1 Integration with the global economy

	Merchandise trade		Trade in services		Growth in real trade less growth in real GDP	Gross private capital flows		Foreign direct investment			
								% of GDP			
	% of GDP		% of GDP		percentage points	% of GDP		Net inflows		Net outflows	
	1990	2005	1990	2005	1990–2005	1990	2005	1990	2005	1990	2005
Afghanistan	..	51.4	..	..	..	..	..	..	..	..	..
Albania	29.0	39.0	2.9	30.4	12.5	18.0	7.3	2.8	3.1	0.0	0.0
Algeria	36.6	64.9	2.9	..	0.1	2.6	..	0.0	1.1	0.0	..
Angola	53.5	96.2	18.7	21.2	..	10.1	29.5	−3.3	−4.0	0.0	0.2
Argentina	11.6	37.5	3.9	7.6	4.0	8.2	9.1	1.3	2.6	0.0	0.2
Armenia	..	55.4	..	14.7	−6.9	..	10.5	81.4	5.3	..	0.1
Australia	25.6	31.6	7.5	7.9	3.1	9.0	32.5	2.5	−4.7	0.3	2.7
Austria	54.8	81.7	22.7	33.7	3.4	9.6	51.9	0.4	3.0	1.0	2.5
Azerbaijan	..	94.3	..	26.6	13.8	..	87.0	0.0	13.4	..	13.9
Bangladesh	17.6	38.5	3.6	5.7	4.2	0.9	2.9	0.0	1.3	0.0	0.0
Belarus	..	110.5	..	10.9	−1.5	..	5.4	0.0	1.0	..	0.0
Belgium	110.2[a]	176.1	25.5[a]	28.9	2.2	78.8[a]	382.1[a]	3.7[a]	8.6	2.9[a]	5.1
Benin	30.0	33.9	13.9	12.4	−2.4	10.7	8.1	3.4	0.5	0.0	0.1
Bolivia	33.1	53.7	9.4	12.5	1.7	3.1	14.1	0.6	−3.0	0.0	0.0
Bosnia and Herzegovina	..	95.5	..	14.8	−2.7	..	28.0	..	3.0	..	0.0
Botswana	98.4	74.6	15.4	16.6	−2.3	9.0	12.3	2.5	2.7	0.2	2.5
Brazil	11.7	24.6	2.4	5.1	4.4	1.9	5.9	0.2	1.9	0.1	1.6
Bulgaria	48.9	112.2	6.9	29.2	5.9	39.2	34.9	0.0	9.8	0.0	−0.9
Burkina Faso	22.0	34.8	9.1	..	−1.2	1.0	..	0.0	0.4	0.0	..
Burundi	27.0	47.2	12.9	18.4	..	3.7	3.0	0.1	0.1	0.0	0.0
Cambodia	22.4	109.9	5.7	28.1	9.7	3.2	13.6	1.7	6.1	..	0.2
Cameroon	30.5	33.9	12.8	11.3	1.8	15.5	14.4	−1.0	0.1	0.1	..
Canada	43.7	61.0	8.3	10.6	3.1	8.1	14.3	1.3	3.1	0.9	4.8
Central African Republic	18.4	20.4	16.0	..	..	2.2	..	0.0	0.4	0.3	..
Chad	27.2	70.1	15.5	..	3.3	5.6	..	0.5	12.9	0.0	..
Chile	51.1	63.4	12.4	13.0	3.5	14.4	20.4	2.1	5.8	0.0	1.0
China	32.5	63.6	2.9	7.1	6.3	2.5	10.9	1.0	3.5	0.2	0.1
Hong Kong, China	217.4	333.3	..	53.2	3.6	..	78.4	..	20.2	..	24.0
Colombia	30.7	34.6	8.3	6.1	2.7	3.1	16.3	1.2	8.5	0.0	0.1
Congo, Dem. Rep.	43.5	59.5	..	..	9.6	..	..	0.2	5.7	..	..
Congo, Rep.	57.2	126.0	31.0	35.3	3.8	6.6	34.2	−0.5	14.2	0.0	0.0
Costa Rica	46.4	84.1	15.7	20.6	3.2	5.4	16.9	2.2	4.3	0.0	0.3
Côte d'Ivoire	47.9	79.3	20.5	17.6	0.5	3.5	6.8	0.4	1.6	0.0	0.0
Croatia	88.8	71.0	..	34.6	4.1	..	23.1	..	4.6	..	1.0
Cuba	..	..	..	..	..	..	..	..	..	..	..
Czech Republic	83.6	124.6	..	16.7	8.4	..	22.0	0.0	4.1	..	0.5
Denmark	51.7	62.3	17.0	31.0	3.2	14.8	27.9	0.8	2.0	1.1	−4.1
Dominican Republic	73.2	53.4	21.7	18.2	0.2	5.0	6.6	1.9	3.5	0.0	0.0
Ecuador	44.2	55.9	13.0	8.6	2.1	11.0	14.3	1.2	4.5	0.0	0.0
Egypt, Arab Rep.	36.8	34.1	22.6	28.1	−1.1	6.8	16.4	1.7	6.0	0.0	0.2
El Salvador	38.4	59.8	13.4	13.9	5.8	2.0	11.7	0.0	3.0	0.0	0.0
Eritrea	77.0	52.1	..	..	−2.6	53.0	..	..	1.2	..	..
Estonia	..	135.1	9.1	40.5	7.2	3.9	93.9	2.1	22.9	0.0	2.4
Ethiopia	11.4	44.8	5.5	19.7	4.1	1.1	5.4	0.1	2.4	0.0	..
Finland	38.8	64.7	8.9	16.7	4.3	17.2	39.2	0.6	2.1	2.0	−0.8
France	36.4	45.0	11.1	10.4	3.8	20.2	32.9	1.1	3.3	2.8	2.3
Gabon	52.5	78.4	21.0	15.2	−1.3	18.0	14.6	1.2	3.7	0.5	0.3
Gambia, The	69.1	52.7	34.5	27.1	−3.2	0.9	15.5	4.5	11.3	0.0	..
Georgia	..	52.5	..	20.7	8.9	..	12.2	..	7.0	..	0.2
Germany	45.5	62.4	8.7	12.8	4.4	10.2	30.7	0.2	1.1	1.4	−0.3
Ghana	35.7	69.9	6.6	21.7	2.9	2.9	5.2	0.3	1.0	0.0	0.0
Greece	32.4	31.5	11.1	21.7	3.3	3.8	38.0	1.2	0.3	0.0	0.3
Guatemala	36.8	50.0	9.7	8.6	2.7	2.9	9.1	0.6	0.7	0.0	0.0
Guinea	49.5	52.0	18.6	8.9	−1.6	3.9	1.5	0.6	3.1	..	0.0
Guinea-Bissau	43.0	73.1	11.0	19.3	4.1	23.0	9.1	0.8	3.3	0.0	0.2
Haiti	17.2	45.1	4.3	13.6	..	1.1	2.6	0.3	0.2	−0.3	0.0

Integration with the global economy 6.1

	Merchandise trade		Trade in services		Growth in real trade less growth in real GDP	Gross private capital flows		Foreign direct investment			
	% of GDP		% of GDP		percentage points	% of GDP		% of GDP Net inflows		% of GDP Net outflows	
	1990	2005	1990	2005	1990–2005	1990	2005	1990	2005	1990	2005
Honduras	57.9	74.5	11.7	19.6	0.3	7.2	7.5	1.4	5.6	0.0	*0.0*
Hungary	61.5	117.3	16.0	22.0	8.4	4.6	26.2	1.9	5.9	0.0	*1.1*
India	13.1	28.5	3.4	*8.2*	4.4	0.8	*5.9*	0.1	0.8	0.0	*0.2*
Indonesia	41.5	54.2	7.5	12.8	0.6	4.1	7.2	1.0	1.8	0.0	..
Iran, Islamic Rep.	34.2	48.5	3.8	..	–2.9	2.7	..	–0.3	0.0	0.0	..
Iraq	*55.4*	*155.9*	..	..	..	..	..	..	..	..	..
Ireland	92.8	88.1	18.0	63.0	6.1	21.9	355.6	1.3	–14.7	0.8	*8.6*
Israel	55.0	72.8	18.1	25.5	1.2	6.5	23.1	0.3	4.5	0.4	*2.7*
Italy	31.1	42.4	8.5	10.2	1.7	10.3	28.3	0.6	1.1	0.7	*1.1*
Jamaica	67.2	62.3	37.5	42.4	..	8.4	50.3	3.0	7.1	0.0	*0.7*
Japan	17.3	24.5	4.2	5.4	2.9	5.4	15.9	0.1	0.1	1.7	*0.7*
Jordan	91.1	116.5	67.5	38.0	–0.7	6.3	20.7	0.9	12.1	–0.8	*0.0*
Kazakhstan	..	79.1	..	17.1	–2.8	..	39.7	*0.4*	3.5	..	*–3.0*
Kenya	37.9	50.4	21.4	16.1	2.2	3.5	6.3	0.7	0.1	0.0	*0.0*
Korea, Dem. Rep.	..	..	..	..	..	..	..	..	..	..	..
Korea, Rep.	51.1	69.3	7.5	13.2	6.4	5.3	7.1	0.3	0.6	0.4	*0.7*
Kuwait	59.8	75.9	25.2	16.8	–3.0	19.3	24.0	0.0	0.3	1.3	*3.2*
Kyrgyz Republic	..	72.9	..	22.4	–1.2	..	9.4	..	1.7	..	*2.0*
Lao PDR	30.5	43.6	5.8	..	..	3.7	..	0.7	1.0	0.0	..
Latvia	..	87.6	*9.2*	23.5	4.8	*2.3*	36.3	*0.6*	4.6	*0.0*	*0.7*
Lebanon	106.5	54.5	..	84.8	0.4	..	..	0.2	11.7	..	..
Lesotho	119.3	140.6	19.8	10.3	–0.2	9.6	6.7	2.8	6.3	0.0	*0.0*
Liberia	374.1	253.5	..	..	..	..	..	58.6	35.4	..	..
Libya	64.2	95.8	5.2	7.4	..	7.3	7.9	..	..	0.4	*–0.7*
Lithuania	..	106.4	..	20.1	8.0	..	29.1	*0.1*	4.0	..	*1.2*
Macedonia, FYR	*103.8*	91.4	..	16.9	4.1	..	11.8	*0.0*	1.7	..	*0.0*
Madagascar	31.5	45.8	12.8	7.5	2.3	1.8	0.8	0.7	0.6	0.0	*0.0*
Malawi	52.7	81.3	16.2	..	–1.7	3.2	..	1.2	0.1	0.0	..
Malaysia	133.4	196.1	21.2	31.9	2.9	10.3	24.1	5.3	3.0	0.0	*1.3*
Mali	39.7	51.3	19.0	*15.9*	1.8	2.0	*8.2*	0.2	3.0	0.0	*0.0*
Mauritania	84.1	71.1	16.0	..	–1.0	48.8	..	0.7	6.2	0.0	..
Mauritius	118.0	84.3	38.0	45.1	–0.5	8.0	13.0	1.7	0.6	0.0	*0.5*
Mexico	32.1	58.0	7.0	4.9	7.7	9.2	7.7	1.0	2.4	0.0	*0.5*
Moldova	..	116.7	..	29.9	11.2	..	13.8	*0.7*	6.8	..	*0.1*
Mongolia	75.7	117.1	9.7	*52.2*	15.7	26.0	*26.1*	0.6	9.7	0.0	*0.0*
Morocco	43.3	60.0	13.4	23.1	2.1	5.5	8.4	0.6	3.0	0.0	*0.0*
Mozambique	40.8	62.6	12.5	14.9	2.8	0.4	6.6	0.4	1.6	0.0	*0.0*
Myanmar	..	..	..	..	..	..	..	..	..	..	..
Namibia	95.6	74.9	20.7	*15.2*	0.0	16.5	*23.5*	..	..	0.1	*–0.4*
Nepal	24.1	36.1	10.2	11.0	..	3.5	4.2	0.2	0.0	0.0	..
Netherlands	83.9	122.0	19.2	24.6	3.5	28.6	94.0	3.5	6.5	4.5	*2.9*
New Zealand	43.0	43.9	13.3	15.3	2.3	17.7	6.0	4.0	1.8	3.6	*–0.8*
Nicaragua	95.9	70.3	17.0	15.0	5.2	9.0	7.8	0.1	4.9	0.0	*0.0*
Niger	27.0	40.3	10.9	*11.6*	..	2.8	*3.7*	1.6	0.4	0.0	*0.0*
Nigeria	67.5	60.2	10.3	11.6	1.7	5.9	25.4	2.1	2.0	0.0	..
Norway	52.8	53.9	21.6	18.9	1.0	11.9	40.1	0.9	1.1	1.3	*0.8*
Oman	71.1	*91.2*	6.7	*14.3*	2.5	3.5	*11.1*	1.2	*0.8*	0.0	*0.0*
Pakistan	32.6	37.3	8.8	10.1	–0.5	4.2	4.3	0.6	2.0	0.0	*0.1*
Panama	35.4	33.4	33.5	31.5	–3.5	106.6	56.8	2.6	6.6	0.0	*0.0*
Papua New Guinea	73.6	99.5	18.9	29.7	..	5.7	20.4	4.8	0.7	0.0	..
Paraguay	43.9	73.5	16.2	13.7	–1.4	5.4	7.6	1.5	0.9	0.0	*0.1*
Peru	22.3	37.4	7.5	6.6	3.3	3.2	10.4	0.2	3.2	0.0	*0.0*
Philippines	47.8	89.5	11.3	10.4	2.4	4.4	17.8	1.2	1.1	0.0	*0.5*
Poland	43.9	62.7	10.3	10.1	7.3	11.0	13.6	0.2	3.2	0.0	*0.3*
Portugal	55.4	54.1	12.1	13.7	2.8	10.8	50.9	3.5	1.7	0.2	*3.4*
Puerto Rico	..	..	..	..	–0.5	..	..	..	..	..	..

6.1 Integration with the global economy

	Merchandise trade		Trade in services		Growth in real trade less growth in real GDP	Gross private capital flows		Foreign direct investment			
	% of GDP		% of GDP		percentage points	% of GDP		% of GDP Net inflows		% of GDP Net outflows	
	1990	2005	1990	2005	1990–2005	1990	2005	1990	2005	1990	2005
Romania	32.8	69.2	3.6	10.8	8.5	2.9	16.7	0.0	6.7	0.0	*0.1*
Russian Federation	..	48.3	..	8.4	3.5	..	19.6	*0.3*	2.0	..	*1.8*
Rwanda	15.4	24.5	6.6	20.1	0.5	2.8	1.6	0.3	0.4	0.0	*0.0*
Saudi Arabia	58.6	77.7	21.8	10.9	..	8.8	31.6	..	..	0.0	*0.0*
Senegal	34.7	58.6	20.9	*17.9*	1.6	4.8	*6.2*	1.0	0.7	–0.2	*0.0*
Serbia and Montenegro	..	63.7	..	..	..	..	..	..	5.6	..	..
Sierra Leone	44.2	42.2	20.9	14.1	..	11.0	5.7	5.0	4.9	0.0	*0.0*
Singapore	308.1	368.0	58.2	90.4	..	54.3	95.5	15.1	17.2	5.5	*9.9*
Slovak Republic	*110.8*	145.0	..	*19.4*	6.8	..	*15.5*	0.6	4.1	..	*0.1*
Slovenia	*102.4*	112.7	*18.0*	20.1	2.0	*3.4*	33.3	*0.9*	1.6	*0.0*	*1.7*
Somalia	..	..	*11.2*	..	..	*21.3*	..	0.6	..	*0.0*	..
South Africa	37.4	47.7	6.4	9.7	2.6	2.4	10.6	–0.1	2.6	0.0	*0.7*
Spain	27.5	41.4	8.4	14.1	5.5	11.1	46.0	2.7	2.0	0.7	*4.8*
Sri Lanka	57.3	64.7	13.4	15.5	2.5	13.1	5.9	0.5	1.2	0.0	*0.0*
Sudan	7.5	42.0	3.0	7.1	4.7	0.3	14.6	–0.2	8.4	0.0	*0.0*
Swaziland	138.2	150.2	32.4	27.1	1.0	10.7	7.4	3.4	–0.6	0.9	*0.1*
Sweden	46.2	67.5	12.7	21.9	4.1	33.6	39.0	0.8	3.0	6.0	*4.4*
Switzerland	56.6	70.1	12.8	20.0	2.9	28.1	83.9	2.4	4.2	2.3	*7.2*
Syrian Arab Republic	53.7	52.7	14.3	20.8	2.7	18.0	2.6	0.6	1.6	0.0	*0.0*
Tajikistan	..	96.8	..	17.2	3.3	..	9.2	*0.5*	2.4	..	*0.0*
Tanzania	31.9	34.2	9.8	19.7	–1.2	0.2	5.7	0.0	3.9	0.0	..
Thailand	65.7	129.3	14.9	27.3	2.9	13.5	12.6	2.9	2.6	0.2	*0.1*
Togo	52.1	66.5	24.1	*18.9*	–1.1	9.6	*17.7*	1.1	0.1	0.0	*–0.4*
Trinidad and Tobago	60.6	102.4	15.9	*10.0*	3.2	11.4	*17.1*	2.2	7.7	0.0	*–2.1*
Tunisia	73.5	82.5	20.6	21.6	–0.4	9.5	3.2	0.6	2.5	0.0	*0.0*
Turkey	23.4	52.4	7.4	10.4	6.9	4.3	14.8	0.5	2.7	0.0	*0.3*
Turkmenistan	..	105.7	..	..	12.1	..	..	..	0.8	..	..
Uganda	10.2	30.2	4.5	14.6	2.8	1.1	5.2	–0.1	2.9	0.0	*0.0*
Ukraine	..	85.0	..	20.4	3.2	..	31.4	*0.3*	9.4	..	*0.0*
United Arab Emirates	103.2	151.3	..	..	1.8	..	..	..	..	..	..
United Kingdom	41.2	40.6	10.6	16.5	3.2	35.3	122.8	3.4	7.2	2.0	*3.8*
United States	15.8	21.2	4.6	5.6	3.9	5.6	14.4	0.8	0.9	0.6	*2.2*
Uruguay	32.7	43.4	9.2	13.3	2.3	12.7	26.5	0.4	4.2	0.0	*0.1*
Uzbekistan	..	60.3	..	..	–0.9	..	..	*0.1*	0.3	..	..
Venezuela, RB	52.8	56.9	7.9	4.8	0.6	51.6	17.9	1.0	2.1	0.8	*–0.3*
Vietnam	79.7	129.9	..	18.0	14.2	..	8.3	2.8	3.7	..	..
West Bank and Gaza	..	..	..	..	–1.2	..	..	..	..	..	..
Yemen, Rep.	46.9	70.6	16.3	10.2	2.4	16.2	2.1	–2.7	–1.8	..	*0.0*
Zambia	76.9	61.5	15.0	..	1.6	64.7	..	6.2	3.6	0.0	..
Zimbabwe	40.7	123.1	8.6	..	5.5	1.7	..	–0.1	3.0	0.0	..
World	**32.3 w**	**47.3 w**	**7.8 w**	**11.0 w**	..	**10.3 w**	**32.4 w**	**1.0 w**	**2.2 w**	**1.2 w**	***2.1 w***
Low income	23.6	41.1	6.2	*9.8*	..	2.4	*6.7*	0.4	1.5	0.0	*0.2*
Middle income	34.5	62.1	7.1	10.5	..	6.6	13.3	0.9	3.1	0.1	*0.5*
Lower middle income	31.6	58.9	6.4	10.0	..	4.4	11.5	0.8	3.1	0.1	*0.3*
Upper middle income	*38.3*	66.4	*8.0*	11.1	..	*7.9*	15.7	*1.2*	3.1	*0.3*	*0.7*
Low & middle income	32.5	59.2	7.0	10.6	..	5.9	13.1	0.8	2.9	0.1	*0.5*
East Asia & Pacific	47.1	74.6	7.3	10.3	..	5.0	11.4	1.6	3.2	0.2	*0.1*
Europe & Central Asia	*49.7*	68.6	*7.1*	12.6	..	*5.3*	20.3	*1.0*	3.5	*0.0*	*0.8*
Latin America & Carib.	23.2	44.2	5.7	6.8	..	7.9	9.8	0.8	2.9	0.1	*0.7*
Middle East & N. Africa	43.5	57.6	9.2	..	..	5.0	..	0.3	2.4	0.0	..
South Asia	16.5	31.2	4.2	*8.2*	..	1.4	*5.4*	0.1	1.0	0.0	*0.2*
Sub-Saharan Africa	41.9	57.8	10.8	13.1	..	5.1	14.2	0.4	2.7	0.0	*0.3*
High income	32.3	43.9	7.9	11.1	..	11.0	37.2	1.0	2.1	1.4	*2.4*
Europe EMU	44.0	61.4	11.0	15.9	..	13.5	58.7	1.1	3.2	1.7	*2.7*

a. includes Luxembourg.

About the data

The growing integration of societies and economies has helped reduce poverty in many countries. One indication of increasing global economic integration is the growing importance of trade in the world economy. Another is the increasing size and importance of private capital flows to developing countries that have liberalized their financial markets.

The table presents standardized measures of the size of trade and capital flows relative to gross domestic product (GDP). The numerators on trade and private capital flows are based on gross flows that capture the two-way flow of goods, services, and capital. In conventional balance of payments accounting exports are recorded as a credit and imports as a debit. And in the financial account inward investment is a credit and outward investment a debit. Thus net flows, the sum of credits and debits, represent a balance in which many transactions are canceled out. Gross flows are a better measure of integration because they show the total value of financial transactions during a given period.

Merchandise trade and trade in services (exports and imports) are shown relative to total GDP. Merchandise trade is an important part of global trade. Trade in services (such as transport, travel, finance, insurance, royalties, construction, communications, and cultural services) is an increasingly important element of global integration. The difference between the growth of real trade in goods and services and the growth of GDP helps to identify economies that have integrated with the global economy by liberalizing trade, lowering barriers to foreign investment, and harnessing their abundant labor to gain a competitive advantage in labor-intensive manufactures and services.

This year the table includes net inflows and outflows of foreign direct investment based on balance of payments data reported by the International Monetary Fund (IMF), supplemented by staff estimates using data reported by the United Nations Conference on Trade and Development and official national sources.

The internationally accepted definition of foreign direct investment is provided in the fifth edition of the IMF's *Balance of Payments Manual* (1993). For a more detailed explanation of foreign direct investment, see *About the data* for table 6.8.

Foreign direct investment may be understated in many developing countries. Some countries fail to report reinvested earnings, and the definition of long-term loans differs among countries. Underreporting of FDI outflows is more pervasive, particularly when investors are attempting to avoid controls on capital and foreign exchange or high taxes on investment income. Some countries do not identify FDI outflows in their balance of payments statistics. However, the quality and coverage of the data are improving as a result of continuous efforts by international and national statistics agencies.

Trade and capital flows are converted to U.S. dollars at the IMF's average official exchange rate for the year shown. An alternative conversion factor is applied if the official exchange rate diverges by an exceptionally large margin from the rate effectively applied to transactions in foreign currencies and traded products.

Definitions

• **Merchandise trade** is the sum of merchandise exports and imports divided by the value of GDP, all in current U.S. dollars. • **Trade in services** is the sum of services exports and imports divided by the value of GDP, all in current U.S. dollars. • **Growth in real trade less growth in real GDP** is the difference between annual growth in trade of goods and services and annual growth in GDP. Growth rates are calculated using constant price series taken from national accounts and are expressed as a percentage. • **Gross private capital flows** are the sum of the absolute values of direct, portfolio, and other investment inflows and outflows recorded in the balance of payments financial account, excluding changes in the assets and liabilities of monetary authorities and general government. The indicator is calculated as a ratio to GDP in U.S. dollars. • **Foreign direct investment net inflows** are the net inflows of investment to acquire a lasting management interest in an enterprise operating in an economy other than that of the investor. It is the sum of equity capital, reinvestment of earnings, and other short- and long-term capital, as shown in the balance of payments. This series shows net inflows in the reporting economy and is divided by the value of GDP. • **Foreign direct investment net outflows** are the net outflows of investment from the reporting economy to the rest of the world.

Private capital flows are rising, but they remain below the peak of 2000 6.1a

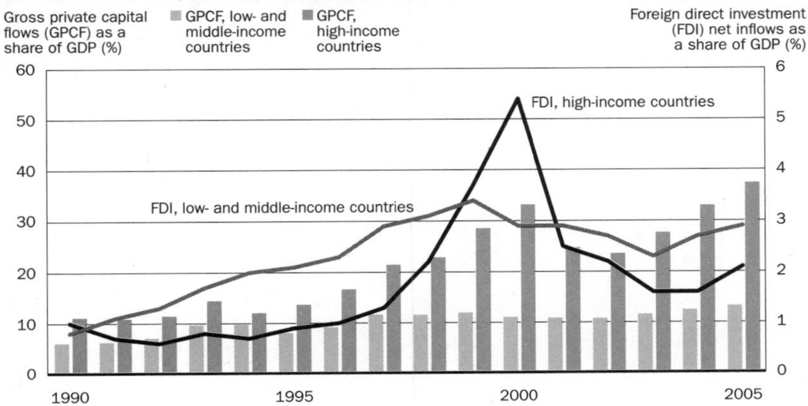

Source: World Bank staff estimates.

Data sources

Data on merchandise trade are from the World Trade Organization. Data on GDP are from the World Bank's national accounts files, converted from national currencies to U.S. dollars using the official exchange rate, supplemented by an alternative conversion factor if the official exchange rate is judged to diverge by an exceptionally large margin from the rate effectively applied to transactions in foreign currencies and traded products. Data on trade in services are from the IMF's Balance of Payments database. Data on real trade and GDP growth are from the World Bank's national accounts files. Gross private capital flows and foreign direct investment are reported in the World Bank Debtor Reporting System and are calculated using mainly the IMF's Balance of Payments database.

6.2 Growth of merchandise trade

	Export volume		Import volume		Export value		Import value		Net barter terms of trade index	
	average annual % growth		average annual % growth		average annual % growth		average annual % growth		2000 = 100	
	1980–90	1990–2005	1980–90	1990–2005	1980–90	1990–2005	1980–90	1990–2005	1990	2005
Afghanistan	..	..	..	..	..	..	..	..	..	..
Albania	..	..	..	..	..	..	..	..	..	..
Algeria	4.7	2.7	–8.0	1.7	–3.1	5.8	–2.7	1.2	74	*126*
Angola	9.0	5.8	–1.9	8.2	6.4	9.6	0.7	9.3	94	*121*
Argentina[a]	..	7.8	..	6.8	..	7.9	..	5.6	85	107
Armenia	..	..	..	..	..	..	..	..	..	..
Australia[a]	6.3	5.6	6.0	7.8	12.1	7.4	12.5	8.9	116	131
Austria[a]	..	..	..	..	..	..	..	..	98	103
Azerbaijan	..	..	..	..	..	..	..	..	..	..
Bangladesh	7.1	10.5	1.8	4.1	7.8	12.4	3.6	8.2	117	*88*
Belarus	..	..	..	..	..	..	..	..	..	..
Belgium[a]	..	5.8	..	5.4	..	8.0	..	8.2	*106*	99
Benin	11.8	3.0	–9.9	5.9	18.8	3.6	–4.9	6.3	107	*93*
Bolivia	3.1	4.9	–1.3	5.2	–1.9	5.6	–0.3	5.8	102	*108*
Bosnia and Herzegovina	..	..	..	..	..	..	..	..	..	..
Botswana	14.8	3.8	11.5	2.3	18.8	3.4	11.1	1.3	98	*92*
Brazil[a]	4.6	5.9	–1.2	2.9	4.9	7.5	–1.9	8.0	138	101
Bulgaria	..	..	..	..	..	..	..	..	..	..
Burkina Faso	–0.3	12.1	3.8	5.0	7.9	10.5	4.3	5.2	119	*98*
Burundi	3.5	8.0	1.0	6.3	2.5	–6.3	2.2	–3.9	128	*84*
Cambodia	..	..	..	..	..	..	..	..	..	..
Cameroon	7.0	3.3	4.8	7.2	1.4	2.7	0.1	4.6	81	*112*
Canada[a]	6.4	6.6	7.4	7.0	7.7	9.1	9.3	8.6	97	111
Central African Republic	0.0	14.7	4.2	1.6	3.5	1.7	7.9	–1.3	238	*99*
Chad	8.6	7.7	11.0	13.0	9.4	7.8	12.6	13.6	112	*101*
Chile	9.2	9.4	–3.0	6.8	8.1	8.2	2.8	7.1	114	*116*
China†	13.6	15.6	11.9	15.1	12.8	15.5	13.5	15.4	102	*92*
Hong Kong, China[a]	15.4	7.9	13.7	7.7	21.7	7.1	19.8	7.0	100	98
Colombia	7.9	4.4	–2.1	6.2	7.7	5.9	0.0	6.6	81	*93*
Congo, Dem. Rep.	9.7	4.4	12.2	11.0	2.7	–3.3	3.1	1.5	86	*94*
Congo, Rep.	7.4	4.5	3.3	6.7	2.1	8.6	5.3	6.1	63	*121*
Costa Rica	3.8	10.1	5.2	11.8	4.6	11.3	4.4	11.0	75	*102*
Côte d'Ivoire	2.6	4.6	–2.1	0.7	1.7	6.0	–1.5	3.0	143	*121*
Croatia	..	..	..	..	..	..	..	..	..	..
Cuba	..	..	..	..	..	..	..	..	..	..
Czech Republic	..	..	..	..	..	..	..	..	..	..
Denmark[a]	4.1	4.9	3.1	5.0	7.3	5.9	5.0	6.1	102	104
Dominican Republic	–0.9	3.5	2.9	8.3	–2.1	4.2	5.4	8.6	96	*96*
Ecuador	7.1	4.7	–1.8	7.6	–0.4	6.2	–1.3	8.8	114	*109*
Egypt, Arab Rep.	13.4	3.4	8.1	–0.5	7.3	4.2	12.6	2.0	101	*107*
El Salvador	–4.6	3.2	4.6	6.6	–4.6	6.9	2.4	9.4	84	*91*
Eritrea	..	–2.8	..	8.1	..	–4.2	..	7.2	*99*	*93*
Estonia	..	..	..	..	..	..	..	..	..	..
Ethiopia	–1.0	9.7	4.0	9.6	–1.1	7.6	4.3	10.2	121	*91*
Finland[a]	..	..	..	..	..	..	..	..	111	86
France[a]	3.6	3.3	3.7	3.5	..	2.9	..	2.7	103	111
Gabon	2.5	5.8	–3.5	1.3	–3.9	2.5	1.1	1.1	157	*125*
Gambia, The	2.2	–9.3	–6.0	–0.8	6.6	–9.1	2.5	–1.3	100	*115*
Georgia	..	..	..	..	..	..	..	..	..	..
Germany[a, b]	..	..	..	..	..	..	..	..	100	101
Ghana	–17.2	4.7	–19.3	6.5	–2.7	6.6	0.6	6.6	100	*123*
Greece[a]	5.0	8.9	6.4	9.3	21.4	16.4	26.0	16.4	97	95
Guatemala	–1.1	6.8	0.1	9.8	–2.2	6.7	0.6	10.7	115	*93*
Guinea	..	3.2	..	2.5	4.0	0.2	9.7	–0.5	122	*107*
Guinea-Bissau	–2.0	14.0	–0.3	–4.1	4.2	11.7	5.2	–3.1	146	*94*
Haiti	–0.4	11.6	–4.6	10.8	–1.2	11.2	–2.9	12.4	132	*87*
†Data for Taiwan, China	26.1	2.8	30.3	3.3	14.9	5.8	12.4	6.4	97	*92*

Growth of merchandise trade

	Export volume		Import volume		Export value		Import value		Net barter terms of trade index	
	average annual % growth		average annual % growth		average annual % growth		average annual % growth		2000 = 100	
	1980–90	1990–2005	1980–90	1990–2005	1980–90	1990–2005	1980–90	1990–2005	1990	2005
Honduras	4.1	2.7	1.6	10.5	1.6	4.9	0.6	11.6	78	90
Hungary[a]	3.4	11.8	1.3	11.8	8.3	23.4	7.0	23.8	111	97
India	4.2	11.5	4.7	10.8	7.3	9.7	4.2	10.3	86	76
Indonesia	7.6	5.9	0.3	3.3	–1.3	6.5	2.6	3.2	95	104
Iran, Islamic Rep.	..	..	..	..	..	..	..	..	..	..
Iraq	..	..	..	..	..	..	..	..	..	..
Ireland[a]	9.3	12.1	4.8	8.7	13.5	13.2	7.8	10.1	106	99
Israel[a]	6.9	8.4	5.8	6.3	9.3	8.8	7.1	6.4	90	95
Italy[a]	4.3	2.9	5.3	3.4	10.5	7.4	8.7	7.5	94	101
Jamaica[a]	–1.0	1.5	..	..	15.4	13.7	..	..	..	..
Japan[a]	5.0	2.8	6.6	4.8	1.8	0.8	–1.3	4.3	105	83
Jordan[a]	10.2	7.4	1.5	4.7	14.9	9.3	4.2	7.7	93	89
Kazakhstan	..	..	..	..	..	..	..	..	..	..
Kenya[a]	..	..	0.2	5.9	..	..	11.2	18.2	85	..
Korea, Dem. Rep.	..	..	..	..	..	..	..	..	..	..
Korea, Rep.[a]	12.4	14.8	11.9	8.6	17.1	15.4	14.8	13.1	126	77
Kuwait	..	..	..	..	..	..	..	..	..	..
Kyrgyz Republic	..	..	..	..	..	..	..	..	..	..
Lao PDR	..	..	..	..	..	..	..	..	..	..
Latvia[a]	..	7.5	..	..	..	10.7	..	..	..	..
Lebanon	..	..	..	..	..	..	..	..	..	..
Lesotho	7.2	16.0	3.9	2.8	3.7	14.7	3.5	1.6	100	91
Liberia	..	..	..	..	..	..	..	..	..	..
Libya[a]	2.8	–3.3	–1.8	–1.3	–5.8	5.8	–1.1	3.9	89	186
Lithuania	..	..	..	..	..	..	..	..	..	..
Macedonia, FYR	..	..	..	..	..	..	..	..	..	..
Madagascar	–2.5	4.6	–6.2	4.3	–1.2	7.9	–4.3	5.8	81	82
Malawi	2.4	3.0	–0.1	–0.3	2.0	0.8	3.3	1.0	148	82
Malaysia	4.8	11.4	8.5	8.5	8.6	9.3	7.7	7.2	103	99
Mali	4.4	10.9	3.0	6.2	6.0	8.6	2.7	5.7	135	113
Mauritania	3.9	1.2	–3.1	3.9	8.0	–3.0	–2.1	0.3	97	95
Mauritius[a]	..	3.6	13.6	3.3	..	3.5	12.7	4.2	97	85
Mexico	15.3	12.4	0.9	11.1	5.9	12.9	6.4	11.6	102	98
Moldova	..	..	..	..	..	..	..	..	..	..
Mongolia	..	..	..	..	..	..	..	..	..	..
Morocco[a]	6.0	3.4	3.4	5.2	12.4	4.3	10.4	5.5	97	100
Mozambique	–9.5	21.5	–2.7	2.3	–9.6	16.3	0.1	3.1	175	94
Myanmar	–8.4	18.5	–18.1	8.6	–7.6	16.7	–4.7	14.8	252	102
Namibia	..	1.5	..	4.7	..	0.3	..	1.7	93	97
Nepal	..	..	..	..	..	..	..	..	..	..
Netherlands[a]	4.4	5.9	4.3	5.4	3.7	6.6	3.2	6.3	101	100
New Zealand[a]	3.5	4.2	4.4	6.1	10.7	4.9	9.8	6.4	105	112
Nicaragua	–4.8	8.6	–3.5	7.2	–5.8	7.7	–3.1	9.3	155	91
Niger	–5.2	1.4	–5.2	–0.9	–5.4	0.8	–3.5	1.4	165	131
Nigeria	–4.4	1.9	–20.8	5.2	–8.4	5.7	–15.0	5.8	89	122
Norway[a]	4.2	4.9	3.5	6.5	4.2	8.6	7.1	5.8	67	122
Oman	11.2	2.4	..	..	3.3	7.4	0.7	6.5	..	..
Pakistan[a]	9.1	3.4	2.9	4.4	18.3	11.6	11.8	14.9	109	75
Panama	–0.5	5.1	–6.7	4.2	–0.5	7.0	–3.6	5.3	69	94
Papua New Guinea	–0.6	–6.8	..	..	4.9	1.8	0.7	–0.7	..	..
Paraguay	12.8	1.9	10.4	1.6	11.6	3.6	4.2	2.7	103	112
Peru	2.7	10.0	–2.0	5.4	–1.5	8.9	1.3	5.9	114	110
Philippines[a]	..	2.3	..	–1.9	..	3.9	..	–1.5	88	89
Poland[a]	4.8	11.5	1.5	14.5	56.1	23.1	40.3	25.2	96	107
Portugal[a]	11.9	0.1	15.1	–0.2	22.7	0.1	21.8	0.0	104	102
Puerto Rico	..	..	..	..	..	..	..	..	..	..

6.2 Growth of merchandise trade

	Export volume		Import volume		Export value		Import value		Net barter terms of trade index	
	average annual % growth		average annual % growth		average annual % growth		average annual % growth		2000 = 100	
	1980–90	**1990–2005**	**1980–90**	**1990–2005**	**1980–90**	**1990–2005**	**1980–90**	**1990–2005**	**1990**	**2005**
Romania	..	..	..	..	..	..	..	..	..	..
Russian Federation	..	..	..	..	..	..	..	..	..	..
Rwanda	2.6	–2.6	1.8	–0.2	–0.9	–0.5	2.7	–0.9	40	*89*
Saudi Arabia	–8.3	1.1	..	..	–12.7	5.6	–6.1	2.3	..	..
Senegal	1.2	10.5	0.4	6.1	3.5	4.7	1.4	5.8	172	*96*
Serbia and Montenegro	..	..	..	..	..	..	..	..	..	..
Sierra Leone	..	..	..	..	..	..	..	..	..	*79*
Singapore[a]	12.1	10.3	8.6	7.2	8.6	8.7	6.7	6.7	116	87
Slovak Republic	..	..	..	..	..	..	..	..	..	..
Slovenia	..	..	..	..	..	..	..	..	..	..
Somalia	..	..	..	..	..	..	..	..	..	..
South Africa[a]	2.2	4.5	–0.2	5.7	15.3	13.8	12.6	15.5	112	109
Spain[a]	2.5	9.2	8.8	8.8	9.0	11.4	10.8	10.9	100	102
Sri Lanka[a]	4.2	5.5	1.6	6.9	13.5	15.1	10.7	15.2	75	*101*
Sudan	..	..	..	..	..	..	..	..	..	*121*
Swaziland	7.6	4.0	2.4	2.0	4.7	4.6	–0.5	3.1	100	*94*
Sweden[a]	4.4	7.6	5.0	5.4	10.7	9.3	9.1	8.3	108	90
Switzerland	..	..	..	..	..	..	..	..	..	..
Syrian Arab Republic	..	..	..	..	..	..	..	..	..	..
Tajikistan	..	..	..	..	..	..	..	..	..	..
Tanzania	..	8.6	..	2.0	–5.1	8.7	–0.5	2.7	107	*100*
Thailand[a]	13.8	9.2	11.2	2.6	16.5	15.7	15.1	10.6	118	93
Togo	–1.2	12.6	0.7	0.3	1.1	7.1	2.0	6.3	133	*30*
Trinidad and Tobago	..	..	..	..	..	..	..	..	..	..
Tunisia	3.0	6.6	1.6	5.6	3.5	6.5	2.7	5.5	109	*99*
Turkey[a]	..	11.4	..	10.6	..	10.6	..	10.8	109	101
Turkmenistan	..	..	..	..	..	..	..	..	..	..
Uganda	–13.5	14.4	–6.8	13.2	–4.0	9.8	4.5	12.7	146	*88*
Ukraine	..	..	..	..	..	..	..	..	..	..
United Arab Emirates	..	..	..	..	..	..	..	..	..	..
United Kingdom[a]	4.5	5.0	7.1	6.4	7.7	5.3	11.3	6.6	101	105
United States[a]	3.6	4.7	7.2	7.9	5.7	5.2	8.2	8.4	101	97
Uruguay	4.4	3.4	–0.5	3.4	4.5	2.9	–1.2	3.5	116	*108*
Uzbekistan	..	..	..	..	..	..	..	..	..	..
Venezuela, RB	3.4	2.4	–4.1	1.6	–4.4	5.7	–3.2	2.5	90	*108*
Vietnam	..	..	..	..	..	..	..	..	..	..
West Bank and Gaza	..	..	..	..	..	..	..	..	..	..
Yemen, Rep.	..	..	–7.2	6.3	–3.2	17.0	–5.0	2.9	..	..
Zambia	–0.5	6.5	2.0	6.6	0.9	–0.1	0.0	4.5	207	*119*
Zimbabwe	3.6	7.7	3.4	7.2	2.5	2.6	–0.5	1.9	98	*105*

a. Data are from the International Monetary Fund's International Financial Statistics database. b. Data prior to 1990 refer to the Federal Republic of Germany before unification.

Growth of merchandise trade 6.2

About the data

Data on international trade in goods are available from each country's balance of payments and customs records. While the balance of payments focuses on the financial transactions that accompany trade, customs data record the direction of trade and the physical quantities and value of goods entering or leaving the customs area. Customs data may differ from data recorded in the balance of payments because of differences in valuation and time of recording. The 1993 System of National Accounts and the fifth edition of the International Monetary Fund's (IMF) *Balance of Payments Manual* (1993) attempted to reconcile definitions and reporting standards for international trade statistics, but differences in sources, timing, and national practices limit comparability. Real growth rates derived from trade volume indexes and terms of trade based on unit price indexes may therefore differ from those derived from national accounts aggregates.

Trade in goods, or merchandise trade, includes all goods that add to or subtract from an economy's material resources. Trade data are collected on the basis of a country's customs area, which in most cases is the same as its geographic area. Goods provided as part of foreign aid are included, but goods destined for extraterritorial agencies (such as embassies) are not.

Collecting and tabulating trade statistics are difficult. Some developing countries lack the capacity to report timely data, especially countries that are landlocked and those whose territorial boundaries are porous. Their trade has to be estimated from the data reported by their partners. (For further discussion of the use of partner country reports, see *About the data* for table 6.3.) Countries that belong to common customs unions may need to collect data through direct inquiry of companies. Economic or political concerns may lead some national authorities to suppress or misrepresent data on certain trade flows, such as oil, military equipment, or the exports of a dominant producer. In other cases reported trade data may be distorted by deliberate under- or over-invoicing to effect capital transfers or avoid taxes. And in some regions smuggling and black market trading result in unreported trade flows.

By international agreement customs data are reported to the United Nations Statistics Division, which maintains the Commodity Trade (Comtrade) database. The United Nations Conference on Trade and Development (UNCTAD) compiles international trade statistics, including price and volume indexes, based on Comtrade data. The IMF also compiles data on trade prices and volumes. The growth rates and terms of trade for most low- and middle-income economies shown in the table were calculated from index numbers compiled by UNCTAD. The growth rates and terms of trade for high-income and selected developing countries were calculated from index numbers compiled in the IMF's *International Financial Statistics*. In some cases price and volume indexes from different sources may vary significantly as a result of differences in estimation procedures. All indexes are rescaled to a 2000 base year.

The terms of trade measures the relative prices of a country's exports and imports. There are several ways to calculate it. The most common is the net barter (or commodity) terms of trade index, or the ratio of the export price index to the import price index. When a country's net barter terms of trade index increases, its exports become more valuable or its imports cheaper.

Terms of trade are deteriorating for non-oil-exporting developing countries 6.2a

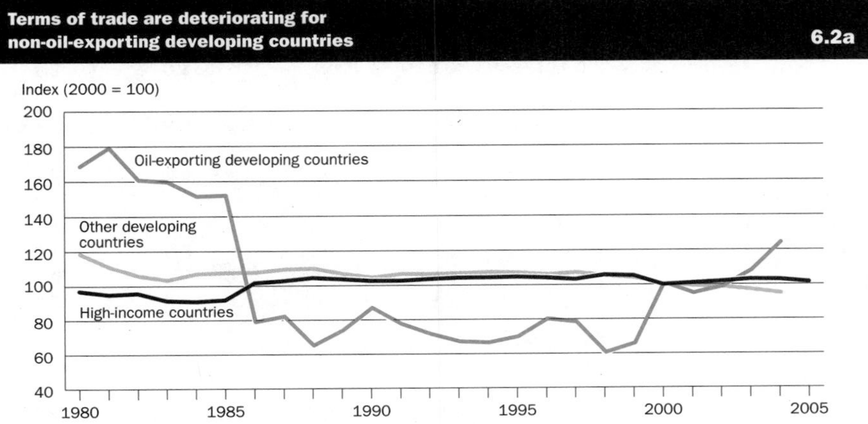

Source: United Nations Conference on Trade and Development and International Monetary Fund.

Definitions

• **Export** and **import volumes** are average annual growth rates calculated for low- and middle-income economies from UNCTAD's quantum index series and for high-income economies from export and import data deflated by the IMF's trade price deflators. • **Export** and **import values** are average annual growth rates calculated from UNCTAD's value indexes or from current values of merchandise exports and imports. • **Net barter terms of trade index** is calculated as the ratio of the export price index to the corresponding import price index measured relative to the base year 2000.

Data sources

The main source of trade indexes data for developing countries is UNCTAD's annual *Handbook of International Trade and Development Statistics*. The IMF's *International Financial Statistics* provides these data for high-income and selected developing economies.

6.3 Direction and growth of merchandise trade

Direction of trade

High-income importers

Source of exports	European Union	Japan	United States	Other high-income	All high-income
	% of world trade, 2005				
High-income economies	28.9	2.8	9.7	12.7	54.0
European Union	22.4	0.5	3.1	3.7	29.7
Japan	0.8	..	1.4	1.9	4.0
United States	1.8	0.6	..	3.6	6.0
Other high-income economies	3.8	1.7	5.3	3.5	14.3
Low- and middle-income economies	8.0	1.8	6.5	5.1	21.5
East Asia & Pacific	1.9	1.4	2.3	3.6	9.2
China	1.3	0.8	1.6	2.4	6.2
Europe & Central Asia	3.8	0.1	0.2	0.4	4.6
Russian Federation	1.1	0.0	0.1	0.2	1.4
Latin America & Caribbean	0.7	0.1	3.0	0.4	4.1
Brazil	0.2	0.0	0.2	0.1	0.6
Middle East & N. Africa	0.9	0.1	0.2	0.3	1.5
Algeria	0.2	0.0	0.1	0.0	0.4
South Asia	0.3	0.0	0.2	0.3	0.9
India	0.2	0.0	0.2	0.3	0.7
Sub-Saharan Africa	0.5	0.1	0.5	0.2	1.2
South Africa	0.2	0.1	0.0	0.1	0.3
World	36.9	4.6	16.2	17.8	75.5

Low- and middle-income importers

Source of exports	East Asia & Pacific	Europe & Central Asia	Latin America & Caribbean	Middle East & N. Africa	South Asia	Sub-Saharan Africa	All low- & middle-income	World
	% of world trade, 2005							
High-income economies	7.3	4.3	1.6	1.3	1.0	0.9	16.4	70.4
European Union	1.0	3.6	0.5	0.8	0.3	0.5	6.7	36.4
Japan	1.4	0.1	0.2	0.1	0.1	0.1	1.8	5.9
United States	0.7	0.2	0.7	0.1	0.1	0.1	1.8	7.8
Other high-income economies	4.3	0.4	0.3	0.3	0.5	0.2	6.0	20.3
Low- and middle-income economies	2.2	2.8	1.2	0.7	0.6	0.6	8.1	29.6
East Asia & Pacific	1.2	0.4	0.2	0.2	0.3	0.2	2.5	11.7
China	0.4	0.4	0.2	0.1	0.2	0.1	1.4	7.5
Europe & Central Asia	0.2	2.1	0.0	0.2	0.1	0.0	2.8	7.3
Russian Federation	0.2	0.8	0.0	0.1	0.0	0.0	1.0	2.4
Latin America & Caribbean	0.2	0.1	0.8	0.1	0.0	0.1	1.3	5.4
Brazil	0.1	0.1	0.2	0.0	0.0	0.0	0.5	1.1
Middle East & N. Africa	0.2	0.1	0.0	0.1	0.0	0.0	0.6	2.1
Algeria	0.0	0.0	0.0	0.0	0.0	0.0	0.1	0.4
South Asia	0.1	0.0	0.0	0.0	0.1	0.1	0.4	1.3
India	0.1	0.0	0.0	0.0	0.1	0.1	0.3	1.0
Sub-Saharan Africa	0.2	0.0	0.1	0.0	0.0	0.2	0.5	1.7
South Africa	0.0	0.0	0.0	0.0	0.0	0.1	0.1	0.5
World	9.6	7.1	2.8	1.9	1.5	1.5	24.5	100.0

Direction and growth of merchandise trade

Nominal growth of trade

High-income importers

annual % growth, 1995–2005

Source of exports	European Union	Japan	United States	Other high-income	All high-income
High-income economies	6.5	3.2	5.9	5.0	5.8
European Union	6.9	2.7	9.0	5.5	6.8
Japan	1.5	..	1.1	3.1	2.0
United States	3.9	–1.5	..	4.3	3.5
Other high-income economies	6.8	5.6	6.0	6.7	6.3
Low- and middle-income economies	12.6	7.7	12.7	11.9	12.0
East Asia & Pacific	14.1	8.2	13.9	11.7	12.0
China	21.3	11.4	20.8	15.5	17.0
Europe & Central Asia	15.1	3.8	10.4	12.2	14.3
Russian Federation	14.9	1.7	3.9	10.1	12.5
Latin America & Caribbean	5.8	2.4	11.3	10.1	9.7
Brazil	6.2	1.1	10.0	12.0	8.0
Middle East & N. Africa	10.6	9.6	22.2	12.6	12.0
Algeria	14.4	–5.1	20.2	22.0	16.2
South Asia	8.7	–0.8	10.6	13.0	9.9
India	9.9	1.1	11.9	15.1	11.6
Sub-Saharan Africa	10.5	20.1	16.7	17.7	13.9
South Africa	5.1	5.1	2.5	4.6	4.5
World	7.5	4.7	8.1	6.6	7.2

Low- and middle-income importers

annual % growth, 1995–2005

Source of exports	East Asia & Pacific	Europe & Central Asia	Latin America & Caribbean	Middle East & N. Africa	South Asia	Sub-Saharan Africa	All low- & middle-income	World
High-income economies	8.7	11.9	2.4	8.2	9.1	6.2	8.4	6.4
European Union	6.7	12.4	1.5	7.8	9.0	6.3	8.9	7.2
Japan	6.0	15.2	0.5	5.7	2.5	0.6	5.4	3.0
United States	7.0	5.8	3.4	3.4	7.5	6.7	5.2	3.8
Other high-income economies	10.6	10.6	3.1	12.1	10.9	8.3	10.1	7.3
Low- and middle-income economies	16.7	12.2	8.8	13.8	14.4	15.8	13.1	12.3
East Asia & Pacific	16.0	21.4	15.2	16.1	16.5	18.7	16.9	12.9
China	18.3	25.9	19.5	23.1	20.3	22.4	21.1	17.6
Europe & Central Asia	12.3	11.1	6.0	13.6	12.0	17.7	11.4	13.1
Russian Federation	11.7	11.1	8.0	17.0	9.9	34.4	11.4	12.0
Latin America & Caribbean	16.8	15.5	6.9	9.2	15.4	13.9	9.2	9.6
Brazil	13.4	15.7	9.1	10.0	10.6	16.4	11.0	9.2
Middle East & N. Africa	21.5	10.3	16.6	14.3	9.2	10.5	14.6	12.7
Algeria	57.3	11.4	26.7	16.2	8.1	9.7	19.3	16.6
South Asia	17.7	6.4	18.6	15.1	14.9	15.2	14.7	11.1
India	19.6	6.7	22.7	20.4	13.0	15.5	15.9	12.8
Sub-Saharan Africa	29.3	15.6	22.6	10.8	8.6	15.6	18.9	15.2
South Africa	3.6	4.8	4.7	8.8	10.7	3.5	4.4	4.5
World	10.1	12.0	4.7	9.8	10.7	9.0	9.7	7.8

6.3 Direction and growth of merchandise trade

About the data

The table provides estimates of the flow of trade in goods between groups of economies. The data are from the International Monetary Fund's (IMF) Direction of Trade database. All developed and 23 developing countries report trade on a timely basis, covering about 80 percent of trade for recent years. Trade by less timely reporters and by countries that do not report is estimated using reports of trading partner countries. Because the largest exporting and importing countries are reliable reporters, a large portion of the missing trade flows can be estimated from partner reports. Partner country data may introduce discrepancies due to smuggling, confidentiality, different exchange rates, overreporting of transit trade, inclusion or exclusion of freight rates, and different points of valuation and times of recording.

In addition, estimates of trade within the European Union (EU) have been significantly affected by changes in reporting methods following the creation of a customs union. The current system for collecting data on trade between EU members—Intrastat, introduced in 1993—has less exhaustive coverage than the previous customs-based system and has resulted in some problems of asymmetry (estimated imports are about 5 percent less than exports). Despite these issues, only a small portion of world trade is estimated to be omitted from the IMF's *Direction of Trade Statistics Yearbook* and Direction of Trade database.

Most countries report their trade data in national currencies, which are converted into U.S. dollars using the IMF's published period average exchange rates (series rf or rh, monthly averages of the market or official rates) for the reporting country or, if those are not available, monthly average rates in New York. Because imports are reported at cost, insurance, and freight (c.i.f.) valuations, and exports at free on board (f.o.b.) valuations, the IMF adjusts country reports of import values by dividing them by 1.10 to estimate equivalent export values. This approximation is more or less accurate, depending on the set of partners and the items traded. Other factors affecting the accuracy of trade data include lags in reporting, recording differences across countries, and whether the country reports trade according to the general or special system of trade. (For further discussion of the measurement of exports and imports, see *About the data* for tables 4.4 and 4.5.)

The regional trade flows shown in the table were calculated from current price values. The growth rates are presented in nominal terms; that is, they include the effects of changes in both volumes and prices.

Three regions account from more than 75 percent of exports to other developing regions, 2005 **6.3a**

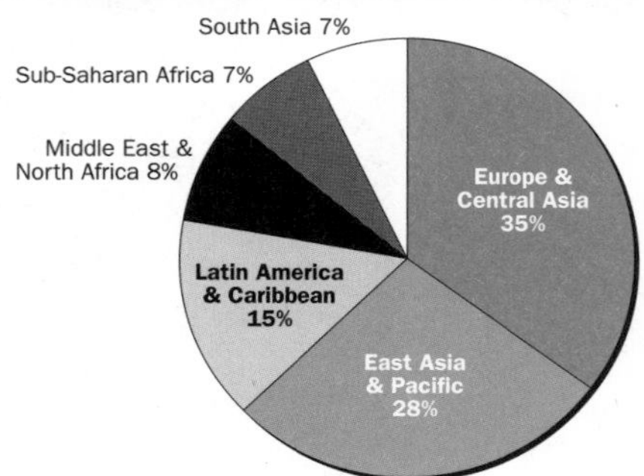

Source: IMF Direction of Trade database.

Definitions

• **Merchandise trade** includes all trade in goods; trade in services is excluded. • **High-income economies** are those classified as such by the World Bank (see inside front cover). • **European Union** is defined as all high-income EU members: Austria, Belgium, Cyprus, Denmark, Finland, France, Germany, Greece, Ireland, Italy, Luxembourg, Malta, the Netherlands, Portugal, Slovenia, Spain, Sweden, and the United Kingdom. • **Other high-income economies** include all high-income economies (OECD and non-OECD) except the European Union, Japan, and the United States. • **Low- and middle-income regional groupings** are based on World Bank classifications and may differ from those used by other organizations.

Data sources

Data on the direction and growth of merchandise trade were calculated using the IMF's Direction of Trade database.

High-income economy trade with low- and middle-income economies 6.4

Exports to low-income economies

	High-income countries		European Union		Japan		United States	
	1995	2005	1995	2005	1995	2005	1995	2005
Total ($ billions)	**67.6**	**134.9**	**33.1**	**58.3**	**9.3**	**12.5**	**7.9**	**16.8**
% of total exports								
Food	8.6	6.0	8.5	6.4	0.5	0.4	20.3	12.1
Cereals	3.1	1.9	2.6	1.5	0.2	0.1	14.4	7.4
Agricultural raw materials	2.7	1.8	1.3	1.4	1.7	1.4	6.7	4.3
Ores and nonferrous metals	2.7	3.3	1.5	3.5	0.7	1.1	3.1	2.5
Fuels	4.3	7.6	2.2	4.3	0.9	0.9	1.5	2.2
Crude petroleum	0.0	0.6	0.0	0.0	0.0	0.0	0.0	0.0
Petroleum products	3.5	5.1	2.2	4.2	0.8	0.8	1.4	1.3
Manufactured goods	79.5	77.4	84.4	81.4	95.1	92.9	64.9	71.7
Chemical products	12.4	11.0	12.2	11.7	6.6	7.2	14.4	10.2
Iron and steel	3.6	3.4	4.3	3.5	6.6	9.3	1.6	1.7
Machinery and transport equipment	45.0	41.0	44.2	40.2	69.2	62.2	38.3	44.3
Furniture	0.2	0.2	0.3	0.3	0.1	0.2	0.1	0.2
Textiles	4.4	3.5	1.7	1.3	3.0	3.6	1.5	2.0
Footwear	0.2	0.1	0.2	0.1	0.0	0.0	0.1	0.1
Other	13.6	18.1	21.4	24.2	9.5	10.4	9.0	13.1
Miscellaneous goods	2.3	3.9	2.0	2.9	1.0	3.3	3.5	7.4

Imports from low-income economies

	High-income countries		European Union		Japan		United States	
	1995	2005	1995	2005	1995	2005	1995	2005
Total ($ billions)	**68.0**	**178.4**	**34.2**	**66.3**	**8.4**	**13.0**	**16.0**	**66.7**
% of total imports								
Food	20.3	10.8	24.8	15.2	25.4	16.5	8.3	5.3
Cereals	0.6	0.6	0.3	0.4	0.2	0.3	0.2	0.1
Agricultural raw materials	6.1	2.0	7.6	3.5	7.1	1.8	1.7	0.8
Ores and nonferrous metals	5.9	3.7	4.9	4.9	16.7	8.7	2.0	0.9
Fuels	19.4	29.8	11.4	16.2	15.2	35.6	33.0	43.6
Crude petroleum	17.9	24.6	10.8	12.0	12.0	28.6	31.6	38.7
Petroleum products	1.3	4.0	0.5	2.0	2.3	5.1	1.5	4.2
Manufactured goods	47.9	53.2	51.2	59.6	35.1	36.9	54.3	48.7
Chemical products	2.7	3.6	2.7	4.1	1.0	2.9	2.3	2.5
Iron and steel	1.3	1.7	0.7	1.9	2.4	1.2	1.3	1.4
Machinery and transport equipment	2.8	5.4	2.8	6.1	0.6	10.3	2.2	3.6
Furniture	0.2	1.5	0.2	1.6	0.5	1.7	0.2	1.8
Textiles	26.0	23.1	26.5	27.4	16.9	9.6	29.8	26.1
Footwear	1.3	3.1	2.1	5.8	0.3	2.3	0.6	1.4
Other	13.6	14.8	16.1	12.6	13.4	8.9	18.0	11.9
Miscellaneous goods	0.4	0.6	0.2	0.7	0.5	0.5	0.6	0.7

Simple applied tariff rates on imports from low-income economies (%)

	High-income countries		European Union		Japan		United States	
	1995	2005	1995	2005	1995	2005	1995	2005
Food	9.7	7.1	11.6	6.8	12.9	12.8	3.8	3.4
Cereals	16.5	11.7	65.6	20.5	14.4	42.7	5.2	2.4
Agricultural raw materials	2.0	2.4	0.3	0.2	2.8	1.2	0.6	0.4
Ores and nonferrous metals	1.8	1.6	0.5	0.5	2.7	0.6	0.4	0.4
Fuels	4.7	1.7	0.1	0.1	1.3	1.0	2.5	0.7
Crude petroleum	7.6	1.1	0.0	0.0	0.0	0.5	0.0	0.1
Petroleum products	5.3	1.9	0.3	0.2	1.7	1.7	3.1	1.1
Manufactured goods	5.4	3.4	1.6	1.1	4.3	2.2	6.7	4.8
Chemical products	3.0	2.4	1.2	1.8	1.1	0.7	1.8	0.9
Iron and steel	3.3	2.1	0.5	0.3	0.3	0.2	3.6	0.2
Machinery and transport equipment	2.4	1.7	0.4	0.4	0.0	0.0	0.9	0.4
Furniture	4.1	2.6	0.2	0.0	0.2	0.0	5.6	1.4
Textiles	9.7	6.0	4.2	2.5	6.7	4.8	13.2	10.3
Footwear	10.3	6.7	4.5	2.5	11.0	9.1	19.0	10.7
Other	6.6	4.0	2.2	1.3	5.3	3.0	8.3	6.1
Miscellaneous goods	10.4	1.1	0.6	0.4	0.0	0.0	1.4	0.2
Average	4.9	3.5	2.8	1.7	2.8	2.4	6.0	4.4

6.4 High-income economy trade with low- and middle-income economies

Exports to middle-income economies

	High-income countries		European Union		Japan		United States	
	1995	2005	1995	2005	1995	2005	1995	2005
Total ($ billions)	**681.0**	**1,501.9**	**263.4**	**609.5**	**103.4**	**177.6**	**147.0**	**285.3**
% of total exports								
Food	7.5	4.6	9.3	5.0	0.3	0.4	10.9	8.1
Cereals	2.0	0.9	1.5	0.7	0.0	0.0	4.8	2.2
Agricultural raw materials	2.3	1.8	1.4	1.4	1.0	0.9	3.9	3.4
Ores and nonferrous metals	2.1	2.9	1.6	2.0	1.3	2.6	1.9	3.1
Fuels	2.3	3.4	1.7	2.1	0.5	1.0	2.3	4.0
Crude petroleum	0.2	0.2	0.3	0.0	0.0	0.0	0.0	0.0
Petroleum products	1.7	2.7	1.2	1.9	0.5	0.9	1.5	3.4
Manufactured goods	83.3	84.3	82.7	86.0	95.7	91.6	77.4	77.6
Chemical products	11.0	12.1	11.8	13.3	6.6	9.0	11.4	11.7
Iron and steel	3.0	3.2	2.8	3.6	6.5	6.8	1.2	1.1
Machinery and transport equipment	47.4	50.5	45.7	48.3	68.1	61.3	46.1	47.9
Furniture	0.5	0.5	0.9	0.8	0.1	0.2	0.6	0.4
Textiles	6.4	4.2	5.7	4.5	2.7	2.1	4.5	3.5
Footwear	0.3	0.2	0.4	0.3	0.0	0.0	0.1	0.0
Other	14.7	13.7	15.4	15.2	11.6	12.2	13.5	13.0
Miscellaneous goods	2.5	3.0	3.2	3.4	1.2	3.6	3.7	3.8

Imports from middle-income economies

	High-income countries		European Union		Japan		United States	
	1995	2005	1995	2005	1995	2005	1995	2005
Total ($ billions)	**746.9**	**2,194.9**	**257.5**	**801.5**	**99.4**	**210.6**	**221.1**	**722.1**
% of total imports								
Food	11.5	6.4	14.5	7.8	16.7	9.2	8.2	4.7
Cereals	0.3	0.3	0.2	0.3	0.2	0.3	0.2	0.1
Agricultural raw materials	3.7	1.5	4.9	2.0	5.9	2.1	1.9	1.0
Ores and nonferrous metals	6.0	4.1	7.7	4.5	11.0	8.4	3.5	2.3
Fuels	13.2	17.9	16.8	21.8	17.4	16.6	11.9	18.7
Crude petroleum	8.7	11.9	10.8	14.7	9.5	7.8	9.1	13.9
Petroleum products	2.2	3.4	2.9	4.1	1.2	1.6	2.5	3.6
Manufactured goods	63.8	68.6	53.4	62.1	47.9	62.5	72.3	71.4
Chemical products	3.8	3.3	5.2	3.3	2.8	3.6	2.7	2.8
Iron and steel	3.0	2.5	3.4	2.9	2.5	1.6	2.3	1.9
Machinery and transport equipment	22.3	32.9	14.1	28.0	11.8	27.6	31.5	35.1
Furniture	1.4	2.3	1.6	2.1	1.6	1.6	1.6	3.3
Textiles	13.9	9.5	13.9	9.5	14.6	10.9	12.4	8.8
Footwear	2.9	1.7	1.6	1.4	1.5	1.2	4.1	2.2
Other	16.5	16.4	13.6	14.8	13.0	15.9	17.7	17.3
Miscellaneous goods	1.8	1.5	2.7	1.8	1.2	1.2	2.1	2.0

Simple applied tariff rates on imports from low-income economies (%)

	High-income countries		European Union		Japan		United States	
	1995	2005	1995	2005	1995	2005	1995	2005
Food	15.4	9.5	24.7	11.7	14.4	13.2	3.1	3.4
Cereals	21.6	15.3	63.3	28.8	22.8	34.2	2.7	2.0
Agricultural raw materials	2.0	1.9	1.0	0.3	1.5	1.6	0.6	0.4
Ores and nonferrous metals	1.7	1.1	1.8	0.7	0.5	0.1	0.5	0.5
Fuels	4.1	1.5	0.7	0.1	0.6	0.8	1.1	0.6
Crude petroleum	13.8	1.2	0.0	0.0	0.0	0.5	0.0	0.2
Petroleum products	4.5	1.9	1.1	0.2	1.1	1.6	1.7	1.0
Manufactured goods	5.6	3.2	4.1	1.1	1.8	2.2	3.9	3.0
Chemical products	3.6	2.2	3.6	1.8	1.4	0.8	1.4	1.0
Iron and steel	3.1	1.3	1.7	0.2	0.6	0.2	3.5	0.2
Machinery and transport equipment	3.2	1.8	2.0	0.4	0.0	0.0	0.6	0.3
Furniture	5.0	3.1	1.8	0.0	0.0	0.0	0.5	0.3
Textiles	11.0	6.6	8.9	2.9	4.7	6.7	11.0	8.8
Footwear	12.1	7.7	9.6	3.0	15.0	17.7	14.7	9.2
Other	6.8	3.9	5.0	1.4	2.5	3.2	5.3	4.2
Miscellaneous goods	7.6	1.1	2.0	0.4	0.0	0.0	1.0	0.4
Average	5.5	3.5	5.8	2.1	2.5	2.6	3.6	2.9

High-income economy trade with low- and middle-income economies

About the data

Developing countries are becoming increasingly important in the global trading system. Since the early 1990s trade between high-income countries and low- and middle-income economies has grown faster than trade among high-income economies. The increased trade benefits consumers and producers. But as the World Trade Organization's (WTO) Ministerial Conferences in Doha, Qatar, in October 2001, Cancun, Mexico, in September 2003, and Hong Kong, China, in December 2005 showed, achieving a more pro-development outcome from trade remains a challenge. Meeting it will require strengthening international consultation. Negotiations after the Doha meetings were launched on services, agriculture, manufactures, WTO rules, the environment, dispute settlement, intellectual property rights protection, and disciplines on regional integration. At the most recent negotiations in Hong Kong, China, trade ministers agreed to eliminate subsidies of agricultural exports by 2013; to abolish cotton export subsidies in 2006 and grant unlimited export access to selected cotton-growing countries in Sub-Saharan Africa; to cut more domestic farm supports in the European Union, Japan, and the United States; and to offer more aid to developing countries to help them compete in global trade.

Trade flows between high-income countries and low- and middle-income economies reflect the changing mix of exports to and imports from developing economies. While food and primary commodities have continued to fall as a share of high-income countries' imports, the share of manufactures in goods imports from both low- and middle-income countries has grown. Moreover, trade between developing countries has grown substantially over the past decade. This growth has resulted from many factors, including developing countries' increasing share of world output and the liberalization of their trade.

Yet trade barriers remain high. The table includes information about tariff rates by selected product groups. Applied tariff rates are the tariffs in effect for partners in preferential trade agreements such as the North American Free Trade Agreement. When these are unavailable, most favored nation rates are used. The difference between most favored nation and applied rates can be substantial. Simple averages of applied rates are shown because they are generally a better indicator of tariff protection.

The data are from the United Nations Conference on Trade and Development (UNCTAD). Partner country reports by high-income countries were used for both exports and imports. Exports are recorded free on board (f.o.b.); imports include insurance and freight charges (c.i.f.). Because of differences in sources of data, timing, and treatment of missing data, the numbers in the table may not be fully comparable with those used to calculate the direction of trade statistics in table 6.3 or the aggregate flows in tables 4.4, 4.5, and 6.2. Data are classified using the Harmonized System of trade at the six- or eight-digit level. Tariff line data were matched to Standard International Trade Classification (SITC) revision 1 codes to define commodity groups. For further discussion of merchandise trade statistics, see *About the data* for tables 4.4, 4.5, 6.2, and 6.3, and for information about tariff barriers, see table 6.7.

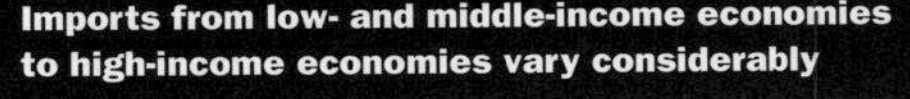

Imports from low- and middle-income economies to high-income economies vary considerably **6.4a**

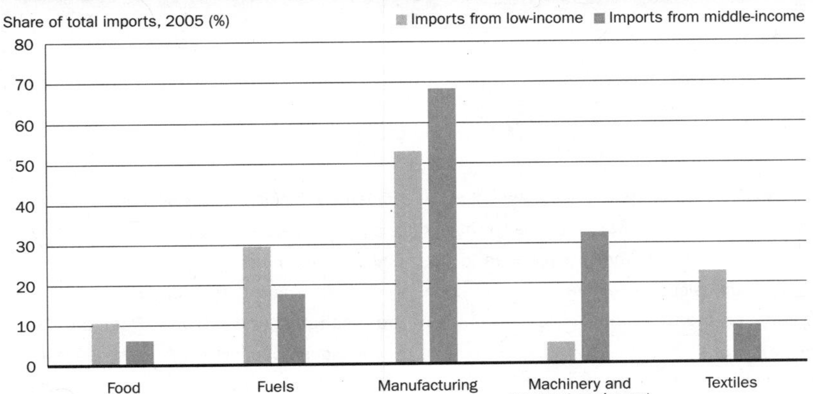

The major manufactured imports of high-income economies from developing countries are manufactured textiles from low-income economies and machinery and transport equipment from middle-income economies.

Source: United Nations Statistics Division's Comtrade database.

Definitions

The product groups in the table are defined in accordance with the SITC revision 1: **food** (0, 1, 22, and 4) and **cereals** (04); **agricultural raw materials** (2 excluding 22, 27, and 28); **ores and nonferrous metals** (27, 28, and 68); **fuels** (3), **crude petroleum** (331), and **petroleum products** (332); **manufactured goods** (5–8 excluding 68), **chemical products** (5), **iron and steel** (67), **machinery and transport equipment** (7), **furniture** (82), **textiles** (65 and 84), **footwear** (85), and **other** manufactured goods (6 and 8 excluding 65, 67, 68, 82, 84, and 85); and **miscellaneous goods** (9). • **Exports** are all merchandise exports by high-income countries to low-income and middle-income economies as recorded in the United Nations Statistics Division's Comtrade database. • **Imports** are all merchandise imports by high-income countries from low-income and middle-income economies as recorded in the United Nations Statistics Division's Comtrade database. • **High-, middle-, and low-income economies** are those classified as such by the World Bank (see inside front cover). • **European Union** is defined as all high-income EU members: Austria, Belgium, Cyprus, Denmark, Finland, France, Germany, Greece, Ireland, Italy, Luxembourg, Malta, the Netherlands, Portugal, Slovenia, Spain, Sweden, and the United Kingdom.

Data sources

Trade values are from United Nations Statistics Division's Comtrade database. Tariff data are from UNCTAD's Trade Analysis and Information System database and are calculated by World Bank staff using the World Integrated Trade Solution system.

6.5 Primary commodity prices

	1970	1980	1990	1995	2000	2001	2002	2003	2004	2005	2006
World Bank commodity price index (1990 = 100)											
Nonenergy commodities	156	159	100	104	89	84	89	91	100	114	138
Agriculture	163	175	100	112	90	84	93	95	98	106	115
Beverages	203	230	100	129	91	76	91	87	88	109	111
Food	166	177	100	100	87	91	97	96	103	103	109
Raw materials	130	133	100	116	93	81	89	98	99	107	124
Fertilizers	108	164	100	88	109	105	108	106	118	126	130
Metals and minerals	144	120	100	87	85	80	78	82	105	133	195
Petroleum	19	204	100	64	127	113	117	126	154	218	254
Steel products[a]	111	100	100	91	79	71	73	79	114	129	122
MUV G-5 index	28	79	100	117	97	94	93	100	107	107	110
Commodity prices (1990 prices)											
Agricultural raw materials											
Cotton (cents/kg)	225	260	182	182	134	112	109	140	128	114	115
Logs, Cameroon ($/cu. m)[a]	153	319	344	290	283	282	..	..	..	..	..
Logs, Malaysian ($/cu. m)	154	248	177	218	195	169	175	187	184	190	217
Rubber (cents/kg)	145	181	86	135	69	61	82	108	122	140	191
Sawnwood, Malaysian ($/cu. m)	625	503	533	632	612	510	565	550	543	616	678
Tobacco ($/mt)	3,836	2,887	3,392	2,258	3,063	3,185	2,947	2,643	2,560	2,606	2,672
Beverages (cents/kg)											
Cocoa	240	330	127	122	93	113	191	175	145	144	144
Coffee, robustas	330	411	118	237	94	64	71	81	74	104	135
Coffee, Arabica	409	440	197	285	198	146	146	141	166	237	228
Tea, avg., 3 auctions	298	211	206	127	193	169	162	151	157	154	170
Energy											
Coal, Australian ($/mt)	..	51	40	34	27	34	27	26	49	44	44
Coal, U.S. ($/mt)	..	55	42	33	34	48	43	..	..	..	..
Natural gas, Europe ($/mmbtu)	..	4	3	2	4	4	3	4	4	6	8
Natural gas, U.S. ($/mmbtu)	1	2	2	1	4	4	4	5	6	8	6
Petroleum ($/bbl)	4	47	23	15	29	26	27	29	35	50	58

About the data

Primary commodities—raw or partially processed materials that will be transformed into finished goods—are often the most significant exports of developing countries, and revenues obtained from them have an important effect on living standards. Price data for primary commodities are collected from a variety of sources, including trade journals, international study groups, government market surveys, newspaper and wire service reports, and commodity exchange spot and near-term forward prices.

The table is based on frequently updated price reports. When possible, the prices received by exporters are used; if export prices are unavailable, the prices paid by importers are used. Annual price series are generally simple averages based on higher frequency data. The constant price series in the table is deflated using the manufactures unit value (MUV) index for the Group of Five (G-5) countries (see below).

The commodity price indexes are calculated as Laspeyres index numbers, in which the fixed weights are the 1987–89 export values for low- and middle-income economies, rebased to 1990. Each index represents a fixed basket of primary commodity exports. The nonenergy commodity price index contains 37 price series for 31 nonenergy commodities. Separate indexes are compiled for petroleum and steel products, which are not included in the nonenergy commodity price index.

The MUV index is a composite index of prices for manufactured exports from the five major (G-5) industrial countries (France, Germany, Japan, the United Kingdom, and the United States) to low- and middle-income economies, valued in U.S. dollars. The index covers products in groups 5–8 of the Standard International Trade Classification revision 1. To construct the MUV G-5 index, unit value indexes for each country are combined using weights determined by each country's export share.

Primary commodity prices

	1970	1980	1990	1995	2000	2001	2002	2003	2004	2005	2006
Commodity prices (continued)											
(1990 prices)											
Fertilizers ($/mt)											
Phosphate rock	39	59	41	30	45	44	43	38	38	39	40
TSP	152	229	132	128	142	135	143	149	174	188	186
Food											
Fats and oils ($/mt)											
Coconut oil	1,417	855	337	572	463	337	452	467	617	576	549
Groundnut oil	1,350	1,090	964	846	734	721	738	1,242	1,085	991	878
Palm oil	927	740	290	536	319	303	419	443	440	394	433
Soybeans	417	376	247	221	218	208	228	264	286	257	243
Soybean meal	367	332	200	168	195	192	188	211	225	200	189
Soybean oil	1,021	758	447	534	348	375	488	553	576	509	542
Grains ($/mt)											
Sorghum	185	164	104	102	91	101	109	106	103	90	111
Maize	208	159	109	105	91	95	107	105	104	92	110
Rice	450	521	271	274	208	183	206	197	222	267	276
Wheat	196	219	136	151	117	134	159	146	147	142	174
Other food											
Bananas ($/mt)	590	481	541	380	436	618	568	374	490	563	613
Beef (cents/kg)	465	350	256	163	199	226	226	198	235	245	231
Oranges ($/mt)	599	496	531	454	374	631	606	680	803	817	751
Sugar, EU domestic (cents/kg)	40	62	58	59	57	56	59	60	63	62	58
Sugar, U.S. domestic (cents/kg)	59	84	51	43	44	50	50	47	42	44	44
Sugar, world (cents/kg)	29	80	28	25	19	20	16	16	15	20	30
Metals and minerals											
Aluminum ($/mt)	1,982	1,847	1,639	1,542	1,594	1,531	1,449	1,430	1,603	1,774	2,327
Copper ($/mt)	5,038	2,768	2,662	2,508	1,866	1,673	1,674	1,777	2,678	3,437	6,086
Iron ore (cents/dmtu)	35	36	33	24	30	32	31	32	35	61	70
Lead (cents/kg)	108	115	81	54	47	50	49	51	83	91	117
Nickel ($/mt)	10,148	8,270	8,864	7,028	8,888	6,303	7,271	9,617	12,915	13,776	21,960
Tin (cents/kg)	1,310	2,128	609	531	559	475	436	489	795	690	795
Zinc (cents/kg)	105	97	151	88	116	94	84	83	98	129	297

a. Series not included in the nonenergy index.

Definitions

• **Nonenergy commodity price index** covers the 31 nonenergy primary commodities that make up the agriculture, fertilizer, and metals and minerals indexes. • **Agriculture** includes beverages, food, and agricultural raw materials. • **Beverages** include cocoa, coffee, and tea. • **Food** includes rice, wheat, maize, sorghum, soybeans, soybean oil, soybean meal, palm oil, coconut oil, groundnut oil, bananas, beef, oranges, and sugar. • **Agricultural raw materials** include cotton, timber (logs and sawnwood), natural rubber, and tobacco. • **Fertilizers** include phosphate rock and triple superphosphate (TSP). • **Metals and minerals** include aluminum, copper, iron ore, lead, nickel, tin, and zinc. • **Petroleum price index** refers to the average spot price of Brent, Dubai, and West Texas Intermediate crude oils, equally weighted. • **Steel products price index** is the composite price index for eight steel products based on quotations free on board (f.o.b.) Japan excluding shipments to China and the United States, weighted by product shares of apparent combined consumption (volume of deliveries) for Germany, Japan, and the United States. • **MUV G-5 index** is the manufactures unit value index for G-5 country exports to low- and middle-income economies. • **Commodity prices**—for definitions and sources, see "Commodity Price Data" (also known as the "Pink Sheet") at the Global Prospects Web site (www.worldbank.org/prospects, click on Products).

Data sources

Data on commodity prices and the MUV G-5 index are compiled by the World Bank's Development Prospects Group. Monthly updates of commodity prices are available on the Web at www.worldbank.org/prospects.

6.6 Regional trade blocs

Merchandise exports within bloc

	Year of creation	$ millions 1990	1995	1999	2000	2001	2002	2003	2004	2005
High-income and low- and middle-income economies										
APEC[a]	1989	901,560	1,688,708	1,896,213	2,261,791	2,070,973	2,168,700	2,420,739	2,905,271	3,286,979
CEFTA	1992	4,235	12,118	13,226	15,123	17,054	19,180	25,309	37,541	48,726
CIS	1991	..	29,943	20,842	27,043	22,262	28,029	36,540	40,446	55,521
EMFTA	1995	1,089,631	1,488,243	1,700,902	1,744,696	1,737,269	1,857,562	2,253,496	2,706,304	2,883,467
European Union	1957	1,011,019	1,385,805	1,579,070	1,608,174	1,612,634	1,721,082	2,087,311	2,482,418	2,642,578
FTAA	1994	300,700	525,346	734,848	855,659	810,360	787,232	826,281	967,653	1,110,730
NAFTA	1994	226,273	394,472	581,161	676,141	639,419	626,020	651,060	737,591	824,550
Latin America and the Caribbean										
ACS	1994	5,398	11,049	11,199	16,267	15,699	15,769	15,138	20,058	25,071
Andean Group	1969	1,312	4,812	3,929	5,300	5,609	5,065	5,036	7,261	9,453
CACM	1961	667	1,594	2,175	2,586	2,739	2,763	3,156	3,574	4,064
CARICOM	1973	448	867	1,136	1,050	1,420	1,184	1,410	1,734	2,078
Central American Group of Four	1993	399	1,026	1,369	1,765	1,886	1,906	2,036	2,315	2,631
Group of Three	1995	1,046	3,460	2,912	3,721	4,178	3,839	3,167	5,669	7,437
LAIA (ALADI)	1980	12,331	35,299	34,785	42,901	40,780	36,054	39,863	55,826	70,430
Mercosur	1991	4,127	14,199	15,313	17,829	15,156	10,228	12,732	17,354	21,118
OECS	1981	29	39	37	38	37	40	48	60	68
Middle East and Asia										
Arab Common Market	1964	911	1,368	951	1,312	1,728	1,998	1,797	6,303	7,138
ASEAN	1967	27,365	79,544	77,889	98,060	86,331	91,684	101,054	122,914	142,955
Bangkok Agreement	1975	4,476	12,066	14,463	16,844	16,733	17,957	21,808	24,925	29,506
EAEC	1990	281,067	634,606	612,415	772,423	698,552	779,384	940,950	1,177,286	1,335,003
ECO	1985	1,243	4,746	3,903	4,518	4,498	5,014	7,468	9,978	13,993
GAFTA	1997	13,313	13,129	13,752	16,238	17,528	19,195	21,511	35,554	44,777
GCC	1981	6,906	6,832	7,306	7,958	8,103	8,899	9,580	12,532	16,507
SAARC	1985	863	2,024	2,180	2,593	2,827	3,402	4,873	5,706	7,062
UMA	1989	958	1,109	919	1,094	1,137	1,202	1,338	1,375	1,926
Sub-Saharan Africa										
CEMAC	1994	139	120	127	97	118	136	148	176	201
CEPGL	1976	7	8	9	10	11	13	15	19	22
COMESA	1994	963	1,386	1,348	1,653	1,819	2,031	2,436	2,849	3,330
Cross Border Initiative	1992	613	1,002	964	1,166	1,070	1,373	1,536	1,705	1,913
EAC	1996	230	530	438	595	664	685	706	750	857
ECCAS	1983	163	163	179	191	203	199	198	238	272
ECOWAS	1975	1,557	1,936	2,364	2,835	2,371	3,229	3,140	4,499	5,673
Indian Ocean Commission	1984	73	127	91	106	134	105	179	155	159
MRU	1973	0	1	4	5	4	5	5	6	6
SADC	1992	1,630	3,373	4,224	4,282	3,771	4,316	5,377	6,384	6,384
UDEAC	1964	139	120	126	96	117	134	146	174	198
UEMOA	1994	621	560	805	741	775	857	1,076	1,233	1,390

Note: Regional bloc memberships are as follows: **Asia Pacific Economic Cooperation (APEC),** Australia, Brunei Darussalam, Canada, Chile, China, Hong Kong (China), Indonesia, Japan, the Republic of Korea, Malaysia, Mexico, New Zealand, Papua New Guinea, Peru, the Philippines, the Russian Federation, Singapore, Taiwan (China), Thailand, the United States, and Vietnam; **Central European Free Trade Area (CEFTA)**, Bulgaria, the Czech Republic, Hungary, Poland, Romania, the Slovak Republic, and Slovenia; **Commonwealth of Independent States (CIS)**, Armenia, Azerbaijan, Belarus, Georgia, Kazakhstan, the Kyrgyz Republic, Moldova, the Russian Federation, Tajikistan, Ukraine, and Uzbekistan; **Euro-Mediterranean Free Trade Area (EMFTA)**, European Union, Algeria, Cyprus, Egypt, Israel, Jordan, Lebanon, Malta, Morocco, Syrian Arab Republic, Tunisia, Turkey, and West Bank and Gaza; **European Union (EU; formerly European Economic Community and European Community)**, Austria, Belgium, Denmark, Finland, France, Germany, Greece, Ireland, Italy, Luxembourg, the Netherlands, Portugal, Spain, Sweden, and the United Kingdom; **Free Trade Areas of the Americas (FTAA)**, Antigua and Barbuda, Argentina, Bahamas, Barbados, Belize, Bolivia, Brazil, Canada, Chile, Colombia, Costa Rica, Dominica, Dominican Republic, Ecuador, El Salvador, Grenada, Guatemala, Guyana, Haiti, Honduras, Jamaica, Mexico, Nicaragua, Panama, Paraguay, Peru, Republica Bolivariana de Venezuela, St. Kitts and Nevis, St. Lucia, St. Vincent and the Grenadines, Suriname, Trinidad and Tobago, the United States, and Uruguay; **North American Free Trade Agreement (NAFTA)**, Canada, Mexico, and the United States; **Economic and Monetary Community of Central Africa (CEMAC)**, Cameroon, the Central African Republic, Chad, the Republic of Congo, Equatorial Guinea, Gabon, and São Tomé and Principe; **Economic Community of the Countries of the Great Lakes (CEPGL)**, Burundi, the Democratic Republic of Congo, and Rwanda; **Common Market for Eastern and Southern Africa (COMESA)**, Angola, Burundi, Comoros, the Democratic Republic of Congo, Djibouti, the Arab Republic of Egypt, Eritrea, Ethiopia, Kenya, Madagascar, Malawi, Mauritius, Namibia, Rwanda, Seychelles, Sudan, Swaziland, Uganda, Tanzania, Zambia, and Zimbabwe; **Cross Border Initiative**, Burundi, Comoros, Kenya, Madagascar, Malawi, Mauritius, Namibia, Rwanda, Seychelles, Swaziland, Tanzania, Uganda, Zambia, and Zimbabwe; **East African Community (EAC)**, Kenya, Tanzania, and Uganda; **Economic Community of Central African States (ECCAS)**, Angola, Burundi, Cameroon, the Central African Republic, Chad, the Democratic Republic of Congo, the Republic of Congo, Equatorial Guinea, Gabon, Rwanda, and São Tomé and Principe; **Economic Community of West African States (ECOWAS)**, Benin, Burkina Faso, Cape Verde, Côte d'Ivoire, the Gambia, Ghana, Guinea, Guinea-Bissau, Liberia, Mali, Mauritania, Niger, Nigeria, Senegal, Sierra Leone, and Togo; **Indian Ocean Commission**, Comoros, Madagascar, Mauritius, Réunion, and Seychelles; **Mano River Union (MRU)**, Guinea, Liberia, and Sierra Leone; **Southern African Development Community**

a. No preferential trade agreement.

Merchandise exports within bloc

	Year of creation	% of total bloc exports								
		1990	1995	1999	2000	2001	2002	2003	2004	2005
High-income and low- and middle-income economies										
APEC[a]	1989	68.3	71.7	71.8	73.1	72.6	73.3	72.6	72.0	70.7
CEFTA	1992	16.3	14.8	13.8	9.9	8.0	7.3	14.6	14.2	14.6
CIS	1991	..	27.6	20.7	19.2	18.2	18.8	19.6	16.6	17.1
EMFTA	1995	69.6	68.7	70.4	69.3	68.3	68.5	69.4	69.2	68.3
FTAA	1994	46.6	52.5	59.7	60.7	60.5	60.8	60.0	60.0	60.3
European Union	1957	66.8	66.1	67.8	66.8	66.2	66.3	67.2	66.8	66.0
NAFTA	1994	41.4	46.2	54.6	55.7	55.5	56.6	56.1	55.9	55.8
Latin America and the Caribbean										
ACS	1994	8.4	8.5	5.6	6.7	6.9	6.9	6.3	6.9	7.2
Andean Group	1969	4.1	12.0	8.8	8.7	10.5	9.5	8.9	8.6	8.2
CACM	1961	15.3	21.8	13.6	19.1	22.8	19.5	20.2	20.9	18.9
CARICOM	1973	8.1	12.0	16.9	14.7	16.5	13.7	12.3	12.5	11.8
Central American Group of Four	1993	13.7	22.2	14.6	23.0	27.0	21.4	21.4	21.4	18.2
Group of Three	1995	2.0	3.2	1.7	1.7	2.1	1.9	1.5	2.3	2.5
LAIA (ALADI)	1980	10.8	17.1	12.7	12.8	12.8	11.2	11.4	12.6	13.2
Mercosur	1991	8.9	20.3	20.6	20.0	17.1	11.5	11.9	12.7	12.9
OECS	1981	8.1	12.6	13.1	10.0	6.0	4.0	7.6	11.7	11.3
Middle East and Asia										
Arab Common Market	1964	2.7	6.7	3.3	2.9	4.4	5.1	4.1	7.9	8.6
ASEAN	1967	18.9	24.5	21.7	23.0	22.4	22.7	22.1	22.3	22.7
Bangkok Agreement	1975	3.7	4.9	5.1	5.1	5.5	5.5	5.7	5.2	5.4
EAEC		39.7	47.9	43.8	46.6	46.6	48.1	49.4	49.8	49.2
ECO	1985	3.2	7.9	5.8	5.6	5.5	5.9	6.6	6.7	7.6
GAFTA	1997	10.3	9.9	8.9	7.2	8.4	9.3	8.5	10.0	9.8
GCC	1981	8.0	6.8	6.7	4.8	5.2	5.9	5.1	5.0	4.8
SAARC	1985	3.2	4.4	4.0	4.1	4.3	4.8	5.7	5.6	5.5
UMA	1989	2.9	3.8	2.5	2.3	2.6	2.8	2.4	1.9	2.0
Sub-Saharan Africa										
CEMAC	1994	2.3	2.1	1.7	1.1	1.4	1.5	1.4	1.3	0.9
CEPGL	1976	0.5	0.5	0.8	0.8	0.8	0.9	1.2	1.2	1.3
COMESA	1994	6.6	7.7	7.4	6.1	7.9	7.4	7.4	6.8	5.9
Cross Border Initiative	1992	10.3	11.9	12.1	11.8	11.5	14.5	13.0	13.8	14.0
EAC	1996	13.4	17.4	14.4	20.5	21.4	19.3	18.2	16.6	15.0
ECCAS	1983	1.4	1.5	1.3	1.1	1.3	1.1	1.0	0.9	0.6
ECOWAS	1975	7.9	9.0	10.4	7.9	8.5	10.9	8.6	9.4	9.5
Indian Ocean Commission	1984	4.1	6.0	4.8	4.4	5.6	4.3	6.2	4.3	4.6
MRU	1973	0.0	0.1	0.4	0.4	0.3	0.2	0.3	0.3	0.3
SADC	1992	17.0	31.6	11.9	9.3	8.6	9.5	9.8	9.5	7.7
UDEAC	1964	2.3	2.1	1.7	1.0	1.4	1.4	1.4	1.2	0.9
UEMOA	1994	13.0	10.3	13.1	13.1	12.7	12.2	13.3	12.9	13.4

(SADC; formerly Southern African Development Coordination Conference), Angola, Botswana, the Democratic Republic of Congo, Lesotho, Malawi, Mauritius, Mozambique, Namibia, Seychelles, South Africa, Swaziland, Tanzania, Zambia, and Zimbabwe; **Central African Customs and Economic Union (UDEAC; formerly Union Douanière et Economique de l'Afrique Centrale)**, Cameroon, the Central African Republic, Chad, the Republic of Congo, Equatorial Guinea, and Gabon; **West African Economic and Monetary Union (UEMOA)**, Benin, Burkina Faso, Côte d'Ivoire, Guinea-Bissau, Mali, Niger, Senegal, and Togo; **Association of Caribbean States (ACS)**, Antigua and Barbuda, the Bahamas, Barbados, Belize, Colombia, Costa Rica, Cuba, Dominica, the Dominican Republic, El Salvador, Grenada, Guatemala, Guyana, Haiti, Honduras, Jamaica, Mexico, Nicaragua, Panama, St. Kitts and Nevis, St. Lucia, St. Vincent and the Grenadines, Suriname, Trinidad and Tobago, and República Bolivariana de Venezuela; **Andean Group**, Bolivia, Colombia, Ecuador, Peru, and República Bolivariana de Venezuela; **Central American Common Market (CACM)**, Costa Rica, El Salvador, Guatemala, Honduras, and Nicaragua; **Caribbean Community and Common Market (CARICOM)**, Antigua and Barbuda, the Bahamas (part of the Caribbean Community but not of the Common Market), Barbados, Belize, Dominica, Grenada, Guyana, Jamaica, Montserrat, St. Kitts and Nevis, St. Lucia, St. Vincent and the Grenadines, Suriname, and Trinidad and Tobago; **Central American Group of Four**, El Salvador, Guatemala, Honduras, and Nicaragua; **Group of Three**, Colombia, Mexico, and República Bolivariana de Venezuela; **Latin American Integration Association (LAIA; formerly Latin American Free Trade Area)**, Argentina, Bolivia, Brazil, Chile, Colombia, Ecuador, Mexico, Paraguay, Peru, Uruguay, and República Bolivariana de Venezuela; **Common Market of the South (Mercosur)**, Argentina, Brazil, Paraguay, and Uruguay; **Organization of Eastern Caribbean States (OECS)**, Antigua and Barbuda, Dominica, Grenada, Montserrat, St. Kitts and Nevis, St. Lucia, and St. Vincent and the Grenadines; **Arab Common Market**, the Arab Republic of Egypt, Iraq, Jordan, Libya, Mauritania, the Syrian Arab Republic, and the Republic of Yemen; **Association of South-East Asian Nations (ASEAN)**, Brunei, Cambodia, Indonesia, the Lao People's Democratic Republic, Malaysia, Myanmar, the Philippines, Singapore, Thailand, and Vietnam; Bangkok Agreement, Bangladesh, India, the Republic of Korea, the Lao People's Democratic Republic, the Philippines, Sri Lanka, and Thailand; **East Asia Economic Caucus (EAEC; formerly East Asia Economic Group)**, Brunei, China, Hong Kong (China), Indonesia, Japan, the Republic of Korea, Malaysia, the Philippines, Singapore, Taiwan (China), and Thailand; **Economic Cooperation Organization (ECO)**, Afghanistan, Azerbaijan, the Islamic Republic of Iran, Kazakhstan, the Kyrgyz Republic, Pakistan, Tajikistan, Turkey, Turkmenistan, and Uzbekistan; **Gulf Cooperation Council (GCC)**, Bahrain, Kuwait, Oman, Qatar, Saudi Arabia, and the United Arab Emirates; **South Asian Association for Regional Cooperation (SAARC)**, Bangladesh, Bhutan, India, Maldives, Nepal, Pakistan, and Sri Lanka; and **Arab Maghreb Union (UMA)**, Algeria, Libya, Mauritania, Morocco, and Tunisia.

Regional trade blocs

Total merchandise exports by bloc

	Year of creation	% of world exports								
		1990	1995	1999	2000	2001	2002	2003	2004	2005
High-income and low- and middle-income economies										
APEC[a]	1989	39.0	46.3	46.6	48.5	46.5	46.0	44.5	44.2	45.0
CEFTA	1992	1.3	1.6	1.9	1.9	2.2	2.4	2.7	2.9	3.1
CIS	1991	..	2.1	1.8	2.2	2.0	2.3	2.5	2.7	3.1
EMFTA	1995	46.3	42.7	42.7	39.4	41.4	42.2	43.3	42.9	40.8
FTAA	1994	19.1	19.7	21.7	22.1	21.8	20.2	18.4	17.7	17.8
European Union	1957	44.8	41.3	41.1	37.7	39.7	40.4	41.5	40.8	38.7
NAFTA	1994	16.2	16.8	18.8	19.0	18.7	17.2	15.5	14.5	14.3
Latin America and the Caribbean										
ACS	1994	1.9	2.6	3.5	3.8	3.7	3.6	3.2	3.2	3.4
Andean Group	1969	0.9	0.8	0.8	0.9	0.9	0.8	0.8	0.9	1.1
CACM	1961	0.1	0.1	0.3	0.2	0.2	0.2	0.2	0.2	0.2
CARICOM	1973	0.2	0.1	0.1	0.1	0.1	0.1	0.2	0.2	0.2
Central American Group of Four	1993	0.1	0.1	0.2	0.1	0.1	0.1	0.1	0.1	0.1
Group of Three	1995	1.5	2.1	3.0	3.3	3.2	3.1	2.7	2.7	2.9
LAIA (ALADI)	1980	3.4	4.1	4.8	5.3	5.2	5.0	4.7	4.8	5.1
Mercosur	1991	1.4	1.4	1.3	1.4	1.4	1.4	1.4	1.5	1.6
OECS	1981	0.0	0.0	0.0	0.0	0.0	0.0	0.0	0.0	0.0
Middle East and Asia										
Arab Common Market	1964	1.0	0.4	0.5	0.7	0.6	0.6	0.6	0.9	0.8
ASEAN	1967	4.3	6.4	6.3	6.7	6.3	6.3	6.1	6.0	6.1
Bangkok Agreement	1975	3.6	4.8	5.0	5.2	4.9	5.1	5.1	5.3	5.3
EAEC	1990	20.9	26.1	24.7	26.0	24.4	25.2	25.4	25.9	26.2
ECO	1985	1.1	1.2	1.2	1.3	1.3	1.3	1.5	1.6	1.8
GAFTA	1997	3.8	2.6	2.7	3.5	3.4	3.2	3.4	3.9	4.4
GCC	1981	2.6	2.0	1.9	2.6	2.5	2.3	2.5	2.7	3.3
SAARC	1985	0.8	0.9	1.0	1.0	1.1	1.1	1.1	1.1	1.3
UMA	1989	1.0	0.6	0.6	0.8	0.7	0.7	0.7	0.8	0.9
Sub-Saharan Africa										
CEMAC	1994	0.2	0.1	0.1	0.1	0.1	0.1	0.1	0.2	0.2
CEPGL	1976	0.0	0.0	0.0	0.0	0.0	0.0	0.0	0.0	0.0
COMESA	1994	0.4	0.4	0.3	0.4	0.4	0.4	0.4	0.5	0.5
Cross Border Initiative	1992	0.2	0.2	0.1	0.2	0.2	0.1	0.2	0.1	0.1
EAC	1996	0.1	0.1	0.1	0.0	0.1	0.1	0.1	0.0	0.1
ECCAS	1983	0.3	0.2	0.2	0.3	0.3	0.3	0.3	0.3	0.4
ECOWAS	1975	0.6	0.4	0.4	0.6	0.5	0.5	0.5	0.5	0.6
Indian Ocean Commission	1984	0.1	0.0	0.0	0.0	0.0	0.0	0.0	0.0	0.0
MRU	1973	0.1	0.0	0.0	0.0	0.0	0.0	0.0	0.0	0.0
SADC	1992	0.3	0.2	0.6	0.7	0.7	0.7	0.7	0.7	0.8
UDEAC	1964	0.2	0.1	0.1	0.1	0.1	0.1	0.1	0.2	0.2
UEMOA	1994	0.1	0.1	0.1	0.1	0.1	0.1	0.1	0.1	0.1

About the data

Trade blocs are groups of countries that have established special preferential arrangements governing trade between members. Although in some cases the preferences—such as lower tariff duties or exemptions from quantitative restrictions—may be no greater than those available to other trading partners, such arrangements are intended to encourage exports by bloc members to one another—sometimes called intratrade.

Most countries are members of a regional trade bloc, and more than a third of the world's trade takes place within such arrangements. While trade blocs vary widely in structure, they all have the same main objective: to reduce trade barriers between member countries. But effective integration requires more than reducing tariffs and quotas. Economic gains from competition and scale may not be achieved unless other barriers that divide markets and impede the free flow of goods, services, and investments are lifted. For example, many regional trade blocs retain contingent protections or restrictions on intrabloc trade. These include antidumping, countervailing duties, and "emergency protection" to address balance of payments problems or to protect an industry from surges in imports. Other barriers include differing product standards, discrimination in public procurement, and cumbersome and costly border formalities.

Membership in a regional trade bloc may reduce the frictional costs of trade, increase the credibility of reform initiatives, and strengthen security among partners. But making it work effectively is challenging for any government. All sectors of an economy may be affected, and some sectors may expand while others contract, so it is important to weigh the potential costs and benefits that membership may bring.

The table shows the value of merchandise intratrade for important regional trade blocs (service exports are excluded) as well as the size of intratrade relative to each bloc's total exports of goods and the share of the bloc's total exports in world exports. Although the Asia Pacific Economic Cooperation (APEC) has no preferential arrangements, it is included in the table because of the volume of trade between its members.

The data on country exports are drawn from the International Monetary Fund's (IMF) Direction of Trade database and should be broadly consistent with those from other sources, such as the United Nations Statistics Division's Commodity Trade (Comtrade) database. However, trade flows between many developing countries, particularly in Sub-Saharan Africa, are not well recorded. Thus the value of intratrade for certain groups may be understated. Data on trade between developing and high-income countries are generally complete.

Membership in the trade blocs shown is based on the most recent information available, from the World Bank Policy Research Report *Trade Blocs* (2000a), from the World Bank's *Global Economic Prospects 2005*, and from consultation with the World Bank's international trade unit. The date of each trade bloc's creation is also included. Although bloc exports have been calculated back to 1990 on the basis of current membership, several of the blocs came into existence in later years and their membership may have changed over time. For this reason, and because systems of preferences also change over time, intratrade in earlier years may not have been affected by the same preferences as in recent years. In addition, some countries belong to more than one trade bloc, so shares of world exports exceed 100 percent. Exports of blocs include all commodity trade, which may include items not specified in trade bloc agreements. Differences from previously published estimates may be due to changes in bloc membership or to revisions in the underlying data.

Definitions

• **Merchandise exports within bloc** are the sum of merchandise exports by members of a trade bloc to other members of the bloc. They are shown both in U.S. dollars and as a percentage of total merchandise exports by the bloc. • **Total merchandise exports by bloc** as a share of world exports are the ratio of the bloc's total merchandise exports (within the bloc and to the rest of the world) to total merchandise exports by all economies in the world.

Preferential regional trade agreements have a mixed impact on trade **6.6a**

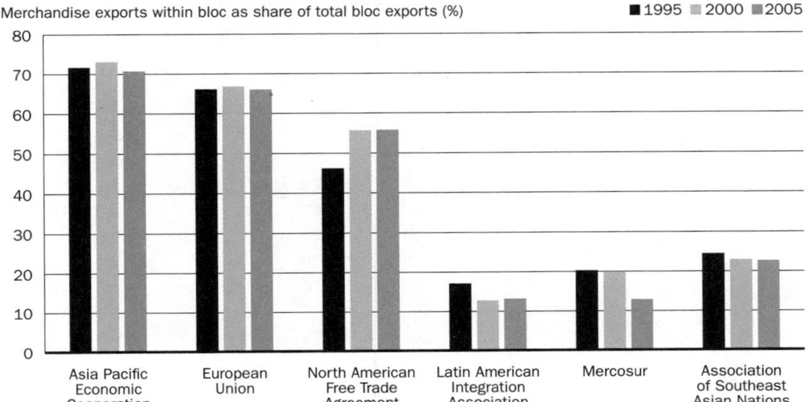

Regional trade agreements do not necessarily create net trade gains among bloc members.

Source: International Monetary Fund's Direction of Trade database.

Data sources

Data on merchandise trade flows are published in the IMF's *Direction of Trade Statistics Yearbook* and *Direction of Trade Statistics Quarterly*; the data in the table were calculated using the IMF's Direction of Trade database. The United Nations Conference on Trade and Development (UNCTAD) publishes data on intratrade in its *Handbook of International Trade and Development Statistics*. The information on trade bloc membership is from the World Bank Policy Research Report *Trade Blocs* (2000a), the World Bank's *Global Economic Prospects 2005*, and the World Bank's international trade unit.

6.7 Tariff barriers

	Most recent year	All products %						Primary products %		Manufactured products %	
		Binding coverage	Simple mean bound rate	Simple mean tariff	Weighted mean tariff	Share of lines with international peaks	Share of lines with specific rates	Simple mean tariff	Weighted mean tariff	Simple mean tariff	Weighted mean tariff
Afghanistan	..	..	..	..	..	..	..	..	..	..	..
Albania	2005[a]	100.0	7.0	6.3	7.1	0.0	0.0	7.3	6.5	6.1	7.2
Algeria	2005	..	..	15.8	10.6	38.6	0.0	15.3	9.0	15.7	11.0
Angola	2005	100.0	59.2	7.6	6.0	10.3	0.0	12.0	13.1	6.8	4.4
Argentina	2005[a]	100.0	31.9	10.6	5.2	22.6	0.0	8.0	1.8	10.8	5.7
Armenia	2001	100.0	8.5	3.3	2.5	0.0	0.0	6.6	3.4	2.8	1.5
Australia	2005[a]	97.1	10.0	4.3	3.1	6.0	0.2	1.6	0.7	4.6	3.7
Azerbaijan	2005	..	..	10.4	5.8	0.0	0.0	12.0	5.4	10.1	5.9
Bangladesh	2005	14.9	162.1	16.8	55.8	36.0	0.0	21.8	19.4	16.0	76.7
Belarus	2002	0.0	11.3	8.9	16.4	0.0	11.1	7.1	11.3	10.4	
Benin	2005	39.1	28.6	14.4	12.4	57.6	0.0	15.4	12.0	14.2	12.8
Bolivia	2005[a]	100.0	40.0	7.2	5.5	0.0	0.0	7.5	5.2	7.2	5.6
Bosnia and Herzegovina	2001[a]	..	..	5.3	5.1	0.0	0.0	3.8	5.3	5.5	5.0
Botswana	2005[a]	96.3	19.0	9.9	11.2	23.6	0.2	5.1	1.0	10.1	12.9
Brazil	2005[a]	100.0	31.4	12.3	7.1	27.7	0.0	7.9	1.5	12.6	9.2
Bulgaria	2005[a]	100.0	24.7	10.7	9.1	26.8	1.9	15.9	10.0	10.0	8.8
Burkina Faso	2005	39.3	41.9	13.1	11.7	48.6	0.0	13.6	10.1	13.0	12.6
Burundi	2005	20.9	67.5	19.6	19.9	46.5	0.0	26.1	25.5	18.5	18.7
Cambodia	2003[a]	..	..	16.0	16.4	25.9	0.0	17.4	15.6	15.8	16.6
Cameroon	2005	12.6	79.9	18.4	16.5	52.6	0.0	20.9	19.5	18.0	15.5
Canada	2005[a]	99.7	5.1	4.5	1.5	7.7	3.5	6.4	3.4	4.1	1.0
Central African Republic	2005	..	..	17.9	16.8	58.0	0.0	21.8	24.8	17.4	13.2
Chad	2005	..	..	17.2	12.5	48.7	0.0	22.1	25.0	16.5	10.3
Chile	2005[a]	100.0	25.1	4.9	3.9	0.0	0.0	4.4	2.8	4.9	4.4
China	2005[a]	100.0	10.0	9.2	4.9	19.1	0.0	8.8	3.4	9.2	5.3
Colombia	2005[a]	100.0	42.8	11.9	9.6	21.5	0.0	11.5	9.5	11.9	9.5
Congo, Dem. Rep.	2003	..	..	13.1	13.0	42.7	0.0	14.7	12.4	12.8	13.3
Congo, Rep.	2005	..	..	19.1	17.7	56.4	0.0	22.9	22.1	18.5	16.2
Costa Rica	2005	100.0	42.9	7.0	4.1	0.5	0.0	10.4	6.1	6.6	3.6
Côte d'Ivoire	2005	33.2	11.2	12.6	10.3	44.3	0.0	14.9	11.2	12.2	9.9
Croatia	2005[a]	100.0	5.9	2.4	1.2	3.0	0.0	4.9	2.3	2.1	0.7
Cuba	2005[a]	31.0	21.3	10.5	9.6	11.0	0.0	10.8	8.6	10.4	10.1
Czech Republic	2003	100.0	5.0	5.0	4.4	4.8	0.0	5.6	4.1	4.9	4.3
Dominican Republic	2005[a]	100.0	34.9	9.0	8.5	27.2	0.0	12.5	7.6	8.5	8.8
Ecuador	2005[a]	99.9	21.8	11.8	8.7	23.8	0.0	11.0	6.6	11.8	9.1
Egypt, Arab Rep.	2005[a]	99.1	36.6	18.9	12.0	21.8	0.0	85.8	16.4	11.6	10.5
El Salvador	2005[a]	100.0	36.6	6.4	6.7	2.5	0.0	10.4	8.3	5.8	5.8
Estonia	2003	100.0	8.7	1.0	0.9	5.4	0.0	8.1	4.0	0.0	0.0
Ethiopia	2002	..	..	19.7	13.5	52.9	0.0	22.1	6.7	19.4	15.7
European Union[b]	2005[a]	100.0	4.2	2.7	2.0	6.7	9.0	7.9	2.3	1.7	1.8
Gabon	2005	100.0	21.4	19.9	16.8	60.6	0.0	22.9	19.4	19.3	15.8
Gambia, The	2003	13.0	101.8								
Georgia	2004	100.0	7.2	7.5	9.5	5.4	0.7	11.8	13.2	6.8	7.1
Ghana	2004	13.5	92.1	13.2	11.0	45.3	0.0	17.4	17.1	12.3	8.8
Guatemala	2005[a]	100.0	42.2	6.7	5.8	1.0	0.0	8.8	5.5	6.4	5.9
Guinea	2005	39.0	20.1	14.2	12.7	58.6	0.0	16.3	14.3	13.9	11.2
Honduras	2005[a]	100.0	32.5	6.7	6.0	0.2	0.0	9.7	7.2	6.3	5.3
Hong Kong, China	2005	45.7	0.0	0.0	0.0	0.0	0.0	0.0	0.0	0.0	0.0
Hungary	2002	96.2	9.8	8.9	7.9	10.9	0.0	17.9	6.7	7.7	8.0
India	2005[a]	73.8	49.6	17.0	14.5	15.5	3.5	24.4	16.5	15.9	12.8
Indonesia	2005[a]	96.6	37.1	6.5	6.0	8.7	0.0	7.2	3.5	6.4	6.7
Iran, Islamic Rep.	2004	..	..	18.7	13.8	43.4	0.0	14.9	11.2	18.9	14.5
Iraq	..	..	..	..	..	..	..	..	..	..	..
Israel	2005[a]	76.3	20.9	2.7	1.7	1.5	1.1	6.9	3.9	2.1	0.9
Jamaica	2003	100.0	49.6	9.4	9.8	36.5	0.0	15.7	11.0	8.4	9.3
Japan	2005[a]	99.7	3.0	3.3	2.5	8.1	2.7	8.4	3.8	2.3	1.4
Jordan	2005[a]	100.0	16.3	12.4	7.6	34.5	0.0	15.6	4.0	11.9	9.9
Kazakhstan	2004	..	..	2.3	1.9	0.0	0.0	3.3	3.1	2.2	1.6
Kenya	2005	14.0	95.1	12.1	7.5	36.4	0.0	15.9	8.6	11.6	6.7

Tariff barriers 6.7

	Most recent year	All products %						Primary products %		Manufactured products %	
		Binding coverage	Simple mean bound rate	Simple mean tariff	Weighted mean tariff	Share of lines with international peaks	Share of lines with specific rates	Simple mean tariff	Weighted mean tariff	Simple mean tariff	Weighted mean tariff
Korea, Rep.	2004[a]	94.5	15.7	9.0	9.3	5.6	0.0	20.3	17.7	7.2	4.5
Kuwait	2005	..	..	4.7	4.5	0.0	0.0	3.9	3.0	4.8	4.8
Kyrgyz Republic	2003	99.9	7.4	4.3	4.3	0.1	2.2	6.7	6.2	3.8	2.9
Lao PDR	2005[a]	..	..	9.2	14.0	23.5	0.0	18.5	29.7	8.5	10.3
Latvia	2001	100.0	12.8	3.3	2.6	3.0	0.0	8.1	5.4	2.5	1.5
Lebanon	2005[a]	..	..	7.2	6.3	12.2	0.0	14.2	6.1	6.1	6.3
Lesotho	2005[a]	..	..	9.9	16.8	24.1	0.8	7.4	3.3	10.0	17.6
Libya	2002	..	..	20.2	25.2	46.6	0.0	19.2	15.1	20.1	28.5
Lithuania	2003[a]	100.0	9.2	1.3	0.7	3.3	0.0	3.5	1.3	1.0	0.4
Macedonia, FYR	2005	100.0	6.9	4.1	3.3	12.2	0.0	10.0	6.4	3.5	1.7
Madagascar	2005	29.7	27.4	11.6	5.2	37.1	0.0	16.9	4.1	11.0	5.9
Malawi	2001[a]	30.2	74.9	13.5	10.2	42.4	0.0	13.4	9.0	13.4	10.7
Malaysia	2005[a]	83.7	14.5	7.5	4.4	22.4	0.0	3.4	2.3	8.2	4.8
Mali	2005	40.7	28.8	12.4	10.7	43.7	0.0	14.4	11.7	12.2	10.4
Mauritania	2001	39.4	19.6	12.8	9.9	51.1	0.0	12.6	10.0	12.8	9.9
Mauritius	2005	18.0	94.0	8.5	4.7	19.7	0.0	9.0	5.3	8.3	4.2
Mexico	2005[a]	100.0	35.0	9.2	3.0	12.4	0.0	8.5	2.2	9.2	3.1
Moldova	2001	..	..	4.8	2.9	0.2	0.4	8.4	2.7	4.1	3.0
Mongolia	2005	100.0	17.5	4.2	4.3	0.0	0.0	5.0	5.1	4.1	3.7
Morocco	2005	100.0	41.3	19.4	13.7	57.0	0.0	23.3	12.1	18.8	14.3
Mozambique	2005[a]	..	..	13.1	8.6	38.2	0.0	16.4	9.1	12.6	8.5
Myanmar	2005[a]	16.5	83.3	4.5	4.1	5.3	0.0	7.6	4.8	4.2	3.8
Namibia	2005[a]	96.3	19.4	5.6	1.3	15.2	0.0	3.7	0.5	5.9	1.6
Nepal	2005[a]	..	..	14.7	14.3	21.6	0.0	13.9	9.3	14.7	16.4
New Zealand	2005[a]	100.0	10.3	5.0	4.6	10.0	4.8	9.9	8.7	4.3	3.4
Nicaragua	2005[a]	100.0	41.7	6.8	5.4	0.5	0.0	10.6	5.4	6.3	5.4
Niger	2005	96.8	44.3	12.7	12.8	47.6	0.0	14.9	14.7	12.4	12.1
Nigeria	2005	18.2	117.8	11.6	10.8	41.0	0.0	14.9	14.9	11.3	9.3
Norway	2003[a]	100.0	3.0	2.6	1.9	4.2	5.7	17.8	8.6	0.5	0.2
Oman	2005[a]	100.0	13.8	3.8	3.2	0.1	0.0	4.1	2.9	3.8	3.3
Pakistan	2005[a]	44.8	52.2	14.6	12.4	42.6	0.0	13.8	8.6	14.6	14.5
Panama	2005[a]	99.9	23.4	7.4	6.9	1.8	0.0	11.2	7.9	7.0	6.4
Papua New Guinea	2005	100.0	31.7	6.1	2.2	25.3	0.3	14.9	3.1	4.8	1.7
Paraguay	2005[a]	100.0	33.6	8.3	5.8	16.8	0.0	6.3	1.5	8.5	7.2
Peru	2005[a]	100.0	30.1	9.2	8.3	11.1	0.0	10.7	9.8	9.1	7.6
Philippines	2005[a]	67.0	25.6	5.4	3.1	4.8	0.0	6.9	5.1	5.1	2.7
Poland	2003[a]	96.2	11.9	5.5	3.4	9.9	3.3	27.8	12.6	2.5	1.2
Romania	2005[a]	100.0	39.9	6.6	3.1	21.0	0.0	13.3	7.2	5.7	1.8
Russian Federation	2005	0.0	11.4	9.6	17.9	16.0	10.7	12.2	11.5	8.9	
Rwanda	2005[a]	100.0	89.5	17.2	9.7	47.0	0.0	12.7	5.5	17.7	12.2
Saudi Arabia	2005[a]	..	..	4.1	4.1	0.0	0.0	3.2	2.7	4.3	4.4
Senegal	2005	100.0	30.0	14.0	9.2	53.8	0.0	14.9	8.2	13.8	10.4
Serbia and Montenegro	2005	..	..	8.2	7.9	20.0	0.0	13.2	10.7	7.4	7.0
Sierra Leone	2004	100.0	47.4								
Singapore	2005[a]	69.3	6.9	0.1	0.0	0.1	0.1	0.3	0.1	0.0	0.0
Slovak Republic	2002	100.0	5.0	22.1	21.2	50.8	0.0	19.2	12.8	22.3	23.5
Slovenia	2003[a]	100.0	23.7	4.4	1.8	11.4	0.0	7.0	3.9	3.9	1.2
South Africa	2005[a]	96.3	19.4	8.5	5.4	21.3	1.0	5.4	1.7	8.8	6.5
Sri Lanka	2005[a]	36.8	29.6	11.3	7.7	23.4	0.4	18.2	9.5	10.3	6.8
Sudan	2002	..	..	21.1	19.6	43.8	0.0	28.2	24.0	20.5	18.9
Swaziland	2005[a]	96.3	19.4	10.8	10.5	26.6	0.0	10.3	4.3	10.8	10.8
Sweden	1989	..	..	5.4	4.3	3.6	0.0	1.4	1.0	6.0	5.0
Switzerland	2005[a]	99.8	0.0	2.7	1.4	8.7	35.1	14.0	8.1	0.6	0.1
Syrian Arab Republic	2002	..	..	14.7	15.5	23.3	0.0	14.4	11.7	14.5	16.6
Tajikistan	2002	..	..	7.6	6.1	6.8	1.7	9.6	5.7	7.3	6.6
Tanzania	2005[a]	13.4	120.0	12.9	8.4	38.0	0.0	18.7	10.6	12.2	7.7
Thailand	2005[a]	74.8	25.8	10.6	4.9	22.1	0.9	13.1	2.3	10.0	5.7
Togo	2005	13.2	80.0	14.6	10.4	55.3	0.0	15.4	9.7	14.4	11.0
Trinidad and Tobago	2003	100.0	55.8	9.8	5.5	36.6	0.0	15.5	4.8	8.8	5.9

6.7 Tariff barriers

	Most recent year	All products % Binding coverage	Simple mean bound rate	Simple mean tariff	Weighted mean tariff	Share of lines with international peaks	Share of lines with specific rates	Primary products % Simple mean tariff	Weighted mean tariff	Manufactured products % Simple mean tariff	Weighted mean tariff
Tunisia	2005[a]	57.9	57.7	13.4	9.1	31.0	0.0	27.4	13.8	12.0	7.5
Turkey	2005[a]	47.7	29.6	2.4	1.6	4.8	0.0	12.6	2.6	1.4	1.2
Turkmenistan	2002	..	..	5.4	2.9	14.8	2.8	14.8	12.6	3.8	1.1
Uganda	2005[a]	14.9	73.5	12.4	9.0	38.3	0.0	16.7	10.1	11.9	8.4
Ukraine	2002	..	..	7.6	3.9	11.2	0.0	6.9	1.5	7.6	6.4
United Arab Emirates	2005[a]	..	..	4.8	4.8	0.2	0.0	4.9	4.7	4.8	4.8
United States	2005[a]	100.0	3.6	3.2	1.6	6.1	5.9	2.8	0.8	3.3	1.8
Uruguay	2005[a]	100.0	31.6	9.9	3.5	26.1	0.0	6.3	1.2	10.1	4.8
Uzbekistan	2001	..	..	10.4	5.8	26.7	0.0	10.5	4.2	10.5	6.2
Venezuela, RB	2005[a]	99.9	36.8	12.8	12.7	23.7	0.0	12.2	11.3	12.8	12.9
Vietnam	2005[a]	..	..	13.2	13.6	34.1	0.0	17.7	14.9	12.3	12.8
Yemen, Rep.	2000	..	..	12.8	11.8	11.2	0.0	13.6	10.8	12.7	12.4
Zambia	2005[a]	15.9	105.7	14.6	9.4	34.5	0.0	14.9	9.3	14.5	9.4
Zimbabwe	2003	20.8	90.7	16.7	17.3	38.8	0.0	19.5	19.8	16.2	14.7
World	..	77.4	30.8	7.7	3.3	13.8	0.5	9.9	3.3	7.4	3.2
Low income	..	48.2	47.1	13.0	14.2	30.1	0.8	15.9	14.1	12.6	14.2
Middle income	..	88.5	31.0	8.8	5.3	16.5	0.7	11.8	4.6	8.3	5.5
Lower middle income	..	86.6	31.5	9.6	5.8	18.1	1.3	12.5	4.4	9.2	6.2
Upper middle income	..	90.8	30.4	7.9	4.7	15.0	0.8	11.2	5.0	7.4	4.6
Low & middle income	..	76.2	34.8	9.4	6.1	17.8	0.9	12.3	5.9	9.0	6.1
East Asia & Pacific	..	79.0	32.4	9.0	5.0	18.4	0.1	9.6	3.5	8.8	5.4
Europe & Central Asia	..	85.6	11.9	6.3	4.9	10.2	1.5	9.9	6.0	5.8	4.5
Latin America & the Carib.	..	97.1	42.8	9.6	5.3	17.4	0.0	11.9	3.9	9.3	5.6
Middle East & N. Africa	..	93.4	34.8	10.6	8.9	23.7	0.0	15.8	8.9	9.8	8.8
South Asia	..	61.1	42.6	15.2	16.1	31.4	1.6	18.4	15.1	14.6	16.8
Sub-Saharan Africa	..	48.7	43.0	12.2	8.1	33.7	0.0	14.3	8.1	11.9	8.1
High-income	..	83.0	13.3	3.4	1.9	4.1	0.2	4.6	2.1	3.2	1.8
OECD	..	98.6	7.4	3.1	2.0	3.7	0.0	3.7	2.1	3.0	1.9
Non-OECD	..	67.3	21.3	4.1	1.2	5.0	0.8	6.3	1.9	3.7	1.1

Note: Tariff rates include ad valorem equivalents of specific rates unavailable in previous years.
a. Rates are either partially or fully recorded applied rates. All other simple and weighted tariff rates are most favored nation rates. b. Data refer to all 25 member states of the European Union.

About the data

Poor people in developing countries work primarily in agriculture and labor-intensive manufactures, sectors that confront the greatest trade barriers. Removing barriers to merchandise trade could increase growth by about 0.8 percent a year in these countries—even more if trade in services (retailing, business, financial, and telecommunications services) were also liberalized.

In general, tariffs in high-income countries on imports from developing countries, though low, are twice the size of those collected from other high-income countries. But protection is also an issue for developing countries, which maintain high tariffs on agricultural commodities, labor-intensive manufactures, and other products and services. In some developing regions new trade policies could make the difference between achieving important Millennium Development Goals—reducing poverty, lowering maternal and child mortality rates, improving educational attainment—and falling far short.

Countries use a combination of tariff and nontariff measures to regulate imports. The most common form of tariff is an ad valorem duty, based on the value of the import, but tariffs may also be levied on a specific, or per unit, basis or may combine ad valorem and specific rates. Tariffs may be used to raise fiscal revenues or to protect domestic industries from foreign competition—or both. Nontariff barriers, which limit the quantity of imports of a particular good, include quotas, prohibitions, licensing schemes, export restraint arrangements, and health and quarantine measures.

Nontariff barriers are generally considered less desirable than tariffs because changes in an exporting country's efficiency and costs no longer result in changes in market share in the importing country. Further, the quotas or licenses that regulate trade become very valuable, and resources are often wasted in attempts to acquire these assets. A high percentage of products subject to nontariff barriers suggests a protectionist trade regime, but the frequency of nontariff barriers does not measure how much they restrict trade. Moreover, a wide range of domestic policies and regulations (such as health regulations) may act as nontariff barriers. Based on the difficulty of combining nontariff barriers into an aggregate indicator, they are not included in this table.

The tariff rates used in calculating the indicators in the table are most favored nation rates unless they are specified as applied rates. Effectively applied rates are those in effect for partners in preferential trade agreements such as the North American Free Trade Agreement. The difference between most favored nation and applied rates can be substantial. As more countries report their free trade agreements, suspensions of tariffs, or other special preferences, *World Development Indicators* will include their effectively applied rates. All estimates are calculated using the most up-to-date information, which is not necessarily updated every year. As a result, data for the same year may differ from data in last year's publication.

Three measures of average tariffs are shown: simple bound rates and the simple and the weighted mean tariffs. The most favored nation or applied rates are calculated using all traded items, while bound rates are based on all products in a country's tariff schedule. Weighted mean tariffs are weighted by the value of the country's trade with each trading partner. Simple averages are often a better indicator of tariff protection than weighted averages, which are biased downward because higher tariffs discourage trade and reduce the weights applied to these tariffs. Bound rates have resulted from trade negotiations that are incorporated into a country's schedule of concessions and are thus enforceable. If a contracting party raises a tariff to a higher level than its bound rate, beneficiaries of the earlier binding have a right to receive compensation, usually as reduced tariffs on other products they export to the country. If the beneficiaries are not compensated, they may retaliate by raising their own tariffs against an equivalent value of the original country's exports.

Some countries set fairly uniform tariff rates across all imports. Others are more selective, setting high tariffs to protect favored domestic industries. The share of tariff lines with international peaks (those for which ad valorem tariff rates exceed 15 percent) provides an indication of how selectively tariffs are applied. The effective rate of protection—the degree to which the value added in an industry is protected—may exceed the nominal rate if the tariff system systematically differentiates among imports of raw materials, intermediate products, and finished goods.

The share of tariff lines with specific rates shows the extent to which countries use tariffs based on physical quantities or other, non–ad valorem measures. Some countries apply only specific duties. Specific duties are not included in the table, except for Switzerland. Work is under way to complete the estimations for ad valorem equivalents of specific duties for all countries.

The indicators were calculated from data supplied by the United Nations Conference on Trade and Development (UNCTAD) and the World Trade Organization (WTO). Data are classified using the Harmonized System of trade at the six- or eight-digit level. Tariff line data were matched to Standard International Trade Classification (SITC) revision 2 codes to define commodity groups and import weights. Import weights were calculated using the United Nations Statistics Division's Commodity Trade (Comtrade) database. Data are shown only for the last year for which complete data are available. To conserve space, data for the European Union are shown instead of data for individual members.

Definitions

• **Binding coverage** is the percentage of product lines with an agreed bound rate. • **Simple mean bound rate** is the unweighted average of all the lines in the tariff schedule in which bound rates have been set. • **Simple mean tariff** is the unweighted average of effectively applied rates or most favored nation rates for all products subject to tariffs calculated for all traded goods. • **Weighted mean tariff** is the average of effectively applied rates or most favored nation rates weighted by the product import shares corresponding to each partner country. • **Share of lines with international peaks** is the share of lines in the tariff schedule with tariff rates that exceed 15 percent. • **Share of lines with specific rates** is the share of lines in the tariff schedule that are set on a per unit basis or that combine ad valorem and per unit rates. • **Primary products** are commodities classified in SITC revision 2 sections 0–4 plus division 68 (nonferrous metals). • **Manufactured products** are commodities classified in SITC revision 2 sections 5–8 excluding division 68.

Data sources

All indicators in the table were calculated by World Bank staff using the World Integrated Trade Solution system. Data on tariffs were provided by UNCTAD and the WTO. Data on global imports are from the United Nations Statistics Division's Comtrade database.

6.8 Global private financial flows

	Foreign direct investment		Portfolio investment flows				Bank and trade-related lending	
	$ millions		$ millions				$ millions	
			Bonds		Equity			
	1990	2005	1990	2005	1990	2005	1990	2005
Afghanistan	..	..	..	..	..	..	..	..
Albania	..	262	..	0	0	..	..	34
Algeria	0	1,081	–15	0	0	..	–409	–821
Angola	–335	–1,304	0	0	0	..	570	1,550
Argentina	1,836	4,730	–857	1,872	0	–48	–1,195	–824
Armenia	1,836	258	..	0	0	1	..	83
Australia	8,111	–34,420	..	..	..	..	..	..
Austria	653	9,057	..	..	..	..	..	..
Azerbaijan	4	1,680	..	0	0	0	..	9
Bangladesh	3	802	0	0	0	1	55	–9
Belarus	..	305	..	0	0	1	..	42
Belgium	8,047[a]	31,959	..	..	..	..	..	..
Benin	62	21	0	0	0	..	..	–4
Bolivia	27	–277	0	0	0	..	–24	314
Bosnia and Herzegovina	..	299	..	0	..	..	..	282
Botswana	96	279	0	0	0	62	–18	–2
Brazil	989	15,193	129	3,580	103	6,451	–555	–1,708
Bulgaria	4	2,614	..	–1,257	0	92	..	2,421
Burkina Faso	0	19	0	0	0	..	..	..
Burundi	1	1	0	0	0	0	–6	–5
Cambodia	..	379	0	0	..	..	..	..
Cameroon	–113	18	0	0	0	..	–14	–44
Canada	7,581	34,146	..	..	..	..	..	..
Central African Republic	1	6	0	0	0	..	–1	..
Chad	9	705	0	0	0	..	–1	–1
Chile	661	6,667	–7	584	367	1,635	1,194	2,593
China	3,487	79,127	–48	2,702	0	20,346	4,668	2,442
Hong Kong, China	..	35,897	..	..	..	..	..	..
Colombia	500	10,375	–4	496	0	86	–151	–768
Congo, Dem. Rep.	23	402	0	–1	..	..	–12	–2
Congo, Rep.	–14	724	0	0	0	..	–100	0
Costa Rica	163	861	–42	–32	0	0	–99	287
Côte d'Ivoire	48	266	–1	0	0	35	10	–163
Croatia	..	1,761	..	–785	..	113	..	2,429
Cuba	..	..	..	..	..	..	..	..
Czech Republic	0	..	..	–201	0	..	669	–4,524
Denmark	1,132	5,238	..	..	..	..	..	..
Dominican Republic	133	1,023	0	–20	0	0	–3	195
Ecuador	126	1,646	0	650	0	2	58	–80
Egypt, Arab Rep.	734	5,376	–1	1,554	0	729	–65	2,936
El Salvador	2	517	0	375	0	..	5	78
Eritrea	..	11	..	0	..	..	..	..
Estonia	..	2,997	..	0	..	–1,349	..	425
Ethiopia	12	265	0	0	0	0	–57	116
Finland	812	3,978	..	..	..	..	..	..
France	13,183	70,686	..	..	..	..	..	..
Gabon	73	300	0	0	0	..	29	6
Gambia, The	14	52	0	0	0	..	–7	..
Georgia	..	450	..	0	..	3	..	46
Germany	3,004	32,034	..	..	..	..	..	..
Ghana	15	107	0	0	0	0	–23	13
Greece	1,005	640	..	..	..	..	..	..
Guatemala	48	208	–11	0	0	..	1	–15
Guinea	18	102	0	0	..	..	–19	..
Guinea-Bissau	2	10	0	0	0	..	..	..
Haiti	8	10	0	0	0	0	..	..

Global private financial flows

	Foreign direct investment		Portfolio investment flows				Bank and trade-related lending	
	$ millions		$ millions				$ millions	
			Bonds		Equity			
	1990	2005	1990	2005	1990	2005	1990	2005
Honduras	44	464	0	0	0	0	32	57
Hungary	623	6,436	921	2,978	0	–16	–1,379	2,124
India	237	6,598	147	–3,959	0	11,968	1,458	4,338
Indonesia	1,093	5,260	26	3,791	0	–165	1,804	–2,306
Iran, Islamic Rep.	–362	30	0	0	0	..	–30	644
Iraq	..	..	..	..	..	..	..	..
Ireland	627	–29,730	..	..	..	..	..	..
Israel	151	5,585	..	..	..	..	..	..
Italy	6,411	19,585	..	..	..	..	..	..
Jamaica	138	682	0	919	0	..	–46	22
Japan	1,777	3,214	..	..	..	..	..	..
Jordan	38	1,532	0	134	0	60	214	11
Kazakhstan	..	1,975	..	3,050	..	170	..	3,557
Kenya	57	21	0	0	0	3	65	–8
Korea, Dem. Rep.	..	..	..	..	..	..	..	..
Korea, Rep.	789	4,339	..	..	..	..	..	..
Kuwait	0	250	..	..	..	..	..	..
Kyrgyz Republic	..	43	..	0	..	0	..	..
Lao PDR	6	28	0	0	0	..	..	228
Latvia	..	730	..	125	..	27	..	2,352
Lebanon	6	2,573	0	1,070	..	1,436	6	–37
Lesotho	17	92	0	0	0	..	0	–8
Liberia	225	194	0	0	..	..	..	0
Libya	..	..	..	..	..	..	..	..
Lithuania	..	1,032	..	–405	..	130	..	374
Macedonia, FYR	..	100	..	187	..	52	..	–79
Madagascar	22	29	0	0	0	..	–15	–1
Malawi	23	3	0	0	1	..	2	–3
Malaysia	2,332	3,966	–1,239	492	0	–1,200	–617	–1,396
Mali	6	159	0	0	0	9	–1	3
Mauritania	7	115	0	0	0	..	–1	14
Mauritius	41	39	0	0	0	36	44	–36
Mexico	2,549	18,772	661	–839	1,995	3,353	4,396	1,705
Moldova	..	199	..	–6	..	1	..	90
Mongolia	..	182	..	0	0	..	..	0
Morocco	165	1,552	0	–41	0	64	318	115
Mozambique	9	108	0	0	0	..	26	–21
Myanmar	163	300	0	0	0	..	–8	–26
Namibia	..	..	..	..	..	..	..	..
Nepal	6	2	0	0	0	..	–14	..
Netherlands	10,676	40,416	..	..	..	..	..	..
New Zealand	1,735	1,979	..	..	..	..	..	..
Nicaragua	1	241	0	0	0	0	20	17
Niger	41	12	0	0	..	..	10	–7
Nigeria	588	2,013	0	0	0	..	–121	–171
Norway	1,003	3,285	..	..	..	..	..	..
Oman	142	715	0	0	0	10	..	–524
Pakistan	245	2,183	0	1,092	0	451	–63	–158
Panama	136	1,027	–2	529	–1	0	–4	–148
Papua New Guinea	155	34	0	0	0	..	49	–164
Paraguay	77	64	0	0	0	..	–9	2
Peru	41	2,519	0	2,640	0	766	18	–981
Philippines	530	1,132	395	1,081	0	1,461	–286	66
Poland	89	9,602	0	11,384	0	1,341	–18	2,717
Portugal	2,610	3,200	..	..	..	..	..	..
Puerto Rico	..	..	..	..	..	..	..	..

6.8 Global private financial flows

	Foreign direct investment		Portfolio investment flows				Bank and trade-related lending	
	$ millions		$ millions				$ millions	
			Bonds		Equity			
	1990	2005	1990	2005	1990	2005	1990	2005
Romania	0	6,630	0	249	0	229	4	7,066
Russian Federation	..	15,151	..	10,033	..	–215	..	33,290
Rwanda	8	8	0	..	0	0	–2	..
Saudi Arabia	..	..	..	..	..	..	..	..
Senegal	57	54	0	0	1	..	–15	18
Serbia and Montenegro	..	1,481	..	0	..	..	..	2,071
Sierra Leone	32	59	0	0	0	..	4	..
Singapore	5,575	20,071	..	..	..	..	..	..
Slovak Republic	93	1,908	..	–934	..	..	..	–1,380
Slovenia	..	541	..	..	..	..	..	..
Somalia	6	24	0	0	..	..	..	..
South Africa	–76	6,257	..	406	389	7,230	..	587
Spain	13,984	22,789	..	..	..	..	..	..
Sri Lanka	43	272	0	0	0	–216	10	–89
Sudan	–31	2,305	0	0	0	0	..	64
Swaziland	30	–16	0	0	–2	0	–2	11
Sweden	1,982	10,679	..	..	..	..	..	..
Switzerland	5,545	15,420	..	..	..	..	..	..
Syrian Arab Republic	71	427	0	0	0	..	–9	–3
Tajikistan	..	54	..	0	..	0	..	–3
Tanzania	0	473	0	0	0	3	5	3
Thailand	2,444	4,527	–87	1,156	440	5,665	1,574	–1,565
Togo	18	3	0	0	4	..	0	..
Trinidad and Tobago	109	1,100	–52	–150	0	..	–126	..
Tunisia	76	723	–60	–136	5	12	–137	4
Turkey	684	9,805	597	3,212	89	5,669	466	14,588
Turkmenistan	..	62	..	..	..	..	..	–85
Uganda	–6	257	0	0	0	2	16	3
Ukraine	..	7,808	..	576	..	82	..	3,284
United Arab Emirates	..	..	..	..	..	..	..	..
United Kingdom	33,504	158,801	..	..	..	..	..	..
United States	48,490	109,754	..	..	..	..	..	..
Uruguay	42	711	–16	573	0	20	–176	–234
Uzbekistan	..	45	..	0	..	..	..	–240
Venezuela, RB	451	2,957	345	5,365	0	91	–922	–512
Vietnam	180	1,954	0	724	..	..	..	–43
West Bank and Gaza	..	..	..	..	..	..	..	..
Yemen, Rep.	–131	–266	0	0	..	..	161	24
Zambia	203	259	0	0	0	..	–9	127
Zimbabwe	–12	103	–30	0	0	..	127	–16
World	**203,236 s**	**974,283 s**	**.. s**	**.. s**	**.. s**	**.. s**	**.. s**	**.. s**
Low income	2,343	20,522	116	–2,144	7	12,471	1,623	3,902
Middle income	22,237	260,273	966	57,254	3,383	54,209	13,172	77,231
Lower middle income	11,999	150,874	388	21,431	545	35,662	6,437	11,838
Upper middle income	10,238	109,399	577	35,823	2,838	18,547	6,735	65,393
Low & middle income	24,580	280,795	1,082	55,110	3,390	66,680	14,795	81,134
East Asia & Pacific	10,512	96,898	–952	9,947	440	26,108	7,180	–2,772
Europe & Central Asia	3,333	73,687	1,893	28,406	89	6,328	3,612	75,498
Latin America & Carib.	8,242	70,017	101	16,640	2,464	12,351	2,430	–75
Middle East & N. Africa	741	13,765	–76	2,581	5	2,311	–350	2,350
South Asia	542	9,869	147	–2,868	1	12,204	1,446	4,086
Sub-Saharan Africa	1,210	16,559	–31	405	393	7,379	477	2,046
High income	178,656	693,488	..	..	..	..	..	..
Europe EMU	61,012	315,043	..	..	..	..	..	..

a. Includes Luxembourg.

Global private financial flows

About the data

The data on foreign direct investment (FDI) are based on balance of payments data reported by the International Monetary Fund (IMF), supplemented by staff estimates using data reported by the United Nations Conference on Trade and Development and official national sources.

The internationally accepted definition of FDI is provided in the fifth edition of the IMF's *Balance of Payments Manual* (1993). Under this definition FDI has three components: equity investment, reinvested earnings, and short- and long-term intercompany loans between parent firms and foreign affiliates. Distinguished from other kinds of international investment, FDI is made to establish a lasting interest in or effective management control over an enterprise in another country. As a guideline, the IMF suggests that investments should account for at least 10 percent of voting stock to be counted as FDI. In practice, many countries set a higher threshold. Also, many countries fail to report reinvested earnings, and the definition of long-term loans differs among countries.

FDI data do not give a complete picture of international investment in an economy. Balance of payments data on FDI do not include capital raised locally, which has become an important source of financing for investment projects in some developing countries. In addition, FDI data capture only cross-border investment flows involving equity participation and thus omit nonequity crossborder transactions such as intrafirm flows of goods and services. For a detailed discussion of the data issues, see the World Bank's *World Debt Tables 1993–94* (vol. 1, chap. 3).

Portfolio flow data are compiled from several market and official sources, including Euromoney databases and publications; Micropal; Lipper Analytical Services; published reports of private investment houses, central banks, national securities and exchange commissions, and national stock exchanges; and the World Bank's Debtor Reporting System.

Gross statistics on international bond and equity issues are produced by aggregating individual transactions reported by market sources. Transactions of public and publicly guaranteed bonds are reported through the Debtor Reporting System by World Bank member economies that have received either loans from the International Bank for Reconstruction and Development or credits from the International Development Association. Information on private nonguaranteed bonds is collected from market sources, because official national sources reporting to the Debtor Reporting System are not asked to report the breakdown between private nonguaranteed bonds and private nonguaranteed loans. Information on transactions by nonresidents in local equity markets is gathered from national authorities, investment positions of mutual funds, and market sources.

The volume of portfolio investment reported by the World Bank generally differs from that reported by other sources because of differences in sources, classification of economies, and method used to adjust and disaggregate reported information. Differences in reporting arise particularly for foreign investments in local equity markets because clarity, adequate disaggregation, and comprehensive and periodic reporting are lacking in many developing economies. By contrast, capital flows through international debt and equity instruments are well recorded, and for these the differences in reporting lie primarily in classification of economies, exchange rates used, whether particular installments of the transactions are included, and treatment of certain offshore issuances.

Net private capital flows—calculated as the sum of foreign direct investment, portfolio investment flows, and bank and trade-related lending—are no longer included in the table because they are likely to be overestimated. The source of overestimation is the possible double counting of intercompany lending, which is a debt liability but may also be included in foreign direct investment flows. There is currently no practical way to know when double counting has occurred and therefore to adjust for it.

Private capital flows to developing countries are rising **6.8a**

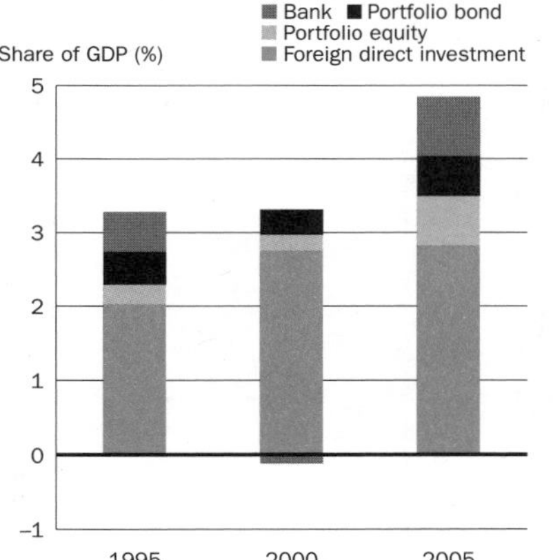

Economic integration over the past decade has favored foreign direct investment inflows to developing countries whose investment climate has improved markedly. Other private capital flows have also surged.

Source: World Bank Debtor Reporting System.

Definitions

• **Foreign direct investment** is net inflows of investment to acquire a lasting management interest in an enterprise operating in an economy other than that of the investor. It is the sum of equity capital, reinvestment of earnings, other long-term capital, and short-term capital, as shown in the balance of payments. • **Portfolio investment flows** are net and include portfolio debt flows (public and publicly guaranteed and private nonguaranteed bond issues purchased by foreign investors) and non-debt-creating portfolio equity flows (the sum of country funds, depository receipts, and direct purchases of shares by foreign investors). • **Bank and trade-related lending** covers commercial bank lending (public and publicly guaranteed and private nonguaranteed) and other private credits.

Data sources

Data are compiled from a variety of public and private sources, including the World Bank's Debtor Reporting System, the IMF's International Financial Statistics and Balance of Payments databases, and other sources mentioned in *About the data*. These data are also published in the World Bank's *Global Development Finance 2007*.

6.9 Financial flows from Development Assistance Committee members

Net disbursements

	Official development assistance[a]				Other official flows[a]	Private flows[a]					Net grants by NGOs[a]	Total net flows[a]
	Total 2005	Bilateral grants 2005	Bilateral loans 2005	Contributions to multilateral institutions 2005	2005	Total 2005	Foreign direct investment 2005	Bilateral portfolio investment 2005	Multilateral portfolio investment 2005	Private export credits 2005	2005	2005
$ millions												
Australia	1,680	1,449	..	231	74	2,786	1,588	1,066	..	132	825	5,366
Austria	1,573	1,244	–12	341	310	2,192	2,090	0	..	102	139	4,215
Belgium	1,963	1,328	–20	655	391	539	1,422	..	..	–884	249	3,142
Canada	3,756	2,853	–20	923	–534	9,178	6,647	1,744	..	787	973	13,373
Denmark	2,109	1,384	–27	751	–8	33	33	..	..	..	81	2,215
Finland	902	591	6	305	..	723	149	736	..	–161	16	1,642
France	10,026	7,707	–468	2,787	–1,390	7,107	6,856	1,163	..	–911	..	15,744
Germany	10,082	8,248	–801	2,635	7,055	11,399	12,986	–1,504	47	–131	1,523	30,059
Greece	384	207	..	178	..	325	325	..	..	..	1	709
Ireland	719	482	..	237	..	4,271	..	4,271	..	..	308	5,298
Italy	5,091	2,213	57	2,821	–1,125	44	951	–2,358	..	1,451	94	4,103
Japan	13,147	9,195	1,212	2,740	–2,421	12,278	14,472	1,158	81	–3,433	255	23,259
Luxembourg	256	187	..	69	..	..	..	..	..	..	8	265
Netherlands	5,115	3,696	–13	1,432	152	17,091	2,348	4,604	–474	10,614	422	22,781
New Zealand	274	224	..	50	7	26	26	..	..	..	94	401
Norway	2,786	1,968	64	754	5	..	..	..	..	..	..	2,791
Portugal	377	201	17	159	–3	728	556	0	..	172	6	1,109
Spain	3,018	2,020	–157	1,155	67	3,716	4,158	0	..	–442	..	6,801
Sweden	3,362	2,247	9	1,106	–4	159	430	0	..	–271	29	3,545
Switzerland	1,767	1,380	20	367	..	5,375	6,827	0	–722	–729	332	7,474
United Kingdom	10,767	8,244	–80	2,603	–99	34,924	29,865	5,683	..	–625	726	46,318
United States	27,622	26,042	–762	2,343	–1,048	69,206	18,965	50,091	255	–104	8,629	104,410
Total	**106,777**	**83,109**	**–976**	**24,644**	**1,430**	**182,100**	**110,695**	**66,652**	**–814**	**5,567**	**14,712**	**305,019**

Official development assistance

	Net disbursements[b]				Gross disbursements[b]		Commitments[b]		Net disbursements[a]			
	total $ millions		per capita $		total $ millions		total $ millions		% of GNI		% of general government disbursement	
	2000	2005	2000	2005	2000	2005	2000	2005	2000	2005	2000	2005
Australia	1,424	1,557	74	77	1,424	1,557	1,653	1,907	0.27	0.25	0.73	0.68
Austria	632	1,539	78	187	635	1,553	823	1,586	0.23	0.52	0.44	1.04
Belgium	1,191	1,924	116	184	1,223	1,975	1,223	2,062	0.36	0.53	0.72	1.06
Canada	2,165	3,410	70	105	2,195	3,429	2,477	3,395	0.25	0.34	0.59	0.85
Denmark	2,441	2,076	457	382	2,467	2,140	2,313	2,446	1.06	0.81	1.93	1.54
Finland	522	883	101	168	532	888	497	1,117	0.31	0.46	0.63	0.92
France	5,931	9,893	101	163	7,223	11,377	6,774	11,970	0.30	0.47	0.60	0.88
Germany	7,089	10,013	86	121	8,182	11,515	8,061	12,435	0.27	0.36	0.59	0.77
Greece	348	372	32	34	348	372	348	372	0.20	0.17	0.38	0.37
Ireland	365	703	96	176	365	703	365	703	0.29	0.42	0.77	1.05
Italy	2,073	4,958	36	85	2,409	5,127	2,435	5,489	0.13	0.29	0.27	0.60
Japan	12,786	13,534	101	106	15,429	19,190	16,199	19,934	0.28	0.28	0.74	0.78
Luxembourg	179	248	406	552	179	248	179	248	0.71	0.82	1.61	1.63
Netherlands	4,774	5,036	300	308	4,914	5,120	5,240	4,367	0.84	0.82	1.86	1.79
New Zealand	184	251	48	61	184	251	195	340	0.25	0.27	0.54	0.62
Norway	1,766	2,494	393	538	1,775	2,494	1,572	2,535	0.76	0.94	1.77	2.20
Portugal	417	371	41	36	642	376	642	376	0.26	0.21	0.56	0.43
Spain	1,895	2,911	47	67	2,202	3,393	2,202	3,393	0.22	0.27	0.53	0.70
Sweden	2,407	3,377	271	373	2,408	3,377	1,925	3,749	0.80	0.94	1.31	1.67
Switzerland	1,258	1,757	175	236	1,261	1,764	1,281	1,707	0.34	0.44	1.07	1.32
United Kingdom	6,031	10,640	103	177	6,099	11,030	6,099	11,030	0.32	0.47	0.83	1.09
United States	10,861	26,888	39	91	11,851	27,682	13,757	27,926	0.10	0.22	0.30	0.60
Total	**66,740**	**104,835**	**79**	**119**	**73,945**	**115,561**	**76,258**	**119,086**	**0.22**	**0.33**	**0.57**	**0.80**

Note: Components may not sum to totals because of gaps in reporting.
a. At current prices and exchange rates. b. At 2004 prices and exchange rates.

Financial flows from Development Assistance Committee members 6.9

About the data

The flows of official and private financial resources from the members of the Development Assistance Committee (DAC) of the Organisation for Economic Co-operation and Development (OECD) to developing economies are compiled by DAC, based principally on reporting by DAC members using standard questionnaires issued by the DAC Secretariat.

DAC exists to help its members coordinate their development assistance and to encourage the expansion and improve the effectiveness of the aggregate resources flowing to recipient economies. In this capacity DAC monitors the flow of all financial resources, but its main concern is official development assistance (ODA). Grants or loans to countries and territories on the DAC list of aid recipients have to meet three criteria to be counted as ODA. They are undertaken by the official sector. They promote economic development and welfare as the main objective. And they are provided at concessional financial terms (if a loan they have a grant element of at least 25 percent, calculated at a discount rate of 10 percent). The DAC Statistical Reporting Directives provide the most detailed explanation of this definition and all ODA-related rules.

This definition excludes nonconcessional flows from official creditors, which are classified as "other official flows," and aid for military purposes. Transfer payments to private individuals, such as pensions, reparations, and insurance payouts, are in general not counted. In addition to financial flows, technical cooperation is included in ODA. Most expenditures for peacekeeping under UN mandates and assistance to refugees are counted in ODA. Also included are contributions to multilateral institutions, such as the United Nations and its specialized agencies, and concessional funding to multilateral development banks. In 1999, to avoid double counting of extrabudgetary expenditures reported by DAC countries and flows reported by the United Nations, all UN agencies revised their data to include only regular budgetary expenditures since 1990 (except for the World Food Programme and the United Nations High Commissioner for Refugees, which revised their data from 1996 onward).

DAC has revised the list of countries and territories that are counted as aid recipients. These revisions will govern aid reporting for three years, starting with 2005 flows. In the past DAC distinguished aid going to Part I and Part II countries. Part I countries, the recipients of ODA, comprised many of the countries classified by the World Bank as low- and middle-income economies. Part II countries, whose assistance was designated official aid, included the more advanced countries of Central and Eastern Europe, countries of the former Soviet Union, and certain advanced developing countries and territories. This distinction has been dropped. ODA recipients now comprise all low- and middle-income countries, except those that are members of the Group of Eight or the European Union (including countries with a firm date for EU accession).The content and structure of tables 6.9 through 6.12 have been revised to reflect this change. Because official aid flows are quite small relative to ODA, the net effect of these changes is believed to be minor.

Flows are transfers of resources, either in cash or in the form of commodities or services measured on a cash basis. Short-term capital transactions (with one year or less maturity) are not counted. Repayments of the principal (but not interest) of ODA loans are recorded as negative flows. Proceeds from official equity investments in a developing country are reported as ODA, while proceeds from their later sale are recorded as negative flows.

Because the table is based on donor country reports, it does not provide a complete picture of the resources received by developing economies for two reasons. First, flows from DAC members are only part of the aggregate resource flows to these economies. Second, the data that record contributions to multilateral institutions measure the flow of resources made available to those institutions by DAC members, not the flow of resources from those institutions to developing and transition economies.

Aid as a share of gross national income (GNI), aid per capita, and ODA as a share of the general government disbursements of the donor are calculated by the OECD. The denominators used in calculating these ratios may differ from corresponding values elsewhere in this book because of differences in timing or definitions.

Definitions

• **Official development assistance** comprises flows that meet the DAC definition of ODA and are made to countries and territories on the DAC list of aid recipients. • **Bilateral grants** are transfers of money or in kind for which no repayment is required. • **Bilateral loans** are loans extended by governments or official agencies that have a grant element of at least 25 percent (calculated at a rate of discount of 10 percent). • **Contributions to multilateral institutions** are concessional funding received by multilateral institutions from DAC members in the form of grants or capital subscriptions. • **Other official flows** are transactions by the official sector whose main objective is other than development or whose grant element is less than 25 percent. • **Private flows** consist of flows at market terms financed from private sector resources in donor countries. They include changes in holdings of private long-term assets by residents of the reporting country. • **Foreign direct investment** is investment by residents of DAC member countries to acquire a lasting management interest (at least 10 percent of voting stock) in an enterprise operating in the recipient country. The data reflect changes in the net worth of subsidiaries in recipient countries whose parent company is in the DAC source country. • **Bilateral portfolio investment** covers bank lending and the purchase of bonds, shares, and real estate by residents of DAC member countries in recipient countries. • **Multilateral portfolio investment** records the transactions of private banks and nonbanks in DAC member countries in the securities issued by multilateral institutions. • **Private export credits** are loans extended to recipient countries by the private sector in DAC member countries to promote trade; they may be supported by an official guarantee. • **Net grants by nongovernmental organizations (NGOs)** are private grants by nongovernmental organizations, net of subsidies from the official sector. • **Total net flows** comprise ODA or official aid flows, other official flows, private flows, and net grants by nongovernmental organizations. • **Net disbursements** are gross disbursements of grants and loans minus repayments of principal on earlier loans. • **Gross disbursements** are the actual international transfer of financial resources and goods and services (valued at the cost to the donor). • **Commitments** are firm obligations, expressed in writing and backed by the necessary funds, undertaken by an official donor to provide specified assistance to a recipient country or a multilateral organization. • **Aid as a percentage of GNI** is the donor's contribution of ODA as a share of its gross national income. • **Aid as a percentage of general government disbursements** is the donor's contribution of ODA as a share of public spending.

Data sources

Data on financial flows are compiled by OECD-DAC and published in its annual statistical report, *Geographical Distribution of Financial Flows to Aid Recipients* and its annual *Development Cooperation Report*. Data are available electronically on the OECD's *International Development Statistics* CD-ROM and at www.oecd.org/dac/stats/idsonline.

6.10 Allocation of bilateral aid from Development Assistance Committee members

Aid by purpose and tying status

	Total		Share of bilateral ODA commitment %									
	$ millions[a]		Investment projects, program aid, and other resource provisions		Debt-related aid		Emergency assistance and developmental food aid		Technical cooperation and administrative charges		Untied aid[b]	
	2000	2005	2000	2005	2000	2005	2000	2005	2000	2005	2000	2005
Australia	758	1,449	14.9	7.3	1.1	1.4	14.2	22.4	60.0	56.3	77.4	71.9
Austria	378	1,260	18.8	4.2	32.9	69.4	8.5	8.0	26.7	15.7	59.2	88.7
Belgium	498	1,360	14.5	11.5	10.6	35.1	8.1	9.1	69.0	40.2	85.7	95.7
Canada	1,412	2,816	10.9	36.3	0.9	16.7	19.9	14.1	26.1	33.2	24.9	59.4
Denmark	940	1,739	67.1	50.0	0.0	3.8	10.8	2.2	13.3	9.0	80.5	86.5
Finland	200	693	15.8	33.1	..	0.2	16.8	21.6	37.5	9.5	89.5	95.1
France	3,412	8,862	27.0	19.3	23.4	42.4	5.2	8.2	43.5	30.2	68.0	94.7
Germany	2,968	9,236	26.1	28.6	2.9	42.7	6.6	4.1	61.4	24.1	93.2	93.0
Greece	99	207	40.5	12.5	..	0.0	7.7	13.5	22.6	51.7	23.5	73.6
Ireland	154	482	66.3	67.2	..	0.1	12.7	17.6	5.1	9.1	..	100.0
Italy	729	2,686	42.1	21.7	29.7	62.6	15.0	3.1	6.6	5.5	38.2	92.1
Japan	13,854	17,265	87.1	46.4	10.4	32.9	1.0	3.9	24.9	15.0	86.4	89.6
Luxembourg	93	187	80.1	68.7	..	0.0	12.6	12.8	3.6	8.0	96.7	99.1
Netherlands	2,834	3,529	32.2	55.8	6.7	2.5	13.9	16.3	18.5	22.0	95.3	96.2
New Zealand	85	224	90.4	48.9	..	0.0	3.4	29.3	8.8	25.0	..	92.3
Norway	795	2,033	44.0	48.0	0.9	0.1	25.6	20.3	18.1	22.5	97.7	99.6
Portugal	320	224	1.5	26.3	53.6	1.5	1.1	5.7	29.5	58.1	98.2	60.7
Spain	913	2,362	17.9	21.6	6.6	38.7	4.6	6.1	17.1	26.1	47.2	86.6
Sweden	1,093	2,256	58.9	58.3	3.3	2.3	20.2	17.9	13.9	11.8	85.4	98.3
Switzerland	630	1,407	52.4	41.0	0.9	15.9	23.1	23.4	16.7	13.1	93.6	97.4
United Kingdom	2,759	8,509	42.5	16.8	5.6	41.5	12.5	7.4	31.4	14.9	91.5	100.0
United States	10,030	25,836	24.3	24.4	1.3	16.3	21.0	18.1	56.0	41.9	..	..
Total	**44,954**	**94,623**	**47.7**	**30.8**	**7.8**	**27.5**	**10.5**	**11.0**	**35.5**	**26.5**	**81.1**	**91.8**

Aid by sector

	Social infrastructure and services						Economic infrastructure and services		Production sectors		Multi-sector or cross-cutting	Total sector allocable
	Total	Education	Health	Population	Water supply and sanitation	Government and civil society	Total	Transport and communications	Total	Agriculture		
Share of bilateral ODA commitment (%)	2005	2005	2005	2005	2005	2005	2005	2005	2005	2005	2005	2005
Australia	45.2	5.6	6.1	2.9	2.4	21.4	3.8	3.0	6.6	5.3	14.1	69.8
Austria	15.2	7.6	2.2	0.1	1.3	3.3	0.7	0.1	1.9	0.8	1.6	19.4
Belgium	32.9	8.9	6.2	1.4	2.8	7.5	6.2	2.7	4.8	3.8	3.3	47.1
Canada	39.8	8.8	10.3	1.5	1.5	15.6	4.3	0.8	5.5	4.4	6.0	55.6
Denmark	41.3	7.4	5.6	0.9	10.3	13.9	14.9	10.5	18.3	13.2	10.2	84.6
Finland	36.5	7.1	4.0	1.0	6.2	16.1	9.2	1.4	7.4	6.2	16.6	69.6
France	25.2	16.5	3.1	0.1	1.3	1.2	9.4	6.4	2.2	1.4	4.9	41.7
Germany	18.2	4.4	1.3	0.8	4.1	5.3	12.0	1.7	3.1	2.3	16.2	49.4
Greece	55.5	18.4	15.3	0.2	0.3	18.6	8.9	8.5	1.2	0.4	5.3	70.9
Ireland	54.0	12.0	20.0	2.0	3.5	14.9	1.5	1.1	3.8	3.4	4.2	63.6
Italy	10.5	2.0	3.8	0.4	2.6	1.4	10.9	0.3	1.3	0.7	4.4	27.1
Japan	20.0	4.9	1.2	0.0	12.3	0.6	23.4	17.1	7.7	5.8	3.1	54.3
Luxembourg	51.8	14.9	18.4	4.6	6.6	2.5	2.9	0.6	5.4	3.8	10.5	70.6
Netherlands	37.6	14.1	3.4	3.3	5.4	8.8	8.8	1.2	4.7	3.9	14.3	65.4
New Zealand	34.7	14.9	5.0	2.3	1.0	9.9	1.2	0.5	4.0	2.2	3.5	43.3
Norway	43.0	9.5	7.7	2.1	2.1	16.1	7.9	0.6	5.5	4.0	10.5	66.9
Portugal	55.8	28.6	4.4	0.0	1.1	11.1	13.1	12.2	2.7	1.3	8.4	80.0
Spain	26.8	9.2	4.9	1.2	2.5	4.5	8.5	3.2	4.4	3.0	8.2	47.9
Sweden	36.5	4.9	4.8	4.1	3.0	16.2	5.9	2.6	4.9	2.9	7.2	54.5
Switzerland	19.6	2.9	2.6	0.3	2.5	10.2	6.2	2.2	7.7	4.4	13.4	46.8
United Kingdom	25.3	3.9	3.3	3.6	0.5	12.8	2.7	1.7	3.2	1.9	3.9	35.1
United States	42.8	2.7	4.9	5.2	3.9	18.3	7.8	4.7	5.4	2.5	4.4	60.4
Average	**30.5**	**6.1**	**3.8**	**2.3**	**4.8**	**9.7**	**10.6**	**5.2**	**5.2**	**3.3**	**6.5**	**52.8**

a. At current prices and exchange rates. b. Excludes technical cooperation and administrative charges.

Allocation of bilateral aid from Development Assistance Committee members 6.10

About the data

Aid can be used in many ways. The sectoral destination to which aid goes, the form that aid takes, and the procurement restrictions attached to aid are among important factors that influence aid effectiveness. The data on allocation of official development assistance (ODA) presented in this table are based principally on reporting by members of the Organisation for Economic Co-operation and Development (OECD) Development Assistance Committee (DAC). For more detailed explanation of ODA, see *About the data* for table 6.9.

The sector of destination for an ODA contribution is defined as the specific area of the recipient country's economic or social structure that the transfer is intended to foster. The DAC sector classification comprises a hierarchy of three levels. The top level is grouped by themes, including social infrastructure and services, economic infrastructure and services, production sectors, and multisector cross-cutting areas. The second level includes six sectors under social infrastructure and services (for example, education and health), five sectors under economic infrastructure and services (for example, transport and storage), and three production sectors (for example, agriculture). The third level comprises subsectors, such as basic education and basic health. Some contributions are not susceptible to allocation by sectors and are reported as nonsector allocable aid. Examples include aid for general development purposes, balance of payment support, aid relating to debt, emergency assistance, administrative costs of donors, and support to nongovernmental organizations.

The form in which an ODA contribution reaches the benefiting sector or the economy in general is also important. A distinction is made between technical cooperation and resource provision. Aid in the form of technical cooperation includes grants to nationals of aid recipient countries receiving education or training at home or abroad, and payments to consultants, advisers, and similar personnel as well as teachers and administrators serving in recipient countries (including the cost of associated equipment). Because technical cooperation is spent mostly in the donor economy, it is combined with the administrative costs of donor aid programs. Resource provision involves mainly cash or in-kind transfers and financing of capital projects, with deliverables being financial support and the provision of commodities and supplies.

Two other types of aid are presented because they serve distinctive purposes. Debt-related aid aims to provide debt relief on liabilities that recipient countries have difficulty servicing. Thus, this type of aid may not provide a full value of new resource flows for development, in particular for heavily indebted poor countries. Emergency assistance and development food aid aim to provide humanitarian relief to lessen the adverse impact of sudden disasters and to support food programs in nonemergency situations. These types of aid do not generally contribute to financing long-term development.

The proportion of untied aid is reported here because tying arrangements may prevent recipients from obtaining the best value for their money and so reduces the value of the aid received. Tying arrangements require recipients to purchase goods and services from the donor country or from a specified group of countries. Such arrangements may be justified on the grounds that they prevent a recipient from misappropriating or mismanaging aid receipts, but they may also be motivated by a desire to benefit suppliers in the donor country. The same volume of aid may have different purchasing power depending on the relative costs of suppliers in countries to which the aid is tied and the degree to which each recipient's aid basket is untied.

Reporting on the sectoral destination and the form of aid by donors may not be complete. Furthermore, measures of aid allocation may differ from the perspectives of donors and recipients because of difference in classification, availability of information, and time of recording.

Definitions

• **Bilateral (ODA) commitments** are firm obligations, expressed in writing and backed by the necessary funds, undertaken by official bilateral donors to provide specified assistance to a recipient country or a multilateral organization. Bilateral commitments are recorded in the full amount of expected transfer, irrespective of the time required for completing disbursements. • **Investment projects, program aid, and other resource provisions** are aid contributions in the form of cash transfers, aid in kind, and the financing of capital projects. Their aim is to increase or improve the recipient's stock of physical capital and to support recipient's development plans and other activities with finance and commodity supply. • **Debt-related aid** groups all actions relating to debt, including forgiveness, swaps, buybacks, rescheduling, and refinancing. • **Emergency assistance and developmental food aid** comprise emergency and distress relief (including aid to refugees and assistance for disaster preparedness) as well as all food aid–related costs. • **Technical cooperation** refers to the provision of resources whose main aim is to augment the stock of human intellectual capital, such as the level of knowledge, skills, technical know-how, and productive aptitude of the population in the aid recipient country (including the cost of associated equipment). Contributions mainly take the form of the supply of human resources from donors or action directed to human resources (such as training or advice). Assistance provided specifically to facilitate implementation of a capital project is not included. • **Administrative charges** include the total current budget outlays of institutions responsible for the formulation and implementation of donor's aid programs as well as other administrative costs incurred by donors in the process of aid delivery. • **Untied aid** is the share of ODA that is not subject to restrictions by donors on procurement sources. • **Social infrastructure and services** refer to efforts to develop the human resources potential of aid recipients. • **Education** includes general teaching and instruction at all levels, as well as construction specifically to improve or adapt educational establishments. Training in a particular field, such as agriculture, is reported against the sector concerned. • **Health** covers assistance to hospitals, clinics, other medical and dental services, public health administration, and medical insurance programs. • **Population** covers all activities related to family planning and research into population problems. • **Water supply and sanitation** cover assistance for water supply and use, sanitation, and water resources development (including rivers). • **Government and civil society** include assistance to strengthen the administrative apparatus and government planning, and activities promoting good governance and strengthening civil society. • **Economic infrastructure and services** group assistance for networks, utilities, and services that facilitate economic activity. • **Transport and communications** cover road, rail, water, and air transport and post and telecommunications, radio, television, and print media. • **Production sectors** refer to contributions to all directly productive sectors. • **Agriculture** includes agricultural sector policy, agricultural development and inputs, crop and livestock production, and agricultural credit, cooperatives, and research. • **Multisector or cross-cutting** includes support for projects that straddle several sectors. • **Total sector allocable** is the sum of aid that can be assigned to a specific sector or multisector.

Data sources

Data on aid flows are published by OECD-DAC in its annual statistical report, *Geographical Distribution of Financial Flows to Aid Recipients*, and its annual *Development Cooperation Report*. Data are available electronically on the OECD's *International Development Statistics* CD-ROM and at www.oecd.org/dac/stats/idsonline.

6.11 Aid dependency

	Net official development assistance		Aid per capita		Aid dependency ratios							
					Aid as % of GNI		Aid as % of gross capital formation		Aid as % of imports of goods and services		Aid as % of central government expenditure	
	$ millions		$									
	2000	2005	2000	2005	2000	2005	2000	2005	2000	2005	2000	2005
Afghanistan	136	2,775	..	..	..	37.8	..	151.6	..	..	..	316.9
Albania	317	319	104	102	8.4	3.7	32.5	16.1	21.0	8.1	..	..
Algeria	201	371	7	11	0.4	0.4	1.5	1.2	..	..	1.8	..
Angola	302	442	22	28	4.1	1.5	22.0	17.9	4.1	2.3	..	..
Argentina	53	100	1	3	0.0	0.1	0.1	0.3	0.1	0.2	..	..
Armenia	216	193	70	64	11.0	3.9	60.6	13.3	21.2	8.4	..	21.7
Australia												
Austria												
Azerbaijan	139	223	17	27	2.8	2.0	12.8	4.7	5.8	2.5	..	..
Bangladesh	1,168	1,321	9	9	2.4	2.1	10.8	9.0	11.7	8.6	..	..
Belarus	40	54	4	5	0.3	0.2	1.2	0.6	0.5	0.3	1.5	0.6
Belgium												
Benin	238	349	33	41	10.6	8.2	55.9	41.6	31.7	..	..	32.9
Bolivia	472	583	57	63	5.8	6.5	31.0	45.4	19.3	17.3	..	23.5
Bosnia and Herzegovina	737	546	192	140	13.1	5.2	68.8	28.6	17.4	6.7	..	15.2
Botswana	31	71	17	40	0.5	0.7	1.4	2.2	1.0	1.4	..	..
Brazil	232	192	1	1	0.0	0.0	0.2	0.1	0.2	0.2	..	..
Bulgaria[a]	311	..	39	..	2.5	..	13.5	..	3.7	..	7.6	..
Burkina Faso	335	660	30	50	12.9	12.8	56.8	61.8	48.5	..	..	108.9
Burundi	93	365	14	48	12.8	46.8	212.5	378.2	55.8	97.7	..	..
Cambodia	396	538	31	38	11.2	9.1	64.2	44.2	16.1	11.0	..	112.6
Cameroon	379	414	26	25	4.0	2.5	22.5	11.6	12.8	..	..	..
Canada												
Central African Republic	75	95	20	24	8.0	7.0	72.8	..	..	..	..	..
Chad	130	380	16	39	9.5	8.6	40.4	39.8	..	..	..	..
Chile	49	152	3	9	0.1	0.1	0.3	0.6	0.2	0.3	..	0.7
China	1,728	1,757	1	1	0.1	0.1	0.4	0.2	0.6	0.2	..	..
Hong Kong, China[a]	4	..	1	..	0.0	..	0.0	..	0.0	..	..	..
Colombia	187	511	4	11	0.2	0.4	1.6	2.2	1.1	1.6	..	1.3
Congo, Dem. Rep.	177	1,828	4	32	4.5	26.9	118.7	181.2	..	..	15.2	..
Congo, Rep.	33	1,449	10	362	1.5	36.8	4.9	118.1	1.6	35.7	..	..
Costa Rica	11	30	3	7	0.1	0.2	0.4	0.6	0.1	0.3	0.3	0.7
Côte d'Ivoire	351	119	21	7	3.6	0.8	31.2	6.8	7.9	1.5	..	4.3
Croatia	66	125	15	28	0.4	0.3	1.8	1.0	0.6	0.5	0.8	0.8
Cuba	44	88	4	8	..	..	..	..	..	..	..	..
Czech Republic[a]	438	..	43	..	0.8	..	2.6	..	1.1	..	2.3	..
Denmark												
Dominican Republic	56	77	7	9	0.3	0.3	1.2	1.3	0.5	0.6	2.1	..
Ecuador	146	210	12	16	1.0	0.6	4.6	2.4	2.3	1.5	..	..
Egypt, Arab Rep.	1,328	926	20	13	1.3	1.0	6.8	5.7	5.6	2.6	6.6	..
El Salvador	180	199	29	29	1.4	1.2	8.1	7.6	3.0	2.4	..	58.0
Eritrea	176	355	49	81	27.7	36.9	86.9	182.2	34.5	..	..	..
Estonia[a]	64	..	47	..	1.2	..	4.2	..	1.2	..	..	..
Ethiopia	686	1,937	11	27	8.8	17.4	42.7	66.0	41.0	39.2	..	..
Finland												
France												
Gabon	12	54	9	39	0.3	0.7	0.9	3.3	0.5	..	..	..
Gambia, The	49	58	37	38	12.2	13.0	66.9	50.4	..	19.6	..	..
Georgia	169	310	36	69	5.3	4.8	25.7	18.4	13.6	8.9	47.9	27.9
Germany												
Ghana	600	1,120	30	51	12.4	10.6	50.5	36.0	17.3	16.4	..	..
Greece												
Guatemala	263	254	24	20	1.4	0.8	7.7	4.2	4.4	2.5	12.5	7.3
Guinea	153	182	18	19	5.0	5.6	22.4	46.1	15.7	..	..	..
Guinea-Bissau	80	79	59	50	39.5	27.4	329.8	180.0	..	..	..	..
Haiti	208	515	26	60	5.5	12.1	20.8	..	15.1	28.7	..	..

Aid dependency

	Net official development assistance		Aid per capita		Aid dependency ratios							
	$ millions		$		Aid as % of GNI		Aid as % of gross capital formation		Aid as % of imports of goods and services		Aid as % of central government expenditure	
	2000	2005	2000	2005	2000	2005	2000	2005	2000	2005	2000	2005
Honduras	449	681	70	94	7.7	8.6	24.5	27.5	12.8	12.4	..	..
Hungary[a]	252	..	25	..	0.6	..	1.8	..	0.6	..	1.3	..
India	1,463	1,724	1	2	0.3	0.2	1.3	0.6	1.8	..	2.0	..
Indonesia	1,654	2,524	8	11	1.1	0.9	4.5	4.0	2.5	2.5	..	..
Iran, Islamic Rep.	130	104	2	2	0.1	0.1	0.4	0.2	0.7	..	0.2	0.3
Iraq	100	21,654	..	..	..	..	..	..	..	..	..	..
Ireland												
Israel[a]	800	..	127	..	0.7	..	3.2	..	1.4	..	1.5	..
Italy												
Jamaica	10	36	4	13	0.1	0.4	0.5	1.2	0.2	0.5	0.4	1.1
Japan												
Jordan	552	622	114	114	6.4	4.8	30.9	20.7	8.7	5.1	24.1	13.9
Kazakhstan	189	229	13	15	1.1	0.4	5.7	1.5	1.8	0.7	7.5	2.2
Kenya	510	768	17	22	4.1	4.1	23.0	24.4	12.9	11.4	23.9	..
Korea, Dem. Rep.	73	81	3	4	..	..	..	..	..	..	..	..
Korea, Rep.[a]	–198	..	–4	..	0.0	..	–0.1	..	–0.1	..	–0.2	..
Kuwait[a]	3	..	1	..	0.0	..	0.1	..	0.0	..	..	..
Kyrgyz Republic	215	268	44	52	16.7	11.4	78.3	76.5	28.5	18.0	99.2	..
Lao PDR	282	296	53	50	17.0	11.4	77.7	32.2	44.1	..	..	..
Latvia[a]	91	..	38	..	1.2	..	4.9	..	2.3	..	4.1	..
Lebanon	199	243	59	68	1.2	1.1	5.9	5.5	..	1.3	3.8	..
Lesotho	37	69	21	38	3.4	3.9	10.1	11.7	4.4	4.8	..	..
Liberia	67	236	22	72	17.4	54.1	..	270.9	..	..	..	..
Libya	14	24	3	4	..	0.1	0.3	..	0.2	0.2	..	..
Lithuania[a]	99	..	28	..	0.9	..	4.4	..	1.6	..	3.2	..
Macedonia, FYR	251	230	125	113	7.1	4.0	31.5	20.0	10.6	6.1	..	..
Madagascar	322	929	20	50	8.4	18.7	55.1	82.4	20.3	127.9	15.6	..
Malawi	446	575	39	45	26.1	28.4	188.7	191.1	65.7	..	..	..
Malaysia	45	32	2	1	0.1	0.0	0.2	0.1	0.0	0.0	0.3	..
Mali	359	691	31	51	15.0	13.6	60.4	57.5	34.4	..	..	..
Mauritania	211	190	80	62	19.4	9.9	101.0	23.1	..	..	..	..
Mauritius	20	32	17	26	0.5	0.5	1.8	2.2	0.7	0.7	2.2	2.5
Mexico	–56	189	–1	2	0.0	0.0	0.0	0.1	0.0	0.1	–0.1	..
Moldova	123	192	29	46	9.4	5.9	39.7	22.1	11.3	6.7	32.9	21.9
Mongolia	217	212	91	83	23.1	11.6	63.5	31.8	27.5	..	..	..
Morocco	419	652	15	22	1.3	1.3	5.3	4.9	3.1	2.7	..	4.0
Mozambique	876	1,286	49	65	24.7	20.7	69.1	95.2	49.7	38.4	..	..
Myanmar	106	145	2	3	..	..	..	..	4.0	..	..	..
Namibia	152	123	80	61	4.4	2.0	22.8	7.9	8.2	..	14.1	..
Nepal	387	428	16	16	7.0	5.8	29.0	20.0	21.2	15.3	..	34.4
Netherlands												
New Zealand												
Nicaragua	561	740	114	144	15.0	15.4	47.2	51.3	23.6	21.6	74.2	71.7
Niger	208	515	18	37	11.7	15.2	101.4	81.8	43.0	..	..	..
Nigeria	174	6,437	1	49	0.4	7.4	1.9	31.2	1.1	20.1	..	..
Norway												
Oman	45	31	18	12	0.2	..	1.9	..	0.6	0.2	0.9	..
Pakistan	692	1,666	5	11	1.0	1.5	5.4	8.9	4.8	5.2	5.6	10.4
Panama	16	20	5	6	0.1	0.1	0.6	0.6	0.2	0.2	0.6	..
Papua New Guinea	275	266	52	45	8.2	..	..	..	13.7	8.2	26.2	..
Paraguay	82	51	15	9	1.2	0.7	6.1	3.2	2.3	1.2	..	4.2
Peru	398	398	15	14	0.8	0.5	3.7	2.7	3.4	1.9	4.2	2.9
Philippines	575	562	8	7	0.7	0.5	3.6	3.7	1.1	1.0	4.3	3.2
Poland[a]	1,396	..	36	..	0.8	..	3.3	..	2.3	..	..	..
Portugal												
Puerto Rico												

Aid dependency

	Net official development assistance		Aid per capita		Aid dependency ratios							
					Aid as % of GNI		Aid as % of gross capital formation		Aid as % of imports of goods and services		Aid as % of central government expenditure	
	$ millions		$									
	2000	2005	2000	2005	2000	2005	2000	2005	2000	2005	2000	2005
Romania[a]	432	..	19	..	1.2	..	6.0	..	2.9	..	..	..
Russian Federation[a]	1,561	..	11	..	0.6	..	3.2	..	2.2	..	..	..
Rwanda	321	576	40	64	17.9	27.1	101.3	119.5	71.2	82.0	..	..
Saudi Arabia	22	26	1	1	0.0	0.0	0.1	0.1	0.0	0.0	..	..
Senegal	423	689	41	59	9.9	8.5	46.2	35.8	21.9	..	70.9	..
Serbia and Montenegro	1,134	1,132	139	140	13.2	4.4	92.9	23.5	..	..	..	..
Sierra Leone	181	343	40	62	29.4	29.6	356.3	191.6	68.8	67.5	98.8	..
Singapore[a]	1	..	0	..	0.0	..	0.0	..	0.0	..	0.0	..
Slovak Republic[a]	113	..	21	..	0.6	..	2.1	..	0.7	..	..	..
Slovenia[a]	61	..	31	..	0.3	..	1.2	..	0.5	..	0.8	..
Somalia	101	236	14	29	..	..	..	..	..	..	..	..
South Africa	487	700	11	15	0.4	0.3	2.3	1.6	1.3	0.9	1.3	1.0
Spain												
Sri Lanka	276	1,189	14	61	1.8	5.1	6.0	19.3	3.2	11.4	7.3	24.1
Sudan	220	1,829	7	50	2.1	7.1	9.7	28.5	8.5	19.9	..	..
Swaziland	13	46	13	41	0.9	1.7	4.8	9.1	0.9	2.0	..	..
Sweden												
Switzerland												
Syrian Arab Republic	158	78	9	4	0.9	0.3	5.0	1.5	2.4	0.7	..	..
Tajikistan	124	241	20	37	13.1	10.9	109.9	73.0	..	13.9	160.3	..
Tanzania	1,019	1,505	29	39	11.4	12.5	63.7	65.8	45.7	36.6	..	..
Thailand	698	–171	11	–3	0.6	–0.1	2.5	–0.3	0.9	–0.1	..	–0.6
Togo	70	87	13	14	5.4	4.0	29.4	22.4	10.5	..	..	25.5
Trinidad and Tobago	–2	–2	–1	–2	0.0	0.0	–0.1	..	0.0	..	..	..
Tunisia	222	376	23	38	1.2	1.4	4.2	5.6	2.1	2.3	4.1	4.5
Turkey	327	464	5	6	0.2	0.1	0.7	0.5	0.5	0.4	0.5	..
Turkmenistan	31	28	7	6	1.2	0.4	3.1	1.5	..	..	..	..
Uganda	817	1,198	34	42	14.1	14.0	69.1	64.8	51.9	42.9	92.4	..
Ukraine	541	410	11	9	1.8	0.5	8.5	2.6	2.8	0.9	6.4	1.3
United Arab Emirates[a]	3	..	1	..	0.0	..	0.0	..	..	..	..	..
United Kingdom												
United States												
Uruguay	17	15	5	4	0.1	0.1	0.6	0.7	0.3	0.3	0.3	0.3
Uzbekistan	186	172	8	7	1.4	1.2	8.3	5.4	..	..	..	..
Venezuela, RB	76	49	3	2	0.1	0.0	0.3	0.2	0.3	0.1	0.3	0.1
Vietnam	1,681	1,905	21	23	5.5	3.7	18.2	10.3	9.3	4.7	..	..
West Bank and Gaza	637	1,102	215	304	13.3	25.0	47.4	106.7	..	..	..	..
Yemen, Rep.	263	336	15	16	3.0	2.5	14.3	8.3	6.2	4.7	..	..
Zambia	795	945	74	81	25.8	13.9	131.4	50.3	53.6	..	..	..
Zimbabwe	176	368	14	28	2.5	11.4	17.5	78.6	..	..	..	..
World	57,760 s	106,372 s	10 w	17 w	0.2 w	0.2 w	0.8 w	.. w	0.6 w	0.7 w	.. w	.. w
Low income	18,718	40,353	9	17	2.3	2.9	9.8	9.9	9.2	..	..	..
Middle income	24,895	46,913	8	15	0.5	0.6	1.9	2.0	1.5	1.5	..	..
Lower middle income	17,560	43,146	7	17	0.6	0.9	2.2	2.7	2.0	2.5	..	..
Upper middle income	6,176	2,776	11	5	0.3	0.1	1.2	0.3	0.7	0.2	..	..
Low & middle income	55,970	106,338	11	20	0.9	1.1	3.7	3.8	2.9	2.9	..	..
East Asia & Pacific	8,589	9,497	5	5	0.5	0.3	1.6	0.8	1.4	0.8	..	..
Europe & Central Asia	11,203	5,731	23	11	1.1	0.2	5.0	1.0	2.6	0.5	..	..
Latin America & Carib.	4,841	6,309	9	11	0.3	0.3	1.2	1.2	0.9	0.9	..	..
Middle East & N. Africa	4,534	26,946	16	88	1.0	3.9	4.1	15.1	3.3	11.2	..	..
South Asia	4,194	9,260	3	6	0.7	0.9	2.9	3.0	3.6	..	..	..
Sub-Saharan Africa	13,194	32,620	20	44	4.1	5.5	21.6	27.3	10.9	13.4	..	..
High income												
Europe EMU												

Note: Regional aggregates include data for economies not specified elsewhere. World and income group totals include aid not allocated by country or region.
a. Starting with 2005 flows, official development assistance will not be reported for these countries.

About the data

Ratios of aid to gross national income (GNI), gross capital formation, imports, and government spending provide a measure of the recipient country's dependency on aid. But care must be taken in drawing policy conclusions. For foreign policy reasons, some countries have traditionally received large amounts of aid. Thus aid dependency ratios may reveal as much about a donor's interest as they do about a recipient's needs. Ratios in Sub-Saharan Africa are generally much higher than those in other regions, and they increased in the 1980s. These high ratios are due only in part to aid flows. Many African countries saw severe erosion in their terms of trade in the 1980s, which, along with weak policies, contributed to falling incomes, imports, and investment. Thus the increase in aid dependency ratios reflects events affecting both the numerator and the denominator.

As defined here, aid includes official development assistance (ODA; see *About the data* for table 6.9). The data cover loans and grants from Development Assistance Committee (DAC) member countries, multilateral organizations, and non-DAC donors. They do not reflect aid given by recipient countries to other developing countries. As a result, some countries that are net donors (such as Saudi Arabia) are shown in the table as aid recipients (see table 6.10a).

The table does not distinguish among different types of aid (program, project, or food aid; emergency assistance; postconflict peacekeeping assistance; or technical cooperation), each of which may have very different effects on the economy. Expenditures on technical cooperation do not always directly benefit the economy to the extent that they defray costs incurred outside the country on the salaries and benefits of technical experts and the overhead costs of firms supplying technical services.

In 1999, to avoid double counting extrabudgetary expenditures reported by DAC countries and flows reported by the United Nations, all UN agencies revised their data since 1990 to include only regular budgetary expenditures (except for the World Food Programme and the United Nations Office of the High Commissioner for Refugees, which revised their data from 1996 onward). These revisions have affected net ODA and official aid and, as a result, aid per capita and aid dependency ratios.

Because the table relies on information from donors, it is not necessarily consistent with information recorded by recipients in the balance of payments, which often excludes all or some technical assistance—particularly payments to expatriates made directly by the donor. Similarly, grant commodity aid may not always be recorded in trade data or in the balance of payments. Moreover, DAC statistics exclude purely military aid.

The nominal values used here may overstate the real value of aid to the recipient. Changes in international prices and in exchange rates can reduce the purchasing power of aid. The practice of tying aid, still prevalent though declining in importance, also tends to reduce its purchasing power (see *About the data* for table 6.10).

The values for population, GNI, gross capital formation, imports of goods and services, and central government expenditure used in computing the ratios are taken from World Bank and International Monetary Fund (IMF) databases. The aggregates also refer to World Bank definitions. Therefore the ratios shown may differ somewhat from those computed and published by the Organisation for Economic Co-operation and Development (OECD). Aid not allocated by country or region—including administrative costs, research on development issues, and aid to nongovernmental organizations—is included in the world total. Thus regional and income group totals do not sum to the world total.

Official development assistance from non-DAC donors, 2001–05 — 6.11a

Net disbursements ($ millions)

	2001	2002	2003	2004	2005
OECD members (non-DAC)					
Czech Republic	26	45	91	108	135
Hungary	..	..	21	70	100
Iceland	10	13	18	21	27
Korea, Rep.	265	279	366	423	752
Poland	36	14	27	118	205
Slovak Republic	8	7	15	28	56
Turkey	64	73	67	339	601
Arab countries					
Kuwait	73	20	138	209	547
Saudi Arabia	490	2,478	2,391	1,734	..
United Arab Emirates	127	156	188	181	141
Other donors					
Israel[a]	93	131	112	84	85
Other donors	2	3	4	22	87
Total	1,194	3,218	3,436	3,759	3,231

Note: China also provides aid, but does not disclose the amount.
a. Includes $50.1 million in 2001, $87.8 million in 2002, $68.8 million in 2003, $47.9 million in 2004, and $49.2 million in 2005 for first-year sustenance expenses for people arriving from developing countries (many of which are experiencing civil war or severe unrest) or people who have left their country for humanitarian or political reasons.
Source: Organisation for Economic Co-operation and Development.

Definitions

• **Net official development assistance** comprises flows (net of repayment of principal) that meet the DAC definition of ODA and are made to countries and territories on the DAC list of aid recipients. See *About the data* for table 6.9. • **Aid per capita** is ODA divided by population. • **Aid dependency ratios** are calculated using values in U.S. dollars converted at official exchange rates. For definitions of GNI, gross capital formation, imports of goods and services, and central government expenditure, see *Definitions* for tables 1.1, 4.8, and 4.11.

Data sources

Data on financial flows are compiled by DAC and published in its annual statistical report, *Geographical Distribution of Financial Flows to Aid Recipients*, and in its annual *Development Cooperation Report*. Data are available in electronic format on the OECD's *International Development Statistics* CD-ROM and at www.oecd.org/dac/stats/idsonline. Data on population, GNI, gross capital formation, imports of goods and services, and central government expenditure are from World Bank and IMF databases.

6.12 Distribution of net aid by Development Assistance Committee members

	Total $ millions 2005	Ten major DAC donors ($ millions) United States 2005	Japan 2005	United Kingdom 2005	Germany 2005	France 2005	Netherlands 2005	Italy 2005	Canada 2005	Sweden 2005	Spain 2005	Other DAC donors $ millions 2005
Afghanistan	2,191.7	1,341.8	71.1	219.9	99.2	19.5	79.1	27.4	89.5	44.2	19.0	181.1
Albania	190.0	42.6	17.6	3.8	30.5	12.6	9.1	8.6	0.6	8.6	7.8	48.1
Algeria	289.7	1.4	1.9	..	2.6	255.0	0.1	9.5	1.9	2.2	–4.0	19.2
Angola	258.2	64.1	26.3	14.1	12.2	23.6	12.8	11.6	4.0	11.2	16.1	62.3
Argentina	77.9	1.5	11.0	..	13.0	12.3	0.3	21.6	3.5	0.4	12.3	2.0
Armenia	148.1	53.6	5.4	6.2	30.0	25.2	11.6	1.2	1.0	1.6	0.4	11.9
Australia												
Austria												
Azerbaijan	109.7	44.1	8.3	0.0	19.1	15.1	5.5	1.2	1.4	1.2	0.1	13.7
Bangladesh	562.9	49.7	–1.0	203.3	46.1	12.2	60.7	1.9	50.8	23.9	0.2	115.3
Belarus	33.7	1.7	0.4	0.1	13.9	3.8	0.2	0.1	0.2	5.7	1.8	5.8
Belgium												
Benin	206.9	23.6	17.9	..	27.6	42.9	22.7	0.0	10.8	1.4	0.5	59.6
Bolivia	388.3	90.6	40.6	–24.3	51.4	16.5	46.7	4.6	14.9	20.8	66.7	59.9
Bosnia and Herzegovina	287.6	46.1	16.7	6.6	26.1	28.5	21.1	2.7	7.7	46.9	6.1	79.2
Botswana	51.9	39.8	–0.9	0.3	3.5	1.4	1.0	..	1.9	0.3	0.2	4.5
Brazil	170.9	–29.6	30.8	6.5	77.0	28.7	15.4	1.5	8.6	2.4	10.2	19.4
Bulgaria												
Burkina Faso	338.5	20.0	18.9	2.6	29.7	79.6	53.8	1.5	16.5	15.2	2.9	97.9
Burundi	180.7	54.7	0.5	14.8	11.4	14.5	22.9	3.4	5.1	5.3	0.7	47.6
Cambodia	344.4	67.5	100.6	21.5	24.8	30.1	8.0	1.9	8.5	14.8	0.7	66.0
Cameroon	336.0	13.6	19.3	4.6	183.0	21.5	17.5	0.8	34.9	8.7	–5.6	37.7
Canada												
Central African Republic	62.2	17.2	0.1	..	3.0	35.0	0.4	0.4	1.6	1.3	0.6	2.7
Chad	166.6	61.8	2.1	–0.7	24.0	44.9	1.6	0.1	6.2	2.5	1.6	22.7
Chile	75.6	–0.1	10.6	1.1	35.2	14.4	0.8	–1.3	3.8	2.4	4.1	4.7
China	1,689.4	19.6	1,064.3	55.5	255.1	153.6	27.8	–12.8	30.0	10.1	8.4	78.0
Hong Kong, China												
Colombia	457.9	334.3	–2.2	1.3	21.5	–2.0	29.9	–6.0	9.1	14.6	31.0	26.7
Congo, Dem. Rep.	1,034.3	141.4	376.3	77.6	51.1	88.0	46.2	1.0	24.8	23.7	9.2	195.1
Congo, Rep.	1,359.5	15.1	0.2	0.6	63.7	1,014.3	6.1	61.2	22.3	2.2	134.2	39.6
Costa Rica	25.0	–12.1	–1.4	5.9	5.4	4.9	3.3	–0.4	3.0	1.0	2.3	13.2
Côte d'Ivoire	151.0	32.7	1.4	3.1	13.2	67.9	2.4	1.2	6.5	3.6	3.6	15.4
Croatia	61.3	21.2	0.5	1.8	7.1	3.5	0.3	–1.5	0.4	5.6	0.3	22.0
Cuba	68.7	10.1	5.8	9.0	3.5	3.5	1.3	0.1	8.0	0.9	15.2	11.3
Czech Republic												
Denmark												
Dominican Republic	56.6	18.9	3.0	0.5	14.7	–5.9	1.3	–4.4	2.5	0.2	21.4	4.3
Ecuador	174.8	53.2	6.2	0.3	17.0	2.6	13.2	0.1	4.5	1.1	48.2	28.5
Egypt, Arab Rep.	658.8	397.4	–36.1	6.2	109.2	80.4	7.8	–2.8	15.7	1.6	28.5	51.0
El Salvador	162.4	46.8	22.7	0.0	8.9	3.4	6.2	0.2	4.4	6.0	42.6	21.3
Eritrea	226.4	141.5	7.2	3.1	4.9	1.7	5.8	25.0	4.2	3.1	0.3	29.4
Estonia												
Ethiopia	1,201.7	625.2	34.2	75.5	49.9	15.9	58.7	86.9	64.9	68.4	4.5	117.7
Finland												
France												
Gabon	29.8	1.8	6.1	..	1.9	16.8	0.0	0.1	2.6	..	0.2	0.2
Gambia, The	15.0	2.0	4.4	1.5	1.4	0.6	0.3	0.3	2.5	0.7	0.2	1.2
Georgia	198.4	73.3	7.3	3.3	51.1	17.5	12.0	1.3	3.5	4.2	0.1	24.8
Germany												
Ghana	602.7	66.8	44.2	119.7	66.4	39.2	70.5	3.5	51.7	26.7	38.9	75.1
Greece												
Guatemala	218.5	37.8	32.8	0.1	18.1	3.4	26.4	–1.6	8.1	15.2	38.9	39.3
Guinea	127.8	42.8	12.0	1.5	19.3	32.4	1.0	..	11.5	1.3	0.6	5.6
Guinea-Bissau	39.4	1.4	0.0	..	0.7	15.6	2.6	0.2	2.0	..	2.3	14.7
Haiti	354.4	154.0	0.9	1.4	3.7	82.0	3.3	..	81.7	1.6	10.3	15.4

Distribution of net aid by Development Assistance Committee members

	Total $ millions	Ten major DAC donors ($ millions) United States	Japan	United Kingdom	Germany	France	Netherlands	Italy	Canada	Sweden	Spain	Other DAC donors $ millions
	2005	2005	2005	2005	2005	2005	2005	2005	2005	2005	2005	2005
Honduras	456.1	88.1	103.5	30.2	24.0	4.5	16.3	23.5	28.6	20.3	95.0	22.0
Hungary												
India	846.3	53.3	71.5	579.2	-68.8	-8.0	72.8	3.5	34.0	16.5	11.2	81.1
Indonesia	2,247.2	160.8	1,223.1	24.1	164.7	29.3	176.0	3.4	95.9	21.6	33.7	314.7
Iran, Islamic Rep.	78.2	3.8	-2.5	0.7	40.6	14.8	6.8	0.6	..	0.2	0.4	13.0
Iraq	21,426.6	10,829.7	3,502.9	1,317.5	2,019.7	635.8	120.5	953.7	385.5	11.3	191.8	1,458.2
Ireland												
Israel												
Italy												
Jamaica	11.2	17.5	-17.9	23.1	-13.8	-1.3	-4.0	-3.4	7.6	0.3	0.2	2.9
Japan												
Jordan	440.8	353.9	23.6	6.1	21.9	1.1	0.8	14.4	7.9	0.6	3.2	7.4
Kazakhstan	153.3	57.1	66.2	1.7	14.1	4.1	2.4	..	1.2	0.8	1.1	4.7
Kenya	494.6	137.8	60.9	86.3	49.6	8.1	28.3	-10.5	21.6	42.1	1.5	69.1
Korea, Dem. Rep.	39.4	7.9	..	..	5.2	-0.4	0.7	0.8	1.6	5.5	..	18.2
Korea, Rep.												
Kuwait												
Kyrgyz Republic	126.4	41.4	21.0	9.4	27.6	1.7	3.1	..	0.7	2.5	0.1	19.0
Lao PDR	159.0	7.4	54.1	0.2	15.0	22.6	2.9	..	3.7	15.0	..	38.2
Latvia												
Lebanon	129.8	38.4	1.0	0.6	12.9	57.9	0.2	0.5	3.4	0.4	2.5	12.2
Lesotho	39.1	1.9	6.7	7.6	5.0	-1.3	0.1	..	3.7	0.0	..	15.3
Liberia	148.6	90.0	..	7.5	1.3	1.6	7.2	0.0	2.9	14.8	1.5	21.7
Libya	16.8	0.1	0.3	..	3.7	2.4	0.2	9.3	..	..	0.1	0.7
Lithuania												
Macedonia, FYR	167.1	45.3	11.3	2.8	28.9	3.0	29.7	2.6	0.3	11.2	0.9	31.2
Madagascar	500.5	80.4	39.6	13.5	11.0	91.2	1.0	51.0	2.2	0.0	135.4	75.2
Malawi	322.1	53.1	19.7	102.0	25.3	2.4	19.4	0.0	17.0	19.3	1.2	62.6
Malaysia	20.1	3.4	-2.1	1.3	7.9	-4.1	0.3	..	1.5	0.7	0.5	10.7
Mali	378.2	58.0	23.2	1.3	29.0	90.0	65.8	..	35.5	21.7	5.3	48.5
Mauritania	124.5	21.5	14.7	..	12.5	47.5	0.6	1.9	3.4	0.6	15.7	6.1
Mauritius	22.2	1.2	16.6	-0.8	-0.9	3.6	0.0	..	1.6	0.0	..	1.0
Mexico	160.6	128.6	11.8	-9.7	25.3	19.4	0.2	0.1	5.8	0.3	-24.5	3.1
Moldova	106.1	30.5	3.7	3.0	7.8	25.8	8.3	..	0.6	8.5	0.1	17.8
Mongolia	131.9	18.1	56.5	0.3	28.2	6.8	7.5	0.1	1.5	2.5	..	10.5
Morocco	289.3	-13.2	-54.2	..	61.8	197.6	1.6	39.4	4.5	0.6	29.0	22.2
Mozambique	770.8	96.0	14.8	80.8	42.6	13.7	64.5	21.6	56.2	79.3	29.4	272.1
Myanmar	77.8	4.1	25.5	10.6	4.4	1.6	0.7	0.3	0.5	4.5	..	25.7
Namibia	98.8	39.5	0.4	1.3	21.4	3.4	3.2	0.0	1.5	5.4	7.6	15.0
Nepal	348.7	54.7	63.4	61.6	63.1	-1.7	12.0	0.0	10.2	1.2	0.1	84.1
Netherlands												
New Zealand												
Nicaragua	509.5	102.4	49.2	6.1	24.5	1.9	33.9	81.0	9.0	40.9	60.1	100.4
Niger	255.7	30.6	23.7	8.0	24.8	70.2	7.6	0.8	17.0	1.6	16.2	55.3
Nigeria	5,966.3	120.5	69.2	2,200.9	1,180.9	1,436.1	202.0	529.6	19.2	0.6	1.9	205.5
Norway												
Oman	3.9	-1.2	3.7	..	0.2	0.9	..	0.0	..	..	0.0	0.2
Pakistan	832.2	362.4	73.8	63.1	34.1	26.0	43.1	-0.8	51.1	9.1	4.6	165.6
Panama	17.3	7.5	2.1	0.1	1.1	0.3	0.1	..	1.1	..	4.5	0.4
Papua New Guinea	245.3	0.0	-5.2	..	2.4	0.1	2.5	..	0.4	0.1	..	244.9
Paraguay	55.3	9.4	27.5	-0.2	2.5	0.4	1.9	0.1	3.2	1.9	7.1	1.6
Peru	310.2	76.4	43.5	3.3	39.0	6.8	13.5	1.2	15.4	3.6	65.5	42.1
Philippines	526.4	98.4	276.4	6.4	49.4	-8.5	22.3	-8.6	19.4	2.5	10.4	58.2
Poland												
Portugal												
Puerto Rico												

6.12 Distribution of net aid by Development Assistance Committee members

	Total $ millions 2005	Ten major DAC donors ($ millions) United States 2005	Japan 2005	United Kingdom 2005	Germany 2005	France 2005	Netherlands 2005	Italy 2005	Canada 2005	Sweden 2005	Spain 2005	Other DAC donors $ millions 2005
Romania												
Russian Federation												
Rwanda	292.0	63.3	2.9	82.0	18.5	14.0	28.4	0.2	10.0	23.4	0.9	48.6
Saudi Arabia	13.8	1.2	5.2	..	1.2	6.1	0.1	..	..	..	..	0.1
Senegal	440.1	39.8	28.0	6.9	34.3	158.2	20.5	11.7	23.5	0.6	82.5	34.3
Serbia and Montenegro	808.2	181.5	121.6	93.0	67.8	57.5	10.8	16.1	9.2	35.5	16.3	199.0
Sierra Leone	130.4	21.0	2.1	60.6	6.4	4.2	7.2	0.7	6.9	2.1	2.4	16.9
Singapore												
Slovak Republic												
Slovenia												
Somalia	146.1	36.9	..	10.7	5.1	1.7	14.2	11.1	6.0	12.9	0.1	47.3
South Africa	486.0	136.6	16.1	70.3	37.0	28.3	55.5	3.2	14.6	22.9	0.4	101.3
Spain												
Sri Lanka	857.1	58.9	312.9	13.7	75.2	40.7	56.2	20.8	45.7	51.7	3.5	177.7
Sudan	1,472.0	771.5	2.1	196.5	44.9	23.0	154.8	16.8	21.8	45.5	9.7	185.6
Swaziland	20.2	0.9	25.9	–9.3	–1.2	0.2	0.1	0.3	3.8	..	..	–0.5
Sweden												
Switzerland												
Syrian Arab Republic	5.9	0.4	–45.3	0.2	12.9	26.3	2.2	0.4	1.9	0.2	1.1	5.8
Tajikistan	105.9	57.6	9.9	4.4	8.3	0.7	0.9	..	6.5	4.6	0.0	13.0
Tanzania	871.0	108.9	36.1	215.9	49.9	4.5	90.2	4.7	33.0	91.8	4.1	232.0
Thailand	–219.9	15.0	–313.9	0.3	9.2	2.1	7.9	1.5	7.8	6.5	0.8	43.0
Togo	59.4	3.0	0.8	0.9	8.4	30.5	5.3	0.0	3.3	0.4	2.0	5.0
Trinidad and Tobago	6.1	0.5	2.0	0.1	0.4	1.2	0.0	..	1.8	..	0.1	0.0
Tunisia	269.1	–15.2	51.1	21.2	29.0	182.3	–1.9	–9.2	1.0	0.5	5.6	4.7
Turkey	51.8	–13.9	–62.3	–1.1	–33.6	114.6	4.5	–5.0	–2.4	2.5	12.4	36.0
Turkmenistan	11.8	9.6	0.1	0.1	1.2	0.7	0.0	..	0.1	..	..	0.2
Uganda	704.3	242.3	14.4	55.6	51.4	7.7	80.1	3.9	12.8	47.9	–0.6	188.5
Ukraine	252.1	113.4	2.5	10.8	53.2	15.5	0.6	0.0	18.6	10.6	0.5	26.5
United Arab Emirates												
United Kingdom												
United States												
Uruguay	2.8	–1.5	2.2	..	0.7	3.7	0.0	–2.8	2.1	0.4	2.3	–4.3
Uzbekistan	124.1	37.5	54.4	0.6	17.0	3.8	0.5	..	0.9	1.0	0.1	8.4
Venezuela, RB	20.8	9.0	4.3	0.2	2.0	6.7	0.1	0.2	1.8	0.1	–5.4	2.0
Vietnam	1,252.1	27.1	602.7	96.6	82.9	96.8	56.1	–3.2	28.4	41.9	9.1	213.7
West Bank and Gaza	569.4	180.2	5.8	23.5	39.8	30.6	29.9	15.9	15.9	36.9	39.4	151.5
Yemen, Rep.	134.7	17.6	8.4	20.3	41.8	6.3	31.9	2.9	1.1	0.6	0.1	3.8
Zambia	835.9	124.2	131.9	165.7	118.2	15.8	55.9	0.2	49.7	34.2	0.2	139.8
Zimbabwe	178.8	33.4	4.1	45.5	13.5	3.8	13.6	1.1	13.5	15.1	0.8	34.4
World	82,133.3 s	25,279.5 s	10,406.1 s	8,164.0 s	7,446.8 s	7,239.2 s	3,682.7 s	2,269.5 s	2,832.8 s	2,255.9 s	1,863.0 s	10,693.7 s
Low income	26,746.4	5,685.2	2,280.5	4,932.4	2,471.1	2,822.0	1,555.5	803.2	941.5	799.2	433.1	4,022.8
Middle income	39,752.9	14,537.6	6,862.5	1,851.5	4,011.0	3,657.2	989.5	1,268.7	989.2	497.1	1,110.2	3,978.5
Lower middle income	37,437.8	13,962.1	6,799.7	1,695.4	3,811.0	3,092.9	852.0	1,232.9	891.1	436.6	1,043.8	3,620.4
Upper middle income	1,646.6	376.5	43.5	138.6	122.8	504.1	67.2	24.8	68.5	37.1	36.6	227.0
Low & middle income	82,112.6	25,278.5	10,395.5	8,164.0	7,445.6	7,233.1	3,682.7	2,269.5	2,831.3	2,255.9	1,863.0	10,693.6
East Asia & Pacific	7,665.1	773.3	3,222.5	225.4	667.8	439.8	324.5	–16.7	205.9	147.2	83.0	1,592.5
Europe & Central Asia	2,973.8	842.7	284.9	150.3	370.0	338.3	120.5	30.6	50.3	151.0	48.0	587.3
Latin America & Carib.	4,589.8	1,344.8	409.5	154.6	433.5	250.1	272.5	121.9	368.9	170.8	584.2	479.1
Middle East & N. Africa	24,468.5	11,801.1	3,468.4	1,398.7	2,418.8	1,528.4	218.7	1,037.7	445.8	66.3	319.2	1,765.5
South Asia	5,735.4	1,921.9	632.6	1,142.7	251.0	89.1	332.3	52.8	288.0	146.8	38.7	839.6
Sub-Saharan Africa	23,066.3	4,192.2	1,133.1	3,745.8	2,444.2	3,892.2	1,400.2	872.7	977.1	793.2	563.8	3,051.8
High income												
Europe EMU												

Note: Regional aggregates include data for economies not specified elsewhere. World and income group totals include aid not allocated by country or region.

Distribution of net aid by Development Assistance Committee members

About the data

The table shows net bilateral aid to low- and middle-income economies from members of the Development Assistance Committee (DAC) of the Organisation for Economic Co-operation and Development (OECD). The DAC compilation of the data includes aid to some countries and territories not shown in the table and aid to unspecified economies that is recorded only at the regional or global level. Aid to countries and territories not shown in the table has been assigned to regional totals based on the World Bank's regional classification system. Aid to unspecified economies has been included in regional totals and, when possible, in income group totals. Aid not allocated by country or region—including administrative costs, research on development issues, and aid to nongovernmental organizations—is included in the world total. Thus regional and income group totals do not sum to the world total.

In 1999 all UN agencies revised their data since 1990 to include only regular budgetary expenditures (except for the World Food Programme and the United Nations Office of the High Commissioner for Refugees, which revised their data from 1996 onward). They did so to avoid double counting extrabudgetary expenditures reported by DAC countries and flows reported by the United Nations.

The table is based on donor country reports of bilateral programs, which may differ from reports by recipient countries. Recipients may lack access to information on such aid expenditures as development-oriented research, stipends and tuition costs for aid-financed students in donor countries, and payment of experts hired by donor countries. Moreover, a full accounting would include donor country contributions to multilateral institutions, the flow of resources from multilateral institutions to recipient countries, and flows from countries that are not members of DAC.

The expenditures that countries report as official development assistance (ODA) have changed. For example, some DAC members have reported as ODA the aid provided to refugees during the first 12 months of their stay within the donor's borders.

Some of the aid recipients shown in the table are also aid donors. See table 6.10a for a summary of ODA from non-DAC countries.

The flow of bilateral aid from DAC members reflects global events and priorities — 6.12a

Total bilateral aid, 2005

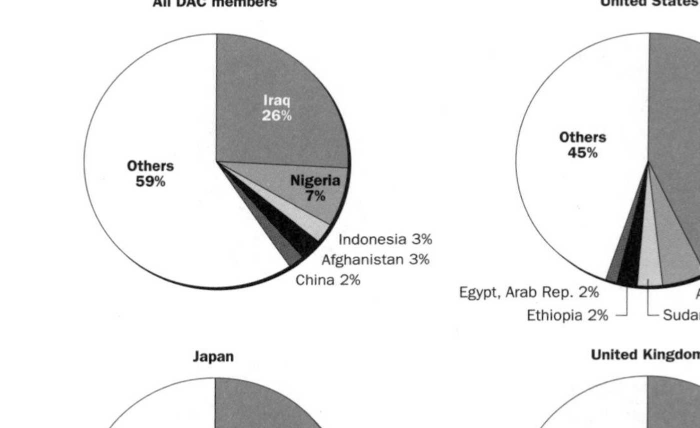

Japan

Others 34%
Iraq 34%
Indonesia 12%
China 10%
Congo, Dem. Rep. 4%
Vietnam 6%

United Kingdom

Nigeria 27%
Others 44%
Iraq 16%
India 7%
Tanzania 3%
Afghanistan 3%

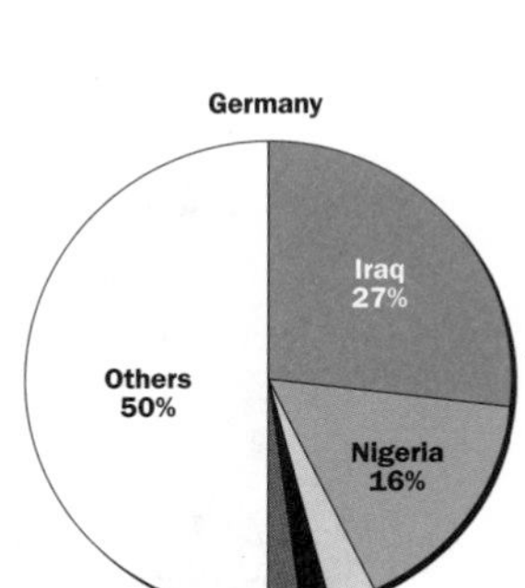

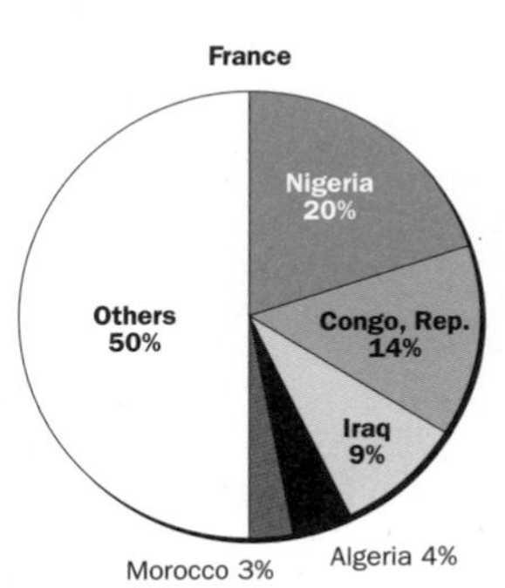

The figure shows the distribution of aid from all DAC members and the top five donors to the top five recipients in 2005.

Source: Organisation for Economic Co-operation and Development, Development Assistance Committee.

Definitions

• **Net aid** comprises net bilateral official development assistance to part I recipients and net bilateral official aid to part II recipients (see *About the data* for table 6.9). • **Other DAC donors** are Australia, Austria, Belgium, Denmark, Finland, Greece, Ireland, Luxembourg, New Zealand, Norway, Portugal, and Switzerland.

Data sources

Data on financial flows are compiled by DAC and published in its annual statistical report, *Geographical Distribution of Financial Flows to Aid Recipients*, and its annual *Development Cooperation Report*. Data are available electronically on the OECD's *International Development Statistics* CD-ROM and at www.oecd.org/dac/stats/idsonline.

6.13 Net financial flows from multilateral institutions

	International financial institutions ($ millions)							United Nations ($ millions)					Total
	World Bank		IMF		Regional development banks								
	IDA	IBRD	Concessional	Non-concessional	Concessional	Non-concessional	Others	UNDP	UNFPA	UNICEF	WFP	Others	$ millions
	2005	2005	2005	2005	2005	2005	2005	2005	2005	2005	2005	2005	2005
Afghanistan	..	..	..	..	..	..	..	7.1	4.9	17.1	..	26.3	55.3
Albania	29.6	0.0	2.7	0.0	0.0	11.5	21.4	1.5	0.4	1.1	1.3	1.9	71.3
Algeria	0.0	–125.3	0.0	–611.6	0.0	–211.6	–493.3	1.0	0.7	1.1	3.7	5.6	–1,429.7
Angola	25.3	0.0	0.0	0.0	0.4	–1.6	1.8	5.9	1.9	7.8	9.1	15.6	66.2
Argentina	0.0	–566.4	0.0	–3,571.2	0.0	60.9	0.0	0.6	0.5	0.6	..	3.2	–4,071.8
Armenia	31.4	–0.6	–22.6	–2.1	0.0	–7.9	–0.4	1.3	0.6	0.8	1.0	2.7	4.1
Australia													
Austria													
Azerbaijan	45.6	0.0	–5.2	–23.9	0.5	–11.8	5.0	2.9	0.7	1.2	1.9	3.6	20.5
Bangladesh	394.5	0.0	97.4	0.0	57.3	86.1	–13.8	16.0	5.4	11.6	18.2	10.2	682.7
Belarus	0.0	–8.9	0.0	–8.6	0.0	–10.9	–14.9	0.6	0.3	0.8	..	0.8	–41.0
Belgium													
Benin	42.8	0.0	–6.2	0.0	34.0	–0.3	–13.0	3.2	2.7	3.1	2.7	4.5	73.4
Bolivia	62.2	0.0	–22.5	–3.5	98.1	–60.8	76.5	0.9	1.5	1.8	3.2	2.2	159.5
Bosnia and Herzegovina	55.6	–23.6	0.0	–39.4	0.0	–3.8	61.8	0.9	0.3	0.9	..	9.0	61.7
Botswana	–0.5	–1.1	0.0	0.0	–1.8	17.6	–13.8	0.6	0.9	1.0	..	4.3	7.1
Brazil	0.0	–255.4	0.0	–23,809.8	0.0	722.8	87.7	0.7	1.1	2.7	..	5.4	–23,245.0
Bulgaria	0.0	114.8	0.0	–443.4	0.0	1.0	–9.1	..	..	..	..	..	–336.8
Burkina Faso	102.0	0.0	11.5	0.0	55.6	0.0	15.7	5.9	2.7	6.8	2.1	3.5	205.8
Burundi	18.9	0.0	21.1	0.0	5.9	–2.7	–2.2	6.5	1.1	5.1	1.7	2.7	58.1
Cambodia	33.7	0.0	–8.7	0.0	82.2	0.0	8.6	4.5	2.0	4.8	1.2	3.3	131.6
Cameroon	19.0	–31.5	–34.7	0.0	20.4	–17.6	–14.8	4.5	2.8	3.2	1.2	5.8	–42.0
Canada													
Central African Republic	0.0	0.0	–4.9	0.0	0.0	0.0	–0.4	2.6	2.3	2.7	3.1	5.2	10.7
Chad	59.6	–1.8	–7.2	0.0	19.6	0.0	9.7	5.2	2.1	8.4	12.8	3.7	112.2
Chile	–0.7	–151.2	0.0	0.0	–1.4	–29.8	0.0	0.7	0.2	0.5	..	1.9	–179.8
China	–146.7	273.7	0.0	0.0	0.0	688.3	–0.3	9.4	4.7	14.4	8.0	12.4	863.8
Hong Kong, China	..	..	..	..	..	..	..	..	..	..	..	..	..
Colombia	–0.7	486.9	0.0	0.0	–20.7	–1,145.9	75.7	1.3	1.1	1.4	2.9	2.8	–595.3
Congo, Dem. Rep.	225.9	0.0	39.4	0.0	22.5	0.0	–10.9	14.9	7.0	21.6	0.5	12.9	333.8
Congo, Rep.	29.7	0.0	7.5	–7.8	9.9	–30.5	–2.3	1.4	0.6	1.1	2.0	6.5	18.1
Costa Rica	–0.2	–12.1	0.0	0.0	–11.2	–156.0	–25.5	0.4	0.6	0.7	..	2.5	–200.7
Côte d'Ivoire	0.0	0.0	–91.1	0.0	0.1	–0.3	–14.5	3.5	1.6	4.4	2.9	9.0	–84.5
Croatia	0.0	11.0	0.0	0.0	0.0	51.9	57.2	0.6	..	0.2	..	4.4	125.3
Cuba	..	..	..	..	..	..	..	1.0	0.7	0.7	3.9	2.0	8.3
Czech Republic	0.0	–19.2	0.0	0.0	0.0	0.0	–48.9	..	..	..	..	..	–68.0
Denmark													
Dominican Republic	–0.7	26.4	0.0	219.9	–21.0	86.1	0.1	0.7	0.8	1.1	0.0	2.0	315.4
Ecuador	–1.1	–35.2	0.0	–195.0	–26.6	–80.4	54.5	1.3	0.9	1.1	0.2	2.9	–277.5
Egypt, Arab Rep.	27.8	19.8	0.0	0.0	–0.4	–91.4	125.5	1.2	1.8	2.7	4.1	5.1	96.2
El Salvador	–0.8	88.4	0.0	0.0	–23.1	16.7	28.4	0.7	0.8	1.1	0.7	1.5	114.3
Eritrea	56.7	0.0	0.0	0.0	12.3	0.0	–5.5	3.3	2.0	2.5	4.4	8.6	84.3
Estonia	0.0	–5.1	0.0	0.0	0.0	0.0	–3.8	..	..	..	..	..	–8.9
Ethiopia	161.8	0.0	–4.0	0.0	127.0	–7.6	33.1	12.1	4.2	24.1	14.1	13.1	377.8
Finland													
France													
Gabon	0.0	–7.0	0.0	–24.7	–0.2	–35.5	17.4	0.6	0.1	0.6	..	5.2	–43.4
Gambia, The	15.6	0.0	–2.0	0.0	7.2	0.0	21.0	2.2	0.6	1.1	1.7	2.9	50.2
Georgia	52.1	0.0	–9.5	–3.4	0.0	–2.3	0.6	1.9	0.5	0.9	0.8	4.1	45.7
Germany													
Ghana	290.8	–2.2	7.4	0.0	57.7	–3.4	19.7	4.2	3.7	4.5	3.3	8.9	394.5
Greece													
Guatemala	0.0	1.4	0.0	0.0	–17.6	–7.0	8.9	1.0	1.5	1.0	3.6	2.5	–4.7
Guinea	22.1	0.0	–25.7	0.0	4.3	–7.4	–24.5	2.3	1.4	3.7	3.0	13.6	–7.2
Guinea-Bissau	10.6	0.0	–2.9	–0.3	3.5	0.0	2.7	2.7	1.0	1.6	2.1	2.0	23.1
Haiti	–5.1	0.0	–4.5	15.3	53.6	0.0	–1.6	4.8	4.2	3.0	1.8	1.8	73.3

Net financial flows from multilateral institutions 6.13

	International financial institutions							United Nations					Total
	$ millions							$ millions					$ millions
	World Bank		IMF		Regional development banks								
	IDA	IBRD	Concessional	Non-concessional	Concessional	Non-concessional	Others	UNDP	UNFPA	UNICEF	WFP	Others	
	2005	2005	2005	2005	2005	2005	2005	2005	2005	2005	2005	2005	2005
Honduras	142.9	–69.7	–0.4	0.0	52.1	–21.1	31.4	1.1	2.7	1.3	1.1	1.2	142.7
Hungary	0.0	–39.5	0.0	0.0	0.0	–6.7	–121.7	..	..	..	..	..	–167.9
India	571.9	715.8	0.0	0.0	0.0	419.5	–12.8	15.4	13.7	34.7	9.7	14.5	1,782.3
Indonesia	40.1	–805.2	0.0	–1,144.7	48.2	465.4	–38.3	8.2	15.7	6.4	7.6	11.5	–1,385.0
Iran, Islamic Rep.	0.0	102.1	0.0	0.0	0.0	0.0	1.0	0.6	1.5	2.1	0.4	9.8	117.5
Iraq	..	..	..	..	..	..	..	..	4.7	1.9	..	2.1	8.7
Ireland													
Israel	..	..	..	..	..	..	..	..	..	..	..	..	..
Italy													
Jamaica	0.0	–22.0	0.0	–0.9	–5.3	–35.0	11.0	0.7	..	1.1	..	1.7	–48.7
Japan													
Jordan	–2.6	–25.0	0.0	–77.1	0.0	0.0	19.3	0.6	0.3	1.2	0.3	104.6	21.7
Kazakhstan	0.0	–621.0	0.0	0.0	0.1	–181.3	–30.4	0.9	0.6	1.4	..	2.2	–827.5
Kenya	–20.1	–1.1	66.5	0.0	19.0	–5.7	–14.8	5.7	3.8	4.9	11.9	26.9	97.0
Korea, Dem. Rep.	..	..	..	..	..	..	..	2.6	1.0	2.6	8.4	3.0	17.6
Korea, Rep.	..	..	..	..	..	..	..	..	..	..	..	..	..
Kuwait	..	..	..	..	..	..	..	..	..	..	..	..	..
Kyrgyz Republic	29.5	0.0	–13.0	0.0	29.6	–8.8	3.8	2.4	0.8	1.1	..	2.8	48.2
Lao PDR	26.1	0.0	–6.1	0.0	57.4	11.1	–2.7	4.3	1.2	2.2	2.9	2.2	98.6
Latvia	0.0	–61.8	0.0	0.0	0.0	–5.9	9.3	..	..	..	..	..	–58.3
Lebanon	0.0	–6.2	0.0	0.0	0.0	0.0	–8.3	0.7	0.6	0.8	..	68.6	56.3
Lesotho	8.1	–3.5	0.0	0.0	–2.1	–1.7	–3.1	0.9	0.1	1.3	4.9	2.1	7.0
Liberia	0.0	0.0	0.0	–0.1	0.0	0.0	0.0	4.1	0.8	3.8	..	16.6	25.2
Libya	..	..	..	..	..	..	..	..	..	..	1.1	1.8	3.0
Lithuania	0.0	–97.4	0.0	–24.8	0.0	–2.6	–7.1	..	..	..	..	..	–132.0
Macedonia, FYR	5.6	43.2	–8.1	12.8	0.0	6.4	–0.6	1.2	0.0	1.1	..	3.1	64.8
Madagascar	209.2	0.0	6.5	0.0	18.4	0.0	–2.0	6.0	1.5	5.9	3.7	2.6	251.8
Malawi	32.6	–0.2	–3.3	–3.2	25.9	–1.9	1.7	7.7	3.7	6.1	5.5	4.4	78.9
Malaysia	0.0	–92.3	0.0	0.0	0.0	–39.4	13.2	0.6	0.5	0.4	..	3.8	–113.3
Mali	102.0	0.0	–14.8	0.0	53.0	0.0	21.3	4.3	1.7	6.9	5.7	3.1	183.2
Mauritania	40.1	0.0	–9.6	0.0	7.1	–1.4	39.3	2.8	2.2	1.8	6.4	2.5	91.2
Mauritius	–0.6	–6.3	0.0	0.0	–0.1	–8.2	14.5	0.2	0.0	..	..	1.7	1.0
Mexico	0.0	–381.8	0.0	0.0	0.0	346.4	0.0	1.0	2.2	1.2	..	4.0	–27.1
Moldova	23.6	–13.4	0.0	–21.5	0.0	–13.5	–7.4	1.8	0.4	1.1	..	1.2	–27.8
Mongolia	12.1	0.0	–5.9	0.0	26.3	0.0	4.4	1.4	1.1	1.1	..	3.3	43.7
Morocco	–1.4	–46.3	0.0	0.0	0.9	292.8	196.8	1.0	2.8	1.6	0.0	3.0	451.2
Mozambique	221.6	0.0	–10.5	0.0	76.6	12.7	31.9	7.4	5.9	8.7	6.4	5.3	366.0
Myanmar	0.0	0.0	0.0	0.0	0.0	0.0	–1.9	11.5	4.0	8.6	1.1	6.8	30.2
Namibia	0.0	0.0	0.0	0.0	0.0	0.0	0.0	0.7	0.7	1.1	0.6	5.0	8.1
Nepal	2.5	0.0	0.0	0.0	17.6	0.0	5.1	6.3	6.6	4.9	5.5	9.5	57.9
Netherlands													
New Zealand													
Nicaragua	63.1	0.0	–8.9	0.0	120.9	–8.0	17.7	3.3	2.5	1.2	1.8	1.5	195.0
Niger	64.6	0.0	12.1	0.0	14.7	–2.5	41.7	6.5	3.3	8.2	15.8	3.0	167.4
Nigeria	245.9	–223.6	0.0	0.0	9.1	–82.7	0.0	8.0	7.9	23.7	..	8.0	–3.7
Norway													
Oman	0.0	0.0	0.0	0.0	0.0	0.0	–182.8	..	0.2	0.0	..	1.1	–181.5
Pakistan	513.0	–94.4	–76.8	–160.5	158.0	187.5	–10.8	11.6	9.5	14.0	10.7	22.6	584.5
Panama	0.0	–30.5	0.0	–9.8	–8.9	12.8	–8.4	0.7	0.5	0.5	..	1.7	–41.5
Papua New Guinea	–3.6	–2.9	0.0	–61.1	–1.3	3.5	–2.6	2.2	0.7	1.7	..	3.6	–59.8
Paraguay	–1.5	–8.2	0.0	0.0	–15.2	3.6	–2.9	0.5	0.8	1.0	..	1.0	–21.0
Peru	0.0	–17.3	0.0	–39.5	–9.5	268.3	–1.0	0.7	22.0	1.7	3.5	2.2	231.0
Philippines	–6.8	–246.6	0.0	–317.4	–18.4	5.0	–4.3	2.2	5.7	2.9	..	3.0	–574.8
Poland	0.0	78.9	0.0	0.0	0.0	0.0	0.0	..	..	..	..	..	78.9
Portugal													
Puerto Rico													

6.13 Net financial flows from multilateral institutions

	International financial institutions							United Nations					Total
	$ millions							$ millions					$ millions
	World Bank		IMF		Regional development banks								
	IDA	IBRD	Concessional	Non-concessional	Concessional	Non-concessional	Others	UNDP	UNFPA	UNICEF	WFP	Others	
	2005	2005	2005	2005	2005	2005	2005	2005	2005	2005	2005	2005	2005
Romania	0.0	76.6	0.0	–151.9	18.8	–43.9	461.2	..	..	..	..	..	360.8
Russian Federation	0.0	–528.3	0.0	–3,388.7	0.0	86.9	0.0	..	..	..	..	..	–3,830.0
Rwanda	46.7	0.0	–2.0	0.0	35.1	0.0	–3.2	4.0	1.9	4.3	4.2	5.9	96.7
Saudi Arabia	..	..	..	..	..	..	..	..	..	0.2	..	1.8	2.0
Senegal	170.5	0.0	–28.4	0.0	19.6	–0.2	31.4	3.9	2.4	3.6	3.2	4.4	210.4
Serbia and Montenegro	88.4	–19.6	0.0	–21.7	0.0	49.8	137.2	..	..	1.1	..	20.7	255.8
Sierra Leone	18.6	0.0	18.2	0.0	19.0	0.0	11.9	5.0	1.7	4.6	5.4	14.3	98.7
Singapore	..	..	..	..	..	..	..	..	..	..	..	..	..
Slovak Republic	0.0	–55.5	0.0	0.0	0.0	–1.6	8.2	..	..	..	..	..	–48.8
Slovenia	..	..	..	..	..	..	..	..	..	..	..	..	..
Somalia	0.0	0.0	0.0	0.0	0.0	0.0	0.0	6.3	0.3	7.9	5.2	5.2	24.9
South Africa	0.0	8.3	0.0	0.0	0.0	52.2	0.0	2.3	0.9	1.4	0.0	6.1	71.2
Spain													
Sri Lanka	73.6	–1.0	0.0	114.5	129.1	37.1	24.9	2.6	2.9	0.7	6.7	6.0	397.0
Sudan	–1.3	0.0	0.0	–28.3	0.0	–2.2	100.4	11.6	8.1	13.0	43.8	6.8	151.8
Swaziland	–0.3	0.0	0.0	0.0	–1.0	22.3	42.4	0.5	0.5	0.8	0.6	1.9	67.9
Sweden													
Switzerland													
Syrian Arab Republic	–1.5	0.0	0.0	0.0	0.0	0.0	–40.8	1.5	2.0	1.0	1.8	38.4	2.4
Tajikistan	34.8	0.0	15.1	0.0	26.1	0.5	0.4	3.7	0.8	1.9	1.7	1.6	86.5
Tanzania	260.5	0.0	–38.1	0.0	122.8	0.0	17.2	7.8	5.1	10.9	5.7	5.0	396.8
Thailand	–3.4	–97.5	0.0	0.0	–2.4	–368.3	–12.7	2.2	2.1	1.3	..	12.1	–466.6
Togo	0.0	0.0	–11.2	0.0	0.0	–1.4	9.2	1.7	0.6	1.7	0.3	2.1	2.9
Trinidad and Tobago	0.0	–13.0	0.0	0.0	–0.1	–9.6	–7.5	0.7	..	..	..	0.9	–28.5
Tunisia	–2.1	–54.5	0.0	0.0	0.0	–8.5	250.0	0.7	0.4	0.7	..	2.2	189.0
Turkey	–5.9	–294.0	0.0	–5,319.9	0.0	0.0	286.9	0.7	1.1	1.8	..	7.5	–5,321.9
Turkmenistan	0.0	–1.8	0.0	0.0	0.0	0.0	–2.9	1.0	0.5	0.9	..	1.2	–1.0
Uganda	111.7	0.0	–30.2	0.0	63.7	–1.6	17.8	6.1	3.8	9.6	..	9.6	190.6
Ukraine	0.0	316.0	0.0	–299.6	0.0	22.0	–65.8	2.8	0.7	1.4	..	3.6	–18.9
United Arab Emirates	..	..	..	..	..	..	..	..	..	..	..	..	..
United Kingdom													
United States													
Uruguay	0.0	30.3	0.0	–171.7	–2.4	25.4	–0.1	0.6	0.5	0.5	..	0.8	–116.2
Uzbekistan	7.1	4.3	0.0	–18.4	0.0	64.3	0.0	3.1	0.9	2.3	..	2.6	66.0
Venezuela, RB	0.0	–92.9	0.0	0.0	0.0	–182.3	–75.5	0.5	0.8	0.9	..	2.3	–346.2
Vietnam	377.7	0.0	–53.5	0.0	217.6	–2.2	–2.5	6.5	7.6	5.1	..	5.6	561.8
West Bank and Gaza	..	..	..	..	..	..	..	..	..	1.9	..	307.4	309.3
Yemen, Rep.	102.2	0.0	–44.3	–11.4	0.0	0.0	56.2	5.8	3.6	5.3	7.1	6.8	131.4
Zambia	75.8	0.0	–62.8	0.0	17.8	–9.2	4.9	5.3	1.8	4.5	7.4	10.1	55.5
Zimbabwe	0.0	–1.7	0.0	–164.7	0.0	0.0	3.4	3.1	4.4	2.0	125.4	4.3	–23.7
World	.. s	.. s	.. s	.. s	.. s	.. s	.. s	398.9 s	386.4 s	710.8 s	554.5 s	1,410.2 s	.. s
Low income	4,692.4	392.1	–271.9	–432.7	1,589.8	643.7	374.6	291.5	165.3	348.1	380.8	366.1	8,539.7
Middle income	699.2	–3,302.8	–75.6	–39,380.9	364.9	512.0	999.6	96.6	114.8	105.0	83.0	849.5	–38,934.7
Lower middle income	698.4	–1,062.8	–79.1	–26,717.8	373.0	385.7	576.4	81.6	96.2	91.3	81.9	658.7	–24,816.4
Upper middle income	0.8	–2,240.0	3.5	–12,663.2	–8.1	126.2	423.2	13.0	11.1	12.8	1.1	126.4	–14,193.1
Low & middle income	5,391.6	–2,910.6	–347.5	–39,813.6	1,594.6	1,155.7	1,374.2	398.9	386.4	710.5	554.5	1,408.3	–29,737.0
East Asia & Pacific	340.1	–973.1	–74.2	–1,523.2	410.5	774.3	–40.1	61.0	49.5	57.1	29.3	117.4	–771.6
Europe & Central Asia	397.4	–1,125.8	–40.5	–9,754.7	75.2	–6.6	788.9	29.2	10.4	19.9	6.6	100.4	–9,499.7
Latin America & Carib.	267.6	–1,024.1	–13.1	–27,566.7	206.3	–202.5	292.5	25.6	50.8	30.6	23.5	84.6	–27,824.9
Middle East & N. Africa	125.8	–135.5	–45.1	–700.1	1.1	–18.7	–59.3	13.8	21.1	21.9	20.4	597.7	–156.9
South Asia	1,566.8	620.4	20.6	–39.9	377.5	730.1	–2.3	62.2	46.8	84.7	54.9	93.0	3,614.9
Sub-Saharan Africa	2,693.9	-272.6	–195.1	–229.0	884.1	–120.9	394.5	196.4	115.2	245.1	342.4	346.2	4,400.2
High income													
Europe EMU													

Note: The aggregates for the regional development banks, United Nations, and total net financial flows include amounts for economies not specified elsewhere.

Net financial flows from multilateral institutions 6.13

About the data

The table shows concessional and nonconcessional financial flows from the major multilateral institutions—the World Bank, the International Monetary Fund (IMF), regional development banks, UN agencies, and regional groups such as the Commission of the European Communities. Much of the data comes from the World Bank's Debtor Reporting System.

The multilateral development banks fund their nonconcessional lending operations primarily by selling low-interest, highly rated bonds (the World Bank, for example, has a AAA rating) backed by prudent lending and financial policies and the strong financial support of their members. These funds are then on-lent at slightly higher interest rates and with relatively long maturities (15–20 years) to developing countries. Lending terms vary with market conditions and the policies of the banks.

Concessional flows from bilateral donors are defined by the Development Assistance Committee (DAC) of the Organisation for Economic Co-operation and Development (OECD) as financial flows containing a grant element of at least 25 percent. The grant element of loans is evaluated assuming a nominal market interest rate of 10 percent. The grant element is nil for a loan carrying a 10 percent interest rate, and it is 100 percent for a grant, which requires no repayment. Concessional flows from multilateral development agencies are credits provided through their concessional lending facilities. The cost of these loans is reduced through subsidies provided by donors or drawn from other resources available to the agencies. Grants provided by multilateral agencies are not included in the net flows.

All concessional lending by the World Bank is carried out by the International Development Association (IDA). Eligibility for IDA resources is based on gross national income (GNI) per capita; countries must also meet performance standards assessed by World Bank staff. Since July 1, 2005, the GNI per capita cutoff has been set at $825, measured in 2003 using the *World Bank Atlas* method (see *Users guide*). In exceptional circumstances IDA extends eligibility temporarily to countries that are above the cutoff and are undertaking major adjustment efforts but are not creditworthy for lending by the International Bank for Reconstruction and Development (IBRD). An exception has also been made for small island economies. Lending by the International Finance Corporation is not included in this table.

The IMF makes concessional funds available through its Poverty Reduction and Growth Facility, which replaced the Enhanced Structural Adjustment Facility in 1999, and through the IMF Trust Fund. Eligibility is based principally on a country's per capita income and eligibility under IDA, the World Bank's concessional window.

Regional development banks also maintain concessional windows for funds. Loans from the major regional development banks—the African Development Bank, Asian Development Bank, and Inter-American Development Bank—are recorded in the table according to each institution's classification.

In 1999 all UN agencies revised their data since 1990 to include only regular budgetary expenditures (except for the World Food Programme and the United Nations Office of the High Commissioner for Refugees, which revised their data from 1996 onward). They did so to avoid double counting extrabudgetary expenditures reported by DAC countries and flows reported by the United Nations.

Maintaining financial flows from multilateral institutions to developing countries 6.13a

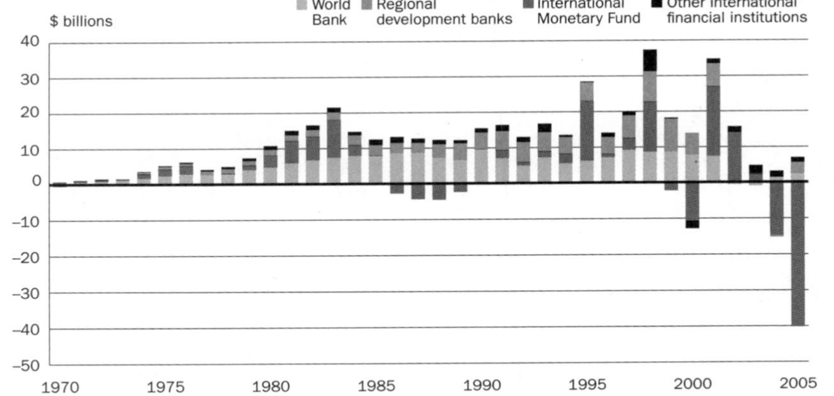

As developing countries pay off loans from international financial institutions, net disbursements from these institutions have fallen greatly in recent years.

Source: World Bank Debtor Reporting System.

Definitions

• **Net financial flows** are disbursements of public or publicly guaranteed loans and credits, less repayments of principal. • **IDA** is the International Development Association, the concessional loan window of the World Bank. • **IBRD** is the International Bank for Reconstruction and Development, the founding and largest member of the World Bank Group. • **IMF** is the International Monetary Fund. Its nonconcessional lending consists of the credit it provides to its members, mainly to meet their balance of payments needs. It provides concessional assistance through the Poverty Reduction and Growth Facility and the IMF Trust Fund. • **Regional development banks** include the African Development Bank, in Tunis, Tunisia, which lends to all of Africa, including North Africa; the Asian Development Bank, in Manila, Philippines, which serves countries in South and Central Asia and East Asia and Pacific; the European Bank for Reconstruction and Development, in London, United Kingdom, which serves countries in Europe and Central Asia; the European Development Fund, in Brussels, Belgium, which serves countries in Africa, the Caribbean, and the Pacific; and the Inter-American Development Bank, in Washington, D.C., which is the principal development bank of the Americas. Concessional financial flows cover disbursements made through concessional lending facilities. Nonconcessional financial flows cover all other disbursements. • **Others** is a residual category in the World Bank's Debtor Reporting System. It includes such institutions as the Caribbean Development Bank and the European Investment Bank. • **United Nations** includes the United Nations Development Programme (UNDP), United Nations Population Fund (UNFPA), United Nations Children's Fund (UNICEF), World Food Programme (WFP), and other UN agencies, such as the Office of the High Commissioner for Refugees, United Nations Relief and Works Agency for Palestine Refugees in the Near East, and United Nations Regular Programme for Technical Assistance.

Data sources

Data on net financial flows from international financial institutions are from the World Bank's Debtor Reporting System. These data are published in the World Bank's *Global Development Finance 2007* and electronically as *GDF Online*. Data on aid from UN agencies are from the DAC annual *Development Cooperation Report*. Data are available in electronic format on the OECD's *International Development Statistics* CD-ROM and at www.oecd.org/dac/stats/idsonline.

6.14 Movement of people

	Net migration		Migration stock		Refugees				Workers' remittances and compensation of employees			
	thousands		thousands		thousands				$ millions			
					By country of origin		By country of asylum		Received		Paid	
	1990–95	2000–05	1990	2005	1996	2005	1996	2005	1990	2005	1990	2005
Afghanistan	3,313	2,140	29	43	2,674.2	2,166.1	18.8	0.0	..	..	..	..
Albania	–423	–100	66	83	5.8	12.7	4.9	0.1	*0*	1,290	..	7
Algeria	–58	–100	274	242	2.2	12.0	190.3	94.1	352	1,950	31	..
Angola	143	145	34	56	249.7	215.8	9.4	14.0	..	..	150	215
Argentina	50	–100	1,650	1,500	..	..	10.4	3.1	*15*	413	21	279
Armenia	–500	–100	659	235	203.2	14.0	219.0	219.6	..	940[a]	..	146
Australia	390	500	3,984	4,097	..	..	67.3	65.0	2,370	2,858	674	1,358
Austria	262	100	473	1,234	..	..	89.1	21.2	635	2,941	320	2,543
Azerbaijan	–116	–100	361	182	236.1	233.7	233.7	3.0	..	693	..	268
Bangladesh	–260	–350	882	1,032	58.0	7.3	30.7	21.1	779	4,251	..	6
Belarus	15	–10	1,271	1,191	0.5	8.9	30.5	0.7	..	370	..	94
Belgium	85	67	899	719	..	..	36.1	15.3	3,583	7,155	2,310	2,758
Benin	105	99	76	175	..	..	6.0	30.3	101	63[a]	21	7[a]
Bolivia	–100	–100	60	116	..	..	0.7	0.5	5	338	8	66
Bosnia and Herzegovina	–1,000	40	56	41	993.9	109.9	40.0	10.6	..	1,844	..	40
Botswana	–7	–6	27	80	..	..	0.2	3.1	86	125	119	123
Brazil	–184	–130	804	641	..	..	2.2	3.5	573	3,540	12	498
Bulgaria	–309	–50	22	104	..	..	1.4	4.4	..	2,130	..	13
Burkina Faso	–128	100	345	773	..	..	28.4	0.5	140	50[a]	81	44[a]
Burundi	–250	192	333	100	428.7	438.7	20.7	20.7	..	..	6	1[a]
Cambodia	194	–10	38	304	62.2	17.8	0.0	0.1	*9*	200	*14*	144
Cameroon	–5	13	171	137	2.1	9.1	46.4	52.0	23	11[a]	111	63[a]
Canada	643	1,050	4,319	6,106	..	..	138.4	147.2	..	..	..	..
Central African Republic	37	–45	63	76	0.2	42.9	36.6	24.6	..	..	36	..
Chad	20	271	74	437	58.4	48.4	0.1	275.4	*1*	..	39	..
Chile	90	30	108	231	12.8	0.9	0.3	0.8	1	3	7	6
China	–1,281	–1,950	380	596	105.8	124.1	290.1	301.0	210	22,492[a]	5	2,602
Hong Kong, China	300	300	2,218	2,999	..	..	1.3	1.9	..	240	..	335
Colombia	–200	–200	102	123	2.2	60.5	0.2	0.2	495	3,346	44	56
Congo, Dem. Rep.	1,208	–322	919	539	158.8	430.9	676.0	204.3	..	..	..	..
Congo, Rep.	14	–14	130	288	0.2	24.4	20.5	66.1	*4*	11	55	45
Costa Rica	62	84	418	441	..	..	23.2	11.3	12	421	..	209
Côte d'Ivoire	200	–371	1,953	2,371	0.3	18.3	327.7	41.6	44	160	471	592
Croatia	153	100	475	661	310.1	119.1	165.4	2.9	..	1,222	..	62
Cuba	–100	–160	100	74	25.5	19.0	1.7	0.7	..	..	..	..
Czech Republic	38	50	424	453	1.0	3.6	2.3	1.8	..	1,017	..	2,135
Denmark	58	61	220	389	..	..	66.4	44.4	*464*	1,075[a]	*160*	1,226[a]
Dominican Republic	–220	–140	103	156	..	..	0.6	..	315	2,717	..	26
Ecuador	–50	–250	78	114	..	..	0.2	10.1	51	2,038	2	38
Egypt, Arab Rep.	–600	–450	176	166	1.2	6.3	6.0	88.9	4,284	5,017	27	57
El Salvador	–57	–38	47	24	19.6	4.3	0.2	0.0	366	2,842	3	24
Eritrea	–359	280	12	15	332.2	144.1	2.1	4.4	..	..	..	..
Estonia	–117	–10	382	202	..	..	..	0.0	..	265	..	50
Ethiopia	888	–150	1,155	555	96.3	65.5	390.5	100.8	5	174	*1*	16
Finland	43	41	61	156	..	..	11.4	11.8	63	695	16	249
France	424	300	5,907	6,471	..	..	151.3	137.3	4,035	12,742	6,949	4,867
Gabon	20	–15	128	245	..	..	0.8	8.5	..	6[a]	147	110[a]
Gambia, The	45	31	118	232	..	..	6.9	7.3	10	58	..	1[a]
Georgia	–560	–248	338	191	48.5	7.3	0.1	2.5	..	346	..	29
Germany	2,688	1,100	5,936	10,144	..	..	1,266.0	700.0	4,876	6,542	6,856	12,519
Ghana	40	12	717	1,669	15.1	18.4	35.6	53.5	6	99	4	6[a]
Greece	470	179	412	974	..	..	5.8	2.4	1,817	1,220	122	809
Guatemala	–360	–300	264	53	40.3	3.4	1.6	0.4	119	3,033	14	33
Guinea	350	–299	402	406	0.5	5.8	663.9	63.5	*27*	42[a]	20	48[a]
Guinea-Bissau	20	1	14	19	0.9	1.1	15.4	7.6	1	28[a]	12	5[a]
Haiti	–105	–105	19	30	15.1	13.5	..	..	61	985	*63*	59

Movement of people

	Net migration		Migration stock		Refugees				Workers' remittances and compensation of employees			
	thousands		thousands		thousands				$ millions			
					By country of origin		By country of asylum		Received		Paid	
	1990–95	2000–05	1990	2005	1996	2005	1996	2005	1990	2005	1990	2005
Honduras	–40	–30	270	26	..	..	0.1	0.0	63	1,796	..	1
Hungary	101	50	348	316	..	..	7.5	8.0	..	300	..	155
India	–1,407	–1,400	7,493	5,700	7.6	16.3	233.4	139.3	2,384	23,725[a]	106	1,008[a]
Indonesia	–725	–1,000	466	160	11.4	34.4	0.1	0.1	166	1,883	..	1,178
Iran, Islamic Rep.	–1,512	–1,379	3,809	1,959	104.1	99.4	2,030.4	974.3	*1,200*	1,032[a]	..	..
Iraq	170	240	84	28	714.7	262.3	113.0	50.2	..	..	..	..
Ireland	–1	194	230	585	..	..	0.1	7.1	286	651	165	1,128
Israel	484	158	1,633	2,661	..	..	*0.0*	0.6	812	851	850	2,349
Italy	573	600	1,346	2,519	..	..	64.7	20.7	5,075	2,398	3,764	5,815
Jamaica	–100	–100	21	18	..	..	0.0	..	229	1,783	27	394
Japan	248	270	877	2,048	..	..	5.3	1.9	*508*	1,080	290	1,281
Jordan[b]	495	100	1,146	2,225	..	..	0.9	1.0	499	2,500	71	349
Kazakhstan	–1,509	–600	3,619	2,502	40.2	4.3	15.6	7.3	..	178	..	1,670
Kenya	222	–212	146	345	9.4	4.6	223.6	251.3	139	524	7	56
Korea, Dem. Rep.	0	0	34	37	..	..	..	..	..	..	..	..
Korea, Rep.	–115	–80	572	551	..	..	0.0	0.1	1,037	808	364	3,336
Kuwait	–626	240	1,551	1,669	..	..	3.8	1.5	..	..	770	2,648
Kyrgyz Republic	–273	–75	623	288	17.1	3.1	16.7	2.6	..	322	..	122
Lao PDR	–10	–7	23	25	46.9	24.4	0.0	..	11	1[a]	..	1[a]
Latvia	–174	–12	805	449	..	..	*0.0*	0.0	..	381	..	20
Lebanon[b]	178	–35	520	657	10.9	18.3	2.4	1.1	1,818	4,924	..	4,233[a]
Lesotho	–84	–36	7	6	..	..	..	..	428	327	..	17
Liberia	–283	–245	81	50	784.0	231.1	120.1	10.2	..	..	..	..
Libya	10	10	457	618	..	..	7.7	12.2	..	15	446	914
Lithuania	–100	–20	349	165	..	..	*0.0*	0.5	..	534	..	47
Macedonia, FYR	–27	–10	95	121	13.0	8.6	5.1	1.3	..	226	..	16
Madagascar	–6	0	58	63	..	..	..	..	8	3	18	8
Malawi	–835	–20	1,157	279	..	..	1.3	4.2	..	1[a]	..	1[a]
Malaysia	230	150	1,014	1,639	..	..	5.3	33.7	325	1,281[a]	230	5,679
Mali	–260	–134	60	46	55.2	0.5	18.2	11.2	107	155[a]	45	64[a]
Mauritania	–15	30	94	66	83.2	31.7	15.9	0.6	14	2[a]	31	..
Mauritius	–7	0	9	21	..	..	..	..	..	215[a]	1	11[a]
Mexico	–1,800	–2,000	702	644	..	..	34.6	3.2	3,098	21,772	..	..
Moldova	–121	–40	579	440	5.8	12.1	..	0.1	..	920	..	68
Mongolia	–60	–50	7	9	..	..	..	..	..	202[a]	..	49[a]
Morocco	–300	–400	85	132	..	..	0.1	0.2	2,006	4,589	16	40
Mozambique	650	–20	122	406	34.7	0.1	0.2	2.0	70	57	25	21
Myanmar	–126	70	101	117	143.0	164.9	..	..	6	117[a]	..	25[a]
Namibia	3	–6	119	143	..	..	2.2	5.3	13	16[a]	30	17[a]
Nepal	–101	–100	413	819	..	..	126.8	126.4	*0*	1,211	..	65
Netherlands	190	150	1,192	1,638	..	..	102.6	118.2	709	2,227	1,393	5,678
New Zealand	79	78	529	642	..	..	3.8	5.3	762	739	367	936
Nicaragua	–110	–100	41	28	22.8	1.5	0.6	0.2	*0*	600	..	..
Niger	5	–10	115	124	10.4	0.7	25.8	0.3	14	60[a]	66	25[a]
Nigeria	–96	–170	447	971	4.8	22.1	8.5	9.0	10	3,329	9	18
Norway	42	58	185	344	..	..	48.4	43.0	158	429	295	953
Oman	25	–160	452	628	..	..	..	0.0	39	39	856	2,257
Pakistan	–2,611	–1,810	6,556	3,254	7.5	29.9	1,202.7	1,084.7	2,006	4,280	1	3
Panama	8	8	62	102	..	..	0.9	1.7	110	126	22	91
Papua New Guinea	0	0	33	25	..	..	10.2	10.0	5	13	43	135
Paraguay	–25	–25	183	168	..	..	0.1	0.1	34	268	..	..
Peru	–450	–300	56	42	6.7	4.9	0.7	0.8	87	1,440	75	164
Philippines	–900	–900	164	374	0.6	0.5	0.7	0.1	1,465	13,566	5	15
Poland	–77	–80	1,127	703	12.9	19.6	0.6	4.6	..	3,549	..	598
Portugal	–7	250	436	764	..	..	0.3	0.4	4,479	3,017	77	1,151
Puerto Rico	–4	–3	322	418	..	..	..	..	..	..	..	..

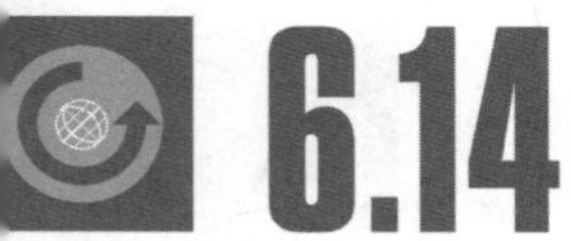

6.14 Movement of people

	Net migration		Migration stock		Refugees				Workers' remittances and compensation of employees			
	thousands		thousands		thousands				$ millions			
					By country of origin		By country of asylum		Received		Paid	
	1990–95	2000–05	1990	2005	1996	2005	1996	2005	1990	2005	1990	2005
Romania	–529	–150	143	133	11.9	11.5	0.3	2.1	..	4,733	..	34
Russian Federation	1,858	400	11,525	12,080	173.7	103.0	246.7	1.5	..	3,117	..	7,651
Rwanda	–1,714	45	73	121	469.1	100.3	25.3	45.2	3	21	21	35
Saudi Arabia	–325	250	4,743	6,361	..	..	9.9	240.7	..	..	11,221	14,318
Senegal	–100	–100	293	326	17.6	8.7	65.0	20.7	142	633[a]	79	77[a]
Serbia and Montenegro	200	–100	130	512	104.0	190.0	563.2	148.3	..	4,650[a]	..	..
Sierra Leone	–380	438	112	119	375.1	40.5	13.5	60.0	..	2	..	2
Singapore	250	200	727	1,843	..	..	0.0	0.0	..	..	..	..
Slovak Republic	9	5	41	124	..	..	1.4	0.4	..	424[a]	..	16[a]
Slovenia	38	10	178	167	..	..	10.0	0.3	38	264	2	95
Somalia	–1,083	170	633	282	637.0	395.6	0.7	0.5	..	..	..	..
South Africa	1,125	50	1,225	1,106	..	..	22.6	29.7	136	658	1,199	1,055
Spain	500	2,025	766	4,790	..	..	5.7	5.4	2,186	7,927	254	7,733
Sri Lanka	–182	–160	461	368	109.6	108.1	0.0	0.1	401	2,088	..	257
Sudan	–158	–519	1,273	639	475.3	693.6	393.9	147.3	62	1,016	2	2
Swaziland	–38	–6	73	45	..	..	0.6	0.8	113	81	4	11
Sweden	151	157	781	1,117	..	..	191.2	74.9	153	630	654	611
Switzerland	80	40	1,376	1,660	..	..	84.4	48.0	924	1,910	8,168	13,200
Syrian Arab Republic[b]	–30	–30	711	985	8.6	16.4	27.8	26.1	385	823	..	40
Tajikistan	–313	–345	426	306	107.5	54.8	1.2	1.0	..	466	..	145
Tanzania	591	–345	574	792	..	..	498.7	548.8	..	16	..	41
Thailand	–88	–50	391	1,050	..	..	108.0	117.1	973	1,187	199	..
Togo	–122	–4	163	183	25.6	51.1	12.6	9.3	27	148[a]	13	34[a]
Trinidad and Tobago	–24	–20	51	38	..	..	..	..	3	87[a]	22	..
Tunisia	–22	–20	38	38	..	..	0.2	0.1	551	1,393	13	15
Turkey	71	–250	1,150	1,328	50.4	170.6	8.2	2.4	3,246	851	..	..
Turkmenistan	50	–10	307	224	..	..	15.6	12.0	..	..	..	..
Uganda	135	–15	550	518	28.3	34.2	264.3	257.3	..	476	..	374
Ukraine	598	–700	7,097	6,833	6.1	84.2	3.6	2.3	..	595	..	34
United Arab Emirates	340	960	1,330	3,212	..	..	0.5	0.1	..	..	..	..
United Kingdom	381	686	3,753	5,408	..	..	98.6	303.2	2,099	6,722	2,034	3,087
United States	5,200	5,800	23,251	38,355	..	..	607.0	379.3	1,170	2,924	11,850	41,072
Uruguay	–20	–10	98	84	..	..	0.1	0.1	..	78	..	2
Uzbekistan	–340	–300	1,653	1,268	69.7	8.3	2.9	44.0	..	..	..	..
Venezuela, RB	40	40	1,024	1,010	..	..	1.6	0.4	1	148	701	211
Vietnam	–270	–200	28	21	518.3	358.3	34.4	2.4	..	4,000[a]	..	..
West Bank and Gaza[b]	–5	–40	911	1,680	80.2	349.7	..	..	..	436[a]	..	..
Yemen, Rep.	650	–100	107	265	..	..	53.5	81.9	1,498	1,283	106	109
Zambia	–7	–65	280	275	..	..	131.1	155.7	..	..	17	24[a]
Zimbabwe	–182	–50	804	511	0.0	11.3	0.6	13.9	1	..	16	..
World	..[c]	..[c]	154,688 s	190,206 s	11,701.6[d] s	8,300.6[d] s	13,357.1[d, e] s	8,662.0[d, e] s	68,584 s	262,489 s	66,295 s	178,677 s
Low income	–3,286	–4,000	31,745	27,120	7,935.2	5,811.7	5,762.5	3,895.6	7,664	48,188	1,305	3,379
Middle income	–9,673	–11,987	51,290	50,804	3,766.4	2,488.9	4,523.9	2,364.2	23,474	144,716	4,770	34,784
Lower middle income	–10,872	–10,086	26,469	24,999	3,182.8	2,042.2	3,972.8	2,230.4	14,370	97,779	959	8,759
Upper middle income	1,200	–1,901	24,821	25,804	583.6	446.7	551.1	133.8	9,104	46,937	3,811	26,025
Low & middle income	–12,958	–15,987	83,035	77,923	11,701.6	8,300.6	10,286.4	6,259.8	31,138	192,904	6,075	38,163
East Asia & Pacific	–3,072	–3,939	2,748	4,432	888.3	724.6	450.7	464.5	3,263	45,053	527	9,918
Europe & Central Asia	–3,398	–2,665	34,071	31,137	2,411.3	1,179.3	1,545.8	483.8	3,246	31,363	..	13,420
Latin America & Carib.	–3,776	–4,012	6,343	5,777	145.1	107.9	88.4	37.7	5,763	48,201	996	2,288
Middle East & N. Africa	–1,030	–2,374	8,828	9,642	940.1	765.0	2,457.3	1,340.5	11,432	24,001	1,566	8,014
South Asia	–1,368	–1,679	15,845	11,229	2,963.6	2,434.3	1,612.4	1,371.6	5,572	35,558	115	1,338
Sub-Saharan Africa	–314	–1,318	15,200	15,706	4,353.1	3,089.5	4,131.9	2,561.6	1,862	8,728	2,871	3,185
High income	12,929	15,970	71,653	112,282	..	..	3,070.7	2,402.2	37,446	69,585	60,220	140,514
Europe EMU	5,285	5,036	17,950	30,335	..	..	1,743.7	1,041.8	27,744	48,981	22,226	51,944

a. World Bank staff estimates. b. Palestinian refugees under the mandate of the United Nations Relief and Works Agency for Palestine Refugees in the Near East are not included in statistics from the United Nations Office of the High Commissioner for Refugees (UNHCR). c. World totals computed by the United Nations sum to zero, but because the aggregates shown here refer to World Bank definitions, regional and income group totals do not equal zero. d. World totals include refugees without a specified country or region, which are classified by UNHCR in the category "various." e. World totals come from UNHCR. Thus regional and income group totals do not add up to the world total.

About the data

Movement of people, most often through migration, is a significant part of integration. Migrants contribute to the economies of both their host country and their country of origin. Yet reliable statistics on migration are difficult to collect and are often incomplete, making international comparisons a challenge.

The United Nations Population Division provides data on net migration and migration stock. To derive estimates of net migration, the organization takes into account the past migration history of a country or area, the migration policy of a country, and the influx of refugees in recent periods. The data to calculate these official estimates come from a variety of sources, including border statistics, administrative records, surveys, and censuses. When no official estimates can be made due to insufficient data, net migration is derived through the balance equation, which is the difference between overall population growth and the natural increase during the 1990–2000 intercensal period.

The data used to estimate the international migrant stock at a particular point in time are obtained mainly from population censuses. The estimates are derived from the data on foreign-born population—those who have residence in one country but who were born in another country. When data on the foreign-born population are not available, data on foreign population are used as estimates.

After the breakup of the Soviet Union in 1991, people living in one of the newly independent countries who were born in another of the countries were classified as international migrants. Estimates of migration stock in the newly independent states from 1990 on are based on the 1989 census of the Soviet Union.

For countries with information on the international migration stock for at least two points in time, interpolation or extrapolation was used to estimate the international migrant stock on July 1 of the reference years. For countries with only one observation, estimates for the reference years were derived using rates of change in the migrant stock in the years preceding or following the single observation available. A model was used to estimate migration for countries that had no data.

Registration, together with other sources—including estimates and surveys—are the main sources of refugee data. Yet there are difficulties in collecting accurate statistics. Although refugees are often registered individually, the accuracy of registrations varies greatly. Many refugees may not be aware of the need to register or may choose not to do so. And administrative records tend to overestimate the number of refugees because it is easier to register than to de-register. Palestinian refugees under the mandate of the United Nations Relief and Works Agency for Palestine Refugees in the Near East are not included in the statistics of the United Nations Office of the High Commissioner for Refugees (UNHCR).

Workers' remittances and compensation of employees are World Bank staff estimates based on data from the International Monetary Fund's (IMF) *Balance of Payments Yearbook*. The IMF data are supplemented by World Bank staff estimates for missing data for countries where workers' remittances are important. The data reported here are the sum of three items defined in the IMF *Balance of Payments Manual* (fifth edition). These are workers' remittances, compensation of employees, and migrants' transfers.

The distinction between these three items is not always consistent in the data reported by countries to the IMF. In some cases, countries compile data on the basis of the citizenship of migrant workers rather than their residency status. Some countries also report remittances entirely as workers' remittances or compensation of employees. Following the fifth edition of the *Balance of Payments Manual* in 1993, migrants' transfers are considered a capital transaction but in previous editions they were regarded as current transfers. For these reasons the figures presented in the table take all three items into account.

High-skill workers in developing countries are increasingly emigrating to high-income countries — 6.14a

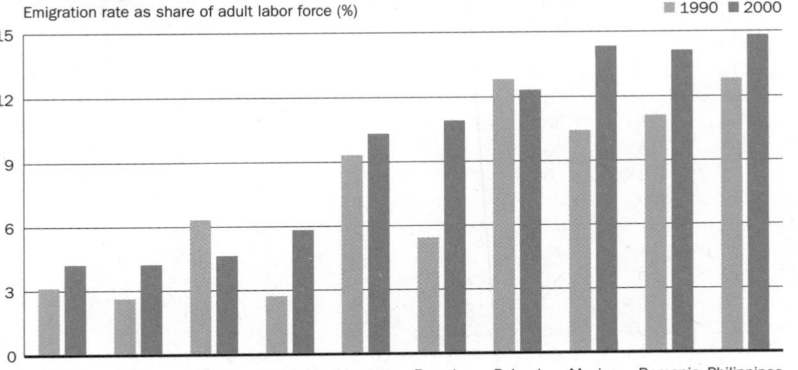

The increase in migration among high-skill workers is due partly to selective immigration policies in Organisation for Economic Co-operation and Development countries and partly to rising skill premiums in these labor markets.

Source: Docquier and Marfouk 2004.

Definitions

• **Net migration** is the net total of migrants during the period, that is, the total number of immigrants less the total number of emigrants, including both citizens and noncitizens. Data are five-year estimates. • **Migration stock** is the number of people born in a country other than that in which they live. It includes refugees. • **Refugees** are people who are recognized as refugees under the 1951 Convention Relating to the Status of Refugees or its 1967 Protocol, the 1969 Organization of African Unity Convention Governing the Specific Aspects of Refugee Problems in Africa, people recognized as refugees in accordance with the UNHCR statute, people granted a refugee-like humanitarian status, and people provided with temporary protection. Asylum seekers are people who have applied for asylum or refugee status and who have not yet received a decision or who are otherwise registered as asylum seekers. • **Country of origin** generally refers to the nationality or country of citizenship of a claimant. • **Country of asylum** is the country where an asylum claim was filed. • **Workers' remittances and compensation of employees**, **received** and **paid** comprise current transfers by migrant workers and wages and salaries earned by nonresident workers. Workers' remittances are classified as current private transfers from migrant workers who are residents of the host country to recipients in their country of origin. They include only transfers made by workers who have been living in the host country for more than a year, irrespective of their immigration status. Compensation of employees is the income of migrants who have lived in the host country for less than a year. Migrants' transfers are defined as the net worth of migrants who are expected to remain in the host country for more than one year that is transferred from one country to another at the time of migration.

Data sources

Data on net migration come from the United Nations Population Division's *World Population Prospects: The 2006 Revision*. Data on migration stock come from the United Nations Population Division's *Trends in Total Migrant Stock: The 2005 Revision*. Data on refugees are from the United Nations Office of the High Commissioner for Refugees' *Statistical Yearbook 2005*. Data on remittances are World Bank staff estimates based on IMF balance of payments data.

6.15 Travel and tourism

	International tourists (thousands)				Tourism expenditure in the country				Tourism expenditure in other countries			
	Inbound		Outbound		$ millions		% of exports		$ millions		% of imports	
	1995	**2005**	**1995**	**2005**	**1995**	**2005**	**1995**	**2005**	**1995**	**2005**	**1995**	**2005**
Afghanistan	..	..	..	..	..	..	..	..	1	..	..	..
Albania	40	46	12	2,097	70	880	23.2	48.3	19	808	2.3	20.9
Algeria	520	1,443	1,090	1,513	32	*178*	..	..	186	*394*	..	..
Angola	9	210	3	..	27	*82*	0.7	*0.6*	113	*86*	3.2	*0.8*
Argentina	2,289	3,895	3,815	4,002	2,550	3,241	10.2	7.0	4,013	3,572	15.4	10.2
Armenia	12	319	..	269	14	161	4.7	12.0	12	146	1.7	7.4
Australia	3,726	5,497	2,519	4,754	11,900	20,637	17.1	15.2	7,272	15,076	9.7	10.1
Austria	17,173	19,952	*3,713*	6,564	14,529	19,310	16.2	11.3	11,686	12,755	12.7	7.8
Azerbaijan	93	1,177	*432*	1,830	88	100	11.2	1.2	165	188	12.8	2.7
Bangladesh	156	208	830	1,767	..	78	..	0.7	*251*	371	*3.4*	2.6
Belarus	161	91	626	572	28	346	0.5	1.9	101	672	1.8	3.8
Belgium	5,560	6,747	*5,645*	9,318	..	10,879	..	3.4	..	16,636	..	5.4
Benin	138	*174*	..	..	*79*	*108*	*12.1*	*15.1*	48	*53*	5.4	*4.9*
Bolivia	284	504	249	312	92	346	7.5	11.0	72	258	4.6	9.0
Bosnia and Herzegovina	*115*	*190*	..	..	..	604	..	16.8	..	160	..	2.0
Botswana	521	*1,523*	..	..	176	*550*	7.3	*12.4*	153	*280*	7.5	*7.7*
Brazil	1,991	5,358	2,600	4,696	1,085	4,169	2.1	3.1	3,982	5,905	6.3	6.0
Bulgaria	3,466	4,837	3,524	4,235	662	3,026	9.8	18.8	312	1,836	4.8	8.9
Burkina Faso	124	*222*	..	..	..	..	..	..	..	..	..	..
Burundi	34	148	36	..	2	2	1.9	2.1	..	62	..	17.6
Cambodia	220	1,422	31	*239*	71	927	7.3	23.1	22	138	1.6	3.0
Cameroon	100	*190*	..	..	75	*162*	3.7	*5.6*	140	*294*	8.7	*9.1*
Canada	16,932	18,770	18,206	21,101	9,176	15,830	4.2	3.7	12,658	23,061	6.3	6.0
Central African Republic	26	*8*	..	*7*	4	*4*	..	..	43	*32*	..	..
Chad	19	29	..	..	43	..	..	..	38	..	..	..
Chile	1,540	2,027	1,070	*2,343*	1,186	1,779	6.1	3.7	934	1,381	5.1	3.6
China	20,034	46,809	4,520	31,026	*12,626*	31,842	*6.1*	3.8	*9,220*	24,715	*5.6*	3.5
Hong Kong, China	10,200	23,359	3,023	4,957	..	13,586	..	3.9	..	..	..	..
Colombia	1,433	933	1,057	1,553	887	1,570	7.2	6.4	1,162	1,562	7.3	6.3
Congo, Dem. Rep.	35	61	..	..	..	..	..	..	..	..	..	..
Congo, Rep.	37	..	..	..	15	*23*	1.1	*0.6*	69	*176*	5.1	*8.9*
Costa Rica	785	*1,453*	273	*425*	763	1,804	17.1	18.6	336	556	7.1	5.2
Côte d'Ivoire	188	..	..	..	103	*76*	2.4	*1.2*	312	*551*	8.2	*11.0*
Croatia	1,485	8,467	..	..	..	7,625	..	40.4	..	786	..	3.6
Cuba	742	2,261	72	*115*	963	1,920	..	..	..	..	..	..
Czech Republic	3,381	6,336	44,873	*36,650*	..	5,580	..	6.3	..	2,605	..	3.0
Denmark	2,124	*3,358*	*5,035*	*4,630*	..	..	..	..	..	..	..	..
Dominican Republic	1,776	3,691	168	419	..	..	..	..	267	494	4.4	4.4
Ecuador	440	861	271	661	315	488	6.1	4.3	331	616	5.8	5.2
Egypt, Arab Rep.	2,871	8,244	2,683	*3,644*	2,954	7,206	22.3	23.5	1,371	1,932	8.0	5.6
El Salvador	235	1,154	348	1,397	152	838	7.5	18.3	99	430	2.7	5.6
Eritrea	315	83	..	..	58	66	..	..	..	..	..	..
Estonia	530	1,900	1,764	*2,075*	452	1,207	17.6	11.0	121	538	4.2	4.6
Ethiopia	103	227	120	..	177	533	23.1	27.6	30	*59*	2.1	*1.6*
Finland	1,779	2,080	5,147	6,035	2,384	3,055	5.0	3.7	2,853	3,529	7.6	5.0
France	60,033	76,001	18,686	22,270	31,295	..	8.6	..	20,699	..	6.2	..
Gabon	125	*222*	..	*236*	94	*74*	3.2	*1.8*	183	*275*	10.6	*12.8*
Gambia, The	45	111	..	387	*67*	57	*30.5*	31.6	16	7	6.9	2.7
Georgia	85	560	228	..	*75*	288	*13.1*	13.3	*171*	238	*12.1*	7.2
Germany	14,847	21,500	*55,800*	77,400	24,052	38,381	4.0	3.4	66,527	80,276	11.2	8.1
Ghana	286	*584*	..	..	30	827	1.9	21.4	74	472	3.5	7.1
Greece	10,130	14,276	..	..	4,182	13,697	26.9	26.4	1,495	3,046	6.0	4.6
Guatemala	563	1,316	333	982	216	883	7.7	17.9	167	500	4.5	5.2
Guinea	*12*	45	..	..	1	*32*	0.1	*4.3*	29	*29*	2.9	*3.0*
Guinea-Bissau	..	5	..	..	..	*2*	..	*2.6*	6	*22*	6.7	*17.3*
Haiti	145	*96*	..	..	..	..	..	..	..	173	..	9.9

6.15 Travel and tourism

	International tourists				Tourism expenditure in the country				Tourism expenditure in other countries			
	thousands											
	Inbound		Outbound		$ millions		% of exports		$ millions		% of imports	
	1995	2005	1995	2005	1995	2005	1995	2005	1995	2005	1995	2005
Honduras	271	749	149	301	85	476	5.2	13.9	99	315	5.3	6.3
Hungary	2,878	3,446	13,083	18,622	2,938	4,581	14.9	6.2	1,501	3,037	7.5	4.0
India	2,124	3,915	3,056	*6,200*	..	*4,128*	..	*5.0*	..	*4,758*	..	*5.1*
Indonesia	4,324	5,002	1,782	4,106	..	5,092	..	5.1	..	4,741	..	5.4
Iran, Islamic Rep.	489	*1,659*	1,000	..	205	*1,324*	1.1	..	247	*4,353*	1.6	..
Iraq	61	..	..	..	..	..	..	..	..	..	..	..
Ireland	4,818	7,333	2,547	6,113	2,698	6,722	5.5	4.2	..	6,168	..	4.5
Israel	2,215	1,903	2,259	3,687	3,491	3,414	12.7	5.9	2,626	3,780	7.4	6.6
Italy	31,052	36,513	*18,173*	*23,349*	30,426	38,264	10.3	8.3	17,219	26,459	6.9	5.7
Jamaica	1,147	1,479	..	..	1,199	1,783	35.3	44.6	173	291	4.6	4.9
Japan	3,345	6,728	15,298	17,404	4,894	15,555	1.0	2.3	46,966	48,102	11.2	7.9
Jordan	1,075	2,987	1,128	1,523	973	1,759	28.0	26.7	719	653	14.7	5.5
Kazakhstan	..	*3,073*	*523*	*3,915*	155	793	2.6	2.6	296	854	4.9	3.3
Kenya	896	*1,199*	..	..	590	969	20.0	18.9	183	..	5.2	..
Korea, Dem. Rep.	..	..	..	..	..	..	..	..	..	..	..	..
Korea, Rep.	3,753	6,022	3,819	10,078	6,670	8,148	4.5	2.4	6,947	16,831	4.5	5.4
Kuwait	72	*91*	878	*1,928*	309	*414*	2.2	*1.2*	2,513	*4,150*	19.9	*21.6*
Kyrgyz Republic	36	315	42	*239*	..	94	..	10.0	*7*	71	*0.7*	5.1
Lao PDR	60	672	..	..	52	..	12.8	..	34	..	4.5	..
Latvia	539	1,116	1,812	2,959	37	446	1.8	5.9	62	655	2.8	6.6
Lebanon	450	1,140	..	..	710	5,869	..	45.0	..	3,535	..	21.8
Lesotho	87	..	..	..	29	..	14.6	..	17	36	1.6	2.7
Liberia	..	..	..	..	..	..	..	..	..	..	..	..
Libya	56	*149*	484	..	4	*261*	0.1	*1.5*	98	*789*	1.7	*7.4*
Lithuania	650	2,000	1,925	*3,502*	102	975	3.2	6.6	107	757	2.7	4.5
Macedonia, FYR	147	197	..	..	*35*	92	*2.7*	3.7	*30*	94	*1.7*	2.6
Madagascar	75	*229*	39	*67*	106	*265*	14.2	*51.5*	79	*184*	8.0	*24.0*
Malawi	192	*471*	..	..	22	36	4.7	..	53	58	8.0	..
Malaysia	7,469	16,431	20,642	*30,761*	5,044	10,389	6.1	6.4	2,722	4,339	3.1	3.3
Mali	42	143	..	..	26	*142*	4.9	*11.7*	74	*126*	7.5	*7.8*
Mauritania	..	..	..	..	..	..	..	..	30	..	5.9	..
Mauritius	422	761	107	183	616	1,189	26.2	31.6	184	295	7.5	7.1
Mexico	20,241	21,915	8,450	13,305	6,847	12,801	7.7	5.6	3,587	8,951	4.4	3.7
Moldova	32	23	71	57	71	163	8.0	10.7	73	197	7.3	7.2
Mongolia	108	*301*	..	..	33	*205*	6.5	*16.9*	22	*207*	4.2	*14.7*
Morocco	2,602	5,843	1,317	*1,746*	1,469	5,426	16.2	28.9	356	999	3.2	4.4
Mozambique	..	*470*	..	..	..	138	..	6.6	..	187	..	6.5
Myanmar	117	232	..	..	169	*98*	12.9	*3.1*	*38*	*32*	*1.5*	*1.3*
Namibia	272	*695*	..	..	..	*426*	..	*18.4*	..	..	..	..
Nepal	363	375	100	373	232	160	22.5	12.5	167	221	10.3	8.2
Netherlands	6,574	10,012	12,313	17,086	10,611	..	4.4	..	13,151	..	6.1	..
New Zealand	1,409	2,365	920	1,872	..	..	..	..	..	..	..	..
Nicaragua	281	712	255	740	51	211	7.7	11.3	56	161	4.9	4.9
Niger	35	*55*	10	..	*26*	*29*	*7.1*	*7.0*	26	*39*	5.7	*5.7*
Nigeria	656	*962*	..	..	47	*49*	0.4	*0.1*	939	*1,469*	7.3	*7.0*
Norway	2,880	3,859	590	3,122	2,730	3,884	4.9	2.9	4,481	*8,788*	9.6	*12.2*
Oman	279	1,116	..	..	..	679	..	3.5	..	838	..	7.6
Pakistan	378	798	..	..	582	827	5.7	4.3	654	1,748	4.6	6.0
Panama	345	702	185	285	372	1,108	4.9	10.3	181	388	2.3	3.6
Papua New Guinea	42	69	51	..	..	..	..	..	..	..	..	..
Paraguay	438	341	427	188	162	96	3.4	2.4	173	129	3.3	3.1
Peru	479	1,486	508	1,841	521	1,371	7.9	7.1	428	900	4.5	5.9
Philippines	1,760	2,623	1,615	2,144	1,141	2,620	4.3	5.9	551	1,547	1.7	2.9
Poland	19,215	15,200	36,387	40,841	6,927	7,127	19.4	6.3	5,865	4,686	17.3	4.1
Portugal	9,511	*11,617*	..	..	5,646	9,222	17.5	17.3	2,540	3,763	6.4	5.4
Puerto Rico	3,131	3,686	1,237	1,410	1,828	3,239	..	..	1,155	1,663	..	..

Travel and tourism

	International tourists				Tourism expenditure in the country				Tourism expenditure in other countries			
	thousands											
	Inbound		Outbound		$ millions		% of exports		$ millions		% of imports	
	1995	2005	1995	2005	1995	2005	1995	2005	1995	2005	1995	2005
Romania	2,757	..	5,737	7,140	689	1,310	7.3	4.0	749	1,022	6.6	2.4
Russian Federation	10,290	22,201	21,329	28,416	..	7,402	..	2.8	..	18,795	..	11.4
Rwanda	..	..	..	..	4	..	5.4	..	13	..	3.5	..
Saudi Arabia	3,325	9,100	..	*3,811*	..	6,111	..	3.4	..	3,763	..	4.7
Senegal	280	387	..	..	168	*269*	11.2	*14.7*	154	*129*	8.5	*4.9*
Serbia and Montenegro	228	725	..	..	..	..	..	..	..	..	..	..
Sierra Leone	38	40	6	63	..	..	..	..	51	34	19.4	7.4
Singapore	6,070	7,080	2,867	*5,165*	..	..	..	..	..	..	..	..
Slovak Republic	903	1,515	218	486	630	*932*	5.7	*3.5*	338	*903*	3.2	*2.6*
Slovenia	732	1,555	..	*2,800*	1,128	1,894	10.9	8.6	606	1,019	5.6	4.6
Somalia	..	..	..	..	..	..	..	..	..	..	..	..
South Africa	4,488	7,369	2,520	..	2,655	8,448	7.7	12.7	2,414	4,813	7.2	7.0
Spain	34,920	55,577	3,648	*5,121*	27,369	52,960	20.4	18.4	5,826	18,440	4.3	5.3
Sri Lanka	403	549	504	727	367	729	7.9	9.2	279	553	4.7	5.5
Sudan	29	*61*	195	..	..	..	..	..	..	..	..	..
Swaziland	300	839	..	1,082	54	*109*	5.3	*4.9*	45	*54*	3.5	*2.4*
Sweden	2,310	..	10,127	12,598	4,390	8,584	4.6	4.8	6,816	11,847	8.4	7.9
Switzerland	6,946	7,229	11,148	..	11,354	12,961	9.2	6.6	9,478	11,060	8.7	6.5
Syrian Arab Republic	815	..	1,746	4,564	..	2,283	..	23.4	..	593	..	5.5
Tajikistan	..	..	..	..	..	10	..	0.8	..	..	..	..
Tanzania	285	*566*	157	..	*344*	836	*28.4*	28.9	*424*	577	*21.6*	15.1
Thailand	6,952	11,567	1,820	3,047	9,257	12,629	13.2	9.7	4,791	5,790	5.8	4.3
Togo	53	81	..	..	..	*25*	..	*3.3*	41	*38*	6.1	*3.5*
Trinidad and Tobago	260	463	261	..	232	661	8.3	*7.8*	91	288	4.3	*2.7*
Tunisia	4,120	6,378	1,778	2,241	1,838	2,782	23.0	19.2	294	443	3.3	3.0
Turkey	7,083	20,273	3,981	8,246	..	..	..	..	..	..	..	..
Turkmenistan	218	12	21	33	*13*	..	*0.7*	..	*74*	..	*4.1*	..
Uganda	160	468	*148*	189	..	357	..	26.6	..	137	..	5.3
Ukraine	3,716	*15,629*	6,552	*15,488*	*448*	3,542	*2.2*	8.0	*405*	3,078	*1.9*	7.0
United Arab Emirates	2,315	*5,871*	..	..	632	2,200	..	..	..	5,300	..	..
United Kingdom	23,537	29,971	41,345	66,494	27,577	39,573	8.6	6.7	30,749	73,786	9.4	11.0
United States	43,490	49,209	51,285	63,502	93,700	122,944	11.8	9.6	60,924	99,624	6.8	5.0
Uruguay	2,022	1,808	*562*	658	725	690	20.7	13.6	332	328	9.3	7.1
Uzbekistan	92	*262*	*246*	*455*	*15*	*57*	..	..	..	..	..	..
Venezuela, RB	700	706	534	1,067	995	713	4.8	1.3	1,852	1,837	11.0	6.3
Vietnam	1,351	3,468	..	..	..	1,880	..	5.1	..	..	..	..
West Bank and Gaza	*220*	88	..	..	..	..	..	..	..	..	..	..
Yemen, Rep.	61	336	..	..	..	..	..	..	..	224	..	4.2
Zambia	163	*515*	..	..	47	*161*	*6.1*	..	*83*	..	*6.2*	..
Zimbabwe	1,363	..	256	..	145	99	..	..	106	..	..	..
World	524,060 t	736,109 t	427,305 t	568,830 t	497,633 t	787,293 t	8.0 w	6.5 w	383,191 t	621,415 t	7.9 w	6.3 w
Low income	10,879	*17,998*	..	*9,317*	..	*12,490*	..	5.9	..	*11,060*	..	6.2
Middle income	159,782	265,628	208,088	*273,023*	93,536	187,387	8.2	6.4	43,377	126,571	5.6	5.1
Lower middle income	66,091	123,098	38,567	*88,101*	*49,702*	104,938	*7.6*	6.1	*31,176*	62,312	*5.4*	4.3
Upper middle income	93,691	142,530	169,521	*184,922*	50,435	83,641	8.9	6.6	26,008	64,259	6.9	6.0
Low & middle income	170,661	279,291	213,011	*282,340*	101,738	205,221	*8.1*	6.4	46,653	131,051	*5.7*	5.1
East Asia & Pacific	44,254	91,295	36,006	*81,084*	*35,094*	66,121	*7.1*	5.0	*20,679*	39,432	*4.9*	3.7
Europe & Central Asia	58,037	90,756	142,185	*161,107*	..	..	..	6.1	..	41,223	..	6.8
Latin America & Carib.	39,667	54,142	21,025	32,407	20,620	38,687	7.1	5.7	18,505	29,372	6.5	5.2
Middle East & N. Africa	13,420	27,605	11,226	*14,092*	11,096	25,288	12.3	23.0	3,287	9,217	4.3	7.1
South Asia	3,744	6,254	4,522	*8,792*	..	*6,343*	..	4.6	..	*6,951*	..	5.1
Sub-Saharan Africa	12,119	*17,247*	..	..	6,385	17,893	6.8	*9.2*	5,739	*8,670*	7.0	*6.7*
High income	353,399	456,818	214,294	365,507	393,204	580,977	7.9	6.5	336,538	490,364	8.2	6.8
Europe EMU	197,165	250,904	*124,665*	174,788	175,291	253,742	8.2	7.1	141,996	171,072	8.2	6.6

About the data

Tourism is defined as the activities of people traveling to and staying in places outside their usual environment for no more than one year for leisure, business, and other purposes not related to an activity remunerated from within the place visited. The social and economic phenomenon of tourism has grown substantially over the past quarter century. Past descriptions of tourism focused on the characteristics of visitors, such as the purpose of their visit and the conditions in which they traveled and stayed. Now, there is a growing awareness of the direct, indirect, and induced effects of tourism on employment, value added, personal income, government income, and the like.

Statistical information on tourism is based mainly on data on arrivals and overnight stays along with balance of payments information. But these data do not completely capture the economic phenomenon of tourism or give governments, businesses, and citizens the information needed for effective public policies and efficient business operations. Credible data are needed on the scale and significance of tourism. Information on the role tourism plays in national economies throughout the world is particularly deficient. Although the World Tourism Organization reports that progress has been made in harmonizing definitions and measurement units, differences in national practices still prevent full international comparability.

The data in the table are from the World Tourism Organization, a specialized agency of the United Nations. The data on international inbound and outbound tourists refer to the number of arrivals and departures of visitors within the reference period, not to the number of people traveling. Thus a person who makes several trips to a country during a given period is counted each time as a new arrival. International visitors include tourists (overnight visitors), same-day visitors, cruise passengers, and crew members.

The World Tourism Organization is improving its coverage of tourism expenditure data. It is now using balance of payments data from the International Monetary Fund (IMF), supplemented by data received from individual countries. The new data, shown in the table, now include travel and passenger transport items as defined in the IMF's *Balance of Payments Manual*.

Aggregates are based on the World Bank's classification of countries and differ from those in the World Tourism Organization's publications. Countries not shown in the table but for which data are available are included in the regional and income group totals. The aggregates in the table are calculated using the World Bank's weighted aggregation methodology (see *Statistical methods*) and differ from aggregates provided by the World Tourism Organization.

Definitions

• **International inbound tourists** (overnight visitors) are the number of tourists who travel to a country other than that in which they have their usual residence, but outside their usual environment, for a period not exceeding 12 months and whose main purpose in visiting is other than an activity remunerated from within the country visited. • **International outbound tourists** are the number of departures that people make from their country of usual residence to any other country for any purpose other than a remunerated activity in the country visited. • **Tourism expenditure in the country** is expenditures by international inbound visitors, including payments to national carriers for international transport. These receipts include any other prepayment made for goods or services received in the destination country. They also may include receipts from same-day visitors, except in cases where these are important enough to justify separate classification. Their share in exports is calculated as a ratio to exports of goods and services (for definition of exports of goods and services see *Definitions* for table 4.8). • **Tourism expenditure in other countries** is expenditures of international outbound visitors in other countries, including payments to foreign carriers for international transport. These expenditures may include those by residents traveling abroad as same-day visitors, except in cases where these are important enough to justify separate classification. Their share in imports is calculated as a ratio to imports of goods and services (for definition of imports of goods and services see *Definitions* for table 4.8).

International tourism generated more than $2 billion a day in 2005 **6.15a**

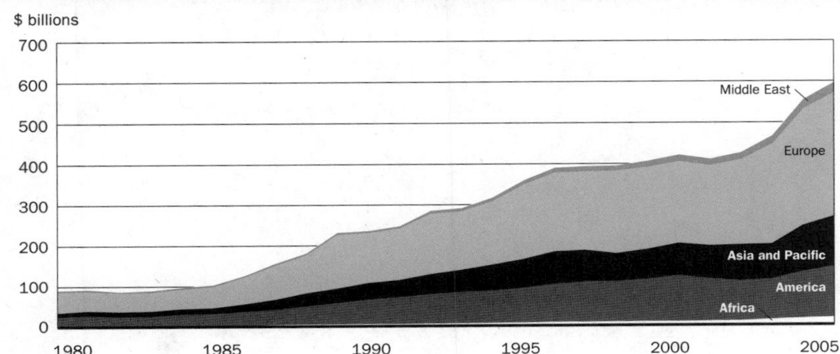

International tourism has become an important pillar of some economies and accounted for 40 percent of global services trade in recent years. In 2005 Africa recorded the highest growth rate in international tourism receipts (8.5 percent), followed by Asia and Pacific (4.3 percent).

Source: World Tourism Organization.

Data sources

Data on visitors and tourism expenditure are available in the World Tourism Organization's *Yearbook of Tourism Statistics* and *Compendium of Tourism Statistics 2007*. Data in the table are updated from electronic files provided by the World Tourism Organization. Data on exports and imports are from the IMF's *International Financial Statistics* and World Bank staff estimates.

PRIMARY DATA DOCUMENTATION

The World Bank is not a primary data collection agency for most areas other than business and investment climate surveys, living standards surveys, and external debt. As a major user of socioeconomic data, however, the World Bank recognizes the importance of data documentation to inform users of differences in the methods and conventions used by the primary data collectors—usually national statistical agencies, central banks, and customs services—and by international organizations, which compile the statistics that appear in the World Development Indicators database. These differences may give rise to significant discrepancies over time both within countries and across them. Delays in reporting data and the use of old surveys as the base for current estimates may further compromise the quality of data reported here.

The tables in this section provide information on sources, methods, and reporting standards of the principal demographic, economic, and environmental indicators in *World Development Indicators.* Additional documentation is available from the World Bank's Country Statistical Information Database at www.worldbank.org/data.

The demand for good quality statistical data is increasing. Timely and reliable statistics are key to the broad development strategy often referred to as "managing for results." Monitoring and reporting on publicly agreed indicators is central to implementing poverty reduction strategies and lies at the heart of the Millennium Development Goals and the new Results Measurement System adopted for the 14th replenishment of the International Development Association.

A global action plan to improve national and international statistics was agreed on during the Second Roundtable on Managing for Development Results in February 2004 in Marrakech, Morocco. The plan, now referred to as the Marrakech Action Plan for Statistics, or MAPS, has been widely endorsed and forms the overarching framework for statistical capacity building. The Third Roundtable conference, held in February 2007 in Hanoi, Vietnam, reaffirmed MAPS as the guiding strategy for improving the capacity of the national and international statistical systems. See www.mfdr.org/RT3 for reports from the conference.

PRIMARY DATA DOCUMENTATION

	Currency	National accounts						Balance of payments and trade			Government finance	IMF data dissemination standard
		Base year	Reference year	System of National Accounts	SNA price valuation	Alternative conversion factor	PPP survey year	Balance of Payments Manual in use	External debt	System of trade	Accounting concept	
Afghanistan	Afghan afghani	2002/03			VAB						B	
Albania	Albanian lek	[a]	1996	[b]	VAB		1996	BPM5	Actual	G	C	G
Algeria	Algerian dinar	1980			VAB			BPM5	Actual	S	B	
Angola	Angolan kwanza	1997			VAP	1991–96		BPM4	Preliminary	S		G
Argentina	Argentine peso	1993		[b]	VAB	1971–84	1996	BPM5	Actual	S	C	S
Armenia	Armenian dram	[a]	1996	[b]	VAB	1990–95	2000	BPM5	Actual	S	C	S
Australia	Australian dollar	[a]	2000	[b]	VAB		2002	BPM5		G	C	S
Austria	Euro	2000		[b]	VAB		2002	BPM5		S	C	S
Azerbaijan	New Azeri manat	[a]	2003	[b]	VAB	1992–95	2000	BPM5	Actual	G	C	G
Bangladesh	Bangladesh taka	1995/96		[b]	VAB		1996	BPM5	Actual	G	C	G
Belarus	Belarusian rubel	[a]	2000	[b]	VAB	1990–95	2000	BPM5	Actual	G	C	S
Belgium	Euro	2000		[b]	VAB		2002	BPM5		S	C	S
Benin	CFA franc	1985			VAP	1992	1996	BPM5	Preliminary	S	B	G
Bolivia	Boliviano	1990		[b]	VAB	1960–85	1996	BPM5	Actual	S	C	G
Bosnia and Herzegovina	Konvertible mark	[a]	1996	[b]	VAB			BPM5	Actual		C	
Botswana	Botswana pula	1993/94		[b]	VAB		1996	BPM5	Actual	G	B	G
Brazil	Brazilian real	1990		[b]	VAB		1996	BPM5	Actual	S	C	S
Bulgaria	Bulgarian lev	[a]	2002	[b]	VAB	1978–89, 1991–92	2002	BPM5	Actual	G	C	S
Burkina Faso	CFA franc	1990			VAP	1992–93		BPM4	Actual	G	B	G
Burundi	Burundi franc	1980			VAB			BPM5	Actual	S	C	
Cambodia	Cambodian riel	2000			VAB			BPM5	Actual	G	C	G
Cameroon	CFA franc	2000		[b]	VAB		1996	BPM5	Preliminary	S	B	G
Canada	Canadian dollar	2000		[b]	VAB		2002	BPM5		G	C	S
Central African Republic	CFA franc	1987			VAB			BPM4	Preliminary	S	B	G
Chad	CFA franc	1995			VAB			BPM5	Actual	S	C	G
Chile	Chilean peso	1996		[b]	VAB		1996	BPM5	Actual	S	C	S
China	Chinese yuan	2000	1990	[b]	VAP	1978–93	1986	BPM5	Preliminary	S	B	G
Hong Kong, China	Hong Kong dollar	2000		[b]	VAB		1996	BPM5		G	C	S
Colombia	Colombian peso	1994		[b]	VAB	1992–94		BPM5	Actual	S	C	S
Congo, Dem. Rep.	Congo franc	1987			VAB	1999–2001		BPM5	Preliminary	S	C	G
Congo, Rep.	CFA Franc	1978			VAP		1996	BPM5	Preliminary	S	C	G
Costa Rica	Costa Rican colon	1991		[b]	VAB			BPM5	Actual	S	C	S
Côte d'Ivoire	CFA franc	1996			VAP		1996	BPM5	Estimate	S	C	G
Croatia	Croatian kuna	[a]	1997	[b]	VAB		2002	BPM5	Actual	G	C	S
Cuba	Cuban peso	1984			VAP					G		
Czech Republic	Czech koruna	2000	1995	[b]	VAB		2002	BPM5		G	C	S
Denmark	Danish krone	2000		[b]	VAB		2002	BPM5		G	C	S
Dominican Republic	Dominican peso	1990			VAP			BPM5	Actual	G	C	G
Ecuador	U.S. dollar	2000		[b]	VAB		1996	BPM5	Preliminary	S	B	S
Egypt, Arab Rep.	Egyptian pound	1991/92			VAB		1996	BPM5	Actual	S	B	S
El Salvador	U.S. dollar	1990			VAB	1982–90		BPM5	Actual	S	C	S
Eritrea	Eritrean nakfa	1992			VAB			BPM4	Actual			
Estonia	Estonian kroon	2000		[b]	VAB	1991–95	2002	BPM5	Actual	G	C	S
Ethiopia	Ethiopian birr	1999/2000		[b]	VAB			BPM5	Actual	G	C	G
Finland	Euro	2000		[b]	VAB		2002	BPM5		G	C	S
France	Euro	[a]	2000	[b]	VAB		2002	BPM5		S	C	S
Gabon	CFA franc	1991			VAP	1993	1996	BPM5	Preliminary	S	B	G
Gambia, The	Gambian dalasi	1987			VAB			BPM5	Actual	G	B	G
Georgia	Georgian lari	[a]	1994	[b]	VAB	1990–95	2000	BPM5	Actual	G	C	G
Germany	Euro	2000		[b]	VAB		2002	BPM5		S	C	S
Ghana	Ghanaian cedi	1975			VAP	1973–87		BPM5	Actual	G	B	G
Greece	Euro	[a]	2000		VAB		2002	BPM5		S	C	S
Guatemala	Guatemalan quetzal	1958			VAP		1980	BPM5	Actual	S	B	G
Guinea	Guinean franc	1996	1994		VAB		1996	BPM5	Estimate	S	B	G
Guinea-Bissau	CFA franc	1986			VAB			BPM5	Estimate	G		G
Haiti	Haitian gourde	1975/76			VAB	1991		BPM5	Actual	G		

PRIMARY DATA DOCUMENTATION

	Latest population census	Latest demographic, education, or health household survey	Source of most recent income and expenditure data	Vital registration complete	Latest agricultural census	Latest industrial data	Latest trade data	Latest water withdrawal data
Afghanistan	1979	MICS, 2003					1977	1987
Albania	2001	RHS, 2002	LSMS, 2004	Yes	1998	1990	2005	1995
Algeria	1998	MICS, 2000	HLSS, 1995		2001	2004	2004	1995
Angola	1970	MICS, 2001			1964–65		1991	1987
Argentina	2001		EPH, 2003	Yes	2002	2001	2005	1995
Armenia	2001	DHS, 2000	ILCS, 2003	Yes			2005	1994
Australia	2001		SIHC, 1994	Yes	2001	2004	2005	1985
Austria	2001		Microcensus 2000	Yes	1999–2000	2004	2005	1991
Azerbaijan	1999	RHS, 2001	HBS, 2003	Yes			2005	1995
Bangladesh	2001	DHS, 2004	HES, 2000		1996	2004	2004	1990
Belarus	1999		IES, 2002	Yes	1994		2005	1990
Belgium	2001		ECHP, 2000	Yes	1999–2000[c]	2004	2005	
Benin	2002	DHS, 2001	CWIQ, 2003		1992	1999	2005	1994
Bolivia	2001	DHS, 2003	MECOVI, 2002		1984–88	2001	2005	1987
Bosnia and Herzegovina	1991	MICS, 2000	LSMS, 2001	Yes		1991	2005	1995
Botswana	2001	MICS, 2000	HIES, 1993–94		1993	2003	2003	1992
Brazil	2000	DHS, 1996	PNAD, 2004		1996	1995	2005	1992
Bulgaria	2001		HBS, 2003	Yes		2003	2005	1988
Burkina Faso	1996	DHS, 2003	EVCBM, 2003		1993	2004	2004	1992
Burundi	1990	MICS, 2000	Priority survey, 1998			2004	2005	1987
Cambodia	1998	DHS, 2005	SES, 2004				2004	1987
Cameroon	1987	DHS, 2004	Priority survey, 2001		1984	2002	2005	1987
Canada	2001		EBC, 2001	Yes	1996/2001	2004	2005	1991
Central African Republic	2003	MICS, 2000	SLID, 2000		1985	2004	2005	1987
Chad	1993	DHS, 2004	EPI, 1993			1975	1995	1987
Chile	2002		CASEN, 2003	Yes	1996–97	2004	2005	1987
China	2000	Intercensal survey 1995	HHS (Rural/Urban), 2004		1997	2003	2005	1993
Hong Kong, China	2006			Yes		2002	2005	
Colombia	2005	DHS, 2005	ECV, 2003		2001	2004	2005	1996
Congo, Dem. Rep.	1984	MICS, 2001			1990		1986	1990
Congo, Rep.	1996	DHS, 2005			1985–86	1988	1995	1987
Costa Rica	2000	RHS, 1993	EHPM, 2003	Yes	1973	2004	2005	1997
Côte d'Ivoire	1998	MICS, 2000; AIS, 2005	LSMS, 2002		2001	1997	2005	1987
Croatia	2001		HBS, 2001	Yes	2003	1992	2005	1996
Cuba	2002	MICS, 2000		Yes		1989	2004	1995
Czech Republic	2001	RHS, 1993	Microcensus 1996/97	Yes	2000	1998	2005	1991
Denmark	2001		Income Tax Register 1997	Yes	1999–2000	2004	2005	1990
Dominican Republic	2002	DHS, 2002	ENFT, 2004		1971	2004	2001	1994
Ecuador	2001	RHS, 2004	LSMS, 1998		1999–2000	2004	2005	1997
Egypt, Arab Rep.	1996	DHS, 2005	HECS, 2000	Yes	1999–2000		2004	1996
El Salvador	1992	RHS, 2002/03	EHPM, 2002	Yes	1970–71	2004	2004	1992
Eritrea	1984	DHS, 2002				2003	2003	
Estonia	2000		HBS, 2003	Yes	2001	2003	2005	1995
Ethiopia	1994	DHS, 2005	ICES, 2000		2001–02	2002	2003	1987
Finland	2000		IDS, 2000	Yes	1990–2000	2004	2005	1991
France	1999		HBS, 1994/95	Yes	1999–2000	2004	2005	1999
Gabon	2003	DHS, 2000			1974–75		2004	1987
Gambia, The	2003	MICS, 2000	HHS, 1998		2001–02	1982	2005	1982
Georgia	2002	MICS, 1999; RHS, 1999	SGH, 2003	Yes			2005	1990
Germany	2004		GSOEP, 2000	Yes	1999–2000	2003	2005	1991
Ghana	2000	SPA, 2002; DHS, 2003	LSMS, 1998/99		1984	2004	2004	1997
Greece	2001		ECHP, 2000	Yes	1999–2000	2004	2005	1980
Guatemala	2002	RHS, 2002	ENEI-2, 2002	Yes	2003	2004	2005	1992
Guinea	1996	DHS, 2005	LSMS, 1994		2000		2002	1987
Guinea-Bissau	1991	MICS, 2000	IES, 1993		1988		1995	1991
Haiti	2003	DHS, 2000	ECVH, 2001		1971	1996	1997	1991

PRIMARY DATA DOCUMENTATION

	Currency	National accounts						Balance of payments and trade			Government finance	IMF data dissemination standard
		Base year	Reference year	System of National Accounts	SNA price valuation	Alternative conversion factor	PPP survey year	Balance of Payments Manual in use	External debt	System of trade	Accounting concept	
Honduras	Honduran lempira	1978			VAB	1988–89		BPM5	Actual	S		G
Hungary	Hungarian forint	[a]	2000	[b]	VAB		2002	BPM5	Actual	S	C	S
India	Indian rupee	1999/2000		[b]	VAB			BPM5	Actual	G	C	S
Indonesia	Indonesian rupiah	2000			VAP		1996	BPM5	Preliminary	S	C	S
Iran, Islamic Rep.	Iranian rial	1997/98			VAB	1980–90	1996	BPM5	Actual	G	C	
Iraq	Iraqi dinar	1997			VAB					S		
Ireland	Euro	2000		[b]	VAB		2002	BPM5		G	C	S
Israel	Israeli new shekel	2000		[b]	VAP		2002	BPM5		S	C	S
Italy	Euro	2000		[b]	VAB		2002	BPM5		S	C	S
Jamaica	Jamaica dollar	1996			VAB		1996	BPM5	Preliminary	G	C	G
Japan	Japanese yen	2000			VAB		2002	BPM5		G	C	S
Jordan	Jordan dinar	1994			VAB		1996	BPM5	Actual	G	B	G
Kazakhstan	Kazakh tenge	[a]	1995	[b]	VAB	1987–95	2000	BPM5	Actual	G	C	S
Kenya	Kenya shilling	2001		[b]	VAB		1996	BPM5	Preliminary	G	B	G
Korea, Dem. Rep.	Democratic Republic of Korea won							BPM5				
Korea, Rep.	Korean won	2000		[b]	VAB		2002	BPM5		S	C	S
Kuwait	Kuwaiti dinar	1995			VAP			BPM5		S	C	G
Kyrgyz Republic	Kyrgyz som	[a]	1995	[b]	VAB	1990–95	2000	BPM5	Actual	G	B	S
Lao PDR	Lao kip	1990			VAB		1993	BPM5	Preliminary	G		
Latvia	Latvian lat	2000		[b]	VAB	1991–95	2002	BPM5	Actual	S	C	S
Lebanon	Lebanese pound	2003			VAB		1996	BPM4	Actual	G	B	G
Lesotho	Lesotho loti	1995		[b]	VAB			BPM5	Actual	G	C	G
Liberia	Liberian dollar	1992			VAB				Estimate			G
Libya	Libyan dinar	1975			VAB	1986		BPM5		G		
Lithuania	Lithuanian litas	2000		[b]	VAB	1990–95	2002	BPM5	Actual	G	C	S
Macedonia, FYR	Macedonian denar	1997	1995	[b]	VAB		2002	BPM5	Actual	G		G
Madagascar	Malagasy ariary	1984			VAB		1996	BPM5	Actual	S	C	G
Malawi	Malawi kwacha	1994			VAB		1996	BPM5	Actual	G	B	G
Malaysia	Malaysian ringgit	1987			VAP		1993	BPM5	Estimate	G	C	S
Mali	CFA franc	1987			VAB		1996	BPM4	Actual	G		G
Mauritania	Mauritanian ouguiya	1985			VAB			BPM4	Actual	G		G
Mauritius	Mauritian rupee	1997/98			VAB		1996	BPM5	Actual	G	C	G
Mexico	Mexican new peso	1993		[b]	VAB		2002	BPM5	Actual	G	C	S
Moldova	Moldovan leu	[a]	1996	[b]	VAB	1987–95	2000	BPM5	Actual	G	C	S
Mongolia	Mongolian tugrik	2000		[b]	VAB		2000	BPM5	Actual	S	C	G
Morocco	Moroccan dirham	1980			VAP		1996	BPM5	Actual	S	C	S
Mozambique	Mozambican metical	1995			VAB	1992–95		BPM5	Actual	S		G
Myanmar	Myanmar kyat	1985/86			VAP			BPM5	Estimate	G	C	
Namibia	Namibia dollar	1995/96		[b]	VAB			BPM5			B	G
Nepal	Nepalese rupee	1994/95			VAB		1996	BPM5	Actual	S	C	G
Netherlands	Euro	[a]	2000	[b]	VAB		2002	BPM5		S	C	S
New Zealand	New Zealand dollar	2000/01			VAB		2002	BPM5		G	C	
Nicaragua	Nicaraguan gold cordoba	1994		[b]	VAB	1965–93		BPM5	Actual	S	C	G
Niger	CFA franc	1987			VAP	1993		BPM5	Preliminary	S		G
Nigeria	Nigerian naira	1987			VAB	1971–98	1996	BPM5	Preliminary	G		G
Norway	Norwegian krone	[a]	2000	[b]	VAB		2002	BPM5		G	C	S
Oman	Rial Omani	1988			VAP		1996	BPM5	Actual	G	B	G
Pakistan	Pakistan rupee	1999/2000		[b]	VAB		1996	BPM5	Actual	G	C	G
Panama	Panamanian balboa	1996		[b]	VAB		1996	BPM5	Actual	S	C	G
Papua New Guinea	Papua New Guinea kina	1983			VAB	1989		BPM5	Actual	G	B	
Paraguay	Paraguayan guarani	1994		[b]	VAP	1982–88		BPM5	Actual	S	B	G
Peru	Peruvian new sol	1994			VAB	1985–91	1996	BPM5	Actual	S	C	S
Philippines	Philippine peso	1985			VAP		1996	BPM5	Actual	G	B	S
Poland	Polish zloty	[a]	2002	[b]	VAB		2002	BPM5	Actual	S	C	S
Portugal	Euro	2000		[b]	VAB		2002	BPM5		S	C	S
Puerto Rico	U.S. dollar	1954			VAP					G		

PRIMARY DATA DOCUMENTATION

	Latest population census	Latest demographic, education, or health household survey	Source of most recent income and expenditure data	Vital registration complete	Latest agricultural census	Latest industrial data	Latest trade data	Latest water withdrawal data
Honduras	2001	DHS, 2005	EPHPM, 2003		1993	2004	2005	1992
Hungary	2001		FBS, 2002	Yes	2000	2004	2005	1991
India	2001	MICS, 2000	NSS, 2004/05		1995–96/ 2000–01	2004	2005	1990
Indonesia	2000	DHS, 2002	SUSENAS, 2002		2003	2003	2005	1990
Iran, Islamic Rep.	1996	DHS, 2000	SECH, 1998	Yes	2003	2004	2005	1993
Iraq	1997	MICS, 2000			1981	2004	1976	1990
Ireland	2006		ECHP, 2000	Yes	2000	2004	2005	1980
Israel	1995		HES, 2001	Yes	1981	2004	2005	1997
Italy	2001		SHIW, 2000	Yes	2000	2003	2005	1998
Jamaica	2001	RHS, 2002/03	LSMS, 2004		1978–79	2004	2004	1993
Japan	2005			Yes	2000	2004	2005	1992
Jordan	2004	DHS, 2002	HIES, 1997		1997	2004	2005	1993
Kazakhstan	1999	DHS, 1999	HBS, 2003	Yes			2005	1993
Kenya	1999	DHS, 2003; SPA, 2004	WMS II, 1997		1977–79	2004	2004	1990
Korea, Dem. Rep.	1993	MICS, 2000						1987
Korea, Rep.	2000		NSFIE, 1998/99	Yes	2000	2004	2005	1994
Kuwait	1995	FHS, 1996		Yes	1970	2001	2001	1994
Kyrgyz Republic	1999	DHS, 1997	HBS, 2003	Yes	2002		2005	1994
Lao PDR	2005	MICS, 2000	ECS I, 2002		1998–99		1974	1987
Latvia	2000		HBS, 2003	Yes	2001	2003	2005	1994
Lebanon	1970	MICS, 2000			1998–99		2004	1996
Lesotho	1996	DHS, 2004	HBS, 1995		1999–2000	1985	2002	1987
Liberia	1984	MICS, 1995					1984	1987
Libya	1995	MICS, 2000			2001	2004	2004	1999
Lithuania	2001		HBS, 2003	Yes	1994	2003	2005	1995
Macedonia, FYR	2002		HBS, 2003	Yes	1994	1996	2005	1996
Madagascar	1993	DHS, 2003/04	Priority survey, 2001		1984–85	2003	2004	1984
Malawi	1998	DHS, 2004	HHS, 2004/05		1993	2004	2005	1994
Malaysia	2000		HIBAS, 1997	Yes		2002	2005	1995
Mali	1998	DHS, 2001	EMCES, 2001		1984		2001	1987
Mauritania	2000	DHS, 2000/01	LSMS, 2000		1984–85	1978	1996	1985
Mauritius	2000			Yes		2004	2005	
Mexico	2000	ENPF, 1995	ENIGH, 2004		1991	2000	2005	1998
Moldova	2004	DHS, 2005	HBS, 2003	Yes		2003	2005	1992
Mongolia	2000	MICS, 2000	LSMS/Integrated Survey, 2002	Yes		1995	2005	1993
Morocco	2004	DHS, 2003/04	LSMS, 1998/99		1996	2001	2005	1998
Mozambique	1997	DHS, 2003	NHS, 2002/03		1999–2000	2004	2005	1992
Myanmar	1983	MICS, 2000			2003		1993	1987
Namibia	2001	DHS, 2000	NHIES, 1993		1996–97	1994	2003	1991
Nepal	2001	DHS, 2001	LSMS, 2003/04		2002	2002	2003	1994
Netherlands	2001		ECHP, 1999	Yes	1999–2000[c]	2004	2005	1991
New Zealand	2006			Yes	2002	2004	2005	1991
Nicaragua	2005	DHS, 2001	LSMS, 2001		2001	2004	2005	1998
Niger	2001	MICS, 2000			1980	2002	2005	1988
Nigeria	2006	DHS, 2003	LSMS, 2003		1960		2003	1987
Norway	2001		IF 2000	Yes	1999	2004	2005	1985
Oman	2003	FHS, 1995			1978–79	2003	2005	1991
Pakistan	1998	RHS, 2000/01	PIHS, 2002		2000	2004	2005	1991
Panama	2000	LSMS, 2003	EH, 2003		2001	2004	2005	1990
Papua New Guinea	2000	DHS, 1996	HGS, 1996			2004	2003	1987
Paraguay	2002	RHS, 2004	EIH, 2003		1991	2004	2004	1987
Peru	2005	DHS, 2004	ENAHO, 2003		1994	1996	2005	1992
Philippines	2000	DHS, 2003	FIES, 2003	Yes	2002	2004	2005	1995
Poland	2002		HBS, 2002	Yes	1996/2002	2004	2005	1991
Portugal	2001			Yes	1999	2004	2005	1990
Puerto Rico	2000	RHS, 1995/96		Yes	1997/2002	2002		

PRIMARY DATA DOCUMENTATION

	Currency	National accounts						Balance of payments and trade			Government finance	IMF data dissemination standard
		Base year	Reference year	System of National Accounts	SNA price valuation	Alternative conversion factor	PPP survey year	Balance of Payments Manual in use	External debt	System of trade	Accounting concept	
Romania	New Romanian leu	[a]	1999	[b]	VAB	1987–89, 1992	2002	BPM5	Actual	S	C	S
Russian Federation	Russian ruble	2000		[b]	VAB	1987–95	2002	BPM5	Preliminary	G	C	S
Rwanda	Rwanda franc	1995			VAP			BPM5	Preliminary	G	C	G
Saudi Arabia	Saudi Arabian riyal	1999			VAP			BPM4		G		
Senegal	CFA franc	1999	1987	[b]	VAP		1996	BPM5	Preliminary	S	B	G
Serbia and Montenegro	Yugoslav new dinar	1998			VAB				Actual		C	
Sierra Leone	Sierra Leonean leone	2001	1990	[b]	VAB		1996	BPM5	Actual	G	B	G
Singapore	Singapore dollar	1995		[b]	VAB		1996	BPM5		G	C	S
Slovak Republic	Slovak koruna	2000	1995	[b]	VAP		2002	BPM5	Actual	G	C	S
Slovenia	Slovenian tolar	[a]	2000	[b]	VAB		2002	BPM5		S	C	S
Somalia	Somali shilling	1985			VAB	1977–90			Estimate			
South Africa	South African rand	2000		[b]	VAB			BPM5	Preliminary	S	C	S
Spain	Euro	2000		[b]	VAB		2002	BPM5		S	C	S
Sri Lanka	Sri Lankan rupee	1996			VAB		1996	BPM5	Actual	G	B	G
Sudan	Sudanese dinar	1981/82[d]	1982		VAB			BPM5	Actual	G	B	G
Swaziland	Lilangeni	1985			VAB		1996		Actual		B	G
Sweden	Swedish krona	[a]	2000		VAB		2002	BPM5		G	C	S
Switzerland	Swiss franc	2000			VAB		2002	BPM5		S	C	S
Syrian Arab Republic	Syrian pound	2000			VAB	1970–2005	1996	BPM5	Estimate	S	C	
Tajikistan	Tajik somoni	[a]	1997	[b]	VAB	1990–95	2000	BPM5	Preliminary	G	C	G
Tanzania	Tanzania shilling	1992			VAB		1996	BPM5	Estimate	S		G
Thailand	Thai baht	1988			VAP		1996	BPM5	Preliminary	G	C	S
Togo	CFA franc	1978			VAP			BPM5	Actual	S	B	G
Trinidad and Tobago	Trinidad and Tobago dollar	2000		[b]	VAB		1996	BPM5	Actual	S	C	G
Tunisia	Tunisian dinar	1990			VAP		1996	BPM5	Actual	G	C	S
Turkey	Turkish lira	1987			VAB		2002	BPM5	Actual	S	B	S
Turkmenistan	Turkmen manat	[a]	1987	[b]	VAB	1987–95, 1997–2005	2000	BPM5	Actual	G		
Uganda	Uganda shilling	1997/98			VAB			BPM5	Actual	G	B	G
Ukraine	Ukrainian hryvnia	[a]	2003	[b]	VAB	1990–95	2000	BPM5	Actual	G	C	S
United Arab Emirates	U.A.E. dirham	1995			VAB			BPM4		G	C	
United Kingdom	Pound sterling	2000		[b]	VAB		2002	BPM5		G	C	S
United States	U.S. dollar	[a]	2000		VAB		2002	BPM5		G	C	S
Uruguay	Uruguayan peso	1983			VAB		1996	BPM5	Actual	S	C	S
Uzbekistan	Uzbek sum	[a]	1997	[b]	VAB	1990–95	2000	BPM5	Actual	G		
Venezuela, RB	Venezuelan bolivar	1984			VAB		1996	BPM5	Actual	G	C	G
Vietnam	Vietnamese dong	1994		[b]	VAP	1991	1996	BPM4	Actual	G	C	G
West Bank and Gaza	Israeli new shekel	1997			VAB						B	G
Yemen, Rep.	Yemen rial	1990			VAP	1991–96	1996	BPM5	Actual	G	B	G
Zambia	Zambian kwacha	1994			VAB	1990–92	1996	BPM5	Actual	G	B	G
Zimbabwe	Zimbabwe dollar	1990			VAB	1991, 1998	1996	BPM5	Actual	G	C	G

PRIMARY DATA DOCUMENTATION

	Latest population census	Latest demographic, education, or health household survey	Source of most recent income and expenditure data	Vital registration complete	Latest agricultural census	Latest industrial data	Latest trade data	Latest water withdrawal data
Romania	2002	RHS, 1999	LSMS, 2003	Yes	2002		2005	1994
Russian Federation	2002	RHS, 1996	LMS, Round 9, 2002	Yes	1994–95	2000	2005	1994
Rwanda	2002	DHS, 2005	LSMS, 1999/2000		1984	2004	2003	1993
Saudi Arabia	2004	Demographic survey, 1999			1999	1989	2005	1992
Senegal	2002	DHS, 2005	ESASM 1995		1998–99	1997	2005	1987
Serbia and Montenegro	Serbia 2002, Montenegro 2003	MICS, 2000		Yes		2002	2004	
Sierra Leone	2004	MICS, 2000	SHEHEA, 1989–90		1984–85	1993	2002	1987
Singapore	2000	General household, 2005		Yes		2004	2005	1975
Slovak Republic	2001		Microcensus, 1996	Yes	2001	1999	2005	1991
Slovenia	2002		HBS, 1998	Yes	2000	2003	2005	1996
Somalia	1987	MICS, 1999				2003	1982	1987
South Africa	2001	DHS, 1998	IES, 2000			2003	2005	1990
Spain	2001		ECHP, 2000	Yes	1999	2004	2005	1997
Sri Lanka	2001	DHS, 1987	HIEs, 2002	Yes	2002	2001	2005	1990
Sudan	1993	MICS, 2000				2001	2005	1995
Swaziland	1997	MICS, 2000	SHIES, 2000/01		2000	2004	2002	
Sweden	2005		HINK, 2000	Yes	1999–2000	2004	2005	1991
Switzerland	2000		EVE, 2000	Yes	2000	1997	2005	1991
Syrian Arab Republic	1994	MICS, 2000			1981	2004	2004	1995
Tajikistan	2000	MICS, 2000	LSMS, 2003	Yes	1994		2000	1994
Tanzania	2002	DHS, 2004	HIES, 2000/01		2003	2004	2005	1994
Thailand	2000	DHS, 1987	SES, 2002		2003	2002	2005	1990
Togo	1981	MICS, 2000			1996	2004	2005	1987
Trinidad and Tobago	2000	MICS, 2000	LSMS, 1992	Yes	2004	2004	2005	1997
Tunisia	2004	MICS, 2000	LSMS, 2000		2004	2004	2005	1996
Turkey	2000	DHS, 1998	LSMS, 2002		2001	2004	2005	1997
Turkmenistan	1995	DHS,2000	LSMS, 1998	Yes			2000	1994
Uganda	2002	DHS, 2000/01; AIS, 2004	NIHS III, 2002		1991	2004	2005	1970
Ukraine	2001	MICS, 2000	HBS, 2003	Yes			2005	1992
United Arab Emirates	2005				1998	2004	2001	1995
United Kingdom	2001		FRS, 1999	Yes	1999–2000[c]	2004	2005	1991
United States	2000	CPS (monthly)	CPS, 2000	Yes	1997/2002	2004	2005	1990
Uruguay	1996		ECH, 2003	Yes	2000	1997	2005	1965
Uzbekistan	1989	MICS, 2000; DHS special, 2002	FBS, 2003	Yes				1994
Venezuela, RB	2001	MICS, 2000	EHM, 2003	Yes	1997	2003	2005	1970
Vietnam	1999	DHS 2002; AIS 2005	LSMS, 2004		2001	2000	2003	1990
West Bank and Gaza	1997	Health Survey, 2000			1971			
Yemen, Rep.	2004	DHS, 1997	HBS, 1998		2002	2003	2005	1990
Zambia	2000	DHS, 2001/02; SPA, 2005	LCMS II, 2004		1990	2004	2005	1994
Zimbabwe	2002	DHS, 1999	LCMS III, 1995		1960	2004	2004	1987

Note: For explanation of the abbreviations used in the table see notes following the table.
a. Original chained constant price data are rescaled. b. Country uses the 1993 System of National Accounts methodology. c. Conducted annually. d. Reporting period switch from fiscal year to calendar year from 1996. Pre-1996 data converted to calendar year.

• **Base year** is the year used as the base or pricing period for constant price calculations in the country's national accounts. Price indexes derived from national accounts aggregates, such as the implicit deflator for gross domestic product (GDP), express the price level relative to prices in the base year. • **Reference year** is the year in which the local currency, constant price series of a country is valued. In most cases the reference year is same as the base year used to report the constant price series. However, when the constant price data are chain linked, the base year is changed annually, so the data are rescaled to a specific reference year to provide a consistent time series. In a few other cases, when the country has not rescaled following a change in base year, World Bank staff rescale the data to maintain a longer historical series. To allow for cross-country comparison and aggregation of the data, constant price data reported in *World Development Indicators* are rescaled to a common reference year (2000) and currency (U.S. dollars). • **System of National Accounts** identifies countries that use the 1993 System of National Accounts (1993 SNA), the terminology applied in *World Development Indicators* since 2001, to compile their national accounts. Although more and more countries are adopting the 1993 SNA, many countries continue to follow the 1968 SNA, and some low-income countries still use concepts from the 1953 SNA. • **SNA price valuation** shows whether value added in the national accounts is reported at basic prices (VAB) or at producer prices (VAP). Producer prices include the value of taxes paid by producers and thus tend to overstate the actual value added in production. However, the VAB prices can be higher than VAP prices in countries that have high agricultural subsidies. See *About the data* for tables 4.1 and 4.2 for further discussion of national accounts valuation. • **Alternative conversion factor** identifies the countries and years for which a World Bank–estimated conversion factor has been used in place of the official exchange rate (line rf in the International Monetary Fund's [IMF] *International Financial Statistics*). See *Statistical methods* for further discussion of the use of alternative conversion factors . • **Purchasing power parity (PPP) survey year** refers to the latest available survey year for the International Comparison Program's estimates of PPPs. For a more detailed description of PPPs see *About the data* for table 1.1. • **Balance of Payments Manual in use** refers to the classification system used for compiling and reporting data on balance of payments items in table 4.15. BPM4 refers to the 4th edition of the IMF's *Balance of Payments Manual* (1977), and BPM5 to the 5th edition (1993). • **External debt** shows debt reporting status for 2005 data. *Actual* indicates that data are as reported; *preliminary* indicates that data are preliminary and include an element of staff estimation; and *estimate* indicates that data are World Bank staff estimates. • **System of trade** refers to the United Nations general trade system (G) or the special trade system (S). For imports under the general trade system both goods entering directly for domestic consumption and goods entered into customs storage are recorded as imports at the time of arrival; under the special trade system goods are recorded as imports when they are declared for domestic consumption whether at the time of entry or on withdrawal from customs storage. Exports under the general system comprise outward-moving goods: (a) national goods wholly or partly produced in the country; (b) foreign goods, neither transformed nor declared for domestic consumption in the country, that move outward from customs storage; and (c) nationalized goods that have been declared from domestic consumption and move outward without having been transformed. Under the special system of trade exports comprise categories (a) and (c). In some compilations categories (b) and (c) are classified as re-exports. Direct transit trade, consisting of goods entering or leaving for transport purposes only, is excluded from both import and export statistics. See *About the data* for tables 4.4, 4.5, and 6.2 for further discussion. • **Government finance accounting concept** describes the accounting basis for reporting central government financial data. For most countries government finance data have been consolidated (C) into one set of accounts capturing all the central government's fiscal activities. Budgetary central government accounts (B) exclude some central government units. See *About the data* for tables 4.10, 4.11, and 4.12 for further details. • **IMF data dissemination standard** shows the countries that subscribe to the IMF's Special Data Dissemination Standard (SDDS) or General Data Dissemination System (GDDS). S refers to countries that subscribe to the SDDS and have posted data on the Dissemination Standards Bulletin Board web site (posted data are at http://dsbb.imf.org). G refers to countries that subscribe to the GDDS. The SDDS was established by the IMF for member countries that have or that might seek access to international capital markets to guide them in providing their economic and financial data to the public. The GDDS helps countries disseminate comprehensive, timely, accessible, and reliable economic, financial, and sociodemographic statistics. IMF member countries voluntarily elect to participate in either the SDDS or the GDDS. Both the SDDS and the GDDS are expected to enhance the availability of timely and comprehensive data and therefore contribute to the pursuit of sound macroeconomic policies. The SDDS is also expected to improve the functioning of financial markets. • **Latest population census** shows the most recent year in which a census was conducted and in which at least preliminary results have been released. It includes registration-based censuses. Some countries with complete population registration systems produce similar tables every 5 or 10 years instead of conducting regular censuses. • **Latest demographic, education, or health household survey** gives information on the household surveys used in compiling the demographic, education, and health data in section 2. AIS is the AIDS indicator Survey, CPS is Current Population Survey, DHS is Demographic and Health Survey, ENPF is National Family Planning Survey (Encuesta Nacional de Planificacion Familiar), FHS is Family Health Survey, MICS is Multiple Indicator Cluster Survey, RHS is Reproductive Health Survey; and SPA is Service Provision Assessments. Detailed information for AIS, DHS, and SPA are available at www.measuredhs.com/aboutsurveys; for MICS at www.childinfo.org; and for RHS at www.cdc.gov/reproductivehealth/surveys. • **Source of most recent income and expenditure data** shows household surveys that collect income and expenditure data. HBS is Household Budget Survey; ICES is Income, Consumption, and Expenditure Survey; IES is Income and Expenditure Survey; LSMS is Living Standards Measurement Study; and SES is Socio-Economic Survey. • **Vital registration complete** identifies countries judged to have at least 90 percent complete registries of vital (birth and death) statistics by the United Nations Department of Economic and Social Affairs Statistics Division and reported in *Population and Vital Statistics Reports*. Countries with complete vital statistics registries may have more accurate and more timely demographic indicators than other countries. • **Latest agricultural census** shows the most recent year in which an agricultural census was conducted and reported to the Food and Agriculture Organization of the United Nations. • **Latest industrial data** refer to the most recent year for which manufacturing value added data at the three-digit level of the International Standard Industrial Classification (ISIC, revision 2 or revision 3) are available in the United Nations Industrial Development

Organization database. • **Latest trade data** show the most recent year for which structure of merchandise trade data from the United Nations Statistical Division's Commodity Trade (Comtrade) database are available. • **Latest water withdrawal data** show the most recent year for which data on freshwater withdrawals have been compiled from a variety of sources. See *About the data* for table 3.5 for more information.

Exceptional reporting periods

In most economies the **fiscal year** is concurrent with the calendar year. The exceptions are shown in this table. The fiscal year ending date reported here refers to the fiscal year of the central government. Fiscal years for other levels of government and the reporting years for statistical surveys may differ. Further, some countries that follow a fiscal year report their national accounts data on a calendar year basis as shown in the *reporting period* column.

The **reporting period for national accounts data** is designated as either calendar year basis (CY) or fiscal year basis (FY). Most economies report their national accounts and balance of payments data using calendar years, but some use fiscal years that straddle two calendar years. In *World Development Indicators* fiscal year data are assigned to the calendar year that contains the larger share of the fiscal year. If a country's fiscal year ends before June 30, the data are shown in the first year of the fiscal period; if the fiscal year ends on or after June 30, the data are shown in the second year of the period. Balance of payments data are reported in *World Development Indicators* by calendar year and so are not comparable to the national accounts data of the countries that report their national accounts on a fiscal year basis.

	Fiscal year end	Reporting period for national accounts data
Afghanistan	Mar. 20	FY
Australia	Jun. 30	FY
Bangladesh	Jun. 30	FY
Botswana	Jun. 30	FY
Canada	Mar. 31	CY
Egypt, Arab Rep.	Jun. 30	FY
Ethiopia	Jul. 7	FY
Gambia, The	Jun. 30	CY
Haiti	Sep. 30	FY
India	Mar. 31	FY
Indonesia	Mar. 31	CY
Iran, Islamic Rep.	Mar. 20	FY
Japan	Mar. 31	CY
Kenya	Jun. 30	CY
Kuwait	Jun. 30	CY
Lesotho	Mar. 31	CY
Malawi	Mar. 31	CY
Mauritius	Jun. 30	FY
Myanmar	Mar. 31	FY
Namibia	Mar. 31	CY
Nepal	Jul. 14	FY
New Zealand	Mar. 31	FY
Pakistan	Jun. 30	FY
Puerto Rico	Jun. 30	FY
Sierra Leone	Jun. 30	CY
Singapore	Mar. 31	CY
South Africa	Mar. 31	CY
Swaziland	Mar. 31	CY
Sweden	Jun. 30	CY
Thailand	Sep. 30	CY
Uganda	Jun. 30	FY
United States	Sep. 30	CY
Zimbabwe	Jun. 30	CY

STATISTICAL METHODS

This section describes some of the statistical procedures used in preparing the World Development Indicators. It covers the methods employed for calculating regional and income group aggregates and for calculating growth rates, and it describes the *World Bank Atlas* method for deriving the conversion factor used to estimate gross national income (GNI) and GNI per capita in U.S. dollars. Other statistical procedures and calculations are described in the *About the data* sections following each table.

Aggregation rules

Aggregates based on the World Bank's regional and income classifications of economies appear at the end of most tables. The countries included in these classifications are shown on the flaps on the front and back covers of the book. Most tables also include the aggregate Europe EMU. This aggregate includes the member states of the Economic and Monetary Union (EMU) of the European Union that have adopted the euro as their currency: Austria, Belgium, Finland, France, Germany, Greece, Ireland, Italy, Luxembourg, Netherlands, Portugal, Slovenia, and Spain. Other classifications, such as the European Union and regional trade blocs, are documented in *About the data* for the tables in which they appear.

Because of missing data, aggregates for groups of economies should be treated as approximations of unknown totals or average values. Regional and income group aggregates are based on the largest available set of data, including values for the 152 economies shown in the main tables, other economies shown in table 1.6, and Taiwan, China. The aggregation rules are intended to yield estimates for a consistent set of economies from one period to the next and for all indicators. Small differences between sums of subgroup aggregates and overall totals and averages may occur because of the approximations used. In addition, compilation errors and data reporting practices may cause discrepancies in theoretically identical aggregates such as world exports and world imports.

Five methods of aggregation are used in *World Development Indicators:*

- For group and world totals denoted in the tables by a *t*, missing data are imputed based on the relationship of the sum of available data to the total in the year of the previous estimate. The imputation process works forward and backward from 2000. Missing values in 2000 are imputed using one of several proxy variables for which complete data are available in that year. The imputed value is calculated so that it (or its proxy) bears the same relationship to the total of available data. Imputed values are usually not calculated if missing data account for more than a third of the total in the benchmark year. The variables used as proxies are GNI in U.S. dollars, total population, exports and imports of goods and services in U.S. dollars, and value added in agriculture, industry, manufacturing, and services in U.S. dollars.
- Aggregates marked by an *s* are sums of available data. Missing values are not imputed. Sums are not computed if more than a third of the observations in the series or a proxy for the series are missing in a given year.
- Aggregates of ratios are denoted by a *w* when calculated as weighted averages of the ratios (using the value of the denominator or, in some cases, another indicator as a weight) and denoted by a *u* when calculated as unweighted averages. The aggregate ratios are based on available data, including data for economies not shown in the main tables. Missing values are assumed to have the same average value as the available data. No aggregate is calculated if missing data account for more than a third of the value of weights in the benchmark year. In a few cases the aggregate ratio may be computed as the ratio of group totals after imputing values for missing data according to the above rules for computing totals.
- Aggregate growth rates are denoted by a *w* when calculated as a weighted average of growth rates. In a few cases growth rates may be computed from time series of group totals. Growth rates are not calculated if more than half the observations in a period are missing. For further discussion of methods of computing growth rates see below.
- Aggregates denoted by an *m* are medians of the values shown in the table. No value is shown if more than half the observations for countries with a population of more than 1 million are missing.

Exceptions to the rules occur throughout the book. Depending on the judgment of World Bank analysts, the aggregates may be based on as little as 50 percent of the available data. In other cases, where missing or excluded values are judged to be small or irrelevant, aggregates are based only on the data shown in the tables.

Growth rates

Growth rates are calculated as annual averages and represented as percentages. Except where noted, growth rates of values are computed from constant price series. Three principal methods are used to calculate growth rates: least squares, exponential endpoint, and geometric endpoint. Rates of change from one period to the next are calculated as proportional changes from the earlier period.

Least-squares growth rate. Least-squares growth rates are used wherever there is a sufficiently long time series to permit a reliable calculation. No growth rate is calculated if more than half the observations in a period are missing. The least-squares growth rate, *r*, is estimated by fitting a linear regression trend line to the logarithmic annual values of the variable in the relevant period. The regression equation takes the form

$$\ln X_t = a + bt$$

which is equivalent to the logarithmic transformation of the compound growth equation,

$$X_t = X_o (1 + r)^t.$$

In this equation X is the variable, t is time, and $a = \ln X_o$ and $b = \ln (1 + r)$ are parameters to be estimated. If b^* is the least-squares estimate of b, then the average annual growth rate, r, is obtained as $[\exp(b^*) - 1]$ and is multiplied by 100 for expression as a percentage. The calculated growth rate is an average rate that is representative of the available observations over the entire period. It does not necessarily match the actual growth rate between any two periods.

Exponential growth rate. The growth rate between two points in time for certain demographic indicators, notably labor force and population, is calculated from the equation

$$r = \ln(p_n/p_0)/n$$

where p_n and p_0 are the last and first observations in the period, n is the number of years in the period, and ln is the natural logarithm operator. This growth rate is based on a model of continuous, exponential growth between two points in time. It does not take into account the intermediate values of the series. Nor does it correspond to the annual rate of change measured at a one-year interval, which is given by $(p_n - p_{n-1})/p_{n-1}$.

Geometric growth rate. The geometric growth rate is applicable to compound growth over discrete periods, such as the payment and reinvestment of interest or dividends. Although continuous growth, as modeled by the exponential growth rate, may be more realistic, most economic phenomena are measured only at intervals, in which case the compound growth model is appropriate. The average growth rate over n periods is calculated as

$$r = \exp[\ln(p_n/p_0)/n] - 1.$$

Like the exponential growth rate, it does not take into account intermediate values of the series.

World Bank Atlas method

In calculating GNI and GNI per capita in U.S. dollars for certain operational purposes, the World Bank uses the *Atlas* conversion factor. The purpose of the *Atlas* conversion factor is to reduce the impact of exchange rate fluctuations in the cross-country comparison of national incomes.

The *Atlas* conversion factor for any year is the average of a country's exchange rate (or alternative conversion factor) for that year and its exchange rates for the two preceding years, adjusted for the difference between the rate of inflation in the country and that in Japan, the United Kingdom, the United States, and the Euro Zone. A country's inflation rate is measured by the change in its GDP deflator.

The inflation rate for Japan, the United Kingdom, the United States, and the Euro Zone, representing international inflation, is measured by the change in the SDR deflator. (Special drawing rights, or SDRs, are the International Monetary Fund's unit of account.) The SDR deflator is calculated as a weighted average of these countries' GDP deflators in SDR terms, the weights being the amount of each country's currency in one SDR unit. Weights vary over time because both the composition of the SDR and the relative exchange rates for each currency change. The SDR deflator is calculated in SDR terms first and then converted to U.S. dollars using the SDR to dollar *Atlas* conversion factor. The *Atlas* conversion factor is then applied to a country's GNI. The resulting GNI in U.S. dollars is divided by the midyear population to derive GNI per capita.

When official exchange rates are deemed to be unreliable or unrepresentative of the effective exchange rate during a period, an alternative estimate of the exchange rate is used in the *Atlas* formula (see below).

The following formulas describe the calculation of the *Atlas* conversion factor for year t:

$$e_t^* = \frac{1}{3}\left[e_{t-2}\left(\frac{p_t}{p_{t-2}} \Big/ \frac{p_t^{S\$}}{p_{t-2}^{S\$}}\right) + e_{t-1}\left(\frac{p_t}{p_{t-1}} \Big/ \frac{p_t^{S\$}}{p_{t-1}^{S\$}}\right) + e_t\right]$$

and the calculation of GNI per capita in U.S. dollars for year t:

$$Y_t^{\$} = (Y_t/N_t)/e_t^*$$

where e_t^* is the *Atlas* conversion factor (national currency to the U.S. dollar) for year t, e_t is the average annual exchange rate (national currency to the U.S. dollar) for year t, p_t is the GDP deflator for year t, $p_t^{S\$}$ is the SDR deflator in U.S. dollar terms for year t, $Y_t^{\$}$ is the *Atlas* GNI per capita in U.S. dollars in year t, Y_t is current GNI (local currency) for year t, and N_t is the midyear population for year t.

Alternative conversion factors

The World Bank systematically assesses the appropriateness of official exchange rates as conversion factors. An alternative conversion factor is used when the official exchange rate is judged to diverge by an exceptionally large margin from the rate effectively applied to domestic transactions of foreign currencies and traded products. This applies to only a small number of countries, as shown in *Primary data documentation*. Alternative conversion factors are used in the *Atlas* methodology and elsewhere in *World Development Indicators* as single-year conversion factors.

CREDITS

Credits

World Development Indicators draws on a wide range of World Bank reports and numerous external sources, listed in the bibliography following this section. Many people inside and outside the World Bank helped in writing and producing this book. The team would like to particularly acknowledge the help and encouragement of François Bourguignon, Senior Vice President and Chief Economist of the World Bank, and Shaida Badiee, Director, Development Data Group. The team is also grateful to the people who provided valuable comments on the entire book. This note identifies many of those who made specific contributions. Numerous others, too many to acknowledge here, helped in many ways for which the team is extremely grateful.

1. World view

The introduction to section 1 was prepared by Sebastien Dessus and Eric Swanson. Alan Gelb, Sarwar Lateef, and Jeffrey Lewis provided valuable suggestions. Changqing Sun and Raymond Muhula provided the decomposition of poverty rates. K.M. Vijayalakshmi prepared tables 1.1 and 1.6. Changqing Sun prepared the estimates of gross national income in purchasing power parity terms and table 1.4. Tables 1.2, 1.3, and 1.5 were prepared by Masako Hiraga. Dorte Domeland-Narvaez of the World Bank's Economic Policy and Debt Department provided the estimates of debt relief for the Heavily Indebted Poor Countries Debt Initiative and Multilateral Debt Relief Initiative. The team is grateful to Yasmin Ahmad and Aimee Nichols at the Organisation for Economic Co-operation and Development for data and advice on official development assistance flows and agricultural support estimates.

2. People

Section 2 was prepared by Masako Hiraga and Sulekha Patel in partnership with the World Bank's Human Development Network and the Development Research Group in the Development Economics Vice Presidency. Mehdi Akhlaghi and William Prince provided invaluable assistance in data and table preparation, and Kiyomi Horiuchi prepared the demographic estimates and projections under the guidance of Eduard Bos. Sulekha Patel wrote the introduction with valuable comments from Davidson Gwatkin, Sarwar Lateef, Jeffrey Lewis, and Eric Swanson. The poverty estimates were prepared by Shaohua Chen and and Prem Sangraula of the World Bank's Poverty Monitoring Group with help from Changquin Sun. The data for table 2.19 on health gaps by income and gender were based on data prepared by Darcy Gallucio and Davidson Gwatkin of the Human Development Network. Other contributions were provided by Eduard Bos and Emi Suzuki (population, health, and nutrition); Montserrat Pallares-Miralles (vulnerability and security); Raymond Muhula, Juan Cruz Perusia, and Lianqin Wang of the United Nations Educational, Scientific, and Cultural Organization Institute for Statistics (education); and Lucia Fort and Juan Carlos Guzman Roa (gender).

3. Environment

Section 3 was prepared by Mehdi Akhlaghi and M. H. Saeed Ordoubadi in partnership with the World Bank's Sustainable Development Network. Important contributions were made by Edward Gillin and Carola Fabi of the Food and Agriculture Organization of the United Nations; Ricardo Quercioli of the International Energy Agency; Amay Cassara, Christian Layke, Daniel Prager, and Robin White of the World Resources Institute; Laura Battlebury of the World Conservation Monitoring Centre; and Gerhard Metchies of German Technical Cooperation (GTZ). The World Bank's Environment Department devoted substantial staff resources to the book, for which the team is very grateful. M.H. Saeed Ordoubadi wrote the introduction with valuable comments from Sarwar Lateef, Jeffrey Lewis, and Eric Swanson. Other contributions were made by Kiran Pandey (biodiversity); Susmita Dasgupta, Craig Meisner, Kiran Pandey, and David Wheeler (air and water pollution); Solly Angel, Augusto Clavijo, Maria Emilia Ferire, Mahyar Eshragh-Tabary, Christine Kessides, and Micah Perlin (urban housing conditions); and Kirk Hamilton, Beat Hintermann, and Giovanni Ruta (adjusted savings).

4. Economy

Section 4 was prepared by K.M. Vijayalakshmi in close collaboration with the Macroeconomic Data Team of the World Bank's Development Data Group, led by Soong Sup Lee. K.M. Vijayalakshmi and Eric Swanson wrote the introduction with valuable suggestions from Sarwar Lateef and Sebastien Dessus. Contributions to the section were provided by Azita Amjadi (trade) and Ibrahim Levent (external debt). The national accounts data for low- and middle-income economies were gathered by the World Bank's regional staff through the annual Unified Survey. Maja Bresslauer, Mahyar Eshragh-Tabary, Victor Gabor, and Soong Sup Lee worked on updating, estimating, and validating the databases for national accounts. The team is grateful to the International Monetary Fund, World Trade Organization, United Nations Industrial Development Organization, and the Organisation for Economic Co-operation and Development for access to the databases.

5. States and markets

Section 5 was prepared by David Cieslikowski and Raymond Muhula, in partnership with the World Bank's Financial and Private Sector Development Network, Sustainable Development Network, Poverty Reduction and Economic Management Network, the International Finance Corporation, and external partners. Brian Pascual assisted in data and table preparation. David Cieslikowski wrote the introduction to the section with valuable comments from Rui Coutinho, Steve Knack, Aart Kraay, Sarwar Lateef, Raymond Muhula, and Eric Swanson. Other contributors include Ada Karina Izaguirre (privatization and infrastructure projects); Michael Ingram (micro, small, and medium-size enterprises); David Stewart (investment climate); Caralee McLeish (business environment); Alka Banerjee and Isilay Cabuk (Standard & Poor's global stock market indexes); Himmat Kalsi (financial); Rui Coutinho (public policies and institutions); Nigel Adderley of the International Institute for Strategic Studies (military personnel); Bjorn Hagelin and Petter Stålenheim of the Stockholm International Peace Research Institute (military expenditures and arms transfers); Henrich Bofinger, Tsukasa Hattori, and Peter Roberts (transport); Jane Degerlund of

Containerisation International (ports); Vanessa Grey and Esperanza Magpantay of the International Telecommunication Union, and Mark Williams (communications and information); Ernesto Fernandez Polcuch of the United Nations Educational, Scientific, and Cultural Organization Institute for Statistics (research and development, researchers, and technicians); and Anders Halvorsen of the World Information Technology and Services Alliance (information and communication technology expenditures).

6. Global links

Section 6 was prepared by Changqing Sun and Azita Amjadi in partnership with the World Bank's Development Research Group (trade), Prospects Group (commodity prices), and external partners. Many thanks to Amy Heyman, Sarwar Lateef, Ibrahim Levent, and Eric Swanson for initial comments and feedback about possible revisions to the section. Substantial input for the data came from Azita Amjadi, Jerzy Rozanski (tariffs), Gloria Moreno, and Ibrahim Levent (financial data). Other contributors include David Cristallo and Henri Laurencin of the United Nations Conference on Trade and Development, Francis Ng, and Dominique van der Mensbrugghe (trade); Betty Dow (commodity prices); Dilek Aykut (foreign direct investment flows); Brian Hammond, Aimee Nichols, and Yasmin Ahmad of the Organisation for Economic Co-operation and Development (aid); Khassoum Diallo and Henrik Pilgaard of the United Nations Office of the High Commissioner for Refugees; Bela Hovy and Francois Pelletier of the United Nations Population Division (migration); K.M. Vijayalatshmi (remittances); and John Kester and Teresa Ciller of the World Tourism Organization (tourism). Mehdi Akhlaghi and William Prince provided valuable technical assistance.

Other parts of the book

Jeff Lecksell of the World Bank's Map Design Unit coordinated preparation of the maps on the inside covers. David Cieslikowski prepared the *Users guide*. Eric Swanson wrote *Statistical methods*. K.M. Vijayalakshmi coordinated preparation of *Primary data documentation*, and Uranbileg Batjargal assisted in updating the *Primary data documentation* table. Richard Fix prepared *Partners* and *Index of indicators*.

Database management

Mehdi Akhlaghi coordinated management of the integrated World Development Indicators database with assistance from William Prince. Operation of the database management system was made possible by the Systems Upgrade team under the leadership of Reza Farivari.

Design, production, and editing

Richard Fix and Azita Amjadi coordinated all stages of production with Communications Development Incorporated, which provided overall design direction, editing, and layout, led by Meta de Coquereaumont, Bruce Ross-Larson, and Christopher Trott. Elaine Wilson created the graphics and typeset the book. Amy Ditzel, Laura Peterson Nussbaum, and Zachary Schauf provided copyediting, proofreading, and production assistance. Communications Development's London partner, Peter Grundy of Peter Grundy Art & Design, provided art direction and design. Staff from External Affairs oversaw printing and dissemination of the book.

Client services

The Development Data Group's Client Services Team (Azita Amjadi, Uranbileg Batjargal, Richard Fix, and William Prince) contributed to the design and planning of *World Development Indicators* and helped coordinate work with the Office of the Publisher.

Administrative assistance and office technology support

Estela Zamora and Awatif Abuzeid provided administrative assistance. Jean-Pierre Djomalieu, Gytis Kanchas, Nacer Megherbi, and Shahin Outadi provided information technology support.

Publishing and dissemination

The Office of the Publisher, under the direction of Dirk Koehler, provided valuable assistance throughout the production process. Stephen McGroarty, Randi Park, and Nora Ridolfi coordinated printing and supervised marketing and distribution. Merrell Tuck-Primdahl of the Development Economics Vice President's Office managed the communications strategy.

World Development Indicators CD-ROM

Programming and testing were carried out by Reza Farivari and his team: Azita Amjadi, Uranbileg Batjargal, Ying Chi, Ramgopal Erabelly, Nacer Megherbi, Shahin Outadi, and William Prince. Masako Hiraga produced the social indicators tables. William Prince coordinated user interface design and overall production and provided quality assurance. Photo credits: Curt Carnemark, Julio Etchart, Alan Gignoux, John Isaac, and Bill Lyons (World Bank).

The interactive World Development Indicators 2007 was designed and programmed for this CD-ROM by Dohatec New Media.

WDI Online

Design, programming, and testing were carried out by Reza Farivari and his team: Mehdi Akhlaghi, Azita Amjadi, Uranbileg Batjargal, Saurabh Gupta, Nacer Megherbi, Gonca Okur, and Shahin Outadi. William Prince coordinated production and provided quality assurance. Valentina Kalk and Triinu Tombak of the Office of the Publisher were responsible for implementation of *WDI Online* and management of the subscription service.

Client feedback

The team is grateful to the many people who have taken the time to provide comment on its publications. Their feedback and suggestions have helped improve this year's edition.

BIBLIOGRAPHY

AbouZahr, Carla, and Tessa Wardlaw. 2003. *Maternal Mortality in 2000: Estimates Developed by WHO, UNICEF, and UNFPA*. Geneva: World Health Organization.

African Union and UNECA (United Nations Economic Commission for Africa). 2005. "Transport and the Millennium Development Goals in Africa." Background working document prepared for the meeting of experts for the African Transport Ministers on the Role of Transport in Achieving the Millennium Development Goals, April 4–5, Addis Ababa. [www4.worldbank.org/afr/ssatp/Resources/PapersNotes/transport_mdg.pdf]

Ahmad, Sultan. 1992. "Regression Estimates of Per Capita GDP Based on Purchasing Power Parities." Policy Research Working Paper 956. World Bank, International Economics Department, Washington, D.C.

———. 1994. "Improving Inter-Spatial and Inter-Temporal Comparability of National Accounts." *Journal of Development Economics* 44 (1): 53–75.

Ashford, Lori S., Davidson R. Gwatkin, and Abdo S. Yazbeck. 2006. *Designing Health and Population Programs to Reach the Poor.* Population Reference Bureau, Washington D.C.

Baeza, Cristian C. and Truman G. Packard. 2006. *Beyond Survival: Protecting Households from Health Shocks in Latin America.* Washington, D.C.: World Bank.

Ball, Nicole. 1984. "Measuring Third World Security Expenditure: A Research Note." *World Development* 12 (2): 157–64.

Barro, Robert J. 1991. "Economic Growth in a Cross-Section of Countries." *Quarterly Journal of Economics* 106 (2): 407–43.

Beck, Thorsten, and Ross Levine. 2001. "Stock Markets, Banks, and Growth: Correlation or Causality?" Policy Research Working Paper 2670. World Bank, Development Research Group, Washington, D.C.

Bhalla, Surjit. 2002. *Imagine There Is No Country: Poverty, Inequality, and Growth in the Era of Globalization*. Washington, D.C.: Institute for International Economics.

Bilsborrow, R. E., Graeme Hugo, A. S. Oberai, and Hania Zlotnik. 1997. *International Migration Statistics*. Geneva: International Labour Office.

Bloom, David E., and Jeffrey G. Williamson. 1998. "Demographic Transitions and Economic Miracles in Emerging Asia." *World Bank Economic Review* 12 (3): 419–55.

Brown, Lester R., Michael Renner, Christopher Flavin. 1998. *Vital Signs 1998: The Environmental Trends That Are Shaping Our Future*. New York: W.W. Norton.

Brown, Lester R., Michael Renner, and Brian Halweil. 1999. *Vital Signs 1999: The Environmental Trends That Are Shaping Our Future*. New York: W.W. Norton.

Brown, Lester R., Christopher Flavin, Hilary F. French, and others. 1998. *State of the World 1998: A Worldwatch Institute Report on Progress toward a Sustainable Society*. New York: W.W. Norton.

Bulatao, Rodolfo. 1998. *The Value of Family Planning Programs in Developing Countries.* RAND Monograph Report. Santa Monica, Calif.: RAND Corporation.

Caiola, Marcello. 1995. *A Manual for Country Economists*. Training Series 1. Vol. 1. Washington, D.C.: International Monetary Fund.

CAWMA (Comprehensive Assessment of Water Management in Agriculture). 2007. *Water for Food, Water for Life.* London: Earthscan.

Carr, Dara. 2004. "Improving the Health of the World's Poorest People." Health Bulletin 1. Population Reference Bureau, Washington, D.C.

CELADE (Centro Latinoamericano de Demografia). Various issues. *Boletín Demografico*.

Chen, Shaohua, and Martin Ravallion. 2004. "How Have the World's Poorest Fared since the 1980s?" *World Bank Research Observer* 19 (2): 141–69.

Chomitz, Kenneth M., Piet Buys, and Timothy S. Thomas. 2005. "Quantifying the Rural-Urban Gradient in Latin America and the Caribbean." Policy Research Working Paper 3634. World Bank, Development Research Group, Washington, D.C.

CIESIN (Center for International Earth Science Information Network). Gridded Population of the World. Columbia University and Centro Internacional de Agricultura Tropical (http://sedac.ciesin.columbia.edu/gpw/).

Claessens, Stijn, Daniela, Klingebiel, and Sergio L. Schmukler. 2002. "Explaining the Migration of Stocks from Exchanges in Emerging Economies to International Centers." Policy Research Working Paper 2816. World Bank, Development Research Group, Washington, D.C.

Collier, Paul, and David Dollar. 1999. "Aid Allocation and Poverty Reduction." Policy Research Working Paper 2041. World Bank, Development Research Group, Washington, D.C.

———. 2001. "Can the World Cut Poverty in Half? How Policy Reform and Effective Aid Can Meet the International Development Goals." Policy Research Working Paper 2403. World Bank, Development Research Group, Washington, D.C.

Commission of the European Communities, IMF (International Monetary Fund), OECD (Organisation for Economic Co-operation and Development), United Nations, and World Bank. 2002. *System of Environmental and Economic Accounts: SEEA 2000*. New York.

Containerisation International. 2007. *Containerisation International Yearbook 2007*. London: Informa Maritime and Transport.

Corrao, Marlo Ann, G. Emmanuel Guindon, Namita Sharma, and Donna Fakhrabadi Shokoohi, eds. 2000. *Tobacco Control Country Profiles*. Atlanta, Ga.: American Cancer Society.

CSD (Commission on Sustainable Development). 1997. *Comprehensive Assessment of the Freshwater Resources of the World.* Report of the Secretary-General. New York.

Dasgupta, Susmita, Denoit Laplante, Craig Meisner, David Wheeler, and Jianping Yan. 2007. "The Impact of Sea Level Rise on Developing Countries: A Comparative Analysis." Policy Research Working Paper 4136. World Bank, Development Research Group, Washington, D.C.

Deaton, Angus. 2002. "Counting the World's Poor: Problems and Possible Solutions." *World Bank Research Observer* 16 (2): 125–47.

Demirgüç-Kunt, Asli, and Ross Levine. 1996. "Stock Market Development and Financial Intermediaries: Stylized Facts." *World Bank Economic Review* 10 (2): 291–321.

De Onis, Mercedes, and Monika Blössner. 2000. "The WHO Global Database on Child Growth and Malnutrition: Methodology and Applications." *International Journal of Epidemiology* 32: 518–26.

De Onis, Mercedes, Adelheid W Onyango, Elaine Borghi, Cutberto Garza, and Hong Yang. 2006. "Comparison of the World Health Organization (WHO) Child Growth Standards and the National Center for Health Statistics/WHO International

Growth Reference: Implications for Child Health Programmes." *Public Health Nutrition* 9 (7): 942–47.

Development Committee. 2003. "Supporting Sound Policies with Adequate and Appropriate Financing: Implementing the Monterrey Consensus at the Country Level." SecM2003-0370. World Bank and International Monetary Fund. Washington, D.C.

Disease Control Priorities Project. 2006. *Global Burden of Disease and Risk Factors.* Washington, D.C.

DKT International. 1998. "1997 Contraceptive Social Marketing Statistics." Washington, D.C.

Doyle, John J., and Gabrielle J. Persley, eds. 1996. *Enabling the Safe Use of Biotechnology: Principles and Practice.* Environmentally Sustainable Development Studies and Monographs Series 10. Washington, D.C.: World Bank.

Drucker, Peter F. 1994. "The Age of Social Transformation." *Atlantic Monthly,* November.

Easterly, William. 2000. "Growth Implosions, Debt Explosions, and My Aunt Marilyn: Do Growth Slowdowns Cause Public Debt Crises?" Policy Research Working Paper 2531. World Bank, Development Research Group, Washington, D.C.

Eurostat (Statistical Office of the European Communities). Various years. *Demographic Statistics.* Luxembourg.

———. Various years. *Statistical Yearbook.* Luxembourg.

Evenson, Robert E., and Carl E. Pray. 1994. "Measuring Food Production (with Reference to South Asia)." *Journal of Development Economics* 44 (1): 173–97.

Faiz, Asif, Christopher S. Weaver, and Michael P. Walsh. 1996. *Air Pollution from Motor Vehicles: Standards and Technologies for Controlling Emissions.* Washington, D.C.: World Bank.

Fankhauser, Samuel. 1995. *Valuing Climate Change: The Economics of the Greenhouse.* London: Earthscan.

FAO (Food and Agriculture Organization). 1976. *Programme for the 1980 World Census of Agriculture.* Rome.

———. 1986a. "Inter-Country Comparisons of Agricultural Production Aggregates." Economic and Social Development Paper 61. Rome.

———. 1986b. *Programme for the 1990 World Census of Agriculture.* FAO Statistical Development Series 5. Rome.

———. 1995. *Programme for the World Census of Agriculture 2000.* FAO Statistical Development Series 5. Rome.

———. 1996. *Food Aid in Figures 1994.* Vol. 12. Rome.

———. 2001. *Agriculture: Towards 2015/30.* Rome.

———. 2003. *State of the World's Forests 2003.* Rome.

———. 2005. *Global Forest Resources Assessment 2005.* Rome.

———. Various years. *Fertilizer Yearbook.* FAO Statistics Series. Rome.

———. Various years. *Production Yearbook.* FAO Statistics Series. Rome.

———. Various years. *State of Food Insecurity in the World.* Rome.

———. Various years. *Trade Yearbook.* FAO Statistics Series. Rome

Filmer, Deon. 2003. "Determinants of Health and Education Outcomes." Background note for *World Development Report 2004: Making Services Work for Poor People.* World Bank, Washington D.C.

Frankel, Jeffrey. 1993. "Quantifying International Capital Mobility in the 1990s." In *On Exchange Rates.* Cambridge, Mass.: MIT Press.

Frankhauser, Pierre. 1994. "Fractales, tissus urbains et reseaux de transport." *Revue d'economie politique* 104: 435–55.

Fredricksen, Birger. 1993. *Statistics of Education in Developing Countries: An Introduction to Their Collection and Analysis.* Paris: United Nations Educational, Scientific, and Cultural Organization.

Gallup, John L., and Jeffrey D. Sachs. 1998. "The Economic Burden of Malaria." Harvard Institute for International Development, Cambridge, Mass.

Gannon, Colin, and Zmarak Shalizi. 1995. "The Use of Sectoral and Project Performance Indicators in Bank-Financed Transport Operations." TWU Discussion Paper 21. World Bank, Transportation, Water, and Urban Development Department, Washington, D.C.

Gardner-Outlaw, Tom, and Robert Engelman. 1997. "Sustaining Water, Easing Scarcity: A Second Update." Population Action International, Washington, D.C.

Goldfinger, Charles. 1994. *L'utile et le futile: L'économie de l'immatériel.* Paris: Editions Odile Jacob.

GTZ (German Agency for Technical Cooperation). 2004. *Fuel Prices and Taxation.* Eschborn, Germany.

Gupta, Sanjeev, Hamid Davoodi, and Erwin Tiongson. 2000. "Corruption and the Provision of Health Care and Education Services." IMF Working Paper 00/116. International Monetary Fund, Washington, D.C.

Gupta, Sanjeev, Brian Hammond, and Eric Swanson. 2000. "Setting the Goals." *OECD Observer* 223: 15–17.

Gwatkin, Davidson R., Shea Rutstein, Kiersten Johnson, Eldaw Suliman, Adam Wagstaff, and Agbessi Amouzou. 2007. *Socio Economic Differences in Health, Nutrition, and Population.* Washington, D.C.: World Bank.

Habyarimana, James, Jishnu Das, Stefan Dercon, and Pramila Krishnan. 2003. "Sense and Absence: Absenteeism and Learning in Zambian Schools." World Bank, Washington, D.C.

Hamilton, Kirk, and Michael Clemens. 1999. "Genuine Savings Rates in Developing Countries." *World Bank Economic Review* 13 (2): 333–56.

Hanushek, Eric. 2002. *The Long-Run Importance of School Quality.* NBER Working Paper 9071. Cambridge, Mass.: National Bureau of Economic Research.

Happe, Nancy, and John Wakeman-Linn. 1994. "Military Expenditures and Arms Trade: Alternative Data Sources." IMF Working Paper 94/69. International Monetary Fund, Policy Development and Review Department, Washington, D.C

Harrison, Ann. 1995. "Factor Markets and Trade Policy Reform." World Bank, Washington, D.C.

Hatzichronoglou, Thomas. 1997. "Revision of the High-Technology Sector and Product Classification." STI Working Paper 1997/2. Organisation for Economic Co-operation and Development, Directorate for Science, Technology, and Industry, Paris.

Heck, W. W. 1989. "Assessment of Crop Losses from Air Pollutants in the U.S." In J. J. McKenzie and M. T. El Ashry, eds., *Air Pollution's Toll on Forests and Crops.* New Haven, Conn.: Yale University Press.

Heston, Alan. 1994. "A Brief Review of Some Problems in Using National Accounts Data in Level of Output Comparisons and Growth Studies." *Journal*

BIBLIOGRAPHY

of Development Economics 44 (1): 29–52.

Hettige, Hemamala, Muthukumara Mani, and David Wheeler. 1998. "Industrial Pollution in Economic Development: Kuznets Revisited." Policy Research Working Paper 1876. World Bank, Development Research Group, Washington, D.C.

IEA (International Energy Agency). 2002. *World Energy Outlook: Energy and Poverty*. Paris.

———. Various years. *Energy Balances of OECD Countries*. Paris.

———. Various years. *Energy Statistics and Balances of Non-OECD Countries*. Paris.

———. Various years. *Energy Statistics of OECD Countries*. Paris.

ILO (International Labour Organization). Various years. *Key Indicators of the Labour Market*. Geneva: International Labour Office.

———. Various years. *Yearbook of Labour Statistics*. Geneva: International Labour Office.

———. 2006. *The End of Child Labour within Reach*. Geneva.

IMF (International Monetary Fund). 1977. *Balance of Payments Manual*. 4th ed. Washington, D.C.

———. 1993. *Balance of Payments Manual*. 5th ed. Washington, D.C.

———. 1995. *Balance of Payments Compilation Guide*. Washington, D.C.

———. 1996. *Balance of Payments Textbook*. Washington, D.C.

———. 2000. *Monetary and Financial Statistics Manual*. Washington, D.C.

———. 2001. *Government Finance Statistics Manual*. Washington, D.C.

———. 2004a. *Compilation Guide on Financial Soundness Indicators*. Washington, D.C.

———. 2004b. *World Economic Outlook*. Chapter 3. Washington, DC.

———. 2006. *Global Financial Stability Report*. Washington, D.C.

———. Various issues. *Direction of Trade Statistics*.

———. Various issues. *International Financial Statistics*.

———. Various years. *Balance of Payments Statistics Yearbook*. Parts 1 and 2. Washington, D.C.

———. Various years. *Direction of Trade Statistics Yearbook*. Washington, D.C.

———. Various years. *Government Finance Statistics Yearbook*. Washington, D.C.

———. Various years. *International Financial Statistics Yearbook*. Washington, D.C.

International Budget Project. 2006. "Open Budget Initiative" website. [www.openbudgetindex.org].

International Civil Aviation Organization. 2005. Civil Aviation Statistics of the World database. Montreal.

International Diabetes Federation. Various years. *Diabetes Atlas*. Brussels.

International Institute for Strategic Studies. 2007. *The Military Balance 2007*. London: Oxford University Press.

International Road Federation. 2006. *World Road Statistics 2006*. Geneva.

International Working Group of External Debt Compilers (Bank for International Settlements, International Monetary Fund, Organisation for Economic Co-operation and Development, and World Bank). 1987. *External Debt Definitions*. Washington, D.C.

Inter-Secretariat Working Group on National Accounts (Commission of the European Communities, International Monetary Fund, Organisation for Economic Co-operation and Development, United Nations, and World Bank). 1993. *System of National Accounts*. Brussels, Luxembourg, New York, and Washington, D.C.

IPCC (Intergovernmental Panel on Climate Change). 2001a. *Climate Change 2001*. Cambridge, U.K.: Cambridge University Press.

———. 2001b. *Climate Change 2001: The Scientific Basis; Contribution of Working Group I to the Third Assessment Report of the Intergovernmental Panel on Climate Change*. Cambridge, U.K.: Cambridge University Press.

———. 2001c. *Climate Change 2001: Impacts, Adaptation, and Vulnerability; Contribution of Working Group II to the Third Assessment Report of the Intergovernmental Panel on Climate Change*. Cambridge, U.K.: Cambridge University Press.

———. 2001d. *Climate Change 2001: Mitigation; Contribution of Working Group II to the Third Assessment Report of the Intergovernmental Panel on Climate Change*. Cambridge, U.K.: Cambridge University Press.

ITU (International Telecommunication Union). 2006. World Telecommunication Indicators Database. Geneva.

IUCN (World Conservation Union). 2004. *2003 IUCN Red List of Threatened Plants*. Gland, Switzerland.

———. 2000. *2000 IUCN Red List of Threatened Animals*. Gland, Switzerland.

Izaguirre, Ada Karina. 2005. "Private Infrastructure: Emerging Market Sponsors Dominate Private Flows". Public Policy for the Private Sector Note 299. World Bank, Private Sector Development, Washington, D.C.

Jamison, Dean T., Joel G. Breman, Anthony R. Measham, George Alleyne, Mariam Claeson, David B. Evans, Prabhat Jha, Anne Mills, and Philip Musgrove, eds. 2006. *Priorities in Health*. Washington, D.C.: World Bank.

Joint Learning Initiative. 2004. *Human Resources for Health: Overcoming the Crisis*. Boston, Mass.

Kaufmann, Daniel. 2005. "Click Refresh Button: Investment Climate Reconsidered." *Development Outreach*, March.

Kaufmann, Daniel, Aart Kraay, and Massimo Mastruzzi. 2005. "Governance Matters IV: Governance Indicators for 1996–2004." Policy Research Working Paper 3630. World Bank, Washington, D.C.

Knack, Steve. 2006. "Global Monitoring Report 2006 and Governance and Growth." Presented at the workshop on Governance and Development, November 11–12, Dhaka.

Knetter, Michael. 1994. *Why Are Retail Prices in Japan So High? Evidence from German Export Prices*. NBER Working Paper 4894. Cambridge, Mass.: National Bureau of Economic Research.

Kozak, Marta. 2005. "Micro, Small, and Medium Enterprises: A Collection of Published Data." International Finance Corporation, Washington, D.C.

Kunte, Arundhati, Kirk Hamilton, John Dixon, and Michael Clemens. 1998. "Estimating National Wealth: Methodology and Results." Environmental Economics Series 57. World Bank, Environment Department, Washington, D.C.

Lanjouw, Jean O., and Peter Lanjouw. 2001. "The Rural Non-Farm Sector: Issues and Evidence from Developing Countries." *Agricultural Economics* 26 (1): 1–23.

Lanjouw, Peter, and Gershon Feder. 2001. "Rural Nonfarm Activities and Rural Development: From Experience toward Strategy." Rural Strategy Discussion

Paper 4. World Bank, Washington, D.C.

Lewis, Karen K. 1995. "Puzzles in International Financial Markets." In Gene Grossman and Kenneth Rogoff, eds., *Handbook of International Economics*. Vol. 3. Amsterdam: North Holland.

Lewis, Stephen R., Jr. 1989. "Primary Exporting Countries." In Hollis Chenery and T. N. Srinivasan, eds., *Handbook of Development Economics*. Vol. 2. Amsterdam: North Holland.

Lopez, Alan D., Colin D. Mathers, Majad Ezzati, Dean T. Jamison, and Christopher J. L. Murray. 2006. *Global Burden of Disease and Risk Factors*. Washington, D.C.: World Bank.

Lovei, Magdolna. 1997. "Toward Effective Pollution Management." *Environment Matters* (Fall): 52–53.

Lucas, R. E. 1988. "On the Mechanics of Economic Development." *Journal of Monetary Economics* 22: 3–42.

Mani, Muthukumara, and David Wheeler. 1997. "In Search of Pollution Havens? Dirty Industry in the World Economy, 1960–95." World Bank, Policy Research Department, Washington, D.C.

McCarthy, F. Desmond, and Holger Wolf. 2001. "Comparative Life Expectancy in Africa." Policy Research Working Paper 2668. World Bank, Development Research Group, Washington, D.C.

McCay, J., M. Erkson, and O. Shafey. 2006. *Tobacco Atlas*. 2nd ed. Atlanta, Ga.: American Cancer Society.

Midgley, Peter. 1994. "Urban Transport in Asia: An Operational Agenda for the 1990s." Technical Paper 224. World Bank, Washington, D.C.

Morgenstern, Oskar. 1963. *On the Accuracy of Economic Observations*. Princeton, N.J.: Princeton University Press.

Morisset, Jacques. 2000. "Foreign Direct Investment in Africa: Policies Also Matter" Policy Research Working Paper 2481. World Bank, Washington D.C.

National Science Board. 2006. *Science and Engineering Indicators 2006*. Arlington, Va.: National Science Foundation.

Netcraft. 2006. "Netcraft Secure Server Survey." [www.netcraft.com/].

Newfarmer, Richard, ed. 2006. *Trade, Doha, and Development: A Window into the Issues*. Washington, D.C.: World Bank.

NRI (National Research Institute) and World Bank. 2003. "Public Expenditure and Service Delivery in Papua New Guinea: Draft." Washington, D.C.

Obstfeldt, Maurice. 1995. "International Capital Mobility in the 1990s." In P.B. Kenen, ed., *Understanding Interdependence: The Macroeconomics of the Open Economy*. Princeton, N.J.: Princeton University Press.

Obstfeldt, Maurice, and Kenneth Rogoff 1996. *Foundations of International Macroeconomics*. Cambridge, Mass.: MIT Press.

OECD (Organisation for Economic Co-operation and Development). 1985. *Measuring Health Care 1960–1983: Expenditure, Costs, Performance*. Paris.

———. 1996. *Trade, Employment, and Labour Standards: A Study of Core Workers' Rights and International Trade*. Paris.

———. 1997. *Employment Outlook*. Paris.

———. 2003. *Agricultural Policies in OECD Countries: Monitoring and Evaluation 2003*. Paris

———. 2006. *OECD Health Data 2006*. Paris.

———. Various issues. *Main Economic Indicators*. Paris.

———. Various years. *International Development Statistics*. CD-ROM. Paris

———. Various years. *National Accounts*. Vol. 1, Main Aggregates. Paris

———. Various years. *National Accounts*. Vol. 2, Detailed Tables. Paris.

———. Various years. *Trends in International Migration: Continuous Reporting System on Migration*. Paris

OECD (Organisation for Economic Co-operation and Development) DAC (Development Assistance Committee). 2006. Procurement Online website. [www.oecd.org/department/0,2688,en_2649_19101395_1_1_1_1_1,00.html].

———. Various years. *Development Cooperation Report*. Paris

———. Various years. *Geographical Distribution of Financial Flows to Aid Recipients: Disbursements, Commitments, Country Indicators*. Paris

O'Meara, Molly. 1999. "Reinventing Cities for People and the Planet." Worldwatch Paper 147. Worldwatch Institute, Washington, D.C.

Özden, Çaglar, and Maurice Schiff, eds. 2005. *International Migration, Remittances, and the Brain Drain*. New York: Palgrave Macmillan.

Palacios, Robert, and Montserrat Pallares-Miralles. 2000. "International Patterns of Pension Provision." Social Protection Discussion Paper 0009. World Bank, Human Development Network, Washington, D.C.

Pandey, Kiran D., Piet Buys, Kenneth Chomitz, and David Wheeler. 2006a. "Biodiversity Conservation Indicators: New Tools for Priority Setting at the Global Environmental Facility." World Bank, Development Economics Research Group and Environment Department, Washington, D.C.

Pandey, Kiran D., Bart Ostro, David Wheeler, Uwe Deichmann, Kirk Hamilton, and Katie Bolt. 2006b. "Ambient Particulate Matter Concentrations in Residential and Pollution Hotspots of World Cities: New Estimates Based on the Global Model of Ambient Particulates (GMAPS)." World Bank, Development Economics Research Group and Environment Department, Washington, D.C.

Pandey, Kiran Dev, Katharine Bolt, Uwe Deichmann, Kirk Hamilton, Bart Ostro, and David Wheeler. 2003. "The Human Cost of Air Pollution: New Estimates for Developing Countries." World Bank, Development Research Group and Environment Department, Washington, D.C.

Pearce, David, and Giles Atkinson. 1993. "Capital Theory and the Measurement of Sustainable Development: An Indicator of Weak Sustainability." *Ecological Economics* 8 (2): 103–08.

Pilling, David. 1999. "In Sickness and in Wealth." *Financial Times*, October 22.

Plucknett, Donald L. 1991. "Saving Lives through Agricultural Research." Issues in Agriculture 16. World Bank, Consultative Group on International Agricultural Research, Washington, D.C.

PricewaterhouseCoopers. 2006. *Worldwide Summaries Online*. New York. [www.pwc.com/extweb/pwcpublications.nsf/docid/9B2B76032544964C8525717E00606CBD].

Princeton University Press. Forthcoming. *Guide to the Mammals of China*. Princeton, N.J.

The PRS Group. 2006. *International Country Risk Guide*. East Syracuse, N.Y. [www.prsgroup.com].

BIBLIOGRAPHY

Public Expenditure and Financial Accountability (PEFA) Program. 2006. [www.pefa.org].

Rama, Martin, and Raquel Artecona. 2002. "A Database of Labor Market Indicators across Countries." World Bank, Development Research Group, Washington, D.C.

Ratha, Dilip, and William Shaw. 2007. "South-South Migration and Remittances." World Bank, Development Prospects Group, Washington, D.C.

Ravallion, Martin, and Shaohua Chen. 1996. "What Can New Survey Data Tell Us about the Recent Changes in Living Standards in Developing and Transitional Economies?" World Bank, Policy Research Department, Washington, D.C.

Ravallion, Martin, Gaurav Datt, and Dominique van de Walle. 1991. "Quantifying Absolute Poverty in the Developing World." *Review of Income & Wealth* 37 (4): 345–61.

Rodrik, Dani. 1996. "Labor Standards in International Trade: Do They Matter and What Do We Do About Them?" Overseas Development Council, Washington, D.C.

Rodrik, Dani, and Arvind Subramanian. 2003. "The Primacy of Institutions (and What This Does and Does Not Mean)." *Finance & Development* 40 (2): 31–34.

Romer, P. M. 1986. "Increasing Returns and Long-Run Growth." *Journal of Political Economy* 94 (5): 1002–37.

Rosengrant, M. W. and P. B. R. Hazel. 2000. *Transforming the Rural Asia Economy: The Unfinished Revolution.* Hong Kong, China: Oxford University Press.

Rouen, Ren, and Kai Chen. 1995. "China's GDP in U.S. Dollars, Based on Purchasing Power Parity." Policy Research Working Paper 1415. Washington, D.C.

Ruggles, Robert. 1994. "Issues Relating to the UN System of National Accounts and Developing Countries." *Journal of Development Economics* 44 (1): 77–85.

Ryten, Jacob. 1998. "Fifty Years of ISIC: Historical Origins and Future Perspectives." ECA/STAT.AC. 63/22. United Nations, Statistics Division, New York.

Saghir, Jamal. 2005. "Energy and Poverty: Myths, Links, and Policy Issues. Energy Working Notes 4. World Bank, Washington, D.C.

Sala-i-Martin, Xavier. 2002. *The Disturbing "Rise" in Global Income Inequality.* NBER Working Paper 8904. Cambridge, Mass.: National Bureau of Economic Research.

Salomon, Joshua A., Daniel R. Hogan, John Stover, Karen A. Stanecki, Neff Walker, Peter D. Ghys, and Bernhard Schwartländer. 2005. "Integrating HIV Prevention and Treatment: From Slogans to Impact." *PLoS Medicine* 2 (1): e16.

Scherr, Sara J. 1999. "Soil Degradation: A Threat to Developing-Country Food Security by 2020." 2020 Vision for Food, Agriculture, and Environment Discussion Paper 27. International Food Policy Research Institute, Washington, D.C.

Shiklovanov, Igor. 1993. "World Fresh Water Resources." In Peter H. Gleick, ed., *Water in Crisis: A Guide to Fresh Water Resources.* New York: Oxford University Press.

SIPRI (Stockholm International Peace Research Institute). 2006. *SIPRI Yearbook 2006: Armaments, Disarmament, and International Security.* Oxford, U.K.: Oxford University Press.

Smith, Lisa, and Laurence Haddad. 2000. "Overcoming Child Malnutrition in Developing Countries: Past Achievements and Future Choices." 2020 Brief 64. International Food Policy Research Institute, Washington, D.C.

Srinivasan, T. N. 1994a. "Database for Development Analysis: An Overview." *Journal of Development Economics* 44 (1): 3–28.

———. ed. 1994b. Special Issue on Database for Development Analysis. *Journal of Development Economics* 44 (1).

Standard & Poor's. 2000. *The S&P Emerging Market Indices: Methodology, Definitions, and Practices.* New York.

———. 2006. *Global Stock Markets Factbook 2006.* New York.

Stern, Nicholas. 2006. *The Economics of Climate Change: The Stern Review.* London: Cambridge University Press.

Tarmann, Allison. 2002. Response to Hunger Tests New Priorities. *Population Today,* November/December 2001.

Taylor, Alan M. 1996a. *International Capital Mobility in History: Purchasing Power Parity in the Long Run.* NBER Working Paper 5742. Cambridge, Mass.: National Bureau of Economic Research.

———. 1996b. *International Capital Mobility in History: The Saving-Investment Relationship.* NBER Working Paper 5743. Cambridge, Mass.: National Bureau of Economic Research.

Transparency International. 2007. "Corruption Perceptions Index." [www.transparency.org]

UNACC/SCN (United Nations Administrative Committee on Coordination, Subcommittee on Nutrition). Various years. *Update on the Nutrition Situation.* Geneva.

UNAIDS (Joint United Nations Programme on HIV/AIDS) and WHO (World Health Organization). 2005. *AIDS Epidemic Update: December 2005.* Geneva.

———. Various years. *Report on the Global AIDS Epidemic.* Geneva.

UNCTAD (United Nations Conference on Trade and Development). 2003. *The Least Developed Countries Report.* Geneva

———. Various years. *Handbook of International Trade and Development Statistics.* Geneva.

UNDP (United Nations Development Programme). 2006. *Human Development Report 2006: Beyond Scarcity: Power, Poverty and Global Water Crisis.* New York.

UNEP (United Nations Environment Programme). 1991. *Urban Air Pollution.* Nairobi.

———. 2002. *Global Environment Outlook 3.* London: Earthscan.

UNESCO (United Nations Educational, Scientific, and Cultural Organization). 1997. *International Standard Classification of Education.* Paris

———. 2005. *Literacy for Life.* Paris.

———. 2006. *EFA Global Monitoring Report.* Paris.

UNESCO (United Nations Educational, Scientific, and Cultural Organization) Institute for Statistics. Various years. *Global Education Digest.* Paris.

———. Online database [www.uis.unesco.org/].

UNESCWA (United Nations Economic and Social Commission for Western Asia). 1997. "Purchasing Power Parities: Volume and Price Level Comparisons for the Middle East, 1993." E/ESCWA/STAT/1997/2. Amman, Jordan.

UNFCCC (United Nations Framework Convention on Climate Change). 2005. "Kyoto Protocol to the United Nations Framework Convention on Climate Change." Bonn, Germany.

UN-HABITAT (United Nations Human Settlements Programme). 2003. *Global Report on Human Settlements.* Nairobi.

UNHCR (United Nations High Commissioner for Refugees). Various years. *Statistical Yearbook*. Geneva.

UNICEF (United Nations Children's Fund). Various years. *State of the World's Children*. New York: Oxford University Press.

UNIDO (United Nations Industrial Development Organization). Various years. *International Yearbook of Industrial Statistics*. Vienna.

UNIFEM (United Nations Development Fund for Women). 2005. *Progress of the World's Women*. New York.

United Nations. 1947. *Measurement of National Income and the Construction of Social Accounts*. New York.

———. 1968. "A System of National Accounts: Studies and Methods." Series F, no. 2, rev. 3. New York.

———. 1990. *International Standard Industrial Classification of All Economic Activities, Third Revision*. Statistical Papers Series M, no. 4, rev. 3. New York.

———. 1992. "Handbook of the International Comparison Programme." Studies in Methods Series F, no. 62. New York.

———. 1993. "SNA Handbook on Integrated Environmental and Economic Accounting." Series F, no. 61. Statistical Office, New York.

———. 1999. "Integrated Environmental and Economic Accounting: An Operational Manual." Studies in Methods Series F, no. 78. New York.

———. 2000. *We the Peoples: The Role of the United Nations in the 21st Century*. New York.

———. 2004. "Trends in Total Migrant Stock: The 2003 Revision." POP/DB/MIG/Rev.2003. Department of Economic and Social Affairs, New York.

———. 2005a. "The Energy Challenge for Achieving the Millennium Development Goals." New York.

———. 2005b. *The Millennium Development Goals Report*. New York.

United Nations Millennium Project. 2005. *Taking Action: Achieving Gender Equality and Empowering Women*. Task Force on Education and Gender Equality. London: Earthscan.

United Nations Population Division. 2002. *International Migration Report 2002*. New York.

———. Various years. *Levels and Trends of Contraceptive Use*. New York.

———. Various years. *Trends in Total Migrant Stock*. New York.

———. Various years. *World Population Prospects*. Department of Economic and Social Affairs, New York.

———. Various years. *World Urbanization Prospects*. New York.

United Nations Statistics Division. 1985. *National Accounts Statistics: Compendium of Income Distribution Statistics*. New York.

———. Various issues. *Monthly Bulletin of Statistics*. New York.

———. Various years. *Energy Statistics Yearbook*. New York.

———. Various years. *International Trade Statistics Yearbook*. New York

———. Various years. *National Accounts Statistics: Main Aggregates and Detailed Tables*. Parts 1 and 2. New York.

———. Various years. *National Income Accounts*. New York.

———. Various years. *Population and Vital Statistics Report*. New York.

———. Various years. *Statistical Yearbook*. New York

U.S. Environmental Protection Agency. 1995. *National Air Quality and Emissions Trends Report 1995*. Washington, D.C.

Walsh, Michael P. 1994. "Motor Vehicle Pollution Control: An Increasingly Critical Issue for Developing Countries." World Bank, Washington, D.C.

Watson, Robert, John A. Dixon, Steven P. Hamburg, Anthony C. Janetos, and Richard H. Moss. 1998. *Protecting Our Planet, Securing Our Future: Linkages among Global Environmental Issues and Human Needs*. Nairobi and Washington, D.C.: United Nations Environment Programme, U.S. National Aeronautics and Space Administration, and World Bank.

Whitehouse, Edward. 2007. *Pensions Panorama: Retirement-Income Systems in 53 Countries*. Washington, D.C.: World Bank.

WHO (World Health Organization). 1983. *International Classification of Diseases*. 10th rev. Geneva.

———. 2003. "Poverty and Health: Report by the Director-General." Geneva. [www.who.int/gb/EB_WHA/PDF/EB105/ee5.pdf].

———. 2006. *Global Atlas of the Health Work Force*. Geneva.

———. Various years. *Global Tuberculosis Control Report*. Geneva.

———. Various years. *World Health Report*. Geneva.

———. Various years. *World Health Statistics*. Geneva.

WHO (World Health Organization) and UNICEF (United Nations Children's Fund). 2003. *The Africa Malaria Report 2003*. Geneva.

———. 2004. *Beyond the Numbers: Reviewing Maternal Deaths and Complications to Make Pregnancy Safer*. Geneva.

———. 2006. *Meeting the MDG Drinking Water and Sanitation Target*. Geneva.

WHO (World Health Organization) and World Bank. 2004. *World Report on Road Traffic Injury Prevention*. Geneva.

WIPO (World Intellectual Property Organization). 2006. *WIPO Patent Report: Statistics on Worldwide Patent Activity*. Geneva.

WITSA (World Information Technology and Services Alliance). 2006. "Digital Planet 2006: The Global Information Economy." Vienna, Va.

Wolf, Holger C. 1997. *Patterns of Intra- and Inter-State Trade*. NBER Working Paper 5939. Cambridge, Mass.: National Bureau of Economic Research.

World Bank. 1990. *World Development Report 1990: Poverty*. New York: Oxford University Pres

———. 1991. *Managing Development: The Governance Dimension*. Discussion Paper 34899. World Bank, Task Force from Operations; Policy, Research and External Affairs; Legal; Corporate Planning and Budget; and Finance Complexes, Washington, D.C.

———. 1992. *World Development Report 1992: Development and the Environment*. New York: Oxford University Press.

———. 1996a. *Environment Matters* (summer). Environment Department, Washington, D.C.

———. 1996b. "Livable Cities for the 21st Century: A Directions in Development book." Washington, D.C.

———. 1996c. "National Environmental Strategies: Learning from Experience." Environment Department, Washington, D.

———. 1997a. *Can the Environment Wait? Priorities for East Asia*. Washington, D.C.

BIBLIOGRAPHY

———. 1997b. "Expanding the Measure of Wealth: Indicators of Environmentally Sustainable Development." Environmentally Sustainable Development Studies and Monographs Series, no. 17. Washington, D.C.

———. 1997c. "Rural Development: From Vision to Action." Environmentally Sustainable Development Studies and Monographs Series, no. 12. Washington, D.C.

———. 1997d. *World Development Report 1997: The State in a Changing World.*

———. 1999a. "Fuel for Thought: Environmental Strategy for the Energy Sector." Environment Department, Energy, Mining, and Telecommunications Department and International Finance Corporation, Washington, D.C.

———. 1999b. *Greening Industry: New Roles for Communities, Markets, and Governments*. New York: Oxford University Press.

———. 2000a. *Trade Blocs*. New York: Oxford University Press.

———. 2000b. *World Development Report 2000/2001: Attacking Poverty*. New York: Oxford University Press.

———. 2001. *World Development Report 2002: Building Institutions for Markets*. New York: Oxford University Press.

———. 2002a. *A Case for Aid: Building a Consensus for Development Assistance*. Washington, D.C.

———. 2002b. "The Environment and the Millennium Development Goals." Washington, D.C.

———. 2002c. "Financial Impact of the HIPC Initiative: First 24 Country Cases." Washington, D.C.

———. 2002d. *Globalization, Growth, and Poverty: Building an Inclusive World Economy*. New York: Oxford University Press.

———. 2002e. *World Development Report 2003: Sustainable Development in a Dynamic World.* New York: Oxford University Press.

———. 2003a. "The Millennium Development Goals for Health: Rising to the Challenges." Washington, D.C.

———. 2003b. *World Bank Atlas*. Washington, D.C.

———. 2003c. *World Development Report 2004: Making Services Work for the Poor*. New York: Oxford University Press.

———. 2004a. "Measuring Results: Improving National Statistics in IDA Countries." International Development Association, Washington, D.C. [http://siteresources.worldbank.org/IDA/Resources/MeasuringResultsStatistics.pdf].

———. 2004b. *Partnerships in Development: Progress in the Fight against Poverty*. Washington, D.C.

———. 2004c. *World Bank Atlas*. Washington, D.C.

———. 2005a. "Country Policy and Institutional Assessments, 2005 Assessment Querstionnaire." Operational Policy and Country Services, Washington, D.C.

———. 2005b. "Meeting the Challenge of Africa's Development: A World Bank Group Action Plan." Africa Region, World Bank, Washington, D.C.

———. 2005c. *Rolling Back Malaria: The World Bank Global Strategy and Booster Program*. Washington, D.C.

———. 2005d. *World Development Report 2006: Equity and Development*. New York: Oxford University Press.

———. 2006a. "Anticorruption Diagnostic Surveys." World Bank Institute's Governance Diagnostic Capacity Building Program website. [www.worldbank.org/wbi/governance].

———. 2006b. "Debt Relief for the Poorest: An Evaluation Update of the HIPC Initiative." Intependent Evaluation Group, Washington, D.C.

———. 2006c. *Doing Business 2007: How to Reform*. Washington, D.C.

———. 2006d. *Private Participation in Infrastructure Project Database.* [http://ppi.worldbank.org/].

———. 2006e. *Where is the Wealth of Nations? Measuring Capital for the 21st Century*. Washington, D.C.

———. 2006f. *Health Financing Revisited.*

———. 2007a. "Enterprise Surveys Online" [www.enterprisesurveys.org]."

———. 2007b. "Performance Assessments and Allocation of IDA Resources". Online database [www.worldbank.org/ida]. Washington, D.C.

———. Forthcoming. *Progress Report of Pension Indicators*. Washington, D.C. [www.worldbank.org/pensions].

———. Various issues. *Global Commodity Markets*.

———. Various years. *Global Development Finance*. Washington, D.C.

———. Various years. *Global Economic Prospects and the Developing Countries*. Washington, D.C.

———. Various years. *World Debt Tables*. Washington, D.C.

———. Various years. *World Development Indicators*. Washington, D.C.

World Bank and International Monetary Fund. 2005a. *Global Monitoring Report 2005: Millennium Development Goals; From Consensus to Momentum*. Washington, D.C.

———. 2005b. "HIPC (Heavily Indebted Poor Countries) Public Expenditure Management Assessment and Action Plans." Washington, D.C. [www.worldbank.org/hipc].

———. 2006a. *Global Monitoring Report 2006: Strengthening Mutual Accountability, Aid, Trade, and Governance*. Washington, D.C.

———. 2006b. "Heavily Indebted Poor Countries (HIPC) Initiative and Multilateral Debt Relief Initiative (MDRI)—Status of Implementation." Washington, D.C.

World Bank and European Bank for Reconstruction and Development. 2006. Business Environment and Enterprise Performance Survey (BEEPS), BEEPS Interactive Dataset. [http://info.worldbank.org/governance/beeps/].

World Energy Council. 1995. *Global Energy Perspectives to 2050 and Beyond*. London.

World Resources Institute, UNEP (United Nations Environment Programme), UNDP (United Nations Development Programme), and World Bank. Various years. *World Resources: A Guide to the Global Environment*. New York: Oxford University Press.

World Tourism Organization. Various years. *Compendium of Tourism Statistics*. Madrid.

———. Various years. *Yearbook of Tourism Statistics*. Vols. 1 and 2. Madrid.

WTO (World Trade Organization). Various years. *Annual Report*. Geneva.

INDEX OF INDICATORS

References are to table numbers.

INDEX OF INDICATORS

D

INDEX OF INDICATORS

F

G

INDEX OF INDICATORS

I

INDEX OF INDICATORS

INDEX OF INDICATORS

INDEX OF INDICATORS

INDEX OF INDICATORS

U

V

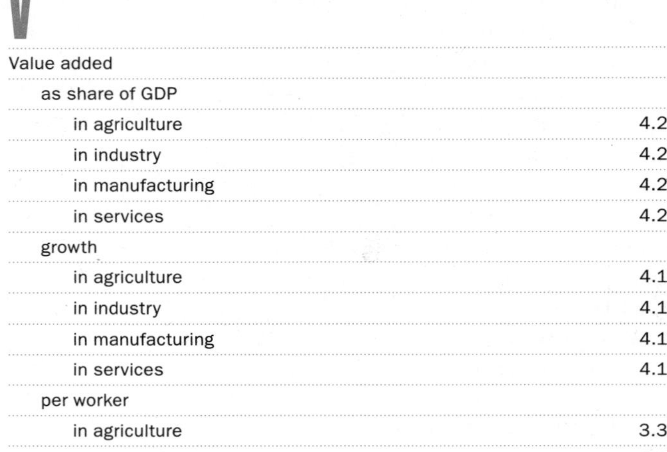

W

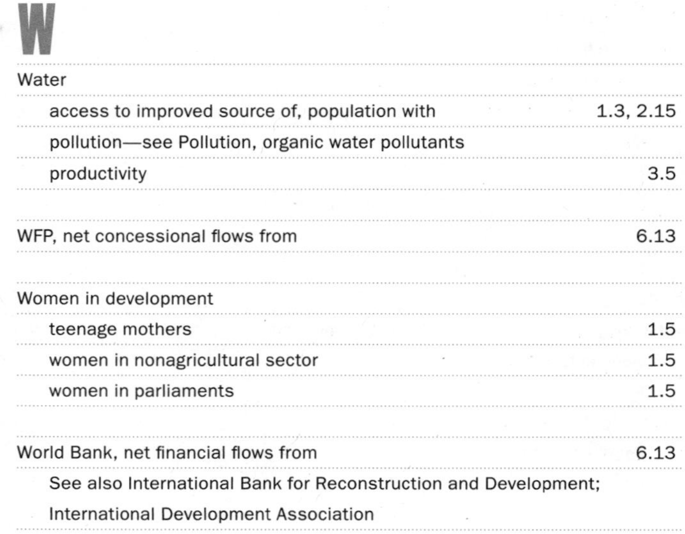